The Rise and Fall
of the Great Powers

THE
RISE AND FALL
OF THE
GREAT POWERS

Economic Change
and Military Conflict
from 1500 to 2000

BY PAUL KENNEDY

Random House
New York

Grateful acknowledgment is made to the following
for permission to reprint previously published material:

Lexington Books, D C Heath and Company: An illustration from *American Defense Annual, 1987–1988*. Reprinted by permission of Lexington Books, D C Heath and Company, edited by Kruzel (Lexington, MA). Copyright © 1987 D C Heath.

Library of Congress Cataloging-in-Publication Data
Kennedy, Paul M., 1945-
The rise and fall of the great powers.

Includes index.
1. History, Modern. 2. Economic history.
3. Military history, Modern. 4. Armaments—Economic
aspects. 5. Balance of power. I. Title.
D210.K46 1988   909.82   87-9690
ISBN 0-394-54674-1

Book design by Charlotte Staub
Maps by Jean Paul Tremblay

Manufactured in the United States of America
68975

To Cath

Acknowledgments

Whatever the weaknesses of this book, they would have been far greater without the kind help of friends. J. R. Jones and Gordon Lee went through the entire manuscript, asking questions all the way. My colleague Jonathan Spence endeavored (I fear with only partial success) to curb the cultural assumptions which emerged in the first two chapters. John Elliott was encouraging about Chapter 2, despite its being very evidently "not my period." Paddy O'Brien and John Bosher sought to make my comments on eighteenth-century British and French finance a little less crude. Nick Rizopoulos and Michael Mandelbaum not only scrutinized the later chapters, but also invited me to present my ideas at a series of meetings at the Lehrman Institute in New York. Many, many scholars have heard me give papers on subthemes in this book, and have provided references, much-needed criticism, and encouragement.

The libraries and staffs at the universities of East Anglia and Yale were of great assistance. My graduate student Kevin Smith helped me in the search for historical statistics. My son Jim Kennedy prepared the maps. Sheila Klein and Sue McClain came to the rescue with typing and word processing, as did Maarten Pereboom with the bibliography. I am extremely grateful for the sustained support and encouragement which my literary agent, Bruce Hunter, has provided over the years. Jason Epstein has been a firm and patient editor, repeatedly getting me to think of the general reader—and also recognizing earlier than the author did how demanding it would be to deal with themes of this magnitude.

My family has provided support and, more important still, light relief. The book is dedicated to my wife, to whom I owe so much.

Paul Kennedy
Hamden, Connecticut, 1986

CONTENTS

MAPS

TABLES & CHARTS

TABLES

CHARTS

Introduction

This is a book about national and international power in the "modern"—that is, post-Renaissance—period. It seeks to trace and to explain how the various Great Powers have risen and fallen, relative to each other, over the five centuries since the formation of the "new monarchies" of western Europe and the beginnings of the transoceanic, global system of states. Inevitably, it concerns itself a great deal with wars, especially those major, drawn-out conflicts fought by coalitions of Great Powers which had such an impact upon the international order; but it is not strictly a book about military history. It also concerns itself with tracing the changes which have occurred in the global economic balances since 1500; and yet it is not, at least directly, a work of economic history. What it concentrates upon is the *interaction* between economics and strategy, as each of the leading states in the international system strove to enhance its wealth and its power, to become (or to remain) both rich and strong.

The "military conflict" referred to in the book's subtitle is therefore always examined in the context of "economic change." The triumph of any one Great Power in this period, or the collapse of another, has usually been the consequence of lengthy fighting by its armed forces; but it has also been the consequence of the more or less efficient utilization of the state's productive economic resources in wartime, and, further in the background, of the way in which that state's economy had been rising or falling, *relative* to the other leading nations, in the decades preceding the actual conflict. For that reason, how a Great Power's position steadily alters in peacetime is as important to this study as how it fights in wartime.

The argument being offered here will receive much more elaborate analysis in the text itself, but can be summarized very briefly:

The relative strengths of the leading nations in world affairs never remain constant, principally because of the uneven rate of growth among different societies and of the technological and organizational breakthroughs which bring a greater advantage to one society than to another. For example, the coming of the long-range gunned sailing ship and the rise of the Atlantic trades after 1500 was not *uniformly* beneficial to all the states of Europe—it boosted some much more than others. In the same way, the later development of steam power and of the coal and metal resources upon which it relied massively increased the relative power of certain nations, and thereby decreased the relative power of others. Once their productive capacity was enhanced, countries would normally find it easier to sustain the burdens of paying for large-scale armaments in peacetime and of maintaining and supplying large armies and fleets in wartime. It sounds crudely mercantilistic to express it this way, but wealth is usually needed to underpin military power, and military power is usually needed to acquire and protect wealth. If, however, too large a proportion of the state's resources is diverted from wealth creation and allocated instead to military purposes, then that is likely to lead to a weakening of national power over the longer term. In the same way, if a state overextends itself strategically—by, say, the conquest of extensive territories or the waging of costly wars—it runs the risk that the potential benefits from external expansion may be outweighed by the great expense of it all—a dilemma which becomes acute if the nation concerned has entered a period of relative economic decline. The history of the rise and later fall of the leading countries in the Great Power system since the advance of western Europe in the sixteenth century—that is, of nations such as Spain, the Netherlands, France, the British Empire, and currently the United States—shows a very significant correlation *over the longer term* between productive and revenue-raising capacities on the one hand and military strength on the other.

The story of "the rise and fall of the Great Powers" which is presented in these chapters may be briefly summarized here. The first chapter sets the scene for all that follows by examining the world around 1500 and by analyzing the strengths and weaknesses of each of the "power centers" of that time—Ming China; the Ottoman Empire and its Muslim offshoot in India, the Mogul Empire; Muscovy; Tokugawa Japan; and the cluster of states in west-central Europe. At the beginning of the sixteenth century it was by no means apparent that the last-named region was destined to rise above all the rest. But however imposing and organized some of those oriental empires appeared by comparison with Europe, they all suffered from the consequences of having a centralized authority which insisted upon a uniformity of belief and practice, not only in official state religion but also in such areas as commercial activities and weapons development. The lack of any such supreme authority in Europe and the warlike rivalries among its various kingdoms and city-states stimulated a constant search for military improvements, which interacted fruitfully with the newer technological and commercial advances that were also being thrown up in this competitive, entrepreneurial environment. Possessing fewer obstacles to change, European societies entered into a constantly upward spiral of economic growth and enhanced military effectiveness which, over time, was to carry them ahead of all other regions of the globe.

While this dynamic of technological change and military competitiveness drove Europe forward in its usual jostling, pluralistic way, there still remained the possibility that one of the contending states might acquire sufficient resources to surpass the others, and then to dominate the continent. For about 150 years after 1500, a dynastic-religious bloc under the Spanish and Austrian Habsburgs seemed to threaten to do just that, and the efforts of the other major European states to check this "Habsburg bid for mastery" occupy the whole of Chapter 2. As is done throughout this book, the strengths and weaknesses of each of the leading Powers are analyzed *relatively,* and in the light of the broader economic and technological changes affecting western society as a whole, in order that the reader can understand better the outcome of the many wars of this period. The chief theme of this chapter is that despite the great resources possessed by the Habsburg monarchs, they steadily overextended themselves in the course of repeated conflicts and became militarily top-heavy for their weakening economic base. If the other European Great Powers also suffered immensely in these prolonged wars, they managed—though narrowly—to maintain the balance between their material resources and their military power better than their Habsburg enemies.

The Great Power struggles which took place between 1660 and 1815, and are covered in Chapter 3, cannot be so easily summarized as a contest between one large bloc and its many rivals. It was in this complicated period that while certain former Great Powers like Spain and the Netherlands were falling into the second rank, there steadily emerged five major states (France, Britain, Russia, Austria, and Prussia) which came to dominate the diplomacy and warfare of eighteenth-century Europe, and to engage in a series of lengthy coalition wars punctuated by swiftly changing alliances. This was an age in which France, first under Louis XIV and then later under Napoleon, came closer to controlling Europe than at any time before or since; but its endeavors were always held in check, in the last resort at least, by a combination of the other Great Powers. Since the cost of standing armies and national fleets had become horrendously great by the early eighteenth century, a country which could create an advanced system of banking and credit (as Britain did) enjoyed many advantages over financially backward rivals. But the factor of geographical position was also of great importance in deciding the fate of the Powers in their many, and frequently changing, contests—which helps to explain why the two "flank" nations of Russia and Britain had become much more important by 1815. Both retained the capacity to intervene in the struggles of west-central Europe while being geographically sheltered from them; and both expanded into the *extra*-European world as the eighteenth century unfolded, even as they were ensuring that the continental balance of power was upheld. Finally, by the later decades of the century, the Industrial Revolution was under way in Britain, which was to give that state an enhanced capacity both to colonize overseas and to frustrate the Napoleonic bid for European mastery.

For an entire century after 1815, by contrast, there was a remarkable absence of lengthy coalition wars. A strategic equilibrium existed, supported by all of the leading Powers in the Concert of Europe, so that no single nation was either able or willing to make a bid for dominance. The prime concerns of government in these post-1815 decades were with domestic instability and (in the case of Russia and the United States) with further expansion across their continental landmasses. This relatively stable international scene allowed the British Empire to rise to its zenith as a global power, in naval and colonial and commercial terms, and also interacted favorably with its virtual monopoly of steam-driven industrial production. By the second half of the nineteenth century, however, industrialization was spreading to certain other regions, and was beginning to tilt the international power balances away from the older leading nations and toward those countries with both the resources and organization to exploit the newer means of production and technology. Already, the few major conflicts of this era—the Crimean War to some degree but more especially the American Civil War and the Franco-Prussian War—were bringing defeat upon those societies which failed to modernize their military systems, and which lacked the broad-based industrial infrastructure to support the vast armies and much more expensive and complicated weaponry now transforming the nature of war.

As the twentieth century approached, therefore, the pace of technological change and uneven growth rates made the international system much more unstable and complex than it had been fifty years earlier. This was manifested in the frantic post-1880 jostling by the Great Powers for additional colonial territories in Africa, Asia, and the Pacific, partly for gain, partly out of a fear of being eclipsed. It also manifested itself in the increasing number of arms races, both on land and at sea, and in the creation of fixed military alliances, even in peacetime, as the various governments sought out partners for a possible future war. Behind the frequent colonial quarrels and international crises of the pre-1914 period, however, the decade-by-decade indices of economic power were pointing to even more fundamental shifts in the global balances—indeed, to the eclipse of what had been, for over three centuries, essentially a *Eurocentric* world system. Despite their best efforts, traditional European Great Powers like France and Austria-Hungary, and a recently united one like Italy, were falling out of the race. By contrast, the enormous, continent-wide states of the United States and Russia were moving to the forefront, and this despite the inefficiencies of the czarist state. Among the western European nations only Germany, possibly, had the muscle to force its way into the select league of the future world Powers. Japan, on the other hand, was intent upon being dominant in East Asia, but not farther afield. Inevitably, then, all these changes posed considerable, and ultimately insuperable, problems for a British Empire which now found it much more difficult to defend its global interests than it had a half-century earlier.

Although the major development of the fifty years after 1900 can thus be seen as the coming of a bipolar world, with its consequent crisis for the "middle" Powers (as referred in the titles of Chapters 5 and 6), this metamorphosis of the entire system was by no means a smooth one. On the contrary, the grinding, bloody mass battles of the First World War, by placing a premium upon industrial organization and national efficiency, gave imperial Germany certain advantages over the swiftly modernizing but still backward czarist Russia. Within a few months of Germany's victory on the eastern front, however, it found itself facing defeat in the west, while its allies were similarly collapsing in the Italian, Balkan, and Near Eastern theaters of the war. Because of the late addition of American military and especially economic aid, the western alliance finally had the resources to prevail over its rival coalition. But it had been an exhausting struggle for all the original belligerents. Austria-Hungary was gone, Russia in revolution, Germany defeated; yet France, Italy, and even Britain itself had also suffered heavily in their victory. The only exceptions were Japan, which further augmented its position in the Pacific; and, of course, the United States, which by 1918 was indisputably the strongest Power in the world.

The swift post-1919 American withdrawal from foreign engagements, and the parallel Russian isolationism under the Bolshevik regime, left an international system which was more out of joint with the fundamental economic realities than perhaps at any time in the five centuries covered in this book. Britain and France, although weakened, were still at the center of the diplomatic stage, but by the 1930s their position was being challenged by the militarized, revisionist states of Italy, Japan, and Germany—the last intent upon a much more deliberate bid for European hegemony than even in 1914. In the background, however, the United States remained by far the mightiest manufacturing nation in the world, and Stalin's Russia was quickly

transforming itself into an industrial superpower. Consequently, the
dilemma for the *revisionist* "middle" Powers was that they had to
expand soon if they were not to be overshadowed by the two continental giants. The dilemma for the status quo middle Powers was that in
fighting off the German and Japanese challenges, they would most
likely weaken themselves as well. The Second World War, for all its
ups and downs, essentially confirmed those apprehensions of decline.
Despite spectacular early victories, the Axis nations could not in the
end succeed against an imbalance of productive resources which was
far greater than that of the 1914–1918 war. What they did achieve was
the eclipse of France and the irretrievable weakening of Britain—
before they themselves were overwhelmed by superior force. By 1943,
the bipolar world forecast decades earlier had finally arrived, and the
military balance had once again caught up with the global distribution
of economic resources.

The last two chapters of this book examine the years in which a
bipolar world did indeed seem to exist, economically, militarily, and
ideologically—and was reflected at the political level by the many
crises of the Cold War. The position of the United States and the USSR
as Powers in a class of their own also appeared to be reinforced by the
arrival of nuclear weapons and long-distance delivery systems, which
suggested that the strategic as well as the diplomatic landscape was
now entirely different from that of 1900, let alone 1800.

And yet the process of rise and fall among the Great Powers—of
differentials in growth rates and technological change, leading to shifts
in the global economic balances, which in turn gradually impinge
upon the political and military balances—had not ceased. Militarily,
the United States and the USSR stayed in the forefront as the 1960s
gave way to the 1970s and 1980s. Indeed, because they both interpreted
international problems in bipolar, and often Manichean, terms, their
rivalry has driven them into an ever-escalating arms race which no
other Powers feel capable of matching. Over the same few decades,
however, the global productive balances have been altering faster than
ever before. The Third World's share of total manufacturing output
and GNP, depressed to an all-time low in the decade after 1945, has
steadily expanded since that time. Europe has recovered from its wartime batterings and, in the form of the European Economic Community, has become the world's largest trading unit. The People's
Republic of China is leaping forward at an impressive rate. Japan's
postwar economic growth has been so phenomenal that, according to
some measures, it recently overtook Russia in total GNP. By contrast,
both the American and Russian growth rates have become more sluggish, and their shares of global production and wealth have shrunk
dramatically since the 1960s. Leaving aside all the smaller nations,

therefore, it is plain that there already exists a *multi*polar world once more, if one measures the economic indices alone. Given this book's concern with the interaction between strategy and economics, it seemed appropriate to offer a final (if necessarily speculative) chapter to explore the present disjuncture between the military balances and the productive balances among the Great Powers; and to point to the problems and opportunities facing today's five large politico-economic "power centers"—China, Japan, the EEC, the Soviet Union, and the United States itself—as they grapple with the age-old task of relating national means to national ends. The history of the rise and fall of the Great Powers has in no way come to a full stop.

Since the scope of this book is so large, it is clear that it will be read by different people for different purposes. Some readers will find here what they had hoped for: a broad and yet reasonably detailed survey of Great Power politics over the past five centuries, of the way in which the relative position of each of the leading states has been affected by economic and technological change, and of the constant interaction between strategy and economics, both in periods of peace and in the tests of war. By definition, it does not deal with *small* Powers, nor (usually) with small, bilateral wars. By definition also, the book is heavily Eurocentric, especially in its middle chapters. But that is only natural with such a topic.

To other readers, perhaps especially those political scientists who are now so interested in drawing general rules about "world systems" or the recurrent pattern of wars, this study may offer less than what they desire. To avoid misunderstanding, it ought to be made clear at this point that the book is not dealing with, for example, the theory that major (or "systemic") wars can be related to Kondratieff cycles of economic upturn and downturn. In addition, it is not centrally concerned with general theories about the *causes* of war, and whether they are likely to be brought about by "rising" or "falling" Great Powers. It is also not a book about theories of empire, and about how imperial control is effected (as is dealt with in Michael Doyle's recent book *Empires*), or whether empires contribute to national strength. Finally, it does not propose any general theory about which sorts of society and social/governmental organizations are the most efficient in extracting resources in time of war.

On the other hand, there obviously is a wealth of material in this book for those scholars who wish to make such generalizations (and one of the reasons why there is such an extensive array of notes is to indicate more detailed sources for those readers interested in, say, the financing of wars). But the problem which historians—as opposed to political scientists—have in grappling with general theories is that the evidence of the past is almost always too varied to allow for "hard" scientific conclusions. Thus, while it is true that some wars (e.g., 1939) can be linked to decision-makers' fears about shifts taking place in the overall power balances, that would not be so useful in explaining the struggles which began in 1776 (American Revolutionary War) or 1792 (French Revolutionary) or 1854 (Crimean War). In the same way, while one could point to Austria-Hungary in 1914 as a good example of a "falling" Great Power helping to trigger off a major war, that still leaves the theorist to deal with the equally critical roles played then by those "rising" Great Powers Germany and Russia. Similarly, any general theory about whether empires pay, or whether imperial control is affected by a measurable "power-distance" ratio, is likely—from the conflicting evidence available—to produce the banal answer sometimes yes, sometimes no.

Nevertheless, if one sets aside *a priori* theories and simply looks at the historical record of "the rise and fall of the Great Powers" over the past five hundred years, it is clear that some generally valid conclusions can be drawn—while admitting all the time that there may be individual exceptions. For example, there is detectable a causal relationship between the shifts which have occurred over time in the general economic and productive balances and the position occupied by individual Powers in the international system. The move in trade flows from the Mediterranean to the Atlantic and northwestern Europe from the sixteenth century onward, or the redistribution in the shares of world manufacturing output away from western Europe in the decades after 1890, are good examples here. In both cases, the economic shifts heralded the rise of new Great Powers which would one day have a decisive impact upon the military/territorial order. This is why the move in the global productive balances toward the "Pacific rim" which has taken place over the past few decades cannot be of interest merely to economists alone.

Similarly, the historical record suggests that there is a very clear connection *in the long run* between an individual Great Power's economic rise and fall and its growth and decline as an important military power (or world empire). This, too, is hardly surprising, since it flows from two related facts. The first is that economic resources are necessary to support a large-scale military establishment. The second is that, so far as the international system is concerned, both wealth and power are always *relative* and should be seen as such. Three hundred years ago, the German mercantilist writer von Hornigk observed that

> whether a nation be today mighty and rich or not depends not on
> the abundance or security of its power and riches, but principally
> on whether its neighbors possess more or less of it.

In the chapters which follow, this observation will be borne out time and again. The Netherlands in the mid-eighteenth century was richer in *absolute* terms than a hundred years earlier, but by that stage was much less of a Great Power because neighbors like France and Britain had "more . . . of it" (that is, more power and riches). The France of 1914 was, absolutely, more powerful than that of 1850—but this was little consolation when France was being eclipsed by a much stronger Germany. Britain today has far greater wealth, and its armed forces possess far more powerful weapons, than in its mid-Victorian prime; that avails it little when its share of world product has shrunk from about 25 percent to about 3 percent. If a nation has "more . . . of it," things are fine; if "less of it," there are problems.

This does not mean, however, that a nation's relative economic and military power will rise and fall *in parallel.* Most of the historical examples covered here suggest that there is a noticeable "lag time" between the trajectory of a state's relative economic strength and the trajectory of its military/territorial influence. Once again, the reason for this is not difficult to grasp. An economically expanding Power— Britain in the 1860s, the United States in the 1890s, Japan today—may well prefer to become rich rather than to spend heavily on armaments. A half-century later, priorities may well have altered. The earlier economic expansion has brought with it overseas obligations (dependence upon foreign markets and raw materials, military alliances, perhaps bases and colonies). Other, rival Powers are now economically expanding at a faster rate, and wish in their turn to extend their influence abroad. The world has become a more competitive place, and market shares are being eroded. Pessimistic observers talk of decline; patriotic statesmen call for "renewal."

In these more troubled circumstances, the Great Power is likely to find itself spending much *more* on defense than it did two generations earlier, and yet still discover that the world is a less secure environment—simply because other Powers have grown faster, and are becoming stronger. Imperial Spain spent much more on its army in the troubled 1630s and 1640s than it did in the 1580s, when the Castilian economy was healthier. Edwardian Britain's defense expenditures were far greater in 1910 than they were at, say, the time of Palmerston's death in 1865, when the British economy was relatively at its peak; but which Britons by the later date felt more secure? The same problem, it will be argued below, appears to be facing both the United States and the USSR today. Great Powers in relative decline instinctively respond by spending more on "security," and thereby divert potential resources from "investment" and compound their long-term dilemma.

Another general conclusion which can be drawn from the five-hundred-year record presented here is that there is a very strong correlation between the eventual outcome of the *major coalition wars* for

European or global mastery, and the amount of productive resources mobilized by each side. This was true of the struggles waged against the Spanish-Austrian Habsburgs; of the great eighteenth-century contests like the War of Spanish Succession, the Seven Years War, and the Napoleonic War; and of the two world wars of this century. A lengthy, grinding war eventually turns into a test of the relative capacities of each coalition. Whether one side has "more . . . of it" or "less of it" becomes increasingly significant as the struggle lengthens.

One can make these generalizations, however, without falling into the trap of crude economic determinism. Despite this book's abiding interest in tracing the "larger tendencies" in world affairs over the past five centuries, it is *not* arguing that economics determines every event, or is the sole reason for the success and failure of each nation. There simply is too much evidence pointing to other things: geography, military organization, national morale, the alliance system, and many other factors can all affect the relative power of the members of the states system. In the eighteenth century, for example, the United Provinces were the richest parts of Europe, and Russia the poorest—yet the Dutch fell, and the Russians rose. Individual folly (like Hitler's) and extremely high battlefield competence (whether of the Spanish regiments in the sixteenth century or of the German infantry in this century) also go a long way to explain individual victories and defeats. What does seem incontestable, however, is that in a long-drawn-out Great Power (and usually coalition) war, victory has repeatedly gone to the side with the more flourishing productive base—or, as the Spanish captains used to say, to him who has the last escudo. Much of what follows will confirm that cynical but essentially correct judgment. And it is precisely because the power position of the leading nations has closely paralleled their relative economic position over the past five centuries that it seems worthwhile asking what the implications of today's economic and technological trends might be for the current balance of power. This does not deny that men make their own history, but they do make it within a historical circumstance which can restrict (as well as open up) possibilities.

An early model for the present book was the 1833 essay of the famous Prussian historian Leopold von Ranke upon *die grossen Mächte* ("the great powers"), in which he surveyed the ups and downs of the international power balances since the decline of Spain, and tried to show why certain countries had risen to prominence and then fallen away. Ranke concluded his essay with an analysis of his contemporary world, and what was happening in it following the defeat of the French bid for supremacy in the Napoleonic War. In examining the "prospects" of each of the Great Powers, he, too, was tempted from the historian's profession into the uncertain world of speculating upon the future.

To write an essay upon "the Great Powers" is one thing; to tell the story in book form is quite another. My original intention was to produce a brief, "essayistic" book, presuming that the readers knew (however vaguely) the background details about the changing growth rates, or the particular geostrategical problems facing this or that Great Power. As I began sending out the early chapters of this book for comments, or giving trial-run talks about some of its themes, it became increasingly clear to me that that was a false presumption: what most readers and listeners wanted was *more* detail, *more* coverage of the background, simply because there was no study available which told the story of the shifts that occurred in the economic and strategical power balances. Precisely because neither economic historians nor military historians had entered this field, the story itself had simply suffered from neglect. If the abundant detail in both the text and notes which follow has any justification, it is to fill that critical gap in the history of the rise and fall of the Great Powers.

STRATEGY &
ECONOMICS
IN THE
PREINDUSTRIAL
WORLD

1
The Rise of
the Western World

In the year 1500, the date chosen by numerous scholars to mark the divide between modern and premodern times,[1] it was by no means obvious to the inhabitants of Europe that their continent was poised to dominate much of the rest of the earth. The knowledge which contemporaries possessed about the great civilizations of the Orient was fragmentary and all too often erroneous, based as it was upon travelers' tales which had lost nothing in their retelling. Nevertheless, the widely held image of extensive eastern empires possessing fabulous wealth and vast armies was a reasonably accurate one, and on first acquaintance those societies must have seemed far more favorably endowed than the peoples and states of western Europe. Indeed, placed alongside these other great centers of cultural and economic activity, Europe's relative weaknesses *were* more apparent than its strengths. It was, for a start, neither the most fertile nor the most populous area in the world; India and China took pride of place in each respect. Geopolitically, the "continent" of Europe was an awkward shape, bounded by ice and water to the north and west, being open to frequent landward invasion from the east, and vulnerable to strategic circumvention in the south. In 1500, and for a long time before and after that, these were not abstract considerations. It was only eight years earlier that Granada, the last Muslim region of Spain, had succumbed to the armies of Ferdinand and Isabella; but that signified the end of a regional campaign, not of the far larger struggle between Christendom and the forces of the Prophet. Over much of the western world there still hung the shock of the fall of Constantinople in 1453, an event which seemed the more pregnant because it by no means marked the limits of the Ottoman Turks' advance. By the end of the century they had taken Greece and the Ionian Islands, Bosnia, Albania, and much of the rest of the Balkans; and worse was to come in the 1520s when their formidable janissary armies pressed toward Budapest and Vienna. In the south, where Ottoman galleys raided Italian ports, the

3

popes were coming to fear that Rome's fate would soon match that of Constantinople.[2]

Whereas these threats seemed part of a coherent grand strategy directed by Sultan Mehmet II and his successors, the response of the Europeans was disjointed and sporadic. Unlike the Ottoman and Chinese empires, unlike the rule which the Moguls were soon to establish in India, there never was a united Europe in which all parts acknowledged one secular or religious leader. Instead, Europe was a hodgepodge of petty kingdoms and principalities, marcher lordships and city-states. Some more powerful monarchies were arising in the west, notably Spain, France, and England, but none was to be free of internal tensions and all regarded the others as rivals, rather than allies in the struggle against Islam.

Nor could it be said that Europe had pronounced advantages in the realms of culture, mathematics, engineering, or navigational and other technologies when compared with the great civilizations of Asia. A considerable part of the European cultural and scientific heritage was, in any case, "borrowed" from Islam, just as Muslim societies had borrowed for centuries from China through the media of mutual trade, conquest, and settlement. In retrospect, one can see that Europe was accelerating both commercially and technologically by the late fifteenth century; but perhaps the fairest general comment would be that each of the great centers of world civilization about that time was at a roughly similar stage of development, some more advanced in one area, but less so in others. Technologically and, therefore, militarily, the Ottoman Empire, China under the Ming dynasty, a little later northern India under the Moguls, and the European states system with its Muscovite offshoot were all far superior to the scattered societies of Africa, America, and Oceania. While this does imply that Europe in 1500 was one of the most important cultural power centers, it was not at all obvious that it would one day emerge at the very top. Before investigating the causes of its rise, therefore, it is necessary to examine the strengths and the weaknesses of the other contenders.

Ming China

Of all the civilizations of premodern times, none appeared more advanced, none felt more superior, than that of China.[3] Its considerable population, 100–130 million compared with Europe's 50–55 million in the fifteenth century; its remarkable culture; its exceedingly fertile and irrigated plains, linked by a splendid canal system since the eleventh century; and its unified, hierarchic administration run by a well-educated Confucian bureaucracy had given a coherence and sophistication to Chinese society which was the envy of foreign visi-

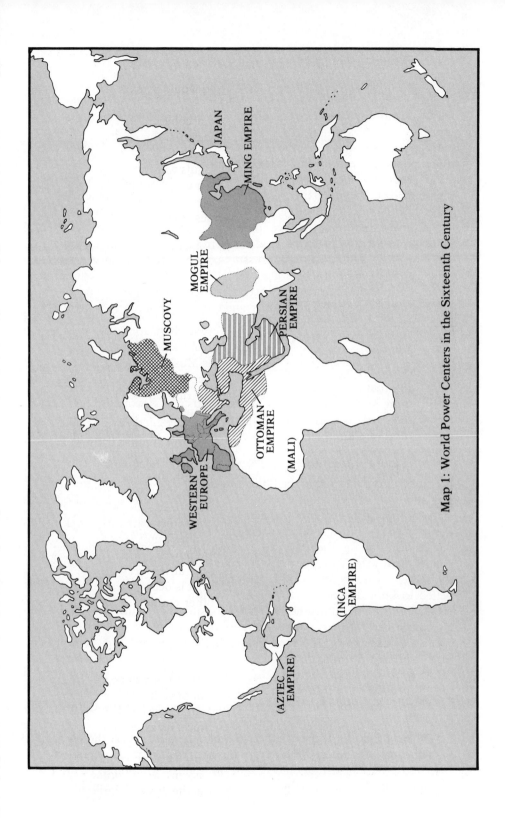

Map 1: World Power Centers in the Sixteenth Century

tors. True, that civilization had been subjected to severe disruption from the Mongol hordes, and to domination after the invasions of Kublai Khan. But China had a habit of changing its conquerors much more than it was changed by them, and when the Ming dynasty emerged in 1368 to reunite the empire and finally defeat the Mongols, much of the old order and learning remained.

To readers brought up to respect "western" science, the most striking feature of Chinese civilization must be its technological precocity. Huge libraries existed from early on. Printing by movable type had already appeared in eleventh-century China, and soon large numbers of books were in existence. Trade and industry, stimulated by the canal-building and population pressures, were equally sophisticated. Chinese cities were much larger than their equivalents in medieval Europe, and Chinese trade routes as extensive. Paper money had earlier expedited the flow of commerce and the growth of markets. By the later decades of the eleventh century there existed an enormous iron industry in north China, producing around 125,000 tons per annum, chiefly for military and governmental use—the army of over a million men was, for example, an enormous market for iron goods. It is worth remarking that this production figure was far larger than the British iron output in the early stages of the Industrial Revolution, seven centuries later! The Chinese were also probably the first to invent true gunpowder; and cannons were used by the Ming to overthrow their Mongol rulers in the late fourteenth century.[4]

Given this evidence of cultural and technological advance, it is also not surprising to learn that the Chinese had turned to overseas exploration and trade. The magnetic compass was another Chinese invention, some of their junks were as large as later Spanish galleons, and commerce with the Indies and the Pacific islands was *potentially* as profitable as that along the caravan routes. Naval warfare had been conducted on the Yangtze many decades earlier—in order to subdue the vessels of Sung China in the 1260s, Kublai Khan had been compelled to build his own great fleet of fighting ships, equipped with projectile-throwing machines—and the coastal grain trade was booming in the early fourteenth century. In 1420, the Ming navy was recorded as possessing 1,350 combat vessels, including 400 large floating fortresses and 250 ships designed for long-range cruising. Such a force eclipsed, but did not include, the many privately managed vessels which were already trading with Korea, Japan, Southeast Asia, and even East Africa by that time, and bringing revenue to the Chinese state, which sought to tax this maritime commerce.

The most famous of the *official* overseas expeditions were the seven long-distance cruises undertaken by the admiral Cheng Ho between 1405 and 1433. Consisting on occasions of hundreds of ships and tens of thousands of men, these fleets visited ports from Malacca and Cey-

lon to the Red Sea entrances and Zanzibar. Bestowing gifts upon deferential local rulers on the one hand, they compelled the recalcitrant to
acknowledge Peking on the other. One ship returned with giraffes from
East Africa to entertain the Chinese emperor; another with a Ceylonese
chief who had been unwise enough not to acknowledge the supremacy
of the Son of Heaven. (It must be noted, however, that the Chinese
apparently never plundered nor murdered—unlike the Portuguese,
Dutch, and other European invaders of the Indian Ocean.) From what
historians and archaeologists can tell us of the size, power, and seawor-
thiness of Cheng Ho's navy—some of the great treasure ships appear
to have been around 400 feet long and displaced over 1,500 tons—they
might well have been able to sail around Africa and "discover" Portugal several decades before Henry the Navigator's expeditions began
earnestly to push south of Ceuta.[5]

But the Chinese expedition of 1433 was the last of the line, and three
years later an imperial edict banned the construction of seagoing
ships; later still, a specific order forbade the existence of ships with
more than two masts. Naval personnel would henceforth be employed
on smaller vessels on the Grand Canal. Cheng Ho's great warships were
laid up and rotted away. Despite all the opportunities which beckoned
overseas, China had decided to turn its back on the world.

There was, to be sure, a plausible strategical reason for this decision. The northern frontiers of the empire were again under some
pressure from the Mongols, and it may have seemed prudent to concentrate military resources in this more vulnerable area. Under such
circumstances a large navy was an expensive luxury, and in any case,
the attempted Chinese expansion southward into Annam (Vietnam)
was proving fruitless and costly. Yet this quite valid reasoning does not
appear to have been reconsidered when the disadvantages of naval
retrenchment later became clear: within a century or so, the Chinese
coastline and even cities on the Yangtze were being attacked by Japanese pirates, but there was no serious rebuilding of an imperial navy.
Even the repeated appearance of Portuguese vessels off the China coast
did not force a reassessment.* Defense on land was all that was required, the mandarins reasoned, for had not all maritime trade by
Chinese subjects been forbidden in any case?

Apart from the costs and other disincentives involved, therefore, a
key element in China's retreat was the sheer conservatism of the Confucian bureaucracy[6]—a conservatism heightened in the Ming period
by resentment at the changes earlier forced upon them by the Mongols.
In this "Restoration" atmosphere, the all-important officialdom was
concerned to preserve and recapture the past, not to create a brighter

---

*For a brief while, in the 1590s, a somewhat revived Chinese coastal fleet helped the
Koreans to resist two Japanese invasion attempts; but even this rump of the Ming navy declined
thereafter.

future based upon overseas expansion and commerce. According to the Confucian code, warfare itself was a deplorable activity and armed forces were made necessary only by the fear of barbarian attacks or internal revolts. The mandarins' dislike of the army (and the navy) was accompanied by a suspicion of the trader. The accumulation of private capital, the practice of buying cheap and selling dear, the ostentation of the *nouveau riche* merchant, all offended the elite, scholarly bureaucrats—almost as much as they aroused the resentments of the toiling masses. While not wishing to bring the entire market economy to a halt, the mandarins often intervened against individual merchants by confiscating their property or banning their business. *Foreign* trade by Chinese subjects must have seemed even more dubious to mandarin eyes, simply because it was less under their control.

This dislike of commerce and private capital does not conflict with the enormous technological achievements mentioned above. The Ming rebuilding of the Great Wall of China and the development of the canal system, the ironworks, and the imperial navy were for *state* purposes, because the bureaucracy had advised the emperor that they were necessary. But just as these enterprises could be started, so also could they be neglected. The canals were permitted to decay, the army was periodically starved of new equipment, the astronomical clocks (built c. 1090) were disregarded, the ironworks gradually fell into desuetude. These were not the only disincentives to economic growth. Printing was restricted to scholarly works and not employed for the widespread dissemination of practical knowledge, much less for social criticism. The use of paper currency was discontinued. Chinese cities were never allowed the autonomy of those in the West; there were no Chinese burghers, with all that that term implied; when the location of the emperor's court was altered, the capital city had to move as well. Yet without official encouragement, merchants and other entrepreneurs could not thrive; and even those who did acquire wealth tended to spend it on land and education, rather than investing in protoindustrial development. Similarly, the banning of overseas trade and fishing took away another potential stimulus to sustained economic expansion; such foreign trade as did occur with the Portuguese and Dutch in the following centuries was in luxury goods and (although there were doubtless many evasions) controlled by officials.

In consequence, Ming China was a much less vigorous and enterprising land than it had been under the Sung dynasty four centuries earlier. There were improved agricultural techniques in the Ming period, to be sure, but after a while even this more intensive farming and the use of marginal lands found it harder to keep pace with the burgeoning population; and the latter was only to be checked by those Malthusian instruments of plague, floods, and war, all of which were very difficult to handle. Even the replacement of the Mings by the more vigorous Manchus after 1644 could not halt the steady relative decline.

One final detail can summarize this tale. In 1736—just as Abraham Darby's ironworks at Coalbrookdale were beginning to boom—the blast furnaces and coke ovens of Honan and Hopei were abandoned entirely. They had been great before the Conqueror had landed at Hastings. Now they would not resume production until the twentieth century.

The Muslim World

Even the first of the European sailors to visit China in the early sixteenth century, although impressed by its size, population, and riches, might have observed that this was a country which had turned in on itself. That remark certainly could not then have been made of the Ottoman Empire, which was then in the middle stages of its expansion and, being nearer home, was correspondingly much more threatening to Christendom. Viewed from the larger historical and geographical perspective, in fact, it would be fair to claim that it was the Muslim states which formed the most rapidly expanding forces in world affairs during the sixteenth century. Not only were the Ottoman Turks pushing westward, but the Safavid dynasty in Persia was also enjoying a resurgence of power, prosperity, and high culture, especially in the reigns of Ismail I (1500–1524) and Abbas I (1587–1629); a chain of strong Muslim khanates still controlled the ancient Silk Road via Kashgar and Turfan to China, not unlike the chain of West African Islamic states such as Bornu, Sokoto, and Timbuktu; the Hindu Empire in Java was overthrown by Muslim forces early in the sixteenth century; and the king of Kabul, Babur, entering India by the conqueror's route from the northwest, established the Mogul Empire in 1526. Although this hold on India was shaky at first, it was successfully consolidated by Babur's grandson Akbar (1556–1605), who carved out a northern Indian empire stretching from Baluchistan in the west to Bengal in the east. Throughout the seventeenth century, Akbar's successors pushed farther south against the Hindu Marathas, just at the same time as the Dutch, British, and French were entering the Indian peninsula from the sea, and of course in a much less substantial form. To these secular signs of Muslim growth one must add the vast increase in numbers of the faithful in Africa and the Indies, against which the proselytization by Christian missions paled in comparison.

But the greatest Muslim challenge to early modern Europe lay, of course, with the Ottoman Turks, or, rather, with their formidable army and the finest siege train of the age. Already by the beginning of the sixteenth century their domains stretched from the Crimea (where they had overrun Genoese trading posts) and the Aegean (where they were dismantling the Venetian Empire) to the Levant. By 1516, Ottoman forces had seized Damascus, and in the following year they entered Egypt, shattering the Mamluk forces by the use of Turkish cannon. Having thus closed the spice route from the Indies, they moved up the Nile and pushed through the Red Sea to the Indian Ocean, countering the Portuguese incursions there. If this perturbed Iberian sailors, it was nothing to the fright which the Turkish armies were giving the princes and peoples of eastern and southern Europe. Already the Turks held Bulgaria and Serbia, and were the predominant influence in Wallachia and all around the Black Sea; but, following the southern drive against Egypt and Arabia, the pressure against Europe was resumed under Suleiman (1520–1566). Hungary, the great eastern bastion of Christendom in these years, could no longer hold off the superior Turkish armies and was overrun following the battle of Mohacs in 1526—the same year, coincidentally, as Babur gained the victory at Panipat by which the Mughal Empire was established. Would all of Europe soon go the way of northern India? By 1529, with the Turks besieging Vienna, this must have appeared a distinct possibility to some. In actual fact, the line then stabilized in northern Hungary and the Holy Roman Empire was preserved; but thereafter the Turks presented a constant danger and exerted a military pressure which could never be fully ignored. Even as late as 1683, they were again besieging Vienna.[7]

Almost as alarming, in many ways, was the expansion of Ottoman naval power. Like Kublai Khan in China, the Turks had developed a navy only in order to reduce a seagirt enemy fortress—in this case, Constantinople, which Sultan Mehmet blockaded with large galleys and hundreds of smaller craft to assist the assault of 1453. Thereafter, formidable galley fleets were used in operations across the Black Sea, in the southward push toward Syria and Egypt, and in a whole series of clashes with Venice for control of the Aegean islands, Rhodes, Crete, and Cyprus. For some decades of the early sixteenth century Ottoman sea power was kept at arm's length by Venetian, Genoese, and Habsburg fleets; but by midcentury, Muslim naval forces were active all the way along the North African coast, were raiding ports in Italy, Spain, and the Balearics, and finally managed to take Cyprus in 1570–1571, before being checked at the battle of Lepanto.[8]

The Ottoman Empire was, of course, much more than a military machine. A conquering elite (like the Manchus in China), the Ottomans had established a unity of *official* faith, culture, and language over an area greater than the Roman Empire, and over vast numbers of subject peoples. For centuries before 1500 the world of Islam had been culturally and technologically ahead of Europe. Its cities were large, well-lit, and drained, and some of them possessed universities and libraries and stunningly beautiful mosques. In mathematics, cartography, medicine, and many other aspects of science and industry—in mills, guncasting, lighthouses, horsebreeding—the Muslims had enjoyed a lead. The Ottoman system of recruiting future janissaries from Christian youth in the Balkans had produced a dedicated, uniform corps of troops. Tolerance of other races had brought many a talented Greek, Jew, and Gentile into the sultan's service—a Hungarian was Mehmet's chief gun-caster in the Siege of Constantinople. Under a successful leader like Suleiman I, a strong bureaucracy supervised fourteen million subjects—this at a time when Spain had five million and England a mere two and a half million inhabitants. Constantinople in its heyday was bigger than any European city, possessing over 500,000 inhabitants in 1600.

Yet the Ottoman Turks, too, were to falter, to turn inward, and to lose the chance of world domination, although this became clear only a century after the strikingly similar Ming decline. To a certain extent it could be argued that this process was the natural consequence of earlier Turkish successes: the Ottoman army, however well administered, might be able to maintain the lengthy frontiers but could hardly expand farther without enormous cost in men and money; and Ottoman imperialism, unlike that of the Spanish, Dutch, and English later, did not bring much in the way of economic benefit. By the second half of the sixteenth century the empire was showing signs of strategical overextension, with a large army stationed in central Europe, an expensive navy operating in the Mediterranean, troops engaged in North Africa, the Aegean, Cyprus, and the Red Sea, and reinforcements needed to hold the Crimea against a rising Russian power. Even in the Near East there was no quiet flank, thanks to a disastrous religious split in the Muslim world which occurred when the Shi'ite branch, based in Iraq and then in Persia, challenged the prevailing Sunni practices and teachings. At times, the situation was not unlike that of the contemporary religious struggles in Germany, and the sultan could maintain his dominance only by crushing Shi'ite dissidents with force. However, across the border the Shi'ite kingdom of Persia under Abbas the Great was quite prepared to ally with European states against the Ottomans, just as France had worked with the "infidel" Turk against the Holy Roman Empire. With this array of adversaries, the Ottoman Empire would have needed remarkable leadership to have maintained its growth; but after 1566 there reigned thirteen incompetent sultans in succession.

External enemies and personal failings do not, however, provide the full explanation. The system as a whole, like that of Ming China, increasingly suffered from some of the defects of being centralized, despotic, and severely orthodox in its attitude toward initiative, dissent, and commerce. An idiot sultan could paralyze the Ottoman Empire in the way that a pope or Holy Roman emperor could never do for all Europe. Without clear directives from above, the arteries of the bureaucracy hardened, preferring conservatism to change, and stifling innovation. The lack of territorial expansion and accompanying booty after 1550, together with the vast rise in prices, caused discontented janissaries to turn to internal plunder. Merchants and entrepreneurs (nearly all of whom were foreigners), who earlier had been encouraged, now found themselves subject to unpredictable taxes and outright seizures of property. Ever higher dues ruined trade and depopulated towns. Perhaps worst affected of all were the peasants, whose lands and stock were preyed upon by the soldiers. As the situation deteriorated, civilian officials also turned to plunder, demanding bribes and confiscating stocks of goods. The costs of war and the loss of Asiatic trade during the struggle with Persia intensified the government's desperate search for new revenues, which in turn gave greater powers to unscrupulous tax farmers.[9]

To a distinct degree, the fierce response to the Shi'ite religious challenge reflected and anticipated a hardening of official attitudes toward all forms of free thought. The printing press was forbidden because it might disseminate dangerous opinions. Economic notions remained primitive: imports of western wares were desired, but exports were forbidden; the guilds were supported in their efforts to check innovation and the rise of "capitalist" producers; religious criticism of traders intensified. Contemptuous of European ideas and practices, the Turks declined to adopt newer methods for containing plagues; consequently, their populations suffered more from severe epidemics. In one truly amazing fit of obscurantism, a force of janissaries destroyed a state observatory in 1580, alleging that it had caused a plague.[10] The armed services had become, indeed, a bastion of conservatism. Despite noting, and occasionally suffering from, the newer weaponry of European forces, the janissaries were slow to modernize themselves. Their bulky cannons were not replaced by the lighter cast-iron guns. After the defeat at Lepanto, they did not build the larger European type of vessels. In the south, the Muslim fleets were simply ordered to remain in the calmer waters of the Red Sea and Persian Gulf, thus obviating the need to construct oceangoing vessels on the Portuguese model. Perhaps technical reasons help to explain these decisions, but cultural and technological conservatism also played a role (by contrast, the irregular Barbary corsairs swiftly adopted the frigate type of warship).

The above remarks about conservatism could be made with equal or even greater force about the Mogul Empire. Despite the sheer size of the kingdom at its height and the military genius of some of its emperors, despite the brilliance of its courts and the craftsmanship of its luxury products, despite even a sophisticated banking and credit network, the system was weak at the core. A conquering Muslim elite lay on top of a vast mass of poverty-stricken peasants chiefly adhering to Hinduism. In the towns themselves there were very considerable numbers of merchants, bustling markets, and an attitude toward manufacture, trade, and credit among Hindu business families which would make them excellent examples of Weber's Protestant ethic. As against this picture of an entrepreneurial society just ready for economic "takeoff" before it became a victim of British imperialism, there are the gloomier portrayals of the many indigenous retarding factors in Indian life. The sheer rigidity of Hindu religious taboos militated against modernization: rodents and insects could not be killed, so vast amounts of foodstuffs were lost; social mores about handling refuse and excreta led to permanently insanitary conditions, a breeding ground for bubonic plagues; the caste system throttled initiative, instilled ritual, and restricted the market; and the influence wielded over Indian local rulers by the Brahman priests meant that this obscurantism was effective at the highest level. Here were social checks of the deepest sort to any attempts at radical change. Small wonder that later many Britons, having first plundered and then tried to govern India in accordance with Utilitarian principles, finally left with the feeling that the country was still a mystery to them.[11]

But the Mogul rule could scarcely be compared with administration by the Indian Civil Service. The brilliant courts were centers of conspicuous consumption on a scale which the Sun King at Versailles might have thought excessive. Thousands of servants and hangers-on, extravagant clothes and jewels and harems and menageries, vast arrays of bodyguards, could be paid for only by the creation of a systematic plunder machine. Tax collectors, required to provide fixed sums for their masters, preyed mercilessly upon peasant and merchant alike; whatever the state of the harvest or trade, the money had to come in. There being no constitutional or other checks—apart from rebellion—upon such depredations, it was not surprising that taxation was known as "eating." For this colossal annual tribute, the population received next to nothing. There was little improvement in communications, and no machinery for assistance in the event of famine, flood, and plague—which were, of course, fairly regular occurrences. All this makes the Ming dynasty appear benign, almost progressive, by comparison. Technically, the Mogul Empire was to decline because it became increasingly difficult to maintain itself against the Marathas in the south, the Afghanis in the north, and, finally, the East India Company. In reality, the causes of its decay were much more internal than external.

Two Outsiders—Japan and Russia

By the sixteenth century there were two other states which, although nowhere near the size and population of the Ming, Ottoman, and Mogul empires, were demonstrating signs of political consolidation and economic growth. In the Far East, Japan was taking forward steps just as its large Chinese neighbor was beginning to atrophy. Geography gave a prime strategical asset to the Japanese (as it did to the British), for insularity offered a protection from overland invasion which China did not possess. The gap between the islands of Japan and the Asiatic mainland was by no means a complete one, however, and a great deal of Japanese culture and religion had been adapted from the older civilization. But whereas China was run by a unified bureaucracy, power in Japan lay in the hands of clan-based feudal lordships and the emperor was but a cipher. The centralized rule which had existed in the fourteenth century had been replaced by a constant feuding between the clans—akin, as it were, to the strife among their equivalents in Scotland. This was not the ideal circumstance for traders and merchants, but it did not check a very considerable amount of economic activity. At sea, as on land, entrepreneurs jostled with warlords and military adventurers, each of whom detected profit in the East Asian maritime trade. Japanese pirates scoured the coasts of China and Korea for plunder, while simultaneously other Japanese welcomed the chance to exchange goods with the Portuguese and Dutch visitors from the West. Christian missions and European wares penetrated Japanese society far more easily than they did an aloof, self-contained Ming Empire.[12]

This lively if turbulent scene was soon to be altered by the growing use of imported European armaments. As was happening elsewhere in the world, power gravitated toward those individuals or groups who possessed the resources to commandeer a large musket-bearing army and, most important of all, cannon. In Japan the result was the consolidation of authority under the great warlord Hideyoshi, whose aspirations ultimately led him twice to attempt the conquest of Korea. When these failed, and Hideyoshi died in 1598, civil strife again threatened Japan; but within a few years all power had been consolidated in the hands of Ieyasu and fellow shoguns of the Tokugawa clan. This time the centralized military rule could not be shaken.

In many respects, Tokugawa Japan possessed the characteristics of the "new monarchies" which had arisen in the West during the preceding century. The great difference was the shogunate's abjuration of overseas expansion, indeed of virtually all contact with the outside world. In 1636, construction of oceangoing vessels was stopped and Japanese subjects were forbidden to sail the high seas. Trade with

Europeans was restricted to the permitted Dutch ship calling at De-shima in Nagasaki harbor; the others were tumbled out. Even earlier, virtually all Christians (foreign and native) were ruthlessly murdered at the behest of the shogunate. Clearly, the chief motive behind these drastic measures was the Tokugawa clan's determination to achieve unchallenged control; foreigners and Christians were thus regarded as potentially subversive. But so, too, were the other feudal lords, which is why they were required to spend half the year in the capital; and why, during the six months they were allowed to reside on their estates, their families had to remain at Yedo (Tokyo), virtually hostages.

This imposed uniformity did not, of itself, throttle economic devel-opment—nor, for that matter, did it prevent outstanding artistic achievements. Nationwide peace was good for trade, the towns and overall population were growing, and the increasing use of cash pay-ments made merchants and bankers more important. The latter, how-ever, were never permitted the social and political prominence they gained in Italy, the Netherlands, and Britain, and the Japanese were obviously unable to learn about, and adopt, new technological and industrial developments that were occurring elsewhere. Like the Ming dynasty, the Tokugawa shogunate deliberately chose, with a few excep-tions, to cut itself off from the rest of the world. This may not have retarded economic activities in Japan itself, but it did harm the relative power of the Japanese state. Disdaining to engage in trade, and forbid-den to travel or to display their weapons except on ceremonial occa-sions, the samurai warriors attached to their lords lived a life of ritual and boredom. The entire military system ossified for two centuries, so that when Commodore Perry's famous "black ships" arrived in 1853, there was little that an overawed Japanese government could do except grant the American request for coaling and other facilities.

At the beginning of its period of political consolidation and growth, Russia appeared similar to Japan in certain respects. Geographically far removed from the West—partly on account of poor communica-tions, and partly because periodic clashes with Lithuania, Poland, Swe-den, and the Ottoman Empire interrupted those routes which did exist—the Kingdom of Muscovy was nevertheless deeply influenced by its European inheritance, not least through the Russian Orthodox Church. It was from the West, moreover, that there came the lasting solution to Russia's vulnerability to the horsemen of the Asian plains: muskets and cannon. With these new weapons, Moscow could now establish itself as one of the "gunpowder empires" and thus expand. A westward drive was difficult, given that the Swedes and Poles also possessed such armaments, but colonial expansion against the tribes and khanates to the south and east was made much easier by this military-technological advantage. By 1556, for example, Russian troops had reached the Caspian Sea. This military expansionism was accompanied, and often eclipsed, by the explorers and pioneers who steadily pushed east of the Urals, through Siberia, and had actually reached the Pacific coast by 1638.[13] Despite its hard-won military superiority over Mongol horsemen, there was nothing easy or inevitable about the growth of the Russian Empire. The more peoples that were conquered, the greater was the likelihood of internal dissension and revolt. The nobles at home were often restive, even after the purge of their numbers by Ivan the Terrible. The Tartar khanate of the Crimea remained a powerful foe; its troops sacked Moscow in 1571, and it remained independent until the late eighteenth century. Challenges from the West were even more threatening; the Poles, for example, occupied Moscow between 1608 and 1613.

A further weakness was that despite certain borrowings from the West, Russia remained technologically backward and economically underdeveloped. Extremes of climate and the enormous distances and poor communications partly accounted for this, but so also did severe social defects: the military absolutism of the czars, the monopoly of education in the hands of the Orthodox Church, the venality and unpredictability of the bureaucracy, and the institution of serfdom, which made agriculture feudal and static. Yet despite this relative backwardness, and despite the setbacks, Russia continued to expand, imposing upon its new territories the same military force and autocratic rule which was used to command the obedience of the Muscovites. Enough had been borrowed from Europe to give the regime the armed strength to preserve itself, while all possibility of western social and political "modernization" was firmly resisted; foreigners in Russia, for example, were segregated from the natives in order to prevent subversive influences. Unlike the other despotisms mentioned in this chapter, the empire of the czars would manage to survive and Russia would one day grow to be a world power. Yet in 1500, and even as late as 1650, this was scarcely obvious to many Frenchmen, Dutchmen, and Englishmen, who probably knew as much about the Russian ruler as they did about the legendary Prester John.[14]

The "European Miracle"[15]

Why was it among the scattered and relatively unsophisticated peoples inhabiting the western parts of the Eurasian landmass that there occurred an unstoppable process of economic development and technological innovation which would steadily make it the commercial and military leader in world affairs? This is a question which has exercised scholars and other observers for centuries, and all that the following paragraphs can do is to present a synthesis of the existing knowledge. Yet however crude such a summary must be, it possesses the incidental advantage of exposing the main strands of the argument which permeate this entire work: namely, that there was a *dynamic* involved, driven chiefly by economic and technological advances, although always interacting with other variables such as social structure, geography, and the occasional accident; that to understand the course of world politics, it is necessary to focus attention upon the material and long-term elements rather than the vagaries of personality or the week-by-week shifts of diplomacy and politics; and that power is a relative thing, which can only be described and measured by frequent comparisons between various states and societies.

The one feature of Europe which immediately strikes the eye when looking at a map of the world's "power centers" in the sixteenth century is its political fragmentation (see Maps 1 and 2). This was not an accidental or short-lived state of affairs, such as occurred briefly in China after the collapse of one empire and before its successor dynasty could gather up again the strings of centralized power. Europe had *always* been politically fragmented, despite even the best efforts of the Romans, who had not managed to conquer much farther north of the Rhine and the Danube; and for a thousand years after the fall of Rome, the basic political power unit had been small and localized, in contrast to the steady expansion of the Christian religion and culture. Occasional concentrations of authority, like that of Charlemagne in the West or of Kievan Russia in the East, were but temporary affairs, terminated by a change of ruler, internal rebellion, or external invasions.

For this political diversity Europe had largely to thank its geography. There were no enormous plains over which an empire of horsemen could impose its swift dominion; nor were there broad and fertile river zones like those around the Ganges, Nile, Tigris and Euphrates, Yellow, and Yangtze, providing the food for masses of toiling and easily conquerable peasants. Europe's landscape was much more fractured, with mountain ranges and large forests separating the scattered population centers in the valleys; and its climate altered considerably from north to south and west to east. This had a number of important consequences. For a start, it both made difficult the establishment of unified control, even by a powerful and determined warlord, and minimized the possibility that the continent could be overrun by an external force like the Mongol hordes. Conversely, this variegated landscape encouraged the growth, and the continued existence, of decentralized power, with local kingdoms and marcher lordships and highland clans and lowland town confederations making a political map of Europe drawn at any time after the fall of Rome look like a patchwork quilt. The patterns on that quilt might vary from century to century, but no single color could ever be used to denote a unified empire.[16]

Europe's differentiated climate led to differentiated products, suit-

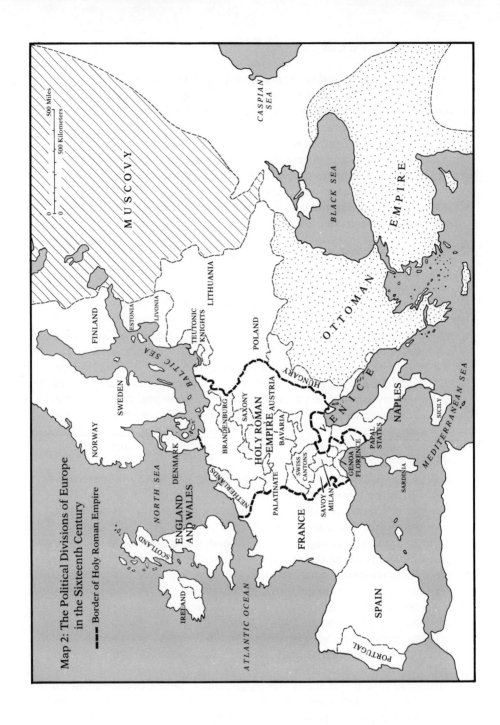

Map 2: The Political Divisions of Europe
in the Sixteenth Century

▬▬▬ Border of Holy Roman Empire

able for exchange; and in time, as market relations developed, they were transported along the rivers or the pathways which cut through the forests between one area of settlement and the next. Probably the most important characteristic of this commerce was that it consisted primarily of *bulk* products—timber, grain, wine, wool, herrings, and so on, catering to the rising population of fifteenth-century Europe, rather than the luxuries carried on the oriental caravans. Here again geography played a crucial role, for water transport of these goods was so much more economical and Europe possessed many navigable rivers. Being surrounded by seas was a further incentive to the vital shipbuilding industry, and by the later Middle Ages a flourishing maritime commerce was being carried out between the Baltic, the North Sea, the Mediterranean, and the Black Sea. This trade was, predictably, interrupted in part by war and affected by local disasters such as crop failures and plagues; but in general it continued to expand, increasing Europe's prosperity and enriching its diet, and leading to the creation of new centers of wealth like the Hansa towns or the Italian cities. Regular long-distance exchanges of wares in turn encouraged the growth of bills of exchange, a credit system, and banking on an international scale. The very existence of mercantile credit, and then of bills of insurance, pointed to a basic *predictability* of economic conditions which private traders had hitherto rarely, if ever, enjoyed anywhere in the world.[17]

In addition, because much of this trade was carried through the rougher waters of the North Sea and Bay of Biscay—and also because long-range fishing became an important source of nutrient and wealth—shipwrights were forced to build tough (if rather slow and inelegant) vessels capable of carrying large loads and finding their motive power in the winds alone. Although over time they developed more sail and masts, and stern rudders, and therefore became more maneuverable, North Sea "cogs" and their successors may not have appeared as impressive as the lighter craft which plied the shores of the eastern Mediterranean and the Indian Ocean; but, as we shall see below, they were going to possess distinct advantages in the long run.[18]

The political and social consequences of this decentralized, largely unsupervised growth of commerce and merchants and ports and markets were of the greatest significance. In the first place, there was no way in which such economic developments could be fully suppressed. This is not to say that the rise of market forces did not disturb many in authority. Feudal lords, suspicious of towns as centers of dissidence and sanctuaries of serfs, often tried to curtail their privileges. As elsewhere, merchants were frequently preyed upon, their goods stolen, their property seized. Papal pronouncements upon usury echo in many ways the Confucian dislike of profit-making middlemen and money-lenders. But the basic fact was that there existed no uniform authority

in Europe which could effectively halt this or that commercial development; no central government whose changes in priorities could cause
the rise and fall of a particular industry; no systematic and universal
plundering of businessmen and entrepreneurs by tax gatherers, which
so retarded the economy of Mogul India. To take one specific and
obvious instance, it was inconceivable in the fractured political circumstances of Reformation Europe that everyone would acknowledge
the pope's 1494 division of the overseas world into Spanish and Portuguese spheres—and even less conceivable that an order banning
overseas trade (akin to those promulgated in Ming China and
Tokugawa Japan) would have had any effect.

The fact was that in Europe there were always some princes and
local lords willing to tolerate merchants and their ways even when
others plundered and expelled them; and, as the record shows, op-
pressed Jewish traders, ruined Flemish textile workers, persecuted
Huguenots, moved on and took their expertise with them. A Rhineland
baron who overtaxed commercial travelers would find that the trade
routes had gone elsewhere, and with it his revenues. A monarch who
repudiated his debts would have immense difficulties raising a loan
when the next war threatened and funds were quickly needed to equip
his armies and fleets. Bankers and arms dealers and artisans were
essential, not peripheral, members of society. Gradually, unevenly,
most of the regimes of Europe entered into a symbiotic relationship
with the market economy, providing for it domestic order and a nonar-
bitrary legal system (even for foreigners), and receiving in taxes a
share of the growing profits from trade. Long before Adam Smith had
coined the exact words, the rulers of certain societies of western
Europe were tacitly recognizing that "little else is requisite to carry a
state to the highest degree of opulence from the lowest barbarism, but
peace, easy taxes, and tolerable administration of justice. . . ."[19] From
time to time the less percipient leaders—like the Spanish administrators of Castile, or an occasional Bourbon king of France—would virtually kill the goose that laid the golden eggs; but the consequent decline
in wealth, and thus in military power, was soon obvious to all but the
most purblind.

Probably the only factor which might have led to a centralization
of authority would have been such a breakthrough in firearms technology by one state that all opponents were crushed or overawed. In the
quickening pace of economic and technical development which occurred in fifteenth-century Europe as the continent's population recovered from the Black Death and the Italian Renaissance blossomed, this
was by no means impossible. It was, as noted above, in this broad
period from 1450 to 1600 that "gunpowder empires" were established
elsewhere. Muscovy, Tokugawa Japan, and Mogul India provide excellent examples of how great states could be fashioned by leaders who

secured the firearms and the cannon with which to compel all rivals to obedience.

Since, furthermore, it was in late-medieval and early modern Europe that new techniques of warfare occurred more frequently than elsewhere, it was not implausible that one such breakthrough could enable a certain nation to dominate its rivals. Already the signs pointed to an increasing concentration of military power.[20] In Italy the use of companies of crossbowmen, protected when necessary by soldiers using pikes, had brought to a close the age of the knight on horseback and his accompanying ill-trained feudal levy; but it was also clear that only the wealthier states like Venice and Milan could pay for the new armies officered by the famous *condottieri.* By around 1500, moreover, the kings of France and England had gained an artillery monopoly at home and were thus able, if the need arose, to crush an overmighty subject even if the latter sheltered behind castle walls. But would not this tendency finally lead to a larger transnational monopoly, stretching across Europe? This must have been a question many asked around 1550, as they observed the vast concentration of lands and armies under the Emperor Charles V.

A fuller discussion of that specific Habsburg attempt, and failure, to gain the mastery of Europe will be presented in the next chapter. But the more general reason why it was impossible to impose unity across the continent can briefly be stated here. Once again, the existence of a *variety* of economic and military centers of power was fundamental. No one Italian city-state could strive to enhance itself without the others intervening to preserve the equilibrium; no "new monarchy" could increase its dominions without stirring rivals to seek compensation. By the time the Reformation was well and truly under way, religious antagonisms were added to the traditional balance-of-power rivalries, thus making the prospects of political centralization even more remote. Yet the real explanation lies a little deeper; after all, the simple existence of competitors, and of bitter feelings between warring groups, was evident in Japan, India, and elsewhere, but that of itself had not prevented eventual unification. Europe was different in that each of the rival forces was able to gain access to the new military techniques, so that no single power ever possessed the decisive edge. The services of the Swiss and other mercenaries, for example, were on offer to anyone who was able to pay for them. There was no single center for the production of crossbows, nor for that of cannon—whether of the earlier bronze guns or of the later, cheaper cast-iron artillery; instead, such armaments were being made close to the ore deposits on the Weald, in central Europe, in Málaga, in Milan, in Liège, and later in Sweden. Similarly, the proliferation of shipbuilding skills in various ports ranging from the Baltic to the Black Sea made it extremely difficult for any one country to monopolize maritime power, which in turn helped to prevent the conquest and elimination of rival centers of armaments production lying across the sea.

To say that Europe's decentralized states system was the great obstacle to centralization is not, then, a tautology. Because there existed a number of competing political entities, *most of which possessed or were able to buy the military means to preserve their independence,* no single one could ever achieve the breakthrough to the mastery of the continent.

While this competitive interaction between the European states seems to explain the absence of a unified "gunpowder empire" there, it does not at first sight provide the reason for Europe's steady rise to global leadership. After all, would not the forces possessed by the new monarchies in 1500 have seemed puny if they had been deployed against the enormous armies of the sultan and the massed troops of the Ming Empire? This was true in the early sixteenth century and, in some respects, even in the seventeenth century; but by the latter period the balance of military strength was tilting rapidly in favor of the West. For the explanation of this shift one must again point to the decentralization of power in Europe. What it did, above all else, was to engender a primitive form of arms race among the city-states and then the larger kingdoms. To some extent, this probably had socioeconomic roots. Once the contending armies in Italy no longer consisted of feudal knights and their retainers but of pikemen, crossbowmen, and (flanking) cavalry paid for by the merchants and supervised by the magistrates of a particular city, it was almost inevitable that the latter would demand value for money—despite all the best maneuvers of *condottieri* not to make themselves redundant; the cities would require, in other words, the sort of arms and tactics which might produce a swift victory, so that the expenses of war could then be reduced. Similarly, once the French monarchs of the late fifteenth century had a "national" army under their direct control and pay, they were anxious to see this force produce decisive results.[21]

By the same token, this free-market system not only forced the numerous *condottieri* to compete for contracts but also encouraged artisans and inventors to improve their wares, so as to obtain new orders. While this armaments spiral could already be seen in the manufacture of crossbows and armor plate in the early fifteenth century, the principle spread to experimentation with gunpowder weapons in the following fifty years. It is important to recall here that when cannon were first employed, there was little difference between the West and Asia in their design and effectiveness. Gigantic wrought-iron tubes that fired a stone ball and made an immense noise obviously looked impressive and at times had results; it was that type which was used by the Turks to bombard the walls of Constantinople in 1453. Yet it seems to have been only in Europe that the impetus existed for constant improvements: in the gunpowder grains, in casting much smaller (yet equally powerful) cannon from bronze and tin alloys, in the shape and texture of the barrel and the missile, in the gun mountings and carriages. All of this enhanced to an enormous degree the power and the mobility of artillery and gave the owner of such weapons the means to reduce the strongest fortresses—as the Italian city-states found to their alarm when a French army equipped with formidable bronze guns invaded Italy in 1494. It was scarcely surprising, therefore, that inventors and men of letters were being urged to design some counter to these cannon (and scarcely less surprising that Leonardo's notebooks for this time contain sketches for a machine gun, a primitive tank, and a steam-powered cannon).[22]

This is not to say that other civilizations did not improve their armaments from the early, crude designs; some of them did, usually by copying from European models or persuading European visitors (like the Jesuits in China) to lend their expertise. But because the Ming government had a monopoly of cannon, and the thrusting leaders of Russia, Japan, and Mogul India soon acquired a monopoly, there was much less incentive to improve such weapons once their authority had been established. Turning in upon themselves, the Chinese and the Japanese neglected to develop armaments production. Clinging to their traditional fighting ways, the janissaries of Islam scorned taking much interest in artillery until it was too late to catch up to Europe's lead. Facing less-advanced peoples, Russian and Mogul army commanders had no compelling need for improved weaponry, since what they already possessed overawed their opponents. Just as in the general economic field, so also in this specific area of military technology, Europe, fueled by a flourishing arms trade, took a decisive lead over the other civilizations and power centers.

Two further consequences of this armaments spiral need to be mentioned here. One ensured the political plurality of Europe, the other its eventual maritime mastery. The first is a simple enough story and can be dealt with briefly.[23] Within a quarter-century of the French invasion of 1494, and in certain respects even before then, some Italians had discovered that raised earthworks inside the city walls could greatly reduce the effects of artillery bombardment; when crashing into the compacted mounds of earth, cannonballs lost the devastating impact they had upon the outer walls. If these varied earthworks also had a steep ditch in front of them (and, later, a sophisticated series of protected bastions from which muskets and cannon could pour a crossfire), they constituted a near-insuperable obstacle to the besieging infantry. This restored the security of the Italian city-states, or at least of those which had not fallen to a foreign conqueror and which possessed the vast amounts of manpower needed to build and garrison such complex fortifications. It also gave an advantage to the armies engaged in holding off the Turks, as the Christian garrisons in Malta and in northern Hungary soon discovered. Above all, it hindered the easy conquest of rebels and rivals by one overweening power in Europe, as the protracted siege warfare which accompanied the Revolt of the Netherlands attested. Victories attained in the open field by, say, the formidable Spanish infantry could not be made decisive if the foe possessed heavily fortified bases into which he could retreat. The authority acquired through gunpowder by the Tokugawa shogunate, or by Akbar in India, was not replicated in the West, which continued to be characterized by political pluralism and its deadly concomitant, the arms race.

The impact of the "gunpowder revolution" at sea was even more wide-ranging.[24] As before, one is struck by the relative similarity of shipbuilding and naval power that existed during the later Middle Ages in northwest Europe, in the Islamic world, and in the Far East. If anything, the great voyages of Cheng Ho and the rapid advance of the Turkish fleets in the Black Sea and eastern Mediterranean might well have suggested to an observer around 1400 and 1450 that the future of maritime development lay with those two powers. There was also little difference, one suspects, between all three regions in regard to cartography, astronomy, and the use of instruments like the compass, astrolabe, and quadrant. What was different was *sustained organization.* Or, as Professor Jones observes, "given the distances covered by other seafarers, the Polynesians for example, the [Iberian] voyages are less impressive than Europe's ability to rationalize them and to develop the resources within her reach."[25] The systematic collection of geographical data by the Portuguese, the repeated willingness of Genoese merchant houses to fund Atlantic ventures which might ultimately compensate for their loss of Black Sea trade, and—farther north—the methodical development of the Newfoundland cod fisheries all signified a sustained readiness to reach outward which was not evident in other societies at that time.

But perhaps the most important act of "rationalization" was the steady improvement in ships' armaments. The siting of cannon on sailing vessels was a natural enough development at a time when sea warfare so resembled that on land; just as medieval castles contained archers along the walls and towers in order to drive off a besieging army, so the massive Genoese and Venetian and Aragonese trading vessels used men, armed with crossbows and sited in the fore and aft "castles," to defend themselves against Muslim pirates in the Mediterranean. This could cause severe losses among galley crews, although not necessarily enough to save a becalmed merchantman if its attackers were really determined. However, once sailors perceived the advances which had been made in gun design on land—that is, that the newer bronze cannon were much smaller, more powerful, and less dangerous to the gun crew than the enormous wrought-iron bombards—it was predictable that such armaments would be placed on board. After all, catapults, trebuchets, and other sorts of missile-throwing instruments had already been mounted on warships in China and the West. Even when cannon became less volatile and dangerous to their crews, they still posed considerable problems; given the more effective gunpowder, the recoil could be tremendous, sending a gun backward right across the deck if not restrained, and these weapons were still weighty enough to unbalance a vessel if sufficient numbers of them were placed on board (especially on the castles). This was where the stoutly built, rounder-hulled, all-weather three-masted sailing vessel had an inherent advantage over the slim oared galleys of the inland waters of the Mediterranean, Baltic, and Black seas, and over the Arab dhow and even the Chinese junk. It could in any event fire a larger broadside while remaining stable, although of course disasters also occurred from time to time; but once it was realized that the siting of such weapons amidships rather than on the castles provided a much safer gun platform, the *potential power* of these caravels and galleons was formidable. By comparison, lighter craft suffered from the twin disadvantage of less gun-carrying capacity and greater vulnerability to cannonballs.

One is obliged to stress the words "potential power" because the evolution of the gunned long-range sailing ship was a slow, often uneven development. Many hybrid types were constructed, some carrying multiple masts, guns, *and* rows of oars. Galley-type vessels were still to be seen in the English Channel in the sixteenth century. Moreover, there were considerable arguments in favor of continuing to deploy galleys in the Mediterranean and the Black Sea; they were swifter on many occasions, more maneuverable in inshore waters, and thus easier to use in conjunction with land operations along the coast—which, for the Turks, outweighed the disadvantages of their being short-ranged and unable to act in heavy seas.[26]

In just the same way, we should not imagine that as soon as the first Portuguese vessels rounded the Cape of Good Hope, the age of unchallenged western dominance had begun. What historians refer to as the "Vasco da Gama epoch" and the "Columbian era"—that is, the three or four centuries of European hegemony after 1500—was a very gradual process. Portuguese explorers might have reached the shores of India by the 1490s, but their vessels were still small (often only 300 tons) and not all that well armed—certainly not compared with the powerful Dutch East Indiamen which sailed in those waters a century later. In fact, the Portuguese could not penetrate the Red Sea for a long while, and then only precariously, nor could they gain much of a footing in China; and in the late sixteenth century they lost some of their East African stations to an Arab counteroffensive.[27]

It would be erroneous, too, to assume that the non-European powers simply collapsed like a pack of cards at the first signs of western
expansionism. This was precisely what did happen in Mexico, Peru,
and other less developed societies of the New World when the Spanish
adventurers landed. Elsewhere, the story was very different. Since the
Chinese government had voluntarily turned its back upon maritime
trade, it did not really care if that commerce fell into the hands of the
barbarians; even the quasi-official trading post which the Portuguese
set up at Macao in 1557, lucrative though it must have been to the local
silk merchants and conniving administrators, does not seem to have
disturbed Peking's equanimity. The Japanese, for their part, were
much more blunt. When the Portuguese sent a mission in 1640 to
protest against the expulsion of foreigners, almost all its members
were killed; there could be no attempt at retribution from Lisbon.
Finally, Ottoman sea power was holding its own in the eastern Mediterranean, and Ottoman land power remained a massive threat to central
Europe. In the sixteenth century, indeed, "to most European statesmen
the loss of Hungary was of far greater import than the establishment
of factories in the Orient, and the threat to Vienna more significant
than their own challenges at Aden, Goa and Malacca; only governments bordering the Atlantic could, like their later historians, ignore
this fact."[28]

Yet when all these reservations are made, there is no doubt that
the development of the long-range armed sailing ship heralded a fundamental advance in Europe's place in the world. With these vessels,
the naval powers of the West were in a position to control the oceanic trade routes and to overawe all societies vulnerable to the workings of sea power. Even the first great clashes between the Portuguese
and their Muslim foes in the Indian Ocean made this clear. No doubt
they exaggerated in retrospect, but to read the journals and reports of
da Gama and Albuquerque, describing how their warships blasted
their way through the massed fleets of Arab dhows and other light
craft which they encountered off the Malabar coast and in the Ormuz
and Malacca roads, is to gain the impression that an extraterrestrial,
superhuman force had descended upon their unfortunate opponents.
Following the new tactic that "they were by no means to board, but
to fight with the artillery," the Portuguese crews were virtually invin-
cible at sea.[29] On land it was quite a different matter, as the fierce
battles (and occasional defeats) at Aden, Jiddah, Goa, and elsewhere
demonstrated; yet so determined and brutal were these western invaders that by the mid-sixteenth century they had carved out for
themselves a chain of forts from the Gulf of Guinea to the South
China Sea. Although never able to monopolize the spice trade from
the Indies—much of which continued to flow via the traditional
channels to Venice—the Portuguese certainly cornered considerable

portions of that commerce and profited greatly from their early lead in the race for empire.[30]

The evidence of profit was even greater, of course, in the vast land empire which the conquistadores swiftly established in the western hemisphere. From the early settlements in Hispaniola and Cuba, Spanish expeditions pushed toward the mainland, conquering Mexico in the 1520s and Peru in the 1530s. Within a few decades this dominion extended from the River Plate in the south to the Rio Grande in the north. Spanish galleons, plying along the western coast, linked up with vessels coming from the Philippines, bearing Chinese silks in exchange for Peruvian silver. In their "New World" the Spaniards made it clear that they were there to stay, setting up an imperial administration, building churches, and engaging in ranching and mining. Exploiting the natural resources—and, still more, the native labor—of these territories, the conquerors sent home a steady flow of sugar, cochineal, hides, and other wares. Above all, they sent home silver from the Potosí mine, which for over a century was the biggest single deposit of that metal in the world. All this led to "a lightning growth of transatlantic trade, the volume increasing eightfold between 1510 and 1550, and threefold again between 1550 and 1610."[31]

All the signs were, therefore, that this imperialism was intended to be permanent. Unlike the fleeting visits paid by Cheng Ho, the actions of the Portuguese and Spanish explorers symbolized a commitment to alter the world's political and economic balances. With their ship-borne cannon and musket-bearing soldier, they did precisely that. In retrospect it sometimes seems difficult to grasp that a country with the limited population and resources of Portugal could reach so far and acquire so much. In the special circumstances of European military and naval superiority described above, this was by no means impossible. Once it was done, the evident profits of empire, and the desire for more, simply accelerated the process of aggrandizement.

There are elements in this story of "the expansion of Europe" which have been ignored, or but briefly mentioned so far. The personal aspect has not been examined, and yet—as in all great endeavors—it was there in abundance: in the encouragements of men like Henry the Navigator; in the ingenuity of ship craftsmen and armorers and men of letters; in the enterprise of merchants; above all, in the sheer courage of those who partook in the overseas voyages and endured all that the mighty seas, hostile climates, wild landscapes, and fierce opponents could place in their way. For a complex mixture of motives—personal gain, national glory, religious zeal, perhaps a sense of adventure—men were willing to risk everything, as indeed they did in many cases. Nor has there been much dwelling upon the awful cruelties inflicted by these European conquerors upon their many victims in Africa, Asia, and America. If these features are hardly mentioned here, it is because many societies in their time have thrown up individuals and groups willing to dare all and do anything in order to make the world their oyster. What distinguished the captains, crews, and explorers of Europe was that they possessed the ships and the firepower with which to achieve their ambitions, and that they came from a political environment in which competition, risk, and entrepreneurship were prevalent.

The benefits accruing from the expansion of Europe were widespread and permanent, and—most important of all—they helped to accelerate an already-existing dynamic. The emphasis upon the acquisition of gold, silver, precious metals, and spices, important though such valuables were, ought not to obscure the worth of the less glamorous items which flooded into Europe's ports once its sailors had breached the oceanic frontier. Access to the Newfoundland fisheries brought an apparently inexhaustible supply of food, and the Atlantic Ocean also provided the whale oil and seal oil vital for illumination, lubrication, and many other purposes. Sugar, indigo, tobacco, rice, furs, timber, and new plants like the potato and maize were all to boost the total wealth and well-being of the continent; later on, of course, there was to come the flow of grain and meats and cotton. But one does not need to anticipate the cosmopolitan world economy of the later nineteenth century to understand that the Portuguese and Spanish discoveries were, within decades, of great and ever-growing importance in enhancing the prosperity and power of the western portions of the continent. Bulk trades like the fisheries employed a large number of hands, both in catching and in distribution, which further boosted the market economy. And all of this gave the greatest stimulus to the European shipbuilding industry, attracting around the ports of London, Bristol, Antwerp, Amsterdam, and many others a vast array of craftsmen, suppliers, dealers, insurers. The net effect was to give to a considerable proportion of western Europe's population—and not just to the elite few—an abiding material interest in the fruits of overseas trade.

When one adds to this list of commodities the commerce which attended the landward expansion of Russia—the furs, hides, wood, hemp, salt, and grain which came from there to western Europe—then scholars have some cause in describing this as the beginnings of a "modern world system."[32] What had started as a number of separate expansions was steadily turning into an interlocking whole: the gold of the Guinea coast and the silver of Peru were used by the Portuguese, Spaniards, and Italians to pay for spices and silks from the Orient; the firs and timber of Russia helped in the purchase of iron guns from England; grain from the Baltic passed through Amsterdam on its way to the Mediterranean. All this generated a continual interaction—of further European expansion, bringing fresh discoveries and thus trade opportunities, resulting in additional gains, which stimulated still more expansion. This was not necessarily a smooth upward progression: a great war in Europe or civil unrest could sharply reduce activities overseas. But the colonizing powers rarely if ever gave up their acquisitions, and within a short while a fresh wave of expansion and exploration would begin. After all, if the established imperial nations did not exploit their positions, others were willing to do it instead.

This, finally, was the greatest reason why the dynamic continued to operate as it did: the manifold rivalries of the European states, already acute, were spilling over into transoceanic spheres. Try as they might, Spain and Portugal simply could not keep their papally assigned monopoly of the outside world to themselves, the more especially when men realized that there was no northeast or northwest passage from Europe to Cathay. Already by the 1560s, Dutch, French, and English vessels were venturing across the Atlantic, and a little later into the Indian and Pacific oceans—a process quickened by the decline of the English cloth trade and the Revolt of the Netherlands. With royal and aristocratic patrons, with funding from the great merchants of Amsterdam and London, and with all the religious and nationalist zeal which the Reformation and Counter-Reformation had produced, new trading and plundering expeditions set out from northwest Europe to secure a share of the spoils. There was the prospect of gaining glory and riches, of striking at a rival and boosting the resources of one's own country, and of converting new souls to the one true faith; what possible counterarguments could hold out against the launching of such ventures?[33]

The fairer aspect of this increasing commercial and colonial rivalry was the parallel upward spiral in knowledge—in science and technology.[34] No doubt many of the advances of this time were spinoffs from the arms race and the scramble for overseas trade; but the eventual benefits transcended their inglorious origins. Improved cartography, navigational tables, new instruments like the telescope, barometer, backstaff, and gimbaled compass, and better methods of shipbuilding helped to make maritime travel a less unpredictable form of travel. New crops and plants not only brought better nutrition but also were a stimulus to botany and agricultural science. Metallurgical skills, and indeed the whole iron industry, made rapid progress; deep-mining techniques did the same. Astronomy, medicine, physics, and engineering also benefited from the quickening economic pace and the enhanced value of science. The inquiring, rationalist mind was observing more, and experimenting more; and the printing presses, apart from producing vernacular Bibles and political treatises, were spreading these findings. The cumulative effect of this explosion of knowledge was to buttress Europe's technological—and therefore military—superiority still further. Even the powerful Ottomans, or at least their front-line soldiers and sailors, were feeling some of the consequences of this by the end of the sixteenth century. On other, less active societies, the effects were to be far more serious. Whether or not certain states in Asia would have taken off into a self-driven commercial and industrial revolution had they been left undisturbed seems open to considerable doubt;[35] but what was clear was that it was going to be extremely difficult for other societies to ascend the ladder of world power when the more advanced European states occupied all the top rungs.

This difficulty would be compounded, it seems fair to argue, because moving up that ladder would have involved not merely the acquisition of European equipment or even of European techniques: it would also have implied a wholesale borrowing of those general features which distinguished the societies of the West from all the others. It would have meant the existence of a market economy, if not to the extent proposed by Adam Smith then at least to the extent that merchants and entrepreneurs would not be consistently deterred, obstructed, and preyed upon. It would also have meant the existence of a plurality of power centers, each if possible with its own economic base, so that there was no prospect of the imposed centralization of a despotic oriental-style regime—and every prospect of the progressive, if turbulent and occasionally brutal, stimulus of competition. By extension, this lack of economic and political rigidity would imply a similar lack of cultural and ideological orthodoxy—that is, a freedom to inquire, to dispute, to experiment, a belief in the possibilities of improvement, a concern for the practical rather than the abstract, a rationalism which defied mandarin codes, religious dogma, and traditional folklore.[36] In most cases, what was involved was not so much positive elements, but rather the reduction in the number of *hindrances* which checked economic growth and political diversity. Europe's greatest advantage was that it had fewer *dis*advantages than the other civilizations.

Although it is impossible to prove it, one suspects that these various general features related to one another, by some inner logic as it were, and that all were necessary. It was a combination of economic laissez-faire, political and military pluralism, and intellectual liberty—however rudimentary each factor was compared with later ages—which had been in constant interaction to produce the "European miracle." Since the miracle was historically unique, it seems plausible to assume that only a replication of all its component parts could have produced a similar result elsewhere. Because that mix of critical ingredients did not exist in Ming China, or in the Muslim empires of the Middle East and Asia, or in any other of the societies examined above, they appeared to stand still while Europe advanced to the center of the world stage.

2
The Habsburg Bid for Mastery, 1519–1659

By the sixteenth century, then, the power struggles within Europe were also helping it to rise, economically and militarily, above the other regions of the globe. What was not yet decided, however, was whether any one of the rival European states could accumulate sufficient resources to surpass the rest, and then dominate them. For about a century and a half after 1500, a continent-wide combination of kingdoms, duchies, and provinces ruled by the Spanish and Austrian members of the Habsburg family threatened to become the predominant political and religious influence in Europe. The story of this prolonged struggle and of the ultimate defeat of these Habsburg ambitions by a coalition of other European states forms the core of this chapter. By 1659, when Spain finally acknowledged defeat in the Treaty of the Pyrenees, the political *plurality* of Europe—containing five or six major states, and various smaller ones—was an indisputable fact. Which of those leading states was going to benefit most from further shifts within the Great Power system can be left to the following chapter; what at least was clear, by the mid-seventeenth century, was that no single dynastic-military bloc was capable of becoming the master of Europe, as had appeared probable on various occasions over the previous decades.

The interlocking campaigns for European predominance which characterize this century and a half differ both in degree and kind, therefore, from the wars of the pre-1500 period. The struggles which had disturbed the peace of Europe over the previous hundred years had been *localized* ones; the clashes between the various Italian states, the rivalry between the English and French crowns, and the wars of the Teutonic Knights against the Lithuanians and the Poles were typical examples.[1] As the sixteenth century unfolded, however, these traditional regional struggles in Europe were either subsumed into or eclipsed by what seemed to contemporaries to be a far larger contest for the mastery of the continent.

The Meaning and Chronology of the Struggle

Although there were always specific reasons why any particular state was drawn into this larger context, two more general causes were chiefly responsible for the transformation in both the intensity and geographical scope of European warfare. The first of these was the coming of the Reformation—sparked off by Martin Luther's personal revolt against papal indulgences in 1517—which swiftly added a fierce new dimension to the traditional dynastic rivalries of the continent. For particular socioeconomic reasons, the advent of the Protestant Reformation—and its response, in the form of the Catholic Counter-Reformation against heresy—also tended to divide the southern half of Europe from the north, and the rising, city-based middle classes from the feudal orders, although there were, of course, many exceptions to such general alignments.[2] But the basic point was that "Christendom" had fractured, and that the continent now contained large numbers of individuals drawn into a *transnational* struggle over religious doctrine. Only in the mid-seventeenth century, when men recoiled at the excesses and futility of religious wars, would there arrive a general, if grudging, acknowledgment of the confessional division of Europe.

The second reason for the much more widespread and interlinked pattern of warfare after 1500 was the creation of a dynastic combination, that of the Habsburgs, to form a network of territories which stretched from Gibraltar to Hungary and from Sicily to Amsterdam, exceeding in size anything which had been seen in Europe since the time of Charlemagne seven hundred years earlier. Stemming originally from Austria, Habsburg rulers had managed to get themselves regularly elected to the position of Holy Roman emperor—a title much diminished in real power since the high Middle Ages but still sought after by princes eager to play a larger role in German and general European affairs.

More practically, the Habsburgs were without equal in augmenting their territories through marriage and inheritance. One such move, by Maximilian I of Austria (1493–1519, and Holy Roman emperor 1508–1519), had brought in the rich hereditary lands of Burgundy and, with them, the Netherlands in 1477. Another, consequent upon a marriage compact of 1515, was to add the important territories of Hungary and Bohemia; although the former was not within the Holy Roman Empire and possessed many liberties, this gave the Habsburgs a great bloc of lands across central Europe. But the most far-reaching of Maximilian's dynastic link-ups was the marriage of his son Philip to Joan, daughter of Ferdinand and Isabella of Spain, whose own earlier union had brought together the possessions of Castile and Aragon (which included Naples and Sicily). The "residuary legatee"[3] to all these marriage compacts was Charles, the eldest son of Philip and Joan. Born in 1500, he became Duke of Burgundy at the age of fifteen and Charles I of Spain a year later, and then—in 1519—he succeeded his paternal grandfather Maximilian I both as Holy Roman emperor and as ruler of the hereditary Habsburg lands in Austria. As the Emperor Charles V, therefore, he embodied all four inheritances until his abdications of 1555–1556 (see Map 3). Only a few years later, in 1526, the death of the childless King Louis of Hungary in the battle of Mohacs against the Turks allowed Charles to claim the crowns of both Hungary and Bohemia.

The sheer heterogeneity and diffusion of these lands, which will be examined further below, might suggest that the Habsburg imperium could never be a real equivalent to the uniform, centralized empires of Asia. Even in the 1520s, Charles was handing over to his younger brother Ferdinand the administration and princely sovereignty of the Austrian hereditary lands, and also of the new acquisitions of Hungary and Bohemia—a recognition, well before Charles's own abdication, that the Spanish and Austrian inheritances could not be effectively ruled by the same person. Nonetheless, that was *not* how the other princes and states viewed this mighty agglomeration of Habsburg power. To the Valois kings of France, fresh from consolidating their own authority internally and eager to expand into the rich Italian peninsula, Charles V's possessions seemed to encircle the French state—and it is hardly an exaggeration to say that the chief aim of the French in Europe over the next two centuries would be to break the influence of the Habsburgs. Similarly, the German princes and electors, who had long struggled against the emperor's having any real authority within Germany itself, could not but be alarmed when they saw Charles V's position was buttressed by so many additional territories, which might now give him the resources to impose his will. Many of the popes, too, disliked this accumulation of Habsburg power, even if it was often needed to combat the Turks, the Lutherans, and other foes.

Given the rivalries endemic to the European states system, therefore, it was hardly likely that the Habsburgs would remain unchallenged. What turned this potential for conflict into a bitter and prolonged reality was its conjunction with the religious disputes engendered by the Reformation. For the fact was that the most prominent and powerful Habsburg monarchs over this century and a half—the Emperor Charles V himself and his later successor, Ferdinand II (1619–1637), and the Spanish kings Philip II (1556–1598) and Philip IV (1621–1665)—were also the most militant in the defense of Catholicism. As a consequence, it became virtually impossible to separate the power-political from the religious strands of the European rivalries which racked the continent in this period. As any contempo-

Map 3: Charles V's Inheritance, 1519

From his paternal grandfather, Maximilian of Austria

From his paternal grandmother, Mary of Burgundy

From his maternal grandfather, Ferdinand of Aragón

From his maternal grandmother, Isabella of Castile

NORTH SEA

BALTIC SEA

ATLANTIC OCEAN

NETHERLANDS

AUSTRIA

CASTILE

ARAGÓN

SARDINIA

NAPLES

SICILY

MEDITERRANEAN SEA

0   500 Miles

0   500 Kilometers

rary could appreciate, had Charles V succeeded in crushing the Protestant princes of Germany in the 1540s, it would have been a victory not only for the Catholic faith but also for Habsburg influence—and the same was true of Philip II's efforts to suppress the religious unrest in the Netherlands after 1566; and true, for that matter, of the dispatch of the Spanish Armada to invade England in 1588. In sum, national and dynastic rivalries had now fused with religious zeal to make men fight on where earlier they might have been inclined to compromise.

Even so, it may appear a little forced to use the title "The Habsburg Bid for Mastery" to describe the entire period from the accession of Charles V as Holy Roman emperor in 1519 to the Spanish acknowledgment of defeat at the Treaty of the Pyrenees in 1659. Obviously, their enemies *did* firmly believe that the Habsburg monarchs were bent upon absolute domination. Thus, the Elizabethan writer Francis Bacon could in 1595 luridly describe the "ambition and oppression of Spain":

> France is turned upside down. . . . Portugal usurped. . . . The Low Countries warred upon. . . . The like at this day attempted upon Aragon. . . . The poor Indians are brought from free men to be slaves.[4]

But despite the occasional rhetoric of some Habsburg ministers about a "world monarchy,"[5] there was no conscious plan to dominate Europe in the manner of Napoleon or Hitler. Some of the Habsburg dynastic marriages and successions were fortuitous, at the most inspired, rather than evidence of a long-term scheme of territorial aggrandizement. In certain cases—for example, the frequent French invasions of northern Italy—Habsburg rulers were more provoked than provoking. In the Mediterranean after the 1540s, Spanish and imperial forces were repeatedly placed on the defensive by the operations of a revived Islam.

Nevertheless, the fact remains that had the Habsburg rulers achieved all of their limited, regional aims—even their *defensive* aims—the mastery of Europe would virtually have been theirs. The Ottoman Empire would have been pushed back, along the North African coast and out of eastern Mediterranean waters. Heresy would have been suppressed within Germany. The revolt of the Netherlands would have been crushed. Friendly regimes would have been maintained in France and England. Only Scandinavia, Poland, Muscovy, and the lands still under Ottoman rule would not have been subject to Habsburg power and influence—and the concomitant triumph of the Counter-Reformation. Although Europe even then would not have approached the unity enjoyed by Ming China, the political and religious principles favored by the twin Habsburg centers of Madrid and Vienna would have greatly eroded the pluralism that had so long been the continent's most important feature.

The chronology of this century and a half of warfare can be summarized briefly in a work of analysis like this. What probably strikes the eye of the modern reader much more than the names and outcome of various battles (Pavia, Lützen, etc.) is the sheer length of these conflicts. The struggle against the Turks went on decade after decade; Spain's attempt to crush the Revolt of the Netherlands lasted from the 1560s until 1648, with only a brief intermission, and is referred to in some books as the Eighty Years War; while the great multidimensional conflict undertaken by both Austrian and Spanish Habsburgs against successive coalitions of enemy states from 1618 until the 1648 Peace of Westphalia has always been known as the Thirty Years War. This obviously placed a great emphasis upon the relative *capacities* of the different states to bear the burdens of war, year after year, decade after decade. And the significance of the material and financial underpinnings of war was made the more critical by the fact that it was in this period that there took place a "military revolution" which transformed the nature of fighting and made it much more expensive than hitherto. The reasons for that change, and the chief features of it, will be discussed shortly. But even before going into a brief outline of events, it is as well to know that the military encounters of (say) the 1520s would appear very small-scale, in terms of both men and money deployed, compared with those of the 1630s.

The first series of major wars focused upon Italy, whose rich and vulnerable city-states had tempted the French monarchs to invade as early as 1494—and, with equal predictability, had produced various coalitions of rival powers (Spain, the Austrian Habsburgs, even England) to force the French to withdraw.[6] In 1519, Spain and France were still quarreling over the latter's claim to Milan when the news arrived of Charles V's election as Holy Roman emperor and of his combined inheritance of the Spanish and Austrian territories of the Habsburg family. This accumulation of titles by his archrival drove the ambitious French king, Francis I (1515–1547), to instigate a whole series of countermoves, not just in Italy itself, but also along the borders of Burgundy, the southern Netherlands, and Spain. Francis I's own plunge into Italy ended in his defeat and capture at the battle of Pavia (1525), but within another four years the French monarch was again leading an army into Italy—and was again checked by Habsburg forces. Although Francis once more renounced his claims to Italy at the 1529 Treaty of Cambrai, he was at war with Charles V over those possessions both in the 1530s and in the 1540s.

Given the imbalance in forces between France and the Habsburg territories at this time, it was probably not too difficult for Charles V to keep blocking these French attempts at expansion. The task became the harder, however, because as Holy Roman emperor he had inherited many other foes. Much the most formidable of these were the Turks, who not only had expanded across the Hungarian plain in the 1520s (and were besieging Vienna in 1529), but also posed a naval threat against Italy and, in conjunction with the Barbary corsairs of North Africa, against the coasts of Spain itself.[7] What also aggravated this situation was the tacit and unholy alliance which existed in these decades between the Ottoman sultan and Francis I against the Habsburgs: in 1542, French and Ottoman fleets actually combined in an assault upon Nice.

Charles V's other great area of difficulty lay in Germany, which had been torn asunder by the Reformation and where Luther's challenge to the old order was now being supported by a league of Protestant princely states. In view of his other problems, it was scarcely surprising that Charles V could not concentrate his energies upon the Lutheran challenge in Germany until after the mid-1540s. When he did so, he was at first quite successful, especially by defeating the armies of the leading Protestant princes at the battle of Mühlberg (1547). But any enhancement of Habsburg and imperial authority always alarmed Charles V's rivals, so that the northern German princes, the Turks, Henry II of France (1547–1559), and even the papacy all strove to weaken his position. By 1552, French armies had moved into Germany, in support of the Protestant states, who were thereby able to resist the centralizing tendencies of the emperor. This was acknowledged by the Peace of Augsburg (1555), which brought the religious wars in Germany to a temporary end, and by the Treaty of Cateau-Cambresis (1559), which brought the Franco-Spanish conflict to a close. It was also acknowledged, in its way, by Charles V's own abdications—in 1555 as Holy Roman emperor to his brother Ferdinand I (emperor, 1555–1564), and in 1556 as king of Spain in favor of his son Philip II (1556–1598). If the Austrian and Spanish branches remained closely related after this time, it now was the case (as the historian Mamatey puts it) that "henceforth, like the doubleheaded black eagle in the imperial coat of arms, the Habsburgs had two heads at Vienna and at Madrid, looking east and west."[8]

While the eastern branch under Ferdinand I and his successor Maximilian II (emperor, 1564–1576) enjoyed relative peace in their possession (save for a Turkish assault of 1566–1567), the western branch under Philip II of Spain was far less fortunate. The Barbary corsairs were attacking the coasts of Portugal and Castile, and behind them the Turks were resuming their struggle for the Mediterranean. In consequence, Spain found itself repeatedly committed to major new wars against the powerful Ottoman Empire, from the 1560 expedition to Djerba, through the tussle over Malta in 1565, the Lepanto campaign of 1571, and the dingdong battle over Tunis, until the eventual truce of 1581.[9] At virtually the same time, however, Philip's policies of religious intolerance and increased taxation had kindled the discontents in the Habsburg-owned Netherlands into an open revolt. The breakdown of Spanish authority there by the mid-1560s was answered by the dispatch northward of an army under the Duke of Alba and by the imposition of a military despotism—in turn provoking full-scale resistance in the seagirt, defensible Dutch provinces of Holland and Zeeland, and causing alarm in England, France, and northern Germany about Spanish intentions. The English were even more perturbed when, in 1580, Philip II annexed neighboring Portugal, with its colonies and its fleet. Yet, as with all other attempts of the Habsburgs to assert (or extend) their authority, the predictable result was that their many rivals felt obliged to come in, to prevent the balance of power becoming too deranged. By the 1580s, what had earlier been a local rebellion by Dutch Protestants against Spanish rule had widened into a new international struggle.[10] In the Netherlands itself, the warfare of siege and countersiege continued, without spectacular results. Across the Channel, in England, Elizabeth I had checked any internal (whether Spanish or papal-backed) threats to her authority and was lending military support to the Dutch rebels. In France, the weakening of the monarchy had led to the outbreak of a bitter religious civil war, with the Catholic League (supported by Spain) and their rivals the Huguenots (supported by Elizabeth and the Dutch) struggling for supremacy. At sea, Dutch and English privateers interrupted the Spanish supply route to the Netherlands, and took the fight farther afield, to West Africa and the Caribbean.

At some periods in the struggle, especially in the late 1580s and early 1590s, it looked as if the powerful Spanish campaign would succeed; in September 1590, for example, Spanish armies were operating in Languedoc and Britanny, and another army under the outstanding commander the Duke of Parma was marching upon Paris from the north. Nevertheless, the lines of the anti-Spanish forces held, even under that sort of pressure. The charismatic French Huguenot claimant to the crown of France, Henry of Navarre, was flexible enough to switch from Protestantism to Catholicism to boost his claims—and then to lead an ever-increasing part of the French nation against the invading Spaniards and the discredited Catholic League. By the 1598 Peace of Vervins—the year of the death of Philip II of Spain—Madrid agreed to abandon all interference in France. By that time, too, the England of Elizabeth was also secure. The great Armada of 1588, and two later Spanish invasion attempts, had failed miserably—as had the effort to exploit a Catholic rebellion in Ireland, which Elizabeth's armies were steadily reconquering. In 1604, with both Philip II and Elizabeth dead, Spain and England came to a compromise peace. It would take another five years, until the truce of 1609, before Madrid negotiated with the Dutch rebels for peace; but well before then it had become clear that Spanish power was insufficient to crush the Netherlands, either by sea or through the strongly held land (and watery) defenses manned by Maurice of Nassau's efficient Dutch army. The continued existence of all three states, France, England, and the United Provinces of the Netherlands, each with the potential to dispute Habsburg pretensions in the future, again confirmed that the Europe of 1600 would consist of many nations, and not of one hegemony.

The third great spasm of wars which convulsed Europe in this period occurred after 1618, and fell very heavily upon Germany. That land had been spared an all-out confessional struggle in the late sixteenth century, but only because of the weakening authority and intellect of Rudolf II (Holy Roman emperor, 1576–1612) and a renewal of a Turkish threat in the Danube basin (1593–1606). Behind the facade of German unity, however, the rival Catholic and Protestant forces were maneuvering to strengthen their own position and to weaken that of their foes. As the seventeenth century unfolded, the rivalry between the Evangelical Union (founded in 1608) and the Catholic League (1609) intensified. Moreover, because the Spanish Habsburgs strongly supported their Austrian cousins, and because the head of the Evangelical Union, the Elector Palatine Frederick IV, had ties with both England and the Netherlands, it appeared as if most of the states of Europe were lining up for a final settlement of their political-religious antagonisms.[11]

The 1618 revolt of the Protestant estates of Bohemia against their new Catholic ruler, Ferdinand II (emperor 1619–1637), therefore provided the spark needed to begin another round of ferocious religious struggles: the Thirty Years War of 1618–1648. In the early stages of this contest, the emperor's forces fared well, ably assisted by a Spanish-Habsburg army under General Spinola. But, in consequence, a heterogeneous combination of religious and worldly forces entered the conflict, once again eager to adjust the balances in the opposite direction. The Dutch, who ended their 1609 truce with Spain in 1621, moved into the Rhineland to counter Spinola's army. In 1626, a Danish force under its monarch Christian IV invaded Germany from the north. Behind the scenes, the influential French statesman Cardinal Richelieu sought to stir up trouble for the Habsburgs wherever he could. However, none of these military or diplomatic countermoves were very successful, and by the late 1620s the Emperor Ferdinand's powerful lieutenant, Wallenstein, seemed well on the way to imposing an all-embracing, centralized authority on Germany, even as far north as the Baltic shores.[12]

Yet this rapid accumulation of imperial power merely provoked the House of Habsburg's many enemies to strive the harder. In the early

1630s by far the most decisive of them was the attractive and influential Swedish king, Gustavus Adolphus II (1611–1632), whose well-
trained army moved into northern Germany in 1630 and then burst
southward to the Rhineland and Bavaria in the following year. Although Gustavus himself was killed at the battle of Lützen in 1632, this
in no way diminished the considerable Swedish role in Germany—or,
indeed, the overall dimensions of the war. On the contrary, by 1634 the
Spaniards under Philip IV (1621–1665) and his accomplished first minister, the Count-Duke of Olivares, had decided to aid their Austrian
cousins much more thoroughly than before; but their dispatch into the
Rhineland of a powerful Spanish army under its general, Cardinal-
Infante, in turn forced Richelieu to decide upon direct French involve-
ment, ordering troops across various frontiers in 1535. For years
beforehand, France had been the tacit, indirect leader of the anti-
Habsburg coalition, sending subsidies to all who would fight the imperial and Spanish forces. Now the conflict was out in the open, and each
coalition began to mobilize even more troops, arms, and money. The
language correspondingly became stiffer. "Either all is lost, or else
Castile will be head of the world," wrote Olivares in 1635, as he planned
the triple invasion of France in the following year.[13]

The conquest of an area as large as France was, however, beyond
the military capacities of the Habsburg forces, which briefly approached Paris but were soon hard stretched across Europe. Swedish
and German troops were pressing the imperial armies in the north. The
Dutch and the French were "pincering" the Spanish Netherlands.
Moreover, a revolt by the Portuguese in 1640 diverted a steady flow of
Spanish troops and resources from northern Europe to much nearer
home, although they were never enough to achieve the reunification of
the peninsula. Indeed, with the parallel rebellion of the Catalans—
which the French gladly aided—there was some danger of a disintegration of the Spanish heartland by the early 1640s. Overseas, Dutch
maritime expeditions struck at Brazil, Angola, and Ceylon, turning the
conflict into what some historians describe as the first global war.[14] If
the latter actions brought gains to the Netherlands, most of the other
belligerents were by this time suffering heavily from the long years of
military effort; the armies of the 1640s were becoming smaller than
those of the 1630s, the financial expedients of governments were the
more desperate, the patience of the people was much thinner and their
protests much more violent. Yet precisely because of the interlinked
nature of the struggle, it was difficult for any one participant to withdraw. Many of the Protestant German states would have done just that,
had they been certain that the Swedish armies would also cease
fighting and go home; and Olivares and other Spanish statesmen would
have negotiated a truce with France, but the latter would not desert the
Dutch. Secret peace negotiations at various levels were carried out in

parallel with military campaigns on various fronts, and each power consoled itself with the thought that another victory would buttress its claims in the general settlement.

The end of the Thirty Years War was, in consequence, an untidy affair. Spain suddenly made peace with the Dutch early in 1648, finally recognizing their full independence; but this was done to deprive France of an ally, and the Franco-Habsburg struggle continued. It became purely a Franco-Spanish one later in the year when the Peace of Westphalia (1648) at last brought tranquillity to Germany, and allowed the Austrian Habsburgs to retire from the conflict. While individual states and rulers made certain gains (and suffered certain losses), the essence of the Westphalian settlement was to acknowledge the religious and political *balance* within the Holy Roman Empire, and thus to confirm the limitations upon imperial authority. This left France and Spain engaged in a war which was all to do with national rivalries and nothing to do with religion—as Richelieu's successor, the French minister, Mazarin, clearly demonstrated in 1655 by allying with Cromwell's Protestant England to deliver the blows which finally caused the Spaniards to agree to a peace. The conditions of the Treaty of the Pyrenees (1659) were not particularly harsh, but in forcing Spain to come to terms with its great archenemy, they revealed that the age of Habsburg predominance in Europe was over. All that was left as a "war aim" for Philip IV's government then was the preservation of Iberian unity, and even this had to be abandoned in 1668, when Portugal's independence was formally recognized.[15] The continent's political fragmentation thus remained in much the same state as had existed at Charles V's accession in 1519, although Spain itself was to suffer from further rebellions and losses of territory as the seventeenth century moved to its close (see Map 4)—paying the price, as it were, for its original strategical overextension.

Strengths and Weaknesses of the Habsburg Bloc

Why did the Habsburgs fail?[16] This issue is so large and the process was so lengthy that there seems little point in looking for personal reasons like the madness of the Emperor Rudolf II, or the incompetence of Philip III of Spain. It is also difficult to argue that the Habsburg dynasty and its higher officers were especially deficient when one considers the failings of many a contemporary French and English monarch, and the venality or idiocy of some of the German princes. The puzzle appears the greater when one recalls the vast accumulation of material power available to the Habsburgs:

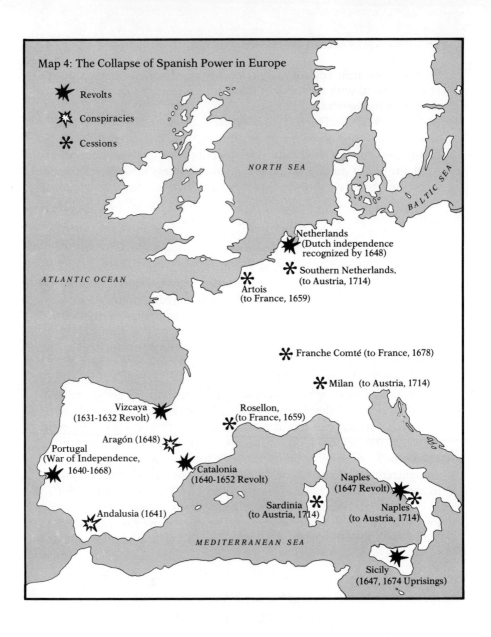

Map 4: The Collapse of Spanish Power in Europe

Revolts

Conspiracies

Cessions

NORTH SEA

BALTIC SEA

ATLANTIC OCEAN

Netherlands
(Dutch independence
recognized by 1648)

Southern Netherlands,
(to Austria, 1714)

Artois
(to France, 1659)

Franche Comté (to France, 1678)

Milan (to Austria, 1714)

Vizcaya
(1631-1632 Revolt)

Rosellon,
(to France, 1659)

Aragón (1648)

Portugal
(War of Independence,
1640-1668)

Catalonia
(1640-1652 Revolt)

Naples
(1647 Revolt)

Andalusia (1641)

Sardinia
(to Austria, 1714)

Naples
(to Austria, 1714)

MEDITERRANEAN SEA

Sicily
(1647, 1674 Uprisings)

Charles V's inheritance of the crowns of four major dynasties, Castile, Aragon, Burgundy, and Austria, the later acquisitions by his house of the crowns of Bohemia, Hungary, Portugal, and, for a short time, even of England, and the coincidence of these dynastic events with the Spanish conquest and exploitation of the New World— these provided the house of Habsburg with a wealth of resources that no other European power could match.[17]

Given the many gaps and inaccuracies in available statistics, one should not place too much reliance upon the population figures of this time; but it would be fair to assume that about one-quarter of the peoples of early modern Europe were living in Habsburg-ruled territory. However, such crude totals* were less important than the wealth of the regions in question, and here the dynastic inheritance seemed to have been blessed with riches.

There were five chief sources of Habsburg finance, and several smaller ones. By far the most important was the Spanish inheritance of Castile, since it was directly ruled and regular taxes of various sorts (the sales tax, the "crusade" tax on religious property) had been conceded to the crown by the Cortes and the church. In addition, there were the two richest trading areas of Europe—the Italian states and the Low Countries—which could provide comparatively large funds from their mercantile wealth and mobile capital. The fourth source, increasingly important as time went on, was the revenue from the American empire. The "royal fifth" of the silver and gold mined there, together with the sales tax, customs duties, and church levies in the New World, provided a vast bonus to the kings of Spain, not only directly but also indirectly, for the American treasures which went into private hands, whether Spanish or Flemish or Italian, helped those individuals and concerns to pay the increasing state taxes levied upon them, and in times of emergency, the monarch could always borrow heavily from the bankers in the expectation of paying off his debts when the silver fleet arrived. The fact that the Habsburg territories contained the leading financial and mercantile houses—those of southern Germany, of certain of the Italian cities, and of Antwerp—must be counted as an additional advantage, and as the fifth major source of income.[18] It was certainly more readily accessible than, say, revenues from Germany, where the princes and free cities represented in the Reichstag voted money to the emperor only if the Turks were at the door.[19]

In the postfeudal age, when knights were no longer expected to perform individual military service (at least in most countries) nor coastal towns to provide a ship, the availability of ready cash and the possession of good credit were absolutely essential to any state en-

*As a rough figure, this would mean about 25 million out of the total European population of 105 million in 1600.

gaged in war. Only by direct payment (or promise of payment) could the necessary ships and naval stores and armaments and foodstuffs be mobilized within the market economy to furnish a fleet ready for combat; only by the supply of provisions and wages on a reasonably frequent basis could one's own troops be steered away from mutiny and their energies directed toward the foe. Moreover, although this is commonly regarded as the age when the "nation-state" came into its own in western Europe, all governments relied heavily upon foreign mercenaries to augment their armies. Here the Habsburgs were again blessed, in that they could easily recruit in Italy and the Low Countries as well as in Spain and Germany; the famous Army of Flanders, for example, was composed of six main nationalities, reasonably loyal to the Catholic cause but still requiring regular pay. In naval terms, the Habsburg inheritance could produce an imposing conglomeration of fighting vessels: in Philip II's later years, for example, Mediterranean galleys, great carracks from Genoa and Naples, and the extensive Portuguese fleet could reinforce the armadas of Castile and Aragon.

But perhaps the greatest military advantage possessed by the Habsburgs during these 140 years was the Spanish-trained infantry. The social structure and the climate of ideas made Castile an ideal recruiting ground; there, notes Lynch, "soldiering had become a fashionable and profitable occupation not only for the gentry but for the whole population."[20] In addition, Gonzalo de Córdoba, the "Great Captain," had introduced changes in the organization of infantry early in the sixteenth century, and from then until the middle of the Thirty Years War the Spanish *tercio* was the most effective unit on the battlefields of Europe. With these integrated regiments of up to 3,000 pikemen, swordsmen, and arquebusiers, trained to give mutual support, the Spanish army swept aside innumerable foes and greatly reduced the reputation—and effectiveness—of French cavalry and Swiss pike phalanxes. As late as the battle of Nördlingen (1634), Cardinal-Infante's infantry resisted fifteen charges by the formidable Swedish army and then, like Wellington's troops at Waterloo, grimly moved forward to crush their enemy. At Rocroi (1643), although surrounded by the French, the Spaniards fought to the death. Here, indeed, was one of the strongest pillars in the Habsburg edifice; and it is significant that Spanish power *visibly* cracked only in the mid-seventeenth century, when its army consisted chiefly of German, Italian, and Irish mercenaries with far fewer warriors from Castile.

Yet, for all these advantages, the Spanish-Austrian dynastic alliance could never prevail. Enormous though its financial and military resources appeared to contemporaries, there was never sufficient to meet requirements. This critical deficiency was itself due to three factors which interacted with each other over the entire period—and which, by extension, provide major lessons for the study of armed conflict.

The first of these factors, mentioned briefly above, was the "military revolution" of early modern Europe: that is to say, the massive increase in the scale, costs and organization of war which occurred in the 150 years roughly following the 1520s.[21] This change was itself the result of various intertwined elements, tactical, political, and demographic. The blows dealt to the battlefield dominance of cavalry—first by the Swiss pikemen and then by mixed formations of men bearing pikes, swords, crossbows, and arquebuses—meant that the largest and most important part of an army was now its infantry. This conclusion was reinforced by the development of the *trace italienne,* that sophisticated system of city fortifications and bastions mentioned in the previous chapter. To man such defensive systems, or to besiege them, required a very large number of troops. Of course, in a major campaign a well-organized commander would be successfully employing consider- able numbers of cavalry and artillery as well, but those two arms were much less ubiquitous than regiments of foot soldiers. It was not the case, then, that nations scrapped their cavalry forces, but that the infantry proportion in their armies rose markedly; being cheaper to equip and feed, foot soldiers could be recruited in larger numbers, especially since Europe's population was rising. Naturally, all this placed immense organizational strains upon governments, but not so great that they would necessarily overwhelm the bureaucracies of the "new monarchies" of the West—just as the vast increase in the size of the armies would not inevitably make a general's task impossible, provided that his forces had a good command structure and were well drilled.

The Spanish Empire's army probably provides the best example of the "military revolution" in action. As its historian notes, "there is no evidence that any one state fielded more than 30,000 effectives" in the Franco-Spanish struggle for Italy before 1529; but:

In 1536–7 the Emperor Charles V mobilized 60,000 men in Lom- bardy alone for the defense of his recent conquest, Milan, and for the invasion of French Provence. In 1552, assailed on all fronts at once—in Italy, Germany, the Netherlands and Spain, in the Atlantic and the Mediterranean—Charles V raised 109,000 men in Germany and the Netherlands, 24,000 more in Lombardy and yet more in Sicily, Naples and Spain. The emperor must have had at his com- mand, and therefore at his cost, about 150,000 men. The upward trend continued. In 1574 the Spanish Army of Flanders alone num- bered 86,000 men, while only half a century later Philip IV could proudly proclaim that the armed forces at his command in 1625 amounted to no less than 300,000 men. In all these armies the real increase in numbers took place among the infantry, especially among the pikemen.[22]

What was happening on land was to a large extent paralleled at sea. The expansion in maritime (especially transoceanic) commerce, the rivalries among the contending fleets in the Channel, the Indian Ocean, or off the Spanish Main, the threats posed by the Barbary corsairs and the Ottoman galley fleets, all interacted with the new technology of shipbuilding to make vessels bigger and much better armed. In those days there was no strict division between a warship and a merchantmen; virtually all fair-sized trading vessels would carry guns, in order to beat off pirates and other predators. But there was a trend toward the creation of *royal* navies, so that the monarch would at least possess a number of regular warships to form the core around which a great fleet of armed merchantmen, galleasses, and pinnaces could gather in time of war. Henry VIII of England gave considerable support to this scheme, whereas Charles V tended to commandeer the privately owned galleons and galleys of his Spanish and Italian possessions rather than to build his own navy. Philip II, under far heavier pressure in the Mediterranean and then in the Atlantic, could not enjoy that luxury. He had to organize, and pay for, a massive program of galley construction, in Barcelona, Naples, and Sicily; by 1574 he was supporting a total of 146 galleys, nearly three times the number a dozen years before.[23] The explosion of warfare in the Atlantic during the following decade necessitated an even greater effort there: oceangoing warships were needed to protect the routes to the West Indies and (after Portugal was absorbed in 1580) to the East, to defend the Spanish coastline from English raids, and, ultimately, to convey an invading army to the British Isles. After the Anglo-Spanish peace of 1604, a large fleet was still required by Spain to ward off Dutch attacks on the high seas and to maintain communications with Flanders. And, decade by decade, such warships became heavier-armed and much more expensive.

It was these spiraling costs of war which exposed the real weakness of the Habsburg system. The general inflation, which saw food prices rise fivefold and industrial prices threefold between 1500 and 1630, was a heavy enough blow to government finances; but this was compounded by the doubling and redoubling in the size of armies and navies. In consequence, the Habsburgs were involved in an almost continual struggle for solvency. Following his various campaigns in the 1540s against Algiers, the French, and the German Protestants, Charles V found that his ordinary *and* extraordinary income could in no way match expenditures, and his revenues were pledged to the bankers for years ahead. Only by the desperate measure of confiscating the treasure from the Indies and seizing all specie in Spain could the monies be found to support the war against the Protestant princes. His 1552 campaign at Metz cost 2.5 million ducats alone—about ten times the emperor's normal income from the Americas at that time. Not surprisingly, he was driven repeatedly to raise fresh loans, but always on worse terms: as the crown's credit tumbled, the interest rates charged by the bankers spiraled upward, so that much of the ordinary revenue had to be used simply to pay the interest on past debts.[24] When Charles abdicated, he bequeathed to Philip II an official Spanish debt of some 20 million ducats.

Philip also inherited a state of war with France, but one which was so expensive that in 1557 the Spanish crown had to declare itself bankrupt. At this, great banking houses like the Fuggers were also brought to their knees. It was a poor consolation that France had been forced to admit its own bankruptcy in the same year—the major reason for each side agreeing to negotiate at Cateau-Cambresis in 1559—for Philip had then immediately to meet the powerful Turkish foe. The twenty-year Mediterranean war, the campaign against the Moriscos of Granada, and then the interconnected military effort in the Netherlands, northern France, and the English Channel drove the crown to search for all possible sources of income. Charles V's revenues had tripled during his reign, but Philip II's "doubled in the period 1556–73 alone, and more than redoubled by the end of the reign."[25]

His outgoings, however, were far larger. In the Lepanto campaign (1571), it was reckoned that the maintenance of the Christian fleets and soldiers would cost over 4 million ducats annually, although a fair part of this burden was shared by Venice and the papacy.[26] The payments to the Army of Flanders were already enormous by the 1570s, and nearly always overdue: this in turn provoking the revolts of the troops, particularly after Philip's 1575 suspension of payments of interest to his Genoese bankers.[27] The much larger flow of income from American mines—around 2 million ducats a year by the 1580s compared with one-tenth of that four decades earlier—rescued the crown's finances, and credit, temporarily; but the armada of 1588 cost 10 million ducats and its sad fate represented a financial as well as a naval disaster. By 1596, after floating loans at an epic rate, Philip again defaulted. At his death two years later his debts totaled the enormous sum of 100 million ducats, and interest payments on this sum equaled about two-thirds of all revenues.[28] Although peace with France and England soon followed, the war against the Dutch ground away until the truce of 1609, which itself had been precipitated by Spanish army mutinies and a further bankruptcy in 1607.

During the few years of peace which followed, there was no substantial reduction in Spanish governmental expenditures. Quite apart from the massive interest payments, there was still tension in the Mediterranean (necessitating a grandiose scheme for constructing coastal fortifications), and the far-flung Spanish empire was still subject to the depredations of privateers (necessitating considerable defense outlays in the Philippines and the Caribbean as well as on the high seas fleet).[29] The state of armed truce in Europe which existed after 1610 hardly suggested to Spain's proud leaders that they could reduce arms expenditures. All that the outbreak of the Thirty Years

War in 1618 did, therefore, was to convert a cold war into a hot one, and to produce an increased flow of Spanish troops and money into Flanders and Germany. It is interesting to note that the run of early Habsburg victories in Europe and the successful defense of the Americas in this period largely coincided with—and was aided by—significant increases in bullion deliveries from the New World. But by the same token, the reduction in treasure receipts after 1626, the bankruptcy declaration of the following year, and the stupendous Dutch success in seizing the silver fleet in 1628 (costing Spain and its inhabitants as much as 10 million ducats) caused the war effort to peter out for a while. And despite the alliance with the emperor, there was no way (except under Wallenstein's brief period of control) that German revenues could make up for this Spanish deficiency.

This, then, was to be the Spanish pattern for the next thirty years of war. By scraping together fresh loans, imposing new taxes, and utilizing any windfall from the Americas, a major military effort like, say, Cardinal-Infante's intervention in Germany in 1634–1635 could be supported; but the grinding costs of war always eventually eroded these short-term gains, and within a few more years the financial position was worse than ever. By the 1640s, in the aftermath of the Catalan and Portuguese revolts, and with the American treasure flow much reduced, a long, slow decline was inevitable.[30] What other fate was due to a nation which, although providing formidable fighters, was directed by governments which consistently spent two or three times more than the ordinary revenues provided?

The second chief cause of the Spanish and Austrian failure must be evident from the narrative account given above: the Habsburgs simply had too much to do, too many enemies to fight, too many fronts to defend. The stalwartness of the Spanish troops in battle could not compensate for the fact that these forces had to be dispersed, in homeland garrisons, in North Africa, in Sicily and Italy, and in the New World, as well as in the Netherlands. Like the British Empire three centuries later, the Habsburg bloc was a conglomeration of widely scattered territories, a political-dynastic *tour de force* which required enormous sustained resources of material and ingenuity to keep going. As such, it provides one of the greatest examples of strategical overstretch in history; for the price of possessing so many territories was the existence of numerous foes, a burden also carried by the contemporaneous Ottoman Empire.[31]

Related to this is the very significant issue of the chronology of the Habsburg wars. European conflicts in this period were frequent, to be sure, and their costs were a terrible burden upon all societies. But all the other states—France, England, Sweden, even the Ottoman Empire—enjoyed certain periods of peace and recovery. It was the Habsburg's, and more especially Spain's, fate to have to turn immediately from a struggle against one enemy to a new conflict against another; peace with France was succeeded by war with the Turks; a truce in the Mediterranean was followed by extended conflict in the Atlantic, and that by the struggle for northwestern Europe. During some awful periods, imperial Spain was fighting on three fronts simultaneously, and with her enemies consciously aiding each other, diplomatically and commercially if not militarily.[32] In contemporary terms, Spain resembled a large bear in the pit: more powerful than any of the dogs attacking it, but never able to deal with all of its opponents and growing gradually exhausted in the process.

Yet how could the Habsburgs escape from this vicious circle? Historians have pointed to the chronic dispersion of energies, and suggested that Charles V and his successors should have formulated a clear set of defense priorities.[33] The implication of this is that some areas were expendable; but which ones?

In retrospect, one can argue that the Austrian Habsburgs, and Ferdinand II in particular, would have been wiser to have refrained from pushing forward with the Counter-Reformation in northern Germany, for that brought heavy losses and few gains. Yet the emperor would still have needed to keep a considerable army in Germany to check princely particularism, French intrigues, and Swedish ambition; and there could also be no reduction in this Habsburg armed strength so long as the Turks stood athwart Hungary, only 150 miles from Vienna. The Spanish government, for its part, could allow the demise of their Austrian cousins neither at the hands of the French and Lutherans nor at the hands of the Turks, because of what it might imply for Spain's own position in Europe. This calculation, however, did not seem to have applied in reverse. After Charles V's retirement in 1556 the empire did not usually feel bound to aid Madrid in the latter's wars in western Europe and overseas; but Spain, conscious of the higher stakes, *would* commit itself to the empire.[34] The long-term consequences of this disparity of feeling and commitment are interesting. The failure of Habsburg Spain's European aims by the mid-seventeenth century was clearly related to its internal problems and relative economic decline; having overstrained itself in all directions, it was now weak at heart. In Habsburg Austria's case, on the other hand, although it failed to defeat Protestantism in Germany, it did achieve a *consolidation* of powers in the dynastic lands (Austria, Bohemia, and so on)—so much so that on this large territorial base and with the later creation of a professional standing army,[35] the Habsburg Empire would be able to reemerge as a European Great Power in the later decades of the seventeenth century, just as Spain was entering a period of even steeper decline.[36] By that stage, however, Austria's recuperation can hardly have been much of a consolation to the statesmen in Madrid, who felt they had to look elsewhere for allies.

It is easy to see why the possessions in the New World were an area of vital importance to Spain. For well over a century, they provided that regular addition to Spain's wealth, and thus to its military power, without which the Habsburg effort could not have been so extensively maintained. Even when the English and Dutch attacks upon the Hispano-Portuguese colonial empire necessitated an ever-increasing expenditure on fleets and fortifications overseas, the direct and indirect gains to the Spanish crown from those territories remained considerable. To abandon such assets was unthinkable.

This left for consideration the Habsburg possessions in Italy and those in Flanders. Of the two, a withdrawal from Italy had less to recommend itself. In the first half of the sixteenth century, the French would have filled the Great Power vacuum there, and used the wealth of Italy for their own purposes—and to Habsburg detriment. In the second half of that century Italy was, quite literally, the outer bulwark of Spain's own security in the face of Ottoman expansion westward. Quite apart from the blow to Spanish prestige and to the Christian religion which would have accompanied a Turkish assault upon Sicily, Naples, and Rome, the loss of this bulwark would have been a grave strategical setback. Spain would then have had to pour more and more money into coastal fortifications and galley fleets, which in any case were consuming the greater part of the arms budget in the early decades of Philip II's reign. So it made good military sense to commit these existing forces to the active defense of the central Mediterranean, for that kept the Turkish enemy at a distance; and it had the further advantage that the costs of such campaigning were shared by the Habsburg possessions in Italy, by the papacy, and, on occasions, by Venice. Withdrawal from this front brought no advantages and many potential dangers.

By elimination, then, the Netherlands was the only area in which Habsburg losses might be cut; and, after all, the costs of the Army of Flanders in the "Eighty Years War" against the Dutch were, thanks to the difficulties of the terrain and the advances in fortifications,[37] quite stupendous and greatly exceeded those on any other front. Even at the height of the Thirty Years War, five or six times as much money was allocated to the Flanders garrison as to forces in Germany. "The war in the Netherlands," observed one Spanish councillor, "has been the total ruin of this monarchy." In fact, between 1566 and 1654 Spain sent at least 218 million ducats to the Military Treasury in the Netherlands, considerably more than the sum total (121 million ducats) of the crown's receipts from the Indies.[38] Strategically, too, Flanders was much more difficult to defend: the sea route was often at the mercy of the French, the English, and the Dutch—as was most plainly shown when the Dutch admiral Tromp smashed a Spanish fleet carrying troop reinforcements in 1639—but the "Spanish Road" from Lombardy via the Swiss valleys or Savoy and Franche-Comté up the eastern frontiers of France to the lower Rhine also contained a number of very vulnerable choke points.[39] Was it really worthwhile to keep attempting to control a couple of million recalcitrant Netherlanders at the far end of an extensive line of communications, and at such horrendous cost? Why not, as the representatives of the overtaxed Cortes of Castile slyly put it, let the rebels rot in their heresy? Divine punishment was assured them, and Spain would not have to carry the burden any longer.[40]

The reasons given against an imperial retreat from that theater would not have convinced those complaining of the waste of resources, but they have a certain plausibility. In the first place, if Spain no longer possessed Flanders, it would fall either to France or to the United Provinces, thereby enhancing the power and prestige of one of those inveterate Habsburg enemies; the very idea was repellent to the directors of Spanish policy, to whom "reputation" mattered more than anything else. Secondly, there was the argument advanced by Philip IV and his advisers that a confrontation in that region at least took hostile forces away from more sensitive places: "Although the war which we have fought in the Netherlands has exhausted our treasury and forced us into the debts that we have incurred, it has also diverted our enemies in those parts so that, had we not done so, it is certain that we would have had war in Spain or somewhere nearer."[41] Finally, there was the "domino theory"—if the Netherlands were lost, so also would be the Habsburg cause in Germany, smaller possessions like Franche-Comté, perhaps even Italy. These were, of course, hypothetical arguments; but what is interesting is that the statesmen in Madrid, and their army commanders in Brussels, perceived an interconnected strategical whole, which would be shattered if any one of the parts fell:

> The first and greatest dangers [so the reasoning went in the critical year of 1635] are those that threaten Lombardy, the Netherlands and Germany. A defeat in any of these three is fatal for this Monarchy, so much so that if the defeat in those parts is a great one, the rest of the monarchy will collapse; for Germany will be followed by Italy and the Netherlands, and the Netherlands will be followed by America; and Lombardy will be followed by Naples and Sicily, without the possibility of being able to defend either.[42]

In accepting this logic, the Spanish crown had committed itself to a widespread war of attrition, which would last until victory was secured, or a compromise peace was effected, or the entire system was exhausted.

Perhaps it is sufficient to show that the sheer costs of continuous war and the determination not to abandon any of the four major fronts were bound to undermine Spanish-Imperial ambitions in any case. Yet the evidence suggests that there was a third, related cause: namely, that the Spanish government in particular failed to mobilize available resources in the most efficient way and, by acts of economic folly, helped to erode its own power.

Although foreigners frequently regarded the empire of Charles V or that of Philip II as monolithic and disciplined, it was in fact a congeries of territories, each of which possessed its own privileges and was proud of its own distinctiveness.[43] There was no central administration (let alone legislature or judiciary), and the only real connecting link was the monarch himself. The absence of such institutions which might have encouraged a sense of unity, and the fact that the ruler might never visit the country, made it difficult for the king to raise funds in one part of his dominions in order to fight in another. The taxpayers of Sicily and Naples would willingly pay for the construction of a fleet to resist the Turks, but they complained bitterly at the idea of financing the Spanish struggle in the Netherlands; the Portuguese saw the sense of supporting the defense of the New World, but had no enthusiasm for German wars. This intense localism had contributed to, and was reflected by, jealously held fiscal rights. In Sicily, for example, the estates resisted early Habsburg efforts to increase taxation and had risen against the Spanish viceroy in 1516 and 1517; being poor, anarchical, and possessing a parliament, Sicily was highly unlikely to provide much for the general defense of Habsburg interests.[44] In the kingdom of Naples and in the newer acquisition of Milan, there were fewer legislative obstacles to Spanish administrators under pressure from Madrid to find fresh funds. Both therefore *could* provide considerable financial aid during Charles V's reign; but in practice the struggle to retain Milan, and the wars against the Turks, meant that this flow was usually reversed. To hold its Mediterranean "bulwark," Spain had to send millions of ducats to Italy, to add to those raised there. During the Thirty Years War the pattern was reversed again, and Italian taxes helped to pay for the wars in Germany and the Netherlands; but, taking this period 1519–1659 as a whole, it is hard to believe that the Habsburg possessions in Italy contributed substantially more—if at all—to the common fund than they themselves took out for their own defense.[45]

The Netherlands became, of course, an even greater drain upon general imperial revenues. In the early part of Charles V's reign, the States General provided a growing amount of taxes, although always haggling over the amount and insisting upon recognition of their privileges. By the emperor's later years, the anger at the frequent extraordinary grants which were demanded for wars in Italy and Germany had fused with religious discontents and commercial difficulties to produce a widespread feeling against Spanish rule. By 1565 the state debt of the Low Countries reached 10 million florins, and debt payments plus the costs of normal administration exceeded revenues, so that the deficit had to be made up by Spain.[46] When, after a further decade of mishandling from Madrid, these local resentments burst into open revolt, the

Netherlands became a colossal drain upon imperial resources, with the 65,000 or more troops of the Army of Flanders consuming one-quarter of the total outgoings of the Spanish government for decade after decade.

But the most disastrous failure to mobilize resources lay in Spain itself, where the crown's fiscal rights were in fact very limited. The three realms of the crown of Aragon (that is, Aragon, Catalonia, and Valencia) had their own laws and tax systems, which gave them a quite remarkable autonomy. In effect, the only guaranteed revenue for the monarch came from royal properties; additional grants were made rarely and grudgingly. When, for example, a desperate ruler like Philip IV sought in 1640 to make Catalonia pay for the troops sent there to defend the Spanish frontier, all this did was to provoke a lengthy and famous revolt. Portugal, although taken over from 1580 until its own 1640 rebellion, was completely autonomous in fiscal matters and contributed no regular funds to the general Habsburg cause. This left Castile as the real "milch cow" in the Spanish taxation system, although even here the Basque provinces were immune. The landed gentry, strongly represented in the Castilian Cortes, was usually willing to vote taxes from which they were exempt. Furthermore, taxes such as the *alcabala* (a 10 percent sales tax) and the customs duties, which were the ordinary revenues, together with the *servicios* (grants by the Cortes), *millones* (a tax on foodstuffs, also granted by the Cortes), and the various church allocations, which were the main extraordinary revenues, all tended to hit at trade, the exchange of goods, and the poor, thus spreading impoverishment and discontent, and contributing to depopulation (by emigration).[47]

Until the flow of American silver brought massive additional revenues to the Spanish crown (roughly from the 1560s to the late 1630s), the Habsburg war effort principally rested upon the backs of Castilian peasants and merchants; and even at its height, the royal income from sources in the New World was only about one-quarter to one-third of that derived from Castile and its six million inhabitants. Unless and until the tax burdens could be shared more equitably within that kingdom and indeed across the entirety of the Habsburg territories, this was virtually bound to be too small a base on which to sustain the staggering military expenditures of the age.

What made this inadequacy absolutely certain was the retrograde economic measures attending the exploitation of the Castilian taxpayers.[48] The social ethos of the kingdom had never been very encouraging to trade, but in the early sixteenth century the country was relatively prosperous, boasting a growing population and some significant industries. However, the coming of the Counter-Reformation and of the Habsburgs' many wars stimulated the religious and military elements in Spanish society while weakening the commercial ones. The economic incentives which existed in this society all suggested the wisdom of acquiring a church benefice or purchasing a patent of minor nobility. There was a chronic lack of skilled craftsmen—for example, in the armaments industry—and mobility of labor and flexibility of practice were obstructed by the guilds.[49] Even the development of agriculture was retarded by the privileges of the Mesta, the famous guild of sheep owners whose stock were permitted to graze widely over the kingdom; with Spain's population growing in the first half of the sixteenth century, this simply led to an increasing need for imports of grain. Since the Mesta's payments for these grazing rights went into the royal treasury, and a revocation of this practice would have enraged some of the crown's strongest supporters, there was no prospect of amending the system. Finally, although there were some notable exceptions —the merchants involved in the wool trade, the financier Simon Ruiz, the region around Seville—the Castilian economy on the whole was also heavily dependent upon imports of foreign manufactures and upon the services provided by non-Spaniards, in particular Genoese, Portuguese, and Flemish entrepreneurs. It was dependent, too, upon the Dutch, even during hostilities; "by 1640 three-quarters of the goods in Spanish ports were delivered in Dutch ships,"[50] to the profit of the nation's greatest foes. Not surprisingly, Spain suffered from a constant trade imbalance, which could be made good only by the re-export of American gold and silver.

The horrendous costs of 140 years of war were, therefore, imposed upon a society which was economically ill-equipped to carry them. Unable to raise revenues by the most efficacious means, Habsburg monarchs resorted to a variety of expedients, easy in the short term but disastrous for the long-term good of the country. Taxes were steadily increased by all manner of means, but rarely fell upon the shoulders of those who could bear them most easily, and always tended to hurt commerce. Various privileges, monopolies, and honors were sold off by a government desperate for ready cash. A crude form of deficit financing was evolved, in part by borrowing heavily from the bankers on the credit of future Castilian taxes or American treasure, in part by selling interest-bearing government bonds *(juros)*, which in turn drew in funds that might otherwise have been invested in trade and industry. But the government's debt policy was always done in a hand-to-mouth fashion, without regard for prudent limitations and without the control which a central bank arguably might have imposed. Even by the later stages of Charles V's reign, therefore, government revenues had been mortgaged for years in advance; in 1543, 65 percent of ordinary revenue had to be spent paying interest on the *juros* already issued. The more the crown's "ordinary" income became alienated, the more desperate was its search for extraordinary revenues and new taxes. The silver coinage, for example, was repeatedly debased with copper *vellon.* On occasions, the government simply seized incoming American silver destined for private individuals and forced the latter to accept *juros* in compensation; on other occasions, as has been mentioned above, Spanish kings suspended interest repayments and declared themselves temporarily bankrupt. If this latter action did not always ruin the financial houses themselves, it certainly reduced Madrid's credit rating for the future.

Even if some of the blows which buffeted the Castilian economy in these years were not man-made, their impact was the greater because of human folly. The plagues which depopulated much of the countryside around the beginning of the seventeenth century were unpredictable, but they added to the other causes—extortionate rents, the actions of the Mesta, military service—which were already hurting agriculture. The flow of American silver was bound to cause economic problems (especially price inflation) which no society of the time had the experience to handle, but the conditions prevailing in Spain meant that this phenomenon hurt the productive classes more than the unproductive, that the silver tended to flow swiftly out of Seville into the hands of foreign bankers and military provision merchants, and that these new transatlantic sources of wealth were exploited by the crown in a way which worked against rather than for the creation of "sound finance." The flood of precious metals from the Indies, it was said, was to Spain as water on a roof—it poured on and then was drained away.

At the center of the Spanish decline, therefore, was the failure to recognize the importance of preserving the economic underpinnings of a powerful military machine. Time and again the wrong measures were adopted. The expulsion of the Jews, and later the Moriscos; the closing of contacts with foreign universities; the government directive that the Biscayan shipyards should concentrate upon large warships to the near exclusion of smaller, more useful trading vessels; the sale of monopolies which restricted trade; the heavy taxes upon wool exports, which made them uncompetitive in foreign markets; the *internal* customs barriers between the various Spanish kingdoms, which hurt commerce and drove up prices—these were just some of the ill-considered decisions which, in the long term, seriously affected Spain's capacity to carry out the great military role which it had allocated to itself in European (and extra-European) affairs. Although the decline of Spanish power did not fully reveal itself until the 1640s, the causes had existed for decades beforehand.

International Comparisons

Yet this Habsburg failure, it is important to emphasize, was a *relative* one. To abandon the story here without examination of the experiences of the other European powers would leave an incomplete analysis. War, as one historian has argued, "was by far the severest test

that faced the sixteenth-century state."[51] The changes in military techniques which permitted the great rise in the size of armies and the
almost simultaneous evolution of large-scale naval conflict placed
enormous new pressures upon the organized societies of the West.
Each belligerent had to learn how to create a satisfactory administrative structure to meet the "military revolution"; and, of equal importance, it also had to devise new means of paying for the spiraling costs
of war. The strains which were placed upon the Habsburg rulers and
their subjects may, because of the sheer number of years in which their
armies were fighting, have been unusual; but, as Table 1 shows, the
challenge of supervising and financing bigger military forces was common to all states, many of which seemed to possess far fewer resources
than did imperial Spain. How did they meet the test?

Table 1. Increase in Military Manpower, 1470–1660[52]

Date	Spain	United Provinces	France	England	Sweden
1470s	20,000		40,000	25,000	
1550s	150,000		50,000	20,000	
1590s	200,000	20,000	80,000	30,000	15,000
1630s	300,000	50,000	150,000		45,000
1650s	100,000		100,000	70,000	70,000

Omitted from this brief survey is one of the most persistent and
threatening foes of the Habsburgs, the Ottoman Empire, chiefly because its strengths and weaknesses were discussed in the previous
chapter; but it is worth recalling that many of the problems and deficiencies with which Turkish administrators had to contend—strategical
overextension, failure to tap resources efficiently, the crushing of commercial entrepreneurship in the cause of religious orthodoxy or military prestige—appear similar to those which troubled Philip II and his
successors. Also omitted will be Russia and Prussia, as nations whose
period as great powers in European politics had not yet arrived; and,
further, Poland-Lithuania, which despite its territorial extent was too
hampered by ethnic diversity and the fetters of feudalism (serfdom, a
backward economy, an elective monarchy, "an aristocratic anarchy
which was to make it a byword for political ineptitude"[53]) to commence its own takeoff to becoming a modern nation-state. Instead, the
countries to be examined are the "new monarchies" of France, England, and Sweden and the "bourgeois republic" of the United Provinces.

Because France was the state which ultimately replaced Spain as
the greatest military power, it has been natural for historians to focus
upon the former's many advantages. It would be wrong, however, to
antedate the period of French predominance; throughout most of the

years covered in this chapter, France looked—and was—decidedly weaker than its southern neighbor. In the few decades which followed the Hundred Years War, the consolidation of the crown's territories vis-à-vis England, Burgundy, and Britanny, the habit of levying direct taxation (especially the *taille,* a poll tax), without application to the States General, the steady administrative work of the new secretaries of state, and the existence of a "royal" army with a powerful artillery train made France appear to be a successful, unified, postfeudal monarchy.[54] Yet the very fragility of this structure was soon to be made clear. The Italian wars, besides repeatedly showing how short-lived and disastrous were the French efforts to gain influence in that peninsula (even when allied with Venice or the Turks), were also very expensive: it was not only the Habsburgs but also the French crown which had to declare bankruptcy in the fateful year of 1557. Well before that crash, and despite all the increase in the *taille* and in indirect taxes like the *gabelle* and customs, the French monarchy was already resorting to heavy borrowings from financiers at high rates of interest (10–16 percent), and to dubious expedients like selling offices. Worse still, it was in France rather than Spain or England that religious rivalries interacted with the ambitions of the great noble houses to produce a bloody and long-lasting civil war. Far from being a great force in international affairs, France after 1560 threatened to become the new cockpit of Europe, perhaps to be divided permanently along religious borders as was to be the fate of the Netherlands and Germany.[55]

Only after the accession of Henry of Navarre to the French throne as Henry IV (1589–1610), with his policies of internal compromise and external military actions against Spain, did matters improve; and the peace which he secured with Madrid in 1598 had the great advantage of maintaining France as an independent power. But it was a country severely weakened by civil war, brigandage, high prices, and interrupted trade and agriculture, and its fiscal system was in pieces. In 1596 the national debt was almost 300 million livres, and four-fifths of that year's revenue of 31 million livres had already been assigned and alienated.[56] For a long time thereafter, France was a recuperating society. Yet its natural resources were, comparatively, immense. Its population of around sixteen million inhabitants was twice that of Spain and four times that of England. While it may not have been as advanced as the Netherlands, northern Italy, and the London region in urbanization, commerce, and finance, its agriculture was diversified and healthy, and the country normally enjoyed a food surplus. The latent wealth of France was clearly demonstrated in the early seventeenth century, when Henry IV's great minister Sully was supervising the economy and state finances. Apart from the *paulette* (which was the sale of, and tax on, hereditary offices), Sully introduced no new fiscal devices; what he did do was to overhaul the tax-collecting machinery, flush out thousands of individuals illegally claiming exemption, recover crown lands and income, and renegotiate the interest rates on the national debt. Within a few years after 1600, the state's budget was in balance. In addition, Sully—anticipating Louis XIV's minister, Colbert—tried to aid industry and agriculture by various means: reducing the *taille*, building bridges, roads, and canals to assist the transport of goods, encouraging cloth production, setting up royal factories to produce luxury wares which would replace imports, and so on. Not all of these measures worked to the extent hoped for, but the contrast with Philip III's Spain was a marked one.[57]

It is difficult to say whether this work of recovery would have continued had not Henry IV been assassinated in 1610. What was clear was that none of the "new monarchies" could properly function without adequate leadership, and between the time of Henry IV's death and Richelieu's consolidation of royal power in the 1630s, the internal politics of France, the disaffection of the Huguenots, and the nobility's inclination toward intrigue once again weakened the country's capacity to act as a European Great Power. Furthermore, when France eventually did engage openly in the Thirty Years War it was not, as some historians have tended to portray it, a unified, healthy power but a country still suffering from many of the old ailments. Aristocratic intrigue remained strong and was only to reach its peak in 1648–1653; uprisings by the peasantry, by the unemployed urban workers, and by the Huguenots, together with the obstructionism of local officeholders, all interrupted the proper functioning of government; and the economy, affected by the general population decline, harsher climate, reduced agricultural output, and higher incidence of plagues which seems to have troubled much of Europe at this time,[58] was hardly in a position to finance a great war.

From 1635 onward, therefore, French taxes had to be increased by a variety of means: the sale of offices was accelerated; and the *taille*, having been reduced in earlier years, was raised so much that the annual yield from it had doubled by 1643. But even this could not cover the costs of the struggle against the Habsburgs, both the direct military burden of supporting an army of 150,000 men and the subsidies to allies. In 1643, the year of the great French military victory over Spain at Rocroi, government expenditure was almost double its income and Mazarin, Richelieu's successor, had been reduced to even more desperate sales of government offices and an even stricter control of the *taille*, both of which were highly unpopular. It was no coincidence that the rebellion of 1648 began with a tax strike against Mazarin's new fiscal measures, and that such unrest swiftly led to a loss in the government's credit and to its reluctant declaration of bankruptcy.[59]

Consequently, in the eleven years of Franco-Spanish warfare which remained after the general Peace of Westphalia in 1648, the two contestants resembled punch-drunk boxers, clinging to each other in a state of near-exhaustion and unable to finish the other off. Each was suffering from domestic rebellion, widespread impoverishment, and dislike of the war, and was on the brink of financial collapse. It was true that, with generals like d'Enghien and Turenne and military reformers like Le Tellier, the French army was slowly emerging to be the greatest in Europe; but its naval power, built up by Richelieu, had swiftly disintegrated because of the demands of land warfare;[60] and the country still needed a solid economic base. In the event, it was France's good fortune that England, resurgent in its naval and military power under Cromwell, elected to join the conflict, thereby finally tilting the balance against a distressed Spain. The Treaty of the Pyrenees which followed was symbolic less of the greatness of France than of the relative decline of its overstretched southern neighbor, which had fought on with remarkable tenacity.[61]

In other words, each of the European powers possessed a mixture of strengths and weaknesses, and the real need was to prevent the latter from outweighing the former. This was certainly true of the "flank" powers in the west and north, England and Sweden, whose interventions helped to check Habsburg ambitions on several critical occasions. It was hardly the case, for example, that England stood poised and well prepared for a continental conflict during these 140 years. The key to the English recovery following the Wars of the Roses had been Henry VII's concentration upon domestic stability and financial prudence, at least after the peace with France in 1492. By cutting down on his own expenses, paying off his debts, and encouraging the wool trade, fishing, and commerce in general, the first Tudor monarch provided a much-needed breathing space for a country hit by civil war and unrest; the natural productivity of agriculture, the flourishing cloth trade to the Low Countries, the increasing use of the rich offshore fishing grounds, and the general bustle of coastal trade did the rest. In the area of national finances, the king's recovery of crown lands and seizure of those belonging to rebels and rival contenders to the throne, the customs yield from growing trade, and the profits from the Star Chamber and other courts all combined to produce a healthy balance.[62]

But political and fiscal stability did not necessarily equal *power*. Compared with the far greater populations of France and Spain, the three to four million inhabitants of England and Wales did not seem much. The country's financial institutions and commercial infrastructures were crude, compared with those in Italy, southern Germany, and the Low Countries, although considerable industrial growth was to occur in the course of the "Tudor century."[63] At the military level, the gap was much wider. Once he was secure upon the throne, Henry

VII had dissolved much of his own army and forbade (with a few exceptions) the private armies of the great magnates; apart from the "Yeomen of the Guard" and certain garrison troops, there was no regular standing army in England during this period when Franco-Habsburg wars in Italy were changing the nature and dimensions of military conflict. Consequently, such forces as did exist under the early Tudors were still equipped with traditional weapons (longbow, bill) and raised in the traditional way (county militia, volunteer "companies," and so on). However, this backwardness did not keep his successor, Henry VIII, from campaigning against the Scots or even deter his interventions of 1513 and 1522–1523 against France, since the English king could hire large numbers of "modern" troops—pikemen, arquebusiers, heavy cavalry—from Germany.[64]

If neither these early English operations in France nor the two later invasions in 1528 and 1544 ended in military disaster—if, indeed, they often forced the French monarch to buy off the troublesome English raiders—they certainly had devastating financial consequences. Of the total expenditures of £700,000 by the Treasury of the Chamber in 1513, for example, £632,000 was allocated toward soldiers' pay, ordnance, warships, and other military outgoings.* Soon, Henry VII's accumulated reserves were all spent by his ambitious heir, and Henry VIII's chief minister, Wolsey, was provoking widespread complaints by his efforts to gain money from forced loans, "benevolences," and other arbitrary means. Only with Thomas Cromwell's assault upon church lands in the 1530s was the financial position eased; in fact, the English Reformation doubled the royal revenues and permitted large-scale spending upon defensive military projects—fortresses along the Channel coast and Scottish border, new and powerful warships for the Royal Navy, the suppression of rebellions in Ireland. But the disastrous wars against France and Scotland in the 1540s cost an enormous £2,135,000, which was about ten times the normal income of the crown. This forced the king's ministers into the most desperate of expedients: the sale of religious properties at low rates, the seizure of the estates of nobles on trumped-up charges, repeated forced loans, the great debasement of the coinage, and finally the recourse to the Fuggers and other foreign bankers.[65] Settling England's differences with France in 1550 was thus a welcome relief to a near-bankrupt government.

What this all indicated, therefore, was the very real limits upon England's power in the first half of the sixteenth century. It was a

---

*My colleague Prof. Robert Ashton warns me that any stated figures of English (and presumably other) state revenues and expenditures in this entire period must be regarded as *nominal;* the amounts deducted by officeholders, bribery, corruption, and inefficient bookkeeping drastically reduced the stated "allocations" to the army and navy. In much the same way, only a portion of the king's "income" ever reached the monarch. The statistics given here are, therefore, indicative and not authoritative.

centralized and relatively homogeneous state, although much less so in the border areas and in Ireland, which could always distract royal resources and attention. Thanks chiefly to the interest of Henry VIII, it was defensively strong, with some modern forts, artillery, dock-yards, a considerable armaments industry, and a well-equipped navy. But it was militarily backward in the quality of its army, and its finances could not fund a large-scale war. When Elizabeth I became monarch in 1558, she was prudent enough to recognize these limita-tions and to achieve her ends without breaching them. In the danger-ous post-1570 years, when the Counter-Reformation was at its height and Spanish troops were active in the Netherlands, this was a difficult task to fulfill. Since her country was no match for any of the real "superpowers" of Europe, Elizabeth sought to maintain England's in-dependence by diplomacy and, even when Anglo-Spanish relations worsened, to allow the "cold war" against Philip II to be conducted at sea, which was at least economical and occasionally profitable.[66] Al-though needing to provide monies to secure her Scottish and Irish flanks and to give aid to the Dutch rebels in the late 1570s, Elizabeth and her ministers succeeded in building up a healthy surplus during the first twenty-five years of her reign—which was just as well, since the queen sorely needed a "war chest" once the decision was taken in 1585 to dispatch an expeditionary force under Leicester to the Nether-lands.

The post-1585 conflict with Spain placed both strategical and finan-cial demands upon Elizabeth's government. In considering the strategy which England should best employ, naval leaders like Hawkins, Ra-leigh, Drake, and others urged upon the queen a policy of intercepting the Spanish silver trade, raiding the enemy's coasts and colonies, and in general exploiting the advantages of sea power to wage war on the cheap—an attractive proposition in theory, although often difficult to implement in practice. But there was also the need to send troops to the Netherlands and northern France to assist those fighting the Span-ish army—a strategy adopted not out of any great love of Dutch rebels or the French Protestants but simply because, as Elizabeth argued, "whenever the last day of France came it would also be the eve of the destruction of England."[67] It was therefore vital to preserve the Euro-pean balance, if need be by active intervention; and this "continental commitment" continued until the early seventeenth century, at least in a personal form, for many English troops stayed on when the expedi-tionary force was merged into the army of the United Provinces in 1594.

In performing the twin function of checking Philip II's designs on land and harassing his empire at sea, the English made their own contribution to the maintenance of Europe's political plurality. But the strain of supporting 8,000 men abroad was immense. In 1586 monies sent to the Netherlands totaled over £100,000, in 1587 £175,000, each being about half of the entire outgoings for the year; in the Armada year, allocations to the fleet exceeded £150,000. Consequently, Elizabeth's annual expenditures in the late 1580s were between two and three times those of the early 1580s. During the next decade the crown spent over £350,000 each year, and the Irish campaign brought the annual average to over £500,000 in the queen's last four years.[68] Try as it might to raise funds from other sources—such as the selling of crown lands, and of monopolies—the government had no alternative but to summon the Commons on repeated occasions and plead for extra grants. That these (totaling some £2 million) were given, and that the English government neither declared itself bankrupt nor failed to pay its troops, was testimony to the skill and prudence of the monarch and her councillors; but the war years had tested the entire system, left debts to the first Stuart king, and placed him and his successor in a position of dependence upon a mistrustful Commons and a cautious London money market.[69]

There is no space in this story to examine the spiraling conflict between crown and Parliament which was to dominate English politics for the four decades after 1603, in which finance was to play the central part.[70] The inept and occasional interventions by English forces in the great European struggle during the 1620s, although very expensive to mount, had little effect upon the course of the Thirty Years War. The population, trade, overseas colonies, and general wealth of England grew in this period, but none of this could provide a sure basis for state power without domestic harmony; indeed, the quarrels over such taxes as Ship Money—which in theory could have enhanced the nation's armed strength—were soon to lead crown and Parliament into a civil war which would cripple England as a factor in European politics for much of the 1640s. When England did reemerge, it was to challenge the Dutch in a fierce commercial war (1652–1654), which, whatever the aims of each belligerent, had little to do with the general European balance.

Cromwell's England of the 1650s could, however, play a Great Power role more successfully than any previous government. His New Model Army, which emerged from the civil war, had at last closed the gap that traditionally existed between English troops and their European counterparts. Organized and trained on modern lines established by Maurice of Nassau and Gustavus Adolphus, hardened by years of conflict, well disciplined, and (usually) paid regularly, the English army could be thrown into the European balance with some effect, as was evident in its defeat of Spanish forces at the battle of the Dunes in 1658. Furthermore, the Commonwealth navy was, if anything, even more advanced for the age. Favored by the Commons because it had generally declared against Charles I during the civil war, the fleet underwent a renaissance in the late 1640s: its size was more than doubled from thirty-nine vessels (1649) to eighty (1651), wages and conditions were improved, dockyard and logistical support were bettered, and the funds for all this regularly voted by a House of Commons which believed that profit and power went hand in hand.[71] This was just as well, because in its first war against the Dutch the navy was taking on an equally formidable force commanded by leaders—Tromp and de Ruyter—who were as good as Blake and Monk. When the service was unleashed upon the Spanish Empire after 1655, it was not surprising that it scored successes: taking Acadia (Nova Scotia) and, after a fiasco at Hispaniola, Jamaica; seizing part of the Spanish treasure fleet in 1656; blockading Cádiz and destroying the *flota* in Santa Cruz in 1657.

Yet, while these English actions finally tilted the balance and forced Spain to end its war with France in 1659, this was not achieved without domestic strains. The profitable Spanish trade was lost to the neutral Dutch in these years after 1655, and enemy privateers reaped a rich harvest of English merchant ships along the Atlantic and Mediterranean routes. Above all, paying for an army of up to 70,000 men and a large navy was a costly business; one estimate suggests that out of a total government expenditure of £2,878,000 in 1657, over £1,900,000 went on the army and £742,000 on the navy.[72] Taxes were imposed, and efficiently extorted, at an unprecedented level, yet they were never enough for a government which was spending "four times as much as had been thought intolerable under Charles I" before the English Revolution.[73] Debts steadily rose, and the pay of soldiers and sailors was in arrears. These few years of the Spanish war undoubtedly increased the public dislike of Cromwell's rule and caused the majority of the merchant classes to plead for peace. It was scarcely the case, of course, that England was altogether ruined by this conflict—although it no doubt would have been had it engaged in Great Power struggles as long as Spain. The growth of England's inland and overseas commerce, plus the profits from the colonies and shipping, were starting to provide a solid economic foundation upon which governments in London could rely in the event of another war; and precisely because England— together with the United Provinces of the Netherlands—had developed an efficient market economy, it achieved the rare feat of combining a rising standard of living with a growing population.[74] Yet it still remained vital to preserve the proper balance between the country's military and naval effort on the one hand and the encouragement of the national wealth on the other; by the end of the Protectorate, that balance had become a little too precarious.

This crucial lesson in statecraft emerges the more clearly if one compares England's rise with that of the other "flank" power, Sweden.[75] Throughout the sixteenth century, the prospects for the northern kingdom looked poor. Hemmed in by Lübeck and (especially) by Denmark from free egress to western Europe, engaged in a succession of struggles on its eastern flank with Russia, and repeatedly distracted by its relationship with Poland, Sweden had enough to do simply to maintain itself; indeed, its severe defeat by Denmark in the war of 1611–1613 hinted that decline rather than expansion would be the country's fate. In addition, it had suffered from internal fissures, which were constitutional rather than religious, and had resulted in confirming the extensive privileges of the nobility. But Sweden's greatest weakness was its economic base. Much of its extensive territory was Arctic waste, or forest. The scattered peasantry, largely self-sufficient, formed 95 percent of a total population of some 900,000; with Finland, about a million and a quarter—less than many of the Italian states. There were few towns and little industry; a "middle class" was hardly to be detected; and the barter of goods and services was still the major form of exchange. Militarily and economically, therefore, Sweden was a mere pigmy when the youthful Gustavus Adolphus succeeded to the throne in 1611.

Two factors, one external, one internal, aided Sweden's swift growth from these unpromising foundations. The first was foreign entrepreneurs, in particular the Dutch but also Germans and Walloons, for whom Sweden was a promising "undeveloped" land, rich in raw materials such as timber and iron and copper ores. The most famous of these foreign entrepreneurs, Louis de Geer, not only sold finished products to the Swedes and bought the raw ores from them; he also, over time, created timber mills, foundries, and factories, made loans to the king, and drew Sweden into the mercantile "world system" based chiefly upon Amsterdam. Soon the country became the greatest producer of iron and copper in Europe, and these exports brought in the foreign currency which would soon help to pay for the armed forces. In addition, Sweden became self-sufficient in armaments, a rare feat, thanks again to foreign investment and expertise.[76]

The internal factor was the well-known series of reforms instituted by Gustavus Adolphus and his aides. The courts, the treasury, the tax system, the central administration of the chancery, and education were but some of the areas made more efficient and productive in this period. The nobility was led away from faction into state service. Religious solidarity was assured. Local as well as central government seemed to work. On these firm foundations, Gustavus could build a Swedish navy so as to protect the coasts from Danish and Polish rivals and to ensure the safe passage of Swedish troops across the Baltic. Above all, however, the king's fame rested upon his great military reforms: in developing the national standing army based upon a form of conscription, in training his troops in new battlefield tactics, in his improvements of the cavalry and introduction of mobile, light artillery, and finally in the discipline and high morale which his leadership gave to the army, Gustavus had at his command perhaps the best fighting force in the world when he moved into northern Germany to aid the Protestant cause during the summer of 1630.[77]

Such advantages were all necessary, since the dimensions of the European conflict were far larger, and the costs far heavier, than anything experienced in the earlier local wars against Sweden's neighbors. By the end of 1630 Gustavus commanded over 42,000 men; twelve months later, double that number; and just before the fateful battle of Lützen, his force had swollen to almost 150,000. While Swedish troops formed a *corps d'élite* in all the major battles and were also used to garrison strategic strongpoints, they were insufficient in number to form an army of that size; indeed, four-fifths of that "Swedish" army of 150,000 consisted of foreign mercenaries, Scots, English, and Germans, who were fearfully expensive. Even the struggles against Poland in the 1620s had strained Swedish public finance, but the German war threatened to be far more costly. Remarkably, however, the Swedes managed to make others pay for it. The foreign subsidies, particularly those paid by France, are well known but they covered only a fraction of the costs. The real source was Germany itself: the various princely states, and the free cities, were required to contribute to the cause, if they were friendly; if they were hostile, they had to pay ransoms to avoid plunder. In addition, this vast Swedish-controlled army exacted quarter, food, and fodder from the territories on which it was encamped. To be sure, this system had already been perfected by the emperor's lieutenant, Wallenstein, whose policy of exacting "contributions" had financed an imperial army of over 100,000 men;[78] but the point here is that it was *not* the Swedes who paid for the great force which helped to check the Habsburgs from 1630 until 1648. In the very month of the Peace of Westphalia itself, the Swedish army was looting in Bohemia; and it was entirely appropriate that it withdrew only upon the payment of a large "compensation."

Although this was a remarkable achievement by the Swedes, in many ways it gave a false picture of the country's real standing in Europe. Its formidable war machine had been to a large degree *parasitic;* the Swedish army in Germany had to plunder in order to live—otherwise the troops mutinied, which hurt the Germans more. Naturally, the Swedes themselves had had to pay for their navy, for home defenses, and for forces employed elsewhere than in Germany; and, as in all other states, this had strained governmental finances, which led to desperate sales of crown lands and revenues to the nobility, thus reducing long-term income. The Thirty Years War had also taken a heavy toll in human life, and the extraordinary taxes burdened the peasantry. Furthermore, Sweden's military successes had given it a variety of trans-Baltic possessions—Estonia, Livonia, Bremen, most of Pomerania—which admittedly brought commercial and fiscal benefits, but the costs of maintaining them in peacetime or defending them in wartime from jealous rivals was to bring a far higher charge upon the Swedish state than had the great campaigning across Germany in the 1630s and 1640s.

Sweden was to remain a considerable power, even after 1648, but only at the regional level. Indeed, under Charles X (1654–1660) and Charles XI (1660–1697), it was arguably at its height in the Baltic arena, where it successively checked the Danes and held its own against Poland, Russia, and the rising power of Prussia. The turn toward absolutism under Charles XI augmented the royal finances and thus permitted the upkeep of a large peacetime standing army. Nonetheless, these were measures to strengthen Sweden as it slowly declined from the first ranks. In Professor Roberts's words:

> For a generation Sweden had been drunk with victory and bloated with booty: Charles XI led her back into the grey light of everyday existence, gave her policies appropriate to her resources and her real interests, equipped her to carry them out, and prepared for her a future of weight and dignity as a second-class power.[79]

These were not mean achievements, but in the larger European context they had limited significance. And it is interesting to note the extent to which the balance of power in the Baltic, upon which Sweden no less than Denmark, Poland, and Brandenburg depended, was being influenced and "manipulated" in the second half of the seventeenth century by the French, the Dutch, and even the English, for their own purposes, by subsidies, diplomatic interventions, and, in 1644 and 1659, a Dutch fleet.[80] Finally, while Sweden could never be called a "puppet" state in this great diplomatic game, it remained an economic midget compared with the rising powers of the West, and tended to become dependent upon their subsidies. Its foreign trade around 1700 was but a small fraction of that possessed by the United Provinces or England; its state expenditure was perhaps only one-fiftieth that of France.[81] On this inadequate material base, and without the possibility of access to overseas colonies, Sweden had little chance—despite its admirable social and administrative stability—of maintaining the military predominance that it had briefly held under Gustavus Adolphus. In the coming decades, in fact, it would have its work cut out merely seeking to arrest the advances of Prussia in the south and Russia in the east.

The final example, that of Dutch power in this period, offers a remarkable contrast to the Swedish case. Here was a nation created in the confused circumstances of revolution, a cluster of seven heterogenous provinces separated by irregular borders from the rest of the Habsburg-owned Netherlands, a mere part of a part of a vast dynastic empire, restricted in population and territorial extent, which swiftly became a great power inside and *outside* Europe for almost a century. It differed from the other states—although not from its Italian forerunner, Venice—in possessing a republican, oligarchic form of government; but its most distinctive characteristic was that the foundations of its strength were firmly anchored in the world of trade, industry, and finance. It was, to be sure, a formidable military power, at least in defense; and it was the most effective naval power until eclipsed by England in the later seventeenth century. But those manifestations of armed might were the consequences, rather than the essence, of Dutch strength and influence.

It was hardly the case, of course, that in the early years of their revolt the 70,000 or so Dutch rebels counted for much in European affairs; indeed, it was not for some decades that they regarded themselves as a separate nation at all, and not until the early seventeenth century that the boundaries were in any way formed. The so-called Revolt of the Netherlands was in the beginning a sporadic affair, during which different social groups and regions fought against each other as well as opposing—and sometimes compromising with—their Habsburg rulers; and there were various moments in the 1580s when the Duke of Parma's superbly conducted policy of recovering the territories for Spain looked on the verge of success. But for the subsidies and military aid from England and other Protestant states, the importation of large numbers of English guns, and the frequent diversion of the Spanish armies into France, the rebellion then might have been brought to an end. Yet since the ports and shipyards of the Netherlands were nearly all in rebel hands, and Spain found it impossible to gain control of the sea, Parma could reconquer only by slow, landward siege operations which lost their momentum whenever he was ordered to march his armies into France.[82]

By the 1590s, then, the United Provinces had survived and could, in fact, reconquer most of the provinces and towns which had been lost in the east. Its army was by that stage well trained and led by Maurice of Nassau, whose tactical innovations and exploitation of the watery terrain made him one of the great captains of the age. To call it a Dutch army would be a misnomer: in 1600 it consisted of forty-three English, thirty-two French, twenty Scots, eleven Walloon, and nine German companies, and only seventeen Dutch companies.[83] Despite this large (but by no means untypical) variety of nationalities, Maurice molded his forces into a coherent, standardized whole. He was undoubtedly aided in this, however, by the financial underpinning provided by the Dutch government; and his army, more than most in Europe, was regularly paid, just as the government continually provided for the maintenance of its substantial navy.

It would be unwise to exaggerate the wealth and financial stability of the Dutch republic or to suggest that it found it easy to pay for the prolonged conflict, especially in its early stages. In the eastern and southern parts of the United Provinces, the war caused considerable damage, loss of trade, and decline in population. Even the prosperous province of Holland found the tax burdens enormous; in 1579 it had to provide 960,000 florins for the war, in 1599 almost 5.5 million florins. By the early seventeenth century, with the annual costs of the war against Spain rising to 10 million florins, many wondered how much longer the struggle could be maintained without financial strain. Fortunately for the Dutch, Spain's economy—and its corresponding ability to pay the mutiny-prone Army of Flanders—had suffered even more, and at last caused Madrid to agree to the truce of 1609.

Yet if the conflict had tested Dutch resources, it had not exhausted them; and the fact was that from the 1590s onward, its economy was growing fast, thus providing a solid foundation of "credit" when the government turned—as all belligerent states had to turn—to the money market. One obvious reason for this prosperity was the interaction of a growing population with a more entrepreneurial spirit, once the Habsburg rule had been cast off. In addition to the natural increase in numbers, there were tens (perhaps hundreds) of thousands of refugees from the south, and many others from elsewhere in Europe. It seems clear that many of these immigrants were skilled workers, teachers, craftsmen, and capitalists, with much to offer. The sack of Antwerp by Spanish troops in 1576 gave a boost to Amsterdam's chances in the international trading system, yet it was also true that the Dutch took every opportunity offered them for commercial advancement. Their domination of the rich herring trade and their reclamation of land from the sea provided additional sources of wealth. Their vast mercantile marine, and in particular their *fluyts* (simple, robust freighters), earned them the carrying trade of much of Europe by 1600: timber, grain, cloth, salt, herrings were transported by Dutch vessels along every waterway. To the disgust of their English allies, and of many Dutch Calvinist divines, Amsterdam traders would willingly supply such goods to their mortal enemy, Spain, if the profits outweighed the risks. At home, raw materials were imported in vast quantities and then "finished" by the various trades of Amsterdam, Delft, Leyden, and so on. With "sugar refining, melting, distilling, brewing, tobacco cutting, silk throwing, pottery, glass, armament manufacture, printing, paper making"[84] among the chief industries, it was hardly surprising that by 1622 around 56 percent of Holland's population of 670,000 lived in medium-sized towns. Every other region in the world must have seemed economically backward by comparison.

Two further aspects of the Dutch economy enhanced its military power. The first was its overseas expansion. Although this commerce did not compare with the humbler but vaster bulk trade in European waters, it was another addition to the republic's resources. "Between 1598 and 1605, on average twenty-five ships sailed to West Africa, twenty to Brazil, ten to the East Indies, and 150 to the Caribbean every year. Sovereign colonies were founded at Amboina in 1605 and Ternate in 1607; factories and trading posts were established around the Indian Ocean, near the mouth of the Amazon and (in 1609) in Japan."[85] Like England, the United Provinces were now benefiting from that slow shift in the economic balances from the Mediterranean to the Atlantic world which was one of the main secular trends of the period 1500–1700; and which, while working at first to the advantage of Portugal and Spain, was later galvanizing societies better prepared to extract the profits of global commerce.[86]

The second feature was Amsterdam's growing role as the center of international finance, a natural corollary to the republic's function as the shipper, exchanger, and commodity dealer of Europe. What its financiers and institutions offered (receiving deposits at interest, transferring monies, crediting and clearing bills of exchange, floating loans) was not different from practices already established in, say, Venice and Genoa; but, reflecting the United Provinces' trading wealth, it was on a larger scale and conducted with a greater degree of certainty—the more so since the chief investors were a part of the government, and wished to see the principles of sound money, secure credit, and regular repayment of debt upheld. In consequence of all this, there was usually money available for government loans, which gave the Dutch Republic an inestimable advantage over its rivals; and since its credit rating was firm because it promptly repaid debts, it could borrow more cheaply than any other government—a major advantage in the seventeenth century and, indeed, at all times!

This ability to raise loans easily was the more important after the resumption of hostilities with Spain in 1621, for the cost of the armed forces rose steadily, from 13.4 million florins (1622) to 18.8 million florins (1640). These were large sums even for a rich population to bear, and the more particularly since Dutch overseas trade was being hurt by the war, either through direct losses or by the diversion of commerce into neutral hands. It was therefore politically easier to permit as large a part of the war as possible to be financed from public loans. Although this led to a massive increase in the official debt—the Province of Holland's debt was 153 million florins in 1651—the economic strength of the country and the care with which interest was repaid meant that the credit system was never in danger of collapse.[87] While this demonstrates that even wealthy states winced at the cost of military expenditures, it also confirmed that as long as success in war

depended upon the length of one's purse, the Dutch were always likely
to outstay the others.

War, Money, and the Nation-State

Let us now summarize the chief conclusions of this chapter. The
post-1450 waging of war was intimately connected with "the birth of
the nation-state."[88] Between the late fifteenth and the late seventeenth
centuries, most European countries witnessed a centralization of political and military authority, usually under the monarch (but in some
places under the local prince or a mercantile oligarchy), accompanied
by increased powers and methods of state taxation, and carried out by
a much more elaborate bureaucratic machinery than had existed when
kings were supposed to "live of their own" and national armies were
provided by a feudal levy.

There were various causes for this evolution of the European nation-state. Economic change had already undermined much of the old
feudal order, and different social groups had to relate to each other
through newer forms of contract and obligation. The Reformation, in
dividing Christendom on the basis *cuius regio, eius religio,* that is, of
the rulers' religious preferences, merged civil and religious authority,
and thus extended secularism on a national basis. The decline of Latin
and the growing use of vernacular language by politicians, lawyers,
bureaucrats, and poets accentuated this secular trend. Improved
means of communication, the more widespread exchange of goods, the
invention of printing, and the oceanic discoveries made man more
aware not only of other peoples but also of differences in language,
taste, cultural habits, and religion. In such circumstances, it was no
wonder that many philosophers and other writers of the time held the
nation-state to be the natural and best form of civic society, that its
powers should be enhanced and its interests defended, and that its
rulers and ruled needed—whatever the specific constitutional form
they enjoyed—to work harmoniously for the common, national
good.[89]

But it was war, and the consequences of war, that provided a much
more urgent and continuous pressure toward "nation-building" than
these philosophical considerations and slowly evolving social tendencies. Military power permitted many of Europe's dynasties to keep
above the great magnates of their land, and to secure political uniformity and authority (albeit often by concessions to the nobility). Military
factors—or better, geostrategical factors—helped to shape the territorial boundaries of these new nation-states, while the frequent wars
induced national consciousness, in a negative fashion at least, in that
Englishmen learned to hate Spaniards, Swedes to hate Danes, Dutch
rebels to hate their former Habsburg overlords. Above all, it was war—

and especially the new techniques which favored the growth of infantry armies and expensive fortifications and fleets—which impelled belligerent states to spend more money than ever before, and to seek out a corresponding amount in revenues. All remarks about the general rise in government spending, or about new organizations for revenue-collecting, or about the changing relationship between kings and estates in early-modern Europe, remain *abstract* until the central importance of military conflict is recalled.[90] In the last few years of Elizabeth's England, or in Philip II's Spain, as much as three-quarters of all government expenditures was devoted to war or to debt repayments for previous wars. Military and naval endeavors may not always have been the *raison d'être* of the new nation-states, but it certainly was their most expensive and pressing activity.

Yet it would be wrong to assume that the functions of raising revenues, supporting armies, equipping fleets, sending instructions, and directing military campaigns in the sixteenth and seventeenth centuries were carried out in the manner which characterized, say, the Normandy invasion of 1944. As the preceding analysis should have demonstrated, the military machines of early-modern Europe were cumbersome and inefficient. Raising and controlling an army in this period was a frighteningly difficult enterprise: ragtag troops, potentially disloyal mercenaries, inadequate supplies, transport problems, unstandardized weapons, were the despair of most commanders. Even when sufficient monies were allocated to military purposes, corruption and waste took their toll.

Armed forces were not, therefore, predictable and reliable instruments of state. Time and again, large bands of men drifted out of control because of supply shortages or, more serious, lack of pay. The Army of Flanders mutinied no less than forty-six times between 1572 and 1607; but so also, if less frequently, did equally formidable forces, like the Swedes in Germany or Cromwell's New Model Army. It was Richelieu who sourly observed, in his *Testament Politique:*

> History knows many more armies ruined by want and disorder than by the efforts of their enemies; and I have witnessed how all the enterprises which were embarked on in my day were lacking for that reason alone.[91]

This problem of pay and supply affected military performance in all sorts of ways: one historian has demonstrated that Gustavus Adolphus's stunningly mobile campaigns in Germany, rather than being dictated by military-strategic planning in the Clausewitzian sense, reflected a simple but compelling search for food and fodder for his enormous force.[92] Well before Napoleon's aphorism, commanders knew that an army marched upon its stomach.

But these physical restrictions applied at the national level, too, especially in raising funds for war. No state in this period, however prosperous, could pay immediately for the costs of a prolonged conflict; no matter what fresh taxes were raised, there was always a gap between governmental income and expenditure which could only be closed by loans—either from private bankers like the Fuggers or, later, through a formally organized money market dealing in government bonds. Again and again, however, the spiraling costs of war forced monarchs to default upon debt repayments, to debase the coinage, or to attempt some other measure of despair, which brought short-term relief but long-term disadvantage. Like their commanders frantically seeking to keep troops in order and horses fed, early-modern governments were engaged in a precarious hand-to-mouth living. Badgering estates to grant further extraordinary taxes, pressing rich men and the churches for "benevolences," haggling with bankers and munitions suppliers, seizing foreign treasure ships, and keeping at arm's length one's many creditors were more or less permanent activities forced upon rulers and their officials in these years.

The argument in this chapter is *not,* therefore, that the Habsburgs failed utterly to do what other powers achieved so brilliantly. There are no stunning contrasts in evidence here; success and failure are to be measured by very narrow differences.[93] All states, even the United Provinces, were placed under severe strain by the constant drain of resources for military and naval campaigns. All states experienced financial difficulties, mutinies of troops, inadequacies of supply, domestic opposition to higher taxes. As in the First World War, these years also witnessed struggles of endurance, driving the belligerents closer and closer to exhaustion. By the final decade of the Thirty Years War, it was noticeable that neither alliance could field armies as large as those commanded by Gustavus and Wallenstein, for each side was, literally, running out of men and money. The victory of the anti-Habsburg forces was, then, a marginal and relative one. They had managed, but only just, to maintain the balance between their material base and their military power better than their Habsburg opponents. At least some of the victors had seen that the sources of national wealth needed to be exploited carefully, and not recklessly, during a lengthy conflict. They may also have admitted, however reluctantly, that the trader and the manufacturer and the farmer were as important as the cavalry officer and the pikeman. But the margin of their appreciation, and of their better handling of the economic elements, was slight. It had been, to borrow the later words of the Duke of Wellington, a "damned close-run thing." Most great contests are.

3
Finance, Geography, and the Winning of Wars, 1660–1815

The signing of the Treaty of the Pyrenees did not, of course, bring to an end the rivalries of the European Great Powers, or their habit of settling these rivalries through war. But the century and a half of international struggle which occurred after 1660 was different, in some very important respects, from that which had taken place in the preceding hundred years; and, as such, these changes reflected a further stage in the evolution of international politics.

The most significant feature of the Great Power scene after 1660 was the maturing of a genuinely *multipolar* system of European states, each one of which increasingly tended to make decisions about war and peace on the basis of "national interests" rather than for transnational, religious causes. This was not, to be sure, an instant or absolute change: the European states prior to 1660 had certainly maneuvered with their secular interests in mind, and religious prejudice still fueled many international quarrels of the eighteenth century. Nevertheless, the chief characteristic of the 1519–1659 era—that is, an Austro-Spanish axis of Habsburg powers fighting a coalition of Protestant states, plus France—now disappeared, and was replaced by a much looser system of short-term, shifting alliances. Countries which had been foes in one war were often to find themselves partners in the next, which placed an emphasis upon calculated *Realpolitik* rather than deeply held religious conviction in the determination of policy.

The fluctuations in both diplomacy and war that were natural to this volatile, multipolar system were complicated by something which was not new, but was common to all ages: the rise of certain states and the decline of others. During this century and a half of international rivalry between Louis XIV's assumption of full authority in France in 1660–1661 and Napoleon Bonaparte's surrender after Waterloo in 1815, certain leading nations of the previous period (the Ottoman Empire, Spain, the Netherlands, Sweden) fell back into the second rank, and Poland was eclipsed altogether. The Austrian Habsburgs, by various territorial and structural adjustments in their hereditary lands, managed to remain in the first order; and in the north of Germany, Brandenburg-Prussia pulled itself up to that status from unpromising beginnings. In the west, France after 1660 swiftly expanded its military might to become the most powerful of the European states—to many observers, almost as overwhelming as the Habsburg forces had appeared a half-century earlier. France's capacity to dominate west-central Europe was held in check only by a combination of maritime and continental neighbors during a series of prolonged wars (1689–1697; 1702–1714; 1739–1748; 1756–1763); but it was then refashioned in the Napoleonic era to produce a long line of Gallic military victories which were brought to an end only by a coalition of four other Great Powers. Even in its defeat in 1815, France remained one of the leading states. Between it in the west and the two Germanic countries of Prussia and the Habsburg Empire in the east, therefore, a crude trilateral equilibrium slowly emerged within the European core as the eighteenth century unfolded.

But the really significant alterations in the Great Power system during that century occurred on the *flanks* of Europe, and even farther afield. Certain of the western European states steadily converted their small, precarious enclaves in the tropics into much more extensive domains, especially in India but also in the East Indies, southern Africa, and as far away as Australia. The most successful of these colonizing nations was Britain, which, domestically "stabilized" after James II was replaced by William and Mary in 1688, steadily fulfilled its Elizabethan potential as the greatest of the European maritime empires. Even its loss of control over the prosperous North American colonies in the 1770s—from which there emerged an independent United States of formidable defensive strength and considerable economic power—only temporarily checked this growth of British global influence. Equally remarkable were the achievements of the Russian state, which expanded eastward and southward, across the steppes of Asia, throughout the eighteenth century. Moreover, although sited on the western and eastern margins of Europe, both Britain and Russia had an interest in the fate of the center—with Britain being involved in German affairs because of its dynastic links to Hanover (following George I's accession in 1714) and Russia being determined to have the chief voice in the fate of neighboring Poland. More generally, the governments in London and St. Petersburg wanted a balance of power on the European continent, and were willing to intervene repeatedly in order to secure an equilibrium which accorded with their interests. In other words, the European states system was becoming one of *five* Great Powers—France, the Habsburg Empire, Prussia, Britain, and Russia—as well as lesser countries like Savoy and declining states such as Spain.[1]

Why was it that those five Powers in particular—while obviously not possessing exactly the same strengths—were able to remain in (or to enter) the "major league" of states? Purely military explanations are not going to get us very far. It is hard to believe, for example, that the rise and fall of Great Powers in this period was caused chiefly by changes in military and naval technology, such as might benefit one country more than another.* There were, of course, many small-scale improvements in weaponry: the flintlock rifle (with ring bayonet) eliminated the pikeman from the battlefield; artillery became much more mobile, especially after the newer types designed by Gribeauval in France during the 1760s; and the stubby, shorter-ranged naval gun known as the carronade (first built by the Carron Company, of Scotland, in the late 1770s) enhanced the destructive power of warships. There were also improvements in tactical thought and, in the background, steady increases in population and in agricultural output which would permit the organization of far larger military units (the division; the corps) and their easier sustenance upon rich farmlands by the end of the eighteenth century. Nonetheless, it is fair to say that Wellington's army in 1815 was not significantly different from Marlborough's in 1710, nor Nelson's fleet much more advanced technologically than that which had faced Louis XIV's warships.[2]

Indeed, the most significant changes occurring in the military and naval fields during the eighteenth century were probably in *organization,* because of the enhanced activity of the state. The exemplar of this shift was undoubtedly the France of Louis XIV (1661–1715), where ministers such as Colbert, Le Tellier, and others were intent upon increasing the king's powers at home as well as his glories abroad. The creation of a French war ministry, with intendants checking upon the financing, supply, and organization of troops while Martinet as inspector general imposed new standards of training and discipline; the erection of barracks, hospitals, parade grounds, and depots of every sort on land, to sustain the Sun King's enormous army, together with the creation of a centrally organized, enormous fleet at sea—all this forced the other powers to follow suit, if they did not wish to be eclipsed. The monopolization and bureaucratization of military power by the state is clearly a central part of the story of "nation-building"; and the process was a reciprocal one, since the enhanced authority and resources of the state in turn gave to their armed forces a degree of *permanence* which had often not existed a century earlier. Not only were there "professional," "standing" armies and "royal" navies, but there was also a much more developed infrastructure of war academies, barracks, ship-repair yards, and the like, with administrators to run them.

*For example, in the way in which the coming of steam-driven warships after 1860 benefited Britain (which had plenty of coal) over France (which had little).

Power was now *national* power, whether expressed through the enlightened despotisms of eastern Europe, the parliamentary controls of Britain, or the later demogogic forces of revolutionary France.[3] On the other hand, such organizational improvements could be swiftly copied by other states (the most dramatic example being Peter the Great's transformation of Russia's army in the space of a couple of decades after 1698), and by themselves provided no guarantee of maintaining a country's Great Power position.

Much more important than any of these strictly military developments in explaining the relative position occupied by the Great Powers in the years 1660–1815 were two other factors, *finance* and *geography*. Taken together—for the two elements frequently interacted—it is possible to gain some larger sense of what at first sight appears as a bewildering pattern of successes and failures produced by the many wars of this period.

The "Financial Revolution"

The importance of finance and of a productive economic base which created revenues for the state was already clear to Renaissance princes, as the previous chapter has illustrated. The rise of the *ancien régime* monarchies of the eighteenth century, with their large military establishments and fleets of warships, simply increased the government's need to nurture the economy and to create financial institutions which could raise and manage the monies concerned.[4] Moreover, like the First World War, conflicts such as the seven major Anglo-French wars fought between 1689 and 1815 were struggles of endurance. Victory therefore went to the Power—or better, since both Britain and France usually had allies, to the Great Power coalition—with the greater capacity to maintain credit and to keep on raising supplies. The mere fact that these were *coalition* wars increased their duration, since a belligerent whose resources were fading would look to a more powerful ally for loans and reinforcements in order to keep itself in the fight. Given such expensive and exhausting conflicts, what each side desperately required was—to use the old aphorism—"money, money, and yet more money." It was this need which formed the background to what has been termed the "financial revolution" of the late seventeenth and early eighteenth centuries,[5] when certain western European states evolved a relatively sophisticated system of banking and credit in order to pay for their wars.

There was, it is true, a second and nonmilitary reason for the financial changes of this time. That was the chronic shortage of specie, particularly in the years before the gold discoveries in Portuguese Brazil in 1693. The more European commerce with the Orient developed in the seventeenth and eighteenth centuries, the greater the out-flow of silver to cover the trade imbalances, causing merchants and dealers everywhere complain of the scarcity of coin. In addition, the steady increases in European commerce, especially in essential pro-ducts such as cloth and naval stores, together with the tendency for the seasonal fairs of medieval Europe to be replaced by permanent centers of exchange, led to a growing regularity and predictability of financial settlements and thus to the greater use of bills of exchange and notes of credit. In Amsterdam especially, but also in London, Lyons, Frank-furt, and other cities, there arose a whole cluster of moneylenders, commodity dealers, goldsmiths (who often dealt in loans), bill mer-chants, and jobbers in the shares of the growing number of joint-stock companies. Adopting banking practices which were already in evi-dence in Renaissance Italy, these individuals and financial houses steadily created a structure of national and international credit to underpin the early modern world economy.

Nevertheless, by far the largest and most sustained boost to the "financial revolution" in Europe was given by war. If the difference between the financial burdens of the age of the Philip II and that of Napoleon was one of degree, it still was remarkable enough. The cost of a sixteenth-century war could be measured in millions of pounds; by the late-seventeenth century, it had risen to *tens* of millions of pounds; and at the close of the Napoleonic War the outgoings of the major combatants occasionally reached a hundred million pounds *a year.* Whether these prolonged and frequent clashes between the Great Powers, when translated into economic terms, were more of a benefit to than a brake upon the commercial and industrial rise of the West can never be satisfactorily resolved. The answer depends, to a great extent, upon whether one is trying to assess the *absolute* growth of a country as opposed to its *relative* prosperity and strength before and after a lengthy conflict.[6] What is clear is that even the most thriving and "modern" of the eighteenth-century states could not immediately pay for the wars of this period out of their ordinary revenue. Moreover, vast rises in taxes, even if the machinery existed to collect them, could well provoke domestic unrest, which all regimes feared—especially when facing foreign challengers at the same time.

Consequently, the only way a government could finance a war ade-quately was by borrowing: by selling bonds and offices, or better, nego-tiable long-term stock paying interest to all who advanced monies to the state. Assured of an inflow of funds, officials could then authorize payments to army contractors, provision merchants, shipbuilders, and the armed services themselves. In many respects, this two-way system of raising and *simultaneously* spending vast sums of money acted like a bellows, fanning the development of western capitalism and of the nation-state itself.

Yet however natural all this may appear to later eyes, it is important to stress that the success of such a system depended on two critical factors: reasonably efficient machinery for raising loans, and the maintenance of a government's "credit" in the financial markets. In both respects, the United Provinces led the way—not surprisingly, since the merchants there were part of the government and desired to see the affairs of state managed according to the same principles of financial rectitude as applied in, say, a joint-stock company. It was therefore appropriate that the States General of the Netherlands, which efficiently and regularly raised the taxes to cover governmental expenditures, was able to set interest rates very low, thus keeping down debt repayments. This system, superbly reinforced by the many financial activities of the city of Amsterdam, soon gave the United Provinces an international reputation for clearing bills, exchanging currency, and providing credit, which naturally created a structure—and an atmosphere—within which long-term funded state debt could be regarded as perfectly normal. So successfully did Amsterdam become a center of Dutch "surplus capital" that it soon was able to invest in the stock of foreign companies and, most important of all, to subscribe to a whole variety of loans floated by foreign governments, especially in wartime.[7]

The impact of these activities upon the economy of the United Provinces need not be examined here, although it is clear that Amsterdam would not have become the financial capital of the continent had it not been supported by a flourishing commercial and productive base in the first place. Furthermore, the very long-term consequence was probably disadvantageous, since the steady returns from government loans turned the United Provinces more and more away from a manufacturing economy and into a *rentier* economy, whose bankers were somewhat disinclined to risk capital in large-scale industrial ventures by the late eighteenth century; while the ease with which loans could be raised eventually saddled the Dutch government with an enormous burden of debt, paid for by excise duties which increased both wages and prices to uncompetitive levels.[8]

What is more important for the purposes of our argument is that in subscribing to *foreign* government loans, the Dutch were much less concerned about the religion or ideology of their clients than about their financial stability and reliability. Accordingly, the terms set for loans to European powers like Russia, Spain, Austria, Poland, and Sweden can be seen as a measure of their respective economic potential, the collateral they offered to the bankers, their record in repaying interest and premiums, and ultimately their prospects of emerging successfully from a Great Power war. Thus, the plummeting of Polish governmental stock in the late eighteenth century and, conversely, the remarkable—and frequently overlooked—strength of Austria's credit for decade after decade mirrored the relative durability of those states.[9]

But the best example of this critical relationship between financial strength and power politics concerns the two greatest rivals of this period, Britain and France. Since the result of their conflict affected the entire European balance, it is worth examining their experiences at some length. The older notion that eighteenth-century Great Britain exhibited adamantine and inexorably growing commercial and industrial strength, unshakable fiscal credit, and a flexible, upwardly mobile social structure—as compared with an *ancien régime* France founded upon the precarious sands of military hubris, economic backwardness, and a rigid class system—seems no longer tenable. In some ways, the French taxation system was less regressive than the British. In some ways, too, France's economy in the eighteenth century was showing signs of movement toward "takeoff" into an industrial revolution, even though it had only limited stocks of such a critical item as coal. Its armaments production was considerable, and it possessed many skilled artisans and some impressive entrepreneurs.[10] With its far larger population and more extensive agriculture, France was much wealthier than its island neighbor; the revenues of its government and the size of its army dwarfed those of any western European rival; and its *dirigiste* regime, as compared with the party-based politics of Westminster, seemed to give it a greater coherence and predictability. In consequence, eighteenth-century Britons were much more aware of their own country's relative weaknesses than its strengths when they gazed across the Channel.

For all this, the English system possessed key advantages in the financial realm which enhanced the country's power in wartime and buttressed its political stability and economic growth in peacetime. While it is true that its *general* taxation system was more regressive than that of France—that is, it relied far more upon indirect than direct taxes—particular features seem to have made it much less resented by the public. For example, there was in Britain nothing like the vast array of French tax farmers, collectors, and other middlemen; many of the British duties were "invisible" (the excise duty on a few basic products), or appeared to hurt the foreigner (customs); there were no *internal* tolls, which so irritated French merchants and were a disincentive to domestic commerce; the British land tax—the chief direct tax for so much of the eighteenth century—allowed for no privileged exceptions and was also "invisible" to the greater part of society; and these various taxes were discussed and then authorized by an elective assembly, which for all its defects appeared more representative than the *ancien régime* in France. When one adds to this the important point that per capita income was already somewhat higher in Britain than in France even by 1700, it is not altogether surprising that the population of the island state was willing and able to pay proportionately larger taxes. Finally, it is possible to argue—although more difficult to prove statistically—that the comparatively light burden of direct taxation in Britain not only increased the propensity to save among the better-off in society (and thus allowed the accumulation of investment capital during years of peace), but also produced a vast reserve of taxable wealth in *wartime,* when higher land taxes and, in 1799, direct income tax were introduced to meet the national emergency. Thus, by the period of the Napoleonic War, despite a population less than half that of France, Britain was for the first time ever raising more revenue from taxes each year in *absolute* terms than its larger neighbor.[11]

Yet however remarkable that achievement, it is eclipsed in importance by the even more significant difference between the British and French systems of public credit. For the fact was that during most of the eighteenth-century conflicts, almost three-quarters of the *extra* finance raised to support the additional wartime expenditures came from loans. Here, more than anywhere else, the British advantages were decisive. The first was the evolution of an institutional framework which permitted the raising of long-term loans in an efficient fashion and simultaneously arranged for the regular repayment of the interest on (and principal of) the debts accrued. The creation of the Bank of England in 1694 (at first as a wartime expedient) and the slightly later regularization of the national debt on the one hand and the flourishing of the stock exchange and growth of the "country banks" on the other boosted the supply of money available to both governments and businessmen. This growth of paper money in various forms *without* severe inflation or the loss of credit brought many advantages in an age starved of coin. Yet the "financial revolution" itself would scarcely have succeeded had not the obligations of the state been guaranteed by successive Parliaments with their powers to raise additional taxes; had not the ministries—from Walpole to the younger Pitt—worked hard to convince their bankers in particular and the public in general that they, too, were actuated by the principles of financial rectitude and "economical" government; and had not the steady and in some trades remarkable expansion of commerce and industry provided concomitant increases in revenue from customs and excise. Even the onset of war did not check such increases, provided the Royal Navy protected the nation's overseas trade while throttling that of its foes. It was upon these solid foundations that Britain's "credit" rested, despite early uncertainties, considerable political opposition, and a financial near-disaster like the collapse of the famous South Seas Bubble of 1720. "Despite all defects in the handling of English public finance," its historian has noted, "for the rest of the century it remained more honest, as well as more efficient, than that of any other in Europe."[12]

The result of all this was not only that interest rates steadily dropped,* but also that British government stock was increasingly attractive to foreign, and particularly Dutch, investors. Regular dealings in these securities on the Amsterdam market thus became an important part of the nexus of Anglo-Dutch commercial and financial relationships, with important effects upon the economies of both countries.[13] In *power-political* terms, its value lay in the way in which the resources of the United Provinces repeatedly came to the aid of the British war effort, even when the Dutch alliance in the struggle against France had been replaced by an uneasy neutrality. Only at the time of the American Revolutionary War—significantly, the one conflict in which British military, naval, diplomatic, and trading weaknesses were most evident, and therefore its credit-worthiness was the lowest—did the flow of Dutch funds tend to dry up, despite the higher interest rates which London was prepared to offer. By 1780, however, when the Dutch entered the war on France's side, the British government found that the strength of its own economy and the availability of domestic capital were such that its loans could be almost completely taken up by domestic investors.

The sheer dimensions—and ultimate success—of Britain's capacity to raise war loans can be summarized as in Table 2.

Table 2. British Wartime Expenditure and Revenue, 1688–1815
(pounds)

Inclusive Years	Total Expenditure	Total Income	Balance Raised by Loans	Loans as % of Expenditure
1688–97	49,320,145	32,766,754	16,553,391	33.6
1702–13	93,644,560	64,239,477	29,405,083	31.4
1739–48	95,628,159	65,903,964	29,724,195	31.1
1756–63	160,573,366	100,555,123	60,018,243	37.4
1776–83	236,462,689	141,902,620	94,560,069	39.9
1793–1815	1,657,854,518	1,217,556,439	440,298,079	26.6
Totals	2,293,483,437	1,622,924,377	670,559,060	33.3

And the strategical consequence of these figures was that the country was thereby enabled "to spend on war out of all proportion to its tax revenue, and thus to throw into the struggle with France and its allies the decisive margin of ships and men without which the resources previously committed might have been committed in vain."[14] Although many British commentators throughout the eighteenth century trembled at the sheer size of the national debt and its possible consequences, the fact remained that (in Bishop Berkeley's words) credit

---

*By the time of the War of Austrian Succession (1739–1747), the government was able to borrow large sums at 3 or 4 percent, half the rate of interest which had prevailed in Marlborough's time.

was "the principal advantage that England hath over France." Finally, the great growth in state expenditures and the enormous, sustained demand which Admiralty contracts in particular created for iron, wood, cloth, and other wares produced a "feedback loop" which assisted British industrial production and stimulated the series of technological breakthroughs that gave the country yet another advantage over the French.[15]

Why the French failed to match these British habits is now easy to see.[16] There was, to begin with, no proper system of *public* finance. From the Middle Ages onward, the French monarchy's financial operations had been "managed" by a cluster of bodies—municipal governments, the clergy, provincial estates, and, increasingly, tax farmers—which collected the revenues and supervised the monopolies of the crown in return for a portion of the proceeds, and which simultaneously advanced monies to the French government—at handsome rates of interest—on the expected income from these operations. The venality of this system applied not only to the farmers general who gathered in the tobacco and salt dues; it was also true of that hierarchy of parish collectors, district receivers, and regional receivers general responsible for direct taxes like the *taille.* Each of them took his "cut" before passing the monies on to a higher level; each of them also received 5 percent interest on the price he had paid for office in the first place; and many of the more senior officials were charged with paying out sums directly to government contractors or as wages, without first handing their takings in to the royal treasury. These men, too, loaned funds—at interest—to the crown.

Such a lax and haphazard organization was inherently corrupt, and much of the taxpayers' monies ended in private hands. On occasions, especially after wars, investigations would be launched against financiers, many of whom were induced to pay "compensations" or accept lower interest rates; but such actions were mere gestures. "The real culprit," one historian has argued, "was the system itself."[17] The second consequence of this inefficiency was that at least until Necker's reforms of the 1770s, there existed no overall sense of national accounting; annual tallies of revenue and expenditure, and the problem of deficits, were rarely thought to be of significance. Provided the monarchy could raise funds for the immediate needs of the military and the court, the steady escalation of the national debt was of little import.

While a similar sort of irresponsibility had earlier been shown by the Stuarts, the fact was that by the eighteenth century Britain had evolved a parliamentary-controlled form of public finance which gave it numerous advantages in the duel for primacy. Not the least of these seems to have been that while the rise in government spending and in the national debt did not hurt (and may indeed have boosted) British investment in commerce and industry, the prevailing conditions in

France seem to have encouraged those with surplus capital to purchase an office or an annuity rather than to invest in business. On some occasions, it was true, there were attempts to provide France with a national bank, so that the debt could be properly managed and cheap credit provided; but such schemes were always resisted by those with an interest in the existing system. The French government's financial policy, if indeed it deserves that name, was therefore always a hand-to-mouth affair.

France's commercial development also suffered in a number of ways. It is interesting to note, for example, the disadvantages under which a French port like La Rochelle operated compared with Liverpool or Glasgow. All three were poised to exploit the booming "Atlantic economy" of the eighteenth century, and La Rochelle was particularly well sited for the triangular trade to West Africa and the West Indies. Alas for such mercantile aspirations, the French port suffered from the repeated depredations of the crown, "insatiable in its fiscal demands, unrelenting in its search for new and larger sources of revenue." A vast array of "heavy, inequitable and arbitrarily levied direct and indirect taxes on commerce" retarded economic growth; the sale of offices diverted local capital from investment in trade, and the fees levied by those venal officeholders intensified that trend; monopolistic companies restricted free enterprise. Moreover, although the crown compelled the Rochelais to build a large and expensive arsenal in the 1760s (or have the city's entire revenues seized!), it did not offer a *quid pro quo* when wars occurred. Because the French government usually concentrated upon military rather than maritime aims, the frequent conflicts with a superior Royal Navy were a disaster for La Rochelle, which saw its merchant ships seized, its profitable slave trade interrupted, and its overseas markets in Canada and Louisiana eliminated—all at a time when marine insurance rates were rocketing and emergency taxes were being imposed. As a final blow, the French government often felt compelled to allow its overseas colonists to trade with neutral shipping in wartime, but this made those markets ever more difficult to recover when peace was concluded. By comparison, the Atlantic sector of the British economy grew steadily throughout the eighteenth century, and if anything benefited in wartime (despite the attacks of French privateers) from the policies of a government which held that profit and power, trade and dominion, were inseparable.[18]

The worst consequence of France's financial immaturity was that in time of war its military and naval effort was eroded, in a number of ways.[19] Because of the inefficiency and unreliability of the system, it took longer to secure the supply of (say) naval stores, while contractors usually needed to charge more than would be the case with the British or Dutch admiralties. Raising large sums in wartime was always more of a problem for the French monarchy, even when it drew increasingly upon Dutch money in the 1770s and 1780s, for its long history of currency revaluations, its partial repudiations of debt, and its other arbitrary actions against the holders of short-term and long-term bills caused bankers to demand—and a desperate French state to agree to—rates of interest far above those charged to the British and many other European governments.* Yet even this willingness to pay over the odds did not permit the Bourbon monarchs to secure the sums which were necessary to sustain an all-out military effort in a lengthy war.

The best illustration of this relative French weakness occurred in the years following the American Revolutionary War. It had hardly been a glorious conflict for the British, who had lost their largest colony and seen their national debt rise to about £220 million; but since those sums had chiefly been borrowed at a mere 3 percent interest, the annual repayments totaled only £7.33 million. The actual costs of the war to France were considerably smaller; after all, it had entered the conflict at the halfway stage, following Necker's efforts to balance the budget, and for once it had not needed to deploy a massive army. Nonetheless, the war cost the French government at least a billion livres, virtually all of which was paid by floating loans at rates of interest at least double that available to the British government. In both countries, servicing the debt consumed half the state's annual expenditures, but after 1783 the British immediately embarked upon a series of measures (the Sinking Fund, a consolidated revenue fund, improved public accounts) in order to stabilize that total and strengthen its credit—the greatest, perhaps, of the younger Pitt's achievements. On the French side, by contrast, large new loans were floated each year, since "normal" revenues could never match even peacetime expenditures; and with yearly deficits growing, the government's credit weakened still further.

The startling statistical consequence was that by the late 1780s France's national debt may have been almost the same as Britain's—around £215 million—but the interest payments each year were nearly double, at £14 million. Still worse, the efforts of succeeding finance ministers to raise fresh taxes met with stiffening public resistance. It was, after all, Calonne's proposed tax reforms, leading to the Assembly of Notables, the moves against the *parlements,* the suspension of payments by the treasury, and then (for the first since 1614) the calling of the States General in 1789 which triggered off the final collapse of the *ancien régime* in France.[20] The link between national bankruptcy and revolution was all too clear. In the desperate circumstances which followed, the government issued ever more notes (to the value of 100

---

*In the early years of Louis XIV, by contrast, France had been able to borrow at cheaper rates of interest than the Stuarts, or even William III.

million livres in 1789, and 200 million in 1790), a device replaced by the Constituent Assembly's own expedient of seizing church lands and issuing paper money on their estimated worth. All this led to further inflation, which the 1792 decision for war only exacerbated. And while it is true that later administrative reforms within the treasury itself and the revolutionary regime's determination to know the true state of affairs steadily produced a unified, bureaucratic, revenue-collecting structure akin to those existing in Britain and elsewhere, the internal convulsions and external overextension that were to last until 1815 caused the French economy to fall even further behind that of its greatest rival.

This problem of raising revenue to pay for current—and previous—wars preoccupied *all* regimes and their statesmen. Even in peacetime, the upkeep of the armed services consumed 40 or 50 percent of a country's expenditures; in wartime, it could rise to 80 or even 90 percent of the far larger whole! Whatever their internal constitutions, therefore, autocratic empires, limited monarchies, and bourgeois republics throughout Europe faced the same difficulty. After each bout of fighting (and especially after 1714 and 1763), most countries desperately needed to draw breath, to recover from their economic exhaustion, and to grapple with the internal discontents which war and higher taxation had all too often provoked; but the competitive, egoistic nature of the European states system meant that *prolonged* peace was unusual and that within another few years preparations were being made for further campaigning. Yet if the financial burdens could hardly be carried by the French, Dutch, and British, the three richest peoples of Europe, how could they be borne by far poorer states?

The simple answer to this question was that they couldn't. Even Frederick the Great's Prussia, which drew much of its revenues from the extensive, well-husbanded royal domains and monopolies, could not meet the vast demands of the war of the Austrian Succession and Seven Years War without recourse to three "extraordinary" sources of income: profits from debasement of the coinage; plunder from neighboring states such as Saxony and Mecklenburg; and, after 1757, considerable subsidies from its richer ally, Britain. For the less efficient and more decentralized Habsburg Empire, the problems of paying for war were immense; but it is difficult to believe that the situation was any better in Russia or in Spain, where the prospects for raising monies—other than by further squeezes upon the peasantry and the underdeveloped middle classes—were not promising. With so many orders (e.g., Hungarian nobility, Spanish clergy) claiming exemptions under the *anciennes régimes,* even the invention of elaborate indirect taxes, debasements of the currency, and the printing of paper money were hardly sufficient to maintain the elaborate armies and courts in peacetime; and while the onset of war led to extraordinary fiscal measures for the national emergency, it also meant that increasing reliance had to be placed upon the western European money markets or, better still, direct subsidies from London, Amsterdam, or Paris which could then be used to buy mercenaries and supplies. *Pas d'argent, pas de Suisses* may have been a slogan for Renaissance princes, but it was still an unavoidable fact of life even in Frederician and Napoleonic times.[21]

This is not to say, however, that the financial element *always* determined the fate of nations in these eighteenth-century wars. Amsterdam was for much of this period the greatest financial center of the world, yet that alone could not prevent the United Provinces' demise as a leading Power; conversely, Russia was economically backward and its government relatively starved of capital, yet the country's influence and might in European affairs grew steadily. To explain that seeming discrepancy, it is necessary to give equal attention to the second important conditioning factor, the influence of geography upon national strategy.

Geopolitics

Because of the inherently competitive nature of European power politics and the volatility of alliance relationships throughout the eighteenth century, rival states often encountered remarkably different circumstances—and sometimes extreme variations of fortune—from one major conflict to the next. Secret treaties and "diplomatic revolutions" produced changing conglomerations of powers, and in consequence fairly frequent shifts in the European equilibrium, both military and naval. While this naturally caused great reliance to be placed upon the expertise of a nation's diplomats, not to mention the efficiency of its armed forces, it also pointed to the significance of the geographical factor. What is meant by that term here is not merely such elements as a country's climate, raw materials, fertility of agriculture, and access to trade routes—important though they all were to its overall prosperity—but rather the critical issue of strategical *location* during these multilateral wars. Was a particular nation able to concentrate its energies upon one front, or did it have to fight on several? Did it share common borders with weak states, or powerful ones? Was it chiefly a land power, a sea power, or a hybrid—and what advantages and disadvantages did that bring? Could it easily pull out of a great war in Central Europe if it wished to? Could it secure additional resources from overseas?

The fate of the United Provinces in this period provides a good example of the influences of geography upon politics. In the early seventeenth century it possessed many of the domestic ingredients for national growth—a flourishing economy, social stability, a well-trained army, and a powerful navy; and it had not then seemed disadvantaged by geography. On the contrary, its river network provided a barrier (at least to some extent) against Spanish forces, and its North Sea position gave it easy access to the rich herring fisheries. But a century later, the Dutch were struggling to hold their own against a number of rivals. The adoption of mercantilist policies by Cromwell's England and Colbert's France hurt Dutch commerce and shipping. For all the tactical brilliance of commanders like Tromp and de Ruyter, Dutch merchantmen in the naval wars against England had either to run the gauntlet of the Channel route or to take the longer and stormier route around Scotland, which (like their herring fisheries) was still open to attack in the North Sea; the prevailing westerly winds gave the battle advantage to the English admirals; and the shallow waters off Holland restricted the draft—and ultimately the size and power—of the Dutch warships.[22] In the same way as its trade with the Americas and Indies became increasingly exposed to the workings of British sea power, so, too, was its Baltic *entrepôt* commerce—one of the very foundations of its early prosperity—eroded by the Swedes and other local rivals. Although the Dutch might temporarily reassert themselves by the dispatch of a large battle fleet to a threatened point, there was no way in which they could permanently preserve their extended and vulnerable interests in distant seas.

This dilemma was made worse by Dutch vulnerability to the landward threat from Louis XIV's France from the late 1660s onwards. Since this danger was even greater than that posed by Spain a century earlier, the Dutch were forced to expand their own army (it was 93,000 strong by 1693) and to devote ever more resources to garrisoning the southern border fortresses. This drain upon Dutch energies was twofold: it diverted vast amounts of money into military expenditures, producing the upward spiral in war debts, interest repayments, increased excise duties, and high wages that undercut the nation's commercial competitiveness in the long term; and it caused a severe loss of life during wartime to a population which, at about two million, was curiously static throughout this entire period. Hence the justifiable alarm, during the fierce toe-to-toe battles of the War of Spanish Succession (1702–1713), at the heavy losses caused by Marlborough's willingness to launch the Anglo-Dutch armies into bloody frontal assaults against the French.[23]

The English alliance which William III had cemented in 1689 was simultaneously the saving of the United Provinces and a substantial contributory factor in its decline as an independent great power—in rather the same way in which, over two hundred years later, Lend-Lease and the United States alliance would both rescue and help undermine a British Empire which was fighting for survival under

Marlborough's distant relative Winston Churchill. The inadequacy of Dutch resources in the various wars against France between 1688 and 1748 meant that they needed to concentrate about three-quarters of defense expenditures upon the military, thus neglecting their fleet— whereas the British assumed an increasing share of the maritime and colonial campaigns, and of the commercial benefits therefrom. As London and Bristol merchants flourished, so, to put it crudely, Amsterdam traders suffered. This was exacerbated by the frequent British efforts to prevent *all* trade with France in wartime, in contrast to the Dutch wish to maintain such profitable links—a reflection of how much more involved with (and therefore dependent upon) *external* commerce and finance the United Provinces were throughout this period, whereas the British economy was still relatively self-sufficient. Even when, by the Seven Years War, the United Provinces had escaped into neutrality, it availed them little, for an overweening Royal Navy, refusing to accept the doctrine of "free ships, free goods," was determined to block France's overseas commerce from being carried in neutral bottoms.[24] The Anglo-Dutch diplomatic quarrel of 1758–1759 over this question was repeated during the early years of the American Revolutionary War and eventually led to open hostilities after 1780, which did nothing to help the seaborne commerce of either Britain or the United Provinces. By the time of the French Revolutionary and Napoleonic struggles, the Dutch found themselves ground ever more between Britain and France, suffering from widespread debt repudiations, affected by domestic fissures, and losing colonies and overseas trade in a global contest which they could neither avoid nor take advantage of. In such circumstances, financial expertise and reliance upon "surplus capital" was simply not enough.[25]

In much the same way, albeit on a grander scale, France also suffered from being a hybrid power during the eighteenth century, with its energies diverted between continental aims on the one hand and maritime and colonial ambitions on the other. In the early part of Louis XIV's reign, this strategical ambivalence was not so marked. France's strength rested firmly upon *indigenous* materials: its large and relatively homogeneous territory, its agricultural self-sufficiency, and its population of about twenty million, which permitted Louis XIV to increase his army from 30,000 in 1659 to 97,000 in 1666 to a colossal 350,000 by 1710.[26] The Sun King's foreign-policy aims, too, were land-based and traditional: to erode still further the Habsburg positions, by moves in the south against Spain and in the east and north against that vulnerable string of Spanish-Habsburg and German territories Franche Comté, Lorraine, Alsace, Luxembourg, and the southern Netherlands. With Spain exhausted, the Austrians distracted by the Turkish threat, and the English at first neutral or friendly, Louis enjoyed two decades of diplomatic success; but then the very hubris of French claims alarmed the other powers.

The chief strategical problem for France was that although massively strong in defensive terms, she was less well placed to carry out a decisive campaign of conquest: in each direction she was hemmed in, partly by geographical barriers, partly by the existing claims and interests of a number of great powers. An attack on the southern (that is, Habsburg-held) Netherlands, for example, involved grinding campaigns through territory riddled with fortresses and waterways, and provoked a response not merely from the Habsburg powers themselves but also from the United Provinces and England. French military efforts into Germany were also troublesome: the border was more easily breached, but the lines of communication were much longer, and once again there was an inevitable coalition to face—the Austrians, the Dutch, the British (especially after the 1714 Hanoverian succession), and then the Prussians. Even when, by the mid-eighteenth century, France was willing to seek out a strong German partner—that is, either Austria or Prussia—the natural consequence of any such alliance was that the *other* German power went into opposition and, more important, strove to obtain support from Britain and Russia to neutralize French ambitions.

Furthermore, every war against the maritime powers involved a certain division of French energies and attention from the continent, and thus made a successful land campaign less likely. Torn between fighting in Flanders, Germany, and northern Italy on the one hand and in the Channel, West Indies, Lower Canada, and the Indian Ocean on the other, French strategy led repeatedly to a "falling between stools." While never willing to make the all-out financial effort necessary to challenge the Royal Navy's supremacy,* successive French governments allocated funds to the marine which—had France been *solely* a land power—might have been used to reinforce the army. Only in the war of 1778–1783, by supporting the American rebels in the western hemisphere but abstaining from any moves into Germany, did France manage to humiliate its British foe. In all its other wars, the French never enjoyed the luxury of strategical concentration—and suffered as a result.

In sum, the France of the *ancien régime* remained, by its size and population and wealth, always the greatest of the European states; but it was not big enough or efficiently organized enough to be a "superpower," and, restricted on land and diverted by sea, it could not prevail

---

*During the 1689–1697 and 1702–1714 conflicts, for example, France allocated less than 10 percent of total expenditure to its navy, and between 57 percent and 65 percent to its army. (The corresponding British figures were 35 percent to the navy and 40 percent to the army.) In 1760 the French navy received only one-quarter of the sums allocated to the army. Even when monies were forthcoming, France's geographical position meant that it was often extremely difficult to get naval stores from the Baltic in wartime, to keep the fleet in good order.

against the coalition which its ambitions inevitably aroused. French actions confirmed, rather than upset, the plurality of power in Europe. Only when its national energies were transformed by the Revolution, and then brilliantly deployed by Napoleon, could it impose its ideas upon the continent—for a while. But even there its success was temporary, and no amount of military genius could ensure permanent French control of Germany, Italy, and Spain, let alone of Russia and Britain.

France's geostrategical problem of having to face potential foes on a variety of fronts was not unique, even if that country had made matters worse for itself by a repeated aggressiveness and a chronic lack of direction. The two great German powers of this period—the Habsburg Empire and Brandenburg-Prussia—were also destined by their geographical position to grapple with the same problem. To the Austrian Habsburgs, this was nothing new. The awkwardly shaped conglomeration of territories they ruled (Austria, Bohemia, Silesia, Moravia, Hungary, Milan, Naples, Sicily, and, after 1714, the southern Netherlands—see Map 5) and the position of other powers in relation to those lands required a nightmarish diplomatic and military juggling act merely to retain the inheritance; increasing it demanded either genius or good luck, and probably both.

Thus, while the various wars against the Turks (1663–1664, 1683–1699, 1716–1718, 1737–1739, 1788–1791) showed the Habsburg armies generally enhancing their position in the Balkans, this struggle against a declining Ottoman Empire consumed most of Vienna's energies in those selected periods.[27] With the Turks at the gates of his imperial capital in 1683, for example, Leopold I was bound to stay neutral toward France despite the provocations of Louis XIV's "reunions" of Alsace and Luxembourg in that very year. This Austrian ambivalence was somewhat less marked during the Nine Years War (1689–1697) and the subsequent War of the Spanish Succession (1702–1713), since Vienna had by that time become part of a gigantic anti-French alliance; but it never completely disappeared even then. The course of many later eighteenth-century wars seemed still more volatile and unpredictable, both for the defense of general Habsburg interests in Europe and for the specific preservation of those interests within Germany itself following the rise of Prussia. From at least the Prussian seizure of the province of Silesia in 1740 onward, Vienna always had to conduct its foreign and military policies with one eye firmly on Berlin. This in turn made Habsburg diplomacy more elaborate than ever: to check a rising Prussia within Germany, the Austrians needed to call upon the assistance of France in the west and, more frequently, Russia in the east; but France itself was unreliable and needed in turn to be checked by an Anglo-Austrian alliance at times (e.g., 1744–1748). Furthermore,

Russia's own steady growth was a further cause of concern, particularly when czarist expansionism threatened the Ottoman hold upon Balkan lands desired by Vienna. Finally, when Napoleonic imperialism challenged the independence of *all* other powers in Europe, the Habsburg Empire had no choice but to join any available grand coalition to contest French hegemony.

The coalition war against Louis XIV at the beginning of the eighteenth century and those against Bonaparte at its end probably give us less of an insight into Austrian weakness than do the conflicts in between. The lengthy struggle against Prussia after 1740 was particularly revealing: it demonstrated that for all the military, fiscal, and administrative reforms undertaken in the Habsburg lands in this period, Vienna could not prevail against another, smaller German state which was considerably more efficient in its army, revenue collection, and bureaucracy. Furthermore, it became increasingly clear that the non-German powers, France, Britain, and Russia, desired neither the Austrian elimination of Prussia nor the Prussian elimination of Austria. In the larger European context, the Habsburg Empire had already become a *marginal* first-class power, and was to remain such until 1918. It certainly did not slip as far down the list as Spain and Sweden, and it avoided the fate which befell Poland; but, because of its decentralized, ethnically diverse, and economically backward condition, it defied attempts by succeeding administrations in Vienna to turn it into the greatest of the European states. Nevertheless, there is a danger in anticipating this decline. As Olwen Hufton observes, "the Austrian Empire's persistent, to some eyes perverse, refusal conveniently to disintegrate" is a reminder that it possessed hidden strengths. Disasters were often followed by bouts of reform—the *rétablissements*—which revealed the empire's very considerable resources even if they also demonstrated the great difficulty Vienna always had in getting its hands upon them. And every historian of Habsburg decline has somehow to explain its remarkably stubborn and, occasionally, very impressive military resistance to the dynamic force of French imperialism for almost fourteen years of the period 1792–1815.[28]

Prussia's situation was very similar to Austria's in geostrategical terms, although quite different internally. The reasons for that country's swift rise to become the most powerful northern German kingdom are well known, and need only be listed here: the organizing and military genius of three leaders, the Great Elector (1640–1688), Frederick William I (1713–1740), and Frederick "the Great" (1740–1786), the efficiency of the Junker-officered Prussian army, into which as much as four-fifths of the state's taxable resources were poured; the (relative) fiscal stability, based upon extensive royal domains and encouragement of trade and industry; the willing use of foreign soldiers and entrepreneurs; and the famous Prussian bureaucrats operating under the General War Commissariat.²⁹ Yet it was also true that Prussia's rise coincided with the collapse of Swedish power, with the disintegration of the chaotic, weakened Polish kingdom, and with the distractions which the many wars and uncertain succession of the Habsburg Empire imposed upon Vienna in the early decades of the eighteenth century. If Prussian monarchs seized their opportunities, therefore, the fact was that the opportunities were there to be seized. Moreover, in filling the "power vacuum" which had opened up in north-central Europe after 1770, the Prussian state also benefited from its position vis-à-vis the other Great Powers. Russia's own rise was helping to distract (and erode) Sweden, Poland, and the Ottoman Empire. And France was far enough away in the west to be not usually a mortal danger; indeed, it could sometimes function as a useful ally against Austria. If, on the other hand, France pushed aggressively into Germany, it was likely to be opposed by Habsburg forces, Hanover (and therefore Britain), and perhaps the Dutch, as well as by Prussia itself. Finally, if that coalition failed, Prussia could more easily sue for peace with Paris than could the other powers; an anti-French alliance was sometimes useful, but not imperative, for Berlin.

Within this advantageous diplomatic and geographical context, the early kings of Prussia played the game well. The acquisition of Silesia—described by some as *the* industrial zone in the east—was in particular a great boost to the state's military-economic capacity. But the limitations of Prussia's real power in European affairs, limitations of size and population, were cruelly exposed in the Seven Years War of 1756–1763, when the diplomatic circumstances were no longer so favorable and Frederick the Great's powerful neighbors were determined to punish him for his deviousness. Only the stupendous efforts of the Prussian monarch and his well-trained troops—assisted by the lack of coordination among his foes—enabled Frederick to avoid defeat in the face of such a frightening "encirclement." Yet the costs of that war in men and material were enormous, and with the Prussian army steadily ossifying from the 1770s onward, Berlin was in no position to withstand later diplomatic pressure from Russia, let alone the bold assault of Napoleon in 1806. Even the later recovery led by Scharnhorst, Gneisenau, and the other military reformers could not conceal the still inadequate bases of Prussian strength by 1813–1815.³⁰ It was by then overshadowed, militarily, by Russia; it relied heavily upon subsidies from Britain, paymaster to the coalition; and it still could not have taken on France alone. The kingdom of Frederick William III (1797–1840) was, like Austria, among the least of the Great Powers and would remain so until its industrial and military transformation in the 1860s.

*   *   *

By contrast, two more distant powers, Russia and the United States, enjoyed a relative invulnerability and a freedom from the strategical ambivalences which plagued the central European states in the eighteenth century. Both of these future superpowers had, to be sure, "a crumbling frontier" which required watching; but neither in the American expansion across the Alleghenies and the great plains nor in the Russian expansion across the steppes did they encounter militarily advanced societies posing a danger to the home base.[31] In their respective dealings with occidental Europe, therefore, they had the advantage of a relatively homogeneous "front." They could each pose a challenge—or, at least, a distraction—to some of the established Great Powers, while still enjoying the invulnerability conferred by their distance from the main European battle zones.

Of course, in dealing with a period as lengthy as 1660 to 1815, it is important to stress that the impact of the United States and Russia was much more in evidence by the end of that era than at the beginning. Indeed, in the 1660s and 1670s, European "America" was no more than a string of isolated coastal settlements, while Muscovy before the reign of Peter the Great (1689–1725) was almost equally remote and even more backward; in commercial terms, each was "underdeveloped," a producer of timber, hemp, and other raw materials and a purchaser of manufactured wares from Britain and the United Provinces. The American continent was, for much of this time, an object to be fought over rather than a power factor in its own right. What changed that situation was the overwhelming British success at the end of the Seven Years War (1763), which saw France expelled from Canada and Nova Scotia, and Spain excluded from West Florida. Freed from the foreign threats which hitherto had induced loyalty to Westminster, American colonists could now insist upon a merely nominal link with Britain and, if denied that by an imperial government with different ideas, engage in rebellion. By 1776, moreover, the North American colonies had grown enormously: the population of two million was by then doubling every thirty years, was spreading out westward, was economically prosperous, and was self-sufficient in foodstuffs and many other commodities. This meant, as the British found to their cost over the next seven years, that the rebel states were virtually invulnerable to merely naval operations and were also too extensive to be subjected by land forces drawn from a home island 3,000 miles away.

The existence of an independent United States was, *over time,* to have two major consequences for this story of the changing pattern of world power. The first was that from 1783 onward there existed an important extra-European center of production, wealth, and—ultimately—military might which would exert long-term influences upon the global power balance in ways which other extra-European (but economically declining) societies like China and India would not.

Already by the mid-eighteenth century the American colonies occupied a significant place in the pattern of maritime commerce and were beginning the first hesitant stages of industrialization. According to some accounts, the emergent nation produced more pig iron and bar iron in 1776 than the whole of Great Britain; and thereafter, "manufacturing output increased by a factor of nearly 50 so that by 1830 the country had become the 6th industrial power of the developed world."[32] Given that pace of growth, it was not surprising that even in the 1790s observers were predicting a great role for the United States within another century. The second consequence was to be felt much more swiftly, especially by Britain, whose role as a "flank" power in European politics was affected by the emergence of a potentially hostile state on its own Atlantic front, threatening its Canadian and West Indian possessions. This was not a constant problem, of course, and the sheer distance involved, together with the United States isolationism, meant that London did not need to consider the Americans in the same serious light as that in which, say, Vienna regarded the Turks or later the Russians. Nevertheless, the experiences of the wars of 1779–1783 and of 1812–1814 demonstrated all too clearly how difficult it would be for Britain to engage fully in European struggles if a hostile United States was at her back.

The rise of czarist Russia had a much more immediate impact upon the international power balance. Russia's stunning defeat of the Swedes at Poltava (1709) altered the other powers to the fact that the hitherto distant and somewhat barbarous Muscovite state was intent upon playing a role in European affairs. With the ambitious first czar, Peter the Great, quickly establishing a navy to complement his new footholds on the Baltic (Karelia, Estonia, Livonia), the Swedes were soon appealing for the Royal Navy's aid to prevent being overrun by this eastern colossus. But it was, in fact, the Poles and the Turks who were to suffer most from the rise of Russia, and by the time Catherine the Great had died in 1796 she had added another 200,000 square miles to an already enormous empire. Even more impressive seemed the temporary incursions which Russian military forces made to the west. The ferocity and frightening doggedness of the Russian troops during the Seven Years War, and their temporary occupation of Berlin in 1760, quite changed Frederick the Great's view of his neighbor. Four decades later, Russian forces under their general, Suvorov, were active in both Italian and Alpine campaigning during the War of the Second Coalition (1798–1802)—a distant operation that was a harbinger of the relentless Russian military advance from Moscow to Paris which took place between 1812 and 1814.[33]

It is difficult to measure Russia's rank accurately by the eighteenth century. Its army was often larger than France's; and in important

manufactures (textiles, iron) it was also making great advances. It was
a dreadfully difficult, perhaps impossible country for any of its rivals
to conquer—at least from the west; and its status as a "gunpowder
empire" enabled it to defeat the horsed tribes of the east, and thus to
acquire additional resources of manpower, raw materials, and arable
land, which in turn would enhance its place among the Great Powers.
Under governmental direction, the country was evidently bent upon
modernization in a whole variety of ways, although the pace and success of this policy have often been exaggerated. There still remained
the manifold signs of backwardness: appalling poverty and brutality,
exceedingly low per capita income, poor communications, harsh climate, and technological and educational retardation, not to mention
the reactionary, feckless character of so many of the Romanovs. Even
the formidable Catherine was unimpressive when it came to economic
and financial matters.

Still, the relative stability of European military organization and
technique in the eighteenth century allowed Russia (by borrowing
foreign expertise) to catch up and then outstrip countries with fewer
resources; and this brute advantage of superior numbers was not really
going to be eroded until the Industrial Revolution transformed the
scale and speed of warfare during the following century. In the period
before the 1840s and despite the many defects listed above, Russia's
army could occasionally be a formidable offensive force. So much
(perhaps three-quarters) of the state's finances were devoted to the
military and the average soldier stoically endured so many hardships
that Russian regiments could mount long-range operations which
were beyond most other eighteenth-century armies. It is true that the
Russian logistical base was often inadequate (with poor horses, an
inefficient supply system, and incompetent officials) to sustain a massive campaign on its own—the 1813–1814 march upon France was
across "friendly" territory and aided by large British subsidies; but
these infrequent operations were enough to give Russia a formidable
reputation and a leading place in the councils of Europe even by the
time of the Seven Years War. In grand-strategical terms, here was yet
another power which could be brought into the balance, thus helping
to ensure that French efforts to dominate the continent during this
period would ultimately fail.

It was, nonetheless, to the *distant* future that early-nineteenth-century writers such as de Tocqueville usually referred when they argued
that Russia and the United States seemed "marked out by the will of
Heaven to sway the destinies of half the globe."[34] In the period between
1660 and 1815 it was a maritime nation, Great Britain, rather than
these continental giants, which made the most decisive advances,
finally dislodging France from its position as the greatest of the pow-

ers. Here, too, geography played a vital, though not exclusive, part. This British advantage of location was described nearly a century ago in Mahan's classic work *The Influence of Sea Power upon History* (1890):

> ... if a nation be so situated that it is neither forced to defend itself by land nor induced to seek extension of its territory by way of land, it has, by the very unity of its aim directed upon the sea, an advantage as compared with a people one of whose boundaries is continental.[35]

Mahan's statement presumes, of course, a number of further points. The first is that the British government would not have distractions on *its* flanks—which after the conquest of Ireland and the Act of Union with Scotland (1707), was essentially correct, though it is interesting to note those occasional later French attempts to embarrass Britain along the Celtic fringes, something which London took very seriously indeed. An Irish uprising was much closer to home than the strategical embarrassment offered by the American rebels. Fortunately for the British, this vulnerability was never properly exploited by foes.

The second assumption in Mahan's statement is the superior status of sea warfare and of sea power over their equivalents on land. This was a deeply held belief of what has been termed the "navalist" school of strategy,[36] and seemed well justified by post-1500 economic and political trends. The steady shift in the main trade routes from the Mediterranean to the Atlantic and the great profits which could be made from colonial and commercial ventures in the West Indies, North America, the Indian subcontinent, and the Far East naturally benefited a country situated off the western flank of the European continent. To be sure, it also required a government aware of the importance of maritime trade and ready to pay for a large war fleet. Subject to that precondition, the British political elite seemed by the eighteenth century to have discovered a happy recipe for the continuous growth of national wealth and power. Flourishing overseas trade aided the British economy, encouraged seamanship and shipbuilding, provided funds for the national Exchequer, and was the lifeline to the colonies. The colonies not only offered outlets for British products but also supplied many raw materials, from the valuable sugar, tobacco, and calicoes to the increasingly important North American naval stores. And the Royal Navy ensured respect for British merchants in times of peace and protected their trade and garnered further colonial territories in war, to the country's political and economic benefit. Trade, colonies, and the navy thus formed a "virtuous triangle," reciprocally interacting to Britain's long-term advantage.

While this explanation of Britain's rise was partly valid, it was not the whole truth. Like so many mercantilist works, Mahan's tended to emphasize the importance of Britain's external commerce as opposed to domestic production, and in particular to exaggerate the importance of the "colonial" trades. Agriculture remained the fundament of British wealth throughout the eighteenth century, and exports (whose ratio to total national income was probably less than 10 percent until the 1780s) were often subject to strong foreign competition and to tariffs, for which no amount of naval power could compensate.[37] The navalist viewpoint also inclined to forget the further fact that British trade with the Baltic, Germany, and the Mediterranean lands was—although growing less swiftly than those in sugar, spices, and slaves—still of great economic importance;* so that a France permanently dominant in Europe might, as the events of 1806–1812 showed, be able to deliver a dreadful blow to British manufacturing industry. Under such circumstances, isolationism from European power politics could be economic folly.

There was also a critically important "continental" dimension to British grand strategy, overlooked by those whose gaze was turned outward to the West Indies, Canada, and India. Fighting a purely maritime war was perfectly logical during the Anglo-Dutch struggles of 1652–1654, 1665–1667, and 1672–1674, since commercial rivalry between the two sea powers was at the root of that antagonism. After the Glorious Revolution of 1688, however, when William of Orange secured the English throne, the strategical situation was quite transformed. The challenge to British interests during the seven wars which were to occur between 1689 and 1815 was posed by an essentially *land-based* power, France. True, the French would take this fight to the western hemisphere, to the Indian Ocean, to Egypt, and elsewhere; but those campaigns, although important to London and Liverpool traders, never posed a direct threat to British national security. The latter would arise only with the prospect of French military victories over the Dutch, the Hanoverians, and the Prussians, thereby leaving France supreme in west-central Europe long enough to amass shipbuilding resources capable of eroding British naval mastery. It was therefore not merely William III's personal union with the United Provinces, or the later Hanoverian ties, which caused successive British governments to intervene militarily on the continent of Europe in these decades. There was also the compelling argument—echoing Elizabeth I's fears about Spain—that France's enemies had to be given assistance *inside* Europe, to contain Bourbon (and Napoleonic) ambitions and thus to preserve Britain's own long-term interests. A "maritime" and a

*Not to mention the *strategic* importance of Baltic naval stores, upon which both the Royal Navy and the mercantile marine relied—a dependency reflected in the frequent dispatch of a British fleet into the Baltic to preserve the balance of power and the free flow of timber and masts.

"continental" strategy were, according to this viewpoint, complementary rather than antagonistic.

The essence of this strategic calculation was nicely expressed by the Duke of Newcastle in 1742:

> France will outdo us at sea when they have nothing to fear on land. I have always maintained that our marine should protect our alliances on the Continent, and so, by diverting the expense of France, enable us to maintain our superiority at sea.[38]

This British support to countries willing to "divert the expense of France" came in two chief forms. The first was direct military operations, either by peripheral raids to distract the French army or by the dispatch of a more substantial expeditionary force to fight alongside whatever allies Britain might possess at the time. The raiding strategy seemed cheaper and was much beloved by certain ministers, but it usually had negligible effects and occasionally ended in disaster (like the expedition to Walcheren of 1809). The provision of a continental army was more expensive in terms of men and money, but, as the campaigns of Marlborough and Wellington demonstrated, was also much more likely to assist in the preservation of the European balance.

The second form of British aid was financial, whether by directly buying Hessian and other mercenaries to fight against France, or by giving subsidies to the allies. Frederick the Great, for example, received from the British the substantial sum of £675,000 each year from 1757 to 1760; and in the closing stages of the Napoleonic War the flow of British funds reached far greater proportions (e.g., £11 million to various allies in 1813 alone, and £65 million for the war as a whole). But all this had been possible only because the expansion of British trade and commerce, particularly in the lucrative overseas markets, allowed the government to raise loans and taxes of unprecedented amounts without suffering national bankruptcy. Thus, while diverting "the expense of France" inside Europe was a costly business, it usually ensured that the French could neither mount a sustained campaign against maritime trade nor so dominate the European continent that they would be free to threaten an invasion of the home islands—which in turn permitted London to finance its wars and to subsidize its allies. Geographical advantage and economic benefit were thus merged to enable the British brilliantly to pursue a Janus-faced strategy: "with one face turned towards the Continent to trim the balance of power and the other directed at sea to strengthen her maritime dominance."[39]

Only after one grasps the importance of the financial and geographical factors described above can one make full sense of the statistics of the growing populations and military/naval strengths of the powers in this period (see Tables 3–5).

Table 3. Populations of the Powers,
1700–1800[40]
(millions)

	1700	1750	1800
British Isles	9.0	10.5	16.0
France	19.0	21.5	28.0
Habsburg Empire	8.0	18.0	28.0
Prussia	2.0	6.0	9.5
Russia	17.5	20.0	37.0
Spain	6.0	9.0	11.0
Sweden		1.7	2.3
United Provinces	1.8	1.9	2.0
United States	—	2.0	4.0

Table 4. Size of Armies, 1690–1814[41]
(men)

	1690	1710	1756/60	1778	1789	1812/14
Britain	70,000	75,000	200,000		40,000	250,000
France	400,000	350,000	330,000	170,000	180,000	600,000
Habsburg Empire	50,000	100,000	200,000	200,000	300,000	250,000
Prussia	30,000	39,000	195,000	160,000	190,000	270,000
Russia	170,000	220,000	330,000		300,000	500,000
Spain		30,000			50,000	
Sweden		110,000				
United Provinces	73,000	130,000	40,000			
United States	—	—	—	35,000	—	—

Table 5. Size of Navies, 1689–1815[42]
(ships of the line)

	1689	1739	1756	1779	1790	1815
Britain	100	124	105	90	195	214
Denmark	29	—	—	—	38	—
France	120	50	70	63	81	80
Russia	—	30	—	40	67	40
Spain	—	34	—	48	72	25
Sweden	40	—	—	—	27	—
United Provinces	66	49	—	20	44	—

As readers familiar with statistics will be aware, such crude figures have to be treated with extreme care. Population totals, especially in the early period, are merely guesses (and in Russia's case the margin for error could be several millions). Army sizes fluctuated widely, depending upon whether the date chosen is at the outset, the midpoint, or the culmination of a particular war; and the total figures often include substantial mercenary units and (in Napoleon's case) even the troops of reluctantly co-opted allies. The number of ships of the line indicated neither their readiness for battle nor, necessarily, the availability of trained crews to man them. Moreover, statistics take no account of generalship or seamanship, of competence or neglect, of national fervor or faintheartedness. Even so, it might appear that the above figures at least *roughly* reflect the chief power-political trends of the age: France and, increasingly, Russia lead in population and military terms; Britain is usually unchallenged at sea; Prussia overtakes Spain, Sweden, and the United Provinces; and France comes closer to dominating Europe with the enormous armies of Louis XIV and Napoleon than at any time in the intervening century.

Aware of the financial and geographical dimensions of these 150 years of Great Power struggles, however, one can see that further refinements have to be made to the picture suggested in these three tables. For example, the swift decline of the United Provinces relative to other nations in respect to army size was not repeated in the area of war finance, where its role was crucial for a very long while. The nonmilitary character of the United States conceals the fact that it could pose a considerable strategical distraction. The figures also understate the military contribution of Britain, since it might be subsidizing 100,000 allied troops (in 1813, 450,000!) as well as providing for its own army, and naval personnel of 140,000 in 1813–1814;[43] conversely, the true strength of Prussia and the Habsburg Empire, dependent on subsidies during most wars, would be exaggerated if one merely considered the size of their armies. As noted above, the enormous military establishments of France were rendered less effective through financial weaknesses and geostrategical obstacles, while those of Russia were eroded by economic backwardness and sheer distance. The strengths and weaknesses of each of these Powers ought to be borne in mind as we turn to a more detailed examination of the wars themselves.

The Winning of Wars, 1660–1763

When Louis XIV took over full direction of the French government in March 1661, the European scene was particularly favorable to a monarch determined to impose his views upon it.[44] To the south, Spain was still exhausting itself in the futile attempt to recover Portugal. Across the Channel, a restored monarchy under Charles II was trying to find its feet, and in English commercial circles great jealousy of the Dutch existed. In the north, a recent war had left both Denmark and Sweden weakened. In Germany, the Protestant princes watched suspiciously for any fresh Habsburg attempt to improve its position, but the imperial government in Vienna had problems enough in Hungary and Transylvania, and slightly later with a revival of Ottoman power. Poland was already wilting under the effort of fending off Swedish and Muscovite predators. Thus French diplomacy, in the best traditions of Richelieu, could easily take advantage of these circumstances, playing off the Portuguese against Spain, the Magyars, Turks, and German princes against Austria, and the English against the Dutch—while buttressing France's own geographical (and army-recruitment) position by its important 1663 treaty with the Swiss cantons. All this gave Louis XIV time enough to establish himself as absolute monarch, secure from the internal challenges which had afflicted French governments during the preceding century. More important still, it gave Colbert, Le Tellier, and the other key ministers the chance to overhaul the administration and to lavish resources upon the army and the navy in anticipation of the Sun King's pursuit of glory.[45]

It was therefore all too easy for Louis to try to "round off" the borders of France in the early stages of his reign, the more especially since Anglo-Dutch relations had deteriorated into open hostilities by 1665 (the Second Anglo-Dutch War). Although France was pledged to support the United Provinces, it actually played little part in the campaigns at sea and instead prepared itself for an invasion of the southern Netherlands, which were still owned by a weakened Spain. When the French finally launched their invasion, in May 1667, town after town quickly fell into their hands. What then followed was an early example of the rapid diplomatic shifts of this period. The English and the Dutch, wearying of their mutually unprofitable war and fearing French ambitions, made peace at Breda in July and, joined by Sweden, sought to "mediate" in the Franco-Spanish dispute in order to limit Louis's gains. The 1668 Treaty of Aix-la-Chapelle achieved just that, but at the cost of infuriating the French king, who eventually made up his mind to be revenged upon the United Provinces, which he perceived to be the chief obstacle to his ambitions. For the next few years, while Colbert waged his tariff war against the Dutch, the French army and navy were further built up. Secret diplomacy seduced England and Sweden from their alliance with the United Provinces and quieted the fears of the Austrians and the German states. By 1672 the French war machine, aided by the English at sea, was ready to strike.

Although it was London which first declared war upon the United Provinces, the dismal English effort in the third Anglo-Dutch conflict of 1672–1674 requires minimal space here. Checked by the brilliant efforts of de Ruyter at sea, and therefore unable to achieve anything on land, Charles II's government came under increasing domestic criticism: evidence of political duplicity and financial mismanagement, and a strong dislike of being allied to an autocratic, Catholic power like France, made the war unpopular and forced the government to pull out of it by 1674. In retrospect, it is a reminder of how immature and uncertain the political, financial, and administrative bases of English power still were under the later Stuarts.[46] London's change of policy was of *international* importance, however, in that it partly reflected the widespread alarm which Louis XIV's designs were now arousing throughout Europe. Within another year, Dutch diplomacy and subsidies found many allies willing to throw their weight against the French. German principalities, Brandenburg (which defeated France's only remaining partner, Sweden, at Fehrbellin in 1675), Denmark, Spain, and the Habsburg Empire all entered the issue. It was not that this coalition of states was strong enough to *overwhelm* France; most of them had smallish armies, and distractions on their own flanks; and the core of the anti-French alliance remained the United Provinces under their new leader, William of Orange. But the watery barrier in the north and the vulnerability of the French army's lines against various foes in the Rhineland meant that Louis himself could make no dramatic gains. A similar sort of stalemate existed at sea; the French navy controlled the Mediterranean, Dutch and Danish fleets held the Baltic, and neither side could prevail in the West Indies. Both French and Dutch commerce were badly affected in this war, to the indirect benefit of neutrals like the British. By 1678, in fact, the Amsterdam merchant classes had pushed their own government into a separate peace with France, which in turn meant that the German states (reliant upon Dutch subsidies) could not continue to fight on their own.

Although the Nymegen peace treaties of 1678–1679 brought the open fighting to an end, Louis XIV's evident desire to round off France's northern borders, his claim to be "the arbiter of Europe," and the alarming fact that he was maintaining an army of 200,000 troops in peacetime disquieted Germans, Dutchmen, Spaniards, and Englishmen alike.[47] This did not mean an immediate return to war. The Dutch merchants preferred to trade in peace; the German princes, like Charles II of England, were tied to Paris by subsidies; and the Habsburg Empire was engaged in a desperate struggle with the Turks. When Spain endeavored to protect its Luxembourg territories from France in 1683, therefore, it had to fight alone and suffer inevitable defeat.

From 1685, however, things began to swing against France. The persecution of the Huguenots shocked Protestant Europe. Within another two years, the Turks had been soundly defeated and driven away from Vienna; and the Emperor Leopold, with enhanced prestige and military strength, could at last turn some of his attention to the west. By September 1688, a now-nervous French king decided to invade Germany, finally turning this European "cold" war into a hot one. Not only did France's action provoke its continental rivals into declaring hostilities, it also gave William of Orange the opportunity to slip across the Channel and replace the discredited James II on the English throne.

By the end of 1689, therefore, France stood alone against the United Provinces, England, the Habsburg Empire, Spain, Savoy, and the major German states.[48] This was not as alarming a combination as it seemed, and the "hard core" of the Grand Alliance really consisted of the Anglo-Dutch forces and the German states. Although a disparate grouping in certain respects, they possessed sufficient determination, financial resources, armies, and fleets to balance the Sun King's France. Ten years earlier, Louis might possibly have prevailed, but French finances and trade were now much less satisfactory after Colbert's death, and neither the army nor the navy—although numerically daunting—was equipped for sustained and distant fighting. A swift defeat of one of the major allies could break the deadlock, but where should that thrust be directed, and had Louis the will to order bold measures? For three years he dithered; and when in 1692 he finally assembled an invasion force of 24,000 troops to dispatch across the Channel, the "maritime powers" were simply too strong, smashing up the French warships and barges at Barfleur–La Hogue.[49]

From 1692 onward, the conflict at sea became a slow, grinding, mutually ruinous war against trade. Adopting a commerce-raiding strategy, the French government encouraged its privateers to prey upon Anglo-Dutch shipping while it reduced its own allocations to the battle fleet. The allied navies, for their part, endeavored to increase the pressures on the French economy by instituting a commercial blockade, thus abandoning the Dutch habit of trading with the enemy. Neither measure brought the opponent to his knees; each increased the economic burdens of the war, making it unpopular with merchants as well as peasants, who were already suffering from a succession of poor harvests. The land campaigns were also expensive, slow struggles against fortresses and across waterways: Vauban's fortifications made France virtually impregnable, but the same sort of obstacles prevented an easy French advance into Holland or the Palatinate. With each side maintaining over 250,000 men in the field, the costs were horrendous, even to these rich countries.[50] While there were also extra-European campaigns (West Indies, Newfoundland, Acadia, Pondicherry), none was of sufficient importance to swing the basic continental or maritime balance. Thus by 1696, with Tory squires and Amsterdam burghers complaining about excessive taxes, and with France afflicted by famine, both William and Louis had cause enough to compromise.

In consequence, the Treaty of Ryswick (1697), while allowing Louis some of his earlier border gains, saw a general return to the status quo ante. Nonetheless, the results of the Nine Years War of 1689–1697 were not as insignificant as contemporary critics alleged. French ambitions had certainly been blunted on land, and its naval power eroded at sea. The Glorious Revolution of 1688 had been upheld, and England had secured its Irish flank, strengthened its financial institutions, and rebuilt its army and navy. And an Anglo-Dutch-German tradition of keeping France out of Flanders and the Rhineland was established. Albeit at great cost, the political plurality of Europe had been reasserted.

Given the war-weary mood in most capitals, a renewal of the conflict scarcely seemed possible. However, when Louis's grandson was
offered the succession to the Spanish throne in 1700, the Sun King saw
in this an ideal opportunity to enhance France's power. Instead of
compromising with his potential rivals, he swiftly occupied the southern Netherlands on his grandson's behalf, and also secured *exclusive*
commercial concessions for French traders in Spain's large empire in
the western hemisphere. By these and various other provocations, he
alarmed the British and Dutch sufficiently to cause them to join Austria
in 1701 in another coalition struggle to check Louis's ambitions: the
War of the Spanish Succession.

Once again, the general balance of forces and taxable resources
suggested that each alliance could seriously hurt, but not overwhelm,
the other.[51] In some respects, Louis was in a stronger position than in
the 1689–1697 war. The Spaniards readily took to his grandson, now
their Philip V, and the "Bourbon powers" could work together in many
theaters; French finances certainly benefited from the import of Spanish silver. Moreover, France had been geared up militarily—to the
level, at one period, of supporting nearly half a million troops. However, the Austrians, less troubled on their Balkan flank, were playing
a greater role in this war than they had in the previous one. Most
important of all, a determined British government was to commit its
considerable national resources, in the form of hefty subsidies to German allies, an overpowering fleet, and, unusually, a large-scale continental army under the brilliant Marlborough. The latter, with between
40,000 and 70,000 British and mercenary troops, could join an excellent Dutch army of over 100,000 men and a Habsburg army of a similar
size to frustrate Louis's attempt to impose his wishes upon Europe.

This did not mean, however, that the Grand Alliance could impose
its wishes upon France, or, for that matter, upon Spain. Outside those
two kingdoms, it is true, events turned steadily in favor of the allies.
Marlborough's decisive victory at Blenheim (1704) severely hurt the
Franco-Bavarian armies and freed Austria from a French invasion
threat. The later battle of Ramillies (1706) gave the Anglo-Dutch forces
most of the southern Netherlands, and that at Oudenarde (1708) brutally stopped the French effort to regain ground there.[52]

At sea, with no enemy main fleet to deal with after the inconclusive
battle of Malaga (1704), the Royal Navy and its declining Dutch equivalent could demonstrate the flexibility of superior naval power. The new
ally, Portugal, could be sustained from the sea, while Lisbon in turn
provided a forward fleet base and Brazil a source of gold. Troops could
be dispatched to the western hemisphere to attack French possessions
in the West Indies and North America, and raiding squadrons could
hunt for Spanish bullion fleets. The seizure of Gibraltar not only gave
the Royal Navy a base controlling the exit from that sea, but divided

the Franco-Spanish bases—and fleets. British fleets ensured the capture of Minorca and Sardinia; they covered Savoy and the Italian coasts from French attack; and when the allies went onto the offensive, they shepherded and supplied the imperial armies' invasion of Spain and supported the assault upon Toulon.[53]

This general Allied maritime superiority could not, however, prevent a resumption of French commerce-raiding, and by 1708 the Royal Navy had been forced to institute a convoying system in order to limit the losses to the merchant marine. And just as British frigates could not keep French privateers from slipping in and out of Dunkirk or the Gironde, so also were they unable to effect a commercial blockade, for that would have meant patrolling the entire Franco-Spanish coastline; even the seizure of corn ships off French ports during the dreadful winter of 1709 could not bring Louis's largely self-sufficient empire to its knees.

This allied capacity to wound but not kill was even more evident in the military campaigns against France and Spain. By 1709 the allied invasion army was falling back from a brief occupation of Madrid, unable to hold the country in the face of increasing Spanish assault. In northern France, the Anglo-Dutch armies found no further opportunity for victories like Blenheim; instead, the war was grinding, bloody, and expensive. Moreover, by 1710 a Tory ministry had come into office at Westminster, eager for a peace which secured Britain's maritime and imperial interests and reduced its expenses in a continental war. Finally, the Archduke Charles, who had been the allies' candidate for the Spanish throne, unexpectedly succeeded as emperor, and thus caused his partners to lose any remaining enthusiasm for placing him in control of Spain as well. With Britain's unilateral defection from the war in early 1712, followed later by that of the Dutch, even the Emperor Charles, so eager to be "Carlos III" of Spain, accepted the need for peace after another fruitless year of campaigning.

The peace terms which brought the War of the Spanish Succession to an end were fixed in the treaties of Utrecht (1713) and Rastadt (1714). Considering the settlement as a whole, there was no doubt that the great beneficiary was Britain.[54] Although it had gained Gibraltar, Minorca, Nova Scotia, Newfoundland, and Hudson Bay and trade concessions in the Spanish New World, it did not ignore the European balance. Indeed, the complex of eleven separate treaties which made up the settlement of 1713–1714 produced a satisfying, sophisticated reinforcement of the equilibrium. The French and the Spanish kingdoms were to remain forever separated, whereas the Protestant Succession in Britain was formally recognized. The Habsburg Empire, having failed in Spain, was given the southern Netherlands and Milan (thus building in further checks to France), plus Naples and Sardinia. Dutch independence had been preserved, but the United Provinces were no longer such a formidable naval and commercial power and were now compelled to devote the greater part of their energies to garrisoning their southern borders. Above all, Louis XIV had been finally and decisively checked in his dynastic and territorial ambitions, and the French nation had been chastened by the horrific costs of war, which had, among other consequences, increased total government debts *sevenfold*. The balance of power was secure on land, while at sea Britain was unchallenged. Small wonder that the Whigs, who returned to office on George I's accession in 1714, were soon anxious to preserve the Utrecht settlement and were even willing to embrace a French *entente* once their archenemy Louis died in the following year.

The redistribution of power among the western European states which had occurred in this half-century of war was less dramatic than the changes which took place in the east. The borders there were more fluid than in the west, and enormous tracts of land were controlled by marcher lords, Croatian irregulars, and Cossack hosts rather than by the professional armies of an enlightened monarch. Even when the nation-states went to war against each other, their campaigning would frequently be over great distances and involve the use of irregular troops, hussars, and so on in order to implement some grand strategical stroke. Unlike the campaigning in the Low Countries, success or failure here brought with it tremendous transfers of land, and thus emphasized the more spectacular rises and falls among the Powers. For example, these few decades alone saw the Turks pose their final large-scale military threat to Vienna, but then suffer swift defeat and decline. The remarkable initial response by Austrian, German, and Polish forces not only rescued the imperial city from a Turkish investing army in 1683 but also led to much more extensive campaigning by an enlarged Holy League.[55] After a great battle near Homacs (1687), Turkish power in the Hungarian plain was destroyed forever; if the lines then stabilized because of repeated calls upon German and Habsburg troops against France during the 1689–1697 War, the further defeats of the Turkish army at Zalankemen (1691) and Zenta (1697) confirmed the trend. Provided it could concentrate its resources on the Balkan front and possessed generals of the caliber of Prince Eugene, the Habsburg Empire could now more than hold its own against the Turks. While it could not organize its heterogeneous lands as efficiently as the western monarchies, nonetheless its future as one of the European great states was assured.

Measured by that criterion, Sweden was far less lucky. Once the young Charles XII came to the Swedish throne in 1697, the predatory instincts of the neighboring states were aroused; Denmark, Poland, and Russia each desired parts of Sweden's exposed Baltic empire and agreed in autumn 1699 to combine against it. Yet when the fighting commenced, Sweden's apparent vulnerability was at first more than compensated for by its own very considerable army, a monarch of great military brilliance, and Anglo-Dutch naval support. A combination of all three factors allowed Charles to threaten Copenhagen and force the Danes out of the war by August 1700, following which he transported his army across the Baltic and routed the Russians in a stunning victory at Narva three months later. Having savored the heady joys of battle and conquest, Charles then spent the following years overrunning Poland and moving into Saxony.

With the wisdom of retrospect, historians have suggested that Charles XII's unwise concentration upon Poland and Saxony turned his gaze from the reforms which Peter the Great was forcing upon Russia after the defeat at Narva.[56] Aided by numerous foreign advisers and willing to borrow widely from the military expertise of the west, Peter built up a massive army and navy in the same energetic way in which he created St. Petersburg from the swamps. By the time Charles with a force of 40,000 troops turned to deal with Peter in 1708, it was probably already too late. Although the Swedish army generally performed better in battle, it suffered considerable losses, was never able to crush the main Russian army, and was hampered by inadequate logistics—such difficulties intensifying as Charles's force moved south into the Ukraine and endured the bitter winter of 1708–1709. When the great battle finally occurred, at Poltava in July 1709, the Russian army was vastly superior in numbers and in good defensive positions. Not only did this encounter wipe out the Swedish force, but Charles's subsequent flight into Turkish territory and lengthy exile there gave Sweden's foes nearer home their opportunity. By the time Charles finally returned to Sweden, in December 1715, all his trans-Baltic possessions had gone and parts of Finland were in Russian hands.

After further years of fighting (in which Charles XII was killed in yet another clash with the Danes in 1718), an exhausted, isolated Sweden finally had to admit to the loss of most of its Baltic provinces in the 1721 Peace of Nystad. It had now fallen to the second order of the powers, while Russia was in the first. Appropriately enough, to mark the 1721 victory over Sweden, Peter assumed the title Imperator. Despite the later decline of the czarist fleet, despite the great backwardness of the country, Russia had clearly shown that it, like France and Britain, "had the strength to act independently as a great power without depending on outside support."[57] In the east as in the west of Europe there was now, in Dehio's phrase, a "counterweight to a concentration at the center."[58]

This general balance of political, military, and economic force in Europe was underwritten by an Anglo-French *détente* lasting nearly two decades after 1715.[59] France in particular needed to recuperate after a war which had dreadfully hurt its foreign commerce and so increased the state's debt that the interest payments on it alone equaled the normal revenue. Furthermore, the monarchies in London and Paris, not a little fearful of their own succession, frowned upon any attempts to upset the status quo and found it mutually profitable to cooperate on many issues.[60] In 1719, for example, both powers were using force to prevent Spain from pursuing an expansionist policy in Italy. By the 1730s, however, the pattern of international relations was again changing. By this stage, the French themselves were less enthusiastic about the British link and were instead looking to recover their old position as the leading nation of Europe. The succession in France was now secure, and the years of peace had aided prosperity—and also led to a large expansion in overseas trade, challenging the maritime powers. While France under its minister Fleury rapidly improved its relations with Spain and expanded its diplomatic activities in eastern Europe, Britain under the cautious and isolationist Walpole was endeavoring to keep out of continental affairs. Even a French attack upon the Austrian possessions of Lorraine and Milan in 1733, and a French move into the Rhineland, failed to provoke a British reaction. Unable to obtain any support from the isolationist Walpole and the frightened Dutch, Vienna was forced to negotiate with Paris for the compromise peace of 1738. Bolstered by military and diplomatic successes in western Europe, by the alliance of Spain, the deference of the United Provinces, and the increasing compliance of Sweden and even Austria, France now enjoyed a prestige unequaled since the early decades of Louis XIV. This was made even more evident in the following year, when French diplomacy negotiated an end to an Austro-Russian war against the Ottoman Empire (1735–1739), thereby returning to Turkish possession many of the territories seized by the two eastern monarchies.

While the British under Walpole had tended to ignore these events within Europe, commercial interests and opposition politicians were much more concerned at the rising number of clashes with France's ally, Spain, in the western hemisphere. There the rich colonial trades and conflicting settler expansionisms offered ample materials for a quarrel.[61] The resultant Anglo-Spanish war, which Walpole reluctantly agreed to in October 1739, might merely have remained one of that series of smaller regional conflicts fought between those two countries in the eighteenth century but for France's decision to give all sorts of aid to Spain, especially "beyond the line" in the Caribbean. Compared with the 1702–1713 War of the Spanish Succession, the Bourbon powers were in a far better position to compete overseas, particularly since neither Britain's army nor its navy was equipped to carry out the conquest of Spanish colonies so favored by the pundits at home.

The death of the Emperor Charles VI, followed by Maria Theresa's

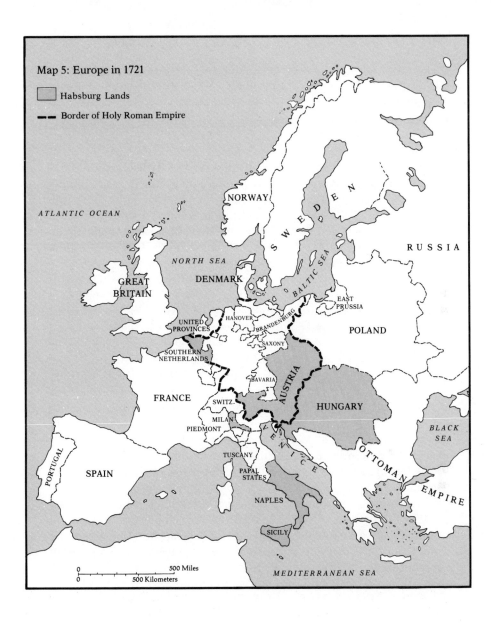

Map 5: Europe in 1721

Habsburg Lands

Border of Holy Roman Empire

NORWAY

SWEDEN

RUSSIA

ATLANTIC OCEAN

NORTH SEA

DENMARK

BALTIC SEA

GREAT
BRITAIN

EAST
PRUSSIA

UNITED
PROVINCES

HANOVER

BRANDENBURG

POLAND

SAXONY

SOUTHERN
NETHERLANDS

BAVARIA

AUSTRIA

FRANCE

SWITZ.

HUNGARY

MILAN

PIEDMONT

VENICE

BLACK
SEA

TUSCANY

OTTOMAN

PORTUGAL

SPAIN

PAPAL
STATES

EMPIRE

NAPLES

SICILY

500 Miles

0

0

500 Kilometers

MEDITERRANEAN SEA

succession and then by Frederick the Great's decision to take advantage of this by seizing Silesia in the winter of 1740–1741, quite transformed the situation and turned attention back to the continent. Unable to contain themselves, anti-Austrian circles in France fully supported Prussia and Bavaria in their assaults upon the Habsburg inheritance. But this in turn led to a renewal of the old Anglo-Austrian alliance, bringing substantial subsidies to the beleaguered Maria Theresa. By offering payments, by meditating to take Prussia (temporarily) and Saxony out of the war, and by the military action at Dettingen in 1743, the British government brought relief to Austria, protected Hanover, and removed French influence from Germany. As the Anglo-French antagonism turned into formal hostilities in 1744, the conflict intensified. The French army pushed northward, through the border fortresses of the Austrian Netherlands, toward the petrified Dutch. At sea, facing no significant challenge from the Bourbon fleets, the Royal Navy imposed an increasingly tight blockade upon French commerce. Overseas, the attacks and counterattacks continued, in the West Indies, up the St. Lawrence river, around Madras, along the trade routes to the Levant. Prussia, which returned to the fight against Austria in 1743, was again persuaded out of the war two years later. British subsidies could be used to keep the Austrians in order, to buy mercenaries for Hanover's protection and even for the purchase of a Russian army to defend the Netherlands. This was, by eighteenth-century standards, an expensive way to fight a war, and many Britons complained at the increasing taxation and the trebling of the national debt; but gradually it was forcing an even more exhausted France toward a compromise peace.

Geography as much as finance—the two key elements discussed earlier—finally compelled the British and French governments to settle their differences at the Treaty of Aix-la-Chapelle (1748). By that time, the French army had the Dutch at its mercy; but would that compensate for the steadily tightening grip imposed on France's maritime commerce or for the loss of major colonies? Conversely, of what use were the British seizure of Louisburg on the St. Lawrence and the naval victories of Anson and Hawke if France conquered the Low Countries? In consequence, diplomatic talks arranged for a general return to the status quo ante, with the significant exception of Frederick's conquest of Silesia. Both at the time and in retrospect, Aix-la-Chapelle was seen more in the nature of a truce than a lasting settlement. It left Maria Theresa keen to be revenged upon Prussia, France wondering how to be victorious overseas as well as on land, and Britain anxious to ensure that its great enemy would next time be defeated as soundly in continental warfare as it could be in a maritime/colonial struggle.

* * *

In the North American colonies, where British and French settlers (each aided by Indians and some local military garrisons) were repeatedly clashing in the early 1750s, even the word "truce" was a misnomer. There the forces involved were almost impossible to control by home governments, the more especially since a "patriot lobby" in each country pressed for support for their colonists and encouraged the view that a fundamental struggle—not merely for the Ohio and Mississippi valley regions, but for Canada, the Caribbean, India, nay, the entire extra-European world—was underway.[62] With each side dispatching further reinforcements and putting its navy on a war footing by 1755, the other states began to adjust to the prospect of another Anglo-French conflict. For Spain and the United Provinces, now plainly in the second rank and fearing that they would be ground down between these two colossi in the west, neutrality was the only solution—despite the inherent difficulties for traders like the Dutch.[63]

For the eastern monarchies of Austria, Prussia, and Russia, however, abstention from an Anglo-French war in the mid-1750s was impossible. The first reason was that although some Frenchmen argued that the conflict should be fought at sea and in the colonies, the natural tendency in Paris was to attack Britain via Hanover, the strategical Achilles' heel of the islanders. This, though, would not only alarm the German states but also compel the British to search for and subsidize military allies to check the French on the continent. The second reason was altogether more important: the Austrians were determined to recover Silesia from Prussia; and the Russians under their Czarina Elizabeth were also looking for a chance to punish the disrespectful, ambitious Frederick. Each of these powers had built up a considerable army (Prussia over 150,000 men, Austria almost 200,000, and Russia perhaps 330,000) and was calculating when to strike; but all of them were going to need subsidies from the west to keep their armies at that size. Finally, it was in the logic of things that if any of these eastern rivals found a "partner" in Paris or London, the others would be impelled to join the opposing side.

Thus, the famous "diplomatic revolution" of 1756 seemed, strategically, merely a reshuffling of the cards. France now buried its ancient differences with the Habsburgs and joined Austria and Russia in their war against Prussia, while Berlin replaced Vienna as London's continental ally. At first sight, the Franco-Austro-Russian coalition looked the better deal. It was decidedly bigger in military terms, and by 1757 Frederick had lost all his early territorial gains and the Duke of Cumberland's Anglo-German army had surrendered, leaving the future of Hanover—and Prussia itself—in doubt. Minorca had fallen to the French, and in the more distant theaters France and its native allies were also making gains. Overturning the treaty of Utrecht, and in Austria's case that of Aix-la-Chapelle, now appeared distinctly possible.

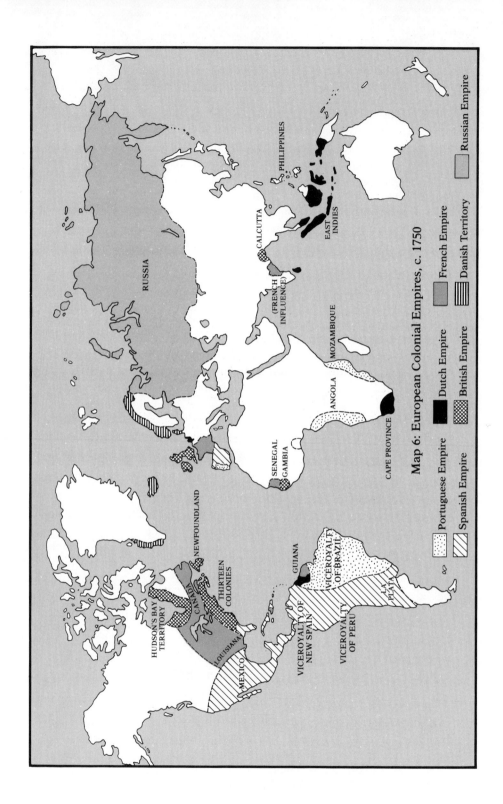

Map 6: European Colonial Empires, c. 1750

Portuguese Empire

Spanish Empire

Dutch Empire

British Empire

French Empire

Danish Territory

Russian Empire

RUSSIA

PHILIPPINES

CALCUTTA

EAST INDIES

(FRENCH INFLUENCE)

MOZAMBIQUE

ANGOLA

SENEGAL

GAMBIA

CAPE PROVINCE

NEWFOUNDLAND

HUDSON'S BAY TERRITORY

CANADA

THIRTEEN COLONIES

LOUISIANA

MEXICO

VICEROYALTY OF NEW SPAIN

GUIANA

VICEROYALTY OF BRAZIL

VICEROYALTY OF PERU

LA PLATA

The reason this did not happen was that the Anglo-Prussian combination remained superior in three vital aspects: leadership, financial staying power, and military/naval expertise.[64] Of Frederick's achievement in harnessing the full energies of Prussia to the pursuit of victory and of his generalship on the field of battle there can be no doubt. But the prize goes, perhaps, to Pitt, who after all was not an absolute monarch but merely one of a number of politicians, who had to juggle with touchy and jealous colleagues, a volatile public, and then a new king, and simultaneously pursue an effective grand strategy. And the measure of that effectiveness could not simply be in sugar islands seized or French-backed nabobs toppled, because all these colonial gains, however valuable, would be only temporary if the foe occupied Hanover and eliminated Prussia. The correct way to a decisive victory, as Pitt gradually realized, was to complement the popular "maritime" strategy with a "continental" one, providing large-scale subsidies to Frederick's own forces and paying for a considerable "Army of Observation" in Germany, to protect Hanover and help contain the French.

But such a policy was in turn very dependent upon having sufficient resources to survive year after year of grinding warfare. Frederick and his tax officials used every device to raise monies in Prussia, but Prussia's capacity paled by comparison with Britain's, which at the height of the struggle possessed a fleet of over 120 ships of the line, had more than 200,000 soldiers (including German mercenaries) on its pay lists, and was also subsidizing Prussia. In fact, the Seven Years War cost the Exchequer over £160 million, of which £60 million (37 percent) was raised on the money markets. While this further great rise in the national debt was to alarm Pitt's colleagues and contribute to his downfall in October 1761, nevertheless the overseas trade of the country increased in every year, bringing enhanced customs receipts and prosperity. Here was an excellent example of profit being converted into power, and of British sea power being used (e.g., in the West Indies) for national profit. As the British ambassador to Prussia was informed, "we must be merchants before we are soldiers. . . . trade and maritime force depend upon each other, and . . . the riches which are the true resources of this country depend upon its commerce."[65] By contrast, the economies of all the other combatants suffered heavily in this war, and even inside France the minister Choiseul had ruefully to admit that

in the present state of Europe it is colonies, trade and in consequence sea power, which must determine the balance of power upon the continent. The House of Austria, Russia, the King of Prussia are only powers of the second rank, as are all those which cannot go to war unless subsidized by the trading powers.[66]

The military and naval expertise displayed by the Anglo-Prussian alliance, at least after the early setbacks, worked in the following way. At sea an enormous Royal Navy under Anson's direction steadily imposed a blockade upon France's Atlantic ports, and had sufficient surplus of force to mask Toulon and regain maritime supremacy in the Mediterranean as well. When fleet actions did occur—at Cartagena, off Lagos, and in Hawke's incomparable gale-battered pursuit of Conflans's fleet into Quiberon Bay—the superiority of British seamanship was made manifest time and again. What was more, this blockading policy—maintained now in all weathers, with the squadrons supplied by a comprehensive provisioning system—not only throttled much of France's maritime trade and thus protected Britain's commerce and its territorial security, but also prevented adequate reinforcements of French troops being sent to the West Indies, Canada, and India. In 1759, the *annus mirabilis,* French colonies were falling into British hands right across the globe, nicely complementing the considerable victory of the Anglo-German troops over two French armies at Minden. When Spain foolishly entered the war in 1762, the same fate befell its colonies in the Caribbean and Philippines.

Meanwhile, the House of Brandenburg had already seen its share of "miracles," and in the battles of Rossbach and Leuthen, Frederick not only ruined a French and an Austrian army respectively, but also blunted the eagerness of those two nations to press into northern Germany; after Frederick caught the Austrians again, at Liegnitz and Torgau in 1760, Vienna was virtually bankrupt. Nevertheless, the sheer costs of all this campaigning were slowly grinding down Prussian power (60,000 soldiers lost in 1759 alone), and the Russian foe proved much more formidable—partly because of Czarina Elizabeth's hatred of Frederick but chiefly because each encounter with the Russian army was such a bloody affair. Yet with the other combatants feeling the pace as well, and France keen to come to terms with a British government now also disposed to peace, Prussia found that it still had enough strength to keep the Austrians and Russians at bay until rescued by Elizabeth's death in 1762. After this, and the new Czar Peter's swift withdrawal from the war, neither Austria nor France could expect anything better than a peace settlement on the basis of a return to the prewar status in Europe—which was, in effect, a defeat for those who had sought to bring Prussia down.

In the 1762–1763 settlements the one obvious beneficiary was again Great Britain. Even after returning various captured territories to France and Spain, it had made advances in the West Indies and West Africa, had virtually eliminated French influence from India, and, most important of all, was now supreme in most of the North American continent. Britain thus had access to lands of far greater extent and potential wealth than Lorraine, Silesia, and those other regions over which the continental states fought so bitterly. In addition, it had helped to check France's diplomatic and military ambitions inside Europe and thereby had preserved the general balance of power. France, by comparison, had not only lost disastrously overseas but had also—unlike in 1748—failed in Europe; indeed, its lackluster military performance suggested that the center of gravity had shifted from western Europe to the east, a fact confirmed by the general disregard of France's wishes during the first partition of Poland in 1772. All this nicely suited British circles, satisfied with their own primacy outside Europe and not eager to be drawn into obligations on the continent.

The Winning of Wars, 1763–1815

The "breathing space" of well over a decade which occurred before the next stage in the Anglo-French struggle gave only a few hints of the turnaround which would occur in British fortunes. The Seven Years War had so overstrained the taxable capacity and social fabric of the Great Powers that most leaders frowned upon a bold foreign policy; introspection and reform tended to be the order of the day. The cost of the war to Prussia (half a million dead, including 180,000 soldiers) had shocked Frederick, who now preferred a quieter life. Although it had lost 300,000 men, the Habsburg Empire's army itself had not done too badly; but the overall governmental system was obviously in need of changes which would doubtless arouse local resentments (especially among the Hungarians) and consume the attentions of Maria Theresa's ministers. In Russia, Catherine II had to grapple with legislative and administrative reforms and then suppress the Pugachev revolt (1773–1775). This did not prevent further Russian expansion in the south or the maneuvers to reduce Poland's independence; but those could still be classed as local issues, and quite distinct from the great *European* combinations which had preoccupied the powers during the Seven Years War. Links with the western monarchies were now less important.

In Britain and France, too, domestic affairs held the center of the stage. The horrendous rise in the national debts of both countries led to a search for fresh sources of revenue and for administrative reform, producing controversies which fueled the already poor relations between George III and the opposition, and between the crown and *parlements* in France. These preoccupations inevitably made British foreign policy in Europe more haphazard and introspective than in Pitt's day, a tendency increased by the rising quarrel with the American colonists over taxation and enforcement of the Acts of Trade and Navigation. On the French side, however, foreign-policy matters were not so fully eclipsed by domestic concerns. Indeed, Choiseul and his successors, smarting from the defeat of 1763, were taking measures to strengthen France's position for the future. The French navy was steadily built up, despite the pressing need to economize; and the "family compact" with Spain was deepened. It is true that Louis XV frowned upon Choiseul's strong encouragement of Spain against Britain in the 1770 clash over the Falkland Islands, since a Great Power war at that point would have been financially disastrous. Nonetheless, French policy remained distinctly anti-British and committed to extracting advantages from any problems which Britain might encounter overseas.[67]

All this meant that when London's quarrel with the American colonists turned into open hostilities, Britain was in a much weaker position, in so many respects, than in 1739 or 1756.[68] A great deal of this was due to personalities. Neither North, nor Shelburne, nor any of the other politicians could offer national leadership and a coherent grand strategy. Political faction, heightened by George III's own interventions and by a fierce debate on the merits of the American colonists' case, divided the nation. In addition, the twin props of British power— the economy and the navy—were eroded in these years. Exports, which had stagnated following the boom period of the Seven Years War, actually declined throughout the 1770s, in part because of the colonists' boycott and then because of the growing conflict with France, Spain, and the Netherlands. The Royal Navy had been systematically weakened during fifteen years of peace, and some of its flag officers were as unseasoned as the timbers which had gone into the building of the ships of the line. The decision to abandon the close blockade strategy when France entered the war in 1778 may have saved wear and tear on British vessels, but it was, in effect, surrendering command of the sea: relief expeditions to Gibraltar, the West Indies, and the North American coast were no real substitute for the effective control of the Western Approaches off the French coast, which would have prevented the dispatch of enemy fleets to those distant theaters in any case. By the time the Royal Navy's strength had been rebuilt and its dominance reasserted, by Rodney's victory at the Saints and Howe's relief of Gibraltar in 1782, the war in America was virtually over.

Yet even if the navy had been better equipped and the nation better led, the 1776–1783 conflict contained two strategical problems which simply did not exist in any of the other eighteenth-century wars fought by Britain. The first of these was that once the American rebellion spread, its suppression involved large-scale *continental* fighting by British forces at a distance of 3,000 miles from the home base. Contrary to London's early hopes, maritime superiority alone could not bring the largely self-sufficient colonists to their knees (though obviously it might have reduced the flow of weapons and recruits from Europe). To conquer and hold the entire eastern territories of America would have been a difficult task for Napoleon's Grand Army, let alone the British-led troops of the 1770s. The distances involved and the consequent delay in communications not only hampered the strategical direction of the war from London or even from New York, but also exacerbated the logistical problem: "every biscuit, man, and bullet required by the British forces in America had to be transported across 3,000 miles of ocean."[69] Despite significant improvements by the British war ministry, the shortages of shipping and the difficulties of procurement were simply too much. Moreover, colonial society was so decentralized that the capture of a city or large town meant little. Only when regular troops were in occupation of the territory in question could British authority prevail; whenever they were withdrawn, the rebels reasserted themselves over the loyalists. If it had taken 50,000 British soldiers, *with substantial colonial support,* to conquer French Canada two decades earlier, how many were needed now to reimpose imperial rule—150,000, perhaps 250,000? "It is probable," one historian has argued, "that to restore British authority in America was a problem beyond the power of military means to solve, however perfectly applied."[70]

The second unprecedented difficulty in the realm of grand strategy was that Britain fought alone, unaided by European partners who would distract the French. To a large degree, of course, this was a diplomatic rather than a military problem. The British were now paying for their break with Prussia after 1762, their arrogance toward Spain, their heavy-handed treatment of the shipping of neutral states like Denmark and the United Provinces, and their failure to secure Russian support. Thus London found itself not only friendless in Europe but also, by 1780, facing a suspicious League of Armed Neutrality (Russia, Denmark, Portugal) and a hostile United Provinces, while it was already overstretched in dealing with American rebels and the Franco-Spanish fleets. But there is more to this story than British diplomatic ineptitude. As noted above, during the 1760s and 1770s the interests of the eastern monarchies had become somewhat detached from those in the West, and were concentrated upon the future of Poland, the Bavarian succession, and relations with the Turks. A France intent upon becoming "arbiter of Europe," as in Louis XIV's day, might have made such detachment impossible; but the relative decline of its army after the Seven Years War and its lack of political engagement in the east meant that London's acute concern about French designs from 1779 onward was not shared by former allies. The Russians under Catherine II were probably the most sympathetic, but even they would not intervene unless there was a real prospect that Britain would be eliminated altogether.

Finally, there was the significant fact that for once France had adopted Choiseul's former argument and now resisted the temptation to attack Hanover or to bully the Dutch. The war against Britain would be fought *only* overseas, thus dislocating the "continental" from the "maritime" arm of traditional British strategy. For the first time ever, the French would concentrate their resources upon a naval and colonial war.

The results were remarkable, and quite confounded the argument of the British isolationists that such a conflict, unencumbered by continental allies and campaigns, was best for the island state. During the Seven Years War, the French navy had been allocated only 30 million livres a year, one-quarter of the French army's allocation and only one-fifth of the monies provided to the Royal Navy each year. From the mid-1770s onward, the French naval budget steadily rose; by 1780 it totaled about 150 million livres, and by 1782 it had reached a staggering 200 million livres.[71] At the time France entered the war, it possessed fifty-two ships of the line, many of them being larger than their British equivalents, and the number was soon increased to sixty-six. To this could be added the Spanish fleet of fifty-eight ships of the line and, in 1780, a Dutch fleet of not more than twenty effectives. While the Royal Navy remained superior to any one maritime rival (in 1778 it had sixty-six ships of the line; in 1779, ninety), it now found itself repeatedly outnumbered. In 1779 it even lost control of the Channel, and a Franco-Spanish invasion looked possible; and in the 1781 encounter between Graves's and de Grasse's fleets off the Chesapeake, French numerical superiority kept the British force at bay and thus led to Cornwallis's surrender at Yorktown and to the effective end of the American campaign. Even when the Royal Navy's size increased and that of its foes fell away (in 1782 it had ninety-four ships of the line to France's seventy-three, Spain's fifty-four, and the United Provinces' nineteen), the margin was still too narrow to do *all* the tasks required: protect the North Atlantic convoys, periodically relieve Gibraltar, guard the exit from the Baltic, send squadrons to the Indian Ocean, and support the military operations in the Caribbean. British naval power was temporary and regional and not, as in previous wars, overwhelming. The fact that the French army was not fighting in Europe had a lot to do with the islanders' unhappy condition.

By 1782, it is true, the financial strain of maintaining such a large navy was hitting the French economy and compelling some retrenchment. Naval stores were now more difficult to obtain, and the shortage of sailors was even more serious. In addition, some of the French ministers feared that the war was unduly diverting attention and resources to areas outside Europe, and thus making it impossible to play any role on the continent. This political calculation, and the parallel fear that the British and Americans might soon settle their differences, caused Paris to hope for an early end to hostilities. Economically, their Dutch and Spanish allies were in an equally bad plight. Nevertheless,

Britain's greater financial stamina, the marked rise in exports from 1782 onward, and the steady improvements in the Royal Navy could not now rescue victory from defeat, nor convince the political factions at home to support the war once America was clearly seen to be lost. Although Britain's concessions at the 1783 Peace of Versailles (Minorca, Florida, Tobago) were hardly a reversal of the great imperial gains of 1763, the French could proclaim themselves well satisfied at the creation of an independent United States and at the blow dealt to Britain's world position. From Paris's perspective, the strategical balance which had been upset by the Seven Years War had now been sensibly restored, albeit at enormous cost.

In eastern Europe, by contrast, the strategical balances were not greatly distorted by the maneuvers of the three great monarchies during the decades after 1763.[72] This was chiefly due to the triangular nature of that relationship: neither Berlin nor Vienna in particular, nor even the more assertive St. Petersburg, wished to provoke the other two into a hostile alliance or to be involved in fighting of the dimensions of the Seven Years War. The brief and ultracautious campaigning in the War of Bavarian Succession (1778–1779), when Prussia opposed Austria's attempt at expansion, merely confirmed this widespread wish to avoid the costs of a Great Power struggle. Further acquisitions of territory could therefore take place only as a result of diplomatic "deals" at the expense of weaker powers, most notably Poland, which was successively carved up in 1772–1773, 1793, and 1795. By the later stages, Poland's fate was increasingly influenced by the French Revolution, that is, by Catherine II's determination to crush the "Jacobins" of Warsaw, and Prussia and Austria's desire to gain compensation in the east for their failures in the west against France; but even this new concern with the French Revolution did not fundamentally change the policies of mutual antagonism and reluctant compromise which the three eastern monarchies pursued toward one another in these years.

Given the geographical and diplomatic confines of this triangular relationship, it was not surprising that Russia's position continued to improve, relative to both Austria and Prussia. Despite Russia's backwardness, it was still far less vulnerable than its western neighbors, both of which strove to placate the formidable Catherine. This fact, and the traditional Russian claims to influence in Poland, ensured that by far the largest portion of that unfortunate state fell to St. Petersburg during the partition. Moreover, Russia possessed an open, "crumbling" frontier to the south, so that during the early 1770s great advances were made at Turkey's expense; the Crimea was formally annexed in 1783, and a fresh round of gains was secured along the northern coast of the Black Sea in 1792. All this confirmed the decline of Ottoman fighting power, and secretly worried both Austria and Prussia almost as much as those states (Sweden in 1788, Britain under the younger Pitt in 1791) which more actively sought to blunt this Russian expansionism. But with Vienna and Berlin eager to keep St. Petersburg's goodwill, and with the western Powers too distracted to play a lasting and effective role in eastern Europe, the growth of the Czarist Empire proceeded apace.

The structure of international relations in the decade or so prior to 1792 therefore gave little sign of the transformation bearing down upon it. For the main part, the occasional quarrels between the major powers had been unconnected regional affairs, and there seemed to exist no threat to the general balance of power. If the future of Poland and the Ottoman Empire preoccupied the great nations of the east, traditional maneuvering over the fate of the Low Countries and over "rival empires of trade" consumed the attention of the western Powers. An Anglo-Spanish clash over Nookta Sound (1790) brought both countries to the brink of war, until Spain reluctantly gave way. While relations between Britain and France were more subdued because of mutual exhaustion after 1783, their commercial rivalry continued apace. Their mutual suspicions also swiftly showed themselves during an internal crisis in the Netherlands in 1787–1788, when the pro-French "Patriot" party was forced out of power by Prussian troops, urged on by the assertive younger Pitt.

Pitt's much more active diplomacy reflected not merely his own personality, but also the significant general recovery which Britain had made in the ranks of the Powers since the setback of 1783. The loss of America had not damaged the country's transatlantic trade; indeed, exports to the United States were booming, and both that market and India's were much more substantial than those in which France had the lead. In the six years 1782–1788 British merchant shipping more than doubled. The Industrial Revolution was under way, fired by consumer demand at home and abroad and facilitated by a spate of new inventions; and the productivity of British agriculture was keeping pace with the food needs of an expanding population. Pitt's fiscal reforms improved the state's finances and restored its credit, yet considerable monies were always voted to the navy, which was numerically strong and well administered. On these firm foundations, the British government felt it could play a more active role abroad when national interests demanded it. On the whole, however, political leaders in Whitehall and Westminster did not envisage a Great Power war occurring in Europe in the foreseeable future.[73]

But the clearest reason why Europe would not be convulsed by a general conflict seemed to lie in the worsening condition of France. For some years after the victory of 1783, its diplomatic position had appeared as strong as ever; the domestic economy, as well as foreign trade with the West Indies and the Levant, was growing rapidly.

Nonetheless, the sheer costs of the 1778–1783 war—totaling more than France's three previous wars together—and the failure to reform national finances interacted with the growing political discontents, economic distress, and social malaise to discredit the *ancien régime*. From 1787 onward, as the internal crisis worsened, France seemed ever less capable of playing a decisive role in foreign affairs. The diplomatic defeat in the Netherlands was caused primarily by the French government's recognition that it simply could not afford to finance a war against Britain and Prussia, while the withdrawal of support for Spain in the Nookta Sound controversy was due to the French assembly's challenge to Louis XVI's right to declare war. All this hardly suggested that France would soon be seeking to overturn the entire "old order" of Europe.

The conflict which was to absorb the energies of much of the continent for over two decades therefore began slowly and unevenly. The French were concerned only with domestic struggles in the period which followed the fall of the Bastille; and although the increasing radicalization of French politics worried some foreign governments, the resultant turmoil in Paris and the provinces suggested that France was of little account in European power politics. For that reason, Pitt was seeking reductions in British military expenditures as late as February 1792, while in the east the three great monarchies were much more interested in the carving up of Poland. Only with the growing rumors about émigré plots to restore the monarchy and the French revolutionaries' own move toward a more aggressive policy on the borders did external and internal events produce an escalation into war. The slow and uncertain maneuvers of the allied armies as they moved across the French frontiers showed how ill prepared they were for this contest, which in turn allowed the revolutionaries to claim victory after the desultory encounter at Valmy (September 1792). It was only in the following year, when the successes of the French armies seemed to threaten the Rhineland, the Low Countries, and Italy and the execution of Louis XVI demonstrated the radical republicanism of the new regime in Paris, that the struggle assumed its full strategical and ideological dimensions. Prussia and the Habsburg Empire, the original combatants, were now joined by an enormous array of other states headed by Britain and Russia and including all of France's neighbors.

Although it is easy in retrospect to see why this First Coalition (1793–1795) against France failed so miserably, the outcome was a surprise and bitter disappointment at the time; after all, the odds were more uneven than in *any* preceding war. In the event, the sheer impetus of the French Revolution led to the adoption of desperate measures—the *levée en masse* and the mobilization of all seizable national resources to fight France's many foes. Moreover, as many writers have pointed out, a very important period of reform had occurred in the French army—in matters of organization, staff planning, artillery, and battle tactics—during the two or three decades before 1789; and what the Revolution did was to sweep aside the aristocratic hindrances to these new ideas and to give the reformers the opportunity (and the weight of numbers) to put their concepts into practice when war broke out. The "total war" methods employed on the home front and the newer tactics on the battlefield seemed as much a reflection of the newly released demagogic energies of the French as the cautious, half-hearted maneuvers of the Coalition armies were symbolic of the habits of the old order.[74] With an army of about 650,000 (July 1793), fired by enthusiasm and willing to take the risks involved in lengthy marches and aggressive tactics, the French were soon overrunning neighboring territories—which meant that from this time onward, the costs of maintaining such an enormous force fell largely upon the populations *outside* France's borders, which in its turn permitted a certain recovery of the French economy.

Any power seeking to blunt this heady expansionism would therefore have to devise the proper means for containing such a new and upsetting form of warfare. This was not an impossible task. The French army's operations under its early leader Dumouriez, and even the much larger and more elaborate campaigns of Napoleon, revealed deficiencies in organization and training and weaknesses in supply and communications, of which a well-trained foe could take great advantage. But where was that well-trained opponent? It was not merely that the elderly generals and slow-moving, baggage-laden troops of the Coalition were tactically inadequate in the face of swarms of skirmishers and hard-hitting columns of the French. The real point was that the necessary political commitment and strategical clarity were also missing among France's enemies. There was, obviously, no transcendent political ideology to fire the soldiers and citizens of the *ancien régime;* indeed, many of them were attracted to the intoxicating ideas of the Revolution, and only when, much later, Napoleon's armies turned "liberation" into conquest and plunder could local patriotism be used to blunt the French hegemony.

Furthermore, at this early stage few members of the Coalition took the French threat seriously. There was no overall agreement as to aims and strategy between the various members of the alliance, whose precarious unity manifested itself in their increasing demands for British subsidies but in not much else. Above all, the first years of the Revolutionary War overlapped with, and were overshadowed by, the demise of Poland. Despite her vitriolic denunciations of the French Revolution, Catherine II was more concerned with eliminating Polish independence than in sending troops to the Rhineland. This caused an anxious Prussian government, already disenchanted by the early cam-

paigns in the west, to switch more and more of its troops from the
Rhine to the Vistula, which in turn compelled Austria to keep 60,000
men on its northern frontier in case Russia and Prussia moved against
the remaining Polish territories. When the third and final partition did
occur, in 1795, it was all too evident that Poland had been a more
effective ally to France in its death throes than as a living, functioning
state. By that time, Prussia had already sued for peace and abandoned
the left bank of the Rhine to the French, leaving Germany in a state
of uneasy neutrality and thus permitting France to turn its attention
elsewhere; most of the smaller German states had followed this Prussian lead; the Netherlands had been overrun, and converted into the
Batavian Republic; and Spain, too, deserting the Coalition, had returned to its early anti-British alignment with France.

This left only Sardinia-Piedmont, which in early 1796 was crushed
by Napoleon; the luckless Habsburg Empire, which was driven out of
much of Italy and forced into the Peace of Campo Formio (October
1797); and Britain. Despite the younger Pitt's wish to imitate his father
in checking French expansionism, the British government also failed
to pursue the war with the necessary determination and strategical
clarity.[75] The expeditionary force sent to Flanders and Holland under
the Duke of York in 1793–1795 had neither the strength nor the expertise to deal with the French army, and its remnants eventually came
home via Bremen. Moreover, as so often happened before and since,
ministers (such as Dundas and Pitt) preferred the "British way in warfare"—colonial operations, maritime blockade, and raids upon the
enemy's coast—to any large-scale continental operation. Given the
overwhelming superiority of the Royal Navy and the disintegration of
its French equivalent, this looked like an attractive and easy option.
But the British troop losses caused by disease in the West Indies operations of 1793–1796 meant that London paid dearly for these strategical
diversions: 40,000 men were killed, another 40,000 rendered unfit for
service—more than all the casualties in the Spanish Peninsular War—
and the campaigns cost at least £16 million. Yet it is doubtful whether
Britain's steadily augmented domination of the extra-European theaters or its peripheral operations against Dunkirk and Toulon compensated for France's growing power within Europe. Finally, the subsidies
demanded by Prussia and Austria to maintain their armies in the field
soared alarmingly, and were impossible to provide. In other words,
British strategy had been simultaneously inefficient *and* expensive,
and in 1797 the foundations of the entire system were shaken—at least
temporarily—by the Bank of England's suspension of cash payments
and by the naval mutinies at Spithead and the Nore. During that troubled period, the exhausted Austrians sued for peace and joined all the
other states which admitted French primacy in western Europe.

If the British could not defeat France, the revolutionary government could not in its turn undermine the enemy's naval mastery. Early attempts to invade Ireland and to raid the western coasts of England had come to little, although that was due as much to the weather as to local defenses. Despite the temporary fright over the 1797 suspension of cash payments, the British credit system held firm. The entry of Spain and the Netherlands into the war on France's side led to the smashing of the Spanish fleet off Cape St. Vincent (February 1797) and to the heavy blows inflicted upon the Dutch at Camperdown (October 1797). France's new allies also had to endure the progressive loss of their colonies overseas—in the East and West Indies, and at Colombo, Malacca, and the Cape of Good Hope, all of which provided new markets for British commerce and additional bases for its naval squadrons. Unwilling to pay the high price demanded by the French government for peace, Pitt and his fellow ministers resolved to fight on, introducing income tax as well as raising fresh loans to pay for what—with French troops assembling along the Channel coast—had become a struggle as much for national survival as for imperial security.

Here, then, was the fundamental strategical dilemma which faced both France and Britain for the next two decades of war. Like the whale and the elephant, each was by far the largest creature in its own domain. But British control of the sea routes could not by itself destroy the French hegemony in Europe, nor could Napoleon's military mastery reduce the islanders to surrender. Furthermore, because France's territorial acquisitions and political browbeating of its neighbors aroused considerable resentment, the government in Paris could never be certain that the other continental powers would permanently accept the French imperium so long as Britain—offering subsidies, munitions, and possibly even troops—remained independent. This, evidently, was also Napoleon's view when he argued in 1797: "Let us concentrate our efforts on building up our fleet and on destroying England. Once that is done Europe is at our feet."[76] Yet that French goal could be achieved only by waging a successful maritime and commercial strategy against Britain, since military gains on land were not enough; just as the British needed to challenge Napoleon's continental domination—by direct intervention and securing allies—since the Royal Navy's mastery at sea was also not enough. As long as the one combatant was supreme on land and the other at sea, each felt threatened and insecure; and each therefore cast around for fresh means, and allies, with which to tilt the balance.

Napoleon's attempt to alter that balance was characteristically bold—and risky: taking advantage of Britain's weak position in the Mediterranean in the summer of 1798, he invaded Egypt with 31,000 troops and thus placed himself in a position to dominate the Levant, the Ottoman Empire, and the route to India. At almost the same time, the British were distracted by yet another French expedition to Ireland. Each of those strokes, had they been fully successful, would have dealt a dreadful blow to Britain's shaky position. But the Irish invasion was small-scale and belated, and was contained in early September, by which time all of Europe was learning of Nelson's defeat of the French fleet at Aboukir and of Napoleon's consequent "bondage" in Egypt. Just as Paris had suspected, such a setback encouraged all who resented French predominance to abandon their neutrality and to join in the war of the Second Coalition (1798–1800). Besides the smaller states of Portugal and Naples, Russia, Austria, and Turkey were now on the British side, assembling their armies and negotiating for subsidies. Losing Minorca and Malta, defeated in Switzerland and Italy by Austro-Russian forces, and with Napoleon himself unable to achieve victory in the Levant, France appeared to be in serious trouble.

Yet the second coalition, like the first, rested upon shaky political and strategical foundations.[77] Prussia was noticeably absent, so that no northern German front could be opened. A premature campaign by the king of Naples led to disaster, and an ill-prepared Anglo-Russian expedition to Holland failed to arouse the local population and eventually had to retire. Far from drawing the conclusion that continental operations needed to be more substantial, and acutely conscious of the financial and political difficulties of raising a large army, the British government fell back upon its traditional policy of "descents" upon the enemy's coastline; but their small-scale attacks upon Belle-Isle, Ferrol, Cádiz, and elsewhere served no useful strategical purpose. Worse still, the Austrians and Russians failed to cooperate in their defense of Switzerland, and the Russians were driven eastward through the mountains; at that, the czar's disenchantment with his allies intensified into a deep suspicion of British policy and a willingness to negotiate with Napoleon, who had slipped back into France from Egypt. The withdrawal of Russia left the Austrians to receive the full weight of the French fury, at Marengo and Hochstadt (both in June 1800), and six months later at Hohenlinden, compelling Vienna once again to sue for peace. With Prussia and Denmark taking advantage of this turn of events to overrun Hanover, and with Spain launching an invasion of Portugal, the British stood virtually alone in 1801, just as they had been three years earlier. In northern Europe, Russia, Denmark, Sweden, and Prussia had come together in a new Armed Neutrality League.

In the maritime and extra-European campaigning, on the other hand, the British had again done rather well. Malta had been captured from the French, providing the Royal Navy with a vital strategical base. The Danish fleet, the first line of the new Armed Neutrality League's scheme to exclude British trade from the Baltic, was smashed off Copenhagen (although the assassination of Czar Paul a few days earlier spelled the end of the league in any case). In that same month of March 1801 a British expedition defeated the French army at Alexandria, which afterward led to a complete French withdrawal from Egypt. Farther afield, British forces in India overwhelmed the French-backed Tipu in Mysore and continued to make additional gains in the north. French, Dutch, Danish, and Swedish possessions in the West Indies also fell into British hands.

Yet the lack of a solid continental ally by 1801 and the inconclusive nature of the Anglo-French campaigning caused many politicians in England to think of peace; and those sentiments were reinforced by the urgings of mercantile circles whose commerce was suffering in the Mediterranean and, to a lesser extent, in the Baltic. Pitt's resignation over Catholic emancipation hastened the move toward negotiations. In Napoleon's calculation, there was little to be lost from a period of peace: the consolidation of French influence in the satellite states would continue, while the British would certainly not be allowed their former commercial and diplomatic privileges in those areas; the French navy, dispersed in various ports, could be concentrated and rebuilt; and the economy could be rested before the next round of the struggle. In consequence of this, British opinion—which did not offer much criticism of the government at the conclusion of the Peace of Amiens (March 1802)—steadily swung in the other direction when it was observed that France was continuing the struggle by other means. British trade was denied entry into much of Europe. London was firmly told to keep out of Dutch, Swiss, and Italian matters. And French intrigues and aggressions were reported from Muscat to the West Indies and from Turkey to Piedmont. These reports, and the evidence of a large-scale French warship-building program, caused the British government under Addington to refuse to hand back Malta and, in May 1803, to turn a cold war into a hot one.[78]

This final round of the seven major Anglo-French wars fought between 1689 and 1815 was to last twelve years, and was the most severely testing of them all. Just as before, each combatant had different strengths and weaknesses. Despite certain retrenchments in the fleet, the Royal Navy was in a very strong position when hostilities recommenced. While powerful squadrons blockaded the French coast, the overseas empires of France and its satellites were systematically recaptured. St. Pierre et Miquelon, St. Lucia, Tobago, and Dutch Guiana were taken before Trafalgar, and further advances were made in India; the Cape fell in 1806; Curaçao and the Danish West Indies in 1807; several of the Moluccas in 1808; Cayenne, French Guiana, San Domingo, Senegal, and Martinique in 1809; Guadeloupe, Mauritius, Amboina, and Banda in 1810; Java in 1811. Once again, this had no *direct* impact upon the European equilibrium, but it did buttress Britain's dominance overseas and provide new "vents" for exports denied their traditional access into Antwerp and Leghorn; and, even in its early stages, it prompted Napoleon to contemplate the invasion of southern England more seriously than ever before. With the Grand Army assembling before Boulogne and a grimly determined Pitt returned to office in 1804, each side looked forward to one final, decisive clash.

In actual fact, the naval and military campaigns of 1805 to 1808, despite containing several famous battles, revealed yet again the strategical constraints of the war. The French army was at least three times larger and much more experienced than its British equivalent, but command of the sea was required before it could safely land in England. Numerically, the French navy was considerable (about seventy ships of the line), a testimony to the resources which Napoleon could command; and it was reinforced by the Spanish navy (over twenty ships of the line) when that country entered the war late in 1804. However, the Franco-Spanish fleets were dispersed in half a dozen harbors, and their juncture could not be effected without running the risk of encountering a Royal Navy of vastly greater battle experience. The smashing defeat of those fleets at Trafalgar in October 1805 illustrated the "quality gap" between the rival navies in the most devastating way. Yet if that dramatic victory secured the British Isles, it could not undermine Napoleon's position on land. For this reason, Pitt had striven to tempt Russia and Austria into a third coalition, paying £1.75 million for every 100,000 men they could put into the field against the French. Even before Trafalgar, however, Napoleon had rushed his army from Boulogne to the upper Danube, annihilating the Austrians at Ulm, and then proceeded eastward to crush an Austro-Russian force of 85,000 men at Austerlitz in December. With a dispirited Vienna suing for peace for the third time, the French could once again assert control in the Italian peninsula and compel a hasty withdrawal of the Anglo-Russian forces there.[79]

Whether or not the news of these great blows caused Pitt's death in early 1806, they revealed once more the difficulty of bringing down a military genius like Napoleon. Indeed, the following few years ushered in the zenith of French predominance in Europe. (See Map 7.) Prussia, whose earlier abstention had weakened the coalition, rashly declared war upon France in October 1806 and was crushed within the month. The large and stubborn Russian armies were an altogether different matter, but after several battles they, too, were badly hurt at the battle of Friedland (June 1807). At the peace treaties of Tilsit, Prussia was turned into a virtual satellite and Russia, while escaping lightly, agreed to ban British trade and promised eventually to join a French alliance. With southern and much of western Germany merged into the Confederation of the Rhine, with western Poland turned into the grand duchy of Warsaw, with Spain, Italy, and the Low Countries subservient, with

Map 7: Europe at the Height of Napoleon's Power, 1810

French Empire

"Greater Empire" subject to Napoleonic controls

Nominal allies of Napoleon

Hostile to Napoleon, protected by British

ATLANTIC OCEAN

GREAT BRITAIN
AND IRELAND

NORWAY
AND
DENMARK

NORTH SEA

SWEDEN

BALTIC SEA

GRAND DUCHY
OF FINLAND

RUSSIAN
EMPIRE

PRUSSIA

GRAND DUCHY
OF WARSAW

CONFEDERATION
OF
THE
RHINE

FRENCH
EMPIRE

SWITZ.

KINGDOM
OF
ITALY

AUSTRIAN
EMPIRE

ILLYRIAN
PROVINCES

BLACK
SEA

SPAIN

PORTUGAL

CORSICA

KINGDOM
OF
SARDINIA

KINGDOM
OF NAPLES

OTTOMAN

EMPIRE

KINGDOM OF
SICILY

0   500 Miles

0   500 Kilometers

MEDITERRANEAN SEA

the Holy Roman Empire at an end, there was no independent state—
and no ally for the British—between Portugal and Sweden. This, in its
turn, gave Napoleon his opportunity to ruin the "nation of shopkeepers" in the most telling fashion: by banning their exports to Europe and
hurting their economy, while accumulating for his own purposes the
timber, masts, and other shipbuilding resources now denied to the
Royal Navy. Indirectly, the British would be weakened before a further
direct assault was mounted. Given Britain's dependence upon European markets for its export industries and upon Baltic masts and Dal-
matian oak for its fleet, the threat was immense. Finally, reduced
earnings from exports would deny London the currency needed to pay
subsidies to any allies and to purchase goods for its own expeditionary
armies.

More than ever before, in this war, therefore, economic factors
intermeshed with strategy. At this central stage in the Anglo-French
duel for supremacy, between Napoleon's Berlin/Milan decrees banning trade with Britain (1806–1807) and the French retreat from Moscow in 1812, the relative merits of the two opposing systems deserve
further analysis. With each seeking to ruin the other economically, any
significant weaknesses would sooner or later emerge—and have dire
power-political consequences.

There is no doubt that Britain's unusually large dependence upon
foreign commerce by this time made it very vulnerable to the trading
ban imposed under Napoleon's "Continental System."[80] In 1808, and
again in 1811–1812, the commercial warfare waged by the French and
their more compliant satellites (e.g., the Danes) was producing a crisis
in British export trades. Vast stocks of manufactures were piled in
warehouses, and the London docks were full to overflowing with colonial produce. Unemployment in the towns and unrest in the counties
increased businessmen's fears and caused many economists to call for
peace; so, too, did the staggering rise in the national debt. When relations with the United States worsened and exports to that important
market tumbled after 1811, the economic pressures seemed almost
unbearable.

And yet, in fact, those pressures were borne, chiefly because they
were never applied long or consistently enough to take full effect. The
revolution in Spain against French hegemony eased the 1808 economic
crisis in Britain, just as Russia's break with Napoleon brought relief to
the 1811–1812 slump, allowing British goods to pour into the Baltic
and northern Europe. Moreover, throughout the entire period large
amounts of British manufactures and colonial re-exports were smug-
gled into the continent, at vast profits and usually with the connivance
of bribed local officials; from Heligoland to Salonika, the banned produce traveled in circuitous ways to its eager customers—as it later

traveled between Canada and New England during the Anglo-American War of 1812. Finally, the British export economy could also be sustained by the great rise in trade with regions untouched by the Continental System or the American "nonintercourse" policy: Asia, Africa, the West Indies, Latin America (despite all the efforts of local Spanish governors), and the Near East. For all these reasons, and despite serious disruption to British trade in *some* markets for *some* of the time, the overall trend was clear: total exports of British produce rose from £21.7 million (1794–1796) to £37.5 million (1804–1806) to £44.4 million (1814–1816).

The other main reason that the British economy did not crumble in the face of external pressures was that, unfortunately for Napoleon, it was now well into the Industrial Revolution. That these two major historical events interacted with each other in many singular ways is clear: government orders for armaments stimulated the iron, steel, coal, and timber trades, the enormous state spending (estimated at 29 percent of gross national product) affected financial practices, and new export markets boosted production of some factories just as the French "counterblockade" depressed it. Exactly how the Revolutionary and Napoleonic wars affected the growth of the British economy *as a whole* is a complex and controversial topic, still being investigated by historians, many of whom now feel that the earlier notions of the swift pace of British industrialization in these decades are exaggerated. What *is* clear, however, is that the economy grew throughout this period. Pig-iron output, a mere 68,000 tons in 1788, had already soared to 244,000 tons in 1806 and rose further to 325,000 tons in 1811. Cotton, virtually a new industry before the war, expanded stupendously in the next two decades, absorbing ever more machinery, steam power, coal, and labor; by 1815, cotton goods had become Britain's greatest export by far. A vast array of new docks and, inland, new canals, turnpikes, and iron rail tracks improved communications and stimulated further production. Regardless of whether this "boom" would have been even greater without the military and naval struggle against France, the fact remains that British productivity and wealth were still rising fast—and could help to bear the burdens which Pitt and his successors imposed in order to pay for the war. Customs and excise receipts, for example, jumped from £13.5 million (1793) to £44.8 million (1815), while the yield from the new income and property taxes rose from £1.67 in 1799 to £14.6 million in the final year of the war. In fact, between 1793 and 1815 the British government secured the staggering sum of £1.217 billion from direct and indirect taxes, and proceeded to raise a further £440 million in loans from the money markets without exhausting its credit—to the amazement of the more fiscally conservative Napoleon. In the critical final few years of the war, the government was borrowing more than £25 million annually, giving itself that decisive extra margin.[81] To be sure, the British were taxed way beyond the limits conceived of by eighteenth-century bureaucrats, and the national debt almost trebled; but the new wealth made such burdens easier to bear— and permitted them, despite their smaller size and population, to endure the costs of war better than the imposing Napoleonic Empire.

The story of France's economy between 1789 and 1815, and of its capacity to sustain large-scale war, is an even more complicated one for historians to unravel.[82] The collapse of the *ancien régime* and the turmoil which followed undoubtedly caused a reduction in French economic activity for a while. On the other hand, the outpouring of public enthusiasm for the Revolution and the mobilization of national resources to meet foreign enemies led to a staggering increase in the output of cannon, small arms, and other military equipment, which in turn stimulated the iron and textile trades. In addition, some of the economic obstacles of the old order such as internal tariffs were swept away, and Napoleon's own legal and administrative reforms aided the prospects for modernization. Even if the coming of the Consulate and the Empire led to the return of many of the features of the monarchical regime (e.g., reliance upon private bankers), this did not check a steady economic growth fueled naturally by population increases, the stimulus of state spending, enhanced tariff protection, and the introduction of certain new technologies.

Nevertheless, there seems no doubt that the rate of growth in the French economy was much slower than in Britain's. The most profound reason for this was that the agricultural sector, the largest by far, changed very little: for the replacement of the seigneur by his peasants was not, of itself, an *agricultural* revolution; and such widely proclaimed policies as the development of sugar beets (in substitution for British colonial cane sugar) had limited results. Poor communications meant that farmers were still tied to local markets, and little stimulus existed for radical innovations. This conservative frame of mind could also be seen in the nascent industrial sector, where new machinery and large-scale enterprises in, say, iron production were the exception rather than the rule. Significant advances were made, of course, but many of them were under the distorting influence of the war and the British naval blockade. Thus, the cotton industry benefited from the Continental System to the extent that it was protected from superior British competition (not to mention the competition from neutral or satellite states, whose goods were excluded by the high French tariffs); and it also benefited from the enhanced domestic market, since Napoleon's conquests of bordering lands increased the number of "Frenchmen" from 25 million in 1789 to 44 million in 1810. But this was offset by the shortage and high price of raw cotton, and by the slowdown in the introduction of new techniques from England. On the whole,

French industry emerged from the war in a distinctly *less competitive* state because of this protection from foreign rivals.

The impact of the naval blockade increased this turning inward of the French economy.[83] Its Atlantic sector, the fastest-growing in the eighteenth century and (as had been the case in Britain) potentially a key catalyst for industrialization, was increasingly cut off by the Royal Navy. The loss of Santa Domingo in particular was a heavy blow to French Atlantic trade. Other overseas colonies and investments were also lost, and after 1806, even trade via neutral bottoms was halted. Bordeaux was dreadfully hurt. Nantes had its profitable French slave trade reduced to nothing. Even Marseilles, with alternative trading partners in the hinterland and northern Italy, saw its industrial output fall to one-quarter between 1789 and 1813. By contrast, regions in the north and east of France, such as Alsace, enjoyed the comparative security of land-based trade. Yet even if those areas, and people within them like winegrowers and cotton-spinners, profited in their protected environment, the *overall* impact upon the French economy was much less satisfactory. "Deindustrialized" in its Atlantic sector, cut off from much of the outside world, it turned inward to its peasants, its small-town commerce, and its localized, uncompetitive, and relatively small-scale industries.

Given this economic conservatism—and, in some cases, definite evidence of retardation—the ability of the French to finance decades of Great Power war seems all the more remarkable.[84] While the popular mobilization in the early to middle 1790s offers a ready reason, it cannot explain the Napoleonic era proper, when a long-service army of over 500,000 men (needing probably 150,000 new recruits each year) had to be paid for. Military expenditures, already costing at least 462 million francs in 1807, had soared to 817 million francs in 1813. Not surprisingly, the normal revenues could never manage to pay for such outlays. Direct taxes were unpopular at home and therefore could not be substantially raised—which chiefly explains Napoleon's return to duties on tobacco, salt, and the other indirect taxes of the *ancien régime;* but neither they nor the various stamp duties and customs fees could prevent an annual deficit of hundreds of millions of francs. It is true that the creation of the Bank of France, together with a whole variety of other financial devices and institutions, allowed the state to conduct a disguised policy of paper money and thus to keep itself afloat on credit—despite the emperor's proclaimed hostility to raising loans. Yet even that was not enough. The gap could only be filled elsewhere.

To a large if incalculable degree, in fact, Napoleonic imperialism was paid for by plunder. This process had begun internally, with the confiscation and sale of the property of the proclaimed "enemies of the Revolution."[85] When the military campaigns in defense of that revolution had carried the French armies into neighboring lands, it seemed altogether natural that the foreigner should pay for it. War, to put it bluntly, would support war. By confiscations of crown and feudal properties in defeated countries; by spoils taken directly from the enemy's armies, garrisons, museums, and treasuries; by imposing war indemnities in money or in kind; and by quartering French regiments upon satellite states and requiring the latter to supply contingents, Napoleon not only covered his enormous military expenditures, he actually produced considerable profits for France—and himself. The sums acquired by the administrators of this *domaine extraordinaire* in the period of France's zenith were quite remarkable and in some ways foreshadow Nazi Germany's plunder of its satellites and conquered foes during the Second World War. Prussia, for example, had to pay a penalty of 311 million francs after Jena, which was equal to half of the French government's ordinary revenue. At each defeat, the Habsburg Empire was forced to cede territories *and* to pay a large indemnity. In Italy between 1805 and 1812 about half of the taxes raised went to the French. All this had the twin advantage of keeping much of the colossal French army *outside* the homeland, and of protecting the French taxpayer from the full costs of the war. Provided that army under its brilliant leader remained successful, the system seemed invulnerable. It was not surprising, therefore, to hear the emperor frequently asserting:

> My power depends on my glory and my glories on the victories I have won. My power will fail if I do not feed it on new glories and new victories. Conquest has made me what I am and only conquest can enable me to hold my position.[86]

How, then, *could* Napoleon be brought down? Britain alone, lacking the military manpower, could not do it. And an attack upon France by any single continental opponent was always doomed to failure. Prussia's ill-timed entry into the war in 1806 proved that point, although it did not stop the frustrated Austrians from renewing hostilities with France once again, early in 1809; yet while Austria fought with great spirit at the battles of Eckmühl and Aspern, its further losses at Wagram once more compelled Vienna to sue for peace and to cede additional lands to France and its allies. The French successes against Austria had, moreover, followed closely upon Napoleon's drive into Spain to crush the revolt there. Thus it seemed that wherever opposition to the emperor's will arose, it was swiftly dealt with. And although at sea the British showed a similar ruthlessness toward enemies, actual or potential, as in their Copenhagen attack (August 1807), they still tended to fritter away military resources in small-scale raids off southern Italy, in an inept attack upon Buenos Aires, and in the disastrous Walcheren operation in the summer of 1809.[87]

Yet it was precisely when Napoleon's system seemed unbeatable that the first significant cracks in the imperial edifice began to appear. Despite the successive military victories, French casualties in these battles had been large—15,000 lost at Eylau and 12,000 at Friedland, 23,000 killed or surrendered at Bailen, a massive 44,000 casualties at Aspern, and another 30,000 at Wagram. Experienced troops were becoming rare, at least outside the exclusive Guard regiments; for example, of the 148,000 men of the Armée de l'Allemagne (exclusive of the Guard) in 1809, 47,000 were underage conscripts.[88] Although Napoleon's army, like Hitler's included many from the conquered territories and the satellites, French manpower stocks were clearly being eroded; whereas the unpredictable czar still had enormous reserves and, even after Wagram, the stubborn and resentful Austrians possessed a very considerable "army in being." All this would have meaning in the near future.

Furthermore, Napoleon's drive into Spain in late 1808 had not "decided" that campaign, as he fondly imagined. In dispersing the formal Spanish armies, he had inadvertently encouraged the local populace to resort to guerrilla warfare, which was altogether more difficult to suppress and which multiplied the logistical problems for the French forces. Denied foodstuffs by the local population, the French army was critically dependent upon its own precarious supply lines. Moreover, in making a battlefield of Spain and, still more, of Portugal, Napoleon had unintentionally chosen one of the few areas in which the still-cautious British could be induced to commit themselves, at first tentatively but then with growing confidence as they saw how Wellington exploited local sympathies, the geography of the peninsula, command of the sea, and—last but not least—his own increasingly professional regiments to contain and erode French *élan*. The 25,000 casualties suffered by Massena's army in his fruitless march against Lisbon in 1810–1811 were an early sign that "the Spanish ulcer" could not be lanced, even when some 300,000 French troops had been dispatched south of the Pyrenees.[89]

Besides weakening France, the Spanish business simultaneously relieved the strain upon Britain, strategically as well as commercially. After all, during most of the preceding Anglo-French wars, Spain had fought on France's side—which not only had posed a landward threat to Gibraltar and a seaward threat (in the form of the Franco-Spanish combined fleets) to British naval mastery, but had also affected export markets in the Peninsula, Latin America, and the Mediterranean generally. A friendly rather than a hostile Spain meant an end to all those pressures. The damage done to British trade by the Continental System was now greatly eased, as the products of Lancashire and the Midlands returned to old markets; by 1810, total British exports had soared to a record £48 million (from £37 million in 1808). Although this relief was but temporary, and was increasingly overshadowed by the closure of the Baltic and by the Anglo-American dispute over impressment and blockade, it was enough. It sustained Napoleon's great *extra*-continental foe, and just at the time when the European continent itself was breaking into revolt.

In effect, the Napoleonic system in Europe rested upon a contradiction. Whatever the merits or demerits of the Revolution within France itself, a nation proclaiming liberty, fraternity, and equality was now—at the direction of its emperor—conquering non-French populations, stationing armies upon them, sequestering their goods, distorting their trade, raising enormous indemnities and taxes, and conscripting their youth.[90] Resentment was also felt at the controls being increasingly imposed under the Continental System, since it was not only Nantes and Bordeaux but also Amsterdam, Hamburg, and Trieste which were being hurt by the economic warfare Napoleon was waging against Britain. Few would openly rise in arms, like the Spaniards, or decide to pull out of the ruinous Continental System, as the Russians did in December 1810.[91] However, once Napoleon's Grand Army was devastated in the Moscow campaigns and the Armée de l'Espagne was being pushed back to the Pyrenees, the opportunity at last beckoned to throw off the French hegemony. What the Prussians, Russians, Swedes, Austrians, and others then needed was a ready supply of the rifles, boots, and clothing—not to mention the money—which the British were already providing to their Portuguese and Spanish allies. Thus, the security of the British Isles and its *relative* prosperity on the one hand, and the overstretched and increasingly grasping nature of French rule on the other, at last interacted to begin to bring down Napoleon's empire.

Such a sweeping analysis of economic and geopolitical factors tends, inevitably, to downplay the more personal aspects of this story, such as Napoleon's own increasing lethargy and self-delusion. It also may underemphasize the very precarious nature of the military equilibrium until almost the final year of the war—for the French even then possessed the resources to build an enormous navy, had they persisted in that course. The British export economy was to receive its severest test only in 1812; and until the battle of Leipzig (October 1813) there appeared good prospects that Napoleon could smash one of his eastern enemies and thus dissolve the coalition against him.

Nonetheless, the French "overstretch," reflecting Napoleon's own hubris, was by this time extreme, and any major setback was bound to affect other parts of the system—simply because these parts had to be drained of troops in order to repair the broken front. By 1811, there were some 353,000 French troops in Spain, and yet, as Wellington observed, they had no authority beyond the spot where they stood; defending their lines of communication consumed most of their efforts, and left them vulnerable to the Anglo-Portuguese-Spanish advance. When, in the year following, Napoleon decided to reduce Russia's independence, a mere 27,000 men could be withdrawn from Spain to join the march upon Moscow. Of the more than 600,000 men in the Grand Army, only 270,000 of that total were Frenchmen, the same number as remained in the Peninsula. Furthermore, since "native" Frenchmen now included the Belgians, Dutch, and many Italians in the annexed territories, troops raised from within the *pre*-1789 French borders were in a decided minority during the Russian campaign. This may not have mattered in the early, successful stages, but it did become important during the retreat, when men were desperate to escape from the bitter weather and marauding Cossacks and to return to their own homes.[92]

The Grand Army's casualties in the Russian campaign were enormous: perhaps as many as 270,000 men were killed and 200,000 captured, and about 1,000 guns and 200,000 horses were lost. The eastern front, more than any other factor, weakened the morale of the French army. Nonetheless, it is important to understand how the eastern European and peninsular campaigns interacted from 1813 onward to produce the eventual downfall: for by then the Russian army had little capacity (and many of its generals little enthusiasm) for pursuing the French across Germany; the British were somewhat distracted by their American war; and Napoleon had raised a fresh force of 145,000 men in the early summer of 1813, which enabled him to hold the line in Saxony and to negotiate an armistice. Although Prussia had prudently switched to the Russian side and Metternich was threatening to intervene with an Austrian army of a quarter of a million men, the eastern powers were still divided and uncertain. Thus, the news that Wellington's troops had smashed Joseph Bonaparte's army at Vitoria (June 1813) and were driving it back to the Pyrenees was important in encouraging the Austrians to declare war and to combine with the Russian, Swedish, and Prussian forces in order to expel the French from Germany. The subsequent battle of Leipzig in October was fought on a scale unknown to the British army—195,000 Frenchmen were overwhelmed in four days of fighting by 365,000 allied troops; but the latter were being economically underpinned by vast British subsidies, as well as being provided with 125,000 muskets, 218 artillery pieces, and much other equipment from the island state.[93]

In turn, the French defeat at Leipzig encouraged Wellington, now north of the Pyrenees, to advance upon Bayonne and Toulouse. As the armies of Prussia and Austria poured across the Rhine and the Cossacks invaded Holland, Napoleon conducted a brilliant tactical defense of northeastern France early in 1814; but his army was drained in strength and contained too many raw recruits. Moreover, the French populace, now that the fighting was on its soil, was (as Wellington had foretold) less than enthusiastic. Stiffened by British urgings to reduce France to its former size and by the pledge of a further £5 million in British subsidies at the Chaumont treaty of March 9, the allied governments kept up their pressure to the end. By March 30, 1814, even Napoleon's marshals had had enough, and within another week the emperor had abdicated.

Compared with these epic events, the Anglo-American war of 1812–1814 was a strategical sideshow.[94] Economically, it might have been far more serious to British interests had it not coincided with the collapse of the Continental System, and had not the New England states, largely dependent upon Anglo-American trade, remained luke-warm (and often neutral) in the conflict. The proclaimed "march on Canada" by American forces soon petered out, and both on land and at sea—despite the raids upon York (Toronto) and Washington, and some impressive single-ship frigate actions—each side demonstrated that it could hurt but not defeat the other. To the British in particular, it showed the importance of the American trades and it revealed the difficulties of maintaining large military and naval establishments overseas at the same time as the armed services were desperately required in the European theater. As was the case in India, trans-oceanic possessions and commerce were simultaneously a strengthen-ing of Britain's power position and a strategical distraction.[95]

Napoleon's final campaign of March to June 1815, while certainly not a sideshow, was a strategical footnote to the great war in Europe.[96] His sudden return to France from exile interrupted the quarrels of the victors over the future of Poland, Saxony, and other lands, but it did not shake the alliance. Even if the hastily assembled French force had not been defeated by Wellington and Blücher at Waterloo, it is difficult to see how it could have resisted the other armies which were being diverted toward Belgium, and still more difficult to see how France could have economically sustained a long war thereafter. Neverthe-less, Napoleon's last escapade was important politically. It reinforced Britain's position in Europe and strengthened the argument that France needed to be surrounded by an array of strong "buffer states" in the future. It demonstrated Prussia's military recovery after Jena, and thus partly readjusted the balances in eastern Europe. And it com-pelled all the powers at Vienna to bury their remaining differences in order to achieve a peace which would enshrine the principles of the balance of power.[97] After two decades of near-constant war and well over a century of Great Power tensions and conflict, the European states system was at last being fashioned along lines which ensured a rough equilibrium.

The final Vienna settlement of 1815 did not, as the Prussians had once suggested, partition France. It did, however, surround Louis XVIII's domain with substantial territorial units—the Kingdom of the Netherlands to the north, an enlarged Kingdom of Sardinia (Piedmont) to the southeast, and Prussia in the Rhineland; while Spain, returned to the Bourbons, was guaranteed in its integrity by the powers. Farther east, the idea of a *balance* of power was also implemented, after heated quarrels between the victors. Because of Austrian objections, Prussia was not permitted to swallow Saxony and instead accepted compensation in Posen and the Rhineland, just as Austria was compensated in Italy and in parts of southeastern Germany for the fact that it retained only the Galician region of Poland. Even Russia, whose claims to the lion's share of Polish territories had finally to be conceded, was considerably shaken at the beginning of 1815 by the threat of an Anglo-French-Austrian alliance to resist dictation over the future of Saxony, and quickly backed down from a confrontation. No power, it appeared, would not be permitted to impose its wishes upon the rest of Europe in the way Napoleon had done. The egoism of the leading states had in no way been evaporated by the events of 1793–1815, but the twin principles of "containment and reciprocal compensation"[98] meant that a unilateral grasp for domination of Europe was now unlikely; and that even small-scale territorial changes would need the approval of a majority of the members of the Concert.

For all the talk about a European "Pentarchy," however, it is important to recall that the five Great Powers were not in the same relationship to one another as they had been in 1750 or even in 1789. Despite Russia's growth, it was fair to say that a rough balance of power existed on land after Napoleon's fall. On the other hand, there was no equivalent at sea, where the British enjoyed a near-monopoly of naval power, which simultaneously reinforced and was underpinned by the economic lead which they had gained over all their rivals. In some cases, like India, this was the result of steady military expansionism and plunder, so that war and profit-seeking had interacted to draw the subcontinent into a purely British orbit by the end of the eighteenth century.[99] Similarly, the seizure of Santo Domingo—which had been responsible for a remarkable three-quarters of France's colonial trade before the Revolution—was by the late 1790s a valuable market for *British* goods and a great source of *British* re-exports. In addition, not only were these overseas markets in North America, the West Indies, Latin America, India, and the Orient growing faster than those in Europe, but such long-haul trades were also usually more profitable and a greater stimulus to the shipping, commodity-dealing, marine insurance, bill-clearing, and banking activities which so enhanced London's position as the new financial center of the world.[100] Despite recent writings which have questioned the rate of growth of the British economy in the eighteenth century and the role of foreign trade in that growth,[101] the fact remains that overseas expansion had given the country unchallenged access to vast new wealth which its rivals did not enjoy. Controlling most of Europe's colonies by 1815, dominating the maritime routes and the profitable re-export trades, and well ahead of other societies in the process of industrialization, the British were now the richest nation in per capita terms. During the next half-century—as will be seen in the following chapter—they would become even richer, as Britain grew to be the "superdominant economy" in the world's trading structure.[102] The principle of equilibrium which Pitt and Castlereagh held so high was one which applied to European territorial arrangements, not to the colonial and commercial spheres.

Little of this can have surprised intelligent early-nineteenth-century observers. Despite his own assumptions of grandeur, Napoleon seems to have become obsessed with Britain at times—with its invulnerability, its maritime dominance, its banks and credit system—and to have yearned to see it all tumble in the dust. Such feelings of envy and dislike doubtless existed, if in a less extreme form, among the Spaniards, Dutch, and others who saw the British monopolizing the outside world. The Russian general Kutusov, wishing to halt his army's westward advance in 1812, once the Grand Army had been driven from the homeland, may have spoken for more than himself when he doubted the wisdom of totally destroying Napoleon, since the "succession would not fall to Russia or to any other continental power, but to the power which already commands the sea, and whose domination would be intolerable."[103] At the end of the day, however, that result was unavoidable: Napoleon's hubris and refusal to compromise ensured not only his downfall, but his greatest enemy's supreme victory. As Gneisenau, another general with a sense of the larger issues, wryly concluded:

> Great Britain has no greater obligation than to this ruffian [Napoleon]. For through the events which he has brought about, England's greatness, prosperity, and wealth have risen high. She is mistress of the sea and neither in this dominion nor in world trade has she now a single rival to fear.[104]

STRATEGY &
ECONOMICS
IN THE
INDUSTRIAL ERA

4

Industrialization and the Shifting Global Balances, 1815–1885

The international system which developed in the half-century and more following Napoleon's downfall possessed an unusual set of characteristics, some merely temporary, while others became permanent features of the modern age.

The first was the steady and then (after the 1840s) spectacular growth of an integrated global economy, which drew ever more regions into a transoceanic and transcontinental trading and financial network centered upon western Europe, and in particular upon Great Britain. These decades of British economic hegemony were accompanied by large-scale improvements in transport and communications, by the increasingly rapid transfer of industrial technology from one region to another, and by an immense spurt in manufacturing output, which in turn stimulated the opening of new areas of agricultural land and raw-materials sources. The erosion of tariff barriers and other mercantilist devices, together with the widespread propagation of ideas about free trade and international harmony, suggested that a new international order had arisen, quite different from the eighteenth-century world of repeated Great Power conflict. The turbulence and costs of the 1793–1815 struggle—known to the nineteenth century as "the Great War"—caused conservatives and liberals alike to opt as far as possible for peace and stability, underpinned by devices as varied as the Concert of Europe or free-trade treaties. These conditions naturally encouraged long-term commercial and industrial investment, thereby stimulating the growth of a global economy.

Secondly, this absence of prolonged Great Power wars did not mean that all interstate conflict came to an end. If anything, the European and North American wars of conquest against less developed peoples intensified, and were in many ways the military concomitant to the economic penetration of the overseas world and to the swift decline in its share of manufacturing output. In addition, there still were regional and individual conflicts among the European powers, especially over questions of nationality and territorial borders; but, as we shall see, open struggles such as the Franco-Austrian War of 1859 or the wars of German unification in the 1860s were limited both in duration and area, and even the Crimean War could hardly be called a major conflict. Only the American Civil War was an exception to this rule, and deserves to be examined as such.

Thirdly, technology deriving from the Industrial Revolution began to make its impact upon military and naval warfare. But the changes were much slower than has sometimes been represented, and it was only in the second half of the century that railways, telegraphs, quick-firing guns, steam propulsion, and armored warships really became decisive indicators of military strength. While the new technology increased the lead in firepower and mobility which the Great Powers enjoyed in the overseas world, it was going to be many decades before military and naval commanders revised their ideas of how to fight a European war. Nevertheless, the twin forces of technical change and industrial development were steadily having an impact, on land and at sea, and also affecting the relative strengths of the Powers.

Although it is difficult to generalize, the shifts in the Great Power balances caused by the uneven pattern of industrial and technological change probably affected the outcome of mid-nineteenth-century wars more than did finance and credit. This was partly because the massive expansion of national and international banking in the nineteenth century and the growth of governmental bureaucracies (treasuries, inspectors, tax collectors) made it easier for most regimes to raise funds from the money markets, unless their credit rating was appallingly bad or there was a temporary liquidity crisis in the international banking system. But it was chiefly due to the fact that most of the wars which occurred were relatively short, so that the emphasis was upon a speedy victory in the field using existing military strength, rather than the long-term mobilization of national resources and the raising of fresh revenues. No amount of newly available funds could, for example, have saved Austria after its battlefield defeats of 1859 and 1866, or a very wealthy France after its armies had been crushed in the war of 1870. It was true that superior finances aided the North in its Civil War victory over the South, and that Britain and France were better able to afford the Crimean War than a near-bankrupt Russia—but that reflected the general superiority of their economies rather than the singular advantage they had in respect of credit and finance. For this reason, there is less to say about the role of war finance in the nineteenth century than there was about the previous period.

This cluster of factors—the growth of the international economy, the productive forces unleashed by the Industrial Revolution, the relative stability of Europe, the modernization of military and naval technology over time, and the occurrence of merely localized and short-term wars—naturally favored some of the Great Powers more than others. Indeed, one of those countries, Britain, benefited so much from the general economic and geopolitical trends of the post-1815 era that it became a different type of Power from the rest. All the other countries were affected, often very seriously, in their relative strength. By the 1860s, however, the further spread of industrialization was beginning to change the balance of world forces once again.

One further feature of this period is worth mentioning. From the early nineteenth century onward, historical statistics (especially of economic indicators) help to trace the shifts in the power balances and to measure more accurately the dynamics of the system. It is important to realize, however, that many of the data are very approximate, particularly for countries lacking an adequate bureaucracy; that certain of the calculations (e.g., shares of world manufacturing output) are merely estimates made by statisticians many years later; and that—the most important caveat of all—economic wealth did not immediately, or always, translate into military power. All that the statistics can do is give rough indications of a country's material potential and of its position in the relative rankings of the leading states.

The "Industrial Revolution," most economic historians are at pains to stress, did not happen overnight. It was, compared with the political "revolutions" of 1776, 1789, and 1917, a gradual, slow-moving process; it affected only certain manufactures and certain means of production; and it occurred region by region, rather than involving an entire country.[1] Yet all these caveats cannot avoid the fact that a fundamentally important transformation in man's economic circumstances began to occur sometime around 1780—not less significant, in the view of one authority, than the (admittedly far slower) transformation of savage Paleolithic hunting man to domesticated Neolithic farming man.[2] What industrialization, and in particular the steam engine, did was to substitute inanimate for animate sources of power; by converting heat into work through the use of machines—"rapid, regular, precise, tireless" machines[3]—mankind was thus able to exploit vast new sources of energy. The consequences of introducing this novel machinery were simply stupendous: by the 1820s someone operating several power-driven looms could produce twenty times the output of a hand worker, while a power-driven "mule" (or spinning machine) had two hundred times the capacity of a spinning wheel. A single railway engine could transport goods which would have required hundreds of packhorses, and do it far more quickly. To be sure, there were many other important aspects to the Industrial Revolution—the factory system, for example, or the division of labor. But the vital point for our purposes was the massive increase in productivity, especially in the textile industries, which in turn stimulated a demand for more machines, more raw materials (above all, cotton), more iron, more shipping, better communications, and so on.

Moreover, as Professor Landes has observed, this unprecedented increase in man's productivity was self-sustaining:

> Where previously an amelioration of the conditions of existence, hence of survival, and an increase in economic opportunity had always been followed by a rise in population that eventually consumed the gains achieved, now for the first time in history, both the economy and the knowledge were growing fast enough to generate a continuing flow of investment and technological innovation, a flow that lifted beyond visible limits the ceiling of Malthus's positive checks.[4]

The latter remark is also vitally important. From the eighteenth century onward, the growth in world population had begun to accelerate: Europe's numbers rose from 140 million in 1750 to 187 million in 1800 to 266 million in 1850; Asia's exploded from over 400 million in 1750 to around 700 million a century later.[5] Whatever the reasons—better climatic conditions, improved fecundity, decline in diseases—increases of that size were alarming; and although agricultural output both in Europe and Asia also expanded in the eighteenth century and was in fact another general reason for the rise in population, the sheer number of new heads (and stomachs) threatened over time to cancel out the benefits of all such additions in agricultural output. Pressure upon marginal lands, rural unemployment, and a vast drift of families into the already overcrowded cities of Europe in the late eighteenth century were but some of the symptoms of this population surge.[6]

What the Industrial Revolution in Britain did (in very crude macroeconomic terms) was to so increase productivity on a sustained basis that the consequent expansion both in national wealth and in the population's purchasing power constantly outweighed the rise in numbers. While the country's population rose from 10.5 million in 1801 to 41.8 million in 1911—an annual increase of 1.26 percent—its national product rose much faster, perhaps as much as fourteenfold over the nineteenth century. Depending upon the area covered by the statistics,* there was an annual average rise in gross national product of between 2 and 2.25 percent. In Queen Victoria's reign alone, product per capita rose two and a half times.

Compared with the growth rates achieved by many nations after 1945, these were not spectacular figures. It was also true, as social historians remind us, that the Industrial Revolution inflicted awful costs upon the new proletariat which labored in the factories and mines and lived in the unhealthy, crowded, jerry-built cities. Yet the fundamental point remains that the sustained increases in productiv-

---

*That is to say, some of the historical statistics refer to Great Britain (minus Ireland), some to the United Kingdom (with Ireland), and some include only northern but not southern Ireland.

ity of the Machine Age brought widespread benefits over time: average real wages in Britain rose between 15 and 25 percent in the years 1815–1850, and by an impressive 80 percent in the next half-century. "The central problem of the age," Ashton has reminded those critics who believe that industrialization was a disaster, "was how to feed and clothe and employ generations of children outnumbering by far those of any earlier time."[7] The new machines not only employed an increasingly large share of the burgeoning population, but also boosted the nation's overall per capita income; and the rising demand of urban workers for foodstuffs and essential goods was soon to be met by a steam-driven communications revolution, with railways and steamships bringing the agricultural surpluses of the New World to satisfy the requirements of the Old.

We can grasp this point in a different way by using Professor Landes's calculations. In 1870, he notes, the United Kingdom was using 100 million tons of coal, which was "equivalent to 800 million million Calories of energy, enough to feed a population of 850 million adult males for a year (actual population was then about 31 million)." Again, the capacity of Britain's steam engines in 1870, some 4 million horsepower, was equivalent to the power which could be generated by 40 million men; but "this many men would have eaten some 320 million bushels of wheat a year—more than three times the annual output of the entire United Kingdom in 1867–71."[8] The use of inanimate sources of power allowed industrial man to transcend the limitations of biology and to create spectacular increases in production and wealth without succumbing to the weight of a fast-growing population. By contrast, Ashton soberly noted (as late as 1947):

> There are today on the plains of India and China men and women, plague-ridden and hungry, living lives little better, to outward appearance, than those of the cattle that toil with them by day and share their places of sleep by night. Such Asiatic standards, and such unmechanised horrors, are the lot of those who increase their numbers without passing through an industrial revolution.[9]

The Eclipse of the Non-European World

Before discussing the effects of the Industrial Revolution upon the Great Power system, it will be as well to understand its impacts farther afield, especially upon China, India, and other non-European societies. The losses they suffered were twofold, both relative and absolute. It was not the case, as was once fancied, that the peoples of Asia, Africa, and Latin America lived a happy, ideal existence prior to the impact of western man. "The elemental truth must be stressed that the charac-

teristic of any country before its industrial revolution and modernization is poverty. . . . with low productivity, low output per head, in
traditional agriculture, any economy which has agriculture as the
main constituent of its national income does not produce much of a
surplus above the immediate requirements of consumption. . . ."[10] On
the other hand, in view of the fact that in 1800 agricultural production
formed the basis of both European and non-European societies, and
of the further fact that in countries such as India and China there also
existed many traders, textile producers, and craftsmen, the differences
in per capita income were not enormous; an Indian handloom weaver,
for example, may have earned perhaps as much as half of his European
equivalent prior to industrialization. What this also meant was that,
given the sheer numbers of Asiatic peasants and craftsmen, Asia still
contained a far larger share of world manufacturing output* than did
the much less populous Europe before the steam engine and the power
loom transformed the world's balances.

Just how dramatically those balances shifted in consequence of
European industrialization and expansion can be seen in Bairoch's two
ingenious calculations (see Tables 6–7).[11]

The root cause of these transformations, it is clear, lay in the staggering increases in productivity emanating from the Industrial Revolution. Between, say, the 1750s and the 1830s the mechanization of
spinning in Britain had increased productivity in that sector alone by a
factor of 300 to 400, so it is not surprising that the British share of total
world manufacturing rose dramatically—and continued to rise as it
turned itself into the "first industrial nation."[12] When other European
states and the United States followed the path to industrialization, their
shares also rose steadily, as did their per capita levels of industrialization and their national wealth. But the story for China and India was
quite a different one. Not only did their shares of total world manufacturing shrink relatively, simply because the West's output was rising so
swiftly; but in some cases their economies declined absolutely, that is,
they de-industrialized, because of the penetration of their traditional
markets by the far cheaper and better products of the Lancashire textile
factories. After 1813 (when the East India Company's trade monopoly
ended), imports of cotton fabrics into India rose spectacularly, from 1
million yards (1814) to 51 million (1830) to 995 million (1870), driving
out many of the traditional domestic producers in the process. Finally—
and this returns us to Ashton's point about the grinding poverty of
"those who increase their numbers without passing through an industrial revolution"—the large rise in the populations of China, India, and
other Third World countries probably reduced their general per capita
income from one generation to the next. Hence Bairoch's remarkable—

---

*Following, at least, the definition of "manufactures" that Bairoch employs (see note 11).

Table 6. Relative Shares of World Manufacturing Output, 1750–1900

	1750	1800	1830	1860	1880	1900
(Europe as a whole)	23.2	28.1	34.2	53.2	61.3	62.0
United Kingdom	1.9	4.3	9.5	19.9	22.9	18.5
Habsburg Empire	2.9	3.2	3.2	4.2	4.4	4.7
France	4.0	4.2	5.2	7.9	7.8	6.8
German States/Germany	2.9	3.5	3.5	4.9	8.5	13.2
Italian States/Italy	2.4	2.5	2.3	2.5	2.5	2.5
Russia	5.0	5.6	5.6	7.0	7.6	8.8
United States	0.1	0.8	2.4	7.2	14.7	23.6
Japan	3.8	3.5	2.8	2.6	2.4	2.4
Third World	73.0	67.7	60.5	36.6	20.9	11.0
China	32.8	33.3	29.8	19.7	12.5	6.2
India/Pakistan	24.5	19.7	17.6	8.6	2.8	1.7

Table 7. Per Capita Levels of Industrialization, 1750–1900
(relative to U.K. in 1900 = 100)

	1750	1800	1830	1860	1880	1900
(Europe as a whole)	8	8	11	16	24	35
United Kingdom	10	16	25	64	87	[100]
Habsburg Empire	7	7	8	11	15	23
France	9	9	12	20	28	39
German States/Germany	8	8	9	15	25	52
Italian States/Italy	8	8	8	10	12	17
Russia	6	6	7	8	10	15
United States	4	9	14	21	38	69
Japan	7	7	7	7	9	12
Third World	7	6	6	4	3	2
China	8	6	6	4	4	3
India	7	6	6	3	2	1

and horrifying—suggestion that whereas the per capita levels of industrialization in Europe and the Third World may have been not too far apart from each other in 1750, the latter's was only one-eighteenth of the former's (2 percent to 35 percent) by 1900, and only one-fiftieth of the United Kingdom's (2 percent to 100 percent).

The "impact of western man" was, in all sorts of ways, one of the most noticeable aspects of the dynamics of world power in the nineteenth century. It manifested itself not only in a variety of economic relationships—ranging from the "informal influence" of coastal traders, shippers, and consuls to the more direct controls of planters, railway builders, and mining companies[13]—but also in the penetrations of explorers, adventurers, and missionaries, in the introduction of western diseases, and in the proselytization of western faiths. It occurred as much in the centers of continents—westward from the Missouri, southward from the Aral Sea—as it did up the mouths of African rivers and around the coasts of Pacific archipelagoes. If it eventually had its impressive monuments in the roads, railway networks, telegraphs, harbors, and civic buildings which (for example) the British created in India, its more horrific side was the bloodshed, rapine, and plunder which attended so many of the colonial wars of the period.[14] To be sure, the same traits of force and conquest had existed since the days of Cortez, but now the pace was accelerating. In the year 1800, Europeans occupied or controlled 35 percent of the land surface of the world; by 1878 this figure had risen to 67 percent, and by 1914 to over 84 percent.[15]

The advanced technology of steam engines and machine-made tools gave Europe decisive economic and military advantages. The improvements in the muzzle-loading gun (percussion caps, rifling, etc.) were ominous enough; the coming of the breechloader, vastly increasing the rate of fire, was an even greater advance; and the Gatling guns, Maxims, and light field artillery put the final touches to a new "firepower revolution" which quite eradicated the chances of a successful resistance by indigenous peoples reliant upon older weaponry. Furthermore, the steam-driven gunboat meant that European sea power, already supreme in open waters, could be extended inland, via major waterways like the Niger, the Indus, and the Yangtze: thus the mobility and firepower of the ironclad *Nemesis* during the Opium War actions of 1841 and 1842 was a disaster for the defending Chinese forces, which were easily brushed aside.[16] It was true, of course, that physically difficult terrain (e.g., Afghanistan) blunted the drives of western military imperialism, and that among non-European forces which adopted the newer weapons and tactics—like the Sikhs and the Algerians in the 1840s—the resistance was far greater. But whenever the struggle took place in open country where the West could deploy its machine guns and heavier weapons, the issue was never in doubt. Perhaps the greatest disparity of all was seen at the very end of the century, during the battle of Omdurman (1898), when in one half-morning the Maxims and Lee-Enfield rifles of Kitchener's army destroyed 11,000 Dervishes for the loss of only forty-eight of their own troops. In consequence, the firepower gap, like that which had opened up in industrial productivity, meant that the leading nations possessed resources fifty or a hundred times greater than those at the bottom. The global dominance of the West, implicit since da Gama's day, now knew few limits.

Britain as Hegemon?

If the Punjabis and Annamese and Sioux and Bantu were the "losers" (to use Eric Hobsbawm's term)[17] in this early-nineteenth-century expansion, the British were undoubtedly the "winners." As noted in the previous chapter, they had already achieved a remarkable degree of global preeminence by 1815, thanks to their adroit combination of naval mastery, financial credit, commercial expertise, and alliance diplomacy. What the Industrial Revolution did was to enhance the position of a country already made supremely successful in the preindustrial, mercantilist struggles of the eighteenth century, and then to transform it into a different sort of power. If (to repeat) the pace of change was gradual rather than revolutionary, the results were nonetheless highly impressive. Between 1760 and 1830, the United Kingdom was responsible for around "two-thirds of Europe's industrial growth of output,"[18] and its share of world manufacturing production leaped from 1.9 to 9.5 percent; in the next thirty years, British industrial expansion pushed that figure to 19.9 percent, despite the spread of the new technology to other countries in the West. Around 1860, which was probably when the country reached its zenith in relative terms, the United Kingdom produced 53 percent of the world's iron and 50 percent of its coal and lignite, and consumed just under half of the raw cotton output of the globe. "With 2 percent of the world's population and 10 percent of Europe's, the United Kingdom would seem to have had a capacity in modern industries equal to 40–45 percent of the world's potential and 55–60 percent of that in Europe."[19] Its energy consumption from modern sources (coal, lignite, oil) in 1860 was five times that of either the United States or Prussia/Germany, six times that of France, and 155 times that of Russia! It alone was responsible for one-fifth of the world's commerce, but for two-fifths of the trade in manufactured goods. Over one-third of the world's merchant marine flew under the British flag, and that share was steadily increasing. It was no surprise that the mid-Victorians exulted at their unique state, being now (as the economist Jevons put it in 1865) the trading center of the universe:

> The plains of North America and Russia are our corn fields; Chicago and Odessa our granaries; Canada and the Baltic are our timber forests; Australasia contains our sheep farms, and in Argentina and on the western prairies of North America are our herds of oxen; Peru sends her silver, and the gold of South Africa and Australia flows to London; the Hindus and the Chinese grow tea for us, and our coffee, sugar and spice plantations are in all the Indies. Spain and France are our vineyards and the Mediterranean our fruit garden; and our cotton grounds, which for long have occupied the

Southern United States, are now being extended everywhere in the warm regions of the earth.[20]

Since such manifestations of self-confidence, and the industrial and commercial statistics upon which they rested, seemed to suggest a position of unequaled dominance on Britain's part, it is fair to make several other points which put this all in a better context. First—although it is a somewhat pedantic matter—it is unlikely that the country's gross national product (GNP) was ever the largest in the world during the decades following 1815. Given the sheer size of China's population (and, later, Russia's) and the obvious fact that agricultural production and distribution formed the basis of national wealth everywhere, even in Britain prior to 1850, the latter's overall GNP never looked as impressive as its per capita product or its stage of industrialization. Still, "by itself the volume of total GNP has no important significance";[21] the physical product of hundreds of millions of peasants may dwarf that of five million factory workers, but since most of it is immediately consumed, it is far less likely to lead to surplus wealth or decisive military striking power. Where Britain was strong, indeed unchallenged, in 1850 was in modern, wealth-producing industry, with all the benefits which flowed from it.

On the other hand—and this second point is not a pedantic one—Britain's growing industrial muscle was not organized in the post-1815 decades to give the state swift access to military hardware and manpower as, say, Wallenstein's domains did in the 1630s or the Nazi economy was to do. On the contrary, the ideology of laissez-faire political economy, which flourished alongside this early industrialization, preached the causes of eternal peace, low government expenditures (especially on defense), and the reduction of state controls over the economy and the individual. It might be necessary, Adam Smith had conceded in *The Wealth of Nations* (1776), to tolerate the upkeep of an army and a navy in order to protect British society "from the violence and invasion of other independent societies"; but since armed forces *per se* were "unproductive" and did not add value to the national wealth in the way that a factory or a farm did, they ought to be reduced to the lowest possible level commensurate with national safety.[22] Assuming (or, at least, hoping) that war was a last resort, and ever less likely to occur in the future, the disciples of Smith and even more of Richard Cobden would have been appalled at the idea of organizing the state for war. As a consequence, the "modernization" which occurred in British industry and communications was not paralleled by improvements in the army, which (with some exceptions)[23] stagnated in the post-1815 decades.

However preeminent the British economy in the mid-Victorian period, therefore, it was probably less "mobilized" for conflict than at any time since the early Stuarts. Mercantilist measures, with their emphasis upon the links between national security and national wealth, were steadily eliminated: protective tariffs were abolished; the ban on the export of advanced technology (e.g., textile machinery) was lifted; the Navigation Acts, designed among other things to preserve a large stock of British merchant ships and seamen for the event of war, were repealed; imperial "preferences" were ended. By contrast, defense expenditures were held to an absolute minimum, averaging around £15 million a year in the 1840s and not above £27 million in the more troubled 1860s; yet in the latter period Britain's GNP totaled about £1 billion. Indeed, for fifty years and more following 1815 the armed services consumed only about 2–3 percent of GNP, and central government expenditures as a whole took much less than 10 percent—proportions which were far less than in either the eighteenth or the twentieth century.[24] These would have been impressively low figures for a country of modest means and ambitions. For a state which managed to "rule the waves," which possessed an enormous, far-flung empire, and which still claimed a large interest in preserving the European balance of power, they were truly remarkable.

Like that of the United States in, say, the early 1920s, therefore, the size of the British economy in the world was not reflected in the country's fighting power; nor could its laissez-faire institutional structures, with a minuscule bureaucracy increasingly divorced from trade and industry, have been able to mobilize British resources for an all-out war without a great upheaval. As we shall see below, even the more limited Crimean War shook the system severely, yet the concern which that exposure aroused soon faded away. Not only did the mid-Victorians show ever less enthusiasm for military interventions in Europe, which would always be expensive, and perhaps immoral, but they reasoned that the equilibrium between the continental Great Powers which generally prevailed during the six decades after 1815 made any full-scale commitment on Britain's part unnecessary. While it did strive, through diplomacy and the movement of naval squadrons, to influence political events along the vital peripheries of Europe (Portugal, Belgium, the Dardanelles), it tended to abstain from intervention elsewhere. By the late 1850s and early 1860s, even the Crimean campaign was widely regarded as a mistake. Because of this lack of inclination and effectiveness, Britain did not play a major role in the fate of Piedmont in the critical year of 1859, it disapproved of Palmerston and Russell's "meddling" in the Schleswig-Holstein affair of 1864, and it watched from the sidelines when Prussia defeated Austria in 1866 and France four years later. It is not surprising to see that Britain's military capacity was reflected in the relatively modest size of its army during this period (see Table 8), little of which could, in any case, be mobilized for a European theater.

Table 8. Military Personnel of the Powers, 1816–1880[25]

	1816	1830	1860	1880
United Kingdom	255,000	140,000	347,000	248,000
France	132,000	259,000	608,000	544,000
Russia	800,000	826,000	862,000	909,000
Prussia/Germany	130,000	130,000	201,000	430,000
Habsburg Empire	220,000	273,000	306,000	273,000
United States	16,000	11,000	26,000	36,000

Even in the extra-European world, where Britain preferred to deploy its regiments, military and political officials in places such as India were almost always complaining of the *inadequacy* of the forces they commanded, given the sheer magnitude of the territories they controlled. However imposing the empire may have appeared on a world map, district officers knew that it was being run on a shoestring. But all this is merely saying that Britain was a different sort of Great Power by the early to middle nineteenth century, and that its influence could not be measured by the traditional criteria of military hegemony. Where it *was* strong was in certain other realms, each of which was regarded by the British as far more valuable than a large and expensive standing army.

The first of these was in the naval realm. For over a century before 1815, of course, the Royal Navy had usually been the largest in the world. But that maritime mastery had frequently been contested, especially by the Bourbon powers. The salient feature of the eighty years which followed Trafalgar was that no other country, or combination of countries, seriously challenged Britain's control of the seas. There was, it is true, the occasional French "scare"; and the Admiralty also kept a wary eye upon Russian shipbuilding programs and upon the American construction of large frigates. But each of those perceived challenges faded swiftly, leaving British sea power to exercise (in Professor Lloyd's words) "a wider influence than has ever been seen in the history of maritime empires."[26] Despite a steady reduction in its own numbers after 1815, the Royal Navy was at some times probably as powerful as the next three or four navies in actual fighting power. And its major fleets *were* a factor in European politics, at least on the periphery. The squadron anchored in the Tagus to protect the Portuguese monarchy against internal or external dangers; the decisive use of naval force in the Mediterranean (against the Algiers pirates in 1816; smashing the Turkish fleet at Navarino in 1827; checking Mehemet Ali at Acre in 1840); and the calculated dispatch of the fleet to anchor before the Dardanelles whenever the "Eastern Question" became acute: these were manifestations of British sea power which, although geographically restricted, nonetheless weighed in the minds of European governments. Outside Europe, where smaller Royal Navy fleets or even individual warships engaged in a whole host of activities—suppressing piracy, intercepting slaving ships, landing marines, and overawing local potentates from Canton to Zanzibar—the impact seemed perhaps even more decisive.[27]

The second significant realm of British influence lay in its expanding colonial empire. Here again, the overall situation was a far less competitive one than in the preceding two centuries, where Britain had had to fight repeatedly for empire against Spain, France, and other European states. Now, apart from the occasional alarm about French moves in the Pacific or Russian encroachments in Turkestan, no serious rivals remained. It is therefore hardly an exaggeration to suggest that between 1815 and 1880 much of the British Empire existed in a power-political vacuum, which is why its colonial army could be kept relatively low. There were, it is true, limits to British imperialism—and certain problems, with the expanding American republic in the western hemisphere as well as with France and Russia in the eastern. But in many parts of the tropics, and for long periods of time, British interests (traders, planters, explorers, missionaries) encountered no foreigners other than the indigenous peoples.

This relative lack of external pressure, together with the rise of laissez-faire liberalism at home, caused many a commentator to argue that colonial acquisitions were unnecessary, being merely a set of "millstones" around the neck of the overburdened British taxpayer. Yet whatever the rhetoric of anti-imperialism within Britain, the fact was that the empire continued to grow, expanding (according to one calculation) at an average annual pace of about 100,000 square miles between 1815 and 1865.[28] Some were strategical/commercial acquisitions, like Singapore, Aden, the Falkland Islands, Hong Kong, Lagos; others were the consequence of land-hungry white settlers, moving across the South African veldt, the Canadian prairies, and the Australian outback—whose expansion usually provoked a native resistance that often had to be suppressed by troops from Britain or British India. And even when formal annexations were resisted by a home government perturbed at this growing list of new responsibilities, the "informal influence" of an expanding British society was felt from Uruguay to the Levant and from the Congo to the Yangtze. Compared with the sporadic colonizing efforts of the French and the more localized internal colonization by the Americans and the Russians, the British as imperialists were in a class of their own for most of the nineteenth century.

The third area of British distinctiveness and strength lay in the realm of finance. To be sure, this element can scarcely be separated from the country's general industrial and commercial progress; money had been necessary to fuel the Industrial Revolution, which in turn produced much more money, in the form of returns upon capital invested. And, as the preceding chapter showed, the British government had long known how to exploit its credit in the banking and stock markets. But developments in the financial realm by the mid-nineteenth century were both qualitatively and quantitatively different from what had gone before. At first sight, it is the quantitative difference which catches the eye. The long peace and the easy availability of capital in the United Kingdom, together with the improvements in the country's financial institutions, stimulated Britons to invest abroad as never before: the £6 million or so which was annually exported in the decade following Waterloo had risen to over £30 million a year by midcentury, and to a staggering £75 million a year between 1870 and 1875. The resultant income to Britain from such interest and dividends, which had totaled a handy £8 million each year in the late 1830s, was over £50 million a year by the 1870s; but most of that was promptly reinvested overseas, in a sort of virtuous upward spiral which not only made Britain ever wealthier but gave a continual stimulus to global trade and communications.

The consequences of this vast export of capital were several, and important. The first was that the returns on overseas investments significantly reduced the annual trade gap on visible goods which Britain always incurred. In this respect, investment income added to the already considerable invisible earnings which came from shipping, insurance, bankers' fees, commodity dealing, and so on. Together, they ensured that not only was there never a balance-of-payments crisis, but Britain became steadily richer, at home and abroad. The second point was that the British economy acted as a vast bellows, sucking in enormous amounts of raw materials and foodstuffs and sending out vast quantities of textiles, iron goods, and other manufactures; and this pattern of visible trade was paralleled, and complemented, by the network of shipping lines, insurance arrangements, and banking links which spread outward from London (especially), Liverpool, Glasgow, and most other cities in the course of the nineteenth century.

Given the openness of the British home market and London's willingness to reinvest overseas income in new railways, ports, utilities, and agricultural enterprises from Georgia to Queensland, there was a general complementarity between visible trade flows and investment patterns.* Add to this the growing acceptance of the gold standard and the development of an international exchange and payments mechanism based upon bills drawn on London, and it was scarcely surprising that the mid-Victorians were convinced that by following the principles of classical political economy, they had discovered the secret

---

*Argentina, for example, would be able to find a ready market in the U.K. for its exports of beef and grain, thereby allowing it not only to pay for imported British manufactures and for the various service fees but also to repay the long-term loans floated in London, and thus to keep its own credit high for further borrowing. The contrast with U.S. loans to Latin America in the twentieth century—lending at short term, and not allowing the importation of agricultural produce—is striking.

which guaranteed both increasing prosperity and world harmony. Although many individuals—Tory protectionists, oriental despots, new-fangled socialists—still seemed too purblind to admit this truth, over time everyone would surely recognize the fundamental validity of laissez-faire economics and utilitarian codes of government.[29]

While all this made Britons wealthier than ever in the short term, did it not also contain elements of strategic danger in the longer term? With the wisdom of retrospect, one can detect at least two consequences of these structural economic changes which would later affect Britain's relative power in the world. The first was the way in which the country was contributing to the long-term expansion of other nations, both by establishing and developing foreign industries and agriculture with repeated financial injections and by building railways, harbors, and steamships which would enable overseas producers to rival its own production in future decades. In this connection, it is worth noting that while the coming of steam power, the factory system, railways, and later electricity enabled the British to overcome natural, physical obstacles to higher productivity, and thus increased the nation's wealth and strength, such inventions helped the United States, Russia, and central Europe even more, because the natural, physical obstacles to the development of their landlocked potential were much greater. Put crudely, what industrialization did was to equalize the chances to exploit one's own indigenous resources and thus to take away some of the advantages hitherto enjoyed by smaller, peripheral, naval-cum-commercial states and to give them to the great land-based states.[30]

The second potential strategical weakness lay in the increasing dependence of the British economy upon international trade and, more important, international finance. By the middle decades of the nineteenth century, exports composed as much as one-fifth of total national income,[31] a far higher proportion than in Walpole's or Pitt's time; for the enormous cotton-textile industry in particular, overseas markets were vital. But foreign imports, both of raw materials and (increasingly) of foodstuffs, were also becoming vital as Britain moved from being a predominantly agricultural to being a predominantly urban/industrial society. And in the fastest-growing sector of all, the "invisible" services of banking, insurance, commodity-dealing, and overseas investment, the reliance upon a world market was even more critical. The world was the City of London's oyster, which was all very well in peacetime; but what would the situation be if ever it came to another Great Power war? Would Britain's export markets be even more badly affected than in 1809 and 1811–1812? Was not the entire economy, and domestic population, becoming too dependent upon imported goods, which might easily be cut off or suspended in periods of conflict? And would not the London-based global banking and financial system collapse at the onset of another world war, since the markets might be closed, insurances suspended, international capital transfers retarded, and credit ruined? In such circumstances, ironically, the advanced British economy might be more severely hurt than a state which was less "mature" but also less dependent upon international trade and finance.

Given the Liberal assumptions about interstate harmony and constantly increasing prosperity, these seemed idle fears; all that was required was for statesmen to act rationally and to avoid the ancient folly of quarreling with other peoples. And, indeed, the laissez-faire Liberals argued, the more British industry and commerce became integrated with, and dependent upon, the global economy, the greater would be the disincentive to pursue policies which might lead to conflict. In the same way, the growth of the financial sector was to be welcomed, since it was not only fueling the midcentury "boom," but demonstrating how advanced and progressive Britain had become; even if other countries followed her lead and did industrialize, she could switch her efforts to servicing that development, and gaining even more profits thereby. In Bernard Porter's words, she was the first frogspawn egg to grow legs, the first tadpole to change into a frog, the first frog to hop out of the pond. She was economically different from the others, but that was only because she was so far ahead of them.[32] Given these auspicious circumstances, fears of strategical weakness appeared groundless; and most mid-Victorians preferred, like Kingsley as he cried tears of pride during the Great Exhibition at the Crystal Palace in 1851, to believe that a cosmic destiny was at work:

> The spinning jenny and the railroad, Cunard's liners and the electric telegraph, are to me . . . signs that we are, on some points at least, in harmony with the universe; that there is a mighty spirit working among us . . . the Ordering and Creating God.[33]

Like all other civilizations at the top of the wheel of fortune, therefore, the British could believe that their position was both "natural" and destined to continue. And just like all those other civilizations, they were in for a rude shock. But that was still some way into the future, and in the age of Palmerston and Macaulay, it was British strengths rather than weaknesses which were mostly in evidence.

The "Middle Powers"

The impact of economic and technological change upon the relative position of the Great Powers of continental Europe was much less dramatic in the half-century or so following 1815, chiefly because the

industrialization which did occur started off from a much lower base
than in Britain. The farther east one went, the more feudal and agricultural the local economy tended to be; but even in western Europe,
which had been close to Britain in many aspects of commercial and
technological development prior to 1790, two decades of war had left
a heavy mark: population losses, changed customs barriers, higher
taxes, the "pastoralization" of the Atlantic sector, the loss of overseas
markets and raw materials, the difficulties of acquiring the latest British inventions, were all setbacks to general economic growth, even
when (for special reasons) certain trades and regions had flourished
during the Napoleonic wars.[34] If the coming of peace meant a resumption of normal trade and also allowed continental entrepreneurs to see
how far behind Great Britain they had fallen, it did not produce a
sudden burst of modernization. There simply was not enough capital,
or local demand, or official enthusiasm, to produce a transformation;
and many a European merchant, craftsman, and handloom weaver
would bitterly oppose the adoption of English techniques, seeing in
them (quite correctly) a threat to their older way of life.[35] In consequence, although the steam engine, the power loom, and the railway
made some headway in continental Europe,

> between 1815 and 1848 the traditional features of the economy
> remained preeminent: the superiority of agriculture over industrial
> production, the absence of cheap and rapid means of transport, and
> the priority given to consumer goods over heavy industry.[36]

As Table 7 above shows, the relative increases in per capita levels of
industrialization for the century after 1750 were not very impressive;
and only in the 1850s and 1860s did the picture begin to change.

The prevailing political and diplomatic conditions of "Restoration
Europe" also combined to freeze the international status quo, or at
least to permit only small-scale alterations in the existing order. Precisely because the French Revolution had been such a frightening
challenge both to the internal social arrangements and to the traditional states system of Europe, Metternich and fellow conservatives
now regarded any new developments with suspicion. An adventurist
diplomacy, running the risk of a general war, was as much to be
frowned upon as a campaign for national self-determination or for
constitutional reform. On the whole, political leaders felt that they had
enough on their hands simply dealing with domestic turbulences and
the agitation of sectional interests, many of which were beginning to
feel threatened by even the early appearances of new machinery, the
growth of urbanization, and other incipient challenges to the guilds,
the crafts, and the protective regulations of a preindustrial society.
What one historian has described as an "endemic civil war that pro-

duced the great outbreaks of insurrection in 1830, as well as a host of intermediate revolts,"[37] meant that statesmen generally possessed neither the energies nor the desires to engage in foreign conflicts which might well weaken their own regimes.

In this connection, it is worth nothing that many of the military actions which did occur were initiated precisely to defend the existing sociopolitical order from revolutionary threat—for example, the Austrian army's crushing of resistance in Piedmont in 1823, the French military's move into Spain in the same year to restore to King Ferdinand his former powers, and, the most notable cause of all, the use of Russian troops to suppress the Hungarian revolution of 1848. If these reactionary measures grew increasingly unpopular to British opinion, that country's insularity meant that it would not intervene to rescue the liberal forces from suppression. As for territorial changes within Europe, they could occur only after the agreement of the "Concert" of the Great Powers, some of which might need to be compensated in one way or another. Unlike either the age of Napoleon preceding it or the age of Bismarck following it, therefore, the period 1815–1865 internationalized most of its tricky political problems (Belgium, Greece), and frowned upon unilateral actions. All this gave a basic, if precarious, stability to the existing states system.

The international position of Prussia in the decades after 1815 was clearly affected by these general political and social conditions.[38] Although greatly augmented territorially by the acquisition of the Rhineland, the Hohenzollern state now seemed much less impressive than it had been under Frederick the Great. It was, after all, only in the 1850s and 1860s that economic expansion took place on Prussian soil faster than virtually anywhere else in Europe. In the first half of the century, by contrast, the country seemed an industrial pigmy, its annual iron production of 50,000 tons being eclipsed by that not only of Britain, France, and Russia but also of the Habsburg Empire. Furthermore, the acquisition of the Rhineland not only split Prussia geographically but also exacerbated the political divisions between the state's more "liberal" western and more "feudal" eastern provinces. For the greater part of this period, domestic tensions were at the forefront of politics; and while the forces of reaction usually prevailed, they were alarmed at the reformist tendencies of 1810–1819, and quite panicked by the revolution of 1848–1849. Even when the military reimposed a profoundly illiberal regime, fear of domestic unrest made the Prussian elite reluctant to contemplate foreign-policy adventures; on the contrary, conservatives felt, they needed to identify as closely as possible with the forces of stability elsewhere in Europe, especially Russia and even Austria.

Prussia's internal-politics disputes were complicated still further by the debate about the "German question," that is to say, about the possibility of an eventual union of the thirty-nine German states, and the means by which that goal could be secured. For not only did the issue predictably divide the liberal-nationalist bourgeoisie of Prussia from most of the conservatives, but it also involved delicate negotiations with the middle- and south-German states and—most important of all—revived the rivalry with the Habsburg Empire that had last been seen in the heated disputes over Saxony in 1814. Although Prussia was the undisputed leader of the increasingly important German Customs Union (Zollverein) which developed from the 1830s onward, and which the Austrians could not join because of the protectionist pressures of their own industrialists, the balance of political advantage generally lay in Vienna's favor during these decades. In the first place, both Frederick William III (1797–1840) and Frederick William IV (1840–1861) feared the results of a clash with the Habsburg Empire more than Metternich and his successor Schwarzenberg did with their northern neighbor. In addition, Austria presided over the German Federation's meetings at Frankfurt; it had the sympathy of many of the smaller German states, not to mention the Prussian old conservatives; and it seemed indisputably a European power, whereas Prussia was little more than a German one. The most noticeable sign of Vienna's greater weight came in the 1850 agreement at Oelmuetz, which temporarily ended their jockeying for advantage in the German question when Prussia agreed to demobilize its army and to abandon its own schemes for unification. A diplomatic humiliation, in Frederick William IV's view, was preferable to a risky war so shortly after the 1848 revolution. And even those Prussian nationalists like Bismarck, smarting at such a retreat before Austrian demands, felt that little could be done elsewhere until "the struggle for mastery in Germany" was finally settled.

One quite vital factor in Frederick William's submission at Oelmuetz had been the knowledge that the Russian czar supported Austria's case in the "German question." Throughout the entire period from 1812 until 1871, in fact, Berlin took pains to avoid provoking the military colossus to the east. Ideological and dynastic reasons certainly helped to justify such obsequiousness, but they did not fully conceal Prussia's continued sense of inferiority, which the Russian acquisition of most of Congress Poland in 1814 had simply accentuated. Expressions of disapproval by St. Petersburg over any moves toward liberalization in Prussia, Czar Nicholas I's well-known conviction that German unification was utopian nonsense (especially if it was to come about, as was attempted in 1848, by a radical Frankfurt assembly offering an emperor's crown to the Prussian king!), and Russia's support of Austria before Oelmuetz were all manifestations of this overshadowing foreign influence. It was scarcely surprising, therefore, that the outbreak of the Crimean War in 1854 found the Prussian government desperately eager to stay neutral, fearing the consequences of going to war against Russia even while it worried at losing the respect of Austria and the western powers. Given its circumstances, Prussia's position was logical, but, because the British and Austrians disliked Berlin's "wavering" policy, Prussian diplomats were not allowed to join the other delegates at the Congress of Paris (1856) until some way into the proceedings. Symbolically, then, it was still being treated as a marginal participant.

In other areas, too—although less persistently—Prussia found itself constrained by foreign powers. Palmerston's denunciations of the Prussian army's move into Schleswig-Holstein in 1848 was the least worrying. Much more disturbing was the potential French threat to the Rhineland, in 1830, again in 1840, and finally in the 1860s. All those periods of tension merely confirmed what the quarrels with Vienna and occasional growls from St. Petersburg already suggested: that Prussia in the first half of the nineteenth century was the least of the Great Powers, disadvantaged by geography, overshadowed by powerful neighbors, distracted by internal and inner-German problems, and quite incapable of playing a larger role in international affairs. This seems, perhaps, too harsh a judgment in the light of Prussia's various strengths: its educational system, from the parish schools to the universities, was second to none in Europe; its administrative system was reasonably efficient; and its army and its formidable general staff were early in studying reforms in both tactics and strategy, especially in the military implications of "railways and rifles."[39] But the point was that this potential could not be utilized until the internal-political crisis between liberals and conservatives was overcome, until there was firm leadership at the top, in place of Frederick William IV's vacillations, and until Prussia's industrial base had been developed. Only after 1860, therefore, could the Hohenzollern state emerge from its near-second-class status.

Yet, as with many other things in life, strategical weakness is relative; and, compared with the Habsburg Empire to the south, Prussia's problems were perhaps not so daunting. If the period 1648–1815 had seen the empire "rising" and "asserting itself,"[40] that expansion had not eliminated the difficulties under which Vienna labored as it strove to carry out a Great Power role. On the contrary, the settlement of 1815 compounded these difficulties, at least in the longer term. For example, the very fact that the Austrians had fought so frequently against Napoleon and emerged on the winning side meant that they required "compensations" in the general shuffling of boundaries which occurred during the negotiations of 1814–1815; and although the Habsburgs wisely agreed to withdraw from the southern Netherlands, southwestern Germany (the Vorlande), and parts of Poland, this was balanced by their large-scale expansion in Italy and by the assertion of their leading role in the newly created German Federation.

Given the general theory of the European equilibrium and especially those versions preferred by British commentators as well as by Metternich himself—this reestablishment of Austrian power was commendable. The Habsburg Empire, sprawled across Europe from the northern-Italian plain to Galicia, would act as the central fulcrum to the balance, checking French ambitions in western Europe and in Italy, preserving the status quo in Germany against both the "greater-German" nationalists and the Prussian expansionists, and posing a barrier to Russian penetration of the Balkans. It was true that each of these tasks was supported by one or more of the other Great Powers, depending upon the context; but the Habsburg Empire was vital to the functioning of this complex five-sided checkmate, if only because it seemed to have the greatest interest of all in freezing the 1815 settlement—whereas France, Prussia, and Russia, sooner or later, wanted some changes, while the British, seeing fewer and fewer strategical and ideological reasons to support Metternich after the 1820s, were consequently less willing to aid Austria's efforts to maintain all aspects of the existing order. In the view of certain historians, indeed, the general peace which prevailed in Europe for decades after 1815 was due chiefly to the position and functions of the Habsburg Empire. When, therefore, it could gain no military support from the other powers to preserve the status quo in Italy and Germany in the 1860s, it was driven out of those two theaters; and when, after 1900, its own survival was in doubt, a great war of succession—with fateful implications for the European balance—was inevitable.[41]

So long as the conservative powers in Europe were united in preserving the status quo—against French resurgence, or the "revolution" generally—this Habsburg weakness was concealed. By appealing to the ideological solidarity of the Holy Alliance, Metternich could usually be assured of the support of Russia and Prussia, which in turn allowed him a free hand to arrange the interventions against any liberal stirrings—whether by sending Austrian troops to put down the Naples insurrection of 1821, or by permitting the French military action in Spain to support the Bourbon regime, or by orchestrating the imposition of the reactionary Carlsbad Decrees (1819) upon the members of the German Federation. In much the same way, the Habsburg Empire's relations with St. Petersburg and Berlin benefited from their shared interest in suppressing Polish nationalism, which for the Russian government was a far more vital issue than the occasional disagreements over Greece or the Straits; the joint suppression of the Polish revolt in Galicia and Austria's incorporation of the Free City of Kracow in 1846 with the concurrence of Russia and Prussia showed

the advantages which could be gained from such monarchical solidarity.

Over the longer term, however, this Metternichian strategy was
deeply flawed. A radical *social* revolution could fairly easily be kept in
check in nineteenth-century Europe; whenever one occurred (1830,
1848, the 1871 Commune), the frightened middle classes defected to
the side of "law and order." But the widespread ideas and movements
in favor of national self-determination, stimulated by the French Revolution and the various wars of liberation earlier in the century, could
not be suppressed forever; and Metternich's attempts to crush independence movements steadily exhausted the Habsburg Empire. By reso-
lutely opposing any stirrings of national independence, Austria quickly
lost the sympathy of its old ally, Britain. Its repeated use of military
force in Italy provoked a reaction among all classes against their Habsburg "jailor," which in turn was to play into the hands of Napoleon III
a few decades later, when that ambitious French monarch was able to
help Cavour in driving the Austrians out of northern Italy. In the same
way, the Habsburg Empire's unwillingness to join the Zollverein for
economic reasons and the constitutional-geographical impossibility of
its becoming part of a "greater Germany" disappointed many German
nationalists, who then began to look to Prussia for leadership. Even the
czarist regime, which generally supported Vienna's efforts to crush
revolutions, occasionally found it easier than Austria to deal with national questions: witness Alexander I's policy, in cooperation with the
British, of supporting Greek independence during the late 1820s despite all Metternich's counterarguments.

The fact was that in an age of increasing national consciousness, the
Habsburg Empire looked ever more of an anachronism. In each of the
other Great Powers, it has been pointed out,

> a majority of the citizenry shared a common language and religion.
> At least 90 percent of Frenchmen spoke French and the same pro-
> portion belonged at least nominally to the Catholic Church. More
> than eight in every ten Prussians were German (the rest were mostly
> Poles) and of the Germans 70 percent were Protestant. The Tsar's
> seventy million subjects included some notable minorities (five mil-
> lion Poles, three and a half million Finns, Ests, Letts and Latvians,
> and three million assorted Caucasians), but that still left fifty mil-
> lions who were both Russian and Orthodox. And the inhabitants of
> the British Isles were 90 percent English-speaking and 70 percent
> Protestant. Countries like this needed little holding together; they
> had an intrinsic cohesion. By contrast the Austrian Emperor ruled
> an ethnic mishmash that must have made him groan every time he
> thought about it. He and eight million of his subjects were German,
> but twice as many were Slavs of one sort or another (Czechs, Slo-
> vaks, Poles, Ruthenians, Slovenes, Croats and Serbs), five million

were Hungarians, five million Italians and two million Romanians.
What sort of nation did that make?

The answer is none at all.[42]

The Habsburg army, regarded as "one of the most important, if not
the most important, single institutions" in the empire, reflected this
ethnic diversity. "In 1865 [that is, the year before the decisive clash
with Prussia for mastery of Germany], the army had 128,286 Germans,
96,300 Czechs and Slovaks, 52,700 Italians, 22,700 Slovenes, 20,700
Rumanians, 19,000 Serbs, 50,100 Ruthenes, 37,700 Poles, 32,500 Magyars, 27,600 Croats, and 5,100 men of other nationalities on its muster
roles."[43] Although this made the army almost as colorful and variegated as the British-Indian regiments under the Raj, it also created all
sorts of disadvantages when compared with the much more homogeneous French or Prussian armies.

This potential military weakness was compounded by the lack of
adequate funding, which was due partly to the difficulties of raising
taxes in the empire, but chiefly caused by the meagerness of its commercial and industrial base. Although historians now speak of "the
economic rise of the Habsburg Empire"[44] in the period 1760–1914, the
fact is that during the first half of the nineteenth century industrialization occurred only in certain western regions, such as Bohemia, the
Alpine lands, and around Vienna itself, whereas the greater part of the
empire remained relatively untouched. While Austria itself advanced,
therefore, the empire *as a whole* fell behind Britain, France, and
Prussia in terms of per capita industrialization, iron and steel production, steam-power capacities, and so on.

What was more, the costs of the French wars "had left the empire
financially exhausted, burdened with a heavy public debt and a mass
of depreciated paper money,"[45] which virtually compelled the government to keep military spending to a minimum. In 1830 the army was
allocated the equivalent of only 23 percent of the total revenues (down
from 50 percent in 1817), and by 1848 that share had sunk to 20
percent. When crises occurred, as in 1848–1849, 1854–1855, 1859–1860,
and 1864, extraordinary increases in military spending were authorized; but they were never enough to bring the army up to anywhere like
full strength, and they were just as swiftly reduced when the crisis was
perceived to be over. For example, the military budget was 179 million
florins in 1860, dropped to 118 million by 1863, rose to 155 million in
the 1864 conflict with Denmark, and was drastically cut back to 96
million in 1865—again, just a year before the war with Prussia. None
of these totals kept pace with the military budgets of France, Britain,
and Russia, or (a little later) that of Prussia; and since the Austrian
military administration was regarded as corrupt and inefficient even
by mid-nineteenth-century standards, the monies which *were* al-

located were not very well spent. In sum, the armed strength of the Habsburg Empire in no way corresponded to the wars it might be called upon to fight.[46]

All this is not to antedate the demise of the empire. Its staying power, as many historians have remarked, was quite extraordinary: having survived the Reformation, the Turks, and the French Revolution, it also proved capable of weathering the events of 1848–1849, the defeat of 1866, and, until the very last stages, the strains of the First World War. While its weaknesses were evident, it also possessed strengths. The monarchy commanded the loyalty not only of the ethnic German subjects but also of many aristocrats and "service" families in the non-German lands; its rule, say, in Poland was fairly benign compared with the Russian and Prussian administrations. Furthermore, the complex, multinational character of the empire, with its array of local rivalries, permitted a certain amount of *divide et impera* from the center, as its careful use of the army demonstrated: Hungarian regiments were stationed chiefly in Italy and Austria and Italian regiments in Hungary, half of the Hussar regiments were stationed abroad, and so on.[47]

Finally, it possessed the negative advantage that none of the other Great Powers—even when engaged in hostilities with the Habsburg Empire—knew what to put in its place. Czar Nicholas I might resent Austrian pretensions in the Balkans, but he was willing enough to lend an army to help crush the Hungarian revolution of 1848; France might intrigue to drive the Habsburgs out of Italy, but Napoleon III also knew that Vienna could be a useful future ally against Prussia or Russia; and Bismarck, though determined to expel all Austrian influence from Germany, was keen to preserve the Habsburg Empire as soon as it capitulated in 1866. As long as that situation existed, the Empire would survive—on sufferance.

Despite its losses during the Napoleonic War, the position of France in the half-century following 1815 was significantly better than that of either Prussia or the Habsburg Empire in many respects.[48] Its national income was much larger, and capital was more readily available; its population was far bigger than Prussia's and more homogeneous than the Habsburg Empire's; it could more easily afford a large army, and could pay for a considerable navy as well. Nonetheless, it is treated here as a "middle power" simply because strategical, diplomatic, and economic circumstances all combined to prevent France from concentrating its resources and gaining a decisive lead in any particular sphere.

The overriding fact about the years 1814–1815, at the power-political level, was that all of the other great states had shown themselves determined to prevent French attempts to maintain a hegemony over

Europe; and not only were London, Vienna, Berlin, and St. Petersburg willing to compose their quarrels on other issues (e.g., Saxony) in order to defeat Napoleon's final bid, but they were also intent upon erecting a postwar system to block France off in the future from its traditional routes of expansion. Thus, while Prussia acted as guardian to the Rhineland, Austria strengthened its position in northern Italy, and British influence was expanded in the Iberian peninsula; behind all this lay a large Russian army, ready to move across Europe in defense of the 1815 settlement. In consequence, however, much Frenchmen of all parties might urge a policy of "recovery,"[49] it was plain that no dramatic improvement was possible. The best that could be achieved was, on the one hand, the recognition that France was an equal partner in the European Concert, and on the other, the restoration of French political influence in neighboring regions *alongside* that of the existing powers. Yet even when the French could achieve parity with, say, the British in the Iberian Peninsula and return to playing a major role in the Levant, they always had to be wary of provoking another coalition against them. Any move by France into the Low Countries, as it became clear in the 1820s and 1830s, instinctively produced an Anglo-Prussian alliance which was too strong to combat.

The other card available to Paris was to establish close relations with *one* of the Great Powers, which could then be exploited to secure French aims.[50] Given the latent rivalries between the other states and the considerable advantages a French alliance could offer (money, troops, weapons), this was a plausible assumption; yet it was flawed in three respects. First, the other power might be able to exploit the French more than France could exploit it—as Metternich did in the mid-1830s, when he entertained French overtures simply to divide London and Paris. Secondly, the changes of regime which occurred in France in these decades inevitably affected diplomatic relations in a period where ideology played so large a role. For example, the long-felt hopes of an alliance with Russia crashed with the coming of the 1830 revolution in France. Finally, there remained the insuperable problem that while several of the other powers wanted to cooperate with France at certain times, none of them in this period desired a change in the status quo: that is, they offered the French only diplomatic friendship, not the promise of territorial gain. Not until after the Crimean War was there any widespread sentiment outside France for a reordering of the 1815 boundaries.

These obstacles might have appeared less formidable had France been as strong vis-à-vis the rest of Europe as it had been under Louis XIV at the height of his power, or under Napoleon at the height of his. But the fact was that France after 1815 was not a particularly dynamic country. Perhaps as many as 1.5 million Frenchmen had died in the wars of 1793–1815,[51] and, more significant still, the French population increase was slower than that of any other Great Power throughout the nineteenth century. Not only had that lengthy conflict distorted the French economy in the various ways mentioned above (see pp. 131–33 above), but the coming of peace exposed it to the commercial challenge of its great British rival. "The cardinal fact for most French producers after 1815 was the existence of an overwhelmingly dominant and powerful industrial producer not only as their nearest neighbor but as a mighty force in all foreign markets and sometimes even in their own heavily protected domestic market."[52] This lack of competitiveness, the existing disincentives within France to modernize (e.g., small size of agricultural holdings, poor communications, essentially local markets, absence of cheap, readily available coal), and the loss of any stimulus from overseas markets meant that between 1815 and 1850 its rate of industrial growth was considerably less than Britain's. At the beginning of the century, the latter's manufacturing output was level with France's; by 1830 it was 182.5 percent of France's; and by 1860 that had risen to 251 percent.[53] Moreover, even when France's rate of railway construction and general industrialization began to quicken in the second half of the nineteenth century, it found to its alarm that Germany was growing even faster.

Yet it is now no longer so clear to historians that France's economy during this century should be airily dismissed as "backward" or "disappointing"; in many respects, the path taken by Frenchmen toward national prosperity was just as logical as the quite different route taken by the British.[54] The social horrors of the Industrial Revolution were less widespread in France; yet by concentration upon high-quality rather than mass-produced goods, the value per capita added to each manufacture was substantially greater. If the French on the whole did not invest domestically in large-scale industrial enterprises, this was often a matter of calculation rather than a sign of poverty or retardation. There was, in fact, considerable surplus capital in the country, much of which went into industrial investments elsewhere in Europe.[55] French governments were not likely to be embarrassed by a shortage of funds, and there *was* investment in munitions and in metallurgical processes related to the armed forces. It was French inventors who produced the shell gun under General Paixhans, the "epoch-making ship designs" of the *Napoleon* and *La Gloire*, and the Minié bullet and rifling.[56]

Nevertheless, the fact remains that France's *relative* power was being eroded in economic terms as well as in other respects. While France was, to repeat, greater than Prussia or the Habsburg Empire, there was no sphere in which it was the decisive leader, as it had been a century earlier. Its army was large, but second in numbers to Russia's. Its fleet, erratically supported by successive French administrations, was usually second in size to the Royal Navy—but the gap between them was enormous. In terms of manufacturing output and national product, France was falling behind its trail-blazing neighbor. Its launching of *La Gloire* was swiftly eclipsed by the Royal Navy's H.M.S. *Warrior,* just as its field artillery fell behind Krupp's newer designs. It did play a role outside Europe, but again its possessions and influence were far less extensive than Britain's.

All this points to another acute problem which made difficult the measurement—and often the deployment—of France's undoubted strength. It remained a classic *hybrid* power,[57] frequently torn between its European and its non-European interests; and this in turn affected its diplomacy, which was already complicated enough by ideological and balance-of-power considerations. Was it more important to check Russia's advance upon Constantinople than to block British pretensions in the Levant? Should it be trying to prize Austria out of Italy, or to challenge the Royal Navy in the English Channel? Should it encourage or oppose the early moves toward German unification? Given the pros and cons attached to each of these policies, it is not surprising that the French were often found ambivalent and hesitating, even when they were regarded as a full member of the Concert.

On the other hand, it must not be forgotten that the general circumstances which constrained France also enabled it to act as a check upon the other Great Powers. If this was especially the case under Napoleon III, it was also true, incipiently, even in the late 1820s. Simply because of its size, France's recovery had implications in the Iberian and Italian peninsulas, in the Low Countries, and farther afield. Both the British and the Russian attempts to influence events in the Ottoman Empire needed to take France into account. It was France, much more than the wavering Habsburg Empire or even Britain, which posed the chief military check to Russia during the Crimean War. It was France which undermined the Austrian position in Italy, and it was chiefly France which, less dramatically, ensured that the British Empire did not have a complete monopoly of influence along the African and Chinese coasts. Finally, when the Austro-Prussian "struggle for mastery in Germany" rose to a peak, both rivals revealed their deep concern over what Napoleon III might or might not do. In sum, following its recovery after 1815 France during the decades following remained a considerable power, very active diplomatically, reasonably strong militarily, and better to have as a friend than as a rival—even if its own leaders were aware that it was no longer so dominant as in the previous two centuries.

The Crimean War and the Erosion
of Russian Power

Russia's *relative* power was to decline the most during the post-1815 decades of international peace and industrialization—although that was not fully evident until the Crimean War (1854–1856) itself. In 1814 Europe had been awed as the Russian army advanced to the west, and the Paris crowds had prudently shouted "Vive l'empéreur Alexandre!" as the czar entered their city behind his brigades of cossacks. The peace settlement itself, with its archconservative emphasis against future territorial and political change, was underwritten by a Russian army of 800,000 men—as far superior to any rivals on land as the Royal Navy was to other fleets at sea. Both Austria and Prussia were overshadowed by this eastern colossus, fearing its strength even as they proclaimed monarchical solidarity with it. If anything, Russia's role as the gendarme of Europe increased when the messianic Alexander I was succeeded by the autocratic Nicholas I (1825–1855); and the latter's position was further enhanced by the revolutionary events of 1848–1849, when, as Palmerston noted, Russia and Britain were the only powers that were "standing upright."[58] The desperate appeals of the Habsburg government for aid in suppressing the Hungarian revolt were rewarded by the dispatch of three Russian armies. By contrast, the waverings of Frederick William IV of Prussia toward internal reform movements, together with the proposals for changes in the German Federation, provoked unrelenting Russian pressure until the court at Berlin accepted policies of domestic reaction and the diplomatic retreat at Oelmuetz. As for the "forces of change" themselves after 1848, all elements, whether defeated Polish and Hungarian nationalists, or frustrated bourgeois liberals, or Marxists, were agreed that the chief bulwark against progress in Europe would long remain the empire of the czars.

Yet at the economic and technological level, Russia was losing ground in an alarming way between 1815 and 1880, at least relative to other powers. This is not to say that there was no economic improvement, even under Nicholas I, many of whose officials had been hostile to market forces or to any signs of modernization. The population grew rapidly (from 51 million in 1816, to 76 million in 1860, to 100 million in 1880), and that of the towns grew the fastest of all. Iron production increased, and the textile industry multiplied in size. Between 1804 and 1860, it was claimed, the number of factories or industrial enterprises rose from 2,400 to over 15,000. Steam engines and modern machinery were imported from the west; and from the 1830s onward a railway network began to emerge. The very fact that historians have quarreled over whether an "industrial revolution" occurred in Russia during these decades confirms that things were on the move.[59]

But the blunt point was that the rest of Europe was moving far faster and that Russia was losing ground. Because of its far bigger population, it had easily possessed the largest *total* GNP in the early nineteenth century. Two generations later, that was no longer the case, as shown in Table 9.

Table 9. GNP of the European Great Powers, 1830–1890[60]
(at market prices, in 1960 U.S. dollars and prices; in billions)

	1830	1840	1850	1860	1870	1880	1890
Russia	10.5	11.2	12.7	14.4	22.9	23.2	21.1
France	8.5	10.3	11.8	13.3	16.8	17.3	19.7
Britain	8.2	10.4	12.5	16.0	19.6	23.5	29.4
Germany	7.2	8.3	10.3	12.7	16.6	19.9	26.4
Habsburg Empire	7.2	8.3	9.1	9.9	11.3	12.2	15.3
Italy	5.5	5.9	6.6	7.4	8.2	8.7	9.4

But these figures were even more alarming when the per capita amount of GNP is studied (see Table 10).

Table 10. Per Capita GNP of the European Great Powers, 1830–1890[61]
(in 1960 U.S. dollars and prices)

	1830	1840	1850	1860	1870	1880	1890
Britain	346	394	458	558	628	680	785
Italy	265	270	277	301	312	311	311
France	264	302	333	365	437	464	515
Germany	245	267	308	354	426	443	537
Habsburg Empire	250	266	283	288	305	315	361
Russia	170	170	175	178	250	224	182

The figures show that the increase in Russia's *total* GNP which occurred during these years was overwhelmingly due to the rise in its population, whether by births or by conquests in Turkestan and elsewhere, and had little to do with real increases in productivity (especially industrial productivity). Russia's per capita income, and national product, had always been behind that of western Europe; but it now fell even further behind, from (for example) one-half of Britain's per capita income in 1830 to one-quarter of that figure sixty years later.

In the same way, the doubling of Russia's iron production in the early nineteenth century compared badly with Britain's *thirtyfold* increase;[62] within two generations, Russia had changed from being Europe's largest producer and exporter of iron into a country increasingly dependent upon imports of western manufactures. Even the improvements in rail and steamship communications need to be put in

perspective. By 1850 Russia had little over 500 miles of railroad, compared with the United States' 8,500 miles; and much of the increase in
steamship trade, on the great rivers or out of the Baltic and Black seas,
revolved around the carriage of grains needed for the burgeoning
home population and to pay for imported manufactured goods by the
dispatch of wheat to Britain. What new developments occurred were
all too frequently in the hands of foreign merchants and entrepreneurs
(the export trade certainly was), and turned Russia ever more into a
supplier of *primary* materials for advanced economies. On closer examination of the evidence, it appears that most of the new "factories"
and "industrial enterprises" employed fewer than sixteen people, and
were scarcely mechanized at all. A general lack of capital, low consumer demand, a minuscule middle class, vast distances and extreme
climates, and the heavy hand of an autocratic, suspicious state made
the prospects for industrial "takeoff" in Russia more difficult than in
virtually anywhere else in Europe.[63]

For a long while, these ominous economic trends did not translate
into a noticeable Russian military weakness. On the contrary, the post-
1815 preference shown by the Great Powers for *ancien régime* structures in general could nowhere be more clearly seen than in the social
composition, weaponry, and tactics of their armies. Still in the shadows cast by the French Revolution, governments were more concerned
about the political and social reliability of their armed forces than
about military reforms; and the generals themselves, no longer facing
the test of a great war, emphasized hierarchy, obedience, and caution—traits reinforced by Nicholas I's obsession with formal parades
and grand marches. Given these general circumstances, the sheer size
of the Russian army and the steadiness of its mass conscripts appeared
more impressive to outside observers than such arcane matters as
military logistics or the general level of education among the officer
corps. What was more, the Russian army *was* active and often successful in its frequent campaigns of expansion into the Caucasus and
across Turkestan—thrusts which were already beginning to worry the
British in India, and to make Anglo-Russian relations in the nineteenth
century much more strained than they had been in the eighteenth.[64]
Equally impressive to outside eyes was the Russian suppression of the
Hungarian rebellion of 1848–1849, and the czar's claim that he stood
ready to dispatch 400,000 troops to quell the contemporaneous revolt
in Paris. What those observers failed to note was the less imposing fact
that the greater part of the Russian army was always pinned down by
internal garrison duties, by "police" actions in Poland and Finland,
and by other activities, such as border patrols and the Military Colonies; and that what was left was not particularly efficient—of the 11,000
casualties incurred in the Hungarian campaign, for example, all but

1,000 were caused by diseases, because of the inefficiency of the army's logistical and medical services.[65]

The campaigning in the Crimea from 1854 until 1855 provided an all too shocking confirmation of Russia's backwardness. Czarist forces could not be concentrated. Allied operations in the Baltic (while never very serious), together with the threat of Swedish intervention, pinned down as many as 200,000 Russian troops in the north. The early campaigning in the Danubian principalities, and the far greater danger that Austria would turn its threats of intervention into reality, posed a danger to Bessarabia, the western Ukraine, and Russian Poland. The fighting against the Turks in the Caucasus placed immense demands upon both troops and supply systems, as did the defense of Russian territories in the Far East.[66] When the Anglo-French assault on the Crimea brought the war to a highly sensitive region of Russian territory, the armed forces of the czar were incapable of repudiating such an invasion.

At sea, Russia possessed a fair-sized navy, with competent admirals, and it was able to destroy completely the weaker Turkish fleet at Sinope in November 1853; but as soon as the Anglo-French fleets entered the fray, the positions were reversed.[67] Many Russian vessels were fir-built and unseaworthy, their firepower was inadequate, and their crews were half-trained. The allies had many more steam-driven warships, some of them armed with shrapnel shells and Congreve rockets. Above all, Russia's enemies had the industrial capacity to build newer vessels (including dozens of steam-driven gunboats), so that their advantage became greater as the war lengthened.

But the Russian army was even worse off. The ordinary infantryman fought well, and, under the inspired leadership of Admiral Nakhimov and the engineering genius of Colonel Todtleben, Russia's prolonged defense of Sevastopol was a remarkable feat. But in all other respects the army was woefully inadequate. The cavalry regiments were unadventurous and their parade-ground horses incapable of strenuous campaigning (here the irregular cossack forces were better). Worse still, the Russian soldiers were wretchedly armed. Their old-fashioned flintlock muskets had a range of 200 yards, whereas the rifles of the Allied troops could fire effectively up to 1,000 yards; thus Russian casualties were far heavier.

Worst of all, even when the hugeness of the task was known, the Russian system *as a whole* was incapable of responding to it. Army leadership was poor, ridden with personal rivalries, and never able to produce a coherent grand strategy—here it simply reflected the general incompetence of the czar's government. There were very few trained and educated officers of the middle rank, such as the Prussian army possessed in abundance, and initiative was totally frowned upon. Astonishingly, there were also very few reservists to call up in the event of a national emergency, since the adoption of a mass short-service system would have involved the demise of serfdom.* One consequence of this system was that Russia's long-service army included many *over-aged* troopers; another even more fatal consequence was that some 400,000 of the new recruits hastily enrolled at the beginning of the war were totally untrained—for there were insufficient officers to do the job—and the withdrawal of that many men from the serf labor market hurt the Russian economy.

Finally, there were the logistical and economic weaknesses. Since there were no railways south of Moscow (!), the horse-drawn supply wagons had to cross hundreds of miles of steppes, which were a sea of mud during the spring thaw and the autumn rains. Furthermore, the horses themselves required so much fodder (which in turn had to be carried by other packhorses, and so on) that an enormous logistical effort produced disproportionately small results: allied troops and reinforcements could be sent from France and England by sea to the Crimea in three weeks, whereas Russian troops from Moscow some-times took three months to reach the front. More alarming still was the collapse of the Russian army's equipment stocks. "At the beginning of the war 1 million guns had been stockpiled; [at the end of 1855] only 90,000 were left. Of the 1,656 field guns, only 253 were available. . . . Stocks of powder and shot were in even worse shape."[68] The longer the war lasted, the greater the allied superiority became, while the British blockade stifled the importation of new weapons.

But the blockade did more than that: it cut off Russia's flow of grain and other exports (except for those going overland to Prussia) and made it impossible for the Russian government to pay for the war other than by heavy borrowing. Military expenditures, which even in peacetime took four-fifths of the state revenue, rose from about 220 million rubles in 1853 to about 500 million in both war years 1854 and 1855. To cover part of the alarming deficit, the Russian treasury bor-rowed in Berlin and Amsterdam, but then the ruble's international value tumbled; to cover the rest, it resorted to printing paper money, which led to large-scale price inflation and increasing peasant unrest. The earlier, brave attempts of the finance ministry to create a silver-based ruble and to ban all promissory notes—which had been the ruination of "sound finance" during the Napoleonic War and the cam-paigns against Persia, Turkey, and the Polish rebels—were now com-pletely wrecked by the war in the Crimea. If Russia persisted in its fruitless struggle, the Crown Council was warned on January 15, 1856, the state would go bankrupt.[69] Negotiations with the Great Powers offered the only way to avoid catastrophe.

---

*It being argued that any man who had competed two or three years in the army could no longer be a serf; and that it was safer to recruit a small proportion of each year's males as *long-service* troops.

All this is not to say that the allies found the Crimean War easy; for them, too, the campaigning involved strain and unpleasant shocks. The least badly affected, interestingly enough, was France, which for once benefited from being a hybrid power—it was less backward industrially and economically than Russia, and less "unmilitarized" than Britain. The armed forces sent eastward under General Saint-Arnaud were well equipped, well trained because of their North African operations, and reasonably experienced in overseas campaigning; their logistical and medical-support systems were as efficient as any which a midcentury administration could produce; and the French officers showed justified bemusement at their amateur British opposite numbers with their overloaded baggage. The French expeditionary force was by far the largest and made most of the major breakthroughs in the war. To some degree, then, the nation recovered its Napoleonic heritage in this fighting.

By the later stages of the campaign, however, France was beginning to reveal signs of strain. Although it was a rich country, its government had to compete for ready funds with railway constructors and others seeking money from the Crédit Mobilier and other bankers. Gold was being drained away to the Crimea and Constantinople, sending up prices at home; and poor grain harvests didn't help. Although the full war losses (100,000) were not known, early French enthusiasm for the conflict quickly evaporated. Popular riots over inflation reinforced the argument, widespread after the news of Sevastopol's fall, that the war was being prolonged only for selfish and ambitious British purposes.[70] By that time, too, Napoleon III was eager to bring the fighting to an end: Russia had been chastised, France's prestige had been boosted (and would rise further following a great international peace conference in Paris), and it was important not to get too distracted from German and Italian matters by escalating the conflict around the Black Sea. Even if he could not substantially redraw the map of Europe in 1856, Napoleon could certainly feel that France's prospects were rosier than at any time since Waterloo. For another decade, the post–Crimean War fissures in the old Concert of Europe would allow that illusion to continue.

The British, by contrast, were far from satisfied with the Crimean War. Despite certain efforts at reform, the army was still in the Wellingtonian mold, and its commander, Raglan, had actually been Wellington's military secretary in the Peninsular War. The cavalry was adequate—as cavalry forces go—but often misused (not just at Balaclava), and could scarcely be deployed in the Sevastopol siegeworks. While the soldiers were toughened old sweats who fought hard, the appalling lack of warm shelter in Crimean rains and winter, the incapacity of the army's primitive medical services to handle large-scale outbreaks of dysentery and cholera, and the paucity of land transport caused needless losses and setbacks which infuriated the British nation. More embarrassing still, since the British army, like the Russian, was a long-service force chiefly useful for garrison duties, there was no trained reserve which could be drawn upon in wartime; but while the Russians could at least forcibly conscript hundreds of thousands of raw recruits, laissez-faire Britain could not, leaving the government in the embarrassing position of advertising for foreign mercenaries with which to fill the shortfall of troops in the Crimea. Yet while its army always remained a junior partner to the French, Britain's navy had no real chance to secure a Nelsonic victory against a foe who prudently withdrew his fleet into fortified harbors.[71]

The explosion of public discontent in Britain at the London *Times'* notorious revelations of military incompetence and of the sufferings of the sick and wounded troops can only be mentioned in passing here; it not only led to a change of ministry, but also provoked an earnest debate upon the difficulties inherent in being "a liberal state at war."[72] More than that, the whole affair revealed that what had seemed to be Britain's peculiar strengths—a low degree of government, a small imperial army, a heavy reliance upon sea power, an emphasis upon individual freedoms and an unfettered press, the powers of Parliament and of individual ministers—quite easily turned into weaknesses when the country was called upon to carry out an extensive military operation throughout all seasons against a major foe.

The British response to this test was (rather like the American response to wars in the twentieth century) to allocate vast amounts of money to the armed forces in order to make up for past neglect; and, once again, the crude figures of the military expenditures of the combatants go a long way toward explaining the eventual outcome of the conflict (see Table 11).

Table 11. Military Expenditures of the Powers in the Crimean War[73]
(millions of pounds)

	1852	1853	1854	1855	1856
Russia	15.6	19.9	31.3	39.8	37.9
France	17.2	17.5	30.3	43.8	36.3
Britain	10.1	9.1	76.3	36.5	32.3
Turkey	2.8	?	?	3.0	?
Sardinia	1.4	1.4	1.4	2.2	2.5

But even when Britain bestirred itself, it could not swiftly create the proper instruments of power: military spending might multiply, hundreds of steam-driven vessels might be ordered, the expeditionary force might enjoy a *surplus* of tents and blankets and ammunition by 1855, and a belligerent Palmerston might assert the need to break up the Russian Empire; yet Britain's small army could do little if France moved toward peace and Austria stayed neutral—which was precisely what happened in the months after the fall of Sevastopol. Only if the British nation and political economy became much more "militarized" could it sustain the war alone against Russia in any meaningful way; but the likely costs were far too high to a political leadership already made uneasy at the strategical, constitutional, and economic difficulties which the Crimean campaign had thrown up.[74] While feeling cheated of a proper victory, therefore, the British also were willing to compromise. What all this did was to make many Europeans (Frenchmen and Austrians as well as Russians) suspicious of London's aims and reliability, just as it made the British public ever more disgusted at being entangled in continental affairs. While Napoleon's France moved to the center of the European stage of 1856, therefore, Britain steadily moved to the edge—a drift which the Indian Mutiny (1857) and domestic reform movements could only intensify.

If the Crimean War had shocked the British, that was nothing compared to the blow which had been delivered to Russia's power and self-esteem—not to mention the losses caused by the 480,000 deaths. "We cannot deceive ourselves any longer," Grand Duke Konstantin Nikolayevich flatly stated. ". . . we are both weaker and poorer than the first-class powers, and furthermore poorer not only in material but also in mental resources, especially in matters of administration."[75] This knowledge drove the reformers in the Russian state toward a whole series of radical changes, most notably the abolition of serfdom. In addition, railway-building and industrialization were given far greater encouragement under Alexander II than under his father. Coal production, iron and steel production, large-scale utilities, and far bigger industrial enterprises were more in evidence from the 1860s onward, and the statistics provided in the economic histories of Russia are impressive enough at first sight.[76]

As ever, however, a change of perspective affects one's judgment. Could this modernization keep pace with, let alone draw ahead of, the vast annual increases in the numbers of poor, uneducated peasants? Could it match the explosive increases in iron and steel production, and manufactures, taking place in the West Midlands, the Ruhr, Silesia, and Pittsburgh during the following two decades? Could it, even with its reorganized army, keep pace with the "military revolution" which the Prussians were about to reveal to the world, and which would emphasize again the *qualitative* over the *quantitative* elements of national strength? The answers to all those questions would disappoint a Russian nationalist, all too aware that his country's place in Europe was substantially reduced from the position of eminence it had occupied in 1815 and 1848.

The United States and the Civil War

As mentioned previously, observers of global politics from de Tocqueville onward felt that the rise of the Russian Empire went in parallel with that of the United States. To be sure, everyone admitted that there were fundamental differences in the political culture and constitutions of those two states, but in World Power terms they seemed very much alike in respect to their geographical size, their "open" and ever-moving frontiers, their fast-growing populations, and their scarcely tapped resources.[77] While much of that is true, the fact remains that throughout the nineteenth century there were important economic discrepancies between the United States and Russia which would have an increasing impact upon their national power. The first of these was in terms of total population, although the gap significantly narrowed between 1816 (Russia 51.2 million, United States 8.5 million) and 1860 (Russia 76 million, United States 31.4 million). What was more pertinent was the character of that population: whereas Russia consisted overwhelmingly of serfs, with low income and low production, Americans on their homesteads or in the swiftly growing cities generally* enjoyed a high standard of living, and of national output, relative to other countries. Already in 1800, wages had been about one-third higher than those in western Europe, and that superiority was to be preserved, if not increased, throughout the century. Despite the vast inflow of European immigrants by the 1850s, the ready availability of land in the west, together with constant industrial growth, caused labor to be relatively scarce and wages to be high, which in turn induced manufacturers to invest in labor-saving machinery, further stimulating national productivity. The young republic's isolation from European power struggles, and the *cordon sanitaire* which the Royal Navy (rather than the Monroe Doctrine) imposed to separate the Old World from the New, meant that the only threat to the United States' future prosperity could come from Britain itself. Yet despite sore memories of 1776 and 1812, and border disputes in the northwest,[78] an Anglo-American war was unlikely; the flow of British capital and manufactures toward the United States and the return flow of American raw materials (especially cotton) tied the two economies ever closer together and further stimulated American economic growth. Instead of having to divert financial resources into large-scale defense expenditures, therefore, a strategically secure United States could concentrate its own (and British) funds upon developing its vast economic potential. Neither conflict with the Indians nor the 1846 war with Mexico was a substantial drain upon such productive investment.

The result of all this was that even before the outbreak of the Civil

---

*Except the black slaves, and the still relatively populous Indians.

War in April 1861, the United States had become an economic giant, although its own distance from Europe, its concentration upon internal development (rather than foreign trade), and the rugged nature of the countryside partly disguised that fact. While its share of world manufacturing output in 1860 was well behind that of Great Britain, it had already surged past Germany and Russia and was on the point of overtaking France. The United States, with only 40 percent of Russia's population in 1860, had an urban population more than twice as large, produced 830,000 tons of iron to Russia's 350,000 tons, had an energy consumption from modern fuel sources fifteen times as large, and a railway mileage thirty times greater (and even three times greater than Britain's). By contrast, the United States possessed a regular army of a mere 26,000 men compared with Russia's gigantic force of 862,000.[79] The disparity between the economic indices and the military indices of the two continent-wide states was perhaps never greater than at this point.

Within another year, of course, the Civil War had begun to transform the amount of national resources which Americans devoted to military purposes. The origins and causes of that conflict are not for discussion here; but since the leadership of both sides had determined upon a fight to the finish, and since each side could call upon hundreds of thousands of men, the struggle was likely to be prolonged. What made it more so was the distances involved, with the "front" ranging from the Virginia coast to the Mississippi, and even farther westward into Missouri and Arkansas—much of this being forest, mountain range, and swamplands. Similarly, the North's naval blockade of its foes' ports involved patrolling a coastline as extensive as that between Hamburg and Genoa. Crushing the South, in other words, would be an extraordinarily difficult logistical and military task, especially for a people which had kept its armed forces to a minimum and had no experience of large-scale war.

Yet while the four years of conflict were exhausting and fearfully bloody—the Union losing about 360,000 men to the Confederacy's 258,000*—they also catalyzed the latent national power which the United States possessed, transforming it (at least for a short while) into the greatest military nation on earth before its post-1865 demobilization. From amateur beginnings, the armed forces of each side turned themselves into mass conscript armies, employing modern rifled artillery and small arms, grinding away in the siege warfare of northern Virginia or being shuttled en masse by rail to the western theaters, communicating by telegraph to army headquarters, and drawing upon the resources of a mobilized war economy; the naval campaigns, more-

---

*About one-third in battle, the rest chiefly through diseases. The grand total of around 620,000 was more than the American losses in World War I, World War II, and the Korean War put together, and was suffered by a much smaller population.

over, witnessed the first use of ironclads, of rotating turrets, of early torpedos and mines, and of swift, steam-driven commerce raiders. Since this conflict much more than either the Crimean struggle or Prussia's wars of unification lays claim to being the first real industrialized "total war" on proto-twentieth-century lines, it is worth noting why the North won.

The first and most obvious reason—assuming that willpower would remain equal on each side—was the disproportion in resources and population. It may have been true that the South enjoyed the morale advantage of fighting for its very existence and (usually) on its own soil; that it could call upon a higher proportion of white males who were used to riding and shooting; that it possessed determined and good-quality generals and that, for a long while, it could import munitions and other supplies to make up for its matériel deficiencies.[80] But none of these could fully compensate for the great numerical imbalance between the North and the South. While the former contained a population of approximately twenty million whites, the Confederacy had only six million. What was more, the Union's total was steadily enhanced by immigrants (more than 800,000 arrived between 1861 and 1865) and by the 1862 decision to enlist black troops—something which the South avoided, predictably enough, until the last few months of the war. Around two million men served in the Union Army, which reached a peak strength of about one million in 1864–1865, whereas only about 900,000 men fought for the Confederate Army, whose maximum strength was never more than 464,500—from which "peak," reached in late 1863, it slowly declined.

But there was, as usual, more to war than sheer numbers. Even to reach the army size it did, the South ran the risk of taking too many men away from agriculture, mines, and foundries, thus weakening its already questionable capacity to fight a prolonged war. From the very beginning, in fact, the Confederates found themselves disadvantaged economically. In 1860 the North possessed 110,000 manufacturing establishments to the South's 18,000 (and many of the latter relied upon Northern technological expertise and skilled laborers); the Confederacy produced only 36,700 tons of pig iron, whereas Pennsylvania's total alone was 580,000 tons; New York State manufactured almost $300 million worth of goods—well over four times the production of Virginia, Alabama, Louisiana, and Mississippi combined. This staggering disparity in the economic base of each belligerent steadily transformed itself into real military effectiveness.

For example, whereas the South could make very few rifles (chiefly from the machinery captured at Harper's Ferry) and heavily relied upon imports, the North massively expanded its home manufactures of rifles, of which nearly 1.7 million were produced. The North's railway system (some 22,000 miles in length, and fanning out from the east to the southwest) could be maintained, and even expanded, during the war; the South's mere 9,000 miles of track, and inadequate supplies of locomotives and rolling stock, was gradually worn out. Similarly, while neither side possessed much of a navy at the outset of the conflict, the South was disadvantaged by having no machine shop which could build marine engines, whereas the North possessed several dozen such establishments. Although it took time for the Union's maritime supremacy to make itself felt—during which period blockade runners brought European-made munitions to the Confederate Army, and Southern commerce raiders inflicted heavy losses upon the North's merchant marine—the net slowly and inexorably tightened around the South's ports. By December 1864 the Union's navy totaled some 671 warships, including 236 steam vessels built since the war's beginning. Northern sea power was also vital in giving its armed forces control of the great inland rivers, especially in the Mississippi-Tennessee region; it was the successful use of *combined* rail and water transport which aided the Union's offensives in the western theater.

Finally, the Confederates found it impossible to pay for the war. Their chief income in peacetime came from the export of cotton; when that trade dried up and when—to the South's disappointment—the European powers did not intervene in the struggle, there was no way to compensate for the loss. There were few banks in the South, and little liquid capital; and taxing land and slaves brought little revenue when the productivity of both was being hard hit by the war. Borrowing from abroad produced little, yet without foreign currency or specie it was difficult to pay for vital imports. Inevitably, perhaps, the Confederate treasury turned to the printing press, but "overabundant paper money combined with severe commodity shortages to create rampant inflation"[81]—which in turn dealt a severe blow to the populace's will to continue the fight. By contrast, the North could always raise enough money, from taxation and loans, to pay for the conflict; and its printing of "greenbacks" in some ways stimulated further industrial and economic growth. Impressively, the Union's productivity surged again during the war, not only in munitions, railway-building, and ironclad construction, but also in agricultural output. By the end of the war, Northern soldiers were probably better fed and supplied than any army in history. If there was going to be a particularly American approach to military conflict—an "American way of war," to use Professor Weigley's phrase[82]—then it was first forged here, in the Union's mobilization and deployment of its massive industrial-technological potential to crush its foe.

If all the above sounds too deterministic an explanation for the outcome of a conflict which seemed to sway backward and forward for nearly four years, then it may be worth stressing the fundamental strategical problem which faced the South. Given the imbalances in size and population, there was no way in which it could overrun the North; the best that could be achieved was to so blunt the enemy's armies, and willpower, that he would abandon his policy of coercion and admit the South's claims (to slavery, or to secede, or both). This strategy would have been greatly aided if the border states like Maryland and Kentucky had overwhelmingly voted to join the Confederacy, which simply didn't happen; and it would have been helped beyond measure if a foreign power like Britain had intervened, but to suppose that was likely was a staggering misreading of British political priorities in the early 1860s.[83] With the exclusion of those two possibilities of swinging the *overall* military balance in favor of the South, the Confederates were simply left with the strategy of resisting the Union's pressures and hoping that a majority of Northerners would tire of the war. But that meant, unavoidably, a long-drawn-out conflict—and the lengthier the war was, the more the Union could mobilize its greater resources, boost its munitions production, lay down hundreds of warships, and inexorably squeeze the South, by naval blockade, by unrelenting military pressure in northern Virginia, by long-range campaigning in the west, and by Sherman's devastating drives through enemy territories. As the South's economy, morale, and front-line forces waned—by the beginning of 1865 its "present for duty" troop total was down to 155,000 men—surrender was the only realistic choice left.

The Wars of German Unification

Although the American Civil War was studied by a number of European military observers,[84] its special features (of distance, of the wilderness, of being a civil conflict) made it appear less of a pointer to general military developments than the armed struggles which were to occur in Europe during the 1860s. There the Crimean War had not only undermined the old-style Concert diplomacy but had also caused each of the "flank" powers to feel less committed to intervention in the center: Russia needed many years to recover from its humiliating defeat; and Britain preferred to concentrate upon imperial and domestic issues. This therefore left European affairs dominated, artificially as it turned out, by France. Prussia, having occupied a seemingly inglorious place under Frederick William IV during the Crimean War, was now convulsed by the constitutional quarrels between his successor William I and the Prussian parliament, especially over the issue of army reform. The Habsburg Empire, for its part, was still juggling with the interrelated problem of preserving its Italian interests against Piedmont and its German interests against Prussia, while at the same time endeavoring to contain Hungarian discontents at home.

France, by contrast, seemed strong and confident under Napoleon III. Banking, railway, and industrial development had all advanced since the early 1850s. Its colonial empire was extended in West Africa, Indochina, and the Pacific. Its fleet was expanded so that at times (e.g., 1859) it caused alarm on the other side of the English Channel. Militarily and diplomatically, it seemed to be the decisive third force in any solution of either the German or the Italian question—as was amply shown in 1859, when France swiftly intervened on Piedmont's behalf in the short-lived war against Austria.[85]

Yet however important the battles of Magenta and Solferino were in compelling the Habsburg Empire to surrender its hold upon Lombardy, acute observers in 1859 would have noticed that it was Austrian military incompetence, not French military brilliance (and certainly not Piedmontese military brilliance!), which decided the outcome. France's army did have the advantage of possessing many more rifles than Austria—this being responsible for the numerous casualties which so unnerved the Emperor Francis Joseph—but French deficiencies were also remarkable: medical and ammunition supplies were sorely lacking, mobilization schedules were haphazard, and Napoleon III's own leadership was less than brilliant. This did not matter so much at the time, since the Habsburg army was weaker and the leadership of General Gyulai was even more dithering.[86] Military effectiveness is, after all, *relative*—which was later demonstrated by the fact that Habsburg forces could still deal easily with the Italians on land (at Custozza, in 1866) and at sea (at Lissa) even when they were incapable of taking on France, or Prussia, or Russia. But this meant, by extension, that France itself would not be automatically superior in a future conflict against a *different* foe. The outcome of that war would depend upon the varying levels of military leadership, weapons systems, and productive base possessed by each side.

Since it was precisely in the era of the 1850s and 1860s that the technological explosion caused by the Industrial Revolution made its first real impacts upon warfare, it is not surprising that armed services everywhere were now found grappling with unprecedented operational problems. What would be the more important arm in battle—the infantry with its new breech-loading rifles, or the artillery with its new steel-barreled, mobile guns? What was the impact of railways and telegraphs upon command in the field? Did the new technology of war give the advantage to the advancing army, or the defending one?[87] The proper answer to such questions was, of course, that it all depends on the circumstances. That is, the outcome would be affected not only by newer weaponry but also by the terrain in which it was used, the morale and tactical competence of the troops, the efficacy of the supply systems, and all of the other myriad factors which help to decide the fate of battles. Since knowing beforehand how everything would work out was an impossibility, the key factor was the possession of a military-political leadership adept at juggling the various elements and a military instrument flexible enough to respond to new circumstances. And in these vital respects, neither the Habsburg Empire nor even France were going to be as successful as Prussia.

The Prussian "military revolution" of the 1860s, soon to produce what Disraeli would grandly term the "German revolution" in European affairs, was based upon a number of interrelated elements. The first of these was a unique short-service system, pushed through by the new King Wilhelm I and his war minister against their Liberal opponents, which involved three years' obligatory service in the regular army and then another four in the reserve before each man passed into the Landwehr—which meant that the fully mobilized Prussian army had seven annual intakes.* Since no substitutes were permitted, and the Landwehr could take over most garrison and "rear area" duties, such a system gave Prussia a far larger front-line army relative to its population than any other Great Power had. This depended, in turn, upon a relatively high level of at least primary education among the people—a rapidly expandable, short-service system, in the opinion of most experts, would be difficult to work in a nation of uneducated peasants—and it depended also upon a superb organization simply to handle such great numbers. There was, after all, little use in raising a force of half a million or a million men if they could not be adequately trained, clothed, armed, and fed, and transported to the decisive battle zone; and it would be even more of a waste of manpower and resources if the army commander could not communicate with and control the sheer masses involved.

The body imparting control to this force was the Prussian General Staff, which rose from obscurity in the early 1860s to be "the brains of the army" under the elder Moltke's genius. Hitherto, most armies in peacetime had consisted of combat units, supported by quartermaster, personnel, engineering, and other branches; actual military staffs were scrambled together only when campaigning began and a command was established. In the Prussian case, however, Moltke had recruited the brightest products of the War Academy and taught them to plan and prepare for possible future conflicts. Operations plans had to be made, and frequently revised, well before the outbreak of hostilities; war games and maneuvers bore careful study, as did historical campaigns and operations carried out by other powers. A special department was created to supervise the Prussian railway system and make sure that troops and supplies could be speeded to their destinations. Above all, Moltke's staff system attempted to inculcate in the officer corps the operational practice of dealing with large bodies of men

---

*And, exceptionally, the first Landwehr annual intake as well.

(army corps or full armies) which would move and fight independently but always be ready to converge upon the scene of the decisive battle. If communication could not be maintained with Moltke's headquarters in the rear, generals at the front were permitted to use their initiative and to act according to a few basic ground rules.

The above is, of course, an idealized model. The Prussian army was not perfect and was to suffer from many teething troubles in actual battle even after the reforms of the early to middle 1860s. Many of the field commanders ignored Moltke's advice and crashed blindly ahead in premature attacks or in the wrong direction—the Austrian campaign of 1866 was full of such blunders.[88] At the tactical level, too, the frontal assault (and heavy loses) of the Prussian Guards at Gravelotte-St. Privat in 1870 demonstrated a crass stupidity. The railway supply system by itself did not guarantee success; often it merely built up a vast stockpile of stores at the frontier, while the armies which needed those stocks had moved away from any nearby lines. Nor could it be said that Prussian scientific planning had ensured that their forces always possessed the best weapons: Austrian artillery was clearly superior in 1866, and the French Chassepot bolt-action rifle was stupendously better in 1870.

The real point about the Prussian system was not that it was free of errors, but that the general staff carefully studied its past mistakes and readjusted training, organization, and weapons accordingly. When the weakness of its artillery was demonstrated in 1866, the Prussian army swiftly turned to the new Krupp breechloader which was going to be so impressive in 1870. When delays occurred in the railway supply arrangements, a new organization was established to improve matters. Finally, Moltke's emphasis upon the deployment of several full armies which could operate independently yet also come to one another's aid meant that even if one such force was badly mauled in detail—as actually occurred in both the Austro-Prussian and Franco-Prussian wars—the overall campaign was not ruined.[89]

It was therefore a combination of factors which gave the Prussians the swift victory over the Austrians in the summer of 1866 that few observers had anticipated. Although Hanover, Saxony, and other northern German states joined the Habsburg side, Bismarck's diplomacy had ensured that none of the Great Powers would intervene in the initial stages of the struggle; and this in turn gave Moltke the opportunity to dispatch three armies through separate mountain routes to converge on the Bohemian plain and assault the Austrians at Sadowa (Koeniggratz). In retrospect, the outcome seems all too predictable. Over one-quarter of the Habsburg forces were needed in Italy (where they were victorious); and the Prussian recruitment system meant that despite Prussia's population being less than half that of its various foes, Moltke could deploy almost as many front-line troops.

The Habsburg army had been underfinanced, had no real staff system, and was ineptly led by Benedek; and however bravely individual units fought, they were slaughtered in open clashes by the far superior Prussian rifles. By October 1866, the Habsburgs had been forced to cede Venetia and to withdraw from any interest in Germany—which was by then well on its way to being reorganized under Bismarck's North German Federation.[90]

The "struggle for mastery in Germany" was almost complete; but the clash over who was supreme in western Europe, Prussia or an increasingly nervous and suspicious France, had been brought much closer, and by the late 1860s each side was calculating its chances. Ostensibly, France still appeared the stronger. Its population was much larger than Prussia's (although the total number of *German-speakers* in Europe was greater). The French army had gained experience in the Crimea, Italy, and overseas. It possessed the best rifle in the world, the Chassepot, which far outranged the Prussian needlegun; and it had a new secret weapon, the *mitrailleuse,* a machine gun which could fire 150 rounds a minute. Its navy was far superior; and help was expected from Austria-Hungary and Italy. When the time came in July 1870 to chastise the Prussians for their effrontery (i.e., Bismarck's devious diplomacy over the future of Luxembourg, and over a possible Hohenzollern candidate to the Spanish throne), few Frenchmen had doubts about the outcome.

The magnitude and swiftness of the French collapse—by September 4 its battered army had surrendered at Sedan, Napoleon III was a prisoner, and the imperial regime had been overthrown in Paris—was a devastating blow to such rosy assumptions. As it turned out, neither Austria-Hungary nor Italy came to France's aid, and French sea power proved totally ineffective. All therefore had depended upon the rival armies, and here the Prussians proved indisputably superior. Although both sides used their railway networks to dispatch large forces to the frontier, the French mobilization was much less efficient. Called-up reservists had to catch up with their regiments, which had already gone to the front. Artillery batteries were scattered all over France, and could not be easily concentrated. By contrast, within fifteen days of the declaration of war, three German armies (of well over 300,000 men) were advancing into the Saarland and Alsace. The Chassepot rifle's advantage was all too frequently neutralized by the Prussian tactic of pushing forward their mobile, quick-firing artillery. The *mitrailleuse* was kept in the rear, and never employed effectively. Marshal Bazaine's lethargy and ineptness were indescribable, and Napoleon himself was little better. By contrast, while individual Prussian units blundered and suffered heavy losses in "the fog of war," Moltke's distant supervision of the various armies and his willingness to rearrange his plans to exploit unexpected circumstances kept up the momentum of the invasion until the French cracked. Although republican forces were to maintain a resistance for another few months, the German grip around Paris and upon northeastern France inexorably tightened; the fruitless counterattacks of the Army of the Loire and the irritations offered by *francs-tireurs* could not conceal the fact that France had been smashed as an independent Great Power.[91]

The triumph of Prussia-Germany was, quite clearly, a triumph of its military system; but, as Michael Howard acutely notes, "the military system of a nation is not an independent section of the social system but an aspect of it in its entirety."[92] Behind the sweeping advances of the German columns and the controlled orchestration of the general staff there lay a nation much better equipped and prepared for the conditions of modern warfare than any other in Europe. In 1870, the German states combined already possessed a larger population than France, and only disunity had disguised that fact. Germany had more miles of railway lines, better arranged for military purposes. Its gross national product and its iron and steel production were just then over-taking the French totals. Its coal production was two and a half times as great, and its consumption from modern energy sources was 50 percent larger. The Industrial Revolution in Germany was creating many more large-scale firms, such as the Krupp steel and armaments combine, which gave the Prusso-German state both military and indus-trial muscle. The army's short-service system was offensive to liberals inside and outside the country—and criticism of "Prussian militarism" was widespread in these years—but it mobilized the manpower of the nation for warlike purposes more effectively than the laissez-faire west or the backward, agrarian east. And behind all this was a people possessing a far higher level of primary and technical education, an unrivaled university and scientific establishment, and chemical lab-oratories and research institutes without an equal.[93]

Europe, to repeat the quip of the day, had lost a mistress and gained a master. Under Bismarck's astonishingly adroit handling, the Great Power system was going to be dominated by Germany for two whole decades after 1870; all roads, diplomats remarked, now led to Berlin. Yet as most people could see, it was not merely the cleverness and ruthlessness of the imperial chancellor which made Germany the most important power on the European continent. It was also German in-dustry and technology, which boomed still faster once national unifi-cation had been accomplished; it was German science and education and local administration; and it was the impressive Prussian army. That the Second German Reich possessed major internal flaws, over which Bismarck constantly fretted, was scarcely noticed by outside observers. Every nation in Europe, even the isolationist British to some degree, felt affected by this new colossus. The Russians, although stay-ing benevolently neutral during the 1870–1871 war and taking advan-

tage of the crisis in western Europe to improve their own position in
the Black Sea,[94] resented the fact that the European center of gravity
was now located in Berlin and secretly worried about what Germany
might do next. The Italians, who had occupied Rome in 1870 while the
French (the pope's protectors) were being crushed in Lorraine, steadily
gravitated toward Berlin. So, too, did the Austro-Hungarian Empire
(as it became known after Vienna's 1867 compromise with the Hungarians), which hoped to find in the Balkans compensation for its loss
of place in Germany and Italy—but was well aware that such an ambition might provoke a Russian reaction. Finally, the shocked and embittered French felt it necessary to reexamine and reform vast areas of
government and society (education, science, railways, the armed
forces, the economy) in what was to be a fruitless attempt to regain
parity with their powerful neighbor across the Rhine.[95] Both at the
time and even more in retrospect, the year 1870 was viewed as a
decisive watershed in European history.

On the other hand, perhaps because most countries felt the need to
draw breath after the turbulences of the 1860s, and because statesmen
operated cautiously under the new order, the *diplomatic* history of the
Great Powers for the decade or so after 1871 was one of a search for
stability. Being concerned respectively with the post–Civil War reconstruction and with the aftermath of the Meiji Revolution, neither the
United States nor Japan were part of the "system," which if anything
was more Eurocentric than before. While there now existed a recast
version of the "European pentarchy," the balances were considerably
altered from those which pertained after 1815. Prussia-Germany,
under Bismarck's direction, was now the most powerful and influential of the European states, in place of a Prussia which had always been
the weakest. There was also another new power, united Italy, but its
desperate condition of economic backwardness (especially the lack of
coal) meant that it was never properly accepted into the major league
of powers, even though it was obviously more important in European
diplomacy than countries such as Spain or Sweden.[96] What it did do,
because of its pretensions in the Mediterranean and North Africa, was
to move into a state of increasing rivalry with France, distracting the
latter power and offering a useful future ally to Germany; secondly,
because of its legacy of liberation wars against Vienna and its own
ambitions in the western Balkans, Italy also disconcerted Austria-Hungary (at least until Bismarck had cemented over those tensions in the
Austro-German-Italian "Triple Alliance" of 1882). This meant that neither Austria-Hungary nor France, the two chief "victims" of Germany's
rise, could concentrate its energies fully upon Berlin, since both now
possessed a vigorous (if not too muscular) Italy in their rear. And
whereas this fact simply added to the Austrian reasons for reconciling
themselves to Germany, and becoming a quasi-satellite in conse-

quence, it also meant that even France's greater degree of national strength and alliance worthiness[97] was compromised in any future struggle against Berlin by the existence of a hostile and unpredictable Italy to the south.

With France isolated, Austria-Hungary cowed, and the intermediate "buffer states" of southern Germany and Italy now merged into their larger national units,[98] the only substantial checks to the further aggrandizement of Germany seemed to lie with the independent "flank" powers of Russia and Great Britain. To British administrations oscillating between a Gladstonian emphasis upon internal reforms (1868–1874) and a Disraelian stress upon the country's "imperial" and "Asian" destinies (1874–1880), this issue of the European equilibrium rarely seemed very pressing. This was probably not the case in Russia, where Chancellor Gorchakov and others resented the transformation of their Prussian client-state into a powerful Germany; but such feelings were mingled with the close dynastic and ideological sympathies that existed between the courts of St. Petersburg and Potsdam after 1871, by the still-pressing Russian need to recover from the Crimean War disasters, by the hope of obtaining Berlin's support for Russian interests in the Balkans, and by the renewal of interest in central Asia. On the whole, however, the flank powers' likelihood of intervening in the affairs of west-central Europe would depend heavily upon what Germany itself did; there was certainly no need to become involved if it could be assumed that the second German Reich was now a satiated power.[99]

This assurance Bismarck himself was all too willing to give after 1871, since he had no wish to create a *gross-deutscher* ("Greater German") state which incorporated millions of Austrian Catholics, destroyed the Austro-Hungarian Empire, and left Germany isolated between a vengeful France and a suspicious Russia.[100] It therefore seemed to him far safer to go along with the creation of the Three Emperors' League (1873), a quasi-alliance which stressed the ideological solidarity of the eastern monarchies (as against "republican" France) and simultaneously cemented over some of the Austro-Russian clashes of interest in the Balkans. And when, during the "war-in-sight" crisis of 1875, indications arose that the German government might be contemplating a preventive war against France, the warnings from both London and (especially) St. Petersburg convinced Bismarck that there would be strong opposition to any further alterations in the European balance.[101] For internal-political as well as external-diplomatic reasons, therefore, Germany remained within the boundaries established in 1871—a "half-hegemonial power," as some historians have termed it—until its military-industrial growth and the political ambitions of a post-Bismarckian leadership would once again place it in a position to question the existing territorial order.[102]

However, to pursue that transformation would take us well into the next chapter. For the period of the 1870s and into the 1880s, Bismarck's own diplomacy ensured the preservation of the status quo which he now deemed essential to German interests. The chancellor was partially helped in this endeavor by the flaring-up, in 1876, of another acute phase in the age-old "eastern question" when Turkey's massacre of the Bulgarian Christians and Russia's military response to it turned all attention from the Rhine to Constantinople and the Black Sea.[103] It was true that the outbreak of hostilities on the lower Danube or the Dardanelles could be dangerous even to Germany, if the crisis was allowed to escalate into a full-scale Great Power war, as seemed quite possible by early 1878. However, Bismarck's diplomatic skills in acting as "honest broker" to bring all the Powers to a compromise at the Congress of Berlin reinforced the pressures for a peaceful solution of the crisis and emphasized again the central—and stabilizing—position in European affairs which Germany now occupied.

But the great Eastern Crisis of 1876–1878 also did a great deal for Germany's *relative* position. While the small Russian fleet in the Black Sea performed brilliantly against the Turks, the Russian army's 1877 campaigning revealed that its post–Crimean War reforms had not really taken effect. Although bravery and sheer numbers produced an eventual Russian victory over the Turks in both the Bulgarian and the Caucasian theaters of operation, there were far too many examples of "extremely inadequate reconnaissance of the enemy positions, lack of coordination between the units, and confusion in the high command";[104] and the threat of British and Austrian intervention on Turkey's behalf compelled the Russian government, once again aware of a looming bankruptcy, to agree to compromise on its demands by late 1877. If the Pan-Slavs in Russia were later to blame Bismarck for supervising the Berlin Conference which formalized those humiliating concessions, the fact remained that many among the St. Petersburg elite were more than ever aware of the need to maintain good relations with Berlin—and even to reenter, in a revised form, another Three Emperors' understanding in 1881. Similarly, although Vienna had threatened to break away from Bismarck's controls at the peak of the crisis in 1879, the secret Austro-German alliance of the following year tied it again to German strings, as did the later Three Emperors' alliance of 1881, and the Triple Alliance between Berlin, Vienna, and Italy of 1882. All of these agreements, moreover, had the effect of drawing the signatories away from France and placing them in some degree of dependence upon Germany.[105]

Finally, the events of the late 1870s had reemphasized the long-standing Anglo-Russian rivalry in the Near East and Asia, which inclined both of those powers to look toward Berlin for benevolent neutrality, and turned public attention even further away from Alsace-

Lorraine and central Europe. This tendency was to become even stronger in the 1880s, when a whole series of events—the French acquisition of Tunis (1881), the British intervention in Egypt (1882), the wholesale "scramble" for tropical Africa (1884 onward), and the renewed threat of an Anglo-Russian war over Afghanistan (1885)—marked the beginnings of the age of the "New Imperialism."[106] Although the longer-term effects of this renewed burst of western colonialism were going to profoundly alter the position of many of the Great Powers, the short-term consequence was to emphasize Germany's diplomatic influence within Europe and thus aid Bismarck's endeavors to preserve the status quo. If the peculiarly tortuous system of treaties and countertreaties which he devised during the 1880s was not likely to produce lasting stability, it nonetheless seemed to ensure that peace prevailed among the European powers at least in the near future.

Conclusions

With the important exception of the American Civil War, the period 1815–1885 had not witnessed any lengthy, mutually exhausting military struggles. The lesser campaigns of this age, like the Franco-Austrian clash in 1859 or the Russian attack upon Turkey in 1877, did little to affect the Great Power system. Even the more important wars were limited in some significant ways: the Crimean War was chiefly a regional one, and concluded before Britain had fully harnessed its resources; and the Austro-Prussian and Franco-Prussian wars were over in one season's campaigning—a remarkable contrast to the far lengthier conflicts of the eighteenth century. No wonder, then, that the vision which military leaders and strategic pundits entertained of Great Power struggles in the future was one of swift knockout victories *à la Prusse* in 1870—of railways and mobilization schedules, of general staff plans for a speedy offensive, of quick-firing guns and mass, short-service armies, all of which would be brought together to overwhelm the foe within a matter of weeks. That the newer, quick-firing weapons might, if used properly, benefit defensive rather than offensive warfare was not appreciated at the time; nor, alas, were the portents of the American Civil War, where a combination of irreconcilable popular principles and extensive terrain had made for a far lengthier and deadlier conflict than any short, sharp European conflict of this period.

Yet all of these wars—whether fought in the Tennessee Valley or the Bohemian plain, in the Crimean Peninsula or the fields of Lorraine—pointed to one general conclusion: the powers which were defeated were those that had failed to adopt to the "military revolution" of the mid-nineteenth century, the acquisition of new weapons, the mobilizing and equipping of large armies, the use of improved communications offered by the railway, the steamship, and the telegraph, and a productive industrial base to sustain the armed forces. In all of these conflicts, grievous blunders were to be committed on the battlefield by the generals and armies of the winning side from time to time—but they were never enough to cancel out the advantages which that belligerent possessed in terms of trained manpower, supply, organization, and economic base.

This leads to a final and more general set of remarks about the period after about 1860. As noted at the beginning of this chapter, the half-century which followed the battle of Waterloo had been characterized by the steady growth of an international economy, by large-scale productive increases caused by industrial development and technical change, by the relative stability of the Great Power system and the occurrence of only localized and short-term wars. In addition, while there had been some modernization of military and naval weaponry, new developments within the armed forces were far less than those occurring in civilian spheres exposed both to the Industrial Revolution and to constitutional-political transformation. The prime beneficiary of this half-century of change had been Britain; in terms both of productive power and of world influence, it probably reached its peak in the late 1860s (even if the policies of the first Gladstone ministry tended to conceal that fact). The prime losers had been the nonindustrialized peasant societies of the extra-European world, which were able to withstand neither the industrial manufactures nor the military incursions of the West. For the same fundamental reason, the less industrialized of the European Great Powers—Russia, the Habsburg Empire—began to lose their earlier place, and a newly united nation, Italy, never really made it into the first rank.

From the 1860s, moreover, these trends were to intensify. The volume of world trade and, even more important, the growth of manufacturing output increased swiftly. Industrialization, formerly confined to Britain and certain parts of continental Europe and North America, was beginning to transform other regions. In particular, it was boosting the positions of Germany, which in 1870 already possessed 13 percent of world *industrial* production, and of the United States, which even then had 23 percent of the total.[107] Thus the chief features of the international system which was emerging by the end of the nineteenth century were already detectable, even if few observers could fully recognize them. On the other hand, the relatively stable Pentarchy of the post-1815 Concert system was dissolving, not merely because its members were more willing to fight against each other by the 1860s than a few decades earlier, but also because some of those states were two or three times more powerful than others. On the other hand, Europe's own monopoly of modern industrial production was being broken across the Atlantic. Steam power, railways, electricity, and other instruments of modernization could benefit any society which had both the will and the freedom to adopt them.

The absence of major conflicts during that post-1871 period in which Bismarck dominated European diplomacy may have suggested that a new equilibrium had been established, following the fissures of the 1850s and 1860s. Yet away from the world of armies and navies and foreign offices, far-reaching industrial and technological developments were under way, changing the global economic balances more swiftly than ever before. And it would not be too long before those alterations in the productive/industrial base would have their impacts upon the military capacities and external policies of the Great Powers.

5

The Coming of a Bipolar World and the Crisis of the "Middle Powers": Part One, 1885–1918

In the winter of 1884–1885, the Great Powers of the world, joined by a few smaller states, met in Berlin in an attempt to reach an agreement over trade, navigation, and boundaries in West Africa and the Congo and the principles of effective occupation in Africa more generally.[1] In so many ways, the Berlin West Africa Conference can be seen, symbolically, as the zenith of Old Europe's period of predominance in global affairs. Japan was not a member of the conference; although modernizing swiftly, it was still regarded by the West as a quaint, backward state. The United States, by contrast, *was* at the Berlin Conference, since the issues of trade and navigation discussed there were seen by Washington as relevant to American interests abroad;[2] but in most other respects the United States remained off the international scene, and it was not until 1892 that the European Great Powers upgraded the rank of their diplomatic representatives to Washington from minister to ambassador—the mark of a first-division nation. Russia, too, was at the conference; but while its interests in Asia were considerable, in Africa it possessed little of note. It was, in fact, in the second list of states to be invited to the conference,[3] and played no role other than generally giving support for France against Britain. The center of affairs was therefore the triangular relationship between London, Paris, and Berlin, with Bismarck in the all-important middle position. The fate of the planet still appeared to rest where it had seemed to rest for the preceding century or more: in the chancelleries of Europe. To be sure, if the conference had been deciding the future of the Ottoman Empire instead of the Congo basin, then countries such as Austria-Hungary and Russia would have played a larger role. But that still would not gainsay what was reckoned at the time to be an incontrovertible truth: that Europe was the center of the world. It was in this same period that the Russian general Dragimirov would declare that "Far Eastern affairs are decided in Europe."[4]

Within another three decades—a short time indeed in the course of the Great Power system—that same continent of Europe would be tearing itself apart and several of its members would be close to collapse. Three decades further, and the end would be complete; much of the continent would be economically devastated, parts of it would be in ruins, and its very future would be in the hands of decision-makers in Washington and Moscow.

While it is obvious that no one in 1885 could accurately forecast the ruin and desolation which prevailed in Europe sixty years later, it *was* the case that many acute observers in the late nineteenth century sensed the direction in which the dynamics of world power were driving. Intellectuals and journalists in particular, but also day-to-day politicians, talked and wrote in terms of a vulgar Darwinistic world of struggle, of success and failure, of growth and decline. What was more, the future world order was already seen to have a certain shape, at least by 1895 or 1900.[5]

The most noticeable feature of these prognostications was the revival of de Tocqueville's idea that the United States and Russia would be the two great World Powers of the future. Not surprisingly, this view had lost ground at the time of Russia's Crimean disaster and its mediocre showing in the 1877 war against Turkey, and during the American Civil War and then in the introspective decades of reconstruction and westward expansion. By the late nineteenth century, however, the industrial and agricultural expansion of the United States and the military expansion of Russia in Asia were causing various European observers to worry about a twentieth-century world order which would, as the saying went, be dominated by the Russian knout and American moneybags.[6] Perhaps because neomercantilist commercial ideas were again prevailing over those of a peaceful, Cobdenite, free-trading global system, there was a much greater tendency than earlier to argue that changing economic power would lead to political and territorial changes as well. Even the usually cautious British prime minister Lord Salisbury admitted in 1898 that the world was divided into the "living" and "dying" powers.[7] The recent Chinese defeat in their 1894–1895 war with Japan, the humiliation of Spain by the United States in their brief 1898 conflict, and the French retreat before Britain over the Fashoda incident on the Upper Nile (1898–1899) were all interpreted as evidence that the "survival of the fittest" dictated the fates of nations as well as animal species. The Great Power struggles were no longer merely over European issues—as they had been in 1830 or even 1860—but over markets and territories that ranged across the globe.

But if the United States and Russia seemed destined by size and population to be among the future Great Powers, who would accompany them? The "theory of the Three World Empires"—that is, the popular belief that only the three (or, in some accounts, four) largest and most powerful nation-states would remain independent—exercised many an imperial statesman.[8] "It seems to me," the British minister for the colonies, Joseph Chamberlain, informed an 1897 audience, "that the tendency of the time is to throw all power into the hands of the greater empires, and the minor kingdoms—those which are non-progressive—seem to fall into a secondary and subordinate place. . . ."[9] It was vital for Germany, Admiral Tirpitz urged Kaiser Wilhelm, to build a big navy, so that it would be one of the "four World Powers: Russia, England, America and Germany."[10] France, too, must be up there, warned a Monsieur Darcy, for "those who do not advance, go backwards and who goes back goes under."[11] For the long-established powers, Britain, France, and Austria-Hungary, the issue was whether they could maintain themselves in the face of these new challenges to the international status quo. For the new powers, Germany, Italy, and Japan, the problem was whether they could break through to what Berlin termed a "world-political freedom" before it was too late.

It need hardly be said that not every member of the human race was obsessed with such ideas as the nineteenth century came to a close. Many were much more concerned about domestic, social issues. Many clung to the liberal, laissez-faire ideals of peaceful cooperation.[12] Nonetheless there existed in governing elites, military circles, and imperialist organizations a prevailing view of the world order which stressed struggle, change, competition, the use of force, and the organization of national resources to enhance state power. The less-developed regions of the globe were being swiftly carved up, but that was only the beginning of the story; with few more territories to annex, the geopolitician Sir Halford Mackinder argued, efficiency and internal development would have to replace expansionism as the main aim of modern states. There would be a far closer correlation than hitherto "between the larger geographical and the larger historical generalizations,"[13] that is, size and numbers would be more accurately reflected in the international balances, provided that those resources were properly exploited. A country with hundreds of millions of peasants would count for little. On the other hand, even a modern state would be eclipsed also if it did not rest upon a large enough industrial, productive foundation. "The successful powers will be those who have the greatest industrial base," warned the British imperialist Leo Amery. "Those people who have the industrial power and the power of invention and science will be able to defeat all others."[14]

*   *   *

Much of the history of international affairs during the following half-century turned out to be a fulfillment of such forecasts. Dramatic changes occurred in the power balances, both inside Europe and without. Old empires collapsed, and new ones arose. The *multipolar* world of 1885 was replaced by a *bipolar* world as early as 1943. The international struggle intensified, and broke into wars totally different from the limited clashes of nineteenth-century Europe. Industrial productivity, with science and technology, became an ever more vital component of national strength. Alterations in the international shares of manufacturing production were reflected in the changing international shares of military power and diplomatic influence. Individuals still counted—who, in the century of Lenin, Hitler, and Stalin, could say they did not?—but they counted in power politics only because they were able to control and reorganize the productive forces of a great state. And, as Nazi Germany's own fate revealed, the test of world power by war was ruthlessly uncaring to any nation which lacked the industrial-technical strength, and thus the military weaponry, to achieve its leader's ambitions.

If the broad outlines of these six decades of Great Power struggles were already being suggested in the 1890s, the success or failure of *individual* countries was still to be determined. Obviously, much depended upon whether a country could keep up or increase its manufacturing output. But much also depended, as always, upon the immutable facts of geography. Was a country near the center of international crises, or at the periphery? Was it safe from invasion? Did it have to face two or three ways simultaneously? National cohesion, patriotism, and the controls exercised by the state over its inhabitants were also important; whether a society withstood the strains of war would very much depend upon its internal makeup. It might also depend upon alliance politics and decision-making. Was one fighting as part of a large alliance bloc, or in isolation? Did one enter the war at the beginning, or halfway through? Did other powers, formerly neutral, enter the war on the opposite side?

Such questions suggest that any proper analysis of "the coming of a bipolar world, and the crisis of the 'middle powers' " needs to consider three separate but interacting levels of causality: first, the changes in the military-industrial productive base, as certain states became materially more (or less) powerful; second, the geopolitical, strategical, and sociocultural factors which influenced the responses of each *individual* state to these broader shifts in the world balances; and third, the diplomatic and political changes which also affected chances of success or failure in the great coalition wars of the early twentieth century.

The Shifting Balance of World Forces

Those *fin de siècle* observers of world affairs agreed that the pace of economic and political change was quickening, and thus likely to make the international order more precarious than before. Alterations had always occurred in the power balances to produce instability and often war. "What made war inevitable," Thucydides wrote in *The Peleponnesian War*, "was the growth of Athenian power and the fear which this caused in Sparta."[15] But by the final quarter of the nineteenth century, the changes affecting the Great Power system were more widespread, and usually swifter, than ever before. The global trading and communications network—telegraphs, steamships, railways, modern printing presses—meant that breakthroughs in science and technology, or new advances in manufacturing production, could be transmitted and transferred from one *continent* to another within a matter of years. Within five years of Gilcrist and Thomas's 1879 invention of a way to turn cheap phosphoric ores into basic steel, there were eighty-four basic converters in operation in western and central Europe,[16] and the process had also crossed the Atlantic. The result was *more* than a shift in the respective national shares of steel output; it also implied a significant shift in military potential.

Military potential is, as we have seen, not the same as military power. An economic giant could prefer, for reasons of its political culture or geographical security, to be a military pigmy, while a state without great economic resources could nonetheless so organize its society as to be a formidable military power. Exceptions to the simplistic equation "economic strength = military strength" exist in this period, as in others, and will need to be discussed below. Yet in an era of modern, industrialized warfare, the link between economics and strategy was becoming tighter. To understand the long-term shifts affecting the international power balances between the 1880s and the Second World War, it is necessary to look at the economic data. These data have been selected with a view to assessing a nation's potential for war, and therefore do not include some well-known economic indices* which are less helpful in that respect.

Population size by itself is never a reliable indicator of power, but Table 12 does suggest how, at least demographically, Russia and the United States could be viewed as a different sort of Great Power from

---

*E.g., shares of world trade, which disproportionately boost the position of maritime, trading nations, and underemphasize the economic power of states with a large degree of self-sufficiency.

the others, with Germany and (later) Japan beginning to draw a little away from the remainder.

Table 12. Total Population of the Powers, 1890–1938[17]
(millions)

		1890	1900	1910	1913	1920	1928	1938	
1	Russia	116.8	135.6	159.3	175.1	126.6	150.4	180.6	1
2	United States	62.6	75.9	91.9	97.3	105.7	119.1	138.3	2
3	Germany	49.2	56.0	64.5	66.9	42.8	55.4	68.5	4
4	Austria-Hungary	42.6	46.7	50.8	52.1	—	—	—	
5	Japan	39.9	43.8	49.1	51.3	55.9	62.1	72.2	3
6	France	38.3	38.9	39.5	39.7	39.0	41.0	41.9	7
7	Britain	37.4	41.1	44.9	45.6	44.4	45.7	47.6	5
8	Italy	30.0	32.2	34.4	35.1	37.7	40.3	43.8	6

There are, however, two ways of "controlling" the raw data of Table 12. The first is to compare the total population of a country with the part of it that is living in urban areas (Table 13), for that is usually a significant indicator of industrial/commercial modernization; the second is to correlate those findings with the per capita levels of industrialization, as measured against the "benchmark" country of Great Britain (Table 14). Both exercises are enormously instructive, and tend to reinforce each other.

Without getting into too detailed an analysis of the figures in Tables 13 and 14 at this stage, several broad generalizations can be made. Once such measures of "modernization" as the size of urban population and the extent of industrialization are introduced, the positions of most of the powers are significantly altered from those in Table 12: Russia drops from first to last, at least until its 1930s industrial expansion, Britain and Germany gain in position, and the United States' unique combination of having both a populous *and* a highly industrialized society stands out. Even at the beginning of this period, the gap between the strongest and the weakest of the Great Powers is large, both absolutely and relatively; by the eve of the Second World War, there still remain enormous differences. The process of modernization might involve all these countries going through the same "phases";[18] it did not mean that, in *power* terms, each would benefit to the same degree.

The important *differences* between the Great Powers emerge yet more clearly when one examines detailed data about industrial productivity. Since iron and steel output has often been taken as an indicator of potential military strength in this period, as well as of industrialization *per se,* the relevant figures are reproduced in Table 15.

But perhaps the best measure of a nation's industrialization is its

Table 13. Urban Population of the Powers (in millions) and as Percentage of the Total Population, 1890–1938[19]

	1890	1900	1910	1913	1920	1928	1938	
1 Britain	11.2	13.5	15.3	15.8	16.6	17.5	18.7	5
(1)	(29.9%)	(32.8%)	(34.9%)	(34.6%)	(37.3%)	(38.2%)	(39.2%)	(1)
2 United States	9.6	14.2	20.3	22.5	27.4	34.3	45.1	1
(2)	(15.3%)	(18.7%)	(22.0)	(23.1%)	(25.9%)	(28.7%)	(32.8%)	(2)
3 Germany	5.6	8.7	12.9	14.1	15.3	19.1	20.7	3
(4)	(11.3%)	(15.5%)	(20.0%)	(21.0%)	(35.7%)	(34.4%)	(30.2%)	(3)
4 France	4.5	5.2	5.7	5.9	5.9	6.3	6.3	7
(3)	(11.7%)	(13.3%)	(14.4%)	(14.8%)	(15.1%)	(15.3%)	(15.0%)	(7)
5 Russia	4.3	6.6	10.2	12.3	4.0	10.7	36.5	2
(8)	(3.6%)	(4.8%)	(6.4%)	(7.0%)	(3.1%)	(7.1%)	(20.2%)	(5)
6 Italy	2.7	3.1	3.8	4.1	5.0	6.5	8.0	6
(5)	(9.0%)	(9.6%)	(11.0%)	(11.6%)	(13.2%)	(16.1%)	(18.2%)	(6)
7 Japan	2.5	3.8	5.8	6.6	6.4	9.7	20.7	3
(6)	(6.3%)	(8.6%)	(10.3%)	(12.8%)	(11.6%)	(15.6%)	(28.6%)	(4)
8 Austria-Hungary	2.4	3.1	4.2	4.6	—	—	—	
(7)	(5.6%)	(6.6%)	(8.2%)	(8.8%)				

Table 14. Per Capita Levels of Industrialization, 1880–1938[20]
(relative to G.B. in 1900 = 100)

	1880	1900	1913	1928	1938	
1 Great Britain	87	[100]	115	122	157	2
2 United States	38	69	126	182	167	1
3 France	28	39	59	82	73	4
4 Germany	25	52	85	128	144	3
5 Italy	12	17	26	44	61	5
6 Austria	15	23	32	—	—	
7 Russia	10	15	20	20	38	7
8 Japan	9	12	20	30	51	6

Table 15. Iron/Steel Production of the Powers, 1890–1938[21]
(millions of tons; pig-iron production for 1890, steel thereafter)

	1890	1900	1910	1913	1920	1930	1938
United States	9.3	10.3	26.5	31.8	42.3	41.3	28.8
Britain	8.0	5.0	6.5	7.7	9.2	7.4	10.5
Germany	4.1	6.3	13.6	17.6	7.6	11.3	23.2
France	1.9	1.5	3.4	4.6	2.7	9.4	6.1
Austria-Hungary	0.97	1.1	2.1	2.6	—	—	—
Russia	0.95	2.2	3.5	4.8	0.16	5.7	18.0
Japan	0.02	—	0.16	0.25	0.84	2.3	7.0
Italy	0.01	0.11	0.73	0.93	0.73	1.7	2.3

energy consumption from modern forms (that is, coal, petroleum, natural gas, and hydroelectricity, but not wood), since it is an indication both of a country's technical capacity to exploit inanimate forms of energy and of its economic pulse rate; these figures are given in Table 16.

Table 16. Energy Consumption of the Powers, 1890–1938[22]
(in millions of metric tons of coal equivalent)

	1890	1900	1910	1913	1920	1930	1938
United States	147	248	483	541	694	762	697
Britain	145	171	185	195	212	184	196
Germany	71	112	158	187	159	177	228
France	36	47.9	55	62.5	65	97.5	84
Austria-Hungary	19.7	29	40	49.4	—	—	—
Russia	10.9	30	41	54	14.3	65	177
Japan	4.6	4.6	15.4	23	34	55.8	96.5
Italy	4.5	5	9.6	11	14.3	24	27.8

Tables 15 and 16 both confirm the swift industrial changes which occurred in *absolute* terms to some of the powers in particular periods—Germany before 1914, Russia and Japan in the 1930s—as well as indicating the slower rates of growth in Britain, France and Italy. This can also be represented in *relative terms* to indicate a country's comparative industrial position over time (Table 17).

Table 17. Total Industrial Potential of the Powers in Relative Perspective, 1880–1938[23]
(U.K. in 1900 = 100)

	1880	1900	1913	1928	1938
Britain	73.3	[100]	127.2	135	181
United States	46.9	127.8	298.1	533	528
Germany	27.4	71.2	137.7	158	214
France	25.1	36.8	57.3	82	74
Russia	24.5	47.5	76.6	72	152
Austria-Hungary	14	25.6	40.7	—	—
Italy	8.1	13.6	22.5	37	46
Japan	7.6	13	25.1	45	88

Finally, it is useful to return in Table 18 to Bairoch's figures on shares of world manufacturing production to show the changes which occurred since the earlier analysis of the nineteenth-century balances in the preceding chapter.

**Table 18. Relative Shares of World Manufacturing
Output, 1880–1938[24]**
(percent)

	1880	1900	1913	1928	1938
Britain	22.9	18.5	13.6	9.9	10.7
United States	14.7	23.6	32.0	39.3	31.4
Germany	8.5	13.2	14.8	11.6	12.7
France	7.8	6.8	6.1	6.0	4.4
Russia	7.6	8.8	8.2	5.3	9.0
Austria-Hungary	4.4	4.7	4.4	—	—
Italy	2.5	2.5	2.4	2.7	2.8

The Position of the Powers, 1885–1914

In the face of such unnervingly specific figures, that a certain power possessed 2.7 percent of world manufacturing production in 1913, or that another had an industrial potential in 1928 which was only 45 percent of Britain's in 1900, it is worth reemphasizing that all these statistics are abstract until placed within a specific historical and geopolitical context. Countries with virtually identical industrial output might nonetheless merit substantially different ratings in terms of Great Power effectiveness, because of such factors as the internal cohesion of the society in question, its ability to mobilize resources for state action, its geopolitical position, and its diplomatic capacities. Given the limitations of space, it will not be possible in this chapter to do for all the Great Powers what Correlli Barnett sought to do in his large-scale study of Britain some years ago. But what follows will try to remain close to Barnett's larger framework, in which he argues that

> the power of a nation-state by no means consists only in its armed forces, but also in its economic and technological resources; in the dexterity, foresight and resolution with which its foreign policy is conducted; in the efficiency of its social and political organization. It consists most of all in the nation itself, the people; their skills, energy, ambition, discipline, initiative; their beliefs, myths and illusions. And it consists, further, in the way all these factors are related to one another. Moreover national power has to be considered not only in itself, in its absolute extent, but relative to the state's foreign or imperial obligations; it has to be considered relative to the power of other states.[25]

There is perhaps no better way of illustrating the diversity of grand-strategical effectiveness than by looking in the first instance at the three relative newcomers to the international system, Italy, Germany, and Japan. The first two had become united states only in 1870–1871;

the third began to emerge from its self-imposed isolation after the Meiji Restoration of 1868. In all three societies there were impulses to emulate the established powers. By the 1880s and 1890s each was acquiring overseas territories; each, too, began to build a modern fleet to complement its standing army. Each was a significant element in the diplomatic calculus of the age and, at the latest by 1902, had become an alliance-partner to an older power. Yet all these similarities can hardly outweigh the fundamental differences in real strength which each possessed.

Italy

At first sight, the coming of a united Italian nation represented a major shift in the European balances. Instead of being a cluster of rivaling small states, partly under foreign sovereignty and always under the threat of foreign intervention, there was now a solid block of thirty million people growing so swiftly that it was coming close to France's total population by 1914. Its army and its navy in this period were not especially large, but as Tables 19 and 20 show, they were still very respectable.

Table 19. Military and Naval Personnel of the Powers, 1880–1914[26]

	1880	1890	1900	1910	1914
Russia	791,000	677,000	1,162,000	1,285,000	1,352,000
France	543,000	542,000	715,000	769,000	910,000
Germany	426,000	504,000	524,000	694,000	891,000
Britain	367,000	420,000	624,000	571,000	532,000
Austria-Hungary	246,000	346,000	385,000	425,000	444,000
Italy	216,000	284,000	255,000	322,000	345,000
Japan	71,000	84,000	234,000	271,000	306,000
United States	34,000	39,000	96,000	127,000	164,000

Table 20. Warship Tonnage of the Powers, 1880–1914[27]

	1880	1890	1900	1910	1914
Britain	650,000	679,000	1,065,000	2,174,000	2,714,000
France	271,000	319,000	499,000	725,000	900,000
Russia	200,000	180,000	383,000	401,000	679,000
United States	169,000	?240,000	333,000	824,000	985,000
Italy	100,000	242,000	245,000	327,000	498,000
Germany	88,000	190,000	285,000	964,000	1,305,000
Austria-Hungary	60,000	66,000	87,000	210,000	372,000
Japan	15,000	41,000	187,000	496,000	700,000

In diplomatic terms, as was noted above,[28] the rise of Italy certainly impinged upon its two Great Power neighbors, France and Austria-Hungary; and while its entry into the Triple Alliance in 1882 ostensibly "resolved" the Italo-Austrian rivalry, it confirmed that an isolated France faced foes on two fronts. Within just over a decade from its unification, therefore, Italy seemed a full member of the European Great Power system, and Rome ranked alongside the other major capitals (London, Paris, Berlin, St. Petersburg, Vienna, Constantinople) as a place to which full embassies were accredited.

But the appearance of Italy's Great Power status covered some stupendous weaknesses, above all the country's economic retardation, particularly in the rural south. Its illiteracy rate—37.6 percent overall and again far greater in the south—was much higher than in any other western or northern European state, a reflection of the backwardness of much of Italian agriculture—smallholdings, poor soil, little investment, sharecropping, inadequate transport. Italy's total output and per capita national wealth were comparable to those of the peasant societies of Spain and eastern Europe rather than those of the Netherlands or Westphalia. Italy had no coal; yet, despite its turn to hydroelectricity, about 88 percent of Italy's energy continued to come from British coal, a drain upon its balance of payments and an appalling strategical weakness. In these circumstances, Italy's rise in population without significant industrial expansion was a mixed blessing, since it slowed its industrial growth in per capita terms relative to the other western Powers,[29] and the comparison would have been even more unfavorable had not hundreds of thousands of Italians (usually the more mobile and able) emigrated across the Atlantic each year. All this made it, in Kemp's phrase, "the disadvantaged latecomer."[30]

This is not to say that there was no modernization. Indeed, it is precisely about this period that many historians have referred to "the industrial revolution of the Giolittian era" and to "a decisive change in the economic life of our country."[31] At least in the north, there was a considerable shift to heavy industry—iron and steel, shipbuilding, automobile manufacturing, as well as textiles. In Gerschrenkon's view, the years 1896–1908 witnessed Italy's "big push" toward industrialization; indeed, Italian industrial growth rose faster than anywhere else in Europe, the population shift from the countryside to the towns intensified, the banking system readjusted itself in order to provide industrial credit, and real national income moved sharply upward.[32] Piedmontese agriculture showed similar steps forward.

However, once the Italian statistics are placed in comparative prospective, the gloss begins to fade. It *did* create an iron and steel industry, but in 1913 its output was one-eighth that of Britain, one-seventeenth that of Germany, and only two-fifths that of Belgium.[33] It did achieve swift rates of industrial growth, but that was from such a very low beginning level that the real results were not impressive. At the outset of the First World War, it had not achieved even one-quarter of the industrial strength which Great Britain possessed in 1900, and its share of world manufacturing production actually dropped, from a mere 2.5 percent in 1900 to 2.4 percent in 1913. Although Italy marginally entered the listings of Great Powers, it is worth noting that—Japan excluded—every other of these powers had two or three times its industrial muscle; some (Germany and Britain) had sixfold the amount, and one (the United States) over thirteen times.

This might have been compensated for somewhat by a relatively greater degree of national cohesion and resolve on the part of the Italian population, but such elements were absent. The loyalties which existed in the Italian body politic were familial and local, perhaps regional, but not national. The chronic gap between north and south, which the industrialization of the former only exacerbated, and the lack of any great contact with the world outside the village community in so many parts of the peninsula were not helped by the hostility between the Italian government and the Catholic Church, which forbade its members to serve the state. The ideals of *risorgimento,* hailed by native and admiring foreign liberals, did not penetrate very far down Italian society. Recruitment for the armed services was difficult, and the actual location of army units according to strategical principles, rather than regional political calculations, was impossible. Civil-military relationships at the top were characterized by a mutual miscomprehension and distrust. The general antimilitarism of Italian society, the poor quality of the officer corps, and the lack of adequate funding for modern weaponry raised doubts about Italian military effectiveness long before the disastrous 1917 battle of Caporetto or the 1940 Egyptian campaign.[34] Its unification wars had relied upon the intervention of France, and then the threat to Austria-Hungary from Prussia. The 1896 catastrophe at Adowa (in Abyssinia) gave Italy the awful reputation of having the only European army defeated by an African society without means of effective response. The Italian government decision to make war in Libya in 1911–1912, which took the Italian general staff itself by surprise, was a financial disaster of the first order. The navy, looking very large in 1890, steadily declined in relative size and was always of questionable efficiency. Successive Mediterranean commander in chiefs of the Royal Navy always hoped that the Italian fleet would be neutral, not allied, if it ever came to a war with France in this period.[35]

The consequences of all this upon Italy's strategical and diplomatic position were depressing. Not only was the Italian general staff acutely aware of its numerical and technical inferiority compared with the French (especially) and the Austro-Hungarians, but it also knew that Italy's inadequate railway network and the deep-rooted regionalism made impossible large-scale, flexible troop deployments in the Prussian manner. And not only was the Italian navy aware of its deficiencies, but Italy's vulnerable and lengthy coastline made its alliance politics extremely ambivalent, and thus made strategic planning more chaotic than ever. The alliance treaty that Italy signed in 1882 with Berlin was comforting at first, particularly when Bismarck seemed to paralyze the French; but even then the Italian government kept pressing for closer ties with Britain, which alone could neutralize the French fleet. When, in the years after 1900, Britain and France moved closer together and Britain and Germany moved from cooperation to antagonism, the Italians felt that they had little alternative but to tack toward the new Anglo-French combination. The residual dislike of Austria-Hungary strengthened this move, just as the respect for Germany and the importance of German industrial finance in Italy checked it from being an open break. Thus by 1914, Italy occupied a position like that of 1871. It was "the least of the Great Powers,"[36] frustratingly unpredictable and unscrupulous in the eyes of its neighbors, and possessing commercial and expansionist ambitions in the Alps, the Balkans, North Africa, and farther afield which conflicted with the interests of both friends and rivals. Economic and social circumstances continued to weaken its power to influence events, and yet it remained a player in the game. In sum, the judgment of most other governments seems to have been that it was better to have Italy as a partner than as a foe; but the margin of benefit was not great.[37]

Japan

Italy was a marginal member of the Great Power system in 1890, but Japan wasn't even in the club. For centuries it had been ruled by a decentralized feudal oligarchy consisting of territorial lords (daimyo) and an aristocratic caste of warriors (samurai). Hampered by the absence of natural resources and by a mountainous terrain that left only 20 percent of its land suitable for cultivation, Japan lacked all of the customary prerequisites for economic development. Isolated from the rest of the world by a complex language with no close relatives and an intense consciousness of cultural uniqueness, the Japanese people remained inward-looking and resistant to foreign influences well into the second half of the nineteenth century. For all these reasons, Japan seemed destined to remain politically immature, economically backward, and militarily impotent in World Power terms.[38] Yet within two generations it had become a major player in the international politics of the Far East.

The cause of this transformation, effected by the Meiji Restoration from 1868 onward, was the determination of influential members of the Japanese elite to avoid being dominated and colonized by the West, as seemed to be happening elsewhere in Asia, even if the reform measures to be taken involved the scrapping of the feudal order and the bitter opposition of the samurai clans.[39] Japan had to be modernized not because individual entrepreneurs wished it, but because the "state" needed it. After the early opposition had been crushed, modernization proceeded with a *dirigisme* and commitment which makes the efforts of Colbert or Frederick the Great pale by comparison. A new constitution, based upon the Prusso-German model, was established. The legal system was reformed. The educational system was vastly expanded, so that the country achieved an exceptionally high literacy rate. The calendar was changed. Dressed was changed. A modern banking system was evolved. Experts were brought in from Britain's Royal Navy to advise upon the creation of an up-to-date Japanese fleet, and from the Prussian general staff to assist in the modernization of the army. Japanese officers were sent to western military and naval academies; modern weapons were purchased from abroad, although a native armaments industry was also established. The state encouraged the creation of a railway network, telegraphs, and shipping lines; it worked in conjunction with emerging Japanese entrepreneurs to develop heavy industry, iron, steel, and shipbuilding, as well as to modernize textile production. Government subsidies were employed to benefit exporters, to encourage shipping, to get a new industry set up. Japanese exports, especially of silk and textiles, soared. Behind all this lay the impressive political commitment to realize the national slogan *fukoken kyohei* ("rich country, with strong army"). For the Japanese, economic power and military/naval power went hand in hand.

But all this took time, and the handicaps remained severe.[40] Although the urban population more than doubled between 1890 and 1913, numbers engaged on the land remained about the same. Even on the eve of the First World War, over three-fifths of the Japanese population was engaged in agriculture, forestry, and fishing; and despite all the many improvements in farming techniques, the mountainous countryside and the small size of most holdings prevented an "agricultural revolution" on, say, the British model. With such a "bottom-heavy" agricultural base, all comparisons of Japan's industrial potential or of per capita levels of industrialization were bound to show it at or close to the lower end of the Great Power lists (see Tables 14 and 17 above). While its pre-1914 industrial spurt can clearly be detected in the large rise of its energy consumption from modern fuels and in the increase in its share of world manufacturing production, it was still deficient in many other areas. Its iron and steel output was small, and it relied heavily upon imports. In the same way, although its shipbuilding industry was greatly expanded, it still ordered some warships elsewhere. It also was very short of capital, needing to borrow increasing amounts from abroad but never having enough to invest in industry, in infrastructure, and in the armed services. Economically, it had performed miracles to become the only nonwestern state to go through an industrial revolution in the age of high imperialism; yet it still remained, compared to Britain, the United States, and Germany, an industrial and financial lightweight.

Two further factors, however, aided Japan's rise to Great Power status and help to explain why it surpassed, for example, Italy. The first was its geographical isolation. The nearby continental shore was held by nothing more threating than the decaying Chinese Empire. And while China, Manchuria, and (even more alarming) Korea might fall into the hands of another Great Power, geography had placed Japan far closer to those lands than any one of the other imperialist states—as Russia was to find to its discomfort when it tried to supply an army along six thousand miles of railway in 1904–1905, and as the British and American navies were to discover several decades later as they wrestled with the logistical problems involved in the relief of the Philippines, Hong Kong, and Malaya. Assuming a steady Japanese growth in East Asia, it would only be by the most extreme endeavors that any other major state could prevent Japan from becoming the predominant power there in the course of time.

The second factor was *moral.* It seems indisputable that the strong Japanese sense of cultural uniqueness, the traditions of emperor worship and veneration of the state, the samurai ethos of military honor and valor, the emphasis upon discipline and fortitude, produced a political culture at once fiercely patriotic and unlikely to be deterred by sacrifices and reinforced the Japanese impulses to expand into "Greater East Asia," for strategical security as well as markets and raw materials. This was reflected in the successful military and naval campaigning against China in 1894, when those two countries quarreled over their claims in Korea.[41] On land and sea, the better-equipped Japanese forces seemed driven by a will to succeed. At the end of that war, the threats of the "triple intervention" by Russia, France, and Germany compelled an embittered Japanese government to withdraw its claims to Port Arthur and the Liaotung Peninsula, but that merely increased Tokyo's determination to try again later. Few, if any, in the government dissented from Baron Hayashi's grim conclusion:

> If new warships are considered necessary we must, at any cost, build them: if the organization of our army is inadequate we must start rectifying it from now; if need be, our entire military system must be changed. . . .
>
> At present Japan must keep calm and sit tight, so as to lull suspicions nurtured against her; during this time the foundations of national power must be consolidated; and we must watch and wait for the opportunity in the Orient that will surely come one day. When this day arrives, Japan will decide her own fate. . . .[42]

Its time for revenge came ten years later, when its Korean and Manchurian ambitions clashed with those of czarist Russia.[43] While naval experts were impressed by Admiral Togo's fleet when it destroyed the Russian ships at the decisive battle of Tsushima, it was the general bearing of Japanese society which struck other observers. The surprise strike at Port Arthur (a habit begun in the 1894 China conflict, and revived in 1941) was applauded in the West, as was the enthusiasm of Japanese nationalist opinion for an outright victory, whatever the cost. More remarkable still seemed the performance of Japan's officers and men in the land battles around Port Arthur and Mukden, where tens of thousands of soldiers were lost as they charged across minefields, over barbed wire, and through a hail of machine-gun fire before conquering the Russian trenches. The samurai spirit, it seemed, could secure battlefield victories with the bayonet even in the age of mass industrialized warfare. If, as all the contemporary military experts concluded, morale and discipline were still vital prerequisites of national power, Japan was rich in those resources.

Even then, however, Japan was not a full-fledged Great Power. Japan had been fortunate to have fought an even more backward China and a czarist Russia which was militarily top-heavy and disadvantaged by the immense distance between St. Petersburg and the Far East. Furthermore, the Anglo-Japanese Alliance of 1902 had allowed it to fight on its home ground without interference from third powers. Its navy had relied upon British-built battleships, its army upon Krupp guns. Most important of all, it had found the immense costs of the war impossible to finance from its own resources and yet had been able to rely upon loans floated in the United States and Britain.[44] As it turned out, Japan was close to bankruptcy by the end of 1905, when the peace negotiations with Russia got under way. That may not have been obvious to the Tokyo public, which reacted furiously to the relatively light terms with which Russia escaped in the final settlement. Nevertheless, with victory confirmed, Japan's armed forces glorified and admired, its economy able to recover, and its status as a Great Power (albeit a regional one) admitted by all, Japan had come of age. No one could do anything significant in the Far East without considering its response; but whether it could expand further without provoking reaction from the more established Great Powers was not at all clear.

Germany

Two factors ensured that the rise of imperial Germany would have a more immediate and substantial impact upon the Great Power balances than either of its fellow "newcomer" states. The first was that, far from emerging in geopolitical isolation, like Japan, Germany had arisen right in the center of the old European states system; its very creation had directly impinged upon the interests of Austria-Hungary

and France, and its existence had altered the relative position of *all* of
the existing Great Powers of Europe. The second factor was the sheer
speed and extent of Germany's further growth, in industrial, commercial, and military/naval terms. By the eve of the First World War its
national power was not only three or four times Italy's and Japan's, it
was well ahead of either France or Russia and had probably overtaken
Britain as well. In June 1914 the octogenarian Lord Welby recalled
that "the Germany they remembered in the fifties was a cluster of
insignificant states under insignificant princelings";[45] now, in one
man's lifetime, it was the most powerful state in Europe, and still
growing. This alone was to make "the German question" the epicenter
of so much of world politics for more than half a century after 1890.

Only a few details of Germany's explosive economic growth can be
offered here.[46] Its population had soared from 49 million in 1890 to 66
million in 1913, second only in Europe to Russia's—but since Germans
enjoyed far higher levels of education, social provision, and per capita
income than Russians, the nation was strong both in the quantity and
the quality of its population. Whereas, according to an Italian source,
330 out of 1,000 recruits entering its army were illiterate, the corresponding ratios were 220/1,000 in Austria-Hungary, 68/1,000 in
France, and an astonishing 1/1,000 in Germany.[47] The beneficiaries
were not only the Prussian army, but also the factories requiring
skilled workers, the enterprises needing well-trained engineers, the
laboratories seeking chemists, the firms looking for managers and
salesmen—all of which the German school system, polytechnical institutes, and universities produced in abundance. By applying the fruits
of this knowledge to agriculture, German farmers used chemical fertilizers and large-scale modernization to increase their crop yields, which
were much higher per hectare than in any of the other Great Powers.[48]
To appease the Junkers and the peasants' leagues, German farming
was given considerable tariff protection in the face of more cheaply
produced American and Russian foodstuffs; yet because of its relative
efficiency, the large agricultural sector did not drag down per capita
national income and output to anything like the degree it did in all the
other continental Great Powers.

But it was in its industrial expansion that Germany really distinguished itself in these years. Its coal production grew from 89 million
tons in 1890 to 277 million tons in 1914, just behind Britain's 292
million and far ahead of Austria-Hungary's 47 million, France's 40
million, and Russia's 36 million. In steel, the increases had been even
more spectacular, and the 1914 German output of 17.6 million tons
was larger than that of Britain, France, and Russia combined. More
impressive still was the German performance in the newer, twentieth-
century industries of electrics, optics, and chemicals. Giant firms like
Siemens and AEG, employing 142,000 people between them, domi-

nated the European electrical industry. German chemical firms, led by Bayer and Hoechst, produced 90 percent of the world's industrial dyes. This success story was naturally reflected in Germany's foreign-trade figures, with exports tripling between 1890 and 1913, bringing the country close to Britain as the leading world exporter; not surprisingly, its merchant marine also expanded, to be the second-largest in the world by the eve of the war. By then, its share of world manufacturing production (14.8 percent) was higher than Britain's (13.6 percent) and two and a half times that of France (6.1 percent). It had become the economic powerhouse of Europe, and even its much-publicized lack of capital did not seem to be slowing it down. Little wonder that nationalists like Friedrich Naumann exulted at these manifestations of growth and their implications for Germany's place in the world. "The German race brings it," he wrote. "It brings army, navy, money and power. . . . Modern, gigantic instruments of power are possible only when an active people feels the spring-time juices in its organs."[49]

That publicists such as Naumann and, even more, such rabidly expansionist pressure groups as the Pan-German League and the German Navy League should have welcomed and urged the rise of German influence in Europe and overseas is hardly surprising. In this age of the "new imperialism," similar calls could be heard in every other Great Power; as Gilbert Murray wickedly observed in 1900, *each* country seemed to be asserting, "We are the pick and flower of nations . . . above all things qualified for governing others."[50] It was perhaps more significant that the German ruling elite after 1895 also seemed convinced of the need for large-scale territorial expansion when the time was ripe, with Admiral Tirpitz arguing that Germany's industrialization and overseas conquests were "as irresistible as a natural law"; with the Chancellor Bülow declaring, "The question is not whether we want to colonize or not, but that we *must* colonize, whether we want it or not"; and with Kaiser Wilhelm himself airily announcing that Germany "had great tasks to accomplish outside the narrow boundaries of old Europe" although he also envisaged it exercising a sort of "Napoleonic supremacy," in a peaceful sense, over the continent.[51] All this was quite a change of tone from Bismarck's repeated insistence that Germany was a "saturated" power, keen to preserve the status quo in Europe and unenthused (despite the colonial bids of 1884–1885) about territories overseas. Even here it may be unwise to exaggerate the particularly aggressive nature of this German "ideological consensus"[52] for expansion; statesmen in France and Russia, Britain and Japan, the United States and Italy were also announcing *their* country's manifest destiny, although perhaps in a less deterministic and frenetic tone.

What *was* significant about German expansionism was that the country either already possessed the instruments of power to alter the status quo or had the material resources to create such instruments.

The most impressive demonstration of this capacity was the rapid
buildup of the German navy after 1898, which under Tirpitz was transformed from being the sixth-largest fleet in the world to being second
only to the Royal Navy. By the eve of war, the High Seas Fleet consisted
of thirteen dreadnought-type battleships, sixteen older ones, and five
battlecruisers, a force so big that it had compelled the British Admiralty gradually to withdraw almost all its capital-ship squadrons from
overseas stations into the North Sea; while there were to be indications
(better internal construction, shells, optical equipment, gunnery control, night training, etc.) that the German vessels were pound for pound
superior.[53] Although Tirpitz could never secure the enormous funds to
achieve his real goal of creating a navy "equally strong as England's,"[54]
he nonetheless had built a force which quite overawed the rival fleets
of France or Russia.

Germany's capacity to fight successfully on land seemed to some
observers less impressive; indeed, at first sight, the Prussian army in
the decade before 1914 appeared eclipsed by the far larger forces of
czarist Russia, and matched by those of France. But such appearances
were deceptive. For complex domestic-political reasons, the German
government had opted to keep the army to a certain size and to allow
Tirpitz's fleet substantially to increase its share of the total defense
budget.[55] When the tense international circumstances of 1911 and 1912
caused Berlin to decide upon a large-scale expansion of the army, the
swift change of gear was imposing. Between 1910 and 1914, its army
budget rose from $204 million to $442 million, whereas France's grew
only from $188 million to $197 million—and yet France was conscripting 89 percent of its eligible youth compared with Germany's 53 percent to achieve that buildup. It was true that Russia was spending some
$324 million on its army by 1914, but at stupendous strain: defense
expenditures consumed 6.3 percent of Russia's national income, but
only 4.6 percent of Germany's.[56] With the exception of Britain, Germany bore the "burden of armaments" more easily than any other
European state. Furthermore, while the Prussian army could mobilize
and equip millions of reservists and—because of their better education
and training—actually deploy them in front-line operations, France
and Russia could not. The French general staff held that their reservists
could only be used behind the lines;[57] and Russia possessed neither the
weapons, boots, and uniforms to equip its theoretical reserve army of
millions nor the officers to supervise them. But even this does not
probe the full depths of the German military capacity, which was also
reflected in such unquantifiable factors as good internal lines of communication, faster mobilization schedules, superior staff training, advanced technology, and so on.

But the German Empire was weakened by its geography and its
diplomacy. Because it lay in the center of the continent, its growth

appeared to threaten a number of other Great Powers simultaneously. The efficiency of its military machine, coupled with Pan-German calls for a reordering of Europe's boundaries, alarmed both the French and the Russians and drove them closer to each other. The swift expansion of the German navy upset Britain, as did the latent German threat to the Low Countries and northern France. Germany, in one scholar's phrase, was "born encircled."[58] Even if German expansionism was directed overseas, where could it go without trespassing upon the spheres of influence of other Great Powers? A venture into Latin America could only be pursued at the cost of war with the United States. Expansion in China had been frowned upon by Russia and Britain in the 1890s and was out of the question after the Japanese victory over Russia in 1905. Attempts to develop the Baghdad Railway alarmed both London and St. Petersburg. Efforts to secure the Portuguese colonies were checked by the British. While the United States could apparently expand its influence in the western hemisphere, Japan encroach upon China, Russia and Britain penetrate into the Middle East, and France "round off" its holdings in northwestern Africa, Germany was to go empty-handed. When Bülow, in his famous "hammer or anvil" speech of 1899, angrily declared, "We cannot allow any foreign power, any foreign Jupiter to tell us: 'What can be done? The world is already partitioned,' " he was expressing a widely held resentment. Little wonder that German publicists called for a redivision of the globe.[59]

To be sure, all rising powers call for changes in an international order which has been fixed to the advantage of the older, established powers.[60] From a *Realpolitik* viewpoint, the question was whether this particular challenger could secure changes without provoking too much opposition. And while geography played an important role here, diplomacy was also significant; because Germany did not enjoy, say, Japan's geopolitical position, its statecraft had to be of an extraordinarily high order. Realizing the unease and jealousy which the Second Reich's sudden emergence had caused, Bismarck strove after 1871 to convince the other Great Powers (especially the flank powers of Russia and Britain) that Germany had no further territorial ambitions. Wilhelm and his advisers, eager to show their mettle, were much less careful. Not only did they convey their dissatisfaction with the existing order, but—and this was the greatest failure of all—the decision-making process in Berlin concealed, behind a facade of high imperial purpose, a chaos and instability which amazed all who witnessed it in close action. Much of this was due to the character weaknesses of Wilhelm II himself, but it was exacerbated by institutional flaws in the Bismarckian constitution; with no body (like a cabinet) collectively possessing responsibility for overall government policy, different departments and interest groups pursued their aims without any check from above or ordering of priorities.[61] The navy thought almost solely of a future war with England; the army planned to eliminate France; financiers and businessmen wished to move into the Balkans, Turkey, and the Near East, eliminating Russian influence in the process. The result, moaned Chancellor Bethmann Hollweg in July 1914, was to "challenge everybody, get in everyone's way and actually, in the course of all this, weaken nobody."[62] This was not a recipe for success in a world full of egoistic and suspicious nation-states.

Finally, there remained the danger that failure to achieve diplomatic or territorial successes would affect the delicate internal politics of Wilhelmine Germany, whose Junker elite worried about the (relative) decline of the agricultural interest, the rise of organized labor, and the growing influence of Social Democracy in a period of industrial boom. It was true that after 1897 the pursuit of *Weltpolitik* was motivated to a considerable extent by the calculation that this would be politically popular and divert attention from Germany's domestic-political fissures.[63] But the regime in Berlin always ran the dual risk that if it backed down from a confrontation with a "foreign Jupiter," German nationalist opinion might revile and denounce the Kaiser and his aides; whereas, if the country became engaged in an all-out war, it was not clear whether the natural patriotism of the masses of workers, soldiers, and sailors would outweigh their dislike of the archconservative Prusso-German state. While some observers felt that a war would unite the nation behind the emperor, others feared it would further strain the German sociopolitical fabric. Again, this needs to be placed in context—for example, German internal weaknesses were hardly as serious as those in Russia or Austria-Hungary, but they did exist, and they certainly could affect the country's ability to engage in a lengthy "total" war.

It has been argued by many historians that imperial Germany was a "special case," following a *Sonderweg* ("special path") which would one day culminate in the excesses of National Socialism. Viewed solely in terms of political culture and rhetoric around 1900, this is a hard claim to detect: Russian and Austrian anti-Semitism was at least as strong as German, French chauvinism as marked as the German, Japan's sense of cultural uniqueness and destiny as broadly held as Germany's. Each of the powers examined here was "special," and in an age of imperialism was all too eager to assert its specialness. From the criterion of power politics, however, Germany did possess unique features which were of great import. It was the one Great Power which combined the modern, industrialized strength of the western democracies with the autocratic (one is tempted to say irresponsible) decision-making features of the eastern monarchies.[64] It was the one "newcomer" Great Power, with the exception of the United States, which really had the strength to challenge the existing order. And it was the one rising Great Power which, if it expanded its borders farther to the east or to the west, could only do so at the expense of powerful neighbors: the one country whose future growth, in Calleo's words, "directly" rather than "indirectly" undermined the European balance.[65] This was an explosive combination for a nation which felt, in Tirpitz's phrase, that it was "a life-and-death question . . . to make up the lost ground."[66]

It seemed a vital matter to the rising states to break through, but it was even more urgent for those established Great Powers now under pressure to try to hold their own. Here again, it will be necessary to point to the very significant differences between the three Powers in question, Austria-Hungary, France, and Britain—and perhaps especially between the first-named and the last. Nonetheless, the charts of their relative power in world affairs would show all of them distinctly weaker by the end of the nineteenth century than they had been fifty or sixty years earlier,[67] even if their defense budgets were larger and their colonial empires more extensive, and if (in the case of France and Austria-Hungary) they still had territorial ambitions in Europe. Furthermore, it seems fair to claim that the leaderships within these nations *knew* the international scene had become more complicated and threatening than that which their predecessors had faced, and that such knowledge was forcing them to consider radical changes of policy in an effort to meet the new circumstances.

Austria-Hungary

Although the Austro-Hungarian Empire was by far the weakest of the established Great Powers—and, in Taylor's words, slipping out of their ranks[68]—this is not obvious from a glance at the macroeconomic statistics. Despite considerable emigration, its population rose from 41 million in 1890 to 52 million in 1914, to go well clear of France and Italy, and some way ahead of Britain. The empire also underwent much industrialization in these decades, though the pace of change was perhaps swifter before 1900 than after. Its coal production by 1914 was a respectable 47 million tons, higher than either France's or Russia's, and even in its steel production and energy consumption it was not significantly inferior to either of the Dual Alliance powers. Its textile industry experienced a surge in output, brewing and sugar-beet production rose, the oilfields of Galicia were exploited, mechanization occurred on the estates of Hungary, the Skoda armaments works multiplied in size, electrification occurred in the major cities, and the state vigorously promoted railway construction.[69] According to one of Bairoch's calculations, the Austro-Hungarian Empire's GNP in 1913 was virtually the same as France's,[70] which looks a little suspect—as does Farrar's claim that its share of "European power" rose from 4.0 percent in 1890 to 7.2 percent in 1910.[71] Nonetheless, it is clear that the empire's growth rates from 1870 to 1913 were among the highest in Europe, and that its "industrial potential" was growing faster even than Russia's.[72]

Once one examines Austria-Hungary's economy and society in more detail, however, significant flaws appear. Perhaps the most fundamental of these was the enormous regional differences in per capita income and output, which to a large degree mirrored socioeconomic and ethnic diversities in a territory stretching from the Swiss Alps to the Bukovina. It was not merely the fact that in 1910 73 percent of the population of Galicia and Bukovina were employed in agriculture compared with 55 percent for the empire as a whole; much more significant and alarming was the enormous disparity of wealth, with per capita income in Lower Austria (850 crowns) and Bohemia (761 crowns) being far in excess of those in Galicia (316 crowns), Bukovina (310 crowns), and Dalmatia (264 crowns).[73] Yet while it was in the Austrian provinces and Czech lands that industrial "takeoff" was occurring, and in Hungary that agricultural improvements were under way, it was in those poverty-stricken Slavic regions that the population was increasing the fastest. In consequence, Austria-Hungary's per capita level of industrialization remained well below that of the leading Great Powers, and despite all the absolute increases in output, its share of world manufacturing production hovered around a mere 4.5 percent in those decades. This was not a strong economic base on which a country with Austria-Hungary's strategical tasks could rest.

This relative backwardness might have been compensated for by a high degree of national-cultural cohesion, such as existed in Japan or France; but, alas, Vienna controlled the most ethnically diverse cluster of peoples in Europe[74]—when war came in 1914, for example, the mobilization order was given in fifteen different languages. The age-old tension between German speakers and Czech speakers in Bohemia was not the most serious of the problems facing Emperor Francis Joseph and his advisers, even if the "Young Czech" movement was making it sound so. The strained relations with Hungary, which despite its post-1867 status as an equal partner clashed with Vienna again and again over such issues as tariffs, treatment of ethnic minorities, "Magyarization" of the army, and so on, were such that by 1899, western observers feared the breakup of the entire empire and the French foreign minister, Delcassé, secretly renegotiated the terms of the Dual Alliance with Russia in order to prevent Germany from succeeding to the Austrian lands and access to the Adriatic coast. By 1905, indeed, the general staff in Vienna was quietly preparing a contingency plan for the military occupation of Hungary should the crisis worsen.[75] Vienna's list of nationality problems did not stop with the Czechs and the Magyars. The Italians in the south resented the stiff Germanization in their territories, and looked over the border for help from Rome—as the captive Rumanians, to a lesser degree, looked eastward to Bucharest. The Poles, by contrast, were quiescent, in part because the rights they enjoyed under the Habsburg Empire were superior to those obtaining in the German- and Russian-dominated territories. But by far the largest danger to the unity of the empire came from the South Slavs, since dissident groups within seemed to be looking toward Serbia and, more distantly, toward Russia. Compromises with South Slav aspirations were urged from time to time, by more liberal circles in Vienna, but they were fiercely resisted by the Magyar gentry, who both opposed any diminution of Hungary's special status and also kept up their strong discrimination of ethnic minorities within Hungary itself. Since a political solution of this issue was denied to the moderates, the door was open for Austro-German nationalists like the chief of staff, General Conrad, to argue that the Serbs and their sympathizers should be dealt with by force. Despite the restraint exercised by Emperor Francis Joseph himself, this always remained a last resort if the Empire's survival did really seem to be threatened.

All of this undoubtedly effected Austria-Hungary's power, and in a whole number of ways. It was not that multi-ethnicity inevitably meant military weakness. The army remained a unifying institution, and extraordinarily adept at using a whole array of languages of command; nor had its old skills of divide and rule been forgotten when it came to garrisons and deployments. But it was increasingly difficult to rely upon the wholehearted cooperation of the Czech or Hungarian regiments in certain circumstances, and even the traditional loyalty of the Croats (used for centuries along the "military border") was eroded by Hungarian persecution. What was more, Vienna's classic answer to all of these particularist grievances was to smother them with committees, with new jobs, tax concessions, additional railway branch lines, and so on. "There were, in 1914, well over 3,000,000 civil servants, running things as diverse as schools, hospitals, welfare, taxation, railways, posts, etc. . . . so . . . that there was not much money left for the army itself."[76] According to Wright's figures, defense appropriations took a far smaller share of "national (i.e., central government) appropriations" in the Austria-Hungarian Empire than in any of the other Great Powers.[77] In consequence, while its fleet never had enough funds to match even the Italian, let alone the French, navy in the Mediterranean, allocations to the army were between one-third and one-half of those which the Russian and Prussian armies enjoyed. The army's weapons, especially artillery, were out-of-date and far too few. Because of lack of funds, only about 30 percent of the available manpower was conscripted, and many of them were sent on "permanent leave" or received only eight weeks training. It was not a system geared to produce masses of competent reserves in wartime.[78]

As the international tensions built up in the decade or so after 1900, the Austro-Hungarian Empire's strategical position appeared parlous indeed. Its internal divisions threatened to split the country asunder, and complicated relations with most of its neighbors. Its economic growth, although marked, was not allowing it to catch up with leading Great Powers such as Britain and Germany. It spent less per capita on defense than many of the other powers, and it conscripted a far smaller ratio of its eligible youth into the army than any of the continental nations. To cap it all, it seemed to have so many possible foes that its general staff had to plan for a whole variety of campaigns—a complication which very few of the other Great Powers were distracted with.

That the Austro-Hungarian Empire had so many potential enemies was itself due to its unique geographical and multinational situation. Despite the Triple Alliance, the tensions with Italy became greater after 1900, and on several occasions Conrad advocated a military blow against this southern neighbor; even if his proposal was firmly rejected by both the foreign ministry and the emperor, the garrisons and fortresses along the Italian frontier were steadily built up. Much farther afield, Vienna had to worry about Rumania, which by 1912 became a distinct threat as it moved into the opposite camp. But the country which attracted the most venom was Serbia, which, with Montenegro, seemed a magnet to the South Slavs within the empire and thus a cancerous growth which had to be eliminated. The only problem with that agreeable solution was that an attack upon Serbia could well provoke a military response from Austria-Hungary's most formidable rival, czarist Russia, which would invade the northeastern front just as the bulk of the Austro-Hungarian army was pushing southward, past Belgrade. Although even the hyperbelligerent Conrad asserted that it was "up to the diplomats"[79] to keep the empire from having to fight all these foes at once, his own pre-1914 war plans reveal the fantastic military juggling act for which the army had to prepare. While a main force (A-Staffel) of nine army corps would be prepared for deployment against either (!) Italy or Russia, a smaller group of three army corps would be mobilized against Serbia-Montenegro (Minimalgruppe Balkan). In addition, a strategic reserve of four army corps (B-Staffel) would hold itself ready "either to reinforce A-Staffel and make it into a powerful offensive force, or, if there were no danger from either Italy or Russia, to join Minimalgruppe Balkan for an offensive against Serbia."[80]

"The heart of the matter," it has been said, "was simply that Austria-Hungary was trying to act the part of a great power with the resources of a second-rank one."[81] The desperate efforts to be strong on all fronts ran a serious risk of making the empire weak everywhere; at the very least, they placed superhuman demands upon the empire's railway system, and upon the staff officers who would control it. More than that, these operational dilemmas confirmed what most observers in

Vienna had reluctantly accepted since 1870: that in the event of a Great Power war, Austria-Hungary needed German support. This would not be the case in a purely Austro-Italian war (although that, despite Conrad's frequent fears, was the least likely contingency); but German military assistance certainly would be required if Austria-Hungary became embroiled in a war with Serbia, and the latter was then aided by Russia; hence the repeated attempts by Conrad prior to 1914 to secure Berlin's assurances on this point. Finally, the baroque nature of this operational planning reflects once again what many contemporaries could see but some later historians have declined to admit:[82] that if the nationalist explosions of discontent in the Balkans, and in the empire itself, continued to go off, the chances of preserving Kaiser Joseph's unique but anachronistic inheritance were well-nigh impossible. And when that happened, the European equilibrium was bound to be undermined.

France

France in 1914 possessed considerable advantages over Austria-Hungary. Perhaps the most important was that it had only one enemy, Germany, against which its entire national resources could be concentrated. This had not been the case in the late 1880s, when France was challenging Britain in Egypt and West Africa and engaged in a determined naval race against the Royal Navy, quarreling with Italy almost to the point of blows, and girding itself for the *revanche* against Germany.[83] Even when more cautious politicians drew the country back from the brink and then moved into the early stages of their alliance with Russia, the French strategical dilemma was still an acute one. Its most formidable foe, clearly, was the German Empire, now more powerful than ever. But the Italian naval and colonial challenge (as the French viewed it) was also disturbing, not only for its own sake, but because a war with Italy would almost certainly involve its German ally. For the army, this meant that a considerable number of divisions would have to be stationed in the southeast; for the navy, it exacerbated the age-old strategical problem of whether to concentrate the fleet in Mediterranean or Atlantic ports or to run the risk of dividing it into two smaller forces.[84]

All this was compounded by the swift deterioration in Anglo-French relations which followed the British occupation of Egypt in 1882. From 1884, the two countries were locked into an escalating naval race, which on the British side was associated with the possible loss of their Mediterranean line of communications and (occasionally) with fears of a French cross-Channel invasion.[85] Even more persistent and threatening were the frequent Anglo-French colonial clashes. Britain and France had quarreled over the Congo in 1884–1885 and over West Africa throughout the entire 1880s and 1890s. In 1893 they seemed to be on the brink of war over Siam. The greatest crisis of all came in 1898, when their sixteen-year rivalry over control of the Nile Valley climaxed in the confrontation between Kitchener's army and Marchand's small expedition at Fashoda. Although the French backed down on that occasion, they were energetic and bold imperialists. Neither the inhabitants of Timbuktu nor those of Tonkin would have regarded France as a power in decline, far from it. Between 1871 and 1900, France had added 3.5 million square miles to its existing colonial territories, and it possessed indisputably the largest overseas empire after Britain's. Although the commerce of those lands was not great, France had built up a considerable colonial army and an array of prime naval bases from Dakar to Saigon. Even in places which France had not colonized, such as the Levant and South China, its influence was large.[86]

France had been able to carry out such a dynamic colonial policy, it has been argued, because the structures of government had permitted a small group of bureaucrats, colonial governors, and *parti colonial* enthusiasts to effect "forward" strategies which the fast-changing ministries of the Third Republic had little chance to control.[87] But if the volatile state of French parliamentary politics had inadvertently given a strength and consistency to its imperial policy—by placing it in the hands of permanent officials and their friends in the colonial "lobby"— it had a far less happy impact upon naval and military affairs. For example, the swift changes of regime brought with them new ministers of marine, some of whom were mere "placemen," others of whom had strongly held (but always varying) opinions on naval strategy. In consequence, although large sums were allocated to the French navy in these decades, the money was not well spent: the building programs reflected the frequent changes from one administration's preference for a *guerre de course* (commerce-raiding) strategy to another's firm support for battleships, leaving the navy itself with a heterogeneous collection of ships which were no match for those of the British or, later, the Germans.[88] But the impact of politics upon the French navy paled by comparison with the effect upon the army, where the strong dislike shown by the officer corps toward republican politicians and a whole host of civil-military clashes (of which the Dreyfus affair was merely the most notorious) weakened the fabric of France and placed in question both the loyalty and the efficiency of the army. Only with the remarkable post-1911 nationalist revival could these civil-military disputes be set aside in the common crusade against the German enemy; but there were many who wondered whether too heavy a dose of politics had not done irreparable damage to the French armed forces.[89]

The other obvious internal constraint upon French power was the state of its economy.[90] The position here is a complex one, and has been made the more so by economic historians' predilections for different indices. On the positive side:

> This period saw a great development in banking and financial institutions participating in industrial investment and in foreign lending. The iron and steel industry was established on modern lines and great new plants were built, especially on the Lorraine orefield. On the coalfields of northern France the familiar, ugly landscape of an industrial society took place. Important strides were made in engineering and the newer industries. . . . France had its notable entrepreneurs and innovators who won a leading place in the late nineteenth and early twentieth century in steel, engineering, motor cars and aircraft. Firms like Schneider, Peugeot, Michelin and Renault were in the vanguard.[91]

Until Henry Ford's mass-production methods were developed, indeed, France was the leading automobile producer in the world. There was a further burst of railway-building in the 1880s, which together with improved telegraphs, postal systems, and inland waterways, increased the trend toward a national market. Agriculture had been protected by the Méline tariff of 1892, and there remained a focus upon producing high-quality goods, with a large per capita added value. Given these indices of absolute economic expansion and the small increase in the number of Frenchmen during these decades, measurement of output which are related to France's population look impressive—e.g., per capita growth rates, per capita value of exports, etc.

Finally, there was the undeniable fact that France was immensely rich in terms of mobile capital, which could be (and systematically was) applied to serve the interests of the country's diplomacy and strategy. The most impressive sign of this had been the very rapid paying off the German indemnity of 1871, which, in Bismarck's erroneous calculation, was supposed to cripple France's strength for many years to come. But in the period following, French capital was also poured out to various countries inside Europe and without. By 1914, France's foreign investments totaled $9 billion, second only to Britain's. While these investments had helped to industrialize considerable parts of Europe, including Spain and Italy, they had also brought large political and diplomatic benefits to France itself. The slow weaning of Italy away from the Triple Alliance at the turn of the century was attended, if not fully caused, by the Italian need for capital. Franco-Russian loans to China, in exchange for railway rights and other concessions, were nearly always raised in Paris and funneled through St. Petersburg. France's massive investments in Turkey and the Balkans—which the frustrated Germans could never manage to match prior to 1914—gave it an edge, not only in politico-cultural terms, but also in securing contracts for French rather than German armaments. Above all, the French poured money into the modernization of their Russian ally, from the floating of the first loan on the Paris market in October 1888 to the critical 1913 offer of lending 500 million francs— on condition that the Russian strategic railway system in the Polish provinces be greatly extended, so that the "Russian steamroller" could be mobilized the faster to crush Germany.[92] This was the clearest demonstration yet of France's ability to use its financial muscle to bolster its own strategic power (although the irony was that the more efficient the Russian military machine became, the more the Germans had to prepare to strike quickly against France).

Yet once again, as soon as comparative economic data are used, this positive image of France's growth fades away. While it was certainly a large-scale investor abroad, there is little evidence that this capital brought the country the optimal return, either in terms of interest earned[93] or in a rise in foreign orders for French products: all too often, even in Russia, German merchants grabbed the lion's share of the import trade. Germany's proportion of exported European manufacturers had already overtaken France's in the early 1880s; by 1911, it was almost twice as high. But this in turn reflected the awkward fact that whereas the French economy had suffered from vigorous British industrial competition a generation or two earlier, it was now being affected by the rise of the German industrial giant. With truly rare exceptions like the automobile industry, the comparative statistics time and time again measure this eclipse. By the eve of war, its total industrial potential was only about 40 percent of Germany's, its steel production was little over one-sixth, its coal production hardly one-seventh. What coal, steel, and iron were produced was usually more expensive, coming from smaller plants and poorer mines. Similarly, for all the alleged advances of the French chemical industry, the country was massively dependent upon German imports. Given its small plants, out-of-date practices, and heavy reliance upon protected local markets, it is not surprising that France's industrial growth in the nineteenth century had been coldly described as "arthritic . . . hesitant, spasmodic, and slow."[94]

Nor were its bucolic charms any consolation, at least in terms of relative power and wealth. The blows dealt by disease to silk and wine production were never fully recovered from; and what the Méline tariff did, in its effort to protect farm incomes and preserve social stability, was to slow down the drift from the land and to support inefficient producers. With agriculture still accounting for 40 percent of the active population around 1910 and still overwhelmingly composed of smallholdings, this was an obvious drag upon both French productivity and overall wealth. Bairoch's data show the French GNP in 1913 only 55 percent of Germany's and its share of world manufacturing production around 40 percent of Germany's; Wright has its national income as being $6 billion in 1914 to Germany's $12 billion.[95] Another war with its eastern neighbor, should France stand alone, could only repeat the result of 1870–1871.

On many of these comparative indices, France had also slipped well behind the United States, Britain, and Russia as well as Germany, so that by the early twentieth century it was only the fifth among the Great Powers. Yet it was the erosion of French power vis-à-vis Germany which mattered, simply because of the bitter relations between the two countries. In this respect, the trends were ominous. Whereas Germany's population rose by nearly eighteen million between 1890 and 1914, France's increased by little over one million. This, together with Germany's greater national wealth, meant that however much the French strained to keep up militarily, they were always outdistanced. By conscripting over 80 percent of its eligible youth, France had produced a staggeringly large army for its size, at least according to certain measurements: for instance, the eighty divisions it could mobilize from a population of 40 million compared favorably with the Austrians' forty-eight divisions from a population of 52 million. But this was to little avail against imperial Germany. Not only could the Prussian general staff, employing its better-trained reserves, mobilize somewhat over one hundred divisions, but it had a vast manpower potential to draw upon—almost ten million men in the requisite age group, compared with France's five million; and it possessed the fantastic figure of 112,000 well-trained NCOs—the key element in an expanding army—compared with France's 48,000. Moreover, although Germany allocated a smaller proportion of its national income to military spending, it devoted much more in absolute terms. Throughout the 1870s and 1880s the French high command had struggled in vain against "a condition of unacceptable inferiority";[96] on the eve of the First World War, the confidential memoranda about the German material superiority were equally alarming: "4,500 machine guns to 2,500 in France, 6,000 77-millimeter cannon to 3,800 French 75s, and an almost total monopoly in heavy artillery."[97] The last aspect in particular showed French weaknesses at their worst.

And yet the French army went into battle in 1914 confident of victory, having dropped its defensive strategy in favor of an all-out offensive, reflecting the heightened emphasis upon morale which Grandmaison and others attempted to inculcate into the army—psychologically, one suspects, as compensation for these very material weaknesses. "Neither numbers nor miraculous machines will determine victory," General Messing preached. "This will go to soldiers with valor and quality—and by this I mean superior physical and moral endurance, offensive strength."[98] This assertiveness was associated with the "patriotic revival" in France which took place after the 1911

Moroccan crisis and which suggested the country would fight far better than it had in 1870, despite the class and political divisions which had made it appear so vulnerable during the Dreyfus affair. Most military experts assumed that the war to come would be short. What mattered, therefore, was the number of divisions which could immediately be put into the field, not the size of the German steel and chemical industries nor the millions of potential recruits Germany possessed.[99]

This revival of national confidence was perhaps most strongly affected by the improvement in France's international position secured by the foreign minister, Delcassé, and his diplomats after the turn of the century.[100] Not only had they nursed and maintained the vital link to St. Petersburg despite all the diplomatic efforts of the Kaiser's government to weaken it, but they had steadily improved relations with Italy, virtually detaching it from the Triple Alliance (and thus easing the strategical problem of having to fight in Savoy as well as Lorraine). Most important of all, the French had been able to compose their colonial differences with Britain in the 1904 *entente,* and then to convince leading members of the Liberal government in London that France's security was a British national interest. Although domestic-political reasons in Britain precluded a fixed alliance, the chances of France obtaining future British support improved with each addition to Germany's High Seas Fleet and with every indication that a German strike westward would go through neutral Belgium. If Britain did come in, the Germans would have to worry not only about Russia but about the effect of the Royal Navy on its High Seas Fleet, the destruction of its overseas trade, and a small but significant British expeditionary force deployed in northern France. Fighting the Boches with Russia and Britain as one's allies had been the French dream since 1871; now it seemed a distinct reality.

France was not strong enough to oppose Germany in a one-to-one struggle, something which all French governments were determined to avoid. If the mark of a Great Power is a country which is willing and able to take on any other, then France (like Austria-Hungary) had slipped to a lower position. But that definition seemed too abstract in 1914 to a nation which felt psychologically geared up for war,[101] militarily stronger than ever, wealthy, and, above all, endowed with powerful allies. Whether even a combination of all those features would enable France to withstand Germany was an open question; but most Frenchmen seemed to think it would.

Great Britain

At first sight, Britain was imposing. In 1900 it possessed the largest empire the world had ever seen, some twelve million square miles of land and perhaps a quarter of the population of the globe. In the preceding three decades alone, it had added 4.25 million square miles

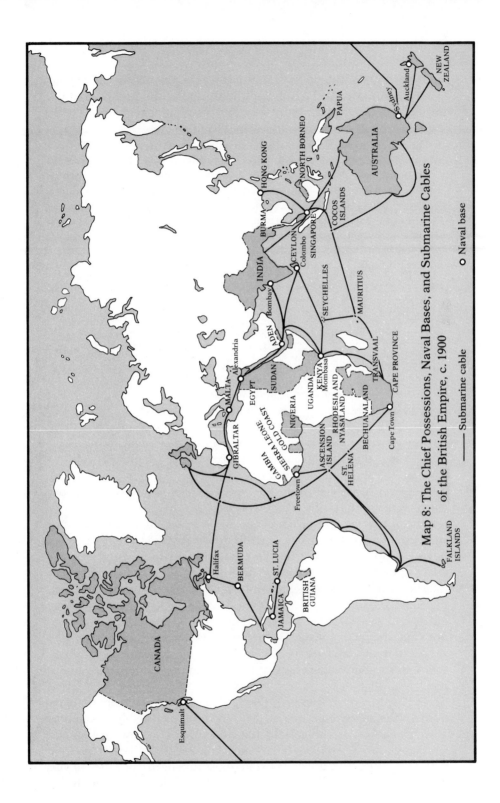

Map 8: The Chief Possessions, Naval Bases, and Submarine Cables of the British Empire, c. 1900

○ Naval base

—— Submarine cable

NEW ZEALAND
Auckland
Sydney
AUSTRALIA
PAPUA
NORTH BORNEO
COCOS ISLANDS
SINGAPORE
HONG KONG
BURMA
CEYLON
Colombo
INDIA
Bombay
SEYCHELLES
MAURITIUS
ADEN
Alexandria
MALTA
EGYPT
SUDAN
GIBRALTAR
GAMBIA
SIERRA LEONE
GOLD COAST
NIGERIA
Freetown
ASCENSION ISLAND
UGANDA
KENYA
Mombasa
RHODESIA AND NYASALAND
ST. HELENA
BECHUANALAND
TRANSVAAL
CAPE PROVINCE
Cape Town
FALKLAND ISLANDS
BRITISH GUIANA
JAMAICA
ST. LUCIA
BERMUDA
Halifax
CANADA
Esquimalt

and 66 million people to the empire. It was not simply a critical later historian but also the French and the Germans, the Ashanti and the Burmese, and many others at the time, who felt as follows:

> There had taken place, in the half-century or so before the [1914] war, a tremendous expansion of British power, accompanied by a pronounced lack of sympathy for any similar ambition on the part of other nations. . . . If any nation had truly made a bid for world power, it was Great Britain. In fact, it had more than made a bid for it. It had achieved it. The Germans were merely talking about building a railway to Bagdad. The Queen of England was Empress of India. If any nation had upset the world's balance of power, it was Great Britain.[102]

There were other indicators of British strength: the vast increases in the Royal Navy, equal in power to the next two largest fleets; the unparalleled network of naval bases and cable stations around the globe; the world's largest merchant marine by far, carrying the goods of what was still the world's greatest trading nation; and the financial services of the City of London, which made Britain the biggest investor, banker, insurer, and commodity dealer in the global economy. The crowds who cheered their heads off during Victoria's Diamond Jubilee festivities in 1897 had some reason to be proud. Whenever the three or four world empires of the coming century were discussed, it—but not France, or Austria-Hungary, or many other candidates—was always on the short list of members.

However, if viewed from other perspectives—say, from the sober calculations of the British "official mind,"[103] or from that of later historians of the collapse of British power—the late nineteenth century was certainly not a time when the empire was making a "bid for world power." On the contrary, that "bid" had been made a century earlier and had climaxed in the 1815 victory, which allowed the country to luxuriate in the consequent half-century of virtually unchallenged maritime and imperial preeminence. After 1870, however, the shifting balance of world forces was eroding British supremacy in two ominous and interacting ways. The first was that the spread of industrialization and the changes in the military and naval weights which followed from it weakened the relative position of the British Empire more than that of any other country, because it was *the* established Great Power, with less to gain than to lose from fundamental alterations in the status quo. Britain had not been as directly affected as France and Austria-Hungary by the emergence of a powerful, united Germany (only after 1904–1905 would London really have to grapple with that issue). But it was *the* state most impinged upon by the rise of American power, since British interests (Canada, naval bases in the

Caribbean, trade and investment in Latin America) were much more prominent in the western hemisphere than those of any other European country;[104] it was *the* country most affected by the expansion of Russian borders and strategic railways in Turkestan, since everyone could see the threat which that posed to British influence in the Near East and Persian Gulf, and ultimately perhaps to its control of the Indian subcontinent;[105] it was *the* country which, by enjoying the greatest share of China's foreign trade, was likely to have its commercial interests the most seriously damaged by a carving up of the Celestial Empire or by the emergence of a new force in that region;[106] similarly, it was *the* power whose relative position in Africa and the Pacific was affected the most by the post-1880 scramble for colonies, since it had (in Hobsbawm's phrase) "exchanged the informal empire over most of the underdeveloped world for the formal empire of a quarter of it"[107]—which was not a good bargain, despite the continued array of fresh acquisitions to Queen Victoria's dominions.

While some of these problems (in Africa or China) were fairly new, others (the rivalry with Russia in Asia, and with the United States in the western hemisphere) had exercised many earlier British administrations. What was different now was that the relative power of the various challenger states was much greater, while the threats seemed to be developing almost simultaneously. Just as the Austro-Hungarian Empire was distracted by having to grapple with a number of enemies within Europe, so British statesmen had to engage in a diplomatic and strategical juggling act that was literally worldwide in its dimensions. In the critical year of 1895, for example, the Cabinet found itself worrying about the possible breakup of China following the Sino-Japanese War, about the collapse of the Ottoman Empire as a result of the Armenian crisis, about the looming clash with Germany over southern Africa at almost exactly the same time as the quarrel with the United States over the Venezuela–British Guiana borders, about French military expeditions in equatorial Africa, and about a Russian drive toward the Hindu Kush.[108] It was a juggling act which had to be carried out in naval terms as well; for no matter how regularly the Royal Navy's budget was increased, it could no longer "rule the waves" in the face of the five or six foreign fleets which were building in the 1890s, as it had been able to do in midcentury. As the Admiralty repeatedly pointed out, it *could* meet the American challenge in the western hemisphere, but only by diverting warships from European waters, just as it *could* increase the size of the Royal Navy in the Far East, but only by weakening its squadrons in the Mediterranean. It could not be strong everywhere. Finally, it was a juggling act which had to be carried out in military terms, by the transfer of battalions from Aldershot to Cairo, or from India to Hong Kong, to meet the latest emergencies— and yet all this had to be done by a small-scale volunteer force that had been completely eclipsed by mass armies on the Prussian model.[109]

The second, interacting weakness was less immediate and dramatic, but perhaps even more serious. It was the erosion of Britain's industrial and commercial preeminence, upon which, in the last resort, its naval, military, and imperial strength rested. Established British industries such as coal, textiles, and ironware increased their output in absolute terms in these decades, but their relative share of world production steadily diminished; and in the newer and increasingly more important industries such as steel, chemicals, machine tools, and electrical goods, Britain soon lost what early lead it possessed. Industrial production, which had grown at an annual rule of about 4 percent in the period 1820 to 1840 and about 3 percent between 1840 and 1870, became more sluggish; between 1875 and 1894 it grew at just over 1.5 percent annually, far less than that of the country's chief rivals. This loss of industrial supremacy was soon felt in the cutthroat competition for customers. At first, British exports were priced out of their favorable position in the industrialized European and North American markets, often protected by high tariff barriers, and then out of certain colonial markets, where other powers competed both commercially and by placing tariffs around their new annexations; and, finally, British industry found itself weakened by an ever-rising tide of imported foreign manufacturers into the unprotected home market— the clearest sign that the country was becoming uncompetitive.

The slowdown of British productivity and the decrease in competitiveness in the late nineteenth century has been one of the most investigated issues in economic history.[110] It involved such complex issues as national character, generational differences, the social ethos, and the educational system as well as more specific economic reasons like low investment, out-of-date plant, bad labor relations, poor salesmanship, and the rest. For the student of grand strategy, concerned with the *relative* picture, these explanations are less important than the fact that the country as a whole was steadily losing ground. Whereas in 1880 the United Kingdom still contained 22.9 percent of total world manufacturing output, that figure had shrunk to 13.6 percent by 1913; and while its share of world trade was 23.2 percent in 1880, it was only 14.1 percent in 1911–1913. In terms of industrial muscle, both the United States and imperial Germany had moved ahead. The "workshop of the world" was now in third place, not because it wasn't growing, but because others were growing faster.

Nothing frightened the thinking British imperialists more than this relative economic decline, simply because of its impact upon British *power*. "Suppose an industry which is threatened [by foreign competition] is one which lies at the very root of your system of National defence, where are you then?" asked Professor W.A.S. Hewins in 1904. "You could not get on without an iron industry, a great Engineering trade, because in modern warfare you would not have the means of producing, and maintaining in a state of efficiency, your fleets and armies."[111] Compared with this development, quarrels over colonial borders in West Africa or over the future of the Samoan Islands were trivial. Hence the imperialists' interests in tariff reform—abandoning the precepts of free trade in order to protect British industries—and in closer ties with the white dominions, in order to secure both defense contributions and an exclusive imperial market. Britain had now become, in Joseph Chamberlain's frightening phrase, "the weary Titan, [staggering] under the too vast orb of its fate."[112] In the years to come, the First Lord of the Admiralty warned, "the United Kingdom by itself will not be strong enough to hold its proper place alongside of the U.S., or Russia, and probably not Germany. We shall be thrust aside by sheer weight."[113]

Yet if the imperialists were undoubtedly right *in the long term*— "will the Empire which is celebrating one centenary of Trafalgar survive for the next?" the influential journalist Garvin asked gloomily in 1905[114]—they nearly all tended to exaggerate the contemporary perils. The iron and steel trades and the machine-tool industry had been overtaken in various markets, but were certainly not wiped out. The textile industry was enjoying an export boom in the years prior to 1914, which only in retrospect would be seen as an Indian summer. The British shipbuilding industry—vital for both the Royal Navy and the flourishing merchant marine—was still in a class of its own, launching over 60 percent of the world's merchant tonnage and 33 percent of its warships in these decades, which offered some consolation to those who feared that Britain had become too dependent upon imported foodstuffs and raw materials in wartime. It *was* true that if Britain became involved in a lengthy, mass-industrialized conflict between the Great Powers, it would find that much of its armaments industry (e.g., shells, artillery, aircraft, ball bearings, optical equipment, magnetos, dyestuffs) was inadequate, reflecting the traditional assumption that the British army was to be deployed and equipped for small colonial wars and not gigantic continental struggles. But for the greater part of this period, those were exactly the sort of conflicts in which the army was involved. And if the exhausting, lengthy "modern" warfare of trenches and machine guns which at least some pundits were already forecasting in 1898 did come to pass, then the British would not be alone in wanting the correct matériel.

That Britain also possessed economic *strengths* in this period ought to be a warning, therefore, against too gloomy and sweeping a portrayal of the country's problems. In retrospect one can assert, "From 1870 to 1970 the history of Britain was one of steady and almost unbroken decline, economically, militarily and politically, relative to other nations, from the peak of prosperity and power which her industrial revolution had achieved for her in the middle of the nineteenth century";[115] but there is also a danger of exaggerating and anticipating the pace of that decline and of ignoring the country's very considerable assets, even in the nonindustrial sphere. It was, in the first place, immensely wealthy, both at home and abroad, though the British Treasury felt itself under heavy pressure in the two decades before 1914 as the newer technology more than doubled the price of an individual battleship. Moreover, the increases in the size of the electorate were leading to considerable "social" spending for the first time. Yet if the increases in payments for "guns and butter" looked alarming in absolute terms, this was because the night-watchman state had been taking so little of an individual's income in taxes, and spending so little of the national income for government purposes. Even in 1913, total central *and* local government expenditure equaled only 12.3 percent of GNP. Thus, although Britain was one of the heaviest spenders on defense prior to 1914, it needed to allocate a smaller share of its national income to that purpose than any other Great Power in Europe;[116] and if archimperialists tended to disparage Britain's *financial* strength as opposed to *industrial* power, it did have the quite fantastic sum of around $19.5 *billion* invested overseas by then, equaling some 43 percent of the world's foreign investments,[117] which were an undoubted source of national wealth. There was no question that it could pay for even a large-scale, expensive war if the need arose; what was more doubtful was whether it could preserve its liberal political culture—of free trade, low government expenditures, lack of conscription, reliance chiefly upon the navy—if it was forced to devote more and more of its national resources to armaments and to modern, industrialized war.[118] But that it had a deep enough purse was indisputable.

Certain other factors also enhanced Britain's position among the Great Powers. Although it was increasingly difficult to think of defending the *landward* borders of the empire in an age when strategic railways and mass armies were undermining the geopolitical security of India and other possessions,[119] the insularity of the British Isles remained as great an advantage as ever—freeing its population from the fears of a sudden invasion by neighboring armies, allowing the emphasis upon sea power rather than land power, and giving its statesmen a much greater freedom of action over issues of war and peace than those enjoyed by the continental states. In addition, although the possession of an extensive and hard-to-defend colonial empire implied immense strategical problems, it also brought with it considerable strategical advantages. The great array of imperial garrisons, coaling stations, and fleet bases, readily reinforceable by sea, placed it in an extremely strong position against European powers in any conflict fought outside the continent. Just as Britain could send aid to its overseas possessions, so they (especially the self-governing dominions and

India) could assist the imperial power with troops, ships, raw materials, and money—and this was an age when politicians in Whitehall were carefully cultivating their kinsmen overseas in the cause of a more organized "imperial defense."[120] Finally, it might cynically be argued that because British power and influence had been extended so much in earlier times, Britain now possessed lots of buffer zones, lots of less-than-vital areas of interest, and therefore lots of room for *compromise*, especially in its spheres of so-called "informal empire."

Much of the public rhetoric of British imperialism does not suggest that concessions and withdrawals were the order of the day. But the careful assessment of British strategic priorities—which the system of interdepartmental consultation and Cabinet decision-making allowed[121]—went on, year after year, examining each problem in the *context* of the country's global commitments, and fixing upon a policy of compromise or firmness. Thus, since an Anglo-American war would be economically disastrous, politically unpopular, and strategically very difficult, it seemed preferable to make concessions over the Venezuela dispute, the isthmian canal, the Alaska boundary, and so on. By contrast, while Britain would be willing to bargain with France in the 1890s over colonial disputes in West Africa, southeast Asia, and the Pacific, it would fight to preserve its hold on the Nile Valley. A decade later, it would make attempts to defuse the Anglo-German antagonism (by proposing agreements over naval ratios, the Portuguese colonies, and the Baghdad Railway); but it was much more suspicious of offering promises concerning neutrality if a continental war should arise. While Foreign Secretary Grey's efforts toward Berlin prior to 1914 were about as successful as Salisbury's earlier bids to reach Asian accords with St. Petersburg, they both revealed a common assumption that diplomacy could solve most problems that arose in world affairs. To suggest, on the one hand, that Britain's global position around 1900 was as weakened as it was to be in the late 1930s, and to argue, on the other, that there had been "a tremendous expansion of British power" prior to 1914, upsetting the world's balances,[122] are equally one-sided portraits of what was a much more complex position.

In the several decades before the First World War, then, Great Britain had found itself overtaken industrially by both the United States and Germany, and subjected to intense competition in commercial, colonial, and maritime spheres. Nonetheless, its combination of financial resources, productive capacity, imperial possessions, and naval strength meant that it was still probably the "number-one" world power, even if its lead was much less marked than in 1850. But this position as number one was also the essential British problem. Britain was now a *mature* state, with a built-in interest in preserving existing arrangements or, at least, in ensuring that things altered slowly and peacefully. It would fight for certain obvious aims—the defense of

India, the maintenance of naval superiority especially in home waters, probably also the preservation of the European balance of power—but each issue had to be set in its larger context and measured against Britain's other interests. It was for this reason that Salisbury opposed a fixed military commitment *with* Germany in 1889 and 1898–1901, and that Grey strove to avoid a fixed military commitment *against* Germany in 1906–1914. While this made Britain's future policy frustratingly ambiguous and uncertain to decision-makers in Paris and Berlin, it reflected Palmerston's still widely held claim that the country had permanent interests but not permanent allies. If the circumstances which allowed such freedom of action were diminishing as the nineteenth century ended, nevertheless the traditional juggling act between Britain's various interests—imperial versus continental,[123] strategic versus financial[124]—continued in the same old fashion.

Russia

The empire of the czars was also, by most people's reckonings, an automatic member of the select club of "world powers" in the coming twentieth century. Its sheer size, stretching from Finland to Vladivostok, ensured that—as did its gigantic and fast-growing population, which was nearly three times that of Germany and nearly four times that of Britain. For four centuries it had been expanding, westward, southward, eastward, and despite setbacks it showed no signs of wanting to stop. Its standing army had been the largest in Europe throughout the nineteenth century, and it was still much bigger than anybody else's in the approach to the First World War, with 1.3 million front-line troops and, it was claimed, up to 5 million reserves. Russia's military expenditures, too, were extremely high and with the "extraordinary" capital grants on top of the fast-rising "normal" expenditures may well have equaled Germany's total. Railway construction was proceeding at enormous speed prior to 1914—threatening within a short time to undermine the German plan (i.e., the so-called Schlieffen Plan) to strike westward first—and money was also being poured into a new Russian fleet after the war with Japan. Even the Prussian General Staff claimed to be alarmed at this expansion of Russian might, with the younger Moltke asserting that by 1916 and 1917 Prussia's "enemies' military power would then be so great that he did not know how he could deal with it."[125] Some of the French observers, by contrast, looked forward with great glee to the day when the Russian "steamroller" would roll westward and flatten Berlin. And a certain number of Britons, especially those connected with the St. Petersburg embassy, were urging their political chiefs that "Russia is rapidly becoming so powerful that we must retain her friendship at almost any cost."[126] From Galicia to Persia to Peking, there was a widespread concern at the growth of Russian might.

Was Russia really on the point of becoming the gendarme of Europe once more, as these statements might suggest? Assessing that country's effective strength has been a problem for western observers from the eighteenth century to the present, and it has always been made the harder by the paucity of reliable runs of comparative data, by the differences between what the Russians said to foreigners and said to themselves, and by the dangers of relying upon sweeping subjective statements in the place of objective fact. Surveys, however thorough, of "how Europe judged Russia before 1914" are *not* the same as an exact analysis of "the power of Russia" itself.[127]

From the plausible evidence which does exist, however, it seems that Russia in the decades prior to 1914 was simultaneously powerful *and* weak—depending, as ever, upon which end of the telescope one peered down. To begin with, it was now much stronger industrially than it had been at the time of the Crimean War.[128] Between 1860 and 1913—a very lengthy period—Russian industrial output grew at the impressive annual average rate of 5 percent, and in the 1890s the rate was closer to 8 percent. Its steel production on the eve of the First World War had overtaken France's and Austria-Hungary's, and was well ahead of Italy's and Japan's. Its coal output was rising even faster, from 6 million tons in 1890 to 36 million tons in 1914. It was the world's second-largest oil producer. While its long-established textile industry also increased—again, it had many more cotton spindles than France or Austria-Hungary—there was also a late development of chemical and electrical industries, not to mention armaments works. Enormous factories, frequently employing thousands of workers, sprang up around St. Petersburg, Moscow, and other major cities. The Russian railway network, already some 31,000 miles in 1900, was constantly augmented, so that by 1914 it was close to 46,000 miles. Foreign trade, stabilized by Russia's going onto the gold standard in 1892, nearly tripled between 1890 and 1914, when Russia became the world's sixth-largest trading nation. Foreign investment, attracted not only by Russian government and railway bonds but also by the potentialities of Russian business, brought enormous amounts of capital for the modernization of the economy. This great stream of funds joined the torrents of money which the state (flushed from increased customs receipts and taxes on vodka and other items of consumption) also poured into economic infrastructure. By 1914, as many histories have pointed out, Russia had become the fourth industrial power in the world. If these trends continued, might it not at last possess the industrial muscle concomitant with its extent of territory and population?

A look through the telescope from the other end, however, produces a quite different picture. Even if there were approximately three million workers in Russian factories by 1914, that represented the appallingly low level of 1.75 percent of the population; and while firms which employed ten thousand workers in one textile factory looked impressive on paper, most experts now agree that those figures may be deceptive, since the spindles were used through the night by fresh "shifts" of men and women in this labor-rich but technology-poor society.[129] What was perhaps even more significant was the extent to which Russian industrialization, despite some indigenous entrepreneurs, was carried out by foreigners—a successful international firm like Singer, for example, or the large numbers of British engineers—or had at the least been created by foreign investors. "By 1914, 90 percent of mining, almost 100 percent of oil extraction, 40 percent of the metallurgical industry, 50 percent of the chemical industry and even 28 percent of the textile industry were foreign-owned."[130] This was not in itself an unusual thing—Italy's position was somewhat similar—but it does show an extremely heavy reliance upon foreign entrepreneurship and capital, which might or might not (as in 1899 and 1905) keep up its interest, rather than upon indigenous resources for industrial growth. By the early twentieth century, Russia had incurred the largest foreign debt in the world and, to keep the funds flowing in, needed to offer above-average market rates to investors; yet the outward payments of interest were increasingly larger than the "visible" trade balances: in sum, a precarious situation.

That was, perhaps, just one more sign of an "immature" economy, as was the fact that the largest part of Russian industry was devoted to textiles and food processing (rather than, say, engineering and chemicals). Its tariffs were the highest in Europe, to protect industries which were simultaneously immature and inefficient, yet the flood of imported manufactures was rising with every increase in the defense budget and railway building. But perhaps the best indication of its underdeveloped status was the fact that as late as 1913, 63 percent of Russian exports consisted of agricultural produce and 11 percent of timber,[131] both desperately needed to pay for the American farm equipment, German machine tools, and the interest on the country's vast foreign debt—which, however, they did not quite manage to do.

Yet the assessment of Russian strength is worse when it comes to *comparative* output. Although Russia was the fourth-largest industrial power before 1914, it was a long way behind the United States, Britain, and Germany. In the indices of its steel production, energy consumption, share of world manufacturing production, and total industrial potential, it was eclipsed by Britain and Germany; and when these figures are related to population size and calculated on a per capita basis, the gap was a truly enormous one. In 1913 Russia's per capita level of industrialization was less than one-quarter of Germany's and less than one-sixth of Britain's.[132]

At base, the Russia which in 1914 overawed the younger Moltke and the British ambassador to St. Petersburg was a peasant society. Some

80 percent of the population derived its livelihood from agriculture, and a good part of the remainder continued to have ties to the village and the commune. This deadening fact needs to be linked to two others. The first is that most of Russia's enormous increase in population—61 million new mouths between 1890 and 1914 alone—occurred in the villages, and in the most backward (and non-Russian) regions, where poor soil, little fertilizer, and wooden plows were common. Secondly, all the comparative international data of this period show how inefficient Russian agriculture was overall—its crop yield for wheat being less than a third of Britain's and Germany's, for potatoes being about half.[133] Although there were modern estates and farms in the Baltic region, in so many other areas the effect of the communal possession of land and the medieval habit of strip-farming was to take away the incentive for individual enterprise. So too did the periodic redistribution of the lands. The best way to increase one's family share of land was simply to breed more and more sons before the next redistribution. This structural problem was not aided by the poor communications, the unpredictable but dreadful impact of the climate upon the crops, and the great disparity between the "surplus" provinces in the south and the overcrowded, less fertile "importing" provinces in old Russia proper. In consequence, while agricultural output did steadily increase over these decades (at about 2 percent annually), its gains were greatly eroded by the rise in population (1.5 percent annually). And because this enormous agricultural sector was increasing its *per capita* output by a mere 0.5 percent annually, the *real national product of Russia* was only expanding at about 1 percent per head[134]—much less than those of Germany, the United States, Japan, Canada, and Sweden, and of course, a quite different figure from the much-quoted annual *industrial* increases of 5 or 8 percent.

The social consequences of all this are also a factor in any assessment of Russian *power*. Professor Grossman observes that "the extraordinarily swift growth of industry tended to be associated with great sluggishness—and even significant reverses—in other sectors, especially in agriculture and personal consumption; it also tended to outpace the modernization of society, if one may be permitted the phrase."[135] It is, in fact, a most seeming phrase. For what was happening was that a country of extreme economic backwardness was being propelled into the modern age by political authorities obsessed by the need "to acquire and retain the status of a European Great Power."[136] Thus, although one certainly can detect considerable self-driven entrepreneurial activities, the great *thrust* toward modernization was state-inspired and related to military needs—railways, iron and steel, armaments, and so on. But in order to afford the vast flow of imported foreign manufactures and to pay interest on the enormous foreign debt, the Russian state had to ensure that agricultural exports (especially wheat) were steadily increased, even in period of great famine, like 1891; the slow increase in farm output did not, in many years, imply a better standard of living for the deprived and undernourished peasantry. By the same token, in order to pay for the state's own extremely heavy capital investments in industrialization and in defense expenditures, high (chiefly indirect) taxes had to be repeatedly raised and personal consumption squeezed. To use an expression of the economic historians, the czarist government was securing "forced" savings from its helpless populace. Hence the staggering fact that "by 1913 the average Russian had 50 percent more of his income appropriated by the state for current defense than did the average Englishman, even though the Russian's income was only 27 percent of that of his British contemporary."[137]

The larger social costs of this unhealthy combination of agrarian backwardness, industrialization, and top-heavy military expenditures are easy to imagine. In 1913, while 970 million rubles were allocated by the Russian government to the armed forces, a mere 154 million rubles were spent upon health and education; and since the administrative structure did not give the localities the fiscal powers of the American states or English local government, that inadequacy could not be made up elsewhere. In the fast-growing cities, the workers had to contend with no sewerage, health hazards, appalling housing conditions, and high rents. There were fantastic levels of drunkenness—a short-term escape from brute reality. The mortality rate was the highest in Europe. Such conditions, the discipline enforced within the factories, and the lack of any appreciable real rise in living standards produced a sullen resentment of the system which in turn offered an ideal breeding ground for the populists, Bolsheviks, anarchosyndicalists, radicals—indeed, for anybody who (despite the censorship) argued for drastic changes. After the epic 1905 unrest, things cooled off for a while; but in the three years 1912–1914 the incidence of strikes, mass protests, police arrests, and killings was spiraling to an alarming degree.[138] Yet that sort of ferment paled by comparison with the issue which has frightened all Russian leaders from Catherine the Great to the present regime—the "peasant question." When bad harvests and high prices occurred, they interacted with the deep resentments against high rents and grim working conditions to produce vast outbreaks of agrarian unrest. After 1900, the historian Norman Stone records:

> The provinces of Poltyra and Tambov were, for the greater part, devastated; manor houses burned down, animals mutilated. In 1901 there were 155 interventions by troops (as against 36 in 1898) and in 1903, 322, involving 295 squadrons of cavalry and 300 battalions of infantry, some with artillery. 1902 was the high point of the whole

thing. Troops were used to crush the peasantry on 365 occasions. In 1903, for internal order, a force far greater than the army of 1812 was mustered. . . . In sixty-eight of the seventy-five districts of the central Black Earth there were "troubles"—fifty-four estates wrecked. The worst area was Saratov.[139]

Yet when the minister for the interior, Stolypin, tried to reduce this discontent by breaking up the peasant communes after 1908, he simply provoked fresh unrest—whether from villages determined to keep their communal system or from newly independent farmers who swiftly went bankrupt. Thus, "Troops were needed on 13,507 occasions in January 1909, and 114,108 occasions that [whole] year. By 1913, there were 100,000 arrests for 'attacks on State power.' "[140] Needless to say, all this strained a reluctant army, which was also busy crushing the resentful ethnic minorities—Poles, Finns, Georgians, Latvians, Estonians, Armenians—who were seeking to preserve the grudging concessions over "Russification" which they had obtained during the regime's weakness in 1905–1906.[141] Any further military defeat would once again see such groups striving to escape Muscovy's domination. Although we do not have the exact breakdown, there was doubtless a heavy proportion of such groups in the staggering total of two million Russians who got married in August 1914—in order to avoid being drafted into the army.

In short, it is not simply from the perspective of the post–Bolshevik Revolution that one can see that Russia before 1914 was a sociopolitical tinderbox, and very likely to produce large conflagrations in the event of further bad harvests, or reductions in the factory workers' standards of living, or—possibly—a great war. One is bound to use the words "very likely" here, since there also existed (alongside these discontents) a deep loyalty to czar and country in many areas, an increasingly nationalistic assembly, broad Pan-Slavic sympathies, and a corresponding hatred of the foreigner. Indeed, there was many a feckless publicist and courtier, in 1914 as in 1904, who argued that the regime could not afford to appear reticent in great international issues. If it came to war, they urged, the nation would firmly support the pursuit of victory.[142]

But could such a victory be assured, given Russia's likely antagonists in 1914? In the war against Japan, the Russian soldier had fought bravely and stolidly enough—as he had in the Crimea and in the 1877 war against Turkey—but incompetent staffwork, poor logistical support, and unimaginative tactics all had had their effect. Could the armed services now take on Austria-Hungary—and, more particularly, the military-industrial powerhouse of imperial Germany—with any better result? Despite all of its own absolute increases in industrial output in this period, the awful fact was that Russia's productive strength was actually *decreasing* relative to Germany's. Between 1900 and 1913, for example, its own steel production rose from 2.2 to 4.8 million tons, but Germany's leaped forward from 6.3 to 17.6 million tons. In the same way, the increases in Russia's energy consumption and total industrial potential were not as large, either absolutely or relatively, as Germany's. Finally, it will be noticed that in the years 1900–1913 Russia's share of world manufacturing production *sank*, from 8.8 percent to 8.2 percent, because of the expansion of the German and (especially) the American shares.[143] There were not encouraging trends.

But, it has been argued, "by the yardstick with which armies were measured in 1914," Russia *was* powerful, since "a war which tested economics and state bureaucratic structures as well as armies" was not anticipated by the military experts.[144] If so, one is left wondering why contemporary references to German military power drew attention to Krupp steel, the shipyards, the dyestuffs industry, and the efficiency of German railways *as well as* front-line forces.[145] Nonetheless, if it is simply the military figures which matter, then the fact that Russia was creating ever more divisions, artillery batteries, strategic railways, and warships did impress. Assuming that a war would be a short one, these sorts of general statistics all pointed to Russia's growing strength.

Once this superficial level of number-counting is discarded, however, even the military issue becomes altogether more problematical. Once again, the decisive factor was Russia's socioeconomic and technical backwardness. The sheer size of its vast peasant population meant that only one-fifth of each annual cohort was actually conscripted into the armed forces; to have taken in every able-bodied man would have caused the system to collapse in chaos. But those peasants who were recruited could hardly be regarded as ideal material for a modern industrialized war. Thanks to the crude and overheavy concentration upon armaments rather than the broader, more subtle areas of national strength (e.g., general levels of education, technological expertise, bureaucratic efficiency), Russia was frightfully backward at the *personnel* level. As late as 1913 its literacy rate was only 30 percent, which, as one expert has tartly remarked, "was a much lower rate than for mid-eighteenth-century England."[146] And while it was all very well to vote vast sums of money for new recruits, would they be of much use if the army possessed too few trained NCOs? The experts in the Russian general staff, looking with "feelings of inferiority and envy" at Germany's strength in that respect, thought not. They were also aware (as were some foreign observers) of the desperate shortages of good officers.[147] Indeed, from the evidence now available, it appears that in almost all respects—heavy artillery, machine guns, handling of large numbers of infantry, levels of technical training, communications, and even its large fleet of aircraft—the Russian military was acutely conscious of its weaknesses.[148]

The same sort of gloomy conclusions arose when Russia's planned mobilization and strategic-railway system were examined in detail. Although the *overall* mileage of the railway network by 1914 seemed impressive, once it was set against the immense distances of the Russian Empire—or compared with the much denser systems of western Europe—its inadequacy became clear. In any case, since many of these lines were built on the cheap, the rails were often too light and the bedding for the track too weak, and there were too few water tanks and crossings. Some locomotives burned coal, others oil, others wood, which further complicated things—but that was a small problem compared with the awkward fact that the army's peacetime locations were quite different from its wartime deployment areas and affected by its deliberate dispersion policy (Poles serving in Asia, Caucasians in the Baltic provinces, etc.). Yet if a great war came, the masses of troops had somehow to be efficiently transported by the inadequate staff of the railway battalions, of whom "over a third were wholly or partly illiterate, while three-quarters of the officers had no technical training."[149]

The mobilization and deployment problem was exacerbated by the almost insuperable difficulty caused by Russia's commitments to France and Serbia. Given the country's less efficient railway system and the vulnerability of the forces deployed in the Polish salient to a possible "pincer" attack from East Prussia and Galicia, it had seemed prudent prior to 1900 for the Russian high command to stay on the defensive at the outset of war and steadily to build up its military strength; and, indeed, some strategists still argued that case in 1912. Many more generals, however, were keen to smash Austria-Hungary (against which they were confident of victory) and, as the tension between Vienna and Belgrade mounted, to help the latter in the event of an Austro-Hungarian invasion of Serbia. Yet for Russia to concentrate its forces on the southern front was made impossible by the fear of what Germany might do. For decades after 1871, the planners had assumed that a Russo-German war would begin with a massive and swift German assault eastward. But when the outlines of the Schlieffen Plan became clear, St. Petersburg came under enormous French pressure to launch offensives against Germany *as soon as it could,* in order to relieve its western ally. Fear of having France eliminated, together with Paris's tough insistence that further loans be tied to improvements in Russia's *offensive* capabilities, compelled the Russian planners to agree to strike westward as quickly as possible. All this had caused enormous wrangles within the general staff in the few years before 1914, with the various schools of thought disagreeing over the number of army corps to be deployed on the northern as opposed to the southern front, over the razing of the old defensive fortresses in Poland (in which, absurdly, so much of the new artillery was sited), and over the feasibility of ordering a partial rather than a complete mobilization. Given Russia's diplomatic obligations, the ambivalence was perhaps understandable; but it did not help the cause of producing a smoothly run military machine which would secure swift victories against its foes.[150]

This catalogue of problems could be extended almost ad nauseam. The fifty divisions of Russian cavalry, thought vital in a country with few modern roads, required so much fodder—there were about one million horses!—that they alone would probably produce a breakdown in the railway system; supplying hay would certainly slow down any sustained offensive operation, or even the movement of reserves. Because of the backwardness of its transport system and the internal-policing roles of the military, literally millions of its soldiers in wartime would not be considered front-line troops at all. And although the sums of money allocated to the army prior to 1914 seemed enormous, much of it was consumed by the basic needs of food, clothing, and fodder. Similarly, despite the large-scale increases in the fleet and the fact that many of the new designs have been described as "excellent,"[151] the navy required a much higher level of technical training as well as more frequent tactical practice among its personnel to be truly effective; since it had neither (the crews were still based mainly on shore) and was forced to divide its fleet between the Baltic and the Black Sea, the prospects for Russian sea power were not good—unless it fought only the Turks.

Finally, no assessment of Russia's overall capacities in this period can avoid some comments upon the regime itself. Although certain foreign conservatives admired its autocratic and centralized system, arguing that it gave a greater consistency and strength to national policies than the western democracies were capable of, a closer examination would have revealed innumerable flaws. Czar Nicholas II was a Potemkin village in person, simple-minded, reclusive, disliking difficult decisions, and blindly convinced of his sacred relationship with the Russian people (in whose real welfare, of course, he showed no interest). The methods of governmental decision-making at the higher levels were enough to give "Byzantinism" a bad name: irresponsible grand dukes, the emotionally unbalanced empress, reactionary generals, and corrupt speculators, outweighing by far the number of diligent and intelligent ministers whom the regime could recruit and who, only occasionally, could reach the czar's ear. The lack of consultation and understanding between, say, the foreign ministry and the military was at times frightening. The court's attitude to the assembly (the Duma) was one of unconcealed contempt. Achieving radical reforms in this atmosphere was impossible, when the aristocracy cared only for its privileges and the czar cared only for his peace of mind. Here was an elite in constant fear of workers' and peasants' unrest, and yet, although government spending was by far the largest in the world in absolute terms, it kept direct taxes on the rich to a minimum (6 percent of the state's revenue) and placed massive burdens upon foodstuffs and vodka (about 40 percent). Here was a country with a delicate balance of payments, but with no chance of preventing (or taxing) the vast outflow of monies which Russian aristocrats spent abroad. Partly because of the traditions of heavy-handed autocracy, partly because of the inordinately flawed class system, and partly because of the low levels of education and pay, Russia lacked those cadres of competent civil servants who made, for example, the German, British, and Japanese administrative systems *work*. Russia was not, in reality, a strong state; and it was still one which, given the drift in leadership, was capable of blundering unprepared into foreign complications, notwithstanding the lessons of 1904.

How then, are we to assess the real power of Russia in these years? That it was growing in both industrial and military terms year by year was undoubted. That it possessed many other strengths—the size of its army, the patriotism and sense of destiny in certain classes of society, the near-invulnerability of its Muscovite heartland—was also true. Against Austria-Hungary, against Turkey, perhaps now even against Japan, it had good prospects of fighting and winning. But the awful thing was that its looming clash with Germany was coming too early for Russia to deal with. "Give the state twenty years of internal and external peace," boasted Stolypin in 1909, "and you will not recognize Russia." That *may* have been true, even if Germany's strength was also likely to increase over the same period. Yet according to the data produced by Professors Doran and Parsons (see Chart 1), the "relative power" of Russia in these decades was just rising from its low point after 1894 whereas Germany's was close to its peak.[152]

And while that may be too schematized a presentation to most readers, it had indeed been true (as mentioned previously) that Russia's power and influence had declined throughout much of the nineteenth century in rough proportion to her increasing economic backwardness. Every major exposure to battle (the Crimean War, the Russo-Japanese War) had revealed both new and old military weaknesses, and compelled the regime to endeavor to close the gap which had opened up between Russia and the western nations. In the years before 1914, it seemed to some observers that the gap was again being closed, although to others manifold weaknesses still remained. Since it could not have Stolypin's required two decades of peace, it would once again have to pass through the test of war to see if it had recovered the position in European power politics which it possessed in 1815 and 1848.

Chart 1. The Relative Power of Russia and Germany

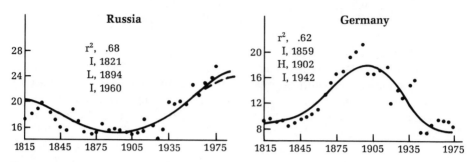

Key:
 L = year of low point
 H = year of high point
 I = year of inflection point

Source: Doran and Parsons

United States

Of all the changes which were taking place in the global power balances during the late nineteenth and early twentieth centuries, there can be no doubt that the most decisive one for the future was the growth of the United States. With the Civil War over, the United States was able to exploit the many advantages mentioned previously—rich agricultural land, vast raw materials, and the marvelously convenient evolution of modern technology (railways, the steam engine, mining equipment) to develop such resources; the lack of social and geographical constraints; the absence of significant foreign dangers; the flow of foreign and, increasingly, domestic investment capital—to transform itself at a stunning pace. Between the ending of the Civil War in 1865 and the outbreak of the Spanish-American War in 1898, for example, American wheat production increased by 256 percent, corn by 222 percent, refined sugar by 460 percent, coal by 800 percent, steel rails by 523 percent, and the miles of railway track in operation by over 567 percent. "In newer industries the growth, starting from near zero, was so great as to make percentages meaningless. Thus the production of crude petroleum rose from about 3,000,000 barrels in 1865 to over 55,000,000 barrels in 1898 and that of steel ingots and castings from less than 20,000 long tons to nearly 9,000,000 long tons."[153] This was not a growth which stopped with the war against Spain; on the contrary, it rose upward at the same meteoric pace throughout the early twentieth century. Indeed, given the advantages listed above, there was a virtual inevitability to the whole process. That is to say, only persistent human ineptitude, or near-constant civil war, or a climatic disaster could have checked this expansion—or deterred the millions of immi-

grants who flowed across the Atlantic to get their share of the pot of gold and to swell the productive labor force.

The United States seemed to have *all* the economic advantages which *some* of the other powers possessed *in part,* but *none* of their disadvantages. It was immense, but the vast distances were shortened by some 250,000 miles of railway in 1914 (compared with Russia's 46,000 miles, spread over an area two and a half times as large). Its agricultural yields per acre were always superior to Russia's; and if they were never as large as those of the intensively farmed regions of western Europe, the sheer size of the area under cultivation, the efficiency of its farm machinery, and the decreasing costs of transport (because of railways and steamships) made American wheat, corn, pork, beef, and other products cheaper than any in Europe. Technologically, leading American firms like International Harvester, Singer, Du Pont, Bell, Colt, and Standard Oil were equal to, or often better than, any in the world; and they enjoyed an enormous domestic market and economies of scale, which their German, British, and Swiss rivals did not. "Gigantism" in Russia was not a good indicator of industrial efficiency;[154] in the United States, it usually was. For example, "Andrew Carnegie was producing more steel than the whole of England put together when he sold out in 1901 to J. P. Morgan's colossal organization, the United States Steel Corporation."[155] When the famous British warship designer Sir William White made a tour of the United States in 1904, he was shaken to discover fourteen battleships and thirteen armored cruisers being built simultaneously in American yards (although, curiously, the U.S. merchant marine remained small). In industry *and* agriculture *and* communications, there was both efficiency and size. It was therefore not surprising that U.S. national income, in absolute figures and per capita, was so far above everybody else's by 1914.[156]

Table 21. National Income, Population, and per Capita Income of the Powers in 1914

	National Income	Population	Per Capita Income
United States	$37 billion	98 million	$377
Britain	11	45	244
France	6	39	153
Japan	2	55	36
Germany	12	65	184
Italy	4	37	108
Russia	7	171	41
Austria-Hungary	3	52	57

The consequences of this rapid expansion are reflected in Table 21, and in the pertinent comparative statistics. In 1914, the United States was producing 455 million tons of coal, well ahead of Britain's 292 million and Germany's 277 million. It was the largest oil producer in the world, and the greatest consumer of copper. Its pig-iron production was larger than those of the next three countries (Germany, Britain, France) combined, and its steel production almost equal[157] to the next four countries (Germany, Britain, Russia, and France). Its energy consumption from modern fuels in 1913 was equal to that of Britain, Germany, France, Russia, and Austria-Hungary together. It produced, and possessed, more motor vehicles than the rest of the world together. It was, in fact an entire rival continent and growing so fast that it was coming close to the point of overtaking all of Europe. According to one calculation, indeed, had these growth rates continued and a world war been avoided, the United States would have overtaken Europe as the region possessing the greatest economic output in the world by 1925.[158] What the First World War did, through the economic losses and dislocations suffered by the older Great Powers, was to bring that time forward, by six years, to 1919.[159] The "Vasco da Gama era"—the four centuries of European dominance in the world—was coming to an end even before the calaclysm of 1914.

The role of foreign trade in the United States' economic growth was small indeed (around 8 percent of its GNP derived from foreign trade in 1913, compared with Britain's 26 percent),[160] but its economic impact upon other countries was considerable. Traditionally, the United States had exported raw materials (especially cotton), imported finished manufactures, and made up the usual deficit in "visible" trade by the export of gold. But the post–Civil War boom in industrialization quite transformed that pattern. Swiftly becoming the world's largest producer of manufactures, the United States began to pour its farm machinery, iron and steel wares, machine tools, electrical equipment, and other products onto the world market. At the same time, the Northern industrialists' lobby was so powerful that it ensured that foreign products would be kept out of the home market by higher and higher tariffs; raw materials, by contrast, or specialized goods (like German dyestuffs) were imported in ever-larger quantities to supply American industry. But while the surge in the country's industrial exports was the most significant change, the "transportation revolution" also boosted American farm exports. With the cost of carrying a bushel of wheat from Chicago to London plummeting from 40 cents to 10 cents in the half-century before 1900, American agricultural produce streamed across the Atlantic. Corn exports peaked in 1897 at 212 million bushels, wheat exports in 1901 at 239 million bushels; this tidal wave also included grain and flour, meat and meat products.[161]

The consequences of this commercial transformation were, of course, chiefly economic, but they also began to affect international relations. The hyperproductivity of American factories and farms caused a widespread fear that even its enormous domestic market might soon be unable to absorb these goods, and led powerful interest groups (midwestern farmers as well as Pittsburgh steel producers) to press the government to give all sorts of aid to opening up, or at least keeping open, markets overseas. The agitation to preserve an "open door" in China and the massive interest shown in making the United States the dominant economic force in Latin America were only two of the manifestations of this concern to expand the country's share of world trade.[162] Between 1860 and 1914 the United States increased its exports more than sevenfold (from $334 million to $2.365 billion), yet because it was so protective of its own market, imports increased only fivefold (from $356 million to $1.896 billion). Faced with this avalanche of cheap American food, continental European farmers agitated for higher tariffs—which they usually got; in Britain, which had already sacrificed its grain farmers for the cause of free trade, it was the flood of American machines, and iron and steel, which produced alarm. While the journalist W. T. Stead wrote luridly of "the Americanization of the world"—the phrase was the title of his book of 1902—Kaiser Wilhelm and other European leaders hinted at the need to combine against the "unfair" American trading colossus.[163]

Perhaps even more destabilizing, although less well understood, was the impact of the United States upon the world's financial system and monetary flows. Because it had such a vast surplus in its trade with Europe, the latter's deficit had to be met by capital transfers—joining the enormous stream of direct European investments into U.S. industry, utilities, and services (which totaled around $7 billion by 1914). Although some of this westward flow of bullion was reversed by the returns on European investments and by American payments for services such as shipping and insurance, the drain was a large one, and constantly growing larger; and it was exacerbated by the U.S. Treasury's policy of accumulating (and then just sitting on) nearly one-third of the world's gold stock. Moreover, although the United States had by now become an integral part of a complete global trading system—running a deficit with raw-materials-supplying countries, and a vast surplus with Europe—its own financial structure was underdeveloped. Most of its foreign trade was done in sterling, for example, and London acted as the lender of last resort for gold. With no central bank able to control the financial markets, with a stupendous seasonal outflow and inflow of funds between New York and the prairie states conditioned solely by the grain harvest and that by a volatile climate, and with speculators able to derange not merely the domestic monetary system but also the frequent calls upon gold in London, the United States in the years before 1914 was already becoming a vast but unpredictable bellows, fanning but also on occasions dramatically cooling the world's trading system. The American banking crisis of 1907 (originally provoked by an attempt by speculators to corner the market in copper), with consequent impacts on London, Amsterdam, and Hamburg, was merely one example of the way the United States was impinging upon the economic life of the other Great Powers, even before the First World War.[164]

This growth of American industrial power and overseas trade was accompanied, perhaps inevitably, by a more assertive diplomacy and by an American-style rhetoric of *Weltpolitik.*[165] Claims to a special moral endowment among the peoples of the earth which made American foreign policy superior to those of the Old World were intermingled with Social Darwinistic and racial arguments, and with the urging of industrial and agricultural pressure groups for secure overseas markets. The traditional, if always exaggerated, alarm about threats to the Monroe Doctrine was accompanied by calls for the United States to fulfill its "Manifest Destiny" across the Pacific. While entangling alliances still had to be avoided, the United States was now being urged by many groups at home into a much more activist diplomacy—which, under the administrations of McKinley and (especially) Theodore Roosevelt, was exactly what took place. The 1895 quarrel with Britain over the Venezuelan border dispute—justified in terms of the Monroe Doctrine—was followed three years later by the much more dramatic war with Spain over the Cuban issue. Washington's demand to have sole control of an isthmian canal (instead of the older fifty-fifty arrangement with Britain), the redefinition of the Alaskan border despite Canadian protests, and the 1902–1903 battlefleet preparations in the Caribbean following the German actions against Venezuela were all indications of U.S. determination to be unchallenged by any other Great Power in the western hemisphere. As a "corollary" of this, however, American administrations showed themselves willing to intervene by diplomatic pressure *and* military means in Latin American countries such as Nicaragua, Haiti, Mexico, and the Dominican Republic when their behavior did not accord with United States norms.

But the really novel feature of American external policy in this period were its interventions and participation in events *outside* the western hemisphere. Its attendance at the Berlin West Africa Conference in 1884–1885 had been anomalous and confused: after grandiose speeches by the U.S. delegation in favor of free trade and open doors, the subsequent treaty was never ratified. Even as late as 1892 the *New York Herald* was proposing the abolition of the State Department, since it had so little business to conduct overseas.[166] The war with Spain in 1898 changed all that, not only by giving the United States a position in the western Pacific (the Philippines) which made it, too, a sort of Asiatic colonial power, but also by boosting the political fortunes of those who had favored an assertive policy. Secretary of State Hay's "Open Door" note in the following year was an early indication that the United States wished to have a say in China, as was the commitment of 2,500 American troops to the international army sent to restore order in China in 1900. Roosevelt showed an even greater willingness to engage in *grosse Politik,* acting as mediator in the talks which brought an end to the Russo-Japanese War, insisting upon American participation in the 1906 conference over Morocco, and negotiating with Japan and the other Powers in an attempt to maintain the "Open Door" in China.[167] Much of this has been seen by later scholars less as being based upon a sober calculation of the country's real interests in the world than as reflecting an immaturity of foreign-policy style, an ethnocentric naïveté, and a wish to impress audiences both at home and abroad—traits which would complicate a "realistic" American foreign policy in the future;[168] but even if that is true, the United States was hardly alone in this age of imperialist bombast and nationalist pride. In any case, except in Chinese affairs, such diplomatic activism was not maintained by Roosevelt's successors, who preferred to keep the United States free from international events occurring outside the western hemisphere.

Along with these diplomatic actions went increases in arms expenditures. Of the two services, the navy got the most, since it was the front line of the nation's defenses in the event of a foreign attack (or a challenge to the Monroe Doctrine) and also the most useful instrument to support American diplomacy and commerce in Latin America, the Pacific, and elsewhere. Already in the late 1880s, the rebuilding of the fleet had commenced, but the greatest boost came at the time of the Spanish-American War. Since the easy naval victories in that conflict seemed to justify the arguments of Admiral Mahan and the "big navy" lobby, and since the strategists worried about the possibility of a war with Britain and then, from 1898 onward, with Germany, the battle fleet was steadily built up. The acquisition of bases in Hawaii, Samoa, the Philippines, and the Caribbean, the use of naval vessels to act as "policemen" in Latin America, and Roosevelt's dramatic gesture of sending his "great white fleet" around the world in 1907 all seemed to emphasize the importance of sea power.

Consequently, while the naval expenditures of $22 million in 1890 represented only 6.9 percent of total federal spending, the $139 million allocated to the navy by 1914 represented 19 percent.[169] Not all of this was well spent—there were too many home fleet bases (the result of local political pressures) and too few escort vessels—but the result was still impressive. Although considerably smaller than the Royal Navy, and with fewer *Dreadnought*-type battleships than Germany, the U.S. Navy was the third largest in the world in 1914. Even the construction of a U.S.-controlled Panama Canal did not stop American planners from agonizing over the strategical dilemma of dividing the fleet, or leaving one of the country's coastlines exposed: and the records of some officers in these years reveal a somewhat paranoid suspicion of foreign powers.[170] In fact, given its turn-of-the-century *rapprochement* with Great Britain, the United States was immensely secure, and even if it feared the rise of German sea power, it really had far less to worry about than any of the other major powers.[171]

The small size of the U.S. military was in many ways a reflection of that state of security. The army, too, had been boosted by the war with Spain, at least to the extent that the public realized how minuscule it actually was, how disorganized the National Guard was, and how close to disaster the early campaigning in Cuba had come.[172] But the tripling of the size of the regular army after 1900 and the additional garrisoning tasks it acquired in the Philippines and elsewhere still left the service looking insignificant compared with that of even a middle-sized European country like Serbia or Bulgaria. Even more than Britain, the United States clung to a laissez-faire dislike of mass standing armies and avoided fixed military obligations to allies. Less than 1 percent of its GNP went to defense. Despite its imperialist activities in the period 1898–1914, therefore, it remained what the sociologist Herbert Spencer termed an "industrial" society rather than a "military" society like Russia. Since many historians have suggested that "the rise of the superpowers" began in this period, it is worth noting the staggering *differences* between Russia and the United States by the eve of the First World War. The former possessed a front-line army about ten times as large as the latter's; but the United States produced six times as much steel, consumed ten times as much energy, and was four times larger in total industrial output (in per capita terms, it was six times more productive).[173] No doubt Russia seemed the more powerful to all those European general staffs thinking of swiftly fought wars involving masses of available troops; but by all other criteria, the United States was strong and Russia weak.

The United States had definitely become a Great Power. But it was not part of the Great Power system. Not only did the division of powers between the presidency and the Congress made an active alliance policy virtually impossible, but it was also clear that no one was in favor of abandoning the existing state of very comfortable isolation. Separated from other strong nations by thousands of miles of ocean, possessing a negligible army, content to have achieved hemispheric dominance and, at least after Roosevelt's departure, less eager to engage in worldwide diplomacy, the United States in 1913 still stood on the edges of the Great Power system. And since most of the other countries after 1906 were turning their attention from Asia and Africa to developments in the Balkans and North Sea, it was perhaps not surprising that they tended to see the United States as less a factor in the international power balances than had been the case around the turn of the century. That was yet another of the common pre-1914 assumptions which the Great War itself would prove wrong.

Alliances and the Drift to War, 1890–1914

The third and final element in understanding the way the Great Power system was changing in these decades is to examine the volatile alliance diplomacy from Bismarck's demise to the outbreak of the First World War. For although the 1890s saw some relatively small-scale conflicts (the Sino-Japanese War, the Spanish-American War, the Boer War), and later one large if still localized encounter in the Russo-Japanese War, the general tendency after that time was for what Felix Gilbert has termed the "rigidification" of the alliance blocs.[174] This was accompanied by the expectation on the part of most governments that if and when the next great war occurred, they would be members of a coalition. This would enhance and complicate assessments of relative national power, since allies brought disadvantages as well as benefits.

The tendency toward alliance diplomacy did not, of course, affect the distant United States at this time, and it impinged upon Japan only in a regional way, through the Anglo-Japanese alliances of 1902 and 1905. But alliance diplomacy increasingly affected all the European Great Powers, even the insular British, because of the mutual fears and rivalries which arose in these years. This creation of fixed military alliances in peacetime—rarely if ever seen before—was begun by Bismarck in 1879, when he sought to "control" Vienna's foreign policy, and to warn off St. Petersburg, by establishing the Austro-German alliance. In the German chancellor's secret calculations, this move was also intended to induce the Russians to abandon their "erratic policy"[175] and to return to the Three Emperor's League—which, for a time, they did; but the longer-lasting legacy of Bismarck's action was that Germany bound itself to come to Austria-Hungary's aid in the event of a Russian attack. By 1882, Berlin had also concluded a similar mutual treaty with Rome in the event of a French attack, and within another year, both Germany and Austria-Hungary had offered another secret alliance, to aid Rumania against Russian aggression. Scholars of this diplomacy insist that Bismarck had chiefly short-term and defensive aims in view—to give comfort to nervous friends in Vienna, Rome, and Bucharest, to keep France diplomatically isolated, to prepare "fall-back" positions should the Russians invade the Balkans. No doubt that is true; but the fact is that he *had* given pledges, and further, that even if the exact nature of these secret treaties was not publicly known, it caused both France and Russia to worry about their own isolation and to suspect that the great wire-puller in Berlin had built up a formidable coalition to overwhelm them in wartime.

Although Bismarck's own "secret wire" to St. Petersburg (the so-called Reinsurance Treaty of 1887) prevented a formal break between Germany and Russia, there was something artificial and desperate in these baroque, double-crossing efforts by the chancellor to prevent the steady drift toward a Franco-Russian alliance in the late 1880s. The respective aspirations of France to recover Alsace-Lorraine and Russia to expand in eastern Europe were chiefly deterred by fear of Germany. There was no other *continental* alliance partner of note for either of them; and there beckoned the mutual benefits of French loans and weaponry for Russia, and Russian military aid for France. While ideological differences between the bourgeois French and the reactionary czarist regime slowed this drift for a while, the retirement of Bismarck in 1890 and the more threatening movements of Wilhelm II's government clinched the issue. By 1894, the Triple Alliance of Germany, Austria-Hungary, and Italy had been balanced by the Franco-Russian Dual Alliance, a political *and* military commitment which would last as long as the Triple Alliance did.[176]

In more ways than one, this new development appeared to stabilize the European scene. A rough equilibrium existed between the two alliance blocs, making the results of a Great Power conflict more incalculable, and thus less likely, than before. Having escaped from their isolation, France and Russia turned away to African and Asian concerns. This was aided, too, by the lessening of tensions in Alsace and in Bulgaria; by 1897, indeed, Vienna and St. Petersburg had agreed to put the Balkans on ice.[177] Furthermore, Germany was also turning toward *Weltpolitik,* while Italy, in its inimitable fashion, was becoming embroiled in Abyssinia. South Africa, the Far East, the Nile Valley, and Persia held people's attention by the mid-1890s. It was also the age of the "new navalism,"[178] with all the powers endeavoring to build up their fleets in the belief that navies and colonies naturally went hand in hand. Not surprisingly, therefore, this was the decade when the British Empire, although generally aloof from European entanglements, felt itself under the heaviest pressure, from old rivals like France and Russia, and then newer challengers like Germany, Japan, and the United States. In such circumstances, the importance of the military clauses of the European alliance blocs seemed less and less relevant, since a general war there would not be triggered off by happenings such as the Anglo-French clash at Fashoda (1898), the Boer War, or the scramble for concessions in China.

Yet, over the slightly longer term, these imperial rivalries were to affect the relations of the Great Powers, even in their European context. By the turn of the century, the pressures upon the British Empire were such that some circles around Colonial Secretary Joseph Chamberlain called for an end to "splendid isolation" and an alliance with Berlin, while fellow ministers such as Balfour and Lansdowne were beginning to accept the need for diplomatic compromises. A whole series of concessions to the United States over the isthmian canal, the Alaska boundary, seal fisheries, etc.—disguised under the term "the Anglo-American *rapprochement*"—took Britain out of a strategically untenable position in the western hemisphere and, more important still, drastically altered what nineteenth-century statesmen had taken for granted: that Anglo-American relations would always be cool, grudging, and occasionally hostile.[179] In forging the Anglo-Japanese Alliance of 1902, British statesmen also hoped to ease a difficult strategical burden in China, albeit at the cost of supporting Japan under certain circumstances.[180] And by 1902–1903, there were influential British circles who thought it possible to compromise over colonial issues with France, which had shown at the earlier Fashoda crisis that it would not go to war over the Nile.

While all these arrangements seemed at first to concern only extra-European affairs, they bore indirectly upon the standing of the Great Powers in Europe. The resolution of Britain's strategical dilemmas in the western hemisphere, plus the support it would gain from the Japanese fleet in the Far East, eased some of the pressures upon the Royal Navy's maritime dispositions and enhanced its prospects of consolidating in wartime; and settling Anglo-French rivalries would mean an even greater boost to Britain's naval security. All this also affected Italy, whose coastlines were simply far too vulnerable to allow itself to be placed in a camp opposite to an Anglo-French combination; in any case, by the early years of the twentieth century, France and Italy had their own good (financial and North African) reasons for improving relations.[181] However, if Italy was drifting away from the Triple Alliance, that was bound to affect its half-submerged quarrels with Austria-Hungary. Finally, even the distant Anglo-Japanese alliance was to have repercussions upon the European states system, since it made it unlikely that any third power would intervene when Japan decided in 1904 to challenge Russia over the future of Korea and Manchuria; moreover, when that war broke out, the specific clauses* of the Anglo-Japanese treaty *and* the Franco-Russian alliance strongly induced the two "seconds," Britain and France respectively, to work with each other to avoid being drawn openly into the conflict. It was not surprising, therefore, that the outbreak of hostilities in the Far East swiftly caused London and Paris to bring their colonial hagglings to an end and to conclude the *entente* of April 1904.[182] The years of Anglo-French rivalry, originally provoked by the British occupation of Egypt in 1882, were now over.

*Britain would be "benevolently neutral" to Japan if the latter was fighting one foe, but had to render military aid if it was fighting more than one; France's agreement to assist Russia was similarly phrased. Unless London and Paris both agreed to stay out, therefore, their new found friendship would be ruined.

Even this might not have caused the famous "diplomatic revolution"[183] of 1904–1905 if not for two other factors. The first was the growing suspicion held by the British and French toward Germany, whose aims, although unclear, looked ambitious and dangerous, as Chancellor Bülow and his imperial master Wilhelm II proclaimed the coming of the "German century." By 1902–1903 the High Seas Fleet, with a range and construction which suggested that it was being built chiefly with Britain in mind, was causing the British Admiralty to contemplate countermoves. In addition, while German aims toward Austria-Hungary were regarded with unease by Paris, its ambitions in Mesopotamia were disliked by British imperialists. Both countries observed with increasing anger Bülow's diplomatic efforts to encourage a Far East war in 1904 and to get them entangled in it—from which event Berlin would be the principal beneficiary.[184]

An even greater influence upon the European balances and relationships resulted from the impressive Japanese naval and military victories during the war, coinciding with the widespread unrest in Russia during 1905. With Russia unexpectedly reduced to a second-class power for some years to come, the military equilibrium in Europe swung decisively in favor of Berlin—against which France would now have worse prospects than in 1870. If ever there was a favorable time for Germany to strike westward, it probably would have been in the summer of 1905. But the Kaiser's concern over social unrest at home, his desire to improve relations with Russia, and his uncertainty about the British, who were redeploying their battleships from China to home waters and considering French pleas for aid if Germany did attack, all had their effect. Rather than plunge into war, Berlin opted instead for diplomatic victories, forcing its archfoe French Foreign Minister Delcassé from office, and insisting upon an international conference to check French pretensions in Morocco. Yet the results of the Algeciras meeting, which saw most of the conference participants supporting France's claim to a special position in Morocco, were a devastating confirmation of just how far Germany's diplomatic influence had declined since Bismarck's day, even as its industrial, naval, and military power had grown.[185]

The first Moroccan crisis returned international rivalries from Africa to the continent of Europe. This trend was soon reinforced by three more important events. The first was the 1907 Anglo-Russian *entente* over Persia, Tibet, and Afghanistan, in itself a regional affair but with wider implications for not only did it eliminate those Asian quarrels between London and St. Petersburg which all powers had taken for granted throughout the nineteenth century, and so ease Britain's defense of India, but it also caused nervous Germans to talk about being "encircled" in Europe. And while there were still many Britons, especially in the Liberal government, who did *not* see themselves as part of an anti-German coalition, their cause was weakened by the second event: the heated Anglo-German "naval race" of 1908–1909, following a further increase in Tirpitz's shipbuilding program and British fears that they would lose their naval lead even in the North Sea. When British efforts over the next three years to try to reduce this competition met with a German demand for London's neutrality in the event of a European war, the suspicious British backed away. They and the French had been nervously watching the Balkan crisis of 1908–1909, in which Russian indignation at Austria-Hungary's formal annexation of the provinces of Bosnia-Herzegovina led to a German demand that Russia accept the *fait accompli* or suffer the consequences.[186] Weakened by their recent war with Japan, the Russians submitted. But this diplomatic bullying produced in Russia a patriotic reaction, an increase in defense expenditures, and a determination to cling closer to one's allies.

Despite occasional attempts at a *détente* between one capital and another after 1909, therefore, the tendency toward "rigidification" increased. The second crisis over Morocco in 1911, when the British strongly intervened for France and against Germany, produced an upsurge of patriotic emotion in both of the latter countries and enormous increases in their army sizes as nationalists talked openly of the coming conflict, while in Britain the crisis had caused the government to confront its divergent military and naval plans in the event of joining a European war.[187] One year later, the failure of the diplomatic mission to Berlin by the British minister, Lord Haldane, and the further increases in the German fleet had driven London into the compromising November 1912 Anglo-French naval agreement. By that time, too, an opportunistic attack upon Turkey by Italian forces had been imitated by the states of the Balkan League, which virtually drove the Ottoman Empire out of Europe before its members then fell out over the spoils. This revival of the age-old "Eastern Question" was the most serious event of all, partly because the passionate strivings for advantage by the rivaling Balkan states could not really be controlled by the Great Powers, and partly because certain of the newer developments seemed to threaten the vital interests of some of those Powers: the rise of Serbia alarmed Vienna, the prospect of increasing German military influence over Turkey terrified St. Petersburg. When the assassination of Archduke Ferdinand in June 1914 provoked Austria-Hungary's actions against Serbia, and then the Russian countermoves, there was indeed much truth in the old cliché that the archduke's death was merely the spark which lit the tinderbox.[188]

The July 1914 assassination is one of the best-known examples in history of a particular event triggering a general crisis, and then a world war. Austria-Hungary's demands upon Serbia, its rejection of the conciliatory Serbian reply, and its attack upon Belgrade led to the

Russian mobilization in aid of its Serbian ally. But that, in turn, led the Prussian General Staff to press for the immediate implementation of the Schlieffen Plan, that is, its preemptive westward strike, via Belgium, against France—which had the further effect of bringing in the British.

While each of the Great Powers in this crisis acted according to its perceived national interests, it was also true that their decision to go to war had been affected by the existing operations plans. From 1909 onward the Germans committed themselves to Austria-Hungary, not just diplomatically but militarily, to a degree which Bismarck had never contemplated. Furthermore, the German operations plan now involved an immediate and massive assault upon France, via Belgium, whatever the specific cause of the war. By contrast, Vienna's military planners still dithered between the various fronts, but the determination to get a first blow in at Serbia was growing. Boosted by French funds, Russia pledged itself to an ever-swifter mobilization and westward strike should war come; while, with even less cause, the French in 1911 adopted the famous Plan XVII, involving a headlong rush into Alsace-Lorraine. And whereas the likelihood that Italy would fight alongside its Triple Alliance partners was now much decreased, a British military intervention in Europe had become the more probable in the event of a German attack upon Belgium and France. Needless to say, in each of the general staffs there was the unquestioned assumption that *speed* was of the essence; that is, as soon as a clash seemed likely, it was vital to mobilize one's own forces and to get them up to and over the border before the foe had a chance to do the same. If this was especially true in Berlin, where the army had committed itself to delivering a knockout blow in the west and then returning to the east to meet the slower-moving Russians, the same sort of thinking prevailed elsewhere. If and when a really great crisis occurred, the diplomats were not going to have much time before the strategic planners took over.[189]

The point about all of these war plans was not merely that they appear, in retrospect, like a line of dominoes which would tumble when the first one fell. What was also important was that since a coalition war was much more likely than in, say, 1859 or 1870, the prospects that the conflict would be prolonged were also that much greater, although few contemporaries appear to have realized it. The notorious miscalculation that the war begun in July/August 1914 would be "over by Christmas" has usually been explained away by the failure to anticipate that quick-firing artillery and machine guns made a *guerre de manœuvre* impossible and forced the masses of troops into trenches, from where they could rarely be dislodged; and that the later resort to prolonged artillery bombardments and enormous infantry offensives provided no solution, since the shelling merely churned up

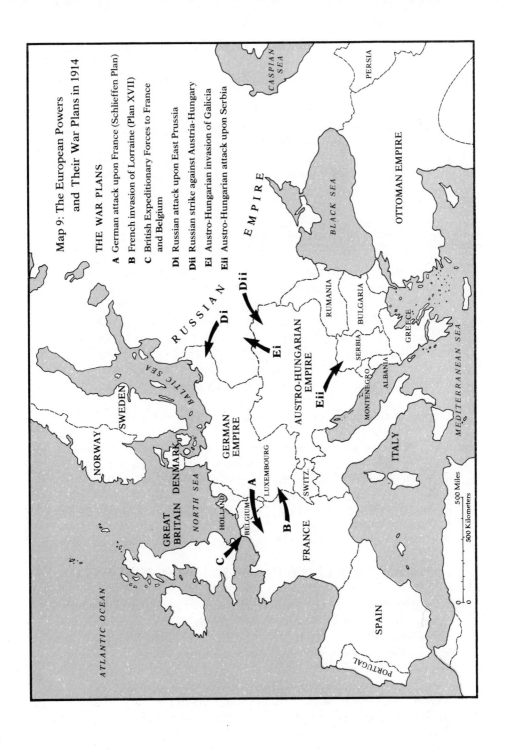

Map 9: The European Powers
and Their War Plans in 1914

THE WAR PLANS

A German attack upon France (Schlieffen Plan)
B French invasion of Lorraine (Plan XVII)
C British Expeditionary Forces to France
and Belgium
Di Russian attack upon East Prussia
Dii Russian strike against Austria-Hungary
Ei Austro-Hungarian invasion of Galicia
Eii Austro-Hungarian attack upon Serbia

the ground and gave the enemy notice of where the attack would take place.[190] In much the same way, it is argued that the admiralties of Europe also misread the war that was to come, preparing themselves for a decisive battle-fleet encounter and not properly appreciating that the geographical contours of the North Sea and Mediterranean and the newer weapons of the mine, torpedo, and submarine would make fleet operations in the traditional style very difficult indeed.[191] Both at sea and on land, therefore, a swift victory was unlikely for technical reasons.

All of this is, of course, true, but it needs to be put in the context of the alliance system itself.[192] After all, had the Russians been allowed to attack Austria-Hungary alone, or had the Germans been permitted a rerun of their 1870 war against France while the other powers remained neutral, the prospects of victory (even if a little delayed) seem incontestable. But these coalitions meant that even if one belligerent was heavily beaten in a campaign or saw that its resources were inadequate to sustain further conflict, it was encouraged to remain in the war by the hope—and promises—of aid from its allies. Looking ahead a little, France could hardly have kept going after the disastrous Nivelle offensive and the 1917 mutinies, Italy could hardly have avoided collapse after its defeat at Caporetto in 1917, and the Austro-Hungarian Empire could hardly have continued after the dreadful losses of 1916 (or even the 1914 failures in Galicia and Serbia) had not each of them received timely support from its allies. Thus, the alliance system itself virtually guaranteed that the war would *not* be swiftly decided, and meant in turn that victory in this lengthy duel would go—as in the great coalition wars of the eighteenth century—to the side whose combination of both military/naval *and* financial/industrial/technological resources was the greatest.

Total War and the Power Balances, 1914–1918

Before examining the First World War in the light of the grand strategy of the two coalitions and of the military and industrial resources available to them, it may be useful to recall the position of each of the Great Powers within the international system of 1914. The United States was on the sidelines—even if its great commercial and financial ties to Britain and France were going to make impossible Wilson's plea that it be "neutral in thought as in deed."[193] Japan liberally interpreted the terms of the Anglo-Japanese Alliance to occupy the German possessions in China and in the central Pacific; neither this nor its naval-escort duties further afield would be decisive, but for the Allies it was obviously far better to have a friendly Japan than a hostile one. Italy, by contrast, chose neutrality in 1914 and in view of its military and socioeconomic fragility would have been wise to maintain that policy: if its 1915 decision to enter the war *against* the Central Powers was a blow to Austria-Hungary, it is difficult to say that it was the significant benefit to Britain, France, and Russia that Allied diplomats had hoped for.[194] In much the same way, it was difficult to say who benefited most from the Turkish decision to enter the war on Berlin's side in November 1914. True, it blocked the Straits, and thus Russia's grain exports and arms imports; but by 1915 it would have been difficult to transport Russian wheat *anywhere,* and there were no "spare" munitions in the west. On the other hand, Turkey's decision opened the Near East to French and (especially) British imperial expansion—though it also distracted the imperialists in India and Whitehall from full concentration along the western front.[195]

The really critical positions, therefore, were those occupied by the "Big Five" powers in Europe. By this stage, it is artificial to treat Austria-Hungary as something entirely separate from Germany, for while Vienna's aims often diverged from Berlin's on many issues, it could make war or peace—and probably survive as a quasi-independent Great Power—only at the behest of its powerful ally.[196] The Austro-German combination was formidable. Its front-line armies were considerably smaller than those of the French and Russian, but they operated on efficient internal lines and could be supplemented by a swelling number of recruits. As can be seen from Table 22 below, they also enjoyed a considerable superiority in industrial and technological strength over the Dual Alliance.

The position of France and Russia was, of course, exactly the converse. Separated from each other by more than half of Europe, France and Russia would find it difficult (to say the least) to coordinate their military strategy. And while they appeared to enjoy a large lead in army strengths at the outset of the war, this was reduced by the clever German use of trained reservists in the front-line fighting, and this lead declined still further after the reckless Franco-Russian offensives in the autumn of 1914. With victory no longer going to the swift, it was more and more likely that it would go to the strong; and the industrial indices were not encouraging. Had the Franco-Russe alone been involved in a lengthy, "total" war against the Central Powers, it is hard to think how it could have won.

But the fact was, of course, that the German decision to launch a preemptive strike upon France by way of Belgium gave the upper hand to British interventionists.[197] Whether it was for the traditional reasons of the "balance of power" or in defense of "poor little Belgium," the British decision to declare war upon Germany was critical, though Britain's small, long-service army could affect the overall military equilibrium only marginally—at least until that force had transformed itself into a mass conscript army on continental lines. But since the war *was* going to last longer than a few months, Britain's strengths were considerable. Its navy could neutralize the German fleet and blockade the Central Powers—which would not bring the latter to their knees, but would deny them access to sources of supply outside continental Europe. Conversely, it ensured free access to supply sources for the Allied Powers (except when later interrupted by the U-boat campaign); and this advantage was compounded by the fact that Britain was such a wealthy trading country, with extensive links across the globe and enormous overseas investments, some of which at least could be liquidated to pay for dollar purchases. Diplomatically, these overseas ties meant that Britain's decision to intervene influenced Japan's action in the Far East, Italy's declaration of neutrality (and later switch), and the generally benevolent stance of the United States. More direct overseas support was provided, naturally enough, by the self-governing dominions and by India, whose troops moved swiftly into Germany's colonial empire and then against Turkey.

In addition, Britain's still-enormous industrial and financial resources could be deployed in Europe, both in raising loans and sending munitions to France, Belgium, Russia, and Italy, and in supplying and paying for the large army to be employed by Haig on the western front. The economic indices in Table 22 show the significance of Britain's intervention in power terms.

Table 22. Industrial/Technological Comparisons of the 1914 Alliances (taken from Tables 15–18 above)

	Germany/Austria-Hungary	France/Russia	+	Britain	=	
Percentages of world manufacturing production (1913)	19.2%	14.3%	+	13.6%	=	27.9%
Energy consumption (1913), metric million tons of coal equivalent	236.4	116.8	+	195.0	=	311.8
Steel production (1913), in million tons	20.2	9.4	+	7.7	=	17.1
Total industrial potential (U.K. in 1900=100)	178.4	133.9	+	127.2	=	261.1

To be sure, this made a significant rather than an overwhelming superiority in matériel possessed by the Allies, and the addition of Italy in 1915 would not weigh the scales much further in their favor. Yet if victory in a prolonged Great Power war usually went to the coalition with the largest productive base, the obvious questions arise as to why the Allies were failing to prevail even after two or three years of fighting—and by 1917 were in some danger of losing—and why they then found it vital to secure American entry into the conflict.

One part of the answer must be that the areas in which the Allies were strong were unlikely to produce a swift or decisive victory over the Central Powers. The German colonial empire in 1914 was economically so insignificant that (apart from Nauru phosphates) its loss meant very little. The elimination of German overseas trade was certainly more damaging, but not to the extent that British devotees of "the influence of sea power" imagined; for the German export trades were redeployed for war production, the Central Powers bloc was virtually self-sufficient in foodstuffs provided its transport system was maintained, military conquests (e.g., of Luxembourg ores, Rumanian wheat and oil) canceled out many raw-materials shortages, and other supplies came via neutral neighbors. The maritime blockade had an effect, but only when it was applied in conjunction with military pressures on all fronts, and even then it worked very slowly. Finally, the other traditional weapon in the British armory, peripheral operations on the lines of the Peninsular War of 1808–1814, could not be used against the German coast, since its sea-based and land-based defenses were too formidable; and when it was employed against weaker powers—at Gallipoli, for example, or Salonika—operational failures on the Allied side and newer weapons (mine fields, quick-firing shore batteries) on the defender's side, blunted their hoped-for impact. As in the Second World War, every search for the "soft underbelly" of the enemy coalition took Allied troops away from fighting in France.[198]

The same points can be made about the overwhelming Allied naval superiority. The geography of the North Sea and the Mediterranean meant that the main Allied lines of communication were secure *without* needing to seek out their enemies' vessels in harbor or to mount a risky close blockade of their shores. On the contrary, it was incumbent upon the German and Austro-Hungarian fleets to come out and challenge the Anglo-French-Italian navies if they wanted to gain "command of the sea"; for if they remained in port, they were useless. Yet neither of the navies of the Central Powers wished to send its battle fleets on a virtual suicide mission against vastly superior forces. Thus, the few surface naval clashes which did occur were chance encounters (e.g., Dogger Bank, Jutland), and were strategically unimportant except insofar as they confirmed the Allied control of the seaways. The prospect of further encounters was reduced by the threat posed to warships by mines, submarines, and scouting aircraft or Zeppelins, which made the commanders of each side increasingly wary of sending out their fleets unless (a highly unlikely condition) the enemy's ships were known to be approaching one's own shoreline. Given this impotence in surface warfare, the Central Powers gradually turned to U-boat attacks upon Allied merchantmen, which was a much more serious threat; but by its very nature, a submarine campaign against trade was a slow, grinding affair, the real success of which could be measured only by setting the tonnage of merchant ships lost against the tonnage being launched in Allied shipyards—and that against the number of U-boats destroyed. It was not a form of war which promised swift victories.[199]

A second reason for the relative impotence of the Allies' numerical and industrial superiority lay in the nature of the military struggle itself. When each side possessed millions of troops sprawling across hundreds of miles of territory, it was difficult (in western Europe, impossible) to achieve a single decisive victory in the manner of Jena or Sadowa; even a "big push," methodically plotted and prepared for months ahead, usually disintegrated into hundreds of small-scale battlefield actions, and was usually also accompanied by a near-total breakdown in communications. While the front line might sway back and forth in certain sections, the absence of the means to achieve a real breakthrough allowed each side to mobilize and bring up reserves, fresh stocks of shells, barbed wire, and artillery in time for the next stalemated clash. Until late in the war, no army was able to discover how to get its own troops through enemy-held defenses often *four miles deep*, without either exposing them to withering counterfire or so churning up the ground by earlier bombardments that it was difficult to advance. Even when an occasional surprise assault overran the first few lines of enemy trenches, there was no special equipment to exploit that advantage; the railway lines were miles in the rear, the cavalry was too vulnerable (and tied to fodder supplies), heavily laden infantrymen could not move far, and the vital artillery arm was restricted by its long train of horse-drawn supply wagons.[200]

In addition to this general problem of achieving a swift battlefield victory, there was the fact that Germany enjoyed two more specific advantages. The first was that by its sweeping advances in France and Belgium in August/September 1914, it had seized the ridges of high ground which overlooked the line of the western front. From that time onward, and with a rare exception like Verdun, it stayed on the defensive in the west, compelling the Anglo-French armies to attack under unfavorable conditions and with forces which, although numerically superior, were not sufficient to outweigh this basic disadvantage. Secondly, the geographical benefits of Germany's position, with good internal means of communication between east and west, to some degree compensated for its "encirclement" by the Allies, by permitting generals such as Falkenhayn and Ludendorff to switch divisions from one front to the next, and, on one occasion, to send a whole army across central Europe in a week.[201]

Consequently, in 1914, even as the bulk of the army was attacking in the west, the Prussian General Staff was nervously redeploying two corps to reinforce its exposed eastern front. This action was not a fatal blow to the westward strike, which was logistically unsound in any case;[202] and it did help the Germans to counter the premature Russian offensive into East Prussia by launching their own operation around the Masurian Lakes. When the bloody fighting at Ypres in November 1914 convinced Falkenhayn of the hopelessness of achieving a swift victory in the west, a further eight German divisions were transferred to the eastern command. Since the Austro-Hungarian forces had suffered a humiliating blow in their Serbian campaign, and since the unreal French Plan XVII of 1914 had ground to a halt in Lorraine with losses of over 600,000 men, it appeared that only in the open lands of Russian Poland and Galicia could a breakthrough be effected—although whether that would be a Russian repeat of their victory over Austria-Hungary at Lemberg or a German repeat of Tannenberg/Masurian Lakes was not at all clear. As the Anglo-French armies were battering away in the west throughout 1915 (where the French lost a further 1.5 million men and the British 300,000), the Germans prepared for a series of ambitious strikes along the eastern front, partly to rescue the beleaguered Austro-Hungarians in Carpathia, but chiefly to destroy the Russian army in the field. In fact, the latter was still so large (and growing) that its destruction was impossible; but by the end of 1915 the Russians had suffered a series of devastating blows at the hands of the tactically and logistically superior Germans, and had been driven from Lithuania, Poland, and Galicia. In the south, German reinforcements had joined the Austrian forces, and the opportunistic Bulgarians, in finally overrunning Serbia. Nothing that the western Allies attempted in 1915—from the operationally mishandled Gallipoli campaign, to the fruitless landing at Salonika, to inducing Italy into the war—really aided the Russians or seemed to challenge the consolidated bloc of the Central Powers.[203]

In 1916, Falkenhayn's unwise reversal of German strategy—shifting units westward in order to bleed the French to death by the repeated assaults upon Verdun—merely confirmed the correctness of the older policy. While large numbers of German divisions were being ruined by the Verdun campaign, the Russians were able to mount their last great offensive under General Brusilov in the east, in June 1916, driving the disorganized Habsburg army all the way back to the Carpathian mountains and threatening its collapse. At almost the same time, the British army under Haig launched its massive offensive at the Somme, pressing for months against the well-held German ridges. As soon as these twin Allied operations had led to the winding-down of the Verdun campaign (and the replacement of Falkenhayn by Hindenburg and Ludendorff in late August 1916), the German strategical position improved. German losses on the Somme were heavy, but were less than Haig's; and the switch to a defensive stance in the West once again permitted the Germans to transfer troops to the east, stiffening the

Austro-Hungarian forces, then overrunning Rumania, and later giving aid to the Bulgarians in the south.[204]

Apart from these German advantages of inner lines, efficient railways, and good defensive positions, there was also the related question of *timing*. The larger total resources which the Allies possessed could not be instantly mobilized in 1914 in the pursuit of victory. The Russian army administration could always draft fresh waves of recruits to make up for the repeated battlefield losses, but it had neither the weapons nor the staff to expand that force beyond a certain limit. In the west, it was not until 1916 that Haig's army totaled more than a million men, and even then the British were tempted to divert their troops into extra-European campaigns, thus reducing the potential pressure upon Germany. This meant that during the first two years of the conflict, Russia and France took the main burden of checking the German military machine. Each had fought magnificently, but by the beginning of 1917 the strain was clearly showing; Verdun had taken the French army close to its limits, as Nivelle's rash assaults in 1917 revealed; and although the Brusilov offensive had virtually ruined the Habsburg army as a fighting force, it had done no damage to Germany itself and had placed even more strains upon Russian railways, food stocks, and state finances as well as expending much of the existing trained Russian manpower. While Haig's new armies made up for the increasing weariness of the French, they did not portend an Allied victory in the west; and if they also were squandered in frontal offensives, Germany might still be able to hold its own in Flanders while indulging in further sweeping actions in the east. Finally, no help could be expected south of the Alps, where the Italians were now desperately calling for assistance.

This pattern of ever-larger military sacrifices made by each side was paralleled, inevitably, in the financial-industrial sphere—but (at least until 1917) with the same stalemated results. Much has been made in recent studies of the way in which the First World War galvanized national economies, bringing modern industries for the first time to many regions and leading to stupendous increases in armaments output.[205] Yet on reflection, this surely is not surprising. For all the laments of liberals and others about the costs of the pre-1914 arms race, only a very small proportion (slightly over 4 percent on average) of national income was being devoted to armaments. When the advent of "total war" caused that figure to rise to 25 or 33 percent—that is, when governments at war took decisive command of industry, labor, and finance—it was inevitable that the output of armaments would soar. And since the generals of *every* army were bitterly complaining by late 1914 and early 1915 of a chronic "shell shortage," it was also inevitable that politicians, fearing the effects of being found wanting, entered into an alliance with business and labor to produce the desired goods.[206] Given the powers of the modern bureaucratic state to float loans and raise taxes, there were no longer the fiscal impediments to sustaining a lengthy war that had crippled eighteenth-century states. Inevitably, then, after an early period of readjustment to these new conditions, armaments production soared in all countries.

It is therefore important to ask where the wartime economies of the various combatants showed weaknesses, since it was most likely that this would lead to collapse, unless aid came from better-endowed allies. In this respect, little space will be given to the two weakest of the Great Powers, Austria-Hungary and Italy, since it is clear that the former, although holding up remarkably well in its extended campaigning (especially on the Italian front), would have collapsed in its war with Russia had it not been for repeated German military interventions which turned the Habsburg Empire ever more into a satellite of Berlin;[207] while Italy, which did not need anywhere like that degree of direct military assistance until the Caporetto disaster, was increasingly dependent upon its richer and more powerful allies for vital supplies of foodstuffs, coal, and raw materials, for shipping, and for the $2.96 billion of loans with which it could pay for munitions and other produce.[208] Its eventual "victory" in 1918, like the eventual defeat and dissolution of the Habsburg Empire, essentially depended upon actions and decisions taken elsewhere.

By 1917, it has been argued,[209] Italy, Austria-Hungary, and Russia were racing each other to collapse. That Russia should actually be the first to go was due, in large part, to two problems from which Rome and Vienna were spared; the first was that it was exposed, along hundreds of miles of border, to the slashing attacks of the much more efficient German army; the second was that even in August 1914 and certainly after Turkey's entry into the war, it was strategically isolated and thus never able to secure the degree of either military or economic aid from its allies necessary to sustain the enormous efforts of its fighting machine. When Russia, like the other combatants, swiftly learned that it was using up its ammunition stocks about ten times faster than the prewar estimates, it had massively to expand its home production—which turned out to be far more reliable than waiting for the greatly delayed overseas orders, even if it also implied diverting resources into the self-interested hands of the Moscow industrialists. But the impressive rise in Russian arms output, and indeed in overall industrial and agricultural production, during the first two and a half years of the war greatly strained the inadequate transport system, which in any case was finding it hard to cope with the shipment of troops, fodder for the cavalry, and so on. Shell stocks therefore accumulated miles from the front; foodstuffs could not be transported to the deficit areas, especially in the cities; Allied supplies lay for months on the harborsides at Murmansk and Archangel. These infrastructural inadequacies could not be overcome by Russia's minuscule and inefficient bureaucracy, and little help came from the squabbling and paralyzed political leadership at the top. On the contrary, the czarist regime helped to dig its own grave by its recklessly unbalanced fiscal policies; having abolished the trade in spirits (which produced one-third of its revenue), losing heavily on the railways (its other great peacetime source of income), and—unlike Lloyd George—declining to raise the income tax upon the better-off classes, the state resorted to floating ever more loans and printing ever more paper in order to pay for the war. The price index spiraled, from a nominal 100 in June 1914 to 398 in December 1916, to 702 in June 1917, by which time an awful combination of inadequate food supplies and excessive inflation triggered off strike after strike.[210]

As in industrial production, Russia's military performance was creditable during the first two or three years of the war—even if it was nothing like those fatuous prewar images of the "Russian steamroller" grinding its way across Europe. Its troops fought in their usual dogged, tough manner, enduring hardships and discipline unknown in the west; and the Russian record against the Austro-Hungarian army, from the September 1914 victory at Lemberg to the brilliantly executed Brusilov offensive, was one of constant success, akin to its Caucasus campaign against the Turks. Against the better-equipped and faster-moving Germans, however, the record was quite the reverse; but even that needs to be put into perspective, since the losses of one campaign (say, Tannenberg/Masurian Lakes in 1914, or the Carpathian fighting in 1915) were made up by drafting a fresh annual intake of recruits, which were then readied for the next season's operations. Over time, of course, the quality and morale of the army was bound to be affected by these heavy losses—250,000 at Tannenberg/Masurian Lakes, 1 million in the early 1915 Carpathian battles, another 400,000 when Mackensen struck at the central Polish salient, as many as 1 million in the 1916 fighting which started with the Brusilov offensive and ended with the debacle in Rumania. By the end of 1916, the Russian army had suffered casualties of some 3.6 million dead, seriously sick, and wounded, and another 2.1 million had been captured by the Central Powers. By that time, too, it had decided to call up the second-category recruits (males who were the sole breadwinners in the family), which not only produced tremendous peasant unrest in the villages, but also brought into the army hundreds of thousands of bitterly discontented conscripts. Almost as important were the dwindling numbers of trained NCOs, the inadequate supplies of weapons, ammunition, and food at the front, and the growing sense of inferiority against the German war machine, which seemed to know in advance all of

Russia's intentions,* to have overwhelming artillery fire, and to move faster than anyone else. By the beginning of 1917 these repeated defeats in the field interacted with the unrest in the cities and the rumors of the distribution of land, to produce a widespread disintegration in the army. Kerensky's July 1917 offensive—once again, initially successful against the Austrians, and then slashed to pieces by Mackensen's counterattack—was the final blow. The army, *Stavka* concluded, "is simply a huge, weary, shabby, and ill-fed mob of angry men united by their common thirst for peace and by common disappointment."[211] All that Russia could look forward to now was defeat and an internal revolution far more serious than that of 1905.

It is idle to speculate how close France, too, came to a similar fate by mid-1917, when hundreds of thousands of soldiers mutinied following Nivelle's senseless offensive;[212] for the fact was that despite the superficial similarities with Russian conditions, the French possessed key advantages which kept them in the fight. The first was the far greater degree of national unity and commitment to drive the German invaders back to the Rhine—although even those feelings might have faded away had France been fighting on its own. The second, and probably crucial, difference was that the French could benefit from fighting a *coalition* war in the way that Russia could not. Since 1871, they had known that they could not stand alone against Germany; the 1914–1918 conflict simply confirmed that judgment. This is not to downgrade the French contribution to the war, either in military or economic items, but merely to put it in context. Given that 64 percent of the nation's pig-iron capacity, 24 percent of its steel capacity, and 40 percent of its coal capacity fell swiftly into German hands, the French industrial renaissance after 1914 was remarkable (suggesting, incidentally, what *could* have been done in the nineteenth century had the political commitment been there). Factories, large and small, were set up across France, and employed women, children, and veterans, and even conscripted skilled workers who were transferred back from the trenches. Technocratic planners, businessmen, and unions combined in a national effort to produce as many shells, heavy guns, aircraft, trucks, and tanks as possible. The resultant surge in output has caused one scholar to argue that "France, more than Britain and far more than America, became the arsenal of democracy in World War I."[213]

Yet this top-heavy concentration upon armaments output—increasing machine-gun production 170-fold, and rifle production 290-fold— could never have been achieved had France not been able to rely upon British and American aid, which came in the form of a steady flow of imported coal, coke, pig iron, steel, and machine tools so vital for the

---

*Not surprisingly, since the Russians were incredibly careless with their wireless transmissions.

new munitions industry; in the Anglo-American loans of over $3.6 billion, so that France could pay for raw materials from overseas; in the allocation of increasing amounts of British shipping, without which most of this movement of goods could not have been carried out; and in the supply of foodstuffs. This last-named category seems a curious defect in a country which in peacetime always produced an agricultural surplus; but the fact was that the French, like the other European belligerents (except Britain), hurt their own agriculture by taking too many men from the land, diverting horses to the cavalry or to army-transport duties, and investing in explosives and artillery to the detriment of fertilizer and farm machinery. In 1917, a bad harvest year, food was scarce, prices were spiraling ominously upward, and the French army's own stock of grain was reduced to a two-day sup-ply—a potentially revolutionary situation (especially following the mutinies), which was only averted by the emergency allocation of British ships to bring in American grain.[214]

In rather the same way, France needed to rely upon increasing amounts of British and, later, American *military* assistance along the western front. For the first two to three years of the war, it bore the brunt of that fighting and took appalling casualties—over 3 million even before Nivelle's offensive of 1917; and since it had not the vast reserves of untrained manpower which Germany, Russia, and the British Empire possessed, it was far harder to replace such losses. By 1916–1917, however, Haig's army on the western front had been ex-panded to two-thirds the size of the French army and was holding over eighty miles of the line; and although the British high command was keen to go on the offensive in any case, there is no doubt that the Somme campaign helped to ease the pressure upon Verdun—just as Passchendaele in 1917 took the German energies away from the French part of the front while Pétain was desperately attempting to rebuild his forces' morale after the mutinies, and waiting for the new trucks, aircraft, and heavy artillery to do the work which massed infan-try clearly could not. Finally, in the epic to-and-fro battles along the western front between March and August 1918, France could rely not only upon British and imperial divisions, but also upon increasing numbers of American ones. And when Foch orchestrated his final counteroffensive in September 1918, he could engage the 197 under-strength German divisions with 102 French, 60 British Empire, 42 (double-sized) American, and 12 Belgian divisions.[215] Only with a *com-bination* of armies could the formidable Germans at last be driven from French soil and the country be free again.

When the British entered the war in August 1914, it was with no sense that they, too, would become dependent upon another Great Power in order to secure ultimate victory. So far as can be deduced from their prewar plans and preparations, the strategists had imagined that while the Royal Navy was sweeping German merchantmen (and perhaps the High Seas Fleet) from the oceans, and while the German colonial empire was being seized by dominion and British Indian troops, a small but vital expeditionary force would be sent across the Channel to "plug" a gap between the French and Belgian armies and to hold the German offensive until such time as the Russian steam-roller and the French Plan XVII were driving deep into the Fatherland. The British, like all the other powers, were not prepared for a long war, although they had taken certain measures to avoid a sudden crisis in their delicate international credit and commercial networks. But unlike the others, they were also not prepared for large-scale operations on the continent of Europe.[216] It was therefore scarcely surprising that one to two years of intense preparation were needed before 1 million British troops stood ready in France, and that the explosion of government spending upon rifles, artillery, machine guns, aircraft, trucks, and ammunition merely revealed innumerable production deficiencies which were only slowly corrected by Lloyd George's Ministry of Munitions.[217] Here again there were fantastic rises in output, as shown in Table 23.

Table 23. U.K. Munitions Production, 1914–1918[218]

	1914	1915	1916	1917	1918
Guns	91	3,390	4,314	5,137	8,039
Tanks	—	—	150	1,110	1,359
Aircraft	200	1,900	6,100	14,700	32,000
Machine guns	300	6,100	33,500	79,700	120,900

But that is scarcely surprising when one realizes that British defense expenditures rose from £91 million in 1913 to £1.956 billion in 1918, by which time it represented 80 percent of total government expenditures and 52 percent of the GNP.[219]

To give full details of the vast growth in the number of British and imperial divisions, squadrons of aircraft, and batteries of heavy artillery seems less important, therefore, than to point to the weaknesses which the First World War exposed in Britain's overall strategical position. The first was that while geography and the Grand Fleet's numerical superiority meant the Allies retained command of the sea in the *surface* conflict, the Royal Navy was quite unprepared to counter the unrestricted U-boat warfare which the Germans were implementing by early 1917. The second was that whereas the cluster of relatively cheap strategical weapons (blockade, colonial campaigns, amphibious operations) did not seem to be working against a foe with the wide-ranging resources of the Central Powers, the alternative strategy of direct military encounters with the German army also seemed incapable of producing results—and was fearfully costly in manpower. By the time the Somme campaign whimpered to a close in November 1916, British casualties in that fighting had risen to over 400,000. Although this wiped out the finest of Britain's volunteers and shocked the politicians, it did not dampen Haig's confidence in ultimate victory. By the middle of 1917 he was preparing for yet a further offensive from Ypres northeastward to Passchendaele—a muddy nightmare which cost another 300,000 casualties and badly hurt morale throughout much of the army in France. It was, therefore, all too predictable that however much Generals Haig and Robertson protested, Lloyd George and the imperialist-minded War Cabinet were tempted to divert ever more British divisions to the Near East, where substantial territorial gains beckoned and losses were far fewer than would be incurred in storming well-held German trenches.[220]

Even before Passchendaele, however, Britain had assumed (despite this imperial campaigning) the leadership role in the struggle against Germany. France and Russia might still have larger armies in the field, but they were exhausted by Nivelle's costly assaults and by the German counterblow to the Brusilov offensive. This leadership role was even more pronounced at the economic level, where Britain functioned as the banker and loan-raiser on the world's credit markets, not only for itself but also by guaranteeing the monies borrowed by Russia, Italy, and even France—since none of the Allies could provide from their own gold or foreign-investment holdings anywhere near the sums required to pay the vast surge of imported munitions and raw materials from overseas. By April 1, 1917, indeed, inter-Allied war credits had risen to $4.3 billion, 88 percent of which was covered by the British government. Although this looked like a repetition of Britain's eighteenth-century role as "banker to the coalition," there was now one critical difference: the sheer size of the trade deficit with the United States, which was supplying billions of dollars' worth of munitions and foodstuffs to the Allies (but not, because of the naval blockade, to the Central Powers) yet required few goods in return. Neither the transfer of gold nor the sale of Britain's enormous dollar securities could close this gap; only borrowing on the New York and Chicago money markets, to pay the American munitions suppliers in dollars, would do the trick. This in turn meant that the Allies became ever more dependent upon U.S. financial aid to sustain their own war effort. In October 1916, the British Chancellor of the Exchequer was warning that "by next June, or earlier, the President of the American Republic would be in a position, if he wishes, to dictate his terms to us."[221] It was an altogether alarming position for "independent" Great Powers to be in.

But what of Germany? Its performance in the war had been staggering. As Professor Northedge points out, "with no considerable assistance from her allies, [it] had held the rest of the world at bay, had beaten Russia, had driven France, the military colossus of Europe for more than two centuries, to the end of her tether, and in 1917, had come within an ace of starving Britain into surrender."[222] Part of this was due to those advantages outlined above: good inner lines of communication, easily defensible positions in the west, and open space for mobile warfare against less efficient foes in the east. It was also due to the sheer fighting quality of the German forces, which possessed an array of intelligent, probing staff officers who readjusted to the new conditions of combat faster than those in any other army, and who by 1916 had rethought the nature of both defensive and offensive warfare.[223]

Finally, the German state could draw upon both a large population and a massive industrial base for the prosecution of "total war." Indeed, it actually mobilized more men than Russia—13.25 million to 13 million—a remarkable achievement in view of their respective overall populations; and always had more divisions in the field than Russia. Its own munitions production soared, under the watchful eye not only of the high command but of intelligent bureaucrat-businessmen such as Walther Rathenau, who set up cartels to allocate vital supplies and avoid bottlenecks. Adept chemists produced ersatz goods for those items (e.g., Chilean nitrates) cut off by the British naval blockade. The occupied lands of Luxembourg and northern France were exploited for their ores and coal, Belgian workers were drafted into German factories, Rumanian wheat and oil were systematically plundered following the 1916 invasion. Like Napoleon and Hitler, the German military leadership sought to make conquest pay.[224] By the first half of 1917, with Russia collapsing, France wilting, and Britain under the "counterblockade" of the U-boats, Germany seemed on the brink of victory. Despite all the rhetoric of "fighting to the bitter end," statesmen in London and Paris were going to be anxiously considering the possibilities of a compromise peace for the next twelve months until the tide turned.[225]

Yet behind this appearance of Teutonic military-industrial might, there lurked very considerable problems. These were not too evident before the summer of 1916, that is, while the German army stayed on the defensive in the west and made sweeping strikes in the east. But the campaigns of Verdun and the Somme were of a new order of magnitude, both in the firepower employed and the losses sustained; and German casualties on the western front, which had been around 850,000 in 1915, leaped to nearly 1.2 million in 1916. The Somme offensive in particular impressed the Germans, since it showed that the British were at last making an all-out commitment of national resources for victory in the field; and it led in turn to the so-called Hindenburg Program of August 1916, which proclaimed an enormous expansion in munitions production and a far tighter degree of controls over the German economy and society to meet the demands of total war. This combination of on the one hand an authoritarian regime exercising all sorts of powers over the population and on the other a great growth in government borrowing and printing of paper money rather than raising income and dividend taxes—which, in turn, produced high inflation—dealt a heavy blow to popular morale—an ingredient in grand strategy which Ludendorff was far less equipped to understand than, say, a politician like Lloyd George or Clemenceau.

Even as an economic measure, the Hindenburg Program had its problems. The announcement of quite fantastic production totals—doubling explosives output, trebling machine-gun output—led to all sorts of bottlenecks as German industry struggled to meet these demands. It required not only many additional workers, but also a massive infrastructural investment, from new blast furnaces to bridges over the Rhine, which further used up labor and resources. Within a short while, therefore, it became clear that the program could be achieved only if skilled workers were returned from military duty; accordingly, 1.2 million were released in September 1916, and a further 1.9 million in July 1917. Given the serious losses on the western front, and the still-considerable casualties in the east, such withdrawals meant that even Germany's large able-bodied male population was being stretched to its limits. In that respect, although Passchendaele was a catastrophe for the British army, it was also viewed as a disaster by Ludendorff, who saw another 400,000 of his troops incapacitated. By December 1917, the German army's manpower totals were consistently under the peak of 5.38 million men it had possessed six months earlier.[226]

The final twist in the Hindenburg Program was the chronic neglect of agriculture. Here, even more than in France or Russia, men and horses and fuel were taken from the land and directed toward the needs of the army or the munitions industry—an insane imbalance, since Germany could not (like France) compensate for such planning errors by obtaining foodstuffs from overseas to make up the difference. While agricultural production plummeted in Germany, food prices spiraled and people everywhere complained about the scarcity of food supplies. In one scholar's severe judgment, "by concentrating lopsidedly on producing munitions, the military managers of the German economy thus brought the country to the verge of starvation by the end of 1918."[227]

But that time was an epoch away from early 1917, when it was the Allies who were feeling the brunt of the war and when, indeed, Russia was collapsing in chaos and both France and Italy seemed not far from that fate. It is in this grand-strategical context, of each bloc being exhausted by the war but of Germany still possessing an overall military advantage, that one must place the high command's inept policies toward the United States in the first few months of 1917. That the

American polity was leaning toward the Allied side even before then was no great secret; despite occasional disagreements over the naval blockade, the general ideological sympathy for the Allied democracies and the increasing dependence of U.S. exporters upon the western European market had made Washington less than completely neutral toward Germany. But the announcement of the unrestricted U-boat campaign against merchant shipping and the revelations of the secret German offers to Mexico of an alliance (in the "Zimmermann Telegram") finally brought Wilson and the Congress to enter the war.[228]

The significance of the American entry into the conflict was not at all a military one, at least for twelve to fifteen months after April 1917, since its army was even less prepared for modern campaigning than any of the European forces had been in 1914. But its productive strength, boosted by the billions of dollars of Allied war orders, was unequaled. Its total industrial potential and its share of world manufacturing output was two and a half times that of Germany's now overstrained economy. It could launch merchant ships in their hundreds, a vital requirement in a year when the U-boats were sinking over 500,000 tons a month of British and Allied vessels. It could build destroyers in the astonishing time of three months. It produced half of the world's food exports, which could now be sent to France and Italy as well as to its traditional British market.

In terms of economic power, therefore, the entry of the United States into the war quite transformed the balances, and more than compensated for the collapse of Russia at this same time. As Table 24 (which should be compared with Table 22) demonstrates, the productive resources now arranged against the Central Powers were enormous.

Table 24. Industrial/Technological Comparisons with the United States but Without Russia

	U.K./U.S./France	Germany/Austria-Hungary
Percentages of world manufacturing production (1913)	51.7	19.2
Energy consumption (1913), million metric tons of coal equivalent	798.8	236.4
Steel production (1913) in million tons	44.1	20.2
Total industrial potential (U.K. in 1900=100)	472.6	178.4

Because of the "lag time" between turning this economic potential into military effectiveness, the immediate consequences of the American entry into the war were mixed. The United States could not, in the short time available, produce its own tanks, field artillery, and aircraft at anything like the numbers needed (and in fact it had to borrow from France and Britain for such heavier weaponry); but it could continue to pour out the small-arms munitions and other supplies upon which London, Paris, and Rome depended so much. And it could take over from the bankers the private credit arrangements to pay for all these goods, and transform them into intergovernmental debts. Over the longer term, moreover, the U.S. Army could be expanded into a vast force of millions of fresh, confident, well-fed troops, to be thrown into the European balance.[229] In the meanwhile, the British had to grind their way through the Passchendaele muds, the Russian army had disintegrated, German reinforcements had permitted the Central Powers to deal a devastating blow to Italy at Caporetto, and Ludendorff was withdrawing some of his forces from the east in order to launch a final strike at the weakened Anglo-French lines. Outside of Europe, it was true, the British were making important gains against Turkey in the Near East. But the capture of Jerusalem and Damascus would be poor compensation for the loss of France, if the Germans at last managed to do in the west what they had done everywhere else in Europe.

This was why the leaderships of all of the major belligerents saw the coming campaigns of 1918 as absolutely decisive to the war as a whole. Although Germany had to leave well over a million troops to occupy its new great empire of conquest in the east, which the Bolsheviks finally acknowledged in the Treaty of Brest-Litovsk (March 1918), Ludendorff had been switching forces westward at the rate of ten divisions a month since early November 1917. By the time the German war machine was poised to strike, in late March 1918, it had a superiority of almost thirty divisions over the Anglo-French forces, and many of its units had been trained by Bruchmüller and other staff officers in the new techniques of surprise "storm trooper" warfare. If they succeeded in punching a hole through the Allied lines and driving to Paris or the Channel, it would be the greatest military achievement in the war. But the risks also were horrendous, for Ludendorff was mobilizing the entire remaining resources of Germany for this single campaign; it was to be "all or nothing," a gamble of epic proportions. Behind the scenes, the German economy was weakening ominously. Its industrial output was down to 57 percent of the 1913 level. Agriculture was more neglected than ever, and poor weather contributed to the decline in output; the further rise in food prices increased domestic discontents. The overworked rolling stock was by now unable to move anything like the amount of raw materials from the eastern territories that had been planned. Of the 192 divisions Ludendorff deployed in the west, 56 were labeled "attack divisions," in its way a disguise for the fact that they would receive the lion's share of the diminishing stocks of equipment and ammunition.[230] It was a gamble which the high command believed had to succeed. But if the attack failed, German resources would be exhausted—and that just at the time when the Americans were at last capable of pouring nearly 300,000 troops a month into France, and the unrestricted U-boat campaign had been completely checked by the Allied convoys.

Ludendorff's early successes—crushing the outnumbered British Fifth Army, driving a wedge between the French and British forces, and advancing by early June 1918 to within thirty-seven miles of Paris in another one of his lunges—frightened the Allies into giving Foch supreme coordination of their Western Front forces, sending reinforcements from England, Italy, and the Near East, and again (privately) worrying about a compromise peace. Yet the fact was that the Germans *had* overextended themselves, and suffered the usual consequences of going from the defensive to the offensive. In the first two heavy blows against the British sector, for example, they had inflicted 240,000 British and 92,000 French casualties, but their own losses had risen to 348,000. By July, "the Germans lost about 973,000 men, and over a million more were listed as sick. By October there were only 2.5 million men in the west and the recruiting situation was desperate."[231] From mid-July onward, the Allies were superior, not simply in fresh fighting men, but even more so in artillery, tanks, and aircraft—allowing Foch to orchestrate a whole series of offensives by British Empire, American, and French armies so that the weakening German forces would be given no rest. At the same time, too, the Allies' military superiority and greater staying power was showing itself in impressive victories in Syria, Bulgaria, and Italy. All at once, in September/October 1918, the entire German-led bloc seemed to a panic-stricken Ludendorff to be collapsing, internal discontent and revolutions now interacting with the defeats at the front to produce surrender, chaos, and political upheaval.[232] Not only was the German military bid finished, therefore, but the Old Order in Europe was ruined as well.

In the light of the awful individual losses, suffering, and devastation which had occurred both in "the face of battle" and on the home fronts,[233] and of the way in which the First World War has been seen as a self-inflicted death blow to European civilization and influence in the world,[234] it may appear crudely materialistic to introduce another statistical table at this point (Table 25). Yet the fact is that these figures point to what has been argued above: that the advantages possessed by the Central Powers—good internal lines, the quality of the German army, the occupation and exploitation of many territories, the isolation and defeat of Russia—could not over the long run outweigh this massive disadvantage in sheer economic muscle, and the considerable disadvantage in the size of total mobilized forces. Just as Ludendorff's despair at running out of able-bodied troops by July 1918 was a reflection of the imbalance of forces, so the average *Frontsoldat's* amaze-

Table 25. War Expenditure and Total Mobilized Forces, 1914–1919[235]

	War Expenditure at 1913 Prices (billions of dollars)	Total Mobilized Forces (millions)
British Empire	23.0	9.5
France	9.3	8.2
Russia	5.4	13.0
Italy	3.2	5.6
United States	17.1	3.8
Other Allies*	− 0.3	2.6
Total Allies	57.7	40.7
Germany	19.9	13.25
Austria-Hungary	4.7	9.00
Bulgaria, Turkey	0.1	2.85
Total Central Powers	24.7	25.10

*Belgium, Rumania, Portugal, Greece, Serbia.

ment at how well provisioned were the Allied units which they overran in the spring of that year was an indication of the imbalance of production.[236]

While it would be quite wrong, then, to claim that the outcome of the First World War was predetermined, the evidence presented here suggests that the overall course of that conflict—the early stalemate between the two sides, the ineffectiveness of the Italian entry, the slow exhaustion of Russia, the decisiveness of the American intervention in keeping up the Allied pressures, and the eventual collapse of the Central Powers—correlates closely with the economic and industrial production and effectively mobilized forces available to each alliance during the different phases of the struggle. To be sure, generals still had to direct (or *mis*direct) their campaigns, troops still had to summon the individual moral courage to assault an enemy position, and sailors still had to endure the rigors of sea warfare; but the record indicates that such qualities and talents existed on both sides, and were not enjoyed in disproportionate measure by one of the coalitions. What *was* enjoyed by one side, particularly after 1917, was a marked superiority in productive forces. As in earlier, lengthy coalition wars, that factor eventually turned out to be decisive.

6

The Coming of a Bipolar World and the Crisis of the "Middle Powers": Part Two, 1919–1942

The Postwar International Order

The statesmen of the greater and lesser powers assembling in Paris at the beginning of 1919 to arrange a peace settlement were confronted with a list of problems both more extensive and more intractable than had been encountered by any of their predecessors in 1856, 1814–1815, and 1763. While many items on the agenda could be settled and incorporated into the Treaty of Versailles itself (June 28, 1919), the confusion prevailing in eastern Europe as rival ethnic groups jostled to establish "successor states," the civil war and interventions in Russia, and the Turkish nationalist reaction against the intended western division of Asia Minor meant that many matters were not fixed until 1920, and in some cases 1923. However, for the purposes of brevity, this group of agreements will be examined as a whole, rather than in the actual chronological order of their settlement.

The most striking change in Europe, measured in territorial-juridical terms, was the emergence of a cluster of nation-states—Poland, Czechoslovakia, Austria, Hungary, Yugoslavia, Finland, Estonia, Latvia, and Lithuania—in place of lands which were formerly part of the Habsburg, Romanov, and Hohenzollen empires. While the ethnically coherent Germany suffered far smaller territorial losses in eastern Europe than either Soviet Russia or the totally dissolved Austro-Hungarian Empire, its power was hurt in other ways: by the return of Alsace-Lorraine to France, and by border rectifications with Belgium and Denmark; by the Allied military occupation of the Rhineland, and the French economic exploitation of the Saarland; by the unprecedented "demilitarization" terms (e.g., minuscule army and coastal-defense navy, no air force, tanks, or submarines, abolition of Prussian General Staff); and by an enormous reparations bill. In addition, Germany also lost its extensive colonial empire to Britain, the self-governing dominions, and France—just as Turkey found its Near East territories turned into British and French mandates, distantly

Map 10: Europe After the First World War

supervised by the new League of Nations. In the Far East, Japan inherited the former German island groups north of the equator, although it returned Shantung to China in 1922. At the 1921–1922 Washington Conference, the powers recognized the territorial status quo in the Pacific and Far East, and agreed to restrict the size of their battle fleets according to relative formulae, thereby heading off an Anglo-American-Japanese naval race. In both the West and the East, therefore, the international system appeared to have been stabilized by the early 1920s—and what difficulties remained (or might arise in the future) could now be dealt with by the League of Nations, which met regularly at Geneva despite the surprise defection of the United States.[1]

The sudden American retreat into at least relative diplomatic isolationism after 1920 seemed yet another contradiction to those world-power trends which, as detailed above, had been under way since the 1890s. To the prophets of world politics in that earlier period, it was self-evident that the international scene was going to be increasingly influenced, if not dominated, by the three rising powers of Germany, Russia, and the United States. Instead, the first-named had been decisively defeated, the second had collapsed in revolution and then withdrawn into its Bolshevik-led isolation, and the third, although clearly the most powerful nation in the world by 1919, also preferred to retreat from the center of the diplomatic stage. In consequence, international affairs during the 1920s and beyond still seemed to focus either upon the actions of France and Britain, even though both countries had been badly hurt by the First World War, or upon the deliberations of the League, in which French and British statesmen were preeminent. Austria-Hungary was now gone. Italy, where the National Fascist Party under Mussolini was consolidating its hold after 1922, was relatively quiescent. Japan, too, appeared tranquil following the 1921–1922 Washington Conference decisions.

In a curious and (as will be seen) artificial way, therefore, it still seemed a Eurocentered world. The diplomatic histories of this period focus heavily upon France's "search for security" against a future German resurgence. Having lost a special Anglo-American military guarantee at the same time as the U.S. Senate rejected the Treaty of Versailles, the French sought to create a variety of substitutes: encouraging the formation of an "antirevisionist" bloc of states in eastern Europe (the so-called Little Entente of 1921); concluding individual alliances with Belgium (1920), Poland (1921), Czechoslovakia (1924), Rumania (1926), and Yugoslavia (1927); maintaining a very large army and air force to overawe the Germans and intervening—as in the 1923 Ruhr crisis—when Germany defaulted on the reparation payments; and endeavoring to persuade successive British administrations to provide a new military guarantee of France's borders, something which was achieved only indirectly in the multilateral

Locarno Treaty of 1925.[2] It was also a period of intense financial diplomacy, since the interacting problem of German reparations and Allied war debts bedeviled relations not only between the victors and the vanquished, but also between the United States and its former European allies.[3] The financial compromise of the Dawes Plan (1924) eased much of this turbulence, and in turn prepared the ground for the Locarno Treaty the following year; that was followed by Germany's entry into the League and then the amended financial settlement of the Young Plan (1929). By the late 1920s, indeed, with prosperity returning to Europe, with the League apparently accepted as an important new element in the international system, and with a plethora of states solemnly agreeing (under the 1928 Pact of Paris) not to resort to war to settle future disputes, the diplomatic stage seemed to have returned to normal. Statesmen such as Stresemann, Briand, and Austen Chamberlain appeared, in their way, the latter-day equivalents of Metternich and Bismarck, meeting at this or that European spa to settle the affairs of the world.

Despite these superficial impressions, however, the underlying structures of the post-1919 international system were significantly different from, and much more fragile than, those which influenced diplomacy a half-century earlier. In the first place, the population losses and economic disruptions caused by four and a half years of "total" war were immense. Around 8 million men were killed in actual fighting, with another 7 million permanently disabled and a further 15 million "more or less seriously wounded"[4]—the vast majority of these being in the prime of their productive life. In addition, Europe *excluding* Russia probably lost over 5 million civilian casualties through what has been termed "war-induced causes"—"disease, famine and privation consequent upon the war as well as those wrought by military conflict";[5] the Russian total, compounded by the heavy losses in the civil war, was much larger. The wartime "birth deficits" (caused by so many men being absent at the front, and the populations thereby not renewing themselves at the normal prewar rate) were also extremely high. Finally, even as the major battles ground to a halt, fighting and massacres occurred during the postwar border conflicts in, for example, eastern Europe, Armenia, and Poland; and none of these war-weakened regions escaped the dreadful influenza epidemic of 1918–1919, which carried off further millions. Thus, the final casualty list for this extended period might have been as much as 60 million people, with nearly half of these losses occurring in Russia, and with France, Germany, and Italy also being badly hit. There is no known way of measuring the personal anguish and the psychological shocks involved in such a human catastrophe, but it is easy to see why the participants—statesmen as well as peasants—were so deeply affected by it all.

The material costs of the war were also unprecedented and seemed, to those who viewed the devastated landscapes of northern France, Poland, and Serbia, even more shocking: hundreds of thousands of houses were destroyed, farms gutted, roads and railways and telegraph lines blown up, livestock slaughtered, forests pulverized, and vast tracts of land rendered unfit for farming because of unexploded shells and mines. When the shipping losses, the direct and indirect costs of mobilization, and the monies raised by the combatants are added to the list, the total charge becomes so huge as to be virtually incomprehensible: in fact, some $260 billion, which, according to one calculation, "represented about six and a half times the sum of all the national debt accumulated in the world from the end of the eighteenth century up to the eve of the First World War."[6] After decades of growth, world manufacturing production turned sharply down; in 1920 it was still 7 percent less than in 1913, agricultural production was about one-third below normal, and the volume of exports was only around half what it was in the prewar period. While the growth of the European economy as a whole had been retarded, perhaps as much as by eight years,* individual countries were much more severely affected. Predictably, Russia in the turmoil of 1920 recorded the lowest industrial output, equal to a mere 13 percent of the 1913 figure; but in Germany, France, Belgium, and much of eastern Europe, industrial output was at least 30 percent lower than before the conflict.[7]

If some societies were the more heavily affected by the war, then others of course escaped lightly—and many improved their position. For the fact was that modern war, and the industrial productivity generated by it, also had positive effects. In strictly economic and technological terms, these years had seen many advances: in automobile and truck production, in aviation, in oil refining and chemicals, in the electrical and dyestuff and alloy-steel industries, in refrigeration and canning, and in a whole host of other industries.[8] Naturally, it proved easier to develop and to benefit commercially from such advances if one's economy was far from the disruption of the front line; which is why the United States itself, but also Canada, Australia, South Africa, India, and parts of South America, found their economies stimulated by the industrial, raw-material, and foodstuffs demand of a Europe convulsed by a war of attrition. As in previous mercantilist conflicts, one country's loss was often another's gain—provided the

---

*That is to say, its output in 1929 totaled what it probably would have reached in 1921, had there been no war and had the pre-1913 growth rates continued.

**Table 26. World Indices of
Manufacturing Production, 1913–1925**[9]

	1913	1920	1925
World	100	93.6	121.6
Europe*	100	77.3	103.5
USSR	100	12.8	70.1
United States	100	122.2	148.0
Rest of World	100	109.5	138.1

*U.K., France, Belgium, Netherlands, Germany,
Denmark, Norway, Sweden, Finland, Switzerland,
Austria, Italy, Czechoslovakia, Hungary, Poland,
Rumania, Greece, and Spain.

latter avoided the costs of war, or was at least protected from the full
blast of battle.

Such figures on world manufacturing production are very illuminating in this respect, since they record the extent to which
Europe (and especially the USSR) were hurt by the war, while other
regions gained substantially. To some degree, of course, the spread of
industrialization from Europe to the Americas, Japan, India, and Australasia, and the increasing share of these latter territories in world
trade, was simply the continuation of economic trends which had been
in evidence since the late nineteenth century. Thus, according to one
arcane calculation already mentioned earlier, the United States pre-
1914 growth was such that it probably would have overtaken Europe
in total output in the year 1925;[10] what the war did was to accelerate
that event by a mere six years, to 1919. On the other hand, unlike the
1880–1913 changes, these particular shifts in the global economic balances were *not* taking place in peacetime over several decades and in
accord with market forces. Instead, the agencies of war and blockade
created their own peremptory demands and thus massively distorted
the natural patterns of world production and trade. For example, shipbuilding capacity (especially in the United States) had been enormously increased in the middle of the war to counter the sinkings by
U-boats; but after 1919–1920, there were excess berths across the globe.
Again, the output of the steel industries of continental Europe had
fallen during the war, whereas that of the United States and Britain
had risen sharply; but when the European steel producers recovered,
the excess capacity was horrific. This problem also affected an even
greater sector of the economy—agriculture. During the war years,
farm output in continental Europe had shriveled and Russia's prewar
export trade in grain had disappeared, whereas there had been large
increases in output in North and South America and in Australasia,
whose farmers were the decided (if unpremeditating) beneficiaries of
the archduke's death. But when European agriculture recovered by the
late 1920s, producers across the world faced a fall-off in demand, and
tumbling prices.[11] These sorts of structural distortions affected all re-

gions, but were felt nowhere as severely as in east-central Europe, where the fragile "successor states" grappled with new boundaries, dislocated markets, and distorted communications. Making peace at Versailles and redrawing the map of Europe along (roughly) ethnic lines did not of itself guarantee a restoration of economic stability.

Finally, the financing of the war had caused economic—and later political—problems of unprecedented complexity. Very few of the belligerents (Britain and the United States were among the exceptions) had tried to pay for even part of the costs of the conflict by increasing taxes; instead most states relied almost entirely on borrowing, assuming that the defeated foe would be forced to meet the bill—as had happened to France in 1871. Public debts, now uncovered by gold, rose precipitously; paper money, pouring out of the state treasuries, sent prices soaring.[12] Given the economic devastation and territorial dislocations caused by the war, no European country was ready to follow the United States back onto the gold standard in 1919. Lax monetary and fiscal policies caused inflation to keep on increasing, with disastrous results in central and eastern Europe. Competitive depreciations of the national currency, carried out in a desperate attempt to boost exports, simply created more financial instability—as well as political rivalry. This was all compounded by the intractable related issues of intra-Allied loans and the victors' (especially France's) demand for substantial German reparations. All the European allies were in debt to Britain, and to a lesser extent to France; while those two powers were heavily in debt to the United States. With the Bolsheviks' repudiating Russia's massive borrowings of $3.6 billion, with the Americans asking for their money back, with France, Italy, and other countries refusing to pay off their debts until they had received reparations from Germany, and with the Germans declaring that they could not possibly pay the amounts demanded of them, the scene was set for years of bitter wrangling, which sharply widened the gap in political sympathies between western Europe and a disgruntled United States.[13]

If it was true that these quarrels seemed smoothed over by the Dawes Plan of 1924, the political and social consequences of this turbulence had been immense, especially during the German hyperinflation of the previous year. What was equally alarming, although less well understood at the time, was that the apparent financial and commercial stabilization of the world economy by the mid-1920s rested on far more precarious foundations than had existed prior to the First World War. Although the gold standard was being restored in most countries by then, the subtle (and almost self-balancing) pre-1914 mechanism of international trade and monetary flows based upon the City of London had not. London had, in fact, made desperate attempts to recover that role—including the 1925 fixing of the sterling convertibility rate at the prewar level of £1:$4.86, which badly hurt British exporters; and it also had resumed large-scale lending overseas. Nonetheless, the fact was that the center of world finance had naturally moved across the Atlantic between 1914 and 1919, as Europe's international debts increased and the United States became the world's greatest creditor nation. On the other hand, the quite different structure of the American economy—less dependent upon foreign commerce and much less integrated into the world economy, protectionist-inclined (especially in agriculture) rather than free-trading, lacking a full equivalent to the Bank of England, fluctuating much more wildly in its booms and busts, with politicians much more directly influenced by domestic lobbies—meant that the international financial and commercial system revolved around a volatile and flawed central point. There was now no real "lender of last resort," offering long-term loans for the infrastructural development of the world economy and stabilizing the temporary disjunctions in the international accounts.[14]

These structural inadequacies were concealed in the late 1920s, when vast amounts of dollars flowed out of the United States in short-term loans to European governments and municipalities, all willing to offer high interest rates in order to use such funds—not always wisely—both for development and to close the gap in their balance of payments. With short-term money being thus employed for long-term projects, with considerable amounts of investment (especially in central and eastern Europe) still going into agriculture and thus increasing the downward pressures on farm prices, with the costs of servicing these debts rising alarmingly and, since they could not be paid off by exports, being sustained only by further borrowings, the system was already breaking down in the summer of 1928, when the American domestic boom (and the Federal Reserve's reactive increase in interest rates) sharply curtailed the outflow of capital.

The ending of that boom in the "Wall Street crash" of October 1929 and the further reduction in American lending then instigated a chain reaction which appeared uncontrollable: the lack of ready credit reduced both investment and consumption; depressed demand among the industrialized countries hurt producers of foodstuffs and raw materials, who responded desperately by increasing supply and then witnessing the near-total collapse of prices—making it impossible for them in turn to purchase manufactured goods. Deflation, going off gold and devaluing the currency, restrictive measures on commerce and capital, and defaults upon international debts were the various expedients of the day; each one dealt a further blow to the global system of trade and credit. The archprotectionist Smoot-Hawley Tariff, passed (in the calculation of aiding American farmers) by the only country with a substantial trade surplus, made it even more difficult for other countries to earn dollars—and led to the inevitable reprisals, which devastated American exports. By the summer of 1932, industrial production in many countries was only half that of 1928, and world trade had shrunk by one-third. The value of European trade ($58 billion in 1928) was still down at $20.8 billion in 1935—a decline which in turn hit shipping, shipbuilding, insurance, and so on.[15]

Given the severity of this worldwide depression and the massive unemployment caused by it, there was no way international politics could escape from its dire effects. The fierce competition in manufactures, raw materials, and farm produce increased national resentments and impelled many a politician, aware of his constituents' discontents, into trying to make the foreigner pay; more extreme groups, especially of the right, took advantage of the economic dislocation to attack the entire liberal-capitalist system and to call for assertive "national" policies, backed if necessary by the sword. The more fragile democracies, in Weimar Germany especially but also in Spain, Rumania, and elsewhere, buckled under these politico-economic strains. The cautious conservatives who ruled Japan were edged out by nationalists and militarists. If the democracies of the West weathered these storms better, their statesmen were forced to concentrate upon domestic economic management, increasingly tinged with a beggar-thy-neighbor attitude. Neither the United States nor France, the main gold-surplus countries, were willing to bail out debtor states; indeed, France inclined more and more to use its financial strength to try to control German behavior (which merely intensified resentments on the other side of the Rhine) and to aid its own European diplomacy. Similarly, the "Hoover moratorium" on German reparations, which so infuriated the French, could not be separated from the issue of reductions in (and ultimately defaults on) war debts, which made the Americans bitter. Competitive devaluations in currency, and disagreements at the 1933 World Economic Conference about the dollar-sterling rate, completed this gloomy picture.

By that time, the cosmopolitan world order had dissolved into various rivaling subunits: a sterling block, based upon British trade patterns and enhanced by the "imperial preferences" of the 1932 Ottawa Conference: a gold block, led by France; a yen block, dependent upon Japan, in the Far East; a U.S.-led dollar block (after Roosevelt also went off gold); and, completely detached from these convulsions, a USSR steadily building "socialism in one country." The trend toward autarky was thus already strongly developed even before Adolf Hitler commenced his program of creating a self-sufficient, thousand-year Reich in which foreign trade was reduced to special deals and "barter" agreements. With France having repeatedly opposed the Anglo-Saxon powers over the treatment of German reparations, with Roosevelt claiming that the United States always lost out in deals with the British, and with Neville Chamberlain already convinced of his later remark that the American policy was all "words,"[16] the democracies were in no frame of mind to cooperate in handling the pressures building up for territorial charges in the flawed 1919 world order.

The Old World statesmen and foreign offices had always found it difficult either to understand or to deal with economic issues; but perhaps an even more disruptive feature, to those fondly looking back at the cabinet diplomacy of the nineteenth century, was the increasing influence of mass public opinion upon international affairs during the 1920s and 1930s. In some ways, of course, this was inevitable. Even before the First World War, political groups across Europe had been criticizing the arcane, secretive methods and elitist preconceptions of the "old diplomacy," and calling instead for a reformed system, where the affairs of state were open to the scrutiny of the people and their representatives.[17] These demands were greatly boosted by the 1914–1918 conflict, partly because the leaderships who demanded the total mobilization of society realized that society, in turn, would require compensations for its sacrifices and a say in the peace; partly because the war, fondly proclaimed by Allied propagandists as a struggle for democracy and national self-determination, did indeed smash the autocratic empires of east-central Europe; and partly because the powerful and appealing figure of Woodrow Wilson kept up the pressures for a new and enlightened world order even as Clemenceau and Lloyd George were proclaiming the need for total victory.[18]

But the problem with "public opinion" after 1919 was that many sections of it did *not* match that fond Gladstonian and Wilsonian vision of a liberal, educated, fair-minded populace, imbued with internationalist ideas, utilitarian assumptions, and respect for the rule of law. As Arno Mayer has shown, "the old diplomacy" which (it was widely claimed) had caused the World War was being challenged after 1917 not only by Wilsonian reformism, but also by the Bolsheviks' much more systematic criticism of the existing order—a criticism of considerable attraction to the organized working classes in *both* belligerent camps.[19] While this caused nimble politicians such as Lloyd George to invent their own "package" of progressive domestic and foreign policies, to neutralize Wilson's appeal and to check labor's drift toward socialism,[20] the impact upon more conservative and nationalist figures in the Allied camp was quite different. In their view, Wilsonian principles must be firmly rejected in the interests of national "security," which could only be measured in the hard cash of border adjustments, colonial acquisitions, and reparations; while Lenin's threat, which was much more frightening, had to be ruthlessly smashed, in its Bolshevik heartland and (especially) in the imitative soviets which sprang up in the West. The politics and diplomacy of the peacemaking,[21] in other words, was charged with background ideological and domestic-political elements to a degree unknown at the congresses of 1856 and 1878.

There was more. In the western democracies, the images of the First World War which prevailed by the late 1920s were of death, destruction, horror, waste, and the futility of it all. The "Carthaginian peace" of 1919, the lack of those benefits promised by wartime politicians in return for the people's sacrifices, the millions of maimed veterans and of war widows, the economic troubles of the 1920s, the loss of faith and the breakdown in Victorian social and personal relationships, were all blamed upon the folly of the July 1914 decisions.[22] But this widespread public recoil from fighting and militarism, mingled in many quarters with the hope that the League of Nations would render impossible any repetition of that disaster, was not shared by all of the war's participants—even if Anglo-American literature gives that impression.[23] To hundreds of thousands of former *Frontsoldaten* across the continent of Europe, disillusioned by the unemployment and inflation and boredom of the postwar bourgeois-dominated order, the conflict had represented something searing but positive: martial values, the camaraderie of warriors, the thrill of violence and action. To such groups, especially in the defeated nations of Germany and Hungary and in the bitterly dissatisfied victor nation of Italy, but also among the French right, the ideas of the new fascist movements—of order, discipline, and national glory, of the smashing of the Jews, Bolsheviks, intellectual decadents, and self-satisfied liberal middle classes—had great appeal. In their eyes (and in the eyes of their equivalents in Japan), it was struggle and force and heroism which were the enduring features of life, and the tenets of Wilsonian internationism which were false and outdated.[24]

What this meant was that international relations during the 1920s and 1930s continued to be complicated by ideology, and by the steady fissuring of world society into political blocs which only partly overlapped with the economic subdivisions mentioned earlier. On the one hand, there were the western democracies, especially in the English-speaking world, recoiling from the horror of the First World War, concentrating upon domestic (especially socioeconomic) issues, and massively reducing their defense establishments; and while the French leadership kept up a large army and air force out of fear of a revived Germany, it was evident that much of its public shared this hatred of war and desire for social reconstruction. On the other hand, there was the Soviet Union, isolated in so many ways from the global politico-economic system yet attracting admirers in the West because it offered, purportedly, a "new civilization" which *inter alia* escaped the Great Depression,[25] though the USSR was also widely detested. Finally, there were, at least by the 1930s, the fascistic "revisionist" states of Germany, Japan, and Italy, which were not only virulently anti-Bolshevik but also denounced the liberal-capitalist status quo that had been reestablished in 1919. All this made the conduct of foreign policy inordinately difficult for democratic statesmen, who possessed little grasp of either the fascist or the Bolshevik frame of mind, and yearned merely to return to that state of Edwardian "normalcy" which the war had so badly destroyed.

Compared with these problems, the post-1919 challenges to the Eurocentric world which were beginning to arise in the tropics were less threatening—but still important. Here, too, one can detect precedents prior to 1914, such as Arabi Pasha's revolt in Egypt, the young Turks' breakthrough after 1908, Tilak's attempts to radicalize the Indian Congress movement, and Sun Yat-sen's campaign against western dominance in China; by the same token, historians have noted how events such as the Japanese defeat of Russia in 1905 and the abortive Russian revolution of that same year fascinated and electrified proto-nationalist forces elsewhere in Asia and the Middle East.[26] Ironically, yet predictably, the more that colonialism penetrated underdeveloped societies, drew them into a global network of trade and finance, and brought them into contact with western ideas, the more this provoked an indigenous reaction; whether it came in the form of tribal unrest against restrictions upon their traditional patterns of life and trade or, more significantly, in the form of western-educated lawyers and intellectuals seeking to create mass parties and campaigning for national self-determination, the result was an increasing challenge to European colonial controls.

The First World War accelerated these trends in all sorts of ways. In the first place, the intensified economic exploitation of the raw materials in the tropics and the attempts to make the colonies contribute—both with manpower and with taxes—to the metropolitan powers' war effort inevitably caused questions to be asked about "compensation," just as it was doing among the working classes of Europe.[27] Furthermore, the campaigning in West, Southwest, and East Africa, in the Near East, and in the Pacific raised questions about the viability and permanence of colonial empires in general—a tendency reinforced by Allied propaganda about "national self-determination" and "democracy," and German counterpropaganda activities toward the Maghreb, Ireland, Egypt, and India. By 1919, while the European powers were establishing their League of Nations mandates—hiding their imperial interests behind ever more elaborate fig leaves, as A.J.P. Taylor once described it—the Pan African Congress had been meeting in Paris to put its point of view, the Wafd Party was being founded in Egypt, the May Fourth Movement was active in China, Kemal Ataturk was emerging as the founder of modern Turkey, the Destour party was reformulating its tactics in Tunisia, the Sarehat Islam had reached a membership of 2.5 million in Indonesia, and Gandhi was catalyzing the many different strands of opposition to British rule in India.[28]

More important still, this "revolt against the West" would no longer find the Great Powers united in the supposition that whatever their own differences, a great gulf lay between themselves and the less-developed peoples of the globe; this, too, was another large difference from the time of the Berlin West Africa Conference. Such unity had already been made redundant by the entry into the Great Power club of the Japanese, some of whose thinkers were beginning to articulate notions of an East Asian "co-prosperity sphere" as early as 1919.[29] And it was overtaken altogether by the coming of the two versions of the "new diplomacy" proposed by Lenin and Wilson—for whatever the political differences between those charismatic leaders, they had in common a dislike of the old European colonial order and a desire to transform it into something else. Neither of them, for a variety of reasons, could prevent the further extension of that colonial order under the League mandates; but their rhetoric and influence seeped across imperial demarcation zones and interacted with the mobilization of indigenous nationalists. This was evident in China by the late 1920s, where the old European order of treaty privileges, commercial penetration, and occasional gunboat actions was beginning to lose ground to competing alternative "orders" proposed by Russia, the United States, and Japan, and to wilt in the face of the resurgent Chinese nationalism.[30]

This did not mean that western colonialism was about to collapse. The sharp British response at Amritsar in 1919, the Dutch imprisonment of Sukarno and other Indonesian nationalist leaders and breaking-up of the trade unions in the late 1920s, the firm French reaction to Tonkinese unrest at the intense agricultural development of rice and rubber, all testified to the residual power of European armies and weaponry.[31] And the same could be said, of course, of Italy's belated imperial thrust into Abyssinia in the mid-1930s. Only the far larger shocks administered by the Second World War would really loosen these imperial controls. Nevertheless, this colonial unrest was of some importance to international relations in the 1920s and especially in the 1930s. First of all, it distracted the attention (and the resources) of certain of the Great Powers from their concern with the European balance of power. This was preeminently the case with Britain, whose leaders worried far more about Palestine, India, and Singapore than about the Sudetenland or Danzig—such priorities being reflected in their post-1919 "imperial" defense policy;[32] but involvements in Africa also affected France to the same degree, and of course quite distracted the Italian military. Furthermore, in certain instances the reemergence of extra-European and colonial issues was cutting right across the former 1914–1918 alliance structure. Not only did the question of imperialism cause Americans to be ever more distrustful of Anglo-French policies, but events such as the Italian invasion of Abyssinia and the Japanese aggression into mainland China divided Rome and

Tokyo from London and Paris by the 1930s—and offered possible partners to German revisionists. Here again, international affairs had become that bit more difficult to manage according to the prescriptions of the "old diplomacy."

The final major cause of postwar instability was the awkward fact that the "German question" had not been settled, but made more intractable and intense. The swift collapse of Germany in October 1918 when its armies still controlled Europe from Belgium to the Ukraine came as a great shock to nationalist, right-wing forces, who tended to blame "traitors within" for the humiliating surrender. When the terms of the Paris settlement brought even more humiliations, vast numbers of Germans denounced both the "slave treaty" and the Weimar-democratic politicians who had agreed to such terms. The reparations issue, and the related hyperinflation of 1923, filled the cup of German discontents. Very few were as extreme as the National Socialists, who appeared as a cranky demagogic fringe movement for much of the 1920s; but very few Germans were *not* revisionists, in one form or another. Reparations, the Polish corridor, restrictions on the armed forces, the separation of German-speaking regions from the Fatherland were not going to be tolerated forever. The only questions were how soon these restrictions could be abolished and to what extent diplomacy should be preferred to force in order to alter the status quo. In this respect, Hitler's coming to power in 1933 merely intensified the German drive for revisionism.[33]

The problem of settling Germany's "proper" place in Europe was compounded by the curious and unbalanced distribution of international power after the First World War. Despite its territorial losses, military restrictions, and economic instability, Germany after 1919 was still *potentially* an immensely strong Great Power. A more detailed analysis of its strengths and weaknesses will be given below, but it is worth noting here that Germany still possessed a much larger population than France and an iron-and-steel capacity which was around three times as big. Its internal communications network was intact, as were its chemical and electrical plants and its universities and technical institutes. "At the moment in 1919, Germany was down-and-out. The immediate problem was German weakness; but given a few years of 'normal' life, it would again become the problem of German strength."[34] Furthermore, as Taylor points out, the old balance of power on the European continent which had helped to restrain German expansionism was no more. "Russia had withdrawn; Austria-Hungary had vanished. Only France and Italy remained, both inferior in manpower and still more in economic resources, both exhausted by the war."[35] And, as time went on, first the United States and then Britain showed an increasing distaste for interventions in Europe, and an increasing disapproval of French efforts to keep Germany down.

Yet it was precisely this apprehension that France was *not* secure which drove Paris into seeking to prevent a revival of German power by all means possible: insisting on the full payment of reparations; maintaining its own large and costly armed forces; endeavoring to turn the League of Nations into an organization dedicated to preserving the status quo; and resisting all suggestions that Germany be admitted to "arm up" to France's level[36]—all of which, predictably, fueled German resentments and helped the agitations of the right-wing extremists.

The other device in France's battery of diplomatic and political weapons was its link with the eastern European "successor states." On the face of it, support for Poland, Czechoslovakia, and the other beneficiaries of the 1919–1921 settlements in that region was both a plausible and a promising strategy;[37] by it, German expansionism would be checked on each flank. In reality, the scheme was fraught with difficulties. Because of the geographical dispersion of the various populations under the former multinational empires, it had not been possible in 1919 to create a territorial settlement which was ethnically coherent; large groups of minorities therefore lived on the wrong side of every state's borders, offering a source not only of internal weakness but also of foreign resentments. In other words, Germany was not alone in desiring a revision of the Paris treaties; and even if France was eager to insist upon no changes in the status quo, it was aware that neither Britain nor the United States felt any great commitment to the hastily arranged and irregular boundaries in this region. As London made clear in 1925, there would be no Locarno-type guarantees in eastern Europe.[38]

The economic scene in eastern and central Europe made matters even worse, since the erection of customs and tariff barriers around these newly created countries increased regional rivalries and hindered general development. There were now twenty-seven separate currencies in Europe instead of fourteen as before the war, and an extra 12,500 miles of frontiers; many of the borders separated factories from their raw materials, ironworks from their coalfields, farms from their market. What was more, although French and British bankers and enterprises moved into these successor states after 1919, a much more "natural" trading partner for those nations was Germany, once it had recovered its own economic stability in the 1930s. Not only was it closer to, and better connected by road and rail with, the eastern European market, but it could readily absorb the area's agricultural surpluses in the way that farm-surplus France and imperial-preference Britain could not, offering in return for Hungarian wheat and Rumanian oil much-needed machinery and (later) armaments. Moreover, these countries, like Germany itself, had currency problems and thus found it easier to trade on a "barter" basis. Economically, therefore, Mitteleuropa could again steadily become a German-dominated zone.[39]

Many of the participants at the Paris negotiations of 1919 were aware of some (though obviously not all) of the problems mentioned above. However, they felt that, like Lloyd George, they could look to the newly created League of Nations "to remedy, to repair, and to redress. . . . [It] will be there as a Court of Appeal to readjust crudities, irregularities, injustices."[40] Surely any outstanding political or economic quarrel between states could now be settled by reasonable men meeting around a table in Geneva. That again seemed a plausible supposition to make in 1919, but it was to founder on hard reality. The United States would not join the League. The Soviet Union was treated as a pariah state and kept out of the League. So, too, were the defeated powers, at least for the first few years. When the revisionist states commenced their aggressions in the 1930s, they soon thereafter left the League.

Furthermore, because of the earlier disagreements between the French and British versions of what the League should be—a policeman or a conciliator—the body lacked enforcement powers and had no real machinery of collective security. Ironically, therefore, the League's actual contribution turned out to be not deterring aggressors, but confusing the democracies. It was immensely popular with war-wearied public opinion in the West, but its very creation then permitted many the argument that there was no need for national defense forces since the League would somehow prevent future wars. In consequence, the existence of the League caused cabinets and foreign ministers to wobble between the "old" and the "new" diplomacy, usually securing the benefits of neither, as the Manchurian and Abyssinian cases amply demonstrated.

In the light of all of the above difficulties, and of the overwhelming fact that Europe plunged into another great war only twenty years after signing the Treaty of Versailles, it is scarcely surprising that historians have seen this period as a "twenty years' truce" and portrayed it as a gloomy and fractured time—full of crises, deceits, brutalities, dishonor. But with book titles like *A Broken World, The Lost Peace*, and *The Twenty Years' Crisis* describing these entire two decades,[41] there is a danger that the great differences between the 1920s and the 1930s may be ignored. To repeat a remark made earlier, by the late 1920s, the Locarno and Kellogg-Briand (Pact of Paris) treaties, the settling of many Franco-German differences, the meetings of the League, and the general revival of prosperity seemed to indicate that the First World War was at last over as far as international relations were concerned. Within another year or two, however, the devastating financial and industrial collapse had shaken that harmony and had begun to interact with the challenges which the Japanese and German (and later Italian) nationalists would pose to the existing order. In a remarkably short space of time, the clouds of war returned. The system was under threat, in a fundamental way, just at a moment when the democracies were least prepared, psychologically and militarily, to meet it; and just as they were less coordinated than at any time since the 1919 settlement. Whatever the deficiencies and follies of any particular "appeaser" in the unhappy 1930s, therefore, it is as well to bear in mind the unprecedented complexities with which the statesmen of that decade had to grapple.

Before seeing how the international crises of this period unfolded into war, it is important once again to examine the particular strengths and weaknesses of each of the Great Powers, all of which had been affected not only by the 1914–1918 conflict but also by the economic and military developments of the interwar years. In this latter respect, Tables 12–18 above, showing the shifts in the productive balances between the powers, will be referred to again and again. Two further preliminary remarks about the economics of rearmament should be made at this point. The first concerns differential growth rates, which were much more marked during the 1930s than they had been, say, in the decade prior to 1914; the dislocation of the world economy into various blocs and the remarkably different ways in which national economic policy was pursued (from four-year plans and "new deals" to classic deflationary budgets) meant that output and wealth could be rising in one country while dramatically slowing down in another. Secondly, the interwar developments in military technology made the armed forces more dependent than ever upon the productive forces of their nations. Without a flourishing industrial base and, more important still, without a large, advanced scientific community which could be mobilized by the state in order to keep pace with new developments in weaponry, victory in another great war was inconceivable. If the future lay (to use Stalin's phrase) in the hands of the big battalions, they in turn increasingly rested upon modern technology and mass production.

The Challengers

The economic vulnerability of a Great Power, however active and ambitious its national leadership, is nowhere more clearly seen than in the case of Italy during the 1930s. On the face of it, Mussolini's fascist regime had brought the country from the hinterlands to the forefront of the diplomatic world. With Britain, it was one of the outside guarantors of the 1925 Locarno agreement; with Britain, France and Germany, it was also a signatory to the 1938 Munich settlement. Italy's claim to primacy in the Mediterranean had been asserted by the attack upon Corfu (1923), by intensifying the "pacification" of Libya, and by the very large intervention (of 50,000 Italian troops) in the Spanish Civil War. Between 1935 and 1937, Mussolini avenged the defeat of Adowa by his ruthless conquest of Abyssinia, boldly defying the League's sanctions and hostile western opinion. At other times, he supported the status quo, moving troops up to the Brenner in 1934 to deter Hitler from taking over Austria, and readily signing the anti-German accord at Stresa in 1935. His tirades against Bolshevism won him the admiration of many foreigners (Churchill included) in the 1920s, and he was wooed by all sides during the decade following—with Chamberlain traveling to Rome as late as January 1939 in an effort to stop Italy from drifting completely into the German camp.[42]

But diplomatic prominence was not the only measure of Italy's new greatness. This fascist state, with its elimination of factious party politics, its "corporatist" planning for the economy in the place of disputes between capital and labor, its commitment to government action, seemed to offer a new model to a disenchanted postwar European society—and one attractive to those who feared the alternative "model" being offered by the Bolsheviks. Because of Allied investments, industrialization had proceeded apace from 1915 to 1918, at least in those heavy industries related to arms production. Under Mussolini, the state committed itself to an ambitious modernization program, which ranged from draining the Pontine marshes, to the impressive development of hydroelectricity, to the improvements in the railway system. The electrochemical industry was furthered, and rayon and other artificial fibers were developed. Automobile production was increased, and the Italian aeronautical industry seemed to be among the most innovative in the world, its aircraft gaining a whole series of speed and altitude records.[43]

Military power, too, seemed to give good indications of Italy's rising status. Although he had not spent much on the armed services in the 1920s, Mussolini's belief in force and conquest and his rising desire to expand Italy's territories led to significant increases in defense spending during the 1930s. Indeed, a little over 10 percent of national income and as much as one-third of government income was devoted to the armed forces by the mid-1930s, which in absolute figures was more than was spent by Britain or France, and much more than the American totals. Smart new battleships were being laid down, to rival the French navy and the British Mediterranean Fleet, and to support Mussolini's claim that the Mediterranean was indeed *mare nostrum*. When Italy entered the war it possessed 113 submarines—"the largest submarine force in the world except perhaps that of the Soviet Union."[44] Even larger sums were being allocated to the air force, the Regia Aeronautica, in the years leading up to 1940, in keeping perhaps with early fascism's emphasis upon modernity, science, speed, and glamour. Both in Abyssinia and, even more, in Spain, the Italians demonstrated the uses of air power and convinced themselves—and many foreign observers—that they possessed the most advanced air force in the world. This buildup of the navy and the air force left fewer funds for the Italian army, but its thirty divisions were being substantially restructured in the late 1930s, and new tanks and artillery were being planned. Besides, Mussolini felt, there were the masses of fascist *squadristi* and trained bands, so that in another total war the nation might well possess the claimed "eight million bayonets." All this boded well for the creation of a second Roman Empire.

Alas for such dreams, fascist Italy was, in power-political terms, spectacularly weak. The key problem was that even "at the end of the First World War Italy, economically speaking, was a semideveloped country."[45] Its per capita income in 1920 was probably equal to that achieved by Britain and the United States in the early *nineteenth* century, and by France a few decades later. National income data concealed the fact that per capita income in the north was 20 percent above, in the south 30 percent below, the average; and the gap, if anything, was widening. Thanks to a continued flow of emigrants, Italy's population in the interwar years increased by only around 1 percent a year; since the gross domestic product grew by 2 percent a year, the average per capita rose by a mere 1 percent a year, which was not disastrous, but hardly an economic miracle. At the root of Italy's weakness was the continued reliance upon small-scale agriculture, which in 1920 accounted for 40 percent of GNP and absorbed 50 percent of the total working population.[46] It was a further sign of this economic backwardness that even as late as 1938 over half a family's expenditure went on food. Far from reducing these proportions, fascism, with its heavy emphasis upon the virtues of rural life, endeavored to support agriculture by a battery of measures, including protective tariffs, widespread land reclamation, and, finally, complete control of the wheat market. Important in the regime's calculations was the desire to reduce dependence upon foreign food producers and the strong wish to prevent a further drift of peasants into the towns, where they would boost the unemployment totals and add to the social problem. The consequence was a very heavy *under*employment in the countryside, with all of the corresponding features: low productivity, illiteracy, immense regional disparities.

Given the relatively backward nature of the Italian economy and the state's willingness to spend money both on armaments and on the preservation of village agriculture, it is not surprising that the amount of savings for entrepreneurial investment was low. If the First World War had already reduced the stock of domestic capital, the economic depression and the turn to protectionism were further blows. To be sure, companies boosted by government orders for aircraft or trucks could make a good profit, but it is unlikely that Italy's industrial development benefited (on the whole) from attempts at autarky; tariffs merely gave protection to inefficient producers, while the general neo-mercantilism of the age reduced the flow of foreign investments which had done much to stimulate Italian industrialization earlier. By 1938 Italy still possessed only 2.8 percent of world manufacturing production, produced 2.1 percent of its steel, 1.0 percent of its pig iron, 0.7 percent of its iron ore, and 0.1 percent of its coal, and consumed energy from modern sources at a rate far below that of any of the other Great Powers. Finally, in the light of Mussolini's evident eagerness to go to war against France, and sometimes even France and Britain combined, it is worth noting that Italy remained embarrassingly dependent upon imported fertilizer, coal, oil, scrap iron, rubber, copper, and other vital raw materials—80 percent of which had to come past Gibraltar or Suez, and much of which was carried in British ships. It was typical of the regime that no contingency plan had been prepared in the event of these imports ceasing, and that a policy of stockpiling such strategic materials was out of the question, since by the late 1930s Italy didn't even have the foreign currency to cover its current needs. This chronic currency shortage also helps to explain why the Italians also could not afford to pay for the German machine tools so vital for the production of the more modern aircraft, tanks, guns, and ships which were being developed in the years after 1935 or so.[47]

Economic backwardness also explains why, despite all the attention and resources which Mussolini's regime devoted to the armed forces, their actual performance and condition were poor—and getting worse. The navy was probably the best-equipped of the three services, but probably too weak to drive the Royal Navy out of the Mediterranean. It possessed no aircraft carriers—Mussolini had forbidden their construction—and was forced instead to rely upon the Regia Aeronautica, a poor arrangement given the lack of interservice cooperation. Its cruisers were fair-weather vessels, and its great array of submarines proved to be a heavy investment in obsolescence: "The boats lacked attack computers, their air-conditioning systems gave off poisonous gases when tubing ruptured under depth-charge attack, and they were relatively slow in diving, which proved embarrassing when enemy aircraft approached."[48] Similar signs of obsolescence could be seen in the Italian air force, which had shown itself capable of bombing (if not always hitting) Abyssinian tribesmen, and had then impressed many observers by its Spanish Civil War performances. But by the late 1930s the Fiat CR42 biplane was totally eclipsed by the newer British and German monoplanes; and even the bomber force suffered from having only light to medium bombers, with weak engines and stupendously ineffective bombs. Yet both the above services had secured increasing shares of the defense budget. The army, by contrast, saw its share drop from 58.2 percent in 1935–1936 to 44.5 percent in 1938–1939, and that at a time when it desperately needed modern tanks, artillery, trucks, and communications systems. The "main battle tank" of the Italian army, when it entered the Second World War, was the Fiat L.3, of three and a half tons, with no radio, little vision, and only two machine guns—this at a time when the latest German and French tank designs were close upon twenty tons and had much heavier weaponry.

Given the almost irremediable weaknesses which afflicted the Italian economy under fascism, it would be rash to suggest that it could ever have won a war against another proper Great Power; but its prospects were made the bleaker by the fact that its armed forces were the victims of early rearmament—and swift obsolescence. Since this was a common problem in the 1930s, affecting France and Russia to almost the same degree, it is important to go into it in a little more detail before returning to our specific analysis of Italy's weaknesses.

The key factor was the intense application of science and technology to military developments in this period, which was transforming weapon systems in all the services. Fighter aircraft, for example, were swiftly changing from maneuverable (but lightly armed and fabric-covered) biplanes which could do about 200 mph to "duraluminum monoplane aircraft laden with multiple heavy machine guns and cannon, cockpit armor and self-sealing fuel tanks"[49] which flew at up to 400 mph and required much more powerful engines. Bomber aircraft were changing—in those nations which could afford the move—from two-engined, shorter-range medium bombers to the massively expensive four-engined types capable of carrying large bomb loads and with a radius of over two thousand miles. Post–Washington Treaty battleships (e.g., of the *King George V, Bismarck,* and *North Carolina* sort), were much faster, better-armored, and equipped with far heavier antiaircraft defenses than their predecessors. The newer aircraft carriers were large, well-designed types, with a much greater striking power than the updated seaplane carriers and converted battle cruisers of the 1920s. Tank developers were rushing ahead with heavier, better-armed, and better-armored models which required far more powerful engines than those which had driven the light experimental prototypes of the pre-1935 years. Furthermore, all of these weapon systems were just beginning to be affected by the changes in electrical communications, by improvements in navigational devices and antisubmarine detection equipment, by early radar and improved radio equipment—which not only made the newer weapons so much more expensive, but also complicated the procurement process. Did one have enough of the new machine tools, gauges, and jigs to switch to these improved models? Could armaments works and electrical suppliers meet the rising demand? Did they have enough spare plant, and trained engineers? Dare one *stop* producing the tried but perhaps obsolescent older models while waiting for the newer types to be tested and then built? Finally—and critically—how did these desperate rearmament efforts relate to the state of the nation's economy, its access to overseas as well as domestic resources, its ability to pay its way? These were, of course, not new dilemmas—but they pressed upon the decision-makers of the 1930s with a far greater urgency than ever before.

It is in this technological-economic context (as well as in the diplomatic context) that the varying patterns of Great Power rearmament in the 1930s can best be understood. There are many disparities in the compilation of the actual annual totals of defense expenditures by individual nations in this decade, but Table 27 can serve as a fair guide to what was happening.

Table 27. Defense Expenditures of the Great Powers, 1930–1938[50]
(millions of current dollars)

	Japan	Italy	Germany	USSR	U.K.	France	U.S.
1930	218	266	162	722	512	498	699
1933	183	351	452	707	333	524	570
	(356)	(361)	(620)	(303)	(500)	(805)	(792)
	[387]						
1934	292	455	709	3479	540	707	803
	(384)	(427)	(914)	(980)	(558)	(731)	(708)
	[427]						
1935	300	966	1,607	5,517	646	867	806
	(900)	(966)	(2,025)	(1,607)	(671)	(849)	(933)
	[463]						
1936	313	1,149	2,332	2,933	892	995	932
	(440)	(1,252)	(3,266)	(2,903)	(911)	(980)	(1,119)
	[488]						
1937	940	1,235	3,298	3,446	1,245	890	1,032
	(1,621)	(1,015)	(4,769)	(3,430)	(1,283)	(862)	(1,079)
	[1,064]						
1938	1,740	746	7,415	5,429	1,863	919	1,131
	(2,489)	(818)	(5,807)	(4,527)	(1,915)	(1,014)	(1,131)
	[1,706]						

Seen in this comparative light, the Italian problem becomes clearer. It had not been a great spender on armaments in absolute terms during the first half of the 1930s, although even then it had needed to devote a higher proportion of its national income to the armed services than probably all other states except the USSR. But the extended Abyssinian campaign, overlapped by the intervention in Spain, led to greatly increased expenditures between 1935 and 1937. Thus part of Italian defense spending in those years was devoted to current operations, and not to the buildup of the services or the armaments industry. On the contrary, the Abyssinian and Spanish adventures gravely weakened

Italy, not only because of losses in the field, but also because the longer it fought, the more it needed to import—and pay for—vital strategic raw materials, causing the Bank of Italy's reserves to shrink to almost nothing by 1939. Unable to afford the machine tools and other equipment needed to modernize the air force and the army, the country was probably getting *weaker* in the two to three years prior to 1940. The army was not helped by its own reorganization, since the device of creating half again as many divisions by simply reducing each division from three to two regiments led to many officer promotions but to no real increase in efficiency. The air force, supported (if that is the right word) by an industry which was *less* productive than that of 1915–1918, claimed that it had over 8,500 planes; further investigations reduced that total to 454 bombers and 129 fighters, few of which would be regarded as first-rate in other air forces.[51] Without proper tanks or antiaircraft guns or fast fighters or decent bombs or aircraft carriers or radar or foreign currency or adequate logistics, Mussolini in 1940 threw his country into another Great Power war, on the assumption that it was already won. In fact, only a miracle, or the Germans, could prevent a debacle of epic proportions.

All of this emphasis upon weaponry and numbers does, of course, ignore the elements of leadership, quality of personnel, and national proclivity for combat; but the sad fact was that, far from compensating for Italy's matériel deficiencies, those elements merely added to its relative weakness. Despite superficial fascist indoctrination, nothing in Italian society and political culture had altered between 1900 and 1930 to make the army a more attractive career to talented, ambitious males; on the contrary, its collective inefficiency, lack of initiative, and concern for personal career prospects was stultifying—and amazed the German attachés and other military observers. The army was not the compliant tool of Mussolini; it could, and often did, obstruct his wishes, offering innumerable reasons why things could not be done. Its fate was to be thrust, often without prior consultation, into conflicts where something *had* to be done. Dominated by its cautious and inadequately trained senior officers, and lacking a backbone of experienced NCOs, the army's plight in the event of a Great Power war was hopeless; and the navy (except for the enterprising midget submarines) was little better off. If the officer corps and crews of the Regia Aeronautica were better educated and better trained, that would avail them little when they were still flying obsolescent aircraft, whose engines succumbed to the desert sands, whose bombs were hopeless, and whose firepower was pathetic. Perhaps it hardly needs saying that there was no chiefs of staff committee to coordinate plans between the services, or to discuss (let alone settle) defense priorities.

Finally, there was Mussolini himself, a strategical liability of the first order. He was not, it has been argued, the all-powerful leader on the lines of Hitler which he projected himself as being. King Victor Emmanuel III strove to preserve his prerogatives, and succeeded in keeping the loyalties of much of the bureaucracy and the officer corps. The papacy was also an independent, and rival, focus of authority for many Italians. Neither the great industrialists nor the recalcitrant peasantry were enthusiastic about the regime by the 1930s; and the National Fascist Party itself, or at least its regional bosses, seemed more concerned with the distribution of jobs than the pursuit of national glory.[52] But even had Mussolini's rule been absolute, Italy's position would be no better, given Il Duce's penchant for self-delusion, resort to bombast and bluster, congenital lying, inability to act and think effectively, and governmental incompetence.[53]

In 1939 and 1940, the western Allies frequently considered the pros and cons of having Italy fighting on Germany's side rather than remaining neutral. On the whole, the British chiefs of staff preferred Italy to be kept out of the war, so as to preserve peace in the Mediterranean and Near East; but there were powerful counterarguments, which seem in retrospect to have been correct.[54] Rarely in the history of human conflict has it been argued that the entry of an additional foe would hurt one's enemy more than oneself; but Mussolini's Italy was, in that way at least, unique.

The challenge to the status quo posed by Japan was also of a very individual sort, but needed to be taken much more seriously by the established Powers. In the world of the 1920s and 1930s, heavily colored by racist and cultural prejudices, many in the West tended to dismiss the Japanese as "little yellow men"; only during the devastating attacks upon Pearl Harbor, Malaya, and the Philippines was this crude stereotype of a myopic, stunted, unmechanical people revealed for the nonsense it was.[55] The Japanese navy trained hard, both for day and night fighting, and learned well; its attachés fed a continual stream of intelligence back to the planners and ship designers in Tokyo. Both the army and the naval air forces were also well trained, with a large stock of competent pilots and dedicated crewmen.[56] As for the army proper, its determined and hyperpatriotic officer corps stood at the head of a force imbued with the *bushido* spirit; they were formidable troops both in offensive and defensive warfare. The fanatical zeal which led to the assassination of (allegedly) weak ministers could easily be transformed into battlefield effectiveness. While other armies merely talked of fighting to the last man, Japanese soldiers took the phrase literally, and did so.

But what distinguished the Japanese from, say, Zulu warriors was that by this period the former possessed military-technical superiority as well as sheer bravery. The pre-1914 process of industrialization had been immensely boosted by the First World War, partly because of

Allied contracts for munitions and a strong demand for Japanese shipping, partly because its own exporters could step into Asian markets
which the West could no longer supply.[57] Imports and exports tripled
during the war, steel and cement production more than doubled, and
great advances were made in chemical and electrical industries. As
with the United States, Japan's foreign debts were liquidated during
the war and it became a creditor. It also became a major shipbuilding
nation, launching 650,000 tons in 1919 compared with a mere 85,000
tons in 1914. As the League of Nations *World Economic Survey*
showed, the war had boosted its manufacturing production even more
than that of the United States, and the continuation of that growth
during the 1919–1938 period meant that it was second only to the
Soviet Union in its overall rate of expansion (See Table 28).

Table 28. Annual Indices of Manufacturing Production, 1913–1938[58]
(1913 = 100)

	World	U.S.	Germany	U.K.	France	USSR	Italy	Japan
1913	100.0	100.0	100.0	100.0	100.0	100.0	100.0	100.0
1920	93.2	122.2	59.0	92.6	70.4	12.8	95.2	176.0
1921	81.1	98.0	74.7	55.1	61.4	23.3	98.4	167.1
1922	99.5	125.8	81.8	73.5	87.8	28.9	108.1	197.9
1923	104.5	141.4	55.4	79.1	95.2	35.4	119.3	206.4
1924	111.0	133.2	81.8	87.8	117.9	47.5	140.7	223.3
1925	120.7	148.0	94.9	86.3	114.3	70.2	156.8	221.8
1926	126.5	156.1	90.9	78.8	129.8	100.3	162.8	264.9
1927	134.5	154.5	122.1	96.0	115.6	114.5	161.2	270.0
1928	141.8	162.8	118.3	95.1	134.4	143.5	175.2	300.2
1929	153.3	180.8	117.3	100.3	142.7	181.4	181.0	324.0
1930	137.5	148.0	101.6	91.3	139.9	235.5	164.0	294.9
1931	122.5	121.6	85.1	82.4	122.6	293.9	145.1	288.1
1932	108.4	93.7	70.2	82.5	105.4	326.1	123.3	309.1
1933	121.7	111.8	79.4	83.3	119.8	363.2	133.2	360.7
1934	136.4	121.6	101.8	100.2	111.4	437.0	134.7	413.5
1935	154.5	140.3	116.7	107.9	109.1	533.7	162.2	457.8
1936	178.1	171.0	127.5	119.1	116.3	693.3	169.2	483.9
1937	195.8	185.8	138.1	127.8	123.8	772.2	194.5	551.0
1938	182.7	143.0	149.3	117.6	114.6	857.3	195.2	552.0

By 1938, in fact, Japan had not only become much stronger
economically than Italy, but had also overtaken France in all of the
indices of manufacturing and industrial production (see Tables 14–18
above). Had its military leaders not gone to war in China in 1937 and,
more disastrously, in the Pacific in 1941, one is tempted to conclude
that it would also have overtaken British output well before actually
doing so, in the mid-1960s.

This is not to say that Japan had effortlessly overcome all of its
economic problems, but merely that it was growing markedly
stronger. Because of its primitive banking system, it had not found it

easy to adjust to becoming a creditor nation during the First World War, and its handling of the money supply had caused great inflation—not to mention the "rice riots" of 1919.[59] As Europe resumed its peacetime production of textiles, merchant vessels, and other goods, Japan felt the pressure of renewed competition; the cost of its manufacturing, at this stage, was still generally higher than in the West. Furthermore, a heavy proportion of the Japanese population remained in small-plot agriculture, and these groups suffered not only from rising rice imports from Taiwan and Korea, but also from the collapse of the vital silk export trade when American demand fell away after 1930. Seeking to alleviate these miseries by imperial expansion was always a temptation for worried or ambitious Japanese politicians—the conquest of Manchuria, for example, meant economic benefits as well as military gains. On the other hand, when Japanese industry and commerce recovered during the 1930s, partly through rearmament and partly through the exploitation of captive East Asian markets, so its dependence upon imported raw materials grew (in this respect, at least, it was similar to Italy). As the Japanese steel industry expanded, it required larger amounts of pig iron and ore from China and Malaya. Domestic supplies of coal and copper were also inadequate for industry's requirements; but even that was less critical than the country's near-total reliance upon petroleum fuels of all sorts. Japan's quest for "economic security"[60]—a self-evident good in the eyes of its fervent nationalists and the military rulers—drove it ever forward, but with mixed results.

Despite—and, of course, in some ways because of—these economic difficulties, the finance ministry under Takahashi was willing to borrow recklessly in the early 1930s in order to allocate more to the armed services, whose share of government spending rose from 31 percent in 1931–1932 to 47 percent in 1936–1937;[61] when he finally took alarm at the economic consequences and sought to modify further increases, he was promptly assassinated by the militarists, and armaments expenditures spiraled upward. By the following year, the armed services were taking 70 percent of government expenditure and Japan was thus spending, in absolute terms, more than any of the far wealthier democracies. Thus the Japanese armed services were in a far better position than those of Italy by the late 1930s, and possibly also those of France and Britain. The Imperial Japanese Navy, legally restricted by the Washington Treaty to slightly over half the size of either the British or American navy, was in reality much more powerful than that. While the two leading naval powers economized during the 1920s and early 1930s, Japan built right up to the treaty limits—and, indeed, secretly went far beyond them. Its heavy cruisers, for example, displaced closer to 14,000 tons than the 8,000 tons required by the treaty. All of the Japanese major warships were fast and very heavily armed; its older battleships had been modernized, and by the late 1930s it was laying down the gigantic *Yamato*-class vessels, larger than anything else in the world. The most important element of all, although the battleship admirals didn't properly realize it, was Japan's powerful and efficient naval air service, with 3,000 aircraft and 3,500 pilots, which centered upon the ten carriers in the fleet but also included some deadly-efficient bomber and torpedo-carrying squadrons on land. Japanese torpedoes were of unequaled power and quality. Finally, the country also possessed the world's third-largest merchant marine, although (curiously) the navy itself virtually neglected antisubmarine warfare.[62]

Because of conscription, the Japanese army had ready access to manpower and could ingrain the recruits into its traditions of absolute obedience and mass maximum effort. While it had kept the size of the army limited in earlier years, its expansion program saw the 24 divisions and 54 air squadrons of 1937 grow to 51 active service divisions and 133 air squadrons by 1941. In addition, there were 10 depot divisions (for training), and a large number of independent brigade and garrison troops, probably equal to another 30 divisions. By the eve of war, therefore, Japan had an army of over 1 million men, backed by nearly 2 million trained reserves. It was not strong in tanks, for which neither the terrain nor the wooden bridges of much of East Asia were suitable, but it had good mobile artillery and was well trained for jungle work, river crossings, and amphibious landings. The army's 2,000 first-line aircraft (like the navy's) included the formidable Zero fighter, as fast and maneuverable as anything produced in Europe at the time.[63]

Japan's military effectiveness, therefore, was extremely high; but it was not free of weaknesses. Government decision-making in the 1930s was rendered erratic and, at times, incoherent by clashes between the various factions, by civil-military disputes, and by assassinations. In addition, there was the lack of proper coordination between the army and the navy—not a unique situation by any means, but the more dangerous in Japan's case since each service had a quite different enemy *and* area of operations in mind. While the navy anticipated a future war with either Britain or the United States, the army's eyes were fixed exclusively upon the Asian continent and the threat to Japanese interests there posed by the Soviet Union. Since the army was much more influential in Japanese politics and also dominated imperial general headquarters, its views generally prevailed. There was no effective opposition, from either the navy or the foreign office, although both were reluctant, when in 1937 the army insisted upon taking further action against China following the contrived Marco Polo Bridge incident. Despite a large-scale invasion of northern China from Manchurian soil, and landings along the Chinese coast, the Japanese army found it impossible to achieve a decisive victory. While

losing great numbers of troops, Chiang Kai-shek kept up the struggle
and moved even farther inland, pursued by Japanese striking columns
and aircraft. The problem for Imperial General Headquarters was not
so much the losses this campaigning involved—the army probably
suffered only 70,000 casualties—but the stupendous costs of such inconclusive and extended warfare. By the end of 1937, there were over
700,000 Japanese troops in China, a number which steadily increased
(though Willmott's figure of 1.5 million by 1938 seems far too high)[64]
without ever managing to force the Chinese to surrender. The "China
Incident," as Tokyo referred to it, was now costing $5 million a day and
causing an even larger rise in defense spending. Rationing was introduced in 1938, as were a whole series of enactments which virtually
put Japan onto a "total war" mobilization. The national debt spiraled
upward at an alarming rate as the government borrowed more and
more to pay for the enormous defense expenditures.[65]

What made this strategy even more difficult to sustain was Japan's
shrinking stocks of foreign currency and raw materials, and her increasing dependence upon imports from the disapproving Americans,
British, and Dutch. After her air forces had used up large amounts of
fuel in the China campaigns, "factories were ordered to reduce their
fuel by 37 percent, ships by 15 percent and automobiles by 65 percent."[66] This situation was the more intolerable to the Japanese since
they believed that Chiang Kai-shek's forces were only able to keep up
their resistance because of the flow of western supplies, via the Burma
Road, French Indochina, or other routes. Logically, inexorably, the
conviction grew that Japan would have to strike south, both to isolate
China and to gain a firm grip upon the oil and other raw materials of
Southeast Asia, the Dutch East Indies, and Borneo. This was, of course,
the direction which the Japanese navy had always favored; yet even the
army, despite its prior concern about the Soviet Union and its extensive operations in China, was forced slowly to admit that action was
necessary to ensure Japan's economic security.

This led to the gravest problem of all. Given the armed strength
which they had built up by the late 1930s, the Japanese could easily
sweep the French out of Indochina and the Dutch out of the East
Indies. Even the British Empire would have found it difficult to hold
its own against Japan, as the strategic planners in Whitehall secretly
admitted during the 1930s; and by the time war had broken out in
Europe, a full British commitment to the Far East was impossible. It
was quite another thing, however, for the Japanese to go to war against
either Russia or the United States. In the prolonged and bloody border
clashes with the Red Army around Nomonhan between May and August 1939, for example, Imperial General Headquarters was alarmed
at the clear superiority of Soviet artillery and aircraft, and at the firepower of the much larger Russian tanks.[67] With the Kwantung (Man-

churia) army possessing only half the number of divisions that the Russians had placed in Mongolia and Siberia, and with large forces increasingly bogged down in China, even the more extremist army officers recognized that war against the USSR had to be avoided—at least until the international circumstances were more favorable.

But if a northern war would expose Japan's limitations, would not a southern one also, if it ran the risk of bringing in the United States? And would the Roosevelt administration, which so strongly disapproved of the Japanese actions in China, stand idly by while Tokyo helped itself to the Dutch East Indies and Malaya, thereby escaping from American economic pressure? The "moral embargo" upon the export of aeronautical materials in June 1938, the abrogation of the American-Japanese trade treaty in the following year, and, most of all, the British-Dutch-U.S. ban of oil and iron-ore exports following the Japanese takeover of Indochina in July 1941 made it clear that "economic security" could be achieved only at the price of war with the United States. But the United States had nearly twice the population of Japan, and *seventeen* times the national income, produced five times as much steel, and seven times as much coal, and made eighty times as many motor vehicles each year. Its industrial potential, even in a poor year like 1938, was seven times larger than Japan's;[68] it might in other years be nine or ten times as large. Even granted the high level of Japanese patriotic fervor and the memory of its staggering successes against far larger opponents in 1895 (China) and 1905 (Russia), what it was now planning bordered on the incredible—and the absurd. Indeed, to such sober strategists as Admiral Yamamoto, an attack upon a country as powerful as the United States seemed folly, especially when it became clear that most of the Japanese army would remain in China; yet *not* to take on the United States after July 1941 would leave Japan exposed to western economic blackmail, which was also an intolerable notion. Unable to go back, the Japanese military leaders prepared to plunge forward.[69]

In the 1920s, Germany appeared to be by far the weakest and most troubled of those Great Powers which felt dissatisfied by the postwar territorial and economic arrangements. Shackled by the military provisions of the Versailles Treaty, burdened by the need to pay reparations, constrained strategically by the transfer of border regions to France and Poland, and convulsed internally by inflation, class tension, and the corresponding volatility and confusion of the electorate and the parties, Germany possessed nothing like the freedom of action in foreign affairs enjoyed by Italy and Japan. While things had vastly improved by the late 1920s in consequence of the general prosperity and of Stresemann's successes in enhancing Germany's position by diplomacy, the country still was a politically troubled "half-free" Great

Power when the financial and commercial crises of 1929–1933 devastated both its precarious economy and its much-disliked Weimar democracy.[70]

If the advent of Hitler transformed Germany's position in Europe within a matter of years, it is important to recall the points made earlier: that virtually every German was a "revisionist" to a greater or lesser degree and much of the early Nazi foreign-policy program represented a *continuity* with the past ambitions of German nationalists and the suppressed armed forces; that the 1919–1922 border settlements in east-central Europe were seen as unsatisfactory by many other nations and ethnic groups, who pressed for changes long before the Nazis seized power, and were willing to join Berlin in amending them; that Germany, despite its losses of territory, population, and raw materials, retained the industrial potential to be the greatest of the European powers; and that the international balances which were needed to contain a resurgence of German aggrandizement were now far more disparate, and much less coordinated, than prior to 1914. That Hitler soon achieved staggering successes in his scheme to improve Germany's diplomatic and military position is undoubted; but it is also clear that many existing circumstances favored his ruthless exploitation of opportunities.[71]

Hitler's "specialness," so far as the themes pursued in this book are concerned, lay in two areas. The first was the peculiarly intense and manic nature of the National Socialist Germany which he intended to create: a society racially "purified" by the elimination of Jews, gypsies, and any other allegedly non-Teutonic elements; a people whose minds and souls were given over to unquestioned support of the regime, which would thereby replace the older loyalties of class, church, region, and family; an economy mobilized and controlled for the purposes of expanding *Deutschtum* whenever or wherever the leader decreed that to be necessary, and against however many of the Great Powers; an ideology of force and struggle and hatred, which rejoiced in smashing foes and scorned the very idea of compromise.[72] Given the size and complexity of twentieth-century German society, it hardly needs remarking that this was an unreal vision: there were "limits to Hitler's power"[73] across the country; there were individuals, and interest groups, which supported him in 1932–1933, and even until 1938–1939, but with decreasing enthusiasm; and no doubt for all those who openly opposed the regime there were many others who developed a mentally internalized resistance. But despite such exceptions, there was also no question that the National Socialist regime was immensely popular and—even more important—absolutely unchallenged in respect to its disposition of national resources. With a political culture bent upon war and conquest and a political economy distorted to the extent that by 1938 52 percent of government expenditure and a massive 17 percent of gross national product was being poured into armaments, Germany had entered a different league from any of the other western European states. In the year of Munich, indeed, Germany was spending more upon weapons than Britain, France, and the United States combined. Insofar as the state apparatus could concentrate them, all German national energies were being mobilized for a renewed struggle.[74]

The second major feature of German rearmament was the frighteningly precarious state of the national economy as it heated up during this expansion. As has been noted above, both the Italian and the Japanese economies manifested similar problems by the late 1930s—and the same would happen to France and Britain when they sought to respond to the fantastic pace of arms increases. But in none of those countries was the buildup of the armed forces as sudden as in Germany. In January 1933 its army was, legally, supposed to be no more than 100,000 men, although well before Hitler's accession the military had secret plans to expand from a seven-division force to a twenty-one division force—just as it had privately prepared for the reestablishment of an air force, tank formations, and other elements banned by the Versailles Treaty. Hitler's general instruction of February 1933 to von Fritsch, "to create an army of the greatest possible strength,"[75] was simply taken by the planners to be the go-ahead to turn the earlier scheme into effect, free at last from financial and manpower restrictions. By 1935, however, conscription was announced and the army's ceiling raised to thirty-six divisions. The acquisition of Austrian units in 1938, the takeover of the Rhineland military police, the creation of armored divisions, and the reorganization of the Landwehr sent that figure ever higher. In the crisis period of late 1938, the army totaled forty-two active, eight reserve, and twenty-one Landwehr divisions; by the next summer, when the war began, the German field army's order of battle listed 103 divisions—a jump of thirty-two within one year.[76] The Luftwaffe's expansion was even greater and faster. German aircraft production of a mere thirty-six planes in 1932 rose to 1,938 in 1934 and 5,112 in 1936, and the service's twenty-six squadrons (July 1933 directive) rose to 302 squadrons, with over 4,000 front-line aircraft, at the outset of war.[77] If the navy was less impressive in size, then that was to a large degree due to the fact that (as Tirpitz earlier discovered) the creation of a powerful battle fleet took at least one to two decades. Nonetheless, by 1939 Admiral Raeder commanded a number of fast, modern warships, the navy had five times the number of personnel that it possessed in 1932, and it was spending twelve times as much as before Hitler came to power.[78] At sea, as well as on land and in the air, the German rearmament program was intent upon altering the balance of power as soon as possible.

While all this looked impressive from the outside, it was decidedly shaky within. The blows the German economy had received from the Versailles territorial arrangements, the great inflation of 1923, the payment of reparations, and the difficulty of reentering pre-1914 foreign markets meant that it was only in 1927–1928 that Germany's output equaled that achieved prior to the First World War. But this recovery was promptly ruined by the great economic crisis of the following few years, which hit Germany more severely than most other countries; by 1932, industrial production was only 58 percent that of 1928, exports and imports had been more than halved, the gross national product had fallen from 89 billion to 57 billion reichsmarks, and unemployment had swollen from 1.4 to 5.6 million people.[79] Much of Hitler's early popularity stemmed from the fact that the widespread programs of roadbuilding, electrification, and industrial investment greatly reduced the unemployment totals even before conscription did the rest.[80] By 1936, however, the economic recovery was being increasingly affected by the fantastic expenditure upon armaments. In the short term, this spending was yet another quasi-Keynesian government boost to capital investment and industrial growth. In the medium, let alone the long, term, the economic consequences were frightening. Probably only the U.S. economy could, without major difficulty, have withstood the strain placed upon it by this level of arms spending; the German economy certainly could not.

The first serious problem, little perceived by foreign observers at the time, was the quite chaotic structure of National Socialist decision-making, something which Hitler seems to have encouraged in order to retain ultimate authority. Despite the pronouncements of the Four-Year Plan, there was no coherent national program to relate the arms buildup to Germany's economic capacity and to allocate priorities between the services; Goering, nominally in charge of the plan, was a hopeless administrator. Instead, each branch pursued its own breakneck expansion, setting new (often preposterous) targets and then competing for the necessary allocations of capital investment and, especially, raw materials. To be sure, the situation would have been even more chaotic had the government not imposed strict controls upon labor, compelled private industry to reinvest its profits into manufactures approved of by the state and, through high taxation, deficit borrowing, checking wages and personal consumption, also forced an increasing amount of the national product into capital investment for the arms industry. But even when government expenditure soared to 33 percent of GNP by 1938 (and much "private" investment was by then really done at the state's request), there were insufficient resources to meet the overlapping and sometimes megalomaniacal demands of the armed services. The Z-Plan fleet being built for the German navy would have needed 6 million tons of fuel oil (equal to Germany's entire consumption in 1938); the Luftwaffe's plan to have 19,000 (!) front-line and reserve aircraft by 1942 would require "85 percent of the existing *world* production of oil."[81] In the meantime, each service struggled to get a larger share of skilled manpower, steel, ball bearings, petroleum, and other vital strategic materials.

Finally, this frantic arms buildup clashed with Germany's acute dependence upon imported raw materials. Rich only in coal, the Reich required vast amounts of iron ore, copper, bauxite, nickel, petroleum, rubber, and many other items upon which modern industry—and modern weapons systems—relied.[82] By contrast, the United States, the British Empire, and the Soviet Union were well endowed in all those respects. Before 1914, Germany had paid for such imports by its booming export of manufactures: in the 1930s, this was no longer possible, since German industry was now being redirected into the production of tanks, guns, and aircraft for the Wehrmacht's consumption. Furthermore, the costs of the First World War and of later reparations, together with the collapse in the traditional export trades, had drained Germany of virtually all foreign currency; in 1938, it possessed only 1 percent of the world's gold and financial reserves, compared with the United States' 54 percent and France's and Britain's 11 percent each.[83] Hence the strict regime of currency controls, barter arrangements, and other special "deals" instituted by Reich agencies in order to pay for vital imports without transferring gold or currency. Hence, too, the much proclaimed efforts to escape from such dependence by the production of synthetic substitutes (oil, fertilizer, etc.) under the Four-Year Plan. Each of these devices helped; none of them, or even all of them together, could balance the demands made by the arms buildup. This explains the recurrent crises within the German armaments industry, as the national stockpiles of raw materials were exhausted and funds ran out to pay for fresh supplies. In 1937, Raeder warned that the entire naval construction would have to be halted unless more materials were secured. And in January 1939, Hitler himself ordered massive reductions in allocations to the Wehrmacht of steel, copper, rubber, and other materials while the economy waged an "export battle" to raise foreign currency.[84]

There were three related consequences of the above for German power and policies. The first was that Germany was not as strong, militarily, by 1938–1939 as Hitler liked to boast and the western democracies feared. The field army, claiming a strength of 2.75 million men at the outset of war, contained a small number of mobile, well-armed divisions and a very long tail of underequipped reserve divisions; experienced officers and NCOs were almost overwhelmed by the need to train such a mass of raw soldiery. Munitions stocks were slim. Even the famed panzer units had fewer tanks than the Anglo-French totals at the onset of hostilities. The navy, which was planning for a war in the mid-1940s, described itself as "completely inadequately armed for the great conflict with Britain"[85]—a fair summary in respect to surface warships, even if the U-boats were going to help redress the balance. As for the Luftwaffe, it was strong chiefly because its foes were so chronically weak—but it always suffered from a lack of reserves and supporting services. In the international crises of the late 1930s, it had never been as powerful as its opponents had imagined—and both its aircraft industry and its aircrews had found it very difficult to adjust to the "second generation" of planes. For example, the number of aircraft crews "fully operational" was far fewer than those defined as "front-line" during the Munich crisis—and the very idea of bombing London to a cinder was absurd.[86]

Still, it may be unwise to go all the way with recent revisionist literature about Germany's unreadiness for war in 1939. At the end of the day, military effectiveness is relative. Few, if any, armed services claim that all their needs are satisfied; and the German weaknesses have to be measured against those of their foes. When that is done, the picture seems far more favorable to Berlin, especially because of the efficiency of its armed services *in operational doctrine:* its army was prepared to concentrate its tank forces, and then to allow them initiative on the battlefield, keeping in touch by radio; its air force, despite tendencies toward "strategic" missions, was trained to give assistance to the army's thrusts; its U-boat arm, though small, was flexible as to tactics. All this was important compensation for, say, meager stocks of rubber.[87]

This brings us to the second consequence. Because the German armed forces had rearmed so rapidly that they severely strained the economy, there was a massive temptation on Hitler's part to resort to war in order to obviate such economic difficulties. As he well knew, the acquisition of Austria brought with it not only another five divisions of troops, some iron ore and oil fields, and a considerable metal industry, but also $200 million in gold and foreign-exchange reserves.[88] The Sudetenland was less useful economically (though it did have coal deposits), and by early 1939 the Reich's foreign currency position was critical. It was scarcely surprising, therefore, that Hitler was greedily eyeing the rest of Czechoslovakia and rushed to Prague in March 1939 to examine the booty once the occupation occurred. Apart from the gold and currency assets held by the Czech national bank, the Germans also seized large stocks of ores and metals, which were swiftly used to aid German industry; while the large and profitable Czech arms industry could now be exploited to earn currency for Germany by selling (or bartering) its products to clients in the Balkans. The aircraft, tanks, and weapons of the substantial Czech army were also taken, partly to equip new German divisions, and partly to be sold for foreign currency. All this, together with Czechoslovakia's industrial production, was a great boost to German power in Europe, and permitted Hitler's hectic (if somewhat hand-to-mouth) rearmament program to continue—until the next crisis. As Tim Mason has pointed out, "the only 'solution' open to this regime of the structural tensions and crises produced by dictatorship and rearmament was more dictatorship and rearmament. . . . A war for the plunder of manpower and materials lay square in the dreadful logic of German economic development under National Socialism."[89]

The third consequence—and problem—was this: just how far could Germany maintain such a policy of conquest and plunder without overextending itself? Once the initial German rearmament was under way, and its armed services were equipped with modern weapons, the pattern of overcoming weak neighbors and gaining fresh territories, raw materials, and currency seemed self-fulfilling; by April/May 1939, it was clear that Poland was the next stage. But even if that country could be swiftly conquered, was Germany capable of facing France and Britain—that is, engaging in a war which would be much more challenging to a Greater German economy still heavily dependent upon imported raw materials? The evidence suggests that while he was willing to take the risk of fighting the western democracies in 1939, Hitler hoped that they would once again back down and allow him another limited war of plunder, against Poland alone; and this in turn would help the German economy to prepare its first Great Power war, somewhere in the mid-1940s.[90] Given the weakened economic and strategic power of France and Britain, and the hesitancy of their political leaderships by 1939, even a premature struggle with those powers may have seemed worth the risk—although if the military operations were stalemated on the lines of the 1914–1918 war, Germany's initial lead in modern armaments would probably be slowly eroded. Victory for the Führer and his regime would, however, be much more problematical if the United States should lend its aid to the Allies; or if operations were extended into Russia, where the sheer size of the country implied lengthy, drawn-out fighting which placed a premium on economic stamina.

On the other hand, since the Nazi regime lived upon conquest, and Hitler was driven forward from one acquisition to the next, how and where could a halt be called? The full logic of his megalomania implied that no other state should be a challenge to Germany in Europe, and possibly in the world. Only by this means would his foes be crushed, the "Jewish problem" solved, and the Thousand-Year Reich established on a firm footing.[91] Despite all the lines of continuity, the German Führer was quite different from his Frederickian and Bismarckian forebears in his fantastic schemes for world power and his ultimate disregard for all the obstacles which stood in the way of this design. Impelled as much by these manic, long-term ambitions as by the need to escape from short-term crises, Hitler, like the Japanese, was committed to altering the international order as soon as possible.

France and Britain

The position of both France and Britain in the face of this gathering storm was one of acute and increasing difficulty. Although there were many important differences between them, both were liberal-capitalist democracies which had been badly hurt by the war, which were unable (despite their best efforts) to recover in any sustained way the rosy Edwardian political economy of their memories, which felt under large and growing pressure from the labor movement at home, and which possessed a public opinion eager to avoid another conflict and overwhelmingly concerned with domestic, "social" issues rather than foreign affairs. This is by no means to say that the diplomacy of London and Paris was identical; because of their quite different geographical-strategical positions, and the varying pressures brought to bear upon their respective governments, the two democracies frequently differed about how to handle the "German problem."[92] But while they quarreled as to the means, both were unanimous over the end; in the troubled post-1919 years, France and Britain were unquestionably status quo powers.

At the beginning of the 1930s, it was France which seemed the stronger and the more influential, at least on the all-important European scene. Throughout these years it possessed the second-largest army among the Great Powers (after the Soviet Union) and also the second-largest air force (again, the Russian totals were larger). Diplomatically, it was immensely influential, especially at Geneva and in eastern Europe. It had suffered severe economic turbulence in the years immediately following 1919, when the franc had to readjust to the awkward facts that it could no longer rely upon Anglo-American subsidies and that German reparations would be far less than expected. But Poincaré's 1926 stabilization of the currency found French industry in the middle of a remarkable boom; pig-iron production soared from 3.4 million tons in 1920 to 10.3 million tons in 1929, steel output from 3 to 9.7 million, automobiles from 40,000 to 254,000; while chemicals, dyestuffs, and electrical products had all escaped from the pre-war German domination. The favorable fixing of the franc helped French trade, and the Bank of France's large stockpile of gold gave it an influence throughout central and eastern Europe. Even when the "Great Crash" came, France seemed the least affected—partly because of its gold holdings and advantageously placed currency, partly because the French economy was much less dependent upon the international market than, say, Britain's.[93]

After 1933, however, the French economy began to collapse in a steady, systematic, frightening way. The vain attempts to avoid a devaluation of the franc when all of the other major trading countries had gone "off" gold meant that French exports became less and less competitive, and its foreign trade collapsed: "imports went down by 60 percent and exports by 70 percent."[94] After some years of paralysis, the 1935 decision to deflate heavily dealt a blow to the sagging French industrial sector, which was further hit when the 1936 Popular Front administration forced through a forty-hour working week and an increase in wages. That action, and the massive devaluation of the franc in October 1936, accelerated the already enormous flow of gold out of France, badly hurting its international credit. In the agriculture sector, which still employed half of the French nation, and whose yields were still the least efficient in western Europe, surplus production kept prices down and worsened the already low per capita income, a trend accelerated by the drift back to the villages of those losing their jobs in industry; the only (very dubious) benefit of this return to the land was that, as in Italy, it disguised the true level of unemployment. Housebuilding fell off dramatically. The newer industries, like automobiles, stagnated in France just as they were recovering elsewhere. In 1938, the franc was only 36 percent of its 1928 level, French industrial production was only 83 percent of that a decade earlier, steel output a mere 64 percent, building 61 percent. Perhaps the most awful figure—in view of the implications for French *power*—was that its national income in the year of Munich was 18 percent less than that in 1929;[95] and this in the face of a Germany which was fantastically more dangerous, and at a time when massive rearmament was vital.

It would be very easy, therefore, to explain the collapse of French military effectiveness in the 1930s solely in economic terms. Aided by the relative prosperity of the late 1920s, and worried about clandestine German rearmament, France had sharply increased her defense expenditures (especially upon the army) in the budget years 1929–1930 and 1930–1931. Alas, the false hopes placed in the Geneva disarmament talks, followed by the effects of the depression; both had their toll. By 1934, defense expenditures still represented the 4.3 percent of national income which they had done in 1930–1931, but the absolute sum was over 4 million francs less, since the economy was sinking so fast.[96] Although the Popular Front government of Léon Blum sought to reverse this decline in arms expenditures, it was not until 1937 that the 1930 defense estimates were exceeded—and most of that increase went into repairing the more obvious deficiencies in the field army, and into further fortifications. In these critical years, therefore, Germany bounded ahead, both economically and militarily:

France had fallen behind Britain and Germany in automobile production; it had slumped into fourth place in aircraft manufacturing, from first to fourth in less than a decade; its steel production had

increased by a miserly 30 percent between 1932 and 1937, compared
to the 300 percent increase enjoyed by German industry; its coal
production showed a significant decline over the same five-year
period, a development which is largely explained by the return of
the Saar coal fields in early 1935 and the consequent increase in
German production.[97]

With this swiftly weakening economy, and with the debt charges and
the outlay for 1914–1918 war pensions composing *half* the total public
expenditure, it was impossible for France to reequip its three armed
forces satisfactorily even when, as in 1937 and 1938, it spent over 30
percent of its budget upon defense. Ironically, the ungrateful French
navy was probably the best catered for, and possessed a well-balanced
and modern fleet by 1939—which was of little help in stemming a
German blow on land. Of all the services, the most badly affected was
the French air force, which was continually starved of funds and for
which a small-scale, scattered aeronautics industry eked out a living by
producing a mere fifty or seventy planes a month between 1933 and
1937, about one-tenth of the German total. In 1937, for example, Germany built 5,606 aircraft, whereas France produced only 370 (or 743,
depending upon the source one uses).[98] Only in 1938 did the government begin pouring money into the aircraft industry, thus producing
all the inevitable bottlenecks which come with a too-sudden expansion,
not to mention the design—and flying—difficulties caused by the move
to newer, high-performance aircraft. The first eighty of the promising
Dewoitine 520 fighters were accepted by the air force only in January–
April 1940, for example, and its pilots were just beginning to practice
flying the plane, when the Blitzkrieg struck.[99]

But behind these economic and production difficulties, most historians concede, lay deeper-seated social and political problems.
Shocked by the losses of the Great War, depressed by repeated economic blows and disappointments, divided by class and ideological
concerns which intensified as politicians struggled unsuccessfully with
the problems of devaluation, deflation, the forty-hour work week,
higher taxes, and rearmament, French society witnessed a severe collapse in public morale and cohesion as the 1930s advanced. Far from
producing a *union sacrée,* the rise of fascism in Europe had caused—at
least by the time of the Spanish Civil War—further divisions of French
opinion, with the extreme right preferring (as the street chant went)
Hitler to Blum, and with many among the left disliking both a rise in
arms spending and the proposed abrogation of the forty-hour week.
Such ideological clashes interacted with the volatility of the parties and
the chronic instability of French interwar governments (twenty-four
changes between 1930 and 1940) to give the impression of a society
sometimes on the brink of civil war. At the very least, it was hardly

capable of standing up to Hitler's bold moves and to Mussolini's distractions.[100]

As so often before in French politics, all this affected civil-military relations and the standing of the army in society.[101] But quite apart from the general atmosphere of suspicion and gloom in which France's leaders had to operate, there existed a whole array of specific weaknesses. No effective body existed, like the Committee of Imperial Defence or the Chiefs of Staff Sub-Committee in Great Britain, to bring together the military and the nonmilitary branches of government for strategic planning in a systematic way, or even to coordinate the views of the rival services. The leading figures in the army, Gamelin, Georges, Weygand, and (in the background) Pétain, were in their sixties and seventies, defensive-minded, cautious, uninterested in tactical innovations. While flatly rejecting de Gaulle's proposals for a smaller, modernized, tank army, they did not themselves grapple with alternative ways of using the newer weapons of war. The policy of combined arms was not practiced. Problems of battle control and communications (e.g., by radio) were ignored. The role of aircraft was downgraded. Although French intelligence provided lots of information about what the Germans were thinking, it was all ignored; there was open disbelief in the efficacy of using large-scale armored formations, as the Germans were doing in their maneuvers; and all the copies of translations of Guderian's *Achtung Panzer* sent to every garrison library in France remained unread.[102] What this meant was that even when French industry was galvanized into producing considerable numbers of tanks—many, like the SOMUA-35, of very good quality—there was no proper doctrine for their use.[103] Given such failures in command and training, it was going to be extraordinarily difficult for the French army to compensate for the country's sociopolitical malaise and economic decline if ever it came to another great war.

Nor could such weaknesses be overcome, as was the case prior to 1914, by successes in French diplomacy and an advantageous alliance strategy. On the contrary, as the 1930s unfolded, the contradictions in France's external policy became more open. The first of these had already been there, of course, in the irreconcilability of the post-Locarno adoption of the strategic defensive behind the Maginot Line, and the desire to stop German expansion in eastern Europe, if need be by going *forward* to aid France's continental allies as the treaties demanded. The German recovery of the Saarland in 1935 and Hitler's reoccupation of the demilitarized Rhineland zone made a French advance less possible, even had its army leaders been willing to contemplate offensive operations. But that was nothing to the blows which rained upon France's diplomatic and strategic position in 1936: the quarrel over the Abyssinian Crisis with Italy, turning the latter from a potential ally against Germany into a potential foe; the beginning of the Spanish Civil War, with its prospect of another fascist power being established in France's rear; and Belgium's withdrawal into neutrality, with its strategical implications. At the end of that calamitous year, France could no longer concentrate upon its northeast frontier alone; and the idea of its rushing into the Rhineland in order to help an eastern ally had become remote. At the time of the Munich crisis, therefore, many leading Frenchmen were petrified at the prospect of having to fulfill their obligation to Czechoslovakia.[104] Finally, once the Munich agreement had been signed, Paris found the USSR much more hostile to collaboration with the West, and unwilling any longer to take seriously the Franco-Russian pact of 1935.

In such gloomy diplomatic, military, and economic circumstances, it was scarcely surprising that French strategy essentially came to rest upon gaining full-scale British support in any future war with Germany. There were obvious economic reasons for this. France was heavily dependent upon imported coal (30 percent), copper (100 percent), oil (99 percent), rubber (100 percent), and other vital raw materials, much of which came from the British Empire and was carried by the British merchant fleet. If "total war" came, the sagging franc might again need the Bank of England's help to pay its way in the world; indeed, by 1936–1937, France already felt heavily dependent upon Anglo-American financial support.[105] Conversely, only with the Royal Navy's aid could Germany once more be cut off from overseas supplies. By the late 1930s, the assistance of the Royal Air Force was also required—as was the commitment of a fresh British expeditionary force. In all these respects, it has been argued, there was a long-term logic in the French policy of strategic passivism; assuming that any German strike on the west could be halted as in 1914, the superior resources of the Anglo-French empires would eventually prevail—and no doubt also compel the recovery of the Czech and Polish territories temporarily lost in the east.[106]

Yet it could hardly be said that this French strategy of "waiting for Britain" was an unqualified blessing. Obviously, it handed the initiative to Hitler, who after 1934 repeatedly showed that he knew how to take it. In addition, it tied France's hands (although there is considerable evidence that people like Bonnet and Gamelin preferred to be so constrained). Since 1919, the British had been urging the French to adopt a softer, more conciliatory policy toward Germany and strongly disliked what they perceived to be Gallic intransigence; and for years after Hitler's seizure of power, both Britain's government and its people exhibited little appreciation of France's security dilemma. More specifically, the British strongly disapproved of French military commitments to the "successor states" of eastern Europe, and when Anglo-French cooperation became unavoidable, they pressured Paris to repudiate its obligations. Even before the Czech crisis, Britain had dislocated and undermined the old, hard-line French policy toward Berlin—without, however, offering anything substantive in its place. Only in the spring of 1939 did the two countries really come together into a proper military alliance, and even then their mutual political suspicions had not fully dissolved.[107] As we shall see below, it seems fair to argue that Albion was not so much "perfidious" as it was myopic, wishful-thinking, and obsessed with a score of domestic and imperial problems; but that merely confirms the fact that it was a weak and uncertain reed for French policy to rest upon if German expansionism was to be contained.

Perhaps the greatest miscalculation of France was that Britain in the late 1930s was as capable of helping check the German challenge as it had been in 1914. Britain was still a considerable power, of course, enjoying many strategical advantages and with a manufacturing output and industrial potential twice as large as France's; but its own position, too, was less substantial and assured than it had been two decades earlier. Psychologically, the British nation had been badly scarred by the First World War and disenchanted by the fruitlessness (so far as the populace could see it) of the "Carthaginian" peace which followed. This public turnaway from militarism, continental involvements, and any concern for the balance of power coincided both with the full advent of parliamentary democracy (through the 1918 and 1928 franchise extensions) and with the rise of the Labour Party. Even more, perhaps, than in France, national politics in these decades seemed to revolve around the "social" question—a fact reflected in the small amount (10.5 percent) of public expenditure being devoted to the armed forces by 1933 compared with the sums allocated the social services (46.6 percent).[108] This was not a climate, Baldwin and Chamberlain frequently reminded their Cabinet colleagues, in which votes could be gained by interfering in the intractable problems of east-central Europe, whose boundaries were (in Whitehall's eyes) less than sacred.

Even to those political groups and strategic planners who concerned themselves more with foreign affairs than with social issues or electoral maneuvering, the post-1919 international scene suggested caution and noncommitment. As soon as the war was over, the self-governing dominions had pressed for a redefinition of their status. When that had been effected, through the 1926 Balfour Declaration and the 1931 Statute of Westminister, they had evolved into virtually independent states, with (if they wished) separate foreign policies. None of them was eager to fight over European issues; some, like Eire, South Africa, and even Canada, were reluctant to fight over anything. If Britain wished to maintain the image of imperial unity, it followed that it could go to war only over an issue which would attract the support of the dominions; and even when such separatism was modified as the threat from Germany, Italy, and Japan increased, London remained aware of the important *extra*-European dimension to all its foreign-policy decisions.[109] More important still, in strictly military terms, were the "imperial-policing" activities in which the British army, and also the RAF, were engaged in India, Iraq, Egypt, Palestine, and elsewhere. For much of the interwar years, in fact, the British army found itself reverting to a Victorian role: the Russian threat to India was perceived as the greatest (if rather abstract) strategic danger; and keeping the natives quiet was the day-to-day operational activity.[110] Finally, this imperial strand in British grand strategy was powerfully reinforced by the Royal Navy's obsession with sending a "main fleet to Singapore" and with Whitehall's justifiable concern about defending its distant and vulnerable possessions against the Japanese.[111]

It was true that this strategical ambivalence of the British "Janus" was centuries old; but what was altogether more frightening was that it now had to be carried out with a much weakened industrial base. British manufacturing output had been sluggish in the 1920s, in part because of the return of sterling to the gold standard at too high a level. Although it did not suffer as dramatically as Germany and the United States, Britain's ailing economy was shaken to its roots by the worldwide slump after 1929. Textile production, which still provided 40 percent of British exports, was cut by two-thirds; coal, which provided another 10 percent of exports, dropped by one-fifth; shipbuilding was so badly hit that in 1933 production fell to 7 percent of its prewar figure; steel production fell by 45 percent in the three years 1929–1932 and pig-iron production by 53 percent. With international trade drying up and being replaced by currency blocs, Britain's share of global commerce continued in a downward trend, from 14.15 percent (1913) to 10.75 percent (1929) to 9.8 percent (1937). Moreover, the *invisible* earnings from shipping, insurance, and overseas investment, which for over a century had handsomely covered the *visible* trade gap, no longer could do so; by the early 1930s, Britain was living on its capital. The trauma of the 1931 crisis, involving the collapse of the Labour government and the decision to go off gold, made politicians all too aware of the country's economic vulnerability.[112]

To some degree, indeed, those leaders' apprehension may have been exaggerated. By 1934, the economy was slowly beginning to recover. While older industries in the north languished, newer ones—aircraft, automobiles, petrochemicals, electrical goods—were growing.[113] Trade within the "sterling block" provided a certain crutch to British exporters. The drop in food and raw materials prices aided the British consumer. But such palliatives were not sufficient to a Treasury worried about Britain's delicate credit abroad and about further runs on sterling. In their view, the overwhelming priority was for the country to pay its way in the world, which meant balancing the government's books, keeping taxes to a minimum, and controlling state spending. Even when the Manchurian crisis caused the government in 1932 to give up the famous Ten-Year Rule,* the Treasury was swift to insist that "this must not be taken to justify an expanding expenditure by the Defense Services without regard to the very serious financial and economic situation which still obtains."[114]

This combination of domestic-political and economic pressures ensured that, like France, Britain was cutting its defense expenditures during the early 1930s just when the dictator states were beginning to increase theirs. Not until 1936, following several years of studying the country's "defense deficiencies" and the twin shock of Hitler's open rearmament followed by the Abyssinian crisis, did British spending upon the armed services take its first substantial upward rise; but that year's allocation was less than Italy's and only one-third or one-quarter of Germany's. Even at that stage, Treasury controls and politicians' worries about domestic opinion prevented full-scale rearmament, which only really began in the crisis year of 1938. Well before that date, however, the armed services were warning of the impossibility of safeguarding "our trade, territory and vital interests against Germany, Italy and Japan at the same time," and urging the government "to reduce the number of our potential enemies and to gain the support of potential allies."[115] In other words, diplomacy—the diplomacy of appeasement—was required in order to defend this economically weakened, strategically overstretched empire from threats in the Far East, the Mediterranean, and Europe itself. In no foreign theater of war, the chiefs of staff felt, was Britain strong enough; and even that dismal fact was overshadowed by the alarming rise of the Luftwaffe, which made the inhabitants of the island state directly vulnerable for the first time to the military operations of an enemy.[116]

There is some evidence that the British chiefs of staff, too, were excessively gloomy about their country's prospects,[117] like the military professionals in virtually every other state; the First World War had made them cautious and pessimistic.[118] But there *was* no doubt that Britain had been overtaken in the air by Germany by 1936–1937, that its minuscule long-service army could do little on the continent of Europe, and that its navy would find it impossible to control European waters *and* to send a main fleet to Singapore. Perhaps even more perturbing to British decision-makers was that it was now extremely difficult to find those "potential allies" which the chiefs of staff demanded. The coalitions which Britain had woven together to counter Napoleon, the successful *ententes* and *rapprochements* which had been effected in the years after 1900, could no longer be found. Japan

---

*That is, the post-1919 directive that the armed services should frame their estimates on the assumption that they would not be engaged in a major war within the next ten years.

had drifted from being an ally to being a foe; the same had happened to Italy. Russia, the other "flank" power (to use Dehio's term)[119] which traditionally had joined Britain in opposing a continental hegemon, was now in diplomatic isolation and deeply suspicious of the western democracies. Almost as inscrutable and unpredictable, at least to frustrated Whitehall minds, was the policy of the United States in the early to middle 1930s; avoiding all diplomatic and military commitments, still unwilling to join the League, strongly opposed to the various British efforts to buy off the revisionist states (e.g., by admitting Japan's special place in East Asia, or offering special payments and exchange arrangements to Germany), and making it impossible—through the 1937 neutrality legislation—to borrow on the American markets in the way Britain had done to sustain its war effort between 1914 and 1917, the United States was persistently dislocating British grand strategy in the same, perhaps inadvertent, way that Britain was dislocating France's eastern European strategy.[120] This left, then, as potential allies only France itself, and the rest of the British Empire. France's diplomatic needs, however, drew Britain into commitments in Central Europe, which the dominions strongly opposed and which the whole structure of "imperial defense" was incapable of defending; on the other hand, the *extra-*European concerns of the empire took away the attention and resources required to contain the German threat. In consequence, the British during the 1930s found themselves engaged in a global diplomatic and strategical dilemma to which there was no satisfactory solution.[121]

This is not to deny that Baldwin, Chamberlain and their colleagues could have done more, or to claim that the determinants of British appeasement policy were such that all alternative policies proposed by Churchill and other critics were impracticable. There was a persistent willingness on the British government's part, despite all the counterevidence, to trust in "reasonable" approaches toward the Nazi regime. The emotional dislike of Communism was such that Russia's potential as a member of an antifascist coalition was always ignored or downgraded. Vulnerable eastern European states, like Czechoslovakia and Poland, were all too often regarded as nuisances, and the lack of sympathy for France's problems showed a fatal meanness of spirit. Germany's and Italy's power was consistently overrated, on the basis of slim evidence, whereas all British defense weaknesses were seized upon as a reason for inaction. Whitehall's views of the European balance of power were self-serving and short-term. Critics of the appeasement policy such as Churchill were systematically censored and neutralized, even as the government proclaimed that it could only follow (rather than give a lead to) public opinion.[122] For all the plausible, objectively valid grounds behind the British government's desire to avoid standing up to the dictator states, therefore, there is much in its ungenerous, narrow attitude that looks dubious, even at this distance in time.

On the other hand, any investigation of the economic and strategical realities ought also to admit that by the late 1930s, the basic problems affecting British grand strategy were not soluble merely by a change of attitude, or even of prime ministers. Indeed, the more Chamberlain was compelled—by Hitler's further aggressions, and by the outrage of British opinion—to abandon appeasement, the more the fundamental contradictions became evident. Though the chiefs of staff insisted upon massive increases in defense spending, the Treasury argued that such spending would be economically ruinous. Already in 1937, Britain, like France, was spending more of its GNP upon defense than either of those countries had done in the crisis years prior to 1914, but without any significant improvement in security—simply because of the far higher arms spending of the manically driven, overheated German state. But as British defense expenditures soared further—roughly, from 5.5 percent of GNP in 1937 to 8.5 percent in 1938, to 12.5 percent in 1939—its delicate economy also began to suffer. Even when money was released for arms increases, the inadequacy of British industrial plant and the critical shortage of skilled engineers slowed down the hoped-for production of aircraft, tanks, and ships; but this in turn compelled the services to place ever-larger orders for weapons, sheet steel, ball bearings, and other items with neutral countries such as Sweden and the United States, which further drained foreign-currency reserves and threatened the balance of payments. As the country's stocks of gold and dollars shrank, its international credit became shakier than ever. "If we were under the impression that we were as well able as in 1914 to conduct a long war," the Treasury coldly pointed out in response to the fresh rearmament measures of April 1939, "we were burying our head in the sand."[123] This was not a pleasant forecast for a power whose strategic planners assumed that they had no chance of winning a short war, but somehow hoped to prevail in a drawn-out conflict.

Equally serious contradictions were also surfacing in the military sphere on the eve of war. While Britain's 1939 decision to accept once again a formal "continental commitment" to France and its almost parallel decision to give the Mediterranean priority over Singapore in terms of naval deployments settled some long-standing strategical issues, they also left British interests in the Far East totally exposed to the next act of Japanese aggression. In a similarly contradictory way, Britain's swift guarantees to Poland in the spring of 1939, followed by further guarantees to Greece, Rumania, and Turkey, were signs of Whitehall's rediscovery of the importance of eastern Europe and the Balkans within the continental balance of power; but the fact was that the British armed forces had little prospect of defending those lands against determined German attack.

In sum, neither Chamberlain's stiffer policies toward Germany after March 1939 nor even his replacement by Churchill in May 1940 "solved" Britain's strategical and economic dilemmas; all they did was to redefine the problems. For an overstretched global empire at this late stage in its history—still controlling one-quarter of the globe but with only 9 to 10 percent of its manufacturing strength and "war potential"[124]—both appeasement and anti-appeasement brought disadvantages; there was only a choice of evils.[125] That the right choice was made in 1939, to stand up to Hitler's further act of aggression, is undoubted. But by that stage the balance of forces aligned against British interests in Europe and even more in the Far East had become so unfavorable that it was difficult to see how a clear-cut victory against fascism could be secured without the intervention of the neutral Great Powers. And that, too, would bring its problems.

The Offstage Superpowers

As noted above, one of the greatest difficulties which faced British and French decision-makers as they wrestled with the diplomatic and strategical challenges of the 1930s was the uncertainty which surrounded the stance of those two giant and somewhat detached Powers, Russia and the United States. Was it worth making further efforts to persuade them into an alliance against the fascist states, even if this involved substantial concessions to Moscow's and Washington's requirements, and provoked criticism at home? Which of these should be wooed more ardently, and in what respects? Would an open move, say, toward Russia merely provoke rather than deter a German or Japanese reaction? From the viewpoint of Berlin and Tokyo (less so of Rome), the attitude of Russia and the United States was equally important. Would these Powers remain aloof while Hitler reordered the boundaries of central Europe? How would they react to further Japanese expansion in China or operations against the old European empires in Southeast Asia? Would the United States give at least economic aid to the western democracies, as occurred between 1914 and 1917? And would the USSR be bought off, by economic and territorial deals? Finally, did those two enigmatic, introspective polities *really matter*? How strong were they, in fact? How important in the changing international order?

It was harder to attempt an answer to such questions in the case of a "closed" society like the Soviet Union. Nonetheless the outlines of Soviet economic growth and military power in that era now seem evident. The first and most obvious point was that Russia had been dreadfully reduced in strength, more than any of the other Great Powers, by the 1914–1918 conflict and then by the revolution and civil war. Its population had plummeted from 171 million in 1914 to 132 million in 1921. The loss of Poland, Finland, and the Baltic states removed many of the country's industrial plants, railways, and farms, and the prolonged fighting destroyed much that remained. The stupendous decline in manufacturing—down to 13 percent of its 1913 output by 1920—concealed the even greater collapse of certain key commodities: "thus only 1.6 percent of the prewar iron ore was being produced, 2.4 percent of the pig iron, 4.0 percent of the steel, and 5 percent of the cotton."[126] Foreign trade had disappeared altogether, the gross yield of crops was less than half the prewar figure, and per capita national income declined by more than 60 percent to a truly horrendous level. However, since the extreme severity of these falls was chiefly caused by the social and political chaos of the years 1917–1921, it followed that the establishment of Soviet rule (or indeed *any* rule) was bound to effect a recovery of sorts. The prewar and wartime development of Russian industry had bequeathed to the Bolsheviks an array of factories, railway works, and steel mills. There was a basic infrastructure of railways, roads, and telegraph lines. There were industrial workers who could return to the factories once the civil war was over. And there was an established pattern of agricultural production, and the sale of foodstuffs to the towns and cities, which could be restored once Lenin had decided (under the New Economic Policy of 1921) to abandon the fruitless attempts to "communize" the peasantry and instead to permit individual farming. By 1926, therefore, agricultural output had returned to its prewar level, followed two years later by industrial output. The war and revolution had cost Russia thirteen years of economic growth, but it now stood ready to resume its upward surge.

But that "surge" was unlikely to be swift enough—certainly not to the increasingly autocratic Stalin—while Russia labored under its traditional economic weaknesses. With no foreign investment available, capital had somehow to be raised from domestic sources to finance the development of large-scale industry *and* the creation of substantial armed forces in a hostile world. Given the elimination of a middle class, which could either have been encouraged to create capital or plundered for its existing wealth; given, too, the fact that 78 percent of Russian population (1926) remained in a bottom-heavy agricultural sector, which was still overwhelmingly in private hands, there seemed to Stalin only one way for the state to raise money and simultaneously increase the switch from farming to industry: that is, by the collectivization of agriculture, forcing the peasants into communes, destroying the kulaks, controlling the output from the land, and fixing both the wages paid to farm workers and the (far higher) prices of food for resale. In a frighteningly draconian way, the state thus interposed itself between rural producers and urban consumers, and extracted money from each to a degree that the czarist regime had never dared to do. This was accentuated by the deliberate price inflation, a variety of taxes and dues, and the pressures to show one's loyalty by buying state bonds. The overall result, represented in the crude macroeconomic statistics, was that the share of Russian GNP devoted to private consumption, which in other countries going through the "takeoff" to industrialization was around 80 percent, was driven down to the appalling level of 51 or 52 percent.[127]

There were two contrary, yet predictable economic consequences from this extraordinary attempt at a socialist "command economy." The first was the catastrophic decline in Soviet agricultural production, as kulaks (and others) resisted the forced collectivization and then were eliminated. The horrific preemptive slaughter of farm animals—"the number of horses fell from 33.5 million in 1928 to 16.6 million in 1935; and the number of cattle from 70.5 to 38.4 million"[128]—in turn produced a staggering decline in meat and grain outputs and in an already miserable standard of living, not to be recovered until Khrushchev's time. Esoteric calculations have been attempted as to the proportion of the national income which was later returned to agriculture in the form of tractors or electrification—as opposed to the amount siphoned off by collectivization and price controls[129]—but this is an arcane exercise for our purposes, since (for example) tractor factories, once established, were designed to be converted to the production of light tanks; peasants, of course, were not so useful in checking the Wehrmacht. What *was* incontrovertible was that for the moment, Soviet agricultural output collapsed. The casualties, especially during the 1933 famine, could be reckoned in millions of lives. When output began to recover in the late 1930s, it was expedited by hundreds of thousands of tractors, hordes of agricultural scientists, and armies of tightly controlled collectives. But the cost, in human terms, was immeasurable.

The second consequence was altogether brighter, at least for the purposes of Soviet economic-military power. Having driven private consumption's share of the GNP down to a level probably unmatched in modern history—and certainly far lower than, say, the Nazis could ever contemplate in Germany—the USSR was able to deploy the fantastic proportion of around 25 percent of GNP for industrial investment and still possess considerable sums for education, science, and the armed services. While the workplace of much of the Russian people was being transformed at a staggering rate, with the number employed in agriculture dropping from 71 percent to 51 percent in the twelve years 1928–1940, that population was also being educated at an unprecedented pace. This was vital at two levels, since Russia had always suffered—in comparison, say, with Germany or the United

States—from having a poorly trained and illiterate industrial work force, and in possessing only a minuscule number of engineers, scientists, and managers necessary for the higher direction and *steady improvement* of the manufacturing sector. With millions of workers now being trained, either in factory schools or in technical colleges, and then (slightly later) with a vast expansion in university numbers, the country was at last acquiring the trained cadres necessary for sustained growth; the number of graduate engineers in the "national economy" rose, for example, from 47,000 in 1928 to 289,900 in 1941.[130] Many of the figures touted by Soviet propagandists in this period were doubtless inflated and concealed various weak points, but the deliberate allocation of resources to growth was unquestionable. So, too, was the creation of enormous new power plants, steelworks, and factories beyond the Urals, invulnerable to attack from either the West or Japan.

The resulting upturn in manufacturing output and national income—even if one accepts the more cautious estimates—was something unprecedented in the history of industrialization. Because the actual volume and value of output in earlier years (e.g., 1913, let alone 1920) was so low, the percentage changes are almost meaningless— even if Table 28 above serves the useful point of showing how the USSR's manufacturing production was expanding during the Great Depression. However, if one examines only the period of the two Five-Year Plans (1928 to 1937), Russian national income rose from 24.4 to 96.3 billion rubles, coal output increased from 35.4 to 128 million tons and steel production from 4 to 17.7 million tons, electricity output rose sevenfold, machine-tool figures over twentyfold, and tractors nearly fortyfold.[131] By the late 1930s, indeed, Russia's industrial output had not only soared well past that of France, Japan, and Italy but had probably overtaken Britain's as well.[132]

Behind this impressive buildup, however, there still lurked many deficiencies. Although farm output slowly rose in the mid-1930s, Russian agriculture was now less capable than before of feeding the nation, let alone producing a surplus for export; and the yields per acre were still appallingly low. Despite fresh investment in railways, the communications system remained primitive and inadequate for the country's growing needs. In many industries there was a heavy dependence upon foreign firms and foreign expertise, especially from the United States. The "gigantism" of the plants and of the entire manufacturing processes made difficult any swift adjustments of the product mix or the introduction of new designs. There were inevitable bottlenecks, too, because the planned expansion of certain industries did not match the existing stocks of raw materials or skilled manpower. After 1937, the reorientation of the Soviet economy toward a massive armament program was bound to affect industrial continuity and to distort the earlier planning. Above all, there were the great purges.

Whatever the reasons for Stalin's manic, paranoid assault upon so many of his own people, the economic results were serious: "civil servants, managers, technicians, statisticians, even foremen"[133] were swept away into the camps, making Russia's shortage of trained personnel more acute than ever. While the terror no doubt drove many to demonstrate a Stakhanovite loyalty to the system, it also greatly inhibited innovation, experimentation, open discussion, and constructive criticism: "the simplest thing to do was to avoid responsibility, to seek approval from one's superior for any act, to obey mechanically any order received, regardless of local conditions."[134] It saved one's skin; but it did not help the growth of a complex economy.

Having been born out of a war, and feeling acutely threatened by potential enemies—Poland, Japan, Britain—the USSR devoted a large share of the state budget (12–16 percent) to defense expenditures for much of the 1920s. That share fell away during the early years of the first Five-Year Plan, by which time the regular Soviet armed forces had settled down to about 600,000 men, backed by a large but inefficient militia twice that size. The Manchurian crisis and Hitler's accession to power led to swift increases in the size of the army, to 940,000 in 1934 and 1.3 million in 1935. With the rise in industrial output and national income deriving from the Five-Year Plans, large numbers of tanks and aircraft were built. Innovative officers around Tukhachevsky were willing to study (if not fully accept) ideas from Douhet, Fuller, Liddell Hart, Guderian, and other western theorists of warfare, and by the early 1930s the USSR possessed not only a tank army but also a large paratroop force. While the Soviet navy remained small and ineffective, a large aircraft industry was created in the late 1920s, which for a while produced more planes each year than all the other powers combined (see Table 29).

Table 29. Aircraft Production of the Powers, 1932–1939[135]

	1932	1933	1934	1935	1936	1937	1938	1939
France	(600)	(600)	(600)	785	890	743	1,382	3,163
Germany	36	368	1,968	3,183	5,112	5,606	5,235	8,295
Italy	(500)	(500)	(750)	(1,000)	(1,000)	(1,500)	1,850	(2,000)
Japan	691	766	688	952	1,181	1,511	3,201	4,467
U.K.	445	633	740	1,140	1,877	2,153	2,827	7,940
United States	593	466	437	459	1,141	949	1,800	2,195
USSR	2,595	2,595	2,595	3,578	3,578	3,578	7,500	10,382

But these figures, too, concealed alarming weaknesses. The predictable corollary of Russian "gigantism" was an excessive emphasis upon quantity. Given the attributes of a command economy, this had resulted in the production of enormous numbers of aircraft and tanks by the early 1930s; by 1932, indeed, the USSR was producing over 3,000

tanks and over 2,500 aircraft—fantastically more than any other country in the world. Given the tremendous growth of the regular army after 1934, it must have been extraordinarily difficult to find sufficient highly trained officers and NCOs to supervise the tank battalions and air squadrons. It was even more difficult, in a country with a surplus of peasants and desperately short of skilled workers, to man a modern army and air force; despite the massive educational program, the country's chief weakness in the 1930s probably still lay in the poor training of many of its workers and soldiers. Furthermore, Russia, like France, was a victim of heavy investment in aircraft and tank types of the early 1930s. When the Spanish Civil War showed the limits, in speed, maneuverability, range, and toughness, of these first-generation weapons, the race to build faster aircraft and more powerful tanks was accelerated. But the Soviet arms industry, like a large vessel at sea, could not change course swiftly; and it seemed folly to stop production on existing types while newer models were being built and tested. (In this connection, it is interesting to note that "of the 24,000 Russian tanks operational in June 1941, only 967 were of a new design equivalent or superior to the German tanks of that time.")[136] On top of this, there came the purges. The decapitation of the Red Army—90 percent of all generals and 80 percent of all colonels suffered in Stalin's manic drive—not only had the overall effect of destroying so many trained officers, but had specific results which badly hurt the armed forces. By wiping out Tukhachevsky and the "modern warfare" enthusiasts, by eliminating those who studied German methods and British theories, the purges left the army in the hands of such politically safe but intellectually retarded figures as Voroshilov and Kuluk. One early result was the disbanding of the seven mechanized corps, a decision influenced by the argument that the Spanish Civil War had shown that tank formations could play no independent offensive role on the battlefield and that the vehicles should be distributed to rifle battalions in order to support the infantry. In much the same way it was decided that the TB-3 strategic bombers were of little use to the USSR.

With much of its air force obsolescent and its armored units disbanded, with the services cowed into blind obedience by the purges, Russia was much weaker at the end of the 1930s than it had been five or ten years earlier—and in the meantime both Germany and Japan had greatly increased their arms output and were becoming more aggressive. The post-1937 Five-Year Plan clearly involved an enormous arms buildup, equal to and in many areas—e.g., aircraft production— larger than Germany's own. But until that investment had translated itself into far larger and better-equipped armed forces, Stalin felt Russia to be passing through a "danger zone" at least as threatening as the years 1919–1922. These external circumstances help explain the various changes in Soviet diplomacy during the 1930s. Worried by the

Japanese aggression in Manchuria and perhaps even more by Hitler's Germany, Stalin faced the prospect of a potential two-front war in theaters thousands of miles apart (exactly the strategical dilemma which paralyzed British decision-makers). Yet his diplomatic tacking toward the West, which included Russia's 1934 entry into the League of Nations and the 1935 treaties with France and Czechoslovakia, did not bring the desired increase in collective security. Without a Polish agreement, there was really little Russia could do to aid France or Czechoslovakia—and vice versa. And the British frowned at these efforts to create a diplomatic "popular front" against Germany, which in part explains Stalin's caution during the Spanish Civil War; a triumphant socialist republic in Spain, Moscow feared, might drive Britain and France to the right, as well as embroil Russia in open conflict with Franco's supporters, Italy and Germany.

By 1938–1939, the external situation must have appeared more threatening than ever in Stalin's eyes (which makes his purges even more foolish and inexplicable). The Munich settlement not only seemed to confirm Hitler's ambitions in east-central Europe but—more worryingly—revealed that the West was not prepared to oppose them and might indeed prefer to divert German energies farther eastward. Since these two years also saw substantial border clashes between Soviet and Japanese armies in the Far East (necessitating the heavy reinforcement of the Russian divisions in Siberia), it was not surprising that Stalin, too, decided to follow an "appeasement" policy toward Berlin even if that meant sitting down with his ideological foe. Given the USSR's own political ambitions in eastern Europe, Moscow had far fewer reservations about a carving up of the independent states in that region, provided that its own share was substantial. The surprise Nazi-Soviet pact of August 1939 at least provided Russia with a buffer zone on its western border and more time for rearmament while the West fought Germany in consequence of Hitler's attack upon Poland. Feeding morsels to the crocodile (to use Churchill's phrase) seemed much better than being devoured by it.[137]

All this makes it inordinately difficult to measure Soviet power by the end of the 1930s, especially since statistics on "relative war potentials"[138] reflect neither internal morale nor quality of armed forces nor geographical position. Clearly, the Red Army no longer resembled that "formidable modern force of great weight with advanced equipment and exceptionally tough fighting men" (except in the latter respect) which Mackintosh described the 1936 army as being;[139] but how far it had lost ground was not clear. The 1939–1940 "Winter War" against Finland appeared to confirm its precipitous decline, yet the less-well-known 1939 clashes with Japan at Nomonhan showed a cleverly led, modern force in action.[140] It is also evident that Stalin was aghast at the devastating Blitzkrieg-style victories of the German army in 1940, and more than ever anxious not to provoke Hitler into a war. His other great and obvious worry was where Tokyo would decide to strike in the East—not that Japan was so mortal a foe, but the defense of Siberia was logistically very exhausting and would further weaken Russia's capacity against the German threat. The swift recall of Zhukov's armor, to join in the invasion of eastern Poland in September 1939, once a border truce in the east had been arranged with Japan, was illustrative of this precarious strategical juggling act.[141] On the other hand, by that time the damage inflicted upon the Red Army was being hastily repaired and its numbers increased (to 4,320,000 men by 1941), the entire Soviet economy was being deployed toward war production, massive new factories were being built in central Russia, and improved aircraft and tanks (including the formidable T-34) were being tested. The 16.5 percent of the budget allocated to defense spending in 1937 had jumped to 32.6 percent in 1940.[142] Like most of the other Great Powers in this period, therefore, the USSR was racing against time. More even than in 1931, Stalin needed to urge his fellow countrymen to close the productive gap with the West. "To slacken the tempo would mean falling behind. And those who fall behind get beaten. . . ." The Russia of the czars had suffered "continual beatings" because it had fallen behind in industrial productivity and military strength.[143] Under its even more autocratic and ruthless leader, the Soviet regime was determined to catch up fast. Whether Hitler would let it do so was impossible to say.

The relative power of the United States in world affairs during the interwar years was, curiously, in inverse ratio to that of both the USSR and Germany. That is to say, it was inordinately strong in the 1920s, but then declined more than any other of the Great Powers during the depressed 1930s, recovering only (and partially) at the very end of this period. The reason for its preeminence in the first of these decades has been made clear above. The United States was the only major country, apart from Japan, to benefit from the Great War. It became the world's greatest financial and creditor nation, in addition to its already being the largest producer of manufactures and foodstuffs. It had by far the largest stocks of gold. It had a domestic market so extensive that massive economies of scale could be practiced by giant firms and distributors, especially in the booming automobile industry. Its high standard of living and its ready availability of investment capital interacted in a mutually beneficial fashion to spur on further heavy investments in manufacturing industry, since consumer demand could absorb virtually all of the goods which increased productivity offered. In 1929, for example, the United States produced over 4.5 million motor vehicles, compared with France's 211,000, Britain's 182,000, and Germany's 117,000.[144] It was hardly surprising that there were fantastic leaps in the import of rubber, tin, petroleum, and other raw materials to feed this manufacturing boom; but exports, especially of cars, agricultural machinery, office equipment, and similar wares, also expanded throughout the 1920s, the entire process being aided by the swift growth of American overseas investments.[145] Yet even if this is well known, it still remains staggering to note that the United States in those years was producing "a larger output than that of the other six Great Powers *taken together*" and that "her overwhelming productive strength was further underlined by the fact that the gross value of manufactures produced per head of population in the United States was nearly twice as high as in Great Britain or Germany, and more than ten to eleven times as high as in the USSR or Italy."[146]

While it is also true, as the author of the above lines immediately notes, "that the United States' political influence in the world was in no respect commensurate with her extraordinary industrial strength,"[147] that may not have been so important in the 1920s. In the first place, the American people decidedly rejected a leading role in world politics, with all the diplomatic and military entanglements which such a posture would inevitably produce; provided American commercial interests were not deleteriously affected by the actions of other states, there was little cause to get involved in foreign events—especially those arising in eastern Europe or the Horn of Africa. Secondly, for all the *absolute* increases in American exports and imports, their place in its national economy was not large, simply because the country was so self-sufficient; in fact, "the proportion of manufactured goods exported in relation to their total production decreased from a little less than 10 percent in 1914 to a little under 8 percent in 1929," and the book value of foreign direct investments as a share of GNP remained unaltered[148]—which helps to explain why, despite a widespread acceptance of world-market ideas *in principle*, American economic policy was much more responsive to domestic needs. Except in respect to certain raw materials, the world outside was not that important to American prosperity. Finally, international affairs in the decade after 1919 did not suggest the existence of a major threat to American interests: the Europeans were still quarreling but much less so than in the early 1920s, Russia was isolated, Japan quiescent. Naval rivalry had been contained by the Washington treaties. In such circumstances, the United States could reduce its army to a very small size (about 140,000 regulars), although it did allow the creation of a reasonably large and modern air force, and the navy was permitted to develop its aircraft-carrier and heavy-cruiser programs.[149] While the generals and admirals predictably complained about receiving insufficient resources from Congress, and certain damaging measures were done to national security (like Stimson's 1929 decision to wind up the code-breaking service on the grounds that "gentlemen do not read each others mail"),[150] the fact was that this was a decade in which the United

States still could remain an economic giant but a military middle-weight. It was perhaps symptomatic of this period of tranquillity that the United States still did not possess a superior civil-military body for considering strategic issues, like the Committee of Imperial Defence in Britain or its own later National Security Council. What need was there for one when the American people had decisively rejected the ideas of war?

The leading role of the United States in bringing about the financial collapse of 1929 has been described above.[151] What is even more significant, for the purposes of measuring comparative national power, was that the subsequent depression and tariff wars hurt it much more than any other advanced economy. If this was partly due to the relatively uncontrolled and volatile nature of American capitalism, it was also affected by the fatal decision to opt for protectionism by the Smoot-Hawley tariffs of 1930. Despite the complaints by U.S. farmers and some industrial lobbies about unfair foreign competition, the country's industrial and agricultural productivity was such—as the surplus of exports over imports clearly showed—that a breakup of the open world trading order would hurt its exporters more than any others. "The nation's GNP had plummeted from $98.4 billion in 1929 to barely half that three years later. The value of manufactured goods in 1933 was less than one-quarter what it had been in 1929. Nearly fifteen million workers had lost their jobs and were without any means of support. . . . During this same period the value of American exports had decreased from $5.24 billion to $1.61 billion, a fall of 69 percent."[152] With other nations scuttling hastily into protective trading blocs, those American industries which did rely heavily upon exports were devastated. "Wheat exports, which had totaled $200 million ten years earlier, slumped to $5 million in 1932. Auto exports fell from $541 million in 1929 to $76 million in 1932."[153] World trade collapsed generally, but the U.S. share of foreign commerce contracted even faster, from 13.8 percent in 1929 to less than 10 percent in 1932. What was more, while certain other major powers steadily recovered output by the middle to late 1930s, the United States suffered a further severe economic convulsion in 1937 which lost much of the ground gained over the preceding five years. But because of what has been termed the "disarticulated world economy"[154]—that is, the drift toward trading blocs which were much more self-contained than in the 1920s—this second American slump did not hurt other countries so severely. The overall consequence was that in the year of the Munich crisis, the U.S. share of world manufacturing output was lower than at any time since around 1910 (see Table 30).

Because of the severity of this slump, and because of the declining share of foreign trade in the GNP, American policy under Hoover and especially under Roosevelt became even more introspective. In view of

Table 30. Shares of World Manufacturing
Output, 1929–1938[155]
(percent)

	1929	1932	1937	1938
United States	43.3	31.8	35.1	28.7
USSR	5.0	11.5	14.1	17.6
Germany	11.1	10.6	11.4	13.2
U.K.	9.4	10.9	9.4	9.2
France	6.6	6.9	4.5	4.5
Japan	2.5	3.5	3.5	3.8
Italy	3.3	3.1	2.7	2.9

the strength of isolationist opinion and Roosevelt's pressing set of problems at home, it could hardly be expected that he would give to international affairs the concentrated attention which both Cordell Hull and the State Department wished from him. Nevertheless, because of the crucial position which the United States continued to occupy in the world economy, there remains some substance in the criticism of "the occupation with domestic recovery" and the "desire for the appearance of immediate action and results [and] a national habit of policy formation that gave little sustained thought to the impact American programs might have on other nations."[156] The 1934 ban upon loans to any foreign government which had defaulted on its war debts, the 1935 arms embargo in the event of war, and the slightly later prohibition of loans to any belligerent power simply made the British and French more cautious than ever about standing up to the fascist states. The 1935 denunciations of Italy were accompanied by enormous increases in American petroleum supplies to Mussolini's regime, to the consternation of the British Admiralty. The various commercial restrictions upon Germany and Japan, in partial response to their aggression, "served to antagonize [both] without providing meaningful aid to the opponents of these nations. FDR's economic diplomacy created enemies without winning friends or supporting prospective allies."[157] Perhaps the most serious consequence—although the responsibility needs to be shared—was the mutual suspicions which arose between Whitehall and Washington precisely at a time when the dictator states were making their challenge.[158]

By 1937 and 1938, however, Roosevelt himself seems to have become more worried by the fascist threats, even if American public opinion and economic difficulties restrained him from taking the lead. His messages to Berlin and Tokyo became firmer, his encouragement of Britain and France somewhat warmer (even if that hardly helped those two democracies in the short term). By 1938, secret Anglo-American naval talks were taking place about how to deal with the twin challenges of Japan and Germany. The president's "quarantine" speech was an early sign that he would move toward economic discrimination against the dictator states. Above all, Roosevelt now pressed for large-scale increases in defense expenditures. As the figures in Table 26 above show, even in 1938 the United States was spending less on armaments than Britain or Japan, and only a fraction of the sums spent by Germany and the Soviet Union. Nonetheless, aircraft production virtually doubled between 1937 and 1938, and in the latter year Congress passed a "Navy Second to None" Act, allowing for a massive expansion in the fleet. By that time, too, tests were taking place on the prototype B-17 bomber, the Marines Corps was refining its doctrine of amphibious warfare, and the army (while not yet possessing a decent tank) was grappling with the problems of armored warfare and planning to mobilize a vast force.[159] When war broke out in Europe, none of the services was at all ready; but they were in better shape, relative to the demands of modern warfare, than they had been in 1914.

Even these rearmament measures scarcely disturbed an economy the size of the United States. The key fact about the American economy in the late 1930s was that it was greatly *underutilized.* Unemployment was around ten million in 1939, yet industrial productivity per man-hour had been vastly improved by investments in conveyor belts, electric motors (in place of steam engines), and better managerial techniques, although little of this showed through in *absolute* output figures because of the considerable reduction in work hours by the labor force. Given the depressed demand, which the 1937–1938 recession did not help, the various New Deal schemes were insufficient to stimulate the economy and take advantage of this underutilized productive capacity. In 1938, for example, the United States produced 26.4 million tons of steel, well ahead of Germany's 20.7 million, the USSR's 16.5 million, and Japan's 6.0 million; yet the steel industries of those latter three countries were working to full capacity, whereas *two-thirds* of American steel plants were idle. As it turned out, this underutilization was soon going to be changed by the enormous rearmament programs.[160] The 1940 authorization of a doubling (!) of the navy's combat fleet, the Army Air Corps' plan to create eighty-four groups with 7,800 combat aircraft, the establishment (through the Selective Service and Training Act) of an army of close to 1 million men—all had an effect upon an economy which was not, like those of Italy, France, and Britain, suffering from severe structural problems, but was merely underutilized because of the Depression. Precisely because the United States had an enormous spare capacity whereas other economies were overheating, perhaps the most significant statistics for understanding the outcome of the future struggle were not the 1938 figures of actual steel or industrial output, but those which attempt to measure national income (Table 31) and, however imprecise, "relative war potential" (Table 32). For in each case they remind us that if the United States had suffered disproportionately during the Great

Depression, it nonetheless remained (in Admiral Yamamoto's words) a sleeping giant.

Table 31. National Income of the Powers in 1937 and Percentage Spent on Defense[161]

	National Income (billions of dollars)	Percentage on Defense
United States	68	1.5
British Empire	22	5.7
France	10	9.1
Germany	17	23.5
Italy	6	14.5
USSR	19	26.4
Japan	4	28.2

Table 32. Relative War Potential of the Powers in 1937[162]

United States	41.7%
Germany	14.4%
USSR	14.0%
U.K.	10.2%
France	4.2%
Japan	3.5%
Italy	2.5%
(seven Powers	90.5%)

The awakening of this giant after 1938, and especially after 1940, provides a final confirmation the crucial issue of *timing* in the arms races and strategical calculations of this era. Like Britain and the USSR a little earlier, the United States was now endeavoring to close the armaments gap which had been opened up by the prior and heavy defense spending of the fascist states. That it could outspend any other country, if the political will existed at home, was clear from the statistics: even as late as 1939, U.S. defense composed only 11.7 percent of total expenditures and a mere 1.6 percent of GNP[163]—percentages far, far less than in any of the other Great Powers. An increase in the defense-spending share of the American GNP to bring it close to the proportions devoted to armaments by the fascist states would automatically make the United States the most powerful military state in the world. There are, moreover, many indications that Berlin and Tokyo realized how such a development would constrict their opportunities for future expansion. In Hitler's case, the issue is complicated by his scorn for the United States as a degenerate, miscegenated power, but he also sensed that he dared not wait until the mid-1940s to resume his conquests, since the military balance would by then have decisively swung to the Anglo-French-American camp.[164] On the Japanese side, because the United States was taken more seriously, the calculations were more precise: thus, the Japanese navy estimated that whereas its warship strength would be a respectable 70 percent of the American navy in late 1941, "this would fall to 65 percent in 1942, to 50 percent in 1943, and to a disastrous 30 percent in 1944."[165] Like Germany, Japan also had a powerful strategical incentive to move soon if it was going to escape from its fate as a middleweight nation in a world increasingly overshadowed by the superpowers.

The Unfolding Crisis, 1931–1942

When the relative strengths and weaknesses of each of the Great Powers are viewed in their entirety, and also integrated into the economic and technological-military dynamics of the age, the course of international diplomacy during the 1930s becomes more comprehensible. This is not to imply that the *local* roots of the various crises— whether in Mukden, Ethiopia, or the Sudetenland—were completely irrelevant, or that there would have been no international problems if the Great Powers had been in harmony. But it is clear that when a regional crisis arose, the statesmen in each of the leading capitals were compelled to view such events in the light both of the larger diplomatic scene and, perhaps especially, of their pressing domestic problems. The British prime minister, MacDonald, put this nicely to his colleague Baldwin, after the 1931 Manchurian affair had interacted with the sterling crisis and the collapse of the second Labor government:

> We have all been so distracted by day to day troubles that we never had a chance of surveying the whole situation and hammering out a policy regarding it, but have had to live from agitation to agitation.[166]

It is a good reminder of the way politicians' concerns were often immediate and practical, rather than long-term and strategic. But even after the British government had recovered its breath, there is no sign that it contemplated a change in its circumspect policy toward Japan's conquest of Manchuria. Quite apart from the continued need to deal with economic problems, and the public's unrelenting dislike of entanglements in the Far East, British leaders were also aware of dominion pressures for peace and of the very rundown state of imperial defenses in a region where Japan enjoyed the strategical advantage. In any case, there were various Britons who approved of Tokyo's decision to deal with the irritating Chinese nationalists and many more who wanted to maintain good relations with Japan. Even when those sentiments waned, after further Japanese aggressions, the only way in which

Whitehall might be moved to stronger action would be in conjunction with the League and/or the other Great Powers.

But the League itself, however admirable its principles, had no effective means for preventing Japanese aggression in Manchuria other than the armed forces of its leading members. Thus its recourse to an investigative committee (the Lytton Commission) merely gave the Powers an excuse to delay action while at the same time Japan continued its conquest. Of the major states, Italy had no real interests in the Far East. Germany, although enjoying commercial and military ties with China, preferred to sit back and observe whether Japan's "revisionism" could offer a useful precedent in Europe. The Soviet Union *was* concerned about Japanese aggression, but was unlikely to be invited to cooperate with the other powers and had no intention of being pushed forward alone. The French, predictably, were caught in a dilemma: they had no wish to see precedents being set for altering existing territorial boundaries and flouting League resolutions; on the other hand, being increasingly worried about clandestine German rearmament and the need to maintain the status quo in Europe, the French were appalled at the idea of complications arising in the Far East which would direct attention, and possibly military resources, away from the German problem. While Paris publicly stood firm alongside League principles, it privately let Tokyo know that it understood Japan's problems in China.[167] By contrast, the U.S. government—at least as represented by Secretary of State Stimson—in no way condoned Japanese actions, rightly seeing in them a threat to the open-door world upon which, in theory, the American way of life was so dependent. But Stimson's high-principled condemnations attracted neither Hoover, who feared the consequent entanglements, nor the British government, which preferred trimming to crusading. The result was a Stimson-Hoover quarrel in their respective memoirs, and (more significant) a legacy of mistrust between Washington and London. All this offered a depressing and convincing example of what one scholar has termed "the limits of foreign policy."[168]

Whether or not the Japanese military's move into Manchuria in 1931 was carried out[169] without the home government's knowledge was less important than the fact that this action succeeded, and was expanded upon, without the West being able to do anything substantial. The larger consequences were that the League had been shown to be an ineffective instrument for preventing aggression, and that the three western democracies were incapable of united action. This was also evident in the contemporaneous discussion at Geneva concerning land and air disarmament; here, of course, the United States was missing, but the Anglo-French differences over how to respond to German demands for "equality" and the continued British evasion of any guarantee to ease France's fears meant that Hitler's new regime could walk out of the talks and denounce the existing treaties without fear of any retribution.[170]

The revival of a German threat by 1933 placed further strains upon Anglo-French-American diplomatic cooperation at a time when the World Economic Conference had broken down and the three democracies were erecting their own currency and trading blocs. Although France was the more directly threatened by Germany, it was Britain which felt that its freedom of maneuver had been more substantially impinged upon. By 1934 both the Cabinet and its Defence Requirements Committee conceded that while Japan was the more immediate danger, Germany was the greater long-term threat. But since it was not possible to be strong against both, it was important to achieve a reconciliation in one of those regions. Whereas some circles favored improving relations with Japan so as to be better able to stand up to Germany, the Foreign Office argued that an Anglo-Japanese understanding in the Far East would ruin London's delicate relations with the United States. On the other hand, it could be pointed out to those imperial and naval circles who wanted to give priority to strengthening British defenses in the Orient that it was impossible to turn one's back upon French concern over German revisionism and (after 1935) fatal to ignore the growing threat from the Luftwaffe. For the rest of the decade the decision-makers in Whitehall sought to escape from this strategical dilemma of facing potential enemies at opposite ends of the globe.[171]

In 1934 and 1935, however, such a dilemma seemed disturbing but not acute. If Hitler's regime was clearly an unpleasant one, he had shown himself surprisingly willing to negotiate a settlement with Poland; in any case, Germany was still considerably weaker in military terms than either France or Russia. Furthermore, the German effort to move into Austria following Dollfuss's assassination in 1934 had provoked Mussolini to deploy troops on the Brenner Pass as a warning. The prospect of Italy being associated with the status quo powers was especially comforting to France, which sought to bring an anti-German coalition together in the "Stresa Front" of April 1935. At almost the same time, Stalin indicated that he, too, wished to associate with the "peace-loving" states, and by 1935 the Soviet Union had not only joined the League of Nations but had instituted its security pacts with Paris and Prague. Although Hitler had made plain his opposition to an "eastern Locarno," it looked as if Germany was nicely contained on all sides. And in the Far East, Japan was quiet.[172]

By the second half of 1935, however, this encouraging scene was disintegrating fast without Hitler having lifted a finger. The differing Anglo-French perceptions of the "security problem" were already revealed in the British unease at France's renewed links with Russia on the one hand and the French dismay at the Anglo-German naval agreement of June 1935 on the other. Both measures had been taken unilat-

erally to gain extra security, France desiring to bring the USSR into the
European balance, Britain eager to reconcile its naval needs in European waters and the Far East; but each step seemed to the other neighbor to give a wrong signal to Berlin.[173] Even so, such contradictions
were damaging but not catastrophic, which could not be said of Mussolini's decision to invade Abyssinia following a series of local clashes
and in vain pursuit of his own ambition to create a new Roman Empire. This, too, was a good example of a regional quarrel having extraordinarily broader ramifications. To the French, aghast at the idea
of turning a new potential ally against Germany into a bitter foe, the
whole Abyssinian episode was an unmitigated disaster: to allow a
flagrant transgression of the League's principles was disturbing, as was
Mussolini's muscle-flexing (for where might he strike next?); on the
other hand, to drive Italy into the German camp would be an appalling
act of folly in strictly *Realpolitik* terms—but the latter consideration
was unlikely to sway the idealistic British.[174] Yet Whitehall's dilemma
was at least as large, since it not only had to handle even greater public
unease about Italy's blatant transgression of League principles, but
also had to worry about what Japan might do in the Far East if the West
was engaged in a Mediterranean imbroglio. Whereas France feared
that quarreling with Italy would tempt Hitler into the Rhineland, Britain suspected that it would encourage Japan to expand farther into
Asia, the more especially since, at that exact time, Tokyo was on the
point of denouncing the naval treaties and going for an unrestricted
fleet buildup.[175] In a larger sense, both were right; the difficulty, as
usual, was in reconciling the immediate problem with the longer-term
implication.

The French fears were proved correct first. The 1935 Anglo-French
offer of a territorial readjustment in Northeastern Africa to Italy's
favor (the Hoare-Laval Pact) had caused British public opinion in
particular to explode in moral indignation. Yet while the London and
Paris governments were torn between responding to that mood, and
still in private facing the overwhelmingly plausible strategic and economic reasons why they should not go to war with Italy, Hitler chose
to order a reoccupation of the demilitarized Rhineland (March 1936).
In strictly military terms, that was not such a blow; it was highly
unlikely by then that France could have launched an offensive strike
against Germany, and quite impossible for the British to have done
so.[176] But this further weakening of the Versailles settlement—and the
total abandonment of the Locarno Treaty—raised the general issue of
what was, or was not, an internationally acceptable way of altering the
status quo. Because of the failure of its leading members to halt Mussolini's aggression in 1935–1936, the League was now pretty much
discredited; it played little or no role, for example, either in the Spanish
Civil War or in Japan's open assault upon China in 1937. If further

changes in the existing territorial order were going to be checked, or at least controlled, that could only be done by determined moves against the "revisionist" states by the major "status quo" powers.

To none of the latter, however, did the threat to resort to arms seem a practical possibility. Indeed, just as the fascist countries were coming closer together (in November 1937 Germany and Japan signed their anti-Comintern pact, shortly after Mussolini had proclaimed the Rome-Berlin axis), their potential opponents were becoming even more introspective and disunited.[177] Despite American resentments at the Japanese invasion of China and the bombing of the U.S.S. *Panay*, 1937 was not a good year for Roosevelt to take decisive steps in overseas affairs even had he wished to: the economy had been hit by a renewed slump, and Congress was passing ever tighter neutrality legislation. Since all Roosevelt could offer was words of condemnation without any promise of action, his policies merely "tended to strengthen Anglo-French doubts about American reliability."[178] In a quite different way, Stalin also was concentrating upon domestic affairs, since his purges and show trials were then at their height. Although he cautiously extended aid to the Spanish republic in the Civil War, he was aware that many in the West disliked the "redshirts" even more than the "blackshirts," and that it would be highly dangerous to be pushed forward into an open conflict with the Axis. Japan's actions in the Far East, and the signing of the anti-Comintern pact, made him more cautious still.

Yet the Power worst affected of all in the years 1936–1937 was undoubtedly France. Not only was its economy sagging and its political scene so divided that some observers thought it close to civil war, but its own elaborate security system in Europe had been almost totally destroyed in a series of shattering blows. The German reoccupation of the Rhineland removed any lingering possibility that the French army could undertake offensive actions to put pressure upon Berlin; the country now seemed dangerously vulnerable to the Luftwaffe, just as the French air force was becoming obsolescent; the Abyssinian affair and the Rome-Berlin axis turned Italy from a potential ally into a most unpredictable and threatening foe; Belgium's retreat into isolation dislocated existing plans for the defense of France's northern frontiers, and there was no way (due to the cost) that the Maginot Line could be extended to close this gap; the Spanish Civil War raised the awful prospect of a fascist, pro-Axis state being created in France's rear; and in eastern Europe, Yugoslavia was tacking closer toward Italy and the Little Entente seemed moribund.[179]

In these gloomy, near-paralyzing circumstances, the role of Great Britain became of critical importance, as Neville Chamberlain (in May 1937) replaced Baldwin as prime minister. Concerned at his country's economic and strategical vulnerability and personally horrified at the prospect of war, Chamberlain was determined to head off any future crisis in Europe by making "positive" offers toward satisfying the dictators' grievances. Suspicious of the Soviet Union, disdainful of Roosevelt's "verbiage," impatient at what he felt was France's confused diplomacy of intransigence and passivity, and regarding the League as totally ineffective, the prime minister embarked upon his own strategy to secure lasting peace by appeasement. Even before then, London had been making noises to Berlin about commercial and colonial concessions; Chamberlain's contribution was to increase the pace by being willing to consider territorial changes in Europe itself. At the same time, and precisely because he saw in Germany the greatest danger, the prime minister was eager to improve relations with Italy in the hope of detaching that country from the Axis.[180] All this was bound to be controversial—it caused, *inter alia,* the resignation of Chamberlain's foreign secretary (Eden) early in 1938, criticism from the small but growing number of anti-appeasers at home, and increased suspicion in Washington and Moscow—but on the other hand it could well be argued that so many bold moves in the past history of diplomacy were also controversial. The real flaw in Chamberlain's strategy, understood by some in Europe but not by the majority, was that Hitler was fundamentally *unappeasable* and determined upon a future territorial order which small-scale adjustments alone could never satisfy.

If that conclusion became clear by 1939, and still more by 1940–1941, it was not evident either to the British or even the French government in the crisis year of 1938. The takeover of Austria in the spring of that year was an unpleasant instance of Hitler's fondness for unannounced moves, but could one really object to the principle of joining Germans with Germans? If anything, it merely intensified Chamberlain's conviction that the issue of the German-speaking minority in Czechoslovakia had to be settled before that crisis brought the Powers up to, and over, the brink of war. Admittedly, the question of the Sudetenland was a much more contentious one—Czechoslovakia, too, had rights to a sovereignty which had been internationally guaranteed, and the western Powers' desire to satisfy Hitler now seemed more influenced by negative selfish fears than by positive ideals—but the fact was that the Führer was the only leader at this time prepared to fight, and was indeed irritated that the prospect of smashing the Czechs was removed by the concessions he gained at the Munich conference. As ever, it took two to make a Great Power war; and in 1938 there was no willing opponent to Hitler.[181]

Because the political and public will for war was lacking in the west, it makes little sense here to enter into the long-lasting debate about what might have happened had Britain and France fought on Czechoslovakia's behalf, although it is worth noting that the military balance was not as favorable to Germany as the various apologists of appeasement suggested.[182] What is clear, however, is that that balance swung even more in Hitler's favor following the Munich settlement. The elimination of Czechoslovakia as a substantial middleweight European force by March 1939, the German acquisition of Czech armaments, factories, and raw materials, and Stalin's increasing suspicion of the West outweighed the factors working in favor of London and Paris such as the considerable increases in British arms output, the more intimate Anglo-French military cooperation, or the swing in British and dominion opinion in favor of standing up to Hitler. At the same time, Chamberlain failed (January 1939) to detach Italy from the Axis, or to deter it from its own aggressions in the Balkans—even if Mussolini, for urgent reasons of his own, would not fight immediately alongside his fellow dictator in a Great Power war against the western nations.

When Hitler began to apply pressure upon Poland in the late spring of 1939, therefore, the possibilities of avoiding a conflict were less than in the previous year—and the prospects of an Anglo-French victory should war break out were *much* less. Germany's annexation of the "rump" state of Czechoslovakia in March 1939 and Italy's move into Albania a month later had led the democracies, under mounting public pressure to "stop Hitler," to offer guarantees to Poland, Greece, Rumania, and Turkey, thus tying western Europe to the fate of eastern Europe to a degree which the British at least had never before contemplated. Yet Poland could not be directly assisted by the western countries, and any *indirect* assistance was going to be small in a period when the French army had assumed the strategic defensive and the British were concentrating so much of their resources upon improved aerial defenses at home. The only direct aid which could be given to Poland must come from the east, and if Chamberlain's government was unenthusiastic about agreements with Moscow, the Poles for their part were adamantly opposed to having the Red Army on their territory. Since Stalin's overwhelming concern was to buy time and avoid a war, and Hitler's need was to increase the pressure upon the western nations to abandon Poland, both dictators had a secular interest in doing a "deal" at Warsaw's expense, whatever their own ideological differences. The shock announcement of the Molotov-Ribbentrop pact (August 23, 1939) not only enhanced Germany's strategical position but also made a war over Poland virtually inevitable. This time "appeasement" was not an option open to London and Paris, even if the economic and military circumstances pointed (perhaps more than in the preceding years) to the avoidance of a Great Power conflict.[183]

The outbreak of the Second World War thus found Britain and France once again opposing Germany, and, as in 1914, a British expeditionary force was dispatched across the Channel while the Anglo-French navies imposed their maritime blockade.[184] In so many other respects, however, the strategical contours of this war were quite different from the previous one, and disadvantageous to the Allies. Not only was there no eastern front, but the political agreement between Berlin and Moscow to carve up Poland also led to commercial arrangements, so that an increasing flow of raw materials sent from Russia steadily obviated any effects which the blockade might have had upon the German economy. It was true that in the first year of the war, stocks of oil and other raw materials were still desperately low in Germany, but ersatz production, Swedish iron ore, and the growing supplies from Russia helped to bridge the gap. In addition, Allied inertia on the western front meant that there was little pressure upon German holdings of petroleum and ammunitions. Finally, there were no encumbrancing allies for Germany to prop up, like Austria-Hungary in the 1914–1918 war. Had Italy also joined in the conflict in September 1939, its own economic deficiencies might have posed an excessive strain upon the Reich's slender stocks and, arguably, dislocated the chances for the German westward strike in 1940. To be sure, Italy's participation would have complicated the Anglo-French position in the Mediterranean, but not perhaps by much, and Rome's neutrality made it a useful conduit for German trade—which is why many of the planners in Berlin hoped that Mussolini would remain on the sidelines.[185]

While the "phony war" did not put Germany's economic vulnerability to the test, it did allow Germany to perfect those elements of national strategy in which the Wehrmacht was so superior—that is, operational doctrine, combined arms, tactical air power, and decentralized offensive warfare. The Polish campaign in particular confirmed the efficacy of Blitzkrieg warfare, exposed a number of weaknesses (which could then be corrected), and strengthened German confidence in being able to overrun foes by rapid, surprise assaults and the proper concentration of aerial and armored power. This was again easily demonstrated in the swift overrunning of Denmark and the Netherlands, although geography made Norway both inaccessible to German panzer divisions and subject to the influence of British sea power, which is why that campaign was touch-and-go for a while until the Luftwaffe's dominance was established. But the best example of the superiority of German military doctrine and operational tactical ability came in the French campaign of May-June 1940, when the larger but less well organized Allied infantry and armored forces were torn apart by Guderian's clusters of tanks and motorized infantry. In all of these encounters, the attacker enjoyed a considerable air superiority. Unlike the 1914–1916 battles, therefore, in which neither side showed much skill in grappling with the newer condition of warfare, these 1940 campaigns revealed German advantages which seemed to obviate Germany's long-term economic vulnerability.[186]

What was more, by winning so decisively in 1939–1940 the German war machine greatly expanded its available sources of oil and raw materials. Not only could it (and did it!) plunder heavily from its defeated foes, but the elimination of France and Britain's obvious incapacity to launch a major military campaign also meant that there would be no serious drain upon the Wehrmacht's stocks through extensive campaigning. A land line had been made to Spanish raw materials, Swedish ores were now safe from Allied expeditions, and Russia, secretly appalled at Hitler's swift successes, was increasing its supplies. In these circumstances, Italy's entry into the war just as France was collapsing was not the economic embarrassment it might have been— and, indeed, distracted British resources away from Europe to the Near East, even if Italy's spectacularly unsuccessful campaigning showed how overrated it had been throughout the 1930s.[187]

Had the war continued simply with these three belligerents, it is difficult to say how long it might have gone on. The British Empire under Churchill was determined to continue the struggle and was mobilizing large numbers of men and stocks of munitions— outbuilding Germany both in aircraft and tank production in 1940, for example.[188] And while Britain's own holdings of gold and dollars were by then insufficient to pay for American supplies, Roosevelt was managing to undo the damaging neutrality legislation and to persuade Congress that it was in the country's own security interests to sustain Britain—by Lend-Lease, the "destroyers for bases" deal, convoy protection, and so on.[189] The overall result was to leave the two major combatants in the position of being unable to damage the other decisively. If the Battle of Britain had rendered impossible a German cross-Channel invasion, the imbalance of land forces made a British military entry into Europe quite out of the question. Bomber Command's raids upon Germany were good for British morale, but did little real damage at this stage. Despite occasional raids into the North Atlantic, the German surface fleet was in no position to take on the Royal Navy; on the other hand, the U-boat campaign was as threatening as ever, thanks to Doenitz's newer tactics and additional boats. In North Africa, Somalia, and Abyssinia, British Empire forces found it easy to take Italian-held positions, but extremely difficult to cope with the explosive form of warfare practiced by Rommel's Afrika Korps or by the German invading forces in Greece. The second year of what has been termed "the last European war" was, therefore, characterized by defensive victories and small-scale gains rather than by epic encounters and conquests.[190]

Inevitably, then, Hitler's fateful decision to invade Russia in June 1941 changed the entire dimensions of the conflict. Strategically, it meant that Germany now had to fight on several fronts and thus revert to its dilemma of 1914–1917—this being a particularly heavy strain for the Luftwaffe, which had its squadrons thinly spread between the west, the east, and the Mediterranean. It also ensured that the British Empire's position in the Middle East—which could surely have been over-run had Hitler dispatched there one-quarter of the troops and aircraft used for Operation Barbarossa—would remain, like the home islands, as a springboard for an enemy counteroffensive in the future. Most important of all, however, the sheer geographical extent and logistical demands of campaigning hundreds of miles deep into Russia under-mined the Wehrmacht's greatest advantage: its ability to launch shock attacks within limited confines, so as to overwhelm the enemy before its own supplies began to run out and its war machine slowed down. In contrast to the stupendous array of front-line strength assembled by Germany and its allies in June 1941, the supporting and follow-on resources were minimal, especially in the light of the poor road system; no thought had been given to winter warfare, since it was assumed that the struggle would be over within three months; German aircraft pro-duction in 1941 was significantly smaller than that of Britain or Russia, let alone the United States; the Wehrmacht had far fewer tanks than Russia; and the supplies of petroleum and ammunition were quickly run down in the extensive campaigning.[191] Even when the Wehrmacht was spectacularly successful in the field—and Stalin's inept deploy-ment orders in the face of the impending attack allowed the Germans to kill or capture three million Russians in the first four months of fighting—that did not of itself solve the problem. Russia could suffer appalling losses of men and equipment, and cede a million square miles of territory, and still not be defeated; the capture of Moscow, or perhaps even of Stalin himself, might not have forced a surrender, given the country's extraordinarily large reserves. In sum, this was a limitless war, and the Third Reich, for all its imposing successes and operational brilliance, was not properly equipped to fight it.

Whether Russia could have survived the German army at the gates of Moscow *and* a heavy attack by Japan upon Siberia in December 1941 is quite another matter, fascinating to speculate upon and impos-sible to answer. In signing both the Tripartite Pact (September 1940) with Germany and Italy and the later (April 1941) neutrality treaty with the Soviet Union, Japan had hoped to deter the USSR while con-centrating on its southern expansion; but many in Tokyo were tempted again to a war against Russia at the news of the German advance upon Moscow. If indeed the Japanese army had struck against its traditional foe in Asia instead of agreeing to the southern operations, it might still have been difficult for Roosevelt to persuade the American people to enter fully into such a war, and the assistance which the British could have given Russia in the Far East (had Churchill alone entered that conflict) would have been minimal. Instead of facing that dreadful two-front scenario, Stalin was able to switch his well-trained, winter-hardy divisions from Siberia in late 1941 to help blunt the German offensive and then to drive it back.[192] Seen from Tokyo's viewpoint, however, the decision to expand southward was utterly logical. The West's embargo on trade with Japan and freezing of its assets in July 1941 (following Tokyo's seizure of French Indochina) made both the army and the navy acutely aware that unless they gave in to American political demands *or* attempted to seize the oil and raw materials supplies of Southeast Asia, they would be economically ruined within a matter of months. From July 1941, therefore, a northern war against Russia became virtually impossible and southern operations virtually inevitable—but since the Americans were judged hardly likely to stand by while Japan helped itself to Borneo, Malaya, and the Dutch East Indies, their military installations in the western Pacific—and their fleet base at Pearl Harbor—also needed to be eliminated. Simply to keep up the momentum of their "China incident," the Japanese generals now found it necessary to support large-scale operations thousands of miles from home against targets they had scarcely heard of.[193]

December 1941 marked the second major turning point in a war which had now become global. The Russian counterattacks around Moscow in the same month confirmed that here, at least, the Blitzkrieg had failed. And if the stunning array of Japanese successes in the first six months of the Pacific war dealt heavy blows to the Allies, none of the territories lost (not even Singapore or the Philippines) was really vital in grand-strategical terms. What was much more important was that Japan's actions, and Hitler's gratuitous declaration of war upon the United States, at last brought into the conflict the most powerful country in the world. To be sure, industrial productivity alone could not ensure military effectiveness—and German operational skills in particular meant that simple man-to-man and dollar-to-dollar comparisons were foolish[194]—but the Grand Alliance, as Churchill fondly called it, was so superior in matériel terms to the Axis and its productive bases were so far away from the German and Japanese armed forces that it had the resources and the opportunity to build up an overwhelming military strength which none of the earlier opponents of fascist aggression could have hoped to possess. Within another year, in fact, de Tocqueville's forecast of 1835 concerning the emergence of a bipolar world was at last on the point of being realized.

STRATEGY &
ECONOMICS
TODAY &
TOMORROW

7

Stability and Change in a Bipolar World, 1943-1980

At the news of the U.S. entry into the war, Winston Churchill openly rejoiced—and with good reason. As he later explained it, "Hitler's fate was sealed. Mussolini's fate was sealed. As for the Japanese, they would be ground to powder. All the rest was merely the proper application of overwhelming force."[1] Yet such confidence must have seemed wildly misplaced to more cautious minds on the Allied side during 1942 and until the first half of 1943. For six months after Pearl Harbor, Japanese forces had run rampant in the Pacific and Southeast Asia, overwhelming the European colonial empires, encircling China from the south, and threatening India, Australia, and Hawaii. In the Russo-German war, the Wehrmacht resumed its brutal offensives once the winter of 1941-1942 had passed and battled its way toward the Caucasus; at almost the same time, the far smaller German force under Rommel in North Africa had pushed to within fifty-five miles of Alexandria. The U-boat assault upon Allied convoys was proving deadlier than ever, with the highest losses of merchantmen occurring in the spring of 1943; yet the Anglo-American "counterblockade" of the German economy by means of strategic bombing was failing to achieve its purpose and was leading to severe casualties among the aircrews. If the fate of the Axis Powers *was* sealed after December 1941, there was little indication that they knew it.

"The Proper Application of Overwhelming Force"

Nevertheless, Churchill's basic assumption was correct. The conversion of the conflict from a European war to a truly global war may have complicated Britain's own strategical juggling act—as many historians have pointed out, the loss of Singapore was the result of the British concentration of aircraft and trained divisions in the Mediterranean theater[2]—but it totally altered the overall balance of forces

347

once the newer belligerents were properly mobilized. In the meantime, the German and Japanese war machines could still continue their conquests; yet the further they extended themselves the less capable they were of meeting the counteroffensives which the Allies were steadily preparing.

The first of these came in the Pacific, where Nimitz's carrier-based aircraft had already blunted the Japanese drive into the Coral Sea (May 1942) and toward Midway (June 1942) and showed how vital naval air power was in the vast expanses of that ocean. By the end of the year, Japanese troops had been pulled out of Guadalcanal and Australian-American forces were pushing forward in New Guinea. When the counteroffensive through the central Pacific began late in 1943, the two powerful American battle fleets covering the Gilberts invasion were themselves protected by *four* fast-carrier task forces (twelve carriers) with overwhelming control of the air.[3] An even greater imbalance of force had permitted the British Empire divisions to crash through the German positions at El Alamein in October 1942 and to drive Rommel's units back toward Tunisia; when Montgomery ordered the attack, he had six times as many tanks as his opponent, three times as many troops, and almost complete command of the air. In the month following, Eisenhower's Anglo-American army of 100,000 men landed in French North Africa to begin a "pincer movement" from the west against the German-Italian forces, which would culminate in the latter's mass surrender in May 1943.[4] By that time, too, Doenitz had been compelled to withdraw his U-boat wolf packs from the North Atlantic, where they had suffered very heavy losses against Allied convoys now protected by very-long-range Liberators, escort carriers, and hunter-killer escort groups equipped with the latest radar and depth charges—and alerted by "Ultra" decrypts as to the U-boats' movements.[5] If it was to take longer for the Allies to achieve "command of the air" over Europe to complement their command of the sea, the solution was being swiftly developed in the form of the long-range Mustang fighter, which first accompanied the USAAF's bomber fleets in December 1943; within another few months, the Luftwaffe's capacity to defend the airspace above the Third Reich's soldiers, factories, and civilian population had been weakened beyond recovery.[6]

Even more ominous to the Wehrmacht high command was the changing balance of advantage along the eastern front. As early as August 1941, when many observers felt that Russia was in the process of being finished off as a Great Power, General Halder was gloomily confiding in the War Staff diary:

> We reckoned with about 200 enemy divisions. Now we have already counted 360 . . . not armed and equipped to our standards, and their

tactical leadership is often poor. But . . . if we smash a dozen of them, the Russians simply put up another dozen. . . . Time . . . favors them, as they are near their own resources, while we are moving farther and farther away from ours.[7]

In this sort of mass, reckless, brutalized fighting, the casualty figures were making even First World War totals seem modest. In the first five months of campaigning, the Germans claimed to have killed, wounded, or captured well over 3 million Russians.[8] Yet at that particular moment, when Stalin and the Stavka were planning the first counteroffensive around Moscow, the Red Army still had 4.2 million men in its field armies, and was numerically superior in tanks and aircraft.[9] To be sure, it could not match the professional expertise of the Germans either on land or in the air—even as late as 1944 the Russians were losing five or six men for every one German soldier[10]—and when the fearful winter of 1941–1942 passed, Hitler's war machine could again commence its offensive, this time toward Stalingrad and then disaster. After Stalingrad, in the summer of 1943, the Wehrmacht tried again, pulling together its armored forces to produce the fantastic total of seventeen panzer divisions for the encirclement of Kursk. Yet in what was to be by far the greatest tank battle of the Second World War, the Red Army countered with thirty-four armored divisions, some 4,000 vehicles to the German's 2,700. While the numbers of Soviet tanks had been reduced by over one-half within a week, they had smashed the greater part of Hitler's *Panzerarmee* in the process and were now ready for the unrelenting counteroffensive toward Berlin. At that point, news of the Allied landing in Italy provided Hitler with the excuse for withdrawing from what had been an unmitigated disaster, as well as confirming the extent to which the Reich's enemies were closing the ring.[11]

Was all this, then, merely the "proper application of overwhelming force"? Clearly, economic power was never the *only* influence upon military effectiveness, even in the mechanized, total war of 1939–1945; economics, to paraphrase Clausewitz, stood in about the same relationship to combat as the craft of the swordsmith to the art of fencing. And there were far too many examples of where the German and Japanese leadership made grievous political or strategical errors after 1941 which were to cost them dear. In the German case, this ranged from relatively small-scale decisions, like pouring reinforcements into North Africa in early 1943, just in time for them to be captured, to the appallingly stupid as well as criminal treatment of the Ukrainian and other non-Russian minorities in the USSR, who were happy to escape from the Stalinist embrace until checked by Nazi atrocities. It ran from the arrogance of assuming that the Enigma codes could never be broken to the ideological prejudice against employing German women in munitions factories, whereas all Germany's foes willingly exploited that largely untapped labor pool. It was compounded by rivalries within the higher echelons of the army itself, which made it ineffective in resisting Hitler's manic urge for overambitious offensives like Stalingrad and Kursk. Above all, there was what scholars refer to as the "polycratic chaos" of rivaling ministries and subempires (the army, the SS, the Gauleiter, the economics ministry), which prevented any coherent assessment and allocation of resources, let alone the hammering-out of what elsewhere would be termed a "grand strategy." This was not a serious way to run a war.[12]

While Japanese strategical mistakes were less egregious and counterproductive, they were nonetheless amazing. Because Japan was carrying out a "continental" strategy in which the army's influence predominated, its operations in the Pacific and Southeast Asia had been implemented with a minimum of force—only eleven divisions, compared with the thirteen in Manchuria and the twenty-two in China. Yet even when the American counteroffensive in the central Pacific was under way, Japanese troop and aerial reinforcements to that region were far too tardy and far too small—especially as compared with the resources allocated for the massive China offensives of 1943–1944. Ironically, even when Nimitz's forces were closing upon Japan in early 1945, and its cities were being pulverized from the air, there were still 1 million soldiers in China and another 780,000 or so in Manchuria—now incapable of being withdrawn because of the effectiveness of the American submarine campaign.

Yet the Imperial Japanese Navy, too, needs to take its share of the blame. The operational handling of key battles like Midway was riddled with errors, but even when the aircraft carrier was proving itself supreme in Pacific warfare, many Japanese admirals after Yamamoto's death were wedded to the battleship and still looked for the chance to fight a second Tsushima—as the 1944 Leyte Gulf operation and, even more symbolically, the one-way suicide trip of the *Yamato* revealed. Japanese submarines, with their formidable torpedoes, were utterly misused as scouts for the battle fleet or in running supplies to beleaguered island garrisons, rather than being deployed against the enemy's lines of communication. By contrast, the navy failed to protect its own merchant marine, and was quite backward in developing convoy systems, antisubmarine techniques, escort carriers, and hunter-killer groups, although Japan was even more dependent than Britain upon imported materials.[13] It was symptomatic of this battle-fleet obsession that while the navy was allocating resources to the construction of giant *Yamato*-class vessels, it built *no* destroyer escorts between 1941 and 1943—in contrast to the Americans' 331 ships.[14] Japan also completely lost the battle of intelligence, codes, and decrypts.[15] All of this was about as helpful to the preserva-

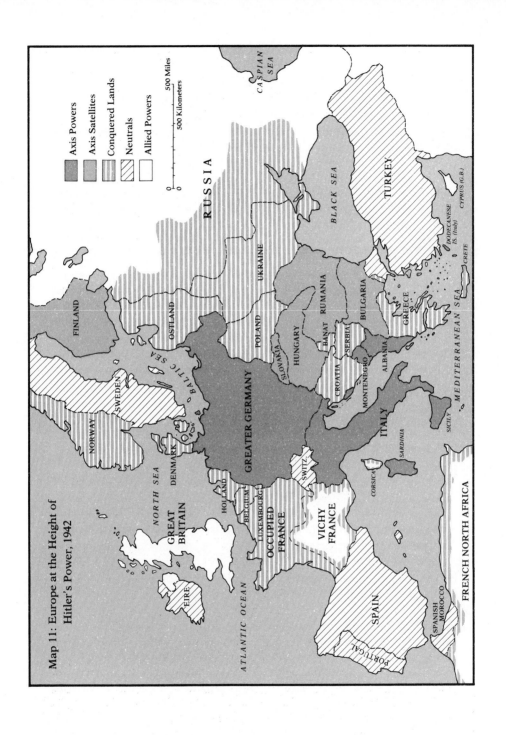

Map 11: Europe at the Height of Hitler's Power, 1942

Axis Powers
Axis Satellites
Conquered Lands
Neutrals
Allied Powers

tion of a Greater East Asia Co-prosperity Sphere as German mistakes were to the maintenance of the Thousand-Year Reich.

There is, obviously, no known way of "factoring out" those errors (to use the economists' inelegant term) and thus discovering how the Axis Powers might have fared had such follies been avoided. But unless the Allies for their part had committed equally serious strategical and political mistakes, it is difficult to see how their productive superiority would not have prevailed in the long term. Obviously, a successful German occupation of Moscow in December 1941 would have been damaging to Russia's war effort (and to Stalin's regime); but would the USSR's population have surrendered then and there when its only fate would have been extermination—and when it still had large productive and military reserves thousands of miles to the east? Despite the economic losses dealt by Operation Barbarossa—coal production down by 57 percent, pig iron by 68 percent, and so on[16]—it is worth noting that Russia produced 4,000 more aircraft than Germany in 1941 and 10,000 more in 1942, and this was for one front, as opposed to Germany's three.[17] Given its increasing superiority in men, tanks, artillery, and planes, by the second year of the conflict the Red Army could actually afford to sustain losses at a rate of five or six to one (albeit at an appalling cost to its own troops) and still push forward against the weakening Germans. By the beginning of 1945, on the Belorussian and Ukrainian fronts alone, "Soviet superiority was both absolute and awesome, fivefold in manpower, fivefold in armor, over sevenfold in artillery and seventeen times the German strength in the air."[18]

Since the Anglo-American forces in France a few months earlier were enjoying "an effective superiority of 20 to 1 in tanks and 25 to 1 in aircraft,"[19] the amazing fact is that the Germans did so well for so long; even at the close of 1944, just as in September 1918, they were still occupying territories far larger than the Reich's own boundaries at the onset of war. To this question military historians have offered a virtually unanimous response: that German operational doctrine, emphasizing flexibility and decentralized decision-making at the *battlefield* level, proved far superior to the cautious, set-piece tactics of the British, the bloody, full-frontal assaults of the Russians, and the enthusiastic but unprofessional forward rushes of the Americans; that German "combined-arms" experience was better than anybody else's; and that the caliber and training of both the staff officers and the NCOs was extraordinarily high, even in the final year of the war.

Yet our contemporary admiration for the German operational performance, which seems to be rising book by book,[20] ought not to obscure the obvious fact that Berlin, like Tokyo, had overstretched itself. In November 1943, General Jodl estimated that 3.9 million Germans (together with a mere 283,000 Axis-allied troops) were trying to hold off 5.5 million Russians on the eastern front. A further 177,000

German troops were in Finland, while Norway and Denmark were garrisoned by 486,000 men. There were 1,370,000 occupation troops in France and Belgium. "Another 612,000 men were tied down in the Balkans, and there were 412,000 men in Italy. . . . Hitler's armies were scattered the length and breadth of Europe and were inferior in numbers and equipment on every front."[21] The same could be said of the Japanese divisions, spread thinly across the Far East from Burma to the Aleutian Islands.

Even in those campaigns which seemingly "changed the course of the war," one wonders whether an Axis victory rather than an Allied one would not merely have postponed the eventual outcome. Had, say, Nimitz lost more than one carrier at Midway, they would have been replaced, in that same year, by three new fleet carriers, three light fleet carriers, and fifteen escort carriers; in 1943, by five fleet carriers, six light fleet carriers, and twenty-five escort carriers; and in 1944, by nine fleet carriers and thirty-five escort carriers.[22] Similarly, in the critical years of the Battle of the Atlantic, the Allies lost 8.3 million tons of shipping overall in 1942 and 4 million tons in 1943, but those frightening totals were compensated for by Allied launchings of 7 million and 9 million tons of new merchant ships respectively. This was chiefly due to the fantastic explosion in American shipbuilding output, which by mid-1942 was already launching vessels faster than the U-boats could sink them—causing one notable authority to conclude, "In World War II, the German submarine campaign may have postponed, but did not affect the outcome."[23] On land, also—and the Second World War in Europe was preeminently a gunner's war and a tank crew's war—Germany's production of artillery pieces, self-propelled guns and tanks was considerably less than Russia's, let alone the combined Allied totals (see Table 33).

Table 33. Tank Production in 1944[24]

Germany	17,800
Russia	29,000
Britain	5,000
United States	17,500 (in 1943, 29,500)

But the most telling statistics of all relate to aircraft production (Table 34), for everyone could see that without command of the air it was impossible for armies and navies to operate effectively; *with* command of the air, one could not only achieve campaign victories, but also deal heavy blows at the foe's wartime economy.

Such figures, moreover, disguise the fact that the Anglo-American totals include a large number of heavy four-engined bombers, so that the Allied superiority is even more marked when the number of engines or the structure weight of the aircraft is compared with the Axis

Table 34. Aircraft Production of the Powers, 1939–1945[25]

	1939	1940	1941	1942	1943	1944	1945
United States	5,856	12,804	26,277	47,836	85,898	96,318	49,761
USSR	10,382	10,565	15,735	25,436	34,900	40,300	20,900
Britain	7,940	15,049	20,094	23,672	26,263	26,461	12,070
British Commonwealth	250	1,100	2,600	4,575	4,700	4,575	2,075
TOTAL ALLIES	24,178	39,518	64,706	101,519	151,761	167,654	84,806
Germany	8,295	10,247	11,776	15,409	24,807	39,807	7,540
Japan	4,467	4,768	5,088	8,861	16,693	28,180	11,066
Italy	1,800	1,800	2,400	2,400	1,600	—	—
TOTAL AXIS	14,562	16,815	19,264	26,670	43,100	67,987	18,606

totals.[26] Here was the ultimate reason why, despite extraordinary efforts by the Germans to retain command of the air,[27] their cities and factories and railway lines were increasingly devastated—as was, even more so, the almost totally unprotected Japanese homeland. Here, too, was the reason why Doenitz's U-boats had to keep below the surface; why Slim's Burma Army could reinforce Imphal; why American carriers could launch repeated attacks upon Japanese bases all over the western Pacific; and why Allied soldiers, whenever stopped by a stubborn German defense, could always call for aircraft to crush the enemy and get the offensive going again. On D-Day itself (June 6, 1944), it may be worth noting, the Germans could muster 319 aircraft against the Allies 12,837 in the west. To turn Clausewitz's phrase around, the art of fencing (like the art of war) indeed required skill and experience; but that would avail the fighter little if he ran out of stocks of swords. In the battle of the swordsmiths, the Allies were very clearly winning.

For the simple fact was that even after the expansion of the German and Japanese empires, the economic and productive forces ranged upon each side were *much more disproportionate* than in the First World War. According to the rough approximations which we have already seen,[28] the Greater Germany of 1938 had a share of the world's manufacturing output and a "relative war potential" which were both about equal to that of Britain and France combined. It was probably inferior to the total resources and war potential of the British and French *empires* combined; but those lands had not been mobilized to Germany's degree when war broke out, and, as discussed previously, the Allies were less than competent in the vital matter of operational expertise. Germany's acquisitions of territory in 1939 and (especially) in 1940 put it decisively ahead of the isolated and somewhat mauled Power which Churchill took control of. France's collapse and Italy's entry into the conflict therefore left the British Empire facing an agglomeration of military force which, in terms of war potential, was probably twice as strong; militarily, the Berlin-Rome Axis was unassailable on land, still inferior at sea, and about equal in the air—hence the British preference for fighting in North Africa rather than Europe. The German attack upon the USSR did not at first seem to change this balance, if only because of the disastrous casualties suffered by the Red Army, which were then compounded by the losses of Soviet territory and plant.

On the other hand, the decisive events of December 1941 entirely altered these balances: the Russian counterattack at Moscow showed that it would not fall to Blitzkrieg warfare; and the entry of Japan and the United States into what was now a global conflict brought together a "Grand Alliance" of enormous industrial-productive staying power. It could not *immediately* affect the course of the military campaigns, since Germany was still strong enough to renew its offensive in Russia during the summer of 1942, and Japan was enjoying its first six months of easy victories against the unprepared forces of the United States, the Dutch, and the British Empire. Yet all this could not obviate the fact that the Allies possessed *twice* the manufacturing strength (using the distorted 1938 figures, which downplay the U.S.' share), *three* times the "war potential," and *three* times the national income of the Axis powers, even when the French shares are added to Germany's total.[29] By 1942 and 1943, these figures of *potential* power were being exchanged into the hard currency of aircraft, guns, tanks, and ships; indeed, by 1943–1944 the United States alone was producing one ship a day and one aircraft every five minutes! What is more, the Allies were producing many newer *types* of weapons (Superfortresses, Mustangs, light fleet carriers), whereas the Axis powers could only produce advanced weapons (jet fighters, Type 23 U-boats) in relatively small quantities.

The best measure of this decisive shift in the balances comes from Wagenführ's figures for the armaments-production totals of the major combatants (see Table 35).

Table 35. Armaments Production of the Powers, 1940–1943[30]
(billions of 1944 dollars)

	1940	1941	1943
Britain	3.5	6.5	11.1
USSR	(5.0)	8.5	13.9
United States	(1.5)	4.5	37.5
Total of Allied *combatants*	3.5	19.5	62.5
Germany	6.0	6.0	13.8
Japan	(1.0)	2.0	4.5
Italy	0.75	1.0	—
Total of Axis *combatants*	6.75	9.0	18.3

Thus, in 1940 British armaments production was significantly behind Germany's but still growing fast, so that it was slightly superior by the following year—the last year in which the German economy was being operated at relative leisure. The twin military shocks of Stalingrad and North Africa, and Speer's assumption of the economics ministry, led to an enormous boost in German arms production by 1943;[31] and Japan, too, more than doubled its output. Even so, the increases in combined British and Soviet production during those two years equaled the rise in Axis output (G.B./USSR, $10 billion increase, 1941–1943; cf. Axis, $9.8 billion increase), and kept them still superior in total armaments production. But the most staggering change came with the *more than eightfold* rise in American arms output between 1941 and 1943, which meant that by the latter year the Allied total was over three times that of its foes—thereby finally realizing that imbalance in "war potential" and national income which had existed embryonically at the very beginning. No matter how cleverly the Wehrmacht mounted its tactical counterattacks on both the western and eastern fronts until almost the last months of the war, it was to be ultimately overwhelmed by the sheer mass of Allied firepower. By 1945, the thousands of Anglo-American bombers pounding the Reich each day and the hundreds of Red Army divisions poised to blast through to Berlin and Vienna were all different manifestations of the same blunt fact. Once again, in a protracted and full-scale coalition war, the countries with the deepest purse had prevailed in the end.

This was also true of Japan's own collapse in the Pacific war. It is now clear that the dropping of the atomic bombs in 1945 marked a watershed in the military history of the world, and one which throws into doubt the viability of mankind should a Great Power war with atomic weaponry ever be fought. Yet in the context of the 1945 campaigning, it was but one of a series of military tools which the United States then could employ to compel Japan to surrender. The successful American submarine campaign was threatening to starve Japan; the swarms of B-29 bombers were pounding its towns and cities to ashes (the Tokyo "fire raid" of March 9, 1945, caused approximately 185,000 casualties and destroyed 267,000 buildings); and the American planners and their allies were preparing for a massive invasion of the home islands. The mix of motives which, despite certain reservations, pushed toward the decision to drop the bomb—the wish to save Allied casualties, the desire to send a warning to Stalin, the need to justify the vast expenses of the atomic project—are still debated today;[32] but the point being made here is that it was the United States alone which at this time had the productive and technological resources not only to wage two large-scale conventional wars but also to invest the scientists, raw materials, and money (about $2 billion) in the development of a new weapon which might or might not work. The devastation inflicted upon Hiroshima, together with Berlin's fall into the hands of the Red

Army, not only symbolized the end of another war, it also marked the beginning of a new order in world affairs.

The New Strategic Landscape

The outlines of that new order were already being described by American military planners even as the conflict was at its height. As one of their policy papers expressed it:

> The successful termination of the war against our present enemies will find a world profoundly changed in respect of relative national military strengths, a change more comparable indeed with that occasioned by the fall of Rome than with any other change occurring during the succeeding fifteen hundred years. . . . After the defeat of Japan, the United States and the Soviet Union will be the only military powers of the first magnitude. This is due in each case to a combination of geographical position and extent, and vast munitioning potential.[33]

While historians might quibble at the claim that nothing of a comparable nature had occurred during the past fifteen hundred years, it was becoming clear that the global balance of power after the war would be totally different from that preceding it. Former Great Powers—France, Italy—were already eclipsed. The German bid for mastery in Europe was collapsing, as was Japan's bid in the Far East and Pacific. Britain, despite Churchill, was fading. The bipolar world, forecast so often in the nineteenth and early twentieth centuries, had at last arrived; the international order, in DePorte's words, now moved "from one system to another."[34] Only the United States and the USSR counted, so it seemed; and of the two, the American "superpower" was vastly superior.

Simply because much of the rest of the world was either exhausted by the war or still in a stage of colonial "underdevelopment," American power in 1945 was, for want of another term, *artificially* high, like, say, Britain's in 1815. Nonetheless, the actual dimensions of its might were unprecedented in absolute terms. Stimulated by the vast surge in war expenditures, the country's GNP measured in constant 1939 dollars rose from $88.6 billion (1939) to $135 billion (1945), and much higher ($220 billion) in current dollars. At last, the "slack" in the economy which the New Deal had failed to eradicate was fully taken up, and underutilized resources and manpower properly exploited: "During the war the size of the productive plant within the country grew by nearly 50 percent and the physical output of goods by more than 50 percent."[35] Indeed, in the years 1940 to 1944, industrial expansion in the United States rose at a faster pace—over 15 percent a year—than at any period before or since. Although the greater part of this growth was caused by war production (which soared from 2 percent of total output in 1939 to 40 percent in 1943), nonwar goods also increased, so that the civilian sector of the economy was not encroached upon as in the other combatant nations. Its standard of living was higher than any other country's, but so was its per capita productivity. Among the Great Powers, the United States was the only country which became richer— in fact, much richer—rather than poorer because of the war. At its conclusion, Washington possessed gold reserves of $20 billion, almost two-thirds of the world's total of $33 billion.[36] Again, ". . . more than half the total manufacturing production of the world took place within the U.S.A., which, in fact, turned out a third of the world production of goods of all types."[37] This also made it by far the greatest exporter of goods at the war's end, and even a few years later it supplied one-third of the world's exports. Because of the massive expansion of its shipbuilding facilities, it now owned half of the world supply of shipping. Economically, the world was its oyster.

This economic power was reflected in the military strength of the United States, which at the end of the war controlled 12.5 million service personnel, including 7.5 million overseas. Although this total was naturally going to shrink in peacetime (by 1948, the army's personnel was only one-ninth what it had been four years earlier), that merely reflected political choices, not real military potential. Given the early postwar assumptions about the limited overseas roles of the United States, a better indication of its strength lay in the tallies of its modern weaponry. By this stage, the U.S. Navy was unquestionably "second to none," its fleet of 1,200 major warships (centered upon dozens of aircraft carriers rather than battleships) now being considerably larger than the Royal Navy's, with no other significant maritime force existing. In both its carrier task forces and its Marine Corps divisions, the United States had amply demonstrated its capacity to project its power across the globe to any region accessible from the sea. Even more imposing was the American "command of the air"; the 2,000-plus heavy bombers which had pounded Hitler's Europe and the 1,000 ultra-long-range B-29s which had reduced many Japanese cities to ashes were to be supplemented by even more powerful jet-propelled strategic bombers like the B-36. Above all, the United States possessed a monopoly of atomic bombs, which promised to unleash a devastation upon any future enemy as horrific as that which had occurred at Hiroshima and Nagasaki.[38] As later analyses have pointed out, American military power may actually have been less than it seemed (there were very few A-bombs in stock, and dropping them had large political implications), and it was difficult to use it to influence the conduct of a country as distant, inscrutable, and suspicious as the USSR; but the image of ineffable superiority remained undisturbed until the Korean War, and was reinforced by the pleas of so many nations for American loans, weapons, and promises of military support.

Given the extraordinarily favorable economic and strategical position which the United States thus occupied, its post-1945 outward thrust could come as no surprise to those familiar with the history of international politics. With the traditional Great Powers fading away, it steadily moved into the vacuum which their going created; having become number one, it could no longer contain itself within its own shores, or even its own hemisphere. To be sure, the war itself had been the primary cause of this projection outward of American power and influence; because of it, for example, in 1945 it had sixty-nine divisions in Europe, twenty-six in Asia and the Pacific, and none in the continental United States.[39] Simply because it was politically committed to the reordering of Japan and Germany (and Austria), it was "over there"; and because it had campaigned via island groups in the Pacific, and into North Africa, Italy, and western Europe, it had forces in those territories also. There were, however, many Americans (especially among the troops) who expected that they would all be home within a short period of time, returning U.S. armed-forces deployments to their pre-1941 position. But while that idea alarmed the likes of Churchill and attracted isolationist Republicans, it proved impossible to turn the clock back. Like the British after 1815, the Americans in their turn found their informal influence in various lands hardening into something more formal—and more entangling; like the British, too, they found "new frontiers of insecurity" whenever they wanted to draw the line. The "Pax Americana" had come of age.[40]

The economic aspects of this new order were, at least, predictable enough. During the war, internationalists like Cordell Hull had argued, with some reason, that the global crisis of the 1930s had been in large part caused by a malfunctioning of the international economy: by protective tariffs, unfair economic competition, restricted access to raw materials, autarkic governmental policies. This eighteenth-century Enlightenment belief that "unhampered trade dovetails with peace"[41] was joined by the pressures exerted by export-oriented industries, which feared that a postwar slump might follow the decline in U.S. government spending unless new overseas markets were opened up to absorb the products of America's enhanced productivity. To this was added a determined, and perhaps excessive, advocacy by the military to ensure American control of (or unrestricted access to) strategically critical materials such as oil, rubber, and metal ores.[42] All this combined to make the United States committed to the creation of a new world order beneficial to the needs of western capitalism and, of course, to the most flourishing of the western capitalist states—though with the longer-term, Adam Smithian assurance that "the more efficient distribution of resources brought about by unimpeded trade would raise productivity all around and thus increase everybody's purchasing power."[43] Hence the package of international arrangements hammered out between 1942 and 1946—the setting-up of the International Monetary Fund, of the International Bank for Reconstruction and Development—and then the later General Agreement on Tariffs and Trade (GATT). Those countries wishing to secure some of the monies available for reconstruction and development under this new economic regime found themselves obliged to conform to American requirements on free convertibility of currencies and open competition (as the British did, despite their efforts to preserve imperial preference)[44]—or to stand clear of the entire system (as the Russians did, when they perceived how incompatible this was with socialist controls).

The practical flaws in such arrangements were, first, that the amount of money available was simply insufficient to deal with the devastation caused by six years of total war; and, secondly, that a laissez-faire system inevitably works to the advantage of the country in the most competitive position—in this case, the undamaged, hyperproductive United States—and to the detriment of those less well equipped to compete—nations devastated by war, with boundaries altered, masses of refugees, bombed-out housing, worn-out machinery, ruinous debts, lost markets. Only the later American perception of the twin dangers of widespread social discontent in Europe and growing Soviet influence, which stimulated the creation of the Marshall Plan, permitted funds to be released for the substantial industrial redevelopment of the "free world." By that time, however, the expansion of American economic influence was going hand in hand with the erection of an array of military-base and security treaties across the globe (below, pp. 389–90). Here, too, there are many parallels with the expansion of British bases and treaty relationships after 1815; but the most noticeable difference was that Britain, on the whole, was able to avoid the plethora of fixed and entangling alliances with other sovereign countries which the United States was now assuming. Almost all of these American commitments were, it is true, "a response to events"[45] as the Cold War unfolded; but regardless of the justification, the blunt fact was that they involved the United States in a degree of global overstretch totally at variance with its own earlier history.

Little of this seems to have worried the decision-makers of 1945, many of whom appear to have felt not only that this was the working out of "manifest destiny," but that they now had a golden opportunity to put right what the former Great Powers had managed to mess up. "American experience," exulted Henry Luce of *Life* magazine, "is the key to the future. . . . America must be the elder brother of nations in the brotherhood of man."[46] Not only China, in which extremely high hopes were placed, but all of the other countries of what was soon to be termed the Third World were encouraged to emulate American ideals of self-help, entrepreneurship, free trade, and democracy. "All these principles and policies are so beneficial and appealing to the sense of justice, of right and of the well-being of free peoples everywhere," Hull prophesized, "that in the course of a few years the entire international machinery should be working fairly satisfactorily."[47] Whoever was so purblind as not to appreciate that fact—whether old-fashioned British and Dutch imperialists, or leftward-tending European political parties, or the grim-faced Molotov—would be persuaded, by a mixture of sticks and carrots, in the right direction. As one American official put it, "It is now our turn to bat in Asia";[48] and, he might have added, nearly everywhere else as well.

The one area where American influence was highly unlikely to penetrate was that controlled by the Soviet Union, which in 1945 (and ever since) claimed to be the true victor of the fight against fascism. According to the Red Army's statistics, it had smashed a total of 506 German divisions; and of the 13.6 million German casualties and prisoners lost during the Second World War, 10 million met their fate on the eastern front.[49] Yet even before the Third Reich had collapsed, Stalin was switching dozens of divisions to the Far East, ready to unleash them upon Japan's denuded Kwantung Army in Manchuria when the time was ripe; which turned out to be, perhaps unsurprisingly, three days after Hiroshima. The extended campaign on the western front more than reversed the disastrous post-1917 slump in Russia's position in Europe; indeed, it actually restored it to something akin to that of the period 1814–1848, when its great army had been the gendarme of east-central Europe. Russian territorial boundaries expanded, in the north at the expense of Finland, in the center at the expense of Poland; and in the south, recovering Bessarabia, at the expense of Rumania. The Baltic states of Estonia, Latvia, and Lithuania were reincorporated into Russia. Part of East Prussia was taken, and a slice of eastern Czechoslovakia (Ruthenia, or Subcarpathian Ukraine) was also thoughtfully added, so that there was direct access to Hungary. To the west and southwest of this enhanced Russia lay a new *cordon sanitaire* of satellite states, Poland, East Germany, Czechoslovakia, Hungary, Rumania, Bulgaria, and (until they wriggled free) Yugoslavia and Albania. Between them and the West, the proverbial "iron curtain" was falling; behind that curtain, Communist party cadres and secret police were determining that the entire region would operate under principles totally at variance with Cordell Hull's hopes. The same was true in the Far East, where the swift occupation of Manchuria, North Korea, and Sakhalin not only avenged the war of 1904–1905, but allowed a link-up with Mao's Chinese Communists, who were also unlikely to swallow the gospel of laissez-faire capitalism.

But if this growth of Soviet influence looked imposing, its economic base had been badly hurt by the war—in contrast to the United States' undisturbed boom. Russia's population losses were appalling: 7.5 million in the armed forces; 6–8 million civilians killed by the Germans; plus the "indirect" war losses caused by the reduced food rations, forced labor, and vastly increased hours of work, so that "altogether probably some 20–25 million Soviet citizens died premature deaths between 1941 and 1945."[50] Since the casualties were mainly men, the consequent imbalance between the sexes greatly affected the country's demographic structure and caused a severe drop in the birthrate. The material damage done in the German-occupied parts of European Russia, the Ukraine, and Belorussia was so large as to be beyond normal imaginings:

> Of the 11.6 million horses in occupied territory, 7 million were killed or taken away, as were 20 out of 23 million pigs. 137,000 tractors, 49,000 grain combines and large numbers of cowsheds and other farm buildings were destroyed. Transport was hit by the destruction of 65,000 kilometers of railway track, loss of or damage to 15,800 locomotives, 428,000 goods wagons, 4,280 river boats, and half of all the railway bridges in the occupied territory. Almost 50 percent of all urban living space in this territory, 1.2 million houses, were destroyed, as well as 3.5 million houses in rural areas.
>
> Many towns lay in ruins. Thousands of villages were smashed. People lived in holes in the ground.[51]

It was scarcely surprising, therefore, that when the Russians moved into their "occupation zone" in Germany, they attempted to strip it of all movable assets, factory plant, rail lines, etc., as well as demanding compensations from other eastern European territories (Rumanian oil, Finnish timber, Polish coal).

It was true that the Soviet Union had outproduced Greater Germany in the armaments battle as well as outfighting it at the front; but it had done so by an incredibly single-minded concentration upon military-industrial production and by drastic decreases in every other sector—consumer goods, retail trade, and agricultural supplies (though the decline in food output was chiefly caused by German plunderings).[52] In essence, therefore, the Russia of 1945 was a military giant and, at the same time, economically poor, deprived, and unbalanced. With Lend-Lease cut off, and having rejected later American monies because of the political conditions attached to them, the Soviet Union reverted to its post-1928 program of enforced economic growth from its own resources—with the same strong emphasis upon producer goods (heavy industry, coal, electricity, cement) and transport to the detriment of consumer goods and agriculture, and with a natural reduction in military expenditures from their wartime levels. The result, after initial difficulties, was "a minor economic miracle"[53] so far as heavy industry was concerned, with output nearly doubling between 1945 and 1950. Obsessed by the need to rebuild the sinews of national power, the Stalinist regime had no problems in achieving that crude aim or in keeping the standard of living for most Russians down at pre-Revolution levels. Yet it also ought to be noted that, as with the post-1922 growth, much of the "recovery" of industrial production consisted of getting back to the *prewar* output; in the Ukraine, for example, metallurgical and electrical output around 1950 had reached, or just exceeded, the 1940 figures. Once again, because of war, Russia's economic growth had been choked back by a decade or so. More serious still, in the longer term, was the continued failure of the vital agricultural sector: with the emergency wartime incentive measures suppressed, and because of the totally inadequate (and misdirected) investment, farming wilted and food output slumped. Until his death, Stalin maintained his bitter vendetta against the peasantry's preference for private plots, thereby ensuring that the traditional low productivity and high inefficiency of Russian agriculture would continue.[54]

By contrast, Stalin was clearly intent upon maintaining a high level of military security in the postwar world. Given the need to rebuild the economy, it was not surprising that the enormous Red Army was reduced by two-thirds after 1945, to the still very substantial total of 175 divisions, supported by 25,000 front-line tanks and 19,000 aircraft. It still would remain, therefore, the largest defense establishment in the world—a fact justified (in Soviet eyes, at least) by its need to deter future aggressors and, more prosaically, to keep control of its newly acquired satellites in Europe as well as its conquests in the Far East. Although this was an enormous force, many of its divisions existed only in skeleton form, or were essentially garrison troops.[55] Moreover, the service ran the danger which had befallen the gigantic Russian army in the decades after 1815—increasing obsolescence, in the face of new military advances. This was to be combated not only by a substantial reorganization and modernization of the army's divisions,[56] but also by committing the economic and scientific resources of the Soviet state to the development of new weapon systems. By 1947–1948, the formidable MiG-15 jet fighter was going into service, and—in imitation of the Americans and British—a long-range strategic air force had been created. Captured German scientists and technicians were being used to develop a variety of guided missiles. Even during the war, resources had been allocated for the development of a Soviet A-bomb. And the Russian navy, which had been a mere ancillary arm in the struggle against Germany, was also being transformed, with the addition of new heavy cruisers and even more oceangoing submarines. Much of this weaponry was derivative and, by western standards, unsophisticated. What could not be doubted, however, was the Soviet determination not to be left behind.[57]

The third major element in the buttressing of Russian power was Stalin's renewed emphasis upon the internal discipline and absolute conformism of the late 1930s. Whether this was due to his increasing paranoia or a carefully calculated set of moves to reinforce his own dictatorial position—or a mixture of both—is hard to say; but the events spoke for themselves.[58] Anyone with foreign connections was suspect; returning prisoners-of-war were shot; the creation of the state of Israel, and thus an alternative source of Jewish loyalties, led to renewed anti-Semitic measures within Russia. The army leadership was cut down to size, with the respected Marshal Zhukov being removed as commander of the Soviet ground forces in 1946. Discipline within the Communist party itself, and admission to the same, was tightened; in 1948, the entire party leadership of Leningrad (which Stalin always disliked) was purged. Censorship was intensified, not only over literature and the creative arts, but also over the natural sciences, biology, linguistics. This overall "tightening" of the system naturally fitted in with the reasserted collectivization of agriculture mentioned earlier, and with the rise of Cold War tensions. It was also natural that a similar process of ideological stiffening and totalitarian controls should take place in the Soviet-dominated states of eastern Europe, where the elimination of rival parties, the holdings of show trials, the drive against individual rights and properties, became the order of the day. All this, and in particular the elimination of democracy in Poland and (in 1948) in Czechoslovakia, led to a considerable ebbing of western enthusiasm for the Soviet system. Again, it is unclear whether these measures were all carefully calculated—there was, and is, a crude logic in the Soviet elite's desire to isolate its satellites as well as its own people from the ideas and riches of the West—or whether it simply reflected Stalin's increasing paranoia as his end approached. Whatever the cause, there would be one massive stretch of territory totally immune from the influences of any "Pax Americana," and indeed offering an alternative to it.

This growth of the Soviet Empire appeared to confirm the geopolitical predictions of Mackinder and others that a gigantic military power would control the resources of the Eurasian "Heartland"; and that the further expansion of that state into the periphery or "Rimland" would need to be contested by the great maritime states if they were to preserve a global balance of power.[59] It would still be another few years before U.S. administrations, shaken by the Korean War, completely abandoned their earlier ideas of "One World" and replaced them with the image of an unrelenting superpower struggle across the international arena. Yet to a large extent this was implicit in the circumstances of 1945; the United States and the USSR were the only nations now capable, as de Tocqueville had once put it, of swaying the destinies of half the globe; and both had fallen prey to "globalist" thinking. "The USSR now is one of the mightiest countries of the world. One cannot decide now *any* serious problems of international relations without the USSR . . ." Molotov claimed in 1946,[60] an echo of the earlier American intimation to Moscow (when it seemed that Churchill and Stalin might come to a private agreement over eastern Europe) that "in this global war there is literally no question, political or military, in which the United States is not interested."[61] A serious clash of interests was inevitable.

But what of those former Great Powers, now merely middleweight countries, whose collapse was the obverse side of the rise of the superpowers? It needs to be said immediately that the defeated fascist states of Germany, Japan, and Italy were in a different category from that of Great Britain and, perhaps, of France also in the immediate post-1945 period. When the fighting ceased, the Allies went ahead with their plans to ensure that neither Germany nor Japan would ever again be a threat to the international order. This involved not only the long-term military occupation of both countries but, in the German case, its division into four occupation zones and then, later, into two separate German states. Japan was stripped of its overseas acquisitions (as was Italy in 1943), Germany of its European gains and of its older territories in the east (Silesia, East Prussia, etc.). The devastation caused by the strategic bombing, the overstraining of the transport system, the decline of the housing stock, and the lack of many raw materials and export markets was compounded by the Allied controls upon industry—and, in Germany, by the dismantling of industrial plant. German national income and output in 1946 was less than one-third that of 1938, a horrendous reduction.[62] In Japan, a similar economic regression had occurred; real national income in 1946 was only 57 percent that of 1934–1936 and real manufacturing wages were down to only 30 percent of the same; foreign trade was so minimal that even two years later, exports were only 8 percent and imports 18 percent of the 1934–1936 figure. Japan's shipping had been eliminated by the war, the number of cotton spindles cut from 12.2 million to 2 million, coal output halved, and so on.[63] Economically as well as militarily, their days as powerful nations seemed over.

Although Italy had switched sides in 1943, its economic fate was almost as grim. For two years, Allied forces had fought and bombed their way up the peninsula, severely adding to the damage caused by Mussolini's strategical extravagances. "In 1945 . . . Italy's gross national product had reverted to the 1911 level and had diminished by about 40 percent in real terms, as compared with 1938. The population, despite war losses, had increased largely as a result of repatriation from the colonies and the halt in emigration. The standard of living was alarmingly low, and but for international aid, especially from the United States, many Italians would have died of starvation."[64] Italian real wages were down to 26.7 percent of their 1913 value by 1945.[65] In fact, all of these countries were terribly dependent upon American aid during this period; and, as such, were little more than economic satellites.

It was difficult to tell the difference, in economic terms, between France and Germany. Four years of plundering by the Germans had been followed by months of large-scale fighting in 1944; "most waterways and harbors were blocked, most bridges destroyed, much of the railway system temporarily unusable."[66] Fohlen's indices of French imports and exports shows them plunging to virtually nothing by 1944–1945; France's national income by that time was only half that of 1938, itself a gloomy year.[67] France had no stocks of foreign currency, and the franc itself had not been accepted on the foreign exchanges; its value, when fixed at 50 to the dollar in 1944, was "purely fictitious,"[68] and within a year it had slid to 119 to the dollar; by 1949, when things seemed more stable, it was 420 to the dollar. French party politics, and in particular the role of the Communist party, obviously interacted with these purely economic problems of reconstruction, nationalization, and inflation.

On the other hand, the Free French had been members of the "Grand Alliance" against fascism and had fought in many of the major campaigns, as well as triumphing in their "civil" war against pro-Vichy forces in West Africa, the Levant, and Algeria. Given the German occupation of France and the division in French loyalties during the war, de Gaulle's organization was heavily dependent upon Anglo-American aid—which de Gaulle resented, even as he demanded more. Nonetheless, the British were eager to see France reestablished as a strong military Power in Europe as a check to Russia, rather than a collapsing Germany, and so France acquired many of the accouterments of Great Power status: an occupation zone in Germany, permanent membership in the UN Security Council, and so on. Although it could not regain its former mandates in Syria and Lebanon, it did seek to reassert itself in Indochina and in the protectorates of Tunisia and Morocco; and with its overseas departments and territories, it still possessed the second-largest colonial empire in the world and was determined to hang on to it.[69] To many outside observers, especially the Americans, this attempt to regain the trappings of first-class power status while so desperately weak economically—and so dependent upon American financial support—was nothing more than a *folie de grandeur*. And so, to a large extent, it was. Perhaps its chief consequence was to disguise, at least for some more years, the extent to which the strategical landscape of the globe had been altered by the war.

Although most Britons in 1945 would have felt indignant at the comparison, the continued appearance of their nation and empire as one of the Great Powers of the world also disguised the new strategical balances—as well as making it psychologically difficult for decision-makers in London to readjust to the politics of decline. The British Empire was the only major state which had fought through the Second World War from beginning to end. Under Churchill's leadership, it had been unquestionably one of the "Big Three." Its military performance, at sea, in the air, even on land, had been significantly better than in the First World War. By August 1945, all the possessions of the king-emperor—including Hong Kong—were back in British hands. British troops and airbases were sprawled across North Africa, Italy, Germany, Southeast Asia. Despite heavy losses, the Royal Navy possessed over 1,000 warships, nearly 3,000 minor war vessels, and nearly 5,500 landing craft. RAF Bomber Command was the second-largest strategic air force (by far) in the world. And yet, as Correlli Barnett has forcefully pointed out, "victory" was not

> synonymous with the preservation of British power. The defeat of Germany [and its allies] was only one factor, if a highly important factor, in such a preservation. For Germany might be defeated and yet British power still be brought to an end. What counted was not so much "victory" in itself, but the circumstances of the victory, and in particular the circumstances in which England found herself. . . .[70]

For the blunt fact was that in securing a victorious outcome to the war the British had severely overstrained themselves, running down their gold and dollar reserves, wearing out their domestic machinery, and (despite an extraordinary mobilization of their resources and population) becoming increasingly dependent upon American munitions, shipping, foodstuffs, and other supplies to stay in the fighting. While its need for such imports had risen year by year, its export trade had withered away—by 1944 it was a mere 31 percent of the 1938 figure. When the Labor government entered office in July 1945, one of the first documents it had to read was Keynes's hair-raising memorandum about the "financial Dunkirk" which the country was facing: its colossal trade gap, its weakened industrial base, its enormous overseas establishments, meant that American aid was desperately needed, to replace the cut-off Lend-Lease. Without that help, indeed, "a greater degree of austerity would be necessary than we have experienced at any time during the war. . . ."[71] Once again, as happened after the First World War, the goal of creating a home fit for heroes would have to be modified. But this time, it was impossible to believe that Britain was still at the center of the world politically.

Yet, the illusions of Great Power status lingered on, even among Labor ministers intent upon creating a "welfare state." The history of the next few years therefore involved an earnest British attempt to grapple with these irreconcilables—improving domestic standards of living, moving to a "mixed economy," closing the trade gap, and at the same time supporting a vastly extended array of overseas bases, in Germany, the Near East, and India, and maintaining large armed forces in the face of the worsening relations with Russia. As the detailed studies of the Attlee administration suggest,[72] it was remarkably successful in many respects: industrial productivity rose, the trade gap narrowed, social reforms were enacted, the European scene was stabilized. The Labor government also found it prudent to withdraw from India, to pull out of the chaos in Palestine, and to abandon the guarantees to Greece and Turkey, so that it was relieved of at least some of its more pressing overseas burdens. On the other hand, that economic recovery had itself depended upon the large loan Keynes had negotiated in Washington in 1945, upon the further massive support which came via Marshall Plan aid, and upon the still-devastated state of most of Britain's commercial rivals; it was, therefore, a delicate and conditional economic revival. Equally suspect, over the longer term, was the success of the British withdrawals of 1947. It certainly shed intolerable burdens; but that strategical "fancy footwork" was postulated on the assumption that in abandoning certain regions, Britain could relocate its bases to accord more with its real imperial interests—the Suez Canal rather than Palestine, Arabian oil rather than India. At this stage, there certainly was no intention in Whitehall of giving up the *rest* of the dependent empire, which in economic terms was more important to Britain than ever before.[73] Only further shocks and the rising costs of hanging on would later force another reappraisal of Britain's place in the world. In the meantime, however, it would remain an overextended but still powerful strategical entity, dependent upon the United States for security and yet also that country's most useful ally—and an important strategic collaborator—in a world dividing into two large power blocs.[74]

All the efforts of British and French governments to the contrary, however, there was no doubt about "the passing of the European age." While the U.S. GNP had surged by more than 50 percent in real terms during the war, Europe's as a whole (but minus the Soviet Union) had fallen by about 25 percent.[75] Europe's share of total world manufacturing output was lower than at any time since the early nineteenth century; even by 1953, when most of the war damage had been repaired, it possessed only 26 percent of the whole (compared with the United States' 44.7 percent).[76] Its population was now only about 15–16 percent of the total world population. In 1950 its per capita GNP was only about one-half of the United States'; moreover, the Soviet Union had by then significantly closed the gap, so that the total GNP of the powers was as shown in Table 36.

Table 36. Total GNP and per Capita GNP of the Powers in 1950[77]
(in 1964 dollars)

	Total GNP	Per Capita GNP
United States	381 billion	2,536
USSR	126	699
U.K.	71	1,393 (1951)
France	50	1,172
West Germany	48	1,001
Japan	32	382
Italy	29	626 (1951)

This eclipse of the European powers was reflected even more markedly in military personnel and expenditures. In 1950, for example, the United States spent $14.5 billion on defense and had 1.38 million military personnel, while the USSR spent slightly more ($15.5 billion) on its far larger armed forces of 4.3 million men. In both respects, the superpowers were far ahead of Britain ($2.3 billion; 680,000 personnel), France ($1.4 billion; 590,000 personnel), and Italy ($0.5 billion; 230,000 personnel), and of course Germany and Japan were still demilitarized. The Korean War tensions saw quite significant increases in the defense spending of the middleweight European powers in 1951, but they paled by comparison with the expenditures of the United States ($33.3 billion) and USSR ($20.1 billion). In that year alone, the defense expenditures of Britain, France, and Italy *combined* were less than one-fifth of the United States' and less than one third of the USSR's; and their *combined* military personnel was one-half of the United States' and one-third of Russia's.[78] In both relative economic strength and in military power, the European states seemed decidedly eclipsed.

Such an impression was, if anything, heightened by the coming of nuclear weapons and long-range delivery systems. It is clear from the record that many of the scientists working on the A-bomb were acutely aware that they were reaching toward a watershed in the entire history of warfare, weapon systems, and man's capacity for destruction; the successful test at Alamogordo on July 16, 1945, confirmed to the observers that "there had been brought into being something big and something new that would prove to be immeasurably more important than the discovery of electricity or any of the other great discoveries which have affected our existence." When the "strong, sustained, awesome roar which warned of doomsday"[79] was repeated in the actual

carnage of Hiroshima and Nagasaki, there could be no further doubt
of the weapon's power. Its creation left American decision-makers
wrestling with the many practical consequences for the future. How
did it affect conventional warfare? Should it be used immediately at the
outset of war, or as a weapon of last resort? What were the implications, and potentialities, of developing bigger (H-bombs) and smaller
(tactical) forms of nuclear weapons? Should the knowledge be shared
with others?[80] It also undoubtedly gave a boost to the already existing
Soviet development of nuclear weapons, since Stalin put his formidable security chief, Beria, in charge of the atomic program on the day
after Hiroshima.[81] Although the Russians were clearly behind at this
time, in the creation of both bombs and delivery systems, they caught
up much faster than the Americans estimated they would. For some
years after 1945, it seems fair to assume that the American nuclear
advantage helped to "balance out" the Russian preponderance in conventional forces. But it was not long, certainly in the history of international relations, before Moscow began to catch up and thus to prove
its own claim that the United States' monopoly of this weapon had
been only a passing phase.[82]

The coming of atomic weapons transformed the "strategical landscape," since they gave to any state possessing them the capability of
mass indiscriminate destruction, even of mankind itself. Much more
narrowly, and immediately, the advent of this new level in weapons
technology put increased pressure upon the traditional European
states to catch up—or admit that they were indeed relegated to second-
class status. Of course, in the case of Germany and Japan, and the
economically and technologically weakened Italy, there was no prospect of joining the nuclear club. But to the government in London,
even when Attlee replaced Churchill, it was inconceivable that the
country should not possess those weapons, both as a deterrent and
because they "were a manifestation of the scientific and technological
superiority on which Britain's strength, so deficient if measured in
sheer numbers of men, must depend."[83] They were seen, in other
words, as a relatively *cheap* way of retaining independent Great Power
influence—a calculation which, shortly afterward, appealed equally to
the French.[84] Yet, however attractive that logic appeared to be, it was
weakened by practical factors: that neither state would possess the
weapons, and delivery systems, for some years; and that their nuclear
arsenals would be minor compared with those of the superpowers, and
might indeed be made obsolete by a further leap in technology. For all
the ambitions of London and Paris (and, later on, China) to join the
nuclear club, this striving during the early post-1945 decades was
somewhat similar to the Austro-Hungarian and Italian efforts to possess their own *Dreadnought*-type battleships prior to 1914. It was, in
other words, a reflection of weakness rather than strength.

The final element which seemed to emphasize that the world must now be viewed, strategically and politically, as bipolar rather than in its traditional multipolar form was the heightened role of *ideology*. To be sure, even in the age of classical nineteenth-century diplomacy, ideological factors had played a part in policy—as the actions of Metternich, Nicholas I, Bismarck, and Gladstone amply testified. This seemed much more the case in the interwar years, when a "radical right" and a "radical left" arose to challenge the prevailing assumptions of the "bourgeois-liberal center." Nonetheless, the complex dynamics of multipolar rivalries by the late 1930s (with British Tories like Churchill wanting an alliance with Communist Russia against Nazi Germany, and with liberal Americans wanting to support Anglo-French diplomacy in Europe but to dismantle the British and French empires outside Europe) made difficult all attempts to explain world affairs in ideological terms. During the war itself, moreover, differences on political and social principles could be subsumed under the overriding need to combat fascism. Stalin's suppression of the Communist International in 1943 and the West's admiration for the Russian resistance to Operation Barbarossa also seemed to blur earlier suspicions—especially in the United States, where *Life* magazine in 1943 airily claimed that the Russians "look like Americans, dress like Americans and think like Americans," and the *New York Times* a year later declared that "Marxian thinking in Soviet Russia is out."[85] Such sentiments, however naive, help to explain the widespread American reluctance to accept that the postwar world was not living up to their vision of international harmony—hence, for example, the pained and angry reactions of many to Churchill's famous "Iron Curtain" speech of March 1946.[86]

Yet, within another year or two, the ideological nature of what was now admitted to be the Cold War between Russia and the West was all too evident. The increasing signs that Russia would not permit parliamentary-type democracy in eastern Europe, the sheer size of the Russian armed forces, the civil war raging between Communists and their opponents in Greece, China, and elsewhere, and—last but by no means least—the growing fears of "the Red menace," spy rings, and internal subversion at home led to a massive swing in American sentiment, and one to which the Truman administration responded with alacrity. In his "Truman Doctrine" speech of March 1947, occasioned by the fear that Russia would enter into the power vacuum created by Britain's withdrawal of guarantees to Greece and Turkey, the president portrayed a world faced with a choice between two different sets of ideological principles:

> One way of life is based upon the will of the majority, and is distinguished by free institutions, representative government, free elections, guarantees of individual liberty, freedom of speech and

religion and freedom from political oppression. The second way of
life is based upon the will of a minority forcibly imposed on the
majority. It relies upon terror and oppression, a controlled press,
framed elections and the suppression of personal freedom.[87]

It would be the policy of the United States, Truman continued, "to help
free people to maintain their institutions and their integrity against
aggressive movements that seek to impose upon them totalitarian
regimes." Henceforward, international affairs would be presented, in
even more emotional terms, as a Manichean struggle; in Eisenhower's
words, "Forces of good and evil are massed and armed and opposed
as rarely before in history. Freedom is pitted against slavery, lightness
against dark."[88]

No doubt much of this rhetoric had a domestic purpose—and not
just in the United States, but also in Britain, Italy, France, and wherever it was useful for conservative forces to invoke such language to
discredit their rivals, or to attack their own governments for being
"soft on Communism." What was also true was that it must have deepened Stalin's suspicions of the West, which was swiftly portrayed in the
Soviet press as contesting the Russian "sphere of influence" in eastern
Europe, surrounding the Soviet Union with new foes on all sides,
establishing forward bases, supporting reactionary regimes against
any Communist influences, and deliberately "packing" the United Nations. "The new course of American foreign policy," Moscow claimed,
"meant a return to the old anti-Soviet course, designed to unloose war
and forcibly to institute world domination by Britain and the United
States."[89] This explanation, in turn, could help the Soviet regime to
justify its crackdown upon internal dissidents, its tightening grip upon
eastern Europe, its forced industrialization, its heavy spending upon
armaments. Thus, the foreign and domestic requirements of the Cold
War could feed off each other, mutually covered by an appeal to ideological principles. Liberalism and Communism, being both universal
ideas, were "mutually exclusive";[90] this permitted each side to understand, and to portray, the whole world as an arena in which the ideological quarrel could not be separated from power-political advantage.
One was either in the American-led bloc or the Soviet one. There was
to be no middle way; in an age of Stalin and Joe McCarthy, it was
imprudent to think that there could be. This was the new strategical
reality, to which not merely the peoples of a divided Europe but also
those in Asia, the Middle East, Africa, Latin America, and elsewhere
would have to adjust.

The Cold War and the Third World

As it turned out, a large part of international politics over the following two decades *was* to concern itself with adjusting to that Soviet-American rivalry, and then with its partial rejection. In the beginning, the Cold War was centered upon remaking the boundaries of Europe. Underneath, therefore, it was still to do with the "German problem," since the resolution of that issue would in turn determine the amount of influence which the victorious Powers of 1945 would exert over Europe. The Russians had undoubtedly suffered more than any other country from German aggressions in the first half of the twentieth century, and, reinforced by Stalin's own paranoid demand for security, they were determined to permit no repetitions in the second half. Promoting the Communist world revolution was a secondary but not unconnected consideration, since Russia's strategic and political position was most likely to be enhanced if it could create other Marxist-led states which looked to Moscow for guidance. Such considerations, much more than any centuries-old drive toward warm-water ports, probably ordered the Soviet policy in the post-1945 world, even if it left open the detailed solution of the various issues. There was, in the first place, therefore, a determination to undo the territorial settlements of 1918–1922, with "roundings-off" for strategical purposes; as noted above, this meant the reassertion of Russian control over the Baltic states, the pushing westward of the Polish-Russian border, the elimination of East Prussia, and the acquisition of territories from Finland, Hungary, and Rumania. Little of this worried the West; indeed, much of it had been agreed to during the war. What was more perturbing was the Russian indications of how they intended to ensure that the formerly independent countries of east-central Europe would contain regimes "friendly to Moscow."

In this respect, the fate of Poland was a harbinger of what would occur elsewhere, although it was the more poignant because of Britain's 1939 decision to fight for that country's integrity, and because of the Polish contingents (and government in exile) which had operated in the West. The discovery of the mass grave of Polish officers at Katyn, the Russian disapproval of the Warsaw uprising, Stalin's insistence on altering Poland's boundaries, and the appearance of a pro-Moscow faction of Poles at Lublin made Churchill in particular suspicious of Russia's intentions; within another few years, with the installation of a puppet regime and the virtual elimination of any pro-western Poles from positions of power, those fears were realized.[91]

Moscow's handling of the Polish issue related to the "German problem" in all sorts of ways. Territorially, the westward adjustment of the boundaries not only reduced the size of German lands (as did the swallowing-up of East Prussia), it also gave the Poles an incentive to oppose any future German revision of the Oder-Neisse line. Strategically, the Russian insistence upon making Poland a secure "buffer zone" was intended to ensure that there could be no repetition of Germany's 1941 attack; it was logical, therefore, for Moscow to insist upon determining the fate of the German people as well. Politically, the support of the "Lublin" Poles was paralleled by the grooming of German Communists in exile to play a similar role when they returned to their homeland. Economically, Russia's exploitation of Poland and its eastern European neighbors was a foretaste of the stripping of German assets. When, however, it became obvious to Moscow that it would be impossible to win the German people's goodwill while systematically reducing them to penury, the asset-stripping ceased and Molotov's tone became much more encouraging. But those tactical shifts were of less importance than the obvious message that Russia intended to have a, if not *the*, major say in deciding Germany's future.[92]

Both in the Polish and the German cases, then, Russian policy was bound to clash with that of the West. Politically and economically the Americans, British, and French desired free-market ideas and democratic elections to be the norm throughout Europe (although London and Paris clearly wished the state to occupy a larger place than the laissez-faire Americans preferred). Strategically, the West was just as determined as Moscow to prevent any revival of German militarism, and the French especially were to worry about that until the mid-1950s; but none of them wanted to see the Wehrmacht's domination of Europe merely replaced by the Red Army's. And although both the French and the Italian governments after 1945 contained Communists, there was a deep mistrust of Marxist parties gaining real power anywhere—a feeling confirmed by the steady elimination of non-Communist parties in eastern Europe. Although there were still voices hoping for a reconciliation between Russia and the West, the fact was that their respective aims clashed in all manner of ways. If one side's program succeeded, the other would feel threatened; in that sense, at least, the Cold War seemed inevitable, until both sides agreed to compromise on their universalist assumptions.

For that reason, a step-by-step account of the escalation of the tensions is not necessary here;[93] it would have the same relevance to this analysis of the evolving dynamics of world power as would, say, a detailed account of Metternich's diplomacy in an earlier chapter. The chief features of the Cold War after 1945 are, however, worthy of examination, since they have continued to affect the conduct of international relations to this day.

The first of these was the intensification of the "split" between the two blocs in Europe. That this bifurcation had not occurred immediately in 1945 was understandable: the chief tasks then for the Allied occupation forces, and for the "successor" parties which emerged out of hiding and exile once the Germans had left, were pressing administrative ones—restoring communications and utilities, getting foodstuffs to the cities, housing the refugees, tracking down war criminals. Much of this led to a blurring of ideological positions: in the occupied zones of Germany, the Americans found themselves quarreling as much with the French as with the Russians; in national assemblies and cabinets being formed across Europe, Socialists sat alongside Communists in the east, Communists alongside Christian Democrats in the west. But by late 1946 and early 1947, the gap was widening and becoming more publicized: various plebiscites and regional elections in the German zones were showing "the political complexion of West Germany . . . beginning to differ markedly from that of East Germany";[94] the steady elimination of any non-Communist elements in Poland, Bulgaria, and Rumania was mirrored by the internal political crisis in France in April 1947, when the Communists were forced to resign from the government. A month after, the same happened in Italy. In Yugoslavia, Tito's political domination (in place of the Allied wartime agreements about shared power) was interpreted by the West as a further step in Moscow's planned advance. These disagreements, together with the Soviet Union's unwillingness to join the IMF and International Bank, especially disturbed those Americans who had hoped to preserve good relations with Moscow after the war.

It was only a modest leap in assumptions, therefore, for the West to suspect that Stalin also planned to acquire control in *western* and *southern* Europe when the circumstances were right and, indeed, to hurry those circumstances along. This was unlikely to occur by outright military force, although the increasing Russian pressure upon Turkey was worrying, and prompted Washington to station a naval task force in the eastern Mediterranean by 1946; rather, it might come about through the ability of Moscow's minions to take advantage of the continued economic dislocation and political rivalries caused by the war. The Greek Communist revolt was seen as one sign of this; the Communist-supported strikes in France another. The Russian bids to woo German public opinion were suspicious; so, too, if one really wanted to worry about things, was the strength of the Communists in northern Italy. Historians of each of those movements are nowadays more skeptical of how much they could have been controlled by a Moscow-conceived "master plan." The Greek Communists, Tito, and Mao Tse-tung cared most about their local foes, not a global Marxist order; and the leaders of Communist parties and trade unions in the West had to respond, first and foremost, to their followers' mood. On the other hand, a gain for Communism in any of those countries would undoubtedly have been welcome to Russia, provided it did not lead to a major war; and it is easy to understand why, at the time, Soviet experts like George Kennan were sympathetically heard when they argued the case for "containing" the Soviet Union.

Among all of the varied elements of the fast-evolving "strategy of containment,"[95] two stood out. The first, admitted by Kennan to be negative in nature although increasingly preferred by the military chiefs as offering more solid guarantees of stability, was to indicate to Moscow those regions of the globe which the United States "cannot permit . . . to fall into hands hostile to us."[96] Such states would, therefore, be given military support to build up their powers of resistance; and a Soviet attack on them would be regarded virtually as a *casus belli.* Much more positive, however, was the American recognition that resistance to Russian subversion was weakened because of "the profound exhaustion of physical plant and of spiritual vigor" caused by the Second World War.[97] The most crucial component of any long-term containment policy would therefore be a massive program of U.S. economic aid, to permit the rebuilding of the shattered industries, farms, and cities of Europe and Japan; for that would not only make the latter far less likely to be tempted by Communist doctrines of class struggle and revolution, it would also help to readjust the *power balances* in America's favor. If, to use Kennan's very plausible geopolitical argument, there were only "five centers of industrial and military power in the world which are important to us from the standpoint of national security"[98]—the United States itself, its rival the USSR, Great Britain, Germany and central Europe, and Japan—then it followed that by keeping the three last-named areas in the western camp and by building up their strength, there would be a resultant "correlation of forces" which would ensure that the Soviet Union was permanently inferior. Equally obvious, this strategy would be regarded with profound suspicion by Stalin's Russia, especially since it included the restoration of its two recent enemies, Germany and Japan.

Once again, therefore, an exact chronology of the various steps taken by each side during and after the "watershed year" of 1947 is less important than the general consequences. The U.S. replacement of the British guarantees to Greece and Turkey—symbolically, a transfer of responsibilities from the former global policeman to the rising one, and as much a part of London's logic as of Washington's[99]—was justified by Truman in terms of a "doctrine" which had no regional limitations. In the European context, however, the open American willingness "to help free peoples maintain their institutions" could be linked to the earnest discussions which were taking place about how to deal with the widespread economic distress, the food shortages, and the scarcity of coal which were afflicting the continent. The American administration's solution—the so-called Marshall Plan for massive aid "to place Europe on its feet economically"—was deliberately presented as an offering to *all* European nations, whether Communist or not. But whatever the attractions of receiving that aid may have been to Moscow, it did involve joint cooperation with western Europe, just at a time when the Soviet economy had returned to the most rigid forms of socialization and collectivization; and it took no genius to see that the *raison d'être* for the plan was to convince Europeans everywhere that private enterprise was better able to bring them prosperity than Communism. The result of Molotov's walkout from the Paris talks on the plan, and of the Russian pressure upon Poland and Czechoslovakia not to apply for aid, was that Europe became much more divided than before. In western Europe, boosted by the billions of dollars of American aid (especially to the larger states of Britain, France, Italy, and West Germany), economic growth shot ahead, integrated into a North Atlantic trading network. In eastern Europe, Communist controls were being tightened. The Cominform was set up in 1947, as a sort of reconstituted and only half-disguised Communist International. The pluralist regime in Prague was ended by a Communist coup in 1948. While Tito's Yugoslavia managed to escape from Stalin's claustrophobic embrace, other satellites found themselves subject to purges, and in 1949 they were forced to join Comecon (Council of Mutual Economic Assistance), which, far from being a Soviet Marshall Plan was "simply a new piece of machinery for milking the satellites."[100] Churchill may have been a little premature in his "Iron Curtain" description of 1946; two years later, his words seemed realized.

The intensification of East-West economic rivalries was complemented at the military level, and once again Germany was at the center of the dispute. In March 1947 the British and French had signed the Dunkirk Treaty, whereby each pledged all-out military support to the other signatory in the event of an attack by Germany (even though the Foreign Office in London held that contingency to be "rather academic" and was more concerned about western Europe's internal weaknesses). In March 1948 this pact was extended, by the Brussels Treaty, to include the Benelux countries. The latter agreement did not mention Germany by name, but it is fair to say that many politicians in western Europe (especially France) were still obsessed with the "German problem" at this time rather than the "Russian problem."[101] The antediluvian nature of their concerns was to be shaken up as 1948 unfolded. In the same month as the Brussels Treaty was signed, the Russians walked out of the Four-Power Control Council on Germany, claiming irreconcilable differences with the West over that country's economic and political future. Three months later, in an effort to end the black market and currency chaos in Germany, the three western control powers announced the creation of a new deutsche mark. The Russian response to this unilateral action was not only to ban the West German notes from their zone but to clamp down on movements in and out of Berlin, that island of western influence one hundred miles into their sphere.

If anything brought the extent of the antagonism close to home, it was the Berlin crisis of 1948–1949.[102] Already officials in Washington and London were discussing means whereby a grouping of the European states, the dominions, and the United States could stand together in the event of hostilities with Russia. While—as with the Marshall Plan—the Americans wished the Europeans to come forward first with schemes for military security, there was by this stage no doubt as to how seriously the United States took the Communist challenge. A full-blown "Red scare" at home complemented tougher actions abroad. In March 1948, Truman was even asking Congress to reinstate conscription, a request granted in the Selective Service Act of June of that year. All of these moves were boosted by the Soviet blockade of the land routes to Berlin. While the age of air power enabled the Americans and British to call Stalin's bluff by flying supplies into Berlin for the next eleven months, until the land access was restored, there had been many who argued for sending a military convoy to force its way to the city. It is difficult to believe that such an action would not have provoked a war; as it was, under a new treaty the United States moved a fleet of B-29 bombers to British airfields, a sign of their earnestness in the matter.

In these circumstances, even isolationist senators could be moved to support proposals for the creation of what was to be the North Atlantic Treaty Organization, with full American membership—and, indeed, with its chief strategical purpose being the provision of North American aid to the European states in the event of Russian aggression. In its early years, NATO reflected political concerns more than any exact military calculations, symbolizing as it did the historic shift in American diplomatic traditions as it took over from Britain as the leading western "flank" power, dedicated to maintaining the European equilibrium. In the view of the American and British governments, the chief task had been to tie the United States and Canada to the Brussels Pact signatories, and to extend the promise of mutual support to countries like Norway and Italy, which also felt insecure. On the day that the NATO treaty was signed, in fact, the U.S. Army had a mere 100,000 troops in Europe (compared with 3 million in 1945), and there existed only twelve divisions—seven French, two British, two American, one Belgian—in place to resist a Soviet push westward. Although the Russian forces at this period were nowhere near as large or capable as alarmist voices in the West claimed, the imbalance in each bloc's troop totals was disquieting; slightly later, those fears were increased by the thought that the Communists could sweep over the northern German plain as swiftly as they had crossed the Yalu during the Korean War. This meant that while the NATO strategy increasingly relied upon the "massive retaliation" of American long-range bombers to answer a Soviet invasion, there was a commitment to build up large conventional armed forces as well. In turn, this had the effect of tying all three of the western "flank" Powers—the United States, Canada, and Britain—to permanent military obligations on the continent of Europe to a degree which would have amazed their respective strategic planners in the 1930s.[103]

The NATO alliance did militarily what the Marshall plan had done economically; it deepened the 1945 division of Europe into two camps, with only traditional neutrals (Switzerland, Sweden), Franco's Spain, and certain special cases (Finland, Austria, Yugoslavia) in neither one nor the other. It was to be answered, in due course, by the Soviet-dominated Warsaw Pact. This deepening division, in turn, made the prospects for a reunification of Germany ever more remote. Despite French worries, the West German armed forces began to be built up within the NATO structure by the late 1950s—which was logical enough, if the West really wanted to narrow the gap in troop totals.[104] But that inevitably moved the USSR to develop an East German army, albeit under special controls. With each German state integrated into its respective military alliance, it became inevitable that both blocs would regard any future German attempt to become neutral with alarm and suspicion, as a blow to their own security. In Russia's case, this was reinforced, even after Stalin's death in 1953, by the conviction that any country which had become Communist should not be permitted to abandon that creed (the "Brezhnev Doctrine," to use later parlance). By October 1953, the U.S. National Security Council had privately accepted that the eastern European satellite states "could be freed only by general war or by the Russians themselves." As Bartlett cryptically notes, "Neither was possible."[105] In 1953, too, a rising in East Germany was swiftly put down. In 1956, alarmed at the Hungarian decision to withdraw from the Warsaw Pact, Russia moved its divisions back into that land and suppressed its independence. In 1961, in an admission of defeat, Khrushchev ordered the erection of the Berlin Wall to stem the flow of talent to the West. In 1968, the Czechs suffered the same fate as the Hungarians twelve years earlier, though the bloodshed was less. Each of these measures, taken by a Soviet leadership incapable (despite its official propaganda) of matching either the ideological or the economic appeal of the West, simply added to the division between the two blocs.[106]

The second main feature of the Cold War, its steady *lateral* escalation from Europe itself into the rest of the world, was hardly surprising. During much of the war itself, there had been an almost single-minded concentration of Russian energies upon dealing with the German threat; but that did not mean that Moscow had abandoned its political interest in the future of Turkey, Persia, and the Far East—

as was made plain in August 1945. It was therefore highly unlikely that
Russia's quarrels with the West over European issues would be geographically limited to that continent, especially since the principles in
dispute were of universal application—self-government versus national security, economic liberalism versus socialist planning, and so
on. More important still, the war itself had caused immense social and
political turbulence, from the Balkans to the East Indies; and even in
countries not directly overrun by invading armies (for example, India,
or Egypt), the mobilization of manpower, resources, and *ideas* had led
to profound changes. Traditional social orders lay smashed, colonial
regimes had been discredited, underground nationalist parties had
flourished, and resistance movements had grown up, committed not
only to military victory but also to political transformation.[107] There
was, in other words, an immense degree of political turbulence in the
world situation of 1945, which could be a threat to Great Powers eager
to restore peacetime stability as soon as possible; but this could also
be an opportunity for each of the superpowers, imbued with their
universalist doctrines, to bid for support among the vast swathe of
peoples emerging from the debris of the collapsed older order. During
the war itself, the Allies had given aid to all manner of resistance
movements struggling against their German and Japanese overlords,
and it was natural for those groups to hope for a continuation of such
aid after 1945, even while they engaged in jostling with rival contenders for power. That some of these partisan groups were Communist
and others bitterly anti-Communist made it more difficult than ever for
decision-makers in Moscow and Washington to separate these regional
quarrels from their own global preoccupations. Greece and Yugoslavia
had already demonstrated how a local, internal dispute could swiftly
be given an international significance.

The first of the extra-European disputes between Russia and the
West was very much a legacy of such *ad hoc* wartime arrangements;
in 1941–1943 Iran had been placed under tripartite military protection,
partly to ensure that it remained in the Allied camp, partly to ensure
that none of the Allies gained undue economic influence with the
Teheran regime.[108] When Moscow did not withdraw its garrison in
early 1946, and instead seemed to be encouraging separatist, pro-Com-
munist movements in the north, the traditional British objections to
undue Russian influence in this part of the world were augmented, and
then rather eclipsed, by the Truman administration's strong protests.
The withdrawal of the Russian troops, soon followed by the Iranian
army's suppression of the northern provinces and of the Tudeh (Communist) party itself, gave ample satisfaction in Washington, where it
confirmed Truman's belief in the efficacy of "talking tough" to the
Soviets. The case demonstrated, in Ulam's words, "the meaning of
containment before the doctrine was actually enunciated,"[109] and psy-

chologically prepared Washington to react similarly against news of Russian activities elsewhere. Thus, the continuing civil war in Greece, Moscow's pressure upon the Turks for concessions at the Straits and in the Kars border region, and the British government's 1947 declaration that it could no longer maintain its guarantees to those two nations triggered off a public American response (in the "Truman Doctrine") which was already in embryonic form. As early as April 1946 the State Department was urging the need to give support to "the United Kingdom and the *communications* of the British Commonwealth."[110] The growing acceptance of such views, and the way in which Washington was beginning to link together the various crises along the "northern tier" of those countries which blocked Russian expansion into the eastern Mediterranean and Middle East, indicates how swiftly the idealistic strands in American foreign policy were being joined, if not altogether replaced by geopolitical calculation.

It was with this perception of the *global* advance of Communism that the western Powers also viewed the changes occurring in the Far East. In the case of the Dutch, who were soon to be ejected from their "East Indies" by Sukarno's widely based nationalist movement, or the French, quickly embroiled in an armed struggle with Ho Chi Minh's Vietminh, or the British, soon engaged in counterinsurgency warfare in Malaya, their response as old colonial powers might have been the same even had no Communist existed east of Suez.[111] (On the other hand, by the late 1940s it proved useful in gaining Washington's sympathies, and in France's case military aid also, to claim that the insurgents were master-minded by Moscow.) But the shock to the United States of the "loss" of China was altogether more severe than these challenges farther south. From the time of American missionary endeavors in the nineteenth century onward, enormous amounts of cultural and psychological (much less financial) capital had been invested by the United States in that large and populous land; and this had been blown up to even greater proportions by the press coverage of Chiang Kai-shek's government during the war itself. In more than the religious sense, the United States felt it had a "mission" in China.[112] And while the professionals in the State Department and the military were increasingly aware of the Kuomintang's corruption and inefficiency, their perceptions were not generally shared by public opinion, especially on the Republican right, which by the late 1940s was beginning to see world politics in rigidly black-and-white terms.

The political turbulence and uncertainties which existed throughout the Orient in these years placed Washington in repeated dilemmas. On the one hand, the American republic could not be seen to be the supporter of corrupt Third World regimes or of decaying colonial empires. On the other, it did not want the "forces of revolution" to spread further, since that (it was claimed) would enhance Moscow's influence. It was relatively easy to encourage the British to withdraw from India in 1947, for it simply involved a transfer to a parliamentary, democratic regime under Nehru. The same could be done in pressing the Dutch to leave Indonesia by 1949, although Washington still worried about the growth of Communist insurgency there—as it did in the Philippines (given independence in 1946). But elsewhere the "wobbling" was more in evidence. Instead of pushing ahead with the earlier notions of a full-blown social transformation and demilitarization of Japanese society, for example, Washington planners steadily moved toward ideas of rebuilding the Japanese economy through the giant firms *(zaibatsu),* and even toward encouraging the creation of Japan's own armed forces—partly to ease the United States' economic and military burdens, partly to ensure that Japan would be an anti-Communist bastion in Asia.[113]

This hardening of Washington's position by 1950 was the result of two factors. The first was the increasing attacks upon the more flexible "containment" policies of Truman and Acheson, not only by Republican critics and the fast-rising "red-baiter" Joe McCarthy, but also by newer diehards within the administration itself, such as Louis Johnson, John Foster Dulles, Dean Rusk, and Paul Nitze—compelling Truman to act more assertively in order to protect his domestic political flank. The second was the North Korean attack across the 38th parallel in June 1950, which was swiftly interpreted by the United States as but one part of an aggressive master plan orchestrated by Moscow. Together, these two factors gave the upper hand to those forces in Washington which desired a more active, and even belligerent, policy to stop the rot. "We are losing Asia fast," wrote the influential journalist Stewart Alsop, invoking the homely imagery of a ten-pin bowling game. The Kremlin was the hard-hitting, ambitious bowler.

> The head pin was China. It is down already. The two pins in the second row are Burma and Indochina. If they go, the three pins in the next row, Siam, Malaya, and Indonesia, are pretty sure to topple in their turn. And if all the rest of Asia goes, the resulting psychological, political and economic magnetism will almost certainly drag down the four pins of the fourth row, India, Pakistan, Japan and the Philippines.[114]

The consequences of this change of mind affected American policy throughout East Asia. Its most obvious manifestation was the rapidly escalating military support to South Korea—an unsavory and repressive regime, which must share the blame for the conflict, but was at this time seen as an innocent victim. The early U.S. air and naval support was soon reinforced by army and marine divisions, which permitted MacArthur to launch his impressive counterattack (Inchon) until the northward advance of the United Nations forces in turn provoked China's own intervention in October/November 1950. Denied the use of A-bombs, the Americans were forced to conduct a campaign reminiscent of the trench warfare of 1914–1918.[115] By the time the cease-fire was reached, in June 1953, the United States had spent about $50 billion to fight the war, had sent over 2 million servicemen to the war zone, and had lost over 54,000 of them. While it had contained the North, the United States had also created for itself a long-lasting and substantial military commitment to the South from which it would be difficult, if not impossible, to withdraw.

This fighting also led to significant changes in American policy elsewhere in Asia. By 1949, many in the Truman administration had given up support of Chiang Kai-shek in disgust, viewed the "rump" government in Taiwan with contempt, and were thinking of following the British in recognizing Mao's Communist regime. Within another year, however, Taiwan was being supported and protected by the U.S. fleet, and China itself was regarded as a bitter foe, against which (at least in MacArthur's view) it would be necessary to use atomic weapons to counter its aggressions. In Indonesia, so important for its raw materials and food supplies, the new government would be given aid to fight the Communist insurgents; in Malaya, the British would be encouraged to do the same; and in Indochina, while still pressing the French to establish a more representative form of government, the United States was now prepared to pour in arms and money to combat the Vietminh.[116] No longer convinced that the moral and cultural appeal of American civilization was enough to prevent the spread of communism, the United States turned increasingly to military-territorial guarantees, especially after Dulles became secretary of state.[117] Even by August 1951 a treaty had reaffirmed U.S. air- and naval-base rights to the Philippines and American commitments to the defense of those islands. A few days later, Washington signed its tripartite security treaty with Australia and New Zealand. One week later, the peace treaty with Japan was finally concluded, legally ending the Pacific war and restoring full sovereignty to the Japanese state—but on the same day a security pact was signed, keeping American forces both in the home islands and in Okinawa. Washington's policy toward Communist China remained unrelentingly hostile, and toward Taiwan increasingly supportive, even over such minor outposts as Quemoy and Matsu.

The third major element in the Cold War was the increasing arms race between the two blocs, along with the creation of supportive military alliances. In terms of monies spent, the trend was by no means an even one, as shown in Table 37.

The enormous surge in American defense expenditures for several years after 1950 clearly reflected the costs of the Korean War, *and*

Table 37. Defense Expenditures of the Powers, 1948–1970[118]
(billions of dollars)

Date	U.S.	USSR	West Germany	France	U.K.	Italy	Japan	China
1948	10.9	13.1		0.9	3.4	0.4		
1949	13.5	13.4		1.2	3.1	0.5		2.0
1950	14.5	15.5		1.4	2.3	0.5		2.5
1951	33.3	20.1		2.1	3.2	0.7		3.0
1952	47.8	21.9		3.0	4.3	0.8		2.7
1953	49.6	25.5		3.4	4.5	0.7	0.3	2.5
1954	42.7	28.0		3.6	4.4	0.8	0.4	2.5
1955	40.5	29.5	1.7	2.9	4.3	0.8	0.4	2.5
1956	41.7	26.7	1.7	3.6	4.5	0.9	0.4	5.5
1957	44.5	27.6	2.1	3.6	4.3	0.9	0.4	6.2
1958	45.5	30.2	1.2	3.6	4.4	1.0	0.4	5.8
1959	46.6	34.4	2.6	3.6	4.4	1.0	0.4	6.6
1960	45.3	36.9	2.9	3.8	4.6	1.1	0.4	6.7
1961	47.8	43.6	3.1	4.1	4.7	1.2	0.4	7.9
1962	52.3	49.9	4.3	4.5	5.0	1.3	0.5	9.3
1963	52.2	54.7	4.9	4.6	5.2	1.6	0.4	10.6
1964	51.2	48.7	4.9	4.9	5.5	1.7	0.6	12.8
1965	51.8	62.3	5.0	5.1	5.8	1.9	0.8	13.7
1966	67.5	69.7	5.0	5.4	6.0	2.1	0.9	15.9
1967	75.4	80.9	5.3	5.8	6.3	2.2	1.0	16.3
1968	80.7	85.4	4.8	5.8	5.6	2.2	1.1	17.8
1969	81.4	89.8	5.3	5.7	5.4	2.2	1.3	20.2
1970	77.8	72.0	6.1	5.9	5.8	2.4	1.3	23.7

Washington's belief that it needed to rearm in a threatening world; the post-1953 decline was Eisenhower's attempt to control the "military-industrial complex" before it damaged both society and economy; the 1961–1962 increases reflected the Berlin Wall and Cuban missile crises; and the post-1965 jump in spending showed the increasing American commitment in Southeast Asia.[119] Although the Soviet figures are mere estimates and Moscow's policy was shrouded in mystery, it is probably fair to deduce that its own 1950–1955 buildup was caused by worries that war with the West would lead to devastating aerial attacks upon the Russian homeland unless its numbers of aircraft and missiles were greatly augmented; the 1955–1957 reductions reflect Khrushchev's *détente* diplomacy and efforts to release funds for consumer goods; and the very strong buildup after 1959–1960 reveals the worsening relations with the West, the humiliation over the Cuba crisis, and the determination to be strong in all services.[120] Communist China's more modest buildup was as much a reflection of its own economic growth as of anything else, but the 1960s defense increases suggest that Peking was willing to pay the price for its break with Moscow. As for the western European states, the figures in Table 37 show both Britain and France greatly increasing their defense expenditures at the time of the Korean War, and France's expenditures still rising until 1954 because of its embroilment in Indochina; but thereafter both those powers, and West Germany, Italy, and Japan in their turn, permitted only modest increases (and an occasional decline) in defense spending. Apart from China's growth—and those figures also are very imprecise—the pattern of arms spending in the 1950s and 1960s still conveys the impression of a bipolar world.

Perhaps more significant than figures alone was the multilevel and multisided character of the arms race. Although shocked by the Russian achievement of manufacturing its own A-bomb in 1949, the United States believed that it could inflict far more damage upon the USSR in a nuclear exchange than the USSR could inflict on it. On the other hand, as the strongly ideological NSC-68 (National Security Council Memorandum 68, of January 1950) put it, it was imperative "to increase as rapidly as possible our general air, ground and sea strength and that of our allies to a point where we are militarily not so heavily dependent on atomic weapons."[121] Between 1950 and 1953, in fact, U.S. ground forces tripled in size, and although much of this was due to the calling-up of reserves to fight in Korea, there was also a determination to convert NATO from a set of general military obligations into an *on-the-ground* alliance—to forestall a Soviet overrunning of western Europe which both American and British planners feared likely at this time.[122] Although there was no real prospect of the fantastic total of ninety Allied divisions being created on the lines of the Lisbon Agreement of 1952, there was nonetheless a significant rise in military commitments to Europe—from one to five U.S. divisions by 1953, with Britain agreeing to station four divisions in Germany, so that a reasonable balance had been achieved by the mid-1950s, when the West German army was expanded to compensate for reductions made then by London and Paris. In addition, there were enormous increases in Allied expenditures upon their air forces, so that some 5,200 were available to NATO by 1953. While much less is known about the development of the Soviet army and air force in these years, it is clear that Zhukov was engaged upon significant reorganization once Stalin died—getting rid of masses of half-prepared troops, making units much more powerful, mobile, and compact, replacing artillery with missiles, and, in sum, giving them a much better capacity for offensive action than they had possessed in 1950–1951, when the West's fear of attack was greatest. At the same time, it is clear that Russia, too, was placing the greatest proportion of these budgetary increases upon defensive and offensive air power.[123]

A second and quite new area of the East-West arms race opened up at sea, although this was also in an irregular pattern. The U.S. Navy had finished the Pacific war trailing clouds of glory, because of the impressive performance of its fast-carrier task forces and its submarine fleet; and the Royal Navy also felt that it had had a "good war," and one much more decisively fought than the stalemated 1914–1918 conflict at sea.[124] But the coming of A-bombs (especially in the Bikini trials against a variety of warships) to be carried by long-range strategic bombers or missiles seemed to cast a cloud over the future of the traditional instruments of naval warfare and even over the aircraft carrier itself. In the post-1945 retrenchment of defense expenditures, and "rationalization" of the separate services into a unified defense ministry, both navies came under heavy pressure. They were rescued, at least to some extent, by the Korean War, which again saw amphibious landings, carrier-based air strikes, and the clever exploitation of western sea power. The U.S. Navy was also able to join the nuclear club with the creation of a new class of enormous carriers, possessing strike bombers equipped with atomic weapons, and, by the late 1950s, with the planned construction of nuclear-powered submarines capable of firing long-range ballistic missiles. The British, less able to afford modern carriers, nonetheless retained converted "commando" carriers for what were termed brushfire wars, and, like the French, also strove to create a submarine-based deterrent. If all western navies by 1965 contained fewer ships and men than in 1945, they certainly had a more powerful punch.[125]

But the greatest stimulus to the continued expenditure of these navies was the buildup of the Soviet fleet. During the Second World War itself, the Russian navy had achieved very little, despite its large submarine force, and most of its personnel had fought on land (or assisted at river crossings by the army). After 1945, Stalin permitted the construction of many more submarines, based upon superior German designs and probably to be employed in an extended coastal-defense role; but he also favored the creation of a larger surface navy, including battleships and aircraft carriers. This ambitious scheme was swiftly halted by Khrushchev, who saw no purpose in building large, expensive warships in an age of nuclear missiles; in this his views were identical to those of many politicians and air marshals in the West. What probably shook that assumption was the repeated examples of the use of surface sea power by Russia's most likely foes—the Anglo-French sea-based attack upon Suez in 1956, the landing of U.S. forces in Lebanon in 1958 (thus checking the Russian-backed Syrians), and especially the *cordon sanitaire* which American warships placed around Cuba in the tense confrontation of the missile crisis of 1962. The lesson which the Kremlin (urged on by the influential Admiral Gorschkov) drew from these incidents was that until Russia also possessed a powerful navy, it would continue to be at a serious disadvantage in the world-power stakes—a conclusion reinforced by the U.S. Navy's rapid move to Polaris-missile-carrying submarines in the early 1960s. The result was both a massive expansion in virtually all classes of vessels in the Red Navy—cruisers, destroyers, submarines of all types, hybrid aircraft-carriers—*and* a massive expansion in their deployment overseas, challenging western maritime predominance in, say, the Mediterranean or the Indian Ocean in a manner which Stalin had never attempted.[126]

This form of challenge could, however, be regarded in traditional terms, as was clear by the many comparisons which observers made between Admiral Gorschkov's buildup and Tirpitz's four decades earlier; and even if the Soviet Union appeared committed to a new "naval race," it would be decades (if at all) before it could match the massively expensive carrier task forces of the U.S. Navy. The really *revolutionary* aspect of the post-1945 arms race was occurring elsewhere, in the sphere of atomic weapons and long-range missiles to project them. Despite the horrific casualties caused at Hiroshima and Nagasaki, there still remained many who saw in atomic weapons "just another bomb" rather than a watershed in the history of man's capacity for destruction. Moreover, following the failure of the 1946 Baruch Plan to internationalize atomic-power developments, there was the comforting thought that the United States possessed a nuclear monopoly and that the Strategic Air Command's bombers compensated for (and deterred) the large Soviet superiority in ground forces;[127] the western European states in particular accepted that a Russian military invasion would be answered by American (and later British) airborne bombings with nuclear weapons.

Technological innovations, and Soviet advances especially, changed all that. Russia's successful explosion of an atomic device in 1949 (well before most western estimates had predicted) broke the American monopoly. More alarming still was the construction of long-range Russian bombers, especially of the Bison type, which by the mid-1950s not only were assumed to be capable of reaching the United States but also were (erroneously) supposed to exist in such large numbers that a "bomber gap" existed. While the resultant controversy signified both the difficulty of gaining hard evidence about Russian capabilities and the U.S. Air Force's tendency to exaggerate,[128] it was in fact only to be a few more years before the era of American invulnerability was over. In 1949 Washington had agreed to the production of a new "super" bomb (the H-bomb), of staggeringly larger destructive capacity. This seemed once again to promise to the United States a decisive advantage, and the early to middle 1950s witnessed, both in Foster Dulles's startling speeches and in the Air Force's own plans, a commitment to "massive retaliation" upon Russia or China in the event of the next war.[129] While this doctrine itself produced considerable private unease within both the Truman and Eisenhower administrations—leading to the buildup of conventional forces and tactical (i.e., "battlefield") nuclear weapons, as alternatives to unleashing Armageddon—the chief blow to that strategy came from the Russian side.

In 1953, Russia also tested an H-bomb, a mere nine months after the American test. Moreover, the Soviet government had devoted considerable resources to exploiting German wartime technology on rocketry. By 1955 the USSR was mass-producing a medium-range ballistic missile (the SS-3); by 1957 it had fired an intercontinental ballistic missile over a range of five thousand miles, using the same rocket engine which shot *Sputnik*, the earth's first artificial satellite, into orbit in October of the same year.

Shocked by these Russian advances, and by the implication that both U.S. cities and U.S. bomber forces might be vulnerable to a sudden Soviet strike, Washington committed massive resources to its own intercontinental ballistic missiles in order to close what was predictably termed "the missile gap."[130] But the nuclear arms race was not confined to such systems. From 1960 onward, each side was also swiftly developing the capacity to launch ballistic missiles from submarines; and by that time a whole variety of battlefield nuclear weapons, and shorter-range rockets, had been constructed. All this was attended by the intellectual wrestlings of both strategic planners and civilian analysts in their "think tanks" about how to manage the various stages of escalation in what was now a strategy of "flexible response." However clear the solutions proposed, none of this managed to escape from the awful problem that it was going to be difficult if not impossible to integrate nuclear weapons into the traditional ways of fighting conventional warfare (it was soon realized, for example, that the battlefield "nukes" would blow up most of Germany). Yet if recourse were had to launching high-yield H-bombs upon Russian and American soil, the mutual casualties and damage would be unprecedented. Locked in what Churchill called a mutual balance of terror, and unable to *dis*invent their weapons of mass destruction, Washington and Moscow threw more and more resources into the technology of nuclear warfare.[131] And while both Britain and France were pushing ahead with their own atomic bombs and delivery systems in the 1950s, it still seemed—by all contemporary measure of aircraft, missiles, and nuclear bombs themselves—that in this field, too, only the superpowers counted.

The final major element in this rivalry was the creation by both Russia and the West of alliances across the globe, and the competition to find new partners—or at least to prevent Third World countries from joining the other side. In the early years, this was overwhelmingly an American activity, flowing from its advantageous position in 1945, from the fact that it already had many garrisons and air bases outside the western hemisphere, and from the equally important fact that so many countries were looking to Washington for economic and sometimes military support. By contrast, the USSR was desperately needing to rebuild itself, its chief foreign concern was the stabilization of its own borders on terms favorable to Moscow, and it had neither the economic nor the military instruments of power to project itself farther afield. Despite territorial gains in the Baltic, northern Finland, and the Far East, Russia was still, relatively speaking, a landlocked superpower. Moreover, it now seems clear that Stalin's view of the world outside was one overwhelmingly charged with caution and suspicion—toward the West, which, he feared, would not tolerate open Communist gains (e.g., in Greece in 1947); and also toward those Communist leaders, such as Tito and Mao, who were certainly not "Soviet puppets."[132] The setting-up of the Cominform in 1947 and the strong propaganda about supporting revolutionaries abroad had echoes from the 1930s (and even more, from the 1918–1921 era); but in actual fact Moscow seems to have avoided foreign entanglements in this period.

Yet the view from Washington, as noted above, was that a master plan for world Communist domination was unfolding, step by step, and needed to be "contained." The proffered guarantees to Greece and Turkey in 1947 were the first sign of this change of course, and the 1949 NATO treaty was its most spectacular exemplar. With the further additions to NATO's membership in the 1950s, this meant that the United States was pledged "to the defense of most of Europe and even parts of the Near East—from Spitzbergen to the Berlin Wall and beyond to the Asian borders of Turkey."[133] But that was only the beginning of the American overstretch. The Rio Pact and the special arrangement with Canada meant that it was responsible for the defense of the entire western hemisphere. The ANZUS treaty created obligations in the southwestern Pacific. The confrontations in East Asia during the early 1950s had led to the signing of various bilateral treaties, whereby the United States was pledged to aid countries along the "rim"—Japan, South Korea, and Taiwan, as well as the Philippines. In 1954, this was buttressed further by the establishment of SEATO (the Southeast Asia Treaty Organization), whereby the United States joined Britain, France, Australia, New Zealand, the Philippines, Pakistan, and Thailand in promising mutual support to combat aggression in that vast region. In the Middle East, it was the chief sponsor of another regional grouping, the 1955 Baghdad Pact (later, the Central Treaty Organization, or CENTO), in which Britain, Turkey, Iraq, Iran, and Pakistan stood against subversion and attack. Elsewhere in the Middle East, the United States had evolved or was soon to evolve special agreements with Israel, Saudi Arabia, and Jordan, either because of the strong Jewish-American ties or in consequence of the 1957 "Eisenhower Doctrine," which proffered American aid to Arab states. Early in 1970, one observer noted,

> the United States had more than 1,000,000 soldiers in 30 countries, was a member of four regional defense alliances and an active

participant in a fifth, had mutual defense treaties with 42 nations,
was a member of 53 international organizations, and was furnish-
ing military or economic aid to nearly 100 nations across the face
of the globe.[134]

This was an array of commitments about which Louis XIV or Palmerston would have felt a little nervous. Yet in a world which seemed to
be swiftly shrinking in size and in which each part appeared to relate
to another, these step-by-step pledges all had their logic. Where, in a
bipolar system, could Washington draw the line—especially after it
was claimed that its earlier definition that Korea was *not* vital had
been an invitation to the Communist attack of the following year?[135]
"This has become a very small planet," Dean Rusk argued in May 1965.
"We have to be concerned with all of it—with all of its land, waters,
atmosphere, and with surrounding space."[136]

If the projection of Soviet power and influence into the world outside was far less extensive, the years after Stalin's death nonetheless
saw noteworthy advances. Khrushchev, it is clear, wanted the Soviet
Union to be admired, even loved, rather than feared; he also wanted
to redirect resources from the military to agricultural investment and
consumer goods. His general foreign-policy ideas reflected his hope for
a "thaw" in the Cold War. Overruling Molotov, he removed Soviet
troops from Austria; he handed back the Porkkala naval base to Finland and Port Arthur to China; and he improved relations with Yugoslavia, arguing that there were "separate roads to socialism" (a position
as upsetting to many of his Presidium colleagues as it was to Mao
Tse-tung). Although 1955 saw the formal establishment of the Warsaw
Pact, in response to West Germany's joining of NATO, Khrushchev was
willing to open diplomatic relations with Bonn. He was also keen to
improve relations with the United States, although his own volatility
of manner and the by now chronic distrust with which Washington
interpreted all Russian moves made a real *détente* impossible. In that
same year, Khrushchev traveled to India, Burma, and Afghanistan.
The Third World was from now on going to be taken seriously by the
Soviet Union, just when more and more Afro-Asian states were gaining
independence.[137]

Little of this was as complete or smooth-going a transformation as
the ebullient Khrushchev would have liked. In April 1956, that instrument of Stalinist control the Cominform had been dissolved. Embarrassingly, two months later the Hungarian uprising—a "separate road"
away from socialism—had to be put down with Stalinist resolve. Quarrels with China multiplied and, as will be discussed below, produced
a deep cleft in the Communist world. *Détente* foundered on the rocks
of the U-2 incident (1960), the Berlin Wall crisis (1961), and then the
confrontation with the United States over Soviet missiles in Cuba

(1962). None of this, however, could turn back the Russian move toward world policy; the mere establishment of diplomatic relations with newly emergent countries and contact with their representatives at the United Nations made the growth of Soviet ties with the outside world inevitable. In addition, Khrushchev, eager to demonstrate the innate superiority of the Soviet system over capitalism, was bound to look for new friends abroad; his more pragmatic successors, after 1964, were interested in breaking the American cordon which had been placed around the USSR, *and* in checking Chinese influence. There were, moreover, many Third World countries eager to escape from what they termed "neocolonialism" and to institute a planned economy rather than a laissez-faire one—a preference which usually caused a cessation of western aid. All this fused to give Russian foreign policy a distinct "outward thrust."

This thrust began in a very decisive fashion in December 1953, by the signing of a trade agreement with India (neatly coinciding with Vice-President Nixon's visit to New Delhi), followed up by the 1955 offer to construct the Bhilai steel plant, and then by lots of military aid; this was a connection to the most important of the Third World powers, it simultaneously annoyed the Americans and the Chinese, and it punished Pakistan for its membership in the Baghdad Pact. Almost at the same time, in 1955–1956, the USSR and Czechoslovakia began giving aid to Egypt, replacing Washington in the funding of the Aswan Dam. Soviet loans also went to Iraq, Afghanistan, and North Yemen. Pronounced anti-imperialist states in Africa, such as Ghana, Mali, and Guinea, were also encouraged by Moscow. In 1960, the great breakthrough occurred in Latin America, when the USSR signed its first trade agreement with Castro's Cuba, then already becoming embroiled with an irritated United States. All this set a pattern which was not reversed by Khrushchev's fall. Having waged a strident propaganda campaign against imperialism, the USSR quite naturally offered "friendship treaties," trade credits, military advisers, and the rest to any newly decolonized nation. Russia could also benefit, in the Middle East, from the U.S. support of Israel (hence, for example, Moscow's increasing aid to Syria and Iraq as well as Egypt in the 1960s); it could gain kudos by offering military and economic assistance to North Vietnam; even in distant Latin America, it could proclaim its commitment to national-liberation movements. In this struggle for world influence, the USSR had now come a long way from Stalin's paranoid caution.[138]

But did this competition by Washington and Moscow for the affections of the rest of the globe, this mutual jostling for influence with the aid of treaties, credits, and weapons exports, mean that a bipolar world had indeed come into being, with everything significant in international affairs gravitating around the two opposing *Schwerpunkte* of the

United States and the USSR? From the viewpoint of a Dulles or a
Molotov, that indeed was how the world was ordered. And yet, even
as these two blocs competed across the globe, and in areas unknown
to both in 1941, they were meeting up with a quite different trend. For
a Third World was just at this time coming of age, and many of its
members, having at last thrown off the controls of the traditional
European empires, were in no mood to become mere satellites of a
distant superpower, even if the latter could provide useful economic
and military aid.

What was happening, in fact, was that one major trend in twentieth-
century power politics, the rise of the superpowers, was beginning to
interact with another, newer trend—the political fragmentation of the
globe. In the Social Darwinistic and imperialistic atmosphere that had
prevailed around 1900, it was easy to think that all power was being
concentrated in fewer and fewer capitals of the world (see above, pp.
195–96) Yet the very arrogance and ambitiousness of western imperialism brought with it the seeds of its own destruction; the exaggerated
nationalism of Cecil Rhodes, or the Panslavs, or the Austro-Hungarian
military, provoked reactions among Boers, the Poles, the Serbs, the
Finns; ideas of national self-determination, propagated to justify the
unification of Germany and Italy, or the 1914 Allied decision to assist
Belgium, seeped relentlessly eastward and southward, to Egypt, to
India, to Indochina. Because the empires of Britain, France, Italy, and
Japan had triumphed over the Central Powers in 1918 and had checked
Wilson's ideas for a new world order in 1919, these stirrings of nationalism were only selectively encouraged: it was fine to grant self-determination to the peoples of eastern Europe, because they were
European and thus regarded as "civilized"; but it was *not* fine to extend
these principles to the Middle East, Africa, or Asia, where the imperialist powers extended their territories and held down independence
movements. The shattering of those empires in the Far East after 1941,
the mobilization of the economies and recruitment of the manpower
of the other dependent territories as the war developed, the ideological
influences of the Atlantic Charter, and the decline of Europe all combined to release the forces for change in what by the 1950s was being
called the Third World.[139]

But it was described as a "third" world precisely because it insisted
on its distinction both from the American- and the Russian-dominated
blocs. This did not mean that the countries which met at the original
Bandung conference in April 1955 were free of all ties and obligations
to the superpowers—Turkey, China, Japan, and the Philippines, for
example, were among those attending the conference for whom the
term "nonaligned" would have been inappropriate.[140] On the other
hand, they all pressed for increased decolonization, for the United
Nations to focus upon issues other than the Cold War tensions, and for

measures to change a world which was still economically dominated by white men. When the second major phase of decolonization occurred, in the late 1950s and early 1960s, the original members of the Third World movement could be joined by a large number of new recruits, smarting at the decades (or centuries) of foreign rule and grappling with the hard fact that independence had left them with a host of economic problems. Given the vast swelling of their numbers, they could now begin to dominate the United Nations General Assembly; originally a body of fifty (overwhelmingly European and Latin American) countries, the UN steadily changed into an organization of well over one hundred states with many new Afro-Asian members. This did not restrict the actions of the larger Powers that were permanent members of the Security Council and that possessed a veto—conditions insisted upon by a cautious Stalin. But it did mean that if either of the superpowers wished to appeal to "world opinion" (as the United States had done in getting the United Nations to aid South Korea in 1950), it had to gain the agreement of a body whose membership did not share the preoccupations of Washington and Moscow. Chiefly because the 1950s and 1960s were dominated by issues of decolonization, and by increasing calls to end "underdevelopment," causes which the Russians adroitly espoused, this Third World opinion had a distinctly anti-western flavor, from the Suez crisis of 1956 to the later issues of Vietnam, the Middle East wars, Latin America, and South Africa. Even at the formal summits of the nonaligned countries, the emphasis was increasingly placed upon anticolonialism; and the geographical sitings of those meetings (Belgrade in 1961, Cairo in 1964, and Lusaka in 1970) symbolized this shift away from Eurocentered issues. The agenda of world politics was no longer exclusively in the hands of those powers possessing the greatest military and economic muscle.[141]

The most prominent of the early advocates of nonalignment—Tito, Nasser, Nehru—symbolized this transformation. Yugoslavia was remarkable in breaking with Stalin (it was expelled from the Cominform as early as 1948) and yet maintaining its independence without a Russian invasion occurring. It was a policy firmly maintained after Stalin's death; not for nothing was the first nonaligned summit held in Belgrade.[142] Nasser had risen to fame throughout the Arab world after his 1956 clash with Britain, France, and Israel, was a fierce critic of western imperialism, and willingly accepted Soviet aid; yet he was not a puppet of Moscow—he "treated his home-grown communists badly and between 1959 and 1961 a vigorous anti-Soviet radio and press campaign was launched."[143] Pan-Arabism, and especially Muslim fundamentalism, were not natural partners for atheistic materialism, even if local Marxist intellectuals strove to produce a fusion of the two. As for India, long the symbolic leader of the "moderate" nonaligned states, the repeated infusions of Soviet economic and military aid, which rose to new heights following Sino-Indian and Pakistani-Indian clashes, did not stop Nehru from criticizing Russian actions elsewhere and being very suspicious of the Communist party of India. His condemnations of British policy at Suez was due to his dislike of *all* Great Power interventions abroad.

The very fact that so many new states were entering the international community in these years, and that Russia was eager to wean them away from the West without itself having much knowledge of local conditions, also meant that its diplomatic "gains" were frequently attended by "losses." The most spectacular example of this was China itself, which will be discussed further below; but there were many others. The 1958 change of regime in Iraq allowed Russia to pose as the friend of that Arab state and to offer it loans; four years later, a Ba'athist coup led to the bloody suppression of the Communist party there. Moscow's continued aid to India inevitably angered Pakistan; there was no way it could please the one without losing the other. In Burma, an early promising start foundered when that country banned *all* foreigners. In Indonesia, things were worse; after receiving masses of Russian and eastern-European aid, Sukarno's government had turned from Moscow to Peking by 1963. Two years later, the Indonesian army wiped out the Communist party with great ferocity. Sékou Touré in Guinea sent home the Russian ambassador in 1961 for involving himself in a local strike, and during the Cuban missile crisis he refused to let Soviet planes refuel at the airport they had specially extended at Conakry.[144] Russia's support of Lumumba in the Congo crisis of 1960 undermined his prospects, and his successor Mobutu closed down the Soviet embassy. The most spectacular instance of that sort of setback—and a major blow to Soviet influence—came in 1972, when Sadat ordered 21,000 Russian advisers out of Egypt.

The relationship between the Third World and the "first two worlds" was always, therefore, a complex and shifting one. There were, to be sure, countries which were persistently pro-Russian (Cuba, Angola) and others which were strongly pro-American (Taiwan, Israel), chiefly because they felt under threat from their neighbors. There were some which, following Tito's early lead, genuinely sought to be nonaligned. There were others which, while leaning toward one bloc because it offered them aid, strongly resisted undue dependence. And, finally, there were the frequent revolutions, civil wars, changes of regime, and border conflicts in the Third World which took Moscow and Washington by surprise. Local rivalries in Cyprus, in the Ogaden, along the India-Pakistan border, and in Kampuchea (Cambodia) embarrassed the superpowers, since each of the contending parties sought their aid. Like other Great Powers before them, both Russia and the United States had to grapple with the hard fact that their "universalist" message would not be automatically accepted by other societies and cultures.

The Fissuring of the Bipolar World

As the 1960s moved into the 1970s, there nevertheless remained good reasons why the Washington-Moscow relationship should continue to seem all-important in world affairs. Militarily, the USSR had drawn much closer to the United States, but both were still in a different league from everyone else. In 1974, for example, the United States was spending $85 billion and the USSR was spending $109 billion on defense, which was three to four times what was spent by China ($26 billion) and eight to ten times what was spent by the leading European states (U.K. $9.7 billion; France, $9.9 billion; West Germany, $13.7 billion);[145] and the American and Russian armed forces, of over 2 million and 3 million men, respectively, were much larger than those of the European states, and much better equipped than the 3 million men in the Chinese services. Both superpowers had over 5,000 combat aircraft, more than ten times the number possessed by the former Great Powers.[146] Their total tonnage in warships—the United States had 2.8 million tons, the USSR 2.1 million tons in 1974—was well ahead of Britain (370,000 tons), France (160,000 tons), Japan (180,000 tons), and China (150,000 tons).[147] But the greatest disparity lay in the numbers of nuclear delivery weapons, shown in Table 38.

Table 38. Nuclear Delivery Vehicles of the Powers, 1974[148]

	U.S.	USSR	Britain	France	China
Intercontinental ballistic missiles	1,054	1,575	—	—	—
Intermediate ballistic missiles	—	600	—	18	c. 80
Submarine-based ballistic missiles	656	720	64	48	—
Long-range bombers	437	140	—	—	—
Medium-range bombers	66	800	50	52	100

So capable had each superpower become of obliterating the other (and anyone else besides)—a state of affairs quickly named MAD, or Mutually Assured Destruction—that they began to evolve arrangements for controlling the nuclear arms race in various ways. There was, following the Cuban missile crisis, the installation of a "hot line" to allow each side to communicate in the event of another critical occasion; there was the nuclear test-ban treaty of 1963, also signed by the United Kingdom, which banned testing in the atmosphere, under water, and in outer space; there was the Strategic Arms Limitation Treaty (SALT I) of 1972, which set limits on the numbers of intercontinental ballistic missiles each side could possess and halted the Russian construction of an anti-ballistic-missile system; there was the extension of that agreement at Vladivostock in 1975, and, in the late 1970s, there were negotiations toward a SALT II treaty (signed in June 1979, but never ratified by the U.S. Senate). Yet these various measures of agreement, and the particular economic and domestic-political and foreign-policy motives which pushed each side into them, did not stop the arms race; if anything, the banning or limitation of one weapon system merely led to a transfer of resources to another area. From the late 1950s onward, the USSR steadily and inexorably increased its allocations to the armed forces; and while the pattern of American defense spending was distorted by its expensive war in Vietnam and then the public reaction against that venture, the long-term trend was also toward ever-higher totals. Every few years, newer weapon systems would be added: multiple warheads were fitted to each side's rockets; missile-carrying submarines augmented each side's navy; the nuclear stalemate in *strategic* missiles (provoking a European fear that the United States would not respond to a Soviet attack westward by unleashing long-range American missiles, since that could in turn provoke atomic strikes upon American cities) led to new types of medium-range or "theater" nuclear weapons, like the Pershing II and the cruise missiles being developed as answers to the Russian SS-20. The arms race and arms-control discussions of various sorts were obverse sides of the same coin; but each kept Washington and Moscow at the center of the stage.

In other fields, too, their rivalry appeared central. As mentioned earlier, one of the more notable features of the Soviet arms buildup since 1960 was the enormous expansion of its surface fleet—*physically*, as it constructed ever more powerful, missile-bearing destroyers and cruisers, then medium-sized helicopter carriers, then aircraft carriers;[149] and *geographically*, as the Soviet navy began to send more and more vessels into the Mediterranean and farther afield, to the Indian Ocean, West Africa, Indochina, and Cuba, where it was able to use an increasing number of bases. This last development reflected a very significant extension of American-Russian rivalries into the Third World, chiefly because of Moscow's further success in breaking into regions where foreign influence had hitherto been a western monopoly. The continued tension in the Middle East, and especially the Arab-Israeli wars of 1967 and 1973 (where American arms supplies to Israel were decisive), meant that various Arab states—Syria, Libya, Iraq—would remain looking to Moscow for assistance. The Marxist regimes of Southern Yemen and Somalia provided naval-base facilities to the Russian navy, giving it a new maritime presence in the Red Sea. But, as usual, breakthroughs were accompanied by setbacks: Moscow's apparent preference for Ethiopia led to the expulsion of Soviet personnel and ships from Somalia in 1977, just a few years after the same had happened in Egypt; and Russian advances in this area were countered by the growth of the American presence in Oman and Diego Garcia, naval-base rights in Kenya and Somalia, and increased arms shipments to Egypt, Saudia Arabia, and Pakistan. Farther to the south, however, the Soviet-Cuban military assistance to the MPLA forces in Angola, the frequent attempts of the Soviet-aided Libyan regime of Qaddafi to export revolution elsewhere, and the presence of Marxist governments in Ethiopia, Mozambique, Guinea, Congo, and other West African states suggested that Moscow was winning in the struggle for global influence. Its own military move into Afghanistan in 1979—the first such expansion (outside eastern Europe) since the Second World War—and Cuba's encouragement of leftist regimes in Nicaragua and Grenada furthered this impression that the American-Russian rivalry knew no limits, and provoked additional countermoves and increases in defense spending on Washington's part. By 1980, with a new Republican administration denouncing the Soviet Union as an "evil empire" against which massive defense forces and unbending policies were the only answer, little seemed to have changed since the days of John Foster Dulles.[150]

Yet, for all this focus upon the American-Russian relationship and its many ups and downs between 1960 and 1980, other trends had been at work to make the international power system much *less* bipolar than it had appeared to be in the earlier period. Not only had the Third World emerged to complicate matters, but significant fissures had occurred in what had earlier appeared to be the two monolithic blocs dominated by Moscow and Washington. The most decisive of these by far, with repercussions which are difficult to measure fully even at the present time, was the split between the USSR and Communist China. In retrospect, it may seem self-evident that even the allegedly "scientific" and "universalist" claims of Marxism would founder on the rocks of local circumstances, indigenous cultural strengths, and differing stages of economic development—after all, Lenin himself had had to make massive deviations from the original doctrine of dialectical materialism in order to secure the 1917 Revolution. And some foreign observers of Mao's Communist movement in the 1930s and 1940s were aware that he, at least, was not inclined to adhere slavishly to Stalin's dogmatic position toward the relative importance of workers and peasantry. They were also aware that Moscow, in its turn, had been less than wholehearted in its support of the Chinese Communist Party and had, even as late as 1946 and 1948, tried to balance it off against Chiang Kai-shek's Nationalists. This, in the USSR's view, would avoid the creation of "a vigorous new Communist regime established without the assistance of the Red Army in a country with almost three times the population of Russia [which] would inevitably become a competing pole of attraction within the world Communist movement."[151]

Nonetheless, the sheer extent of the split took most observers by surprise, and was for many years missed by a United States aroused by the fear of a global Communist conspiracy. Admittedly, the Korean War and the subsequent Chinese-American jockeying over Taiwan took attention from the lukewarm state of the Moscow-Peking axis, in which Stalin's relatively small amounts of aid to China were always tendered for a price which emphasized Russia's privileges in Mongolia and Manchuria. Although Mao was able to redress the balance in his 1954 negotiations with the Russians, his hostility to the United States over the offshore islands of Quemoy and Matsu and his more extreme adherence (at least at that time) to the belief in the inevitability of a clash with capitalism made him bitterly suspicious of Khrushchev's early *détente* policies. From Moscow's viewpoint, however, it seemed foolish in the late 1950s to provoke the Americans unnecessarily, especially when the latter had a clear nuclear advantage; it would also be a setback, diplomatically, to support China in its 1959 border clash with India, which was so important to Russia's Third World policy; and it would be highly unwise, given the Chinese proclivity to independent action, to aid their nuclear program without getting some controls over it—all of these being regarded as successive betrayals by Mao. By 1959, Khrushchev had canceled the atomic agreement with Peking and was proffering India far larger loans than had ever been given to China. In the following year, the "split" became open for all to see at the World Communist Parties' meeting in Moscow. By 1962–1963, things were worse still: Mao had denounced the Russians for giving in over Cuba, and then for signing the partial Nuclear Test Ban Treaty with the United States and Britain; the Russians had by then cut off all aid to China and its ally Albania and increased supplies to India; and the first of the Sino-Soviet border clashes occurred (although never as serious as those of 1969). More significant still was the news that in 1964 the Chinese had exploded their first atomic bomb and were hard at work on delivery systems.[152]

Strategically, this split was the single most important event since 1945. In September 1964, *Pravda* readers were shocked to see a report that Mao was not only claiming back the Asian territories which the Chinese Empire had lost to Russia in the nineteenth century, but also denouncing the USSR for its appropriations of the Kurile Islands, parts of Poland, East Prussia, and a section of Rumania. Russia, in Mao's view, had to be reduced in size—in respect to China's claims, by 1.5 million square kilometers![153] How much the opinionated Chinese leader had been carried away by his own rhetoric it is hard to say, but there was no doubt that all this—together with the border clashes and the development of Chinese atomic weapons—was thoroughly alarming to the Kremlin. Indeed, it is likely that at least some of the buildup of the Russian armed forces in the 1960s was due to this perceived new danger to the east as well as the need to respond to the Kennedy administration's defense increases. "The number of Soviet divisions deployed along the Chinese frontier was increased from fifteen in 1967 to twenty-one in 1969 and thirty in 1970"—this latter jump being caused by the serious clash at Damansky (or Chenpao) island in March 1969. "By 1972 forty-four Soviet divisions stood guard along the 4,500-mile border with China (compared to thirty-one divisions in Eastern Europe), while a quarter of the Soviet air force had been deployed from west to east."[154] With China now possessing a hydrogen bomb, there were hints that Moscow was considering a preemptive strike against the nuclear installation at Lop Nor—causing the United States to make its own contingency plans, since it felt that it could not allow Russia to obliterate China.[155] Washington had come a long way since its 1964 ponderings about joining the USSR in "preventative military action" to arrest China's development as a nuclear power![156]

This was hardly to say that Mao's China had emerged as a full-fledged third superpower. Economically, it had enormous problems—which were exacerbated by its leader's decision to initiate the "Cultural Revolution," with all its accompanying discontinuities and uncertainties. And while it might boast the largest army in the world, its people's militias were not likely to be a match for Soviet motor rifle divisions. China's navy was negligible compared with the expanding Russian fleet; its air force, though large, chiefly consisted of older planes; and its nuclear-delivery system was but in its infancy. Nonetheless, unless the USSR was prepared to run the risk of provoking the Americans and offending world opinion by launching a massive nuclear attack upon China, any fighting *at a lesser level* could quickly produce enormous casualties—which the Chinese seemed willing to accept, but Russian politicians in the Brezhnev era were less keen about. It was therefore not surprising that as Russo-Chinese relations worsened, Moscow should not only have shown interest in nuclear-arms-limitation talks with the West but also have quickened the pace of improving relations with countries like the Federal Republic of Germany, which under Willy Brandt seemed much more willing to foster *détente* than in Adenauer's days.

In the political and diplomatic arena, the Sino-Soviet split was even more embarrassing to the Kremlin. Although Khrushchev himself had been willing to tolerate "separate roads to socialism" (always provided those routes were not too divergent!), it was quite another thing for the USSR to be openly accused of having abandoned true Marxist principles; for its satellites and clients to be encouraged to throw off the Russian "yoke"; and for its diplomatic efforts in the Third World to be complicated by Peking's rival aid and propaganda—the more especially since Mao's brand of peasant-based Communism appeared often more appropriate than the Russian emphasis upon an industrial proletariat. This did not mean that the Soviet Empire in eastern Europe was in any real danger of following the Chinese lead—only the eccentric regime in Albania did so.[157] But it remained embarrassing to Moscow to be denounced by Peking for suppressing the Czech liberalization reforms in 1968, and again for its actions against Afghanistan in 1979. In the Third World, moreover, China was somewhat better placed to block Russian influence: it competed hard in North Yemen; it made much of its railway construction scheme in Tanzania; it criticized Moscow for failing to give sufficient support to the Vietminh and the Vietcong against the United States; and as it renewed relations with Japan, it warned Tokyo about a too-heavy economic collaboration with the Russians in Siberia. Once again, this was rarely an equal struggle—Russia could usually offer much more to Third World states in terms of credits and advanced arms, and could also project its influence by using Cuban and Libyan surrogates. But simply having to compete with a fellow Marxist state as well as with the United States was altogether more upsetting than the predictable, bipolar rivalries of two decades earlier.

In all sorts of ways, then, China's assertive and independent line made diplomatic relationships more complicated and baroque, especially in Asia. The Chinese had been stung by Moscow's wooing of India and even more by its dispatch of military supplies to New Delhi following Sino-Indian border clashes; not surprisingly, therefore, Peking gave support to Pakistan in its own clashes with India, and was strongly resentful of the Russian invasion of Afghanistan. China was further alienated by Moscow's support for North Vietnam's expansion in the late 1970s, by the latter's entry into Comecon, and by the increasing Russian naval presence in Vietnamese ports. When Vietnam invaded Cambodia in December 1978, China engaged itself in bloody and not very successful border clashes with its southern neighbor, which was in turn being heavily supplied with Russian weapons. By this stage, Moscow was even looking more favorably toward the Taiwan regime, and Peking was urging the United States to increase its naval forces in the Indian Ocean and western Pacific, to counter the Russian squadrons. A mere twenty years after China was criticizing the USSR for being too soft toward the West, it was pressing NATO to increase its defenses and warning both Japan and the Common Market against strengthening economic ties with Russia![158]

By comparison, the dislocations which occurred in the western camp from the early 1960s onward, caused chiefly by de Gaulle's campaign against American hegemony, were nowhere near as serious in the long term—although they certainly added to the impression that the two blocs were breaking up. With strong memories of the Second World War still in mind, de Gaulle seethed at the fact that he was treated as less than equal by the United States; he resented American policy during the Suez crisis in 1956, not to mention Dulles's habit of threatening a nuclear conflagration over issues like Quemoy. Although de Gaulle had more than enough to keep him busy for several years after 1958 as he sought to extricate France from Algeria, even at that time he criticized western Europe's subservience (as he saw it) to American interests. Like the British a decade earlier, he saw in nuclear weapons a chance to preserve Great Power status; when news of the first French atomic test of 1960 arrived, the general called out, "Hooray for France—since this morning she is stronger and prouder."[159] Determined to have France's nuclear deterrent totally independent, he angrily rejected Washington's offer of a Polaris missile system similar to Britain's because of the conditions the Kennedy administration attached to it. While this meant that France's own nuclear-weapons program would consume a far greater proportion of the total defense budget (perhaps as much as 30 percent) than it did elsewhere, de Gaulle and his successors felt the price was worth paying. At the same time, he began to pull France out of the NATO military structure, expelling that organization's HQ from Paris in 1966 and closing down all American bases on French soil. In parallel with this, he sought to improve France's relations with Moscow—where his actions were warmly applauded—and he ceaselessly proclaimed the need for Europe to stand on its own feet.[160]

De Gaulle's spectacular actions did not rest merely on Gallic rhetoric and cultural pride. Boosted by Marshall Plan aid and other American grants, and benefiting from Europe's general economic recovery after the late 1940s, the French economy had grown swiftly for almost two decades.[161] The colonial wars in Indochina (1950–1954) and Algeria (1956–1962) diverted French resources for a while, but not irremediably. Having negotiated very favorable terms for its national interests at the time of the formation of the European Economic Community in 1957, France was able to benefit from this larger market while restructuring its own agriculture and modernizing its industry. Although critical of Washington and firmly preventing British entry into the EEC, de Gaulle effected a dramatic reconciliation with Adenauer's Germany in 1963. And all the time he spoke of a need for Europe to stand on its own feet, to be free of superpower domination, to remember its glorious past and to cooperate—with France naturally showing the lead—in the pursuit of equally glorious destiny.[162] These were heady words, but they evoked a response on *both* sides of the Iron Curtain, and appealed to many who disliked both the Russian and American political cultures, not to mention their respective foreign policies.

By 1968, however, de Gaulle's own political career had been undermined by the students' and workers' revolt. The strains caused by modernization and the still relatively modest size of the French economy (3.5 percent of world manufacturing production in 1963)[163] meant that the country simply was not strong enough to play the influential role that the general had envisaged; and whatever the special agreements he proffered to the West Germans, the latter dared not abandon their tight links with the United States, upon which, in the final resort, Bonn politicians knew they heavily depended. Moreover, Russia's ruthless crushing of the Czech reforms in 1968 showed that the eastern superpower had no intention of letting the countries in its sphere evolve their own policies, let alone become part of a French-led, European-wide confederation.

Nonetheless, for all his hubris, de Gaulle had symbolized and accelerated trends which could not be stopped. Despite their military weaknesses compared with the United States and the USSR, the armed forces of the western European states were much larger and stronger, relatively speaking, than they had been in the post-1945 years; two of them had nuclear weapons and were developing delivery systems. Economically, as will be discussed in more detail below, the "recovery of Europe" had succeeded splendidly. What was more, despite Russia's 1968 invasion of Czechoslovakia, the era of the Cold War division of Europe into hermetically sealed blocs was being weakened. Willy Brandt's spectacular policy of reconciliation with Russia, with Poland and Czechoslovakia, and especially with the (at first very reluctant) East German regime between 1969 and 1973, chiefly on the basis of accepting the 1945 boundaries as permanent, inaugurated a period of blossoming East-West contacts. Western investments and technology flowed across the Iron Curtain, and this "economic *détente*" spilled over into cultural exchanges, the Helsinki Accords (of 1975) on human rights, and efforts to avert future military misunderstandings and to achieve mutual force reductions. To all this the superpowers, for their own good reasons, and with some inevitable reservations (especially on the Soviet side), gave their blessing. But perhaps the most significant fact had been the persistent pressures by the Europeans themselves to effect the *rapprochement;* even when relations cooled between Moscow and Washington, therefore, it was going to be extremely difficult in the future for either the USSR or the United States to halt this process.[164]

Of the two, the Americans were in a much better position than the Russians to adjust to the new, pluralistic international environment. Whatever de Gaulle's anti-American gestures, they were nowhere near the seriousness of Sino-Soviet border clashes, elimination of bilateral trade, ideological invective, and diplomatic jostling across the globe which, by 1969, were causing some observers to argue that a Russo-Chinese war was inevitable.[165] However much American administrations resented France's actions, they hardly needed to redeploy their armed forces because of such quarrels. In any case, NATO was still permitted to retain overflight rights and the fuel-oil pipeline which ran across France, and Paris kept up its special defense arrangements with West Germany—so that its troops, too, would be available if the Warsaw Pact forces struck westward. Finally, of course, it had been a fundamental axiom of American policy after 1945 that a strong and independent Europe (that is, independent from Russian domination) was in the United States' long-term interests and would help to reduce its defense burdens—even while admitting that such a Europe might also be an economic and perhaps a diplomatic competitor. It was for that reason that Washington had encouraged all moves toward European integration, and was urging Britain to join the EEC. By contrast, Russia might begin not only to feel insecure militarily if a powerful European confederation emerged in the West, but also to worry about the magnetic pull which such a body would exercise upon the Rumanians, Poles, and other satellite peoples. A policy of selective *détente* and economic cooperation with western Europe by Moscow was one thing, partly because it could bring technological and trading benefits, partly because it might draw the Europeans further away from the Americans, and partly because of the China challenge on Russia's Asian front. In the longer term, however, a prosperous, resurgent Europe which would overshadow the USSR in all respects except the military (and perhaps become strong in that area, too) could hardly be in Russia's best interests.[166]

Yet if, in retrospect, the United States was better placed to adjust to the changing patterns of world power, that was not obvious for many years after 1960. In the first place, there was a chronic dislike of "Asian Communism," with Mao's China replacing Khrushchev's Russia as the fomenter of world revolution in the eyes of many Americans. China's border war of 1962 with India, a country which Washington (like Moscow) wished to woo, confirmed the earlier aggressive image emanating from the clashes over Quemoy and Matsu; and *détente* between the United States and China was hardly conceivable in the early 1960s, when Mao's propaganda machine was denouncing the Russians for backing down over Cuba and for signing the limited nuclear-test-ban treaty with the West. Finally, between 1965 and 1968 China was in the convulsions of Mao's Cultural Revolution, which made the country appear chronically unstable as well as even more ideologically abhorrent to administrations in Washington. None of this pointed to "a situation in which much progress towards better relations with the United States was likely."[167]

Above all, of course, the United States in these years was itself increasingly convulsed by the problems emerging from the war in Vietnam. The North Vietnamese, and the Vietcong in the South, appeared to most Americans as but new manifestations of the creeping Asian Communism which had to be forcibly contained before it did even further damage; and since those revolutionary forces were being encouraged and supplied by China and Russia, both of the latter Powers (but perhaps especially the bitterly critical regime in Peking) could only be seen as part of a hostile Marxist coalition lined up against the "free world." Indeed, as the Johnson administration escalated its own buildup in Vietnam, decision-makers in Washington frequently worried about how far they could go *without* provoking the sort of Chinese intervention which had occurred in the Korean War.[168] From the Chinese government's standpoint, it must have been a matter of earnest debate throughout the 1960s about whether the growing clash with the Soviets to the north was as ominous as the ever-escalating American military and aerial operations to the south. Yet while in fact its own relationship with the ethnically different Vietnamese had traditionally been one of rivalry, and it was deeply suspicious of the amount of military hardware which Russia was giving to Hanoi, these tensions were invisible to most western eyes throughout the period of the Kennedy and Johnson administrations.

In so many ways, symbolic as well as practical, it would be difficult to exaggerate the impacts of the lengthy American campaign in Vietnam and other parts of Southeast Asia upon the international power system—or upon the national psyche of the American people themselves, most of whose perceptions of their country's role in the world still remain strongly influenced by that conflict, albeit in different ways. The fact that this was a war fought by an "open society"—and made the more open because of revelations like the Pentagon Papers, and by the daily television and press reportage of the carnage and apparent futility of it all; that this was the first war which the United States had unequivocally lost, that it confounded the victorious experiences of the Second World War and destroyed a whole array of reputations, from those of four-star generals to those of "brightest and best" intellectuals; that it coincided with, and in no small measure helped to cause, the fissuring of a consensus in American society about the nation's goals and priorities, was attended by inflation, unprecedented student protests and inner city disturbances, and was followed in turn by the Watergate crisis, which discredited the presidency itself for a time; that it seemed to many to stand in bitter and ironic contradiction to everything which the Founding Fathers had taught, and made the United States unpopular across most of the globe; and finally that the shamefaced and uncaring treatment of the GIs who came back from Vietnam would produce its own reaction a decade later and thus ensure that the memory of this conflict would continue to prey upon the public consciousness, in war memorials, books, television documentaries, and personal tragedies—all of this meant that the Vietnam War, although far smaller in terms of casualties, impacted upon the American people somewhat as had the First World War upon Europeans. The effects were seen, overwhelmingly, at the *personal* and *psychological* levels; more broadly, they were interpreted as a crisis in American civilization and in its constitutional arrangements. As such, they would continue to have significance quite independent of the strategical and Great Power dimensions of this conflict.

But the latter aspects are the most important ones for our survey, and require further mention here. To begin with, it provided a useful and sobering reminder that a vast superiority in military hardware and economic productivity will not always and automatically translate into military *effectiveness*. That does not undermine the thrust of the present book, which has stressed the importance of economics and technology in large-scale, protracted (and usually coalition) wars between the Great Powers when each combatant has been equally committed to victory. Economically, the United States may have been fifty to one hundred times more productive than North Vietnam; militarily, it possessed the firepower to (as some hawks urged) bomb the enemy back into the stone age—indeed, with nuclear weapons, it had the capacity to obliterate Southeast Asia altogether. But this was *not* a war in which those superiorities could be made properly effective. Fear of domestic opinion, and of world reaction, prevented the use of atomic weapons against a foe who could never be a *vital* threat to the United States itself. Worries about the American public's opposition to heavy casualties in a conflict whose legitimacy and efficacy came increasingly under question had similarly constrained the administration's use of the conventional methods of warfare; restrictions were placed on the bombing campaign; the Ho Chi Minh Trail through neutral Laos could not be occupied; Russian vessels bearing arms to Haiphong harbor could not be seized. It was important not to provoke the two major Communist states into joining the war. This essentially reduced the fighting to a series of small-scale encounters in jungles and paddy fields, terrain which blunted the advantages of American firepower and (helicopter-borne) mobility, and instead placed an emphasis upon jungle-warfare techniques and unit cohesion—which was much less of a problem for the crack forces than for the rapidly turning over contingents of draftees. Although Johnson followed Kennedy's lead in sending more and more troops to Vietnam (it peaked at 542,000, in 1969), it was never enough to meet General Westmoreland's demands; clinging to the view that this was still a limited conflict, the government refused to mobilize the reserves, or indeed to put the economy on a war footing.[169]

The difficulties of fighting the war on terms disadvantageous to the United States' real military strengths reflected a larger political problem—the discrepancy between means and ends (as Clausewitz might have put it). The North Vietnamese and the Vietcong were fighting for what they believed in very strongly; those who were not were undoubtedly subject to the discipline of a totalitarian, passionately nationalistic regime. The South Vietnamese governing system, by contrast, appeared corrupt, unpopular, and in a distinct minority, opposed by the Buddhist monks, unsupported by a frightened, exploited, and war-weary peasantry; those native units loyal to the regime and who often fought well were not sufficient to compensate for this inner corrosion. As the war escalated, more and more Americans questioned the efficacy of fighting for the regime in Saigon, and worried at the way in which all this was corrupting the American armed forces themselves—in the decline in morale, the rise in cynicism, indiscipline, drug-taking, prostitution, the increasing racial sneers at the "gooks," and atrocities in the field, not to mention the corrosion of the United States' own currency or of its larger strategic posture. Ho Chi Minh had declared that his forces were willing to lose men at the rate of ten to one—and when they were rash enough to emerge from the jungles to attack the cities, as in the 1968 Tet offensive, they often did; but, he continued, despite those losses they would still fight on. That sort of willpower was not evident in South Vietnam. Nor was American society itself, increasingly disturbed by the war's contradictions, willing to sacrifice everything for victory. While the latter feeling was quite understandable, given what was at stake for each side, the fact was that it proved impossible for an open democracy to wage a halfhearted war successfully. This was the fundamental contradiction, which neither McNamara's systems analysis nor the B-52 bombers based on Guam could alter.[170]

More than a decade after the fall of Saigon (April 1975), and with books upon all aspects of that conflict still flooding from the presses, it still remains difficult to assess clearly how it may have affected the U.S. position in the world. Viewed from a longer perspective, say, backward from the year 2000 or 2020, it might be seen as having produced a salutory shock to American global hubris (or to what Senator Fulbright called "the arrogance of power"), and thus compelled the country to think more deeply about its political and strategical priorities and to readjust more sensibly to a world already much changed since 1945—in other words, rather like the shock which the Russians received in the Crimean War, or the British received in the Boer War, producing in their turn beneficial reforms and reassessments.

At the time, however, the short-term effects of the war could not be other than deleterious. The vast boom in spending on the war, precisely at a time when domestic expenditures upon Johnson's "Great Society" were also leaping upward, badly affected the American economy in ways which will be examined below (pp. 434–35). Moreover, while the United States was pouring money into Vietnam, the USSR was devoting steadily larger sums to its nuclear forces—so that it achieved a rough strategic parity—and to its navy, which in these years emerged as a major force in global gunboat diplomacy; and this increasing imbalance was worsened by the American electorate's turn against military expenditures for most of the 1970s. In 1978, "national security expenditures" were only 5 percent of GNP, lower than they had been for thirty years.[171] Morale in the armed services plummeted, in consequence both of the war itself and of the postwar cuts. Shakeups in the CIA and other agencies, however necessary to check abuses, undoubtedly cramped their effectiveness. The American concentration upon Vietnam worried even sympathetic allies; its methods of fighting in support of a corrupt regime alienated public opinion, in western Europe as much as in the Third World, and was a major factor in what some writers have termed American "estrangement" from much of the rest of the planet.[172] It led to a neglect of American attention toward Latin America—and a tendency to replace Kennedy's hoped-for "Alliance for Progress" with military support for undemocratic regimes and with counterrevolutionary actions (like the 1965 intervention in the Dominican Republic). The—inevitably—open post-Vietnam War debate over the regions of the globe for which the United States would or *would not* fight in the future disturbed existing allies, doubtless encouraged its foes, and caused wobbling neutrals to consider re-insuring themselves with the other side. At the United Nations debates, the American delegate appeared increasingly beleaguered and isolated. Things had come a long way since Henry Luce's assertion that the United States would be the elder brother of nations in the brotherhood of man.[173]

The other power-political consequence of the Vietnam War was that it obscured, by perhaps as much as a decade, Washington's recognition of the extent of the Sino-Soviet split—and thus its chance to evolve a policy to handle it. It was therefore the more striking that this neglect should be put right so swiftly after the entry into the presidency of that bitter foe of Communism Richard Nixon, in January 1969. But Nixon possessed, to use Professor Gaddis's phrase, a "unique combination of ideological rigidity with political pragmatism"[174]—and the latter was especially manifest in his dealings with foreign Great Powers. Despite Nixon's dislike of domestic radicals and animosity toward, say, Allende's Chile for its socialist policies, the president claimed to be unideological when it came to global diplomacy. To him, there was no great contradiction between ordering a massive increase in the bombing of North Vietnam in 1972—to compel Hanoi to come closer to the American bargaining position for withdrawal from the South—and journeying to China to bury the hatchet with Mao Tse-tung in the same year. Even more significant was to be his choice of Henry Kissinger as his national security adviser (and later secretary of state). Kissinger's approach to world affairs was historicist and relativistic: events had to be seen in their larger context, and related to each other; Great Powers should be judged on what they did, not on their domestic ideology; an absolutist search for security was utopian, since that would make everyone else absolutely insecure—all that one could hope to achieve was relative security, based upon a reasonable balance of forces in world affairs, a mature recognition that the world scene would never be completely harmonious, and a willingness to bargain. Like the statesmen he had written about (Metternich, Castlereagh, Bismarck), Kissinger felt that "the beginning of wisdom in human as well as international affairs was knowing when to stop."[175] His aphorisms were Palmerstonian ("We have no permanent enemies") and Bismarckian ("The hostility between China and the Soviet Union served our purposes best if we maintained closer relations with each side than they did with each other"),[176] and were unlike anything in American diplomacy since Kennan. But Kissinger had a much greater chance to direct policy than his fellow admirer of nineteenth-century European statesmen ever possessed.[177]

Finally, Kissinger recognized the limitations upon American power, not only in the sense that the United States could not afford to fight a protracted war in the jungles of Southeast Asia *and* to maintain its other, more vital interests, but also because both he and Nixon could perceive that the world's balances were altering, and new forces were undermining the hitherto unchallenged domination of the two superpowers. The latter were still far ahead in terms of strictly military power, but in other respects the world had become more of a multipolar place: "In economic terms," he noted in 1973, "there are at least five major groupings. Politically, many more centers of influence have emerged. . . ." With echoes of (and amendments to) Kennan, he identified five important regions, the United States, the USSR, China, Japan, and western Europe; and unlike many in Washington and (perhaps) everyone in Moscow, he welcomed this change. A *concert* of large powers, balancing each other off and with no one dominating another, would be "a safer world and a better world" than a bipolar situation in which "a gain for one side appears as an absolute loss for the other."[178] Confident in his own abilities to defend American interests in such a pluralistic world, Kissinger was urging a fundamental reshaping of American diplomacy in the largest sense of that word.

The diplomatic revolution caused by the steady Sino-American *rapprochement* after 1971 had a profound effect on the "global correlation of forces." Although taken by surprise at Washington's move, Japan felt that it at last was able to establish relations with the People's Republic of China, which thus gave a further boost to its booming Asian trade. The Cold War in Asia, it appeared, was over—or perhaps it would be better to say that it had become more complicated: Pakistan, which had been a diplomatic conduit for secret messages between Washington and Peking, received the support of both those Powers during its clash with India in 1971; Moscow, predictably, gave strong support to New Delhi. In Europe, too, the balances had been altered. Alarmed by China's hostility and taken aback by Kissinger's diplomacy, the Kremlin deemed it prudent to conclude the SALT I treaty and to encourage the various other attempts to improve relations across the Iron Curtain. It also held back when, following its tense confrontation with the United States at the time of the 1973 Arab-Israeli war, Kissinger commenced his "shuttle diplomacy" to reconcile Egypt and Israel, effectively freezing Russia out of any meaningful role.

It is difficult to know how long Kissinger could have kept up his Bismarck-style juggling act had the Watergate scandal not swept Nixon from the White House in August 1974 and made so many Americans even more suspicious of their government. As it was, the secretary of state remained in his post during Ford's tenure of the presidency, but with increasingly less freedom for maneuver. Defense budget requisitions were frequently slashed by Congress. All further aid was cut off to South Vietnam, Cambodia, and Laos in February 1975, a few months before those states were overrun. The War Powers Act sharply pared the president's capacity to commit American troops overseas. Soviet-Cuban interventions in Angola could not, Congress had voted, be countered by sending CIA funds and weapons to the pro-western factions there. With the Republican right growing restive at this decline in American power abroad and blaming Kissinger for ceding away national interests (the Panama Canal) and old friends (Taiwan), the secretary of state's position was beginning to crumble even before Ford was swept out of power in the 1976 election.

As the United States grappled with serious socioeconomic problems throughout the 1970s and as different political groups tried to reconcile themselves to its reduced international position, it was perhaps inevitable that its external policies would be more erratic than was the case in placid times. Nonetheless, there were to be "swings" in policy over the next few years which were remarkable by any standards. Imbued with the most creditable of Gladstonian and Wilsonian beliefs about the need to create a "fairer" global order, Carter breezily entered an international system in which many of the other actors (especially in the world's "trouble spots") had no intention of conducting their policies according to Judeo-Christian principles. Given the Third World's discontent at the economic gap between rich and poor nations, which had been exacerbated by the 1973 oil crisis, there was prudence as well as magnanimity in his push for north-south cooperation, just as there was common sense in the terms of the renegotiated Panama Canal treaty, and in his refusal to equate every Latin American reformist movement with Marxism. Carter also took justified credit for "brokering" the 1978 Camp David agreement between Egypt and Israel—although he ought not to have been so surprised at the critical reaction of the other Arab nations, which in turn was to give Russia the opportunity to strengthen its ties with the more radical states in the Middle East. For all its worthy intentions, however, the Carter government foundered upon the rocks of a complex world which seemed increasingly unwilling to abide by American advice, and upon its own inconsistencies of policy (often caused by quarrels within the administration).[179] Authoritarian, right-wing regimes were berated and pressured across the globe for their human-rights violations, yet Washington continued to support President Mobutu of Zaire, King Hassan of Morocco, and the shah of Iran—at least until the latter's demise in 1979, which led to the hostages crisis, and in turn to the flawed attempt to rescue them.[180] In other parts of the globe, from Nicaragua to Angola, the administration found it difficult to discover democratic-liberal forces worthy of its support, yet hesitated to commit itself against Marxist revolutionaries. Carter also hoped to keep defense expenditures low, and appeared bewildered that *détente* with the USSR had halted neither that country's arms spending nor its actions in the Third World. When Russian troops invaded Afghanistan at the end of 1979, Washington, which was by then engaged in a large-scale defense buildup, withdrew the SALT II treaty, canceled grain sales to Moscow, and began to pursue—especially in Brzezinski's celebrated visits to China and Afghanistan—"balance-of-power" politics which the president had condemned only four years earlier.[181]

If the Carter administration had come into office with a set of simple recipes for a complex world, those of his successor in 1980 were no less simple—albeit drastically different. Suffused by an emotional reaction against all that had "gone wrong" with the United States over the preceding two decades, boosted by an electoral landslide much affected by the humiliation in Iran, charged by an ideological view of the world which at times seemed positively Manichaean, the Reagan government was intent upon steering the ship of state in quite new directions. *Détente* was out, since it merely provided a mask for Russian expansionism. The arms buildup would be increased, in all directions. Human rights were off the agenda; "authoritarian governments" were in favor. Amazingly, even the "China card" was suspect, because of the Republican right's support for Taiwan. As might have been expected, much of this simplemindedness also foundered on the complex realities of the world outside, not to mention the resistance of a Congress and public which liked their president's homely patriotism but suspected his Cold War policies. Interventions in Latin America, or in any place clad in jungles and thus reminiscent of Vietnam, were constantly blocked. The escalation of the nuclear arms race produced widespread unease, and pressure for renewed arms talks, especially when administration supporters talked of being able to "prevail" in a nuclear confrontation with the Soviet Union. Authoritarian regimes in the tropics collapsed, often made more unpopular by association with the American government. The Europeans were bewildered at a logic which forbade them to buy natural gas from the USSR, but permitted American farmers to sell that country grain. In the Middle East, the Reagan administration's inability to put pressure upon Mr. Begin's Israel contradicted its strategy of lining up the Arab world in an anti-Russian front. At the United Nations, the United States seemed more isolated than ever; by 1984, it had withdrawn from UNESCO—a situation which would have amazed Franklin Roosevelt. By more than doubling the defense budget in five years, the United States was certainly going to possess greater military hardware than it did in 1980; but whether the Pentagon was receiving good value for its outpourings was increasingly doubted, as was the question of whether it could control its interservice rivalries.[182] The invasion of Grenada, trumpeted as a great success, was in various *operational* aspects worryingly close to a Gilbert and Sullivan farce. Last but not least, even sympathetic observers wondered if this administration could work out a coherent grand strategy when so many of its members were quarreling with one another (even after Haig's retirement as secretary of state), when its chief appeared to give little attention to critical issues, and when (with rare exceptions) it viewed the world outside through such ethnocentric spectacles.[183]

Many of these issues will be returned to in the final chapter. The point about listing the various troubles of the Carter and Reagan administrations *together* was that they had, taken as a whole, distracted attention from the larger forces which were shaping global power politics—and most particularly that shift from a bipolar to a multipolar world which Kissinger had much earlier detected and begun to adjust to. (As will be seen below, the emergence of three additional centers of political-cum-economic power—western Europe, China, and Japan—did not mean that the latter were free of problems either; but that is not the point here.) More important still, the American concentration upon the burgeoning problems of Nicaragua, Iran, Angola, Libya, and so on was still tending to obscure the fact that the country most affected by the transformations which were occurring in global politics during the 1970s was probably the USSR itself—a consideration which deserves some further brief elaboration before this section concludes.

That the USSR had enhanced its military strength in these years was undoubted. Yet, as Professor Ulam points out, because of other developments, that simply meant that

> the rulers of the Soviet Union were in a position to appreciate the
> uncomfortable discovery made by so many Americans in the forties

and fifties: enhanced power does not automatically, especially in the nuclear age, give a state greater security. From almost every point of view, economically and militarily, in absolute and in relative terms, the USSR under Brezhnev was much more powerful than it had been under Stalin. And yet along with this greatly increased strength came new international developments and foreign commitments that made the Soviet state more vulnerable to external danger and the turbulence of world politics than it had been, say, in 1952.[184]

Moreover, even in the closing years of the Carter administration the United States had resumed a defense buildup which—continued at a massive pace by the succeeding Reagan government—threatened to restore U.S. military superiority in strategic nuclear weaponry, to enhance U.S. maritime supremacy, and to place a heavier emphasis than ever before upon advanced technology. The annoyed Soviet reply that they would not be outspent or outgunned could not disguise the awkward fact that this would place increased pressure upon an economy which had significantly slowed down (pp. 429–32 below) and was not well positioned to indulge in a high-technology race.[185] By the late 1970s, it was in the embarrassing position of needing to import large amounts of foreign *grain,* not to mention technology. Its satellite empire in eastern Europe was, apart from the select Communist party cadres, increasingly disaffected; the Polish discontents in particular were a dreadful problem, and yet a repetition of the 1968 Czech invasion seemed to promise little relief. Far to the south, the threat of losing its Afghan buffer state to foreign (probably Chinese) influences provoked the 1979 coup d'état, which not only turned out to be a military quagmire but had a disastrous impact upon the Soviet Union's standing abroad.[186] Russian actions in Czechoslovakia, Poland, and Afghanistan had much reduced its appeal as a "model" to others, whether in western Europe or in Africa. Muslim fundamentalism in the Middle East was a disturbing phenomenon, which threatened (as in Iran) to vent itself against local Communists as well as against pro-American groupings. Above all, there was the relentless Chinese hostility, which, thanks to the Afghan and Vietnam complications, seemed even more marked at the end of the 1970s than it had at the beginning.[187] If any of the two superpowers had "lost China," it was Russia. Finally, the ethnocentricity and narrow suspiciousness of its aging rulers and the obstructiveness of its domestic elites, the *nomenklatura,* toward sweeping reforms were probably going to make a successful adjustment to the newer world balances even more difficult than for the United States.

All this ought to have been of some consolation in Washington, and acted as a guide to a more relaxed and sophisticated view of foreign-policy problems, even when the latter were unexpected and unpleasant. On some issues, admittedly, such as modifying earlier support for Taiwan, the Reagan administration did become more pragmatic and conciliatory. Yet the language of the 1979–1980 election campaign was difficult to shake off, perhaps because it had not been mere rhetoric, but a fundamentalist view of the world order and of the United States' destined place in it. As had happened so often in the past, the holding of such sentiments always made it difficult for countries to deal with external affairs as they really were, rather than as they thought they should be.

The Changing Economic Balances, 1950 to 1980

In July 1971, Richard Nixon repeated his opinion to a group of news-media executives in Kansas City that there now existed five clusters of world economic power—western Europe, Japan, and China as well as the USSR and the United States. "These are the five that will determine the economic future and, *because economic power will be the key to other kinds of power,* the future of the world in other ways in the last third of this century."[188] Assuming that presidential remark upon the importance of economic power to be valid, it is necessary to get a deeper sense of the transformations which were occurring in the global economy since the early years of the Cold War; for although international trade and prosperity were to be subject to some unusual turbulences (especially in the 1970s), certain basic long-term trends can be detected which seemed likely to shape the state of world politics into the foreseeable future.

As with all of the earlier periods covered in this book, there can be no exactitude in the comparative economic statistics used here. If anything, the growth in the number of professional statisticians employed by governments and by international organizations and the development of much more sophisticated techniques since the days of Mulhall's *Dictionary of Statistics* have tended to show how difficult is the task of making proper comparisons. The reluctance of "closed" societies to publish their figures, differentiated national ways of measuring income and product, and fluctuating exchange rates (especially after the post-1971 decisions to abandon a gold-exchange standard and to adopt floating exchange rates) have all combined to cast doubt upon the correctness of any *one* series of economic data.[189] On the other hand, a *number* of statistical indications can be used, with a reasonable degree of confidence, to correlate with one another and to point to broad trends occurring over time.

The first, and by far the most important, feature has been what Bairoch rightly describes as "a totally unprecedented rate of growth in

world industrial output"[190] during the decades after the Second World
War. Between 1953 and 1975 that growth rate averaged a remarkable
6 percent a year overall (4 percent per capita), and even in the 1973–
1980 period the average increase was 2.4 percent a year, which was
very respectable by historical standards. Bairoch's own calculations of
the "production of world manufacturing industries"—essentially
confirmed by Rostow's figures on "world industrial production"[191]—
give some sense of this dizzy rise (see Table 39).

Table 39. Production of World Manufacturing
Industries, 1830–1980[192]
(1900 = 100)

	Total Production	Annual Growth Rate
1830	34.1	(0.8)
1860	41.8	0.7
1880	59.4	1.8
1900	100.0	2.6
1913	172.4	4.3
1928	250.8	2.5
1938	311.4	2.2
1953	567.7	4.1
1963	950.1	5.3
1973	1730.6	6.2
1980	3041.6	2.4

As Bairoch also points out, "The accumulated world industrial output between 1953 and 1973 was comparable in volume to that of the
entire century and a half which separated 1953 from 1800."[193] The
recovery of war-damaged economies, the development of new technologies, the continued drift from agriculture to industry, the harnessing of national resources within "planned economies," and the spread
of industrialization to the Third World all helped to effect this dramatic
change.

In an even more emphatic way, and for much the same reasons, the
volume of world trade also grew spectacularly after 1945, in contrast
to the distortions of the era of the two world wars:

Table 40. Volume of World Trade,
1850–1971[194]
(1913 = 100)

1850	10.1	1938	103
1896–1900	57.0	1948	103
1913	100.0	1953	142
1921–1925	82	1963	269
1930	113	1968	407
1931–1935	93	1971	520

What was more encouraging, as Ashworth points out, was that by 1957, for the first time ever world trade in manufactured goods exceeded those in primary produce, which itself was a consequence of the fact that the increase in the overall output of manufactures during these decades was considerably larger than the (very impressive) increases in agricultural goods and minerals (see Table 41).

Table 41. Percentage Increases in World Production, 1948–1968[195]

	1948–1958	1958–1968
Agricultural goods	32%	30%
Minerals	40%	58%
Manufactures	60%	100%

To some extent, this disparity can be explained by the great increases in manufacturing and trade *among* the advanced industrial countries (especially those of the European Economic Community); but their rising demand for primary products and the beginnings of industrialization among an increasing number of Third World countries meant that the economies of most of the latter were also growing faster in these decades than at any time in the twentieth century.[196] Notwithstanding the damage which western imperialism did to many of the societies in other parts of the world, the exports and general economic growth of these societies do appear to have benefited most when the industrialized nations were in a period of expansion. Less-developed countries (LDCs), argues Foreman-Peck, grew rapidly in the nineteenth century when "open" economies like Britain's were expanding fast—just as they were the worst hit of all when the industrial world fell into depression in the 1930s. During the 1950s and 1960s, they once again experienced faster growth rates, because the developed countries were booming, raw-materials demand was rising, and industrialization was spreading.[197] After its nadir in 1953 (6.5 percent), Bairoch shows the Third World's share of world manufacturing production rising steadily, to 8.5 percent (1963), then 9.9 percent (1973), and then 12.0 percent (1980).[198] In the CIA's estimates, the less-developed countries' share of "gross world product" has also been increasing, from 11.1 percent (1960), to 12.3 percent (1970), to 14.8 percent (1980).[199]

Given the sheer number of people in the Third World, however, their share of world product was still disproportionately low—and their poverty horrifically manifest. The average GNP per capita in the industrialized countries was $10,660 in 1980, but only $1,580 per capita for the middle-income countries like Brazil, and a shocking $250 per capita for the very poorest Third World countries like Zaire.[200] For the fact was that while their proportion of world product and manufacturing output was arising *as a whole*, the gain was not shared in equal proportion by all of the LDCs. Differences in wealth between some countries in the tropics were large even as the colonialists withdrew—just as they had been, in many cases, before the imperial era. They were exacerbated by the uneven pattern of demand for the countries' products, by the varying levels of aid which each managed to secure, and by the vicissitudes of climate, politics, tampering with the environment, and economic forces quite outside their control. Drought could devastate a country for years. Civil wars, guerrilla activities, or the forced resettlement of peasants could reduce agricultural output and trade. Sinking world prices, say, of peanuts or tin could almost bring a single-product economy to a halt. Soaring interest rates, or a rise in the value of the U.S. dollar, could be body blows. A spiraling population growth, caused by western medical science's success in checking disease, increased the pressure upon food stocks and threatened to wipe out any gains in overall national income. On the other hand, there were states which went through a "green revolution," with agricultural output boosted by improved farming techniques and new strains of plants. In addition, the massive earnings recorded by those countries lucky enough to possess oil in the 1970s turned them into a different economic category—although even these so-called OPEC-LDCs suffered as oil prices tumbled in the early 1980s. Finally, in one of the most significant developments of all, there arose among Third World countries a number of what Rosecrance terms "the trading states"—South Korea, Taiwan, Singapore, and Malaysia, imitating Japan, West Germany, and Switzerland in their entrepreneurship and commitment to produce industrial manufactures for the global market.[201]

This disparity among less-developed nations points to the second major feature of macroeconomic change over the past few decades—the differential growth rates among the various nations of the globe, which was as true of the larger, industrialized Powers as it was of the smaller countries. Since this trend is the one which—on the record of the preceding centuries—has ultimately had the greatest impact upon the international power balances, it is worth examining in some detail how it affected the major nations in these decades.

There can be no doubt that the economic transformation of Japan after 1945 offered the most spectacular example of sustained modernization in these decades, outclassing almost all of the existing "advanced" countries as a commercial and technological competitor, and providing a model for emulation by the other Asian "trading states." To be sure, Japan had already distinguished itself almost a century earlier by becoming the first Asian country to copy the West in both economic and—fatefully for itself—military and imperialist terms. Although badly damaged by the 1937–1945 war, and cut off from its traditional markets and suppliers, it possessed an industrial infrastructure which could be repaired and a talented, well-educated, and socially cohesive population whose determination to improve themselves could now be channeled into peaceful commercial pursuits. For the few years after 1945, Japan was prostrate, an occupied territory, and dependent upon American aid. In 1950, the tide turned—ironically, to a large degree because of the heavy U.S. defense spending in the Korean War, which stimulated Japan's export-oriented companies. Toyota, for example, was in danger of foundering when it was rescued by the first of the U.S. Defense Department's orders for its trucks; and much the same happened to many other companies.[202]

There was, of course, much more to the "Japanese miracle" than the stimulant of American spending during the Korean War and, again, during the Vietnam War; and the effort to explain exactly how the country transformed itself, and how others can imitate its success, has turned into a miniature growth industry itself.[203] One major reason was its quite fanatical belief in achieving the highest levels of quality control, borrowing (and improving upon) sophisticated management techniques and production methods in the West. It benefited from the national commitment to vigorous, high-level standards of universal education, and from possessing vast numbers of engineers, of electronics and automobile buffs, and of small but entrepreneurial workshops as well as the giant *zaibatsu*. There was social ethos in favor of hard work, loyalty to the company, and the need to reconcile management-worker differences through a mixture of compromise and deference. The economy required enormous amounts of capital to achieve sustained growth, and it received just that—partly because there was so little expenditure upon defense by a "demilitarized" country sheltering under the American strategic umbrella, but perhaps even more because of fiscal and taxation policies which encouraged an unusually high degree of personal savings, which could then be used for investment purposes. Japan also benefited from the role played by MITI (its Ministry for International Trade and Industry) in "nursing new industries and technological developments while at the same time coordinating the orderly run-down of aging, decaying industries,"[204] all this in a manner totally different from the American laissez-faire approach.

Whatever the mix of explanations—and other experts upon Japan would point more strongly to cultural and sociological reasons, not to mention that indefinable "plus factor" of national self-confidence and willpower in a people whose time has come—there was no denying the extent of its economic success. Between 1950 and 1973 its gross domestic product grew at the fantastic average of 10.5 percent a year, far in excess of that of any other industrialized nation; and even the oil crisis in 1973–1974, with its profound blow to world expansion, did not prevent Japan's growth rates in subsequent years from staying almost twice as large as those of its major competitors. The range of manufactures in which Japan steadily became the dominant world producer was quite staggering—cameras, kitchen goods, electrical products, musical instruments, scooters, on and on the list goes. Japanese products challenged the Swiss watch industry, overshadowed the German optical industry, and devastated the British and American motorcycle industries. Within a decade, Japan's shipyards were producing over half of the world's tonnage of launchings. By the 1970s, its more modern steelworks were turning out as much as the American steel industry. The transformation of its automobile industry was even more dramatic—between 1960 and 1984 its share of world car production rose from 1 percent to 23 percent—and in consequence Japanese cars and trucks were being exported in their millions all over the world. Steadily, relentlessly, the country moved from low- to high-technology products—to computers, telecommunications, aerospace, robotics, and biotechnology. Steadily, relentlessly, its trade surpluses increased— turning it into a financial giant as well as an industrial one—and its share of world production and markets expanded. When the Allied occupation ended in 1952, Japan's "gross national product was little more than one-third that of France or the United Kingdom. By the late 1970s the Japanese GNP was as large as the United Kingdom's and France's *combined* and more than half the size of America's."[205] Within one generation, its share of the world's manufacturing output, and of GNP, had risen from around 2–3 percent to around 10 percent—and was not stopping. Only the USSR in the years after 1928 had achieved anything like that degree of growth, but Japan had done it far less painfully and in a much more impressive, broader-based way.

By comparison with Japan, *every* other large Power must seem economically sluggish. Nonetheless, when the People's Republic of China (PRC) began to assert itself in the years after its foundation in 1949, there were few observers who did not take it seriously. In part this may have reflected a traditional worry about the "Yellow Peril," since the sleeping giant in the East would clearly be a major force in world affairs just as soon as it had organized its 800 million population for national purposes. More important still was the very prominent, not to say aggressive, role which the PRC adopted toward foreign Powers almost since its inception, even if that may have been a nervous response to its perceived encirclement. The clashes with the United States over Korea and Quemoy and Matsu; the move into Tibet; the border struggles with India; the angry break with the USSR, and military confrontations in the disputed regions; the bloody encounter with North Vietnam; and the generally combative tone of Chinese propaganda (especially under Mao) as it criticized western imperialism and "Russian hegemonism" and urged on people's liberation movements across the globe made it a much more important, but also more incalculable, figure in world affairs than the discreet and subtle Japanese.[206] Simply because China possessed one-quarter of the world's population, its political lurches in one direction or another had to be taken seriously.

Nevertheless, measured on strictly economic criteria, the PRC seemed a classic case of economic backwardness. In 1953, for example, it was responsible for only 2.3 percent of world manufacturing production and had a "total industrial potential" equal only to 71 percent of Britain's in 1900![207] Its population, leaping upward by tens of millions of new mouths each year, consisted overwhelmingly of poor peasants whose per capita output was dreadfully low and rendered the state little in terms of "added value." The disruption caused by the warlords, the Japanese invasion, and then the civil war of the late 1940s was not stopped when the peasant communes took over from the landowners after 1949. Nevertheless, economic prospects were not entirely hopeless. China did possess a basic infrastructure of roads and light railways, its textile industry was substantial, its cities and ports were centers of entrepreneurial activity, and the Manchurian region in particular had been developed by the Japanese during the 1930s.[208] What the country required, if it was to enter the stage of industrial takeoff, was a long period of stability and massive infusions of capital. Both conditions were achieved to some degree—because of the dominance of the Communist Party, and the flow of Russian aid—as the 1950s evolved. The Five-Year Plan of 1953 consciously imitated those Stalinist priorities of developing heavy industry and of increasing steel, iron and coal production. By 1957, industrial output had doubled.[209] On the other hand, the amount of ready capital for industrial investment, whether raised internally or borrowed from Russia, was quite insufficient for a country of China's economic needs—and the Sino-Soviet split brought Russian financial and technical aid to an abrupt halt. In addition, Mao's fatuous decisions to achieve a "Great Leap Forward" by encouraging thousands of cottage-sized steelworks and his campaign for the "Cultural Revolution" (which led to the disgrace of technical experts, professional managers, and trained economists) slowed development considerably. Finally, throughout the 1950s and 1960s, the PRC's confrontationist diplomacy and its military clashes with almost all of its neighbors meant that far too large a proportion of the country's scarce resources had to be devoted to the armed forces.

The period of the Cultural Revolution was not *all* bad in economic terms; it did at least emphasize the importance of the rural areas, stimulating small-scale industries as well as improved farming techniques, and bringing basic medical and social care to the villages.[210] Nevertheless, significant increases in national product could come only from further industrialization, infrastructural improvements, and long-term investments—all of which were aided by the winding down of the Cultural Revolution and by the growth of trade with the United States, Japan, and other advanced economies. China's own coal and oil resources were being swiftly exploited, as were its stocks of many precious minerals. By 1980, its steel output of 37 million tons was well in excess of that of Britain or France, and its consumption of energy from modern sources was twice that of any of the leading European states.[211] By that date, too, its share of world manufacturing production had risen to 5.0 percent (from 3.9 percent in 1973), and was closing upon West Germany's.[212] This heady recent growth has not been unattended by problems, and the party leadership has had to readjust downward the targets for the country's "four modernizations"; it is also worth repeating that when any of China's statistics of wealth or output are presented in per capita terms, its relative economic backwardness is again revealed. Yet, notwithstanding those deficiencies, it became clear over time that the Asian giant was at last on the move and determined to build an economic foundation adequate for its intended role as a Great Power.[213]

The fifth region of economic power identified by Nixon in his July 1971 speech had been "western Europe," which was of course more of a geographical expression than a unified assertive Power like China, the USSR, and the United States. Even the term itself meant different things to different people—it could be all of those countries outside the Russian-dominated sphere (and therefore include Scandinavia, Greece, and Turkey), or it could be the original (or enlarged) European Economic Community, which at least possessed an institutional framework, or it was often used as a shorthand for that cluster of formerly great states (Britain, France, Germany, Italy) which might need to be consulted, say, by the U.S. State Department before the latter initiated a new policy toward Russia or in the Middle East. Even that did not exhaust the possibilities of semantic confusion, since for much of this period the British regarded "Europe" as beginning on the other side of the English Channel; and there were, moreover, many committed European integrationists (not to mention German nationalists) who regarded the post-1945 division of the continent as a merely temporary condition, to be followed in the future by a joining of the countries of both sides into some larger union. Politically and constitutionally, therefore, it has been difficult to use the term "Europe" or even "western Europe" as more than a figure of speech—or a vague cultural-geographical concept.[214]

At the economic level, however, there did seem to be a basic similarity in what was being experienced across Europe in these years. The most outstanding feature was the "sustained and high level of economic growth."[215] By 1949–1950, most countries were back to their prewar levels of output, and some (especially, of course, the wartime neutrals) were significantly ahead. But there then followed year after year of increased manufacturing output, of unprecedented levels of growth in exports, of a remarkable degree of full employment and historically high levels of disposable income as well as of investment capital. The result was to make Europe the fastest-growing region in the world, Japan excepted. "Between 1950 and 1970 European gross domestic product grew on average at about 5.5 percent per annum and 4.4 percent on a per capita basis, as against world average rates of 5.0 and 3.0 percent respectively. Industrial production rose even faster at 7.1 percent compared with a world rate of 5.9 percent. Thus by the latter date output per head in Europe was almost two and a half times greater than in 1950."[216] Interestingly enough, this growth was shared in all parts of the continent—in northwestern Europe's industrial core, in the Mediterranean lands, in eastern Europe; even the sluggish British economy grew faster during this period than it had for decades. Not surprisingly, Europe's relative place in the world economy, which had been declining since the turn of the century, soon began to expand. "During the period 1950 to 1970 her share of world output of goods and services (GDP) rose from 37 to 41 percent, while in the case of industrial production the increase was even greater, from 39 to 48 percent."[217] Both in 1960 and in 1970, the CIA figures were showing—admittedly on statistical evidence that can be disputed[218]— that the "European Community" possessed a larger share of gross world product than even the United States, and that it was twice as large as the Soviet Union's.

The reasons for Europe's economic recovery are, on reflection, not at all surprising. For too long, much of the continent had suffered from invasions, prolonged fighting and foreign occupation, bombings of towns, factories, roads, and railways, shortages of food and raw materials caused by blockade, the call-up of millions of men and killing off of millions of animals. Even before the fighting, Europe's "natural" economic development—that is, growth which evolved region by region, as new sources of energy and production revealed themselves, as new markets took off, as new technology spread—had been distorted by the actions of the nationalistically inclined *Machtstaat.*[219] Ever-higher tariff barriers had separated suppliers from their markets. Government subventions had kept inefficient firms and farmers protected from foreign competition. Increasingly large amounts of national income had been devoted to armaments spending rather than commercial enterprise. It was thus impossible to maximize Europe's economic growth in this "climate of blocks and autarky, of economic nationalism, and of gaining benefits by hurting others."[220] Now, after 1945, there were not only "new Europeans" like Monnet, Spaak, and Hallstein determined to create economic structures which would avoid the mistakes of the past, but there was also a helpful and beneficient United States, willing (through the Marshall Plan and other aid schemes) to finance Europe's recovery provided it was done as a cooperative venture.

Thus, a Europe whose economic potential had been distorted and underutilized by war and politics now had a chance to correct those deficiencies. There was a broad determination to "build anew" in both eastern and western parts of the continent, and a willingness to learn from the follies of the 1930s. State planning, whether of the Keynesian or socialistic variety, gave a concentrated thrust to this desire for social and economic improvement; the collapse (or discrediting) of older structures made innovation easier. The United States not only gave billions of dollars of Marshall Plan aid—"a shot in the arm at a critical time," as it was aptly described[221]—but also provided a defense umbrella under which the European states could shelter. (It was true that both Britain and France spent heavily on defense during the Korean War years and the period before their decolonizations—but they, and all their neighbors, would have had to devote much more of their scarce national resources to armaments had they not been protected by the United States.) Because there were fewer trade barriers, firms and individuals were able to flourish in a much larger market. This was especially so since trade *among* developed countries (in this case, the European states themselves) was always more profitable than trade elsewhere, simply because the mutual demand was greater. If the "foreign" trade of Europe rose faster than anything else in these decades, therefore, it was chiefly because much more buying and selling was going on among neighbors. In one generation after 1950, per capita income increased as much as it had during the century and a half prior to that date![222] The socioeconomic pace of this change was truly remarkable: the share of West Germany's working population engaged in agriculture, forestry and fishing dropped from 24.6 percent in 1950 to 7.5 percent in 1973, and in France it fell from 28.2 percent to 12.2 percent in the same period (and to 8.8 percent in 1980). Disposable incomes boomed as industrialization spread; in West Germany per capita income soared from $320 in 1949 to $9,131 in 1978, and in Italy it rose from $638 in 1960 to $5,142 in 1979. The number of automobiles per 1,000 of population rose from 6.3 in West Germany (1948) to 227 (1970), and in France from 37 to 252.[223] However one measured it, and despite continued regional disparities, the evidence of very real gains was clear.

This combination of general economic growth, together with wide variations in both the rate of change and its effects, can clearly be seen if one examines what happened in each of the former Great Powers. South of the Alps, there occurred what journalists hyperbolically termed "the Italian miracle," with the country's GNP in real terms rising nearly three times as fast after 1948 than it had during the interwar years; indeed, until 1963, when growth slowed, the Italian economy rose faster in these years than that of any other country except Japan and West Germany. Yet perhaps that, too, is not surprising in retrospect. It was always the least developed of the European "Big Four," which is another way of saying that its potential for growth had not been as fully exploited. Freed from the absurdities of fascist economic policies, and benefiting strongly from American aid, Italian manufacturers were able to utilize the country's lower wage costs and strong reputation in design to boost exports at an amazingly fast rate, especially within the Common Market. Hydroelectricity and cheaply imported oil compensated for the lack of indigenous coal supplies. Motor construction was a great stimulant. As local consumption levels boomed, FIAT, the domestic automobile producer, occupied an unchallenged position for many years in this home market, giving it a strong base for its export drive north of the Alps. Traditional manufactures, like shoes and fine clothes, were now joined by newer products; Italian refrigerators outsold any others in Europe by the 1960s. This was not, by any means, a story of unqualified success. The gap between north and south in Italy remained chronic. Social conditions, both in the inner cities and in the poorer rural areas, were far worse than in northern Europe. Governmental instability, a large "black economy," and a high public deficit, together with a higher than average inflation rate, affected the value of the lira and suggested that this economic recovery was a fragile one. Whenever European-wide comparisons of income, or industrialization, were made, Italy did not compare too well with its more advanced neighbors; when *growth* rates were compared, things looked much better. That is simply another way of saying that Italy had started from a long way behind.[224]

By contrast, Great Britain in 1945 was a long way ahead, at least among the larger European states; which may be part of the explanation for its relative economic decline during the four decades following. That is to say, since it (just like the United States) had not been so badly damaged by the war, its rate of growth was unlikely to be as high as in those countries recovering from years of military occupation and damage. Psychologically, too, as has been discussed above,[225] the fact that Britain was undefeated, that it was still one of the "Big Three" at Potsdam, and that it regained all of its worldwide empire made it difficult for people to see the need for drastic reforms in its own economic system. Far from producing newer structures, the war had preserved traditional institutions such as trade unions, the civil service, the ancient universities. Although the Labor administration of 1945–1951 pushed ahead with its plans for nationalization and for the creation of a "welfare state," a more fundamental restructuring of economic practices and of *attitudes* to work did not occur. Confident still in its special place in the world, Britain continued to rely upon captive colonial markets, struggled in vain to preserve the old parity for sterling, maintained extensive overseas garrisons (a great drain on the currency), declined to join in the early moves toward European unity, and spent more on defense than any of the other NATO powers apart from the United States itself.

The frailty of Britain's international and economic position was partially disguised in the early post-1945 period by the even greater weakness of other states, the prudent withdrawals from India and Palestine, the short-term surge in exports, and the maintenance of empire in the Middle East and Africa.[226] The humiliation at Suez in 1956 therefore came as a greater shock, since it revealed not only the weakness of sterling but also the blunt fact that Britain could not operate militarily in the Third World in the face of American disapproval. Nonetheless, it can be argued that the realities of decline were *still* disguised—in defense matters, by the post-1957 policy of relying upon the nuclear deterrent, which was far less expensive than large conventional forces yet suggested a continued Great Power status; and in economic matters, by the fact that Britain also shared in the general boom of the 1950s and 1960s. If its growth rates were about the lowest in Europe, they were nevertheless better than the expansion of previous decades and thus allowed Macmillan to claim to the British electors, "You've never had it so good!" Measured in terms of disposable income, or numbers of washing machines and automobiles, that claim was historically correct.

Measured against the much faster progress being made elsewhere, however, the country appeared to be suffering from what the Germans unkindly termed "the English disease"—a combination of militant trade unionism, poor management, "stop-go" policies by government, and negative cultural attitudes toward hard work and entrepreneurship. The new prosperity brought a massive surge in imports of better-designed European products and of cheaper Asian wares, in turn leading to balance-of-payments difficulties, sterling crises, and devaluations which helped to fuel inflation and thus higher wage demands. Price controls, legislation on wage increases, and fiscal deflation were employed at various times by British governments to check inflation and create the right circumstances for sustained growth. They rarely worked for long. The British automobile industry was steadily undermined by its foreign competitors, the once-booming shipbuilding industry grew to depend almost solely upon Admiralty orders, the producers of electrical goods and motorbikes found that they could no longer compete. Some companies (like ICI) were notable exceptions to this trend; the City of London's financial services held up well, and retailing remained strong—but the erosion of Britain's *industrial* base was remorseless. Joining the Common Market in 1971 did not provide the hoped-for panacea: it exposed the British market to even greater competition in manufactures, while tying Britain into the expensive farm-price policies of the EEC. North Sea oil also proved less than a godsend: it brought Britain massive foreign-currency earnings, but that so drove up the price of sterling that it hurt manufacturing exports.[227]

The economic statistics offer a measure of what Bairoch terms "the acceleration of the industrial decline of Great Britain."[228] Its share of world manufacturing production slipped from 8.6 percent in 1953 to 4.0 percent in 1980. Its share of world trade also fell away swiftly, from 19.8 percent (1955) to 8.7 percent (1976). Its gross national product, third-largest in the world in 1945, was overtaken by West Germany's, then by Japan's, then by France's. Its per capita disposable income was steadily overtaken by a host of smaller but richer European countries; by the late 1970s it was closer to those of Mediterranean states than to those of West Germany, France, or the Benelux countries.[229] To be sure, much of this decline in Britain's *shares* (whether of world trade or world GNP) was due to the fact that special technical and historical circumstances had given the country a disproportionately large amount of global wealth and commerce in earlier decades; now that those special circumstances had gone, and other countries were able to exploit their own potential for industrialization, it was natural that Britain's relative position should slip. Whether it should have slipped so much and so fast is another issue; whether it will slip further, relative to its European neighbors, is equally difficult to say. By the early 1980s, the decline seemed to be leveling off, leaving Britain still with the world's sixth-largest economy, and with very substantial armed forces. By comparison with Lloyd George's time, or even with Clement Attlee's in 1945, however, it was now just an ordinary, moderately large power, not a Great Power.

While the British economy was languishing in relative decline, West Germany was enjoying its *Wirtschaftswunder,* or "economic miracle." Once again, it is worth stressing how "natural," relatively speaking, this development was. Even in its truncated state, the Federal Republic possessed the most developed infrastructure in Europe, contained large internal resources (from coal to machine-tool plants), and had a highly educated population, perhaps especially strong in managers, engineers, and scientists, which was swollen by the emigration of talent from the east. For the past half-century or more, its economic powers had been distorted by the requirements of the German military machine. Now that the national energies could (as in Japan) be concentrated solely upon commercial success, the only question was the extent of the recovery. German big business, which had accommodated itself fairly easily to the Second Reich, to Weimar, and then to the Nazi period of rule, had to adjust to the new circumstances and pick up American management assumptions.[230] The big banks were once again able to play a large role in the direction of industry. The chemical and electrical industries soon reemerged to be the giants of European industry. Massively successful automobile companies, like Volkswagen and Mercedes, had their inevitable "multiplier effects" upon hundreds of small supplier firms. As exports boomed—Germany became second only to the United States in world export trade—increasing number of firms and local communities needed to bring in "guest workers" to meet the crying demand for unskilled labor. Once again, for the third time in a hundred years, the German economy was the powerhouse of Europe's economic growth.[231]

Statistically, then, the story seemed one of unbroken success. Even between 1948 and 1952, German industrial production rose by 110 percent and real GNP by 67 percent.[232] With the country having the highest gross investment levels in Europe, German firms benefited immensely from their ready access to capital. Steel output, virtually nonexistent in 1946, was soon the largest in Europe (over 34 million tons by 1960), and the same was true of most other industries. Year after year, the country had the largest growth in gross domestic product. Its GNP, a mere $32 billion in 1952, was the biggest in Europe (at $89 billion) by a decade later, and was over $600 billion by the late 1970s. Its per capita disposable income, a modest $1,186 in 1960 (when the United States' was $2,491), was an imposing $10,837 in 1979—ahead of the American average of $9,595.[233] Year after year, export surpluses were built up, with the deutsche mark needing frequent upward adjustment, and indeed becoming a sort of reserve currency. Although naturally worried at the competition posed by the even more efficient Japanese, the West Germans were undoubtedly the second most successful among the larger "trading states." This was the more impressive since the country had been separated from 40 percent of its territory and over 35 percent of its population; ironically, the German Democratic Republic was soon to show that it was the most productive and industrialized per capita of all of the eastern European states (including the USSR) despite the loss of millions of its talented labor force to the West. Had it been possible to return to the 1937 boundaries, a united Germany would once again have been far ahead of any economic rival in Europe and, indeed, perhaps not significantly behind the much larger USSR itself.

Precisely because Germany had been defeated and divided, and because its international status (and that of Berlin) continued to be regulated by the "treaty powers," this economic weight did not translate into political might. Feeling a natural responsibility toward Germans in the east, the Federal Republic was peculiarly sensitive to any warming or cooling in the NATO–Warsaw Pact relationship. It had the largest trade with eastern Europe and the USSR, yet it was obviously in the front line should another war occur. Soviet and (only slightly less) French alarm at any revival of "German militarism" meant that it could never become a nuclear Power. It felt guilty toward neighbors like the Poles and the Czechs, vulnerable toward Russia, heavily dependent upon the United States; it welcomed with gratitude the special Franco-German relationship offered by de Gaulle, but rarely felt able to use its economic muscle to control the more assertive policies of the French. Engaged in a profound intellectual confrontation with their own past, the West Germans were very happy to be seen as good team players, but *not* as decisive leaders in international affairs.[234]

This contrasted very markedly, then, with France's role in the postwar world or, more accurately, in the post-1958 world, when de Gaulle took over the helm of the state. As mentioned above (pp. 401–2), the economic progress which the planners around Monnet hoped to achieve after 1945 had been affected by colonial wars, party-political instability, and the weakness of the franc. Yet even at the time of the Indochinese and Algerian campaigns the French economy was growing fast. For the first time in many decades, its population was increasing, and thus fueling domestic demand. France was a rich, varied, but half-developed land, its economy stagnant since the early 1930s. Merely with the coming of peace, the infusion of American aid, the nationalization of utilities, and the stimulus of a larger market, growth was likely. Furthermore, France (like Italy) had a relatively low per capita level of industrialization, because of its small-town, agriculture-heavy economy, which meant that the increases in that regard were quite spectacular: from 95 in 1953, to 167 in 1963, to 259 in 1973 (relative to U.K. in 1900 = 100).[235] The annual rate of growth reached an average of 4.6 percent in the 1950s, and spurted to 5.8 percent in the 1960s, under the impetus of Common Market membership. The particular arrangements of the latter not only protected French agriculture from world-market prices, but gave it a large market within Europe. The general boom in the West aided the export of France's traditional high-added-value wares (clothes, shoes, wines, jewelry), which were now joined by aircraft and automobiles. Between 1949 and 1969, automobile production rose tenfold, aluminum sixfold, tractors and cement fourfold, iron and steel two and a half times.[236] The country had always been relatively rich, if underindustrialized; by the 1970s, it was a lot richer, and looked altogether more modern.

Nevertheless, France's growth was never as broadly based industrially as that of its neighbor across the Rhine, and President Pompidou's hopes that his country would soon overtake West Germany had little prospect of realization. With certain notable exceptions in the electrical, automobile, and aerospace industries, most French firms were still small and undercapitalized, and the prices of their products were too high compared with Germany's. Despite the "rationalization" of agriculture, many smallholdings remained—and were, in fact, sustained by the Common Market subvention policies; yet the pressures upon rural France, together with the social strain of industrial modernization (closing old steelworks, etc.) provoked outbursts of working-class discontent, of which the most famous were the 1968 riots. Poor in indigenous fuel supplies, France became heavily dependent upon imported oil, and (despite its ambitious nuclear-energy program) its balance of payments heavily fluctuated according to the world price of oil. Its trade deficit with West Germany steadily increased, and necessitated regular (if embarrassed) devaluations against the deutsche mark—which was probably a more reliable measure of France's economic standing than the wild fluctuations in the dollar-franc exchange rate. Even in periods of sustained economic growth, then, there was a certain precariousness to the French economy—which, in the event of shock, sent many prudent bourgeois across the Swiss frontier, bearing the family savings.

Yet France always had an impact upon affairs far larger than might be expected from a country with a mere 4 percent of the world GNP— and this was true not merely of the period of de Gaulle's presidency. It may have been due to sheer national-cultural assertiveness,[237] and that coinciding with a time when Anglo-American influences were waning, Russia was appearing more and more unattractive, and Germany was deferential. If western Europe *was* to have a leader and spokesman, France was a more obvious candidate than the isolationist British or the subdued Germans. Furthermore, successive French administrations quickly recognized that their country's modest real power could be buttressed by persuading the Common Market to adopt a particular line—on agricultural tariffs, high technology, overseas aid, cooperation at the United Nations, policy toward the Arab-Israeli conflict, and so on—which effectively harnessed what had become the world's largest trading bloc to positions favored by Paris. None of this restrained France from quite unilateral actions when the occasion seemed to merit it.

The fact that all four of these larger European states grew in wealth and output during these decades, together with their smaller neighbors, was not a guarantee of everlasting happiness. The early hopes toward ever-closer political and constitutional integration foundered upon the still-strong nationalism of its members, shown first of all by de Gaulle's France, and then by those states (Britain, Denmark, Greece) which had only later, and more warily, joined the EEC. Economic disputes, especially over the high cost of the farm-support policy, often paralyzed affairs in Brussels and Strasbourg. With neutral Eire a member, it was not possible to effect a common defense policy, which had to be left to NATO (from whose command structure the French had now absented themselves). The shock of the oil price rises in the 1970s seemed to hit Europe especially badly, and to take the steam out of the earlier optimism; despite widespread alarm, and considerable planning in Brussels, it seemed difficult to evolve high-technology policies to counter the Japanese and American challenges. Yet, notwithstanding these many difficulties, the sheer economic size of the EEC meant that the international landscape was now significantly different from that of 1945 or 1948. The EEC was by far the largest importer and exporter of the world's goods (although much of that was intra-European trade), and it contained, by 1983, by far the largest international currency and gold reserves; it manufactured more automobiles (34 percent) than either Japan (24 percent) or the United States (23 percent) and more cement than anyone else, and its crude-steel production was second only to that of the USSR.[238] With a total population in 1983 significantly larger than the United States' and almost exactly the same as Russia's—each having 272 million—the ten-member EEC had a substantially bigger GNP and share of world manufacturing production than the Soviet state, or the entire Comecon bloc. If politically and militarily the European Community was still immature, it was now a much more powerful presence in the global economic balances than in 1956.

Almost exactly the opposite could be said about the USSR, as it evolved from the 1950s to the 1980s. As has been described above (pp. 385–91), these were decades when the Soviet Union not only maintained a strong army, but also achieved nuclear-strategic parity with the United States, developed an oceangoing navy, and extended its influence in various parts of the world. Yet this persistent drive to achieve equality with the Americans on the global scene was not matched by parallel achievements at the economic level. Ironically (given Marx's stress upon the importance of the productive substructure in determining events), the country which claimed to be the world's original Communist state appeared to be suffering from increasing economic difficulties as time went on.

This is not to gainsay the quite impressive economic progress which was made in the USSR—and throughout the Soviet-dominated bloc—since Stalin's final years. In many respects, the region was even more transformed than western Europe during those few decades, although that may have been chiefly due to the fact that it was so much poorer and "underdeveloped" to begin with. At any event, measured in crude statistical terms, the gains were imposing. Russia's steel output, a mere 12.3 million tons in 1945, soared to 65.3 million tons in 1960, and to 148 million tons in 1980 (making the USSR the world's largest producer); electricity output rose from 43.2 million kilowatt-hours, to 292 million, to 1.294 billion, during the same periods; automobile production jumped from 74,000 units, to 524,000, to 2.2 million units; and this list of increases in products could be added to almost indefinitely.[239] Overall industrial output, averaging over 10 percent growth a year during the 1950s, increased from a notional 100 in 1953 to 421 in 1964,[240] which was a remarkable achievement—as were such obvious manifestations of Russian prowess as the Sputnik, space exploration, and military hardware. By the time of Khrushchev's political demise, the country had a far more prosperous, broader-based economy than under Stalin, and that absolute gain has steadily increased.

There were, however, two serious defects which began to over-shadow these achievements. The first was the steady, long-term *decline* in the rate of growth, with industrial output each year since 1959 dropping from double-digit increases to a lower and lower figure, so that by the late 1970s it was down to 3–4 percent a year and still falling. In retrospect, this was a fairly natural development, since it has now become clear that the early, impressive annual increases were chiefly due to vast infusions of labor and capital. As the existing labor supply began to be fully utilized (and to compete with the requirements of the armed forces, and agriculture), the pace of growth could not help but fall back. As for capital investment, it was heavily directed into large-scale industry and defense-related production, which again empha-sized quantitative rather than qualitative growth, and left many other sectors of the economy undercapitalized. Although the standard of living of the average Russian was improved by Khrushchev and his successors, nonetheless consumer demand could not (as in the West) stimulate growth in an economy in which personal consumption was being deliberately kept low in order to preserve national resources for heavy industry and the military. Above all, perhaps, there remained the chronic structural and climatic weaknesses affecting Soviet agri-culture, the net output of which grew 4.8 percent a year in the 1950s but only 3 percent in the 1960s and 1.8 percent in the 1970s—despite all the attention and capital lavished upon it by anguished Soviet plan-ners and their ministers.[241] Bearing in mind the size of the agricultural sector in the USSR, and the fact that its population rose by 84 million in the three decades after 1950, the overall increases in national prod-uct per capita were significantly less than the rates of *industrial* output, which were in themselves a somewhat "forced" achievement.

The second serious defect was, predictably enough, in terms of the Soviet Union's *relative* economic standing. During the 1950s and early 1960s, with its share both of world manufacturing output and of world trade increasing, Khrushchev's claim that the Marxist mode of produc-tion was superior and would one day "bury capitalism" seemed to have some plausibility to it. Since that time, however, the trend has become more worrying to the Kremlin. The European Community, led by its industrial half-giant West Germany, has become much wealthier and more productive than the USSR. The small island state of Japan grew so fast that its overtaking of Russia's total GNP became merely a matter of time. The United States, despite its own relative industrial decline, kept ahead in total output and wealth. The standard of living of the average Russian, and of his eastern-European confreres, did not close the gap with that in western Europe, toward which the peoples of the

Marxist economies looked with some envy. The newer technology, of computers, robotics, telecommunications, revealed the USSR and its satellites as poorly positioned to compete. And agriculture remained as weak as ever, in productive terms: in 1980, the American farm worker was producing enough food to supply sixty-five people, whereas his Russian equivalent turned out enough to feed only eight.[242] This, in turn, led to the embarrassing Soviet need to import increasing amounts of foodstuffs.

Many of Russia's own economic difficulties have been mirrored by those of its satellites, which also achieved high growth rates in the 1950s and early 1960s—though again from levels which were low compared with those of the West, and by following priorities which similarly emphasized centralized planning, heavy industry, and collectivization of agriculture.[243] While significant differences in prosperity and growth occurred among the eastern European states (and still do occur), the overall tendency was one of early expansion and then slowdown—leaving Marxist planners with a choice of difficult options. In Russia's case, additional farmland could be brought under cultivation, though the limits imposed by the winter ecology in the north and the deserts in the south restricted possibilities in that direction (and easily reminded many of how Khrushchev's confident exploitation of the "virgin lands" soon turned them into dustbowls);[244] similarly, more intensive exploitation of raw materials ran the danger of increasing inefficiencies in dealing with, say, oil stocks,[245] while extractive costs rose swiftly as soon as mining was extended into the permafrost region. More capital might be poured into industry and technology, but only at the cost of diverting resources either from defense—which has remained the number-one priority of the USSR, despite all the changes of leadership—or from consumer goods— slighting of which was seen to be highly unpopular (especially in eastern Europe) at a time when improved communications were making the West's relative prosperity even more obvious. Finally, Russia and its fellow Communist regimes could contemplate a series of reforms, not merely of the regular rooting-out-corruption and shaking-up-the-bureaucracy sort, but of the *system* itself, providing personal incentives, introducing a more realistic price mechanism, allowing increases in private farming, encouraging open discussion and entrepreneurship in dealing with the newer technologies, etc.; in other words, going for "creeping capitalism," such as the Hungarians were adroitly practicing in the 1970s. The difficulty of that strategy, as the Czech experiences of 1968 showed, was that "liberalization" measures threw into question the *dirigiste* Communist regime itself—and were therefore frowned upon by party ideologues and the military throughout the cautious Brezhnev era.[246] Reversing relative economic decline therefore had to be done carefully, which in turn made a striking success unlikely.

Perhaps the only consolation to decision-makers in the Kremlin was that their archrival, the United States, also appeared to be encountering economic difficulties from the 1960s onward and that it was swiftly losing the *relative* share of the world's wealth, production, and trade which it had possessed in 1945. Yet mention of that year is, of course, the most important fact in understanding the American relative decline. As argued above, the United States' favorable economic position at that point in history was both unprecedented and artificial. It was on top of the world partly because of its own productive spurt, but also because of the temporary weakness of other nations. That situation would alter, against the United States, with Europe's and Japan's recovery of prewar level of output; and it would alter still further with the general expansion of world manufacturing production (which rose more than threefold between 1953 and 1973), since it was inconceivable that the United States could maintain its one-half share of 1945 when new factories and industrial plant were being created all over the globe. By 1953, Bairoch calculates, the American percentage had fallen to 44.7 percent; by 1980 to 31.5 percent; and it was still falling.[247] For much the same reason, the CIA's economic indicators showed the United States' share of world GNP dropping from 25.9 percent in 1960 to 21.5 percent in 1980 (although the dollar's short-lived rise in the currency markets would see that share increase over the next few years).[248] The point was not that Americans were producing significantly less (except in industries generally declining in the western world), but that others were producing much more. Automobile production is perhaps the easiest way of illustrating the two trends which make up this story: in 1960, the United States manufactured 6.65 million automobiles, which was a massive 52 percent of the world output of 12.8 million such vehicles; by 1980, it was producing a mere 23 percent of the world output, but since the latter totaled 30 million units, the absolute American production had increased to 6.9 million units.

Yet despite that half-consoling thought—similar to the argument which the British used to half-console themselves seventy years earlier when their shares of world output began to be eroded—there was a worrying aspect to this development. The real question was not "Did the United States have to decline relatively?" but "Did it have to decline *so fast?*" For the fact was that even in the heyday of the Pax Americana, its competitive position was already being eroded by a disturbingly low average annual rate of growth of output per capita, especially as compared with previous decades (see Table 42).

Once again, it may be possible to argue that this was a historically "natural" development. As Michael Balfour remarks, for decades be-

Table 42. Average Annual Rate of
Growth of Output per Capita,
1948–1962[249]

	(1913–50)	1948–62
United States	(1.7)	1.6
U.K.	(1.3)	2.4
Belgium	(0.7)	2.2
France	(0.7)	3.4
Germany/FRG	(0.4)	6.8
Italy	(0.6)	5.6

fore 1950 the United States had increased its output faster than anyone else because it had been a major innovator in methods of standardization and mass production. As a result, it had "gone further than any other country to satisfy human needs and [was] already operating at a high level of efficiency (measured in terms of output per man per hour) so that the known possibilities for increasing output by better methods or better machinery were, in comparison with the rest of the world, smaller."[250] Yet while that was surely true, the United States was not helped by certain other secular trends which were occurring in its economy: fiscal and taxation policies encouraged high consumption, but a low personal savings rate; investment in R&D, except for military purposes, was slowly sinking compared with other countries; and defense expenditures themselves, as a proportion of national product, were larger than anywhere else in the western bloc of nations. In addition, an increasing proportion of the American population was moving from industry to services, that is, into low-productivity fields.[251]

Much of this was hidden during the 1950s and 1960s by the glamour developments of American high technology (especially in the air), by the high prosperity which triggered off consumer demand for flashy cars and color televisions, and by the evident flow of dollars from the United States to poorer parts of the world, as foreign aid, or as military spending, or as investment by banks and companies. It is instructive in this regard to recall the widespread alarm in the mid-1960s at what Servan-Schreiber called le défi Americain—the vast outward surge of U.S. investments into Europe (and, by extension, elsewhere), allegedly turning those countries into economic satellites; the awe, or hatred, with which giant multinationals like Exxon and General Motors were regarded; and, associated with these trends, the respect accorded to the sophisticated management techniques imbued by American business schools.[252] From a certain economic perspective, indeed, this transfer of U.S. investment and production was an indicator of economic strength and modernity; it took advantage of lower labor costs and ensured greater access in overseas markets. Over time, however, these capital flows eventually became so strong that they began to outweigh the surpluses which Americans earned on exports of manufactures, foodstuffs, and "invisible" services. Although this increasing payments deficit did see some gold draining out of the United States by the late 1950s, most foreign governments were content to hold more dollars (that being the leading reserve currency) rather than demand payment in gold.

As the 1960s unfolded, however, this cozy situation evaporated. Both Kennedy and (even more) Johnson were willing to increase American military expenditures overseas, and not just in Vietnam, although that conflict turned the flow of dollars exported into a flood. Both Kennedy and (even more) Johnson were committed to increases in domestic expenditures, a trend already detectable prior to 1960. Neither administration liked the political costs of raising taxes to pay for the inevitable inflation. The result was year after year of federal government deficits, soaring price rises, and increasing American industrial uncompetitiveness—in turn leading to larger balance-of-payments deficits, the choking back (by the Johnson administration) of foreign investments by U.S. firms, and then the latter's turn toward the new instrument of Eurodollars. In the same period, the U.S. share of world (non-Comecon) gold reserves shrank remorselessly, from 68 percent (1950) to a mere 27 percent (1973). With the entire international payments and money-flow system buckling under these interacting problems, and being further weakened by de Gaulle's angry counterattacks against what he regarded as America's "export of inflation," the Nixon administration found it had little choice but to end the dollar's link to gold in private markets, and then to float the dollar against other currencies. The Bretton Woods system, very much a creation of the days when the United States was financially supreme, collapsed when its leading pillar could bear the strains no more.[253]

The detailed story of the ups and downs of the dollar in the 1970s, when it was floating freely, are not for telling here; nor is the zigzag course of successive administrations' efforts to check inflation and to stimulate growth, always without causing too much pain politically. The higher-than-average inflation in the United States generally caused the dollar to weaken vis-à-vis the German and Japanese currencies in the 1970s; oil shocks, which hurt countries more dependent upon OPEC supplies (e.g., Japan, France), political turbulence in various parts of the world, and high American interest rates tended to push the dollar upward, as was the case by the early 1980s. Yet although these oscillations were important, and tended to add to global economic insecurities, they may be less significant for our purposes than the unrelenting longer-term trends, which were the decreasing productivity growth, which in the private sector fell from 2.4 percent (1965–1972), to 1.6 percent (1972–1977), to 0.2 percent (1977–1982);[254] the increasing federal deficits, which could be seen as giving a Keynesian-type "boost" to the economy, but at the cost of sucking in so much cash from abroad (attracted by the higher American interest rates) that it sent the dollar's price to artificially high levels and turned the country from a net lender to a net borrower; and the increasing difficulty American manufacturers found in competing with imported automobiles, electrical goods, kitchenware, and other manufactures. Not surprisingly, American per capita GNP, once the highest in the world, began to slip down the list.[255]

There were still consolations, to those who could see the American economy and its needs in larger terms than selected comparisons with Swiss incomes or Japanese productivity. As Calleo points out, post-1945 American policy did achieve some very basic and significant aims: domestic prosperity, as opposed to a 1930s-type slump; the containing of Soviet expansionism without war; the revival of the economies—and the democratic traditions—of western Europe, later joined by Japan to create "an increasingly integrated economic bloc," with "an imposing battery of multilateral institutions . . . to manage common economic as well as military affairs"; and, finally, "the transformation of the old colonial empires into independent states still closely integrated into a world economy."[256] In sum, it had maintained the liberal international order, upon which it, itself, increasingly depended; and while its share of world production and wealth had shrunk, perhaps faster than need have been the case, the redistribution of global economic balances still left an environment which was not too hostile to its own open-market and capitalist traditions. Finally, if it had seen its productive lead eroded by certain faster-growing economies, it had still maintained a very considerable superiority over the Soviet Union in almost all respects of true national power and—by clinging to its own entrepreneurial creed—remained open to the stimulus of managerial initiative and technological charge which its Marxist rival would have far greater difficulty in accepting.

A more detailed discussion of the implication of these economic movements must await the final chapter. It may, however, be useful to give in statistical form (see Table 43) the essence of the trends examined above, as they concern the global economic balances, namely the partial recovery of the share of world product in the hands of the less-developed countries; the remarkable growth of Japan and, to a lesser extent, of the People's Republic of China; the erosion of the European Economic Community's share even as it remained the largest economic bloc in the world; the stabilization, and then slow decline, of the USSR's share; and the much faster decline, but still far larger economic muscle, of the United States.

Indeed, by 1980, the final year in Table 43, the World Bank's figures of population, GNP per capita, and GNP itself, were very much point-

Table 43. Shares of Gross World Product, 1960–1980[257]
(percent)

	1960	1970	1980
Less-developed countries	11.1	12.3	14.8
Japan	4.5	7.7	9.0
China	3.1	3.4	4.5
European Economic Community	26.0	24.7	22.5
United States	25.9	23.0	21.5
Other developed countries	10.1	10.3	9.7
USSR	12.5	12.4	11.4
Other Communist countries	6.8	6.2	6.1

ing to a *multipolar* distribution of the global economic balances, as shown in Table 44.

Table 44. Population, GNP per Capita, and GNP in 1980[258]

	Population (millions)	GNP per Capita (dollars)	GNP (billions of dollars)
United States	228	11,360	2,590
USSR	265	4,550	1,205
Japan	117	9,890	1,157
EEC (12 states) of which	317	—	2,907
W. Germany	61	13,590	828
France	54	11,730	633
U.K.	56	7,920	443
Italy	57	6,480	369
West and East Germany together	78	—	950
China[259]	980	290 or 450	284 or 441

Finally, it might be useful to recall that these long-term shifts in the productive balances are of importance not so much for their own sake, but for their power-political implications. As Lenin himself noted in 1917–1918, it was the *uneven* economic growth rates of countries which led ineluctably to the rise of specific powers and the decline of others:

Half a century ago, Germany was a miserable, insignificant country, as far as its capitalist strength was concerned, compared with the strength of England at that time. Japan was similarly insignificant compared with Russia. Is it "conceivable" that in ten or twenty years' time the relative strength of the imperialist powers will have remained *un*changed? Absolutely inconceivable.[260]

And for all Lenin's own concentration upon the capitalist/imperialist states, the rule seems common to *all* national units, whatever their favored political economy, that uneven rates of economic growth would, sooner or later, lead to shifts in the world's political and military balances. This, certainly, has been the pattern observed in the four centuries of Great Power development prior to the present one. It therefore follows that the unusually rapid shifts in the centers of world production during the past two or three decades cannot avoid having repercussions upon the grand-strategical future of today's leading Powers, and rightly deserve the attention of one final chapter.

8

To the
Twenty-first Century

History and Speculation

A chapter with a title such as that above implies not merely a change in chronology but also, and much more significantly, a change in *methodology*. Even the very recent past is history, and although problems of bias and source make the historian of the previous decade "hard put to separate the ephemeral from the fundamental,"[1] he is still operating within the same academic discipline. But writings upon how the present may evolve into the future, even if they discuss trends which are already under way, can lay no claim to being historical truth. Not only do the raw materials change, from archivally based monographs to economic *forecasts* and political *projections*, but the validity of what is being written about can no longer be assumed. Even if there always were many methodological difficulties in dealing with "historical facts,"[2] past events like an archduke's assassination or a military defeat *did indeed occur.* Nothing one can say about the future has that certainty. Unforeseen happenings, sheer accidents, the halting of a trend, can ruin the most plausible of forecasts; if they do not, then the forecaster is merely lucky.

What follows, then, can only be provisional and conjectural, based upon a reasoned surmise of how present tendencies in global economics and strategy may work out—but with no guarantee that all (or any) of this will happen. The gyrations which have occurred in the international value of the dollar over the past few years and the post-1984 collapse in oil prices (with its differing implications, for Russia, for Japan, for OPEC) offer a good warning against drawing conclusions from economically based trends; and the world of politics and diplomacy has never been one which followed straight lines. Many a final chapter in works dealing with contemporary affairs has to be changed, only a few years later, in the wisdom of hindsight; it will be surprising if this present chapter survives unscathed.

Perhaps the best way to comprehend what lies ahead is to look *backward* briefly, at the rise and fall of the Great Powers over the past five centuries. The argument in this book has been that there exists a dynamic for change, driven chiefly by economic and technological developments, which then impact upon social structures, political systems, military power, and the position of individual states and empires. The speed of this global economic change has not been a uniform one, simply because the pace of technological innovation and economic growth is itself irregular, conditioned by the circumstance of the individual inventor and entrepreneur as well as by climate, disease, wars, geography, the social framework, and so on. In the same way, different regions and societies across the globe have experienced a faster *or* slower rate of growth, depending not only upon the shifting patterns of technology, production, and trade, but also upon their receptivity to the new modes of increasing output and wealth. As some areas of the world have risen, others have fallen behind—relatively or (sometimes) absolutely. None of this is surprising. Because of man's innate drive to improve his condition, the world has never stood still. And the intellectual breakthroughs from the time of the Renaissance onward, boosted by the coming of the "exact sciences" during the Enlightenment and Industrial Revolution, simply meant that the dynamics of change would be increasingly more powerful and self-sustaining than before.

The second major argument of this book has been that this uneven pace of economic growth has had crucial long-term impacts upon the relative military power and strategical position of the members of the states system. This again is unsurprising, and has been said many times before, although the emphasis and presentation of argument may have been different.[3] The world did not need to wait until Engels's time to learn that "nothing is more dependent on economic conditions than precisely the army and the navy."[4] It was as clear to a Renaissance prince as it is to the Pentagon today that military power rests upon adequate supplies of wealth, which in turn derive from a flourishing productive base, from healthy finances, and from superior technology. As the above narrative has shown, economic prosperity does not *always and immediately* translate into military effectiveness, for that depends upon many other factors, from geography and national morale to generalship and tactical competence. Nevertheless, the fact remains that all of the major shifts in the world's *military-power* balances have followed alterations in the *productive* balances; and further, that the rising and falling of the various empires and states in the international system has been confirmed by the outcomes of the major Great Power wars, where victory has always gone to the side with the greatest material resources.

While what follows is speculation rather than history, therefore, it is based upon the plausible assumption that these broad trends of the past five centuries are likely to continue. The international system, whether it is dominated for a time by six Great Powers or only two, remains anarchical—that is, there is no greater authority than the sovereign, egoistical nation-state.[5] In each particular period of time some of those states are growing or shrinking in their *relative* share of secular power. The world is no more likely to remain frozen in 1987 or 2000 than it was in 1870 or 1660. On the contrary, certain economists would argue that the very *structures* of international production and trade are changing faster than ever before: with agricultural and raw-materials products losing their relative value, with industrial "production" becoming uncoupled from industrial "employment," with knowledge-intensive goods becoming dominant in all advanced societies, and with world capital flows becoming increasingly detached from trade patterns.[6] All this, and the many new developments in science, are bound to influence international affairs. In sum, without the intervention of an act of God, or a disastrous nuclear conflagration, there will continue to be a dynamic of world power, essentially driven by technological and economic change. If the rosy forecasts of the impact of computers, robotics, biotechnology, and so on are correct— and if, in addition, forecasts of the success of a "green revolution" in parts of the Third World (with India and even China becoming regular net exporters of grain)[7] do turn out right—then the world *as a whole* could be a lot richer by the early twenty-first century. Even if technological progress is less dramatic, economic growth is likely to occur. Changing demographic patterns, with their impact upon demand, would ensure that, as would the more sophisticated exploitation of raw materials.

What is also clear is that this growth will be uneven—faster here, slower there, depending upon the conditions for change. It is this, more than anything else, which makes the prognoses that follow so provisional; for there is no guarantee that, for example, Japan's impressive economic expansion over the past four decades will continue during the next two; nor is it impossible for Russian growth rates, which have been declining since the 1960s, to increase again in the 1990s, given changes in that country's economic policy and mechanisms. On the evidence of existing trends, however, neither of those outcomes appears very likely. To put it another way, if it did happen that Japan stagnated and Russia boomed economically between now and the early twenty-first century, then that could only come about from changes in circumstances and policies far more drastic than it is reasonable to assume from the available evidence. Just because estimates of how the world will appear in fifteen or twenty-five years' time may go wrong does not mean that one should prefer implausible outcomes rather than sensible expectations based upon current broad developments.

It is reasonable to expect, for example, that one of the better-known "global trends" of today, the rise of the Pacific region, is likely to continue, simply because that development is so broad-based. It includes not only the economic powerhouse of Japan, but also that swiftly changing giant the People's Republic of China; not only the prosperous and established industrial states of Australia and New Zealand, but also the immensely successful Asian newly industrializing countries like Taiwan, South Korea, Hong Kong, and Singapore—as well as the larger Association of Southeast Asian Nations (ASEAN) lands of Malaysia, Indonesia, Thailand, and the Philippines; by extension, it also includes the Pacific states of the United States and provinces of Canada.[8] Economic growth in this vast area has been stimulated by a happy combination of factors: a spectacular rise in industrial productivity by export-oriented societies, in turn leading to great increases in foreign trade, shipping, and financial services; a marked move into the newer technologies as well as into cheaper, labor-intensive manufactures; and an immensely successful effort to increase agricultural output (especially grains and livestock) faster than total population growth. Each success has beneficially interacted with the others, to produce a rate of economic expansion which has far eclipsed that of the traditional western powers—as well as that of Comecon—in recent years.

In 1960, for example, the combined gross domestic product of the Asian-Pacific countries (i.e., excluding the United States) was a mere 7.8 percent of world GDP; by 1982, it had more than doubled, to 16.4 percent, and since then the area's growth rates have exceeded those of Europe, the United States, and the USSR by ever wider margins. It is very likely to contain over 20 percent of world GDP by the year 2000—the equal of Europe, or the United States; and that achievement will occur even on the basis of growth-rate differentials "much smaller" than those which have existed over the past quarter-century.[9] The dynamism of the Pacific basin has also been felt in the shifting economic balances within the United States itself during that same period. American trade with Asia and the Pacific was only 48 percent of that with Europe (OECD members) in 1960, but had risen to 122 percent of American-European trade by 1983—a change which has been accompanied by a redistribution of both population and income within the United States in the direction of the Pacific.[10] Despite a slowdown in, say, any *one* country's growth, or problems affecting a particular industry, it is evident that these trends are continuing as a whole. It is not surprising, therefore, that one economic expert has confidently predicted that the entire Pacific region, which now possesses 43 percent of the world's GNP, will enjoy a good 50 percent of it by the year 2000; and concludes, "The center of world economic gravity is shifting rapidly towards Asia and the Pacific, as the Pacific takes its place as one of the key centers of world economic power."[11] This sort of language has of course been heard frequently since the nineteenth century; but only with the massive growth of the region's commerce and productivity since 1960 has that forecast become a reality.

Similarly, it is also reasonable to assume that the next few decades will witness a continuation of a much less attractive but even broader trend: the spiraling cost of the arms race, which is fueled by the sheer expensiveness of newer weapon systems as well as by international rivalries. "One of the few constancies in history," it has been observed, "is that the scale of commitment on military spending has always risen."[12] And if that was true (granted some short-term fluctuations) for the wars and arms races of the eighteenth century, when weapons technology changed only slowly, it is much truer of the present century, when each new generation of aircraft, warships, and tanks is vastly more expensive than preceding ones, even when allowance is made for inflation. Edwardian statesmen, appalled that a pre-1914 battleship cost £2.5 million, would be staggered to learn that it now costs the British Admiralty £120 million and more for a replacement *frigate*! American legislators, who had willingly allocated funds for thousands of B-17 bombers in the late 1930s, now understandably wince at the Pentagon's estimate that the new B-1 bomber will cost over $200 billion for a mere one hundred planes. In all areas, the upward spiral is at work:

> Bombers cost two hundred times as much as they did in World War II. Fighters cost one hundred times or more than they did in World War II. Aircraft carriers are twenty times as expensive and battle tanks are fifteen times as expensive as in World War II. A Gato class submarine cost $5,500 per ton in World War II, compared with $1.6 million per ton for the Trident.[13]

Compounding these problems is the evidence that today's armaments industry is becoming increasingly divergent from commercial, free-market manufacturing. The former, usually concentrated in a few gigantic firms enjoying a special relationship with their own department of defense (whether in the United States, Britain, or France, or even more in the "command economy" of the USSR), is frequently protected from marketplace operations by the state's granting of exclusive contracts and cost-overrun guarantees, for products for which only it (and friendly states) will be the consumer. The latter, even in the case of giant companies like IBM and General Motors, has to struggle against cutthroat competition to win merely a *share* of the volatile internal and external markets in which quality, consumer taste, and price are vital variables. The former, driven by military men's desire to have the most advanced "state-of-the-art" weaponry so that their armed services may be able to fight in all possible (if sometimes highly implausible) battle scenarios, produces goods which are increasingly more expensive, more elaborate, and *much less numerous.* The latter, after initial heavy investment in the early prototypes of household goods or office computers, has its average unit costs pushed *downward,* because of market competition and large-scale production.[14] And while it may be true that the explosion in new technological and scientific developments since the late nineteenth century inevitably drove defense manufacturers into a relationship with governments which deviated from "free market" norms,[15] the present pace of this increase is an alarming one. The various proposals about "military reform" in the United States could perhaps prevent the result forecast by the cynics, that the entire Pentagon budget may be swallowed up on *one* aircraft by the year 2020; but even those efforts are unlikely to *reverse* the trend toward ever fewer weapons at ever higher cost.

While much of this is of course due to the growing and inescapable sophistication of weapons—like modern fighter aircraft, which may contain 100,000 separate parts—it is also caused by the continuing array of arms races on land, on and under the oceans, in the air, and in space. If the greatest of those rivalries is between NATO and the Warsaw Pact countries (which, thanks to the two superpowers, spend almost 80 percent of the world's investment in armaments, and possess 60–70 percent of its aircraft and ships), there are smaller yet still significant arms races—not to mention wars—in the Middle East, Africa, Latin America, and across Asia, from Iran to Korea. The consequence has been an explosion in Third World military expenditures, even by the poorest regimes, and large-scale increases in arms sales and transfers to those countries; by 1984, world arms imports of a colossal $35 billion had exceeded the world trade in grain ($33 billion). In the following year, it is also worth noting, world military expenditures had reached a total of about $940 billion, rather more than the entire income of the poorer half of this planet's population. What was more, that expenditure on weapons was rising faster than the global economy and most national economies were expanding. At the head were the United States and the USSR, each devoting well over $250 billion annually to defense and likely to push that total to over $300 billion in the near future. In most countries, spending on the armed forces was taking an increasing share of governmental budgets and of GNP, checked only (with very few exceptions of motive, as in Japan and Luxembourg) by economic weaknesses, shortage of hard currency, etc., rather than by a genuine commitment to reduce arms expenditures.[16] The "militarization of the world economy," as the Worldwatch Institute terms it, is now advancing faster than it has for a generation.[17]

These two trends—the uneven pattern of growth, with the global
productive balances tilting toward the Pacific basin; and the spiraling
costs of weapons and armed forces—are of course separate developments. Yet at the same time it is obvious that they are increasingly
likely to interact and indeed are doing so already. Both of them are
driven by the dynamic of technological and industrial change (even if
individual arms races will have political and ideological motives as
well). Both of them impinge heavily upon the national economy: the
first by boosting wealth and productivity at a faster or slower pace, and
by making certain societies more prosperous than others; the second
by consuming national resources—measured not simply in terms of
investment capital and raw materials, but also (and perhaps even more
importantly) in the share of scientists, engineers, R&D personnel,
engaged in defense-related production as opposed to commercial,
export-oriented growth. Although it has been claimed that defense
expenditures can have certain commercial economic spin-offs, it
seems increasingly difficult to argue against the proposition that *excessive* arms spending will hurt economic growth.[18] The difficulties experienced by contemporary societies which are militarily top-heavy
merely repeat those which, in their time, affected Philip II's Spain,
Nicholas II's Russia, and Hitler's Germany. A large military establishment may, like a great monument, look imposing to the impression-
able observer; but if it is not resting upon a firm foundation (in this
case, a productive national economy), it runs the risk of a future collapse.

By extension, therefore, both of these trends have profound socioeconomic and political implications. Slow growth occurring in a particular country is likely to depress public morale, produce discontents,
and exacerbate the discussion over national spending priorities; on the
other hand, a fast pace of technological and industrial expansion will
also have its consequences, especially upon a hitherto nonindustrialized society. Large-scale armaments spending, for its part, can benefit
specific industries within the national economy; but it can also lead to
a diversion of resources from other groups in society, and it can make
that national economy less capable of handling the commercial challenges of other countries. Unless there is an enemy immediately at the
gate, high defense spending in this century has nearly always provoked
a "guns versus butter" controversy. Less publicly, but of even greater
significance for our purposes, it has provoked a debate upon the proper
relationship of economic strength to military power.[19]

Not for the first time in history, therefore, there looms today a
tension between a nation's existence in an anarchic military-political
world and its existence in a laissez-faire economic world; between on
the one hand its search for strategic security, as represented by its
investment in the latest weapon systems and in its large-scale diversion

of national resources to the armed forces, and on the other hand its search for economic security, as represented by an enhanced national prosperity, which depends upon growth (which in turn flows from new methods of production and wealth creation), upon increased output, and upon flourishing internal and external demand—all of which may be damaged by excessive spending upon armaments. Precisely because a top-heavy military establishment may slow down the rate of economic growth and lead to a decline in the nation's share of world manufacturing output, and therefore wealth, and therefore *power*, the whole issue becomes one of the balancing the short-term security afforded by large defense forces against the longer-term security of rising production and income.

The tension between these conflicting aims is perhaps particularly acute in the late twentieth century because of the publicity given to the existence of various alternative "models" for emulation. On the one hand, there are the extremely successful "trading states"—chiefly in Asia, like Japan and Hong Kong, but also including Switzerland, Sweden, and Austria—which have taken advantage of the great growth in world production and in commercial interdependence since 1945, and whose external policy emphasizes peaceful, trading relations with other societies. In consequence, they have all sought to keep defense spending as low as is compatible with the preservation of national sovereignty, thereby freeing resources for high domestic consumption and capital investment. On the other hand, there are the various "militarized" economies—Vietnam in Southeast Asia, Iran and Iraq as they engage in their lengthy war, Israel and its jealous neighbors in the Near East, and the USSR itself—all of which allocate more (in some cases, much more) than 10 percent of their GNP to defense expenditures each year and, while firmly believing that such levels of spending are necessary to guarantee military security, manifestly suffer from that diversion of resources from productive, peaceful ends. Between the two poles of the merchant and the warrior states, so to speak, there lie most of the rest of the nations of this planet, not convinced that the world is a safe enough place to allow them to reduce arms expenditure to Japan's unusually low level, but also generally uneasy at the high economic and social costs of large-scale spending upon armaments, and aware that there is a certain trade-off between short-term military security and long-term economic security. For countries which have—again, in contrast to Japan—extensive overseas military obligations from which it would be difficult to escape, the problem is further compounded. Moreover, in many of the leading Powers the planners are acutely aware that they have to balance the spiraling cost of weaponry not only against productive investment but also against growing social requirements (especially as their overall population ages), which makes the allocation of spending priorities a more difficult task than ever.

The feat demanded of most if not all governing bodies as the world heads toward the twenty-first century is therefore a *threefold* one: simultaneously to provide military security (or some viable alternative security) for its national interests, *and* to satisfy the socioeconomic needs of its citizenry, *and* to ensure sustained growth, this last being essential both for the positive purposes of affording the required guns and butter at the present, and for the negative purpose of avoiding a relative economic decline which could hurt the people's military and economic security in the future. Achieving all three of those feats over a sustained period of time will be a very difficult task, given the uneven pace of technological and commercial change and the unpredictable fluctuations in international politics. Yet achieving the first two feats— or either one of them—without the third will inevitably lead to relative eclipse over the longer term, which has of course been the fate of all slower-growing societies that failed to adjust to the dynamics of world power. As one economist has soberly pointed out, "It is hard to imagine, but a country whose productivity growth lags 1 percent behind other countries over one century can turn, as England did, from the world's indisputed industrial leader into the mediocre economy it is today."[20]

Just how well (or badly) the leading nations seem placed to carry out this task is the focus of the rest of this chapter. It hardly needs emphasizing that since the varied demands of defense spending/military security, social/consumer needs, and investment for growth involve a triangular competition for resources, there is no absolutely perfect solution to this tension. Probably the best that can be achieved is that all three aims be kept in rough harmony, but just how that balance is reached will always be strongly influenced by national circumstances, not by some theoretical definition of equilibrium. A state surrounded by hostile neighbors will think it better to allocate more to military security than one whose citizens feel relatively unthreatened; a country rich in natural resources will find it easier to pay for guns and butter; a society determined upon economic growth in order to catch up to the others will have different priorities from one on the brink of war. Geography, politics, and culture will all ensure that one state's "solution" will never be exactly the same as another's. Nevertheless, the basic argument remains: without a rough balance between these competing demands of defense, consumption, and investment, a Great Power is unlikely to preserve its status for long.

China's Balancing Act

The competing claims of weapons modernization, the people's social requirements, and the need to channel all available resources into "productive" nonmilitary enterprises is nowhere more pressing than in the People's Republic of China (PRC), which is simultaneously the poorest of the major Powers and probably the least well placed strategically. Yet if the PRC suffers from certain chronic hardships, its present leadership seems to be evolving a grand strategy altogether more coherent and forward-looking than that which prevails in Moscow, Washington, or Tokyo, not to mention western Europe. And while the *material* constraints upon China are great, they are being ameliorated by an economic expansion which, *if it can be kept up*, promises to transform the country within a few decades.

The country's weaknesses are so well known as to require only a brief mention here. Diplomatically and strategically, Peking has regarded itself (with some justification) as being isolated and surrounded. If this was partly due to Mao's policies toward China's neighbors, it was also a consequence of the rivalry and ambitions of other powers in Asia during the preceding decades. The memories of Japan's earlier aggressions have not faded from the Chinese mind, and reinforce the caution with which the leadership in Peking regards that country's explosive growth in recent years. Despite the 1970s thaw in relations with Washington, the United States is also viewed with some suspicion—the more particularly under a Republican regime which seems overenthusiastic about constructing an anti-Russian bloc, which appears to nourish a lingering fondness for Taiwan, and which interferes too readily against Third World countries and revolutionary movements for Peking's liking. The future of Taiwan and the smaller offshore islands remains a thorny problem, and only half-submerged. The PRC's relations with India have stayed cool, being complicated by their respective ties to Pakistan and Russia. Notwithstanding recent "wooing" efforts by Moscow, China feels bound to see in the USSR its chief foreign danger—and not merely because of the masses of Russian divisions and aircraft deployed along the frontier, but also in consequence of the Russian invasion of Afghanistan and, more worryingly, in the military expansionism of the Soviet-supported Vietnamese state to the south. Somewhat like the Germans earlier in this century, therefore, the Chinese think deeply about "encirclement" even as they simultaneously strive to enhance their place in the global system of power.[21]

Moreover, this awkward, multilateral set of diplomatic tasks has to be managed by a country which is not very strong militarily or economically, when measured against its chief rivals. For all the size

of the Chinese Army in *numerical* terms, it remains woefully underequipped in modern instruments of warfare. Most of its tanks,
guns, aircraft, and warships are indigenous versions of Russian or
western models which China acquired years ago, and are certainly not
on a par with later, much more sophisticated types; a lack of hard
currency and an unwillingness to become too dependent upon other
nations have kept purchases of foreign arms to a minimum. Perhaps
even more worrying to Peking's leaders are the weaknesses in China's
combat effectiveness, due to the Maoist attacks upon professionalism
in the army and the preference for peasant militias—such utopian
solutions being of little assistance in the 1979 border war with Vietnam, whose battle-hardened and well-trained troops killed some
26,000 Chinese and wounded 37,000 others.[22] Economically, China
appears still further behind; even when amending its official per capita
GNP figures in a way which better accords with western concepts and
economic measurements,[23] the figure can hardly be more than a mere
$500, compared with well over $13,000 for many of the advanced
capitalist states and a respectable $5,000+ for the USSR. With its
population likely to rise from a billion people today to 1.2 or 1.3 billion
by the year 2000, the prospects of a major increase in personal income
may not be large; even in the next century the average Chinaman will
be poor, relative to the inhabitants of the established Powers. Furthermore, it hardly needs saying that the difficulties of governing such a
populous state, of reconciling the various factions (party, army,
bureaucrats, farmers), and of achieving growth without social and
ideological turbulence will test even the most flexible and intelligent
leadership. China's internal history for the past century does not offer
encouraging precedents for long-term strategies of development.

Nevertheless, the indications of reform and self-improvement in
China which have occurred over the past six to eight years are very
remarkable, and suggest that this period of Deng Xiaoping's leadership
may one day be seen in the way that historians view Colbert's France,
or the early stages of Frederick the Great's reign, or Japan in the
post–Meiji Restoration decades: that is, as a country straining to develop its power (in all senses of that word) by every pragmatic means,
balancing the desire to encourage enterprise and initiative and change
with an *étatiste* determination to direct events so that the national
goals are achieved as swiftly and smoothly as possible. Such a strategy
involves the ability to see how the separate aspects of government
policy relate to each other. It therefore involves a sophisticated balancing act, requiring careful judgments as to the speed at which these
transformations can safely occur, the amount of resources to be allocated to long-term as opposed to short-term needs, the coordination
of the state's internal and external requirements, and—last but not
least in a country which still has a "modified" Marxist system—the

ways by which ideology and practice can be reconciled. Although difficulties have occurred and new ones are likely to emerge in the future,
the record so far is an impressive one.

It can be seen, for example, in the many ways in which the Chinese
armed services are transforming themselves after the convulsions of
the 1960s. The planned reduction of the People's Liberation Army
(which includes the navy and air force) from 4.2 to 3 million personnel
is, in fact, an enhancement of real strength, since far too many of them
were merely support troops, used for railway-building and civic duties.
Those remaining within the armed forces are likely to be of higher
overall quality: new uniforms and the restoration of military ranks
(abolished by Mao as being "bourgeois") are the outward sign of this;
but they will be reinforced by replacing a largely volunteer army with
conscription (to give the state access to high-quality personnel), by
reorganizing the military regions and streamlining the staffs, and by
improving officer training at the academies, which have also emerged
from their period of Maoist disgrace.[24] Along with this will go a large-
scale modernization of China's weaponry, which, although numerically substantial, suffers from considerable obsolescence. Its navy is
being given an array of new vessels, from destroyers and escorts to
fast-attack craft and even hovercraft; and it has built up a very substantial fleet of conventional submarines (107 in 1985), making it the third-
largest such force in the world. Its tanks are now displaying laser
rangefinders; its aircraft are becoming all-weather types, with modern
radar. All this is attended by a willingness to experiment with large-
scale maneuvers under modern battlefield conditions (one such 1981
maneuver involved six or seven Chinese armies backed by aircraft—
which had been missing in the 1979 clash with Vietnam),[25] and to
rethink the strategy of a "forward defense" along the frontiers with
Russia in favor of counterattacks some way behind the long, exposed
borders. The navy, too, is experimenting on a much larger scale: in
1980 an eighteen-vessel task force undertook an eight-thousand-nauti-
cal-mile mission in the South Pacific, in conjunction with China's latest
intercontinental ballistic missile experiments. (Was this, one wonders,
the first significant demonstration of Chinese sea power since Cheng
Ho's cruises of the early fifteenth century? See pp. 6–7 above.)

More impressive still, for China's emergence as a Great Power militarily, has been the extraordinarily rapid development of its nuclear
technology. Although the first Chinese tests occurred in Mao's time, he
had publicly scorned nuclear weapons when preferring the merits of
a "people's war"; the Deng leadership, by contrast, is intent upon taking
China into the ranks of the *modern* military states as swiftly as possible. As early as 1980, China was testing ICBMs with a range of seven
thousand nautical miles (which would encompass not only all of the
USSR but also parts of the United States).[26] A year later, one of its

rockets launched three space satellites, which is an indication of a multiple-warhead rocket technology. Most of China's nuclear forces are *land-based,* and medium-range rather than long-distance; but they are being joined by new ICBMs and, perhaps the most significant step of all (in terms of nuclear deterrence), by a fleet of missile-carrying submarines. Since 1982, China has been testing submarine-launched ballistic missiles and working on improvements of both range and accuracy. There are also reports of Chinese experimentation with tactical nuclear weapons. All this is backed up by large-scale atomic research, and by a refusal to have its nuclear weapons development "frozen" by international limitations agreements, since that would merely aid the existing Great Powers.

As against this evidence of military-technological prowess, it is also easy to point to continuing signs of weakness. There is always a significant time lag between producing an early prototype of a weapon and having large numbers of them, tried and tested, in the possession of the armed forces themselves; and this is particularly so with a country which is not rich in capital or scientific resources. Severe setbacks— including the possible explosion of a Chinese submarine while attempting to launch a missile; the cancellation or slowdown of weapons programs; the lack of expertise in metallic technology, advanced jet engines, and radar, navigation, and communications equipment—continue to hamper China's drive toward real military equality with the USSR and the United States. Its navy, despite the Pacific Ocean exercises, is far from being a "blue water" fleet, and its force of missile-bearing submarines will long remain behind those of the "Big Two," which are pouring funds into the development of gigantic types (*Ohio* class, *Alfa* class) that can dive deeper and run faster than any previous submarine.[27] Finally, the mention of finance is a reminder that as long as China is spending only one-eighth or thereabouts of the amount upon defense as the superpowers, there is no way it can achieve full parity; it cannot, therefore, plan to acquire *every* sort of weapon or to prepare for every conceivable threat.

Nonetheless, even China's existing military capability gives it an influence which is far more substantial than that existing some years ago. The improvements in training, organization, and equipment ought to place the PLA in a better position to meet regional rivals like Vietnam, Taiwan, and India than in the past two decades. Even the military balance vis-à-vis the Soviet Union may no longer be so disproportionately tilted in Moscow's favor. Should future disputes in Asia lead to a Sino-Russian war, the leadership in Moscow may find it politically difficult to consent to launching heavy nuclear strikes at China, both because of world reaction and because of the unpredictability of the American response; but if it did "go nuclear," there is less and less prospect of the Soviet armed forces being able to *guarantee* the destruction of China's growing land-based and (especially) sea-based missile systems before they can retaliate. On the other hand, if there is only conventional fighting, the Soviet dilemma remains acute. The fact that Moscow takes the possibility of war seriously can be gleamed from its deployment of around fifty divisions (including six or seven tank divisions) of Russian troops in its two military districts east of the Urals. And while it may be assumed that such forces can handle the seventy or more PLA divisions similarly stationed in the frontier area, their superiority may hardly be enough to ensure a striking victory—especially if the Chinese trade space for time in order to weaken the effects of a Soviet Blitzkrieg. To many observers, there now exists a "rough equivalence," a "balance of forces," in Central Asia[28]—and, if true, the strategical repercussions of that extend far beyond the immediate region of Mongolia.

But the most significant aspect of China's longer-term war-fighting power lies elsewhere: in the remarkably swift growth of its economy which has occurred during the past few decades and which seems likely to continue into the future. As was mentioned in the preceding chapter (see pp. 418–20), even before the Communists had firmly established their rule, China was a considerable manufacturing power—although that was disguised by the sheer size of the country, the fact that the vast majority of the population consisted of peasant farmers, and the disruptions of war and civil wars. The creation of a Marxist regime and the coming of domestic peace allowed production to shoot ahead, with the state actively encouraging both agricultural and industrial growth—although sometimes doing so (i.e., under Mao) by bizarre and counterproductive means. Writing in 1983–1984, one observer noted that "China has achieved annual growth rates in industry and agriculture since 1952 of around 10 percent and 3 percent respectively, and an overall growth of GNP of 5–6 percent per year."[29] If those figures do not match the achievements of such export-oriented Asian "trading states" as Singapore or Taiwan, they are impressive for a country as large and populous as China, and readily translate into an economic power of some size. By the late 1970s, according to one calculation, the Chinese industrial economy was as large as (if not larger than) those of the USSR and Japan in 1961.[30] Moreover, it is worth remarking once again that these *average* growth rates include the period of the so-called Great Leap Forward of 1958–1959; the break with Russia, and the withdrawal of Soviet funds, scientists, and blueprints in the early 1960s; and the turmoil of the Cultural Revolution, which not only distorted industrial planning but also undermined the entire educational and scientific system for nearly one generation. Had those events *not* occurred, Chinese growth would have been even faster overall—as may be gathered from the fact that over the past five years of Deng-led reforms, agriculture has averaged an 8 percent growth, and industry a spectacular 12 percent.[31]

To a very large degree, the agricultural sector remains both China's opportunity and its weak point. The East Asian methods of wet-rice cultivation are inordinately productive in yields per hectare, but are also extremely labor-intensive—which makes it difficult to effect a switch to, say, the large-scale, mechanized forms of agriculture used on the American prairies. Yet since agriculture forms over 30 percent of China's GDP and employs 70 percent of the population, decay (or merely a slowdown) in that sector will act as a drag upon the entire economy—as has clearly happened in the Soviet Union. This challenge is compounded by the population time bomb. Already China is attempting to feed a billion people on only 250 million acres of arable land (compared with the United States' 400 million acres of crops for its 230 million population);[32] can it possibly manage to feed another 200 million Chinese by the year 2000, without an increasing dependence upon imported food, which has both balance-of-payments and strategic costs? It is difficult to get a clear answer to that crucial question, in part because the experts point to different pieces of evidence. China's traditional export of foodstuffs slowly declined over the past three decades, and in 1980 it became, very briefly, a net *importer*.[33] On the other hand, the Chinese government is devoting massive scientific resources into achieving a "green revolution" on the Indian model, and Deng's encouragement of market-oriented reforms, together with large increases in agricultural purchase prices (without passing the cost on to the cities), have led to tremendous rises in food production over the past half-decade. Between 1979 and 1983—when much of the rest of the globe was suffering from economic depression—the 800 million Chinese in rural areas increased their incomes by about 70 percent, and their calorific intake was nearly as high as that of Brazilians or Malaysians. "In 1985, the Chinese produced 100 million more tons of grain than they did a decade earlier, one of the most productive surges ever recorded."[34] With the population increasing, and turning more and more to meat consumption (which requires yet more grain), the pressure to keep up this expansion in agricultural consumption will become more intense—and yet the acreage available remains restricted, and the growth in yields caused by the applications of fertilizer is bound to slow down. Nonetheless, the evidence suggests that China is managing to maintain this part of its elaborate balancing act with a considerable degree of success.

The future of China's drive toward industrialization is of even greater importance—but is a yet more delicate trick internally. It has been hampered not only by the lack of consumer purchasing power, but also by years of rather heavy-handed planning on the Russian and eastern European model. The "liberalization" measures of the past few years—getting state industries to respond to the commercial realities of quality, price, and market demand, encouraging the creation of privately run, small-scale enterprises, and allowing a great expansion in foreign trade[35]—have led to impressive rises in manufacturing output, but also to many problems. The creation of tens of thousands of private businesses has alarmed party ideologists, and the rise in prices (probably caused as much by the necessary adjustment to market costs as by the frequently denounced "racketeering" and "profiteering") has caused mutterings among urban workers, whose incomes have not risen as fast as either the farmers' or the entrepreneurs'. In addition, the foreign-trade boom quickly led to a sucking in of imported manufactures, and thus to a trade deficit. The statements made in 1986 by Prime Minister Zhao Ziyang that matters may have slipped somewhat "out of control" and that "consolidation" was needed for a while— together with the announced decrease in the hectic growth targets— are indications that internal and ideological problems remain.[36]

It is nevertheless remarkable that even the reduced growth rates are planned to be a very respectable 7.5 percent annually in future years (as opposed to the 10 percent rate since 1981). That itself would *double* China's GNP in less than ten years (a 10 percent rate would do the same in a mere seven years), yet for a number of reasons economic experts seem to feel that such a target can be achieved. In the first place, China's rate of savings and investment has been consistently in excess of 30 percent of GNP since 1970, and while that in turn brings problems (it reduces the proportion available for consumption, which is compensated for by price stability and income equality, which in turn get in the way of entrepreneurship), it also means that there are large funds available for productive investment. Secondly, there are huge opportunities for cost savings: China has been among the most profligate and extravagant countries in its consumption of energy (which caused declines in its quite considerable oil stocks), but its post-1978 energy reforms have substantially reduced the costs of one of industry's main "inputs" and thus freed money for investments elsewhere— or consumption.[37] Moreover, only now is China beginning to shake off the consequences of the Cultural Revolution. After more than a decade during which Chinese universities and research institutes were closed (or compelled to operate in a totally counterproductive way), it was predictable that it would take some time to catch up on the scientific and technological progress made elsewhere. "It is only against this background," it was remarked a few years ago,

> that one can understand the importance of the thousands of scientists who went to the United States and elsewhere in the West in the late 1970s for stays of one or two years and occasionally longer periods. . . . as early as 1985—and certainly by 1990—China will

have a cadre of many thousands of scientists and technicians familiar with the frontiers of their various fields. Tens of thousands more trained at home as well as abroad will staff the institutes and enterprises that will implement the programs required to bring Chinese industrial technology up to the best international standards, at least in strategic areas of activity.[38]

In the same way, it could only be in the post-1978 period of encouraging (albeit selectively) foreign trade and investment in China that its managers and entrepreneurs had the proper opportunity to pick and choose from among the technological devices, patents, and production facilities enthusiastically offered by western governments and companies which quite exaggerated the size of the Chinese market for such items. Despite—or, rather, because of—the Peking government's desire to control the level and contents of overseas trade, it is likely that imports will be deliberately selected to boost economic growth.

The final and perhaps the most remarkable aspect of China's "dash for growth" has been the very firm control upon defense spending, so that the armed forces do not consume resources needed elsewhere. In Deng's view, defense has to remain the fourth of China's much-vaunted "four modernizations"—behind agriculture, industry, and science; and although it is difficult to gain exact figures on Chinese defense spending (chiefly because of different methods of calculation),[39] it seems clear that the proportion of GNP allocated to the armed forces has been tumbling for the past fifteen years—from perhaps 17.4 percent in 1971 (according to one source) to 7.5 percent in 1985.[40] This in its turn may cause grumbling among the military and thus increase the internal debate over economic priorities and policies; and it would clearly have to be reversed if serious border clashes recurred in the north or the south. Nonetheless, the fact that defense spending must take an inferior place is probably the most significant indication to date of China's all-out commitment to economic growth, and stands in stark contrast to both the Soviet obsession with "military security" and the Reagan administration's commitment to pouring funds into the armed services. As many experts have pointed out,[41] given China's existing GNP and amount of national savings and investment within it, there would be no real problem in spending much more than its current c. $30 billion on defense. That it chooses not to do so reflects Peking's belief that long-term security will be assured only when its present output and wealth have been multiplied many times.

In sum: "The only events likely to stop this growth in its tracks would be the outbreak of war with the Soviet Union or prolonged political upheaval on the pattern of the Cultural Revolution. China's management, energy, and agricultural problems are serious, but they are the kinds of problems faced and overcome by all developing nations during the growth process."[42] If that seems a remarkably rosy statement, it pales compared with *The Economist's* recent calculation that if China maintains an average 8 percent annual growth—which it calls "feasible"—it would soar past the British and Italian GNP totals well before 2000 and be vastly in excess of *any* European power by 2020.[43]

Chart 2. GDP Projections of China, India, and Certain Western European States, 1980–2020

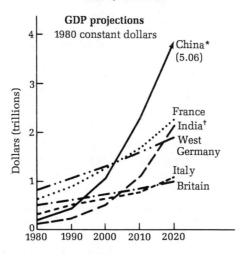

* Assuming 7 percent growth rate 1980-1985 and 8 percent thereafter
† Assuming 5.5 percent growth rate 1980-1985 and 7 percent thereafter
Other countries assuming average annual rates as in 1970-1982

Source: *The Economist*/IMF

The greatest mistake of all would be to assume that this sort of projection, with all the changeable factors that it rests upon, could ever work out with such exactitude. But the general point remains: China will have a very large GNP within a relatively short space of time, barring some major catastrophe; and while it will still be relatively poor in per capita terms, it will be decidedly richer than it is today.

Three further points are worth making about China's future impact upon the international scene. The first, and least important for our purposes, is that while the country's economic growth will boost its foreign trade, it is impossible to transform it into another West Germany or Japan. The sheer size of the domestic market of a continent-wide Power such as China, and of its population and raw-materials base, makes it highly unlikely that it would become as dependent upon overseas commerce as one of the smaller, maritime "trading states."[44] The extent of its labor-intensive agricultural sector and the regime's determination not to become too reliant upon imported foodstuffs will also be a drag upon foreign trade. What *is* likely is that China will become an increasingly important producer of low-cost goods, like textiles, which will help to pay for western—or even Russian—technology; but Peking is clearly determined *not* to become dependent upon foreign capital, manufactures, or markets, or upon any one country or supplier in particular. Acquiring foreign technology, tools, and production methods will all be subject to the larger requirements of China's balancing act. This is not contradicted by China's recent membership in the World Bank and the IMF (and its possible future membership in GATT and the Asian Development Bank)—which are not so much indications of Peking's joining the "free world" as they are of its hard-nosed calculation that it may be better to gain access to foreign markets, and to long-term loans, via international bodies than through unilateral "deals" with a Great Power or private banks. In other words, such moves protect China's status and independence. The second point is separate from, but interrelates with, the first. It is that whereas in the 1960s Mao's regime seemed almost to relish in the frequent border clashes, Peking now prefers to maintain peaceful relations with its neighbors, even those it regards with suspicion. As noted above, peace is central to Deng's economic strategy; war, even of a regional sort, would divert resources into the armed services and alter the order of priority among China's "four modernizations." It may also be the case, as has been argued recently,[45] that China feels more relaxed about relations with Moscow simply because its own military improvements have created a rough equilibrium in central Asia. Having achieved a "correlation of forces," or at least a decent defensive capacity, China can concentrate more upon economic development.

Yet if its intentions are peaceable, China also emphasizes how determined it is to preserve its own complete independence, and how much it disapproves of the two superpowers' military interventions abroad. Even toward Japan the Chinese have kept a wary eye, restricting its share of the import/export trade and yet also warning Tokyo not to get too heavily involved in developing Siberia.[46] Toward Washington and Moscow, China has been much more studied—and critical. All of the Soviet suggestions for improving relations and even the return of Soviet engineers and scientists to China in early 1986 have not altered Peking's fundamental position: that a real improvement cannot take place until Moscow makes concessions in some, if not all, of the three outstanding issues—the Russian invasion of Afghanistan, the Russian support of Vietnam, and the long-standing question of central Asian boundaries and security.[47] On the other hand, U.S. policies in Latin America and the Middle East have come in for repeated attack from Peking (as, to be sure, have similar Russian adventures in the tropics). Being economically one of the "less-developed countries" and inherently suspicious of the white races' domination of the globe makes China a natural critic of superpower intervention, even if it is not a formal member of the Third World movement and even if those criticisms are nowadays fairly mild compared to Mao's fulminations of the 1960s. And despite its earlier (and still powerful) hostility to Russian pretensions in Asia, the Chinese remain suspicious of the earnest American discussion of how and when to play the "China card."[48] In Peking's view, it may be necessary to incline toward Russia or (more frequently, since the Sino-Soviet quarrels) toward the United States, by measures including the joint monitoring of Russian nuclear testing and exchanging information over Afghanistan and Vietnam; but the ideal position is to be equidistant between the two, and to have them both wooing the Middle Kingdom.

To this extent, China's importance as a truly independent actor in the present (and future) international system is enhanced by what, for want of a better word, one might term its "style" of relating to the other Powers. This has been put so nicely by Jonathan Pollack that it is worth repeating *in extenso:*

> [W]eapons, economic strength, and power potential alone cannot explain the imputed significance of China in a global power equation. If its strategic significance is judged modest and its economic performance has been at best mixed, this cannot account for the considerable importance of China in the calculations of both Washington and Moscow, and the careful attention paid to it in other key world capitals. The answer lies in the fact that, notwithstanding its self-characterization as a threatened and aggrieved state, China has very shrewdly and even brazenly used its available political, economic, and military resources. Towards the superpowers, Peking's overall strategy has at various times comprised confrontation and armed conflict, partial accomodation, informal alignment, and a detachment bordering on disengagement, sometimes interposed with strident, angry rhetoric. As a result, China becomes all things to all nations, with many left uncertain and even anxious about its long-term intentions and directions.
>
> To be sure, such an indeterminate strategy has at times entailed substantial political and military risks. Yet the same strategy has lent considerable credibility to China's position as an emergent major power. China has often acted in defiance of the preferences or demands of both superpowers; at other times it has behaved far differently from what others expect. Despite its seeming vulnerability, China has not proven pliant and yielding toward either Moscow or Washington. . . . For all these reasons, China has assumed a singular international position, both as a participant in many of the central political and military conflicts in the post war era and as a

state that resists easy political or ideological categorization. . . .
Indeed, in a certain sense China must be judged as a candidate
superpower in its own right—not in imitation or emulation of either
the Soviet Union or the United States, but as a reflection of Peking's
unique position in global politics. In a long-term sense, China represents a political and strategic force too significant to be regarded as
an adjunct to either Moscow or Washington or simply as an intermediate power.[49]

As a final point, it needs to be stressed again that although China
is keeping a tight hold upon military expenditures at the moment, it
has no intention of remaining a strategical "lightweight" in the future.
On the contrary, the more that China pushes forward with its economic expansion in a Colbertian, *étatiste* fashion, the more that development will have power-political implications. This is the more likely
when one recalls the attention China is giving to expanding its scien-
tific/technological base, and the impressive achievements already
made in rocketry and nuclear weapons when that base was so much
smaller. Such a concern for enhancing the country's economic substructure at the expense of an immediate investment in weapons will
hardly satisfy China's generals (who, like military groups everywhere,
prefer short-term to long-term means of security). Yet as *The Economist* has nicely remarked:

> For [China's] military men with the patience to see the [economic]
> reforms through, there is a payoff. If Mr. Deng's plans for the econ-
> omy as a whole are allowed to run their course, and the value of
> China's output quadruples, as planned, between 1980 and 2000 (ad-
> mittedly big ifs), then 10 to 15 years down the line the civilian
> economy should have picked up enough steam to haul the military
> sector along more rapidly. That is when China's army, its neighbors
> and the big powers will really have something to think about.[50]

It is only a matter of time.

The Japanese Dilemma

The very fact that Peking is so purposeful about what is to happen
in East Asia increases the pressures now bearing down upon Japan's
(self-proclaimed) "omnidirectional peaceful diplomacy"—or what
might more cynically be described as "being all things to all men."[51]
The Japanese dilemma may perhaps be best summarized as follows:
Due to its immensely successful growth since 1945, the country
enjoys a unique and very favorable position in the global economic and
power-political order, yet that is also—the Japanese feel—an extremely

delicate and vulnerable position, which could be badly deranged if international circumstances changed. The best thing that could happen from Tokyo's viewpoint, therefore, would be for the continuation of those factors which caused "the Japanese miracle" in the first place. But precisely because this is an anarchic world in which "dissatisfied" powers jostle alongside "satisfied" ones, and because the dynamic of technological and commercial change is driving so fast, the likelihood is that those favorable factors will diminish—or even disappear altogether. Given Japan's belief in the delicacy and vulnerability of its own position, it finds it hard openly to resist the pressures for change; instead, the latter must be slowed down, or deflected, by diplomatic compromise. Hence its constant advocacy of the peaceful solution to international problems, its alarm and embarrassment when it finds itself in a political crossfire between other countries, and its evident wish to be on good terms with everyone while it gets steadily richer.

The reasons for Japan's phenomenal economic success have already been discussed (see above, pp. 416–18). For over forty years the Japanese homeland has been protected by American nuclear and conventional forces, and its sea lanes by the U.S. Navy. Thus enabled to redirect its national energies from militaristic expansion and its resources from high defense spending, Japan has devoted itself to the pursuit of sustained economic growth, especially in export markets. This success could not have been achieved without its own people's commitment to entrepreneurship, quality control, and hard work, but it was also aided by certain special factors: the holding-down of the yen to an artificially low level for decade after decade in order to boost exports; the restrictions, both formal and informal, upon the purchase of imported foreign manufactures (although not, of course, of the vital raw materials which industry needed); and the existence of a liberal international trading order which placed few obstacles in the way of Japanese goods—and which was kept "open," despite the increasing burdens upon itself, by the United States. For the past quarter-century, therefore, Japan has been able to enjoy all of the advantages of evolving into a global economic giant, but without any of the political responsibilities and territorial disadvantages which have, historically, followed from such a growth. Little wonder that it prefers things to remain as they are.

Since the foundations of Japan's present success lie exclusively in the economic sphere, it is not surprising that this also is the field which worries Tokyo most. On the one hand (as will be discussed below), technological and economic growth offers fresh glittering prizes to the country whose political economy is best positioned for the coming twenty-first century; and only a few dispute the contention that Japan is in that favorable position.[52] On the other hand, its very success is already provoking a "scissors effect" reaction against its export-led expansion. The one "blade" of those scissors is the emulation of Japan by other ambitious Asian NICs (newly industrialized countries), such as South Korea, Singapore, Taiwan, Thailand, etc.—not to mention China itself at the lower end of the product scale (e.g., textiles).[53] All of these countries have far lower labor costs than Japan,* and are challenging strongly in fields in which the Japanese no longer enjoy decisive advantages—textiles, toys, domestic goods, shipbuilding, even (to a much less degree) steel and automobiles. This does not, of course, mean that Japan's production of ships, cars, trucks, and steel is doomed, but to the extent that it is increasingly necessary for them to move "up-market" (e.g., to higher-grade steels, or more sophisticated and larger-sized automobiles) they are withdrawing from the bottom end of a production spectrum where previously they were unchallenged; and one of the more important tasks of MITI (the Ministry for International Trade and Industry) is to plan the phasing out of industries which are no longer competitive—not only to make the decline less traumatic but also to arrange for the transfer of resources and personnel into other, more competitive sectors of the international economy.

The second, even more worrying blade of the scissors has been the increasingly hostile reaction of Americans and Europeans to the seemingly inexorable penetration of their domestic markets by Japanese products. Year after year, the populations of these prosperous markets have bought Japanese steel, machine tools, motorcycles, automobiles, and TV sets and other electrical goods. Year after year, Japan's trading surpluses with the EEC and the United States have widened. The European reaction has been the tougher one, ranging from import quotas to bureaucratic obstructionism (such as the French requirement that Japanese electrical goods be admitted only via an understaffed customs house in Poitiers).[54] Because of its own belief in an open world trading system, American administrations have hesitated to ban or otherwise restrict Japanese imports apart from dubious "voluntary" limits. But even the staunchest American advocates of laissez-faire have grown uneasy at a situation in which, essentially, the United States supplies Japan with foodstuffs and raw materials and receives Japanese manufactures in return—a sort of "colonial" or "underdevelopment" trading status it has not known for a century and a half. Moreover, the growing U.S. trade deficits with Japan—$62 billion in the fiscal year ending March 31, 1986—and the pressures from beleaguered American industries which have felt the brunt of this transpacific competition have increased Washington's demand for measures to reduce the imbalance—e.g., to encourage a rise in the exchange value of the yen, a substantial increase in American imports

---

*Which is why even Japanese firms are building factories there.

into Japan, and so on. As the western world drifts toward quasi-protectionism, moreover, its tendency to put limits upon the *total* amount of textiles or televisions imported implies that Japan will have to divide that shrunken market with its Asian rivals.

It is scarcely surprising, therefore, that some Japanese spokesmen deny that things are good, and point to an alarming conjunction of threats to their present market shares and prosperity: the increasing challenge by Asian NICs in so many industries; the restrictions upon Japanese exports by western governments; the pressures to change Japan's tax laws, divert monies from savings to consumption, and ensure a large increase in imports; finally, the swift rise in the value of the yen. All of these, it is claimed, could mean the end of Japan's export-led boom, a decline in its payments surpluses, a slowing-down in its growth rate (which has already been decelerating as its economy becomes more "mature" and its potential for spectacular expansion diminishes). In that connection, Japan worries that it is not only its economy which is maturing: because of the age structure of its population, by 2010 it will have "the lowest ratio of working-age people (those 15 to 64 years old) among the leading industrial nations," which will require high social security outlays and could lead to a loss of dynamism.[55] Moreover, all the attempts to get the Japanese consumer to buy foreign-made manufactures (except those with a certain prestige, like Mercedes cars) lead to domestic political controversy,[56] which might in turn cause a possible breakdown in the consensus politics which has been an integral part of Japan's sustained export-led expansion in the past.

Yet while it may be true that Japan's economic growth is slowing down as it enters a more mature phase, and while it is certainly true that other countries are unwilling to permit Japan to keep the economic advantages which aided its previous explosion of exports, there nevertheless remain considerable substantive reasons why it is likely to expand faster than the other *major* Powers in the future. In the first place, as a country so incredibly dependent upon imported raw materials (99 percent of its oil, 92 percent of its iron, 100 percent of its copper), it benefits enormously from the changing terms of trade which have reduced the prices of so many ores, fuels, and foodstuffs; the drop in world oil prices after 1980–1981, which saves Japan billions of dollars of foreign currency each year, is only the most spectacular of the falls in raw-materials and foodstuffs prices.[57] Furthermore, while a rapid appreciation in the value of the yen is likely to cut some of the country's exports overseas (depending always upon the elasticity of demand), it also greatly reduces the cost of imports—and thus helps industry to stay competitive and inflation to remain low. In addition, the 1973 oil crisis stimulated the Japanese into searching for all sorts of energy economies, which contribute to the still greater efficiency of its industry; in the past decade alone, Japan has reduced its dependence on oil by 25 percent. In addition, that same crisis impelled Japan into a sustained search for new sources of raw materials and a heavy investment in such areas (somewhat akin to Britain's investments overseas in the nineteenth century). None of this makes it *absolutely* certain that Japan can rely upon a continued flow of low-priced raw materials; but the auguries for that are good.

More significant still is the continued surge of Japanese industry toward the most promising (and, ultimately, most profitable) sectors of the economy for the early twenty-first century: that is, high technology. In other words, as Japan steadily pulls out of the production of textiles, shipbuilding, basic steel—leaving them to countries with lower labor costs—it clearly intends to be a (if not *the*) leading force in those scientifically advanced manufactures which have a much higher added value. Its achievements in the computing field are already so well known as to be legendary. Borrowing heavily from American technology in the first instance, Japanese companies were able to exploit all their native advantages (a protected home market, MITI support, better quality control, a favorable yen-to-dollar ratio) as well as—most probably—"dumping" at below-cost prices to drive most American companies out of the production of semiconductors, whether of the 16k RAM, the 64k RAM, or the later 256k RAM.[58]

Even more worrying to the American computer industry is the evidence of Japan's determined move into two fresh (and much more profitable) fields. The first is the production of advanced computers themselves, particularly the sophisticated and extremely expensive "fifth generation" supercomputers, which can work hundreds of times faster than the largest existing machines and promise to give their owners enormous benefits in everything from codebreaking to designing aircraft shapes. Already American experts are stunned by the speed at which Japan has moved into this area, and at the amount of research capital which MITI and large companies like Hitachi and Fujitsu are pouring into it.[59] Yet the same is also happening in the field of computer *software*, where again American firms (and a few European firms) were unchallenged until the early 1980s.[60] To be sure, the successful production both of supercomputers and of software is a much larger task than making semiconductors, and will test Japan's designers to the utmost; and in the meantime both American and European companies (the latter strongly supported by the in governments) are preparing to meet the commercial challenge, while the U.S. Department of Defense will give its massive backing to ensuring that its national firms remain ahead in the development of supercomputers. Nonetheless, those bodies would be very sanguine to assume that Japan can be permanently held off in these fields.

Since respected journals like *The Economist,* the *Wall Street Jour-*

nal, the *New York Times,* and many others frequently carry articles about Japan's move into further areas of high technology, it would be superfluous to repeat the details here. Mitsubishi's link-up with Westinghouse has been seen as evidence of Japan's increasing interest in the nuclear-power industry.[61] Biotechnology is also a large Japanese concern, especially with its implications for enhancing crop yields. So, too, is ceramics. The reports that the Japanese Aircraft Development Corporation has joined up with Boeing to produce a new generation of fuel-efficient aircraft for the 1990s—denounced by one American expert as a "Faustian bargain" whereby Japan will provide cheap finance and acquire U.S. technology and expertise[62]—may be even more significant for the future. But perhaps the most important (in terms of sheer output) will be the already impressive lead which Japan has in the field of industrial robots and its development of (experimental) entire factories virtually controlled by computers, lasers, and robots: the ultimate solution to the country's decreasing labor force! The latest figures show that "Japan continued to introduce about as many industrial robots as the rest of the world combined, several times the rate of introduction in the United States." Another survey indicates that the Japanese use their robots much more efficiently than Americans do.[63]

Behind all of these high-technology ventures are a cluster of broader, structural factors which continue to give Japan marked advantages over its chief rivals. The role of MITI as a sort of economic equivalent to the famous Prussian General Staff may have been exaggerated by foreigners,[64] but there seems little doubt that the broad direction which it gives to Japanese economic development by arranging research and funding for growth industries and a gentle euthanasia for declining ones has worked better to date than the uncoordinated laissez-faire approach of the United States. The second strength—one of the most important of all in explaining the rise and fall of particular firms and industries—is the large (and increasing) amount of money which is allocated to research and development in Japan. "The proportion of GNP devoted to R&D will virtually double this decade, rising from 2 percent of GNP in 1980 to an expected 3.5 percent by 1990. The United States has stabilized R&D expenses at about 2.7 percent of GNP. However, if military research is excluded, Japan is already devoting about as many man-hours to R&D as the United States and will soon be spending about as much for it. If present trends continue, Japan will take the lead in nonmilitary R&D spending by the early 1990s."[65] Even more interesting, perhaps, is the fact that a far higher proportion of Japanese R&D is paid for and done by industry itself than in Europe and the United States (where so much is done by governments or universities). In other words, it is aimed directly at the marketplace and is expected to pay its way quickly. "Pure" science is left to others, and tapped only when its commercial relevance becomes clear.

The third advantage is the very high level of national savings in Japan, which is especially marked compared with that in the United States. This is partly explained by the differences in tax systems, which in the United States have traditionally encouraged personal borrowing and consumer spending—and in Japan encourage private savings. On average, too, the individual in Japan has to save much more for his or her old age, since the pension schemes are usually less generous. What all this means is that Japanese banks and insurance companies are awash with funds and can provide industry with masses of low-interest capital. The share of GNP which is collected in Japan both as income tax *and* social security payments is much lower than in the other major capitalist-cum-"welfare state" societies, and the Japanese evidently intend to keep it that way, in order to free the money for investment capital.[66] Europeans who would like to imitate "the Japanese way" would first of all have to massively reduce their social welfare spending. Americans enamored of Japan's system would have to slash both defense and social expenditures, *and* to alter their taxation laws even more drastically than they have done so far.

The fourth strength is that Japanese firms have a virtually guaranteed home market in all except prestige and specialized manufactures—a situation no longer enjoyed by most American firms or (despite their protectionist efforts) by the majority of European companies. While much of this was aided by in-built bureaucratic practices and regulations designed to favor Japanese producers in their home market, even the abolition of such mercantilistic devices is unlikely to persuade Japan's consumers to "buy foreign," other than raw materials and basic foodstuffs; the high quality and familiarity of Japanese products, a strong cultural pride, and the complex structure of domestic distribution and sales will ensure that.

Finally, there is the very high quality of the Japanese work force— at least as measured by various mathematical and scientific aptitude tests—which is not only groomed in an intensely competitive public education system but also systematically trained by the companies themselves. Even fifteen-year-olds in Japan show a marked superiority in testable subjects (e.g., mathematics) over most of their western counterparts. In the higher reaches of learning, the balance is different: Japan has a dearth of Nobel Prize scientists, but it produces many more engineers than any western country (about 50 percent more than the United States itself). It also has nearly 700,000 R&D workers, which is more than Britain, France, and West Germany have combined.[67]

No statistically quantifiable assessment can be made of the combined effects of the above five factors, compared with conditions in other leading nations; but, taken together, they obviously give Japanese industry an immensely strong bedrock. So, too, does the docility and diligence of the Japanese work force and the harmony which seems to prevail in the industrial-relations system, where there are only company unions, a search for consensus, and virtually no strikes. There are, clearly, unattractive features here as well: longer hours of work, the all-pervading conformism to the company ethos (from the early-morning physical exercises onward), the absence of truly independent trade unions, the cramped housing conditions, the emphasis upon hierarchy and deference. Moreover, Japan also contains, outside the factory gates, a radicalized student body. Such facts, and other disturbing traits in Japanese society, have been commented on by many western observers[68]—some of whom appear to view the country with the same sort of horror and awe that continental Europeans manifested toward the "factory system" of early-nineteenth-century Britain. In other words, what is clearly a more effective arrangement of workers, and of society, in terms of *output* (and thus wealth creation) involves a disturbing challenge to traditional norms and individualist ways of behavior. And it is because the emulation of the Japanese industrial miracle would involve not merely the copying of this or that piece of technology or management but the imitation of much of the Japanese social system that observers such as David Halberstam argue, "This is America's newest and . . . most difficult challenge for the rest of the century . . . a much harder and more intense competition than . . . the political-military competition with the Soviet Union. . . ."[69]

As if these industrial strengths were not enough, they have been complemented by the amazingly swift emergence of Japan as the world's leading creditor nation, exporting tens of billions of dollars each year. This transformation, which has been under way since MITI's 1969 dismantling of export controls upon Japanese lending and its creation of financial inducements for overseas investments, is rooted in two basic causes. The first of these is the inordinately high level of personal savings in Japan—over 20 percent of Japanese wages are saved, so that by 1985 "the average total savings of Japanese households exceeded the average annual income for the first time"[70]—which has left financial institutions flush with funds that are increasingly invested abroad to gain a higher return. The second reason has been the unprecedentedly large trade surpluses occurring for Japan in recent years because of the explosion in its earnings from exports. Fearing that such surpluses would fuel domestic inflation (if returned home), the Japanese finance ministry has been encouraging the giant banks to invest vast sums overseas.[71] In 1983, the net outflow of Japanese capital was $17.7 billion; in 1984, it leaped to $49.7 billion; and in 1985, it leaped again, to $64.5 billion, turning Japan into the world's largest net creditor nation. By 1990, the director of the Institute for

International Economics forecasts, the rest of the world will owe Japan a staggering $500 billion; and by 1995, the Nomura Research Institute predicts, Japan's gross overseas assets will exceed $1 trillion.[72] Not surprisingly, Japanese banks and securities firms are rapidly becoming the largest and most successful in the world.[73]

The consequences of this vast surge in Japanese capital exports contain dangers as well as benefits for the world economy, and perhaps also for Japan itself. A considerable amount of these funds is invested into infrastructures around the globe (e.g., the English Channel tunnel) or into the opening of new iron-ore fields (e.g., in Brazil), which will benefit Tokyo indirectly or directly. Other monies are being channeled by Japanese companies and their balances into the creation of overseas subsidiaries (especially for production)—either to have Japanese goods manufactured in low-labor-cost countries so that they can remain competitive, or to place such plants within the territories of, say, EEC countries and the United States in order to obviate protectionist tariffs. The greater part of this capital flow has, however, gone into short-term bonds (especially U.S. Treasury bonds), which if ever recalled back to Japan in large amounts could unsettle the international financial system—just as in 1929—and place tremendous pressures upon U.S. dollars *and* the U.S. economy, since much of this money is going to finance the huge budget deficits incurred by the Reagan administration. On the whole, however, Tokyo is much more likely to keep recycling its surplus capital into new ventures overseas than to bring it home.

The rise of Japan in the past few years to be the world's leading net creditor nation—combined with the transformation of the United States from being the biggest lender to being the biggest borrower—has occurred so swiftly that it is still difficult to work out its full implications. Since "historically a creditor nation has led growth in each period of global economic expansion, and Japan's era is just arriving,"[74] it may well be that Tokyo's emergence as the leading world banker gives a further middle-to-long-term boost to international commerce and finance, following the earlier examples provided by the Netherlands, Britain, and the United States. What seems remarkable at this stage is that the surge in Japan's "invisible" financial role is occurring *before* there is any significant erosion of its immense "visible" industrial lead, as happened (for example) in the British case. Perhaps that may change, and swiftly, if the value of the yen soars too high and Japan experiences long-term "maturity" and slowdown in its manufacturing base and in its rate of productive growth. Yet even if this does happen—and there are reasons (as given above) to think that any decline of Japan as a manufacturing nation will be a slow process—one fact is clear: with the forecast amount of overseas assets in its hands by the year 2000, its current-account balances are bound to be handsomely supplemented by a vast flow of earnings from abroad. In all ways, therefore, Japan seems destined to get much richer.

Just how powerful, economically, will Japan be in the early twenty-first century? Barring large-scale war, or ecological disaster, or a return to a 1930s-style world slump and protectionism, the consensus answer seems to be: *much* more powerful. In computers, robotics, telecommunications, automobiles, trucks, and ships, and possibly also in biotechnology and even in aerospace, Japan will be either the leading or the second nation. In finance, it may by then be in a class of its own. Already it is reported that its per capita GNP has sailed past those of the United States and western Europe, giving it almost the highest standard of living on earth. What its share of world manufacturing output or of total world GNP will be is impossible to say. It is worth recalling that in 1951, Japan's total GNP was one-third of Britain's and one-twentieth (!) of the United States'; yet within three decades it had risen to be double Britain's and nearly half the United States'. To be sure, its rate of growth over those decades was unusually swift, because of special conditions. Yet according to many assessments,[75] the Japanese economy is still likely to expand about 1½ to 2 percent a year faster than the other large economies (except, of course, China) over the next several decades.* It is for that reason that scholars such as Herman Kahn and Ezra Vogel have argued that Japan will be "number one" economically in the early twenty-first century, and it is not surprising that many Japanese are fired by that very prospect. For a country which possesses only 3 percent of the world population and only 0.3 percent of its habitable land, it seems an almost unbelievable achievement; and but for the possibilities inherent in the new technology, one would be tempted to assume that Japan was already close to maximizing the potential of its people and land and that, like other relatively small peripheral or island states (Portugal, Venice, the Netherlands, even Britain in its time) it would one day be eclipsed by nations which had far larger resources and merely needed to copy its successful habits. For the foreseeable future, however, Japan's trajectory continues to rise upward.

No matter how one measures Japan's present and future economic strength, two facts are overriding. The first is that it is enormously

---

*Assuming that to be the case, it is still difficult for technical reasons to suggest what that means in exact figures. Many of the statistics commonly used (e.g., by the CIA) in international comparisons are based upon U.S. dollars and market exchange rates; thus the tumbling of the value of the dollar vis-à-vis the yen by nearly 40 percent in 1985–1986 could, by that reckoning, massively boost Japan's GNP total as compared with the United States' (and also as compared with the USSR's, since its GNP is often calculated in "geometric mean dollars").[76] Simply a rise in the yen from its present exchange value to 120 or even 100 to the dollar—which some economic experts think is its "true" rate[77]—would give Japan a total GNP close to the United States' and well in excess of Russia's. It is because of the problems caused by rapidly fluctuating exchange rates that some economists prefer to use "purchasing parity ratios," although that measurement also has its problems.

productive and prosperous, and getting much more so. The second is that its *military* strength, and defense spending, bears no relation to its place in the international economic order of things. It possesses a reasonable-sized navy (including thirty-one destroyers and eighteen frigates), a home-defense air force, and a modest army, but it is clearly much less of a military power, relative to others, than it was in the 1930s, or even in the 1910s. More pertinent still for the debate upon "burden-sharing"[78] is the fact that Japan allocates so relatively little for defense. According to the figures in *The Military Balance*, in 1983 Japan spent $11.6 billion on defense, compared with $21–24 billion spent by France, West Germany, and Britain, and a colossal $239 billion by the United States; per capita, therefore, the average Japanese inhabitant had had to pay only $98 for defense that year, compared with the average Briton's $439 and the average American's $1,023.[79] Given its current prosperity, Japan seems to be getting off lightly from the costs of defense—and in two related ways: the first is that it shelters under the protection of others, namely, the United States; the second is that its low defense outlays help it to keep down public spending and thus provide more resources for the Japanese manufacturing effort which is so hurting American and European competitors.[80]

Were Japan indeed to respond to the pressures of the U.S. government and of other western critics and to increase its defense spending to the level allocated by the European NATO members—averaging around 3–4 percent of GNP—the transformation would be dramatic and would turn it (along with China) into the third-largest military power in the world, with expenditures on defense of over $50 billion a year. Nor is there any doubt, given Japan's technological and productive resources, that it could build, for example, carrier task forces for its navy, or long-range missiles as a deterrent. That would certainly benefit domestic firms like Mitsubishi, as well as providing a counter to Soviet power in the Far East, thus rendering help to an overstretched United States.

What is much more likely to happen, however, is that Tokyo will endeavor to escape those external pressures, or at least to maintain defense spending as low as it possibly can without provoking a rupture with Washington. The chief reason has not been the purely symbolic one of wishing to keep Japanese expenditures on defense within the ceiling of 1 percent of GNP; by NATO definitions (i.e., by including military pensions), it had already broken that barrier, and in any case, it spent a considerably larger percentage of its GNP upon defense in the early 1950s. Nor has it much to do with the conditions of the 1951 U.S.-Japan security treaty, which is the legal basis for the American military presence in Japan, and which further encouraged Tokyo to think of trade rather than strategic power; for the circumstances of the 1980s are now quite different from those of the Korean War. The real reasons, in the view of the Japanese government, are the domestic and regional objections to a massive increase in its defense spending, and to a revision of the constitution, which forbids sending troops (or even selling arms) abroad. The memory of the militaristic excesses of the 1930s, of the wartime losses, and (especially) of the horrors of the A-bombs has ingrained upon the Japanese consciousness a dislike and suspicion of war and of the instruments of war which is at least as strong as western pacifism after the First World War; and while that may change in time, with the coming of a younger, more assertive generation, the prevailing opinion in the near future is much more likely to constrain the Tokyo government to keep increases in spending on the aptly named "self-defense forces" to modest levels.[81]

To these moral and ideological reasons there can be added economic ones. Among Japanese businessmen and politicians there is considerable opposition to increasing public spending (which, as mentioned above, is much lower in Japan than in any of the other OECD countries): to them, a doubling or trebling of defense expenditures must be paid for by either adding to the large public-sector deficit or raising taxes—and both are acutely disliked. Besides, it is argued, a large army and navy did not bring Japan "security," whether of the military or the economic sort, in the 1930s; and it is difficult to see at present how an increase in defense spending could prevent a possible cutoff of Arab oil—which is a far greater danger to Japan strategically than, say, the hypothetical nuclear winter, and explains Tokyo's desperate efforts to "lie low and say nothing" whenever there is a crisis in the Middle East. Is it not better, then, for Japan to abjure the use of force and to resolve all international disputes peacefully, as a cosmopolitan "trading state" should? Since modern war is so costly and is usually counterproductive, the Japanese feel that there is a lot of merit in their *zenhoi heiwa gaiko* ("omnidirectional peaceful diplomacy").

These feelings are no doubt reinforced by Tokyo's awareness that many of its neighbors would react with alarm to a large-scale buildup of Japanese military power. That would obviously be the response of the Russians—against whom, after all, the United States wants Japan to "burden-share" in defense matters, and who are still in dispute with Tokyo over the islands north of Hokkaido, and who probably feel that they have enough on their hands in the Far East with the expansion of Chinese power. But it would also be the response of those lands previously subjected to Japanese occupation—Korea, Taiwan, the Philippines, Malaysia, Indonesia—as well as Australia and New Zealand, all of which have reacted nervously to any signs of a revival of Japanese nationalism and *bushido* mentality, and which have encouraged Tokyo to "focus on productive nonmilitary ways to enhance Southeast Asian peace and security."[82] Above all, perhaps, there looms for Tokyo the difficulty of assuaging the suspicions of a touchy Peking, which still nurses memories of the Japanese atrocities of 1937–1945, and has also warned Japan not to get too heavily involved in developing Siberia (which in turn complicates the Tokyo-Moscow relationship) or to support Taiwan.

Even Japan's economic expansion (while bringing with it much-needed investments, plus some development aid and tourism) has left many of its neighbors suspicious, feeling that they are being sucked into a newer and more subtle version of the "Greater East Asia Co-Prosperity Sphere" once again—the more especially since Japan does not import very much (except raw materials) from those countries, yet sells a great deal of its own manufactures to them. Here, too, China has been the most outspoken, at first welcoming the late 1970s boom in Japanese trade and investments, then sharply curtailing them, partly because of its own balance-of-payments deficit, partly to avoid economic dependency upon any single foreign country which might take undue advantage of it; America's trade with China, Deng urged in 1979, "must come equal to Japan's,"[83] and thus prevent any possibility of a Japanese variant of "the imperialism of free trade."

All of these are, at the moment, merely straws in the wind, but they make politicians in Tokyo worry about how best to evolve a coherent external strategy for Japan as it moves toward the twenty-first century. There is no doubt that with its economic power expanding, it could become a second Venice—in the sense not just of extensive trading, but also of protecting its maritime sea lanes and of creating quasi-dependencies overseas; yet the internal and external objections to a strong Japan are such that not only will it avoid any move toward territorial acquisitions along old-fashioned imperialist lines, but it is also unlikely to increase its defense forces by very much. This latter conclusion, however, will increasingly irritate American circles who are pressing for "burden sharing" in the western Pacific. Ironically, therefore, Japan will be criticized if it does not substantially increase its spending upon arms, and it will be denounced if it does. Either way spells trouble to what has been nicely termed Japan's "maximal gain/minimum risk foreign policy."[84] This suggests, once again, a Japanese preference for as little change as possible in the military and political affairs of East Asia, even as the pace of economic growth quickens. That, too, compounds the dilemma, for even a non-Marxist would be puzzled to imagine how the profound economic transformation of Asia could avoid being attended by far-reaching changes in other spheres as well.

The deepest worries of the Japanese, therefore, are probably those which are rarely if ever discussed publicly—partly out of diplomatic discretion, partly to avoid bringing such developments about—and concern the future balance of power in East Asia itself. "Omnidirectional peaceful diplomacy" is all very well for the present, but how useful will it be if an overextended United States does withdraw from its Asian commitments, or finds it impossible to protect the flow of oil from Arabia to Yokohama? How useful if there is another Korean war? How useful if China begins to dominate the region? How useful if a declining and nervous USSR takes aggressive actions? There is, of course, no way of answering such hypothetical and alarming questions; yet even a mere "trading state" with small "self-defense forces" may one day find it unavoidable to provide some answers. As other nations have discovered in the past, commercial expertise and financial wealth sometimes no longer suffice in the anarchic world of international power politics.

The EEC—Potential and Problems

Of the five main concentrations of economic and military power in the world today, the only one that is not a sovereign nation-state is Europe—which at once defines the chief problem facing this region as it moves toward the emerging Great Power system of the early twenty-first century. Even if our consideration of the continent's future prospects excludes the Communist-controlled regimes in the east (as, for practical reasons, it must), we are still left with some states which are members of an economic-political organization (the EEC) but not of the chief military alliance (NATO), with others which adhere to the latter but not the former, and with important neutrals which are members of neither. Because of such anomalies, this section will focus upon the European Economic Community (and upon the policies of some of its leading members) rather than upon non-Communist Europe as a whole—for it is only in the EEC that an organization and structure exists, at least *potentially*, for a fifth world power.

But it is precisely because we are examining the EEC's *potential* rather than its present reality that the problem of guessing what it may be like in the year 2000 or 2020 is compounded. In some ways the situation is similar to that which, on a smaller scale, faced the members of the German Federation in the mid-nineteenth century.[85] A customs union existed which had proved to be so successful in stimulating trade and industry that it rapidly attracted new members, and it was clear that if that enlarged economic community was able to turn itself into a Power state it would be a major new actor in the international system—to which the established Great Powers would have to adjust accordingly. But so long as that transformation did not occur; so long as there were divisions among the members of the customs union about further economic integration and, still more, about political and military integration; so long as there were quarrels about which state should take the lead and disputes between the various parties and pressure groups about the benefits (or losses) accruing to them, then just so long would it stay divided, unable to realize its potential, and incapable of dealing as an equal with the other Great Powers. For all the differences of time and circumstance, the "German question" of the last century was a microcosm of the "European problem" of the present.

In its *potential*, the EEC clearly has the size, the wealth, and the productive capacity of a Great Power. With the adherence of Spain and Portugal, its twelve-member population now totals around 320 million—which is 50 million more than the USSR and almost half as big again as the U.S. population. Moreover, it is a highly trained population, with hundreds of universities and colleges across Europe and millions of scientists and engineers. While its average per capita income conceals great gulfs—say, between West German and Portuguese incomes—it is much richer on the whole than Russia, and some of its member states are richer per capita than the United States. As was pointed out earlier, it is by far the largest trading block in the world, although much of that is intra-European trade. Perhaps a better measure of its economic strength lies in its productive output, in automobiles, steel, cement, etc., which puts it ahead of the United States, Japan, and (except in steel) the USSR. Depending upon the annual statistics, and upon the wild swings in the value of the dollar relative to European currencies over the past six years, the total GNP of the EEC is about equal (1980, 1986) to that of the USA, or about two-thirds as big (1983–1984 figures). It is certainly far larger than Russia, Japan, or China in its share of world GNP or manufacturing output.

In military terms also, the European member states are far from negligible. Taking only the four largest countries (West Germany, France, Britain, Italy) into account, one finds their combined regular-army size to be over a million men, with a further 1.7 million in reserves[86]—a total which is of course smaller than the Russian and Chinese armies, but considerably larger than the U.S. Army. In addition, these four states possess hundreds of major surface warships and submarines and thousands of tanks, artillery, and aircraft. Finally, both France and Britain possess nuclear weapons, and delivery systems—sea-based and land-based. The implications and effectiveness of these military forces will be discussed below; the point being made here is simply that, *once combined*, the totals are very substantial. What is more, the spending upon these forces represents around 4 percent of the GNP, as a rough average. Were those countries, or, more significant still, the entire EEC, spending around 7 percent of total GNP on defense, as the United States is today, the sums allocated would be equal to hundreds of billions of dollars—that is, roughly the same amount as the two military superpowers spend.

And yet Europe's real power and effectiveness in the world is much less than the crude total of its economic and military strength would suggest—simply because of disunity. The armed forces, for example, not only suffer from a multitude of languages (a problem which the German Federation's members never had to face), but are equipped with many different weapons and have very marked differences in quality and training—between, say, the West German and the Greek armies, or the Royal Navy and the Spanish navy. Despite NATO's many attempts at standardization, one is still talking about a dozen armies, navies, and air forces of varying worth. But even those problems pale beside the obstacles at the *political* level, relating to the foreign and defense policy priorities of Europe. Ireland's traditional (and anachronistic) stance on neutrality prevents the EEC from discussing defense issues—although even if discussions occurred, they would probably soon founder upon Greek objections. Turkey, with its substantial army, is not a member of the EEC; and the Turkish and Greek armed forces often seem more worried about each other than about the Warsaw Pact. France's independent stance has (as will be seen below) military advantages and disadvantages; but it adds to the complications of consultation on defense and foreign-policy matters. Both Britain and France indulge in "out of area" operations and, indeed, still maintain an array of bases and troops overseas. For West Germany, the overriding defense issue—toward which *all* its forces are geared—is the security of its eastern frontier. Evolving a unified European policy toward, say, the Palestinian issue, or even toward the United States itself, is inordinately complex (and often fails), because of the differing interests and traditions of each of the member states.

In terms of economic integration, and of the constitutional and institutional arrangements that exist to implement decisions in the economic field, the EEC is obviously much further ahead; even so, as an "economic community," it is much more splintered than a sovereign state would ever be. Political ideology always affects economic policy and priorities. Coordination is difficult, if not impossible, when socialist regimes are in power in some of the member states and conservative parties are dominant in the others. Although the coordination of currencies is now more successful than it was, the occasional realignments which do take place (usually involving a revaluation of the German mark) are a reminder of the separate fiscal systems—and differentiated credit-worthiness—of the members. Despite proposals from the European Commission, there is as yet little progress toward a common European policy on a whole variety of issues, from full-scale airline deregulation to financial services. At too many of the common frontiers there are still customs posts, and lengthy checks, to the fury of the truck drivers. Even agriculture, the mainstay of the EEC's spending functions and one of the few economic sectors where there is a "common market," has proved to be a bone of contention.

And if it is indeed likely that world foodstuffs production will continue to expand, with India and other Asian countries increasingly entering the export markets, the pressure to reform the EEC's price-support system will build up, until the issue explodes into heated controversy again.

Finally, there is the persistent worry that after its postwar decades of economic growth and success, Europe is beginning to stagnate, and perhaps even to decline. The problems caused by the oil crisis of 1979—the steep rise in fuel prices, the pressure upon balance of payments, the general world depression in demand, output, and trade—seemed to hit the Europeans harder than many of the other major economies of the earth, as is indicated by Table 45.

Table 45. Growth in Real GNP, 1979–1983[87]
(percent)

	1979	1980	1981	1982	1983
United States	2.8	−0.3	2.6	−0.5	2.4
Canada	3.4	1.0	4.0	−4.2	3.0
Japan	5.1	4.9	4.0	3.2	3.0
China	7.0	5.2	3.0	7.4	9.0
EEC (ten)	3.5	1.1	−0.3	0.5	0.8

One of the chief concerns of the European states has been the effect of this slump upon employment levels—the number of people losing their jobs in western Europe in recent years has been much higher than at any time in the post-1945 era (for example, it leaped from 5.9 million to 10.2 million within the EEC between 1978 and 1982) and has shown little sign of coming down—which in turn swells the already extremely high level of social expenditures, leaving less for investment.[88] Nor has there been anything like the creation of new jobs on the scale which has occurred in the United States (chiefly in low-paying service industries) and Japan (in high technology and services) as the 1980s have unfolded. Whether one ascribes this to the lack of business incentives, high costs and immobility of the labor market, and bureaucratic over-regulation (as right-wingers tend to do), or to the failure of the state to plan and invest sufficiently (as the Left usually sees it), or to a fatal combination of both, the result is the same. More alarming still, to many commentators, have been the signs that Europe is falling behind its American and (especially) its Japanese competitors in the high-technology stakes of the future. Thus, the 1984–85 *Annual Economic Report* of the European Commission warned:

> The Community is now having to respond to the challenge of an emerging inferiority, by comparison with the United States and Japan, in industrial capacity in new and fast-growing technologies.

> . . . The deteriorating world trade performance of the Community
> in such fields as computers, micro-electronics, and equipment is
> now generally recognized.[89]

Quite possibly, this picture of "Eurosclerosis" and "Europessimism"
has been painted too gloomily, for there are many other signs of European competitiveness—in quality automobiles, commercial and fighter
aircraft, satellites, chemicals, telecommunications systems, financial
services, etc. Nevertheless, the two most pressing issues remain in
doubt. Is the EEC, because of the sociopolitical diversity of its members, as capable as its overseas competitors of responding to swift and
large-scale shifts in employment patterns? Or is it designed more to
slow down the impact of economic changes upon uncompetitive sectors (agriculture, textiles, shipbuilding, coal, and steel), and, in being
so humane in the short term, disadvantaging itself in the longer term?
And is the EEC capable of mobilizing the scientific and investment
resources to remain a leading contender in the high-technology stakes,
when its own companies are nowhere near as big as the American and
Japanese giants, and when any "industrial strategy" has to be worked
out, not by the likes of MITI, but by *twelve* governments (plus the EEC
Commission), each exhibiting different concerns?

If one turned one's attention from the EEC as a whole to a brief
examination of the situation in which the leading *three* military/politi-
cal countries of Europe find themselves, the sense of "potential" being
threatened by "problems" is only reinforced. No state, arguably, mani-
fests this ambivalence about the future more than the Federal Republic
of Germany, in large part because of its inheritance from the past and
the still "provisional" nature of the present structure of Europe.

Although many Germans fret about the economic prospects for
their country by the early twenty-first century, that can hardly be
regarded as the major concern (especially as compared with the economic difficulties facing other societies). While its total labor force is
only a little higher than Britain's or France's, its GNP is significantly
larger, reflecting an economy whose long-term productive growth has
been extremely impressive. It is the largest producer in the EEC of
steel, chemicals, electrical goods, automobiles, tractors, and (given
Britain's decline) even merchant ships and coal. Because of a remarkably low level both of inflation and of labor disputes, it has kept its
export prices competitive, despite the frequent upward valuations of
the deutsche mark—which are, after all, merely belated acknowledgments by other nations of West Germany's better economic performance. A heavy emphasis upon engineering and design in the German
management tradition (as opposed to the American emphasis upon
finance) has given it an international reputation for quality products.
Year after year, the German economy has notched up a surplus in its

trade balances second only to Japan's. Its international reserves are larger than those of any other country in the world (except, presumably, those of Japan after the latter's recent surge), and the deutsche mark is often used by other nations as a reserve currency.

As against all this, one can point to those factors which give the Germans cause for *Angst.* [90] The EEC's agricultural price-support system, long a drain for the German taxpayer, redistributes resources from the most competitive to the least competitive sectors of the economy—and not just in the Federal Republic itself (where there are a surprisingly large number of small farms), but to the peasantry of southern Europe. This has obvious social value, but it is a burden proportionately much larger than the protection given to American and perhaps even to Japanese agriculture. The persistently high level of unemployment, a sign that the Federal Republic still has too large a proportion of its work force in older industries, is also a major drain upon the economy, keeping social-security payments at a very high proportion of GDP; and while unemployment among the youth can be alleviated by the impressively broad level of training and apprenticeships, and will also be eased by the rapid aging of the German population, this latter trend is perhaps regarded with the greatest unease of all. If it is clearly an exaggeration to believe that the German race will "die out," the steep decline in the birth rate will have obvious repercussions upon the German economy when an even larger share of the population consists of old-age pensioners. Along with this demographic fear goes the much less tangible worry that the "successor generation" will not want to work as earnestly as those who rebuilt Germany from the wartime ashes, and that with higher wage costs and far shorter working weeks than the Japanese, even German productivity growth will not keep up with the challenge from the Pacific basin.

Even so, none of those problems are insuperable, provided the Germans can maintain their "package" of low inflation, quality goods, high investment in new technology, superior design and salesmanship, and labor peace. (At the very least, one can say that if the problems named above affect the German economy, how much more will they hurt the economies of most of its less competitive neighbors!) What is much more difficult to forecast is whether the extraordinarily complex and quite unique contours of the "German question" as they have existed since the late 1940s will continue unchanged into the twenty-first century: that is, whether there will continue to be two "Germanies," separated by hostile alliances, despite the growing intimacy between them; whether the NATO alliance (of which the Federal Republic is such a central part) can defend the German lands without destroying them, should East-West relations worsen into hostilities; and whether, in the event of a diminution in American power and a reduction of its forces in Europe, Germany and its major EEC/NATO partners can provide an adequate substitute for the U.S. strategic umbrella which has served so well for the past forty years. None of these interrelated issues are crying out for an immediate solution, but all of them are giving thoughtful observers grounds for concern.

The "German-German" relationship will probably seem, at this time, the most hypothetical of the cluster. As has been made clear in the preceding chapters, the proper place of the German people within the European states system has troubled statesmen for at least the past century and a half.[91] If all those speaking the German tongue are brought together as one nation-state—as has been the European norm for nearly two centuries—the resultant concentration of population and industrial might would always make Germany the economic power center of west-central Europe. That itself need not *necessarily* turn it into the dominant military-territorial force in Europe as well, in the way that the imperialism of both the Wilhelmine and (even more) the Nazi eras led to a German bid for hegemony. In a bipolar world which, militarily, is still dominated by Washington and Moscow, in an age when major Great Power aggressions run the risk of triggering a nuclear war, and with a post-1945 "de-Nazified" generation of German politicians running affairs in Bonn and East Berlin, the notion of any future Germanic bid for "mastery in Europe" seems anachronistic. Even were it attempted, the balance of European (let alone global) power would prevail against it. In abstract terms, therefore, there is surely nothing wrong *and a lot that is right* with permitting the 62 million "West" Germans and 17 million "East" Germans to reunite, particularly when each population increasingly perceives that it has more in common with the other than with its superpower guardian.

Yet the tragic fact is that however logical that solution is in one sense—and however much the two German peoples are showing signs (despite the ideological gulf) of their common inheritance and culture—the present political realities speak against it, even if it took the form of a loose Germanic federation on the nineteenth-century model, as has been ingeniously suggested.[92] For the blunt fact is that East Germany serves as a strategical barrier for the Soviet control over the buffer states of eastern Europe (not to say the jump-off position for a move to the west); and since the men in the Kremlin still think in terms of imperialist *Realpolitik*, letting the German Democratic Republic gravitate toward (and into) the Federal Republic would be regarded as a major blow. As one authority has recently pointed out, based on present forces alone, a unified Germany could field over 660,000 regular troops plus 1.5 million paramilitary and reservists. The USSR could not view with equanimity a unified German nation with an army of 2 million on its western flank.[93] On the other hand, it seems difficult to see why a *peacefully* united Germany should want to maintain armed forces of that size, forces which reflect present Cold War tensions. It

is also difficult to believe that despite its heavy-handed emphasis upon
the lessons of the Second World War, even the Soviet leadership accepts its own propaganda about German revanchism and neo-Nazism
(which has been an increasingly difficult position to maintain since
Willy Brandt's period of office). But what is also clear is that Moscow
has a congenital dislike of withdrawing from *anywhere,* and also worries deeply about the political consequences of a reunited Germany.
Not only would it be a formidable economic Power in its own right—
with a total GNP dangerously close to the USSR's own, at least in
formal dollar-equivalent terms—but it also would act as a trading
magnet for all of its eastern European neighbors. Even more fundamental a point: how could Russia withdraw from East Germany
without provoking the question of a similar withdrawal from
Czechoslovakia, Hungary, and Poland—leaving as the USSR's western
frontier the dubious Polish/Ukrainian borderline, which is temptingly
close for the fifty million Ukrainians?

What remains, therefore, is a state of suspended animation. Intra-
German trade relations are likely to grow (clouded only by the occasional tension between the superpowers); each German state is likely
to become relatively more productive and richer than its neighbors;
each will swear loyalty to its supranational military (NATO/Warsaw
Pact) and economic (EEC/Comecon) organizations while making special arrangements with its Germanic sister state. It is impossible to
forecast how Bonn would react should the Soviet Union itself be
shaken and upset from within—and should that coincide with serious
unrest in the German Democratic Republic. It is also impossible to
forecast how the "East" Germans would react if there was to be a
Warsaw-Pact offensive westward. Certainly, the special Soviet "control" arrangements over the Democratic Republic's army, and the
shadowing of every one of its divisions by a Russian motor-rifle division, suggest that even the grim men in the Kremlin worry about
setting German against German—as well they should.

But the more concrete and immediate problem which the Federal
Republic faces—and has faced since its existence—has been to discover a viable defense policy in the event of a war in Europe. From the
beginning (see pp. 378–79), the apprehension that a vastly superior Red
Army could strike westward without much hindrance led both the
Germans and their fellow Europeans to rely upon the U.S. nuclear
deterrent as their chief security. Ever since the USSR acquired the
capacity to hit the American homeland with its own ICBMs, however,
that strategy has been in doubt—would Washington really begin a
nuclear interchange in response to a Russian conventional attack on
the northern German plain?—even if it has never been officially abandoned. This is also true of the related question of whether the United
States would unleash strategic nuclear attacks against the Soviet Union

(again, inviting reprisals upon its own cities) if the Russians contented themselves with firing short- or *intermediate*-range missiles (SS-20s) solely at European targets. There has been, to be sure, no lack of proposals for creating a "credible deterrent" to meet such contingencies: installing Pershing II and various forms of cruise-missile systems to counter the Russian SS-20s; producing an enhanced-radiation (or "neutron") bomb, intended to kill off invading Warsaw Pact troops without damage to buildings and infrastructure; and—in the French case—reliance upon a Paris-controlled deterrent force as an alternative to an uncertain American defense system. All of these, however, have their own attendant problems;[94] and, quite apart from the political reactions which they provoke, each of them points to the uniquely contradictory nature of nuclear weapon systems—that having recourse to them is more than likely to lead to the destruction of that which one wishes to defend.

It is scarcely surprising, therefore, that while successive West German administrations have paid lip service to the value of NATO's nuclear-deterrence strategy, and have foresworn the acquisition of nuclear weapons for themselves, they have been to the fore in the creation of a strong *conventional* defense system. As it is, the Bundeswehr has not only the largest of the NATO armies in Europe (335,000 troops, with 645,000 trained reserves)[95] but also one of extremely high quality and with good equipment; provided it did not lose command of the air, it would give an impressive account of itself. On the other hand, the steeply declining birthrate makes it increasingly difficult to maintain the Bundeswehr at full strength, while the government's desire to keep defense spending down to 3.5 to 4 percent of GNP means that it will be difficult for the armed services to procure as much new equipment as they need.[96] At the end of the day, such weakness can be overcome—just as the deficiencies in the less-well-equipped Allied armies stationed in West Germany could be overcome, given the political will. However, this still leaves the Germans facing the uncomfortable (for some, intolerable) dilemma that any outbreak of large-scale hostilities in central Europe would lead to incalculable bloodshed and material loss on their territory.

It is not surprising, therefore, that since at least the time of Willy Brandt's chancellorship the government in Bonn has been to the fore in its pursuit of *détente* in Europe—and not merely with its German sister state, but also with eastern European nations and with the USSR itself, in an endeavor to calm their traditional fears of a too-strong Germany; and that it, more than all its NATO partners, has partaken in and financed East-West trade in the Cobdenite belief that economic interdependence makes war more difficult (and also no doubt because West German banks and industries are so favorably placed to take advantage of that commerce). This does not imply a move into "neu-

tralism" for the two Germanies—as is sometimes proposed by left-wing
Social Democrats and the Green Party—for that would depend upon
securing Moscow's consent to East German neutralism as well, which
is highly unlikely. What it does mean is that West Germany sees its
security problem concentrated almost exclusively in Europe and shuns
any "out-of-area" capability—let alone the occasional extra-European
actions in which the French and British still indulge. By extension,
therefore, it dislikes being forced to take a position on the (in its view)
distracting and distant issues in the Near East and farther afield, and
that in turn leads it into disagreements with a U.S. government which
feels that the preservation of western security cannot be so neatly
limited to central Europe. In its relationship to Moscow and East Berlin on the one hand and to non-European issues on the other, West
Germany finds it difficult if not impossible to conduct a merely bilateral diplomacy; it must, instead, have regard for the reactions of Washington (and, often, of Paris). That, too, is a price which has to be paid
for its awkward and unique position in the international power system.[97]

If the Federal Republic finds the economic challenges less intracti-
ble than foreign- and defense-policy problems, the same cannot be said
for the United Kingdom. It, too, is the legatee of a historical past—and,
of course, of a geographical position—which strongly influences its
policy toward the world outside. But, as we have seen in earlier chapters, it is also the country among the former Great Powers whose
economy and society have found it hardest to adjust to the shifting
patterns of technology and manufacturing in the post-1945 decades
(and in many respects in the decades before). The most devastating
impact of the global changes has been upon manufacturing, a sector
which once earned Britain the title "workshop of the world." It is true
that among many of the advanced economies of the world, manufacturing's share of output and employment has been steadily shrinking
while other sectors (e.g., services) have grown; but in Britain's case the
fall has been much more precipitous. Not only has its proportion of
world manufacturing output continued its remorseless decline *relatively*, but it has also decreased *absolutely*. More shocking still has
been the abrupt switch in the place of manufactures in Britain's foreign trade. While it may be difficult to prove *The Economist*'s tart
observation that "since 1983, Britain's trade balance on manufactures
has been in deficit for the first time since the Romans invaded Britain,"
it is a fact that even in the late 1950s exports of manufactures were
three times as big as imports.[98] Now that surplus has gone. What is
more, the decline in employment occurs not only in older industries
but also in the "sunrise" high-technology firms.[99]

If the fall in Britain's manufacturing competitiveness is a century-
old tale,[100] it has clearly been accelerated by the discovery of North Sea

oil, which while producing earnings to cover the visible trade gap has also had the effect of turning sterling into a "petrocurrency," sending its value to unrealistically high levels for a while and making many of its exports uncompetitive. Even when the oil runs out, causing sterling to decline further, it is not at all clear that that would *ipso facto* lead to a revival in manufacturing: plant has been scrapped, foreign markets lost (perhaps permanently), and international competitiveness eroded by higher than average rises in unit labor costs. Britain's shift into services is somewhat more promising, but it nonetheless remains as true here as in the United States that many services (from window cleaning to fast food) neither earn foreign currency nor are particularly productive. Even in the expanding, high-earning fields of international banking, investment, commodity dealing, and so on, it seems clear that the competition is, if anything, more intense—and in the past thirty years "Britain's share of world trade in services has fallen from 18 percent to 7 percent."[101] As banking and finance become a global business, increasingly dominated by those (chiefly American and Japanese) firms with massive capital resources in New York *and* London *and* Tokyo, the British share may diminish further. Finally, future developments in telecommunications and office equipment are already suggesting that white-collar jobs may soon follow the path already trodden by blue-collar workers in the West.

None of this, one hopes, portends a cataclysm. A general growth in world output and trade would help to keep the British economy afloat, even if its share of the whole gently declined and its per capita GNP was steadily being overtaken by many more nations, from Italy to Singapore. The decline could intensify, if a change of government led to large increases in social spending (rather than productive investment), higher taxation levels, a drop in business confidence, and a flight from sterling; it might slow down, with a government which adopted a less strict monetary policy, evolved a coherent "industrial strategy," and cooperated with fellow Europeans in marketable (and nonprestige) ventures. It also may be true, as one economist maintains,[102] that British manufacturing is now altogether leaner, fitter, and more competitive, having undergone an "industrial renaissance." But the auguries for a spectacular turnaround are not good; the relative immobility and lack of training in the labor market, the high unit costs, and the comparative smallness of even the largest British manufacturing firms are very considerable handicaps. The output of engineers and scientists is still dismally low. Above all, there is the poor level of investment in R&D: for every $1 spent in Britain on R&D in the early 1980s, $1.50 was spent in Germany, $3 in Japan, and $8 in the United States—yet 50 percent of that British R&D was devoted to nonproductive defense activities, compared with Germany's 9 percent and Japan's minuscule amount.[103] By contrast with its chief rivals (except the

United States), British R&D is both much less related to industry's needs and much less paid for by industry itself.

The large proportion devoted to defense-related R&D brings us onto the other horn of the British dilemma. If it was an unambitious, obscure, isolated, pacific state, its slow industrial anemia would be a pity—but irrelevant to the international power system. Yet the fact is that, although much shrunken from its Victorian heyday, Britain still remains—or claims to be—one of the leading "midsized" Powers of the globe. Its defense budget is the third- or fourth-largest (depending upon how one measures China's total), its navy the fourth-largest, its air force the fourth-largest[104]—all of which, it might be thought, is significantly out of proportion to its geographical size (a mere 245,000 square kilometers), its population (56 million) and its modest, declining share of world GNP (3.38 percent in 1983). Furthermore, despite its imperial sunset, it still has very extensive strategical commitments abroad: not only in the 65,000 troops and airmen in Germany as its contribution to NATO's Central Front, but also in garrisons and naval bases across the globe—Belize, Cyprus, Gibraltar, Hong Kong, the Falklands, Brunei, the Indian Ocean. Despite all the premature announcements, it is still not one with Nineveh and Tyre.[105]

This divergence between Britain's shrunken economic state and its overextended strategical posture is probably more extreme than that affecting any other of the larger Powers, except Russia itself. It therefore finds itself particularly vulnerable to the fact that weapon prices are rising 6 to 10 percent faster than inflation, and that every new weapon system is three to five times costlier than that which it is intended to replace. It is made the more vulnerable in consequence of domestic-political constraints upon defense spending; while Conservative administrations feel it necessary to contain arms spending in order to reduce the deficit, any alternative regime would feel inclined to chop defense expenditures in absolute terms. Quite apart from this political dilemma, however, there looms for Britain a fundamental and (soon) unavoidable choice: *either* to cut allocations to all of the armed services, placing each of them in a less than effective state; *or* to cut some of the nation's defense commitments.

Yet as soon as that proposition is stated, the obstacles emerge. Command of the air is taken to be axiomatic (hence the RAF's superior budget), even while the cost of new Euro-fighters is spiraling out of sight. By far the greatest British overseas commitment is to Germany and Berlin (almost $4 billion), but even now those 55,000 troops, 600 tanks, and 3,000 other armored vehicles are, despite high morale, underprovisioned. However, any reduction in the size of the BAOR (British Army on the Rhine) or fancy-footwork scheme to keep half the troops in British rather than German garrisons is likely to trigger off such *political* repercussions—from German grief, to Belgian emulation, to American annoyance—that it could be totally counterproductive. A second alternative is to reduce the size of the surface fleet—the Ministry of Defence solution of 1981, until the Falklands crisis upset that scheme.[106] But while such an alternative probably has the most advocates in Whitehall's corridors of power, it looks ill-timed in the face of Russia's rising naval challenge and the increasing American emphasis upon NATO having an "out-of-area" thrust. (And it is certainly a contradiction for the advocates of enhancing NATO's conventional forces in Europe to agree to reductions in the alliance's second-largest fleet of Atlantic escorts.) A more possible candidate for "cuts" would be Britain's expensive and (while emotionally understandable) vastly overextended commitments in the Falkland Islands: but even that retrenchment would probably only postpone a longer decision for several years. Finally, there is the investment in the very expensive Trident submarine-based ballistic-missile system, the costs of which seem to rise month by month.[107] Given the Conservative government's enthusiasm for an advanced and "independent" deterrent system—not to mention the way in which the Trident boats may actually be altering the overall nuclear balance (see below, p. 506)— that decision is only likely with a radical change of administration in Britain, which in turn might throw more than future defense policy into question.

At the end of the day, however, the awkward choice is there. As the *Sunday Times* has put it, "Unless something is done soon, this country's defense policy will increasingly consist of trying to do the same job with less money, which can only be bad for Britain and NATO."[108] This leaves the politicians (of *any* party) with the alternative of reducing certain commitments, and enduring the consequences thereof; or of increasing defense expenditures still further—and Britain spends proportionately more (5.5 percent of GNP) than any other European NATO partner except Greece—and thereby reducing its own investment in productive growth and its long-term prospects for an economic recovery. As with most decaying Powers, there is only a choice of hard options.

The same dilemma confronts Britain's neighbor across the Channel, even if that has been concealed by the lack of sustained domestic questioning of France's defense policy, and by a significantly better (if still flawed) economic performance since the 1950s. At the end of the day, Paris, like London, has to grapple with the problem of being only a "midsized" Power with extensive national interests and overseas commitments, the defense of which is coming under steadily increased pressure from escalating weapon costs.[109] While its population is the same as Britain's, its total GNP and its per capita GNP are larger. The French produce more cars and more steel than the British and have a very large aerospace industry. Unlike Britain, France remains heavily dependent upon imported oil; on the other hand, it still runs a considerable surplus in agricultural goods, which are heavily subsidized by the EEC. In a number of significant high-technology fields—telecommunications, space satellites, aircraft, nuclear power—the French have shown a strong commitment to keeping abreast with worldwide competition. If France's economy was badly dented by the Socialist administration's dash for growth in the early 1980s (just when all its major trading partners were retrenching fiscally), the stricter policies which followed seem to have reduced inflation, cut the trade gap, and stabilized the franc, all of which ought to allow for a resumption in French economic growth.

But whenever France's economic structure and prospects are compared with those of its powerful neighbor across the Rhine—or with Japan's—the precariousness shows through. While France is still spectacularly adroit in exporting fighter aircraft, wines, and grain, it "remains relatively weak in selling run-of-the-mill manufactured goods abroad."[110] Too many of its customers have been unstable Third World countries that order lavish projects like dams or Mirages and then have difficulty paying for them; by contrast, the "import penetration" of industrial goods, automobiles, and electrical appliances into France indicates broad fields where it is not competitive. Its trade deficit with West Germany grows year by year and, since French prices always rise faster than those in Germany, will in all probability lead to further devaluations of the franc. The northern landscape of France is still scarred with decaying industries—coal, iron, steel, shipbuilding—and much of its automobile industry is also feeling the strain. And while the new technologies seem full of promise, neither can they absorb France's many unemployed nor are they receiving the levels of investment necessary to keep pace with German, Japanese, and American technologies. More worrying still for a country as economically (and, of perhaps greater import, psychologically) attached to agriculture is the looming crisis of global overproduction of grains, dairy produce, fruit, wine, etc.—with its increasing strain upon French and EEC budgets if farm-support prices are maintained and its threat of social unrest if prices are cut. Until a few years ago, Paris could rely upon Community funds to aid in restructuring agriculture; now, most of that cash is likely to go to the peasants of Spain, Portugal, and Greece. All this may leave France without the capital resources necessary for a much larger R&D effort and for sustained, high-tech-based growth over the next two decades.

It is in this larger context, of fixing priorities for France's future, that one needs to view the debate over national defense policy. In many ways, there is much that is impressive about French strategy, and military actions, in recent times. Recognizing (and assertively voicing) the increasing doubts about the credibility of the American strategic nuclear deterrent, France has provided itself with its own "triad" of delivery systems for use in the event of Soviet aggression. By keeping in its own hands every aspect of its nuclear deterrent (from production to targeting), and by insisting that its entire force of missiles will be loosed at Russia if deterrence fails, Paris feels it has a more certain way of holding the Kremlin in check. At the same time, it has maintained one of the largest land armies and has a substantial garrison in south-western Germany and a commitment to come to the Federal Republic's aid; while being outside the NATO command structure, and thus able to proffer an independent "European" voice on strategic issues, it has not dislocated the military need for reinforcing the Central Front in the event of a Russian attack. The French have also maintained an extra-European role and—by means of occasional military interventions overseas, the presence of their garrisons and advisers in Third World countries, and their successful arms-sales policy—offered an alternative influence (and source of supply) to either the USSR or the United States. If this has sometimes irritated Washington—and if French nuclear testing in the South Pacific has rightly annoyed the countries of that region—then Moscow in its turn can hardly be comforted by the various and sometimes unpredictable displays of Gallic independence. Furthermore, since both the right and the left in France support the idea of the nation's playing a distinct role abroad, French claims and actions for that purpose do not provoke the domestic criticism which would occur in virtually all other Western societies. All this had led foreign observers (and, of course, Frenchmen themselves) to describe their policy as logical, hard-nosed, realistic, and so on.

Yet the policy itself is not without its problems—as some French commentators are beginning openly to admit[111]—and must cause the historically minded to recall the gap which existed between the theory and the reality of France's defense policy prior to 1914 and 1939. In the first place, there is a great deal of truth in the cold observation that all of France's posturings of independence have taken place behind the American shield and guarantee to western Europe, both conventional and nuclear. A Gaullist policy of assertiveness was only possible, Raymond Aron pointed out, because for the first time in this century France was not in the front line.[112] But what if that security disappears? That is, what if the American nuclear deterrent is admitted to be non-credible? What if the United States, over time, steadily pulls back its troops, tanks, and aircraft from Europe? Under certain circumstances, both of those eventualities might be seen as welcome. Yet, as the French themselves admit, they can hardly appear so in the light of Moscow's recent policies: steadily building up its own nuclear *and* European-based conventional forces to excessive levels, keeping a tight hold upon its eastern European satellites, and launching "peace offensives" designed perhaps particularly to wean the West German public

out of the NATO alliance and into neutralism. Many of the signs of
what has been termed France's "New Atlanticism"[113]—a stiffer tone
toward the Soviet Union, criticism of neutralist tendencies among the
German Social Democrats, the Franco-German agreement for the forward deployment in Germany (possibly with tactical nuclear weapons)
of the Force d'Action Rapide, the closer links with NATO[114]—are obvious consequences of French concern about the future. Until Moscow
changes, Paris is bound to worry that the USSR might move *into* western Europe when (or even before) the United States has moved *out.*

But if that threat became more likely, what could France do about
it in *practical* terms? Naturally, it could increase its conventional
forces still further, moving toward the creation of an enhanced
Franco-German army strong enough to hold off a Russian assault even
if U.S. forces were diminished (or even absent). In the view of people
like Helmut Schmidt,[115] this is the logical extension not only of the
Paris-Bonn *entente* but also of international trends (e.g., the weakening of American capacities). There are all sorts of political and organizational difficulties in the way of such a scheme—ranging from the
possible attitude of a future left-of-center German administration, to
questions of command, language and deployment, to the touchy issue
of French tactical nuclear weapons[116]—but in any event such a strategy
is likely to founder upon one insuperable reef: lack of money. France
is currently spending about 4.2 percent of its GNP upon defense (compared with the United States' 7.4 percent and Britain's 5.5 percent), but
given the delicate state of the French economy, that percentage cannot
be increased by very much. Moreover, France's independence in
atomic-weapons development means that its nuclear strategic forces
absorb up to 30 percent of the defense budget, far more than elsewhere. What is left is not enough for the AMX battle tank, advanced
aircraft, the new nuclear-powered aircraft carrier, "smart" battlefield
weapons, and so on. While certain increases in the French armed
forces may be likely, that could not possibly satisfy all requirements.[117]
Just as in Britain's case, therefore, the French are being faced with the
awkward choice of either eliminating some weapon systems (and
roles) entirely or forcing economies upon all of them.

Equally worrying are the doubts being raised about France's nuclear deterrent, both at the technical and the (related) strategical level.
Parts of the triad of French nuclear weaponry—the land-based missiles, and especially the aircraft—suffer from deterioration over time
and even their costly upgrading and modernization may not keep pace
with newer weapons technology.[118] This problem may become particularly acute if significant breakthroughs occur in American Strategic
Defense Initiative (SDI) technology, and if the Russians in their turn
develop a much larger system of ballistic-missile defense. Nothing is
more disturbing, from the French viewpoint, than the two superpow-

ers enhancing their potential invulnerability while Europe remains exposed. As against this, there is the significant buildup of the French submarine-launched ballistic-missile system (discussed below, p. 506). However, the general principle remains: advanced technology could render useless existing types of weaponry, and certainly will make the cost of any replacements much more expensive. In any case, the French are caught in the same trap of credibility as all of the other nuclear Powers. If Paris thinks it increasingly unlikely that the United States would risk a strategic nuclear exchange with the USSR because the German frontier had been invaded, how likely is its own promise to "go nuclear" on behalf of the Federal Republic? (The West Germans hardly believe it.) Even the Gaullist tradition of defending the "sanctuary" of France by firing off all its missiles at Russia hangs upon the unproven assumption that the French people prefer obliteration to a possible (or likely) defeat by conventional means. "Tearing an arm off the Russian bear" has always sounded like a good phrase, until it is remembered that one will certainly be devoured by the bear; and that Russia's own antimissile defenses may limit the damage it will suffer. Obviously, the official posture of French nuclear strategy is not going to be altered soon, if at all. But it is worth wondering how realistic it is, should the East-West balance worsen and the United States weaken.[119]

France's problem, then, is that so many demands are pressing upon its own modest national resources. Given demographic and structural-economic trends, the high share of national income consumed by social security is likely to continue, and probably increase. Large funds may soon be needed for the agricultural sector. At the same time, the modernization of the armed forces requires substantial amounts of money. Yet all of these have to be balanced against—and take away from—the pressing need for vastly enlarged investment in R&D and in advanced industrial processes. If it cannot allocate the monies necessary for the last-named purpose, it will over time put into jeopardy the prospects of affording defense, social security, and all the rest. Obviously this dilemma is not France's alone, although it is the French above all who have argued for a distinctively "European" position on international economic and defense issues—and who therefore most clearly articulate European concerns. For this reason, too, it is Paris which has usually taken the lead in initiating new policies—deepening Franco-German military ties, producing European Airbuses and satellites, and so on. Many of these schemes have met with skepticism among France's neighbors at this Gallic fondness for bureaucratic planning and prestige endeavors, or with the suspicion that French companies are likely to be awarded the lion's share of Euro-funded projects. Other schemes, however, have already proved their worth or seem to hold a rich promise.

Europe's "problems" are, of course, more than those considered here: they include aging populations and aging industries, ethnic discontents in the inner cities, the gap between the prosperous north and the poorer south, the political/linguistic tensions in Belgium, Ulster, and northern Spain. Pessimistic observers also occasionally allude to the possibility of a "Finlandization" of certain European states (Denmark, West Germany), which would then become dependent upon Moscow. Since that development could only follow from a leftward political shift in the countries concerned, it is difficult to estimate its likelihood. As it is, if one considers Europe—as represented chiefly by the EEC—as a *power-political* unit in the global system, the most important issues it faces are clearly those discussed above: how to evolve a common defense policy for the coming century which will be viable even in what may be an era of significant change in the international power balances; and how to remain competitive against the very formidable economic challenges posed by new technology and new commercial competitors. In the case of the other four regions and societies examined in this chapter, it is possible to suggest what changes are likely to occur over time in their present position: that Japan and China will probably see their status in the world enhanced, and that the USSR and even the United States will see theirs eroded. But Europe remains an enigma. If the European Community can really act together, it may well improve its position in the world, both militarily and economically. If it does not—which, given human nature, is the more plausible outcome—its relative decline seems destined to continue.

The Soviet Union and Its "Contradictions"

The word "contradiction" in Marxist terminology is a very specific one, and refers to the tensions which (it is argued) inherently exist within the capitalist system of production and will inevitably cause its demise.[120] It may therefore seem deliberately ironic to employ the same expression to describe the position in which the Soviet Union, the world's first Communist state, now finds itself. Nevertheless, as will be described below, in a number of absolutely critical areas there seems to be opening up an ever-widening gap between the aims of the Soviet state and the methods employed to reach them. It proclaims the need for enhanced agricultural and industrial output, yet hobbles that possibility by collectivization and by heavy-handed planning. It asserts the overriding importance of world peace, yet its own massive arms buildup and its link with "revolutionary" states (together with its revolutionary heritage) serve to increase international tensions. It claims to require absolute security along its extensive borders, yet its hitherto unyielding policy toward its neighbors' own security concerns worsens

Moscow's relations—with western and eastern Europe, with Middle East peoples, with China and Japan—and in turn makes the Russians feel "encircled" and *less* secure. Its philosophy asserts the ongoing dialectical process of change in world affairs, driven by technology and new means of production, and inevitably causing all sorts of political and social transformations; and yet its own autocratic and bureaucratic habits, the privileges which cushion the party elites, the restrictions upon the free interchange of knowledge, and the lack of a personal-incentive system make it horribly ill-equipped to handle the explosive but subtle high-tech future which is already emerging in Japan and California. Above all, while its party leaders frequently insist that the USSR will never again accept a position of military inferiority, and even more frequently urge the nation to increase production, it has clearly found it difficult to reconcile those two aims; and, in particular, to check a Russian tradition of devoting too high a share of national resources to the armed forces—with deleterious consequences for its ability to compete with other societies commercially. Perhaps there are other ways of labeling all these problems, but it does not seem inappropriate to term them "contradictions."

Given the emphasis in Marxian philosophy upon the *material* basis of existence, it may seem doubly ironic that the chief difficulties facing the USSR today are located in its economic substructure; and yet the evidence gleaned by western experts—not to mention the increasingly open acknowledgments by the Soviet leadership itself—leave no doubt that that is so. It would be interesting to know how Khrushchev, who in the 1950s confidently forecast that the USSR would overtake the United States economically and "bury" capitalism, would have felt about Mr. Gorbachev's 1986 admissions to the 27th Communist Party Congress:

> Difficulties began to build up in the economy in the 1970s, with the rates of economic growth declining visibly. As a result, the targets for economic development set in the Communist Party program, and even the lower targets of the 9th and 10th 5-year plans were not attained. Neither did we manage to carry out the social program charted for this period. A lag ensued in the material base of science and education, health protection, culture and everyday services.
>
> Though efforts have been made of late, we have not succeeded in fully remedying the situation. There are serious lags in engineering, the oil and coal industries, the electrical engineering industry, in ferrous metals and chemicals in capital construction. Neither have the targets been met for the main indicators of efficiency and the improvement of the people's standard of living.
>
> Acceleration of the country's socio-economic development is the

key to all our problems; immediate and long-term, economic and
social, political and ideological, internal and external.[121]

To which it might be remarked that the final statement could have been
made by *any* government in the world, and that the mere recognition
of economic problems is no guarantee that they will be solved.

The most critical area of weakness in the economy during the entire
history of the Soviet Union has been agriculture, which is the more
amazing when it is recalled that a century ago Russia was one of the
two largest grain exporters in the world. Yet since the early 1970s it has
needed to import tens of millions of tons of wheat and corn each year.
If world food-production trends continue, Russia (and certain other
socialist economies of eastern Europe) will share with parts of Africa
and the Near East the dubious distinction of being the only countries
which have changed from being net food *exporters* to *importers* on a
large-scale and sustained way over recent years.[122] In Russia's case,
this embarrassing stagnation in agricultural output has not been for
want of attention or effort; since Stalin's death, every Soviet leader has
pressed for increases in food production, in order to meet consumer
demand and to fulfill the promised rises in the Russian standard of
living. It would be wrong to assume that such rises have not occurred—
clearly, the average Russian is much better off now than in 1953, when
his situation was desperate. But what is much more depressing is that
after some decades of drawing closer to the West, his standard of living
is falling behind again—despite all the resources which the state com-
mits toward agriculture, which swallows up nearly 30 percent of total
investment (cf. 5 percent in the United States) and employs over 20
percent of the labor force (cf. 3 percent in the United States). Merely
in order to maintain standards of living, the USSR is compelled to
invest approximately $78 billion in agriculture each year, *and* to subsi-
dize food prices by a further $50 billion—despite which it seems "to be
moving further and further away from being the exporter it once
was"[123] and instead needs to pour out further billions of hard currency
to import grain and meats to make up its own shortfalls in agricultural
output.

There are, it is true, certain *natural* reasons for the precariousness
of Soviet agriculture, and for the fact that its productivity is about
one-seventh that of American farming. Although the USSR is often
regarded as geographically rather similar to the United States—both
being continent-wide, northern-hemisphere states—it actually lies
much farther to the north: the Ukraine is on the same latitude as
southern Canada. Not only does this make it difficult to grow corn, but
even the Soviet wheat-growing regions endure far colder winters—and
are subject to more frequent droughts—than states like Kansas and
Oklahoma. The four years 1979–1982 were particularly bad in that

respect, and so embarrassed the government that it stopped giving details of agricultural output (although its average import of 35 million tons of grain each year provided a clue!). Even the "good" year of 1983 did not make the USSR self-sufficient—and it was followed in turn by yet another disastrous year of cold and drought.[124] Moreover, any attempt to increase production by extending the wheat acreage into the "virgin lands" is always constricted by frosts in the north and the arid conditions in the south.

Nevertheless, no outside observers are convinced that it is climate alone which has depressed Soviet agricultural output.[125] By far the biggest problems are simply caused by the "socialization" of agriculture. To keep the Russian populace happy, food prices are held artificially low through subsidies, so that "meat costing the state $4 a pound to produce sells for 80 cents a pound"[126]—which, for example, makes it cheaper for peasants to buy and feed bread and potatoes to their livestock than to use unprocessed grain. The vast amounts of state investment in agriculture are thrown at large-scale projects (dams, drainage) rather than at individual barns or up-to-date small tractors that an ordinary peasant might want. Decisions as to planting, investment, and so on are taken not by those who work the fields but by managers and bureaucrats. The denial of responsibility and initiative to the individual peasants is probably the single greatest reason for disappointing yields, chronic inefficiencies, and enormous wastage— although the wastage is clearly affected also by the inadequate storage facilities and lack of year-round roads, which causes "approximately 20 percent of the grain, fruit and vegetable harvest, and as much as 50 percent of the potato crop [to perish] because of poor storage, transportation and distribution."[127] What could be done if the system were altered in its fundamentals—that is, a massive change away from collectivization towards individual peasant-run farming—is indicated by the fact that the existing private plots produce around 25 percent of Russia's total crop output, yet occupy a mere 4 percent of the country's arable land.[128]

Yet whatever the noises about "reform" from the highest levels, the indications are that the Soviet Union is not contemplating following Mr. Deng's large-scale agricultural changes to anything like the extent of China's "liberalization" (see above), even when it is clear that Russian output is falling far behind that of its adventurous neighbor.[129]

Although the Kremlin is unlikely to explain openly why it prefers the present system of collectivized agriculture despite its manifest inefficiencies, two reasons for this inflexibility stand out. The first is that a massive extension of private plots, the creation of many more private markets, and increases in the prices paid for agricultural produce would imply significant rises in the peasantry's share of national income—to the detriment of the resentful urban population and, per-

Chart 3. Grain Production in the Soviet Union and China, 1950–1984

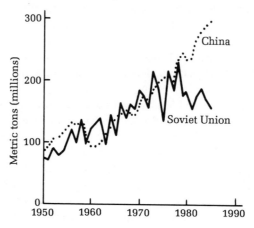

Source: Brown *et. al.*/U.S. Department of Agriculture

haps, of industrial investment. It would mean, in other words, the final triumph of Bukharin's policies (which favored agricultural incentives) and the demise of Stalin's prejudices.[130] Secondly, it would mean a decline in the powers of the bureaucrats and managers who run Soviet agriculture, and thus have implications for all of the other spheres of decision-making. While it is surely true that "individual farmers making day-to-day decisions in response to market signals, changing weather, and the conditions of their crops have a combined intelligence far exceeding that of a centralized bureaucracy, however well designed and competently staffed,"[131] what might that imply for the future of the "centralized bureaucracy"? If it *is* correct that there is a consistent, embarrassing relationship between "socialism and national food deficits,"[132] then that can hardly have escaped the Politburo's attention. But from its own perspective, it may seem better—safer, certainly—to maintain "socialist" (i.e., collectivized) farming even if that implies rising food imports, rather than to admit the failure of the Communist system and to remove the existing controls upon so large a segment of society.

By the same token, it is also difficult for the USSR to amend its industrial sector. To some observers, that may hardly seem necessary, given the remarkable achievements of the Soviet economy since 1945 and the fact that it outproduces the United States in, for example, machine tools, steel, cement, fertilizers, oil, and so on.[133] Yet there are many signs that Soviet industry, too, is stagnating and that the period of relatively easy expansion—caused by fixing ambitious output targets, and then devoting masses of finance and manpower to meeting those figures—is coming to a close. Part of this is due to increasing labor and energy shortages, which are discussed separately below. Equally important, however, are the repeated signs that manufacturing suffers from an excess of bureaucratic planning, from being too concentrated upon heavy industry, and from being unable to respond either to consumer choice or to the need to alter products to meet new demands or markets. Producing masses of cement is not necessarily a good thing, if the excessive investment in it has taken resources from a more needy sector; if the actual cement-production process has been very wasteful of energy; if the final product has to be transported long distances across the country, thus placing further strains upon the overworked railway system; and if the cement itself has to be distributed among the thousands of building projects which Soviet planners authorized but have never been able to complete.[134] The same remarks might be made about the enormous Soviet steel industry, much of the output of which seems to be wasted—causing some scholars to marvel at the "paradox of industrial plenty in the midst of consumer poverty."[135] There are, to be sure, efficient sectors in Soviet industry (usually related to defense, which can command large resources and *must* compete with the West), but the overall system suffers from concentrating upon production without much concern for market prices and consumer demand. Since Soviet factories cannot go out of business, as in the West, they also lack the ultimate stimulus to produce efficiently. However many tinkerings there are to assist industrial growth at a faster rate, it is difficult to believe that they will produce a sustained breakthrough if the existing system of a "planned economy" remains.

Yet if today's levels of Soviet industrial efficiency are scarcely tolerable (or, judging from the harsher tone of the government, increasingly intolerable), the system is likely to be even more damaged by three further pressures bearing down upon it. The first of these concerns energy supplies. It has become increasingly obvious that the great expansion in Soviet industrial output since the 1940s heavily depended upon plentiful supplies of coal, oil and natural gas, almost without regard to cost. In consequence, the "energy waste" and "steel waste" in both the USSR and its chief satellites is extraordinary, compared with western Europe, as shown in Table 46.

In Russia's case, this misuse of "inputs" may have seemed tolerable

**Table 46. Kilos of Coal Equivalent and Steel Used to Produce
$1,000 of GDP in 1979–1980[136]**

	Coal	Steel		Coal	Steel
Russia	1,490	135	Britain	820	38
East Germany	1,356	88	West Germany	565	52
Czechoslovakia	1,290	132	France	502	42
Hungary	1,058	88	Switzerland	371	26

when its energy supplies were so plentiful and (relatively) easily accessible; but the awful fact is that this is no longer the case. It may have
been that the CIA's famous 1977 forecast that Soviet oil production
would soon peak, and then rapidly decline, *was* premature; nonetheless, Russian oil output did drop a little in 1984 and 1985, for the first
time since the Second World War.[137] More alarming still is the fact that
the remaining (and very considerable) stocks of oil—and of natural
gas—are to be found at much deeper levels or in regions, like western
Siberia, badly affected by permafrost. Over the past decade, as Gorbachev reported in 1985, the cost of extracting an additional ton of Soviet
oil had risen by 70 percent and this problem was, if anything, intensifying.[138] Hence, to a large degree, the very extensive commitment by
Russia to building up its nuclear-power output as swiftly as possible,
thus doubling its share of electricity production (from 10 percent to 20
percent) by 1990. It is too soon to know how far the disaster at the
Chernobyl plant will hurt those plans—the four reactors at Chernobyl
produced one-seventh of the total Russian nuclear-generated electricity, so that their shutdown implied an increased use of other fuel
stocks—but what is obvious is that it will both increase costs (because
of additional safety measures) and reduce the pace of the planned
development of the industry.[139] Finally, there is the awkward fact that
the energy sector already absorbs so much capital—about 30 percent
of all industrial investment—and that amount is bound to rise sharply.
It seems difficult to believe the recent report that "a simple continuation of recent investment trends in oil, coal and electric power, combined with the targeted investment increase for natural gas, will
absorb virtually the *entire* available increase in capital resources for
Soviet industry over the period 1981–5,"[140] simply because the implications elsewhere are too severe. Nevertheless, the overall pattern is
clear: merely to keep the economy growing at a modest pace, the
energy sector will require an increased share of the GNP.[141]

Equally problematic, from the viewpoint of the Russian leadership,
is the challenge posed in the high-technology areas of robotics, supercomputers, lasers, optics, telecommunications, and so on, where the
USSR is in danger of increasingly falling behind the West. In the
narrower, strictly military sense, there is the threat that "smart" battlefield weapons and advanced detection systems could neutralize
Russia's *quantitative* advantages in military hardware: thus, supercomputers might be able to decrypt Russian codes, to locate submarines under the ocean's surface, to handle a fast-moving battle scene,
and—last but not least—to protect American nuclear bases (as implied
in President Reagan's "Star Wars" program); while sophisticated
radar, laser, and guidance-control technology might allow western
aircraft and artillery/rocket forces to locate and destroy enemy planes
and tanks with impunity—as Israel regularly does to Syrian (Soviet-

equipped) weapon-systems. Merely to keep up with these advanced technologies requires ever-larger allocations of scientific and engineering resources to Russia's defense-related sector.[142]

In the civilian field, the problem is even greater. Given the limitations which are being reached in such classic "inputs" as labor and capital investment, high technology is rightly perceived as being vital for increasing Russian output. To give but one example, the large-scale use of computers could greatly reduce wastage in the discovery, production, and distribution of energy supplies. But the adoption of this new technology not only implies heavy investments (taken from where?), it also challenges the intensely secretive, bureaucratic, and centralized Soviet system. Computers, word processors, telecommunications, being knowledge-intensive industries, can best be exploited by a society which possesses a technology-trained population that is encouraged to experiment freely and to exchange new ideas and hypotheses in the widest possible way. This works well in California and Japan, but threatens to loosen the Russian state's monopoly of information. If, even today, senior scientists and scholars in the Soviet Union are forbidden to use copying machines personally (the copying departments are staffed by the KGB), then it is hard to see how the country could move toward the widespread use of word processors, interactive computers, electronic mail, etc. without a substantial loosening of police controls and censorship.[143] As in agriculture, therefore, the regime's commitment to "modernization" and its willingness to allocate additional resources of money and manpower are vitiated by an economic substructure and a political ideology which are basic obstacles to change.

By comparison, then, the increasing reliance of the Soviet Union upon imported technologies and machinery—whether legally traded goods, or stolen from the West—is a less fundamental if still serious problem. The extent of the industrial and scientific espionage (whether for military or commercial purposes) can obviously not be quantified, but seems to be yet another indication of Russia's worry that it is falling behind.[144] The more regular trade—importing western technology (and also eastern-European manufactures) in exchange for Russian raw materials—is a traditional way in which the country seeks to "close the gap"; it was done in the 1890–1914 period, and again in the 1920s. In that sense, all that has changed is the more modern nature of the product: oil-drilling machinery, rolled steel, pipe, computers, machine tools, equipment for the chemical/plastics industry, etc. What must be much more worrying to Soviet planners is the accumulating evidence that the imported technology takes longer to set up, and is used much less efficiently than in the West.[145] The second problem is the availability of hard currency for the purchase of such technology. Traditionally, this could be circumvented by importing

manufactured goods from fellow Comecon countries (thus involving
no loss of hard currency), but the latter's products have increasingly
failed to keep up with those from the West, even if they still have to
be accepted to prevent a collapse of their eastern-European economies.[146] And while Russia has normally paid for a large proportion of
western imports through the barter or direct sale of surplus oil, its
prospects (and those of eastern Europe) may be shrinking because of
the uncertainties in oil prices, its own growing energy needs, and the
general change in the terms of trade for raw materials as manufacturing processes become more sophisticated.[147] At the same time as Russian earnings from oil and other raw materials (except, presumably,
gas) shrink, the payments for a variety of imports remain high—all of
which presumably reduces the sums available for investment.

The third major cause for concern about Russia's future economic
growth lies in demographics. The position here is so gloomy that one
scholar began his recent survey "Population and Labor Force" with the
following blunt statement:

> On any basis, short-term or long-term, the prospects for the develop-
> ment of Soviet population and manpower resources until the end of
> the century are quite dismal. From the reduction in the country's
> birthrate to the incredible increase in the death rates beyond all
> reasonable past projections; from the decrease in the supply of new
> entrants to the labor force, compounded by its unequal regional
> distribution, to the relative ageing of the population, not much hope
> lies before the Soviet government in these trends.[148]

While all of these elements are serious—and interacting—the most
shocking trend has been the steady deterioration in both life expect-
ancy and infant mortality rates since the 1970s and perhaps earlier.
Because of a slow erosion in hospital and general health care, poor
standards of sanitation and public hygiene, and the fantastic levels of
alcoholism, death rates in the Soviet Union have increased, especially
among the working males: "Today, the average Soviet man can expect
to live for only about 60 years, six years less than in the mid-1960s."[149]
Equally shocking has been the rise in infant mortality—the only industrialized country where this has occurred—to a point where infant
deaths are, comparatively, over three times the U.S. rate, despite the
enormous numbers of Soviet doctors. Yet if the Russian population is
dying off faster than before, its birthrates are slowing down sharply.
Because (presumably) of urbanization, higher female participation in
the work force, poor housing conditions, and other disincentives, the
crude overall birthrate has been steadily dropping, more particularly
among the *Russian* population of the country. The consequences of all

these trends is that the male Russian population of the country is scarcely increasing at all.

The implications of all this have been disturbing Russia's leaders for some time, and are obviously behind the exhortations to increase family size, the stricter campaign against alcoholism, and the efforts to persuade older workers to remain in the factories. The first is that the country clearly requires a larger proportion of resources to be devoted to health care and social security, especially as the percentage of older population increases: in this the USSR is no different from other industrialized countries (except in its increased death rates), but this again raises the issue of spending priorities. Secondly, there are the implications for both Soviet industry and the armed services, given the drastic fall-off in the rate of growth of the labor force: according to projections, between 1980 and 1990 the labor force will enjoy a net increase of "only 5,990,000 persons, whereas during the preceding ten years the estimated increase in the labor force was 24,217,000."[150] To leave the military's problems until later, this trend reminds us again that a large part of the growth in Russian industrial output in the 1950s to the 1970s was due to an enhanced labor force, rather than increases in efficiency; from now on economic expansion can no longer rely upon a fast-increasing work force in manufacturing. To a considerable extent, of course, this difficulty could be overcome if more able-bodied males were released from agriculture; but the problem there is that an excessive number of youths in the Slavic areas have already left the communes for the city, whereas the surplus which does exist in the non-Slavic republics is more poorly educated, often has little knowledge of the Russian language, and would require an immense investment in training for industry. This brings us to the final trend which makes Moscow planners uneasy: that since the fertility rates in central Asian republics like Uzbekistan are three times larger than among the Slavic and Baltic peoples, a major shift in the long-term population balances is under way. In consequence, the Russian population's share is expected to decline from 52 percent in 1980 to only 48 percent by 2000.[151] For the first time in the history of the USSR, Russians will not be in the majority.

This catalog of difficulties may seem too gloomy to certain commentators. Military-related production in the USSR is often impressive and is constantly driven to improve itself because of the dynamic of the arms-race itself.[152] As one historian (admittedly writing in 1981)[153] points out, the picture cannot be seen as altogether negative, especially if one looks at Soviet economic achievements over the past half-century; and it has been a habit among western observers to exaggerate Russia's strengths in one period and its weaknesses in the next. Nevertheless, however much the USSR has improved itself since Lenin's time, the awkward facts are that it has not caught up with the West and, indeed, that the gap in real standards of living seems to have been widening since the later years of the Brezhnev regime; that it is being overtaken, by all measures of per capita output and industrial efficiency, by Japan and certain other Asian countries; and that its slowdown in rate of growth, its aging population, and its difficulties with climate, energy stocks, and agriculture cast a dark shadow over the claims and exhortations of the Soviet leadership.

It is in this context, then, that Gorbachev's belief that "acceleration of the country's socioeconomic development is the key to all our problems" becomes the more understandable. And yet, quite apart from natural difficulties (permafrost, etc.), two main *political* obstacles stand in the way of producing a "leap forward" on the Chinese model. The first is the entrenched position of the party officials, bureaucrats, and other members of the elite, who enjoy a large array of privileges (depending upon rank) which cushion them from the hardships of everyday life in the Soviet Union, and who monopolize power and influence. To decentralize the planning and pricing system, to free the peasants from communal controls, to allow managers of factories a greater freedom of action, to offer incentives for individual enterprise rather than party loyalty, to close outdated plants, to refuse to accept shoddy products, and to allow a far freer circulation of information would be seen by those in power as dire threats to their own position. Exhortations, more flexible planning, enhanced investments in this or that sector, and disciplinary drives against alcoholism or corrupt management are one thing; but all proposed changes, Soviet party officials have stressed, have to take place "within the framework of scientific socialism" and without "any shifts toward a market economy or private enterprise."[154] In the opinion of one recent visitor, "the Soviet Union needs its inefficiencies to remain Soviet";[155] if that is so, all Mr. Gorbachev's urgings about the need for a "profound transformation" of the system are unlikely to make much impact upon the long-term growth rates.

The second political obstacle lies in the very significant share of GNP devoted by the USSR to defense. How best to calculate the totals and how that measures with western defense spending has exercised many analysts; the CIA's 1975 announcement that the ruble prices of Soviet weaponry were twice as high as previously estimated—and that Russia was probably spending 11–13 percent of GNP upon defense rather than 6–8 percent—led to all sorts of misinterpretations of what that meant.[156] But the exact figures (which may not even be available to Soviet planners) are less significant than the fact that although the growth in armaments spending slowed down after 1976, the Kremlin appears to have allocated around twice as much of the country's product to this area as has the USA, even under Reagan's arms buildup; and this in turn means that the Soviet armed forces have siphoned off vast

stocks of trained manpower, scientists, machinery, and capital investment which could have been devoted to the civilian economy. This
does *not* mean, according to certain economic forecasts, that a large
reduction in defense expenditures would quickly lead to a great surge
in Russia's growth rates, simply because of the fact that it would take
a long time before, say, a T-72 tank-assembly factory could be retooled
to do something else.[157] On the other hand, if the arms race with NATO
over the rest of this century drove up the share of Russian defense
spending from 14 to 17 percent or more of GNP by the year 2000, a
larger and larger amount of equipment such as machine-building and
metalworking tools would be consumed by the military, crowding out
the share of investment capital going to the rest of industry. Yet, while
economists believe that "this will represent a tremendous problem for
Soviet decision-makers,"[158] all the indications are that defense expenditures *will* rise faster than GNP growth—and have the consequent
effect upon prosperity and consumption.

Like every other one of the large Powers, therefore, the USSR has
to make a choice in its allocations of national resources between (1)
the requirements of the military—in this case, with their built-in ability
to articulate Russia's security needs; and (2) the increasing desire of
the Russian populace for consumer goods and better living and working conditions, not to mention improved social services to check the
high death and sickness rates; and (3) the needs of both agriculture and
industry for fresh capital investment, in order to modernize the economy, increase output, keep abreast of the advances of others, and in
the longer term satisfy both the defense and the social requirements
of the country.[159] As elsewhere, this involves difficult choices by the
decision-makers concerned; yet one has the sense that however large
and pressing are the needs both of the Russian consumer and of "modernizing" the economy, the traditional obsession by Moscow with military security means that the fundamental choice has already been
made. Unless the Gorbachev regime really manages to transform
things, guns will always come before butter and, if need be, before
economic growth as well. This, as much as any other characteristic,
makes Russia basically different from Japan and western Europe, and
even from China and the United States.

Historically, then, the Kremlin today follows the tradition of the
Romanov czars, and of Stalin himself, in its desire to have armed
forces equal to (and, if preferable, larger than) those of any other
Power. There is no doubt that at the present time, the military strength
of the USSR is extremely imposing. To try to offer a realistic figure for
annual totals of current Soviet defense expenditures would probably
be a deception: on the one hand, Moscow's *official* figures are absurdly
low, concealing large amounts of defense-related spending under
other headings ("science," the space programs, internal security, civil

defense, and construction); on the other hand, western estimates of the real total are complicated by the artificial dollar-ruble exchange rate, limited understanding of Soviet budgetary procedures, the difficulties in, say, the CIA's effort to put a "dollar cost" on a Russian-made weapon or manpower costs, and institutional/ideological biases. The result is an array of "guestimates," which one can choose according to one's fancy.[160] What is not in question, however, is the massive modernization which has occurred in all branches of the Soviet armed forces, both nuclear and conventional, on land and sea and in the air. Whether one considers the rapid growth of Russian land- and sea-based strategic missile systems, the thousands of aircraft and tens of thousands of main battle tanks, the extraordinary developments in the surface navy and in the submarine fleet, the specialist activities (airborne and amphibious warfare units, chemical warfare, intelligence and "disinformation" activities), the end result is impressive. It may or may not have cost as much in real terms as the Pentagon's own allocations; but it undoubtedly gives the USSR a range of military capabilities which only the rival American superpower possesses. This is *not* a twentieth-century military Potemkin village, ready to collapse at the first serious testing.[161]

On the other hand, the Soviet war machine also has its own weaknesses and problems, and certainly ought not to be presented as an omnipotent force, able to execute with consummate efficiency all of the possible military operations which the Kremlin might require of it. Since the dilemmas which face the strategy-makers of the *other* large Powers of the globe are also being pointed out in this chapter, it is only proper to draw attention to the great variety of difficulties confronting Russia's military-political leadership—without, however, jumping to the opposite conclusion that the Soviet Union is therefore unlikely to "survive" for very long.[162]

Some of the difficulties facing Russian military decision-makers over the middle to longer term derive directly from the economic and demographic problems of the Soviet state which have been outlined above. The first is in technology. Since Peter the Great's time—to repeat a point made in the previous chapters of this book—Russia has always enjoyed its greatest military advantage vis-à-vis the West when the pace of weapons technology has slowed down enough to allow a standardization of equipment and thus of fighting units and tactics—whether that be the eighteenth-century infantry column or the mid-twentieth-century armored division. Whenever an upward spiral in weapons technology has placed an emphasis upon quality rather than quantity, however, the Russian advantage has diminished. And while it is clearly true that Russia has substantially closed the technological gap with the West which existed in czarist times, and that its military enjoys unrivaled access to the scientific and productive resources of a state-run economy, there nonetheless is evidence of significant lag times[163] in a large number of technological processes. One of the two clearest signs of this is the unease with which the Soviet Union has watched its weaponry being repeatedly outclassed by American hardware in the surrogate battles which have taken place in the Middle East and elsewhere over the past few decades. Admittedly, the quality of North Korean, Egyptian, Syrian, and Libyan pilots and tank crews was never of the highest, but even if it had been, there are grounds to doubt if they could have prevailed against American weapons with far superior avionics, radar equipment, miniaturized guidance systems, and so on. It has probably been in response to this that western experts on the Soviet military report a constant effort to upgrade quality[164] and to produce—a few years later—"mirror images" of U.S. weapon systems. But this in turn draws Soviet planners into the same vortex which threatens western defense programs: more sophisticated equipment leads to much longer building times, larger maintenance schedules, heavier (usually) and vastly more expensive (always) hardware, and a decline in production numbers. This is not a comforting trend for a Power which has traditionally relied upon large numbers of weapons to carry out its various and disparate strategical tasks.

The second sign of Soviet unease about technological obsolescence relates to the so-called Strategic Defense Initiative (SDI) of the Reagan administration. It seems difficult at this stage to believe that it would really make the United States completely invulnerable to nuclear attack (for example, it can do nothing against low-flying "cruise" missiles), but the protection it may give to American missile sites and airbases and the added strain upon the Soviet defense budget of producing many more rockets and warheads to swamp the SDI system with sheer numbers can hardly be welcome to the Kremlin. More worrying still, perhaps, are the implications for high-tech *conventional* warfare. One commentator has pointed out:

> A defense that can protect against 99 percent of the Soviet nuclear arsenal may be judged as not good enough, given the destructive potential of the weapons that could survive. . . . [But if] the United States could achieve a technological superiority that would assure destruction of much of the Soviet Union's conventionally armed aircraft, tanks, and ships, the Soviet numerical advantage would be less threatening. Technology judged less than ideal for SDI may be perfectly applicable for nonnuclear combat.[165]

This, in turn, compels a much larger Russian investment into the advanced technologies of lasers, optics, supercomputers, guidance systems, and navigation: in other words, as one Russian spokesman has put it, there will be "a whole new arms race at a much higher technological level."[166] Judging from the 1984 warnings of Marshal Ogarkov, then chief of military staff, about the awful consequences of Russia's failing to match western technology, the Red Army seems less than confident that it could win that sort of race.

At the other end of the spectrum, there lies a potential demographic threat to Russia's traditional advantage in *quantity,* that is, in manpower. As noted above, this is the result of two trends: the overall decline in total USSR birthrate, and the rising share of births in the non-Russian regions. If this is leading to difficulties in the allocation of manpower between agriculture and industry, then it is even more of a long-term problem for military recruitment. In round terms, there ought not to be a problem in taking 1.3 to 1.5 million recruits each year from the 2.1 million males available; but an increasing proportion comes from the Asiatic youth of Turkestan, many of whom are not well versed in the Russian language, have a far lower level of mechanical (let alone electronic) competence, and are sometimes strongly influenced by Islam. All of the studies of the ethnic composition of the Soviet armed forces reveal that the officer corps and NCOs are overwhelmingly Slavic—as are the rocket forces, the air force, the navy, and the technical forces.[167] So, too, unsurprisingly, are the Category I (first-class) divisions of the Red Army. By contrast, the Category II and (especially) Category III divisions and most of service and transport units are manned by non-Slavs, which raises an interesting question about the effectiveness of these "follow-on" divisions in a conventional war against NATO, if the Category I divisions required substantial reinforcement. Labeling this bias "racialistic" and (Great Russian) "nationalistic," as many western commentators do, is less significant in strictly military terms than the fact that a considerable portion of available Soviet manpower is regarded as unreliable and inefficient by the general staff—which is probably a true judgment, given the reports of Muslim fundamentalism throughout southern Russia and the bewilderment of those troops at, say, having to invade Afghanistan.

In other words, like the Austro-Hungarian Empire eighty years ago or, for that matter, the *Czarist* Empire eighty years ago—the Russian leadership faces a "nationality problem"[168] undimmed by the ideology of Marxism. To be sure, the control apparatus now is altogether more formidable than that existing prior to 1914, and one ought perhaps to take with a pinch of salt claims that, for example, the Ukraine is a "hotbed" of disaffection.[169] Nevertheless, long memories about how Ukrainians welcomed the German invaders in 1941, reports of discontent in the Baltic provinces, the forcible (and successful) Georgian protests at the 1978 attempt to make Russian the equal-first language in that republic; above all, perhaps, the straddling across the Sino-Soviet border of millions of Kazakhs and Uighers, and the existence of 48 million Muslims north of the unstable borders with Turkey, Iran, and Afghanistan: these facts seem to prey upon the minds of the Russian leadership and to add to their insecurities. More specifically, they provoke an increasing concern about where to place the shrinking numbers of the more "reliable" Slavic youth. Should they be directed into the armed forces, to the Category I divisions and other prestige services, even if fewer and fewer of them are available for industry and agriculture, both of which desperately need infusions of trained and loyal recruits? Or should the non-Slavic population form a growing proportion of the Red Army, despite the risks to military efficiency, in order to release Russians and fellow Slavs for civilian purposes?[170] Since the Soviet tradition is one of "safety first," probably the former tendency will prevail; but far from solving the dilemma, that merely reflects a choice between evils.

If the economic components of what Soviet strategists term "the correlation of forces"[171] is a cause for concern among the Politburo, those same leaders can hardly draw much encouragement from the more strictly *military* aspects of the fast-changing global balance of power. However imposing and alarming the Soviet military machine appears to outside observers, it is nonetheless worth measuring those forces against the array of strategical tasks which the Soviet military may be called upon to carry out.

In undertaking such an exercise, it is useful to separate a consideration of conventional warfare from that which may involve nuclear weapons. For obvious reasons, *the* item in the military balances which has attracted most attention and the most concern is the armory of strategic nuclear weapons in the hands of the Great Powers, and especially of the United States and the USSR, both of which possess the capacity to devastate the globe. For the record, it may be worth reproducing the 1986 "count" of their strategic nuclear warheads by the International Institute of Strategic Studies (see Table 47).

Table 47. Estimated Strategic Nuclear Warheads[172]

	U.S.	USSR
ICBM-borne warheads	2,118	6,420
SLBM-borne warheads	5,536	2,787+
Aircraft-borne warheads	2,520	680
Totals	10,174	9,987+

Precisely how one reacts to such figures depends upon one's interests. To those concerned with numbers alone, or with the possible misrepresentation of numbers, there will be a keen checking of the subtotals and a reminder of the fact that additional large stocks of *tactical* nuclear weapons are also held by each superpower.[173] To a very considerable number of nonofficial commentators, and to many of the public at large, the sheer extent and destructive capacity of the nuclear weaponry held in these two arsenals is an indication of political incapacity or mental sickness, which threatens all daily life on this planet and should be abolished or greatly reduced as soon as possible.[174] On the other hand, there is that whole cluster of commentators—in think tanks and universities, as well as in defense departments—who have accepted the possibility that nuclear weapons might indeed be *used*, as part of a national strategy; and who therefore devote their intellectual energies to an intensive study of the respective weapon systems, of escalation strategies and war-gaming, of the pros and cons of arms control and verification agreements, of "throw-weights," "footprints," and "equivalent megatonnages," targeting policies, and "second-strike" scenarios.[175]

How to deal with "the nuclear problem"[176] within a five-century survey such as this obviously presents a major difficulty. Is it not the case that the existence of nuclear weapons—or, rather, the possibility of their mass deployment—has made redundant any consideration of war, of strategy, of economics, from a traditional viewpoint? In the event of an all-out exchange of strategic nuclear weapons, would not estimates of their impact on the "shifting power balances" in world affairs be irrelevant to everyone in the northern hemisphere (and perhaps to everyone in the southern hemisphere as well)? Did not the traditional pattern—of Great Power rivalries turning from time to time into open warfare—finally come to an end in 1945?

There is, obviously, no way of answering such questions with certainty. Yet there are indications that today's Great Powers may be returning to more traditional assumptions about the use of force despite—in many ways, *because of*—the existence of nuclear weapons. In the first place, there appears to be now—and probably has been for some years—an essential balance in nuclear armaments between the two superpowers. For all the debate about "windows of opportunity" and the possibilities of one side or the other having a "first-strike capability," it is clear that neither Washington nor Moscow possesses any guarantee that it could obliterate its rival without the likelihood of also suffering devastation; and the coming of a "Star Wars" technology will not significantly alter that fact. In particular, the possession by each side of a great number of *submarine*-launched ballistic missiles, located in underwater craft which are difficult to detect,[177] makes it inconceivable for either side to assume that it could knock out its enemy's nuclear-weapons capacity all at once. This fact, more than—or at least as much as—fears of a "nuclear winter" will stay the hand of decision-makers, unless they are dragged down by some accidentally induced escalation. It therefore follows that each side is locked into a nuclear stalemate from which it cannot retreat—it being practically impossible either to disinvent nuclear technology or for one (or both) superpowers to give up possession of the weapons—and from which it cannot gain real advantage—since each power's new system is countered or imitated by the other, and since it is too risky actually to use the weapons themselves.

In other words, the vast nuclear armories of each superpower will continue to exist, but (barring an accidental "triggering") they are in all likelihood unusable, because they contradict the ancient assumption that in war, as in most other things, there ought to be a balance between means and ends. In a nuclear war, by contrast, the risk is run of inflicting and incurring such damage to mankind that no political, ideological, or economic purpose would be served by it. Although masses of brainpower are devoted to evolving a "nuclear-war-fighting strategy," it is difficult to contest Jervis's observation that "a rational strategy for the employment of nuclear weapons is a contradiction in terms."[178] Once the first missile is unleashed, there would be an end to the "mutual hostage" position into which each side has been locked ever since the United States lost its nuclear monopoly. The results then might be so cataclysmic that no rational political leadership is likely to take the first step across the threshold. Unless there is an inadvertent nuclear war—which is, because of human error or technical malfunction, always possible[179]—each side is likely to be deterred from "going nuclear." If a clash does occur, both the political and the military leaderships will endeavor to "contain" it at the level of conventional fighting.

This does not address what may be a far more serious problem for the two rival superpowers over the next twenty years and beyond: that of nuclear proliferation into countries in the more volatile parts of the world—the Near East, the Indian subcontinent, South Africa, possibly Latin America.[180] Since the states concerned are not part of the Great Power system, the awful possibility of their resorting to nuclear weapons in some regional clash is not considered here: on the whole it seems fair to conclude that the United States and the USSR have a shared interest in halting nuclear proliferation, since it makes global politics more complicated than ever before. If anything, the trend toward proliferation may cause the superpowers to appreciate what they have in common.

In a quite different league—from Moscow's viewpoint, certainly— are the fast-expanding nuclear armories of China, Britain, and France. Until a few years ago, it was commonly assumed that all three of those nations were merely marginal factors in the nuclear balance, and that their nuclear strategy was not at all "credible," since they could only inflict (in all three cases) limited damage upon the USSR in exchange for their own atomic obliteration. But the indications are that that assumption may soon require modification. The most alarming tendency—again, from Moscow's viewpoint—is the increasing nuclear capacity of the People's Republic of China, about which it has been concerned for the past twenty-five years.[181] If the PRC can develop not only a more sophisticated land-based ICBM system but also—as seems its intention—a long-range, submarine-based ballistic-missile system, and if Sino-Soviet disputes are not settled to mutual satisfaction, then the USSR faces the possibility of a future armed clash along the borders which might escalate into a nuclear interchange with its Chinese neighbor. As things are at present, the devastation of the PRC would be immense; but Moscow cannot exclude the possibility that at least a certain number (and, the 1990s, a larger number) of Chinese nuclear missiles would hit the Soviet Union.

More worrying technically, although perhaps less alarming politically, is the buildup of the British and French nuclear delivery and warhead capacities. Until recently, the "deterrent" effect of both of these Powers' strategic weapon systems appeared dubious. In the rather implausible event of their being involved in a nuclear interchange with the USSR, and with the United States neutral (which is, after all, the justification for the British and French systems), it was difficult to see them risking national suicide when they could only inflict partial damage upon Russia from their own modest delivery systems. In the next few years, however, the devastation which each of those midsized Powers could do to the USSR will be multiplied many times, because of the vast enhancement of their submarine-launched ballistic-missile systems. For example, Britain's acquisition of submarines carrying the Trident II missile system—derided by *The Economist* as "the Rolls Royce of nuclear missiles"[182] because of its high cost and excessive striking power—will give that country a nearly invulnerable deterrent force which could destroy more than 350 Soviet targets, instead of the present sixteen-plus targets. In rather the same way, France's new submarine *L'Inflexible,* with the longer-range, multiwarhead M-4 missile, is probably capable of attacking ninety-six Soviet targets—"more than all of France's five earlier nuclear submarines combined"[183]—and when the other boats have been reequipped with the same M-4 missile, France's strategic warheads will have increased *fivefold,* allowing it also to be theoretically capable of hitting hundreds of Russian targets from thousands of miles away.

What this means in real terms it is, of course, impossible to forecast. In Britain itself many prominent figures have found the idea that their country would *independently* use its nuclear weapons against Russia to be, literally, "incredible";[184] and such critics are unlikely to be swayed by the counterargument that the country's own suicide would at least be attended by inflicting much heavier damage upon the USSR than was possible hitherto. In France, too, public opinion—and some strategic commentators—find its declared deterrent policy to be scarcely credible.[185] On the other hand, it seems fair to assume that

Russian military planners, who take nuclear-war-fighting possibilities very seriously indeed, must find these recent developments disturbing. Not only will they face *four* countries—instead of the United States alone—with the potential to inflict heavy (perhaps extraordinarily heavy) damage upon the Soviet heartland, but they must consider what the *subsequent* world military balances would look like if Russia was involved in a nuclear interchange with one of these Powers (say, China) while the others were neutral observers of such mutually inflicted devastation. Hence the Soviets' repeated insistence that in any overall Strategic Arms Limitation Treaty with the United States the Anglo-French systems have to be taken into account, *and* that the USSR must have a certain margin of nuclear force to take care of China. All this, it seems reasonable to suggest, makes nuclear weapons an ever more dubious instrument of *rational* military policy from the Kremlin's viewpoint.

If, however, this leaves conventional weapons as the chief measure of Soviet military power—and the chief tool for securing the political aims of the Soviet state—it is difficult to believe that Russian planners can feel much more assured at the present state of the international military balance. This may seem a bold statement to make in view of the very extensive publicity which has been given to the far larger totals of Soviet aircraft, tanks, artillery, and infantry divisions in assessments of the U.S.-USSR "military balance"—not to mention the frequent assertion that NATO forces, unable to hold their own in a large-scale conventional war in Europe, would be compelled to "go nuclear" within a matter of days. Yet an increasing number of the most recent academic studies of the "balance" are now suggesting that that is precisely what exists—namely, a situation in which "there still appears to be insufficient overall strength on *either* side to guarantee victory."[186] To reach this conclusion involves both very detailed comparative analyses (e.g., of the composition of the U.S. as opposed to Russian tank divisions) and considerations of certain larger and intangible factors (e.g., the role of China, the reliability of the Warsaw Pact), and only a summary of these arguments can be provided here. If, however, this evidence is even roughly correct, it also cannot be very comforting to Soviet planners.

The first and most obvious point to be made is that any analysis of the *conventional* balance of forces needs to measure the rival alliances as a whole, especially in their European context. As soon as that is done, it becomes evident that the non-American parts of NATO are much more significant than the non-Russian parts of the Warsaw Pact. Indeed, as the 1985 British Defence White Paper made pains to point out, "European countries were providing the major part of the ready [NATO] forces stationed in Europe: 90 percent of the manpower, 85 percent of the tanks, 95 percent of the artillery and 80 percent of the combat aircraft; and over 70 percent of the major warships in Atlantic and European waters. . . . The full mobilized strength of European forces was nearly 7 million men as against 3.5 million for the United States."[187] It is, of course, also true that the United States has deployed 250,000 men *in situ* in Germany, that the army divisions and air squadrons which it plans to pour across the Atlantic in the event of a European war would be critical reinforcements, and that NATO as a whole depends upon the American nuclear deterrent and upon American sea power. But the point is that the North Atlantic Alliance is much more evenly balanced between, as it were, the twin pillars of the "arch," than is the Warsaw Pact, which is top-heavy and skewed toward Moscow. It is also worth noting that America's NATO allies spend six times more on defense than Russia's Warsaw Pact allies; indeed, Britain, France, and West Germany *each* spend more than the non-Russian Warsaw Pact countries together.[188]

If, then, the strength of the two alliances is measured as a whole, and without the curious omissions and provisos which have characterized some of the more alarmist western assessments,* a picture emerges of strategical parity in most respects; and even where the Warsaw Pact has the edge in numbers, that does not look decisive. For example, each alliance appears to have roughly similar "total ground forces in Europe"; they also have similar "total ground forces" and "total ground force reserves."[189] In the *roundest* sense of all, the Warsaw Pact's 13.9 million men (6.4 million "main forces" and 7.5 million reserves) is not vastly greater than NATO's 11.9 million men (5 million "main forces" and 6.8 million reserves), the more especially since a large proportion of the Warsaw Pact total consists of Category III units and reserve forces of the Red Army. Even on the critically important Central Front, where NATO forces are most seriously outnumbered by the masses of Russian armored and motor-rifle divisions, the Warsaw Pact's advantage is not a very comforting one—especially when it is recalled how difficult it would be to conduct fast, offensive, "maneuver warfare" in the crowded terrain of northern Germany and when it is realized how many of Russia's 52,000 "main battle tanks" are the obsolescent T-54s—which would simply clog up the roads. Provided NATO has sufficient reserves of ammunition, fuel, replacement weaponry, etc., it certainly seems to be in a much better position to blunt a Soviet conventional offensive than it was in the 1950s.[190]

In addition, there is the incalculable element of the integrity and cohesion of the respective military alliances. That NATO has many weaknesses is undeniable: from the frequent transatlantic disputes

---

*It is, for example, all too easy to show the Warsaw Pact as massively superior by including, say, all of Russia's armed forces (even those deployed against China), and by excluding, say, France's.

over "burden sharing" to the tricky issue of intergovernmental consultation in the event of pressure to launch nuclear missiles. Neutralist and anti-NATO sentiment, detectable in left-of-center parties from West Germany and Britain to Spain and Greece, is also a cause of periodic concern.[191] And if there were to be, at some future time, a "Finlandization" of any of the states lying along the Warsaw Pact's western boundary (especially, of course, West Germany itself), then that would be a massive strategical gain to the USSR as well as providing economic relief. Yet even if such a scenario is possible *in theory*, that can hardly compare with the worries which Moscow must presently entertain about the reliability of its "empire" in eastern Europe. The broad-based popularity of the Solidarity movement in Poland, the evident East German wishes to improve relations with Bonn, the "creeping capitalism" of the Hungarians, the economic woes which are affecting not merely Poland and Rumania but all of eastern Europe, pose extraordinarily difficult problems for the Soviet leadership. They are not issues which can be readily solved by the use of the Red Army; nor, however, does it appear that fresh doses of "scientific socialism" would provide an answer satisfactory to the eastern Europeans. Despite the Kremlin's recent rhetoric about the modernization and reexamination of Marxist economic and social policies, it is difficult to see Russia relinquishing its many controls over eastern Europe. Yet these varied signs of political discontent and economic distress must call ever more into question the reliability of the *non-Russian* armies in the Warsaw Pact.[192] The Polish armed forces, for example, can hardly be reckoned as an addition to the pact's strength; if anything, the reverse is true, since they—and the critically important Polish road and rail lines—would need close Red Army supervision in wartime.[193] Similarly, it is difficult to imagine the Czech and Hungarian armies enthusiastically rushing forward to assault NATO positions upon Moscow's orders. Even the attitudes of East German forces, probably the most effective and modernized of Russia's allies, may be affected by the order to attack westward. It is true that the great bulk (four-fifths) of the Warsaw Pact's forces are Russians, and that Soviet divisions would be the real spearhead in any conventional war with the West; but it will be a considerable task for Red Army commanders both to conduct such a war and to keep an eye upon the million or more eastern European soldiers, most of them not very efficient and some of them not very reliable.[194] The possibility (however remote) that NATO may even seek to respond to a Warsaw Pact offensive by mounting its own counteroffensive, into, say, Czechoslovakia,[195] can only increase an unease which is probably as much political as it is military.

Since the early 1960s, moreover, Russian planners have had to juggle with an even more horrifying problem: the possibility that they might be involved in a large-scale conflict with NATO *and* with China.

If this occurred at the same time, then the prospects of switching reinforcements from one front or to another would be severely limited, if not impossible; but even if the war was being fought only on one front, the Kremlin might well fear to redeploy divisions from a region which, while technically neutral, had large armed forces of a potential foe arrayed along the border. As it is, the USSR is compelled to keep about fifty divisions and 13,000 tanks ready for the eventuality of a Sino-Soviet clash; and although the Russian forces are more modern and mobile than the Chinese, it is hard to envisage how they could ensure a total victory—not to mention a prolonged occupation—against an army four times as large.[196] All this necessarily assumes that the war would remain a conventional one (which, given some Russian hints about how they would crush China, may be a totally flawed assumption); but if there *is* a Russo-Chinese nuclear exchange, Soviet planners would then have to wonder whether their country might be left in a position of inferiority vis-à-vis the still neutral, yet very critical, West. In the same way, a Soviet Union badly hurt by either nuclear or large-scale conventional fighting against NATO must worry about how to handle Chinese pressures if it had been reduced to a "broken-backed" status.[197]

Although China is (apart from NATO) the most serious concern for Soviet planners simply because of its size, it is not difficult to imagine Soviet worries about the entire Asian "flank." In the largest geopolitical sense, it looks as if the age-old tendency of Muscovite/Russian policy, steady territorial expansion across Asia, has come to a halt. The re-emergence of China, the independence (and growing strength) of India, the economic recovery of Japan—not to mention the assertiveness of many smaller Asian states—has surely put to rest the nineteenth-century fear of a Russia gradually taking control of the entire continent. (The very idea nowadays would make the Soviet general staff blanch with alarm!) To be sure, this would still not prevent Moscow from making marginal gains, as in Afghanistan; but the duration of that conflict and the hostility it has provoked elsewhere in the region merely confirm that any further extensions of Russian territory would be at an incalculable military and political cost. By contrast with the self-confident Russian announcements of its "Asian mission" a century ago, the rulers in the Kremlin now have to worry about Muslim fundamentalism seeping across its southern borders from the Middle East, about the Chinese threat, and about complications in Afghanistan, Korea, and Vietnam. Whatever the number of divisions positioned in Asia, it can probably never seem enough to give "security" along such a vast periphery, especially since the Trans-Siberian Railway is still terribly vulnerable to disruption by an enemy rocket strike, which in turn would have dire implications for the Soviet forces in the Far East.[198]

Given the traditional concern of the Russian regime for the safety of the homeland, it is scarcely surprising that Soviet capacities both at sea and in the overseas world are, relatively speaking, much less significant. This is not to deny the very impressive expansion of the Red Navy over the past quarter-century, and the great variety of new and more powerful submarines, surface vessels, and even experimental aircraft carriers which are being laid down. Nor is it to deny the large expansion of the Soviet merchant marine and fishing fleets, and their significant strategical roles.[199] But there is as yet nothing in the USSR's naval armory which has the striking power of the U.S. Navy's fifteen carrier task forces. Moreover, once the comparison is between the fleets of the two *alliances* rather than the two superpowers, the sizable contributions of the non-American NATO navies makes an immense difference.

Table 48. NATO and Warsaw Pact Naval Strengths[200]

	Warsaw Pact			Nato		
	Non-Soviet	*USSR*	*Total*	*Total*	*U.S.*	*Non-U.S.*
Nuclear submarines	—	105	105	97	85	12
Diesel submarines	6	168	174	137	5	132
Major surface warships	3	184	187	376	149	227
Naval aircraft	52	755	807	2533	2250	283

"Even if China is excluded, the Western Allies have twice as many major surface combatants and three times as much naval air power as the Warsaw Pact, and practically as many submarines," as shown in Table 48. If one adds to this the fact that many more of the Warsaw Pact's large surface warships and submarines are over twenty years old, that its capacity to detect enemy submarines is more limited, and that 75 percent of the Red Navy's personnel are conscripts (in contrast to the West's long-service professionals), it is difficult to see how the USSR would be in a position to bid for "command of the sea" in the near future.[201]

Finally, if indeed the real purpose of the newer and larger surface warships of the Soviet navy is to form an "ocean bastion" in, say, the Barents Sea to protect its nuclear-missile submarines from Allied attack—that is, if the Russian fleet is being chiefly designed to guard the country's *strategic deterrent* as it moves offshore[202]—then this clearly gives it little surplus force (apart from its older submarines) to interdict NATO's maritime lines of communication. By extension, therefore, there would be little prospect of the USSR's being able to render help to its scattered overseas bases and troop deployments in the event of a major conflict with the West. As it is, despite all of the publicity given to Russia's penetration of the Third World, it has very few forces stationed overseas (i.e., outside eastern Europe and Afghanistan), and its only major overseas bases are in Vietnam, Ethiopia, South Yemen, and Cuba, all of which require large amounts of direct financial aid, which seems to be being increasingly resented in Russia itself. It may be that the USSR, having recognized the vulnerability of its Trans-Siberian Railway in the event of a war in which China is involved, is systematically attempting to create a sea line of communication (SLOC), via the Indian Ocean, to its Far East territories. As things are at the moment, however, that route must still appear a very precarious one. Not only are the USSR's spheres of influence not comparable with the far larger array of American (plus British and French) bases, troops, and overseas fleets stationed across the globe, but the few Russian positions which do exist, being exposed, are very vulnerable to western pressures in wartime. If China, Japan, and certain smaller pro-western countries are brought into the equation, the picture looks even more unbalanced. To be sure, the forcible exclusion of the Soviet Union from the Third World would not be a great blow economically— since its trade, investments and loans in those lands are minuscule compared with those of the West[203]—but that is simply another reflection of its being *less* than a global Power.

Although all of this may seem to be overstating the odds which are stacked against the Soviet Union, it is worth noting that its own planners clearly do think about "worst-case" analyses; and also that its arms-control negotiators always resist any idea of having a mere *equality* of forces with the United States, arguing instead that Russia needs a "margin" to ensure its security against China and to take account of its eight-thousand-mile border. To any reasonable outside observer, the USSR already has more than enough forces to guarantee its security, and Moscow's insistence upon building ever-newer weapon systems simply induces insecurity in everyone else. To the decision-makers in the Kremlin, heirs to a militaristic and often paranoid tradition of statecraft, Russia appears surrounded by crumbling frontiers—in eastern Europe, along the "northern tier" of the Middle East, and in its lengthy shared border with China; yet having pushed out so many Russian divisions and air squadrons to stabilize those frontiers has not produced the hoped-for invulnerability. Pulling back from eastern Europe or making border concessions to China is also feared, however, not only because of the local consequences but because it may be seen as an indication of Moscow's loss of willpower. And at the same time as the Kremlin wrestles with these traditional problems of ensuring *territorial* security for the country's extensive landward border, it must also try to keep up with the United States in rocketry, satellite-based weapons, space exploration, and so on. Thus, the USSR—or, better, the Marxist system of the USSR—is being tested both quantitatively and qualitatively in the world power stakes; and it does not like the odds.

But those odds (or "correlation of forces") would obviously be better if the economy were healthier, which brings us back to Russia's long-term problem. Economics matters to the Soviet military, not merely because they are Marxist, and not only because it pays for their weapons and wages, but also because they understand its importance for the outcome of a lengthy, Great Power, coalition war. It *might* be true, the *Soviet Military Encyclopedia* conceded in 1979, that a global coalition war would be short, especially if nuclear weapons were used. "However, taking into account the great military and economic potentials of possible coalitions of belligerent states, it is not excluded that it might be protracted also."[204] But if such a war is "protracted," the emphasis will again be upon economic staying power, as it was in the great coalition wars of the past. With that assumption in mind, it cannot be comforting to the Soviet leadership to reflect that the USSR possesses only 12 or 13 percent of the world's GNP (or about 17 percent, if one dares to include the Warsaw Pact satellites as *plus* factors); and that it is not only far behind both the United States and western Europe in the size of its GNP, but it is also being overtaken by Japan and may—if long-term growth rates continue as they are—even find itself being approached by China in the next thirty years. If that seems an extraordinary claim, it is worth recalling the cold observation by *The Economist* that in 1913 "Imperial Russia had a real product per man-hour 3½ times greater than Japan's [but it] has spent its nigh 70 socialist years slipping relatively backwards, to maybe a quarter of Japan's rate now."[205] However one assesses the military strength of the USSR at the moment, therefore, the prospect of its being only the fourth or fifth among the great productive centers of the world by the early twenty-first century cannot but worry the Soviet leadership, simply because of the implications for long-term Russian power.

This does *not* mean that the USSR is close to collapse, any more than it should be viewed as a country of almost supernatural strength. It *does* mean that it is facing awkward choices. As one Russian expert has expressed it, "The policy of guns, butter, and growth—the political cornerstone of the Brezhnev era—is no longer possible . . . even under the more optimistic scenarios . . . the Soviet Union will face an economic crunch far more severe than anything it encountered in the 1960s and 1970s."[206] It is to be expected that the efforts and exhortations to improve the Russian economy will intensify. But since it is highly unlikely that even an energetic regime in Moscow would either abandon "scientific socialism" in order to boost the economy or drastically cut the burdens of defense expenditures and thereby affect the military core of the Soviet state, the prospects of an escape from the contradictions which the USSR faces are not good. Without its massive military power, it counts for little in the world; *with* its massive military power, it makes others feel insecure and hurts its own economic prospects. It is a grim dilemma.[207]

This can hardly be an unalloyed pleasure for the West, however, since there is nothing in the character or tradition of the Russian state to suggest that it could ever accept imperial decline gracefully. Indeed, historically, *none* of the overextended, multinational empires which have been dealt with in this survey—the Ottoman, the Spanish, the Napoleonic, the British—ever retreated to their own ethnic base until they had been defeated in a Great Power war, or (as with Britain after 1945) were so weakened by war that an imperial withdrawal was politically unavoidable. Those who rejoice at the present-day difficulties of the Soviet Union and who look forward to the collapse of that empire might wish to recall that such transformations normally occur at very great cost, and not always in a predictable fashion.

The United States: The Problem of Number One in Relative Decline

It is worth bearing in mind the Soviet Union's difficulties when one turns to analyze the present and the future circumstances of the United States, because of two important distinctions. The first is that while it can be argued that the American share of world power has been declining *relatively* faster than Russia's over the past few decades, its problems are probably nowhere near as great as those of its Soviet rival. Moreover, its *absolute* strength (especially in industrial and technological fields) is still much larger than that of the USSR. The second is that the very unstructured, laissez-faire nature of American society (while not without its weaknesses) probably gives it a better chance of readjusting to changing circumstances than a rigid and *dirigiste* power would have. But that in turn depends upon the existence of a national leadership which can understand the larger processes at work in the world today, and is aware of both the strong and the weak points of the U.S. position as it seeks to adjust to the changing global environment.

Although the United States is at present still in a class of its own economically and perhaps even militarily, it cannot avoid confronting the two great tests which challenge the *longevity* of every major power that occupies the "number one" position in world affairs: whether, in the military/strategical realm, it can preserve a reasonable balance between the nation's perceived defense requirements and the means it possesses to maintain those commitments; and whether, as an intimately related point, it can preserve the technological and economic bases of its power from relative erosion in the face of the ever-shifting patterns of global production. This test of American abilities will be the greater because it, like Imperial Spain around 1600 or the British Empire around 1900, is the inheritor of a vast array of strategical commitments which had been made decades earlier, when the nation's political, economic, and military capacity to influence world affairs seemed so much more assured. In consequence, the United States now runs the risk, so familiar to historians of the rise and fall of previous Great Powers, of what might roughly be called "imperial overstretch": that is to say, decision-makers in Washington must face the awkward and enduring fact that the sum total of the United States' global interests and obligations is nowadays far larger than the country's power to defend them all simultaneously.

Unlike those earlier Powers that grappled with the problem of strategical overextension, the United States also confronts the possibility of nuclear annihilation—a fact which, many people feel, has changed the entire nature of international power politics. If indeed a large-scale nuclear exchange were to occur, then any consideration of the United States' "prospects" becomes so problematical as to make it pointless—even if it also is the case that the American position (because of its defensive systems, and geographical extent) is probably more favorable than, say, France's or Japan's in such a conflict. On the other hand, the history of the post-1945 arms race so far suggests that nuclear weapons, while mutually threatening to East and West, also seem to be mutually unusable—which is the chief reason why the Powers continue to increase expenditures upon their *conventional* forces. If, however, the possibility exists of the major states someday becoming involved in a nonnuclear war (whether merely regional or on a larger scale), then the similarity of strategical circumstances between the United States today and imperial Spain or Edwardian Britain in their day is clearly much more appropriate. In each case, the declining number-one power faced threats, not so much to the security of its own homeland (in the United States' case, the prospect of being conquered by an invading army is remote), but to the nation's interests abroad—interests so widespread that it would be difficult to defend them all at once, and yet almost equally difficult to abandon any of them without running further risks.

Each of those interests abroad, it is fair to remark, was undertaken by the United States for what seemed very plausible (often very pressing) reasons at the time, and in most instances the reason for the American presence has not diminished; in certain parts of the globe, U.S. interests may now appear larger to decision-makers in Washington than they were a few decades ago.

That, it can be argued, is certainly true of American obligations in the Middle East. Here is a region, from Morocco in the west to Afghanistan in the east, where the United States faces a number of conflicts and problems whose mere listing (as one observer put it) "leaves one breathless."[208] It is an area which contains so much of the world's surplus oil supply; which seems so susceptible (at least on the map) to Soviet penetration; toward which a powerfully organized domestic lobby presses for unflinching support for an isolated but militarily efficient Israel; in which Arab states of a generally pro-western inclination (Egypt, Saudi Arabia, Jordan, the Gulf emirates) are under pressure from their own Islamic fundamentalists as well as from external threats such as Libya; and in which all the Arab states, whatever their own rivalries, oppose Israel's policy toward the Palestinians. This makes the region very important to the United States, but at the same time bewilderingly resistant to any simple policy option. It is, in addition, the region in the world which, at least in some parts of it, seems most frequently to resort to war. Finally, it contains the only territory—Afghanistan—which the Soviet Union is attempting to conquer by means of armed force. It is hardly surprising, therefore, that the Middle East has been viewed as requiring constant American attention, whether of a military or a diplomatic kind. Yet the memory of the 1979 debacle in Iran and of the ill-fated Lebanon venture of 1983, the diplomatic complexities of the antagonisms (how to assist Saudi Arabia without alarming Israel), and the unpopularity of the United States among the Arab masses all make it extremely difficult for an American government to conduct a coherent, long-term policy in the Middle East.

In Latin America, too, there are seen to be growing challenges to the United States' national interests. If a major international debt crisis is to occur anywhere in the world, dealing a heavy blow to the global credit system and especially to U.S. banks, it is likely to begin in this region. As it is, Latin America's economic problems have not only lowered the credit rating of many eminent American banking houses, but they have also contributed to a substantial decline in U.S. manufacturing exports to that region. Here, as in East Asia, the threat that the advanced, prosperous countries of the world will steadily increase tariffs against imported, low-labor-cost manufactures, and be ever less generous in their overseas-aid programs, is a cause for deep concern. All this is compounded by the fact that, economically and socially, Latin America has been changing remarkably swiftly over the past few decades;[209] at the same time, its demographic explosion is pressing ever harder upon the available resources, and upon the older conservative governing structures, in a considerable number of states. This has led to broad-based movements for social and constitutional reforms, or even for outright "revolution"—the latter being influenced by the present radical regimes in Cuba and Nicaragua. In turn, these movements have produced a conservative backlash, with reactionary governments proclaiming the need to eradicate all signs of domestic

Communism, and appealing to the United States for help to achieve that goal. These social and political fissures often compel the United States to choose between its desire to enhance democratic rights in Latin America and its wish to defeat Marxism. It also forces Washington to consider whether it can achieve its own purposes by political and economic means alone, or whether it may have to resort to military action (as in the case of Grenada).

By far the most worrying situation of all, however, lies just to the south of the United States, and makes the Polish "crisis" for the USSR seem small by comparison. There is simply no equivalent in the world for the present state of Mexican–United States relations. Mexico is on the verge of economic bankruptcy and default, its internal economic crisis forces hundreds of thousands to drift illegally to the north each year, its most profitable trade with the United States is swiftly becoming a brutally managed flow of hard drugs, and the border for all this sort of traffic is still extraordinarily permeable.[210]

If the challenges to American interests in East Asia are farther away, that does not diminish the significance of this vast area today. The largest share of the world's population lives there; a large and increasing proportion of American trade is with countries on the "Pacific rim"; two of the world's future Great Powers, China and Japan, are located there; the Soviet Union, directly and (through Vietnam) indirectly, is also there. So are those Asian newly industrializing countries, delicate quasi-democracies which on the one hand have embraced the capitalist laissez-faire ethos with a vengeance, and on the other are undercutting American manufacturing in everything from textiles to electronics. It is in East Asia, too, that a substantial number of American military obligations exist, usually as creations of the early Cold War.

Even a mere listing of those obligations cannot fail to suggest the extraordinarily wide-ranging nature of American interests in this region. A few years ago, the U.S. Defense Department attempted a brief summary of American interests in East Asia, but its very succinctness pointed, paradoxically, to the almost limitless extent of those strategical commitments:

> The importance to the United States of the security of East Asia and the Pacific is demonstrated by the bilateral treaties with Japan, Korea, and the Philippines; the Manila Pact, which adds Thailand to our treaty partners; and our treaty with Australia and New Zealand—the ANZUS Treaty. It is further enhanced by the deployment of land and air forces in Korea and Japan, and the forward deployment of the Seventh Fleet in the Western Pacific. Our foremost regional objectives, in conjunction with our regional friends and allies, are:

—To maintain the security of our essential sea lanes and of the United States' interests in the region; to maintain the capability to fulfill our treaty commitments in the Pacific and East Asia; to prevent the Soviet Union, North Korea, and Vietnam from interfering in the affairs of others; to build a durable strategic relationship with the People's Republic of China; and to support the stability and independence of friendly countries.[211]

Moreover, this carefully selected prose inevitably conceals a considerable number of extremely delicate political and strategical issues: how to build a good relationship with the PRC without abandoning Taiwan; how to "support the stability and independence of friendly countries" while trying to control the flood of their exports to the American market; how to make the Japanese assume a larger share of the defense of the western Pacific without alarming its various neighbors; how to maintain U.S. bases in, for example, the Philippines without provoking local resentments; how to reduce the American military presence in South Korea without sending the wrong "signal" to the North . . .

Larger still, at least as measured by military deployments, is the American stake in western Europe—the defense of which is, more than anything else, the strategic rationale of the American army and of much of the air force and the navy. According to some arcane calculations, in fact, 50 or 60 percent of American general-purpose forces are allocated to NATO, an organization in which (critics repeatedly point out) the other members contribute a significantly lower share of their GNP to defense spending even though Europe's total population and income are now larger than the USA's own.[212] This is not the place to rehearse the various European counterarguments in the "burden-sharing" debate (such as the social cost which countries like France and West Germany pay in maintaining conscription), or to develop the point that if western Europe was "Finlandized" the USA would probably spend even more on defense than at the moment.[213] From an American strategical perspective, the unavoidable fact is that this region has always seemed more vulnerable to Russian pressure than, say, Japan—partly because it is *not* an island, and partly because on the other side of the European land frontier the USSR has concentrated the largest proportion of its land and air forces, significantly greater than what may be reasonably needed for internal-security purposes. This still may not give Russia the military capacity to overrun western Europe (see pp. 507–9), but it is not a situation in which it would be prudent to withdraw substantial U.S. ground and air forces unilaterally. Even the outside possibility that the world's largest concentration of manufacturing production *might* fall into the Soviet orbit is enough to convince the Pentagon that "the security of western

Europe is particularly vital to the security of the United States."[214]

Yet however logical the American commitment to Europe may be strategically, that fact itself is no guarantee against certain military and political complications which have led to transatlantic discord. Although the NATO alliance brings the United States and western Europe close together at one level, the EEC itself is, like Japan, a rival in economic terms, especially in the shrinking markets for agricultural products. More significantly, while *official* European policy has always been to stress the importance of being under the American "nuclear umbrella," a broad-based unease exists among the general publics at the implications of siting U.S. weapons (cruise missiles, Pershing IIs, Trident-bearing submarines—let alone neutron bombs) on European soil. But if, to return to an earlier point, both superpowers would try to avoid "going nuclear" in the event of a major clash, that still leaves considerable problems in guaranteeing the defense of western Europe by *conventional* means. In the first place, that is a very expensive proposition. Secondly, even if one accepts the evidence which is beginning to suggest that the Warsaw Pact's land and air forces could in fact be held in check, such an argument is predicated upon a certain enhancement of NATO's current strength. From that perspective, nothing could be more upsetting than proposals to reduce or withdraw U.S. forces in Europe—however pressing that might be for economic reasons or for the purpose of buttressing American deployments elsewhere in the world. Yet carrying out a grand strategy which is both global and flexible is extremely difficult when so large a portion of the American armed forces are committed to one particular region.

In view of the above, it is not surprising that the circles most concerned about the discrepancy between American commitments and American power are the armed services themselves, simply because they would be the first to suffer if strategical weaknesses were exposed in the harsh test of war. Hence the frequent warnings by the Pentagon against being forced to carry out a global logistical juggling act, switching forces from one "hot spot" to another as new troubles emerge. If this was particularly acute in late 1983, when additional U.S. deployments in Central America, Grenada, Chad, and the Lebanon caused the former chairman of the Joint Chiefs of Staff to proclaim that the "mismatch" between American forces and strategy "is greater now than ever before,"[215] the problem had been implicit for years beforehand. Interestingly, such warnings about the American armed forces being "at full stretch" are attended by maps of "Major U.S. Military Deployment Around the World"[216] which, to historians, look extraordinarily similar to the chain of fleet bases and garrisons possessed by that former world power, Great Britain, at the height of its strategic overstretch.[217]

On the other hand, it is hardly likely that the United States would

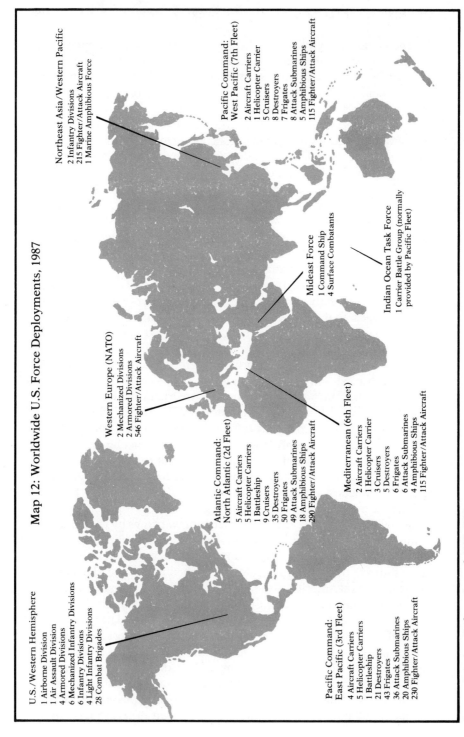

Map 12: Worldwide U.S. Force Deployments, 1987

U.S./Western Hemisphere
1 Airborne Division
1 Air Assault Division
4 Armored Divisions
6 Mechanized Infantry Divisions
6 Infantry Divisions
4 Light Infantry Divisions
28 Combat Brigades

Northeast Asia/Western Pacific
2 Infantry Divisions
215 Fighter/Attack Aircraft
1 Marine Amphibious Force

**Pacific Command:
West Pacific (7th Fleet)**
2 Aircraft Carriers
1 Helicopter Carrier
5 Cruisers
8 Destroyers
7 Frigates
8 Attack Submarines
5 Amphibious Ships
115 Fighter/Attack Aircraft

Western Europe (NATO)
2 Mechanized Divisions
2 Armored Divisions
546 Fighter/Attack Aircraft

**Atlantic Command:
North Atlantic (2d Fleet)**
5 Aircraft Carriers
5 Helicopter Carriers
1 Battleship
9 Cruisers
35 Destroyers
50 Frigates
49 Attack Submarines
18 Amphibious Ships
290 Fighter/Attack Aircraft

Mideast Force
1 Command Ship
4 Surface Combatants

Indian Ocean Task Force
1 Carrier Battle Group (normally
provided by Pacific Fleet)

Mediterranean (6th Fleet)
2 Aircraft Carriers
1 Helicopter Carrier
3 Cruisers
5 Destroyers
6 Frigates
6 Attack Submarines
4 Amphibious Ships
115 Fighter/Attack Aircraft

**Pacific Command:
East Pacific (3rd Fleet)**
4 Aircraft Carriers
5 Helicopter Carriers
1 Battleship
21 Destroyers
43 Frigates
36 Attack Submarines
20 Amphibious Ships
230 Fighter/Attack Aircraft

Source: American Defense Annual, 1987–1988

be called upon to defend *all* of its overseas interests simultaneously and without the aid of a significant number of allies—the NATO members in western Europe, Israel in the Middle East, and, in the Pacific, Japan, Australia, possibly China. Nor are all the regional trends becoming unfavorable to the United States in defense terms; for example, while aggression by the unpredictable North Korean regime is always possible, that would hardly be welcomed by Peking nowadays—and, in addition, South Korea itself has grown to possess over twice the population and four times the GNP of North Korea. In the same way, while the expansion of Russian forces in the Far East is alarming to Washington, that is considerably balanced off by the growing threat posed by the PRC to Russia's land and sea lines of communication with the Orient. The recent, sober admission by the U.S. defense secretary that "we can never afford to buy the capabilities sufficient to meet all of our commitments with one hundred percent confidence"[218] is surely true; but it may be less worrying than at first appears if it is also recalled that the total of potential anti-Soviet resources in the world (United States, western Europe, Japan, PRC, Australasia) is far greater than the total of resources lined up on Russia's side.

Despite such consolations, the fundamental grand-strategical dilemma remains: the United States today has roughly the same massive array of military obligations across the globe as it had a quarter-century ago, when its shares of world GNP, manufacturing production, military spending, and armed forces personnel were so much larger than they are now.[219] Even in 1985, forty years after its triumphs of the Second World War and over a decade after its pull-out from Vietnam, the United States had 520,000 members of its armed forces abroad (including 65,000 afloat).[220] That total is, incidentally, substantially more than the overseas deployments in peacetime of the military and naval forces of the British Empire at the height of its power. Nevertheless, in the strongly expressed opinion of the Joint Chiefs of Staff, and of many civilian experts,[221] it is simply not enough. Despite a near-trebling of the American defense budget since the late 1970s, there has occurred a "mere 5 percent increase in the numerical size of the armed forces on active duty."[222] As the British and French military found in their time, a nation with extensive overseas obligations will always have a more difficult "manpower problem" than a state which keeps its armed forces solely for home defense; and a politically liberal and economically laissez-faire society—aware of the unpopularity of conscription—will have a greater problem than most.[223]

Possibly this concern about the gap between American interests and capabilities in the world would be less acute had there not been so much doubt expressed—since at least the time of the Vietnam War—about the *efficiency* of the system itself. Since those doubts have been repeatedly aired in other studies, they will only be summarized here;

this is not a further essay on the hot topic of "defense reform."[224] One major area of contention, for example, has been the degree of interservice rivalry, which is of course common to most armed forces but seems more deeply entrenched in the American system—possibly because of the relatively modest powers of the chairman of the Joint Chiefs of Staff, possibly because so much more energy appears to be devoted to procurement as opposed to strategical and operational issues. In peacetime, this might merely be dismissed as an extreme example of "bureaucratic politics"; but in actual wartime operations— say, in the emergency dispatch of the Rapid Deployment Joint Task Force, which contains elements from all four services—a lack of proper coordination could be fatal.

In the area of military procurement itself, allegations of "waste, fraud and abuse"[225] have been commonplace. The various scandals over horrendously expensive, *under*performing weapons which have caught the public's attention in recent years have plausible explanations: the lack of proper competitive bidding and of market forces in the "military-industrial complex," and the tendency toward "gold-plated" weapon systems, not to mention the striving for large profits. It is difficult, however, to separate those deficiencies in the procurement process from what is clearly a more fundamental happening: the intensification of the impacts which new technological advances make upon the art of war. Given that it is in the high-technology field that the USSR usually appears most vulnerable—which suggests that American *quality* in weaponry can be employed to counter the superior Russian *quantity* of, say, tanks and aircraft—there is an obvious attraction in what Caspar Weinberger termed "competitive strategies" when ordering new armaments.[226] Nevertheless, the fact that the Reagan administration in its first term spent over 75 percent more on new aircraft than the Carter regime but acquired only 9 percent more planes points to *the* appalling military-procurement problem of the late twentieth century: given the technologically driven tendency toward spending more and more money upon fewer and fewer weapon systems, would the United States and its allies really have enough sophisticated and highly expensive aircraft and tanks in reserve after the early stages of a ferociously fought conventional war? Does the U.S. Navy possess enough attack submarines, or frigates, if heavy losses were incurred in the early stages of a *third* Battle of the Atlantic? If not, the results would be grim; for it is clear that today's complex weaponry simply cannot be replaced in the short times which were achieved during the Second World War.

This dilemma is accentuated by two other elements in the complicated calculus of evolving an effective American defense policy. The first is the issue of budgetary constraints. Unless external circumstances became much more threatening, it would be a remarkable act of political persuasion to get national defense expenditures raised much above, say, 7.5 percent of GNP—the more especially since the size of the federal deficit (see below, pp. 527–28) points to the need to balance governmental spending as the first priority of state. But if there is a slowing-down or even a halt in the increase in defense spending, coinciding with the continuous upward spiral in weapons costs, then the problem facing the Pentagon will become much more acute.

The second factor is the sheer variety of military contingencies that a global superpower like the United States has to plan for—all of which, in their way, place differing demands upon the armed forces and the weaponry they are likely to employ. This again is not without precedent in the history of the Great Powers; the British army was frequently placed under strain by having to plan to fight on the Northwest Frontier of India *or* in Belgium. But even that challenge pales beside the task facing today's "number one." If the critical issue for the United States is preserving a nuclear deterrent against the Soviet Union, at *all* levels of escalation, then money will inevitably be poured into such weapons as the MX missile, the B-1 and "Stealth" bombers, Pershing IIs, cruise missiles, and Trident-bearing submarines. If a large-scale conventional war against the Warsaw Pact is the most probable scenario, then the funds presumably need to go in quite different directions: tactical aircraft, main battle tanks, large carriers, frigates, attack submarines, and logistical services. If it is likely that the United States and the USSR will avoid a direct clash, but that both will become more active in the Third World, then the weapons mix changes again: small arms, helicopters, light carriers, an enhanced role for the U.S. Marine Corps become the chief items on the list. Already it is clear that a large part of the controversy over "defense reform" stems from differing assumptions about the *type* of war the United States might be called upon to fight. But what if those in authority make the wrong assumption?

A further major concern about the efficiency of the system, and one voiced even by strong supporters of the campaign to "restore" American power,[227] is whether the present decision-making structure permits a proper grand strategy to be carried out. This would not merely imply achieving a greater coherence in military policies, so that there is less argument about "maritime strategy" versus "coalition warfare,"[228] but would also involve effecting a synthesis of the United States' long-term political, economic, and strategical interests, in place of the bureaucratic infighting which seems to have characterized so much of Washington's policymaking. A much-quoted example of this is the all-too-frequent *public* dispute about how and where the United States should employ its armed forces abroad to enhance or defend its national interests—with the State Department wanting clear and firm responses made to those who threaten such interests, but the Defense

Department being unwilling (especially after the Lebanon debacle) to get involved overseas except under special conditions.[229] But there also have been, and by contrast, examples of the Pentagon's preference for taking unilateral decisions in the arms race with Russia (e.g., SDI program, abandoning SALT II) without consulting major allies, which leaves problems for the State Department. There have been uncertainties attending the role played by the National Security Council, and more especially individual national security advisers. There have been incoherencies of policy in the Middle East, partly because of the intractibility of, say, the Palestine issue, but also because the United States' strategical interest in supporting the conservative, pro-Western Arab states against Russian penetration in that area has often foundered upon the well-organized opposition of its own pro-Israel lobby. There have been interdepartmental disputes about the use of economic tools—from boycotts on trade and embargoes on technology transfer to foreign-aid grants and weapons sales and grain sales—in support of American diplomatic interests, which affect policies toward the Third World, South Africa, Russia, Poland, the EEC, and so on, and which have sometimes been uncoordinated and contradictory. No sensible person would maintain that the many foreign-policy problems afflicting the globe each possess an obvious and ready "solution"; on the other hand, the preservation of long-term American interests is certainly not helped when the decision-making system is attended by frequent disagreements within.

All this has led to questions by gloomier critics about the overall political culture in which Washington decision-makers have to operate. This is far too large and complex a matter to be explored in depth here. But it has been increasingly suggested that a country needing to reformulate its grand strategy in the light of the larger, uncontrollable changes taking place in world affairs may not be well served by an electoral system which seems to paralyze foreign-policy decision-making every two years. It may not be helped by the extraordinary pressures applied by lobbyists, political action committees, and other interest groups, all of which, by definition, are prejudiced in respect to this or that policy change; nor by an inherent "simplification" of vital but complex international and strategical issues through a mass media whose time and space for such things are limited, and whose *raison d'être* is chiefly to make money and secure audiences, and only secondarily to inform. It may also not be helped by the still-powerful "escapist" urges in the American social culture, which may be understandable in terms of the nation's "frontier" past but is a hindrance to coming to terms with today's more complex, integrated world and with *other* cultures and ideologies. Finally, the country may not always be assisted by its division of constitutional and decision-making powers, deliberately created when it was geographically and strategically isolated from the rest of the world two centuries ago, and possessed a decent degree of time to come to an agreement on the few issues which actually concerned "foreign" policy, but which may be harder to operate when it has become a global superpower, often called upon to make swift decisions vis-à-vis countries which enjoy far fewer constraints. No single one of these presents an insuperable obstacle to the execution of a coherent, long-term American grand strategy; their cumulative and interacting effect is, however, to make it much more difficult than otherwise to carry out needed changes of policy if that seems to hurt special interests and occurs in an election year. It may therefore be here, in the cultural and domestic-political realms, that the evolution of an effective overall American policy to meet the twenty-first century will be subjected to the greatest test.

The final question about the proper relationship of "means and ends" in the defense of American global interests relates to the economic challenges bearing down upon the country, which, because they are so various, threaten to place immense strains upon decision-making in national policy. The extraordinary breadth and complexity of the American economy makes it difficult to summarize what is happening to all parts of it—especially in a period when it is sending out such contradictory signals.[230] Nonetheless, the features which were described in the preceding chapter (pp. 432–35) still prevail.

The first of these is the country's relative industrial decline, as measured against world production, not only in older manufactures such as textiles, iron and steel, shipbuilding, and basic chemicals, but also—although it is far less easy to judge the final outcome of this level of industrial-technological combat—in global shares of robotics, aerospace, automobiles, machine tools, and computers. Both of these pose immense problems: in traditional and basic manufacturing, the gap in wage scales between the United States and newly industrializing countries is probably such that no "efficiency measures" will close it; but to lose out in the competition in future technologies, if that indeed should occur, would be even more disastrous. In late 1986, for example, a congressional study reported that the U.S. trade surplus in high-technology goods had plunged from $27 billion in 1980 to a mere $4 billion in 1985, and was swiftly heading into a deficit.[231]

The second, and in many ways less expected, sector of decline is agriculture. Only a decade ago, experts in that subject were predicting a frightening global imbalance between feeding requirements and farming output.[232] But such a scenario of famine and disaster stimulated two powerful responses. The first was a massive investment into American farming from the 1970s onward, fueled by the prospect of ever-larger overseas food sales; the second was the enormous (western-world-funded) investigation into scientific means of increasing Third World crop outputs, which has been so successful as to turn growing numbers of such countries into food *exporters,* and thus competitors of the United States. These two trends are separate from, but have coincided with, the transformation of the EEC into a major producer of agricultural surpluses, because of its price-support system. In consequence, experts now refer to a "world awash in food," [233] which in turn leads to sharp declines in agricultural prices and in American food exports—and drives many farmers out of business.

It is not surprising, therefore, that these economic problems have led to a surge in protectionist sentiment throughout many sectors of the American economy, and among businessmen, unions, farmers, and their congressmen. As with the "tariff reform" agitation in Edwardian Britain,[234] the advocates of increased protection complain of unfair foreign practices, of "dumping" below-cost manufactures on the American market, and of enormous subsidies to foreign farmers— which, they maintain, can only be answered by U.S. administrations abandoning their laissez-faire policy on trade and instituting tough countermeasures. Many of those individual complaints (e.g., of Japan shipping below-cost silicon chips to the American market) have been valid. More broadly, however, the surge in protectionist sentiment is also a reflection of the erosion of the previously unchallenged U.S. manufacturing supremacy. Like mid-Victorian Britons, Americans after 1945 favored free trade and open competition, not just because they held that global commerce and prosperity would be boosted in the process, but also because they knew that they were most likely to benefit from the abandonment of protectionism. Forty years later, with that confidence ebbing, there is a predictable shift of opinion in favor of protecting the domestic market and the domestic producer. And, just as in that earlier British case, defenders of the existing system point out that enhanced tariffs might not only make domestic products *less* competitive internationally, but that there also could be various external repercussions—a global tariff war, blows against American exports, the undermining of the currencies of certain newly industrializing countries, and a return to the economic crisis of the 1930s.

Along with these difficulties affecting American manufacturing and agriculture there are unprecedented turbulences in the nation's finances. The uncompetitiveness of U.S. industrial products abroad and the declining sales of agricultural exports have together produced staggering deficits in visible trade—$160 billion in the twelve months to May 1986—but what is more alarming is that such a gap can no longer be covered by American earnings on "invisibles," which is the traditional recourse of a mature economy (e.g., Great Britain before 1914). On the contrary, the only way the United States can pay its way in the world is by importing ever-larger sums of capital, which has transformed it from being the world's largest creditor to the world's largest debtor nation *in the space of a few years.*

Compounding this problem—in the view of many critics, *causing* this problem[235]—have been the budgetary policies of the U.S. government itself. Even in the 1960s, there was a tendency for Washington to rely upon deficit finance, rather than additional taxes, to pay for the increasing cost of defense and social programs. But the decisions taken by the Reagan administration in the early 1980s—i.e., large-scale increases in defense expenditures, plus considerable decreases in taxation, but *without* significant reductions in federal spending elsewhere—have produced extraordinary rises in the deficit, and consequently in the national debt, as shown in Table 49.

Table 49. U.S. Federal Deficit, Debt, and Interest, 1980–1985[236]
(billions of dollars)

	Deficit	Debt	Interest on Debt
1980	59.6	914.3	52.5
1983	195.4	1,381.9	87.8
1985	202.8	1,823.1	129.0

The continuation of such trends, alarmed voices have pointed out, would push the U.S. national debt to around $13 *trillion* by the year 2000 (fourteen times that of 1980), and the interest payments on such debt to $1.5 *trillion* (twenty-nine times that of 1980).[237] In fact, a lowering of interest rates could bring down those estimates,[238] but the overall trend is still very unhealthy. Even if federal deficits could be reduced to a "mere" $100 billion annually, the compounding of national debt and interest payments by the early twenty-first century will still cause quite unprecedented totals of money to be diverted in that direction. Historically, the only other example which comes to mind of a Great Power so increasing its indebtedness in *peacetime* is France in the 1780s, where the fiscal crisis contributed to the domestic political crisis.

These American trade and federal deficits are now interacting with a new phenomenon in the world economy—what is perhaps best described as the "dislocation" of international capital movements from the trade in goods and services. Because of the growing integration of the world economy, the volume of trade both in manufactures and in financial services is much larger than ever before, and together may amount to some $3 trillion a year; but that is now eclipsed by the stupendous level of capital flows pouring through the world's money markets, with the London-based Eurodollar market alone having a volume "at least 25 times that of world trade."[239] While this trend was fueled by events in the 1970s (the move from fixed to floating exchange rates, the surplus funds flowing from OPEC countries), it has also been stimulated by the U.S. deficits, since the only way the federal government has been able to cover the yawning gap between its expenditures

and its receipts has been to suck into the country tremendous amounts
of liquid funds from Europe and (especially) Japan—turning the
United States, as mentioned above, into the world's largest debtor
country by far.[240] It is, in fact, difficult to imagine how the American
economy could have got by *without* the inflow of foreign funds in the
early 1980s, even if that had the awkward consequence of sending up
the exchange value of the dollar, and further hurting U.S. agricultural
and manufacturing exports. But that in turn raises the troubling question about what might happen if those massive and volatile funds were
pulled out of the dollar, causing its value to drop precipitously.

The trends have, in turn, produced explanations which suggest that
alarmist voices are exaggerating the gravity of what is happening to the
U.S. economy and failing to note the "naturalness" of most of these
developments. For example, the midwestern farm belt would be much
less badly off had not so many individuals bought land at inflated
prices and excessive interest rates in the late 1970s. Again, the move
from manufacturing into services is an understandable one, which is
occurring in all advanced countries; and it is also worth recalling that
U.S. manufacturing *output* has been rising in absolute terms, even if
employment (especially blue-collar employment) in manufacturing industry has been falling—but that again is a "natural" trend, as the
world increasingly moves from material-based to knowledge-based
production. Similarly, there is nothing wrong in the metamorphosis of
American financial institutions into *world* financial institutions, with
a triple base in Tokyo, London, and New York, to handle (and profit
from) the great volume of capital flows; that can only boost the nation's
earnings from services. Even the large annual federal deficits and the
mounting national debt are sometimes described as being not too serious, after allowance is made for inflation; and there exists in some
quarters a belief that the economy will "grow its way out" of these
deficits, or that measures will be taken by the politicians to close the
gap, whether by increasing taxes or cutting spending or a combination
of both. A too-hasty attempt to slash the deficit, it is pointed out, could
well trigger off a major recession.

Even more reassuring are said to be the positive signs of growth in
the American economy. Because of the boom in the services sector, the
United States has been creating jobs over the past decade faster than
at any time in its peacetime history—and certainly a lot faster than in
western Europe. As a related point, its far greater degree of labor
mobility eases such transformations in the job market. Furthermore,
the enormous American commitment in high technology—not just in
California, but in New England, Virginia, Arizona, and many other
parts of the land—promises ever greater outputs of production, and
thus of national wealth (as well as ensuring a strategical edge over the
USSR). Indeed, it is precisely because of the opportunities that exist in

the American economy that it continues to attract millions of immigrants, and to stimulate thousands of new entrepreneurs; while the floods of capital which pour into the country can be tapped for further investment, especially into R&D. Finally, if the shifts in the global terms of trade are indeed leading to lower prices for foodstuffs and raw materials, that ought to benefit an economy which still imports enormous amounts of oil, metal ores, and so on (even if it hurts particular American producers, like farmers and oilmen).

Many of these individual points may be valid. Since the American economy is so large and variegated, some sectors and regions are likely to be growing at the same time as others are in decline—and to characterize the whole with sweeping generalizations about "crisis" or "boom" is therefore inappropriate. Given the decline in raw-materials prices, the ebbing of the dollar's unsustainably high exchange value of early 1985, the general fall in interest rates—and the impact of all three trends upon inflation and upon business confidence—it is not surprising to find some professional economists being optimistic about the future.[241]

Nevertheless, from the viewpoint of American grand strategy, and of the economic foundation upon which an effective, long-term strategy needs to rest, the picture is much less rosy. In the first place, given the worldwide array of military liabilities which the United States has assumed since 1945, its capacity to carry those burdens is obviously less than it was several decades ago, when its share of global manufacturing and GNP was much larger, its agriculture was not in crisis, its balance of payments was far healthier, the government budget was also in balance, and it was not so heavily in debt to the rest of the world. In that larger sense, there is something in the analogy which is made by certain political scientists between the United States' position today and that of previous "declining hegemons."[242]

Here again, it is instructive to note the uncanny similarities between the growing mood of anxiety among thoughtful circles in the United States today and that which pervaded all political parties in Edwardian Britain and led to what has been termed the "national efficiency" movement: that is, a broad-based debate within the nation's decision-making, business, and educational elites over the various measures which could reverse what was seen to be a growing uncompetitiveness as compared with other advanced societies. In terms of commercial expertise, levels of training and education, efficiency of production, standards of income and (among the less well-off) of living, health, and housing, the "number-one" power of 1900 seemed to be losing its position, with dire implications for the country's long-term *strategic* position; hence the fact that the calls for "renewal" and "reorganization" came at least as much from the Right as from the Left.[243] Such campaigns usually do lead to reforms, here and there; but their very existence is, ironically, a confirmation of decline, in that such an agitation simply would not have been necessary a few decades earlier, when the nation's lead was unquestioned. A strong man, the writer G. K. Chesterton sardonically observed, does not worry about his bodily efficiency; only when he weakens does he begin to talk about health.[244] In the same way, when a Great Power is strong and unchallenged, it will be much less likely to debate its capacity to meet its obligations than when it is relatively weaker.

More narrowly, there could be serious implications for American grand strategy if its industrial base continued to shrink. Were there ever to be a large-scale future war which remained conventional (because of the belligerents' mutual fear of triggering a nuclear holocaust), then one is bound to wonder what the impact upon U.S. productive capacities would be after years of decline in certain key industries, the erosion of blue-collar employment, and so on. In this connection, one is reminded of Hewins's alarmed cry in 1904 about the impact of British industrial decay upon *that* country's power:[245]

> Suppose an industry which is threatened [by foreign competition] is one which lies at the very root of your system of National defence, where are you then? You could not get on without an iron industry, a great Engineering trade, because in modern warfare you would not have the means of producing, and maintaining in a state of efficiency, your fleets and armies.

It is hard to imagine that the decline in American industrial capacity could be so severe: its manufacturing base is simply that much broader than Edwardian Britain's was; and—an important point—the "defense-related industries" have not only been sustained by repeated Pentagon orders, but have paralleled the shift from materials-intensive into knowledge-intensive (high-technology) manufacturing, which over the longer term will also reduce the West's reliance upon critical raw materials. Even so, the very high proportion of, say, semiconductors which are assembled in foreign countries and then shipped to the United States,[246] or—to think of a product as far removed from semiconductors as possible—the erosion of the American shipping and shipbuilding industry, or the closing down of so many American mines and oilfields—such trends cannot but be damaging in the event of another long-lasting, Great Power, coalition war. If, moreover, historical precedents are of any validity at all, the most critical constraint upon any "surge" in wartime production has usually been in the area of skilled craftsmen[247]—which, once again, causes one to wonder about the massive long-term decline in American blue-collar (i.e., usually skilled-craftsmen) employment.

A quite different problem, but one equally important for the sustaining of a proper grand strategy, concerns the impact of slow economic growth upon the American social/political consensus. To a degree which amazes most Europeans, the United States in the twentieth century has managed to avoid ostensible "class" politics. This is due, one imagines, to the facts that so many of its immigrants were fleeing from socially rigid circumstances elsewhere; that the sheer size of the country allowed those who were disillusioned with their economic position to "escape" to the West, and simultaneously made the organization of labor much more difficult than in, say, France or Britain; and that those same geographical dimensions, and the entrepreneurial opportunities within them, encouraged the development of a largely unreconstructed form of laissez-faire capitalism which has dominated the political culture of the nation (despite occasional counterattacks from the left). In consequence, the "earnings gap" between rich and poor in the United States is significantly larger than in any other advanced industrial society; and, by the same token, state expenditures upon social services form a lower share of GNP than in comparable countries (except Japan, which appears to have a much stronger family-based form of support for the poor and the aged).

This lack of "class" politics despite the obvious socioeconomic disparities has obviously been helped by the fact that the United States' overall growth since the 1930s offered the prospect of individual betterment to a majority of the population; and by the more disturbing fact that the poorest *one-third* of American society has not been "mobilized" to become regular voters. But given the differentiated birthrate between the white ethnic groups on the one hand and the black and Hispanic groups on the other—not to mention the changing flow of immigrants into the United States, and given also the economic metamorphosis which is leading to the loss of millions of relatively high-earning jobs in manufacturing, and the creation of millions of poorly paid jobs in services, it may be unwise to assume that the prevailing norms of the American political economy (low government expenditures, low taxes on the rich) would be maintained if the nation entered a period of sustained economic difficulty caused by a plunging dollar and slow growth. What this also suggests is that an American polity which responds to external challenges by increasing defense expenditures, and reacts to the budgetary crisis by slashing the existing social expenditures, may run the risk of provoking an eventual political backlash. As with all of the other Powers surveyed in this chapter, there are no easy answers in dealing with the constant three-way tension between defense, consumption, and investment in settling national priorities.

This brings us, inevitably, to the delicate relationship between slow economic growth and high defense spending. The debate upon "the economics of defense spending" is a highly controversial one, and—

bearing in mind the size and variety of the American economy, the stimulus which can come from large government contracts, and the technical spin-offs from weapons research—the evidence does not point simply in one direction.[248] But what is significant for our purposes is the comparative dimension. Even if (as is often pointed out) defense expenditures formed 10 percent of GNP under Eisenhower and 9 percent under Kennedy, the United States' relative share of global production and wealth was at that time around *twice* what it is today; and, more particularly, the American economy was not then facing the challenges to either its traditional or its high-technology manufactures. Moreover, if the United States at present continues to devote 7 percent or more of its GNP to defense spending while its major economic rivals, especially Japan, allocate a far smaller proportion, then *ipso facto* the latter have potentially more funds "free" for civilian investment; if the United States continues to invest a massive amount of its R&D activities into military-related production while the Japanese and West Germans concentrate upon commercial R&D; and if the Pentagon's spending drains off the majority of the country's scientists and engineers from the design and production of goods for the world market while similar personnel in other countries are primarily engaged in bringing out better products for the civilian consumer, then it seems inevitable that the American share of world manufacturing will steadily decline, and also likely that its economic growth rates will be slower than in those countries dedicated to the marketplace and less eager to channel resources into defense.[249]

It is almost superfluous to say that these tendencies place the United States on the horns of a most acute dilemma over the longer term. Simply because it is *the* global superpower, with far more extensive military commitments than a regional Power like Japan or West Germany, it requires much larger defense forces—in just the same way as imperial Spain felt it needed a far larger army than its contemporaries and Victorian Britain insisted upon a much bigger navy than any other country. Furthermore, since the USSR is seen to be the major military threat to American interests across the globe and is clearly devoting a far greater proportion of *its* GNP to defense, American decision-makers are inevitably worried about "losing" the arms race with Russia. Yet the more sensible among these decision-makers can also perceive that the burden of armaments is debilitating the Soviet economy; and that if the two superpowers continue to allocate ever-larger shares of their national wealth into the unproductive field of armaments, the critical question might soon be: "Whose economy will decline *fastest*, relative to such expanding states as Japan, China, etc.?" A low investment in armaments may, for a globally overstretched Power like the United States, leave it feeling vulnerable everywhere; but a very heavy investment in armaments, while bringing greater security in the short term, may so erode the commercial competitiveness of the American economy that the nation will be *less* secure in the long term.[250]

Here, too, the historical precedents are not encouraging. For it has been a common dilemma facing previous "number-one" countries that even as their relative economic strength is ebbing, the growing foreign challenges to their position have compelled them to allocate more and more of their resources into the military sector, which in turn squeezes out productive investment and, over time, leads to the downward spiral of slower growth, heavier taxes, deepening domestic splits over spending priorities, and a weakening capacity to bear the burdens of defense.[251] If this, indeed, is the pattern of history, one is tempted to paraphrase Shaw's deadly serious quip and say: "Rome fell; Babylon fell; Scarsdale's turn will come."[252]

In the largest sense of all, therefore, the only answer to the question increasingly debated by the public of whether the United States can preserve its existing position is "no"—for it simply has not been given to any one society to remain *permanently* ahead of all the others, because that would imply a freezing of the differentiated pattern of growth rates, technological advance, and military developments which has existed since time immemorial. On the other hand, this reference to historical precedents does *not* imply that the United States is destined to shrink to the relative obscurity of former leading Powers such as Spain or the Netherlands, or to disintegrate like the Roman and Austro-Hungarian empires; it is simply too large to do the former, and presumably too homogeneous to do the latter. Even the British analogy, much favored in the current political-science literature, is not a good one if it ignores the differences in *scale.* This can be put another way: the geographical size, population, and natural resources of the British Isles would suggest that it ought to possess roughly 3 or 4 percent of the world's wealth and power, *all other things being equal;* but it is precisely because all other things are *never* equal that a peculiar set of historical and technological circumstances permitted the British Isles to expand to possess, say, 25 percent of the world's wealth and power in its prime; and since those favorable circumstances have disappeared, all that it has been doing is returning down to its more "natural" size. In the same way, it may be argued that the geographical extent, population, and natural resources of the United States suggest that it ought to possess perhaps 16 or 18 percent of the world's wealth and power, but because of historical and technical circumstances favorable to it, that share rose to 40 percent or more by 1945; and what we are witnessing at the moment is the early decades of the ebbing away from that extraordinarily high figure to a more "natural" share. That decline is being masked by the country's enormous military capabilities at present, and also by its success in "internationalizing" American capitalism and culture.[253] Yet even when it declines to occupy its "natural" share of the world's wealth and power, a long time into the future, the United States will still be a very significant Power in a multipolar world, simply because of its size.

The task facing American statesmen over the next decades, therefore, is to recognize that broad trends are under way, and that there is a need to "manage" affairs so that the *relative* erosion of the United States' position takes place slowly and smoothly, and is not accelerated by policies which bring merely short-term advantage but longer-term disadvantage. This involves, from the president's office downward, an appreciation that technological and therefore socioeconomic change is occurring in the world faster than ever before; that the international community is much more politically and culturally diverse than has been assumed, and is defiant of simplistic remedies offered either by Washington or Moscow to its problems; that the economic and productive power balances are no longer as favorably tilted in the United States' direction as in 1945; and that, even in the military realm, there are signs of a certain redistribution of the balances, away from a bipolar to more of a multipolar system, in which the conglomeration of American economic-cum-military strength is likely to remain larger than that possessed by any one of the others individually, but will not be as disproportionate as in the decades which immediately followed the Second World War. This, in itself, is not a bad thing if one recalls Kissinger's observations about the disadvantages of carrying out policies in what is always seen to be a bipolar world (see pp. 407-8); and it may seem still less of a bad thing when it is recognized how much more Russia may be affected by the changing dynamics of world power. In all of the discussions about the erosion of American leadership, it needs to be repeated again and again that the decline referred to is relative not absolute, and is therefore perfectly natural; and that the only serious threat to the real interests of the United States can come from a failure to adjust sensibly to the newer world order.

Given the considerable array of strengths still possessed by the United States, it ought not *in theory* to be beyond the talents of successive administrations to arrange the diplomacy and strategy of this readjustment so that it can, in Walter Lippmann's classic phrase, bring "into balance . . . the nation's commitments and the nation's power."[254] Although there is no obvious, single "successor state" which can take over America's global burdens in the way that the United States assumed Britain's role in the 1940s, it is nonetheless also true that the country has fewer problems than an imperial Spain besieged by enemies on all fronts, or a Netherlands being squeezed between France and England, or a British Empire facing a bevy of challengers. The tests before the United States as it heads toward the twenty-first century are certainly daunting, perhaps especially in the economic sphere; but the nation's resources remain considerable, *if* they can be properly organized, and *if* there is a judicious recognition of both the limitations and the opportunities of American power.

Viewed from one perspective, it can hardly be said that the dilemmas facing the United States are unique. Which country in the world, one it tempted to ask, is *not* encountering problems in evolving a viable military policy, or in choosing between guns and butter and investment? From another perspective, however, the American position is a very special one. For all its economic and perhaps military decline, it remains, in Pierre Hassner's words, "the decisive actor in every type of balance and issue."[255] Because it has so much power for good or evil, because it is the linchpin of the western alliance system and the center of the existing global economy, what it does, *or does not do,* is so much more important than what any of the other Powers decides to do.

Epilogue

After a five-hundred-year survey of the rise and fall of the Great Powers within the international system, there is a case for concluding with a substantial final section on *theory* and *methodology,* in which the author would engage the proliferating theories upon "war and the cycle of relative power,"[1] "global wars, public debts, and the long cycle,"[2] "the size and duration of empires,"[3] and the various other attempts[4] by political scientists to make some sense of the whole and—usually—to suggest implications for the future. But this is not a work of political science, even if it hopes to have offered a large body of detailed facts and commentaries to those scholars in that discipline who are investigating the larger patterns of war and change in the international order.

This section will also not attempt to offer a conclusive summary of where we stand now, for that would contradict one of the chief messages of this book, which is that the international system is subject to constant changes, not only those caused by the day-to-day actions of statesmen and the ebb and flow of political and military events, but also those caused by the deeper transformations in the foundations of world power, which in time make their way through to the surface.

Nevertheless, it is proper to offer a few general observations before closing this study. It has been argued throughout the book that so far as the international system is concerned, wealth and power, or economic strength and military strength, are always relative and should be seen as such. Since they are relative, and since all societies are subject to the inexorable tendency to change, then the international balances can *never* be still, and it is a folly of statesmanship to assume that they ever would be. Given the anarchic and competitive nature of rivalries between nations, the history of international affairs over the past five centuries has all too frequently been a history of warfare, or at least of preparation for warfare—both of which consume resources which societies might use for other "goods," whether public or private. Whatever the stage of economic and scientific development reached,

536

each century has therefore witnessed a debate about the extent to which national wealth ought to be used for military purposes. It has also recorded a debate about how best to enhance national prosperity, not only because of the individual benefits which increased wealth brings, but also because of the recognition that economic growth, productivity, flourishing finances, will all affect a Great Power's relative prospects if another international conflict occurs. Indeed, the outcome of all of the major, lengthy wars among the Great Powers which have been surveyed here repeatedly points to the crucial influences of productive economic forces—both during the struggle itself, and during those periods *between* wars when differentiated growth rates cause the various Powers to become relatively stronger or weaker. To a large degree, the outcome of the great coalition wars of the period 1500–1945 confirms the shifts which have been taking place, over a longer period, at the economic level. The new territorial order established at the end of each war thus reflects the redistribution of power which has been taking place within the international system. The coming of peace, however, does not stop this process of continual change; and the differentiated pace of economic growth among the Great Powers ensures that they will go on, rising and falling, relative to each other.

Whether the existence of "rising" and "falling" Powers in an anarchical world order must always lead to war is not certain. Most of the historical literature assumed that "war" and "the Great Power system" go hand in hand. Mackinder, one of the founding fathers of neomercantilist and geopolitical thought, held that "the great wars of history . . . are the outcome, direct or indirect, of the unequal growth of nations."[5] But did this pattern cease in 1945? It may indeed be the case that the advent of nuclear weapons, with their built-in threat to turn any exchange of fire into mutual devastation, has finally checked the habit of resorting to armed conflict in response to secular shifts in the Great Power balances, leaving only indirect, small-scale, "surrogate" wars. However, it might also be the case that the mutual apprehensions of nuclear weapons merely ensure that future conflicts, if they occur between the Great Powers, would remain conventional—although even they would be dreadfully bloody affairs, given modern battlefield weaponry.

Obviously, no one knows the answer to such critical questions. Those who assume that mankind would not be so foolish as to become involved in another ruinously expensive Great Power war perhaps need reminding that that belief was also widely held for much of the nineteenth century; and, indeed, Norman Angell's book *The Great Illusion,* which became an international bestseller with its argument that war would be economically disastrous to both victors and vanquished, appeared as late as 1910, as the European general staffs were quietly finalizing their war plans.

Whatever the likelihood of nuclear or conventional clashes between the major states, it is clear that important transformations in the balances *are* occurring, and will continue, probably at a faster pace than before. What is more, they are occurring at the two separate but interacting levels of economic production and strategic power. Unless the trends of the past two decades alter (but why should they?), the *pattern* of world politics looks roughly as follows:

First, there will be a shift, both in shares of total world product and total world military spending, from the five largest concentrations of strength to many more nations; but that will be a gradual process, and no other state is likely to join the present "pentarchy" of the United States, the USSR, China, Japan, and the EEC in the near future.

Secondly, the global productive balances between these five have already begun to tilt in certain directions: away from Russia and the United States, away also from the EEC, to Japan and China. This does not make for a *balanced* five-sided arrangement in economic terms, for the United States and the EEC have roughly the same productive and trading muscle (though the former gains immensely by being a military state); the USSR and Japan are also roughly equal (though Japan is growing the faster), with each having only around two-thirds of the productive power of the previous two; and the PRC is still a long way behind, but growing fastest of all.

Thirdly, in military terms there still exists a bipolar world, in that only the United States and the USSR have the capacity to ensure each other's destruction—and the destruction of any other country. Nevertheless, that bipolarity may be being slowly eroded, both at the *nuclear* level, either because such weapons are unusable under most circumstances, or because China, France, and Britain are each acquiring massive additions to their own nuclear arsenals; and at the *conventional* level, because of the steady buildup of Chinese strength, plus the growing realization that a West German–French (with, possibly, British and Italian) agglomeration of land, sea, and air forces would be an extremely large combination of power, if those nations really could work together effectively. For domestic-political reasons, that is not likely to happen in the near future; but the very fact that such a potential exists places a further uncertainty over the "bipolar" system, at least at the conventional level. By contrast, no one is at present suggesting that Japan will transform itself into a great military Power; yet all acquainted with the pattern of "war and change in world politics" would find it unsurprising if, one day, a different political leadership in Tokyo decided to turn its economic strength into a larger degree of military strength.

If Japan did decide to become a more active military presence in world affairs, it would presumably be because it felt it could no longer preserve its interests by acting simply as a "trading state";[6] in strengthening its armed forces, it would therefore be hoping to enhance its power and influence internationally to an extent that could not be achieved by nonmilitary measures. Yet the history of the past five hundred years of international rivalry demonstrates that military "security" alone is never enough. It may, over the shorter term, deter or defeat rival states (and that, for most political leaders and their publics, is perfectly satisfactory). But if, by such victories, the nation over-extends itself geographically and strategically; if, even at a less imperial level, it chooses to devote a large proportion of its total income to "protection," leaving less for "productive investment," it is likely to find its economic output slowing down, with dire implications for its long-term capacity to maintain both its citizens' consumption demands and its international position.[7] Already this is happening in the case of the USSR, the United States, and Britain; and it is significant that both China and West Germany are struggling to avoid an excessive investment in military spending, both suspecting that it would affect their long-term growth prospects.

We therefore return to the conundrum which has exercised strategists and economists and political leaders from classical times onward. To be a Great Power—by definition, a state capable of holding its own against any other nation[8]—demands a flourishing economic base. In List's words, "War or the very possibility of war makes the establishment of a manufacturing power an indispensable requirement for a nation of the first rank. . . ."[9] Yet by going to war, or by devoting a large share of the nation's "manufacturing power" to expenditures upon "unproductive" armaments, one runs the risk of eroding the national economic base, especially vis-à-vis states which are concentrating a greater share of their income upon productive investment for long-term growth.

All of this was fully recognized by the classical writers on political economy. Those who followed Adam Smith's preferences inclined to keep defense expenditures low; those sympathetic to List's notion of *Nationaloekonomie* wanted to see the state possess greater instruments of force. All of them, if they were honest, admitted that it was really a matter of choice, and a difficult choice at that.[10] Ideally, of course, "profit" and "power" should go hand in hand. Far too often, however, statesmen found themselves confronted with the usual dilemma: between buying military security, at a time of real or perceived danger, which then became a burden upon the national economy; or keeping defense expenditures low, but finding one's interests sometimes threatened by the actions of other states.[11]

The present large Powers in the international system are thus compelled to grapple with the twin challenges which have confronted all their predecessors: first, with the uneven pattern of economic growth, which causes some of them to become wealthier (and, usually, stronger), relative to others; and second, with the competitive and occasionally dangerous scene abroad, which forces them to choose between a more immediate military security and a longer-term economic security. *No* general rule will provide the decision-makers of the time with a universally applicable course of action. If they neglect to provide adequate military defenses, they may be unable to respond if a rival Power takes advantage of them; if they spend too much on armaments—or, more usually, upon maintaining at growing cost the military obligations they had assumed in a previous period—they are likely to overstrain themselves, like an old man attempting to work beyond his natural strength. None of this is made easier by the "law of the increasing cost of war."[12] Even if, to take the most often cited example, one actually can prevent the entire U.S. Air Force budget from being consumed by the production of a *single* aircraft in the year 2020, the cost escalation of modern weaponry is an alarming tendency for all governments—and their taxpayers.

Each of today's large Powers—the United States, the USSR, China, Japan, and (putatively) the EEC—is therefore left grappling with the age-old dilemmas of rise and fall, with the shifting pace of productive growth, with technological innovation, with changes in the international scene, with the spiraling cost of weapons, with alterations in the power balances. Those are not developments which can be controlled by any one state, or individual. To paraphrase Bismarck's famous remark, all of these Powers are traveling on "the stream of Time," which they can "neither create nor direct," but upon which they can "steer with more or less skill and experience."[13] How they emerge from that voyage depends, to a large degree, upon the wisdom of the governments in Washington, Moscow, Tokyo, Peking, and the various European capitals. The above analysis has tried to suggest what the prospects are likely to be for each of those polities and, in consequence, for the Great Power system as a whole. But that still leaves an awful lot depending upon the "skill and experience" with which they manage to sail on "the stream of Time."

Notes

CHAPTER ONE
The Rise of the Western World

1. W. H. McNeill, *A World History* (London, 1979 edn.), p. 295; idem, *The Rise of the West* (Chicago, 1967), p. 565; J. M. Roberts, *The Pelican History of the World* (Harmondsworth, Mdssx., 1980), p. 519; G. Barraclough (ed.), *The Times Atlas of World History* (London, 1978), p. 153.
2. For surveys of international relations in Europe around 1500, see *The New Cambridge Modern History* (hereafter *NCMH*), vol. 1, *The Renaissance 1493–1520*, ed. G. R. Potter (Cambridge, 1961), espec. chs. 7–14; vol. 2, *The Reformation 1520–1529*, ed. G. R. Elton (Cambridge, 1958), chs. 10–11 and 16; G. R. Elton, *Reformation Europe 1517–1559* (London, 1963), ch. 2; G. Mattingly, *Renaissance Diplomacy* (Harmondsworth, Mddsx., 1965), pp. 115ff.
3. There are succinct accounts of Ming China in McNeill, *Rise of the West*, pp. 524–34; and Roberts, *History of the World*, pp. 424–44. For more detail, C. O. Hucker, *China's Imperial Past* (Stanford, Calif., 1975), pp. 303ff; J. A. Harrison, *The Chinese Empire* (New York, 1972); W. Eberhard, *A History of China* (2nd edn., London, 1960), pp. 232–70; M. Elvin, *The Pattern of the Chinese Past* (London, 1973).
4. Y. Shiba, *Commerce and Society in Sung China* (Ann Arbor, Mich., 1970); J. Needham, *The Development of Iron and Steel Technology in China* (London, 1958); L.-S. Yang, *Money and Credit in China* (Cambridge, Mass., 1952); and espec. W. H. McNeill, *The Pursuit of Power: Technology, Armed Forces and Society Since 1000 A.D.* (Chicago, 1983), ch. 2.
5. The great source (in English) for the above is J. Needham, *Science and Civilization in China*, vol. 4, pt. 3, *Civil Engineering and Nautics* (Cambridge, 1971), espec. pp. 379–536; but see also Lo Jung-pang, "The Emergence of China as a Sea Power During the Late Sung and Early Yuan Periods," *Far Eastern Quarterly*, vol. 14 (1955), pp. 489–503; C. G. Reynolds, *Command of the Sea: The History and Strategy of Maritime Empires* (New York, 1974), pp. 98–104.
6. For what follows, see McNeill, *World History*, pp. 254–55; Needham, *Science and Civilization in China*, vol. 4, pt. 3, pp. 524ff; R. Dawson, *Imperial China* (London, 1972), pp. 230ff; Lo Jung-pang, "The Decline of the Early Ming Navy," *Orient Extremus*, vol. 5 (1958), pp. 149–68; and Ho Ping-Ti, "Economic and Institutional Factors in the Decline of the Chinese Empire," in C. C. Cipolla (ed.), *The Economic Decline of Empires* (London, 1970), pp. 274–76, although in general the picture given is less gloomy than other accounts. See also the careful comparisons in J. Needham, *The Grand Titration: Science and Society*

in East and West (London, 1969), passim; and in E. L. Jones, *The European Miracle: Environments, Economies and Geopolitics in the History of Europe and Asia* (Cambridge, 1981).

7. Jones, *European Miracle*, ch. 9; F. Braudel, *The Mediterranean and the Mediterranean World in the Age of Philip II*, 2 vols. (London, 1972), vol. 2, pp. 661ff; P. Wittek, *The Rise of the Ottoman Empire* (London, 1938); H. Inalcik, *The Ottoman Empire: The Classical Age 1300–1600* (New York, 1973); M. A. Cook (ed.), *A History of the Ottoman Empire to 1730* (Cambridge, 1976); M.G.S. Hodgson, *The Venture of Islam*, vols. 2 and 3 (Chicago/London, 1924); C. M. Kortepeter, *Ottoman Imperialism During the Reformation* (London, 1973).

8. A. C. Hess, "The Evolution of the Ottoman Seaborne Empire in the Age of the Oceanic Discoveries, 1453–1525," *American Historical Review*, vol. 75, no. 7 (December 1970), pp. 1892–1919; Braudel, *Mediterranean*, vol. 2, pp. 918ff; Reynolds, *Command of the Sea*, pp. 112ff; and the comments in J. F. Guilmartin, *Gunpowder and Galleys: Changing Technology and Mediterranean Warfare at Sea in the Sixteenth Century* (Cambridge, 1974).

9. Jones, *European Miracle*, pp. 176ff; Cook (ed.), *History of the Ottoman Empire*, espec. pp. 103ff; B. Lewis, "Some Reflections on the Decline of the Ottoman Empire," in Cipolla (ed.), *Economic Decline of Empires*, pp. 215–34; H.A.R. Gibbs and H. Bowen, *Islamic Society and the West*, vol. 1, 2 pts. (London, 1950 and 1957), pt. 1, pp. 273ff.; pt. 2, pp. 1–37. See also H. Inalcik, *The Ottoman Empire: Conquest, Organization and Economy: Collected Studies* (London, 1978), chs. 10–13.

10. Jones, *European Miracle*, p. 182.

11. For the gloomy side, see ibid., ch. 10; Roberts, *History of the World*, pp. 415–23; W. H. Moreland, *From Akbar to Aurangzeb: A Study in Indian Economic History* (London, 1923); M. D. Morris, "Values as an Obstacle to Economic Growth in South Asia," *Journal of Economic History*, vol. 27 (1967), pp. 588–607. For a brighter presentation, A. J. Qaisar, *The Indian Response to European Technology and Culture, A.D. 1498–1707* (Delhi, India, 1982), passim; and, for a slightly later period, C. A. Bayley, *Rulers, Townsmen and Bazaars* (Cambridge, 1983).

12. McNeill, *Rise of the West*, pp. 645–49; Jones, *European Miracle*, pp. 157–59; R. Bendix, *Kings or People: Power and the Mandate to Rule* (Berkeley/Los Angeles, 1978), pp. 431ff; G. B. Sansom, *The Western World and Japan* (London, 1950), pp. 3–208; idem, *A History of Japan*, vols. 2–3 (London, 1961 and 1964); C. R. Boxer, *The Christian Century in Japan 1549–1650* (Berkeley, 1951); J. W. Hall, *Government and Local Power in Japan* (Princeton, 1966); D. M. Brown, "The Impact of Firearms on Japanese Warfare," *Far Eastern Quarterly*, vol. 7 (1947), pp. 236–45; R. P. Toby, *State and Diplomacy in Early Modern Japan* (Princeton, N.J., 1984).

13. McNeill, *World History*, pp. 328–43; Bendix, *Kings or People*, pp. 491ff; I. Wallerstein, *The Modern World System*, vol. 1, *Capitalist Agriculture and the Origins of the European World-Economy in the Sixteenth Century* (New York/London, 1974), pp. 301–24; G. Vernadsky, *The Tsardom of Muscovy 1547–1682* (New Haven, Conn., 1969); R. H. Fisher, *The Russian Fur Trade 1550–1700* (Berkeley, Calif., 1943); M. Florinsky, *Russia: A Short History* (New York, 1964), chs. 3–9; R. J. Kerner, *The Urge to the Sea* (New York, 1971 reprint); T. Szamuely, *The Russian Traditions* (London, 1974); L. Kochan and R. Abraham, *The Making of Modern Russia* (Harmondsworth, Mddsx., 2nd edn., 1983), chs. 3–6.

14. See Roberts, *History of the World*, p. 585: "So little was Russia known even in the [seventeenth] century that a French king could write to the Tsar, not knowing that the prince whom he addressed had been dead for ten years." Note

also the condescending remarks of English traders in Russia in Kochan and Abraham, *Making of Modern Russia*, pp. 56–57.

15. This is the title, of course, of E. L. Jones's impressive book. It, and the important work by W. H. McNeill, *The Pursuit of Power*, have strongly influenced my argument in the following paragraphs. See also McNeill, *Rise of the West*, passim; Wallerstein, *Modern World System*; D. C. North and R. P. Thomas, *The Rise of the Western World* (Cambridge, 1973); J. H. Parry, *The Establishment of the European Hegemony 1415–1715* (3rd edn., New York, 1966); S. Viljoen, *Economic Systems in World History* (London, 1974), passim; P. Chaunu, *European Expansion in the Later Middle Ages* (Amsterdam, 1979).

16. H. C. Darby, "The Face of Europe on the Eve of the Great Discoveries," in *NCMH*, vol. 1, pp. 20–49; N. J. G. Pounds and S. S. Ball, "Core-Areas and the Development of the European States System," *Annals of the Association of American Geographers*, vol. 54 (1964), pp. 24–40; R. G. Wesson, *State Systems: International Relations, Politics and Culture* (New York, 1978), p. 111; Jones, *European Miracle*, ch. 7.

17. N. J. G. Pounds, *An Historical Geography of Europe 1500–1840* (Cambridge, 1979), ch. 1; C. Cipolla, *Before the Industrial Revolution: European Society and Economy 1000–1700* (2nd edn., London, 1980), passim; C. Cipolla (ed.), *The Fontana Economic History of Europe*, vol. 1, *The Middle Ages* (London, 1972), ch. 7; E. Samhaber, *Merchants Make History* (London, 1963), pp. 130ff.; Wallerstein, *Modern World System*, vol. 1, pp. 42ff.; Braudel, *Mediterranean*, vol. 1, pp. 188–224.

18. Roberts, *History of the World*, pp. 505–6; J. H. Parry, *The Age of Reconnaissance* (2nd edn., London, 1966), pp. 60ff.

19. Quoted in Jones, *European Miracle*, p. 235.

20. McNeill, *Pursuit of Power*, ch. 3; J. U. Nef, *War and Human Progress* (New York, 1968 edn.), ch. 2; R. A. Preston, S. F. Wise, and H. O. Werner, *Men in Arms* (London, 1962), ch. 7; C. Cipolla, *Guns and Sails in the Early Phase of European Expansion 1400–1700* (London, 1965), passim; and R. Bean, "War and the Birth of the Nation State," *Journal of Economic History*, vol. 33 (1973), pp. 203–21.

21. One is bound to put quotation marks around the word "national," since so many men in the French army were mercenaries: see V. G. Kiernan, "Foreign Mercenaries and Absolute Monarchy," *Past and Present*, vol. 11 (1957), p. 72. For the general comments above, see McNeill, *Pursuit of Power*, ch. 3; H. Thomas, *History of the World* (New York, 1979 edn.), ch. 24; M. E. Mallet, *Mercenaries and Their Masters: Warfare in Renaissance Italy* (London, 1976); and J. R. Hale, "Armies, Navies and the Art of War," *NCMH*, vol. 2, espec. pp. 486ff; idem, *War and Society in Renaissance Europe 1450–1620* (London, 1985), ch. 2.

22. Cipolla, *Guns and Sails*, passim; Nef, *War and Human Progress*, pp. 46ff.

23. C. Duffy, *Siege Warfare: The Fortress in the Early Modern World 1494–1660* (London, 1979), chs. 1–2; McNeill, *Pursuit of Power*, ch. 3; Wesson, *State Systems*, pp. 112ff; Braudel, *Mediterranean*, vol. 2., pp. 845ff; J. R. Hale, "The Early Development of the Bastion: An Italian Chronology c. 1450—c.1534," in Hale et al. (eds.), *Europe in the Later Middle Ages* (London, 1965), pp. 466–94.

24. For what follows, see Parry, *Age of Reconnaissance*, ch. VII; Reynolds, *Command of the Sea*, pp. 106ff; P. Padfield, *Guns at Sea* (London, 1973), pt. 1; G. V. Scammell, *The World Encompassed: The First European Maritime Empires, c. 800–1650* (Berkeley, Calif., 1981), which places the fifteenth-century voyages in the broader sweep of European expansionism.

25. Jones, *European Miracle*, p. 80. The importance of "efficient economic organi-

zation" is also repeatedly stressed in North and Thomas, *Rise of the Western World*, p. 1 and passim.

26. This is the thrust of Guilmartin's excellent study, *Gunpowder and Galleys*, passim.

27. For the Portuguese experience, see Parry, *Age of Reconnaissance;* P. Padfield, *Tide of Empires: Decisive Naval Campaigns in the Rise of the West*, vol. 1, *1481–1654* (London, 1979), ch. 2; C. R. Boxer, *The Portuguese Seaborne Empire 1415–1825* (London, 1969); V. Magalhaes-Godinho, *L'économie de l'Empire Portugais aux XVe et XVIe siècles* (Paris, 1969); B. W. Diffie and C. D. Winius, *Foundations of the Portuguese Empire 1415–1580* (Minneapolis, 1977); Wallerstein, *Modern World System*, p. 325ff; Braudel, *Mediterranean*, vol. 2, pp. 1174–76; Scammell, *World Encompassed*, ch. 5.

28. P. M. Kennedy, *The Rise and Fall of British Naval Mastery* (London/New York, 1976), p. 18.

29. Padfield, *Tide of Empires*, vol. 1, p. 49.

30. Whether the Portuguese government itself benefited so much is more doubtful: see M. Newitt, "Plunder and the Rewards of Office in the Portuguese Empire," in M. Duffy (ed.), *The Military Revolution and the State 1500–1800* (Exeter Studies in History, Exeter, 1980), pp. 10–28;. and W. Reinhard, *Geschichte der europäischen Expansion*, vol. 1 (Stuttgart, 1983), ch. 3 and 5.

31. Wallerstein, *Modern World System*, p. 170; C. H. Haring, *The Spanish Empire in America* (New York, 1947); Parry, *Spanish Seaborne Empire*, passim; Scammell, *World Encompassed*, ch. 6; C. Gibson, *Spain in America* (New York, 1966).

32. Wallerstein, *Modern World System*. See also Jones, *European Miracle*, ch. 4; Parry, *Age of Reconnaissance*, pt. 3; Roberts, *History of the World*, pp. 600ff; *Cambridge Economic History of Europe*, vol. 4, *The Economy of Expanding Europe in the Sixteenth and Seventeenth Centuries* (Cambridge, 1967), passim. A sensible warning against *anticipating* a real "world system" is contained in R. A. Dodgshon, "A Spatial Perspective," *Peasant Studies*, vol. 6, no. 1 (January 1977), pp. 8–19.

33. For the beginnings of this challenge to the Iberian trading monopoly overseas, see *NCMH*, vol. 1, ch. 16, and vol. 3, ch. 17; Padfield, *Tide of Empires*, ch. 4; Scammell, *World Encompassed*, ch. 7 and 9.

34. K. Mendelsohn, *Science and Western Domination* (London, 1976), passim; Nef, *War and Human Progress*, ch. 3; Elton, *Reformation Europe*, pp. 292ff; McNeill, *Rise of the West*, pp. 592–98; Cipolla (ed.), *Fontana Economic History of Europe*, vol. 2, ch. 3; A. Wolf, *A History of Science, Technology and Philosophy in the Sixteenth and Seventeenth Centuries* (New York, 1935).

35. Jones, *European Miracle*, pp. 170–71 and passim; and cf. A. G. Frank, *World Accumulation 1492–1789* (New York/London, 1978), pp. 137ff.

36. See again Mendelssohn, *Science and Western Domination*, which stresses the importance of scientific observation and prediction; and McNeill, *Rise of the West*, pp. 593–99.

CHAPTER TWO
The Habsburg Bid for Mastery, 1519–1659

1. C. Oman, *A History of the Art of War in the Sixteenth Century* (London, 1937), p. 3. For the earlier wars, see idem, *A History of the Art of War in the Middle Ages*, 2 vols. (London, 1924).

2. See the warning about this in G. R. Elton, *Reformation Europe 1517–1559* (London, 1963), pp. 305ff.

3. Ibid., p. 35.

4. R. A. Stradling, *Europe and the Decline of Spain: A Study of the Spanish System, 1580–1720* (London/Boston, 1981), p. 44.

5. For example, Gattinara's declaration to Charles V that "God has set you on the path towards a world monarchy," quoted in *NCMH*, vol. 2, pp. 301ff.; and the quotations in H. Kamen, *Spain 1469–1714* (London, 1983), p. 67.

6. Oman, *War in the Sixteenth Century*, p. 5. This book remains the best *military* narrative for this period. Useful succinct accounts of these 140 years are in the three relevant volumes of *Fontana History of Europe*: G. R. Elton, *Reformation Europe 1517–1559* (London, 1963); J. H. Elliott, *Europe Divided 1559–1598* (London, 1968); and G. Parker, *Europe in Crisis 1598–1648* (London, 1979). See also *NCMH*, vols. 2–5; and H. G. Koenigsberger, *The Habsburgs and Europe 1516–1660* (Ithaca/London, 1971).

7. *NCMH*, vol. 2, ch. 11 and 17.

8. V. S. Mamatey, *Rise of the Habsburg Empire 1526–1815* (Huntingdon, N.Y., 1978 edn.), p. 9.

9. Details in Oman, *War in the Sixteenth Century*, pp. 703ff; Braudel, *Mediterranean World*, vol. 2, pp. 904–1237.

10. H. C. Koenigsberger, "Western Europe and the Power of Spain," in *NCMH*, vol. 3, pp. 234–318; G. Parker, *Spain and the Netherlands 1559–1659* (London, 1979), passim; C. Wilson, *The Transformation of Europe 1558–1648* (London, 1976), chs. 8–9.

11. The international nature of the rivalry is well covered in Parker, "The Dutch Revolt and the Polarization of International Politics," in *Spain and the Netherlands*, pp. 74ff; and, for a more economic/social interpretation, J. V. Polisensky, *The Thirty Years War* (London, 1971), espec. ch. 4.

12. C. V. Wedgewood, *The Thirty Years War* (London, 1964 edn.), chs. 3–6.

13. Parker, *Europe in Crisis*, p. 252; J. H. Elliott, *The Count-Duke of Olivares* (New Haven, Conn., 1986), p. 495.

14. Parker, *Spain and the Netherlands*, pp. 54–77; C. R. Boxer, *The Dutch Seaborne Empire 1600–1800* (London, 1972), pp. 25–26.

15. For the final years of conflict, see Stradling, *Europe and the Decline of Spain*, chs. 2–4; J. Stoye, *Europe Unfolding 1648–1688* (London, 1969), chs. 3–4.

16. Apart from specific works cited in the notes below, this section has been much influenced by a number of excellent studies of Spanish imperial power, namely: J. H. Elliott, *Imperial Spain 1469–1716* (Harmondsworth, Mddsx., 1970); J. Lynch, *Spain Under the Habsburgs*, 2 vols. (Oxford, 1964 and 1969); Stradling, *Europe and the Decline of Spain*, passim. Also used were two older works, R. Trevor Davies, *The Golden Century of Spain 1501–1621* (London, 1937); and B. Chudoba, *Spain and the Empire 1519–1643* (New York, 1969 edn.). Finally, there is John Elliott's thoughtful article, reproduced in Cipolla (ed.), *Economic Decline of Empires*, as "The Decline of Spain," pp. 168–95.

17. Koenigsberger, *Habsburgs and Europe*, p. xi.

18. R. Ehrenberg, *Das Zeitalter der Fugger: Geldkapital und Creditverkehr im 16. Jahrhundert*, 2 vols. (Jena, 1896); E. Samhaber, *Merchants Make History* (London, 1963), ch. 8; and see the broad recent survey by G. Parker, "The Emergence of Modern Finance in Europe 1500–1730," in Cipolla (ed.), *Fontana Economic History of Europe*, vol. 2, pp. 527–89.

19. *NCMH*, vol. 1, ch. 7; R. A. Kann, *A History of the Habsburg Empire 1526–1918* (Berkeley/Los Angeles/London, 1974), chs. 1–2.

20. Lynch, *Spain Under the Habsburgs*, vol. 1, p. 77.

21. M. Roberts, "The Military Revolution, 1560–1660," in Roberts, *Essays in Swedish History* (London, 1967), pp. 195–225; G. Parker, " 'The Military Revolution,

1560–1660'—a Myth?" in Parker, *Spain and the Netherlands*, pp. 86–105; M. van Creveld, *Supplying War: Logistics from Wallenstein to Patton* (Cambridge, 1977), pp. 5–6; J. R. Hale, "Armies, Navies, and the Art of War," in *NCMH*, vol. 2, pp. 481–509, and vol. 3, pp. 171–208; McNeill, *Pursuit of Power*, ch. 4; R. Bean, "War and the Birth of the Nation State," *Journal of Economic History*, vol. 33 (1973), pp. 203–21.

22. G. Parker, *The Army of Flanders and the Spanish Road 1567–1659: The Logistics of Spanish Victory and Defeat in the Low Countries War* (Cambridge, 1972), p. 6.

23. I.A.A. Thompson, *War and Government in Habsburg Spain 1560–1620* (London, 1976), p. 16; more generally, see Reynolds, *Command of the Sea*, chs. 4–6.

24. Lynch, *Spain Under the Habsburgs*, vol. 1, pp. 53–58.

25. Ibid., p. 128. See also Parker, *Army of Flanders and the Spanish Road*, ch. 6.

26. Braudel, *Mediterranean World*, vol. 2, p. 841; and, for a full breakdown, Parker, "Lepanto (1571): the Costs of Victory," in *Spain and the Netherlands*, pp. 122–34.

27. *NCMH*, vol. 3, pp. 275ff.; Parker, "Why Did the Dutch Revolt Last So Long?", and "Mutiny and Discontent in the Spanish Army of Flanders 1572–1607," in *Spain and the Netherlands*, pp. 45–64, 106–21.

28. Thompson, *War and Government in Habsburg Spain*, ch. 3.

29. Ibid., pp. 36ff, 89ff; Lynch, *Spain Under the Habsburgs*, vol. 2, pp. 30ff.

30. For further details, see J. Regla, "Spain and Her Empire," in *NCMH*, vol. 5, pp. 319–83; Lynch, *Spain Under the Habsburgs*, vol. 2, chs. 4–5; Elliott, *Imperial Spain*, ch. 10; Stradling, *Europe and the Decline of Spain*, chs. 3–5; but see also Kamen, *Spain 1469–1714*, arguing for a later "recovery."

31. See the interesting remarks of Braudel about the disadvantages facing the two "overlarge" empires of Spain and Islam, in *Mediterranean World*, vol. 2, pp. 701–03.

32. The fluctuations of Spanish effort from one theater to another are nicely charted in Parker, "Spain, Her Enemies and the Revolt of the Netherlands, 1559–1648," in *Spain and the Netherlands*, pp. 17–42.

33. Lynch, *Spain Under the Habsburgs*, vol. 1, p. 347.

34. Ibid., vol. 2, p. 70.

35. E. Heischmann, *Die Anfänge des stehenden Heeres in Oesterreich* (Vienna, 1925).

36. *NCMH*, vol. 5, chs. 18 and 20; Kann, *History of the Habsburg Empire*.

37. See the excellent analysis of the war in the Netherlands in Duffy, *Siege Warfare*, ch. 4.

38. Parker, *Spain and the Netherlands*, pp. 185, 188.

39. Idem, *Army of Flanders and the Spanish Road*, pp. 50ff.

40. *NCMH*, vol. 3, p. 308.

41. Cited in Parker, *Europe in Crisis*, p. 238.

42. Ibid., p. 239.

43. For what follows, see Kamen, *Spain 1469–1714*, pp. 81ff, 161ff, 214ff; H. G. Koenigsberger, "The Empire of Charles V in Europe," in *NCMH*, vol. 2, pp. 301–33; and the extended version in Koenigsberger, *Habsburgs and Europe*, passim.

44. H. G. Koenigsberger, *The Government of Sicily Under Philip II* (London, 1951), passim.

45. Idem, *The Habsburgs and Europe*, passim; and see also the excellent new study by D. Stella, *Crisis and Continuity: The Economy of Spanish Lombardy in the Seventeenth Century* (Cambridge, Mass., 1979).

46. Parker, *Spain and the Netherlands*, pp. 21–22.

47. *NCMH*, vol. 1, pp. 450ff, and vol. 2, pp. 320ff; Elliott, *Imperial Spain*, chs. 5 and 8; Lynch, *Spain Under the Habsburgs*, vol. 1, pp. 53ff and passim, and vol. 2, pp. 3ff.

48. For what follows, see Cipolla, *Before the Industrial Revolution*, pp. 250ff; J. V. Vives, "The Decline of Spain in the Seventeenth Century," in Cipolla (ed.), *Economic Decline of Empires*, pp. 121–67, Davies, *Golden Century of Spain*, chs. 3 and 8; Wallerstein, *Modern World System*, vol. 1, pp. 191ff; as well as the books by Elliott and Lynch.

49. Cipolla, *Guns and Sails*, p. 33; Thompson, *War and Government in Habsburg Spain*, p. 25.

50. D. Maland, *Europe in the Seventeenth Century* (London, 1966), p. 214; Lynch, *Spain Under the Habsburgs*, vol. 2, pp. 139ff. But this Spanish policy of tolerating trade with their Dutch enemies was often reversed, as is made clear in Israel's article, note 82 below.

51. Thompson, *War and Government in Habsburg Spain*, p. i; Parker, *Europe in Crisis*, pp. 71–75; more generally, Hale, *War and Society in Renaissance Europe*, chs. 8–9.

52. Parker, *Spain and the Netherlands*, p. 96.

53. *NCMH*, vol. 2, p. 472.

54. Ibid., vol. 1, ch. 10; and espec. M. Wolfe, *The Fiscal System of Renaissance France* (New Haven/London, 1972), chs. 2–3.

55. Oman, *War in the Sixteenth Century*, pp. 393–536, gives the military details of the French wars. For the politics, see J.H.M. Salmon, *Society in Crisis: France in the Sixteenth Century* (London, 1975), passim; and R. Briggs, *Early Modern France 1560–1715* (Oxford, 1977), ch. 1.

56. Nef, *War and Human Progress*, pp. 103ff; Wolfe, *Fiscal System of Renaissance France*, ch. 8; Salmon, *Society in Crisis*, pp. 301ff; E. J. Hamilton, "Origin and Growth of National Debt in Western Europe," *American Economic Review*, vol. 37, no. 2 (1947), pp. 119–20.

57. *NCMH*, vol. 3, pp. 314–17; Wolfe, *Fiscal System of Renaissance France*, ch. 8; Salmon, *Society in Crisis*, ch. 12; Briggs, *Early Modern France*, pp. 80ff; Parker, *Europe in Crisis*, pp. 119–22.

58. Parker, *Europe in Crisis*, pp. 17ff, 246ff; J. B. Wolf, *Toward a European Balance of Power 1620–1715* (Chicago, 1970), pp. 17–19.

59. A. Guery, "Les finances de la monarchie Française," *Annales*, vol. 33, no. 2 (1978), pp. 216–39, espec. pp. 228–30, 236. The similarity of the strains upon both France and Spain is well argued in J. H. Elliott, *Richelieu and Olivares* (Cambridge, 1984), especially chs. 3 and 5–6; and in M. S. Kimmell, "War, State Finance, and Revolution," in P. McGowan and C. W. Kegley (eds.), *Foreign Policy and the Modern World-System* (Beverly Hills, Calif., 1983), pp. 89–124.

60. E. H. Jenkins, *A History of the French Navy* (London, 1973), ch. 4; Briggs, *Early Modern France*, pp. 128–44; Parker, *Europe in Crisis*, pp. 276ff.

61. R. Stradling, "Catastrophe and Recovery: The Defeat of Spain 1639–43," *History*, vol. 64, no. 211 (June 1979), pp. 205–19.

62. On English economic history in this period, see Cipolla, *Before the Industrial Revolution*, pp. 276–96; D. C. Coleman, *The Economy of England 1450–1750* (Oxford, 1977); B. Murphy, *A History of the British Economy* (London, 1973), pt. 1, ch. 4; C. Hill, *Reformation to Industrial Revolution* (Harmondsworth, Mddsx. 1969); R. Davis, *English Overseas Trade 1500–1700* (London, 1973). Among the more prominent political surveys are G. R. Elton, *England Under the Tudors* (London, 1955); D. M. Loades, *Politics and the Nation 1450–1660* (London, 1974), pp. 118ff; and P. Williams, *The Tudor Regime* (Oxford, 1979), espec. chs. 2 and 9. On the crown's finances, see the older work F. C. Dietz,

English Public Finance 1485–1641, vol. 1, *English Government Finance 1485–1558* (London, 1964 edn.).

63. Nef, *War and Human Progress*, pp. 10–12, 71–73, 87–88.

64. C. Barnett, *Britain and Her Army 1509–1970: A Military, Political and Social Survey* (London, 1970), ch. 1; Oman, *War in the Sixteenth Century*, pp. 285ff; G. J. Millar, *Tudor Mercenaries and Auxiliaries 1485–1547* (Charlottesville, Va., 1980). For the later period, see C. G. Cruikshank, *Elizabeth's Army* (2nd edn., Oxford, 1966).

65. Williams, *Tudor Regime*, pp. 64ff; Dietz, *English Government Finance*, chs. 7–14; Hill, *Reformation to Industrial Revolution*, ch. 6; P. S. Crowson, *Tudor Foreign Policy* (London, 1973), ch. 25.

66. K. R. Andrews, *Elizabethan Privateering* (Cambridge, 1964); indem, *Trade, Plunder and Settlement* (Cambridge, 1983); Padfield, *Tide of Empires*, vol. 1, pp. 120ff; D. B. Quinn and A. N. Ryan, *England's Sea Empire, 1550–1642* (London, 1983), ch. 5; Scammell, *World Encompassed*, pp. 465ff.

67. As quoted in Kennedy, *British Naval Mastery*, p. 28. See also M. Howard, "The British Way in Warfare" (Neale Lecture, London, 1975); Barnett, *Britain and Her Army*, pp. 25ff, 51ff; R. B. Wernham, "Elizabethan War Aims and Strategy," in *Elizabethan Government and Society*, ed. S. T. Bindoff, J. Hurstfield, and C. H. Williams (London, 1961), pp. 340–68. See also the two general surveys by Wernham, *Before the Armada: The Growth of English Foreign Policy 1485–1588* (London, 1966), and *The Making of Elizabethan Foreign Policy 1588–1603* (Berkeley/Los Angeles/London, 1980).

68. For these figures, see F. C. Dietz, "The Exchequer in Elizabeth's Reign," *Smith College Studies in History*, vol. 8, no. 2 (January 1923); idem, *English Public Finance 1485–1641*, vol. 2, *1558–1641*, chs. 2–5; W. R. Scott, *The Constitution and Finance of English, Scottish and Irish Joint Stock Companies to 1720*, 3 vols. (Cambridge, 1912), vol. 3, pp. 485–544.

69. Loades, *Politics and the Nation*, pp. 301ff; R. Ashton, *The Crown and the Money Market 1603–1640* (Oxford, 1960), passim, espec. chs. 2 and 7.

70. R. Ashton, *The English Civil War: Conservatism and Revolution 1603–1649* (London, 1979); C. Hill, *The Century of Revolution 1603–1714* (Edinburgh, 1961), pt. 1; C. Russell (ed.), *The Origins of the English Civil War* (London, 1973); L. Stone, *The Causes of the English Revolution 1529–1642* (London, 1972); Loades, *Politics and the Nation*, pp. 327ff.

71. Kennedy, *British Naval Mastery*, pp. 44ff; Barnett, *Britain and Her Army*, pp. 90ff; Hill, *Reformation to Industrial Revolution*, pp. 155ff; J. R. Jones, *Britain and the World 1649–1815* (London, 1980), pp. 51ff. See also two important German studies: B. Martin, "Aussenhandel und Aussenpolitik Englands unter Cromwell," *Historische Zeitschrift*, vol. 218, no. 3 (June 1974), pp. 571–92; and H. C. Junge, *Flottenpolitik und Revolution: Die Entstehung der englischen Seemacht während der Herrschaft Cromwells* (Stuttgart, 1980).

72. M. Ashley, *Financial and Commercial Policy Under the Cromwellian Protectorate* (London, 1962 edn.), p. 48.

73. C. Hill, *Century of Revolution*, p. 161.

74. North and Thomas, *Rise of the Western World*, pp. 118, 150, and passim.

75. What follows relies heavily upon the writings of Michael Roberts, not only his classic *Gustavus Adolphus*, 2 vols. (London, 1958), but also his broader surveys: *Essays in Swedish History* (London, 1967); *Gustavus Adolphus and the Rise of Sweden* (London, 1973); (ed.), *Sweden's Age of Greatness, 1632–1718* (London, 1973); and *The Swedish Imperial Experience 1560–1718* (Cambridge, 1979).

76. Cipolla, *Guns and Sails*, pp. 52ff; Roberts, *Gustavus Adolphus*, vol. 2, pp. 107ff;

Wallerstein, *Modern World System*, vol. 2, pp. 203ff; and E. F. Heckscher, *An Economic History of Sweden* (Cambridge, Mass., 1963), ch. 4, espec. pp. 101ff.

77. There is a brief summary of the reforms in Roberts, *Gustavus Adolphus and the Rise of Sweden*, chs. 6–7; full details in idem, *Gustavus Adolphus*, vol. 2, pp. 63–304.

78. See F. Redlich, "Contributions in the Thirty Years War," *Economic History Review*, 2nd series, vol. 12 (1959), pp. 247–54, as well as his larger work, *The German Military Enterpriser and His Work Force*, 2 vols. (Wiesbaden, 1964). M. Ritter, "Das Kontributionssystem Wallensteins," *Historische Zeitschrift*, vol. 90 (1902), and A. Ernstberger, *Hans de Witte: Finanzmann Wallensteins* (Wiesbaden, 1954), have further details. For Sweden, see Roberts, *Gustavus Adolphus and the Rise of Sweden*, ch. 8; and S. Lundkvist, "Svensk krigsfinansiering 1630–1635," *Historisk tidskrift*, 1966, pp. 377–421, with a German summary.

79. Roberts, "Charles XI," in *Essays in Swedish History*, p. 233.

80. Idem, *Swedish Imperial Experience*, pp. 132–37.

81. Ibid., p. 51.

82. G. Parker, *The Dutch Revolt* (London, 1977), supersedes all other accounts of the sixteenth-century phase of the "Eighty Years War." For the later struggle, see the important article by J. I. Israel, "A Conflict of Empires: Spain and the Netherlands, 1618–1648," *Past and Present*, no. 76 (1977), pp. 34–74; and idem, *The Dutch Republic and the Hispanic World, 1606–1661* (Oxford, 1982).

83. G. Gash, *Renaissance Armies 1480–1650* (Cambridge, 1975), p. 106.

84. C. Wilson, *The Dutch Republic and the Civilization of the Seventeenth Century* (London, 1968), p. 31. See also Wallerstein, *Modern World System*, vol. 1, pp. 199ff; vol. 2, ch. 2.

85. Quoted from Parker, *Dutch Revolt*, p. 249; Reynolds, *Command of the Sea*, pp. 158ff; Boxer, *Dutch Seaborne Empire*, passim; Padfield, *Tide of Empires*, vol. 1, ch. 5; Scammell, *World Encompassed*, ch. 7.

86. On this "shift" from the Mediterranean to the Atlantic world, see Cipolla, *Before the Industrial Revolution*, ch. 10; Braudel, *Mediterranean World*, vol. 2; Wallerstein, *Modern World System*, vols. 1 and 2; and R. T. Rapp, "The Unmaking of the Mediterranean Trade Hegemony," *Journal of Economic History*, vol. 35 (1975), pp. 499–525, with some useful reservations about what was happening.

87. On the losses caused to the United Provinces by the war, see Parker, "War and Economic Change," passim, and Israel, "Conflict of Empires," passim. On Amsterdam's financial role, and official debts, see Parker, "Emergence of Modern Finance in Europe," pp. 549ff, 573ff; V. Barbour, *Capitalism in Amsterdam in the Seventeenth Century* (Baltimore, 1950), passim; André-E. Sayous, "Le rôle d'Amsterdam dans l'histoire du capitalisme commercial et financier," *Revue Historique*, vol. 183, no. 2 (October–December 1938), pp. 242–80.

88. Bean, "War and the Birth of the Nation State," passim. See also S. E. Finer, "State and Nation-Building in Europe: The Role of the Military," in C. Tilly (ed.), *The Formation of National States in Western Europe* (Princeton, 1975), pp. 84–163.

89. *NCMH*, vol. 3, ch. 16; Wesson, *State Systems*, pp. 121ff; O. Ranum (ed.), *National Consciousness, History and Political Culture in Early-Modern Europe* (Baltimore/London, 1975); and E. D. Marcu, *Sixteenth Century Nationalism* (New York, 1976). This was also seen in the "national" economic theories of the time: see G. H. McCormick, "Strategic Considerations in the Development of Economic Thought," pp. 4–8, in G. H. McCormick and R. E. Bissess (eds.), *Strategic Dimensions of Economic Behavior* (New York, 1984).

90. Among the more general interpretations and syntheses, see Tilly (ed.), *Formation of National States in Western Europe*, passim; Bendix, *Kings or People*, pp.

247ff; Wallerstein, *Modern World System*, vol. 1, ch. 3; V. G. Kiernan, "State and Nation in Western Europe," *Past and Present*, vol. 31 (1965), pp. 20–38; J. H. Shennan, *The Origins of the Modern European State 1450–1725* (London, 1974); H. Lubasz (ed.), *The Development of the Modern State* (New York, 1964).

91. Cited in Creveld, *Supplying War*, p. 17.
92. Ibid., pp. 13–17.
93. See again Elliott, *Richelieu and Olivares*, ch. 6.

CHAPTER THREE
Finance, Geography, and the Winning of Wars, 1660–1815

1. For basic political narratives of this period, see D. McKay and H. M. Scott, *The Rise of the Great Powers 1648–1815* (London, 1983), an excellent survey; *NCMH*, vols. 5–9; W. Doyle, *The Old European Order 1660–1800* (Oxford, 1978); E. N. Williams, *The Ancien Regime in Europe 1648–1789* (Harmondsworth, Mddsx., 1979 edn.). Europe in the outside world is treated in J. H. Parry, *Trade and Dominion: The European Overseas Empire in the Eighteenth Century* (London, 1971); G. Williams, *The Expansion of Europe in the Eighteenth Century* (London, 1966). For cartographical representations of these trends, see G. Barraclough (ed.), *Times Atlas of World History*, pp. 192ff.

2. On military and naval developments generally, see Nef, *War and Human Progress*, pt. 2; Ropp, *War in the Modern World*, chs. 1–4; Preston, Wise, and Werner, *Men in Arms*, chs. 9–12; McNeill, *Pursuit of Power*, chs. 4–6; H. Strachan, *European Armies and the Conduct of War* (London/Boston, 1983), chs. 1–4; J. Childs, *Armies and Warfare in Europe 1648–1789* (Manchester, 1982). On navies, see Reynolds, *Command of the Sea*, chs. 6–9; Kennedy, *Rise and Fall of British Naval Mastery*, chs. 3–5; Padfield, *Tide of Empires*, vol. 2.

3. On these developments, see, in addition to the references in note 2 above, A. Corvisier, *Armies and Societies in Europe 1494–1789* (Bloomington, 1979), espec. pt. 2; Howard, *War in European History*, ch. 4; van Creveld, *Supplying War*, pp. 10ff; C. Tilly (ed.), *The Formation of National States in Western Europe* (Princeton, N.J., 1975), espec. S. E. Finer's essay "State-and-Nation-Building in Europe: The Role of the Military," pp. 84–163.

4. G. Parker, "Emergence of Modern Finance in Europe," passim; Tilly (ed.), *Formation of National States in Western Europe*, chs. 3–4; F. Braudel, *The Wheels of Commerce*, vol. 2 of *Civilization and Capitalism, 15th–18th Centuries* (London, 1982); H. van der Wee, "Monetary, Credit and Banking Systems," in E. R. Rich and C. H. Wilson (eds.), *The Cambridge Economic History of Europe*, vol. 5 (Cambridge, 1977), pp. 290–392; P.G.M. Dickson and J. Sperling, "War Finance, 1689–1714," in *NCMH*, vol. 6, ch. 9. Note also K. A. Rasler and W. R. Thompson, "Global Wars, Public Debts, and the Long Cycle," *World Politics*, vol. 35 (1983), pp. 489–516; and C. Webber and A. Wildavsky, *A History of Taxation and Expenditure in the Western World* (New York, 1986), pp. 250ff.

5. The term refers, of course, to the title of P.G.M. Dickson's excellent book *The Financial Revolution in England: A Study in the Development of Public Credit 1688–1756* (London, 1967).

6. This endless debate is covered in W. Sombart, *Krieg und Kapitalismus* (Munich, 1913); Nef, *War and Human Progress;* and many later books and articles. See the useful introduction and bibliography in J. M. Winter (ed.), *War and Economic Development* (Cambridge, 1975).

7. Parker, "Emergence of Modern Finance," passim; Wallerstein, *Modern World System*, vol. 2, pp. 57ff; C. H. Wilson, *Anglo-Dutch Commerce and Finance in*

the Eighteenth Century (Cambridge, 1966 reprint); V. Barbour, *Capitalism in Amsterdam in the Seventeenth Century* (Baltimore, 1950), espec. ch. 6. Above all, see now J. C. Riley, *International Government Finance and the Amsterdam Capital Market 1740–1815* (Cambridge, 1980).

8. See the discussion on this in Wilson, "Decline of the Netherlands," in *Economic History and the Historian: Collected Essays* (London, 1969), pp. 22–47; and idem, *Anglo-Dutch Commerce and Finance;* as well as the references in note 23 below.

9. Riley, *International Government Finance*, chs. 6–7.

10. For general comparisons of the French and British economies, financial policies, and fiscal systems, see Wallerstein, *Modern World System*, vol. 2, chs. 3 and 6; P. Mathias and P. O'Brien, "Taxation in Britain and France, 1715–1810," *Journal of European Economic History*, vol. 5, no. 3 (Winter 1976), pp. 601–49; F. Crouzet, "L'Angleterre et France au XVIIIᵉ siècle: essai d'analyse comparée de deux croissances économiques," *Annales*, vol. 21 (1966), pp. 254–91; McNeill, *Pursuit of Power*, espec. ch. 6; N.F.R. Crafts, "Industrial Revolution in England and France: Some Thoughts on the Question: 'Why was England First?' " *Economic History Review*, 2nd series, vol. 30 (1977), pp. 429–41. There is a brief synopsis in P. Kriedte, *Peasants, Landlords and Merchant Capitalists: Europe and the World Economy, 1500–1800* (Leamington Spa, 1983), pp. 115ff.

11. Mathias and O'Brien, "Taxation in Britain and France," passim; and for the earlier period, see again Dickson and Sperling, "War Finance 1689–1714," passim. There is, however, nothing quite like R. Braun's penetrating comparative essay "Taxation, Sociopolitical Structure, and State-Building," in Tilly (ed.), *Formation of National States in Western Europe*, pp. 243–327.

12. Dickson, *Financial Revolution in England*, p. 198. For the institutional story, see J. H. Clapham, *The Bank of England*, vol. 1, *1694–1797* (Cambridge, 1944); and H. Roseveare, *The Treasury: The Evolution of a British Institution* (London/New York, 1969); and compare with the much less satisfactory (and irregular) situation prior to 1688: C. D. Chandaman, *The English Public Revenue 1660–1688* (Oxford, 1975).

13. Riley, *International Government Finance*, chs. 4 and 6; Wilson, *Anglo-Dutch Commerce and Finance*, passim; A. C. Carter, "Dutch Foreign Investment, 1738–1800," *Economica*, n.s., vol. 20 (November 1953), pp. 322–40. The role of Dutch finance in Britain's growth is also stressed (and perhaps exaggerated) in Wallerstein, *Modern World System*, vol. 2, pp. 279ff; but note also the interesting arguments in L. Neal, "Interpreting Power and Profit in Economic History: A Case Study of the Seven Years War," *Journal of Economic History*, vol. 37 (1977), pp. 34–35.

14. Dickson, *Financial Revolution in England*, p. 9, which is the source for Table 2.

15. Bishop Berkeley's quotation is from ibid., p. 15. For McNeill's argument about the "feedback loop," see *Pursuit of Power*, pp. 178, 206ff.

16. The most useful study here is J. F. Bosher, *French Finances, 1770–1795* (Cambridge, 1970); but see also the articles by Dickson and Sperling, "War Finance," and Mathias and O'Brien, "Taxation in Britain and France," as well as the references in Chapter 2 above to the writings of Bonney, Dent, and Guery. See also the older work R. Mousnier, "L'evolution des finances publiques en France et en Angleterre pendant les guerres de la Ligue d'Augsburg et de la Succession d'Espagne," *Revue Historique*, vol. 44, no. 205 (1951), pp. 1–23.

17. Bosher, *French Finances 1770–1795*, p. 20. This argument is summarized in Bosher's article "French Administration and Public Finance in their European Setting," *NCMH*, vol. 8, ch. 20. For calculations of the amount of taxes siphoned

off into private hands, see Mathias and O'Brien, "Taxation in Britain and France," pp. 643–46.

18. The direct quotations come from J. G. Clark, *La Rochelle and the Atlantic Economy During the Eighteenth Century* (Baltimore/London, 1981), pp. 23, 226; and see in particular chs. 1 and 7, as well as the conclusion. That story can be compared with the British experience, as recounted in R. Davis, *The Rise of the Atlantic Economies* (London, 1975); W. E. Minchinton (ed.), *The Growth of English Overseas Trade in the Seventeenth and Eighteenth Centuries* (London, 1969); A. Calder, *Revolutionary Empire: The Rise of the English-Speaking Empires from the Fifteenth Century to the 1780s* (London, 1981), bks. 2–3; as well as a host of specialized books upon individual ports and trades.

19. See the illuminating detail in the chapters "Finances" and "Supply and Equipment" in L. Kennet, *The French Armies in the Seven Years War: A Study in Military Organization and Administration* (Durham, N.C., 1967). For the navy's weaknesses, particularly with respect to provisions and timber, see P. W. Bamford, *Forests and French Sea Power 1660–1789* (Toronto, 1956), passim; and Jenkins, *History of the French Navy*, ch. 8; and the remarkable analysis by J. F. Bosher, "Financing the French Navy in the Seven Years War: *Beaujon, Goossens et compagnie* in 1759," to be published in *U.S. Naval Institute Proceedings*. For a British comparison, see D. A. Baugh, *British Naval Administration in the Age of Walpole* (Princeton, 1965), passim.

20. For these comparative statistics, see Bosher, *French Finances 1770–1795*, pp. 23–24. This can be supplemented by R. D. Harris, "French Finances and the American War, 1777–1783," *Journal of Modern History*, vol. 46, no. 2 (1976), pp. 233–58; G. Ardent, "Financial Policy and Economic Infrastructure of Modern States and Nations," in Tilly (ed.), *Formation of National States in Western Europe*, pp. 217ff; Hamilton, "Origin and Growth of the National Debt in Western Europe," pp. 122–24. The place of taxation in the French crisis of the late 1780s is delineated in Doyle, *The Old European Order*, pp. 313–20; and *NCMH*, vol. 8, chs. 20–21. For Pitt's reforms, see J. Ehrman, *The Younger Pitt*, 2 vols. to date (London, 1969 and 1983), vol. 1, pp. 239ff; and J.E.D. Binney, *British Public Finance and Administration, 1774–1792* (Oxford, 1958), passim.

21. There is no prospect of giving a satisfactory (let alone an exhaustive) list of references to the war finance of these other states. In general, see Tilly (ed.), *Formation of National States in Western Europe*, chs. 3–4; *NCMH*, vol. 6, pp. 20ff, 284ff; and C. Moraze, "Finance et despotisme, essai sur les despotes eclaires," *Annales*, vol. 3 (1948), pp. 279–96. For Prussia, see the brief remarks in *NCMH*, vol. 7, pp. 296ff, and vol. 8, pp. 7ff, 565ff; and C. Duffy, *The Army of Frederick the Great* (Newton Abbott, 1974), ch. 8. For the Habsburg Empire, see idem, *The Army of Maria Theresa: The Armed Forces of Imperial Austria, 1740–1780* (London, 1977), ch. 10. Even in Russia's case, where conscription operated and the resources of the country were ransacked for military purposes, the earlier self-sufficiency in cash and kind had been replaced by an increasing recourse to foreign loans and paper money by the final decade of the eighteenth century; see idem, *Russia's Military Way to the West: Origins and Nature of Russian Military Power 1700–1800* (London, 1981), pp. 36–38, 179–180.

22. Jones, *Britain and Europe in the Seventeenth Century*, ch. 5; Kennedy, *Rise and Fall of British Naval Mastery*, pp. 50ff.

23. J. G. Stork-Penning, "The Ordeal of the States: Some Remarks on Dutch Politics During the War of the Spanish Succession," *Acta Historiae Neerlandica*, vol. 2 (1967), pp. 107–41; C. R. Boxer, "The Dutch Economic Decline," in Cipolla (ed.), *Economic Decline of Empires;* Wilson, "Taxation and the Decline of Empires:

An Unfashionable Theme," in *Economic History and the Historian*, pp. 114–27; Wolf, *Toward a European Balance of Power*, ch. 7. See also the synopsis in C. P. Kindleberger, "Commercial Expansion and the Industrial Revolution," *Journal of European Economic History*, vol. 4, no. 3 (Winter 1975), pp. 620ff.

24. A. C. Carter, *The Dutch Republic in Europe in the Seven Years War* (London, 1971), especially ch. 7; and, more generally, idem, *Neutrality or Commitment: the Evolution of Dutch Foreign Policy (1667–1795)* (London, 1975), an excellent survey.

25. Carter, *Neutrality or Commitment*, pp. 89ff; and the relevant chapters in E. H. Kossmann, *The Low Countries 1780–1940* (Oxford, 1978).

26. Figures from Doyle, *Old European Order*, p. 242. For France under Louis XIV, see *NCMH*, vols. 5–6; A. de St. Leger and P. Sagnac, *La Prepondérance française, Louis XIV, 1661–1715* (Paris, 1935); R. M. Hatton (ed.), *Louis XIV and Europe* (London, 1976); P. Goubert, *Louis XIV and Twenty Million Frenchmen* (London, 1970); and J. B. Wolf, *Louis XIV* (London, 1968).

27. For excellent analyses of the military-geopolitical problems facing the rulers in Vienna during this period, see K. A. Roider, *Austria's Eastern Question 1700–1790* (Princeton, N.J., 1982); and C. W. Ingrao, "Habsburg Strategy and Geopolitics during the Eighteenth Century," in G. E. Rothenberg, B. K. Kiraly, and P. F. Sugar (eds.), *East Central European Society and War in the Pre-Revolutionary Eighteenth Century* (New York, 1982), pp. 49–96. See also the running commentary in D. Mackay, *Prince Eugene of Savoy* (London, 1977).

28. O. Hufton, *Europe: Privilege and Protest 1730–1789* (London, 1980), p. 155. See also *NCMH*, vol. 8, ch. 10; Kann, *History of the Habsburg Empire*, chs. 3 and 5; and, more generally, E. Wangermann, *The Austrian Achievement* (New York, 1973); and V. S. Mamatey, *Rise of the Habsburg Empire 1526–1815* (New York, 1971). See also the very useful comments in Duffy, *Army of Maria Theresa*, passim.

29. Hufton, *Europe: Privilege and Protest*, ch. 7; Williams, *Ancien Regime in Europe*, chs. 13–16; Wallerstein, *Modern World System*, vol. 2, pp. 225ff; F. L. Carsten, *The Origins of Prussia* (Oxford, 1954), passim; H. Rosenberg, *Bureaucracy, Aristocracy and Autocracy: The Prussian Experience 1660–1815* (Cambridge, Mass., 1958). There is also a good survey of the Prussian reforms and system in *NCMH*, vol. 7, ch. 13.

30. G. Craig, *The Politics of the Prussian Army 1640–1945* (Oxford, 1955), pp. 22ff; Duffy, *Army of Frederick the Great*, passim; T. N. Dupuy, *A Genius for War: The German Army and General Staff, 1807–1945* (Englewood Cliffs, N.J., 1977), pp. 17ff; P. Paret, *Yorck and the Era of Prussian Reform* (Princeton, N.J., 1961), passim.

31. For a brief but very useful analysis, see P. Dukes, *The Emergence of the Super-Powers: A Short Comparative History of the USA and the USSR* (London, 1970), chs. 1–2.

32. Quoted from P. Bairoch, "International Industrialization Levels from 1750 to 1980," *Journal of European Economic History*, vol. 11, no. 2 (Spring 1982), p. 291. See also L. H. Gipson, *The Coming of the Revolution 1763–1775* (New York, 1962), pp. 13–18; R. M. Robertson, *History of the American Economy* (3rd edn., New York, 1973), p. 64.

33. *NCMH*, vol. 7, ch. 14, and vol. 8, ch. 11; Kochan and Abraham, *Making of Modern Russia*, chs. 7–9; Duffy, *Russia's Military Way to the West*, passim; P. Dukes, *The Making of Russian Absolutism 1613–1801* (London, 1982), passim; M. Falkus, *The Industrialization of Russia 1700–1914* (London, 1972), chs. 2–3; M. Raeff, *Imperial Russia 1682–1825* (New York, 1971), passim; and the many

comments on Russia's rise in M. S. Anderson, *Europe in the Eighteenth Century* (London, 1961), espec. ch. 9.

34. A. de Tocqueville, *Democracy in America*, 2 vols. (New York, 1945 edn.), p. 452; and see also the prognostications reported in Dukes, *Emergence of the Super-Powers*, chs. 1–3; H. Gollwitzer, *Geschichte des weltpolitischen Denkens*, 2 vols. (Göttingen, 1972, 1982), vol. 1, pp. 403ff; and the commentary in W. Woodruff, *America's Impact on the World: A Study of the Role of the United States in the World Economy 1750–1970* (New York, 1973).

35. A. T. Mahan, *The Influence of Sea Power upon History 1660–1783* (London, 1965 edn.), p. 29.

36. On which see Kennedy, *The Rise and Fall of the British Naval Mastery*, introduction and chs. 3–5; M. Howard, *The British Way in Warfare* (Neale Lecture, University of London, 1974), passim; Jones, *Britain and the World*, chs. 1–2 and passim.

37. D. E. C. Eversley, "The Home Market and Economic Growth in England 1750–1780," in E. L. Jones and G. E. Mingay (eds.), *Land, Labour and Population of the Industrial Revolution* (London, 1967), pp. 206–59; F. Crouzet, "Toward an Export Economy: British Exports During the Industrial Revolution," *Explorations in Economic History*, vol. 17 (1980), pp. 48–93; P. J. Cain and A. G. Hopkins, "The Political Economy of British Expansion Overseas, 1750–1914," *Economic History Review*, 2nd series, vol. 33, no. 4 (1980), pp. 463–90.

38. Quoted in H. Richmond, *Statesmen and Sea Power* (Oxford, 1946), p. 111; and see further details of this strategical debate in R. Pares, "American versus Continental Warfare 1739–63," *English Historical Review*, vol. 51, no. 103 (1936), pp. 429–65; Wallerstein, *Modern World-System*, vol. 2, pp. 246ff; G. Niedhart, *Handel und Krieg in der britischen Weltpolitik 1738–1763* (Munich, 1979), pp. 64ff.

39. L. Dehio, *The Precarious Balance* (London, 1963), p. 118.

40. These figures—all *approximations*—come from a variety of sources, including Cipolla, *Before the Industrial Revolution*, p. 4; A. Armengaud, "Population in Europe 1700–1914," in C. M. Cipolla (ed.), *Fontana Economic History of Europe*, vol. 3 (1976), pp. 22–76; *NCMH*, vol. 8, p. 714; B. R. Mitchell, *European Historical Statistics, 1750–1970* (London, 1975), pt. A; W. Woodruff, *Impact of Western Man: A Study of Europe's Role in the World Economy 1750–1960* (New York, 1967), p. 104.

41. Corvisier, *Armies and Societies in Europe 1494–1789*, p. 113, gives different figures from Childs, *Armies and Warfare in Europe 1648–1789*, p. 42—and both differ on occasions from data given in specific works on national armies or individual wars.

42. These figures are taken from Anderson, *Europe in the Eighteenth Century*, pp. 144–45, with somewhat different ones given in L. W. Cowie, *Eighteenth-Century Europe* (London, 1963), pp. 141–42. Again, amendments have been made in the light of what seems to be a more authoritative source: thus, the 1779 figures come from J. Dull, *The French Navy and American Independence* (Princeton, N.J., 1975), appendix F; and the 1790 totals from O. von Pivka, *Navies of the Napoleonic Era* (Newton Abbott, 1980), p. 30 (but cf. *NCMH*, vol. 8, p. 190).

43. See pp. 135–37 below.

44. For what follows, see McKay and Scott, *Rise of the Great Powers*, pp. 14ff; Stoye, *Europe Unfolding 1648–1688*, ch. 9; Wolf, *Toward a European Balance of Power*, passim; idem, *The Emergence of the Great Powers 1685–1715* (New York, 1951), chs. 1–7; *NCMH*, vol. 5, ch. 9; St. Leger and Sagnac, *La Prépondérance française*, passim; and Hatton (ed.), *Louis XIV and Europe*, passim.

45. L. Andre, *Michel Le Tellier et Louvois* (Paris, 1943 edn.); C. Jones, "The Military

Revolution and the Professionalization of the French Army under the Ancien Régime," in M. Duffy (ed.), *The Military Revolution and the State 1500–1800* (Exeter Studies in History, no. 1, Exeter, 1980), pp. 29–48; Jenkins, *History of the French Navy*, ch. 5.

46. Jones, *Britain and the World*, pp. 100–110; idem, *Country and Court 1658–1714* (London, 1978), pp. 106ff; Padfield, *Tide of Empires*, vol. 2, ch. 4.

47. McKay and Scott, *Rise of the Great Powers*, pp. 34ff; Hatton (ed.), *Louis XIV and Europe*, passim.

48. *NCMH*, vol. 6, ch. 7; Wolf, *Toward a European Balance of Power*, ch. 4; McKay and Scott, *Rise of the Great Powers*, pp. 43–50.

49. G. Symcox, *The Crisis of French Seapower 1689–1697* (The Hague, 1974), passim; Jenkins, *History of the French Navy*, pp. 69–88; Padfield, *Tide of Empires*, vol. 2, ch. 5.

50. For these remarks, see Symcox, *Crisis of French Seapower*, passim; Kennedy, *Rise and Fall of British Naval Mastery*, pp. 76–80; G. N. Clarke, *The Dutch Alliance and the War Against French Trade 1688–1697* (New York, 1971 edn.), passim; D. G. Chandler, "Fluctuations in the Strength of Forces in English Pay sent to Flanders During the Nine Years War, 1688–1697," *War and Society*, vol. 1, no. 2 (September 1983), pp. 1–20; S. B. Baxter, *William III and the Defense of European Liberty 1650–1702* (Westport, Conn., 1976 reprint), pp. 288ff.

51. McKay and Scott, *Rise of the Great Powers*, pp. 54–63; Wolf, *Toward a European Balance of Power*, ch. 7; *NCMH*, vol. 6, ch. 12.

52. For military events, and tactics, in this war, see G. Chandler, *The Art of Warfare in the Age of Marlborough* (London, 1976); Barnett, *Britain and Her Army*, pp. 152ff; McKay, *Prince Eugene of Savoy*, pp. 58ff.

53. Mahan, *Influence of Sea Power upon History*, ch. 5; Kennedy, *Rise and Fall of British Naval Mastery*, pp. 82–88; Padfield, *Tide of Empires*, vol. 2, pp. 156ff; Jones, *Britain and Europe in the Seventeenth Century*, ch. 7; *NCMH*, vol. 6, chs. 11–13, 15.

54. For the Peace of Utrecht, see McKay and Scott, *Rise of the Great Powers*, pp. 63–66; *NCMH*, vol. 6, ch. 14. On the *Asiento* concession, see G. J. Walker, *Spanish Politics and Imperial Trade, 1700–1789* (Bloomington, 1979), ch. 4.

55. J. W. Stoye, *The Siege of Vienna* (London, 1964); T. M. Barker, *Double Eagle and Crescent* (Albany, N.Y., 1967); McKay, *Prince Eugene of Savoy*, chs. 3 and 5; *NCMH*, vol. 6, ch. 19. For characteristics of military warfare in eastern Europe, see B. K. Kiraly and G. E. Rotherberg (eds.), *War and Society in Eastern Europe*, vol. 1 (New York, 1979), espec. pp. 1–33, 361ff.

56. For Charles XII, see R. M. Hatton, *Charles XII of Sweden* (London, 1968), and her ch. 20(i) in *NCMH*, vol. 6, as well as the comments in Roberts, *Swedish Imperial Experience*. For Peter, see M. S. Anderson, *Peter the Great* (London, 1978); R. Wittram, *Peter I: Czar und Kaiser*, 2 vols. (Göttingen, 1964); B. H. Sumner, *Peter the Great and the Emergence of Russia* (London, 1940); *NCMH*, vol. 6, chs. 20(i) and 21.

57. McKay and Scott, *Rise of the Great Powers*, p. 92.

58. Dehio, *Precarious Balance*, p. 102.

59. McKay and Scott, *Rise of the Great Powers*, ch. 4.

60. *NCMH*, vol. 7, ch. 9. For the policies of the individual powers, see A. M. Wilson, *French Foreign Policy During the Administration of Cardinal Fleury* (Cambridge, Mass., 1936); P. Langford, *The Eighteenth Century, 1688–1815: British Foreign Policy* (London, 1976), pp. 71ff; Kann, *History of the Habsburg Empire*, pp. 90ff.

61. Padfield, *Tide of Empires*, vol. 2, pp. 194ff; R. Pares, *War and Trade in the West Indies 1739–1763* (Oxford, 1936); M. Savelle, *Empires to Nations: Expansion in*

America, 1713–1824 (Minneapolis, 1974), ch. 6; Walker, *Spanish Politics and Imperial Trade*, espec. pt. 3; W. L. Dorn, *Competition for Empire 1740–1763* (New York, 1940). For the War of Austrian Succession, see *NCMH*, vol. 7, ch. 17.

62. Dorn, *Competition for Empire*, passim; Pares, *War and Trade*, passim; idem, "American versus Continental Warfare," passim; *NCMH*, vol. 7, chs. 20 and 22; Padfield, *Tide of Empires*, vol. 2, pp. 224ff; Saville, *Empires to Nations*, pp. 135ff; C. M. Andrews, "Anglo-French Commercial Rivalry, 1700–1750," *American Historical Review*, vol. 20 (1915), pp. 539–56, 761–80; P.L.R. Higonnet, "The Origins of the Seven Years War," *Journal of Modern History*, vol. 40 (1968), pp. 57–90.

63. See again Carter, *Dutch Republic in the Seven Years War*, passim; Walker, *Spanish Politics and Imperial Trade*.

64. On the Seven Years War generally, see *NCMH*, vol. 7, ch. 20; McKay and Scott, *Rise of the Great Powers*, pp. 192–200. British policy is covered in Niedhart, *Handel und Krieg in der britischen Weltpolitik*, pp. 121–38; Jones, *Britain and the World*, pp. 207ff; B. Tunstall, *William Pitt, Earl of Chatham* (London, 1938); J. S. Corbett, *England in the Seven Years War: A Study in Combined Strategy*, 2 vols. (London, 1907); R. Savory, *His Britannic Majesty's Army in Germany During the Seven Years War* (Oxford, 1966). The lackluster French effort is nicely described in Kennett, *French Armies in the Seven Years War;* the improved Austrian performance in Duffy, *Army of Maria Theresa*. Russia's early role is described in H. H. Kaplan, *Russia and the Outbreak of the Seven Years War* (Berkeley, Calif., 1968); and Duffy, *Russia's Military Way to the West*, pp. 92ff. Succinct accounts of Prussia's performance are in Duffy, *Army of Frederick the Great;* and J. Kunisch, *Das Mirakel des Hauses Brandenburg* (Munich, 1978), with useful comparisons.

65. Cited in Kennedy, *Rise and Fall of British Naval Mastery*, p. 106; and see also Pares, "American versus Continental Warfare," passim. On Pitt's difficulties in the ministry of 1757–1762, see R. Middleton, *The Bells of Victory* (Cambridge, 1985).

66. Quoted in H. Rosinski, "The Role of Sea Power in the Global Warfare of the Future," *Brassey's Naval Annual* (1947), p. 103. For French financial weaknesses during the Seven Years War, see again Kennett, *French Armies in the Seven Years War*, and Bosher, "Financing the French Navy in the Seven Years War," passim.

67. For the above, see McKay and Scott, *Rise of the Great Powers*, pp. 253–58; *NCMH*, vol. 8, pp. 254ff; J. F. Ramsay, *Anglo-French Relations 1763–70: A Study of Choiseul's Foreign Policy* (Berkeley, Calif., 1939); H. M. Scott, "The Importance of Bourbon Naval Reconstruction to the Strategy of Choiseul after the Seven Years War," *International History Review*, vol. 1 (1979), pp. 17–35; R. Abarca, "Classical Diplomacy and Bourbon 'Revanche' Strategy, 1763–1770," *Review of Politics*, vol. 32 (1970), pp. 313–37; M. Roberts, *Splendid Isolation 1763–1780* (Stenton Lecture, Reading, 1970).

68. For what follows, see I. R. Christie, *Wars and Revolutions: Britain 1760–1815* (London, 1982), chs. 4–6; P. Mackesy, *The War for America 1775–1783* (London, 1964); B. Donoughue, *British Politics and the American Revolution* (London, 1964); G. S. Brown, *The American Secretary: The Colonial Policy of Lord George Germain 1775–1778* (Ann Arbor, Mich., 1963); *NCMH*, vol. 8, chs. 15–19; and the useful collection of essays in D. Higginbotham (ed.), *Reconsiderations on the Revolutionary War* (Westport, Conn., 1978). There is a good survey of the newer literature in H. M. Scott, "British Foreign Policy in the Age of the American Revolution," *International History Review*, vol. 6 (1984), pp. 113–25.

69. D. Syrett, *Shipping and the American War 1775–83* (London, 1970), p. 243 and passim. See also N. Baker, *Government and Contractors: The British Treasury and War Supplies 1775–1783* (London, 1971); R. A. Bowler, *Logistics and the Failure of the British Army in America 1775–1783* (Princeton, N.J., 1975); E. E. Curtis, *The Organization of the British Army in the American Revolution* (Menston, Yorkshire, 1972 reprint). For the American side, see the excellent survey D. Higginbotham, *The War of American Independence* (Bloomington, Ind., 1977 ed.).

70. Barnett, *Britain and Her Army*, p. 225.

71. Figures are from Kennedy, *Rise and Fall of British Naval Mastery*, p. 111. See also the excellent work by Dull, *French Navy and American Independence;* and A. T. Patterson, *The Other Armada: The Franco-Spanish Attempt to Invade Britain in 1779* (Manchester, 1960). For the diplomatic aspects, see I. de Madariaga, *Britain, Russia and the Armed Neutrality of 1780* (London, 1962); S. F. Bemis, *The Diplomacy of the American Revolution* (New York, 1935); and Higginbotham, *The War of American Independence*, ch. 10; most recently, Dull, *A Diplomatic History of the American Revolution* (New Haven, Conn., 1985).

72. For what follows, see McKay and Scott, *Rise of the Great Powers*, ch. 8; *NCMH*, vol. 8, chs. 9 and 12; I. de Madariaga, *Russia in the Age of Catherine the Great* (London, 1981).

73. Ehrman, *Younger Pitt*, vol. 1, pp. 516–71, and vol. 2, pp. 42ff; Jones, *Britain and the World*, pp. 252ff; Binney, *British Public Finance and Administration;* and, for comparisons with France's economy in the 1780s, see again Crouzet, "Angleterre et France"; Mathias and O'Brien, "Taxation in Britain and France, 1715–1810"; and Nef, *War and Human Progress*, pp. 282ff.

74. For the military reforms, see *NCMH*, vol. 8, pp. 190ff, and vol. 9, ch. 3; McNeill, *Pursuit of Power*, pp. 158ff; Strachan, *European Armies and the Conduct of War*, pp. 25ff; R. S. Quimby, *The Background of Napoleonic Warfare* (New York, 1957); D. Bien, "The Army in the French Enlightenment: Reform, Reaction and Revolution," *Past and Present*, no. 85 (1979), pp. 68–98; and G. Rothenberg, *The Art of Warfare in the Age of Napoleon* (Bloomington, Ind., 1978). For the early stages of the campaigning, see M. Glover, *The Napoleonic Wars: An Illustrated History 1792–1815* (New York, 1979); S. T. Ross, *Quest for Victory: French Military Strategy 1792–1799* (London/New York, 1973), chs. 1–4; G. Rothenberg, *Napoleon's Great Adversaries: The Archduke Charles and the Austrian Army 1792–1814* (London, 1982), ch. 2.

75. British policy and strategy is covered in Jones, *Britain and the World*, pp. 259ff; Ehrman, *Younger Pitt*, vol. 2, pts. 4–5; Christie, *Wars and Revolutions*, pp. 215–326; J. M. Sherwig, *Guineas and Gunpowder: British Foreign Aid in the Wars with France 1793–1815* (Cambridge, Mass., 1969), chs. 1–4; M. Duffy, "British Policy in the War Against Revolutionary France," in C. Jones (ed.), *Britain and Revolutionary France: Conflict, Subversion and Propaganda* (Exeter Studies in History, no. 5, Exeter, 1983); D. Geggus, "The Cost of Pitt's Caribbean Campaigns, 1793–1798," *Historical Journal*, vol. 26, no. 2 (1983), pp. 691–706.

76. Quoted in Glover, *Napoleonic Wars*, p. 50. For Napoleon as strategist and commander, see D. G. Chandler, *The Campaigns of Napoleon* (New York, 1966); C. Barnett, *Napoleon* (London, 1978); Rothenberg, *Art of Warfare in the Age of Napoleon;* and the running commentary in G. Lefevre, *Napoleon*, 2 vols. (London/New York, 1969).

77. See A. B. Rodger, *The War of the Second Coalition, 1798–1801* (Oxford, 1964); P. Mackesy, *Statesmen at War: The Strategy of Overthrow, 1798–1799* (London, 1974); the controversial comments in E. Ingram, *Commitment to Empire:*

Prophecies of the Great Game in Asia, 1797–1800 (Oxford, 1981); Sherwig, *Guineas and Gunpowder,* chs. 6–7; Rothenberg, *Napoleon's Great Adversaries,* ch. 3. For the French side, see Ross, *Quest for Victory,* chs. 5–12; and idem, *European Diplomatic History 1789–1815: France Against Europe* (Malabar, Fla., 1981 reprint), ch. 6. The Russian intervention is covered in A. A. Lobanov-Rostovsky, *Russia and Europe 1789–1825* (Durham, N.C., 1947), pp. 43–64; and Duffy, *Russia's Military Way to the West,* pp. 208ff.

78. Jones, *Britain and the World,* pp. 272–80; C. Emsley, *British Society and the French Wars 1793–1815* (London, 1979), chs. 4–5; Lefevre, *Napoleon,* vol. 1, chs. 5 and 7; Glover, *Napoleonic Wars,* pp. 83–84. See also the comments in E. L. Presseisen, *Amiens and Munich: Comparisons in Appeasement* (The Hague, 1978).

79. Lefevre, *Napoleon,* vol. 1, chs. 7 and 9; Ross, *European Diplomatic History,* ch. 8; Chandler, *Campaigns of Napoleon,* pt. 7; Glover, *Napoleonic Wars,* ch. 3; Rothenberg, *Napoleon's Great Adversaries,* ch. 5; Sherwig, *Guineas and Gunpowder,* chs. 7–8; Jones, *Britain and the World,* pp. 281–87; Marcus, *Naval History of England,* vol. 2, pp. 221–302.

80. For what follows, see Jones, *Britain and the World,* pp. 289ff; F. Crouzet, *L'Economie britannique et le Blocus Continental 1806–1813,* 2 vols. (Paris, 1958); idem, "Wars, Blockade, and Economic Change in Europe 1792–1815," *Journal of Economic History,* vol. 24 (1964), pp. 567–88; Kennedy, *Rise and Fall of British Naval Mastery,* pp. 143–45; *NCMH,* vol. 9, pp. 326ff; E. F. Heckscher, *The Continental System* (Oxford, 1922). For the debate over the impact of the 1793–1815 struggle upon the British economy, see, in addition, Emsley, *British Society and the French Wars,* chs. 7–8; J. E. Cookson, "Political Arithmetic and War 1793–1815," *War and Society,* vol. 1, no. 2 (1983), pp. 37–60; G. Hueckel, "War and the British Economy, 1793–1815: A General Equilibrium Analysis," *Explorations in Economic History,* vol. 10, no. 4 (Summer, 1973), pp. 365–96; P. Deane, "War and Industrialisation," in Winter (ed.), *War and Economic Development,* pp. 91–102; J. L. Anderson, "Aspects of the Effects on the British Economy of the War Against France, 1793–1815," *Australian Economic History Review,* vol. 12 (1972), pp. 1–20.

81. See Table 2, above. For British war finances, see N. J. Silberling, "Financial and Monetary Policy of Great Britain During the Napoleonic Wars," *Quarterly Journal of Economics,* vol. 38 (1923–24), pp. 214–33; E. B. Schumpeter, "English Prices and Public Finance, 1660–1822," *Review of Economic Statistics,* vol. 20 (1938), pp. 21–37; A. Hope-Jones, *Income Tax in the Napoleonic Wars* (Cambridge, 1939); P. O'Brien, *British Financial and Fiscal Policy in the Wars Against France, 1793–1815* (Oxford, 1984).

82. L. Bergeron, *France Under Napoleon* (Princeton, N.J., 1981), pp. 37ff, 159ff; G. Brunn, *Europe and the French Imperium, 1799–1815* (New York, 1938), chs. 4–5; S. B. Clough, *France: A History of National Economics 1789–1939* (New York, 1939), chs. 2–3; Lefevre, *Napoleon,* vol. 2, chs. 1–4; C. Trebilcock, *The Industrialization of the Continental Powers 1780–1914* (London, 1981), pp. 125ff.

83. Bergeron, *France Under Napoleon,* pp. 167ff, 184ff; Crouzet, "Wars, Blockade, and Economic Change," passim.

84. Bergeron, *France Under Napoleon,* pp. 37ff; Lefevre, *Napoleon,* vol. 2, pp. 171ff; Clough, *France,* chs. 2–3.

85. For what follows, see Bergeron, *France Under Napoleon,* pp. 40–41; Lefevre, *Napoleon,* vol. 2, p. 291; McNeill, *Pursuit of Power,* pp. 198ff; Brunn, *Europe and the French Imperium,* pp. 73–75, 110ff; E. J. Hobsbawm, *The Age of Revolution 1789–1848* (London, 1962), p. 97; G. Rudé, *Revolutionary Europe 1783–*

1815 (London, 1964), ch. 13 and espec. pp. 274–75; S. Schama, "The Exigencies of War and the Politics of Taxation in the Netherlands 1795–1810," in Winter (ed.), *War and Economic Development*, pp. 111, 117, 128.

86. Quoted in Glover, *Napoleonic Wars*, p. 129; and compare with Guibert's remarkable pre-Revolution forecast of a people "who, knowing how to make war cheaply and live on the spoils of victory, was not obliged to lay down its arms for reasons of finance"—as cited in *NCMH*, vol. 8, p. 217; and with Spenser Wilkinson's remarks, quoted in Tilly (ed.), *Formation of National States in Western Europe*, pp. 147–48, 152.

87. Glover, *Napoleonic Wars*, pp. 140–41; Jones, *Britain and the World*, pp. 22, 317; Sherwig, *Guineas and Gunpowder*, chs. 9–10.

88. Figures from Glover, *Napoleonic Wars*, p. 152; see also Chandler, *Campaigns of Napoleon*, p. 734. For the Austrian army's campaigning—and recuperation—see Rothenberg, *Napoleon's Great Adversaries*, pp. 123ff.

89. For the Peninsular War, see the relevant parts of Glover, *Campaigns of Napoleon;* J. Weller, *Wellington in the Peninsula* (London, 1962); R. Glover, *Peninsular Preparation: The Reform of the British Army, 1795–1809* (Cambridge, 1963); M. Glover, *The Peninsular War, 1807–1814: A Concise History* (Newton Abbott, 1974); Sherwig, *Guineas and Gunpowder*, pp. 198ff. The French side is covered in J. Thiry, *La Guerre d'Espagne* (Paris, 1966); Ross, *European Diplomatic History*, pp. 276ff; G. H. Lovett, *Napoleon and the Birth of Modern Spain*, 2 vols. (New York, 1965). The importance of the Spanish contribution is rightly stressed in D. Gates, *The Spanish Ulcer: A History of the Peninsula War* (London, 1986).

90. Brunn, *Europe and the French Imperium*, ch. 8; Rudé, *Revolutionary Europe*, chs. 13–14; Lefevre, *Napoleon*, vol. 2, chs. 7–8; J. Godechet, B. F. Hyslop, and D. L. Dowd, *The Napoleonic Era in Europe* (New York, 1971), espec. ch. 8; G. Best, *War and Society in Revolutionary Europe, 1770–1870* (London, 1982), chs. 11–13; R. J. Rath, *The Fall of the Napoleonic Kingdom of Italy* (New York, 1941), chs. 1–2.

91. Crouzet, "Wars, Blockade and Economic Change," passim; Glover, *Napoleonic Wars*, chs. 4–5; O. Connelly, *Napoleon's Satellite Kingdoms* (New York, 1965), passim. For Russian policy, see Chandler, *Campaign of Napoleon*, pp. 739ff; *NCMH*, vol. 9, pp. 512ff; Lobanov-Rostovsky, *Russia in Europe, 1789–1825*, passim; and, earlier, H. Ragsdale, *Détente in the Napoleonic Era: Bonaparte and the Russians* (Lawrence, Kansas, 1980).

92. Chandler, *Campaigns of Napoleon*, pts. 13–14; Glover, *Napoleonic Wars*, pp. 160ff; Ross, *European Diplomatic History*, pp. 310ff; A. Palmer, *Napoleon in Russia* (New York, 1967); C. Duffy, *Borodino and the War of 1812* (London, 1973); Lefevre, *Napoleon*, vol. 2, ch. 9; G. Blond, *La Grande Armée 1804/1815* (Paris, 1979).

93. Glover, *Napoleonic Wars*, p. 193; Sherwig, *Guineas and Gunpowder*, chs. 12–13, espec. pp. 287–88; Rothenberg, *Napoleon's Great Adversaries*, pp. 178ff.

94. Which is perhaps why it is almost completely ignored in so many of the standard military and diplomatic histories of this period. For details, see E. B. Potter (ed.), *Sea Power: A Naval History*, 2nd edn. (Annapolis, Md., 1981), ch. 10, and bibliography on p. 392; B. Perkins, *Prologue to War: England and the United States 1805–1812* (Berkeley, Calif., 1961); A. T. Mahan, *Sea Power in Its Relations to the War of 1812*, 2 vols. (London, 1905); Marcus, *Naval History of England*, vol. 2, ch. 16.

95. Ingram, *Commitment to Empire*, passim; G. J. Adler, "Britain and the Defence of India—The Origins of the Problem, 1798–1815," *Journal of Asian History*, vol. 6 (1972), pp. 14–44.

96. Chandler, *Campaigns of Napoleon*, pt. 17; Glover, *Napoleonic Wars*, pp. 212ff; Lefevre, *Napoleon*, vol. 2, ch. 10; Blond, *La Grand Armée*, ch. 16; H. La-chouque, *Waterloo* (Paris, 1972); U. Pericoli and M. Glover, *1815: The Armies at Waterloo* (London, 1973).

97. For details on the 1814–1815 settlements, see Sherwig, *Guineas and Gunpowder*, ch. 14; *NCMH*, vol. 9, ch. 24; E. V. Gulick, *Europe's Classical Balance of Power* (New York, 1967 edn.), passim; C. K. Webster, *The Foreign Policy of Castlereagh, 1812–1815: Britain and the Reconstruction of Europe* (London, 1931); H. G. Nicolson, *The Congress of Vienna* (London/New York, 1946); D. Dakin, "The Congress of Vienna, 1814–15, and Its Antecedents," in A. Sked (ed.), *Europe's Balance of Power 1815–1848* (London, 1979).

98. Gulick, *Europe's Classical Balance of Power*, p. 304. See also the comments in H. Kissinger, *A World Restored: Metternich, Castlereagh and the Problems of Peace 1812–1822* (Boston, 1957).

99. For a succinct coverage of the extensive literature, see P. J. Marshall, "British Expansion in India in the Eighteenth Century: An Historical Revision," *History*, vol. 60 (1975), pp. 28–43; as well as the remarks in Ingram, *Commitment to Empire*.

100. See Braudel, *Wheels of Commerce*, pp. 403ff, for a useful discussion of the importance of long-distance trade. For the specifically British context, I have benefited from reading Patrick O'Brien's paper "The Impact of the Revolutionary and Napoleonic Wars, 1793–1815, on the Long Run Growth of the British Economy" (Davis Center Paper, 1983).

101. This literature is covered in Crouzet, "Toward an Export Economy," passim; Cain and Hopkins, "The Political Economy of British Expansion Overseas, 1750–1914," passim; R. Davis, *The Industrial Revolution and British Overseas Trade* (Leicester, 1979); N.F.R. Crafts, "British Economic Growth, 1700–1831: A Review of the Evidence," *Economic History Review*, 2nd series, vol. 36 (1983), pp. 177–99.

102. The phrase is used in F. Crouzet, *The Victorian Economy* (London, 1982), p. 1.

103. Glover, *Napoleonic Wars*, pp. 182–83.

104. Quoted in Marcus, *Naval History of England*, vol. 2, p. 501.

CHAPTER FOUR
Industrialization and the Shifting Global Balances, 1815–1885

1. S. Pollard, *Peaceful Conquest: The Industrialization of Europe 1760–1970* (Oxford, 1981), passim. For good treatments of the Industrial Revolution in the West on a *country-by-country* basis, see T. Kemp, *Industrialization in Nineteenth-Century Europe* (London, 1969); W. O. Henderson, *The Industrial Revolution on the Continent: Germany, France, Russia 1800–1914* (London, 1967 edn.); C. Trebilcock, *The Industrialization of the Continental Powers 1780–1914* (London, 1981); C. M. Cipolla (ed.), *Fontana Economic History of Europe*, vol. 3, *The Industrial Revolution* (London, 1973); A. S. Milward and S. B. Saul, *The Economic Development of Continental Europe 1780–1870* (London, 1973).

2. C. M. Cipolla, "Introduction," in Cipolla (ed.), *Industrial Revolution*, p. 7.

3. D. Landes, *The Unbound Prometheus: Technological Change and Industrial Development in Western Europe from 1750 to the Present* (Cambridge, 1969), p. 41.

4. Ibid.

5. Braudel, *Civilization and Capitalism*, vol. 1, pp. 42ff.

6. For details, see McNeill, *Pursuit of Power*, pp. 185ff; G. Rudé, *Paris and London in the Eighteenth Century: Studies in Popular Protest* (New York, 1971), passim.

7. T. S. Ashton, *The Industrial Revolution 1760–1830* (Oxford, 1968 edn.), p. 129. For other excellent studies of British economic change in this period, see Mathias, *First Industrial Nation*, passim; Hobsbawm, *Industry and Empire*, chs. 2–4 and 6; and Crouzet, *Victorian Economy*, pt. 1, from where the population and GNP figures given in the preceding paragraph come.

8. Landes, *Unbound Prometheus*, pp. 97–98.

9. Ashton, *Industrial Revolution*, p. 129.

10. Mathias, *First Industrial Nation*, p. 5.

11. Bairoch, "International Industrialization Levels from 1750 to 1980," pp. 296 and 294 respectively. In the "Methodological Appendix" to this important essay, Bairoch discusses how he reaches these figures. Bairoch's assumptions are by no means uncontested, however: see A. Maddison, "A Comparison of Levels of GDP per Capita in Developed and Developing Countries, 1700–1980," *Journal of Economic History*, vol. 43 (1983), pp. 27–41.

12. Bairoch, "International Industrialization Levels," pp. 290ff; Crouzet, *Victorian Economy*, Introduction.

13. Woodruff, *Impact of Western Man*, passim; D. Fieldhouse, *The Colonial Empires: A Comparative Survey from the Eighteenth Century* (London, 1966), pt. 2; idem, *Economics and Empire 1830–1916* (London, 1973), passim.

14. On which see V. Kiernan, *European Empires from Conquest to Collapse, 1815–1960* (London, 1982); Strachen, *European Armies and the Conduct of War*, ch. 6.

15. Figures from Fieldhouse, *Colonial Empires*, p. 178.

16. This has now been very well covered in D. R. Headrich, *The Tools of Empire: Technology and European Imperialism in the Nineteenth Century* (Oxford, 1981), ch. 2 and passim.

17. E. Hobsbawm, *The Age of Capital 1848–1875* (London, 1975), ch. 7.

18. Bairoch, "International Industrialization Levels," p. 291. For a new study which stresses (and perhaps *over*stresses) the relative slowness of British economic expansion in these decades, see N.F.R. Crafts, *British Economic Growth During the Industrial Revolution* (Oxford, 1985).

19. Crouzet, *Victorian Economy*, pp. 4–5.

20. Quoted in R. Hyam, *Britain's Imperial Century 1815–1914* (London, 1975), p. 47. For further details, see B. Porter, *The Lion's Share: A Short History of British Imperialism 1850–1970* (London, 1976), passim; Cain and Hopkins, "The Political Economy of British Expansion Overseas, 1750–1914," passim; Crouzet, "Towards an Export Economy," passim; J. B. Williams, *British Commercial Policy and Trade Expansion 1750–1850* (Oxford, 1972), passim.

21. P. Bairoch, "Europe's Gross National Product: 1800–1975," *Journal of European Economic History*, vol. 5, no. 2 (Fall 1976), p. 282. And see Table 10 below.

22. D. French, *British Economic and Strategic Planning, 1905–1915* (London, 1982), ch. 1, "Nineteenth-Century Political Economy and the Problem of War," is a good introduction to these ideas.

23. See H. Strachan, *Wellington's Legacy: The Reform of the British Army, 1830–54* (Manchester, 1984).

24. These seem reasonable assumptions, based upon the crude figures of British GNP and government expenditures available in A. T. Peacock and J. Wiseman, *The Growth of Public Expenditure in the United Kingdon* (London, 1967 edn.); and P. Flora (ed.), *State, Economy and Society in Western Europe 1875–1975*, vol. 1 (Frankfurt/London, 1983), especially pt. 4, p. 441.

25. Figures taken from the "Correlates of War" print-out data made available

through the Inter-University Consortium for Political and Social Research at the University of Michigan.

26. C. Lloyd, *The Nation and the Navy* (London, 1961), p. 223.

27. For details, see Kennedy, *Rise and Fall of British Naval Mastery*, ch. 6; and espec. C. J. Bartlett, *Great Britain and Sea Power 1815–1853* (Oxford, 1963), passim. For some regional manifestations: G. S. Graham, *Great Britain in the Indian Ocean: A Study of Maritime Enterprise 1810–1850* (Oxford, 1967); B. Gough, *The Royal Navy and the North West Coast of America 1810–1914* (Vancouver, 1971); G. Fox, *British Admirals and Chinese Pirates 1832–1869* (London, 1940).

28. A.G.L. Shaw (ed.), *Great Britain and the Colonies 1815–1865* (London, 1970), p. 2. Also important here are Hyam, *Britain's Imperial Century*, passim; Porter, *Lion's Share*, passim; J. Gallagher and R. Robinson, "The Imperialism of Free Trade," *Economic History Review*, 2nd series, vol. 6, no. 1 (1953), pp. 1–15.

29. For British assumptions, see B. Porter, *Britain, Europe and the World, 1850–1982: Delusions of Grandeur* (London/Boston, 1983), ch. 1; B. J. Wendt, "Freihandel und Friedenssicherung: Zur Bedeutung des Cobden-Vertrags von 1860 zwischen England und Frankreich," *Vierteljahresschrift fur Sozial- und Wirtschafts-geschichte*, vol. 61 (1974), pp. 29ff. For the economic details, see Cain and Hopkins, "Political Economy of British Expansion Overseas," passim; L. H. Jenks, *Migration of British Capital to 1875* (London, 1963 edn.); Crouzet, *Victorian Economy*, chs. 10–11 and passim; Mathias, *First Industrial Nation*, ch. 11; A. H. Imlah, *Economic Elements in the "Pax Britannica"* (Cambridge, Mass., 1958). The complementarity in the trading/payments relationships is nicely covered in S. B. Saul, *Studies in British Overseas Trade 1870–1914* (Liverpool, 1960); and J. Foreman-Peck, *A History of the World Economy: International Economic Relations since 1850* (Brighton, Sussex, 1983), espec. chs. 1–6.

30. For this argument, see Kennedy, *Rise and Fall of British Naval Mastery*, ch. 7.

31. F. Crouzet, "Towards an Export Economy," p. 70.

32. Porter, *Britain, Europe and the World*, chs. 1–2. For the strategical implications of Britain's increasing reliance upon "service" industries, see P. Kennedy, *Strategy and Diplomacy, 1860–1945: Eight Essays* (London/Boston, 1983), ch. 3; French, *British Economic and Strategic Planning*, passim.

33. Quoted in Higham, *Britain's Imperial Century*, p. 49.

34. See pp. 131–33 above.

35. Kemp, *Industrialization in Nineteenth-century Europe*, chs. 2–3; Pollard, *Peaceful Conquest*, chs. 2–3; T. Hamerow, *Restoration, Revolution, Reaction: Economics and Politics in Germany* (Princeton, N.J., 1958).

36. J. Droz, *Europe Between Revolutions 1815–1848* (London, 1967), p. 18.

37. D. Thomson, *Europe Since Napoleon* (Harmondsworth, Mddsx., 1966 edn.), p. 111; and see also Best, *War and Society in Revolutionary Europe*, pt. 3; A. Sked, "Metternich's Enemies or the Threat from Below," in Sked (ed.), *Europe's Balance of Power 1815–1848* (London, 1979), ch. 8.

38. F. R. Bridge and R. Bullen, *The Great Powers and the European States System 1815–1914* (London, 1980), chs. 2–3; Craig, *Politics of the Prussian Army*, pp. 65ff.; R. Albrecht-Carrié, *A Diplomatic History of Europe Since the Congress of Vienna* (London, 1965 edn.), chs. 1 and 3–4. The best study of Prussian and German-state affairs in this period is now T. Nipperdey, *Deutsche Geschichte 1800–1866* (Munich, 1983).

39. D. Showalter, *Railroads and Rifles: Soldiers, Technology and the Unification of Germany* (Hamden, Conn., 1975), passim; Dupuy, *Genius for War*, chs. 4–6; *NCMH*, vol. 10, *The Zenith of European Power 1830–70*, chs. 12 and 19; L. H.

Addington, *The Patterns of War Since the Eighteenth Century* (Bloomington, Ind., 1984), pp. 39ff.

40. See again Mamatey, *Rise of the Habsburg Empire 1526–1815*, passim; Kann, *A History of the Habsburg Empire*, chs. 3 and 5.

41. A. Sked, "The Metternich System, 1815–48," in Sked (ed.), *Europe's Balance of Power 1815–1848*, ch. 5; Bridge and Bullen, *Great Powers and the European States System*, passim; Albrecht-Carrié, *Diplomatic History*, chs. 3–4; P. W. Schroeder, "World War I as a Galloping Gertie," *Journal of Modern History*, vol. 44 (1972), pp. 319–45—which echoes some of the remarks in his *Austria, Britain and the Crimean War: The Destruction of the European Concert* (Ithaca, N.Y., 1972).

42. Quoted in C. McEvedy, *The Penguin Atlas of Recent History* (Harmondsworth, Mddsx., 1982), p. 8; see also Droz, *Europe Between Revolutions*, pp. 170ff.

43. G. Rothenberg, *The Army of Francis Joseph* (West Lafayette, Ind., 1976), pp. xi, 61. See also A. Sked, *The Survival of the Habsburg Empire: Radetzky, The Imperial Army and the Class War, 1848* (London, 1979), pt. 1.

44. D. F. Good, *The Economic Rise of the Habsburg Empire, 1750–1914* (Berkeley, Calif., 1984) is best here.

45. Rothenberg, *Army of Francis Joseph*, p. 9; and J. Niemeyer, *Das oesterreichische Militärwesen im Umbruch* (Osnabruck, 1979), pp. 43–45.

46. See Rothenberg, *Army of Francis Joseph*, pp. 10, 41, 46, 58, for financial allocations; and G. A. Craig, "Command and Staff Problems in the Austrian Army, 1740–1866," in M. Howard (ed.), *The Theory and Practice of War* (London, 1965), pp. 43–67, for institutional difficulties.

47. Rothenberg, *Army of Francis Joseph*, p. 19; Kann, *History of the Habsburg Empire*, ch. 6; A. Sked, "The Metternich System," in *Europe's Balance of Power 1815–1848*, passim.

48. For a succinct survey, see R. Bullen, "France and Europe, 1815–48: The Problems of Defeat and Recovery," in Sked (ed.), *Survival of the Habsburg Empire*, pp. 122–44. For economic histories, see again Clough, *France; A History of National Economics*, passim; F. Caron, *An Economic History of Modern France* (New York, 1979), pt. 1; T. Kemp, *Economic Forces in French History* (London, 1971), chs. 6–8, 10.

49. Bullen, "France and Europe, 1815–48," pp. 125–26.

50. Ibid.

51. McNeill, *Pursuit of Power*, p. 213, fn. 57.

52. As quoted in Milward and Saul, *Economic Development of Continental Europe 1780–1870*, pp. 307–9. See also Clough, *France*, pp. 41ff; Trebilcock, *Industrialization of the Continental Powers 1780–1914*, pp. 130ff; Kemp, *Economic Forces in French History*, pp. 106ff.

53. Calculated from the figures produced in Table 10 of Bairoch, "International Industrialization Levels from 1750 to 1980," p. 296. See also the figures offered in R. E. Cameron, "Economic Growth and Stagnation in France 1815–1914," *Journal of Modern History*, vol. 30 (1958), pp. 1–13.

54. For these arguments, see Caron, *Economic History of Modern France*, espec. ch. 1. The study by P. O'Brien and C. Keydor, *Economic Growth in Britain and France 1780–1914* (London, 1978), is also a useful corrective to the older literature; but since it is not concerned with what they describe as "the mercantilist jargon of 'national power' " (p. 176), its implications are not so important for our analysis. For a critique of O'Brien and Keydor's handling of comparative statistics, see V. Hentschel, "Produktion, Wachstum und Produktivität in England, Frankreich und Deutschland von der Mitte des 19. Jahrhundert bis zum

Ersten Weltkrieg," *Vierteljahresschrift fur Sozial- und Wirtschaftsgeschichte,* vol. 68 (1981), pp. 457–510.

55. R. Cameron, *France and the Economic Development of Europe 1800–1914* (Princeton, N.J. 1961); Trebilcock, *Industrialization of the Continental Powers,* pp. 176ff; A. Rowley, *Evolution économique de la France de milieu du xixe siècle à 1914* (Paris, 1982), pp. 413ff.

56. McNeill, *Pursuit of Power,* pp. 226ff. French tactical and strategical (as well as technical) innovations are nicely compared in C. E. Hamilton, "The Royal Navy, *La Royale,* and the Militarization of Naval Warfare, 1840–1870," *Journal of Strategic Studies,* vol. 6 (1983), pp. 182–212.

57. In Padfield's definition: see *Tide of Empires,* vol. 1, foreword; and see again Bullen, "France and Europe," passim. France's colonial endeavors are briefly covered in Fieldhouse, *Colonial Empires,* ch. 13.

58. This was Palmerston's phrase of April 1848: see *NCMH,* vol. 10, p. 260. For general surveys of Russia's international position after 1815, see Bridge and Bullen, *Great Powers and the European States System,* passim; Lobanov-Rostovsky, *Russia and Europe 1789–1825,* passim; R. W. Seton-Watson, *The Russian Empire 1801–1917* (Oxford, 1967), ch. 9.

59. See the discussion in M. E. Falkus, *The Industrialization of Russia 1700–1914* (London, 1972), ch. 4; W. C. Blackwell, *The Beginnings of Russian Industralization, 1800–1860* (Princeton, N.J., 1968); and idem, *The Industrialization of Russia: An Historical Perspective* (New York, 1970), chs. 1–2.

60. Bairoch, "Europe's Gross National Product, 1800–1975," Table 4, p. 281.

61. Ibid., Table 6, p. 286.

62. Kochan and Abraham, *Making of Modern Russia,* p. 164.

63. Ibid., chs. 9–10; Trebilcock, *Industrialization of the Continental Powers,* ch. 4; Falkus, *Industrialization of Russia,* chs. 4–5; Dukes, *Emergence of the Super-Powers,* chs. 3–4.

64. J. S. Curtiss, *The Russian Army Under Nicholas I, 1825–1855* (Durham, N.C., 1965), passim; Best, *War and Society in Revolutionary Europe,* ch. 18; Seton-Watson, *Russian Empire,* pp. 289ff; J. Keep, "The Military Style of the Romanov Rulers," *War and Society,* vol. 1, no. 2 (1983), pp. 61–84. For the Anglo-Russian rivalry, see D. Gillard, *The Struggle for Asia 1828–1961* (London, 1977); E. Ingram, *The Beginning of the Great Game in Asia 1828–1834* (Oxford, 1979); Ingram (ed.), "The Great Game in Asia," *International History Review,* vol. 2, no. 2 (April 1980), special issue.

65. Curtiss, *Russian Army Under Nicholas I,* pp. 310–11.

66. By far the best study is J. S. Curtiss, *Russia's Crimean War* (Durham, N.C., 1979); but see also A. Seaton, *The Crimean War: A Russian Chronicle* (London, 1977), passim; idem, *The Russian Army of the Crimea* (Reading, Berkshire, 1973).

67. D. W. Mitchell, *A History of Russian and Soviet Sea Power* (New York, 1974), ch. 8.

68. For these details, see Curtiss, *Russia's Crimean War,* passim; Seaton, *Crimean War,* passim; Seton-Watson, *Russian Empire,* pp. 319ff; Blackwell, *Beginnings of Industrialization in Russia,* pp. 183ff; and the very good summary in W. Baumgart, *The Peace of Paris, 1856* (Santa Barbara, Calif., 1981), pp. 68–80, from where the quotation comes.

69. Baumgart, *Peace of Paris,* pp. 72–74; Seton-Watson, *Russian Empire,* p. 248; W. Pintner, "Inflation in Russia During the Crimean War Period," *American Slavic and East European Review,* vol. 18 (1959), pp. 85-87.

70. Baumgart, *Peace of Paris,* pp. 25–31.

71. Ibid., pp. 31ff.; Barnett, *Britain and Her Army,* pp. 283–91; E. M. Spiers, *The*

Army and Society 1815–1914 (London, 1980), ch. 4; J.A.S. Grenville, *Europe Reshaped 1848–1878* (London, 1976), ch. 10.

72. O. Anderson, *A Liberal State at War* (London, 1967), passim.

73. Figures taken from the "Correlates of War" print-out data, made available through the Inter-University Consortium for Political and Social Research at the University of Michigan.

74. See again MacDonagh, *Liberal State at War*, and compare with Schroeder, *Austria, Britain and the Crimean War*, Baumgart, *The Peace of Paris*, and N. Rich, *Why the Crimean War?: A Cautionary Tale* (Hanover, N.H., 1985), pp. 157ff, which concentrate much more upon Palmerston's belligerent *tone*.

75. Quoted in D.C.B. Lieven, *Russia and the Origins of the First World War* (London, 1983), p. 21. See also D. Beyrau, *Militär und Gesellschaft im vorrevolutionären Russland* (Göttingen, 1984).

76. W. E. Mosse, *Alexander II and the Modernization of Russia* (New York, 1962 edn.), passim; Kochan and Abraham, *Making of Modern Russia*, ch. 10; Seton-Watson, *Russian Empire*, pt. 4; Falkus, *Industrialization of Russia 1700–1914*, ch. 5; Blackwell, *Industrialization of Russia*, ch. 2.

77. See again Dukes, *Emergence of the Super-Powers*, chs. 3–4; Gollwitzer, *Geschichte des weltpolitischen Denkens*, vol. 1, chs. 3–4.

78. Covered in K. Bourne, *Britain and the Balance of Power in North America 1815–1908* (London, 1967).

79. "Correlates of War" print-out data; for the railway mileages, see W. W. Rostow, *The World Economy, History and Prospect* (Austin, Texas, 1978), p. 152. See also W. H. Becker and S. F. Wells, Jr. (eds.), *Economics and World Power: An Assessment of American Diplomacy Since 1789* (New York, 1984), pp. 56ff.

80. The literature upon the American Civil War is staggeringly large. I found most useful H. Hattaway and A. Jones, *How the North Won: A Military History of the Civil War* (Urbana, Ill., 1983); P. J. Parish, *The American Civil War* (New York, 1975); A. R. Millett and P. Maslowski, *For the Common Defense: A Military History of the United States of America* (New York, 1984), chs. 6–7; R. F. Weigley, *History of the United States Army* (Bloomington, Ind., 1984 edn.), chs. 10–11; Ropp, *War in the Modern World*, pp. 175–194; Addington, *Patterns of War*, pp. 62–82.

81. Millett and Maslowski, *For the Common Defense*, p. 155.

82. R. F. Weigley, *The American Way of War: A History of the United States Military Strategy and Policy* (Bloomington, Ind., 1977 edn.); Millett and Maslowski, *For the Common Defense*, passim.

83. For brief details of that position, see K. Bourne, *Victorian Foreign Policy 1830–1902* (Oxford, 1970), pp. 90–96; and, in much more detail, E. D. Adams, *Great Britain and the American Civil War*, 2 vols. (London, 1925).

84. J. Luvaas, *The Military Legacy of the Civil War: The European Inheritance* (Chicago, 1959), passim.

85. For post–Crimean War diplomacy in Europe, see Bridge and Bullen, *Great Powers and the European State System*, pp. 88ff; Albrecht-Carrié, *Diplomatic History*, pp. 94ff; W. E. Mosse, *The Rise and Fall of the Crimean System 1855–71* (London, 1963); *NCMH*, vol. 10, ch. 10, pp. 268ff; A. J. P. Taylor, *The Struggle for Mastery in Europe 1848–1918* (Oxford, 1954), pp. 83ff.

86. Rothenberg, *Army of Francis Joseph*, pp. 52ff.

87. McNeill, *Pursuit of Power*, ch. 7; C. Harvie, *War and Society in the 19th Century*, block 4, unit 10 of *War and Society* (The Open University, Bletchley, 1973); Strachan, *European Armies*, ch. 8; Ropp, *War in the Modern World*, ch. 6; Showalter, *Railroads and Rifles*, passim; *NCMH*, vol. 10, ch. 12; M. Glover, *Warfare from Waterloo to Mons* (London, 1980), pts. 2–3.

88. For Prussian military developments, see again Dupuy, *Genius for War,* pp. 75ff; Showalter, *Railroads and Rifles,* passim; Strachan, *European Armies,* pp. 98ff. For the mistakes made in 1866, see M. van Creveld, *Command in War* (Cambridge, Mass., 1985), ch. 4; G. A. Craig, *The Battle of Koeniggratz* (London, 1965), passim. The Austrian side is summarized in Rothenberg, *Army of Francis Joseph,* pp. 66ff.

89. See again van Creveld, *Command in War,* pp. 140ff; M. Howard, *The Franco-Prussian War* (London, 1981 edn.), passim.

90. For military details, see Craig, *Koeniggratz,* passim; for the diplomatic and political background, O. Pflanze, *Bismarck and the Development of Germany: The Period of Unification 1815–1871* (Princeton, N.J., 1963), chs. 13–15.

91. Howard, *Franco-Prussian War,* offers outstanding coverage of these events. For French military weaknesses, see also R. Holmes, *The Road to Sedan: The French Army, 1866–70* (London, 1984).

92. Howard, *Franco-Prussian War,* p. 1; and Holmes, *Road to Sedan,* passim, for the French side.

93. The raw figures are available in Flora, *State, Economy and Society in Western Europe 1815–1975,* vol. 1; and in B. R. Mitchell, *European Historical Statistics 1750–1975* (2nd edn., New York, 1981), e.g., coal figures on p. 381, etc. For comparative analyses of the two nations' economies, see again Trebilcock, *Industrialization of the Continental Powers,* chs. 2–3; Kemp, *Industrialization in Nineteenth-Century Europe,* chs. 3–4; Landes, *Unbound Prometheus,* ch. 4.

94. The diplomacy of the Franco-Prussian War is covered in Taylor, *Struggle for Mastery in Europe,* pp. 201–17; W. E. Mosse, *The European Powers and the German Question 1848–1870* (Cambridge, 1958); E. Kolb (ed.), *Europa und die Reichsgründung (Historische Zeitschrift,* Beiheft 6, Munich, 1980), passim; Bridge and Bullen, *Great Powers and the European States System,* pp. 108ff.

95. On which see A. Mitchell, *The German Influence in France After 1870: The Formation of the French Republic* (Chapel Hill, N.C., 1979); and idem, *Victors and Vanquished: The German Influence on Army and Church in France after 1870* (Chapel Hill, N.C., 1984).

96. See the revealing figures in Taylor, *Struggle for Mastery in Europe,* pp. xxiv–xxvi (and the remark on p. xxiii, fn. 4); also D. Mack Smith, *Italy: A Modern History* (Ann Arbor, Mich., 1959); and C. J. Lowe and F. Marzari, *Italian Foreign Policy 1870–1940* (London, 1975).

97. To use the terms employed by P. W. Schroeder, "The Lost Intermediaries: The Impact of 1870 on the European System," *International History Review,* vol. 6 (1984), p. 14.

98. On the implications of which, see ibid., passim.

99. Taylor, *Struggle for Mastery in Europe,* pp. 218ff; Bridge and Bullen, *Great Powers and the European State System,* pp. 112ff; W. L. Langer, *European Alliances and Alignments 1871–1890* (New York, 1950 edn.), passim; Grenville, *Europe Reshaped 1848–1878,* ch. 18. British policy is well covered in K. Hildebrand, "Grossbritannien und die deutsche Reichsgründung," in Kolb (ed.), *Europa und die Reichsgründung,* pp. 37ff.

100. For a good discussion, see A. Hillgruber, *Bismarcks Aussenpolitik* (Freiburg, 1972), briefly summarized in idem, *Die gescheiterte Grossmacht: Eine Skizze des Deutschen Reiches 1871–1945* (Düsseldorf, 1980), pp. 17–30.

101. A. Hillgruber, "Die 'Krieg-in-Sicht'-Krise 1875," in E. Schulin (ed.), *Gedenkschrift Martin Göhring, Studien zur europäischen Geschichte* (Wiesbaden, 1968), pp. 239–53; P. Kennedy, *The Rise of the Anglo-German Antagonism, 1860–1914* (London/Boston, 1980), pp. 29–31.

102. Hillgruber, *Die gescheiterte Grossmacht,* pp. 30ff.; and for stimulating discus-

sions of the longer-term issues, see D. Calleo, *The German Problem Reconsidered: Germany and the World Order, 1870 to the Present* (New York/Cambridge, 1978), espec. chs. 2–4; W. D. Gruner, *Die deutsche Frage: Ein Problem der europäischen Geschichte seit 1800* (Munich, 1985), passim; K. Hildebrand, "Staatskunst oder Systemzwang? Die 'Deutsche Frage' als Problem der Weltpolitik," *Historische Zeitschrift*, no. 228 (1979).

103. Taylor, *Struggle for Mastery in Europe*, pp. 228ff; Langer, *European Alliances and Alignments*, chs. 3–5; B. Jelavich, *The Great Powers, the Ottoman Empire, and the Straits Question 1870–1887* (Bloomington, Ind., 1973).

104. Quoted in Seton-Watson, *Russian Empire*, p. 455. For the naval side, see Mitchell, *A History of Russian and Soviet Sea Power*, pp. 184–90. More generally, see B. H. Sumner, *Russia and the Balkans 1870–1880* (London, 1937).

105. See the essays by Beyrau (on Russia) and Rumpler (on Austria-Hungary) in Kolb (ed.), *Europa und die Reichsgründung*; Taylor, *Struggle for Mastery in Europe*, ch. 12; Langer, *European Alliances and Alignments*, chs. 6–7; W. Windelband, *Bismarck und die europäischen Grossmächte 1878–85* (Essen, 1940); B. Waller, *Bismarck at the Crossroads* (London, 1974).

106. Taylor, *Struggle for Mastery in Europe*, ch. 13; Langer, *European Alliances and Alignments*, chs. 7–9; *NCMH*, vol. 11, chs. 20–22.

107. Kennedy, *Rise and Fall of British Naval Mastery*, pp. 189–90.

CHAPTER FIVE
The Coming of a Bipolar World and the Crisis of the "Middle Powers": Part One, 1885–1918

1. For full details, see S. E. Crowe, *The Berlin West African Conference 1884–1885* (Westport, Conn., 1970 reprint). For the general background, see again Langer, *European Alliances and Alignments*, ch. 9; *NCMH*, vol. 11, chs. 20–22; and the various chapters in E. A. Benians et al. (eds.), *The Cambridge History of the British Empire*, vol. 3, *The Empire-Commonwealth 1870–1919* (Cambridge, 1959).

2. See generally D. M. Pletcher, "Economic Growth and Diplomatic Adjustment, 1861–1898," in W. H. Becker and S. F. Wells (eds.), *Economics and World Power: An Assessment of American Diplomacy Since 1789* (New York, 1984), pp. 119–71; M. Plesur, *America's Outward Thrust: Approaches to Foreign Affairs 1865–1890* (DeKalb, Ill., 1971), pp. 151ff; W. A. Williams, *The Roots of the Modern American Empire* (New York, 1969), p. 262.

3. Crowe, *Berlin West Africa Conference*, p. 220.

4. G. F. Hudson, *The Far East in World Affairs* (2nd ed., London, 1939), p. 74.

5. This general story can be followed in G. Barraclough, *An Introduction to Contemporary History* (Harmondsworth, Mddsx., 1967), chs. 3–4; A. de Porte, *Europe Between the Super Powers* (New Haven/London, 1979) chs. 1–5; *NCMH*, vol. 12, *The Shifting Balance of World Forces, 1898–1965*, passim; W. R. Keylor, *The Twentieth-Century World: An International History* (Oxford, 1984), pt. 1; J. Bartlett, *The Global Conflict, 1880–1970: The International Rivalry of the Great Powers* (London, 1984), chs. 1–9: F. H. Hinsley, *Power and the Pursuit of Peace* (Cambridge, 1967), pp. 300ff.

6. Barraclough, *Contemporary History*, ch. 3; F. Fischer, *War of Illusions: German Policies from 1911 to 1914* (London, 1975), ch. 3; Kennedy, *Rise and Fall of British Naval Mastery*, ch. 7.

7. J.A.S. Grenville, *Lord Salisbury and Foreign Policy: The Close of the Nineteenth Century, 1895–1902* (London, 1964), pp. 165–66; and more generally, W. L.

Langer, *The Diplomacy of Imperialism 1890–1902* (2nd ed., New York, 1965), ch. 3 and p. 505.

8. Fischer, *War of Illusions,* pp. 36ff.

9. Ibid., p. 35.

10. Cited in P. Kennedy, *Strategy and Diplomacy 1860–1965: Eight Essays* (London, 1983), pp. 157–58.

11. H. Gollwitzer, *Geschichte des weltpolitischen Denkens,* vol. 2, *Zeitalter des Imperialismus und Weltkriege* (Göttingen, 1982), p. 198.

12. P. Kennedy, *The Rise of the Anglo-German Antagonism, 1860–1914* (London/Boston, 1980), chs. 16–17.

13. Idem, *Strategy and Diplomacy,* p. 46; Keylor, *Twentieth-Century World,* pp. 27ff.

14. Amery comment, on H. J. Mackinder, "The Geographical Pivot of History," *Geographical Journal,* vol. 23, no. 6 (April 1904), p. 441.

15. Thucydides, *The Peleponnesian War* (Harmondsworth, Mddsx., 1954), p. 49. For a discussion of this view, see R. Gilpin, *War and Change in World Politics* (Cambridge, 1981).

16. Landes, *Unbound Prometheus,* p. 259.

17. Figures taken from the "Correlates of War" print-out data made available through the Inter-University Consortium for Political and Social Research at the University of Michigan.

18. C. E. Black et al., *The Modernization of Japan and Russia: A Comparative Study* (New York, 1975), pp. 6–7; and, for the now classic account, W. W. Rostow, *The Process of Economic Growth* (2nd edn., Oxford, 1960).

19. Ibid.

20. Figures from Bairoch, "International Industrialization Levels from 1750 to 1980," pp. 294, 302.

21. "Correlates of War" print-out data.

22. Ibid.

23. Bairoch, "International Industrialization Levels," pp. 292, 299.

24. Ibid., pp. 296, 304.

25. C. Barnett, *The Collapse of British Power* (London/New York, 1972), p. xi.

26. Wright, *Study of War,* pp. 670–71.

27. Ibid. The 1890 total for the United States is given as only 40,000 by Wright, which is clearly a mistake.

28. See pp. 188–89 above.

29. See Table 14 above. Italian history generally in this period is covered in D. Mack Smith, *Italy, A Modern History* (Ann Arbor, 1969), pp. 101ff; C. Seton Watson, *Italy from Liberalism to Fascism* (London, 1967), pp. 129–412. It is noticeable that there is no "Italy" section in the *New Cambridge Modern History,* vol. 11, *1870–98,* and only a few pages, 482–87, in vol. 12, *1898–1945.*

30. Kemp, *Industrialization in Nineteenth-Century Europe,* ch. 6.

31. See the references in A. Tamborra, "The Rise of Italian Industry and the Balkans," *Journal of European Economic History,* vol. 3, no. 1 (1974), pp. 87–120. Other useful studies are G. Mori, "The Genesis of Italian Industrialization," *Journal of European Economic History,* vol. 4, no. 1 (Spring 1975), pp. 79–94; idem, "The Process of Industrialization in Italy: Some Suggestions, Problems and Questions," *Journal of European Economic History,* vol. 8, no. 1 (Spring 1979), pp. 60–82; Trebilcock, *Industrialization of the Continental Powers 1780–1914,* ch. 5; Pollard, *Peaceful Conquest,* pp. 229–32; Seton-Watson, *Italy from Liberalism to Fascism,* pp. 284ff; S. B. Clough, *The Economic History of Modern Italy, 1830–1914* (New York, 1964); L. Cafagua, "The Industrial Revolution in

Italy 1830–1914," in C. Cipolla (ed.), *Fontana Economic History of Europe*, vol. 4, pt. 1, *The Emergence of Industrial Societies*, pp. 287–325.

32. A. S. Milward and S. B. Saul, *The Development of the Economies of Continental Europe 1850–1914* (Cambridge, Mass., 1977), pp. 253ff; J. S. Cohen, "Financing Industrialization in Italy, 1894–1914: The Partial Transformation of a Late-Comer," *Journal of Economic History*, vol. 27 (1967), pp. 363–82; V. Castronovo, "The Italian Takeoff: A Critical Re-examination of the Problem," *Journal of Italian History*, vol. 1 (1978), pp. 492–510.

33. R.J.B. Bosworth, *Italy, the Least of the Great Powers: Italian Foreign Policy Before the First World War* (Cambridge, 1979), p. 4.

34. See the interesting (and thoroughly depressing) collection of articles on "Italian Military Efficiency" in *Journal of Strategic Studies*, vol. 5, no. 2 (1982), pp. 248ff; J. Gooch, "Italy Before 1915: The Quandary of the Vulnerable," in E. R. May (ed.), *Knowing One's Enemies: Intelligence Assessment Before the Two World Wars* (Princeton, N.J., 1984), pp. 205ff; J. Whittam, *The Politics of the Italian Army 1861–1918* (London, 1977), passim; and idem, "War Aims and Strategy: The Italian Government and High Command 1914–1919," in B. Hunt and A. Preston (eds.), *War Aims and Strategic Policy in the Great War* (London, 1977), pp. 85–104.

35. P. Halpern, *The Mediterranean Naval Situation, 1908–1914* (Cambridge, Mass., 1971), ch. 7; A. J. Marder, *The Anatomy of British Sea Power* (Hamden, Conn., 1964 reprint), pp. 174–75.

36. Bosworth, *Italy, the Least of the Great Powers*, passim. See also idem, *Italy and the Approach of the First World War* (London, 1983); Lowe and Marzari, *Italian Foreign Policy, 1870–1940*, passim.

37. P. Kennedy, "The First World War and the International Power System," in S. E. Miller (ed.), *Military Strategy and the Origins of the First World War* (Princeton, N.J., 1985), p. 15.

38. W. R. Keylor, *The Twentieth-Century World*, pp. 14–15. For other general accounts, see *NCMH*, vol. 12, ch. 12; I. Nish, *Japan's Foreign Policy, 1869–1942* (London, 1978); R. Storry, *Japan and the Decline of the West in Asia 1894–1943* (London, 1979).

39. The political and economic modernization of Japan is briefly covered in R. Storry, *A History of Modern Japan* (Harmondsworth, Mddsx., 1982 edn.), ch. 5; and in much more detail in W. H. Beasley, *The Meiji Restoration* (Stanford, Calif., 1972); E. H. Norman, *Japan's Emergence as a Modern State* (New York, 1940); T. Smith, *Political Change and Industrial Development in Japan: Government Enterprise 1868–1880* (Stanford, Calif., 1955).

40. The economic aspects of Japanese modernization can be followed in G. S. Allen, *A Short Economic History of Japan* (London, 1981 edn.), chs. 2–5; L. Klein and K. Ohkawa (eds.), *Economic Growth: The Japanese Experience Since the Meiji Era* (Holmwood, Ill., 1968); Rostow, *World Economy*, pp. 416–25; K. Ohkawa and H. Rosovsky, *Japanese Economic Growth* (Stanford, Calif., 1973).

41. E. B. Potter (ed.), *Sea Power: A Naval History* (Annapolis, Md., 1981), pp. 166–168; Glover, *Warfare from Waterloo to Mons*, pp. 181–84.

42. Quoted in Storry, *Japan and the Decline of the West in Asia*, p. 30.

43. On which see now I. Nish, *The Origin of the Russo-Japanese War* (London, 1985), passim. The conflict itself is best described in J. N. Westwood, *Russia Against Japan, 1904–5: A New Look at the Russo-Japanese War* (London, 1986), and is also covered in Storry, *Japan and the Decline of the West in Asia*, chs. 4–5; S. Okamoto, *The Japanese Oligarchy and the Russo-Japanese War* (New York, 1970); J. A. White, *The Diplomacy of the Russo-Japanese War* (Princeton, N.J., 1964). The war at sea is briefly covered in Potter (ed.), *Sea Power*, pp.

168ff, and P. Padfield, *The Battleship Era* (London, 1972), pp. 167ff; on land, P. Walden, *The Short Victorious War: A History of the Russo-Japanese War, 1904–5* (New York, 1974).

44. See A. J. Sherman, "German-Jewish Bankers in World Politics: The Financing of the Russo-Japanese War," *Leo Baeck Institute Yearbook*, vol. 28 (1983), pp. 59–73.

45. Cited in Kennedy, *Rise of the Anglo-German Antagonism*, p. 464.

46. For general accounts of Germany's economic growth, see Fisher, *War of Illusions*, pt. 1; Calleo, *The German Problem Reconsidered*, ch. 4; N. Stone, *Europe Transformed 1878–1916* (London, 1983), pp. 159ff; W. G. Hoffmann, *Das Wachstum der Deutschen Wirtschaft seit der Mitte des 19. Jahrhunderts*, (Berlin, 1965); W. O. Henderson, *The Rise of German Industrial Power, 1834–1914*, (Berkeley/Los Angeles, 1972), pt. 3; M. Kitchen, *The Political Economy of Germany 1815–1914* (London, 1978).

47. I took this figure from p. 2 of John Gooch's paper "Italy During the First World War," for the forthcoming first volume of *Military Effectiveness*, eds. A. Millett and W. Murray.

48. See the figures in Calleo, *German Problem Reconsidered*, pp. 66, 68.

49. Quoted in J. Steinberg, "The Copenhagen Complex," *Journal of Contemporary History*, vol. 1, pt. 3 (1966), p. 26.

50. Langer, *Diplomacy of Imperialism*, p. 96; and see again Gollwitzer, *Geschichte des weltpolitischen Denkens*, vol. 2, pp. 83–252; idem, *Europe in the Age of Imperialism* (London, 1969), passim; W. Baumgart, *Imperialism: The Idea and Reality of British and French Colonial Expansion 1880–1914* (Oxford, 1982), pt. 3.

51. For these quotations, see respectively, Kennedy, *Rise of the Anglo-German Antagonism*, p. 311; J. C. Röhl, "A Document of 1892 on Germany, Prussia, and Poland," *Historical Journal*, vol. 7 (1964), pp. 144ff; Fisher, *War of Illusions*, ch. 3.

52. I take this term from H.-U. Wehler, *Bismarck und der Imperialismus* (Cologne, 1969), pt. 3, pp. 112ff.

53. See the assessments in A. J. Marder, *From the Dreadnought to Scapa Flow: The Royal Navy in the Fisher Period*, vol. 1, *The Road to War 1904–1914* (London, 1961), ch. 13; Kennedy, *Rise and Fall of British Naval Mastery*, chs. 8–9.

54. Kennedy, *Strategy and Diplomacy*, p. 160.

55. B. F. Schulte, *Die deutsche Armee* (Düsseldorf, 1977); V. R. Berghahn, *Germany and the Approach of War in 1914* (London/New York, 1974), chs. 1 and 6. For good examples of the many fatuous underestimations of German military power (especially as compared with Russia and France), see P. Towle, "The European Balance of Power in 1914," *Army Quarterly and Defense Journal*, vol. 104 (1974), pp. 333–62.

56. All of these figures from Wright, *Study of War*, pp. 670–71.

57. J. K. Tanenbaum, "French Estimates of Germany's Operational War Plans," in May (ed.), *Knowing One's Enemies*, p. 162.

58. Calleo, *German Problem Reconsidered*, introduction.

59. Kennedy, *Rise of the Anglo-German Antagonism*, p. 311.

60. See again Gilpin, *War and Change in World Politics*, passim.

61. For compelling evidence of this, see the articles in J.G.C. Röhl and N. Sombart (eds.), *Kaiser Wilhelm II: New Interpretations* (Cambridge, 1982).

62. Quoted in G. A. Craig, *Germany 1866–1965* (Oxford, 1978), p. 336. There is good evidence of this confusion of purpose in I. N. Lambi, *The Navy and German Power Politics 1862–1914* (London/Boston, 1984).

63. Fisher, *War of Illusions,* passim; Berghahn, *Germany and the Approach of War,* passim.
64. This is explored further in P. Kennedy (ed.), *The War Plans of the Great Powers 1880–1914* (London/Boston 1979), introduction.
65. Calleo, *German Problem Reconsidered,* p. 5.
66. Quoted in Kennedy, *Strategy and Diplomacy,* p. 157.
67. See the charts for France, Great Britain, and Austria-Hungary's "Relative Power" in C. F. Doran and W. Parsons, "War and the Cycle of Relative Power," *American Political Science Review,* vol. 74 (1980), p. 956.
68. Taylor, *Struggle for Mastery in Europe,* p. xxviii.
69. There is a brief coverage in Kann, *History of the Habsburg Empire,* pp. 461ff; a good survey in Milward and Saul, *Development of the Economies of Continental Europe 1850–1914,* pp. 271ff; and a more sophisticated analysis, comparing the empire with Italy and Spain, in Trebilcock, *Industrialization of the Continental Powers,* ch. 5.
70. Bairoch, "Europe's Gross National Product 1800–1975," p. 287.
71. L. L. Farrar, *Arrogance and Anxiety: The Ambivalence of German Powers 1849–1914* (Iowa City, Iowa, 1981), ch. 3, fns. 9 and 18. Farrar calculates "power" by multiplying population and manufacturing production. The early section of this present chapter should indicate that power is a much more complex phenomenon.
72. For comparative growth rates, see Good, *The Economic Rise of the Habsburg Empire 1750–1914,* p. 239; for industrial potential, see Table 17 above.
73. Figures from Good, *Economic Rise of the Habsburg Empire,* p. 150.
74. For what follows, see the brilliant description in Stone, *Europe Transformed,* pp. 303ff; Kann, *History of the Habsburg Empire,* ch. 8; C. A. MacArtney, *The Habsburg Empire 1790–1918* (London, 1969), chs. 14–17; A. J. May, *The Habsburg Monarchy 1862–1916* (Cambridge, Mass., 1960), pp. 343ff.
75. Rothenberg, *Army of Francis Joseph,* ch. 9; Langer, *Diplomacy of Imperialism,* pp. 596–98; and espec. C. Andrew, *Théophile Delcassé and the Making of the Entente Cordiale* (London, 1968), pp. 127ff.
76. Quoted in Stone, *Europe Transformed,* pp. 316–17; see also Rothenberg, *Army of Francis Joseph,* p. 106.
77. Wright, *Study of War,* pp. 670–71, columns 10–12; also useful is Rothenberg, *Army of Francis Joseph,* pp. 125–26, 148, 160, 172.
78. For the state of the Austro-Hungarian navy, see Halpern, *Mediterannean Naval Situation,* ch. 6. The state of the army prior to 1914 is covered in Rothenberg's excellent *Army of Francis Joseph,* chs. 9–12; N. Stone, "Moltke and Conrad: Relations between the Austro-Hungarian and German General Staffs 1909–1914," in Kennedy (ed.), *War Plans of the Great Powers 1880–1914,* pp. 222ff; idem, *The Eastern Front 1914–1917* (London, 1975), ch. 4; idem, "Austria-Hungary," in May (ed.), *Knowing One's Enemies,* pp. 37ff.
79. Rothenberg, *Army of Francis Joseph,* p. 159, also pp. 152, 163.
80. Ibid., p. 159. And see also Stone, "Moltke and Conrad," in Kennedy (ed.), *War Plans of the Great Powers.*
81. Stone, "Austria-Hungary," p. 52.
82. See here P. W. Schroeder's powerful and elegant plea that the Great Powers (Britain especially) should have preserved the Austro-Hungarian Empire in order to save the status quo: "World War I as a Galloping Gertie," *Journal of Modern History,* vol. 44, no.3 (1972), pp. 319–45. It is not unlike pleading that after 1945 the United States and USSR should have tried to preserve the British Empire in order to avoid subsequent instability in the Third World.
83. For French foreign policy, see the older work E. M. Carroll, *French Public*

Opinion and Foreign Affairs 1880–1914 (London, 1931); G. F. Kennan, *The Decline of Bismarck's European Order: Franco-Russian Relations 1875–1890* (Princeton, N.J., 1979); Andrew, *Théophile Delcassé and the Making of the Entente Cordiale;* J.F.V. Keiger, *France and the Origins of the First World War* (London, 1983).

84. There is no comprehensive history of French defense policy in this period; but there are useful details in D. Porch, *The March to the Marne: The French Army 1871–1914* (Cambridge, 1981); P.-M. de la Gorce, *The French Army: A Military Political History* (New York, 1963), chs. 1–5; R. D. Challenor, *The French Theory of the Nation in Arms 1866–1939* (New York, 1955); as well as the references in notes 88–89 below.

85. Marder, *Anatomy of British Sea Power,* pp. 71–3, 86–7, 107–9, 124ff; and the references in Kennedy, *Rise of the Anglo-German Antagonism,* ch. 11, fn. 27.

86. French colonialism and the French colonial empire are covered in A. S. Kanya-Forstner, *The Conquest of the Western Sudan: A Study in French Military Imperialism* (Cambridge, 1969); R. Betts, *Tricouleur: The French Empire* (London, 1978): H. Brunschwig, *French Colonialism, 1871–1916: Myths and Realities* (London, 1966); R. Girardet, *L'idée coloniale en France de 1871 à 1962* (Paris, 1972); J. Ganiage, *L'expansion coloniale de la France sous la Troisième Republique 1871–1914* (Paris, 1968).

87. For a good summary of this argument, see A. S. Kanya-Forstner, "French Expansion in Africa: The Mythical Theory," in R. Owen and R. Sutcliffe (eds.), *Studies in the Theory of Imperialism* (London, 1972), pp. 285ff.

88. French naval policy is covered briefly in Jenkins, *History of the French Navy,* pp. 303ff; Williamson, *Politics of Grand Strategy,* pp. 227ff; Halpern, *Mediterranean Naval Situation,* pp. 47ff; and T. Ropp, *The Development of a Modern Navy: French Naval Policy 1871–1904* (Annapolis, Md., 1987), passim.

89. This may also explain why so many historians have tended to focus upon civil-military relations in France rather than military policy *per se.* For examples, in addition to the works listed in note 84 above, see R. Girardet, *La société militaire dans la France contemporaine* (Paris, 1953); G. Krumeich, *Armaments and Politics in France on the Eve of the First World War* (Leamington Spa, 1986).

90. For what follows, see Milward and Saul, *Development of the Economies of Continental Europe 1850–1914,* ch. 2; Kemp, *Industrialization in Nineteenth-Century Europe,* ch. 3; idem, *Economic Forces in French History,* ch. 9; Trebilcock, *Industrialization of the Continental Powers,* ch. 3 (an excellent and sophisticated survey); Rowley, *Evolution économique de la France du Milieu du XIXᵉ siècle à 1914,* passim; Caron, *Economic History of Modern France,* pt. 1; J. H. Clapham, *The Economic Development of France and Germany, 1815–1914* (Cambridge, 1948); R. Price, *The Economic Modernization of France* (London, 1975).

91. Kemp, *Industrialization in Nineteenth-Century Europe,* pp. 71–72.

92. The literature upon French banking and overseas investment is enormous; for a brief summary, see Kindleberger, *Financial History of Western Europe,* pp. 225ff; Trebilcock, *Industrialization of the Continental Powers,* pp. 173ff; R. Cameron, *France and the Economic Development of Europe* (Princeton, 1961), passim. The Russian loans and Franco-Russian diplomacy are covered in R. Girault, *Emprunts russes et investisements français en Russie, 1887–1914* (Paris, 1973); and Krumeich, *Armaments and Politics in France,* ch. 6.

93. Trebilcock, *Industrialization of the Continental Powers,* p. 182.

94. Ibid., p. 158.

95. Bairoch, "Europe's Gross National Product," p. 281; idem, "International In-

dustrialization Levels," p. 297; Wright, *Study of War*, pp. 670–71. See also the careful comparisons in V. Hentschel, "Produktion, Wachstum and Produktivität in England, Frankreich and Deutschland von der Mitte des 19. Jahrhunderts bis zum Ersten Weltkrieg," *Vierteljahresschrift fur Sozial- und Wirtschaftsgeschichte*, vol. 68 (1981), pp. 457–510. All this quite contradicts Stone, *Europe Transformed*, p. 282.

96. See the overwhelming evidence in Mitchell, *Victors and Vanquished*, chs. 1–5, espec. pp. 109–11.

97. Porch, *March to the Marne*, p. 227.

98. For repeated examples of these sort of claims, see E. Weber, *The Nationalist Revival in France, 1905–1916* (Berkeley, Calif., 1959); H. Contamine, *La Revanche, 1871–1914* (Paris, 1957); Krumeich, *Armament and Politics in France*, passim.

99. Ibid. See also Williamson, *Politics of Grand Strategy*, chs. 5 and 8; B. H. Liddell Hart, "French Military Ideas Before the First World War," in M. Gilbert (ed.), *A Century of Conflict, 1850–1950* (London, 1966), pp. 133–48.

100. For what follows, see Andrew, *Théophile Delcassé and the Making of the Entente Cordiale*, passim; Keiger, *France and the Origins of the First World War*, chs. 1 and 4.

101. J. J. Becker, *1914: Comment les Français sont entrés dans la guerre* (Paris, 1977); J. Joll, *The Origins of the First World War* (London/New York, 1984), ch. 8.

102. J. Remak, "1914—The Third Balkan War: Origins Reconsidered," reprinted in Koch (ed.), *Origins of the First World War*, pp. 89–90.

103. The phrase used first in R. Robinson and J. Gallagher, with A. Denny, *Africa and the Victorian: The Official Mind of Imperialism* (2nd edn., London, 1981). For a discussion of this term, and their other ideas, see P. Kennedy, "Continuity and Discontinuity in British Imperialism 1815–1914," in C. C. Eldridge (ed.), *British Imperialism in the Nineteenth Century* (London, 1984), pp. 20–38.

104. See again Bourne, *Britain and the Balance of Power in North America*, passim. For the settlement of these differences, and other aspects of the relationship, see B. Perkins, *The Great Rapprochement* (New York, 1969).

105. Gillard, *Struggle for Asia*, passim; F. Kazemzadeh, *Russian and Britain in Persia, 1864–1914* (New Haven, Conn., 1968); E. Hölzle, *Die Selbstentmachtung Europas*, pp. 85ff.

106. L. K. Young, *British Policy in China 1895–1902* (Oxford, 1970); P. Lowe, *Britain in the Far East: A Survey from 1819 to the Present* (London, 1981) chs. 3–4.

107. Hobsbawm, *Industry and Empire*, p. 150. See also P. J. Cain, *Economic Foundations of British Overseas Expansion 1815–1914* (London, 1980), ch. 9; W. G. Hynes, *The Economics of Empire: Britain, Africa and the New Imperialism, 1870–95* (London, 1979), passim; Cain and Hopkins, "Political Economy of British Expansion Overseas," pp. 485ff.

108. For details, see the early chapters of Grenville, *Lord Salisbury and Foreign Policy*.

109. Marder, *Anatomy of British Sea Power*, passim; Kennedy, *Rise and Fall of British Naval Mastery*, chs. 7–8; and J. Gooch, *The Plans of War: The General Staff and British Military Strategy c. 1900–1916* (London, 1974), cover naval and military planning.

110. In consequence, the literature is enormous and grows each year. Hobsbawm, *Industry and Empire*, pp. 136–53, 172–85; Landes, *Unbound Prometheus*, pp. 326–58; and Mathias, *First Industrial Nation*, pp. 243–52, 306–34, 365–426, are still very instructive. Crouzet, *Victorian Economy*, pp. 371ff, is a succinct new survey.

111. Cited in Kennedy, *Rise of the Anglo-German Antagonism,* p. 315.
112. Quoted in N. Mansergh, *The Commonwealth Experience* (London, 1969), p. 134.
113. Kennedy, *Rise of the Anglo-German Antagonism,* p. 307, and passim, for similar quotations.
114. Quotation in G. R. Searle, *The Quest for National Efficiency 1899–1914* (Oxford, 1971), p. 5, with a wealth of further detail on this mood.
115. Porter, *Lion's Share,* pp. 353–54.
116. Taylor, *Struggle for Mastery in Europe,* p. xxix; Peacock and Wiseman, *Growth of Public Expenditure in the United Kingdom,* p. 166; Kennedy, *Rise of the Anglo-German Antagonism,* ch. 17.
117. Figures from W. Woodruff, "The Emergence of an Industrial Economy 1700–1914," in Cipolla (ed.), *Fontana Economic History of Europe,* vol. 4, pt. 2, *The Emergence of Industrial Societies,* p. 707.
118. On which theme see Porter's excellent *Britian, Europe and the World,* passim.
119. Kennedy, *Rise and Fall of British Naval Mastery,* pp. 195ff.
120. Mansergh, *Commonwealth Experience,* ch. 5; D. C. Gordon, *The Dominion Partnership in Imperial Defense 1870–1914* (Baltimore, Md., 1965).
121. On which see J. Ehrman, *Cabinet Government and War 1890–1940* (Cambridge, 1958); F. A. Johnson, *Defense by Committee* (London, 1960).
122. See note 102 above.
123. Superbly analyzed in M. Howard, *The Continental Commitment* (London, 1972), passim.
124. French, *British Economic and Strategic Planning,* passim; Kennedy, "Strategy versus Finance in Twentieth-Century Britain," in *Strategy and Diplomacy,* pp. 89–106; and the stimulating treatment in Porter, *Britain, Europe and the World,* ch. 3.
125. Cited in Fischer, *War of Illusions,* p. 402.
126. The words are those of Buchanan, British ambassador to Russia, as quoted in K. Wilson, "British Power in the European Balance, 1906–1914," in D. Dilks (ed.), *Retreat from Power: Studies in Britain's Foreign Policy in the Twentieth Century,* 2 vols. (London, 1981), vol. 1, p. 39.
127. Which are, respectively, the rough subtitle and the main title of R. Ropponen, *Die Kraft Russlands: Wie beurteilte die politische und militarische Führung der europäischen Grossmächte in der Zeit von 1905 bis 1914 die Kraft Russlands?* (Helsinki, 1968), an extraordinarily rich compilation.
128. The following section on the Russian economy prior to 1914 is based upon G. Grossman, "The Industrialization of Russia and the Soviet Union," in Cipolla (ed.), *Fontana Economic History of Europe,* vol. 4, pt. 2, pp. 486ff; R. Munting, *The Economic Development of the USSR* (London, 1982), ch. 1; O. Crisp, *Studies in the Russian Economy Before 1914* (London, 1976), espec. ch. 1, "The Pattern of Industrialization in Russia, 1700–1914"; Seton-Watson, *Russian Empire,* pp. 506ff, 647ff; Blackwell, *Industrialization of Russia,* ch. 2; M. E. Falkus, *Industrialization of Russia 1700–1914,* chs. 7–9; Milward and Saul, *Development of the Economies of Continental Europe,* pp. 365–423; the comparisons in Black (ed.), *Modernization of Japan and Russia,* passim; and the many statistics in the older work of M. S. Miller, *The Economic Development of Russia, 1905–1914* (London, 1926).
129. Crisp, "Pattern of Industrialization," pp. 40–41.
130. Munting, *Economic Development,* p. 34; Girault, *Emprunts russes et Investisements français en Russie,* passim; and J. P. Machay, *Pioneer for Profit: Foreign Entrepreneurs and Russian Industrialization* (Chicago/London, 1970), passim. For indigenous entrepreneurs, see R. Portal, "Muscovite Industrialists: The

Cotton Sector 1861–1914," in W. L. Blackwell (ed.), *Russian Economic Development from Peter the Great to Stalin* (New York, 1974), pp. 161–96.

131. Munting, *Economic Development*, p. 31. More generally, A. Gershrenkon, *Economic Backwardness in Historical Perspective* (Cambridge, Mass., 1962); M. Falkus, "Aspects of Foreign Investment in Tsarist Russia," *Journal of European Economic History*, vol. 8, no. 1 (Spring 1979), pp. 14–16. For the latest, very sophisticated (but therefore very complex) diagnosis, see P. Gatrell, *The Tsarist Economy, 1850–1917* (London, 1986), passim.

132. See Tables 14–18 above; and A. Nove's excellent comparative statistics in *An Economic History of the USSR* (Harmondsworth, Mddsx., 1969), pp. 14–15.

133. Munting, *Economic Development*, pp. 27; Trebilcock, *Industrialization of the Continental Power*, pp. 216ff, 247ff.

134. Grossman, "Industrialization of Russia and the Soviet Union," p. 489.

135. Ibid., p. 486.

136. Lieven, *Russia and the Origins of the First World War*, p. 4. Chs. 1 and 5 of Lieven's book are compelling in this respect, as is T. H. von Laue, *Sergei Witte and the Industrialization of Russia* (New York, 1963).

137. Lieven, *Russia and the Origins of the First World War*, p. 13; H. Rogge, *Russia in the Age of Modernization and Revolution 1881–1917* (London, 1983), pp. 77ff; Falkus, "Aspects of Foreign Investment," p. 10.

138. Stone, *Europe Transformed*, pp. 257ff, is especially good here. See also Seton-Watson, *Russian Empire*, pp. 541ff; Milward and Saul, *Development of the Economies of Continental Europe*, pp. 397ff; J.H.L. Keep, "Russia," in *NCMH*, vol. 9, p. 369.

139. Stone, *Europe Transformed*, pp. 212–13. See also Blackwell, *Industrialization of Russia*, pp. 32ff.

140. Stone, *Europe Transformed*, p. 244.

141. Seton-Watson, *Russian Empire*, pp. 485ff, 607ff, 643ff; Rogge, *Russia in the Age of Modernization and Revolution*, ch. 9. For the army's dislike of internal-police roles, see J. Bushnell, *Mutiny and Repression: Russian Soldiers in the Revolution of 1905–1906* (Bloomington, Ind., 1985), pp. 32ff.

142. Lieven, *Russia and the Origins of the First World War*, ch. 5; Joll, *Origins of the First World War*, pp. 102ff.

143. See Tables 14–18 above.

144. K. Neilson, "Watching the 'Steamroller': British Observers and the Russian Army before 1914," *Journal of Strategic Studies*, vol. 8, no. 2 (June 1985), p. 213.

145. And not surprising, since the War Office's "Military Reports" on foreign countries covered "geography, topography, ethnography, defences, trade, resources, communications, political condition, etc."—see T. G. Ferguson, *British Military Intelligence, 1870–1914* (Frederick, Md., 1984), p. 223.

146. O. Crisp, quoted in Lieven, *Russia and the Origins of the First World War*, p. 9; and see the details in J. Bushnell, "Peasants in Uniform: The Tsarist Army as a Peasant Society," *Journal of Social History*, vol. 13 (1980), pp. 565–76. See also A. K. Wildman, *The End of the Russian Imperial Army* (Princeton, 1980), chs. 1–2.

147. The quotation is from Fuller, "The Russian Empire," in May (ed.), *Knowing One's Enemies*, p. 114, and passim. Also important here is J. Bushnell, "The Tsarist Officer Corps, 1881–1914: Customs, Duties, Inefficiencies," *American Historical Review*, vol. 86 (1981), pp. 753–80; P. Kenez, "Russian Officer Corps Before the Revolution: The Military Mind," *Russian Review*, vol. 31 (1972), pp. 226–36. Bushnell's study *Mutiny and Repression* contains further eye-opening details, as does W. C. Fuller, *Civil-Military Conflict in Imperial Russia 1881–1914* (Princeton, N.J., 1985).

148. Fuller, "Russian Empire," passim; A. K. Wildman, *End of the Russian Imperial Army*, chs. 1–2; W. B. Lincoln, *Passage Through Armageddon: The Russians in the War and Revolution 1914–1918* (New York, 1986), pp. 52ff.

149. Lieven, *Russia and the Origins of the First World War*, pp. 149–50; Stone, *Eastern Front*, p. 134 (from where the quotation comes).

150. The confusions of prewar Russian planning are covered in Stone, *Eastern Front*, pp. 30ff; Lieven, *Russia and the Origins of the First World War*, ch. 5; L.C.F. Turner, "The Russian Mobilization in 1914," rev. version, in Kennedy, *War Plans of the Great Powers*, pp. 252–62; Fuller, "Russian Empire," pp. 111ff.

151. Mitchell, *History of Russian and Soviet Sea Power*, p. 279.

152. Doran and Parsons, "War and the Cycle of Relative Power," p. 956.

153. D. M. Pletcher, "1861–1898: Economic Growth and Diplomatic Adjustments," in W. H. Becker and S. F. Wells (eds.), *Economics and World Power: An Assessment of American Diplomacy Since 1789* (New York, 1984), p. 120. For other surveys of this growth, see M. L. Eysenbach, *American Manufactured Exports 1897–1914: A Study of Growth and Comparative Advantage* (New York, 1976); H. G. Vatter, *The Drive to Industrial Maturity: The U. S. Economy, 1860–1914* (Westport, Conn., 1975 edn.).

154. Stone, *Europe Transformed*, pp. 211ff; cf. R. M. Robertson, *History of American Economy* (New York, 1975 edn.), ch. 13.

155. Barraclough, *Introduction to Contemporary History*, p. 51.

156. Taken from Q. Wright, *Study of War*, pp. 670–71, with my calculations on per capita income.

157. See Tables 15–16 above—but cf. Taylor, *Struggle for Mastery in Europe*, p. xxx.

158. Farrar, *Arrogance and Anxiety*, p. 39, fn. 168.

159. Ibid.; D. H. Aldcroft, *From Versailles to Wall Street: The International Economy in the 1920s* (Berkeley/Los Angeles, 1977), p. 98, Table 4.

160. Keylor, *Twentieth-Century World*, p. 39; cf. Crouzet, *Victorian Economy*, p. 342, fn. 153.

161. Woodruff, *America's Impact on the World*, p. 161.

162. W. LaFeber, *The New Empire: An Interpretation of American Expansion 1860–1898* (Ithaca, N.Y., 1963); W. A. Williams, *The Roots of the Modern American Empire* (New York, 1969). For more general surveys of American foreign policy, see T. A. Bailey, *A Diplomatic History of the American People* (New York, 1974, edn.); R. D. Schulzinger, *American Diplomacy in the Twentieth Century* (New York/Oxford, 1984), chs. 2–3.

163. Pletcher, "1861–1898," pp. 124ff; T. McCormick, *China Market: America's Quest for Informal Empire* (Chicago, 1967); D. G. Munro, *Intervention and Dollar Diplomacy in the Caribbean 1900–1921* (Princeton, N.J., 1964); E. R. May, *Imperial Democracy: The Emergence of America as a Great Power* (New York, 1961), pp. 5–6; Perkins, *Great Rapprochement*, pp. 122ff.

164. For a critical analysis, see M. de Cecco, *Money and Empire: The International Gold Standard 1890–1914* (Oxford, 1974), pp. 110–126; for the 1907 crisis, see J. H. Clapham, *The Economic History of Modern Britain*, 3 vols. (Cambridge, 1938), vol. 3, pp. 55ff.

165. The literature upon the motives and actions of American imperialism between 1895 and 1914 is colossal. Apart from the references in notes 162 and 163 above, see also R. Dallek, *The American Style of Foreign Policy* (New York, 1983), chs. 1–3; E. R. May, *American Imperialism: A Speculative Essay* (New York, 1968); G. F. Linderman, *The Mirror of War: American Society and the Spanish-American War* (Ann Arbor, Mich., 1974); Howard K. Beale, *Theodore Roosevelt and the Rise of America to World Power* (New York, 1962 edn.).

166. Dallek, *American Style of Foreign Policy*, p. 23

167. Beale, *Theodore Roosevelt and the Rise of America to World Power*, passim; Dallek, *American Style of Foreign Policy*, ch. 2; Schulzinger, *American Diplomacy in the Twentieth Century*, pp. 24–38.

168. See especially the criticisms in G. F. Kennan, *American Diplomacy* (Chicago, 1984 edn.), chs. 1–3; and Dallek, *American Style of Foreign Policy*, passim.

169. U.S. naval growth and naval policy in this period are now very well covered. Apart from Potter (ed.), *Sea Power*, chs. 15 and 17–18, see K. J. Hagan (ed.), *In Peace and War: Interpretations of American Naval History, 1775–1978* (Westport, Conn., 1978), chs. 9–10; W. R. Braisted, *The United States Navy in the Pacific*, 2 vols. (Austin, Texas, 1958 and 1971); and the older works H. and M. Sprout, *The Rise of American Naval Power, 1776–1918* (Princeton, N.J., 1946 edn.), and W. Mills, *Arms and Men* (New York, 1956), ch. 2.

170. Apart from Braisted's important works, see R. D. Challenor, *Admirals, Generals and American Foreign Policy 1898–1914* (Princeton, N.J., 1973); J.A.S. Grenville and G. B. Young, *Politics, Strategy and American Diplomacy: Studies in Foreign Policy, 1873–1917* (New Haven, Conn., 1966).

171. Challenor, *Admirals, Generals, and American Foreign Policy*, passim; H. H. Herwig, *Politics of Frustration: The United States in German Naval Planning, 1889–1941* (New York, 1976). For the improvement in Anglo-American relations, see C. S. Campbell, *From Revolution to Rapprochement: The United States and Great Britain, 1783–1900* (New York, 1974), chs. 13–14.

172. Millet and Maslowski, *For the Common Defense*, chs. 9–10. For further details, see D. F. Trask, *The War with Spain in 1898* (New York, 1981); and G. A. Cosmas, *An Army for Empire: The United States Army in the Spanish-American War* (Columbia, Missouri, 1971). Also useful on the change of attitudes is J. L. Abrahamson, *America Arms for a New Century* (New York, 1981); R. Weigley, *History of the United States Army*, chs. 13–14.

173. See again Tables 14–20 above.

174. F. Gilbert, *The End of the European Era, 1890 to the Present* (3rd edn., New York, 1984), p. 110. For detailed analyses of these decades, see Taylor, *Struggle for Mastery in Europe*, pp. 325ff; Bridge and Bullen, *Great Powers and the European States System*, chs. 6–8; Albrecht-Carrié, *Diplomatic History of Europe Since the Congress of Vienna*, pp. 207ff; Bartlett, *Global Conflict*, chs. 2–3.

175. B. Waller, *Bismarck at the Crossroads: The Reorientation of German Foreign Policy After the Congress of Berlin 1878–1880* (London, 1974), p. 195. See also Taylor, *Struggle for Mastery*, pp. 258ff; and Kennan, *Decline of Bismarck's European Order*, pp. 73ff.

176. Kennan, *Decline of Bismarck's European Order*, passim; and idem, *The Fateful Alliance: France, Russia, and the Coming of the First World War* (New York, 1984), passim. The German side is well covered in N. Rich, *Friedrich von Holstein*, 2 vols. (Cambridge, 1965), vol. 1, passim.

177. The argument that the European scene was "stabilized" in the 1890s, permitting the turn toward colonial issues, is best covered in W. L. Langer, *The Diplomacy of Imperialism 1890–1902* (New York, 1951 edn.), passim.

178. Langer's phrase: see ibid., ch. 13; and, more generally, Padfield, *Battleship Era*, ch. 14.

179. On this transformation, see again Perkins, *Great Rapprochement*, passim; Campbell, *From Revolution to Rapprochement*, ch. 14.

180. The standard work here is I. H. Nish, *The Anglo-Japanese Alliance* (London, 1966); but see also C. J. Lowe, *The Reluctant Imperialists: British Foreign Policy 1878–1902*, 2 vols. (London, 1967), vol. 1, ch. 10.

181. Taylor, *Struggle for Mastery in Europe*, ch. 18; Andrew, *Delcassé and the Mak-*

ing of the Entente Cordiale, passim; Albrecht-Carrié, *Diplomatic History,* pp. 232ff. See also the comments in M. Behnen, *Rüstung-Bündnis-Sicherheit* (Tübingen, 1985).

182. This is best covered in Andrew, *Delcassé,* passim; and G. L. Monger, *The End of Isolation; British Foreign Policy 1900–1907* (London, 1963).

183. O. J. Hale, *Germany and the Diplomatic Revolution 1904–1906* (Philadelphia, Pa., 1931); Kennedy, *Rise of the Anglo-German Antagonism,* ch. 14.

184. Kennedy, *Rise of the Anglo-German Antagonism,* pp. 268ff; further details in B. Vogel, *Deutsche Russlandpolitik, 1900–1906* (Düsseldorf, 1973).

185. The complicated events are covered in the works by Taylor, Monger, Andrew, Rich, and Kennedy, cited above. See also H. Raulff, *Zwischen Machtpolitik und Imperialismus: Die deutsche Frankreichpolitik 1904–5* (Düsseldorf, 1976); and Lambi's excellent *Navy and German Power Politics 1862–1914,* ch. 13.

186. Taylor, *Struggle for Mastery,* ch. 19; Z. Steiner, *Britain and the Origins of the First World War* (London, 1977), ch. 2 et seq. For the Russian response to the 1909 humiliation, see Lieven, *Russia and the Origin of the First World War,* pp. 36ff.

187. Steiner, *Britain and the Origins of the First World War,* pp. 200ff; Williamson, *Politics of Grand Strategy,* passim, espec. ch. 7.

188. The most detailed study of these events is L. Albertini, *The Origin of the War of 1914,* 3 vols. (London, 1952–57); but there are good succinct accounts in L.C.F. Turner, *Origins of the First World War* (London, 1970); J. Joll, *Origins of the First World War,* chs. 2–3; and Langhorne, *Collapse of the Concert of Europe,* chs. 6–7.

189. The literature upon pre-1914 war plans is immense; for surveys, see P.M. Kennedy (ed.), *The War Plans of the Great Powers 1880–1914* (London/Boston, 1979); S. E. Miller (ed.), *Military Strategy and the Origins of the First World War* (Princeton, N.J., 1985); J. Snyder, *The Ideology of the Offensive* (Ithaca, N.Y., 1984).

190. Strachan, *European Armies and the Conduct of War,* ch. 9; B. E. Schmitt and H. C. Vedeler, *The World in the Crucible 1914–1919* (New York, 1984), pp. 62ff.

191. Kennedy, *Rise and Fall of British Naval Mastery,* ch. 9.

192. For this argument, see L. L. Farrar, *The Short-War Illusion* (Santa Barbara, Calif., 1973), passim.

193. On which see, briefly, Schulzinger, *American Diplomacy in the Twentieth Century,* pp. 62ff; and, in more detail, D. M. Smith, *The Great Departure: The United States and World War I, 1914–1920* (New York, 1965); P. Devlin, *Too Proud to Fight: Woodrow Wilson's Neutrality* (New York, 1975); E. R. May, *The World War and American Isolation* (Chicago, 1966 edn.); A. S. Link, *Wilson,* 5 vols. to date (Princeton, N.J., 1947–65), vols. 3–5.

194. Bosworth, *Italy, the Least of the Great Powers,* is best here.

195. On which distractions, see P. Guinn, *British Strategy and Politics, 1914–1918* (Oxford, 1965); Beloff, *Imperial Sunset,* vol. 1, ch. 5; and D. French, *British Strategy and War Aims 1914–1916* (London/Boston, 1986), passim.

196. Rothenberg, *Army of Francis Joseph,* chs. 12–14, is an excellent analysis of Austro-Hungarian military policy—including both strengths and weaknesses—during the war.

197. For this argument, see Steiner, *Britain and the Origins of the First World War,* ch. 9; Kennedy, *Rise of the Anglo-German Antagonism,* pp. 458ff.

198. For a more extended argument on these lines, see Kennedy, *British Naval Mastery,* ch. 9.

199. Ibid.

200. Strachen, *European Armies and the Conduct of War,* ch. 9; and see also the

excellent analysis of the problem in S. Bidwell and D. Graham, *Fire-Power: British Army Weapons and Theories of War, 1904–1945* (London, 1982), chs. 4–8. For a succinct survey, see B. Bond, "The First World War," in *NCMH.*, vol. 12, ch. 7.

201. For excellent examples, see Stone, *Eastern Front*, p. 265 and passim.

202. Van Creveld, *Supplying War*, ch. 4, is convincing here. See also the critique in G. Ritter, *The Schlieffen Plan* (New York, 1958), and in L.C.F. Turner, "The Significance of the Schlieffen Plan," in Kennedy (ed.), *War Plans of the Great Powers*, pp. 199–221.

203. For further details, see Stone, *Eastern Front*, chs. 3–8; Schmitt and Vedeler, *World in the Crucible*, chs. 4–5; B. H. Liddell Hart, *History of the First World War* (London, 1970 edn.), chs. 4–5; Lincoln, *Passage Through Armageddon*, chs. 2–4.

204. Schmitt and Vedeler, *World in the Crucible*, ch. 6; J. L. Stokesbury, *A Short History of World War I* (New York, 1981), chs. 11–12.

205. See, for example, Stone on Russia, in *Eastern Front*, ch. 9; Barnett on Britain, in *Collapse of British Power*, pp. 113ff; McNeill on France, in *Pursuit of Power*, pp. 318ff.

206. Apart from McNeill's excellent general survey, see also G. Hardach, *The First World War 1914–1918* (London, 1977), espec. chs. 4 and 6; and A. Marwick, *War and Social Change in the Twentieth Century* (London, 1974), chs. 2–3.

207. See again Rothenberg, *Army of Francis Joseph*, chs. 12–14; for the internal problems, Kann, *History of the Habsburg Empire*, ch. 9; A. J. May, *The Passing of the Habsburg Monarchy, 1914–1918*, 2 vols. (Philadelphia, Pa., 1966), passim.

208. See especially the paper by J. Gooch, "Italy During the First World War," in the forthcoming collection A. Millett and W. Murray (eds.), *Military Effectiveness.*

209. J.A.S. Grenville, *A World History of the Twentieth Century 1900–1945* (London, 1980), vol. 1, pp. 218–19.

210. Stone, *Eastern Front*, passim, has excellent details (even if his case for Russia's industrial successes begs certain questions). See also Seton-Watson, *Russian Empire*, pp. 698ff; and D. R. Jones, "Imperial Russia's Armed Forces at War, 1914–1918: An Analysis of Combat Effectiveness," in Millett and Murray (eds.), *Military Effectiveness.* The role of the Moscow industrialists and their quarrels with the ministries is detailed in L. H. Siegelbaum, *The Politics of Industrial Mobilization in Russia, 1914–1917* (New York, 1984); and there is further massive detail in A. L. Sidorov, *The Economic Position of Russia During the First World War* (Moscow, 1973 trans.). The czar's own efforts are examined in D. R. Jones, "Nicholas II and the Supreme Command," *Sbornik*, vol. 11 (1985), pp. 47–83.

211. Schmitt and Vedeler, *World in the Crucible*, pp. 188–99. This quotation is from N. Golovine, *Russian Army in the World War* (New Haven, 1932), p. 281. For the casualty numbers, and the discontents at the "second-category" call-up, see Wildman, *End of the Russian Imperial Army*, ch. 3; and the nice survey in Lincoln, *Passage Through Armageddon*, passim.

212. G. Pedrocini, *Les mutineries de 1917* (Paris, 1967), is the best of a number of studies on this crisis.

213. McNeill, *Pursuit of Power*, p. 322, with a good synthesis of the literature. See also Hardach, *First World War*, pp. 86ff, 131ff.

214. See the older work M. Ange-Laribé, *L'agriculture pendant la guerre* (Paris, 1925), as well as the coverage in Hardach and McNeill.

215. Figures from Stokesbury, *Short History of World War I*, p. 289.

216. Kennedy, "Great Britain Before 1914," in May (ed.), *Knowing One's Enemies*, pp. 172–204; French, *British Economic and Strategic Planning*, passim.

217. See again Barnett, *Collapse of British Power*, pp. 113ff; Hardach, *First World War*, pp. 77ff; McNeill, *Pursuit of Power*, pp. 325ff; R.J.Q. Adams, *Arms and the Wizard: Lloyd George and the Ministry of Munitions, 1915* (London, 1978), passim.
218. Figures from Hardach, *First World War*, p. 87.
219. Kennedy, *Realities Behind Diplomacy*, p. 146, with the figures drawn from tables in Peacock and Wiseman, *Growth of Public Expenditure in the United Kingdom*.
220. Bond, "First World War," passim in *NCMH*, vol. 12; Guinn, *British Strategy and Politics*, passim: Schmitt and Vedeler, *World in the Crucible*, chs. 6–8; D. R. Woodward, *Lloyd George and the Generals* (Newark, N.J., 1983).
221. Quoted in Beloff, *Imperial Sunset*, vol. 1, p. 255. For full details, see now K. Burk, *Britain, America and the Sinews of War 1914–1918* (London/Boston, 1985).
222. F. S. Northedge, *The Troubled Giant: Britain Among the Great Powers* (London, 1966), p. 623.
223. Well covered in T. Lupfer, "The Dynamics of Doctrine: The Changes in German Tactical Doctrine During the First World War," *Leavenworth Papers*, no. 4 (Fort Leavenworth, Kans., 1981); and Van Creveld, *Command in War*, pp. 168ff.
224. Hardach, *First World War*, pp. 55ff; G. Feldman, *Army, Industry and Labor in Germany 1914–1918* (Princeton, N.J., 1966).
225. See the nervous consideration of this in Beloff, *Imperial Sunset*, pp. 239ff, 246ff, 271.
226. Hardach, *The First World War*, pp. 63ff; McNeill, *The Pursuit of Power*, pp. 338ff; Bond, "The First World War," pp. 198–99, in *NCMH*, vol. 12.
227. Full details are in A. Skalweit, *Die Deutsche Kriegsnährungswirtschaft* (Berlin, 1927), with a summary in Hardach, *First World War*, pp. 112ff. For the impact of the war upon the German people, see J. Kocka, *Facing Total War: German Society 1914–1918* (Leamington Spa, Warwick, 1984), chs. 2 and 4; McNeill, *Pursuit of Power*, p. 340, for the quotation.
228. See the references in note 193 above. For a historiographical summary, see D. M. Smith, "National Interest and American Intervention, 1917: An Historical Appraisal," *Journal of American History*, vol. 52 (1965), pp. 5–24.
229. The American contribution is ably summarized in Millett and Maslowski, *For the Common Defense*, ch. 11; Weigley, *History of the United States Army*, ch. 16; T. K. Nenninger, "American Military Effectiveness in World War I," in Millett and Murray (eds.), *Military Effectiveness* (forthcoming).
230. Strachan, *European Armies and the Conduct of War*, p. 148. See also the useful details in Ritter, *The Sword and the Scepter*, 4 vols. (London, 1975), vol. 4, pp. 119ff, 229ff.
231. Bond, "First World War," *NCMH*, vol. 12, p. 199, which provides these figures; Schmitt and Vedeler, *World in the Crucible*, p. 261. For detailed studies of the 1918 campaigning, see J. Toland, *No Man's Land: The Story of 1918* (London, 1980); H. Essame, *The Battle for Europe, 1918* (New York, 1972); B. Pitt, *1918— The Last Act* (New York, 1962).
232. For details, see Schmitt and Vedeler, *World in the Crucible*, p. 255ff, 376ff; A. J. Ryder, *The German Revolution of 1918* (Cambridge, 1967), passim.
233. J. Keegan, *The Face of Battle* (Harmondsworth, Mddsx., 1978), passim; J. Williams, *The Home Fronts: Britain, France and Germany, 1914–1918* (London, 1972); A. Marwick, *The Deluge—British Society in the First World War* (London, 1965); idem, *War and Social Change in the Twentieth Century*, chs. 2–3.
234. This theme runs through Kennan's books; for example, see *Decline of Bis-*

marck's European Order, p. 3. In a similar vein is Hölzle, *Die Selbstentmachtung Europas*. For surveys of the psychological-cultural impact, referring to the more detailed literature, see Schmitt and Vedeler, *World in the Crucible*, pp. 476ff, and J. Joll, *Europe Since 1870* (London, 1973), espec. ch. 11.

235. War expenditure figures from Hardach, *First World War*, p. 153; total mobilized forces from Barraclough (ed.), *Atlas of World History*, p. 252.

236. See the anecdotes in M. Middlebrook, *The Kaiser's Battle: 21 March 1918* (London, 1978).

CHAPTER SIX
The Coming of a Bipolar World and the Crisis of the "Middle Powers": Part Two, 1919–1942

1. For the 1919–1923 settlements, see the general treatments in *NCMH*, vol. 12, ch. 8; Albrecht-Carrié, *Diplomatic History of Europe*, pp. 360ff; G. Ross, *The Great Powers and the Decline of the European States System 1914–1945* (London, 1983), ch. 3; R. J. Sontag, *A Broken World, 1919–1939* (New York, 1971), chs. 1 and 4; M. L. Dockrill and J. D. Goold, *Peace Without Promise: Britain and the Peace Conferences 1919–23* (London, 1981), passim; S. Marks, *The Illusion of Peace: International Relations in Europe 1918–1933* (London, 1976), ch. 1.

2. Ross, *Great Powers*, ch. 4; Marks, *Illusion of Peace*, ch. 3; A.J.P. Taylor, *The Origins of the Second World War* (Harmondsworth, Mddsx., 1964 edn.), ch. 3; J. Jacobsen, *Locarno Diplomacy: Germany and the West 1925–1929* (Princeton, N.J., 1972); and G. Grun, "Locarno, Ideal and Reality," *International Affairs*, vol. 31 (1955), pp. 477–85, are best here.

3. The literature upon reparations and war debts has now turned into a flood. Among the more important recent works are M. Trachtenberg, *Reparation in World Politics: France and European Diplomacy 1916–1923* (New York, 1980); W. A. McDougall, *France's Rhineland Diplomacy 1914–1924* (Princeton, N.J., 1978); H. Rupieper, *The Cuno Government and Reparations, 1922–1923* (London, 1979); S. A. Shuker, *The End of French Predominance in Europe: The Financial Crisis of 1924 and the Adoption of the Dawes Plan* (Chapel Hill, N.C., 1976); D. P. Silverman, *Reconstructing Europe After the Great War* (Cambridge, Mass., 1982). Marks, *Illusion of Peace*, ch. 2, is also useful, and there is a good summary in Kindleberger, *Financial History of Western Europe*, pt. 4.

4. D. H. Aldcroft, *From Versailles to Wall Street, 1919–1929* (London, 1977), p. 13. This is a good summary of all of the post-1919 studies (often sponsored by the Carnegie Foundation) on "the costs of the war," as well as the more recent literature.

5. Aldcroft, *From Versailles to Wall Street*, p. 14.

6. Aldcroft, *The European Economy 1914–1980* (London, 1978), p. 19.

7. Aldcroft, *From Versailles to Wall Street*, pp. 34–35, 98ff.

8. Rostow, *World Economy*, pp. 194–200, has a good summary; but see also Kenwood and Lougheed, *Growth of the International Economy*, ch. 11; A. S. Milward, *The Economic Effects of the World Wars in Britain* (London, 1970), passim; Landes, *Unbound Prometheus*, ch. 6.

9. I. Svennilson, *Growth and Stagnation in the European Economy*, (Geneva, 1954), pp. 204–05.

10. Farrar, *Arrogance and Anxiety*, p. 39, fn. 17.

11. Aldcroft, *From Versailles to Wall Street*, ch. 1 and pp. 99–101: Kenwood and Lougheed, *Growth of the International Economy*, pp. 176ff. For details of the

collapse in American farm prices after 1919, see Robertson, *History of the American Economy*, p. 515.

12. For a good summary, see Hardach, *First World War*, ch. 6; also Aldcroft, *From Versailles to Wall Street*, pp. 30ff.

13. See the references in note 3 above; and Aldcroft, *From Versailles to Wall Street*, ch. 4.

14. See here the essays in Rowland (ed.), *Balance of Power or Hegemony: The Inter-War Monetary System;* C. P. Kindleberger, *The World in Depression 1929–1939* (California, 1973), passim, but especially chs. 1 and 4; A. Fishlow, "Lessons from the Past: Capital Markets During the 19th Century and the Interwar Period," *International Organization*, vol. 39, no. 3 (1985), especially pp. 415–27. There is also a very good analysis in Kennedy, *Over Here*, pp. 334–47.

15. For an analysis of these events, see Aldcroft, *From Versailles to Wall Street*, chs. 7–11; Kindleberger, *World in Depression*, chs. 3–9; idem, *Financial History of Western Europe*, ch. 20.

16. Kindleberger, *World in Depression*, p. 231; Rowland, "Preparing the American Ascendancy: The Transfer of Economic Power from Britain to the United States, 1933–1944," in Rowland (ed.), *Balance of Power or Hegemony*, pp. 198ff. For Chamberlain's quote, see D. Reynolds, *The Creation of the Anglo-American Alliance, 1937–61* (London, 1981), p. 16 and passim; also C. A. MacDonald, *The United States, Britain and Appeasement 1936–1939* (London, 1980).

17. A.J.P. Taylor, *The Trouble-Makers: Dissent over Foreign Policy, 1789–1939* (London, 1969 edn.), chs. 4–6; Z. S. Steiner, *The Foreign Office and Foreign Policy 1898–1914* (Cambridge, 1969), passim; G. A. Craig and A. L. George, *Force and Statecraft: Diplomatic Problems of Our Time* (Oxford, 1983), ch. 5.

18. See, for example, L. Martin, *Peace Without Victory—Woodrow Wilson and the English Liberals* (New York, 1973 edn.); Taylor, *Trouble-Makers*, ch. 5.

19. A. J. Mayer, *Political Origins of the New Diplomacy* (New York, 1970 edn.), passim; S. R. Grabaud, *British Labour and the Russian Revolution 1917–1924* (Cambridge, Mass., 1956); F. S. Northedge and A. Wells, *Britain and Soviet Communism: The Impact of a Revolution* (London, 1982), ch. 8.

20. G. Schmidt, "Wozu noch politische Geschichte?" *Aus Politik und Zeitgeschichte*, B17/75 (April 1975), pp. 32ff.

21. Mayer, *Politics and Diplomacy of Peacemaking: Containment and Counter-Revolution at Versailles 1918–1919* (London, 1968); Joll, *Europe Since 1870*, ch. 9, "Revolution and Counter-Revolution." There is also good detail upon these fears of revolution in C. S. Maier, *Recasting Bourgeois Europe* (Princeton, N.J., 1975), espec. ch. 1.

22. Joll, *Europe Since 1870*, chs. 9–12; Sontag, *Broken World*, pp. 24ff.

23. Schmitt and Vedeler, *World in the Crucible*, pp. 476ff; B. Bengonzi, *Heroes' Twilight* (New York, 1966); P. Fussell, *The Great War and Modern Memory* (New York, 1975); cf. Barnett, *Collapse of British Power*, pp. 426ff.

24. See again Joll, *Europe Since 1870*, pp. 262ff; Gollwitzer, *Geschichte des Weltpolitischen Denkens*, vol. 2, pp. 538ff.; A. Hamilton, *The Appeal of Fascism* (London, 1971): P. Hayes, *Fascism* (London, 1973), passim; R.A.L. Waite, *Vanguard of Nazism: The Free Corps Movement in Postwar Germany* (Cambridge, Mass., 1952), passim; J. Diehl, *Paramilitary Politics in Weimar Germany* (Bloomington, Ind., 1977).

25. D. Caute, *The Fellow Travellers* (London, 1973); Northedge and Wells, *Britain and Soviet Communism*, chs. 6–8.

26. For what follows, see the excellent analysis in Barraclough, *Introduction to Contemporary History*, ch. 6, "The Revolt Against the West"; and the maps in Barraclough (ed.), *Atlas of World History*, pp. 248, 260–61. See also Gollwitzer,

Geschichte des weltpolitischen Denkens, vol. 2, pp. 575ff; *NCMH,* vol. 12, chs. 10–12; H. Bull and A. Watson, *The Expansion of International Society* (Oxford, 1984), espec. pt. 3; R. F. Holland, *European Decolonization 1918–1981* (London, 1985), ch. 1; H. Griml, *Decolonization: The British, French, Dutch, and Belgian Empires 1919–1963* (London, 1978) chs. 1–3.

27. For a good example on the British side, see B. R. Tomlinson, *The Political Economy of the Raj 1914–1947* (Cambridge, 1979), passim; more generally, Tomlinson, "The Contraction of England: National Decline and the Loss of Empire," *Journal of Imperial and Commonwealth History,* vol. 11 (1982), pp. 58–72; Thornton, *Imperial Idea and its Enemies,* chs. 4–6; Beloff, *Imperial Sunset,* vol. 1, ch. 6.

28. Barraclough, *Introduction to Contemporary History,* pp. 156–58.

29. Storry, *Japan and the Decline of the West in Asia,* pp. 107ff; Grenville, *World History of the Twentieth Century,* pp. 117ff; Keylor, *Twentieth-Century World,* pp. 229ff; Gollwitzer, *Geschichte des weltpolitischen Denkens,* vol. 2, pp. 575ff.

30. A. Iriye, *After Imperialism: The Search for a New Order in the Far East 1921–1931* (New York, 1978 edn.), passim.

31. Kiernan, *European Empires from Conquest to Collapse,* ch. 13; *NCMH,* vol. 12, pp. 319, 324–25; C. M. Andrew and A. S. Kanya-Forstner, *The Climax of French Imperial Expansion 1914–1924* (Stanford, Calif., 1981), p. 246.

32. Howard, *Continental Commitment,* pp. 56ff; B. Bond, *British Military Policy Between the Two World Wars* (Oxford, 1980), chs. 1, 3–4.

33. For discussions of this "continuity" in German policy after 1919, see the general treatments in Calleo, *German Problem Reconsidered,* passim; Gruner, *Die deutsche Frage,* pp. 126ff; Hillgruber, *Germany and the Two World Wars,* passim. See also two important new works: G. Stoakes, *Hitler and the Quest for World Dominion: Nazi Ideology and Foreign Policy in the 1920s* (Leamington Spa, Warwickshire, 1986); M. Lee and W. Michalka, *German Foreign Policy 1917–1933: Continuity or Break?* (Leamington Spa, Warwickshire, 1987).

34. Taylor, *Origins of the Second World War,* p. 48.

35. Ibid. For other surveys of the post-1919 "balance," see DePorte, *Europe Between the Super-Powers,* ch. 3; Thomson, *Europe Since Napoleon,* pp. 622ff.; Ross, *Great Powers and the Decline of the European States System,* chs. 3–6.

36. E. M. Bennett, *German Rearmament and the West, 1932–1933* (Princeton, N.J., 1979), pp. 92ff, is best here.

37. P. Wandycz, *France and Her Eastern Allies 1919–25* (Minneapolis, Minn., 1962), passim; and the classic older work A. Wolfers, *Britain and France Between Two Wars* (New York, 1966 edn.), especially ch. 8. Later French efforts to contain Germany in eastern Europe are explored in L. Radice, *Prelude to Appeasement, East Central European Diplomacy in the early 1930s* (New York, 1981), chs. 3–4.

38. W. N. Medlicott, *British Foreign Policy Since Versailles, 1919–1963* (London, 1968), pp. 61–63; Ross, *Great Powers,* p. 57; A. Orde, *Britain and International Security 1920–1926* (London, 1978), passim. For the continuity of this policy, see P. W. Schroeder, "Munich and the British Tradition," *Historical Journal,* vol. 19 (1976), pp. 223–43.

39. A. Teichova, *An Economic Background to Munich* (Cambridge, 1974) passim; D. Kaiser, *Economic Diplomacy and the Origins of the Second World War* (Princeton, N.J., 1980), passim; B. J. Wendt, "England und der deutsche 'Drang nach Südosten,'" in I. Geiss and B. J. Wendt (eds.), *Deutschland in der Weltpolitik des 19. und 20. Jahrhunderts* (Düsseldorf, 1973), pp. 483–512.

40. Quoted in Northedge, *Troubled Giant,* p. 220. There is a good and succinct survey of the League's activities in *NCMH,* vol. 12, ch. 9; and in Ross, *Great Powers,* ch. 7.

41. E. H. Carr, *The Twenty Years Crisis 1919–1939* (London, 1939); Sontag, *Broken World*, passim; A. Adamthwaite, *The Lost Peace: International Relations in Europe 1918–1939* (London, 1980), passim.
42. D. Mack Smith, *Mussolini: A Biography* (New York, 1982) is a good portrayal of the man, though less so of Italian politics and economy under him. For those aspects, see M. Knox, *Mussolini Unleashed 1939–1941* (Cambridge, 1982), ch. 1; J. Whittam, "The Italian General Staff and the Coming of the Second World War," in A. Preston (ed.), *General Staffs and Diplomacy Before the Second World War* (London, 1978), pp. 77–97; A. Raspin, "Wirtschaftliche und politische Aspekte der italienischen Aufrüstung Anfang der dreissiger Jahre bis 1940," in F. Forstmeier and H. E. Volkmann (eds.), *Wirtschaft und Rüstung am Vorabend des Zweiten Weltkrieges* (Düsseldorf, 1975), pp. 202–21; B. R. Sullivan, "The Italian Armed Forces, 1918–1940," in Millett and Murray (eds.), *Military Effectiveness*, vol. 2 (forthcoming).
43. S. Ricossa, "Italy," in Cipolla (ed.), *Fontana Economic History of Europe*, vol. 6, no. 1, pp. 272ff; R. Higham, *Air Power: A Concise History* (Manhattan, Kan., 1984 edn.), p. 48; J. W. Thompson, *Italian Civil and Military Aircraft 1930–1945* (Fallbrook, Calif., 1963).
44. Knox, *Mussolini Unleashed*, p. 20.
45. Quoted from Ricossa, "Italy," p. 266; see also, Knox, *Mussolini Unleashed*, pp. 30–31, 43.
46. Ricossa, "Italy," p. 270.
47. Knox, *Mussolini Unleashed*, ch. 1; Mack Smith, *Mussolini's Roman Empire*, ch. 13; Raspin, "Wirtschaftliche und Politische Aspekte," passim; W. Murray, *The Change in the European Balance of Power, 1938–1939* (Princeton, N.J., 1984), pp. 110ff.
48. Knox, *Mussolini Unleashed*, p. 48.
49. Ibid., p. 73. More generally, see McNeill, *Pursuit of Power*, pp. 350ff; W. Murray, "German Air Power and the Munich Crisis," in B. Bond and I. Roy (eds.), *War and Society*, vol. 1 (1976), pp. 107–18.
50. The figures with neither parentheses nor brackets come from Hillman, "Comparative Strength of the Powers," in A. J. Toynbee and F. T. Ashton-Gwatkin (eds.), *The World in 1939* (London, 1952), Table VI, p. 454, with currency conversions at the exchange rates he gives in the footnote. The figures in parentheses come from the "Correlates of War" print-out. One suspects that currency changes are responsible for some of the discrepancies, as are different national accounting practices. In Japan's case the matter is further complicated by the distinctions made between regular and "extraordinary" defense spending, and between "forces in homeland" and "others" (e.g., China War). The figures in brackets are from K. Ohkawa and M. Shinohara (eds.), *Patterns of Japanese Economic Development* (New Haven, Conn., 1979), and do *not* include "others."
51. Mack Smith, *Mussolini's Roman Empire*, pp. 177–78.
52. Knox, *Mussolini Unleashed*, pp. 9–16; idem, "Conquest, Foreign and Domestic, in Fascist Italy and Nazi Germany", *Journal of Modern History*, vol. 56 (1986), pp. 1–57.
53. On this, Mack Smith, *Mussolini*, is overwhelming.
54. See below, pp. 340–41.
55. These racial/cultural attitudes are nicely covered in Thorne, *The Issue of War: States, Societies, and the Far Eastern Conflict of 1941–1945* (London, 1985), passim. See also Storry, *Japan and the Decline of the West in Asia*, passim.
56. Howarth, *Fighting Ships of the Rising Sun*, pp. 199ff.
57. Allen, *Short Economic History of Modern Japan*, pp. 100ff.

58. League of Nations, *World Economic Survey* (Geneva, 1945), Table III, p. 134.
59. Allen, *Economic History,* pp. 101–13; Storry, *Japan and the Decline of the West in Asia,* p. 115.
60. On this important theme, see espec. J. B. Crowley, *Japan's Quest for Autonomy: National Security and Foreign Policy 1930–1958* (Princeton, N.J., 1966), passim; M. A. Barnhart, "Japan's Economic Security and the Origins of the Pacific War," *Journal of Strategic Studies,* vol. 4, no. 2 (1981), pp. 105–24; J. W. Morley (ed.), *Dilemmas of Growth in Prewar Japan* (Princeton, N.J., 1971).
61. Allen, *Economic History of Modern Japan,* p. 141.
62. Howarth, *Fighting Ships of the Rising Sun,* pt. 4; H. P. Willmott, *Empires in the Balance* (Annapolis, Md., 1982), ch. 3; A. J. Marder, *Old Friends, New Enemies: The Royal Navy and the Imperial Japanese Navy* (Oxford, 1981), ch. 11; S. E. Pelz, *Race to Pearl Harbor* (Cambridge, Mass., 1974), espec. pts. 1 and 5; C. Bateson, *The War with Japan* (East Lansing, Mich., 1968), ch. 2.
63. Willmott, *Empires in the Balance,* pp. 89ff; R. H. Spector, *Eagle Against the Sun: The American War with Japan* (New York, 1985), chs. 2 and 4; S. Hayashi with A. Coox, *Kogun: The Japanese Army in the Pacific War* (Westport, Conn., 1978 reprint), ch. 1.
64. Willmott, *Empires in the Balance,* p. 55; P. M. Kennedy, "Japan's Strategic Decisions, 1939–45," in Kennedy, *Strategy and Diplomacy 1870–1945,* pp. 182ff; C. Boyd, "Military Organizational Effectiveness: Imperial Japanese Armed Forces Between the World Wars," in Millett and Murray (eds.), *Military Effectiveness,* vol. 2. Pelz, *Race to Pearl Harbor,* ch. 12, is very good on the army-navy quarrels. The China War itself is covered in F. Dorn, *The Sino-Japanese War 1937–1941* (New York, 1974).
65. Barnhart, "Japan's Economic Security," pp. 112–16.
66. Barnhart, "Japan's Economic Security," p. 114, from where the quote comes. See also B. Martin, "Aggressionspolitik als Mobilisierungsfaktor: Der militärische und wirtschaftliche Imperialismus Japans 1931 bis 1941," in F. Forstmeier and H.-E. Volkmann (eds.), *Wirtschaft und Rüstung am Vorabend des Zweiten Weltkrieges* (Düsseldorf, 1975), pp. 234–35.
67. Hayashi and Coox, *Kogun,* pp. 14–17; M. A. Barnhart, "Japanese Intelligence Before the Second World War," in May (ed.), *Knowing One's Enemies,* pp. 435–37; and espec. A. Coox, *Nomonhan,* 2 vols. (Stanford, Calif., 1985), passim.
68. Wright, *Study of War,* p. 672; Overy, *Air War,* p. 151; Bairoch, "World Industrialization Levels," p. 299.
69. For the decision itself, see Willmott, *Empires in the Balance,* ch. 3; Hayashi and Coox, *Kogun,* pp. 19ff; Barnhart, "Japan's Economic Security," pp. 116ff; I. Nobutaka (ed.), *Japan's Decision for War* (Stanford, Calif., 1967), passim; Spector, *Eagle Against the Sun,* ch. 4; R. J. Butow, *Tojo and the Coming of War* (Princeton, N.J., 1961).
70. For general surveys, see Craig, *Germany 1866–1945,* pp. 396ff; A. J. Nicholls, *Weimar and the Rise of Hitler* (London, 1979 edn.), passim. For summaries of the massive historiography, and hotly contested debates upon Germany in the Nazi era, see I. Kershaw, *The Nazi Dictatorship* (London, 1985); and K. Hildebrand, *The Third Reich* (London/Boston, 1984).
71. Taylor, *Origins of the Second World War,* passim; J. Hiden, *Germany and Europe 1919–1939* (London, 1977), espec. ch. 7; F. Fischer, *Bündnis der Eliten* (Düsseldorf, 1979). For details of the "continuity" among the armed forces, see G. Schreiber, *Revisionismus und Weltmachtstreben* (Stuttgart, 1978), passim; J. Dülffer, *Weimar, Hitler und die Marine: Reichspolitik und Flottenbau 1920–1939* (Düsseldorf, 1973); M. Geyer, *Aufrüstung oder Sicherheit* (Wiesbaden, 1980). Also important for what follows is *Das Deutsche Reich und der Zweite*

Weltkrieg, vol. 1, *Ursachen und Voraussetzungen der deutschen Kriegspolitik*, eds. W. Deist et al. (Stuttgart, 1979).

72. A. Bullock, *Hitler: A Study in Tyranny* (London, 1962 edn.); A. Hillgruber, *Germany and the Two World Wars* (Cambridge, Mass., 1981), espec. chs. 5 and 8; N. Rich, *Hitler's War Aims*, 2 vols. (London, 1973–74); G. Weinberg, *The Foreign Policy of Hitler's Germany*, 2 vols. (Chicago, 1970 and 1980); and the literature in M. Hauner, "A Racial Revolution?" *Journal of Contemporary History*, vol. 19 (1984), pp. 669–87; Calleo, *The German Problem Reconsidered*, pp. 85–95; Gruner, *Die deutsche Frage*, pp. 145ff; A. Kuhn, *Hitlers aussenpolitisches Programm* (Stuttgart, 1970); E. Jackel, *Hitler's Weltanschauung* (Middletown, Conn., 1982).

73. The term comes from E. N. Petersen, *The Limits of Hitler's Power* (Princeton, N.J., 1969); but see also Craig, *Germany 1860–1945*, ch. 17; Kershaw, *Nazi Dictatorship*, chs. 4 and 7; Hildebrand, *Third Reich*, pp. 83ff, 152ff; also I. Kershaw, *Popular Opinion and Political Dissent in the Third Reich: Bavaria 1933–1945* (Oxford, 1983).

74. Murray, *Change in the European Balance of Power*, pp. 20–21; Hillman, "Comparative Strength of the Great Powers," p. 454.

75. Quoted in A. Seaton, *The German Army 1933–45* (London, 1982), p. 55. See also Craig, *Politics of the Prussian Army*, pp. 397ff.

76. Seaton, *German Army 1933–45*, chs. 3–4, covers this breakneck expansion, as does W. Deist, *The Wehrmacht and German Rearmament* (London, 1981), chs. 3 and 6, with references to the extensive further literature.

77. For more details, see Deist, *Wehrmacht*, ch. 4; Overy, *Air War*, p. 21; W. Murray, *Luftwaffe* (Baltimore, Md., 1985), ch. 1; E. L. Homze, *Arming the Luftwaffe* (Lincoln, Neb., 1976); K.-H. Volker, *Die deutsche Luftwaffe 1933–1939* (Stuttgart, 1967).

78. Deist, *Wehrmacht*, p. 81; with much more detail in Dülffer, *Weimar, Hitler und die Marine*, passim; and M. Salewski, *Die deutsche Seekriegsleitung 1935–1945*, 3 vols. (Frankfurt, 1970–75).

79. R. J. Overy, *The Nazi Economic Recovery 1932–1938* (London, 1932), pp. 19ff.

80. Ibid., pp. 28ff. Overy's brief work contains full references to further studies on the German economy under the Nazis.

81. Deist, *Wehrmacht*, pp. 89–91 and passim; A. S. Milward, *The German Economy at War* (London, 1965), pp. 17–24.

82. Murray, *Change in the European Balance of Power*, pp. 4ff, is the best summary here; but see also Hillmann, "Comparative Strength of the Powers," pp. 368ff.

83. Murray, *Balance of Power*, p. 15.

84. Ibid., pp. 15–16. See also the important chapter by H.-E. Volkmann, "Die NS-Wirtschaft in Vorbereitung des Krieges," in Deist, et al., *Ursachen und Voraussetzungen der deutschen Kriegspolitik*, espec. pp. 349ff.

85. Deist, *Wehrmacht*, p. 90; Seaton, *German Army*, pp. 93–96.

86. Quoted in Murray, *Luftwaffe*, p. 20; idem., "German Air Power and the Munich Crisis," in Bond and Roy (eds.), *War and Society*, vol. 1, passim; Deist, *Wehrmacht*, pp. 66–69.

87. B. R. Posen, *The Sources of Military Doctrine: France, Britain and Germany Between the World Wars* (Ithaca, N.Y., 1984), passim; W. Murray, "German Army Doctrine, 1918–1939, and the Post-1945 Theory of Blitzkrieg Strategy," in C. Fink et al. (eds.), *German Nationalism and the European Response 1890–1945* (Chapel Hill, N.C., 1985), pp. 71–94; Dupuy, *Genius for War*, ch. 15.

88. Murray, *Balance of Power*, pp. 150–51; and Volkmann, "Die NS-Wirtschaft in Vorbereitung des Krieges," pp. 323ff. Details of the relationship between Germany's economic difficulties and Hitler's "forward" policy are in B. A. Carroll,

Design for Total War: Arms and Economics in the Third Reich (The Hague, 1968); T. W. Mason, "Innere Krise und Angriffskrieg 1938/39," in Forstmeier and Volkmann (eds.), *Wirtschaft und Rüstung am Vorabend des zweiten Weltkrieges*, pp. 158–88; J. Dulffer, "Der Beginn des Krieges 1939," *Geschichte und Gesellschaft*, vol. 2 (1976), pp. 443–70.

89. T. W. Mason, "Some Origins of the Second World War," p. 125, in E. M. Robertson (ed.), *The Origins of the Second World War* (London, 1971); idem, "Innere Krise und Angriffskrieg 1938/39," passim. Murray, *Balance of Power*, pp. 290ff, details the 1938 and 1939 plunder.

90. R. J. Overy, "Hitler's War and the German Economy: A Reinterpretation," *Economic History Review*, 2nd series, vol. 35 (1982), pp. 272–91, is important here.

91. Hillgruber, *Germany and the Two World Wars*, passim; Deist, *Wehrmacht*, ch. 7; Murray, *Luftwaffe*, pp. 81ff; M. Hauner, "Did Hitler Want a World Dominion?" *Journal of Contemporary History*, vol. 13, pp. 15–32; J. Thies, *Architekt der Weltherrschaft: Die "Endziele" Hitlers* (Düsseldorf, 1976), passim; and see the historiographical discussion in Kershaw, *Nazi Dictatorship*, ch. 6.

92. On which see the two older works A. Wolfers, *Britain and France Between the Wars* (New York, 1940); and W. M. Jordan, *Britain, France and the German Problem* (London, 1943); as well as the essays in N. Waites (ed.), *Troubled Neighbours: Franco-British Relations in the Twentieth Century* (London, 1971); and N. Rostow, *Anglo-French Relations 1934–1936* (London, 1984), passim.

93. C. Fohlen, "France," in Cipolla (ed.), *Fontana Economic History of Europe*, vol. 6, no. 1, pp. 80–86; T. Kemp, *The French Economy 1913–39: The History of a Decline* (New York, 1972), chs. 5–7; G. Ziebura, "Determinanten der Aussenpolitik Frankreichs 1932–1939," in K. Rohe (ed.), *Die Westmächte und das Dritte Reich 1933–1939* (Paderborn, 1982), pp. 136ff. There are lots of details (also prejudiced commentary) in A. Sauvy, *Histoire économique de la France entre les deux guerres*, 2 vols. (Paris, 1965–67); and more balance in *Histoire économique et sociale de la France*, vol. 4, pt. 2, *1914–1950*, eds. F. Braudel and E. Labrousse (Paris, 1980).

94. Fohlen, "France," p. 88.

95. Ibid., pp. 86–91; Landes, *Unbound Prometheus*, pp. 388ff; Kemp, *French Economy 1913–39*, chs. 8–12 (with very good details); Caron, *Economic History of Modern France*, pp. 258ff.

96. The best source here is R. Frankenstein, *Le Prix du réarmement français 1935–1939* (Paris, 1939), passim, but p. 303 for the spending totals. The national-income figure is taken from A. Adamthwaite, *France and the Coming of the Second World War* (London, 1977), p. 164. See also B. A. Lee, "Strategy, Arms and the Collapse of France 1939–1940," in R.T.B. Langhorne (ed.), *Diplomacy and Intelligence During the Second World War* (Cambridge, 1985), pp. 63ff.

97. R. J. Young, *In Command of France: French Foreign Policy and Military Planning 1933–1940* (Cambridge, Mass., 1978), ch. 1; see also the essays in *Les Relations franco-allemandes 1933–1939* (Paris, 1976).

98. Frankenstein, *Le Prix du réarmement français*, p. 317; idem, "The Decline of France, and French Appeasement Policies 1936–9," in Mommsen and Kettenacker (eds.) *Fascist Challenge and the Policy of Appeasement*, p. 238; Overy, *Air War*, p. 21. The relatively generous treatment of the navy—and that service's ingratitude—is detailed in R. Chalmers Hood, *Royal Republicans: The French Naval Dynasties Between the World Wars* (Baton Rouge, La., 1985).

99. Frankenstein, *Le Prix des réarmement français*, p. 319; Murray, *Change in the European Balance of Power*, pp. 107–8. The navy's strength by then is assessed

in P. Masson, "La Marine française en 1939–40," *Revue historique des armées,* No. 4 (1979), pp. 57–77.

100. No attempt will be made here to cover all the literature upon French politics and society in the 1930s and its relationship to the 1940 "strange defeat." There are important surveys in J. B. Duroselle, *La Décadence 1932–1939* (Paris, 1979); R. Hohne, "Innere Desintegration und äusserer Machtzerfall: Die französische Politik in den Jahren 1933–36," in Rohe (ed.), *Die Westmächte und das Dritte Reich,* pp. 157ff; H. Dubief, *Le Déclin de la IIIe République 1929–1938* (Paris, 1976); J. Joll (ed.), *The Decline of the Third Republic* (New York, 1959). There is also a useful summary in J. C. Cairns, "Some Recent Historians and the 'Strange Defeat' of 1940," *Journal of Modern History,* vol. 46 (1974), pp. 60–85.

101. For details, see A. Horne, *The French Army and Politics 1870–1970* (London, 1984), ch. 3; P.C.F. Bankwitz, *Maxime Weygand and Civil-Military Relations in Modern France* (Cambridge, Mass., 1967); the more technical details in Frankenstein, *Le Prix du réarmement français,* and H. Dutailly, *Les Problèmes de l'Armée de terre française 1933–1939* (Paris, 1980); and the more cautionary comments in R. A. Doughty, "The French Armed Forces, 1918–1940," in Millett and Murray (eds.), *Military Effectiveness,* vol. 2.

102. Adamthwaite, *France and the Coming of the Second World War,* p. 166; Gorce, *French Army: A Military-Political History,* pp. 270ff; Young, "French Military Intelligence and Nazi Germany," in May (ed.), *Knowing One's Enemies,* pp. 271–309.

103. Posen, *Sources of Military Doctrine,* ch. 4; Doughty, "French Armed Forces, 1918–1940," passim; Murray, *Change in the European Balance of Power,* pp. 97ff; L. Mysyrowicz, *Autopsie d'une Défaite; Origines de l'effondrement militaire français de 1940* (Lausanne, 1973). But the most thorough analysis is now R. A. Doughty, *The Seeds of Disaster: The Development of French Army Doctrine 1919–1939* (Hamden, Conn., 1985).

104. French diplomacy in these critical years is best covered in Adamthwaite, *France and the Coming of the Second World War,* passim; Duroselle, *La Décadence,* passim; and P. Wandycz, *The Twilight of the French Eastern Alliances, 1926–1936* (forthcoming).

105. See R. Girault, "The Impact of the Economic Situation on the Foreign Policy of France, 1936–9," in Mommsen and Kettenacker (eds.), *Fascist Challenge and the Policy of Appeasement,* pp. 209–26.

106. In particular, see Young, "La Guerre de Longue Durée: Some Reflections on French Strategy and Diplomacy in the 1930s," in Preston (ed.), *General Staffs and Diplomacy Before the Second World War,* pp. 41–64; and Posen, *Sources of Military Doctrine,* pp. 112ff, 127ff. For full diplomatic details, see Adamthwaite, *France and the Coming of the Second World War,* especially pt 3; the contributions to *Les Relations Franco-Britanniques 1935–39* (Paris, 1975); and Young, *In Command of France,* chs. 8–9.

107. Apart from the details in Adamthwaite's and Young's books, see also Barnett, *Collapse of British Power;* Howard, *Continental Commitment;* and last but not least, J. C. Cairns, "A Nation of Shopkeepers in Search of a Suitable France," *American Historical Review,* vol. 79 (1974), pp. 710–43.

108. Figures from Kennedy, *Realities Behind Diplomacy,* p. 240. It is impossible to list even one-tenth of the studies upon British "appeasement" policies in the 1930s; but there are very useful summative essays in Mommsen and Kettenacker (eds.), *Fascist Challenge and the Power of Appeasement,* chs. 6–13 and 19–25; and massive detail (and an enormous bibliography) in G. Schmidt, *England in der Krise: Grundzüge und Grundlagen der britischen Appeasement-Politik, 1930–1937* (Opladen, 1981).

109. See especially R. Ovendale, *Appeasement and the English-Speaking World* (Cardiff, 1975), as well as his ch. 23 in Mommsen and Ketternacker (eds.), *Fascist Challenge;* R. F. Holland, *Britain and the Commonwealth Alliance, 1918–1939* (London, 1981).

110. B. Bond, *British Military Policy Between Two World Wars* (Oxford, 1980), espec. chs. 1 and 4, is best here.

111. R. Meyers, "British Imperial Interests and the Policy of Appeasement," and W. R. Louis, "The Road to Singapore: British Imperialism in the Far East 1932–1942," both in Mommsen and Kettenacher (eds.), *Fascist Challenge;* A. J. Marder, *Old Friends, New Enemies: The Royal Navy and the Imperial Japanese Navy* (Oxford, 1981); L. R. Pratt, *East of Malta, West of Suez: Britain's Mediterranean Crisis* (London, 1975); S. W. Roskill, *Naval Policy Between the Wars,* vol. 2 (London, 1976).

112. Kennedy, *British Naval Mastery,* ch. 10. For details of the policy implications, see the varying assessments in G. C. Peden, *British Rearmament and the Treasury 1932–1939* (Edinburgh, 1979); R. P. Shay, *British Rearmament in the Thirties: Politics and Profits* (Princeton, N.J., 1977); Barnett, *Collapse of British Power,* ch. 5; and N. H. Gibbs, *Grand Strategy,* vol. 1 (London, 1976), passim.

113. For the economic recovery and newer industries, see Pollard, *Development of the British Economy,* ch. 3; H. W. Richardson, *Economic Recovery in Britain, 1932–1939* (London, 1967); B.W.E. Alford, *Depression and Recovery? British Economic Growth 1918–1939* (London, 1972).

114. Cited in Howard, *Continental Commitment,* p. 99. For fuller details, see Peden, *British Rearmament and the Treasury,* chs. 3–4; see also R. Meyers, *Britische Sicherheitspolitik 1934–1938* (Düsseldorf, 1976); and Gibbs, *Grand Strategy,* vol. 1, ch. 4.

115. Howard, *Continental Commitment,* pp. 120–21.

116. Details in U. Bialer, *The Shadow of the Bomber: The Fear of Air Attack and British Politics 1932–1939* (London, 1980); M. Smith, *British Air Strategy Between the Wars* (Oxford, 1984), espec. pt. 2.

117. For this argument, see especially Barnett, *Collapse of British Power,* and Murray, *Change in the European Balance of Power.*

118. D. C. Watt, *Too Serious a Business: European Armed Forces and the Approach of the Second World War* (London, 1975), is the key work here.

119. See again Dehio, *Precarious Balance.* For good surveys of the British Cabinet's awareness of the country's strategical dilemmas, see Barnett, *Collapse of British Power;* Howard, *The Continental Commitment;* Posen, *Sources of Military Doctrine,* ch. 5; D. Dilks, "The Unnecessary War? Military Advice and Foreign Policy in Great Britain 1931–1939," in Preston (ed.), *General Staffs and Diplomacy Before the Second World War,* pp. 98–132; and G. Schmidt's thoughtful essay in Rohe (ed.), *Die Westmächte und das Dritte Reich,* pp. 29–56.

120. Schmidt, in Rohe (ed.), *Die Westmächte,* pp. 46ff; C. A. MacDonald, *United States, Britain and Appeasement, 1936–1939,* passim.

121. Schmidt, *England in der Krise,* ch. 1, is best here; but see also the above-named works by Howard, Bond, Barnett, Dilks, Gibbs, and Meyers; and the good summary in G. Niedhart, "Appeasement: Die Britische Antwort auf die Krise des Weltreichs und des internationalen Systems vor dem Zweiten Weltkrieg," *Historische Zeitschrift,* vol. 226 (1978), pp. 68–88.

122. Barnett, *Collapse of British Power,* passim; Murray, *Change in the European Balance of Power,* passim; Kennedy, *Realities Behind Diplomacy,* pp. 290ff; A. Adamthwaite, "The British Government and the Media, 1937–1938," *Journal of Contemporary History,* vol. 18 (1983), pp. 281–97.

123. Cited in Barnett, *Collapse of British Power,* p. 564.

124. Hillmann, "Comparative Strength of the Great Powers," in Toynbee (ed.), *World in March 1939*, pp. 439, 446.

125. For more details of this argument, see Kennedy, "Strategy versus Finance in Twentieth-Century Britain," in *Strategy and Diplomacy*, pp. 100–6; and for an even more deterministic view, Porter, *Britain, Europe and the World*, pp. 86ff, 95ff.

126. Figures from Pollard, *Peaceful Conquest*, p. 294; but see also Munting, *Economic Development of the USSR*, pp. 45ff; Nove, *Economic History of Russia*, chs. 6–10; and the interesting discussion in Grossman, "The Industrialization of Russia and the Soviet Union," in Cipolla (ed.), *Fontana Economic History of Europe*, vol. 4, pt. 2, pp. 501ff.

127. S. H. Cohn, *Economic Development in the Soviet Union* (Lexington, Mass., 1970), pp. 70–71; F. D. Holzmann, "Financing Soviet Economic Development," in Blackwell (ed.), *Russian Economic Development from Peter the Great to Stalin*, pp. 259–76; Kochan and Abraham, *Making of Modern Russia*, pp. 361ff. See also M. Lewin, *Russian Peasants and Soviet Power* (Evanston, Ill., 1968).

128. W. A. Lewis, *Economic Survey 1919–1939* (London, 1949), p. 131; Nove, *Economic History*, ch. 7; Munting, *Economic Development of the USSR*, p. 99; H. J. Ellison, "The Decision to Collectivize Agriculture," in Blackwell (ed.), *Russian Economic Development from Peter the Great to Stalin*, pp. 241–55.

129. On which see Munting, *Economic Development of the USSR*, pp. 106ff.

130. Nove, *Economic History*, p. 232; Lewis, *Economic Survey*, p. 133; M. McCauley, *The Soviet Union Since 1917* (London, 1981), pp. 85–87.

131. Munting, *Economic Development of the Soviet Union*, p. 93; Nove, *Economic History*, pp. 187ff; Blackwell, *Industrialization of Russia*, pp. 132ff; Lewis, *Economic Survey*, p. 125.

132. See Hillmann, "Comparative Strength of the Great Powers," in Toynbee (ed.), *World in March 1939*, pp. 439, 446; Black et al., *Modernization of Japan and Russia*, pp. 195–97; S. H. Cohn, "The Soviet Economy: Performance and Growth," in Blackwell (ed.), *Russian Economic Development from Peter the Great to Stalin*, pp. 321–51.

133. Nove, *Economic History*, p. 236. For further details, see Kochan and Abraham, *Making of Modern Russia*, pp. 382ff; R. Conquest, *The Great Terror* (London, 1968).

134. Nove, *Economic History*, p. 236.

135. Figures from Overy, *Air War*, p. 21. The Italian figures for the years 1932–37 (not available in Overy) were provided by my colleague Brian Sullivan, but are only rough estimates; the same is true of the 1932–34 French figures, generally thought to be about 50 a month—see Young, *In Command of France*, p. 164. Relative neglect of the navy is covered in Mitchell, *History of Russia and Soviet Sea Power*, ch. 17.

136. McNeill, *Pursuit of Power*, p. 350, fn. 77. For the subsequent comments on Soviet military development generally, see J. Erickson, *The Soviet High Command, 1918–1941* (London, 1962), passim; E. F. Ziemke, "The Soviet Armed Forces in the Interwar Period," in Millett and Murray (eds.), *Military Effectiveness*, vol. 1; B. H. Liddell Hart (ed.), *The Red Army* (New York, 1956), chs. 3–9. Russian defense expenditures are detailed in Nove, *Economic History*, pp. 227–28; and Munting, *Economic Development of the USSR*, p. 114.

137. Ulam, *Expansion and Coexistence*, chs. 5–6; J. Haslam, *The Soviet Union and the Struggle for Collective Security in Europe 1933–39* (New York, 1984); and J. Hochmann, *The Soviet Union and the Failure of Collective Security 1934–1938* (Ithaca, N.Y., 1984), are best here.

138. Hillmann, "Comparative Strength of the Great Powers," p. 446.

139. M. Mackintosh, "The Red Army 1920–36," in Liddell Hart (ed.), *Red Army*, p. 63.
140. Erickson, *Soviet High Command*, pp. 532ff, 542ff; K. Dittmar and G. J. Antonov, "The Red Army in the Finnish War," in Liddell Hart (ed.), *Red Army*, pp. 79–92. Above all, Coox, *Nomonhan*, passim.
141. Erickson's works—*The Soviet High Command; The Road to Stalingrad*, early chapters; and "Threat Identification and Strategic Appraisal by the Soviet Union, 1930–1941," in May (ed.), *Knowing One's Enemies*, pp. 375–423—are best here. For diplomatic background, see W. Carr, *Poland to Pearl Harbor* (London, 1985), chs. 3–4.
142. Figures from Nove, *Economic History*, p. 228.
143. Quoted in Munting, *Economic Development of the USSR*, p. 86; see also Ziemke, "Soviet Armed Forces," passim, for the frantic preparations in 1939–1941.
144. Rostow, *World Economy*, p. 210.
145. See the excellent analysis in M. P. Leffler, "Expansionist Impulses and Domestic Constraints, 1921–1932," in Becker and Wells (eds.), *Economics and World Power*, pp. 246–48.
146. Hillmann, "Comparative Strength of the Great Powers," in Toynbee (ed.), *World in March 1939*, pp. 421–22.
147. Ibid., p. 422.
148. Leffler, "Expansionist Impulses and Domestic Constraints," in Becker and Wells (eds.), *Economics and World Power*, p. 258.
149. For a good, succinct survey of American defense policy between the wars, see Millett and Maslowski, *For the Common Defense*, ch. 12.
150. H. Yardley, *The American Black Chamber* (New York, 1931), pp. 262–63.
151. See above, pp. 281–82.
152. R. M. Hathaway, "Economic Diplomacy in a Time of Crisis," in Becker and Wells (eds.), *Economics and World Power*, pp. 277–78.
153. L. Silk, "Protectionist Mood: Mounting Pressure," *New York Times*, Sept. 17, 1985, p. D1; Robertson, *History of the American Economy*, pp. 516ff.
154. Kindleberger, *World in Depression*, ch. 12 and pp. 280–87.
155. Table from Hillman, "Comparative Strength of the Great Powers," in Toynbee (ed.), *World in March 1939*, p. 439.
156. Hathaway, "Economic Diplomacy in a Time of Crisis," in Becker and Wells (eds.), *Economics and World Power*, p. 285.
157. Ibid., pp. 309, 312. For a brief survey, Schulzinger, *America Diplomacy in the Twentieth Century*, pp. 147ff.
158. This is well covered in MacDonald, *United States, Britain and Appeasement 1936–1939*, passim; and Carr, *Poland to Pearl Harbor*, ch. 1. See also D. Reynolds, *Creation of the Anglo-American Alliance 1937–1941*, chs. 1–2; A. Offner, *American Appeasement. United States Foreign Policy and Germany 1933–1938* (Cambridge, Mass., 1969); and N. Graebner, *America as a World Power* (Wilmington, Del., 1984), ch. 2.
159. Millett and Maslowski, *For the Common Defense*, pp. 386ff; Mills, *Arms and Men*, pp. 237ff; J. A. Iseley and P. A. Crowl, *The U. S. Marines and Amphibious War* (Princeton, N.J., 1945); M. H. Gillie, *Forging the Thunderbolt* (Harrisburg, Pa., 1947); M. S. Watson, *Chief of Staff: Pre-War Plans and Preparations* (Washington, D.C., 1950); J. Major, "The Navy Plans for War, 1937–1941," in Hagan (ed.), *In Peace and War*, pp. 237ff; Weighley, *History of the United States Army*, pp. 416ff.
160. Robertson, *History of the American Economy*, pp. 709ff. The steel statistics

come from Hillmann, "Comparative Strength of the Great Powers," in Toynbee (ed.), *World in March 1939,* p. 443 and fn.

161. Figures from Wright, *Study of War,* p. 672.

162. Figures from Hillmann, "Comparative Strength of the Great Powers," in Toynbee (ed.), *World in March 1939,* p. 446.

163. M. S. Kendrick, *A Century and a Half of Federal Expenditures* (New York, 1955), p. 12.

164. The extensive literature upon Hitler's views of the United States are conveniently summarized in Herwig, *Politics of Frustration,* pp. 179ff. See also the commentaries in Weinberg, *Foreign Policy of Hitler's Germany,* vols. 1–2; idem, *World in the Balance* (New Hampshire/London, 1981) pp. 53–136.

165. Cited in Willmott, *Empires in the Balance,* p. 62; see also Pelz, *Race to Pearl Harbor,* pp. 217–18, 224.

166. Cited in Thorne, *Limits of Foreign Policy,* p. 90—a book which makes superfluous all previous studies of the Manchurian crisis.

167. Ibid., pp. 148ff, 231ff.

168. Ibid., passim; Crowley, *Japan's Quest for Autonomy,* pp. 161ff; A. Rappaport, *Henry L. Stimson and Japan, 1931–1933* (Chicago, 1963); Schulzinger, *American Diplomacy,* pp. 148ff.

169. Crowley, *Japan's Quest for Autonomy,* ch. 2; Storry, *History of Modern Japan,* pp. 186ff.

170. Bennett, *German Rearmament and the West,* is best here.

171. See above, pp. 315–20; and Howard, *The Continental Commitment,* ch. 5. The 1934 arguments for and against an Anglo-Japanese understanding are nicely covered in W. R. Louis, "The Road to Singapore: British Imperialism in the Far East 1932–42," in Mommsen and Kettenacker (eds.), *Fascist Challenge and the Policy of Appeasement,* pp. 359ff.

172. Ross, *The Great Powers and the Decline of the European States System,* pp. 85–87; Ulam, *Expansion and Coexistence,* ch. 5.

173. This is now most fully covered in Rostow, *Anglo-French Relations 1934–36,* espec. ch. 5; but see also Taylor, *Origins of the Second World War,* ch. 5; Ross, *Great Powers,* pp. 90ff. The Anglo-German naval agreement is treated in E. Haraszti, *Treaty-Breakers or "Realpolitiker"? The Anglo-German Naval Agreement of June 1935* (Boppard, 1974).

174. F. Hardie, *The Abyssinian Crisis* (London, 1974), passim; A. J. Marder, "The Royal Navy in the Italo-Ethiopian War 1935–36," *American Historical Review,* vol. 75 (1970), pp. 1327–56; R.A.C. Parker, "Great Britain, France and the Ethiopian Crisis 1935–1936," *English Historical Review,* vol. 89 (1974), pp. 293–32; Mack Smith, *Mussolini's Roman Empire,* ch. 5; F. D. Laurens, *France and the Italo-Ethiopian Crisis, 1935–6* (The Hague, 1967); G. Baer, *Test Case: Italy, Ethiopia, and the League of Nations* (Stanford, Calif., 1976).

175. Pelz, *Road to Pearl Harbor,* pt. 4.

176. Now covered in J. T. Emmerson, *The Rhineland Crisis* (London, 1977), and E. Haraszti, *The Invaders: Hitler Occupies the Rhineland* (Budapest, 1983). See also Rostow, *Anglo-French Relations 1934–36,* pp. 233ff.

177. See again Rohe (ed.), *Die Westmächte und das Dritte Reich,* passim.

178. Ross, *Great Powers,* p. 98; see also MacDonald, *The United States, Great Britain, and Appeasement,* passim.

179. See above, pp. 313–14.

180. Although we still await the second volume of D. Dilks's authoritative biography, the literature upon Chamberlain and "appeasement" is already enormous. For surveys, see the relevant chapters in Mommsen and Kettenacher (eds.), *Fascist Challenge and the Policy of Appeasement;* K. Middlemas, *Diplomacy of*

Illusion: The British Government and Germany 1937–39 (London, 1972); M. Cowling, *The Impact of Hitler: British Politics and British Policies 1933–1940,* passim; Barnett, *Collapse of British Power,* ch. 5. Also very important is M. Gilbert, *Winston Churchill,* vol. 5, *1922–1939* (London, 1976).

181. By far the most comprehensive analysis is now T. Taylor, *Munich: The Price of Peace* (New York, 1979); but see also A.J.P. Taylor, *Origins of the Second World War,* ch. 8; Middlemas, *Diplomacy of Illusion,* pp. 211ff; Weinberg, *Foreign Policy of Hitler's Germany,* vol. 2, chs. 10–11; K. Robbins, *Munich, 1938* (London, 1968).

182. W. Murray, "Munich, 1938; The Military Confrontation," *Journal of Strategic Studies,* vol. 2 (1979), pp. 282–302; Barnett, *Collapse of British Power,* pp. 505ff; Kennedy, *Realities Behind Diplomacy,* pp. 291–93.

183. The unfolding of events in 1939 is covered in Murray, *Change in the European Balance of Power,* chs. 8–10; Taylor, *Origins of the Second World War,* chs. 9–11; S. Aster, *1939: The Making of the Second World War* (London, 1973); Weinberg, *Foreign Policy of Hitler's Germany,* vol. 2, pp. 465ff; Barnett, *Collapse of British Power,* pp. 554ff; H. Graml (ed.), *Summer 1939: Die Grossmächte und der europäische Krieg* (Stuttgart, 1979); D. Kaiser, *Economic Diplomacy and the Origins of the Second World War,* pp. 263ff.

184. For the overall strategical dimension in 1939–1940, see Kennedy, *Rise and Fall of British Naval Mastery,* pp. 300ff; Murray, *Change in the European Balance of Power,* pp. 310ff; B. H. Liddell Hart, *History of the Second World War* (London, 1970), pp. 16ff; *Grand Strategy,* vols. 1 (Gibbs) and 2 (Butler).

185. Murray, *Change in the European Balance of Power,* pp. 314–21; cf. Pratt, *East of Malta, West of Suez,* ch. 6; Gibbs, *Grand Strategy,* pp. 664ff; G. Schreiber et al., *Der Mittelmeerraum und Südosteuropa,* vol. 3 of *Das Deutsche Reich und der Zweite Weltkrieg* (Stuttgart, 1984), ch. 1.

186. K. A. Maier et al., *Die Errichtung des Hegemonie auf dem europäischen Continent,* vol. 2 of *Das Deutsche Reich und der Zweite Weltkrieg* (Stuttgart, 1979), passim; Murray, *Change in the European Balance of Power,* ch. 10; idem, *Luftwaffe,* ch. 2; Overy, *Air War,* pp. 26–30; Posen, *Sources of Military Doctrine,* ch. 3; J. A. Gunsberg, *Divided and Conquered: The French High Command and the Defeat of the West, 1940* (Westport, Conn., 1979). For a good analysis of the reasons for the Allied inertia and the German decision to attack, see also J. Mearsheimer, *Conventional Deterrence* (Ithaca, N.Y., 1983), chs. 3–4.

187. Knox, *Mussolini Unleashed,* is best on those repeated Italian disasters; but see also Schreiber et al., *Mittelmeerraum,* pts. 2–3 and 5. For a more sympathetic account of Italy's weaknesses, see J. L. Sadkovich, "Minerals, Weapons and Warfare: Italy's Failure in World War II," accepted for *Storia contemporanea.*

188. Overy, *Air War,* p. 28; Kennedy, *Rise and Fall of British Naval Mastery,* p. 309.

189. Carr, *Poland to Pearl Harbor,* pp. 99ff; Reynolds, *Creation of the Anglo-American Alliance,* pp. 108ff. See also J. Leutze, *Bargaining for Supremacy: Anglo-American Naval Relations 1937–1941* (Chapel Hill, N.C., 1977).

190. J. Lukacs, *The Last European War, September 1939/December 1941* (London, 1977); H. Baldwin, *The Crucial Years 1939–41* (New York, 1976); Carr, *Poland to Pearl Harbor,* passim. For the German side, A. Hillgruber, *Hitler's Strategie: Politik und Kriegsfuhrung 1940–41* (Frankfurt, 1965).

191. Van Creveld, *Supplying War,* ch. 5; Murray, *Luftwaffe,* chs. 3–4; Milward, *German Economy at War,* pp. 39ff. For full details of the early campaigning, see H. Boog et al., *Der Angriff auf die Sowjetunion,* vol. 4 of *Das Deutsche Reich und der Zweite Weltkrieg* (Stuttgart, 1983); and A. Clark, *Barbarossa: The Russo-German Conflict 1941–1945* (London, 1965), pp. 71–216. For the Russian

side, Erickson, *Road to Stalingrad,* passim; A. Seaton, *The Russo-German War 1941–45* (London, 1971).

192. Erickson, *Stalingrad,* pp. 237ff; Carr, *From Poland to Pearl Harbor,* pp. 150ff.

193. Willmott, *Empires in the Balance,* pp. 68ff, is best here; but see also J. Morley (ed.), *The Fateful Choice: Japan's Advance into Southeast Asia, 1939–1941* (New York, 1980).

194. Dupuy, *Genius for War,* appendix E.

CHAPTER SEVEN
Stability and Change in a Bipolar World, 1943–1980

1. Quoted in Spector, *Eagle Against the Sun,* p. 123.

2. For a brief summary, Liddell Hart, *History of the Second World War,* pp. 230–33; J. Neidpath, *The Singapore Naval Base and the Defense of Britain's Eastern Empire 1919–41* (Oxford, 1981), ch. 8; Barclay, *Empire Is Marching,* chs. 8–9.

3. Spector, *Eagle Against the Sun,* chs. 8–12; Liddell Hart, *History of the Second World War,* chs. 23 and 29.

4. Liddell Hart, *History of the Second World War,* chs. 20–22, and 25.

5. Ibid., ch. 24; S. W. Roskill, *The War at Sea,* 3 vols. (London, 1954–1961); F. H. Hinsley et al., *British Intelligence in the Second World War,* vol. 2 (London, 1981), ch. 26.

6. By far the best survey now is Murray, *Luftwaffe,* chs. 5–7; but see also N. Frankland, *The Bomber Offensive Against Germany* (London, 1965).

7. Quoted in Ropp, *War in the Modern World,* p. 336.

8. Ibid., p. 334. For much fuller details, see Erickson, *Road to Stalingrad,* passim; idem, *The Road to Berlin* (London, 1983), passim; E. F. Ziemke, *Stalingrad to Berlin: The German Defeat in the East 1942–1945* (Washington, D.C., 1968); Clark, *Barbarossa,* passim; and Seaton, *Russo-German War 1941–45,* passim.

9. Erickson, *Road to Stalingrad,* p. 272.

10. Dupuy, *Genius for War,* p. 343.

11. Clark, *Barbarossa,* chs. 17–18; Erickson, *Road to Berlin,* ch. 4.

12. These rivalries come out clearly in Clark, *Barbarossa,* passim; and are covered in more detail in Milward, *German Economy at War,* espec. ch. 6; Speer's own *Inside the Third Reich* (New York, 1982 edn.), pts. 2–3; Seaton, *German Army, 1933–45,* chs. 9–11; Hildebrand, *Third Reich,* pp. 49ff.

13. Kennedy, "Japanese Strategic Decisions, 1939–45," in *Strategy and Diplomacy,* pp. 181–95; C. G. Reynolds, "Imperial Japan's Continental Strategy," *U.S. Naval Institute Proceedings,* vol. 109 (August 1983), pp. 65–71; Spector, *Eagle Against the Sun,* passim; and the excellent survey by A. Coox, "The Effectiveness of the Japanese Military Establishment in World War II," in Millett and Murray (eds.), *Military Effectiveness,* vol. 3.

14. Willmott, *Empires in the Balance,* p. 89.

15. R. Lewin, *The American Magic: Codes, Cyphers and the Defeat of Japan* (New York, 1982), is the best synthesis.

16. Clark, *Barbarossa,* p. 228; Erickson, *Road to Stalingrad,* ch. 6. For Soviet war production, see Nove, *Economic History of the USSR.,* ch. 10; Munting, *Economic Development of the USSR,* ch. 5; A. Milward, *War, Economy and Society 1939–1945* (Berkeley, Calif., 1979), pp. 94ff.

17. See Table 34 below; and Overy, *Air War,* pp. 49ff.

18. Erickson, *Road to Berlin,* p. 447. See also the figures in Liddell Hart (ed.), *Red Army,* ch. 13.

19. Liddell Hart, *History of the Second World War*, p. 559.
20. For this trend, see such works as Dupuy, *Genius for War*, passim; M. van Creveld, *Fighting Power: German and U.S. Army Performance, 1939–1945* (Westport, Conn., 1982), passim; M. Hastings, *Overlord: D-Day and the Battle for Normandy* (London, 1984), pp. 14, 370, and passim.
21. Ropp, *War in the Modern World*, p. 342. For details of the Japanese "overstretch," see Hayashi and Coox, *Kogun*. More generally, see the similar argument in A. J. Levine, "Was World War II a Near-Run Thing?" *Journal of Strategic Studies*, vol. 8, no. 1 (March 1985), pp. 38–63.
22. Figures from Willmott, *Empires in the Balance*, p. 98.
23. Ropp, *War in the Modern World*, p. 328, quoting from S. E. Morison, *History of United States Naval Operations*, vol. 10, *The Atlantic Battle Won* (Boston, 1956), p. 64. For further details, see Roskill, *The War at Sea*, 3 vols., passim; Liddell Hart, *History of the Second World War*, ch. 24; Potter (ed.), *Sea Power*, ch. 24; Levine, "Was World War II a Near-Run Thing?" pp. 46ff.
24. For comparisons, see Kennedy, *Rise and Fall of British Naval Mastery*, pp. 309–10; Seaton, *German Army 1933–45*, p. 239 (Seaton includes self-propelled guns with these tank totals).
25. Overy, *Air War*, p. 150. Overy's figures for Italian production in the first half of the war are much less than those given in Table XVIII of James J. Sadkovich's article "Minerals, Weapons and Warfare: Italy's Failure in World War II," *Storia contemporanea* (forthcoming).
26. Overy, *Air War*, p. 150.
27. Murray, *Luftwaffe*, chs. 6–7.
28. See Tables 30 and 32 above.
29. Hillman, "Comparative Strength of the Powers," in Toynbee (ed.), *World in March 1939*, pp. 439, 446; Wright, *Study of War*, p. 672. See also R. W. Goldsmith, "The Power of Victory: Munitions Output in World War II," *Military Affairs*, vol. 10 (Spring 1946), pp. 69–80.
30. Figures from R. Wagenführ, *Die deutsche Industrie im Kriege 1939–1945* (Berlin, 1963), pp. 34, 87. The Italian figures are my own very rough "guestimates," based upon the size of its economy relative to those of the other Powers. For further comparisons, see F. Forstmeier and H. E. Volkmann (eds.), *Kriegswirtschaft und Rüstung 1939–1945* (Düsseldorf, 1977).
31. Milward, *German Economy at War*, pp. 72ff; Wagenführ, *Die deutsche Industrie in Kriege*, ch. 3; and for more general comparisons, Aldcroft, *European Economy 1914–1980*, pp. 124ff.
32. Spector, *Eagle Against the Sun*, ch. 23; L. Giovannetti and F. Freed, *The Decision to Drop the Bomb* (London, 1967), passim; H. Feis, *The Atomic Bomb and the End of World War II* (Princeton, N.J., 1966 edn.), passim; G. Alperowitz, *Atomic Diplomacy: Hiroshima and Potsdam* (London, 1966); M. J. Sherwin, *A World Destroyed: The Atomic Bomb and the Grand Alliance* (New York, 1975).
33. Cited in M. Matloff, *Strategic Planning for Coalition Warfare, 1943–1944* (Washington, D.C., 1959), pp. 523–24.
34. DePorte, *Europe Between the Superpowers*, ch. 4.
35. W. Ashworth, *A Short History of the International Economy Since 1850* (London, 1975), p. 268. See also the figures in Milward, *War, Economy and Society 1939–1945*, p. 63.
36. Rowland (ed.), *Balance of Power or Hegemony*, p. 220.
37. Ashworth, *Short History of the International Economy Since 1850*, p. 268.
38. Apart from the early chapters of L. Freedman, *The Evolution of Nuclear Strategy* (London, 1981), see also D. A. Rosenberg, "The Origins of Overkill: Nuclear Weapons and American Strategy, 1945–1960," *International Security*, vol. 7,

no. 4 (Spring 1983); M. Mandelbaum, *The Nuclear Question: The United States and Nuclear Weapons 1946–1976* (New York, 1979).

39. Figures from W. P. Mako, *U.S. Ground Forces and the Defense of Central Europe* (Washington, D.C., 1983), p. 8.

40. R. Steel, *Pax Americana* (New York, 1977), ch. 2. For the parallels with Britain after 1815, see above, pp. 151–58; and T. Smith, *The Pattern of Imperialism: The United States, Great Britain and the Late-Industrializing World Since 1815* (Cambridge, 1981), pp. 182ff.

41. M. Balfour, *The Adversaries: America, Russia, and the Open World, 1941–62* (London, 1981), p. 14.

42. G. Kolko, *The Politics of War 1943–1945* (New York, 1968), passim; Becker and Wells (eds.), *Economics and World Power*, chs. 6–7; R. Keohane, "State Power and Industry Influence: American Foreign Oil Policy in the 1940s," *International Organization*, vol. 36 (Winter 1982), pp. 165–83; A. E. Eckes, *The United States and the Global Struggle for Minerals* (Austin, Texas, 1979).

43. Balfour, *Adversaries*, p. 15.

44. On which see R. N. Gardner, *Sterling-Dollar Diplomacy* (New York, 1969), passim.

45. The phrase used in Steel, *Pax Americana*, p. 10.

46. Quoted by R. Dallek, "The Postwar World: Made in the USA," in S. J. Ungar (ed.), *Estrangement: America and the World* (New York, 1985), p. 32.

47. Cited in J. W. Spanier, *American Foreign Policy Since World War II* (London, 1972 edn.), p. 26. See also R. A. Divine, *Second Chance: The Triumph of Internationalism in America During World War II* (New York, 1971), passim.

48. Thorne, *Issue of War*, p. 206. See also M. P. Leffler's recent writings: "The American Conception of National Security and the Beginnings of the Cold War, 1945–48," *American Historical Review*, vol. 89 (1984), pp. 349–81; and his Lehrman Institute paper "Security and Containment Before Kennan: The Identification of American Interests at the End of World War II," passim.

49. Erickson, *Road to Berlin*, p. ix.

50. G. Hosking, *A History of the Soviet Union* (London, 1985), p. 296.

51. Nove, *Economic History of the USSR*, p. 285.

52. See the figures in Munting, *Economic Development of the USSR*, p. 118.

53. McCauley, *Soviet Union Since 1917*, p. 138. For further details, see Nove, *Economic History of the USSR*, pp. 140–42.

54. McCauley, *Soviet Union Since 1917*, pp. 140–42.

55. For details, see M. A. Evangelista, "Stalin's Postwar Army Reappraised," *International Security*, vol. 7, no. 3 (1982–83), pp. 110–38.

56. Mackintosh, *Juggernaut: A History of the Soviet Armed Forces*, pp. 272–73.

57. Ibid. See also the relevant chapters in Liddell Hart (ed.), *The Red Army*, pt. 2; D. Holloway, *The Soviet Union and the Arms Race* (New Haven, Conn., 1983), pp. 15ff; Mitchell, *History of Russian and Soviet Sea Power*, pp. 469ff.

58. Hosking, *History of the Soviet Union*, ch. 11, is best here. See also McCauley, *Soviet Union Since 1917*, ch. 5; Nove, *Economic History*, pp. 266ff; Ulam, *Expansion and Coexistence*, pp. 467ff.

59. Spanier, *American Foreign Policy Since World War II*, p. 3; G. Challiand and J.-P. Rageau, *Strategic Atlas: A Comparative Geopolitics of the World's Powers* (New York, 1985), pp. 18ff; J. L. Gaddis, *Strategies of Containment* (New York, 1982), pp. 57ff; and the comments in A. K. Henrikson, "America's Changing Place in the World: From 'Periphery' to 'Center'?" in J. Gottman (ed.), *Center and Periphery* (Beverly Hills, Calif., 1980), pp. 73–100.

60. Ulam, *Expansion and Coexistence*, p. 405.

61. Cited in H. Feis, *Churchill-Roosevelt-Stalin* (Princeton, N.J., 1967), p. 462.

62. Landes, *Unbound Prometheus,* p. 488, fn. 1.
63. Allen, *Short Economic History of Modern Japan,* pp. 187ff, and the relevant tables in appendix B.
64. Ricossa, "Italy 1920–1970," in Cipolla (ed.), *Fontana Economic History of Europe,* vol. 6, pt. 1, p. 240.
65. Ibid., p. 316.
66. Wright, *Ordeal of Total War,* p. 264.
67. Fohlen, "France 1920–1970," in Cipolla (ed.), *Fontana Economic History of Europe,* vol. 6, pt. 1, pp. 92, 109.
68. Ibid., p. 100.
69. De Gaulle's attitude toward the Anglo-Saxon powers is superbly brought out in F. Kersaudy, *Churchill and de Gaulle* (London, 1981), as well as in de Gaulle's own *Memoires de Guerre,* 3 vols. (Paris, 1954–59). For French colonial policy during and after the war, see L. von Albertini, *Decolonization* (New York, 1971 edn.), pp. 358ff; and—with British comparisons—Smith, *Pattern of Imperialism,* ch. 3.
70. Barnett, *Collapse of British Power,* pp. 587–88; and, in a similar tone, Porter, *Britain, Europe and the World 1850–1982,* pp. 111ff.
71. Cited in Kennedy, *Realities Behind Diplomacy,* p. 318, with further details of Britain's economic position. See also Hobsbawm, *Industry and Empire,* pp. 356ff; Barnett, *The Audit of War* (London, 1986), passim.
72. The best of these is K. O. Morgan, *Labour in Power 1945–1951* (Oxford, 1984), passim, and also appendices 3–5. But see also the relevant chapters in K. Harris, *Attlee* (London, 1982), and A. Bullock, *Ernest Bevin: Foreign Secretary* (Oxford, 1983). Economic policy is detailed in A. Cairncross, *Years of Recovery: British Economic Policy 1945–51* (London, 1985), and summarized in D. H. Aldcroft, *The British Economy,* vol. 1 (London, 1986), ch. 8.
73. See especially H. M. Sachar, *Europe Leaves the Middle East 1936–1954* (London, 1972); W. R. Louis, *The British Empire in the Middle East, 1945–1951* (Oxford, 1984); and H. Rahman, "British Post-Second World War Military Planning for the Middle East," *Journal of Strategic Studies,* vol. 5, no. 4 (December 1982), pp. 511–30, for details of the enhanced importance of the region. The post-1945 economic value of the empire is summarized in Porter, *Lion's Share,* pp. 319ff.
74. On this cooperation, see T. H. Anderson, *The United States, Great Britain and the Cold War, 1944–1947* (Columbia, Mo., 1981), for early interchanges; J. Baylis, *Anglo-American Defense Relations 1939–1980* (London, 1981), for a general assessment; and Bartlett, *Global Conflict,* pp. 269ff.
75. See the details in Bairoch, "Europe's Gross National Product, 1800–1975," pp. 291–92.
76. See Bairoch, "International Industrialization Levels," p. 304, cf. p. 296.
77. The per capita GNP figures for 1950 are taken from S. H. Cohn, *Economic Development in the Soviet Union* (Lexington, Mass., 1970), appendix C, Table C-1. To obtain the national GNP figures, I multiplied by the population size given in "The Correlates of War" print-out.
78. "Correlates of War" print-out data.
79. Quotations from Sherwin, *World Destroyed,* p. 314.
80. On which see Freedman, *Evolution of Nuclear Strategy,* passim; and the very useful survey in A. L. Friedberg, "A History of U. S. Strategic 'Doctrine,' 1945–1980," *Journal of Strategic Studies,* vol. 3, no. 3 (December 1983), pp. 40ff. For some early published examples of these ponderings, see B. Brody, *The Absolute Weapon* (New York, 1946); idem, *Strategy in the Nuclear Age* (Princeton, N.J., 1959); H. Kahn, *On Thermonuclear War* (Princeton, N.J., 1960); J. Slessor,

Strategy for the West (London, 1954); P.M.S. Blackett, *Fear, War, and the Bomb* (New York, 1948).

81. Holloway, *Soviet Union and the Arms Race*, ch. 2; J. Prados, *The Soviet Estimate: U.S. Intelligence Analysis and Russian Military Strength* (New York, 1982), pp. 17ff; R. L. Garthoff, *Soviet Strategy in the Nuclear Age* (New York, 1958), passim; H. S. Dinerstein, *War and the Soviet Union* (London, 1962 edn.), especially chs. 1–6.

82. Prados, *Soviet Estimate*, pp. 17–18; Freedman, *Evolution of Nuclear Strategy*, ch. 5 et seq.; T. B. Larson, *Soviet-American Rivalry* (New York, 1978), pp. 178ff.

83. M. Growing, *Independence and Deterrence: Britain and Atomic Energy 1945–1952*, 2 vols. (London, 1974), vol. 1, p. 184. See also L. Freedman, *Britain and Nuclear Weapons* (London, 1980); A. Pierce, *Nuclear Politics: The British Experience with an Independent Strategic Nuclear Force, 1939–1970* (London, 1972); and J. Groom, *British Thinking About Nuclear Weapons* (London, 1974).

84. See below, p. 401; and Freedman, *Evolution of Nuclear Strategy*, ch. 21; W. Kohl, *French Nuclear Diplomacy* (Princeton, N.J., 1971), passim, with fuller references.

85. Dallek, *American Style of Foreign Policy*, p. 130.

86. Ibid., p. 152.

87. Quoted in Balfour, *Adversaries*, p. 71. For the changes in American policy and opinion, see also Anderson, *United States, Great Britain, and the Cold War, 1944–1947*, chs. 6–7; J. L. Gaddis, *The United States and the Origins of the Cold War, 1941–1947* (New York, 1972); and B. R. Kuniholm, *The Origins of the Cold War in the Near East* (Princeton, N.J., 1980), passim.

88. Dallek, *American Style of Foreign Policy*, p. 170.

89. Ulam, *Expansion and Coexistence*, p. 437.

90. G. Lichtheim, *Europe in the Twentieth Century* (London, 1972), p. 351.

91. Balfour, *Adversaries*, pp. 8ff; and for fuller details, L. E. Davis, *The Cold War Begins: Soviet-American Conflict over Eastern Europe* (Princeton, N.J., 1974); Feis, *Churchill-Roosevelt-Stalin*, passim; B. Dovrig, *The Myth of Liberation* (Baltimore, Md., 1973); A. Polonsky, *The Great Powers and the Polish Question 1941–1945* (London, 1976); V. Rothwell, *Britain and the Cold War 1941–47* (London, 1982), espec. ch. 3; R. Douglas, *From War to Cold War 1942–1948* (London, 1981), passim.

92. Ulam, *Expansion and Coexistence*, chs. 7–9; T. Wolfe, *Soviet Power and Europe, 1945–1970* (Baltimore, Md., 1970); M. McCauley (ed.), *Communist Power in Europe, 1944–1949* (London, 1977); W. Taubman, *Stalin's American Policy: From Entente to Detente to Cold War* (New York, 1982), passim.

93. Nor is it proposed to give a full bibliography of the enormous literature upon the Cold War. Balfour, *Adversaries*; Larson, *Soviet-American Rivalry*; Ulam, *Expansion and Coexistence*; and Bartlett, *Global Conflict*, chs. 10–11, all provide surveys with references to the further literature. See also note 87 above.

94. Balfour, *Adversaries*, p. 94; M. Balfour and J. Mair, *Four-Power Control in Germany and Austria 1945–1946* (London, 1956); Rothwell, *Britain and the Cold War*, ch. 6. See also the very important collection J. Foschepoth (ed.), *Kalter Krieg und deutsche Frage* (Göttingen, 1985), espec. pt. 3.

95. A reference to Gaddis's excellent survey, *Strategies of Containment*.

96. Ibid., p. 30.

97. Ibid., p. 31.

98. Ibid., p. 30.

99. Anderson, *United States, Great Britain and the Cold War*, passim; Bullock, *Ernest Bevin: Foreign Secretary*, espec. ch. 10; Kuniholm, *Origins of the Cold War in the Near East*, passim; Keylor, *Twentieth-Century World*, pp. 270–71.

100. Apart from Ulam's book, see also the references in note 92 above; and M. D. Shulman, *Stalin's Foreign Policy Reappraised* (New York, 1969); M. Kaser, *Comecon* (London, 1967); J. K. Hoensch, *Sowjetische Osteuropa-Politik 1945–1974* (Düsseldorf, 1977).

101. See the references in R. Poidevin, "Die Neuorientierung der französischen Deutschlandpolitik in 1948/9," in Foschepoth (ed.), *Kalter Krieg und deutsche Frage;* J. W. Young, *Britain, France and the Unity of Europe 1945–51* (Leicester, 1984), especially ch. 5; Douglas, *From War to Cold War,* pp. 167ff; and, for British ambivalences, see S. Greenwood, "Return to Dunkirk: The Origins of the Anglo-French Treaty of March 1947," *Journal of Strategic Studies,* vol. 6, no. 4 (December 1983), pp. 49–65.

102. Bullock, *Bevin,* pp. 571ff; W. P. Davison, *The Berlin Blockade* (Princeton, N.J., 1958); the relevant chapters in R. Morgan, *The United States and West Germany 1945–73* (London, 1974); J. H. Backer, *Winds of History: The German Years of Lucius DuBignon Clay* (New York, 1983), ch. 10; M. Bell, "Die Blockade Berlins-Konfrontation der Allierten in Deutschland," in Foschepoth (ed.), *Kalter Krieg und deutsche Frage,* pp. 217ff.

103. Evangelista, "Stalin's Postwar Army Reconsidered," passim; W. LaFeber, *America, Russia, and the Cold War 1945–1975* (New York, 1976), pp. 83ff; Lord Ismay, *NATO—the First Five Years, 1949–1954* (Utrecht, 1954); Gaddis, *Strategies of Containment,* pp. 72ff; A. K. Henrikson, "The Creation of the North Atlantic Alliance, 1948–1952," *Naval War College Review,* vol. 32, no. 3 (May/June 1980), pp. 4–39; L. S. Kaplan, *The United States and NATO: The Formative Years* (Lexington, Ky., 1984), passim.

104. On which see A. Grosser, *West Germany from Defeat to Rearmament* (London, 1955); R. McGeehan, *The German Rearmament Question* (Urbana, Ill., 1971); D. Lerner and R. Aron, *France Defeats EDC* (New York, 1957); DePorte, *Europe Between the Superpowers,* pp. 158ff; and T. Schwarz, "The Case of German Rearmament: Alliance Crisis in the 'Golden Age,'" *Fletcher Forum* (Summer 1984), pp. 295–309.

105. Bartlett, *Global Conflict,* p. 312.

106. Ulam, *Expansion and Coexistence,* pp. 544ff; D. J. Dallin, *Soviet Foreign Policy After Stalin* (Philadelphia, Pa., 1961); R. A. Remington, *The Warsaw Pact* (Cambridge, Mass., 1971).

107. On which see again Kolko, *Politics of War,* passim; and Thorne, *Issue of War.*

108. Kolko, *Politics of War,* pp. 298ff; Kuniholm, *Origins of the Cold War in the Near East,* passim; Louis, *British Empire in the Middle East,* pp. 53ff.

109. Ulam, *Expansion and Coexistence,* p. 428; and see also Anderson, *United States, Great Britain and the Cold War,* pp. 103ff.

110. Cited in Bartlett, *Global Conflict,* p. 261 (my emphasis); and see again the works by Anderson, Louis, and Kuniholm above.

111. Griml, *Decolonization,* pp. 183ff, is a good summary; also, Kiernan, *European Empires from Conquest to Collapse,* pp. 210ff; Holland, *European Decolonization 1918–1981,* pp. 86ff.

112. M. Heald and L. S. Kaplan, *Culture and Diplomacy: The American Experience* (Westport, Conn., 1977), chs. 5 and 8; P. A. Varg, *Missionaries, Chinese, and Diplomats . . . 1890–1952* (Princeton, N.J., 1952); A. Iriye, *Across the Pacific* (New York, 1967); and, more specifically, B. W. Tuchman, *Stilwell and the American Experience in China* (New York, 1971); H. Feis, *The China Tangle* (Princeton, N.J., 1953), passim; N. B. Tucker, *Patterns in the Dust: Chinese-American Relations and the Recognition Controversy 1949–50* (New York, 1983).

113. M. Schaller, *The American Occupation of Japan: The Origins of the Cold War*

in Asia (New York, 1985), which places U.S. policy toward Japan in a much wider East Asian and Cold War context; and W. S. Borden, *The Pacific Alliance* (Madison, Wis., 1984), passim.

114. Cited in Schaller, *American Occupation of Japan*, p. 232; see also Smith, *The Pattern of Imperialism*, pp. 193–94. American policy in the region is well covered in W. W. Stueck, *The Road to Confrontation* (Chapel Hill, N.C., 1981); R. M. Blum, *Drawing the Line: The Origin of American Containment Policy in East Asia* (New York, 1982); B. Cumings, *The Origins of the Korean War* (Princeton, N.J., 1981); N. Yonosuke and A. Iriye (eds.), *The Origins of the Cold War in Asia* (New York, 1977). See also R. Dingman, "Strategic Planning and the Policy Process: American Plans for War in East Asia, 1945–50," *Naval War College Review*, vol. 32, no. 6 (1979), pp. 4–21.

115. There is a succinct account of the Korean War in Millett and Maslowski, *For the Common Defense*, pp. 484ff; and much more detail in D. Rees, *Korea: The Limited War* (New York, 1966); F. H. Heller, (ed.), *The Korean War: A 25-Year Perspective* (Kansas, 1977); as well as the U. S. official histories.

116. N. A. Graebner, *America as a World Power* (Wilmington, Del., 1984), ch. 7, "Global Containment: The Truman Years"; Tucker, *Patterns in the Dust*, passim; D. Borg and W. Heinrichs (eds.), *Uncertain Years: Chinese-American Relations, 1947–50* (New York, 1980), passim; Schaller, *American Occupation of Japan*, chs. 11–15; E. M. Irving, *The First Indochina War: French and American Policy, 1945–1954* (London, 1975).

117. For the stiffer mood, see Gaddis, *Strategies of Containment*, chs. 5–6. See also the thoughtful piece by R. Jervis, "The Impact of the Korean War on the Cold War," *Journal of Conflict Resolution*, vol. 24, no. 4 (December 1980), pp. 563–92.

118. "Correlates of War" print-out data.

119. See also the chart in R. W. DeGrasse, *Military Expansion, Economic Decline* (Armonk, NY, 1983), p. 119.

120. Holloway, *Soviet Union and the Arms Race*, pp. 43, 115ff. It is, of course, impossible to obtain reliable Soviet spending figures, and the "explicit" defense-expenditure share of the budget is much too low; see F. D. Holzman, *Financial Checks on Soviet Defense Expenditures* (Lexington, Mass., 1975), passim.

121. Cited in Gaddis, *Strategies of Containment*, p. 100. See also S. F. Wells, "Sounding the Tocsin: NSC-68 and the Soviet Threat," *International Security*, vol. 4 (Fall 1979), pp. 116–38, and Paul Nitze's reply, "The Development of NSC-68," *International Security*, Spring 1980, pp. 159–69; Paul Y. Hammond, "NSC-68: Prologue to Rearmament," in W. R. Schilling et al., *Strategy, Politics, and Defense Budgets* (New York, 1962), pp. 267–378.

122. See Bartlett, *Global Conflict*, pp. 303ff; and the details on NATO's build-up in Ismay, *NATO*, passim; T. P. Ireland, *Creating the Entangling Alliance* (London, 1981); and Kaplan, *United States and NATO*, pp. 143ff.

123. Mackintosh, *Juggernaut*, pp. 292ff; the various essays in Liddell Hart (ed.), *Red Army*, pt. 2; Wolfe, *Soviet Power and Europe*, passim; A. Lee, *The Soviet Air Force* (London, 1961); R. Kilmarx, *A History of Soviet Air Power* (London, 1962).

124. Reynolds, *Command of the Sea*, pp. 530–43; Kennedy, *Rise and Fall of British Naval Mastery*, ch. 11.

125. Reynolds, *Command of the Sea*, pp. 545ff; Hagan (ed.), *In Peace and War: Interpretations of American Naval History 1775–1978*, chs. 15–16; Potter (ed.), *Sea Power*, chs. 31–32; J. Woods (pseud.), "The Royal Navy Since World War II," *U.S. Naval Institute Proceedings*, vol. 108, no. 3 (March 1982), pp. 82ff.

126. Mitchell, *History of Russian and Soviet Sea Power*, chs. 21–22, covers the post-1945 buildup. See also N. Polmar, *Soviet Naval Developments, 1982* (4th edn., Annapolis, Md., 1981), pp. 3–13; R. W. Herrick, *Soviet Naval Strategy* (Annapolis, Md., 1968); L. L. Whetton, "The Mediterranean Threat," *Survival*, no. 8 (August 1980), pp. 252–58; G. Jukes, "The Indian Ocean in Soviet Naval Policy," *Adelphi Papers*, no. 87 (May 1972). Very important in this connection are the works of M. MccGwire, *Soviet Naval Developments* (New York, 1973), *Soviet Naval Policy* (New York, 1975), and *Soviet Naval Influence* (New York, 1977), summarized in idem, "The Rationale for the Development of Soviet Seapower," in J. Baylis and G. Segal (eds.), *Soviet Strategy* (London, 1981), pp. 210ff.

127. On which see G. Herken, *The Winning Weapon: The Atomic Bomb in the Cold War 1945–1950* (New York, 1980); Freedman, *Evolution of Nuclear Strategy*, pp. 38ff; but see also H. R. Borowski, *A Hollow Threat: Strategic Air Power and Containment before Korea* (Westport, Conn., 1982). For implications and comparisons, M. Mandelbaum, *The Nuclear Revolution: International Politics Before and After Hiroshima* (New York, 1981).

128. Prados, *Soviet Estimate*, ch. 4, is best here.

129. Gaddis, *Strategies of Containment*, chs. 4–5, gives the overall context. See also D. A. Rosenberg, "American Atomic Strategy and the Hydrogen Bomb Decision," *Journal of American History*, vol. 66 (June 1979), pp. 62–87; idem, " 'A Smoking Radiating Ruin at the End of Two Hours': Documents on American Plans for Nuclear War with the Soviet Union, 1954–55," *International Security*, vol. 6, no. 3 (Winter 1981–82), pp. 3–38; Freedman, *Evolution of Nuclear Strategy*, ch. 6; Weigley, *The American Way of War*, ch. 17.

130. Prados, *Soviet Estimate*, chs. 5–8; also E. Bottome, *The Missile Gap* (Rutherford, N.J., 1971), passim.

131. Freedman, *Evolution of Nuclear Strategy*, pp. 175ff; Friedberg, "A History of the U.S. Strategic 'Doctrine,' 1945 to 1980," pp. 41ff. Also very useful is John Gaddis, "The Origins of Self-Deterrence: The United States and the Non-Use of Nuclear Weapons, 1945–1958" (ms.). The strategic thinkers are discussed in G. Herken, *Counsels of War* (New York, 1985), and F. Kaplan, *The Wizards of Armageddon* (New York, 1983).

132. R. V. Daniels, *Russia, The Roots of Confrontation* (Cambridge, Mass., 1985), p. 234; McCauley, *The Soviet Union Since 1917*, pp. 155ff; Ulam, *Expansion and Coexistence*, chs. 9–10.

133. Steele, *Pax Americana*, p. 9; and, in more detail, R. E. Osgood, *NATO: The Entangling Alliance* (Chicago, Ill., 1962), passim; DePorte, *Europe Between the Superpowers*, pp. 115ff; Kaplan, *United States and NATO*.

134. Steele, *Pax Americana*, p. 134. See also R. Aron, *The Imperial Republic* (London, 1975); D. Horowitz, *The Free World Colossus* (New York, 1971 edn.); Schulzinger, *American Diplomacy in the Twentieth Century*, chs. 11–12.

135. Keylor, *Twentieth-Century World*, p. 375; J. L. Gaddis, "The Strategic Perspective: The Rise and Fall of the 'Defensive Perimeter' Concept," in Borg and Heinrichs (eds.), *Uncertain Years*, pp. 61–118; and—with some very good quotations—Schaller, *The American Occupation of Japan*, pp. 279ff.

136. Quoted in Woodruff, *America's Impact on the World*, p. 65.

137. Ulam, *Expansion and Coexistence*, pp. 539ff; McCauley, *Soviet Union Since 1917*, pp. 198ff; Daniels, *Russia: The Roots of Confrontation*, pp. 333ff.

138. The literature on this topic is now overwhelming. Among the more important studies are G. Jukes, *The Soviet Union in Asia* (Berkeley, Calif., 1973); H. D. Cohn, *Soviet Policy Toward Black Africa* (New York, 1972); R. H. Donaldson, *Soviet Policy Toward India* (Cambridge, Mass., 1974); R. Kanet (ed.), *The Soviet*

Union and the Developing Nations (Baltimore, Md., 1974); E. Taborsky, *Communist Penetration of the Third World* (New York, 1963).

139. P. Lyon, "The Emergence of the Third World," in H. Bull and A. Watson (eds.), *The Expansion of International Society* (Oxford, 1984), pp. 229ff, as well as the other essays in sec. 3; Barraclough, *Introduction to Contemporary History,* ch. 6; R. Emerson, *From Empire to Nation: The Rise to Self-Assertion of Asian and African Peoples* (Cambridge, Mass., 1962), passim.

140. Lyon, "Emergence of the Third World," in Bull and Watson (eds.), *Expansion of International Society,* p. 229; idem, *Neutralism* (Leicester, 1963); G. H. Jansen, *Afro-Asia and Non-Alignment* (London, 1966).

141. Apart from the works in note 139 above, see also L. S. Stavrianos, *Global Rift: The Third World Comes of Age* (New York, 1981); R. A. Mortimer, *The Third World Coalition in International Politics* (New York, 1980); R. L. Rothstein, *The Weak in the World of the Strong: The Developing Countries in the International System* (New York, 1977); idem, *The Third World and U.S. Foreign Policy* (Boulder, Colo., 1981).

142. Balfour, *Adversaries,* pp. 157ff; Ulam, *Expansion and Coexistence,* pp. 461ff; D. Rusinov, *The Yugoslav Experiment, 1948–1974* (London, 1977); Lyon, "Emergence of the Third World," passim.

143. McCauley, *Soviet Union Since 1917,* p. 204. More generally, see the references in note 138 above, and R. C. Horn, *The Soviet Union and India: The Limits of Influence* (New York, 1981); R. H. Donaldson (ed.), *The Soviet Union in the Third World: Successes and Failures* (Boulder, Colo., 1981); M. H. Haykal, *The Sphinx and the Commissar: The Rise and Fall of Soviet Influence in the Middle East* (London, 1978); K. Dawisha, *Soviet Foreign Policy Towards Egypt* (London, 1979), passim.

144. McCauley, *Soviet Union Since 1917,* p. 210; Donaldson (ed.), *Soviet Union in the Third World: Successes and Failures,* passim; A. Dawisha and K. Dawisha (eds.), *The Soviet Union in the Middle East* (New York, 1982).

145. "Correlates of War" print-out data, which is more reliable than *Military Balance* (see following note) figures for the early 1970s.

146. *The Military Balance 1974–75* (London, 1974), pp. 7, 10; cf. pp. 19, 22.

147. H. Pemsel, *Atlas of Naval Warfare* (London, 1977), p. 159.

148. *Military Balance 1974–75,* pp. 75–77; for China, pp. 48–49.

149. See the references in note 126 above.

150. For Soviet-American relations in the 1970s, see Keylor, *Twentieth-Century World,* pp. 364ff, 405ff; Schulzinger, *American Diplomacy in the Twentieth Century,* pp. 299ff; S. Hoffman, *Primacy or World Order* (New York, 1978), passim; Lawson, *Soviet-American Rivalry,* passim; McCauley, *Soviet Union Since 1917,* pp. 238ff; Daniels, *Russia: The Roots of Confrontation,* pp. 321ff, and the full bibliography on pp. 394–96. Above all, there is now R. L. Garthoff, *Détente and Confrontation: American-Soviet Relations from Nixon to Reagan* (Washington, D.C., 1985), with enormous detail.

151. Keylor, *Twentieth-Century World,* p. 371.

152. For what follows see R. C. Thornton, *The Bear and the Dragon* (New York, 1972); R. C. North, *Moscow and the Chinese Communists* (Stanford, Calif. 1953); R. R. Simmons, *The Strained Alliance* (New York, 1975); G. Ginsburgs and C. F. Pinkele, *The Sino-Soviet Territorial Dispute, 1949–64* (New York, 1978); D. Floyd, *Mao Against Khrushchev* (New York, 1964); A. D. Low, *The Sino-Soviet Dispute* (Rutherford, N.J., 1976); and a good brief summary in Bartlett, *Global Conflict,* pp. 325ff.

153. Ulam, *Expansion and Coexistence,* p. 693; O. E. Clubb, *China and Russia: The "Great Game"* (New York, 1971), passim, gives more details, as does J. Camil-

leri, *Chinese Foreign Policy: The Maoist Era and Its Aftermath* (Seattle, Wash., 1980).

154. Keylor, *Twentieth-Century World,* p. 398.

155. H. Kissinger, *The White House Years* (Boston, 1979), pp. 172ff; and the important analysis in D. L. Strode, "Arms Control and Sino-Soviet Relations," *Orbis,* vol. 28, no. 1 (Spring 1984), pp. 163–88.

156. Gaddis, *Strategies of Containment,* p. 210, fn.

157. W. E. Griffith (ed.), *Communism in Europe: Continuity, Change and the Sino-Soviet Dispute,* 2 vols. (Cambridge, Mass., 1964–66); J. G. Whelan, *World Communism, 1967–1969: Soviet Attempts to Reestablish Control* (Library of Congress, Legislative Reference Service, Washington, D.C., 1970); Z. Brzezinski, *The Soviet Bloc: Unity and Conflict* (Cambridge, Mass., 1967 edn.).

158. See the nice, brief survey by C. Bell, "China and the International Order," in Bull and Watson (ed.), *Expansion of International Society,* ch. 17; more detailed in M. B. Yahuda, *China's Role in World Affairs* (New York, 1978).

159. Cited in W. L. Kohl, *French Nuclear Diplomacy* (Princeton, N.J., 1971), p. 103. See also W. Mendl, *Deterrence and Persuasion: French Nuclear Armament in the Context of National Policy, 1945–1969* (London, 1970); M. M. Harrison, *Reluctant Ally: France and Atlantic Security* (Baltimore, Md., 1981); and espec. E. Kolodziej, *French International Policy Under de Gaulle and Pompidou: The Politics of Grandeur* (Ithaca, N.Y., 1974).

160. Kolodziej, *French International Policy,* passim; A. Grosser, *The Western Alliance: European-American Relations since 1945* (London, 1980), pp. 183ff, 209ff.

161. See below, pp. 427–28.

162. There is a succinct survey of de Gaulle's policies in De Porte, *Europe Between the Superpowers,* pp. 229ff; and Keylor, *Twentieth-Century World,* pp. 346ff.

163. Bairoch, "International Industrialization Levels," p. 304.

164. Keylor, *Twentieth-Century World,* pp. 354ff, 408ff; A. Bronke and D. Novak (eds.), *The Communist States in the Era of Detente, 1971–1977* (Oakville, Ont., 1979); R. L. Tokes, *Euro-Communism and Détente* (New York, 1978); G. B. Ginsburgs and A. Z. Rubinstein (eds.), *Soviet Foreign Policy Towards Western Europe* (New York, 1978); L. L. Whetten, *Germany's Ostpolitik* (London, 1971); and W. E. Griffith, *The Ostpolitik of the Federal Republic of Germany* (Cambridge, Mass., 1978), cover the German aspects.

165. H. Salisbury, *The Coming War Between Russia and China* (London, 1969), passim.

166. Some of these concerns are discussed in E. Morton and G. Segal (eds.), *Soviet Strategy Toward Western Europe* (London, 1984).

167. Bartlett, *Global Conflict,* p. 355. See also G. Segal, *The Great Power Triangle* (London, 1982); R. Sutter, *China Watch: Toward Sino-American Reconciliation* (Baltimore, Md., 1978), passim; and the essays in R. H. Solomon (ed.), *The China Factor: Sino-American Relations and the Global Scene* (New York, 1981), and G. Segal (ed.), *The China Factor: Peking and the Superpowers* (London, 1982), espec. B. Garrett, "The United States and the Great Power Triangle," pp. 76–104.

168. Gaddis, *Strategies of Containment,* pp. 249–50, 259.

169. A. Kendrick, *The Wound Within: America in the Vietnam Years, 1945–1974* (Boston, 1974); T. Powers, *The War at Home: Vietnam and the American People, 1964–1968* (New York, 1973); F. Fitzgerald, *Fire in the Lake: The Vietnamese and the Americans in Vietnam* (Boston, 1972); W. O'Neill, *Coming Apart* (New York, 1971); R. J. Lifton, *Home from the War: Vietnam Veterans* (New York, 1973); L. Baskir and P. Strauss, *Chance and Circumstance: The War, The Draft, and the Vietnam Generation* (New York, 1978); and G. Kolko,

Vietnam: Anatomy of a War, 1940–1975 (New York, 1986), are among some of the welter of good books on these themes.

170. Again, the literature on the American strategy and conduct of the war is already overwhelming. Millett and Maslowski, *For the Common Defense,* ch. 17, is a good summary. H. G. Summers, *On Strategy: A Critical Analysis of the Vietnam War* (New York, 1972) examines the war through Clausewitzian spectacles. B. Palmer, *The 25-Year War: America's Military Role in Vietnam* (New York, 1984), espec. pt. 2, "Assessment"; S. Karnow, *Vietnam: A History* (New York, 1984); G. C. Herring, *America's Longest War: The United States and Vietnam, 1950–1975* (New York, 1979), are all important.

171. Figures from Gaddis, *Strategies of Containment,* p. 359; see also Millett and Maslowski, *For the Common Defense,* pp. 565ff.

172. See again Ungar (ed.), *Estrangement: America and the World,* passim; but especially G. Hodgson, "Disorder Within, Disorder Without."

173. This may be seen, *inter alia,* in the titles of many American studies on the international system and the United States' place in it. Apart from Ungar (ed.), *Estrangement,* see also K. A. Oye et al. (eds.), *Eagle Entangled: U.S. Foreign Policy in a Complex World* (New York, 1979); R. D. Keohane, *After Hegemony* (Princeton, N.J., 1974); J. Kwitny, *Endless Enemies* (New York, 1984); and the important earlier work S. Hoffman, *Gulliver's Troubles* (New York, 1968).

174. Gaddis, *Strategies of Containment,* p. 275. And see again the references in note 167 above, and the very useful survey in Garthoff, *Détente and Confrontation,* pp. 24ff.

175. Gaddis, *Strategies of Containment,* p. 179. See also Kissinger's own *White House Years;* and H. Starr, *Henry Kissinger: Perceptions of International Politics* (Lexington, Ky., 1982), passim. Dallek, *American Style of Foreign Policy,* ch. 9, is much more critical.

176. Gaddis, *Strategies of Containment,* pp. 284, 297.

177. Compare Kennan, *Decline of Bismarck's European Order,* with Kissinger, "The White Revolutionary: Reflections on Bismarck," *Daedelus,* vol. 97 (Summer 1968), pp. 888–924.

178. Gaddis, *Strategies of Containment,* pp. 280–82; and, in more detail, two fine studies: C. Bell, *The Diplomacy of Détente: The Kissinger Era* (New York, 1977); and R. S. Litwak, *Détente and the Nixon Doctrine: American Foreign Policy and the Pursuit of Stability, 1969–1975* (Cambridge, 1984).

179. Apart from the (often contradictory) memoirs of Carter, his secretary of state, Vance, and his national security adviser, Brzezinski, see the coverage in Garthoff, *Détente and Confrontation,* pp. 563ff; and, much more briefly, Ambrose, *Rise to Globalism,* ch. 15; Schulzinger, *American Diplomacy,* pp. 316ff; and John Gaddis's final thoughts in the "Epilogue" to *Strategies of Containment.* Above all, see G. Smith, *Morality, Reason and Power: American Diplomacy in the Carter Years* (New York, 1986), passim, but espec. pp. 241ff.

180. B. Rubin, *Paved with Good Intentions: The United States and Iran* (New York, 1980), passim; G. Sick, *All Fall Down: America's Tragic Encounter with Iran* (New York, 1985); and Smith, *Morality, Reason and Power,* ch. 9, are best here.

181. Garthoff, *Détente and Confrontation,* chs. 26–27, is best here.

182. See, *inter alia,* J. S. Gansler, *The Defense Industry* (Cambridge, Mass., 1980), passim; J. Fallows, *National Defense* (New York, 1981), especially ch. 3; R. W. DeGrasse, *Military Expansion, Economic Decline* (Armonk, N.Y., 1983); J. Coates and M. Kilian, *Heavy Losses* (New York, 1985 edn.), passim.

183. See the biting comments in Schulzinger, *American Diplomacy,* pp. 339ff; S. Talbott, *Deadly Gambits: The Reagan Administration and the Stalemate in Nuclear Arms Control* (New York, 1984), with revealing details; Haig's own

memoir, *Caveat* (New York, 1984); E. Luttwak, *The Pentagon and the Art of War* (New York, 1985).

184. Ulam, *Dangerous Relations: The Soviet Union in World Politics 1970–1982* (New York, 1983), p. 39.

185. D. Holloway, *The Soviet Union and the Arms Race* (New Haven, 1984, 2nd ed.), pp. 134ff; and the more technical analysis is A. Bergson, "Technological Progress," in Bergson and H. S. Levine (eds.), *The Soviet Economy: Toward the Years 2000* (London, 1983), pp. 34–78.

186. Garthoff, *Détente and Confrontation*, pp. 887ff, is excellent here. See also H. S. Bradsher, *Afghanistan and the Soviet Union* (Durham, N.C., 1983), passim; and T. T. Hammond, *Red Flag over Afghanistan* (Boulder, Colo., 1984), passim.

187. Garthoff, *Détente and Confrontation*, pp. 982ff. See also the works cited in note 167 above, as well as B. Garrett, "China Policy and the Constraints of Triangular Logic," in K. A. Oye et al. (eds.), *Eagle Defiant: United States Foreign Policy in the 1980s* (Boston, 1983), espec. pp. 245ff.

188. Gaddis, *Strategies of Containment*, p. 280 (my emphasis).

189. This is most critically the case, of course, in respect to *Russian* data: see F. D. Holzmann, "Soviet Military Spending: Assessing the Numbers Game," *International Security*, vol. 6, no. 4 (Spring 1982), pp. 78–101, which is a good introduction to this subject.

190. Bairoch, "International Industrialization Levels," p. 276.

191. Rostow, *World Economy*, p. 662. (The chief difference is that Rostow uses a 1913 = 100 baseline, whereas Bairoch has chosen 1900.)

192. Bairoch, "International Industrialization Levels," p. 273.

193. Ibid., p. 276.

194. From Rostow, *World Economy*, p. 669.

195. Ashworth, *Short History of the International Economy*, pp. 287–88.

196. Ibid., p. 289; and the more detailed discussion in Bairoch, *The Economic Development of the Third World Since 1900* (Berkeley, Calif., 1975), passim.

197. Foreman-Peck, *History of the World Economy*, p. 376.

198. Bairoch, "International Industrialization Levels," p. 304.

199. See the table in Oye et al. (eds.), *Eagle Defiant*, p. 8.

200. G. Blackburn, *The West and the World Since 1945* (New York, 1985), p. 96; and Bairoch, *Economic Development*, passim, with a good bibliography on pp. 250–52.

201. R. Rosecrance, *The Rise of the Trading State* (New York, 1985), espec. ch. 7; and M. Smith et al., *Asia's New Industrial World* (New York, 1985).

202. See Schaller, *American Occupation of Japan*, p. 289.

203. Of which perhaps the most important study has been E. F. Vogel, *Japan as Number One: Lessons for America* (New York, 1980 edn.).

204. Smith et al., p. 18; C. Johnson, *MITI and the Japanese Miracle* (Stanford, Calif., 1982), passim.

205. Vogel, *Japan as Number One*, pp. 9–10 (my emphasis). Allen, *A Short Economic History of Modern Japan*, pt. 2, is very valuable here. The automobile statistics come from *The Economist*, November 2, 1985, p. 111.

206. Most of the writings upon China after 1945 seem to have focused upon Mao or upon cultural/ideological issues, rather than its external policy: but there is Bell, "China and the International Order," in Bull and Watson (eds.), *The Expansion of International Society*, pp. 255–67; H. Harding (ed.), *China's Foreign Relations in the 1980s* (New Haven, Conn., 1984), espec. chs. 1 and 5–6; A. D. Barnett, *China and the Major Powers in East Asia* (Washington, D.C., 1977); M. Yahuda, *China's Role in World Affairs* (New York, 1978); P. Van Ness, *Revolution and Chinese Foreign Policy* (Berkeley, Calif., 1971); and R. H. Sol-

omon (ed.), *The China Factor: Sino-American Relations and the Global Scene* (Englewood Cliffs, N.J., 1981), with some very useful chapters.

207. Bairoch, "International Industrialization Levels," pp. 299, 302.
208. Rostow, *World Economy*, pp. 525ff; and D. H. Perkins (ed.), *China's Modern Economy in Historical Perspective* (Stanford, Calif., 1975), passim.
209. Blackburn, *West and the World Since 1945*, p. 77.
210. Ibid.; and Bairoch, *Economic Development of the Third World*, pp. 188ff, 201ff, which comments approvingly on the attention the Chinese gave to agriculture.
211. "Correlates of War" print-out data for 1980.
212. Bairoch, "International Industrialization Levels," p. 304.
213. D. H. Perkins, "The International Consequences of China's Economic Development," in Solomon (ed.), *China Factor*, pp. 114–136, is important here.
214. Some of Europe's dilemmas are discussed in DePorte, *Europe Between the Superpowers*, passim; J. R. Wegs, *Europe Since 1945* (New York, 1984, 2nd edn.), espec. chs. 8–15; S. Holt, *The Common Market: The Conflict of Theory and Practice* (London, 1967).
215. Aldcroft, *European Economy 1914–1980*, p. 161.
216. Ibid.; and see also Landes, *Unbound Prometheus*, ch. 7; Pollard, *Peaceful Conquest*, ch. 9; Maddison, "Economic Policy and Performance in Europe 1913–1970," in Cipolla (ed.), *Fontana Economic History of Europe*, vol. 5, pt. 2, pp. 476ff. For the early period, there are detailed studies: M. M. Postan, *An Economic History of Western Europe, 1945–1964* (London, 1967); and A. S. Milward, *The Reconstruction of Western Europe, 1945–1951* (London, 1984).
217. Aldcroft, *European Economy*, pp. 161–62.
218. Oye et al. (eds.), *Eagle Defiant*, p. 8, and notes in Table 1-1.
219. For this argument, see again Pollard, *Peaceful Conquest*, passim.
220. Ibid., p. 305
221. Ibid., p. 171.
222. Aldcroft, *European Economy*, p. 161.
223. See the data in Wegs, *Europe Since 1945*, ch. 9; A. S. Deaton, "The Structure of Demand 1920–1970," in Cipolla (ed.), *Fontana Economic History of Europe*, vol. 5, pt. 1.
224. Ricossa, "Italy, 1920–1970," in Cipolla (ed.), *Fontana Economic History of Europe*, vol. 6, pt. 1, pp. 290ff; G. Scimone, "The Italian Miracle," in J. Hennessy et al., *Economic "Miracles"* (London, 1964); G. H. Hildebrand, *Growth and Structure in the Economy of Modern Italy* (Cambridge, Mass., 1965).
225. See above, pp. 367–68.
226. Porter, *Britain, Europe and the World*, ch. 5; Kennedy, *Realities behind Diplomacy*, chs. 7–8.
227. The literature on Britain's post-1945 relative economic decline is enormous. See, *inter alia*, Gamble, *Britain in Decline*, passim; Kirby, *Decline of British Economic Power Since 1870*, ch. 5; F. Blackaby (ed.), *De-industrialization* (London, 1979), passim; W. Beckerman (ed.), *Slow Growth in Britain: Causes and Consequences* (Oxford, 1979); J. Eatwell, *Whatever Happened to Britain?* (London, 1982), passim.
228. Bairoch, "International Industrialization Levels," p. 303.
229. Wegs, *Europe Since 1945*, p. 161. The figures for world manufacturing production are from Bairoch, those for shares of world trade from Kirby, *Decline*, p. 149, table 15.
230. V. Berghahn, *Unternehmer und Politik in der Bundesrepublik* (Frankfurt, 1985), passim; K. Hardach, *The Political Economy of Germany in the Twentieth Century* (Berkeley, Calif., 1980), pp. 140ff.
231. For fuller details, Hardach, *Political Economy of Germany*, pp. 178ff; L. Er-

hard's satisfied account, *The Economics of Success* (Princeton, N.J., 1963), passim; Hardach, "Germany 1914–1970," in Cipolla (ed.), *Fontana Economic History of Europe*, vol 6., pt. 1, pp. 217ff; Landes, *Unbound Prometheus*, pp. 502ff, 531ff; Balfour, *Adversaries*, pp. 122ff.

232. Hardach, "Germany 1914–1970," in Cipolla (ed.), *Fontana Economic History of Europe*, vol. 6, pt. 1, p. 221.

233. Wegs, *Europe Since 1945*, p. 161.

234. The Federal Republic's diplomatic and security concerns, and the attitude of other Powers to them, are examined in DePorte, *Europe Between the Superpowers*, pp. 1180ff; C. M. Kelleher, *Germany and the Politics of Nuclear Weapons* (New York, 1975); W. F. Hanrieden, *West German Foreign Policy 1949–1963* (Stanford, Calif., 1967); Willis, *France, Germany and the New Europe*, passim; Calleo, *The German Problem Reconsidered*, pp. 161ff; P. Windsor, *German Reunification* (London, 1969), passim; Kaiser, *German Foreign Policy in Transition*, passim; Gruner, *Die deutsche Frage*, pp. 176ff.

235. Bairoch, "International Industrialization Levels," p. 302.

236. Fohlen, "France 1920–1970," in Cipolla (ed.), *Fontana Economic History of Europe*, vol. 6, pt. 1, pp. 100ff; E. Malinraud, *La Croissance française* (Paris, 1972), passim; M. Parodi, *L'économie et la société française de 1945 à 1970* (Paris, 1971); Caron, *Economic History of Modern France*, pp. 182ff; R. F. Kuisel, *Capitalism and the State in Modern France* (Cambridge, 1981), chs. 7–9; and Kindleberger, "The Postwar Resurgence of the French Economy," in S. Hoffman (ed.), *In Search of France* (Cambridge, Mass., 1963).

237. See again Kolodziej, *French International Policy Under de Gaulle and Pompidou: The Politics of Grandeur*.

238. See the statistics in the CIA's *Handbook of Economic Statistics, 1984*, pp. 16ff.

239. See, for example, Hosking, *History of the Soviet Union*, appendix C ("Selected Indices of Industrial and Agricultural Production"), p. 483; Munting, *Economic Development of the USSR*, p. 133; Nove, *Economic History of the USSR*, pp. 340, 387; J. P. Nettl, *The Soviet Achievement* (London, 1967), ch. 6.

240. Munting, *Economic Development of the USSR*, p. 133.

241. The problems of Soviet agriculture have been the focus of massive attention in the scholarly literature; see, in particular, the useful essays 4 and 5 in Bergson and Levine (eds.), *Soviet Economy: Toward the Year 2000*; D. M. Schooner, "Soviet Agricultural Policies," in *Soviet Economy in a Time of Change* (Washington, D.C., 1979; Papers, Joint Economic Committee, U.S. Congress), pp. 87–115; and Munting, *Economic Development of the USSR*, pp. 142ff, 160ff.

242. CIA, *Handbook of Economic Statistics, 1984*, p. 27.

243. Cipolla (ed.), *Fontana Economic History of Europe*, vol. 5, pt. 2, pp. 476ff, and vol. 6, pt. 2, pp. 593ff; N. Spulber, *The State and Economic Development in Eastern Europe* (New York, 1966), passim; Kaser, *Comecon*, passim; and an excellent summary in Aldcroft, *European Economy 1914–1980*, ch. 6.

244. Nove, *Economic History*, pp. 330ff, 363ff; Bergson and Levine (eds.), *Soviet Economy: Toward the Year 2000*, p. 148.

245. Details in M. I. Goldman, *The Enigma of Soviet Petroleum* (London/Boston, 1980), which has a rosier view of the future of Russian oil production than the CIA, but acknowledges the problem of waste.

246. Much of this will be discussed again in the final chapter, but see Bergson and Levine (eds.), *Soviet Economy: Toward the Year 2000*, espec. pp. 402ff; H. S. Rowen, "Living with a Sick Bear," *National Interest*, no. 2 (Winter 1985–86), pp. 14–26; M. I. Goldman, *USSR in Crisis: The Failure of an Economic System* (New York, 1983); P. Dibb, *The Soviet Union: The Incomplete Super-power*

(London, 1985), ch. 3; T. J. Colton, *The Dilemma of Reform in the Soviet Union* (New York, 1984), passim. For eastern Europe's problems, see the "Cracks in the Soviet Empire?" issue of *International Security*, vol. 6, no. 3 (Winter 1981–82).

247. Bairoch, "International Industrialization Levels," p. 304.

248. See Table 43 below; and cf. CIA, *Handbook of Economic Statistics, 1984*, p. 4—which (being computed in U.S. dollars) will presumably have quite altered figures for 1987, because of the decline in the value of the American currency.

249. Balfour, *Adversaries*, p. 204.

250. Ibid., p. 193.

251. L. Thurow, "America Among Equals," in Ungar (ed.), *Estrangement*, pp. 159–78; idem, *The Zero-Sum Game* (New York, 1980), passim, but espec. chs. 1 and 4; DeGrasse, *Military Expansion, Economic Decline*, espec. ch. 2.

252. See, in particular, Grosser, *Western Alliance*, pp. 217ff; J. J. Servan-Schreiber, *The American Challenge* (Harmondsworth, Middlesex, 1969 edn.), espec. pt. 2; R. Barnet, *Global Reach* (New York, 1974), passim; S. Rolfe, *The International Corporation* (Paris, 1969); as well as Woodruff, *America's Impact on the World*, ch. 4.

253. Becker and Wells (ed.), *Economics and World Power*, chs. 7–8; D. Calleo, *The Imperious Economy* (Cambridge, Mass., 1982), passim; J. Gowa, *Closing the Gold Window: Domestic Politics and the End of Bretton Woods* (Ithaca, N.Y., 1983); G. Epstein, "The Triple Debt Crisis," *World Policy Journal*, vol. 2, no. 4 (Fall 1985), pp. 628ff; *Economist*, October 5, 1985, "Monetary Reform" Survey, p. 11.

254. Thurow, "America Among Equals," in Ungar (ed.), *Estrangement*, p. 163.

255. Idem, *Zero-Sum Society*, pp. 3–4. (The U.S. figures presumably looked better with the dollar's rise, 1983–1985, and worsened again with the currency's post-1985 decline.)

256. Calleo, "Since 1961: American Power in a New World," in Becker and Wells (eds.), *Economics and World Power*, pp. 391–93.

257. Oye et al. (eds), *Eagle Defiant*, p. 8 (with a note about the sources used).

258. I have taken the population and GNP per capita figures from Chaliand and Gageau, *Strategic Atlas*, pp. 214–20, which bases its figures on the World Bank's *Report on World Development, 1982*. The total GNP is my extrapolation.

259. Given the assertion by Perkins, in Solomon (ed.), *China Factor*, pp. 118–119, that China's per capita GNP in 1979 was more likely between $400 and $500 than the official conversion figure of $266, I have included a calculation for 1980 based on $450 per capita.

260. Cited in Gilpin, *War and Change in World Politics*, pp. 76–77.

CHAPTER EIGHT
To the Twenty-first Century

1. Keylor, *Twentieth-Century World*, p. 405.

2. The classic statement here is E. H. Carr, *What Is History?* (Harmondsworth, Mddsx., 1964), ch. 1, "The Historian and his Facts"; but see also D. Thomson, *The Aims of History* (London, 1969), ch. 4.

3. See, *inter alia*, Gilpin, *War and Change in World Politics;* G. Modelski, "The Long Cycle of Global Politics and the Nation-State," *Comparative Studies in Society and History*, vol. 20 (April 1978), pp. 214–35; Rasler and Thompson, "Global Wars, Public Debts, and the Long Cycle," passim; McNeill, *Pursuit of Power*, passim; Rosecrance, *Action and Reaction in World Politics*, passim.

4. As in the well-known quotation in *Herr Eugen Dühring's Revolution in Science* (London, 1936), p. 188.
5. The political-science literature here is overwhelming. For a sampling, see M. Wight, *Power Politics* (Harmondsworth, Mddsx., 1979); K. Waltz, *Man, the State and War* (New York, 1959); H. Bull, *The Anarchical Society* (New York, 1977).
6. See, for example, P. F. Drucker, "The Changed World Economy," *Foreign Affairs*, vol. 64, no. 4 (Spring 1986), pp. 768–91—a remarkable article. See also the figures given in "Beyond Factory Robots," *Economist*, July 5, 1986, p. 61.
7. Drucker, "Changed World Economy," pp. 771–72; "China and India," *Economist*, Dec. 21, 1985, pp. 66–67.
8. Again, the literature on this theme is immense. For good general introductions, see S. B. Linder, *The Pacific Century* (Stanford, Calif., 1986); J. W. Morley (ed.), *The Pacific Basin* (New York, 1986); M. Smith et al., *Asia's New Industrial World* (London, 1985); K. E. Calder, "The Making of a Trans-Pacific Economy," *World Policy Journal*, vol. 2, no. 4 (Fall 1985), pp. 593–623.
9. Linder, *Pacific Century*, pp. 13–14.
10. Ibid., pp. 6, 15.
11. P. Drysdale, "The Pacific Basin and Its Economic Vitality," in Morley (ed.), *Pacific Basin*, p. 11.
12. Mathias, *First Industrial Nation*, p. 44.
13. M. Kaldor, *The Baroque Arsenal* (London, 1982), p. 18. For further examples— from a quite different source—see F. Cooper, "Affordable Defense: In Search of a Strategy," *Journal of the Royal United Services Institute for Defense Studies*, vol. 130, no. 4 (December 1985), p. 4. Also very useful is the special survey "Defense Technology," *Economist*, May 21, 1983.
14. The key work here (by an in-house expert) is J. S. Gansler, *The Defense Industry* (Cambridge, Mass., 1980).
15. On which see McNeill, *Pursuit of Power*, passim; and Kaldor, *Baroque Arsenal*, passim.
16. *The Military Balance 1985–86*, pp. 170–73; and the SIPRI (Stockholm International Peace Research Institute) publication *The Arms Race and Arms Control* (London, 1982), especially chs. 2–3.
17. L. Brown et al., *State of the World, 1986* (New York, 1986), p. 196.
18. "Excessive" is, of course, a haphazard term; for if a country feels under acute pressure from foreign foes (e.g., Israel), it seems inappropriate to employ that term. On the other hand, the historical record suggests that if a particular nation is allocating *over the long term* more than 10 percent (and in some cases—when it is structurally weak—more than 5 percent) of GNP to armaments, that is likely to limit its growth rate.
19. For some examples of this, see Cipolla (ed.), *Economic Decline of Empires*, passim; Kennedy, *Strategy and Diplomacy*, ch. 3; F. Lewis, "Military Spending Questioned," *New York Times*, Nov. 11, 1986, pp. D1, D5.
20. Reported in "The Elusive Boom in Productivity," *New York Times*, April 8, 1984, business section, pp. 1, 26. See also "Richer Than You," *Economist*, Oct. 25, 1986, pp. 13–14.
21. See T. Fingar (ed.), *China's Quest for Independence* (Boulder, Colo., 1980), passim; G. Segal and W. Tow (eds.), *Chinese Defense Policy* (London, 1984); Chaliand and Rageau, *Strategic Atlas*, p. 143; and the important essays in R. H. Solomon (ed.), *The China Factor: Sino-American Relations and the Global Scene* (Englewood Cliffs, N. J., 1981); and J. Camilleri, *Chinese Foreign Policy: The Maoist Era and Its Aftermath* (Seattle, Wash., 1980).
22. G. Segal, *Defending China* (London, 1985), covers in detail the decline in

Chinese combat effectiveness; see also H. W. Jencks, *From Missiles to Muskets: Politics and Professionalism in the Chinese Army 1945–1981* (Boulder, Colo., 1982).

23. See D. H. Perkins, "The International Consequences of China's Economic Development," in Solomon (ed.), *China Factor*, p. 118.

24. See the important article "A New Long March in China," *Economist*, Jan. 25, 1986, pp. 29–31; J. T. Dreyer, "China's Military Modernization," *Orbis*, vol. 27, no. 4 (Winter 1984), pp. 1011–26; *Military Balance 1985–1986*, pp. 111–15; M. Y. M. Kan, "Deng's Quest for Military Modernization and National Security," in *Mainland China's Modernization: Its Prospects and Problems* (Berkeley, Calif., 1982), pp. 227–44.

25. Dreyer, "China's Military Modernization," p. 1017.

26. Ibid., p. 1016. See also J. D. Pollack, "China as a Nuclear Power," in W. H. Overholt (ed.), *Asia's Nuclear Future* (Boulder, Colo., 1977), passim.

27. For a brief survey of these weaknesses, see again Dreyer, "China's Military Modernization," pp. 1017ff. On submarine developments, see *New York Times*, April 1, 1986, pp. C1, C3.

28. "As China Grows Strong," *Economist*, Jan. 25, 1986, p. 11; and espec. G. Segal, "Defense Culture and Sino-Soviet Relations," *Journal of Strategic Studies*, vol. 8, no. 2 (June 1985), pp. 180–98, with fuller references.

29. B. Reynolds, "China in the International Economy," in H. Harding (ed.), *China's Foreign Relations in the 1980s* (New Haven, Conn., 1984), p. 75.

30. D. H. Perkins, "The International Consequences of China's Economic Development," in Solomon (ed.), *China Factor*, pp. 115–16; and for more detail, Perkins (ed.), *China's Modern Economy in Historical Perspective* (Stanford, Calif., 1975), passim; and A. D. Barnett, *China's Economy in Global Perspective* (Washington, D.C., 1981), passim.

31. *New York Times*, March 27, 1986, p. A14; Rostow, *World Economy*, pp. 532ff.

32. Perkins, "International Consequences," in Solomon (ed.), *China Factor*, p. 128.

33. Reynolds, "China in the International Economy," in Harding (ed.), *China's Foreign Relations in the 1980s*, p. 87.

34. Quoted in Brown et al., *State of the World, 1986*, p. 19; and see also, "China and India: Two Billion People Discover the Joys of the Market," *Economist*, Dec. 21, 1985, pp. 66–67.

35. "China and India"; and see the amazing eyewitness details of the recent transformation in O. Schell, *To Get Rich Is Glorious: China in the 80s* (New York, 1985).

36. *New York Times*, March 27, 1986, p. A14; and, more generally, K. Lieberthal, "Domestic Politics and Foreign Policy," in Harding (ed.), *China's Foreign Relations in the 1980s*, pp. 58ff. See also the CIA report "China: Economic Performance in 1985" (Washington, D.C., 1986); and, finally, the extremely intelligent article by A. D. Barnett, "Ten Years After Mao," *Foreign Affairs*, vol. 65, no. 1 (Fall 1986), pp. 37–65.

37. See again the important article "China and India," *Economist*, Dec. 21, 1985, pp. 65–70, espec. p. 68; and *Ramses, 1982, The State of the World Economy* (Cambridge, Mass., 1982), pp. 286–87.

38. Perkins, "International Consequences," pp. 130–31.

39. *Military Balance 1985–86*, p. 112; Perkins, "The International Consequences . . .", in Solomon (ed.), *China Factor*, p. 132.

40. See the table in Brown et al., *State of the World, 1986*, p. 207.

41. Perkins, "International Consequences," in Solomon (ed.), *China Factor*, pp. 132–33; *Economist*, Jan. 25, 1986, p. 29.

42. Perkins, "International Consequences," in Solomon (ed.), *China Factor*, p. 120.

43. This projection assumes that "the four largest economies in Western Europe grow in 1985–2000 at the same pace as they did in 1970–82" (which the paper admits may be too pessimistic): "China and India," p. 69.

44. *Ramses*, 1982, p. 285; the figures in Morley (ed.), *Pacific Basin*, p. 13; Reynolds, "China in the International Economy," pp. 73–74. By comparison, see again Rosecrance, *Rise of the Trading State*, passim.

45. See again Segal, "Defense Culture and Sino-Soviet Relations," passim.

46. But note R. Taylor, *The Sino-Japanese Axis* (New York, 1985).

47. "Russia and China," *Economist*, March 29, 1986, pp. 34–35. This does not, however, make it automatically a member of an "anti-Soviet united front," as is argued in C. D. McFetridge, "Some Implications of China's Emergence as a Great Power," *Journal of the Royal United Services Institute for Defense Studies*, vol. 128, no. 3 (September 1983), p. 43.

48. On which see J. G. Stoessinger, *Nations in Darkness: China, Russia and America* (New York, 1978), passim; Solomon (ed.), *China Factor*, passim; Segal (ed.), *China Factor*, passim; and Harding (ed.), *China's Foreign Relations in the 1980s*, passim, espec. ch. 6.

49. Pollack, "China and the Global Strategic Balance," in Harding (ed.), *China's Foreign Relations in the 1980s*, pp. 173–74.

50. "A New Long March in China," *Economist*, Jan. 25, 1986, p. 31.

51. For this policy, see in particular E. A. Olsen, *U.S.-Japan Strategic Reciprocity: A Neo-Internationalist View* (Stanford, Calif., 1985), passim; the remarks on Japan in R. A. Scalapino, "China and Northeast Asia," in Solomon (ed.), *China Factor*, pp. 193ff.; Scalapino (ed.), *The Foreign Policy of Modern Japan* (Berkeley, Calif., 1977); T. J. Pempel, "Japanese Foreign Economic Policy," ch. 5 of P. J. Katzenstein (ed.), *Between Power and Plenty: Foreign Economic Policies of Advanced Industrial States* (Madison, Wis., 1978).

52. This is perhaps best argued in Vogel, *Japan as Number One*; but see also his article "Pax Nipponica?" *Foreign Affairs*, vol. 64, no. 4 (Spring 1986), pp. 752–67; and H. Kahn, *The Emerging Japanese Superstate* (London, 1971). For a contrary argument, see "High Technology: Clash of the Titans," *Economist*, Aug. 23, 1986, pp. 318ff, which points to the U.S. advantages.

53. See again Smith et al., *Asia's New Industrial World*; and Linder, *Pacific Century*, passim.

54. For what follows, see Linder, *Pacific Century*, pp. 107ff; E. Wilkinson, *Misunderstanding: Europe versus Japan* (Tokyo, 1981); "Is It Too Late to Stop the Slide to Protectionism?" *Times* (London), Jan. 14, 1982, p. 15; Olsen, *U.S.-Japan Strategic Reciprocity*, ch. 4.

55. "Japan Frets About Tomorrow," *New York Times*, April 30, 1986, pp. D1–D2.

56. "Obstacles to Change in Japan," *New York Times*, April 29, 1986, p. D1.

57. See the figures in the *CIA Handbook of Economic Statistics, 1984*, pp. 50–54; the weekly *Economist* index on commodity prices; and Drucker, "Changed World Economy," passim.

58. See the useful summary in R. B. Reich, "Japan in the Chips," *New York Review of Books*, July 5, 1985; and "Silicon Valley Has a Big Chip About Japan," *Economist*, March 20, 1986, pp. 63–64.

59. "Big Japanese Gain in Computers Seen," *New York Times*, Feb. 13, 1984, pp. A1, A19; "Will Japan Leapfrog America on Superfast Computers?" *Economist*, March 6, 1982, p. 95.

60. "Japan Sets Next Target," *Sunday Times* (London), Nov. 29, 1981.

61. "Westinghouse/Mitsubishi," *Economist*, Feb. 6, 1982, p. 65.

62. R. B. Reich, "A Faustian Bargain with the Japanese," *New York Times*, April

6, 1986, business section, p. 2; "Japanese All Set for Take-off," *Times* (London), Nov. 11, 1981; Smith et al., *Asia's New Industrial World*, pp. 21–24.

63. The quotation is from Vogel, "Pax Nipponica," p. 753. More generally, see "Japanese Technology," *Times* (London), June 14, 1983, "Special Report," pp. i–viii. The more successful Japanese exploitation of robotics technology is outlined in B. J. Feder, "New Challenge in Automation," *New York Times*, Oct. 30, 1986, p. D2.

64. "Reconsider Japan," *Economist*, April 26, 1986, pp. 19–22; but see again Johnson, *MITI and the Japanese Miracle;* Vogel, *Japan as Number One*, pp. 70ff.

65. Vogel, "Pax Nipponica," p. 754.

66. See the tables in *Economist*, July 9, 1983, "Japan Survey" section, p. 7; and Pempel, "Japanese Foreign Economic Policy," pp. 171–72.

67. *Economist*, April 26, 1986, p. 22; Vogel, "Pax Nipponica," p. 753; idem, *Japan as Number One*, ch. 7; Smith et al., *Asia's New Industrial World*, pp. 13ff.

68. For example, S. Kamata, *Japan in the Passing Lane* (New York, 1984); J. Taylor, *Shadows of the Rising Sun: A Critical View of the "Japanese Miracle"* (New York, 1984); "There Can be Clouds Too," *Economist*, July 9, 1983, "Japan Survey."

69. D. Halberstam, "Can We Rise to the Japanese Challenge?" *Parade*, Oct. 9, 1983, pp. 4–5; and the even more alarming piece by T. H. White, "The Danger from Japan," *New York Times Magazine*, July 28, 1985.

70. "The New Global Top Banker: Tokyo and Its Mighty Money," *New York Times*, April 27, 1986, pp. 1, 16.

71. F. Marsh, *Japanese Overseas Investment* (Economist Intelligence Unit, London, 1983); *Times* (London), April 22, 1983.

72. For these figures and forecasts, see "Japan Investing Enormous Sums of Cash Abroad," *New York Times*, March 11, 1986, pp. A1, D12; "The New Global Top Banker," *New York Times*, April 27, 1986, pp. 1, 16.

73. "Japan's Investment Bankers Head for the Big Wide World," *Economist*, April 19, 1986, pp. 91–94; D. Burstein, "When the Yen Leaves the Sky It May Capture the Earth," *New York Times*, Sept. 3, 1986, p. A27.

74. "New Global Top Banker," p. 1.

75. See the table in Linder, *Pacific Century*, p. 12, quoting the *Japan in the Year 2000* study.

76. See CIA, *Handbook of Economic Statistics, 1984*, p. 33, fn. b.

77. "The Yen Also Rises," *New York Times*, March 5, 1986, p. D2.

78. See again the very pertinent study by Olsen, *U.S.-Japan Strategic Reciprocity*, passim.

79. See the figures in *Military Balance 1985–86*, pp. 170–72.

80. Olsen, *U.S.-Japan Strategic Reciprocity*, passim; Z. Brzezinski, "Japan Should Increase Spending for Defense," *New Haven Register*, Aug. 16, 1985, "Forum," p. 15.

81. There is a good flavor of the Japanese antiwar movement in Storry, *History of Modern Japan*, ch. 11. See also *Economist*, Aug. 16, 1985, pp. 21–22.

82. Olsen, *U.S.-Japan Strategic Reciprocity*, p. 149.

83. See the discussion in Reynolds, "China in the International Economy," in Harding (ed.), *China's Foreign Relations in the 1980s*, ch. 3 (and espec., p. 86, from where the quotation comes); Scalapino, "China and Northeast Asia," in Solomon (ed.), *China Factor*, espec. pp. 193ff. On the other hand, see Taylor, *Sino-Japanese Axis*, passim.

84. Scalapino, "China and Northeast Asia," p. 200. See also the comments on Japanese external policy in "Japan Survey," *Economist*, Dec. 7, 1985, pp. 10ff.

85. See again Gruner, *Die deutsche Frage*, espec. ch. 4.

86. I take these totals from *The Military Balance 1985–86,* pp. 40–43, 46–54.
87. CIA, *Handbook of Economic Statistics, 1984,* p. 37.
88. The unemployment figures were taken from *The Economist Diary, 1984,* p. 44. For the rising social expenditures, see the OECD report of March 1985, *Social Expenditures 1960–1990.*
89. Quoted in Linder, *Pacific Century,* p. 108.
90. See the review article, "Down to Earth: A Survey of the West German Economy," *Economist,* Feb. 4, 1984.
91. Calleo, *German Problem Reconsidered,* and Gruner, *Die Deutsche Frage,* are best here; but see also DePorte, *Europe Between the Superpowers,* pp. 180ff.
92. W. Gruner, "Der Deutsche Bund—Modell fur eine Zwischenlösung?" *Politik und Kultur,* vol. 9 (1982), no. 5.
93. P. Dibb, *The Soviet Union: The Incomplete Superpower* (London, 1986), pp. 43–44.
94. The literature on European defense and nuclear weapons is enormous. I have relied upon A. J. Pierre (ed.), *Nuclear Weapons in Europe* (New York, 1984); the debate provoked by M. Bundy et al., "Nuclear Weapons and the Atlantic Alliance," *Foreign Affairs,* vol. 6, no. 4 (Spring 1982), pp. 753–68; and by *Strengthening Conventional Deterrence in Europe: Proposals for the 1980s* (New York, 1983); J. D. Steinbrunner and L. V. Segal (eds.), *Alliance Security: NATO and the No-First-Use Question* (Washington, D.C., 1983); G. Prins (ed.), *The Nuclear Crisis Reader* (New York, 1984).
95. *Military Balance 1985–86,* p. 49.
96. "West German Defense: Early Warnings," *Economist,* June 29, 1985, p. 46.
97. See again the good discussion in Calleo, *German Problem Reconsidered,* chs. 8–9; and J. Dean, "Directions in Inner-German Relations," *Orbis,* vol. 29, no. 3 (Fall 1985), pp. 609–32; and G. F. Treverton, *Making the Alliance Work: The United States and Europe* (Ithaca, N.Y., 1985), passim.
98. "When the Oil Runs Out," *Economist,* Oct. 19, 1985, p. 65; "After the Oil Years," *Economist,* March 6, 1985, p. 57.
99. "Manufacturing," *Economist,* Sept. 28, 1985, p. 57.
100. See again Gamble, *Britain in Decline;* Kirby, *Decline of British Economic Power Since 1870;* Eatwell, *Whatever Happened to Britain;* and S. Pollard, *The Wasting of the British Economy* (London, 1982).
101. "After the Oil Years," *Economist,* March 6, 1986, p. 57.
102. A. Waters, *Britain's Industrial Renaissance* (London, 1986)—Waters having been, of course, Mrs. Thatcher's economic adviser.
103. "Scientists' Lament," *Economist,* Jan. 18, 1986, p. 16.
104. See again the statistics in *Military Balance 1985–86.*
105. The share of world GNP is calculated from CIA, *Handbook of Economic Statistics, 1984,* p. 32. For a devastating attack upon this attempt to maintain an overextended defense posture, see A. Barnett, "The Dangerous Dream," *New Statesman,* June 17, 1983, pp. 9–11. Less critical, but equally sobering, is "Yes, But How Do We Pay for It?" *Times* (London), June 15, 1983.
106. "Navy Wins War of the Frigates," *The Sunday Times* (London), Oct. 17, 1982; C. Wain, "The Navy's Future", *The Listener,* Aug. 19, 1982.
107. See *The Economist'*s frequent assaults upon it for that reason: e.g., "Trident: Bad Money After Bad," Nov. 3, 1984, p. 34; "Not Trident," Feb. 9, 1985, p. 16. The government's rationale for Trident is in *Statement on the Defense Estimates, 1985,* vol. 1 (Cmnd. 9430-1).
108. "Message to the New Defense Secretary: Think Small," *Sunday Times* (London), Jan. 12, 1986, p. 16; see also "Defense Budget Costs Go over the Top," *Daily Telegraph,* Dec. 10, 1985. There are excellent surveys of the problem—

and various proposals to deal with it—in J. Baylis (ed.), *Alternative Approaches to British Defense Policy* (London, 1983), passim.

109. For French defense policy, see generally M. M. Harrison, *The Reluctant Ally: France and Atlantic Security* (Baltimore, Md., 1981); R. F. Laird, *France, the Soviet Union, and the Nuclear Weapons Issue* (Boulder, Col., 1985); and D. S. Yost, *France's Deterrent Posture* (Adelphi Papers, nos. 194 and 195).

110. "France" survey, *Economist*, Feb. 9, 1985, p. 8.

111. See, in particular, the work by P. Lellouche, *L'avenir de la guerre* (Paris, 1985), nicely discussed in D. S. Yost, "Radical Change in French Defense Policy," *Survival*, vol. 28 (Jan./Feb., 1986), pp. 53–68; R. F. Laird, "The French Strategic Dilemma," *Orbis*, vol. 28, no. 2 (Summer 1984), pp. 307–28.

112. R. S. Rudney, "Mitterand's New Atlanticism: Evolving French Attitudes toward NATO," *Orbis*, vol. 28, no. 1 (Spring 1984), p. 99, citing Aron.

113. Ibid., passim.

114. "Chirac Is Pledged to Stick with NATO and Bonn," *New York Times*, April 6, 1986, "The Week in Review" section p. 2.

115. H. Schmidt, *A Grand Strategy for the West* (New Haven, Conn., 1985), pp. 41–43, 55–57. See also J. P. Pigasse, *Le bouclier d'Europe* (Paris, 1982).

116. See the discussion in Yost, "Radical change in French defense policy?"; as well as idem, *France and Conventional Defense in Central Europe* (Boulder, Colo., 1985).

117. "The French are Ready to Cross the Rhine," *Economist*, July 13, 1985, pp. 43–44; "French Defence: Count on Us," *Economist*, Oct. 25, 1986, pp. 50–51.

118. P. Stares, "The Modernization of the French Strategic Nuclear Force," *Journal of the Royal United Services Institute*, vol. 125, no. 4 (December 1980), p. 37.

119. See again Laird, "French Strategic Dilemma," passim; and P. Lellouche, "France and the Euromissiles," *Foreign Affairs*, Winter 1983–84, pp. 318–34.

120. See the analysis in L. Kolakowski, *Main Currents of Marxism*, vol. 1, *The Founders* (Oxford, 1981 edn.), ch. 13, "The Contradictions of Capital"; and Engels's discussion of contradictions in "Socialism: Utopian and Scientific," in *The Essential Left* (London, 1960), pp. 130ff.

121. "Excerpts from Gorbachev's Speech to the Party," *New York Times*, Feb. 26, 1986. See also "Making Mr. Gorbachev Frown," *Economist*, March 8, 1986, p. 67; S. Bialer, "The Harsh Decade: Soviet Policies in the 1980s," *Foreign Affairs*, vol. 59, no. 5 (Summer 1981), pp. 999–1020.

122. Brown et al., *State of the World, 1986*, pp. 14–19; "Focus: Food," *Economist*, April 12, 1986, p. 107.

123. M. I. Goldman, *USSR in Crisis: The Failure of an Economic System* (New York, 1983), p. 86. For further analyses, see Bergson and Levine (eds.), *Soviet Economy: Toward the Year 2000*, chs. 4–5. How swiftly (relatively) the USSR's position has been worsened can be seen by rereading the rosier assessment of the gap between it and the United States being closed by the year 2000 in Larson's very sober *Soviet-American Rivalry* (written in 1976–77?), p. 272.

124. As reported in "Soviet Is Facing Sixth Poor Harvest in a Row," *New York Times*, Aug. 28, 1985, pp. A1, D17. More generally, R. E. M. Mellor, *The Soviet Union and Its Geographical Problems* (London, 1982); Larson, *Soviet-American Rivalry*, pp. 17ff.

125. For what follows, see Hosking, *History of the Soviet Union*, pp. 392ff; J. R. Millar, "The Prospects for Soviet Agriculture," in M. Bornstein (ed.), *The Soviet Economy: Continuity and Change* (Boulder, Colo., 1981), pp. 273–91 (more optimistic than most); Goldman, *USSR in Crisis*, ch. 3.

126. "The Soviet Economy," *New York Times*, March 15, 1985, pp. A1, A6.

127. Goldman, *USSR in Crisis*, p. 81.

128. Ibid., p. 83; and the remarks in Nove, *Economic History of the USSR*, pp. 362ff.
129. Reprinted from Brown et al., *State of the World*, 1986, p. 18.
130. See again Goldman, *USSR in Crisis*, pp. 70–71; and, more broadly, R. W. Tucker, "Swollen State, Spent Society: Stalin's Legacy to Brezhnev's Russia," *Foreign Affairs*, vol. 60, no. 2 (Winter 1981–82), pp. 415ff.
131. Brown et al., *State of the World, 1986*, p. 18.
132. Ibid., p. 11.
133. See the comparative figures in CIA, *Handbook of Economic Statistics, 1984*, pp. 28–30.
134. Goldman, *USSR in Crisis*, p. 40, has some remarkable figures on that inefficiency. See also the extremely thoughtful piece by J. S. Berliner, "Planning and Management," in Bergson and Levine (eds.), *Soviet Economy: Toward the Year 2000*, pp. 350–89.
135. The phrase comes from Daniels, *Russia: The Roots of Confrontation*, p. 289.
136. Taken from "Inputs Misused," *Economist*, July 6, 1985, p. 12, which (itself employing the words "used to produce *even an alleged* $1,000-worth of GDP") clearly suspects that the *real* figures could be worse.
137. This is best discussed in M. I. Goldman, *The Enigma of Soviet Petroleum: Half-Full or Half-Empty* (London, 1980), passim; but see also L. Silk, "Soviet Oil Troubles," *New York Times*, June 5, 1985, p. D2.
138. "Russia Drills Less Oil, OPEC Keeps It Cheap," *Economist*, June 8, 1985, p. 65.
139. *Economist*, May 3, 1986, pp. 55–57; more generally, see R. W. Campbell, "Energy," in Bergson and Levine (eds.), *Soviet Economy: Toward the Year 2000*, pp. 191ff.
140. Dibb, *Soviet Union: The Incomplete Superpower*, p. 93.
141. Campbell, "Energy," pp. 213–14, in Bergson and Levine (eds.), *Soviet Economy: Toward the Year 2000;* see also L. Dienes, "An Energy Crunch Ahead in the Soviet Union?" in Bornstein (ed.), *Soviet Economy*, pp. 313–43.
142. See below, pp. 500–502.
143. Goldman, "A Low-Tech Economy at Home," *New York Times*, Feb. 19, 1984, business section, p. 2; and the interesting details in R. Amann and J. Cooper (eds.), *Industrial Innovation in the Soviet Union* (New Haven, Conn., 1982).
144. "Losing Battle," *Wall Street Journal*, July 25, 1984.
145. Apart from Goldman, *USSR in Crisis*, p. 131, see R. Amann et al. (eds.), *The Technological Level of Soviet Industry* (New Haven, Conn., 1977).
146. Goldman, *USSR in Crisis*, ch. 6; "Shadows over Comecon," *Economist*, May 29, 1982, pp. 84–85; Comecon Survey, *Economist*, April 20, 1985. pp. 3–18.
147. See again Drucker, "Changed World Economy," passim; "Oil's Decline Seen Curbing Soviet Plans," *New York Times*, March 10, 1986; "East European Trade," *Economist*, Oct. 26, 1985, p. 119. The implications for eastern Europe are also analyzed in T. Gustafson, "Energy and the Soviet Union," *International Security*, vol. 6, no. 3 (Winter 1981–82), pp. 65–89.
148. M. Feshbach, "Population and Labor Force," in Bergson and Levine (eds.), *Soviet Economy: Toward the Year 2000*, p. 79. See also Goldman, *USSR in Crisis*, pp. 100ff; and T. J. Colton, *The Dilemma of Reform in the Soviet Union* (New York, 1984), pp. 15ff.
149. "Sick Men of Europe," *Economist*, March 22, 1986, p. 53.
150. Dibb, *Soviet Union: The Incomplete Superpower*, pp. 92–93.
151. Feshbach, "Population and Labor Force," in Bergson and Levine (eds.), *Soviet Economy: Toward the Year 2000*, passim.
152. See the argument in J. W. Kiser, "How the Arms Race Really Helps Moscow," *Foreign Policy*, no. 60 (Fall 1985), pp. 40–51.
153. Munting, *Economic Development of the USSR*, p. 208.

154. "Gorbachev's Plans: Westerners See a Lot of Zeal, but Little Basic Change," *New York Times*, Feb. 23, 1986, p. 16; "Russia Under Gorbachev," *Economist*, Nov. 16, 1985, p. 21.

155. "The Soviet Economy," *New York Times*, March 15, 1985, pp. A1, A6, quoting Leonard Silk; Colton, *Dilemma of Reform in the Soviet Union*, ch. 3; Daniels, *Russia: The Roots of Confrontation*, pp. 273ff; J. F. Hough and M. Fainsod, *How the Soviet Union Is Governed* (Cambridge, Mass., 1979).

156. This is best covered by F. D. Holzman's articles "Are the Soviets Really Outspending the U.S. on Defense?" *International Security*, vol. 4, no. 4 (Spring 1980), pp. 86–104, and "Soviet Military Spending: Assessing the Numbers Game," *International Security*, vol. 6, no. 4 (Spring 1982), pp. 78–101; as well as idem, *Financial Checks on Soviet Defense Expenditures* (Lexington, Mass., 1975). See also Holloway, *Soviet Union and the Arms Race*, pp. 114ff; Dibb, *Soviet Union: The Incomplete Superpower*, pp. 80ff.

157. This point is made both by Colton, *Dilemma of Reform in the Soviet Union*, p. 91; and Bond and Levine, "An Overview," in Bergson and Levine (eds.), *Soviet Economy: Toward the Year 2000*, pp. 19–21.

158. Ibid., p. 20, the source of this quotation; see also; "Can Andropov Control His Generals?" *Economist*, Aug. 6, 1983, pp. 33–35.

159. L. H. Gelb, "A Common Desire for Guns and Butter," *New York Times*, Nov. 10, 1985, "The Week in Review" section, p. 2.

160. See the table in Holloway, *Soviet Union and the Arms Race*, p. 114; and the discussion in *Military Balance 1985–86*, pp. 17–20; Holzman, "Soviet Military Spending," passim; W. T. Lee, *The Estimation of Soviet Defense Expenditures 1955–75* (New York, 1977), passim; G. Adams, "Moscow's Military Costs," *New York Times*, Jan. 10, 1984, p. A23.

161. For details, one can consult the somewhat bloodcurdling annual publication of the U.S. Defense Department *Soviet Military Power*, and the Committee on the Present Danger's *Can America Catch Up?*—views contested by such critics as T. Gervasi, *The Myth of Soviet Military Supremacy* (New York, 1986), and A. Cockburn, *The Threat: Inside the Soviet Military Machine* (New York, 1984 edn.). For details presented nonpolemically, see the annual *Military Balance*, and the annual report by SIPRI (Stockholm International Peace Research Institute). A good general work is J. Steele, *Soviet Power* (New York, 1984), but see also Dibb, *Soviet Union: The Incomplete Superpower;* and Holloway, *Soviet Union and the Arms Race*, as well as the references following.

162. A. Amalrik, *Will the Soviet Union Survive Until 1984?* (New York, 1970). See also M. Garder, *L'Agonie du régime en Russie sovietique* (Paris, 1966), and the subsequent debate in the journal *Problems of Communism;* and Colton, *Dilemma of Reform in the Soviet Union*, passim.

163. See the comparative tables in Bergson, "Technological Progress," in Bergson and Levine (eds.), *Soviet Economy: Toward the Year 2000*, pp. 51ff; Rostow, *World Economy*, p. 434; Holloway, *Soviet Union and the Arms Race*, pp. 134ff.

164. "Soviet Arms: Their Quality Is Upgraded," *New York Times*, Feb. 12, 1984; Cockburn, *The Threat*, pp. 455–56.

165. Alex Gliksman, "Behind Moscow's Fear of 'Star Wars,' " *New York Times*, Feb. 13, 1986.

166. Quoted in Flora Lewis, "Soviet SDI Fears," *New York Times*, March 6, 1986, p. A27.

167. Dibb, *Soviet Union: The Incomplete Superpower*, pp. 51ff; J. Kazokins, "Nationality in the Soviet Army," *Journal of the Royal United Services Institute for Defense Studies*, vol. 130, no. 4 (December 1985), pp. 27–34. For a rosier pic-

ture, E. Jones, "Manning the Soviet Military," *International Security*, vol. 7, no. 1 (Summer 1982), pp. 105–31.

168. On which see Dibb, Soviet Union: *The Incomplete Superpower*, pp. 44ff, "The Nationality Problem"; Hosking, *History of the Soviet Union*, ch. 14; Daniels, *Russia, The Roots of Confrontation*, pp. 315ff; as well as the more detailed studies, like H. Carrere d'Encausse, *Decline of an Empire* (New York, 1979); M. Rywkin, *Moscow's Muslim Challenge* (New York, 1982); A. Bennigsen and M. Broxup, *The Islamic Threat to the Soviet State* (London, 1983); and S. E. Wimbush (ed.), *Soviet Nationalities in Strategic Perspective* (New York, 1985).

169. J. Anderson, "Ukraine a Hotbed of Dissent, Nationalism" (syndicated article), *New Haven Register*, June 13, 1985; but see also P. T. Potichny (ed.), *The Ukraine in the Seventies* (Oakville, Ont., 1982); Hosking, *History of the Soviet Union*, pp. 432ff.

170. Apart from Kazokins, "Nationality in the Soviet Army," passim, see the eye-opening details in Cockburn, *Threat*, pp. 74ff; E. Jones, "Minorities in the Soviet Armed Forces," *Comparative Strategy*, vol. 3, no. 4 (1982), pp. 285–318; and the Rand Corporation studies S. Curran and D. Ponomoreff, *Managing the Ethnic Factor in the Russian and Soviet Armed Forces: An Historical Overview* (Santa Monica, Calif., 1982); and E. Brunner, Jr., *Soviet Demographic Trends and the Ethnic Composition of Draft Age Males, 1980–1985* (Santa Monica, Calif., 1981).

171. On which term see, for example, the coverage in D. Leebaert (ed.), *Soviet Military Thinking* (London, 1981), espec. the essays in pt. 1; J. Baylis and G. Segal (eds.), *Soviet Strategy* (London, 1981), espec. essays 4 and 5.

172. *Military Balance 1985–86*, p. 180.

173. For example, Gervasi, *Myth of Soviet Military Supremacy*, passim, but espec. pp. 116–18.

174. For examples: J. Schell, *The Fate of the Earth* (New York, 1982); H. Caldicott, *Nuclear Madness* (Brookline, Mass., 1979); E. P. Thompson, *Zero Option* (London, 1982).

175. There is a good brief survey of these strategic ideas in E. Bottome, *The Balance of Terror* (Boston, Mass., 1986 edn.), chs. 4–7 (and a glossary of terms, pp. 243–54); A. W. Garfinkle, *The Politics of the Nuclear Freeze* (Philadelphia, Pa., 1984); and T. Powers, *Thinking About Nuclear Weapons* (New York, 1983).

176. Of the vast array of studies on this problem, I prefer M. Mandelbaum, *The Nuclear Future* (Ithaca, N.Y., 1983); R. Jervis, *The Illogic of American Nuclear Strategy* (Ithaca, N.Y., 1984); and S. Zuckerman, *Nuclear Illusion and Reality* (London, 1982). Also useful is S. M. Keeny and W.K.H. Panofsky, "MAD vs. NUTS: the Mutual Hostage Relationship of the Superpowers," *Foreign Affairs*, vol. 60, no. 2 (Winter 1981–82), pp. 287–304.

177. See again "In Battle of Wits, Submarines Evade Advanced Efforts at Detection," *New York Times*, April 1, 1986, p. C1; and the comments in McGwire, "Rationale for the Development of Soviet Seapower," passim, on the difficulties the USSR has had with integrating American SLBMs into its strategic planning.

178. The quote is from Jervis, *Illogic of American Nuclear Strategy*. For an example of "war-fighting" writers, see C. Gray, "Nuclear Strategy: A Case for a Theory of Victory," *International Security*, vol. 4 (Summer 1979), pp. 54–87.

179. See especially P. Bracken, *The Command and Control of Nuclear Weapons* (New Haven, Conn., 1983); also N. Calder, *Nuclear Nightmares* (Harmondsworth, Mddsx., 1981).

180. On which theme, see in particular J. C. Snyder and S. F. Wells (eds.), *Limiting Nuclear Proliferation* (Cambridge, Mass., 1985); Mandelbaum, *Nuclear Future*, ch. 3; G. Quester (ed.), *Nuclear Proliferation: Breaking the Chain* (Madison,

Wis., 1981). By contrast, K. N. Waltz, "Toward Nuclear Peace," Wilson Center, International Security Studies Program, Working Paper no. 16.

181. D. L. Strode, "Arms Control and Sino-Soviet Relations," *Orbis*, vol. 28, no. 1 (Spring 1984), espec. p. 168ff.

182. *The Economist*, 9 February, 1985, "Not Trident," p. 16. See also, Gervasi, *The Myth of Soviet Military Supremacy*, p. 171.

183. "France Tests Longer-Range Sub Missile," *New York Times*, March 6, 1986, p. A3. See also the table outlining the buildup of French nuclear warheads in *New York Times*, April 6, 1986, "The Week in Review" section, p. 2.

184. For example, "Powell Derides Nuclear 'Last Resort,' " *Times* (London), June 1, 1983, p. 4; Lord Carver, "Why Britain Should Reject Trident," *Sunday Times* (London), Feb. 21, 1982.

185. See again Yost, "Radical Change in French Defense Policy?"

186. Dibb, *Soviet Union: The Incomplete Superpower*, p. 161. By contrast, see Gervasi, *Myth of Soviet Military Supremacy*, ch. 26, which argues that NATO numbers are in fact superior. Also important are the *International Security* essays edited by S. E. Miller, *Conventional Forces and American Defense Policy* (Princeton, N. J., 1986).

187. *Statement on the Defense Estimates, 1985*, vol. 1 (Cmnd 9430), summarized in *Survey of Current Affairs*, vol. 15, no. 6 (June 1985), p. 179.

188. As pointed out by F. D. Holzman, "What Defense-Spending Gap?" *New York Times*, March 4, 1986.

189. See Dibb, *Soviet Union: The Incomplete Superpower*, p. 162; *Military Balance 1985–86*, pp. 186–87; R. L. Fischer, *Defending the Central Front: The Balance of Forces* (Adelphi Papers, no. 127, London, 1976).

190. This is a tricky (and highly disputed) topic. For the optimists' view—with which, for what it is worth, this author agrees—see J. Mearsheimer, "Why the Soviets Can't Win Quickly in Central Europe," pp. 121–57, and B. R. Posen, "Measuring the European Conventional Balance," pp. 79–120, both in Miller (ed.), *Conventional Forces and American Defense Policy*. See also Steele, *Soviet Power*, pp. 76ff; and C. N. Donnelly, "Tactical Problems Facing the Soviet Army: Recent Debates in the Soviet Military Press," *International Defense Review*, vol. 11, no. 9 (1978), pp. 1405–12. More sobering assessments are provided by R. A. Mason, "Military Strategy," in E. Moreton and G. Segal (eds.), *Soviet Strategy Toward Western Europe* (London, 1984), pp. 175–202; P. A. Peterson and J. G. Hines, "The Conventional Offensive in Soviet Theater Strategy," *Orbis*, vol. 27, no. 3 (Fall 1983), pp. 695–739; and—calling attention to the possibility of Soviet use of dual-purpose missiles (i.e., tactical nuclear missiles)—D. M. Gormley, "A New Dimension to Soviet Theater Strategy," *Orbis*, vol. 29, no. 3 (Fall 1985), pp. 537–69. There is a good recent survey, "NATO's Central Front," in *Economist*, Aug. 30, 1986.

191. This is now best treated in Treverton, *Making the Alliance Work*, passim; but see also J. Joffe, "European-American Relations: The Enduring Crisis," *Foreign Affairs*, vol. 59 (Spring 1981).

192. V. Bunce, "The Empire Strikes Back: The Evolution of the Eastern Bloc from a Soviet Asset to a Soviet Liability," *International Organization*, vol. 39, no. 1 (Winter 1985), pp. 13–28. See also the articles on "Cracks in the Soviet Empire?" in *International Security*, vol. 6, no. 3 (Winter 1981–82); D. R. Herspring and I. Volgyes, "Political Reliability in the Eastern European Warsaw Pact Armies," *Armed Forces and Society*, vol. 6, no. 2 (Winter 1980), pp. 270–96; A. R. Johnson et al., *East European Military Establishments: The Warsaw Pact Northern Tier* (New York, 1982).

193. D. A. Andelman, "Contempt and Crisis in Poland," *International Security*, vol. 6, no. 3 (Winter 1981–82), pp. 90–104.

194. Herspring and Volgyes, "Political Reliability," passim; B. S. Lambeth, "Uncertainties for the Soviet War Planner," in Miller (ed.), *Conventional Forces and American Defense Policy*, pp. 181–82; W. E. Griffith, "Superpower Problems in Europe: A Comparative Assessment," *Orbis*, vol. 29, no. 4 (Winter 1986), pp. 748–49.

195. See the controversial proposal of S. P. Huntington, "Conventional Deterrence and Conventional Retaliation in Europe," in Miller (ed.), *Conventional Forces and American Defense Policy*, pp. 251–75. And for a wide-ranging consideration of all these issues, see E. R. Alterman, "Central Europe: Misperceived Threats and Unforeseen Dangers," *World Policy Journal*, vol. 2, no. 4 (Fall 1985), pp. 681–709.

196. See the discussion in Dibb, *Soviet Union: The Incomplete Superpower*, pp. 165–66; Segal, *Defending China*, passim; idem, "Defense Culture and Sino-Soviet Relations," passim; and pp. 449–51 above.

197. Dibb, *Soviet Union: The Incomplete Superpower*, pp. 147ff; Segal, "The China Factor," in Moreton and Segal (eds.), *Soviet Strategy Towards Western Europe*, pp. 154–59; Strode, "Arms Control and Sino-Soviet Relations," passim.

198. See Steele, *Soviet Power*, ch. 8, "Asian Anxieties"; also T. B. Millar, "Asia in the Global Balance," in D. H. McMillen (ed.), *Asian Perspectives on International Security* (London, 1984); Segal (ed.), *The Soviet Union in East Asia* (Boulder, Colo., 1983); M. Hauner, "The Soviet Geostrategic Dilemma" (ms. article for Foreign Policy Research Institute).

199. See again McGwire, "Rationale for the Development of Soviet Seapower," in Baylis and Segal (eds.), *Soviet Strategy*, pp. 210–54; Polmar, *Soviet Naval Developments*, passim.

200. Figures from Dibb, *Soviet Union: The Incomplete Superpower*, p. 172.

201. The quotation is from ibid., p. 171; but see also Steele, *Soviet Power*, pp. 33–36; and Cockburn, *Threat*, ch. 15.

202. McGwire, "The Rationale," pp. 226ff; Dibb, *Soviet Union: The Incomplete Superpower*, pp. 167–74.

203. See the comparative statistics in Smith, *Pattern of Imperialism*, p. 215; the argument in Steele, *Soviet Power*, chs. 9–12; F. Fukuyama, "Gorbachev and the Third World," *Foreign Affairs*, vol. 64, no. 4 (Spring 1986), pp. 715–31; K. Menon, *Soviet Power and the Third World* (New York, 1985).

204. Quoted in Dibb, *Soviet Union: The Incomplete Superpower*, p. 160. Note also, N. Eberstadt, " 'Danger' to the Soviet," *New York Times*, Sept. 26, 1983, p. A21, which argues how weak the USSR's influence would be if nuclear weapons did not exist.

205. "If Gorbachev Dares," *Economist*, July 6, 1985.

206. Quotations from Bialer, "Politics and Priorities," in Bergson and Levine (eds.), *Soviet Economy: Toward the Year 2000*, pp. 403, 405.

207. For considerations of Russia's problems and future, see H. S. Rosen, "Living with a Sick Bear," *National Interest*, no. 2 (Winter 1985–86), pp. 14–26; Garthoff, *Détente and Confrontation*, chs. 29–30; Colton, *Dilemma of Reform in the Soviet Union*, passim; Goldman, *USSR in Crisis*, ch. 7; Dibb, *Soviet Union: The Incomplete Superpower*, ch. 8; and the entire issue of *Orbis*, vol. 30, no. 2 (Summer 1986).

208. B. Rubin, "The Reagan Administration and the Middle East," in Oye et al., (eds.), *Eagle Defiant*, p. 367—a good survey. See also H. Saunders, *The Middle East Problem in the 1980s* (Washington, D.C., 1981). For particular problems, see P. Jabber, "Egypt's Crisis, America's Dilemma," *Foreign Affairs*, vol. 64, no.

5 (Summer 1986), pp. 960–80; and R. W. Tucker, "The Arms Balance and the Persian Gulf," in *The Purposes of American Power* (New York, 1981), ch. 4.

209. A. F. Lowenthal, "Ronald Reagan and Latin America: Coping with Hegemony in Decline," in Oye et al. (eds.), *Eagle Defiant*, pp. 311ff; R. Bonachea, "The United States and Central America," in Kaplan, *Global Power*, pp. 209–41; P. A. Armella et al. (eds.), *Financial Policies and the World Capital Markets: The Place of Latin American Countries* (Chicago, Ill., 1983).

210. "An Economy Struggles to Break Its Fall," *New York Times*, June 8, 1986, p. E3; "Hard Times in Mexico Cause Concern in U.S.," *New York Times*, Oct. 19, 1986, pp. 1, 20.

211. *Report of the Secretary of Defense Caspar W. Weinberger to the Congress, on Fiscal Year 1984 Budget* (Washington, D.C., 1983), p. 17.

212. "NATO: Burdens Shared," *Economist*, Aug. 4, 1984, p. 3. See also the discussion of this in Calleo, *Imperious Economy*, pp. 169–71, and in fns. 16–17 on pp. 256–57; E. Conine, "Do the Interests of the U.S. Really Cover the World?" (syndicated column), *New Haven Register*, Feb. 7, 1985, p. 11; M. Kahler, "The United States and Western Europe," in Oye et al. (eds.), *Eagle Defiant*, ch. 9; and, especially, Treverton, *Making the Alliance Work*, passim.

213. There are useful discussions in Mako, *U.S. Ground Forces and the Defense of Central Europe*, passim; Treverton, *Making the Alliance Work*, passim; L. Sullivan, "A New Approach to Burden-Sharing," *Foreign Policy*, no. 60 (Fall 1985), pp. 91ff; K. Knorr, "Burden-Sharing in NATO: Aspects of U.S. Policy," *Orbis*, vol. 29, no. 3 (Fall 1985), pp. 517–36.

214. *Report of the Secretary of Defense . . . Fiscal Year 1984*, p. 17.

215. "Military Forces Stretched Thin, Army Chief Says," *New York Times*, Aug. 10, 1983, pp. A1, A3.

216. "U.S. Forces: Need Arising for More Troops, Ships and Planes," *New York Times*, Oct. 26, 1983, p. A16 (with map).

217. See, for example, the map in the endpapers of Barnett, *Collapse of British Power*, and of Marder, *Anatomy of British Sea Power*.

218. C. W. Weinberger, "U.S. Defense Strategy," *Foreign Affairs*, vol. 64, no. 4 (Spring 1986), p. 678. In this connection, see also B. R. Posen and S. Van Evera, "Defense Policy and the Reagan Administration: Departure from Containment," in Miller (ed.) *Conventional Forces and American Defense Policy*, pp. 19–61.

219. For the statistical evidence of this, see Oye et al. (eds.), *Eagle Defiant*, ch. 1; Bairoch, "International Industrialization Levels from 1750 to 1980," passim. For other measurements, see A. Bergeson and C. Sahoo, "Evidence of the Decline of American Hegemony in World Production," *Review*, vol. 8, no. 4 (Spring 1985), pp. 595–611; and S. D. Krasner, "United States Commercial and Monetary Policy," in Katzenstein (ed.), *Between Power and Plenty*, pp. 58–59, 68–69.

220. *Military Balance 1985–86*, p. 13.

221. For a good example, see E. A. Cohen, "When Policy Outstrips Power—American Strategy and Statecraft," *Public Interest*, no. 75 (Spring 1984), pp. 3–19.

222. Luttwak, *Pentagon and the Art of War*, p. 256.

223. See especially E. A. Cohen, *Citizens and Soldiers: The Dilemma of Military Service* (Ithaca, N.Y., 1985), chs. 7–9; and Canby's interesting remarks on the European experience, in "Military Reform and the Art of War," Wilson Center, International Security Studies Program, working paper no. 41, pp. 8ff.

224. For a sampling, see G. Hart with W. S. Lind, *America Can Win* (Bethesda, Md., 1986); Kaufman, *Reasonable Defense*, passim; Luttwak, *Pentagon and the Art of War*, passim; J. Record, "Reagan's Strategy Gap," *New Republic*, Oct. 29,

1984, pp. 17–21; J. Fallows, *National Defense* (New York, 1981); idem, "The Spend-Up," *Atlantic*, July 1986, pp. 27–31; Gansler, *Defense Industry*, passim; S. L. Canby, "Military Reform and the Art of War," passim; "Forum: Military Reform and Defense Planning," *Orbis*, vol. 27, no. 2 (Summer 1983), pp. 245–300. Also very important in this connection is the powerful exposé of A. T. Hadley, *The Straw Giant: Triumph and Failure: America's Armed Forces* (New York, 1986).

225. Kaufman, *Reasonable Defense*, p. 35; "Bungling the Military Build-Up," *New York Times*, Jan. 27, 1985, business section, pp. 1, 8; Gansler, *Defense Industry*, passim; Fallows, "The Spend-Up," passim; but see also Luttwak, *Pentagon and the Art of War*, ch. 5, for interesting correctives.

226. Weinberger, "U.S. Defense Strategy," p. 694; but see the doubts expressed in Record, "Reagan's Strategy Gap"; Fallows, "The Spend-Up"; and Canby, "Military Reform and the Art of War;" as well as the reasoned defense of high-technology weapons by K. N. Lewis in the *Orbis* forum "Military Reform."

227. Among which I would include Luttwak, *Pentagon and the Art of War;* Canby, "Military Reform and the Art of War"; and Cohen, "When Policy Outstrips Power."

228. See, for example, R. W. Komer, *Maritime Strategy or Coalition Defense?* (Cambridge, Mass., 1984), passim, and the debate in 1986 in journals such as *International Security* upon the Reagan administration's "maritime strategy."

229. Recently spelled out again in Weinberger, "U.S. Defense Strategy," pp. 684ff. See also "Schultz-Weinberger Discord," *New York Times*, Dec. 11, 1984, pp. A1, A12.

230. See, for example, L. C. Thurow, "Losing the Economic Race," *New York Review of Books*, Sept. 27, 1984, pp. 29–31; cf. W. D. Nordhaus, "On the Eve of a Historic Economic Boom," *New York Times*, April 6, 1986, which followed shortly after P. G. Petersen's article in the same paper, "When the Economic Valium Wears Off."

231. S. M. Bodner, "Our Trade Gap Is Really a Standard of Living Gap," *New York Times*, May 6, 1986 (letters); and "Why America Cannot Pay its Way," *Economist*, July 13, 1985, p. 69, both cover the problems facing traditional industries. For the debate upon future technologies, see "High Technology: Clash of the Titans," *Economist*, Aug. 23, 1986. For the congressional study, see "A Disturbing New Deficit," *Time*, Nov. 3, 1986, p. 56.

232. For example, while *The Global 2000 Report to the President* (Washington, D.C., 1980), vol. 1, pp. 18–19, referred to absolute increases in world grain production, it forecast increasing deficits in China, South Asia, and western Europe.

233. "Farmers' Slipping Share of the Market," *New York Times*, May 26, 1986; "Farm Imports Rise as Exports Plunge," *New York Times*, April 20, 1986; "Elephant-High Farm Debts," *Economist*, Sept. 14, 1985, p. 17.

234. For a good brief survey, see P. Cain, "Political Economy in Edwardian England: The Tariff-Reform Controversy," in A. O'Day (ed.), *The Edwardian Age*, (London, 1979), pp. 34–59.

235. Petersen, "When the Economic Valium Wears Off," passim; F. Rohatyn, "The Debtor Economy: A Proposal," *New York Review of Books*, Nov. 8, 1984, pp. 16–21; J. Chace, *Solvency, the Price of Survival* (New York, 1981), chs. 1–2.

236. *President's Private Sector Survey on Cost Control*, report, as reprinted in "Of Debt. Deficits, and the Death of a Republic" (Figgie International advertisement), *New York Times*, April 20, 1986, p. F9. This advertisement misprints the 1985 total of interest as $179 billion; it is in fact $129 billion.

237. Ibid.

238. "Cost of Paying Interest Eases Dramatically for U.S.," *New York Times,* Dec. 28, 1986, pp. 1, 24.

239. The quotation is from Drucker, "Changed World Economy," p. 782. See also M. Shubik and P. Bracken, "Strategic Purpose and the International Economy," in McCormick and Bissell (eds.), *Strategic Dimensions of Economic Behaviour,* p. 212.

240. Drucker, "Changed World Economy," passim; S. Marriss, *Deficits and the Dollar: The World Economy at Risk* (Washington, D.C., 1985); and the comments in "As America Diets, Allies Must Eat" (lead article), *New York Times,* Jan. 17, 1986; "A Nation Hooked on Foreign Funds," *New York Times,* Nov. 18, 1984, business section, pp. 1, 24; "U.S. as Debtor: A Threat to World Trade," *New York Times,* Sept. 22, 1985, business section, p. 3.

241. See again Nordhaus, "On the Eve of a Historic Economic Boom"; the uncharacteristically rosy argument in "America Manufactures Still," *Economist,* April 19, 1986, p. 81; and L. Silk, "Can the U.S. Remain No. 1?" *New York Times,* Aug. 10, 1984, p. D2 (a question, incidentally, which would not have been asked ten to twenty years ago).

242. Rasler and Thompson, "Global Wars, Public Debts, and the Long Cycle," passim; Gilpin, *War and Change in World Politics,* passim.

243. This is best described in G. R. Searle, *The Quest for National Efficiency: A Study in British Politics and British Political Thought, 1899–1914* (Oxford, 1971).

244. Quoted in ibid., p. 101.

245. See above, p. 228–29.

246. See the Brookings study by J. Grunwald and K. Flamm, *The Global Factory: Foreign Assembly in International Trade* (Washington, D.C., 1985); and P. Seabury, "International Policy and National Defense," *Journal of Contemporary Studies,* Spring 1983.

247. See, for example, the British experience in the late 1930s, as detailed in Gibbs, *Grand Strategy,* vol. 1, p. 311.

248. Gansler, *Defense Industry,* pp. 12ff; and especially R. W. DeGrasse, *Military Expansion, Economic Decline* (Armonk, N.Y., 1985 edn.); G. Adama, *The Iron Triangle* (New York, 1981); Thurow, "How to Wreck the Economy," *New York Review of Books,* May 14, 1981, pp. 3–8; Kaufmann, *A Reasonable Defense,* pp. 33–34; more generally, G. Kennedy, *Defense Economics* (London, 1983), espec. ch. 8; S. Chan, "The Impact of Defense Spending on Economic Performance: A Survey of Evidence and Problems," *Orbis,* vol. 29, no. 2 (Summer 1985), pp. 403ff; B. Russett, "Defense Expenditures and National Well-Being," *American Political Science Review,* vol. 76, no. 4 (December 1982), pp. 767–77.

249. Kaldor, *Baroque Arsenal,* passim; DeGrasse, *Military Expansion, Economic Decline,* passim; Thurow, "How to Wreck the Economy," passim; Chace, *Solvency,* ch. 2; E. Rothschild, "The American Arms Boom," in E. P. Thompson and D. Smith (eds.), *Protest and Survive* (Harmondsworth, Mddsx., 1980), pp. 170ff; Rosecrance, *Rise of the Trading State,* chs. 6 and 10.

250. E. Rothschild, "The Costs of Reaganism," *New York Review of Books,* March 15, 1984, pp. 14–17.

251. See again Cipolla, *Economic Decline of Empires;* and Rasler and Thompson, "Global Wars, Public Debts, and the Long Cycle," passim.

252. The quip is from *Misalliance* (1909), and in the original reads "Hindhead's turn will come." As Hobsbawm notes, in *Industry and Empire,* p. 193, this was an obvious jibe at the stockbroker townships south of London, prospering while other parts of the economy were coming under pressure.

253. See above, p. 357. Also useful in this connection is B. Russett, "America's

Continuing Strengths," *International Organization,* vol. 39, no. 2 (Spring 1985), pp. 207–31.

254. W. Lippman, *U.S. Foreign Policy: Shield of the Republic* (Boston, Mass., 1943), pp. 7–8; and see again Cohen, "When Policy Outstrips Power"; and the conclusions in E. Bottome, *The Balance of Terror* (Boston, Mass., 1986 edn.), pp. 235–42.

255. P. Hassner, "Europe and the Contradictions in American Policy," in R. Rosecrance (ed.), *America as an Ordinary Power* (Ithaca, N.Y., 1976), pp. 60–86. See also Helmut Schmidt's insistence, in *Grand Strategy for the West,* p. 147, that "the leadership role can only be assumed by the United States."

EPILOGUE

1. See again Doran and Parsons, "War and the Cycle of Relative Power," passim; G. Modelski, "Wars and the Great Power System," passim; idem, "The Long Cycle of Global Politics and the Nation-State," passim. See also J. Levy, *War in the Modern Great Power System* (Lexington, Ky., 1983).

2. Rasler and Thompson, "Global Wars, Public Debts, and the Long Cycle," passim.

3. L. E. Davis and R. A. Huttenback, "The Cost of Empire," in R. L. Ransom et al. (eds.), *Exploration in the New Economic History* (New York, 1982), pp. 41–69; R. Taagepera, "Size and Duration of Empires: Systematics of Size," *Social Science Research,* vol. 7 (1978), pp. 108–27; idem, "Growth Curves of Empires," *General Systems,* vol. 13 (1968), pp. 171–75.

4. I am thinking here of the various scholars influenced by Wallerstein's "world-system" ideas. For example, A. Bergesen, "Cycles of War in the Reproduction of the World Economy," in P. M. Johnson and W. R. Thompson (eds.), *Rhythms in Politics and Economics* (New York, 1985); E. Friedman (ed.), *Ascent and Decline in the World-System* (Beverly Hills, Calif., 1982); Bergesen (ed.), *Studies in the Modern World-System* (New York, 1980); McGowan and Kegley (eds.), *Foreign Policy and the Modern World-System,* passim.

5. Gilpin, *War and Change in World Politics,* p. 93.

6. Rosecrance, *Rise of the Trading State,* passim.

7. Gilpin, *War and Change in World Politics,* pp. 158–59, has a very good discussion of this point.

8. See the analysis in Wight, *Power Politics,* ch. 3.

9. Quoted by McCormick, on p. 19 of his article "Strategic Considerations in the Development of Economic Thought," in McCormick and Bissell (eds.), *Strategic Dimensions of Economic Behavior.*

10. Ibid.

11. Kennedy, "Strategy versus Finance in Twentieth Century Britain"; and also J. H. Maurer, "Economics, Strategy, and War in Historical Perspective," in McCormick and Bissell (eds.), *Strategic Dimensions of Economic Behavior,* pp. 59–83.

12. Gilpin's term; see *War and Change in World Politics,* p. 162.

13. Cited in Pflanze, *Bismarck and the Development of Germany,* p. 17.

Bibliography

Abarca, R. "Classical Diplomacy and Bourbon 'Revanche' Strategy, 1763–1770," *Review of Politics* 32 (1970).

Abrahamson, J.L. *America Arms for a New Century.* New York, 1981.

Adama, G. *The Iron Triangle.* New York, 1981.

Adams, E.D. *Great Britain and the American Civil War,* 2 vols. London, 1925.

Adams, R.J.Q. *Arms and the Wizard: Lloyd George and the Ministry of Munitions, 1915.* London, 1978.

Adamthwaite, A. *France and the Coming of the Second World War 1936–1939.* Cambridge, 1977.

——, "The British Government and the Media, 1937–1938," *Journal of Contemporary History* 18 (1983).

——. *The Lost Peace: International Relations in Europe 1918–1939.* London, 1980.

Addington, L.H. *The Patterns of War Since the Eighteenth Century.* Bloomington, Ind., 1984.

Adler, G.J., "Britain and the Defence of India—the Origins of the Problem, 1798–1815," *Journal of Asian History* 6 (1972).

Albertini, L. *The Origin of the War of 1914,* 3 vols. London, 1952–57.

Albertini, R. von. *Decolonization.* New York, 1971 edn.

Albrecht-Carrié, R. *A Diplomatic History of Europe Since the Congress of Vienna.* London, 1965 edn.

Aldcroft, D.H. *The British Economy,* vol. 1. London, 1986.

——. *From Versailles to Wall Street: The International Economy in the 1920s.* Berkeley, Calif., 1977.

——. *The European Economy, 1914–1980.*

Alford, B.W.E. *Depression and Recovery: British Economic Growth 1918–1939.* London, 1972.

Allen, G.S. *A Short Economic History of Japan.* London, 1981 edn.

Alperowitz, G. *Atomic Diplomacy: Hiroshima and Potsdam.* London, 1966.

Alterman, E.R., "Central Europe: Misperceived Threats and Unforeseen Dangers," *World Policy Journal* 2 (1985).

Amalrik, A. *Will the Soviet Union Survive until 1984?* New York, 1970.

Amann, R., and J. Cooper, eds. *Industrial Innovation in the Soviet Union.* New Haven, Conn., 1982.

——, et al., eds. *The Technological Level of Soviet Industry.* New Haven, Conn., 1977.

Ambrose, S. *Rise to Globalism: American Foreign Policy Since 1938.* 4th edn., New York, 1985.

Andelman, D.A., "Contempt and Crisis in Poland," *International Security* 6 (1981–2).

Anderson, J.L., "Aspects of the Effects on the British Economy of the War Against France, 1793–1815," *Australian Economic History Review* 12 (1972).

Anderson, M.S. *Europe in the Eighteenth Century*. London, 1961.

——. *Peter the Great*. London, 1978.

Anderson, O. *A Liberal State at War*. London, 1967.

Anderson, T.H. *The United States, Great Britain and the Cold War, 1944–1947*. Columbia, Mo., 1981.

André, L. *Michel le Tellier et Louvois*. Paris, 1943 edn.

Andrew, C.M., and A.S. Kanya-Forstner. *The Climax of French Imperial Expansion 1914–1924*. Stanford, Calif., 1981.

——. *Théophile Delcassé and the Making of the Entente Cordiale*. London, 1968.

Andrews, C.M., "Anglo-French Commercial Rivalry 1700–1750," *American Historical Review* 20 (1915).

Andrews, K.R. *Elizabethan Privateering*. Cambridge, 1964.

——. *Trade, Plunder and Settlement*. Cambridge, 1983.

Ange-Laribe, M. *L'agriculture pendant la guerre*. Paris, 1925.

Armella, P.A., et al., eds. *Financial Policies and the World Capital Markets: The Place of Latin American Countries*. Chicago, 1983.

Aron, R. *The Imperial Republic*. London, 1975.

Ashley, M. *Financial and Commercial Policy under the Cromwellian Protectorate*. London, 1962 edn.

Ashton, R. *The Crown and the Money Market 1603–1640*. Oxford, 1960.

Ashton, T.S. *The Industrial Revolution 1760–1830*. Oxford, 1968 edn.

Ashworth, W. *A Short History of the International Economy Since 1850*. London, 1975.

Aster, S. *1939: The Making of the Second World War*. London, 1973.

Backer, J.H. *Winds of History: The German Years of Lucius DuBignon Clay*. New York, 1983.

Baer, G. *Test Case: Italy, Ethiopia, and the League of Nations*. Stanford, Calif., 1976.

Bailey, T.A. *A Diplomatic History of the American People*. New York, 1974 edn.

Bairoch, P., "International Industrialization Levels from 1750 to 1980," *Journal of European Economic History* 11 (1982).

——, "Europe's Gross National Product: 1800–1975," *Journal of European Economic History* 5 (1976).

——. *The Economic Development of the Third World Since 1900*. Berkeley, Calif., 1975.

Baker, N. *Government and Contractors: The British Treasury and War Supplies 1775–1783*. London, 1971.

Baldwin, H. *The Crucial Years 1939–41*. New York, 1976.

Balfour, M. *The Adversaries: America, Russia, and the Open World, 1941–1962*. London, 1981.

——, and J. Mair. *Four-Power Control in Germany and Austria 1945–1946*. London, 1956.

Bamford, P.W. *Forests and French Sea Power 1660–1780*. Toronto, 1956.

Bankwitz, P.C.F. *Maxime Weygand and Civil-Military Relations in Modern France*. Cambridge, Mass., 1967.

Barbour, V. *Capitalism in Amsterdam in the Seventeenth Century*. Baltimore, 1950.

Barclay, G. *The Empire Is Marching: A Study of the Military Effort of the British Empire*. London, 1976.

Barker, T.M. *Double Eagle and Crescent*. Albany, N.Y., 1967.

Barnet, R. *Global Reach*. New York, 1974.

Barnett, A.D. *China and the Major Powers in East Asia*. Washington, D.C., 1977.

——. *China's Economy in Global Perspective*. Washington, D.C., 1981.

————, "Ten Years After Mao," *Foreign Affairs* 65 (1986).

Barnett, C. *Britain and Her Army 1509–1970: A Military, Political and Social Survey.* London, 1970.

————. *Napoleon.* London, 1978.

————. *The Audit of War.* London, 1986.

————. *The Collapse of British Power.* London, 1972.

Barnhart, M.A., "Japan's Economic Security and the Origins of the Pacific War," *The Journal of Strategic Studies* 4 (1981).

Barraclough, G., ed. *The Times Atlas of World History.* London, 1978.

————. *An Introduction to Contemporary History.* Harmondsworth, Mddsx., 1967.

Bartlett, C.J. *Great Britain and Sea Power 1815–1853.* Oxford, 1963.

————. *The Global Conflict, 1880–1970: The International Rivalry of the Great Powers.* London, 1984.

Baskir, L., and P. Strauss. *Chance and Circumstance: The War, the Draft, and the Vietnam Generation.* New York, 1978.

Bateson, C. *The War with Japan.* East Lansing, Mich., 1968.

Baugh, D.A. *British Naval Administration in the Age of Walpole.* Princeton, N.J., 1965.

Baumgart, W. *Imperialism: The Idea and Reality of British and French Colonial Expansion.* Oxford, 1982.

————. *The Peace of Paris, 1856.* Santa Barbara, Calif., 1981.

Baxter, S.B. *William III and the Defense of European Liberty 1650–1702.* Westport, Conn., 1976 reprint.

Bayley, C.A. *Rulers, Townsmen and Bazaars.* Cambridge, 1983.

Baylis, J., ed. *Alternative Approaches to British Defense Policy.* London, 1983.

————, and G. Segal, eds. *Soviet Strategy.* London, 1981.

————. *Anglo-American Defense Relations 1939–1980.* London, 1981.

Beale, H.K. *Theodore Roosevelt and the Rise of America to World Power.* New York, 1962 edn.

Bean, R., "War and the Birth of the Nation State," *Journal of Economic History* 33 (1973).

Beasley, W.H. *The Meiji Restoration.* Stanford, Calif., 1972.

Becker, J.J. *1914: Comment les Français sont entrés dans la guerre.* Paris, 1977.

Becker, W.H., and S. F. Wells, Jr., eds. *Economics and World Power: An Assessment of American Diplomacy Since 1789.* New York, 1984.

Beckerman, W., ed. *Slow Growth in Britain: Causes and Consequences.* Oxford, 1979.

Behnen, M. *Rüstung-Bündnis-Sicherheit.* Tübingen, 1985.

Bell, C. *The Diplomacy of Détente: The Kissinger Era.* New York, 1977.

Beloff, M. *Imperial Sunset,* vol. i, *Britain's Liberal Empire.* London, 1969.

Bemis, S.F. *The Diplomacy of the American Revolution.* New York, 1935.

Bendix, R. *Kings or People: Power and the Mandate to Rule.* Berkeley, Calif., 1978.

Bengonzi, B. *Heroes' Twilight.* New York, 1966.

Benians, E.A., ed. *The Cambridge History of the British Empire,* vol. iii, *The Empire-Commonwealth 1870–1919.* Cambridge, 1959.

Bennett, E.M. *German Rearmament and the West, 1932–33.* Princeton, N.J., 1979.

Bennigson, A., and M. Broxup. *The Islamic Threat to the Soviet State.* London, 1983.

Bergeron, L. *France under Napoleon.* Princeton, N.J., 1981.

Bergeson, A., ed. *Studies in the Modern World-System.* New York, 1980.

————, and C. Sahoo, "Evidence of the Decline of American Hegemony in World Production," *Review* 8 (1985).

Berghahn, V.R. *Germany and the Approach of War in 1914.* London, 1974.

————. *Unternehmer und Politik in der Bundesrepublik.* Frankfurt, 1985.

Bergson, A., and H. S. Levine, eds. *The Soviet Economy: Toward the Year 2000.* London, 1983.

Best, G. *War and Society in Revolutionary Europe, 1770–1870.* London, 1982.

Betts, R. *Tricouleur: The French Colonial Empire.* London, 1978.

Beyrau, D. *Militär und Gesellschaft im vorrevolutionären Russland.* Göttingen, 1984.

Bialer, S., "The Harsh Decade: Soviet Policies in the 1980s," *Foreign Affairs* 59 (1981).

Bialer, U. *The Shadow of the Bomber: The Fear of Air Attack and British Politics 1932–1939.* London, 1980.

Bidwell, S., and D. Graham. *Fire-Power: British Army Weapons and Theories of War, 1904–1945.* London, 1982.

Bien, D., "The Army in the French Enlightenment: Reform, Reaction and Revolution," *Past and Present* 85 (1979).

Bindoff, S.T., J. Hurstfield, and C.H. Williams, eds. *Elizabethan Government and Society.* London, 1961.

Binney, J.E.D. *British Public Finance and Administration 1774–1792.* Oxford, 1958.

Black, C.E., et al. *The Modernization of Japan and Russia: A Comparative Study.* New York, 1975.

Blackaby, F., ed. *De-industrialization.* London, 1979.

Blackburn, G. *The West and the World Since 1945.* New York, 1985.

Blackett, P.M.S. *Fear, War, and the Bomb.* New York, 1948.

Blackwell, W.L. *The Beginnings of Russian Industrialization, 1800–1860.* Princeton, N.J., 1968.

———. *The Industrialization of Russia: An Historical Perspective.* New York, 1970.

———, ed. *Russian Economic Development from Peter the Great to Stalin.* New York, 1974.

Blond, G. *La Grande Armée 1804/1815.* Paris, 1979.

Blum, R.M. *Drawing the Line: The Origin of American Containment Policy in East Asia.* New York, 1982.

Bond, B. *British Military Policy Between Two World Wars.* Oxford, 1980.

———, "The First World War," *New Cambridge Modern History,* vol. 12 (rev. edn.). Cambridge, 1968.

Boog, H., et al., eds. *Das Deutsche Reich und der Zweite Weltkrieg,* vol. 4, *Der Angriff auf die Sowjetunion.* Stuttgart, 1983.

Borden, W.S. *The Pacific Alliance.* Madison, Wi., 1984.

Borg, D., and W. Heinrichs, eds. *Uncertain Years: Chinese-American Relations, 1947–1950.* New York, 1980.

Bornstein, M., ed. *The Soviet Economy: Continuity and Change.* Boulder, Col., 1981.

Borowski, H.R. *A Hollow Threat: Strategic Air Power and Containment Before Korea.* Westport, Conn., 1982.

Bosher, J.F., "Financing the French Navy in the Seven Years War: Beaujou, Goossens et compagnie in 1759," *U.S. Naval Institute Proceedings,* forthcoming.

———, "French Administration and Public Finance in Their European Setting," *New Cambridge Modern History,* vol. viii. Cambridge, 1965.

———. *French Finances 1770–1795.* Cambridge, 1975.

Bosworth, J.R.B. *Italy and the Approach of the First World War.* London, 1983.

———. *Italy, the Least of the Great Powers: Italian Foreign Policy Before the First World War.* Cambridge, 1979.

Bottome, E. *The Balance of Terror.* Boston, 1986 edn.

———. *The Missile Gap.* Rutherford, N.J., 1971.

Bourne, K. *Britain and the Balance of Power in North America 1815–1908.* London, 1967.

———. *Victorian Foreign Policy 1830–1902.* Oxford, 1970.

Bowler, A. *Logistics and the Failure of the British Army in the America 1775–1783.* Princeton, N.J., 1975.

Boxer, C.R. *The Christian Century in Japan 1549–1650.* Berkeley, Calif., 1951.

———. *The Dutch Seaborne Empire 1600–1800.* London, 1972.

———. *The Portuguese Seaborne Empire 1415–1825.* London, 1969.

Bracken, P. *The Command and Control of Nuclear Weapons.* New Haven, Conn., 1983.

Bradsher, H.S. *Afghanistan and the Soviet Union.* Durham, N.C., 1983.

Braisted, W.R. *The United States Navy in the Pacific,* 2 vols. Austin, Tex., 1958, 1971.

Braudel, F. *The Mediterranean and the Mediterranean World in the Age of Philip II,* 2 vols. London, 1972.

———, and E. Labrousse, eds. *Histoire économique et sociale de la France,* vol. iv. Paris, 1980.

———. *Civilization and Capitalism, 15th–18th Centuries,* 3 vols. London, 1981–84.

Bridge, F.R., and R. Bullen. *The Great Powers and the European States System 1815–1914.* London, 1980.

Briggs, R. *Early Modern France 1560–1715.* Oxford, 1977.

Brodie, B. *Strategy in the Nuclear Age.* Princeton, N.J., 1959.

———. *The Absolute Weapon.* New York, 1946.

Bronke, A., and D. Novak, eds. *The Communist States in the Era of Détente, 1971–1977.* Oakville, Ont., 1979.

Brown, D.M., "The Impact of Firearms on Japanese Warfare," *Far Eastern Quarterly* 7 (1947).

Brown, G.S. *The American Secretary: The Colonial Policy of Lord George Germain 1775–1778.* Ann Arbor, Mich., 1963.

Brown, L., et al. *State of the World, 1986.* New York, 1986.

Brunn, G. *Europe and the French Imperium, 1799–1815.* New York, 1938.

Brunner, E., Jr. *Soviet Demographic Trends and the Ethnic Composition of Draft Age Males, 1980–1995.* Santa Monica, Calif., 1981.

Brunschwig, H. *French Colonialism, 1871–1916: Myths and Realities.* London, 1966.

Brzezinski, Z. *The Soviet Bloc: Unity and Conflict.* Cambridge, Mass., 1967 edn.

Bull, H. *The Anarchical Society.* New York, 1977.

———, and A. Watson, eds. *The Expansion of International Society.* Oxford, 1984.

Bullock, A. *Ernest Bevin, Foreign Secretary.* Oxford, 1983.

———. *Hitler: A Study in Tyranny.* London, 1962 edn.

Bunce, V., "The Empire Strikes Back: The Evolution of the Eastern Bloc from a Soviet Asset to a Soviet Liability," *International Organization* 39 (1985).

Bundy, M., et al., "Nuclear Weapons and the Atlantic Alliance," *Foreign Affairs* 62 (1982).

Burk, K. *Britain, America and the Sinews of War 1914–1918.* London, 1985.

Bushnell, J. *Mutiny and Repression: Russian Soldiers in the Revolution of 1905–1906.* Bloomington, Ind., 1985.

———, "Peasants in Uniform: The Tsarist Army as a Peasant Society," *Journal of Social History* 13 (1980).

———, "The Tsarist Officer Corps, 1881–1915: Customs, Duties, Inefficiencies," *American Historical Review* 86 (1981).

Butler, J.R.M. *Grand Strategy,* vol. ii. London, 1957.

Butow, R.J. *Tojo and the Coming of War.* Princeton, N.J., 1961.

Cain, P.J.. *Economic Foundations of British Overseas Expansion 1815–1914.* London, 1980.

———, and A.G. Hopkins, "The Political Economy of British Expansion Overseas, 1750–1914," *Economic History Review* 33 (1980).

Cairncross, A. *Years of Recovery: British Economic Policy 1945–51.* London, 1985.

Cairns, J.C., "A Nation of Shopkeepers in Search of a Suitable France," *American Historical Review* 79 (1974).

——, "Some Recent Historians and the 'Strange Defeat' of 1940," *Journal of Modern History* 46 (1974).

Calder, A. *Revolutionary Empire: The Rise of the English-Speaking Empires from the Fifteenth Century to the 1780's.* London, 1981.

Calder, K.E., "The Making of a Trans-Pacific Economy," *World Policy Journal* 2 (1985).

Calder, N. *Nuclear Nightmares.* Harmondsworth, Mddsx., 1981.

Caldicott, H. *Nuclear Madness.* Brookline, Mass., 1979.

Calleo, D. *The German Problem Reconsidered: Germany and the World Order, 1870 to the Present.* New York, 1978.

——. *The Imperious Economy.* Cambridge, Mass., 1982.

Cameron, R.E., "Economic Growth and Stagnation in France 1815–1914," *Journal of Modern History* 30 (1958).

——. *France and the Economic Development of Europe 1800–1914.* Princeton, N.J., 1961.

Camilleri, J. *Chinese Foreign Policy: The Maoist Era and Its Aftermath.* Seattle, 1980.

Campbell, C.S. *From Revolution to Rapprochement: The United States and Great Britain, 1783–1900.* New York, 1974.

Canby, S.L., "Military Reform and the Art of War," Wilson Center, International Security Studies Program, working paper 41. Washington, D.C., 1982.

Caron, F. *An Economic History of Modern France.* New York, 1979.

Carr, E.H. *The Twenty Years Crisis 1919–1939.* London, 1939.

——. *What Is History?* Harmondsworth, Mddsx., 1964.

Carr, W. *Poland to Pearl Harbor.* London, 1985.

Carrere d'Encausse, H. *Decline of an Empire.* New York, 1979.

Carroll, B.A. *Design for Total War: Arms and Economics in the Third Reich.* The Hague, 1968.

Carroll, E.M. *French Public Opinion and Foreign Affairs 1880–1914.* London, 1931.

Carsten, F.L. *The Origins of Prussia.* Oxford, 1954.

Carter, A.C., "Dutch Foreign Investment, 1738–1800," *Economica* 20 (1953).

——. *Neutrality or Commitment: The Evolution of Dutch Foreign Policy (1667–1795).* London, 1975.

——. *The Dutch Republic in the Seven Years War.* London, 1971.

Castronovo, V., "The Italian Takeoff: A Critical Re-examination of the Problem," *Journal of Italian History* 1 (1978).

Caute, D. *The Fellow Travellers.* London, 1973.

Cecco, M. de. *Money and Empire: The International Gold Standard 1890–1914.* Oxford, 1974.

Central Intelligence Agency, "China: Economic Performance in 1985." Washington, D.C., 1986.

——. *Handbook of Economic Statistics,* Washington, D.C., 1984.

Chace, J. *Solvency, the Price of Survival.* New York, 1981.

Challenor, R.D. *Admirals, Generals and American Foreign Policy 1898–1914.* Princeton, N.J., 1973.

——. *The French Theory of the Nation in Arms 1866–1939.* New York, 1955.

Challiand, G., and J.-P. Rageau. *Strategic Atlas: A Comparative Geopolitics of the World's Powers.* New York, 1985.

Chalmers Hood, R. *Royal Republicans: The French Naval Dynasties Between the World Wars.* Baton Rouge, La., 1985.

Chan, S., "The Impact of Defense Spending on Economic Performance: A Survey of Evidence and Problems," *Orbis* 29 (1985).

Chandaman, C.D. *The English Public Revenue 1660–1688.* Oxford, 1975.

Chandler, D.G., "Fluctuation in the Strength of Forces in English Pay Sent to Flanders During the Nine Years War, 1688–1697," *War and Society* 1 (1983).

———. *The Art of Warfare in the Age of Marlborough.* London, 1976.

———. *The Campaigns of Napoleon.* New York, 1966.

Chaunu, P. *European Expansion in the Later Middle Ages.* Amsterdam, 1979.

Childs, J. *Armies and Warfare in Europe 1648–1789.* Manchester, 1982.

Christie, I.R. *Wars and Revolutions: Britain 1760–1815.* London, 1982.

Chudoba, B. *Spain and the Empire 1519–1643.* New York, 1969 edn.

Cipolla, C., ed. *The Economic Decline of Empires.* London, 1970.

———. *The Fontana Economic History of Europe,* 6 vols. London, 1972–76.

———. *Before the Industrial Revolution: European Society and Economy 1000–1700,* 2nd edn. London, 1980.

———. *Guns and Sails in the Early Phase of European Expansion 1400–1700.* London, 1965.

Clapham, J.H. *The Bank of England,* vol. i, *1694–1797.* Cambridge, 1944.

———. *The Economic Development of France and Germany, 1815–1914.* Cambridge, 1948.

———. *The Economic History of Modern Britain,* 3 vols. Cambridge, 1938.

Clark, A. *Barbarossa: The Russo-German Conflict 1941–1945.* London, 1965.

Clark, J.G. *La Rochelle and the Atlantic Economy During the Eighteenth Century.* Baltimore, 1981.

Clarke, G.N. *The Dutch Alliance and the War Against French Trade 1688–1697.* New York, 1971 edn.

Clough, S.B. *France: A History of National Economics 1789–1939.* New York, 1939.

———. *The Economic History of Modern Italy, 1830–1914.* New York, 1964.

Clubb, O.E. *China and Russia: The "Great Game."* New York, 1971.

Coates, J., and M. Kilian. *Heavy Losses.* New York, 1985 edn.

Cockburn, A. *The Threat: Inside the Soviet Military Machine.* New York, 1984 edn.

Cohen, E.A. *Citizens and Soldiers: The Dilemma of Military Service.* Ithaca, N.Y., 1985.

———, "When Policy Outstrips Power—American Strategy and Statecraft," *The Public Interest* 75 (1984).

Cohen, J.S., "Financing Industrialization in Italy, 1898–1914: The Partial Transformation of a Latecomer," *Journal of Economic History* 27 (1967).

Cohn, H.D. *Soviet Policy Toward Black Africa.* New York, 1972.

Cohn, S.H. *Economic Development in the Soviet Union.* Lexington, Mass., 1970.

Coleman, D.C. *The Economic History of England 1450–1750.* Oxford, 1977.

Colton, T.J. *The Dilemma of Reform in the Soviet Union.* New York, 1984.

Connelly, O. *Napoleon's Satellite Kingdoms.* New York, 1965.

Conquest, R. *The Great Terror.* London, 1968.

Contamine, H. *La Revanche, 1871–1914.* Paris, 1957.

Cook, M.A., ed. *A History of the Ottoman Empire to 1730.* Cambridge, 1976.

Cookson, J.E., "Political Arithmetic and War 1793–1815," *War and Society* 1 (1983).

Cooper, F., "Affordable Defense: In Search of a Strategy," *Journal of the Royal United Services Institute for Defence Studies* 130 (1985).

Coox, A. *Nomonhan,* 2 vols. Stanford, Calif., 1985.

Corbett, J.S. *England in the Seven Years War: A Study in Combined Strategy,* 2 vols. London, 1907.

Corvisier, A. *Armies and Societies in Europe 1494–1789.* Bloomington, Ind., 1979.

Cosmas, G.A. *An Army for Empire: The United States Army in the Spanish-American War.* Columbia, Mo., 1971.

Cowie, L.W. *Eighteenth-Century Europe.* London, 1963.

Cowling, M. *The Impact of Hitler: British Politics and British Policies 1933–1940.* Cambridge, 1975.

Crafts, N.F.R. *British Economic Growth During the Industrial Revolution.* Oxford, 1985.

——, "British Economic Growth, 1700–1831: A Review of the Evidence," *Economic History Review* 36 (1983).

——, "Industrial Revolution in England and France: Some Thoughts on the Question: 'Why Was England First?' " *Economic History Review* 30 (1977).

Craig, G.A. *Germany 1866–1965.* Oxford, 1978.

——. *The Battle of Koeniggratz.* London, 1965.

——. *The Politics of the Prussian Army 1640–1945.* Oxford, 1955.

——, and A. G. George. *Force and Statecraft: Diplomatic Problems of Our Time.* Oxford, 1983.

Creveld, M. van. *Command in War.* Cambridge, Mass., 1985.

——. *Fighting Power: German and U.S. Army Performance, 1939–1945.* Westport, Conn., 1982.

——. *Supplying War: Logistics from Wallenstein to Patton.* Cambridge, 1977.

Crisp, O. *Studies in the Russian Economy Before 1914.* London, 1976.

Crouzet, F., "L'Angleterre et France au XVIIIᵉ siècle: essai d'analyse comparée de deux croissances économiques," *Annales* 21 (1966).

——. *L'Economie britannique et le Blocus Continental 1806–1813,* 2 vols. Paris, 1958.

——. *The Victorian Economy.* London, 1982.

——, "Toward an Export Economy: British Exports During the Industrial Revolution," *Explorations in Economic History* 17 (1980).

——, "Wars, Blockade and Economic Change in Europe, 1792–1815," *Journal of Economic History* 24 (1964).

Crowe, S.E. *The Berlin West African Conference 1884–1885.* Westport, Conn., 1970 reprint.

Crowley, J.B. *Japan's Quest for Autonomy: National Security and Foreign Policy 1930–1958.* Princeton, N.J., 1966.

Crowson, P.S. *Tudor Foreign Policy.* London, 1973.

Cruikshank, C.G. *Elizabeth's Army.* 2nd edn., Oxford, 1966.

Cumings, B. *The Origins of the Korean War.* Princeton, N.J., 1981.

Curran, S., and D. Ponomoreff. *Managing the Ethnic Factor in the Russian and Soviet Armed Forces: An Historical Overview.* Santa Monica, Calif., 1982.

Curtis, E.E. *The Organization of the British Army in the American Revolution.* Menston, Yorkshire, 1972 reprint.

Curtiss, J.S. *Russia's Crimean War.* Durham, N.C., 1979.

——. *The Russian Army Under Nicholas I, 1825–1855.* Durham, N.C., 1965.

Dallek, R. *The American Style of Foreign Policy.* New York, 1983.

Dallin, D.J. *Soviet Foreign Policy After Stalin.* Philadelphia, 1961.

Daniels, R.V. *Russia, The Roots of Confrontation.* Cambridge, Mass., 1985.

Darby, H.C., "The Face of Europe on the Eve of the Great Discoveries," *New Cambridge Modern History,* vol. i. Cambridge, 1961.

Davies, R.T. *The Golden Century of Spain 1501–1621.* London, 1937.

Davis, L.E. *The Cold War Begins: Soviet-American Conflict over Eastern Europe.* Princeton, N.J., 1974.

Davis, R. *English Overseas Trade 1500–1700.* London, 1973.

——. *The Industrial Revolution and British Overseas Trade.* Leicester, 1979.

——. *The Rise of the Atlantic Economies.* London, 1975.

Davison, W.P. *The Berlin Blockade.* Princeton, N.J., 1958.

Dawisha, A., and K. Dawisha, eds. *The Soviet Union in the Middle East.* New York, 1982.

Dawisha, K. *Soviet Foreign Policy Towards Egypt.* London, 1979.

Dawson, R. *Imperial China.* London, 1972.

Dean, J., "Directions in Inner-German Relations," *Orbis* 29 (1985).

DeGrasse, R.W. *Military Expansion, Economic Decline.* Armonk, N.Y., 1983.

Dehio, L. *The Precarious Balance.* London, 1963.

Deist, W. *The Wehrmacht and German Rearmament.* London, 1981.

———, et al., eds. *Das Deutsche Reich und der Zweite Weltkrieg,* vol. 1, *Ursachen und Voraussetzungen der deutschen Kriegspolitik.* Stuttgart, 1979.

De Gaulle, C. *Mémoires de Guerre,* 3 vols., Paris, 1954–59.

DePorte, A. *Europe Between the Superpowers.* New Haven, Conn., 1979.

de St. Leger, A., and P. Sagnac. *Lá Préponderance française, Louis XIV, 1661–1715.* Paris, 1935.

Devlin, P. *Too Proud to Fight: Woodrow Wilson's Neutrality,* New York, 1975.

Dibb, P. *The Soviet Union: The Incomplete Super-power.* London, 1985.

Dickson, P.G.M. *The Financial Revolution in England: A Study in the Development of Public Credit 1688–1756.* London, 1967.

———, and J. Sperling, "War Finance, 1689–1714," *New Cambridge Modern History,* vol. vi. Cambridge, 1970.

Diehl, J. *Paramilitary Politics in Weimar Germany.* Bloomington, Ind., 1977.

Dietz, F.C. *English Public Finance 1485–1641,* 2 vols. London, 1964 edn.

———, "The Exchequer in Elizabeth's Reign," *Smith College Studies in History* 8 (1923).

Diffie, B.W., and C. D. Winius. *Foundations of the Portuguese Empire 1415–1580.* Minneapolis, 1977.

Dilks, D., ed. *Retreat from Power: Studies in Britain's Foreign Policy in the Twentieth Century,* 2 vols. London, 1981.

Dinerstein, H.S. *War and the Soviet Union.* London, 1962 edn.

Dingman, R., "Strategic Planning and the Policy Process: American Plans for War in East Asia, 1945–50," *Naval War College Review* 32 (1979).

Divine, R.A. *Second Chance: The Triumph of Internationalism in America During World War II.* New York, 1971.

Dockrill, M.L., and J. D. Goold. *Peace Without Promise: Britain and the Peace Conferences 1919–1923.* London, 1981.

Dodgshon, R.A., "A Spatial Perspective," *Peasant Studies* 6 (1977).

Donaldson, R.H., ed. *The Soviet Union in the Third World: Successes and Failures.* Boulder, Col., 1981.

———. *Soviet Policy Toward India.* Cambridge, Mass., 1974.

Donnelly, C.N., "Tactical Problems Facing the Soviet Army: Recent Debates in the Soviet Military Press," *International Defense Review* 11 (1978).

Donoughue, B. *British Politics and the American Revolution.* London, 1964.

Doran, C.F., and W. Parsons, "War and the Cycle of Relative Power," *American Political Science Review* 74 (1980).

Dorn, F. *The Sino-Japanese War 1937–1941.* New York, 1974.

Dorn, W.L. *Competition for Empire 1740–1763.* New York, 1940.

Doughty, R.A. *The Seeds of Disaster: The Development of French Army Doctrine 1919–1939.* Hamden, Conn., 1985.

Douglas, R. *From War to Cold War 1942–1948.* London, 1981.

Dovrig, B. *The Myth of Liberation.* Baltimore, Md., 1973.

Doyle, W. *The Old European Order 1660–1800.* Oxford, 1978.

Dreyer, J.T., "China's Military Modernization," *Orbis* 27 (1984).

Droz, J. *Europe Between Revolutions 1815–1848.* London, 1967.

Drucker, P.F., "The Changed World Economy," *Foreign Affairs* 64 (1986).

Dubief, H. *Le Declin de la IIIᵉ République 1929–1938.* Paris, 1976.

Duffy, C. *Borodino and the War of 1812.* London, 1973.

———. *Russia's Military Way to the West: Origins and Nature of Russian Military Power 1700–1800.* London, 1981.

———. *Siege Warfare: The Fortress in the Early Modern World 1494–1660.* London, 1979.

———. *The Army of Frederick the Great.* Newton Abbott, 1974.

———. *The Army of Maria Theresa: The Armed Forces of Imperial Austria 1740–1780.* London, 1977.

Duffy, M., ed. *The Military Revolution and the State 1500–1800.* Exeter, 1980.

Dukes, P. *The Emergence of the Super-Powers: A Short Comparative History of the USA and the USSR.* London, 1970.

———. *The Making of Russian Absolutism 1613–1801.* London, 1982.

Dülffer, J., "Der Beginn des Krieges 1939," *Geschichte und Gesellschaft* 2 (1976).

———. *Weimar, Hitler und die Marine: Reichspolitik und Flottenbau 1920–1939.* Düsseldorf, 1973.

Dull, J. *A Diplomatic History of the American Revolution.* New Haven, Conn., 1985.

———. *The French Navy and American Independence.* Princeton, N.J., 1975.

Dupuy, N. *A Genius for War: The German Army and General Staff, 1807–1945.* Englewood Cliffs, N.J., 1977.

Duroselle, J.B. *La Décadence 1932–1939.* Paris, 1979.

Dutailly, H. *Les Problèmes de l'Armée de terre française 1933–1939.* Paris, 1980.

Eatwell, J. *Whatever Happened to Britain?* London, 1982.

Eberhard, W. *A History of China,* 2nd edn. London, 1960.

Eckes, A.E. *The United States and the Global Struggle for Minerals.* Austin, Tex., 1979.

Ehrenberg, R. *Das Zeitalter der Fugger: Geldkapital und Creditverkehr im 16. Jahrhundert,* 2 vols. Jena, 1896.

Ehrman, J. *Cabinet Government and War 1890–1940.* Cambridge, 1958.

———. *The Younger Pitt,* 2 vols. London, 1969, 1983.

Eldridge, C.C., ed. *British Imperialism in the Nineteenth Century.* London, 1984.

Elliott, J.H. *Europe Divided 1559–1598.* London, 1968.

———. *Imperial Spain 1469–1716.* Harmondsworth, Mddsx., 1970.

———. *Richelieu and Olivares.* Cambridge, 1984.

———. *The Count-Duke of Olivares.* New Haven, Conn., 1986.

Elton, G.R., ed. *The New Cambridge Modern History,* vol. ii, *The Reformation 1520–1559.* Cambridge, 1958.

———. *England Under the Tudors.* London, 1955.

———. *Reformation Europe 1517–1559.* London, 1963.

Elvin, M. *The Pattern of the Chinese Past.* London, 1963.

Emerson, R. *From Empire to Nation: The Rise to Self-Assertion of Asian and African Peoples.* Cambridge, Mass., 1962.

Emmerson, J.T. *The Rhineland Crisis.* London, 1977.

Emsley, C. *British Society and the French Wars 1793–1815.* London, 1979.

Engels, F. *Herr Eugen Dühring's Revolution in Science.* London, 1936 edn.

———, "Socialism: Utopian and Scientific," in *The Essential Left.* London, 1960.

Epstein, G., "The Triple Debt Crisis," *World Policy Journal* 2 (1985).

Erhard, L. *The Economics of Success.* Princeton, N.J., 1963.

Erickson, J. *The Road to Berlin.* London, 1983.

———. *The Road to Stalingrad.* London, 1975.

———. *The Soviet High Command, 1918–1941.* London, 1962.

Ernstberger, A. *Hans de Witte: Finanzmann Wallensteins.* Wiesbaden, 1954.

Essame, H. *The Battle for Europe, 1918*. New York, 1972.

Evangelista, M.A., "Stalin's Postwar Army Reappraised," *International Security* 7 (1982–3).

Eysenbach, M.L. *American Manufactured Exports 1897–1914: A Study of Growth and Comparative Advantage*. New York, 1976.

Falkus, M. *The Industrialization of Russia 1700–1914*. London, 1972.

——, "Aspects of Foreign Investment in Tsarist Russia," *Journal of European Economic History* 8 (1979).

Fallows, J. *National Defense*. New York, 1981.

Farrar, L.L. *Arrogance and Anxiety: The Ambivalence of German Power 1849–1914*. Iowa City, Ia., 1981.

——. *The Short War Illusion*. Santa Barbara, Calif., 1973.

Feis, H. *Churchill-Roosevelt-Stalin*. Princeton, N.J., 1967.

——. *The Atomic Bomb and the End of World War II*. Princeton, N.J., 1966 edn.

——. *The China Tangle*. Princeton, N.J., 1953.

Feldman, G. *Army, Industry and Labor in Germany 1914–1918*. Princeton, N.J., 1966.

Ferguson, T.G. *British Military Intelligence 1870–1914*. Frederick, Md., 1984.

Fieldhouse, D. *Economics and Empire 1830–1914*. London, 1973.

——. *The Colonial Empires: A Comparative Study from the Eighteenth Century*. London, 1966.

Fingar, T., ed. *China's Quest for Independence*. Boulder, Col., 1980.

Fink, C.L., et al., eds. *German Nationalism and the European Response 1890–1945*. Chapel Hill, N.C., 1985.

Fischer, E. *The Passing of the European Age*. Cambridge, Mass., 1943.

Fischer, F. *Bündnis der Eliten*. Düsseldorf, 1979.

——. *War of Illusions: German Policies from 1911 to 1914*. London, 1975.

Fischer, R.L., "Defending the Central Front: The Balance of Forces," *Adelphi Papers* 127 (1976).

Fisher, R.H. *The Russian Fur Trade 1550–1700*. Berkeley, Calif., 1943.

Fishlow, A., "Lessons from the Past: Capital Markets During the 19th Century and the Interwar Period," *International Organization* 39 (1985).

Fitzgerald, F. *Fire in the Lake: The Vietnamese and the Americans in Vietnam*. Boston, 1972.

Flora, P., ed. *State, Economy and Society in Western Europe 1875–1975*, vol. i. Frankfurt, 1983.

Florinsky, M. *Russia: A Short History*. New York, 1964.

Floyd, D. *Mao Against Khrushchev*. New York, 1964.

Foreman-Peck, J. *A History of the World Economy: International Economic Relations Since 1850*. Brighton, Sussex, 1983.

Forstmeier, F., and H. E. Volkmann, eds. *Kriegswirtschaft und Rüstung 1939–1945*. Düsseldorf, 1977.

——. *Wirtschaft und Rüstung am Vorabend des Zweiten Weltkrieges*. Düsseldorf, 1975.

Foschepoth, J., ed. *Kalter Krieg und deutsche Frage*. Göttingen, 1985.

Fox, G. *British Admirals and the Chinese Pirates 1832–1869*. London, 1940.

Frank, A.G. *World Accumulation 1492–1789*. New York, 1978.

Frankenstein, R. *Le Prix du réarmement français 1935–1939*. Paris, 1939.

Frankland, N. *The Bomber Offensive Against Germany*. London, 1965.

Freedman, L. *Britain and Nuclear Weapons*. London, 1980.

——. *The Evolution of Nuclear Strategy*. London, 1981.

French, D. *British Economic and Strategic Planning, 1905–1915*. London, 1982.

——. *British Strategy and War Aims 1914–1916*. London, 1986.

Friedberg, A.L., "A History of US Strategic 'Doctrine,' 1945–1980," *Journal of Strategic Studies* 3 (1983).

Friedman, E., ed. *Ascent and Decline in the World-System.* Beverly Hills, Calif., 1982.

Fukuyama, F., "Gorbachev and the Third World," *Foreign Affairs* 64 (1986).

Fuller, W.C. *Civil-Military Conflict in Imperial Russia 1881–1914.* Princeton, N.J., 1985.

Fussell, P. *The Great War and Modern Memory.* New York, 1975.

Gaddis, J.L. *Strategies of Containment.* New York, 1982.

———, "The Origins of Self-Deterrence: The United States and the Non-Use of Nuclear Weapons, 1954–1958," forthcoming.

———. *The United States and the Origins of the Cold War, 1941–1947.* New York, 1972.

Gallagher, J., and R. Robinson, "The Imperialism of Free Trade," *Economic History Review* 6 (1953).

Gansler, J.S. *The Defense Industry.* Cambridge, Mass., 1980.

Garder, M. *L'Agonie du régime en Russie soviétique.* Paris, 1966.

Gardner, R.N. *Sterling-Dollar Diplomacy.* New York, 1969.

Garfinkle, A.W. *The Politics of the Nuclear Freeze.* Philadelphia, 1984.

Garthoff, R.L. *Détente and Confrontation: American-Soviet Relations from Nixon to Reagan.* Washington, D.C., 1985.

———. *Soviet Strategy in the Nuclear Age.* New York, 1958.

Gash, G. *Renaissance Armies 1480–1650.* Cambridge, 1975.

Gates, D. *The Spanish Ulcer: A History of the Peninsula War.* London, 1986.

Gatrell, P. *The Tsarist Economy, 1850–1917.* London, 1983.

Geggus, D., "The Cost of Pitt's Caribbean Campaigns, 1793–1798," *Historical Journal* 26 (1983).

Geiss, I., and B. J. Wendt, eds. *Deutschland in der Weltpolitik des 19. und 20. Jahrhunderts.* Düsseldorf, 1973.

Gershrenkon, A. *Economic Backwardness in Historical Perspective.* Cambridge, Mass., 1962.

Gervasi, T. *The Myth of Soviet Military Supremacy.* New York, 1986.

Geyer, M. *Aufrüstung oder Sicherheit.* Wiesbaden, 1980.

Gibbs, H.A.R., and H. Bowen. *Islamic Society and the West,* 2 vols. London, 1950, 1957.

Gibbs, N.H. *Grand Strategy,* vol. i. London, 1976.

Gibson, C. *Spain in America.* New York, 1966.

Gilbert, F. *The End of the European Era, 1890 to the Present,* 3rd edn. New York, 1984.

Gilbert, M., ed. *A Century of Conflict, 1850–1950.* London, 1966.

———. *Winston Churchill,* vol. v, *1922–1939.* London, 1976.

Gillard, D. *The Struggle for Asia 1828–1961.* London, 1977.

Gillie, M.H. *Forging the Thunderbolt.* Harrisburg, Penn., 1947.

Gilpin, R. *War and Change in World Politics.* Cambridge, 1981.

Ginsburgs, G., and C. F. Pinkele. *The Sino-Soviet Territorial Dispute, 1949–64.* New York, 1978.

———, and A. Z. Rubinstein, eds. *Soviet Foreign Policy Towards Western Europe.* New York, 1978.

Giovannetti, L., and F. Freed. *The Decision to Drop the Bomb.* London, 1967.

Gipson, L.H. *The Coming of the Revolution 1763–1775.* New York, 1962.

Girardet, R. *La société militaire dans la France contemporaine.* Paris, 1953.

———. *L'idée coloniale de la France sous la Troisième République 1871–1914.* Paris, 1968.

Girault, R. *Emprunts russes et investisements français en Russie, 1887–1914.* Paris, 1973.

Global 2000 Report to the President, The. Washington, D.C., 1980.

Glover, M. *The Napoleonic Wars: An Illustrated History 1792–1815.* New York, 1979.

———. *The Peninsular War, 1807–1814: A Concise History.* Newton Abbott, 1974.

———. *Warfare from Waterloo to Mons.* London, 1980.

Glover, R. *Peninsular Preparation: The Reform of the British Army, 1795–1809.* Cambridge, 1963.

Godechet, J., B. F. Hyslop, and D. L. Dowd. *The Napoleonic Era in Europe.* New York, 1971.

Goldman, M.I. *The Enigma of Soviet Petroleum: Half-Full or Half-Empty?* London, 1980.

———. *USSR in Crisis: The Failure of an Economic System.* New York, 1983.

Goldsmith, R.W., "The Power of Victory: Munitions Output in World War II," *Military Affairs* 10 (1946).

Gollwitzer, H. *Europe in the Age of Imperialism.* London, 1969.

———. *Geschichte des weltpolitischen Denkens,* 2 vols. Göttingen, 1972, 1982.

Golovine, N. *Russian Army in the World War.* New Haven, Conn., 1932.

Gooch, J. *The Plans of War: The General Staff and British Military Strategy c. 1900–1916.* London, 1974.

Good, D.F. *The Economic Rise of the Habsburg Empire, 1750–1914.* Berkeley, Calif., 1984.

Gorce, P.-M. de la. *The French Army: A Military Political History.* New York, 1963.

Gordon, D.C. *The Dominion Partnership in Imperial Defense 1870–1914.* Baltimore, Md., 1965.

Gormley, D.M., "A New Dimension to Soviet Theater Strategy," *Orbis* 29 (1985).

Gottman, J., ed. *Center and Periphery.* Beverly Hills, Calif., 1980.

Goubert, P. *Louis XIV and Twenty Million Frenchmen.* London, 1970.

Gough, B. *The Royal Navy and the North West Coast of America 1810–1914.* Vancouver, 1971.

Gowa, J. *Closing the Gold Window: Domestic Politics and the End of Bretton Woods.* Ithaca, N.Y., 1983.

Grabaud, S.R. *British Labour and the Russian Revolution 1917–1924.* Cambridge, Mass., 1956.

Graebner, N.A. *America as a World Power.* Wilmington, Del., 1984.

Graham, G.S. *Great Britain in the Indian Ocean: A Study of Maritime Enterprise 1810–1850.* Oxford, 1967.

Graml, H., ed. *Sommer 1939, Die Grossmächte und der europäische Krieg.* Stuttgart, 1979.

Gray, C., "Nuclear Strategy: A Case for a Theory of Victory," *International Security* 4 (1979).

Greenwood, S., "Return to Dunkirk: The Origins of the Anglo-French Treaty of March 1947," *Journal of Strategic Studies* 6 (1983).

Grenville, J.A.S., and G. B. Young. *Politics, Strategy and American Diplomacy: Studies in Foreign Policy, 1873–1917.* New Haven, Conn., 1966.

———. *A World History of the Twentieth Century 1900–1945.* London, 1980.

———. *Europe Reshaped 1848–1878.* London, 1976.

———. *Lord Salisbury and Foreign Policy: The Close of the Nineteenth Century, 1895–1902.* London, 1964.

Griffith, W.E., ed. *Communism in Europe: Continuity, Change and the Sino-Soviet Dispute,* 2 vols. Cambridge, Mass., 1964–66.

———, "Superpower Problems in Europe: A Comparative Assessment," *Orbis* 29 (1986).

———. *The Ostpolitik of the Federal Republic of Germany*. Cambridge, Mass., 1978.

Groom, J. *British Thinking About Nuclear Weapons*. London, 1974.

Grosser, A. *The Western Alliance: European-American Relations Since 1945*. London, 1980.

———. *West Germany from Defeat to Rearmament*. London, 1955.

Growing, M. *Independence and Deterrence: Britain and Atomic Energy 1945–1952*, 2 vols. London, 1974.

Grün, G., "Locarno, Ideal and Reality," *International Affairs* 31 (1955).

Gruner, W., "Der Deutsche Bund—Modell für eine Zwischenlösung?" *Politik und Kultur* 9 (1982).

———. *Die deutsche Frage: Ein Problem der europäischen Geschichte seit 1800*. Munich, 1985.

Grunwald, J., and K. Flamm. *The Global Factory: Foreign Assembly in International Trade*. Washington, D.C., 1985.

Guéry, A., "Les finances de la monarchie française," *Annales* 33 (1978).

Guilmartin, J.F. *Gunpowder and Galleys: Changing Technology and Mediterranean Warfare at Sea in the Sixteenth Century*. Cambridge, 1974.

Guinn, P. *British Strategy and Politics, 1914–1918*. Oxford, 1965.

Gulick, E.V. *Europe's Classical Balance of Power*. New York, 1967 edn.

Gunsberg, J.A. *Divided and Conquered: The French High Command and the Defeat of the West, 1940*. Westport, Conn., 1979.

Gustafson, T., "Energy and the Soviet Union," *International Security* 6 (1981–82).

Hadley, A.T. *The Straw Giant: Triumph and Failure: America's Armed Forces*. New York, 1986.

Hagan, K.J., ed. *In Peace and War: Interpretations of American Naval History, 1775–1978*. Westport, Conn., 1978.

Haig, A. *Caveat*. New York, 1984.

Hale, J.R., ed. *Europe in the Later Middle Ages*. London, 1965.

———, "Armies, Navies and the Art of War," *New Cambridge Modern History*, vol. ii. Cambridge, 1958.

———. *War and Society in Renaissance Europe 1450–1620*. London, 1985.

Hale, O.J. *Germany and the Diplomatic Revolution 1904–1906*. Philadelphia, 1931.

Hall, J.W. *Government and Local Power in Japan*. Princeton, N.J., 1966.

Halpern, P. *The Mediterranean Naval Situation, 1908–1914*. Cambridge, Mass., 1971.

Hamerow, T. *Restoration, Revolution, Reaction: Economics and Politics in Germany*. Princeton, N.J., 1958.

Hamilton, A. *The Appeal of Fascism*. London, 1971.

Hamilton, C.E., "The Royal Navy, *La Royale* and the Militarization of Naval Warfare, 1840–1870," *Journal of Strategic Studies* 6 (1983).

Hamilton, E.J., "Origin and Growth of National Debt in Western Europe," *American Economic Review* 37 (1947).

Hammond, T.T. *Red Flag over Afghanistan*. Boulder, Col., 1984.

Hanrieder, W.F. *West German Foreign Policy 1949–1963*. Stanford, Calif., 1967.

Haraszti, E. *The Invaders: Hitler Occupies the Rhineland*. Budapest, 1983.

———. *Treaty-Breakers or 'Realpolitiker'? The Anglo-German Naval Agreement of June 1935*. Boppard, 1974.

Hardach, G. *The First World War 1914–1918*. London, 1977.

Hardach, K. *The Political Economy of Germany in the Twentieth Century*. Berkeley, Calif., 1980.

Hardie, F. *The Abyssinian Crisis*. London, 1974.

Harding, H., ed. *China's Foreign Relations in the 1980s*. New Haven, Conn., 1984.

Haring, C.H. *The Spanish Empire in America*. New York, 1947.

Harris, K. *Attlee*. London, 1982.

Harris, R.D., "French Finances and the American War, 1777–1783," *Journal of Modern History* 46 (1976).

Harrison, J.A. *The Chinese Empire*. New York, 1972.

Harrison, M.M. *Reluctant Ally: France and Atlantic Security*. Baltimore, 1981.

Hart, G., and W. S. Lind. *America Can Win*. Bethesda, Md., 1986.

Harvie, C. *War and Society in the 19th Century*. Bletchley, 1973.

Haslam, J. *The Soviet Union and the Struggle for Collective Security in Europe 1933–39*. New York, 1984.

Hastings, M. *Overlord: D-Day and the Battle for Normandy*. London, 1984.

Hattaway, H., and A. Jones. *How the North Won: A Military History of the Civil War*. Urbana, Ill., 1983.

Hatton, R.M., ed. *Louis XIV and Europe*. London, 1976.

———. *Charles XII of Sweden*. London, 1968.

Hauner, M., "A Racial Revolution," *Journal of Contemporary History* 19 (1984).

———, "Did Hitler Want a World Dominion?," *Journal of Contemporary History* 13 (1968).

———, "The Soviet Geostrategic Dilemma," Foreign Policy Research Institute, forthcoming.

Hayashi, S., and A. Coox. *Kogun: The Japanese Army in the Pacific War*. Westport, Conn., 1978 reprint.

Hayes, P. *Fascism*. London, 1973.

Haykal, M.H. *The Sphinx and the Commissar: The Rise and Fall of Soviet Influence in the Middle East*. London, 1978.

Headrich, D.R. *The Tools of Empire: Technology and European Imperialism in the Nineteenth Century*. Oxford, 1981.

Heald, M., and L. S. Kaplan. *Culture and Diplomacy: The American Experience*. Westport, Conn., 1977.

Hecksher, E.F. *An Economic History of Sweden*. Cambridge, Mass., 1963.

———. *The Continental System*. Oxford, 1922.

Heischmann, E. *Die Anfänge des stehenden Heeres in Oesterreich*. Vienna, 1925.

Heller, F.H., ed. *The Korean War: A 25-Year Perspective*. Lawrence, Kan., 1977.

Henderson, W.O. *The Industrial Revolution on the Continent: Germany, France, Russia 1800–1914*. London, 1967 edn.

———. *The Rise of German Industrial Power, 1834–1914*. Berkeley, Calif., 1972.

Hennessy, J., et al. *Economic "Miracles."* London, 1964.

Henrickson, A.K., "The Creation of the North Atlantic Alliance, 1948–1952," *Naval War College Review* 32 (1980).

Hentschel, V., "Produktion, Wachstum und Produktivität in England, Frankreich und Deutschland von der Mitte des 19. Jahrhunderts bis zum Ersten Weltkrieg," *Vierteljahresschrift für Sozial- und Wirtschaftsgeschichte* 68 (1981).

Herken, G. *Counsels of War*. New York, 1985.

———. *The Winning Weapon: The Atomic Bomb in the Cold War 1945–1950*. New York, 1980.

Herrick, R.W. *Soviet Naval Strategy*. Annapolis, Md., 1968.

Herring, G. *America's Longest War: The United States and Vietnam, 1950–1975*. New York, 1979.

Herspring, D.R., and I. Volgyes, "Political Reliability in the Eastern European Warsaw Pact Armies," *Armed Forces and Society* 6 (1980).

Herwig, H.H. *Politics of Frustration: The United States in German Naval Planning, 1889–1941*. New York, 1976.

Hess, A.C., "The Evolution of the Ottoman Seaborne Empire in the Age of Oceanic Discoveries, 1453–1525," *American Historical Review* 75 (1970).

Hiden, J. *Germany and Europe 1919–1939*. London, 1977.

Higginbotham, D., ed. *Reconsiderations on the Revolutionary War.* Westport, Conn., 1978.

———. *The War of American Independence.* Bloomington, Ind., 1977 edn.

Higham, R. *Air Power: A Concise History.* Manhattan, Kan., 1984 edn.

Higonnet, P.L.R., "The Origins of the Seven Years War," *Journal of Modern History* 40 (1968).

Hildebrand, G.H. *Growth and Structure in the Economy of Modern Italy.* Cambridge, Mass., 1965.

Hildebrand, K., "Staatskunst oder Systemzwang? Die 'Deutsche Frage' als Problem der Weltpolitik," *Historische Zeitschrift* 228 (1979).

———. *The Third Reich.* London, 1984.

Hill, C. *Reformation to Industrial Revolution.* Harmondsworth, Mddsx., 1969.

———. *The Century of Revolution 1603–1714.* Edinburgh, 1961.

Hillgruber, A. *Bismarcks Aussenpolitik.* Freiburg, 1972.

———. *Die gescheiterte Grossmacht: Eine Skizze des Deutschen Reiches 1871–1945.* Düsseldorf, 1980.

———. *Germany and the Two World Wars.* Cambridge, Mass., 1981.

———. *Hitlers Strategie: Politik und Kriegsführung 1940–41.* Frankfurt, 1965.

Hinsley, F.H., et al. *British Intelligence in the Second World War,* vol. ii. London, 1981.

———. *Power and the Pursuit of Peace.* Cambridge, 1967.

Hobsbawm, E.J. *The Age of Capital 1848–1875.* London, 1975.

———. *Industry and Empire.* Harmondsworth, Mddsx., 1969.

———. *The Age of Revolution 1789–1848.* London, 1962.

Hochmann, J. *The Soviet Union and the Failure of Collective Security 1934–1938.* Ithaca, N.Y., 1984.

Hodgson, M.G.S. *The Venture of Islam.* Chicago, 1924.

Hoensch, J.K. *Sowjetische Osteuropa-Politik 1945–1974.* Düsseldorf, 1977.

Hoffman, S., ed. *In Search of France.* Cambridge, Mass., 1963.

———. *Gulliver's Troubles.* New York, 1968.

———. *Primacy or World Order?* New York, 1978.

Hoffmann, W.G. *Das Wachstum der deutschen Wirtschaft seit der Mitte des 19. Jahrhunderts.* Berlin, 1965.

Holland, R.F. *Britain and the Commonwealth Alliance, 1918–1939.* London, 1981.

———. *European Decolonization: The British, French, Dutch, and Belgian Empires 1919–1963.* London, 1978.

Holloway, D. *The Soviet Union and the Arms Race,* 2nd edn. New Haven, Conn., 1984.

Holmes, R. *The Road to Sedan: The French Army, 1866–1870.* London, 1984.

Holt, S. *The Common Market: The Conflict of Theory and Practice.* London, 1967.

Holzle, E. *Die Selbstentmachtung Europas.* Göttingen, 1975.

Holzman, F.D., "Are the Soviets Really Outspending the US on Defense?," *International Security* 4 (1980).

———. *Financial Checks on Soviet Defense Expenditures.* Lexington, Mass., 1975.

———, "Soviet Military Spending; Assessing the Numbers Game," *International Security* 6 (1982).

Homze, E.L. *Arming the Luftwaffe.* Lincoln, Neb., 1976.

Hope-Jones, A. *Income Tax in the Napoleonic Wars.* Cambridge, 1939.

Horn, R.C. *The Soviet Union and India. The Limits of Influence.* New York, 1981.

Horne, A. *The French Army and Politics 1870–1970.* London, 1984.

Horowitz, D. *The Free World Colossus.* New York, 1971 edn.

Hosking, G. *A History of the Soviet Union.* London, 1985.

Hough, J.F., and M. Fainsod. *How the Soviet Union Is Governed.* Cambridge, Mass., 1979.

Howard, M. ed. *The Theory and Practice of War.* London, 1965.

———. *The British Way in Warfare.* Neale Lecture, London, 1975.

———. *The Continental Commitment.* London, 1972.

———. *The Franco-Prussian War.* London, 1981 edn.

Howarth, S. *The Fighting Ships of the Rising Sun: The Drama of the Imperial Japanese Navy 1895–1945.* New York, 1983.

Hucker, C.O. *China's Imperial Past.* Stanford, Calif., 1975.

Hudson, G.F. *The Far East in World Affairs,* 2nd edn. London, 1939.

Hueckel, G., "War and the British Economy, 1793–1815: A General Equilibrium Analysis," *Explorations in Economic History* 10 (1972).

Hufton, O. *Europe: Privilege and Protest 1730–1789.* London, 1980.

Hunt, B., and A. Preston, eds. *War Aims and Strategic Policy in the Great War.* London, 1977.

Hyam, R. *Britain's Imperial Century 1815–1914.* London, 1975.

Hynes, W.G. *The Economics of Empire: Britain, Africa and the New Imperialism, 1870–95.* London, 1979.

Imlah, A.H. *Economic Elements in the "Pax Britannica."* Cambridge, Mass., 1958.

Inalcik, H. *The Ottoman Empire: Conquest, Organization and Economy: Collected Studies.* London, 1978.

———. *The Ottoman Empire: The Classical Age 1300–1600.* New York, 1973.

Ingram, E., ed., "The Great Game in Asia," *The International History Review* 2 (1980).

———. *Commitment to Empire: Prophecies of the Great Game in Asia, 1797–1800.* Oxford, 1981.

———. *The Beginning of the Great Game in Asia 1828–1834.* Oxford, 1979.

Ireland, T.P. *Creating the Entangling Alliance.* London, 1981.

Iriye, A. *Across the Pacific.* New York, 1967.

———. *After Imperialism: The Search for a New Order in the Far East 1921–1931.* New York, 1978 edn.

Irving, E.M. *The First Indochina War: French and American Policy, 1945–1954.* London, 1975.

Iseley, J.A., and P. A. Crowl. *The U.S. Marines and Amphibious War.* Princeton, N.J., 1945.

Ismay, Lord. *NATO—The First Five Years, 1949–1954.* Utrecht, 1954.

Israel, J.I., "A Conflict of Empires: Spain and the Netherlands, 1618–1648," *Past and Present* 76 (1977).

———. *The Dutch Republic and the Hispanic World, 1606–1661.* Oxford, 1982.

Jabber, P., "Egypt's Crisis, America's Dilemma," *Foreign Affairs* 64 (1986).

Jackel, E. *Hitler's Weltanschauung.* Middletown, Conn., 1982.

Jacobsen, J. *Locarno Diplomacy: Germany and the West 1925–1929.* Princeton, N.J., 1972.

Jansen, G.H. *Afro-Asia and Non-Alignment.* London, 1966.

Jelavich, B. *The Great Powers, the Ottoman Empire, and the Straits Question 1870–1887.* Bloomington, Ind., 1973.

Jencks, H.W. *From Missiles to Muskets: Politics and Professionalism in the Chinese Army 1945–1981.* Boulder, Col., 1982.

Jenkins, E.H. *A History of the French Navy.* London, 1973.

Jenks, L.H. *Migration of British Capital to 1875.* London, 1963 edn.

Jervis, R. *The Illogic of American Nuclear Strategy.* Ithaca, N.Y., 1984.

———, "The Impact of the Korean War on the Cold War," *Journal of Conflict Resolution* 24 (1980).

Joffe, J., "European-American Relations: The Enduring Crisis," *Foreign Affairs* 59 (1981).

Johnson, A.R., et al. *East European Military Establishments: The Warsaw Pact Northern Tier.* New York, 1982.

Johnson, C. *MITI and the Japanese Miracle: The Growth of Industrial Policy 1925–1975.* Stanford, Calif., 1982.

Johnson, F.A. *Defense by Committee.* London, 1960.

Johnson, P.M., and W. R. Thompson, eds. *Rhythms in Politics and Economics.* New York, 1985.

Joll, J., ed. *The Decline of the Third Republic.* New York, 1959.

———. *Europe Since 1870.* London, 1973.

———. *The Origins of the First World War.* London, 1984.

Jones, C., ed. *Britain and Revolutionary France: Conflict, Subversion and Propaganda.* Exeter, 1983.

Jones, D.R., "Nicholas II and the Supreme Command," *Sbornik* 11 (1985).

Jones, E., "Manning the Soviet Military," *International Security* 7 (1982).

———, "Minorities in the Soviet Armed Forces," *Comparative Strategy* 3 (1982).

Jones, E.L., and G. E. Mingay, eds. *Land, Labour and Population of the Industrial Revolution.* London, 1967.

———. *The European Miracle: Environments, Economies and Geopolitics in the History of Europe and Asia.* Cambridge, 1981.

Jones, J.R. *Britain and the World 1649–1815.* London, 1980.

———. *Country and Court 1658–1714.* London, 1978.

Jordan, W.M. *Britain, France and the German Problem.* London, 1943.

Jukes, G., "The Indian Ocean in Soviet Naval Policy," *Adelphi Papers* 87 (1972).

———. *The Soviet Union in Asia.* Berkeley, Calif., 1973.

Junge, C. *Flottenpolitik und Revolution: Die Entstehung der englischen Seemacht während der Herrschaft Cromwells.* Stuttgart, 1980.

Kahn, H. *On Thermonuclear War.* Princeton, N.J., 1960.

———. *The Emerging Japanese Superstate.* London, 1971.

Kaiser, D. *Economic Diplomacy and the Origins of the Second World War.* Princeton, N.J., 1980.

Kaldor, M. *The Baroque Arsenal.* London, 1982.

Kamata, S. *Japan in the Passing Lane.* New York, 1984.

Kamen, H. *Spain 1469–1714.* London, 1983.

Kan, M.Y.M. *Mainland China's Modernization: Its Prospects and Problems.* Berkeley, Calif., 1982.

Kanet, R., ed. *The Soviet Union and the Developing Nations.* Baltimore, 1974.

Kann, R.A. *A History of the Habsburg Empire 1526–1918.* Berkeley, Calif., 1974.

Kanya-Forstner, A.S. *The Conquest of the Western Sudan: A Study in French Military Imperialism.* Cambridge, 1969.

Kaplan, F. *The Wizards of Armageddon.* New York, 1983.

Kaplan, H. *Russia and the Outbreak of the Seven Years War.* Berkeley, Calif., 1968.

Kaplan, L.S. *The United States and NATO: The Formative Years.* Lexington, Ky., 1984.

Karnow, S. *Vietnam: A History.* New York, 1984.

Kaser, M. *Comecon.* London, 1967.

Katzenstein, P.J., ed. *Between Power and Plenty: Foreign Economic Policies of Advanced Industrial States.* Madison, Wi., 1978.

Kazemzadeh, F. *Russia and Britain in Persia 1864–1914.* New Haven, Conn., 1968.

Kazokins, J., "Nationality in the Soviet Army," *Journal of the Royal United Services Institute for Defense Studies* 130 (1985).

Keegan, J. *The Face of Battle.* Harmondsworth, Mddsx., 1978.

Keeny, S.M., and W.K.H. Panofsky, "MAD vs. NUTS: The Mutual Hostage Relationship of the Superpowers," *Foreign Affairs* 60 (1981–82).

Keep, J.H.L., "The Military Style of the Romanov Rulers," *War and Society* 1 (1983).

———, "Russia," *New Cambridge Modern History*, vol. xi. Cambridge, 1962.

Keiger, J.F.V. *France and the Origins of the First World War*. London, 1983.

Kelleher, C.M. *Germany and the Politics of Nuclear Weapons*. New York, 1975.

Kemp, T. *Economic Forces in French History*. London, 1971.

———. *Industrialization in Nineteenth-Century Europe*. London, 1969.

———. *The French Economy 1913–39: The History of a Decline*. New York, 1972.

Kendrick, A. *The Wound Within: America in the Vietnam Years, 1945–1974*. Boston, 1974.

Kendrick, M.S. *A Century and a Half of Federal Expenditures*. New York, 1955.

Kenez, P., "Russian Officer Corps Before the Revolution: The Military Mind," *Russian Review* 31 (1972).

Kennan, G.F. *The Decline of Bismarck's European Order: Franco-Russian Relations 1875–1890*. Princeton, N.J., 1979.

———. *American Diplomacy*. Chicago, 1984 edn.

———. *The Fateful Alliance: France, Russia, and the Coming of the First World War*. New York, 1984.

Kennedy, D. *Over Here: The First World War and American Society*. Oxford, 1980.

Kennedy, G. *Defense Economics*. London, 1983.

Kennedy, P.M., ed. *The War Plans of the Great Powers 1880–1914*. London, 1979.

———. *Strategy and Diplomacy, 1860–1945: Eight Essays*. London, 1983.

———. *The Realities Behind Diplomacy*. London, 1981.

———. *The Rise and Fall of British Naval Mastery*. London, 1976.

———. *The Rise of the Anglo-German Antagonism, 1860–1914*. London, 1980.

Kennet, L. *The French Armies in the Seven Years War: A Study in Military Organization and Administration*. Durham, N.C., 1967.

Keohane, R.O., "State Power and Industry Influence: American Foreign Oil Policy in the 1940s," *International Organization* 36 (1982).

———. *After Hegemony*. Princeton, N.J., 1974.

Kerner, R.J. *The Urge to the Sea*. New York, 1971 reprint.

Kersaudy, F. *Churchill and De Gaulle*. London, 1981.

Kershaw, I. *Popular Opinion and Political Dissent in the Third Reich: Bavaria 1933–1945*. Oxford, 1983.

———. *The Nazi Dictatorship*. London, 1985.

Keylor, W.R. *The Twentieth-Century World: An International History*. Oxford, 1984.

Kiernan, V.G. *European Empires from Conquest to Collapse, 1815–1960*. London, 1982.

———, "Foreign Mercenaries and Absolute Monarchy," *Past and Present* 11 (1957).

———, "State and Nation in Western Europe," *Past and Present* 31 (1965).

Kilmarx, R. *A History of Soviet Air Power*. London, 1962.

Kindleberger, C.P. *A Financial History of Western Europe*. London, 1984.

———, "Commercial Expansion and the Industrial Revolution," *Journal of European Economic History* 4 (1975).

———. *The World in Depression 1929–1939*. Berkeley, Calif., 1973.

Kiraly, B.K., and G. E. Rothenberg, eds. *War and Society in Eastern Europe*, vol. i. New York, 1979.

Kiser, J.W., "How the Arms Race Really Helps Moscow," *Foreign Policy* 60 (1985).

Kissinger, H. *A World Restored: Metternich, Castlereagh and the Problems of Peace 1812–1822*. Boston, 1957.

———. *The White House Years*. Boston, 1979.

———. "The White Revolutionary: Reflections on Bismarck," *Daedelus* 97 (1968).

Kitchen, M. *The Political Economy of Germany 1815–1914*. London, 1978.

Klein, L., and K. Ohkawa, eds. *Economic Growth: The Japanese Experience Since the Meiji Era*. Holmwood, Ill., 1968.

Knorr, K., "Burden-Sharing in NATO: Aspects of US Policy," *Orbis* 29 (1985).

Knox, M., "Conquest, Foreign and Domestic, in Fascist Italy and Nazi Germany," *Journal of Modern History* 56 (1986).

——. *Mussolini Unleashed 1939–1941*. Cambridge, 1982.

Koch, H.W., ed. *The Origins of the First World War*. London, 1982.

Kochan, L., and R. Abraham. *The Making of Modern Russia*. Harmondsworth, Mddsx., 1983 edn.

Kocka, J. *Facing Total War: German Society 1914–1918*. Leamington Spa, 1984.

Koenigsberger, H.G., "The Empire of Charles V in Europe," *New Cambridge Modern History*, vol. ii. Cambridge, 1958.

——, "Western Europe and the Power of Spain," *New Cambridge Modern History*, vol. 3. Cambridge, 1968.

——. *The Government of Sicily Under Philip II*. London, 1951.

——. *The Habsburgs and Europe 1516–1660*. Ithaca, N.Y., 1971.

Kohl, W.L. *French Nuclear Diplomacy*. Princeton, N.J., 1971.

Kolakowski, L. *Main Currents of Marxism*, vol. i, *The Founders*. Oxford, 1981 edn.

Kolb, E. ed. "Europa und die Reichsgründung," *Historische Zeitschrift*, Beiheft 6. Munich, 1980.

Kolko, G. *The Politics of War 1943–1945*. New York, 1968.

——. *Vietnam: Anatomy of a War, 1940–1975*. New York, 1986.

Kolodziej, E. *French International Policy Under De Gaulle and Pompidou: The Politics of Grandeur*. Ithaca, N.Y., 1974.

Komer, R.W. *Maritime Strategy or Coalition Defense?* Cambridge, Mass., 1984.

Kortepeter, C.M. *Ottoman Imperialism During the Reformation*. London, 1973.

Kriedte, P. *Peasants, Landlords and Merchant Capitalists: Europe and the World Economy, 1500–1800*. Leamington Spa, 1983.

Krumeich, G. *Armaments and Politics in France on the Eve of the First World War*. Leamington Spa, 1986.

Kuhn, A. *Hitlers aussenpolitisches Programm*. Stuttgart, 1970.

Kuisel, R.F. *Capitalism and the State in Modern France*. Cambridge, 1981.

Kuniholm, B.R. *The Origins of the Cold War in the Near East*. Princeton, N.J., 1980.

Kunisch, J. *Das Mirakel des Hauses Brandenburg*. Munich, 1978.

Kwitny, J. *Endless Enemies*. New York, 1984.

Lachouque, H. *Waterloo*. Paris, 1972.

LaFeber, W. *America, Russia, and the Cold War 1945–1975*. New York, 1976.

——. *The New Empire: An Interpretation of American Expansion 1860–1898*. Ithaca, N.Y., 1963.

Laird, R.F. *France, the Soviet Union, and the Nuclear Weapons Issue*. Boulder, Col., 1986.

——, "The French Strategic Dilemma," *Orbis* 28 (1984).

Lambi, I.N. *The Navy and German Power Politics 1862–1914*. London, 1984.

Landes, D. *The Unbound Prometheus: Technological Change and Industrial Development in Western Europe from 1750 to the Present*. Cambridge, 1969.

Langer, W.L. *European Alliances and Alignments 1871–1890*. New York, 1950 edn.

——. *The Diplomacy of Imperialism 1890–1902*, 2nd edn. New York, 1965.

Langford, P. *The Eighteenth Century 1688–1815: British Foreign Policy*. London, 1976.

Langhorne, R.T.B., ed. *Diplomacy and Intelligence During the Second World War*. Cambridge, 1985

Larson, T.B. *Soviet-American Rivalry*. New York, 1978.

Laue, T.H. von. *Sergei Witte and the Industrialization of Russia.* New York, 1963.

Laurens, F.D. *France and the Italo-Ethiopian Crisis, 1935–6.* The Hague, 1967.

League of Nations. *World Economic Survey.* Geneva, 1945.

Lee, A. *The Soviet Air Force.* London, 1961.

Lee, M., and W. Michalka. *German Foreign Policy 1917–1933: Continuity or Break?* Leamington Spa, 1987.

Lee, W.T. *The Estimation of Soviet Defense Expenditures 1955–75.* New York, 1977.

Leebaert, D., ed. *Soviet Military Thinking.* London, 1981.

Lefebvre, G. *Napoleon,* 2 vols. London, 1969.

Leffler, M.P., "Security and Containment Before Kennan: The Identification of American Interests at the End of World War II," Lehrman Institute Paper, forthcoming.

——, "The American Conception of National Security and the Beginnings of the Cold War, 1945–48," *American Historical Review* 89 (1984).

Lellouche, P. *L'avenir de la guerre.* Paris, 1985.

——, "France and the Euromissiles," *Foreign Affairs* 62 (1983–84).

Lerner, D., and R. Aron. *France Defeats EDC.* New York, 1957.

Leutze, J. *Bargaining for Supremacy: Anglo-American Naval Relations 1937–1941.* Chapel Hill, N.C., 1977.

Levine, A.J., "Was World War II a Near-Run Thing?," *Journal of Strategic Studies* 8 (1985).

Levy, J. *War in the Modern Great Power System.* Lexington, Ky., 1983.

Lewin, M. *Russian Peasants and Soviet Power.* Evanston, Ill., 1968.

Lewin, R. *The American Magic: Codes, Ciphers and the Defeat of Japan.* New York, 1982.

Lewis, W.A. *Economic Survey 1919–1939.* London, 1949.

Lichtheim, G. *Europe in the Twentieth Century.* London, 1972.

Liddell Hart, B.H., ed. *The Red Army.* New York, 1956.

——. *History of the First World War.* London, 1970 edn.

——. *History of the Second World War.* London, 1970.

Lieven, D.C.B. *Russia and the Origins of the First World War.* London, 1983.

Lifton, R.J. *Home from the War: Vietnam Veterans.* New York, 1973.

Lincoln, W.B. *Passage Through Armageddon: The Russians in the War and Revolution 1914–1918.* New York, 1986.

Linder, S.B. *The Pacific Century.* Stanford, Calif., 1986.

Linderman, G.F. *The Mirror of War: American Society and the Spanish-American War.* Ann Arbor, Mich., 1974.

Link, A.S. *Wilson,* 5 vols. Princeton, N.J., 1947–65.

Lippmann, W. *U.S. Foreign Policy: Shield of the Republic.* Boston, 1943.

Litwak, R.S. *Détente and the Nixon Doctrine: American Foreign Policy and the Pursuit of Stability, 1969–1975.* Cambridge, 1984.

Lloyd, C. *The Nation and the Navy.* London, 1961.

Loades, D.M. *Politics and the Nation 1450–1660.* London, 1974.

Lobonov-Rostovsky, A.A. *Russia and Europe 1789–1825.* Durham, N.C., 1947.

Lo Jung-pang, "The Decline of the Early Ming Navy," *Orient Extremus* 5 (1958).

——, "The Emergence of China as a Sea Power During the Late Sung and Early Yuan Periods," *Far Eastern Quarterly* 14 (1955).

Louis, W.R. *The British Empire in the Middle East, 1945–1951.* Oxford, 1984.

Lovett, G.H. *Napoleon and the Birth of Modern Spain,* 2 vols. New York, 1965.

Low, A.D. *The Sino-Soviet Dispute.* Rutherford, N.J., 1976.

Lowe, C.J., and F. Marzari. *Italian Foreign Policy 1870–1940.* London, 1975.

Lowe, P. *Britain in the Far East: A Survey from 1819 to the Present.* London, 1981.

Lubasz, H., ed. *The Development of the Modern State.* New York, 1964.

Lukacs, J. *The Last European War, September 1939/December 1941.* London, 1977.

Lundkvist, S., "Svensk krigsfinansiering 1630–1635" (with German summary), *Historisk tidskrift* (1966).

Lupfer, T., "The Dynamics of Doctrine: The Changes in German Tactical Doctrine During the First World War," *Leavenworth Papers* 4. Leavenworth, Kan., 1981.

Luttwak, E. *The Pentagon and the Art of War.* New York, 1985.

Luvaas, J. *The Military Legacy of the Civil War: The European Inheritance.* Chicago, 1959.

Lynch, J. *Spain Under the Habsburgs,* 2 vols. Oxford, 1964, 1969.

Lyon, P. *Neutralism.* Leicester, 1963.

Macartney, C.A. *The Habsburg Empire 1790–1918.* London, 1969.

McCauley, M., ed. *Communist Power in Europe, 1944–1949.* London, 1977.

———. *The Soviet Union Since 1917.* London, 1981.

McCormick, T. *China Market: America's Quest for Informal Empire.* Chicago, 1967.

MacDonald, C.A. *The United States, Britain and Appeasement 1936–1939.* London, 1980.

McDougall, W.A. *France's Rhineland Diplomacy 1914–1924.* Princeton, N.J., 1978.

McEvedy, C. *The Penguin Atlas of Recent History.* Harmondsworth, Mddsx., 1982.

McFetridge, C.D., "Some Implications of China's Emergence as a Great Power," *Journal of the Royal United Services Institute for Defence Studies* 128 (1983).

McGeehan, R. *The German Rearmament Question.* Urbana, Ill., 1971.

McGowan, P., and C. W. Kegley, eds. *Foreign Policy and the Modern World-System.* Beverly Hills, Calif., 1983.

Machay, J.P. *Pioneer for Profit: Foreign Entrepreneurs and Russian Industrialization.* Chicago, 1970.

Mack Smith, D. *Italy: A Modern History.* Ann Arbor, Mich., 1959.

———. *Mussolini's Roman Empire.* London, 1976.

———. *Mussolini: A Biography.* New York, 1982.

Mackay, D. *Prince Eugene of Savoy.* London, 1977.

MacKay, D., and H. M. Scott. *The Rise of the Great Powers 1648–1815.* London, 1983.

Mackesy, P. *Statesman at War: The Strategy of Overthrow, 1798–1799.* London, 1974.

———. *The War for America 1775–1783.* London, 1964.

Mackinder, H.J., "The Geographical Pivot of History," *Geographical Journal* 23 (1904).

Mackintosh, M. *Juggernaut: A History of the Soviet Armed Forces.* New York, 1967.

McMillen, D.H., ed. *Asian Perspectives on International Security.* London, 1984.

McNeill, W.H. *A World History.* London, 1979 edn.

———. *The Pursuit of Power: Technology, Armed Forces and Society Since 1000 A.D.* Chicago, 1983.

———. *The Rise of the West.* Chicago, 1967.

Madariaga, I. de. *Britain, Russia and the Armed Neutrality of 1780.* London, 1962.

———. *Russia in the Age of Catherine the Great.* London, 1981.

Maddison, A., "A Comparison of Levels of GDP per Capita in Developed and Developing Countries, 1700–1980," *Journal of Economic History* 43 (1983).

Magalhaes-Godinho, V. *L'économie de l'Empire Portugais aux XVe et XVIe siècles.* Paris, 1969.

Mahan, A.T. *Sea Power in Its Relations to the War of 1812,* 2 vols. London, 1905.

———. *The Influence of Sea Power upon History 1660–1783.* London, 1965 edn.

Maier, C.S. *Recasting Bourgeois Europe.* Princeton, N.J., 1975.

Maier, K.A., et al., eds. *Das Deutsche Reich und der Zweite Weltkrieg,* vol. 2, *Die Errichtung der Hegemonie auf dem europäischen Kontinent.* Stuttgart, 1979.

Mako, W.P. *U.S. Ground Forces and the Defense of Central Europe.* Washington, D.C., 1983.

Maland, D. *Europe in the Seventeenth Century.* London, 1966.

Malinraud, E. *La Croissance française.* Paris, 1972.

Mallet, M.E. *Mercenaries and Their Masters: Warfare in Renaissance Italy.* London, 1976.

Mamatey, V.S. *Rise of the Habsburg Empire 1526–1815.* Huntingdon, N.Y., 1978 edn.

Mandelbaum, M. *The Nuclear Future.* Ithaca, N.Y., 1983.

———. *The Nuclear Question: The United States and Nuclear Weapons 1946–1976.* New York, 1979.

———. *The Nuclear Revolution: International Politics Before and After Hiroshima.* New York, 1981.

Mansergh, N. *The Commonwealth Experience.* London, 1969.

Marder, A.J. *From the Dreadnought to Scapa Flow: The Royal Navy in the Fisher Period,* vol. i, *The Road to War, 1904–1914.* London, 1961.

———. *Old Friends, New Enemies: The Royal Navy and the Imperial Japanese Navy.* Oxford, 1981.

———. *The Anatomy of British Sea Power.* Hamden, Conn., 1964 reprint.

———, "The Royal Navy in the Italo-Ethiopian War 1935–36," *American Historical Review* 75 (1970).

Marks, S. *The Illusion of Peace: International Relations in Europe 1918–1933.* London, 1976.

Marriss, S. *Deficits and the Dollar: The World Economy at Risk.* Washington, D.C., 1985.

Marsh, F. *Japanese Overseas Investment.* London, 1983.

Marshall, P.J., "British Expansion in India in the Eighteenth Century: An Historical Revision," *History* 60 (1975).

Martin, B., "Aussenhandel und Aussenpolitik Englands unter Cromwell," *Historische Zeitschrift* 218 (1974).

Martin, L. *Peace Without Victory—Woodrow Wilson and the English Liberals.* New York, 1973 edn.

Marwick, A. *The Deluge—British Society in the First World War.* London, 1965.

———. *War and Social Change in the Twentieth Century.* London, 1974.

Masson, P., "La Marine française en 1939–40," *Revue historique des armées* 4 (1979).

Mathias, P. *The First Industrial Nation: An Economic History of Britain 1700–1914.* London, 1969.

———, and P. O'Brien. "Taxation in Britain and France, 1715–1810," *Journal of European Economic History* 5 (1976).

Matloff, M. *Strategic Planning for Coalition Warfare, 1943–1944.* Washington, D.C., 1959.

Mattingly, G. *Renaissance Diplomacy.* Harmondsworth, Mddsx., 1965.

May, A.J. *The Habsburg Monarchy 1862–1916.* Cambridge, Mass., 1960.

———. *The Passing of the Habsburg Monarchy, 1914–1918,* 2 vols. Philadelphia, 1966.

May, E.R., ed. *Knowing One's Enemies: Intelligence Assessment Before the Two World Wars.* Princeton, N.J., 1984.

———. *American Imperialism: A Speculative Essay.* New York, 1968.

———. *Imperial Democracy: The Emergence of America as a Great Power.* New York, 1961.

———. *The World War and American Isolation.* Chicago, 1966 edn.

Mayer, A.J. *Political Origins of the New Diplomacy.* New York, 1970 edn.

———. *Politics and Diplomacy of Peacemaking: Containment and Counterrevolution at Versailles 1918–1919.* London, 1968.

MccGwire, M. *Soviet Naval Developments.* New York, 1973.

———. *Soviet Naval Influence.* New York, 1977.

———. *Soviet Naval Policy.* New York, 1975.

Mearsheimer, J. *Conventional Deterrence.* Ithaca, N.Y., 1983.

Medlicott, W.N. *British Foreign Policy Since Versailles, 1919–1963.* London, 1968.

Mellor, R.E.M. *The Soviet Union and Its Geographical Problems.* London, 1982.

Mendelsohn, K. *Science and Western Domination.* London, 1976.

Mendl, W. *Deterrence and Persuasion: French Nuclear Armament in the Context of National Policy, 1945–1969.* London, 1970.

Menon, K. *Soviet Power and the Third World.* New York, 1985.

Meyers, R. *Britische Sicherheitspolitik 1934–1938.* Düsseldorf, 1976.

Middlebrook, M. *The Kaiser's Battle: 21 March 1918.* London, 1978.

Middlemas, K. *Diplomacy of Illusion: The British Government and Germany 1937–39.* London, 1972.

Middleton, R. *The Bells of Victory.* Cambridge, 1985.

Military Balance, The. International Institute of Strategic Studies. London, annual.

Millar, G.J. *Tudor Mercenaries and Auxiliaries 1485–1547.* Charlottesville, Va., 1980.

Miller, M.S. *The Economic Development of Russia, 1905–1914.* London, 1926.

Miller, S.E., ed. *Military Strategy and the Origins of the First World War.* Princeton, N.J., 1985.

———, ed. *Conventional Forces and American Defense Policy.* Princeton, N.J., 1986.

Millett, A.R., and W. Murray, eds. *Military Effectiveness.* Forthcoming.

———, and P. Maslowski. *For the Common Defense: A Military History of the United States of America.* New York, 1984.

Mills, W. *Arms and Men.* New York, 1956.

Milward, A.S. *The Economic Effects of the World Wars in Britain.* London, 1970.

———. *The German Economy at War.* London, 1965.

———. *The Reconstruction of Western Europe, 1945–1951.* London, 1984.

———. *War, Economy and Society 1939–1945.* Berkeley, Calif., 1979.

———, and S. B. Saul. *The Development of the Economies of Continental Europe 1850–1914.* Cambridge, Mass., 1977.

———. *The Economic Development of Continental Europe 1780–1870.* London, 1973.

Minchinton, W.E., ed. *The Growth of English Overseas Trade in the Seventeenth and Eighteenth Centuries.* London, 1969.

Mitchell, A. *The German Influence in France after 1870: The Formation of the French Republic.* Chapel Hill, N.C., 1979.

———. *Victors and Vanquished: The German Influence on Army and Church in France after 1870.* Chapel Hill, N.C., 1984.

Mitchell, B.R. *European Historical Statistics 1750–1970.* London, 1975.

Mitchell, D.W. *A History of Russian and Soviet Sea Power.* New York, 1974.

Modelski, G., "The Long Cycle of Global Politics and the Nation-State," *Comparative Studies in Society and History* 20 (1978).

Mommsen, W.J., and L. Kettenacker, eds. *The Fascist Challenge and the Policy of Appeasement.* London, 1983.

Monger, G.L. *The End of Isolation: British Foreign Policy 1900–1907.* London, 1963.

Morazé, C., "Finance et despotisme, essai sur les despotes éclairés," *Annales* 3 (1948).

Moreland, W.H. *From Akbar to Aurangzeb: A Study in Indian Economic History.* London, 1923.

Moreton, E., and G. Segal, eds. *Soviet Strategy Toward Western Europe.* London, 1984.

Morgan, K.O. *Labour in Power 1945–1951.* Oxford, 1984.

Morgan, R. *The United States and West Germany 1945-1973.* London, 1974.

Mori, G., "The Genesis of Italian Industrialization," *Journal of European Economic History* 4 (1975).

——, "The Process of Industrialization in Italy: Some Suggestions, Problems and Questions," *Journal of European Economic History* 8 (1979).

Morison, S.E. *History of the United States Naval Operations,* vol. x, *The Atlantic Battle Won.* Boston, Mass., 1956.

Morley, J.W., ed. *Dilemmas of Growth in Prewar Japan.* Princeton, N.J., 1971.

——, ed. *The Fateful Choice: Japan's Advance into Southeast Asia, 1939-1941.* New York, 1980.

——, ed. *The Pacific Basin.* New York, 1986.

Morris, M.D., "Values as an Obstacle to Growth in South Asia," *Journal of Economic History* 27 (1967).

Mortimer, R.A. *The Third World Coalition in International Politics.* New York, 1980.

Morton, E., and G. Segal, eds. *Soviet Strategy Toward Western Europe.* London, 1984.

Mosse, W.E. *Alexander II and the Modernization of Russia.* New York, 1962 edn.

——. *The European Powers and the German Question 1848-1870.* Cambridge, 1958.

——. *The Rise and Fall of the Crimean System 1855-1871.* London, 1963.

Mousnier, R., "L'Evolution des finances publiques en France et en Angleterre pendant les guerres de la Ligue d'Augsbourg et de la Succession d'Espagne," *Revue Historique* 44 (1951).

Mowat, C.L., ed. *New Cambridge Modern History,* vol. xii (rev. ed.), *The Shifting Balance of World Forces.* Cambridge, 1968.

Munro, D.G. *Intervention and Dollar Diplomacy in the Caribbean 1900-1921.* Princeton, N.J., 1964.

Munting, R. *The Economic Development of the USSR.* London, 1982.

Murphy, B. *A History of the British Economy.* London, 1973.

Murray, W., "German Air Power and the Munich Crisis," *War and Society* 1 (1976).

——. *Luftwaffe.* Baltimore, Md., 1985.

——, "Munich, 1938: The Military Confrontation," *Journal of Strategic Studies* 2 (1979).

——. *The Change in the European Balance of Power, 1938-1939.* Princeton, N.J., 1984.

Mysyrowics, L. *Autopsie d'une Defaite: Origines de l'effrondrement militaire français de 1940.* Lausanne, 1973.

Neal, L., "Interpreting Power and Profit in Economic History: A Case Study of the Seven Years War," *Journal of Economic History* 37 (1977).

Needham, J. *Science and Civilization in China,* vol. iv, *Civil Engineering and Nautics.* Cambridge, 1971.

——. *The Development of Iron and Steel Technology in China.* London, 1958.

——. *The Grand Titration. Science and Society in East and West.* London, 1969.

Nef, J.U. *War and Human Progress.* New York, 1968.

Neidpath, J. *The Singapore Naval Base and the Defense of Britain's Eastern Empire 1919-1941.* Oxford, 1981.

Neilson, K., "Watching the 'Steamroller': British Observers and the Russian Army Before 1914." *Journal of Strategic Studies* 8 (1985).

Nettl, J.P. *The Soviet Achievement.* London, 1967.

Nicholls, A.J. *Weimar and the Rise of Hitler.* London, 1979 edn.

Nicolson, H.G. *The Congress of Vienna.* London, 1946.

Niedhart, G., "Appeasement: Die britische Antwort auf die Krise des Weltreichs und des internationalen Systems vor dem zweiten Weltkrieg," *Historische Zeitschrift* 226 (1978).

———. *Handel und Krieg in der britischen Weltpolitik 1738–1763.* Munich, 1979.

Niemeyer, J. *Das österreichische Militärwesen im Umbruch.* Osnabrück, 1979.

Nipperdey, T. *Deutsche Geschichte 1800–1866.* Munich, 1983.

Nish, I. *Japan's Foreign Policy, 1869–1942.* London, 1978.

———. *The Anglo-Japanese Alliance.* London, 1966.

———. *The Origins of the Russo-Japanese War.* London, 1985.

Nitze, P., "The Development of NSC-68," *International Security* 5 (1980).

Nobutaka, I, ed. *Japan's Decision for War.* Stanford, Calif., 1967.

Norman, E.H. *Japan's Emergence as a Modern State.* New York, 1940.

North, D.C., and R. P. Thomas. *The Rise of the Western World.* Cambridge, 1973.

North, R.C. *Moscow and the Chinese Communists.* Stanford, Calif., 1953.

Northedge, F.S., and A. Wells. *Britain and Soviet Communism: The Impact of a Revolution.* London, 1982.

———. *The Troubled Giant: Britain Among the Great Powers.* London, 1966.

Nove, A. *An Economic History of the USSR.* Harmondsworth, Mddsx., 1969.

O'Brien, P. *British Financial and Fiscal Policy in the Wars Against France, 1793–1815.* Oxford, 1984.

———, and C. Keydor. *Economic Growth in Britain and France 1780–1914.* London, 1978.

O'Day, A., ed. *The Edwardian Age.* London, 1979.

Offner, A. *American Appeasement, United States Foreign Policy and Germany 1933–1938.* Cambridge, Mass., 1969.

Ohkawa, K., and H. Rosovsky. *Japanese Economic Growth.* Stanford, Calif., 1973.

———, and M. Shinohara, eds. *Patterns of Japanese Economic Development.* New Haven, Conn., 1979.

Okamoto, S. *The Japanese Oligarchy and the Russo-Japanese War.* New York, 1970.

Olsen, E.A. *U.S.-Japan Strategic Reciprocity: A Neo-Internationalist View.* Stanford, Calif., 1985.

Oman, C. *A History of the Art of War in the Middle Ages,* 2 vols. London, 1924.

———. *A History of the Art of War in the Sixteenth Century.* London, 1937.

O'Neill, W. *Coming Apart.* New York, 1971.

Orde, A. *Britain and International Security 1920–1926.* London, 1978.

Osgood, R.E. *NATO: The Entangling Alliance.* Chicago, 1962.

Ovendale, R. *Appeasement and the English-Speaking World.* Cardiff, 1975.

Overholt, W.H., ed. *Asia's Nuclear Future.* Boulder, Col., 1977.

Overy, R.J., "Hitler's War and the German Economy: A Reinterpretation," *Economic History Review* 35 (1982).

———. *The Air War, 1939–1945.* New York, 1980.

———. *The Nazi Economic Recovery 1932–1938.* London, 1982.

Owen, R., and R. Sutcliffe, eds. *Studies in the Theory of Imperialism.* London, 1972.

Oye, K.A., et al., eds. *Eagle Defiant: United States Foreign Policy in the 1980s.* Boston, 1983.

———, et al., eds. *Eagle Entangled: U.S. Foreign Policy in a Complex World.* New York, 1979.

Padfield, P. *Guns at Sea.* London, 1973.

———. *The Battleship Era.* London, 1972.

———. *Tide of Empires: Decisive Naval Campaigns in the Rise of the West,* 2 vols. London, 1979, 1982.

Palmer, A. *Napoleon in Russia.* New York, 1967.

Palmer, B. *The 25-Year War: America's Military Role in Vietnam.* New York, 1984.

Pares, R., "American versus Continental Warfare 1739–1763," *English Historical Review* 51 (1936).

––––. *War and Trade in the West Indies 1739–1763.* Oxford, 1936.

Paret, P. *Yorck and the Era of Prussian Reform.* Princeton, N.J., 1961.

Parish, P.J. *The American Civil War.* New York, 1975.

Parker, G. *Europe in Crisis 1598–1648.* London, 1979.

––––. *Spain and the Netherlands 1559–1659.* London, 1979.

––––. *The Army of Flanders and the Spanish Road 1567–1659: The Logistics of Spanish Victory and Defeat in the Low Countries War.* Cambridge, 1972.

––––. *The Dutch Revolt.* London, 1977.

Parker, R.A.C., "Great Britain, France and the Ethiopian Crisis 1935–1936," *English Historical Review* 89 (1974).

Parodi, M. *L'économie et la société française de 1945 a 1970.* Paris, 1971.

Parry, J.H. *The Age of Reconnaissance*, 2nd edn. London, 1966.

––––. *The Establishment of the European Hegemony 1415–1715*, 3rd edn. New York, 1966.

––––. *Trade and Dominion: The European Overseas Empire in the Eighteenth Century.* London, 1971.

Patterson, A.T. *The Other Armada: The Franco-Spanish Attempt to Invade Britain in 1779.* Manchester, 1960.

Peacock, A.T., and J. Wiseman. *The Growth of Public Expenditure in the United Kingdom.* London, 1967 edn.

Peden, G.C. *British Rearmament and the Treasury 1932–1939.* Edinburgh, 1979.

Pedroncini, G. *Les mutineries de 1917.* Paris, 1967.

Pelz, S.E. *Race to Pearl Harbor.* Cambridge, Mass., 1974.

Pemsel, H. *Atlas of Naval Warfare.* London, 1977.

Pericoli, U., and M. Glover. *1815: The Armies at Waterloo.* London, 1973.

Perkins, B. *Prologue to War: England and the United States 1805–1812.* Berkeley, Calif., 1961.

––––. *The Great Rapprochement.* New York, 1969.

Perkins, D.H., ed. *China's Modern Economy in Historical Perspective.* Stanford, Calif., 1975.

Petersen, E.N. *The Limits of Hitler's Power.* Princeton, N.J., 1969.

Petersen, P.A., and J. G. Hines, "The Conventional Offensive in Soviet Theater Strategy," *Orbis* 27 (1983).

Pflanze, O. *Bismarck and the Development of Germany: The Period of Unification 1815–1871.* Princeton, N.J., 1963.

Pierre, A.J. *Nuclear Politics: The British Experience with an Independent Strategic Nuclear Force, 1939–1970.* London, 1972.

––––, ed. *Nuclear Weapons in Europe.* New York, 1984.

Pigasse, J.P. *Le bouclier d'Europe.* Paris, 1982.

Pintner, W., "Inflation in Russia During the Crimean War Period," *American Slavic and East European Review* 18 (1959).

Pitt, B. *1918—The Last Act.* New York, 1962.

Pivka, O. von. *Navies of the Napoleonic Era.* Newton Abbott, 1980.

Plesur, M. *America's Outward Thrust: Approaches to Foreign Affairs 1865–1890.* DeKalb, Ill., 1971.

Polisensky, J.V. *The Thirty Years War.* London, 1971.

Pollard, S. *Peaceful Conquest: The Industrialization of Europe 1760–1970.* Oxford, 1981.

––––. *The Wasting of the British Economy.* London, 1982.

Polmar, N. *Soviet Naval Developments, 1982*, 4th edn. Annapolis, Md., 1981.

Polonsky, A. *The Great Powers and the Pòlish Question 1941–1945.* London, 1976.

Porch, D. *The March to the Marne: The French Army 1871–1914.* Cambridge, 1981.

Porter, B. *Britain, Europe and the World, 1850–1982: Delusions of Grandeur.* London, 1983.

———. *The Lion's Share: A Short History of British Imperialism 1850–1970.* London, 1976.

Posen, B.R. *The Sources of Military Doctrine: France, Britain and Germany Between the World Wars.* Ithaca, N.Y., 1984.

Postan, M.M. *An Economic History of Western Europe, 1945–1964.* London, 1967.

Potichny, P.T., ed. *The Ukraine in the Seventies.* Oakville, Ont., 1982.

Potter, E.B., ed. *Sea Power: A Naval History.* Annapolis, Md., 1981.

Potter, G.R., ed. *The New Cambridge Modern History,* vol i, *The Renaissance 1493–1520.* Cambridge, 1961.

Pounds, N.J.G. *An Historical Geography of Europe 1500–1840.* Cambridge, 1979.

———, and S. S. Ball, "Core Areas and the Development of the European States System," *Annals of the Association of American Geographers* 54 (1964).

Powers, T. *The War at Home: Vietnam and the American People, 1964–1968.* New York, 1973.

———. *Thinking About Nuclear Weapons.* New York, 1983.

Prados, J. *The Soviet Estimate: U.S. Intelligence Analysis and Russian Military Strength.* New York, 1982.

Pratt, L.R. *East of Malta, West of Suez: Britain's Mediterranean Crisis.* London, 1975.

Presseisen, E.L. *Amiens and Munich: Comparisons in Appeasement.* The Hague, 1978.

Preston, A., ed. *General Staffs and Diplomacy Before the Second World War.* London, 1978.

Preston, R.A., S. F. Wise, and H. O. Werner. *Men in Arms.* London, 1962.

Price, R. *The Economic Modernization of France.* London, 1975.

Prins, G, ed. *The Nuclear Crisis Reader.* New York, 1984.

Qaisar, A.J. *The Indian Response to European Technology and Culture, A.D. 1498–1707.* Delhi, 1982.

Quester, G. *Nuclear Proliferation: Breaking the Chain.* Madison, Wi., 1981.

Quimby, R.S. *The Background of Napoleonic Warfare.* New York, 1957.

Quinn, D.B., and A. N. Ryan. *England's Sea Empire, 1550–1642.* London, 1983.

Radice, L. *Prelude to Appeasement: East Central European Diplomacy in the Early 1930s.* New York, 1981.

Raeff, M. *Imperial Russia 1682–1825.* New York, 1971.

Ragsdale, H. *Détente in the Napoleonic Era: Bonaparte and the Russians.* Lawrence, Kan., 1980.

Rahman, H., "British Post-Second World War Military Planning for the Middle East," *Journal of Strategic Studies* 5 (1982).

Ramsay, J.F. *Anglo-French Relations 1763–70: A Study of Choiseul's Foreign Policy.* Berkeley, Calif., 1939.

Ransom, R.L., et al., eds. *Explorations in the New Economic History.* New York, 1982.

Ranum, O., ed. *National Consciousness, History and Political Culture in Early Modern Europe.* Baltimore, 1975.

Rapp, R.T., "The Unmaking of the Mediterranean Trade Hegemony," *Journal of Economic History* 35 (1975).

Rappaport, A. *Henry L. Stimson and Japan, 1931–1933.* Chicago, 1963.

Rasler, K.A., and W. R. Thompson, "Global Wars, Public Debts, and the Long Cycle," *World Politics* 35 (1983).

Rath, R.J. *The Fall of the Napoleonic Kingdom of Italy.* New York, 1941.

Raulff, H. *Zwischen Machtpolitik und Imperialismus: Die deutsche Frankreichpolitik 1904–5*. Düsseldorf, 1976.

Reamington, R.A. *The Warsaw Pact*. Cambridge, Mass., 1971.

Redlich, F. "Contributions in the Thirty Years War," *Economic History Review* 12 (1959).

——. *The German Military Enterpriser and His Work Force*, 2 vols. Wiesbaden, 1964.

Rees, D. *Korea: The Limited War*. New York, 1966.

Regla, J., "Spain and Her Empire," *New Cambridge Modern History*, vol. v. Cambridge, 1961.

Reinhard, W. *Geschichte der europäischen Expansion*, vol. i. Stuttgart, 1983.

Les Relations franco-allemandes 1933–1939. Paris, 1976.

Les Relations franco-britanniques 1935–39. Paris, 1975.

Reynolds, C.G. *Command of the Sea: The History and Strategy of Maritime Empires*. New York, 1974.

——, "Imperial Japan's Continental Strategy," *U.S. Naval Institute Proceedings* 109 (1983).

Reynolds, D. *The Creation of the Anglo-American Alliance, 1937–1961*. London, 1981.

Rich, N. *Friedrich von Holstein*, 2 vols. Cambridge, 1965.

——. *Hitler's War Aims*, 2 vols. London, 1973–74.

——. *Why the Crimean War?: A Cautionary Tale*. Hanover, N.H., 1985.

Richardson, H.W. *Economic Recovery in Britain, 1932–1939*. London, 1967.

Richmond, H. *Statesmen and Sea Power*. Oxford, 1946.

Riley, J.C. *International Government Finance and the Amsterdam Capital Market 1740–1815*. Cambridge, 1980.

Ritter, G. *The Schlieffen Plan*. New York, 1958.

——. *The Sword and the Scepter*, 4 vols. London, 1975.

Ritter, M., "Das Kontributionssystem Wallensteins," *Historische Zeitschrift* 90 (1902).

Robbins, K. *Munich, 1938*. London, 1968.

Roberts, J.M. *The Pelican History of the World*. Harmondsworth, Mddsx., 1980.

Roberts, M. *Essays in Swedish History*. London, 1967.

——. *Gustavus Adolphus and the Rise of Sweden*. London, 1973.

——. *Gustavus Adolphus*, 2 vols. London, 1958.

——. *Splendid Isolation 1763–1780*. Stenton Lecture, Reading, 1970.

——. *The Swedish Imperial Experience 1560–1718*. Cambridge, 1979.

Robertson, E.M., ed. *The Origins of the Second World War*. London, 1971.

Robertson, R.M. *History of American Economy*. New York, 1975 edn.

Robinson, R., J. Gallagher, and A. Denny. *Africa and the Victorians: The Official Mind of Imperialism*, 2nd edn. London, 1982.

Rodger, A.B. *The War of the Second Coalition, 1798–1801*. Oxford, 1964.

Rogge, H. *Russia in the Age of Modernization and Revolution 1881–1917*. London, 1983.

Rohe, K., ed. *Die Westmächte und das Dritte Reich 1933–1939*. Paderborn, 1982.

Röhl, J.C.G., "A Document of 1892 on Germany, Prussia, and Poland," *Historical Journal* 7 (1964).

——, and N. Sombart, eds. *Kaiser Wilhelm II: New Interpretations*. Cambridge, 1982.

Roider, K.A. *Austria's Eastern Question 1700–1790*. Princeton, N.J., 1982.

Rolfe, S. *The International Corporation*. Paris, 1969.

Ropp, T. *The Development of a Modern Navy: French Naval Policy 1871–1904*. Annapolis, Md., 1987.

——. *War in the Modern World.* Durham, N.C., 1959.

Ropponen, R. *Die Kraft Russlands: Wie beurteilte die politische und militärische Führung der europäischen Grossmächte in der Zeit von 1905 bis 1914 die Kraft Russlands?* Helsinki, 1968.

Rosecrance, R., ed. *America as an Ordinary Power,* Ithaca, N.Y., 1976.

——. *The Rise of the Trading State.* New York, 1985.

Rosenberg, D.A., "A Smoking Radiating Ruin at the End of Two Hours: Documents on American Plans for Nuclear War with the Soviet Union, 1954–55," *International Security* 6 (1981–82).

——, "American Atomic Strategy and the Hydrogen Bomb Decision," *Journal of American History* 66 (1979).

——, "The Origins of Overkill: Nuclear Weapons and American Strategy, 1945–1960," *International Security* 7 (1983).

Rosenberg, H. *Bureaucracy, Aristocracy and Autocracy: The Prussian Experience 1660–1815.* Cambridge, Mass., 1958.

Roseveare, H. *The Treasury: The Evolution of a British Institution.* London, 1969.

Rosinski, H., "The Role of Sea Power in the Global Warfare of the Future," *Brassey's Naval Annual* (1947).

Roskill, S.W. *Naval Policy Between the Wars,* vol. ii. London, 1976.

——. *The War at Sea,* 3 vols. London, 1954–61.

Ross, G. *The Great Powers and the Decline of the European States System 1914–1945.* London, 1983.

Ross, S.T. *European Diplomatic History 1789–1815: France Against Europe.* Malabar, Fla., 1981 reprint.

——. *Quest for Victory: French Military Strategy 1792–1799.* London, 1973.

Rostow, N. *Anglo-French Relations 1934–1936.* London, 1984.

Rostow, W.W. *The Process of Economic Growth,* 2nd edn. Oxford, 1960.

——. *The World Economy: History and Prospect.* Austin, Tex., 1978.

Rothenberg, G.E., B. K. Kiraly, and P. F. Sugar, eds. *East Central European Society and War in the Pre-Revolutionary Eighteenth Century.* New York, 1982.

——. *Napoleon's Great Adversaries: The Archduke Charles and the Austrian Army 1792–1814.* London, 1982.

——. *The Army of Francis Joseph.* West Lafayette, Ind., 1976.

——. *The Art of Warfare in the Age of Napoleon.* Bloomington, Ind., 1978.

Rothstein, R.L. *The Third World and U.S. Foreign Policy.* Boulder, Col., 1981.

——. *The Weak in the World of the Strong: The Developing Countries in the International System.* New York, 1977.

Rothwell, V. *Britain and the Cold War 1941–47.* London, 1982.

Rowen, H.S., "Living with a Sick Bear," *The National Interest* 2 (1985–86).

Rowland, B.M., ed. *Balance of Power or Hegemony: The Inter-War Monetary System.* New York, 1976.

Rowley, A. *Evolution économique de la France de milieu du XIXe siècle à 1914.* Paris, 1982.

Rubin, B. *Paved with Good Intentions: The United States and Iran.* New York, 1980.

Rudé, G. *Paris and London in the Eighteenth Century: Studies in Popular Protest.* New York, 1971.

——. *Revolutionary Europe 1783–1815.* London, 1964.

Rudney, R.S., "Mitterrand's New Atlanticism: Evolving French Attitudes Toward NATO," *Orbis* 28 (1984).

Rupieper, H. *The Cuno Government and Reparations, 1922–1923.* London, 1979.

Rusinov, D. *The Yugoslav Experiment, 1948–1974.* London, 1977.

Russell, C., ed. *The Origins of the English Civil War.* London, 1973.

Russett, B., "America's Continuing Strengths," *International Organization* 39 (1985).

———, "Defense Expenditures and National Well-being," *American Political Science Review* 76 (1982).

Ryder, A.J. *The German Revolution of 1918.* Cambridge, 1967.

Rywkin, M. *Moscow's Muslim Challenge.* New York, 1982.

Sachar, H.M. *Europe Leaves the Middle East 1936–1954.* London, 1972.

Sadkovich, J.J., "Minerals, Weapons and Warfare: Italy's Failure in World War II," *Storia contemporanea*, forthcoming.

Salewski, M. *Die deutsche Seekriegsleitung 1935–1945,* 3 vols. Frankfurt, 1970–75.

Salisbury, H. *The Coming War Between Russia and China.* London, 1969.

Salmon, J.M.H. *Society in Crisis: France in the Sixteenth Century.* London, 1975.

Samhaber, E. *Merchants Make History.* London, 1963.

Sansom, G.B. *A History of Japan,* 3 vols. London, 1958–66.

———. *The Western World and Japan.* London, 1950.

Saul, S.B. *Studies in British Overseas Trade 1870–1914.* Liverpool, 1960.

Saunders, H. *The Middle East Problem in the 1980s.* Washington, D.C., 1981.

Sauvy, A. *Histoire économique de la France entre les deux guerres,* 2 vols. Paris, 1965–67.

Savelle, M. *Empires to Nations: Expansion in America, 1713–1824.* Minneapolis, 1974.

Savory, R. *His Britannic Majesty's Army in Germany During the Seven Years War.* Oxford, 1966.

Sayous, A., "Le role d'Amsterdam dans l'histoire du capitalisme commercial et financier," *Revue Historique* 183 (1938).

Scalapino, R.A., ed. *The Foreign Policy of Modern Japan.* Berkeley, Calif., 1977.

Scammell, G.V. *The World Encompassed: The First European Maritime Empires, c. 800–1650.* Berkeley, Calif., 1981.

Schaller, M. *The American Occupation of Japan: The Origins of the Cold War in Asia.* New York, 1985.

Schell, J. *The Fate of the Earth.* New York, 1982.

Schell, O. *To Get Rich Is Glorious: China in the 80s.* New York, 1985.

Schilling, W.R., et al. *Strategy, Politics, and Defense Budgets.* New York, 1962.

Schmidt, G. *England in der Krise: Grundzüge und Grundlagen der britischen Appeasement-Politik, 1930–1937.* Opladen, 1981.

———, "Wozu noch politische Geschichte?," *Aus Politik und Zeitgeschichte* B17 (1975).

Schmidt, H. *A Grand Strategy for the West.* New Haven, Conn., 1985.

Schmitt, B.E., and H. C. Vedeler. *The World in the Crucible 1914–1919.* New York, 1984.

Schooner, D.M. *Soviet Economy in a Time of Change.* Washington, D.C., 1979.

Schreiber, G., et al., eds. *Das Deutsche Reich und der Zweite Weltkrieg,* vol. iii, *Der Mittelmeerraum und Südosteuropa.* Stuttgart, 1984.

———. *Revisionismus und Weltmachtstreben.* Stuttgart, 1978.

Schroeder, P.W. *Austria, Britain and the Crimean War: The Destruction of the European Concert.* Ithaca, N.Y., 1972.

———, "Munich and the British Tradition," *Historical Journal* (1976).

———, "The Lost Intermediaries: The Impact of 1870 on the European System," *International History Review* 6 (1984).

———, "World War I as a Galloping Gertie," *Journal of Modern History* 44 (1972).

Schulin, E., ed. *Gedenkschrift Martin Göhring: Studien zur europäischen Geschichte.* Wiesbaden, 1968.

Schulte, B.F. *Die deutsche Armee.* Düsseldorf, 1977.

Schulzinger, R.D. *American Diplomacy in the Twentieth Century.* New York, 1984.

Schumpeter, E.B., "English Prices and Public Finance, 1660–1822," *Review of Economic Statistics* 20 (1938).

Schwartz, T., "The Case of German Rearmament: Alliance Crisis in the 'Golden Age,'" *The Fletcher Forum* (1984).

Scott, H.M., "British Foreign Policy in the Age of the American Revolution," *International History Review* 6 (1984).

———, "The Importance of Bourbon Naval Reconstruction to the Strategy of Choiseul after the Seven Years War," *International History Review* 1 (1979).

Scott, W.R. *The Constitution and Finance of English, Scottish and Irish Joint Stock Companies to 1720*, 3 vols. Cambridge, 1912.

Seabury, P., "International Policy and National Defense," *Journal of Contemporary Studies* (1983).

Searle, G.R. *The Quest for National Efficiency: A Study in British Politics and British Political Thought, 1899–1914*. Oxford, 1971.

Seaton, A. *The Crimean War: A Russian Chronicle*. London, 1977.

———. *The German Army 1933–1945*. London, 1982.

———. *The Russian Army of the Crimea*. Reading, Berkshire, 1973.

———. *The Russo-German War 1941–45*. London, 1971.

Segal, G., ed. *The China Factor: Peking and the Superpowers*. London, 1982.

———. *The Soviet Union in East Asia*. Boulder, Col., 1983.

———, and W. Tow, eds. *Chinese Defense Policy*. London, 1984.

———. *Defending China*. London, 1985.

———, "Defense Culture and Sino-Soviet Relations," *Journal of Strategic History* 8 (1985).

———. *The Great Power Triangle*. London, 1982.

Servan-Schreiber, J.J. *The American Challenge*. Harmondsworth, Mddsx., 1969 edn.

Seton-Watson, C. *Italy from Liberalism to Fascism*. London, 1967.

Seton-Watson, R.W. *The Russian Empire 1801–1917*. Oxford, 1967.

Shaw, A.G.L., ed. *Great Britain and the Colonies 1815–1865*. London, 1970.

Shay, R.P. *British Rearmament in the Thirties: Politics and Profits*. Princeton, N.J., 1977.

Shennan, J.H. *The Origins of the Modern European State 1450–1725*. London, 1974.

Sherman, A.J., "German-Jewish Bankers in World Politics: The Financing of the Russo-Japanese War," *Leo Baeck Institute Yearbook* 28 (1983).

Sherwig, J.M. *Guineas and Gunpowder: British Foreign Aid in the Wars with France 1793–1815*. Cambridge, Mass., 1969.

Sherwin, M.J. *A World Destroyed: The Atomic Bomb and the Grand Alliance*. New York, 1975.

Shiba, Y. *Commerce and Society in Sung China*. Ann Arbor, Mich., 1970.

Showalter, D. *Railroads and Rifles: Soldiers, Technology and the Unification of Germany*. Hamden, Conn., 1975.

Shuker, S.A. *The End of French Predominance in Europe: The Financial Crisis of 1924 and the Adoption of the Dawes Plan*. Chapel Hill, N.C., 1976.

Shulman, M.D. *Stalin's Foreign Policy Reappraised*. New York, 1969.

Sick, G. *All Fall Down: America's Tragic Encounter with Iran*. New York, 1985.

Sidorov, A.L. *The Economic Position of Russia During the First World War*. Moscow, 1973.

Siegelbaum, L.H. *The Politics of Industrial Mobilization in Russia, 1914–1917*. New York, 1984.

Silberling, N.J., "Financial and Monetary Policy of Great Britain During the Napoleonic Wars," *Quarterly Journal of Economics* 38 (1923–24).

Silverman, D.P. *Reconstructing Europe After the Great War*. Cambridge, Mass., 1982.

Simmons, R.R. *The Strained Alliance.* New York, 1975.

Skalweit, A. *Die deutsche Kriegsnährungswirtschaft.* Berlin, 1927.

Sked, A., ed. *Europe's Balance of Power 1815–1848.* London, 1979.

———. *The Survival of the Habsburg Empire: Radetsky, the Imperial Army and the Class War, 1848.* London, 1979.

Slessor, J. *Strategy for the West.* London, 1954.

Smith, D.M., "National Interest and American Intervention, 1917: An Historical Appraisal," *Journal of American History* 52 (1965).

———. *The Great Departure: The United States and World War I, 1914–1920.* New York, 1965.

Smith, G. *Morality, Reason and Power: American Diplomacy in the Carter Years.* New York, 1986.

Smith, M., et al. *Asia's New Industrial World.* London, 1985.

———. *British Air Strategy Between the Wars.* Oxford, 1984.

Smith, T. *Political Change and Modern Development in Japan: Government Enterprise 1868–1880.* Stanford, Calif., 1955.

———. *The Pattern of Imperialism: The United States, Great Britain and the Late-Industrializing World Since 1815.* Cambridge, 1981.

Snyder, J. *The Ideology of the Offensive.* Ithaca, N.Y., 1984.

Snyder, J.C., and S. F. Wells, eds. *Limiting Nuclear Proliferation.* Cambridge, Mass., 1985.

Solomon, R.H., ed. *The China Factor: Sino-American Relations and the Global Scene.* Englewood Cliffs, N.J., 1981.

Sombart, W. *Krieg und Kapitalismus.* Munich, 1913.

Sontag, R.J. *A Broken World, 1919–1939.* New York, 1971.

Spanier, J.W. *American Foreign Policy Since World War II.* London, 1972 edn.

Spector, R.H. *Eagle Against the Sun: The American War with Japan.* New York, 1985.

Speer, A. *Inside the Third Reich.* New York, 1982 edn.

Spiers, E.M. *The Army and Society 1815–1914.* London, 1980.

Sprout, H., and M. Sprout. *The Rise of American Naval Power, 1776–1918.* Princeton, N.J., 1946 edn.

Spulber, N. *The State and Economic Development in Eastern Europe.* New York, 1966.

Stares, P., "The Modernization of the French Strategic Nuclear Force," *Journal of the Royal United Services Institute for Defence Studies* 125 (1980).

Starr, H. *Henry Kissinger: Perceptions of International Politics.* Lexington, Ky., 1982.

State of the World Economy, The. Cambridge, Mass., 1982.

Stavrianos, L.S. *Global Rift: The Third World Comes of Age.* New York, 1981.

Steel, R. *Pax Americana.* New York, 1977.

Steele, J. *Soviet Power.* New York, 1984.

Steinberg, J., "The Copenhagen Complex," *Journal of Contemporary History* 1 (1966).

Steinbrunner, D.D., and L. V. Segal, eds. *Alliance Security: NATO and the No-First-Use Question.* Washington, D.C., 1983.

Steiner, Z.S. *Britain and the Origins of the First World War.* London, 1977.

———. *The Foreign Office and Foreign Policy 1898–1914.* Cambridge, 1969.

Stella, D. *Crisis and Continuity: The Economy of Spanish Lombardy in the Seventeenth Century.* Cambridge, Mass., 1979.

Stoakes, G. *Hitler and the Quest for World Dominion: Nazi Ideology and Foreign Policy in the 1920s.* Leamington Spa, 1986.

Stockholm International Peace Research Institute. *The Arms Race and Arms Control.* London, 1982.

Stoessinger, J.G. *Nations in Darkness: China, Russia and America.* New York, 1978.

Stokesbury, J.L. *A Short History of World War I.* New York, 1981.

Stone, L. *The Causes of the English Revolution 1529–1642.* London, 1972.

Stone, N. *Europe Transformed 1878–1919.* London, 1983.

———. *The Eastern Front 1914–1917.* London, 1975.

Stork-Penning, J.G., "The Ordeal of the States: Some Remarks on Dutch Politics During the War of the Spanish Succession," *Acta Historiae Neerlandica* 2 (1967).

Storry, R. *A History of Modern Japan.* Harmondsworth, Mddsx., 1982 edn.

———. *Japan and the Decline of the West in Asia 1894–1943.* London, 1979.

Stoye, J.W. *Europe Unfolding 1648–1688.* London, 1969.

———. *The Siege of Vienna.* London, 1964.

Strachan, H. *European Armies and the Conduct of War.* London, 1983.

———. *Wellington's Legacy: The Reform of the British Army, 1830–1854.* Manchester, 1984.

Stradling, R.A., "Catastrophe and Recovery: The Defeat of Spain 1639–43," *History* 64 (1979).

———. *Europe and the Decline of Spain: A Study of the Spanish System, 1580–1720.* London, 1981.

Strengthening Conventional Deterrence in Europe: Proposals for the 1980s. New York, 1983.

Strode, D.L., "Arms Control and Sino-Soviet Relations," *Orbis* 28 (1984).

Stueck, W.W. *The Road to Confrontation.* Chapel Hill, N.C., 1981.

Sullivan, L., "A New Approach to Burden-Sharing," *Foreign Policy* 60 (1985).

Summers, H.G. *On Strategy: A Critical Analysis of the Vietnam War.* New York, 1972.

Sumner, B.H. *Peter the Great and the Emergence of Russia.* London, 1940.

———. *Russia and the Balkans 1870–1880.* London, 1937.

Sutter, R. *China Watch: Toward Sino-American Reconciliation.* Baltimore, 1978.

Svennilson, I. *Growth and Stagnation in the European Economy.* Geneva, 1954.

Symcox, G. *The Crisis of French Sea Power 1689–1697.* The Hague, 1974.

Syrett, D. *Shipping and the American War 1775–83.* London, 1970.

Szamuely, T. *The Russian Traditions,* London, 1974.

Taagepera, R., "Growth Curves of Empires," *General Systems* 13 (1968).

———, "Size and Duration of Empires: Systematics of Size," *Social Science Research* 7 (1978).

Taborsky, E. *Communist Penetration of the Third World.* New York, 1963.

Talbott, S. *Deadly Gambits: The Reagan Administration and the Stalemate in Nuclear Arms Control.* New York, 1984.

Tamborra, A., "The Rise of Italian Industry and the Balkans," *Journal of European Economic History* 3 (1974).

Taubman, W. *Stalin's American Policy: From Entente to Détente to Cold War.* New York, 1982.

Taylor, A.J.P. *The Origins of the Second World War.* Harmondsworth, Mddsx., 1964 edn.

———. *The Struggle for Mastery in Europe 1848–1918.* Oxford, 1954.

———. *The Trouble-Makers: Dissent over Foreign Policy, 1789–1939.* London, 1969 edn.

Taylor, J. *Shadows of the Rising Sun: A Critical View of the "Japanese Miracle."* New York, 1984.

Taylor, R. *The Sino-Japanese Axis.* New York, 1985.

Taylor, T. *Munich: The Price of Peace.* New York, 1979.

Teichova, A. *An Economic Background to Munich.* Cambridge, 1974.

Thies, J. *Architekt der Weltherrschaft: Die "Endziele" Hitlers.* Düsseldorf, 1976.

Thiry, J. *La Guerre d'Espagne*. Paris, 1966.

Thomas, H. *History of the World*. New York, 1979 edn.

Thompson, E.P. *Zero Option*. London, 1982.

——, and D. Smith, eds. *Protest and Survive*. Harmondsworth, Mddsx., 1980.

Thompson, I.A.A. *War and Government in Habsburg Spain 1560–1620*. London, 1976.

Thompson, J.W. *Italian Civil and Military Aircraft 1930–1935*. Fallbrook, Calif., 1963.

Thomson, D. *Europe Since Napoleon*. Harmondsworth, Mddsx., 1966 edn.

——. *The Aims of History*. London, 1969.

Thorne, C. *The Issue of War: States, Societies, and the Far Eastern Conflict of 1941–1945*. London, 1985.

——. *The Limits of Foreign Policy: The West, the League and the Far Eastern Crisis of 1931–1933*. London, 1972.

Thornton, A.P. *The Imperial Idea and Its Enemies*. London, 1966.

Thornton, R.C. *The Bear and the Dragon*. New York, 1972.

Thucydides. *The Peleponnesian War*. Harmondsworth, Mddsx., 1954 edn.

Thurow, L. *The Zero-Sum Society*. New York, 1980.

Tilly, C., ed. *The Formation of the National States in Western Europe*. Princeton, N.J., 1975.

Toby, R.P. *State and Diplomacy in Early Modern Japan*. Princeton, N.J., 1984.

Tocqueville, A. de. *Democracy in America*, 2 vols. New York, 1945 edn.

Tokes, R.L. *Euro-Communism and Détente*. New York, 1978.

Toland, J. *No Man's Land: The Story of 1918*. London, 1980.

Tomlinson, B.R., "The Contraction of England: National Decline and the Loss of Empire," *Journal of Imperial and Commonwealth History* 11 (1982).

——. *The Political Economy of the Raj 1914–1947*. Cambridge, 1979.

Towle, P., "The European Balance of Power in 1914," *Army Quarterly and Defense Journal* 104 (1974).

Toynbee, A.J., and F. T. Ashton-Gwatkin, eds. *The World in 1939*. London, 1952.

Trachtenberg, M. *Reparation in World Politics: France and European Diplomacy 1916–1923*. New York, 1980.

Trask, D.F. *The War with Spain in 1898*. New York, 1981.

Trebilcock, C. *The Industrialization of the Continental Powers 1780–1914*. London, 1981.

Treverton, G.F. *Making the Alliance Work: The United States and Europe*. Ithaca, N.Y., 1985.

Tuchman, B.W. *Stilwell and the American Experience in China*. New York, 1971.

Tucker, N.B. *Patterns in the Dust: Chinese-American Relations and the Recognition Controversy 1949–50*. New York, 1983.

Tucker, R.W., "Swollen State, Spent Society: Stalin's Legacy to Brezhnev's Russia," *Foreign Affairs* 60 (1981–82).

——. *The Purposes of American Power*. New York, 1981.

Tunstall, B. *William Pitt, Earl of Chatham*. London, 1938.

Turner, L.C.F. *Origins of the First World War*. London, 1970.

Ulam, A. *Dangerous Relations: The Soviet Union in World Politics 1970–1982*. New York, 1983.

——. *Expansion and Coexistence: The History of Soviet Foreign Policy 1917–1973*. New York, 1974.

Ungar, S.J., ed. *Estrangement: America and the World*. New York, 1985.

van der Wee, H., "Monetary, Credit and Banking Systems," *The Cambridge Economic History of Europe*, vol. v. Cambridge, 1977.

Van Ness, P. *Revolution and Chinese Foreign Policy*. Berkeley, Calif., 1971.

Varg, P.A. *Missionaries, Chinese, and Diplomats... 1890–1952.* Princeton, N.J., 1952.

Vatter, H.G. *The Drive to Industrial Maturity: The U.S. Economy, 1860–1914.* Westport, Conn., 1975 edn.

Vernadsky, G. *The Tsardom of Muscovy, 1547–1682.* New Haven, Conn., 1969.

Viljoen, S. *Economic Systems in World History.* London, 1974.

Vogel, B. *Deutsche Russlandpolitik, 1900–1906.* Düsseldorf, 1973.

Vogel, E.F. *Japan as Number One: Lessons for America.* New York, 1980 edn.

———, "Pax Nipponica?," *Foreign Affairs* 64 (1986).

Volcker, K.-H. *Die deutsche Luftwaffe 1933–1939.* Stuttgart, 1967.

Wagenfuhr, R. *Die deutsche Industrie im Kriege 1939–1945.* Berlin, 1963.

Waite, R.A.L. *Vanguard of Nazism: The Free Corps Movement in Postwar Germany.* Cambridge, Mass., 1952.

Waites, N., ed. *Troubled Neighbours: Franco-British Relations in the Twentieth Century.* London, 1971.

Walden, P. *The Short Victorious War: A History of the Russo-Japanese War, 1904–5.* New York, 1974.

Walker, G.J. *Spanish Politics and Imperial Trade 1700–1789.* Bloomington, Ind., 1979.

Waller, B. *Bismarck at the Crossroads: The Reorientation of German Foreign Policy After the Congress of Berlin 1878–1880.* London, 1974.

Wallerstein, I. *The Modern World System,* 2 vols. to date. London, 1974, 1980.

Waltz, K. *Man, the State and War.* New York, 1959.

Waltz, K.N., "Toward Nuclear Peace," Wilson Center, International Security Studies, Working Paper 16.

Wandycz, P. *France and Her Eastern Allies 1919–1925.* Minneapolis, 1962.

———. *The Twilight of the French Eastern Alliances, 1926–1936,* forthcoming.

Wangermann, E. *The Austrian Achievement.* New York, 1973.

Waters, A. *Britain's Industrial Renaissance.* London, 1986.

Watson, M.S. *Chief of Staff: Pre-War Plans and Preparations.* Washington, D.C., 1950.

Watt, D.C. *Too Serious a Business: European Armed Forces and the Approach of the Second World War.* London, 1975.

Webber, C., and A. Wildavsky. *A History of Taxation and Expenditure in the Western World.* New York, 1986.

Weber, E. *The Nationalist Revival in France, 1905–1916.* Berkeley, Calif., 1959.

Webster, C.K. *The Foreign Policy of Castlereagh, 1812–1815: Britain and the Reconstruction of Europe.* London, 1931.

Wedgewood, C.V. *The Thirty Years War.* London, 1964 edn.

Wegs, J.R. *Europe Since 1945,* 2nd edn. New York, 1984.

Wehler, H.-U. *Bismarck und der Imperialismus.* Cologne, 1969.

Weigley, R.F. *History of the United States Army.* Bloomington, Ind., 1984 edn.

———. *The American Way of War: A History of the United States Military Strategy and Policy.* Bloomington, Ind., 1977 edn.

Weinberg, G. *The Foreign Policy of Hitler's Germany,* 2 vols. Chicago, 1970, 1980.

Weinberger, C. *Report of the Secretary of Defense Caspar W. Weinberger to the Congress on Fiscal Year 1984 Budget.* Washington, D.C., 1983.

———, "U.S. Defense Strategy," *Foreign Affairs* 64 (1986).

Weller, J. *Wellington in the Peninsula.* London, 1962.

Wells, S.F., "Sounding the Tocsin: NSC-68 and the Soviet Threat," *International Security* 4 (1979).

Wendt, B.J., "Freihandel und Friedenssicherung: Zur Bedeutung des Cobden-Vertrags von 1860 zwischen England und Frankreich," *Vierteljahresschrift für Sozial- und Wirtschaftsgeschichte* 61 (1974).

Wernham, R.B. *Before the Armada: The Growth of English Foreign Policy 1485–1588.* London, 1966.
———. *The Making of Elizabethan Foreign Policy 1588–1603.* Berkeley, Calif., 1980.
Wesson, R.G. *State Systems: International Relations: Politics and Culture.* New York, 1978.
Westwood, J.N. *Russia Against Japan, 1904–5: A New Look at the Russo-Japanese War.* London, 1986.
Whelan, J.G. *World Communism, 1967–1969: Soviet Attempts to Reestablish Control.* Washington, D.C., 1970.
Whetten, L.L. *Germany's Ostpolitik.* London, 1971.
———, "The Mediterranean Threat," *Survival* 8 (1980).
White, J.A. *The Diplomacy of the Russo-Japanese War.* Princeton, N.J., 1964.
Whittam, J. *The Politics of the Italian Army 1861–1918.* London, 1977.
Wight, M. *Power Politics.* Harmondsworth, Mddsx., 1979.
Wildman, A.K. *The End of the Russian Imperial Army.* Princeton, N.J., 1980.
Wilkinson, E. *Misunderstanding: Europe versus Japan.* Tokyo, 1981.
Williams, E.N. *The Ancien Régime in Europe 1648–1789.* Harmondsworth, Mddsx., 1979 edn.
Williams, G. *The Expansion of Europe in the Eighteenth Century.* London, 1966.
Williams, J. *The Home Fronts: Britain, France and Germany, 1914–1918.* London, 1972.
Williams, J.B. *British Commercial Policy and Trade Expansion 1750–1850.* Oxford, 1972.
Williams, P. *The Tudor Regime.* Oxford, 1979.
Williams, W.A. *The Roots of the Modern American Empire.* New York, 1969.
Willmott, H.P. *Empires in the Balance.* Annapolis, Md., 1982.
Wilson, A.M. *French Foreign Policy During the Administration of Cardinal Fleury.* Cambridge, Mass., 1936.
Wilson, C.H., ed. *Economic History and the Historian: Collected Essays.* London, 1969.
———. *Anglo-Dutch Commerce and Finance in the Eighteenth Century.* Cambridge, 1966 reprint.
———. *The Dutch Republic and the Civilization of the Seventeenth Century.* London, 1968.
———. *The Transformation of Europe 1558–1648.* London, 1976.
Wimbush, W.E., ed. *Soviet Nationalities in Strategic Perspective.* New York, 1985.
Windelband, W. *Bismarck und die europäischen Grossmächte 1878–85.* Essen, 1940.
Windsor, P. *German Reunification.* London, 1969.
Winter, J.M., ed. *War and Economic Development.* Cambridge, 1975.
Wittek, P. *The Rise of the Ottoman Empire.* London, 1938.
Wittram, R. *Peter I. Czar und Kaiser,* 2 vols. Göttingen, 1964.
Wolf, A. *A History of Science, Technology and Philosophy in the Sixteenth and Seventeenth Centuries.* New York, 1935.
Wolf, J.B. *Louis XIV.* London, 1968.
———. *The Emergence of the Great Powers 1685–1715.* New York, 1951.
———. *Toward a European Balance of Power 1620–1715.* Chicago, 1970.
Wolfe, M. *The Fiscal System of Renaissance France.* New Haven, Conn., 1972.
Wolfe, T. *Soviet Power and Europe, 1945–1970.* Baltimore, Md., 1970.
Wolfers, A. *Britain and France Between Two Wars.* New York, 1966 edn.
Woodruff, W. *America's Impact on the World: A Study of the Role of the United States in the World Economy 1750–1970.* New York, 1973.
———. *Impact of Western Man: A Study of Europe's Role in the World Economy 1750–1960.* New York, 1967.

Woods, J. (pseudonym), "The Royal Navy Since World War II," *U.S. Naval Institute Proceedings* 108 (1982).

Woodward, D.R. *Lloyd George and the Generals.* Newark, N.J., 1983.

Wright, G. *The Ordeal of Total War, 1939–1945.* New York, 1968.

Wright, Q. *A Study of War.* Chicago, 1942.

Yahuda, M.B. *China's Role in World Affairs.* New York, 1978.

Yang, L.-S. *Money and Credit in China.* Cambridge, Mass., 1952.

Yardley, H. *The American Black Chamber.* New York, 1931.

Yonosuke, N., and A. Iriye, eds. *The Origins of the Cold War in Asia.* New York, 1977.

Yost, D.S. *France and Conventional Defense in Central Europe.* Boulder, Col., 1985.

———, "France's Deterrent Posture," *Adelphi Papers* 194 and 195 (1985).

Young, J.W. *Britain, France and the Unity of Europe 1945–51.* Leicester, 1984.

Young, L.K. *British Policy in China 1895–1902.* Oxford, 1970.

Young, R.J. *In Command of France: French Foreign Policy and Military Planning 1933–1940.* Cambridge, Mass., 1978.

Ziemke, E.F. *Stalingrad to Berlin: The German Defeat in the East 1942–1945.* Washington, D.C., 1968.

Zuckerman, S. *Nuclear Illusion and Reality.* London, 1982.

Index

Abbas I, 9, 11
Abyssinia (Ethiopia), 287, 292, 293,
    296–97, 313, 336, 341, 396, 397, 512
Acheson, Dean, 382
Achtung Panzer (Guderian), 313
Adenauer, Konrad, 399, 401
AEG, 210–11
Afghanistan, 191, 390, 391, 400, 410, 447,
    510, 516
Afrika Korps, 341
agricultural production:
    green revolution in, 440
    during World War I, 280
    see also specific countries
aircraft production, 324, 353–54
Air Force, U.S., 387
Aix-la-Chapelle, Treaty of (1668), 101
Aix-la-Chapelle, Treaty of (1748), 110
Akbar, Emperor of India, 9, 24
Alba, Duke of (Álvarez de Toledo), 38
Albania, 339, 361
Albuquerque, Afonso de, 26
Aleutian Islands, 353
Alexander I, Czar of Russia, 170
Alexander II, Czar of Russia, 177
Algeria, 366, 401
Allende, Salvador, 407
alliance diplomacy, 249–53, 256
Alliance for Progress, 407
Alsop, Stewart, 382
America, colonial, 74, 93
American Revolution, xxii, 81, 84, 116–19
Amery, Leo, 196
Amiens, Peace of (1802), 126
AMX battle tank, 486
Angell, Norman, 537
Anglo-French War (1750s), 110–11
Anglo-Japanese Alliance (1902), 209, 249,
    251, 256
Anglo-Spanish War (1739), 108, 110
Angola, 40, 397, 409
Annual Economic Report (EEC), 474–75
Anson, George, 114
ANZUS treaty, 389

appeasement diplomacy, 317–19, 337–39
Arab-Israeli wars of 1967 and 1973, 396,
    409
Armed Neutrality League, 125
arms race, 383–89, 395–96
    defense manufacturers and, 442–43
    nuclear vs. conventional forces in, 515
    under Reagan, 410–11, 412
    Soviet economy and, 498–99
    spiraling cost of, 442
    U.S. economy and, 531–33
Army, U.S., 272
Army Air Corps, U.S., 331
Army of Flanders (Spanish), 44, 47, 50,
    53, 68, 71
Aron, Raymond, 485
artillery, 75, 150, 185
Ashton, T. S., 147
Ashworth, W. A., 415
Asian Development Bank, 456
Association of Southeast Asian Nations
    (ASEAN), 441
Aswan Dam, 391
Ataturk, Kemal, 286
Atlantic Charter, 392
atomic weapons, 356–57, 369–70, 385–86,
    398
Attlee, Clement, 370
Augsburg, Peace of (1555), 37
Australasia, 280, 521
Australia, 279, 347, 348, 383, 389, 441,
    469
Austria, 445
Austrian Succession, War of, 85
Austro-Hungarian Empire, 188, 215–19
    army of, 217, 218
    ethnic diversity in, 216–17
    GNP of, 215
    Great Power status of, 215
    industrialization of, 215–16
    socioeconomic disparities in, 216
    in World War I, 257, 261–62, 263
Austro-Russian War against Ottoman
    Empire (1735–1739), 108

663

About the Author

PAUL KENNEDY was born in the north of England, at Wallsend-on-Tyne, in 1945. He attended the University of Newcastle, where he graduated with first class honors in history, and received his doctorate from Oxford.

Professor Kennedy has researched and lectured at a variety of places in Europe and North America. He is a Fellow of the Royal Historical Society, a former Visiting Fellow of the Institute for Advanced Study at Princeton, and of the Alexander von Humboldt Foundation in West Germany. In 1983 Kennedy moved to Yale to become the J. Richardson Dilworth Professor of History, with a focus on modern strategic and international affairs. A frequent reviewer for and contributor to *The New York Times, The New Republic, The Washington Post, The Atlantic* and *The Economist,* Paul Kennedy lives in Hamden, Connecticut, with his wife, Catherine, and their three sons.